Robert G. Watkins

THE OUTLINE OF HISTORY

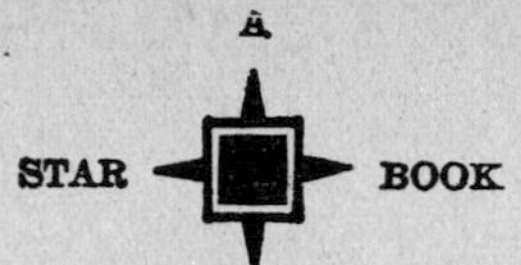

THE OUTLINE OF HISTORY

BEING A PLAIN HISTORY OF LIFE AND MANKIND

By H. G. WELLS

WRITTEN ORIGINALLY WITH THE ADVICE AND EDITORIAL HELP OF MR. ERNEST BARKER, SIR H. H. JOHNSTON, SIR E. RAY LANKESTER, AND PROFESSOR GILBERT MURRAY, AND ILLUSTRATED BY J. F. HORRABIN

COMPLETE IN ONE VOLUME

Containing all maps, charts, illustrations, diagrams, etc. 1200 pages

GARDEN CITY PUBLISHING CO., INC.
GARDEN CITY, NEW YORK

Published in Two Volumes. November, 1920
Reissued in One Volume Edition, September, 1921

Reprinted,	*October,*	*1921*
“	*November,*	“
“	*December,*	“
“	“	“
“	*January,*	*1922*
“	*March,*	“
“	*July,*	“
“	*August,*	“
“	*September,*	“
“	*October,*	“
“	*November,*	“
“	*December,*	“
“	*January,*	*1923*
“	*April,*	“
“	*July,*	“
“	*December,*	“
“	*January,*	*1924*
“	*February,*	“
“	*June,*	“
“	*November,*	“
“	*February,*	*1925*
“	*October,*	“

Reprinted in Star Edition

Reprinted,	*August,*	*1929*
“	*October,*	“
“	*November,*	“
“	*December,*	“
“	*January,*	*1930*
“	***March,***	“
“	*September*	“
“	*October*	“

Printed in the United States of America

INTRODUCTION

"A philosophy of the history of the human race, worthy of its name, must begin with the heavens and descend to the earth, must be charged with the conviction that all existence is one—a single conception sustained from beginning to end upon one identical law."

—FRIEDRICH RATZEL.

THIS *Outline of History,* of which this is a third edition, freshly revised and rearranged, is an attempt to tell, truly and clearly, in one continuous narrative, the whole story of life and mankind so far as it is known to-day. It is written plainly for the general reader, but its aim goes beyond its use as merely interesting reading matter. There is a feeling abroad that the teaching of history considered as a part of general education is in an unsatisfactory condition, and particularly that the ordinary treatment of this "subject" by the class and teacher and examiner is too partial and narrow. But the desire to extend the general range of historical ideas is confronted by the argument that the available time for instruction is already consumed by that partial and narrow treatment, and that therefore, however desirable this extension of range may be, it is in practice impossible. If an Englishman, for example, has found the history of England quite enough for his powers of assimilation, then it seems hopeless to expect his sons and daughters to master universal history, if that is to consist of the history of England, plus the history of France, plus the history of Germany, plus the history of Russia, and so on. To which the only possible answer is that universal history is at once something more and something less than the aggregate of the national histories to which we are accustomed, that it must be approached in a different spirit and dealt with in a different manner. This book seeks to justify that answer. It has been written primarily to show that *history as one whole* is amenable to a more broad and comprehensive handling than is the history of special nations and periods, a broader handling that will bring it within the normal limitations of time and energy set to the reading and education of an ordinary citizen. This outline deals with ages and races and nations, where the ordinary history deals with reigns and pedigrees and campaigns; but it will not be found to be more crowded with names and dates, nor more difficult to follow and understand. History is no exception amongst the sciences; as the gaps fill in, the outline simplifies; as the outlook broadens, the clustering multitude of details dissolves into general laws. And many topics of quite primary interest to mankind, the first appearance and the growth of scientific knowledge for example, and its effects upon human life, the elaboration of the ideas of money and credit, or the story of the origins and spread and influence of Christianity, which must be treated fragmentarily or by elaborate digressions in any partial history, arise and flow completely and naturally in one general record of the world in which we live.

The need for a common knowledge of the general facts of human history throughout the world has become very evident during the tragic happenings of the last few years. Swifter means of communication have brought all men closer to one another for good or for evil. War becomes a universal disaster, blind and monstrously destructive; it bombs the baby in its cradle and sinks the food-ships that cater for the non-combatant and the neutral. There can be no peace now, we realize, but a common peace in all the world; no prosperity but a general prosperity. But *there can be no common peace and prosperity without common historical ideas.* Without such ideas to hold them together in harmonious co-operation, with nothing but narrow, selfish, and conflicting nationalist traditions, races and peoples are bound to drift towards conflict and destruction. This truth, which was apparent to that great philosopher Kant a century or more ago—it is the gist of his tract upon universal peace—is now plain to the man in the street. Our internal policies and our economic and social ideas are profoundly vitiated at present by wrong and fantastic ideas of the origin and historical relationship of social classes. A sense of history as the common adventure of all mankind is as necessary for peace within as it is for peace between the nations.

The writer will offer no apology for making this experiment. His disqualifications are manifest. But such work needs to be done by as many people as possible, he was free to make his contribution, and he was greatly attracted by the task. He has read sedulously and made the utmost use of all the help he could obtain. There is not a chapter that has not been examined by some more competent person than himself and very carefully revised. He has particularly to thank his friends Sir E. Ray Lankester, Sir H. H. Johnston, Professor Gilbert Murray, and Mr. Ernest Barker for much counsel and direction and editorial help. Mr. Philip Guedalla has toiled most efficiently and kindly through all the proofs. Mr. A. Allison, Professor T. W. Arnold, Mr. Arnold Bennett, the Rev. A. H. Trevor Benson, Mr. Aodh de Blacam, Mr. Laurence Binyon, the Rev. G. W. Broomfield, Sir William Bull, Mr. L. Cranmer Byng, Mr. A. J. D. Campbell, Mr. A. Y. Campbell, Mr. L. Y. Chen, Mr. A. R. Cowan, Mr. O. G. S. Crawford, Dr. W. S. Culbertson, Mr. R. Langton Cole, Mr. B. G. Collins, Mr. J. J. L. Duyvendak, Mr. O. W. Ellis, Mr. G. S. Ferrier, Mr. David Freeman, Mr. S. N. Fu, Mr. G. B. Gloyne, Sir Richard Gregory, Mr. F. H. Hayward, Mr. Sydney Herbert, Dr. Fr. Krupicka, Mr. H. Lang Jones, Mr. C. H. B. Laughton, Mr. B. I. Macalpin, Mr. G. H. Mair, Mr. F. S. Marvin, Mr. J. S. Mayhew, Mr. B. Stafford Morse, Professor J. L. Myres, the Hon. W. Ormsby-Gore, Sir Sydney Olivier, Mr. R. I. Pocock, Mr. J. Pringle, Mr. W. H. R. Rivers, Sir Denison Ross, Dr. E. J. Russell, Dr. Charles Singer, Mr. A. St. George Sanford, Dr. C. O. Stallybrass, Mr. G. H. Walsh, Mr. G. P. Wells, Miss Rebecca West, and Mr. George Whale have all to be thanked for help, either by reading parts of the MS. or by pointing out errors in the published parts, making suggestions, answering questions or giving advice. Numerous other helpful correspondents have pointed out printer's errors and minor slips in the serial publication which preceded the book edition, and they have added many useful items of information, and to those writers also the warmest thanks are due. Mr. C. M. Anton Belaiew, Mr. Henry Coates, Mr. J. A. Corry, Mr. Archibald Craig, Mr. W. V. Cruden, Mr. A. H. Dodd, Mr. T. B. Goldsmith, Mr. F. E. Green, Mr. F. S. Hare, Mr. Homer B. Hulbert, Mr. Walter Ingleby, Mr. J. H. Leviton, Mr. H. Comyn Maitland, Mr. Karsten Meyer, Mr. William Platt, Mr. F. Gordon Roe, Mr. Alden Sampson, Mr. Neville H. Smith, Mr. M. Timur, Mr. W. H. Thompson, Mr. A. J. Vogan, Mr. W. A. Voss, Mr. G. F. Wates, and one or two correspondents with illegible signatures, have made valuable suggestions since the publication of the second edition. Pamphlets against the *Outline* by Mr. Gomme and Dr. Downey have also been useful in this later revision. But of course none of these helpers are to be held responsible for the judgments, tone, arrangement or writing of this *Outline*. In the relative importance of the parts, in the moral and political implications of the story, the final decision has necessarily fallen to the writer. The problem of illustrations was a very difficult one for him, for he had had no previous experience in the production of an illustrated book. In Mr. J. F. Horrabin he has had the good fortune to find not only an illustrator but a collaborator. Mr. Horrabin has spared no pains to make this work informative and exact. His maps and drawings are a part of the text, the most vital and decorative part. Some of them represent the reading and inquiry of many laborious days.

The index to this edition is the work of Mr. Strickland Gibson of Oxford. Several correspondents have asked for a pronouncing index and accordingly this has been provided.

The writer owes a word of thanks to that living index of printed books, Mr. J. F. Cox of the London Library. He would also like to acknowledge here the help he has received from Mrs. Wells. Without her labour in typing and re-typing the drafts of the various chapters as they have been revised and amended, in checking references, finding suitable quotations, hunting up illustrations, and keeping in order the whole mass of material for this history, and without her constant help and watchful criticism, its completion would have been impossible.

H. G. Wells.

SCHEME OF CONTENTS

LIST OF MAPS AND ILLUSTRATIONS

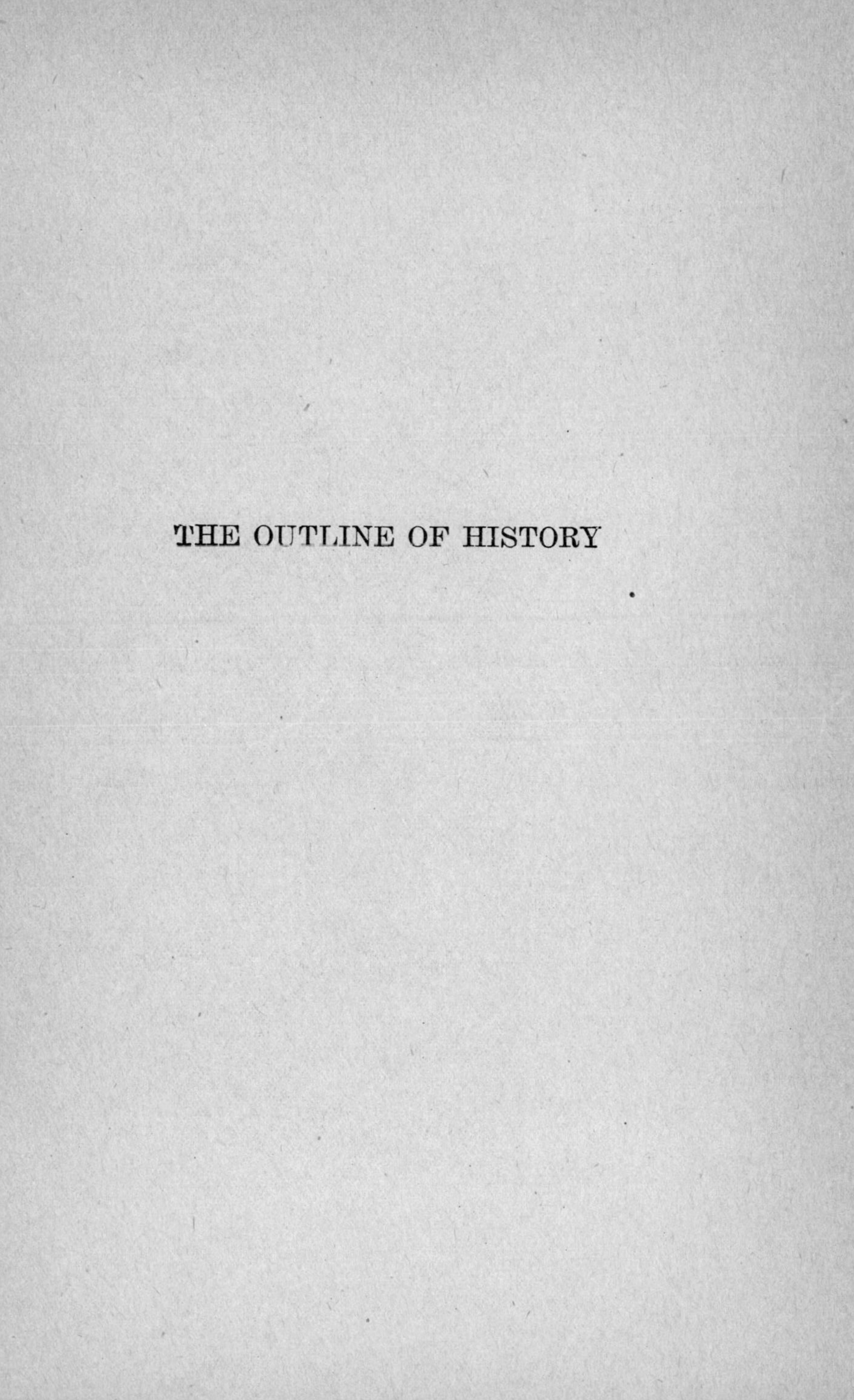

THE OUTLINE OF HISTORY

THE OUTLINE OF HISTORY

I

THE EARTH IN SPACE AND TIME

THE earth on which we live is a spinning globe. Vast though it seems to us, it is a mere speck of matter in the greater vastness of space.

Space is, for the most part, emptiness. At great intervals there are in this emptiness flaring centres of heat and light, the "fixed stars." They are all moving about in space, notwithstanding that they are called fixed stars, but for a long time men did not realize their motion. They are so vast and at such tremendous distances that their motion is not perceived. Only in the course of many thousands of years is it appreciable. These fixed stars are so far off that, for all their immensity, they seem to be, even when we look at them through the most powerful telescopes, mere points of light, brighter or less bright. A few, however, when we turn a telescope upon them are seen to be whirls and clouds of shining vapour which we call nebulæ. They are so far off that a movement of millions of miles would be imperceptible.

One star, however, is so near to us that it is like a great ball of flame. This one is the sun. The sun is itself in its nature like a fixed star, but it differs from the other fixed stars in appearance because it is beyond comparison nearer than they are; and because it is nearer men have been able to learn something of its nature. Its mean distance from the earth is ninety-three million miles. It is a mass of flaming matter, having a diameter of 866,000 miles. Its bulk is a million and a quarter times the bulk of our earth.

These are difficult figures for the imagination. If a bullet fired from a Maxim gun at the sun kept its muzzle velocity unimpaired, it would take seven years to reach the sun. And yet we say the sun is near, measured by the scale of the stars. If the earth were a small ball, one inch in diameter, the sun would be a globe of nine feet diameter; it would fill a small bedroom. It is spinning round on its axis, but since it is an incandescent fluid, its polar regions do not travel with the same velocity as its equator, the surface of which rotates in about twenty-five days. The surface visible to us consists of clouds of incandescent metallic vapour. At what lies below we can only guess. So hot is the sun's atmosphere that iron, nickel, copper, and tin are present in it in a gaseous state. About it at great distances circle not only our earth, but certain kindred bodies called the planets. These shine in the sky because they reflect the light of the sun; they are near enough for us to note their movements quite easily. Night by night their positions change with regard to the fixed stars.

It is well to understand how empty is space. If, as we have said the sun were a ball nine feet across, our earth would, in proportion, be the size of a one-inch ball, and at a distance of 323 yards from the sun. The moon would be a speck the size of a small pea, thirty inches from the earth. Nearer to the sun than the earth would be two other very similar specks, the planets Mercury and Venus, at a distance of 125 and 250 yards respectively. Beyond the earth would come the planets Mars, Jupiter, Saturn, Uranus, and Neptune, at distances of 500, 1,680, 3,000, 6,000, and 9,500 yards respectively. There would also be a certain number of very much smaller specks, flying about amongst these planets, more particularly a number called the asteroids circling between Mars and Jupiter, and occasionally a little puff of more or less luminous vapour and dust would drift into the system from the almost limitless emptiness beyond. Such a puff is what we call a comet. *All the rest of the space about us and around us and for unfathomable distances beyond is cold, lifeless, and void.* The nearest fixed star to us, *on this minute scale,* be it remembered—the earth as a one-inch ball, and the moon a little pea—would be over 40,000 miles away. Most of the fixed stars we see would still be scores and hundreds of millions of miles away.

The science that tells of these things and how men have come to know about them is Astronomy, and to books of astronomy the reader must go to learn more about the sun and stars. The science and description of the world on which we live are called respectively Geology and Geography.

The diameter of our world is a little under 8,000 miles. Its surface is rough, the more projecting parts of the roughness are mountains, and in the hollows of its surface there is a film of water, the oceans and seas. This film of water is about five miles thick at its deepest part—that is to say, the deepest oceans have a depth of five miles. This is very little in comparison with the bulk of the world.

About this sphere is a thin covering of air, the atmosphere. As we ascend in a balloon or go up a mountain from the level of the sea-shore the air is continually less dense, until at last it becomes so thin that it cannot support life. At a height of twenty miles there is scarcely any air at all—not one hundredth part of the density of air at the surface of the sea. The highest point to which a bird can fly is about four miles up—the condor, it is said, can struggle up to that; but most small birds and insects which are carried up by aeroplanes or balloons drop off insensible at a much lower level, and the greatest height to which any mountaineer has ever climbed is under five miles. Men have flown in aeroplanes to a height of over four miles, and balloons with men in them have reached very nearly seven miles, but at the cost of considerable physical suffering. Small experimental balloons, containing not men, but recording instruments, have gone as high as twenty-two miles.

It is in the upper few hundred feet of the crust of the earth, in the sea, and in the lower levels of the air below four miles that life is found. We do not know of any life at all except in these films of air and water upon our planet. So far as we know, all the rest of space is as yet without life. Scientific men have discussed the possibility of life, or of some process of a similar kind, occurring upon such kindred bodies as the planets Venus and Mars. But they point merely to questionable possibilities.

Astronomers and geologists and those who study physics have been able to tell us something of the origin and history of the earth. They consider that, vast ages ago, the sun was a spinning, flaring mass of matter, not yet concentrated into a compact centre of heat and light, considerably larger than it is now, and spinning very much faster, and that as it whirled, a series of fragments detached themselves from it, which become the planets. Our earth is one of these planets. The flaring mass that was the material of the earth broke into two masses as it spun; a larger, the earth itself, and a smaller, which is now the dead, still moon. Astronomers give us convincing reasons for supposing that sun and earth and moon and all that system were then whirling about at a speed much greater than the speed at which they are moving to-day, and that at first our earth was a flaming thing upon which no life could live. The way in which they have reached these conclusions is by a very beautiful and interesting series of observations and reasoning, too long and elaborate for us to deal with here. But they oblige us to believe that the sun, incandescent though it is, is now much cooler than it was, and that it spins more slowly now than it did, and that it continues to cool and slow down. And they also show that the rate at which the earth spins is diminishing and continues to diminish—that is to say, that our day is growing longer and longer, and that the heat at the centre of the earth wastes slowly. There was a time when the day was not a half and not a third of what it is to-day; when a blazing hot sun, much greater than it is now, must have moved visibly—had there been an eye to mark it—from its rise to its setting across the skies. There will be a time when the day will be as long as a year is now, and the cooling sun, shorn of its beams, will hang motionless in the heavens.

It must have been in days of a much hotter sun, a far swifter day and night, high tides, great heat, tremendous storms and earthquakes, that life, of which we are a part, began upon the world. The moon also was nearer and brighter in those days and had a changing face.

II

THE RECORD OF THE ROCKS

§ 1. *The First Living Things.* § 2. *How Old Is the World?*

§ 1

We do not know how life began upon the earth.[1] Biologists, that is to say, students of life, have made guesses about these beginnings, but we will not discuss them here. Let us only note that they all agree that life began where the tides of those swift days spread and receded over the steaming beaches of mud and sand.

The atmosphere was much denser then, usually great cloud masses obscured the sun, frequent storms darkened the heavens. The land of those days, upheaved by violent volcanic forces, was a barren land, without vegetation, without soil. The almost incessant rain-storms swept down upon it, and rivers and torrents carried great loads of sediment out to sea, to become muds that hardened later into slates and shales, and sands that became sandstones. The geologists have studied the whole accumulation of these sediments as it remains today, from those of the earliest ages to the most recent. Of course the oldest deposits are the most distorted and changed and worn, and in them there is now no certain trace to be found of life at all. Probably the earliest forms of life were small and soft, leaving no evidence of their existence behind

[1] Here in this history of life we are doing our best to give only known and established facts in the broadest way, and to reduce to a minimum the speculative element that must necessarily enter into our account. The reader who is curious upon this question of life's beginning will find a very good summary of current suggestions done by Professor L. L. Woodruff in President Lull's excellent compilation *The Evolution of the Earth* (Yale University Press). Professor H. F. Osborn's *Origin and Evolution of Life* is also a very vigorous and suggestive book upon this subject, but it demands a fair knowledge of physics and chemistry. Two very stimulating essays *for the student* are A. H. Church's *Botanical Memoirs*. No. 183, Ox. Univ. Press.

them. It was only when some of these living things developed skeletons and shells of lime and such-like hard material that they left fossil vestiges after they died, and so put themselves on record for examination.

The literature of geology is very largely an account of the fossils that are found in the rocks, and of the order in which layers after layers of rocks lie one on another. The very oldest rocks must have been formed before there was any sea at all, when the earth was too hot for a sea to exist, and when the water that is now sea was an atmosphere of steam mixed with the air. Its higher levels were dense with clouds, from which a hot rain fell towards the rocks below, to be converted again into steam long before it reached their incandescence. Below this steam atmosphere the molten world-stuff solidified as the first rocks. These first rocks must have solidified as a cake over glowing liquid material beneath, much as cooling lava does. They must have appeared first as crusts and clinkers. They must have been constantly remelted and recrystallized before any thickness of them became permanently solid. The name of Fundamental Gneiss is given to a great underlying system of crystalline rocks which probably formed age by age as this hot youth of the world drew to its close. The scenery of the world in the days when the Fundamental Gneiss was formed must have been more like the interior of a furnace than anything else to be found upon earth at the present time.

After long ages the steam in the atmosphere began also to condense and fall right down to earth, pouring at last over these warm primordial rocks in rivulets of hot water and gathering in depressions as pools and lakes and the first seas. Into those seas the streams that poured over the rocks brought with them dust and particles to form a sediment, and this sediment accumulated in layers, or as geologists call them, *strata,* and formed the first Sedimentary Rocks. Those earliest sedimentary rocks sank into depressions and were covered by others; they were bent, tilted up, and torn by great volcanic disturbances and by tidal strains that swept through the rocky crust of the earth. We find these first sedimentary rocks still coming to the surface of the land here and there, either not covered by later strata or exposed after vast ages of concealment by the wearing off of the rock that covered them later—

there are great surfaces of them in Canada especially; they are cleft and bent, partially remelted, recrystallized, hardened and compressed, but recognizable for what they are. And they contain no single certain trace of life at all. They are frequently called *Azoic* (lifeless) Rocks. But since in some of these earliest sedimentary rocks a substance called graphite (black lead) occurs, and also red and black oxide of iron, and since it is asserted that these substances need the activity of living things for their production, which may or may not be the case, some geologists prefer to call these earliest sedimentary rocks *Archæozoic* (primordial life). They suppose that the first life was soft living matter that had no shells or skeletons or any such structure that could remain as a recognizable fossil after its death, and that its chemical influence caused the deposition of graphite and iron oxide. This is pure guessing, of course, and there is at least an equal probability that in the time of formation of the Azoic Rocks, life had not yet begun.

Overlying or overlapping these Azoic or Archæozoic rocks come others, manifestly also very ancient and worn, which do contain traces of life. These first remains are of the simplest description; they are the vestiges of simple plants called algæ, or marks like the tracks made by worms in the sea mud. There are also the skeletons of the microscopic creatures called Radiolaria. This second series of rocks is called the Proterozoic (beginning of life) series, and marks a long age in the world's history. Lying over and above the Proterozoic rocks is a third series, which is found to contain a considerable number and variety of traces of living things. First comes the evidence of a diversity of shellfish, crabs, and such-like crawling things, worms, seaweeds, and the like; then of a multitude of fishes and of the beginnings of land plants and land creatures. These rocks are called the Palæozoic (ancient life) rocks. They mark a vast era, during which life was slowly spreading, increasing, and developing in the seas of our world. Through long ages, through the earliest Palæozoic time, it was no more than a proliferation of such swimming and creeping things in the water. There were creatures called trilobites; they were crawling things like big sea woodlice that were probably related to the American king-crab of to-day. There were also sea scorpions, the prefects of that early world. The individuals of certain species of these were nine feet long. These were the very highest sorts of life. There were abundant different sorts of an order of shellfish called brachiopods. There were plant animals, rooted and joined together like plants, and loose weeds that waved in the waters.

It was not a display of life to excite our imaginations. There was nothing that ran or flew or even swam swiftly or skilfully. Except for the size of some of the creatures, it was not very different from, and rather less various than, the kind of life a student would gather from any summer-time ditch nowadays for miscroscopic examination. Such was the life of the shallow seas through a hundred million years or more in the early Palæozoic period. The land during that time was apparently absolutely barren. We find no trace nor hint of land life. Everything that lived in those days lived under water for most or all of its life.

Between the formation of these Lower Palæozoic rocks in which the sea scorpion and trilobite ruled, and our own time, there have intervened almost immeasurable ages, represented by layers and masses of sedimentary rocks. There are first the Upper Palæozoic rocks, and above these the geologists distinguish two great divisions. Next above the Palæozoic come the Mesozoic (middle life) rocks, a second vast system of fossil-bearing rocks, representing perhaps a hundred millions of swift years, and containing a wonderful array of fossil remains, bones of giant reptiles and the like, which we will presently describe; and above these again are the Cainozoic (recent life) rocks, a third great volume in the history of life, an unfinished volume of which the sand and mud that was carried out to sea yesterday by the rivers of the world, to bury the bones and scales and bodies and tracks that will become at last fossils of the things of to-day, constitute the last written leaf.

These markings and fossils in the rocks and the rocks themselves are our first historical documents. The history of life that men have puzzled out and are still puzzling out from them is called the Record of the Rocks. By studying this record men are slowly piecing together a story of life's beginnings, and of the beginnings of our kind, of which our ancestors a century or so ago had no suspicion. But when we call these rocks and the fossils a record and a history, it must not be supposed that there is any sign of an orderly keeping of a

Note its general resemblance, except for size, to the microscopic summer ditchwater life of to-day.

record. It is merely that whatever happens leaves some trace, if only we are intelligent enough to detect the meaning of that trace. Nor are the rocks of the world in orderly layers one above the other, convenient for men to read. They are not like the books and pages of a library. They are torn, disrupted, interrupted, flung about, defaced, like a carelessly arranged office after it has experienced in succession a bombardment, a hostile military occupation, looting, an earthquake, riots, and a fire. And so it is that for countless generations this Record of the Rocks lay unsuspected beneath the feet of men. Fossils were known to the Ionian Greeks in the sixth century B.C., they were discussed at Alexandria by Erastosthenes and others in the third century B.C., a discussion which is summarised in Strabo's *Geography* (?20-10 B.C.). They were known to the Latin poet Ovid, but he did not understand their nature. He thought they were the first rude efforts of creative power. They were noted by Arabic writers in the tenth century. Leonardo da Vinci, who lived so recently as the opening of the sixteenth century (1452-1519), was one of the first Europeans to grasp the real significance of fossils, and it has been only within the last century and a half that man has begun the serious and sustained deciphering of these long-neglected early pages of his world's history.

§ 2

Speculations about geological time vary enormously. Estimates of the age of the oldest rocks by geologists and astronomers starting from different standpoints have varied between 1,600,000,000, and 25,000,000. That the period of time has been vast, that it is to be counted by scores and possibly by hundreds of millions of years, is the utmost that can be said with certainty in the matter. It is quite open to the reader to divide every number in the appended time diagram by ten or multiply it by two; no one can gainsay him. Of the relative amount of time as between one age and another we have, however, stronger evidence; if the reader cuts down the 800,000,000 we have given here to 400,000,000, then he must reduce the 40,000,000 of the Cainozoic to 20,000,000. And be it noted that whatever the total sum may be, most geologists are in agreement that *half or more than half of the whole of geological time had passed before life had developed to the Later Palæozoic level.* The reader reading quickly through these opening chapters may be apt to think of them

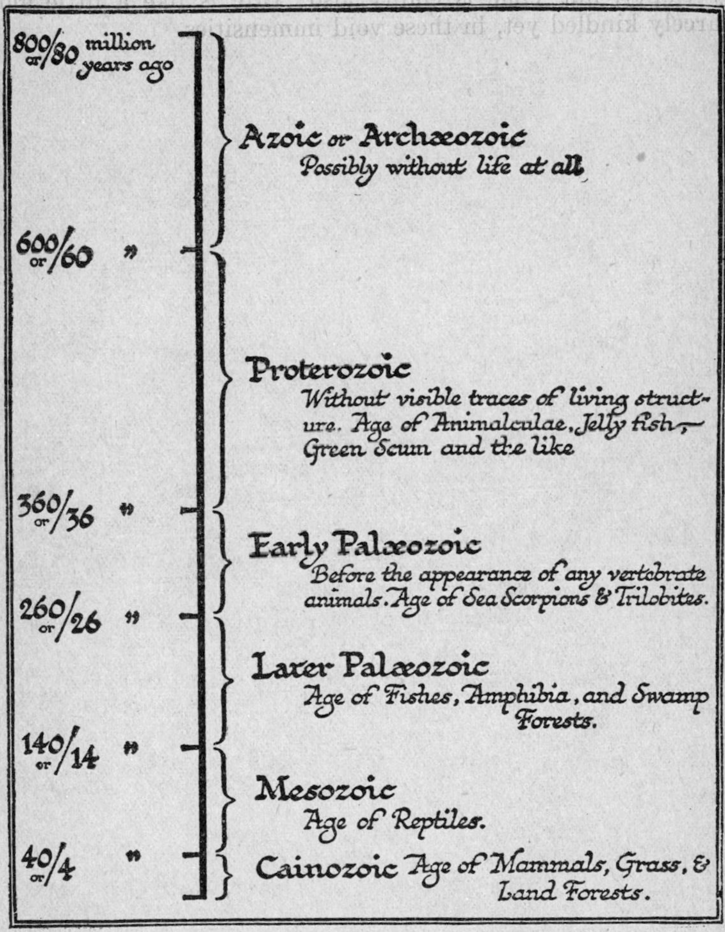

as a mere swift prelude of preparation to the apparently much longer history that follows, but in reality that subsequent history is longer only because it is more detailed and more interesting to us. It looms larger in perspective. For ages that stagger the imagination this earth spun hot and lifeless, and again for ages of equal vastness it held no life above the level of the animalculæ in a drop of ditch-water.

Not only is Space from the point of view of life and humanity empty, but Time is empty also. Life is like a little glow, scarcely kindled yet, in these void immensities.

III

NATURAL SELECTION AND THE CHANGES OF SPECIES

NOW here it will be well to put plainly certain general facts about this new thing, *life,* that was creeping in the shallow waters and intertidal muds of the early Palæozoic period, and which is perhaps confined to our planet alone in all the immensity of space.

Life differs from all things whatever that are without life in certain general aspects. There are the most wonderful differences among living things to-day, but all living things past and present agree in possessing *a certain power of growth,* all living things *take nourishment,* all living things *move about* as they feed and grow, though the movement be no more than the spread of roots through the soil, or of branches in the air. Moreover, living things reproduce; they give rise to other living things, either by growing and then dividing or by means of seeds or spores or eggs or other ways of producing young. *Reproduction* is a characteristic of life.

No living thing goes on living for ever. There seems to be *a limit of growth* for every kind of living thing. Among the very small and simple living things, such as that microscopic blob of living matter the *Amœba,* an individual may grow and then divide completely into two new individuals, which again may divide in their turn. Many other microscopic creatures live actively for a time, grow, and then become quiet and inactive, enclose themselves in an outer covering and break up wholly into a number of still smaller things, spores, which are released and scattered and again grow into the likeness of their parent. Among more complex creatures the reproduction is not usually such simple division, though division does occur even in the case of many creatures big enough to be visible to the unassisted eye. But the rule with almost all larger beings is that the individual grows up to a certain limit of size. Then, before it becomes unwieldy, its growth declines and stops. As it reaches its full size it *matures,* it begins to produce young, which are either born alive or hatched from eggs. But all of its body does not produce young. Only a special part does that. After the individual has lived and produced offspring for some time, it ages and dies. It does so by a sort of necessity. There is a practical limit to its life as well as to its growth. These things are as true of plants as they are of animals. And they are not true of things that do not live. Non-living things, such as crystals, grow, but they have no set limits of growth or size, they *do not move of their own accord* and there is *no stir within them.* Crystals once formed may last unchanged for millions of years. There is *no reproduction* for any non-living thing.

This growth and dying and reproduction of living things leads to some very wonderful consequences. The young which a living thing produces are either directly, or after some intermediate stages and changes (such as the changes of a caterpillar and butterfly), like the parent living thing. But they are never exactly like it or like each other. There is always a slight difference, which we speak of as *individuality.* A thousand butterflies this year may produce two or three thousand next year; these latter will look to us almost exactly like their predecessors, but each one will have just that slight difference. It is hard for us to see individuality in butterflies because we do not observe them very closely, but it is easy for us to see it in men. All the men and women in the world now are descended from the men and women of A.D. 1800, but not one of us now is exactly the same as one of that vanished generation. And what is true of men and butterflies is true of every sort of living thing, of plants as of animals. Every species changes all its individualities in each generation. That is true of all the minute creatures that swarmed and reproduced and died in the Archæozoic and Proterozoic seas, as it is of men to-day.

Every species of living things is continually dying and being born again, as a multitude of fresh individuals.

Consider, then, what must happen to a new-born generation of living things of any species. Some of the individuals will be stronger or sturdier or better suited to succeed in life in some way than the rest, many individuals will be weaker or less suited. In particular single cases any sort of luck or accident may occur, but *on the whole* the better equipped individuals will live and grow up and reproduce themselves and the weaker will *as a rule* go under. The latter will be less able to get food, to fight their enemies and pull through. So that in each generation there is as it were a picking over of a species, a picking out of most of the weak or unsuitable and a preference for the strong and suitable. This process is called *Natural Selection* or the *Survival of the Fittest.*[1]

It follows, therefore, from the fact that living things grow and breed and die, that every species, so long as the conditions under which it lives remain the same, becomes more and more perfectly fitted to those conditions in every generation.

But now suppose those conditions change, then the sort of individual that used to succeed may now fail to succeed and a sort of individual that could not get on at all under the old conditions may now find its opportunity. These species will change, therefore, generation by generation; the old sort of individual that used to prosper and dominate will fail and die out and the new sort of individual will become the rule,—until the general character of the species changes.

Suppose, for example, there is some little furry whitey-brown animal living in a bitterly cold land which is usually under snow. Such individuals as have the thickest, whitest fur will be least hurt by the cold, less seen by their enemies, and less conspicuous as they seek their prey. The fur of this species will thicken and its whiteness increase with every generation, until there is no advantage in carrying any more fur.

Imagine now a change of climate that brings warmth into the land, sweeps away the snows, makes white creatures glaringly visible during the greater part of the year and thick fur an encumbrance. Then every individual with a touch of brown in its colouring and a thinner fur will find itself at an advantage, and very white and heavy fur will be a handicap. There will be a weeding out of the white in favour of the brown in each generation. If this change of climate come about too quickly, it may of course exterminate the species altogether; but if it come about gradually, the species, although it may have a hard time, may yet be able to change

[1] It might be called with more exactness the *Survival of the Fitter.*

Diagram of Life in the Later Palæozoic Age.

Life is creeping out of the water. An insect like a dragon-fly is shown. There were amphibia like gigantic newts and salamanders, and even primitive reptiles in these swamps.

itself and adapt itself generation by generation. This change and adaptation is called the *Modification of Species.*

Perhaps this change of climate does not occur all over the lands inhabited by the species; maybe it occurs only on one side of some great arm of the sea or some great mountain range or such-like divide, and not on the other. A warm ocean current like the Gulf Stream may be deflected, and flow so as to warm one side of the barrier, leaving the other still cold. Then on the cold side this species will still be going on to its utmost possible furriness and whiteness and on the other side it will be modifying towards brownness and a thinner coat. At the same time there will probably be other changes going on; a difference in the paws perhaps, because one half of the species will be frequently scratching through snow for its food, while the other will be scampering over brown earth. Probably also the difference of climate will mean differences in the sort of food available, and that may produce differences in the teeth and the digestive organs. And there may be changes in the sweat and oil glands of the skin due to the changes in the fur, and these will affect the excretory organs and all the internal chemistry of the body. And so through all the structure of the creature. A time will come when the two separated varieties of this formerly single species will become so unlike each other as to be recognizably different species. Such a splitting up of a species in the course of generations into two or more species is called the *Differentiation of Species.*

And it should be clear to the reader that given these elemental facts of life, given growth and death and reproduction with individual variation in a world that changes, life *must* change in this way, modification and differentiation *must* occur, old species *must* disappear, and new ones appear. We have chosen for our instance here a familiar sort of animal, but what is true of furry beasts in snow and ice is true of all life, and equally true of the soft jellies and simple beginnings that flowed and crawled for hundreds of millions of years between the tidal levels and in the shallow, warm waters of the Proterozoic seas.

The early life of the early world, when the blazing sun rose and set in only a quarter of the time it now takes, when the warm seas poured in great tides over the sandy and muddy shores of the rocky lands and the air was full of clouds and steam, must have been modified and varied and species must have developed at a great pace. Life was probably as swift and short as the days and years; the generations, which natural selection picked over, followed one another in rapid succession.

Natural selection is a slower progress with man than with any other creature. It takes twenty years or more before an ordinary human being in western Europe grows up and reproduces. In the case of most animals the new generation is on trial in a year or less. With such simple and lowly beings, however, as first appeared in the primordial seas, growth and reproduction was probably a matter of a few brief hours or even of a few brief minutes. Modification and differentiation of species must accordingly have been extremely rapid, and life had already developed a great variety of widely contrasted forms before it began to leave traces in the rocks. The Record of the Rocks does not begin, therefore, with any group of closely related forms from which all subsequent and existing creatures are descended. It begins in the midst of the game, with nearly every main division of the animal kingdom already represented. Plants are already plants, and animals animals. The curtain rises on a drama in the sea that has already begun, and has been going on for some time. The brachiopods are discovered already in their shells, accepting and consuming much the same sort of food that oysters and mussels do now; the great water scorpions crawl among the seaweeds, the trilobites roll up into balls and unroll and scuttle away. In that ancient mud and among those early weeds there was probably as rich and abundant and active a life of infusoria and the like as one finds in a drop of ditch-water to-day. In the ocean waters, too, down to the utmost downward limit to which light could filter, then as now, there was an abundance of minute and translucent, and in many cases phosphorescent, beings.

But though the ocean and intertidal waters already swarmed with life, the land above the high-tide line was still, so far as we can guess, a stony wilderness without a trace of life.

IV

THE INVASION OF THE DRY LAND BY LIFE

§ 1. *Life and Water.* § 2. *The Earliest Animals.*

§ 1

WHEREVER the shore line ran there was life, and that life went on in and by and with water as its home, its medium, and its fundamental necessity.

The first jelly-like beginnings of life must have perished whenever they got out of the water, as jelly-fish dry up and perish on our beaches to-day. Drying up was the fatal thing for life in those days, against which at first it had no protection. But in a world of rain-pools and shallow seas and tides, any variation that enabled a living thing to hold out and keep its moisture during hours of low tide or drought met with every encouragement in the circumstances of the time. There must have been a constant risk of stranding. And, on the other hand, life had to keep rather near the shore and beaches in the shallows because it had need of air (dissolved of course in the water) and light.

No creature can breathe, no creature can digest its food, without water. We talk of breathing air, but what all living things really do is to breathe oxygen dissolved in water. The air we ourselves breathe must first be dissolved in the moisture in our lungs; and all our food must be liquefied before it can be assimilated. Water-living creatures which are always under water, wave the freely exposed gills by which they breathe in that water, and extract the air dissolved in it. But a creature that is to be exposed for any time out of the water must have its body and its breathing apparatus protected from drying up. Before the seaweeds could creep up out of the Early Palæozoic seas into the intertidal line of the beach, they had to develop a tougher outer skin to hold their moisture.

Before the ancestor of the sea scorpion could survive being left by the tide it had to develop its casing and armour. The trilobites probably developed their tough covering and rolled up into balls, far less as a protection against each other and any other enemies they may have possessed, than as a precaution against drying. And when presently, as we ascend the Palæozoic rocks, the fish appear, first of all the back-boned or vertebrated animals, it is evident that a number of them are already adapted by the protection of their gills with gill covers and by a sort of primitive lung swimming-bladder, to face the same risk of temporary stranding.

Now the weeds and plants that were adapting themselves to intertidal conditions were also bringing themselves into a region of brighter light, and light is very necessary and precious to all plants. Any development of structure that would stiffen them and hold them up to the light, so that instead of crumping and flopping when the waters receded, they would stand up outspread, was a great advantage. And so we find them developing fibre and support, and the beginning of *woody fibre* in them. The early plants reproduced by soft spores, or half-animal "gametes," that were released in water, were distributed by water and could only germinate under water. The early plants were tied, and most lowly plants today are tied, by the conditions of their life cycle, to water. But here again there was a great advantage to be got by the development of some protection of the spores from drought that would enable reproduction to occur without submergence. So soon as a species could do that, it could live and reproduce and spread above the high-water mark, bathed in light and out of reach of the beating and distress of the waves. The main classificatory divisions of the larger plants mark stages in the release of plant life from the necessity of submergence by the development of woody support and of a method of reproduction that is more and more defiant of drying up. The lower plants are still the prisoner attendants of water. The lower mosses must live in damp, and even the development of the spore of the ferns demands at certain stages extreme wetness. The highest plants have carried freedom from water so far that they can live and reproduce if only there is some moisture in the soil below them. They have solved their problem of living out of water altogether.

The essentials of that problem were worked out through the vast æons of the Proterozoic Age and the early Palæozoic Age by nature's method of experiment and trial. Then slowly, but in great abundance, a variety of new plants began to swarm away from the sea and over the lower lands, still keeping to swamp and lagoon and water-course as they spread.

§ 2

And after the plants came the animal life.

There is no sort of land animal in the world, as there is no sort of land plant, whose structure is not primarily that of a water-inhabiting being which has been adapted through the modification and differentiation of species to life out of the water. This adaptation is attained in various ways. In the case of the land scorpion the gill-plates of the primitive sea scorpion are sunken into the body so as to make the lung-books secure from rapid evaporation. The gills of crustaceans, such as the crabs which run about in the air, are protected by the gill-cover extensions of the back shell or carapace. The ancestors of the insects developed a system of air pouches and air tubes, the tracheal tubes, which carry the air all over the body before it is dissolved. In the case of the vertebrated land animals, the gills of the ancestral fish were first supplemented and then replaced by a bag-like growth from the throat, the primitive lung swimming-bladder. To this day there survive certain mudfish which enable us to understand very clearly the method by which the vertebrated land animals worked their way out of the water. These creatures (*e.g.* the African lung fish) are found in tropical regions in which there is a rainy full season and a dry season, during which the rivers become mere ditches of baked mud. During the rainy season these fish swim about and breathe by gills like any other fish. As the waters of the river evaporate, these fish bury themselves in the mud, their gills go out of action, and the creature keeps itself alive until the waters return by swallowing air, which passes into its swimming-bladder. The Australian lung fish, when it is caught by the drying up of the river in stagnant pools, and the water has become deaerated and foul, rises to the surface and gulps air. A newt in a pond does exactly the same thing. These creatures still remain at the transition stage, the stage at which the ancestors of the higher vertebrated animals were released from their restriction to an under-water life.

The amphibia (frogs, newts, tritons, etc.) still show in their life history all the stages in the process of this liberation. They are still dependent on water for their reproduction; their eggs must be laid in sunlit water, and there they must develop. The young tadpole has branching external gills that wave in the water; then a gill cover grows back over them and forms a gill chamber. Then as the creature's legs appear and its tail is absorbed, it begins to use its lungs, and its gills dwindle and vanish. The adult frog can live all the rest of its days in the air, but it can be drowned if it is kept steadfastly below water. When we come to the reptile, however, we find an egg which is protected from evaporation by a tough egg case, and this egg produces young which breathe by lungs from the very moment of hatching. The reptile is on all fours with the seeding plant in its freedom from the necessity to pass any stage of its life cycle in water.

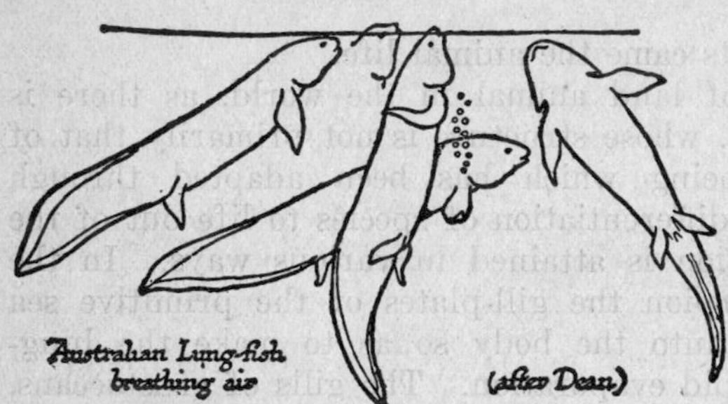
Australian Lung-fish breathing air (after Dean)

The later Palæozoic Rocks of the northern hemisphere give us the materials for a series of pictures of this slow spreading of life over the land. Geographically, all round the northern half of the world it was an age of lagoons and shallow seas very favourable to this invasion. The new plants, now that they had acquired the power to live this new aerial life, developed with an extraordinary richness and variety.

There were as yet no true flowering plants,[1] no grasses nor trees that shed their leaves in winter;[2] the first "flora" consisted of great tree ferns, gigantic equisetums, cycad ferns, and kindred vegetation. Many of these plants took the form of huge-stemmed trees, of which great multitudes of trunks survive fossilized to this day. Some of these trees were over

[1] Phanerogams. [2] Deciduous trees.

a hundred feet high, of orders and classes now vanished from the world. They stood with their stems in the water, in which no doubt there was a thick tangle of soft mosses and green

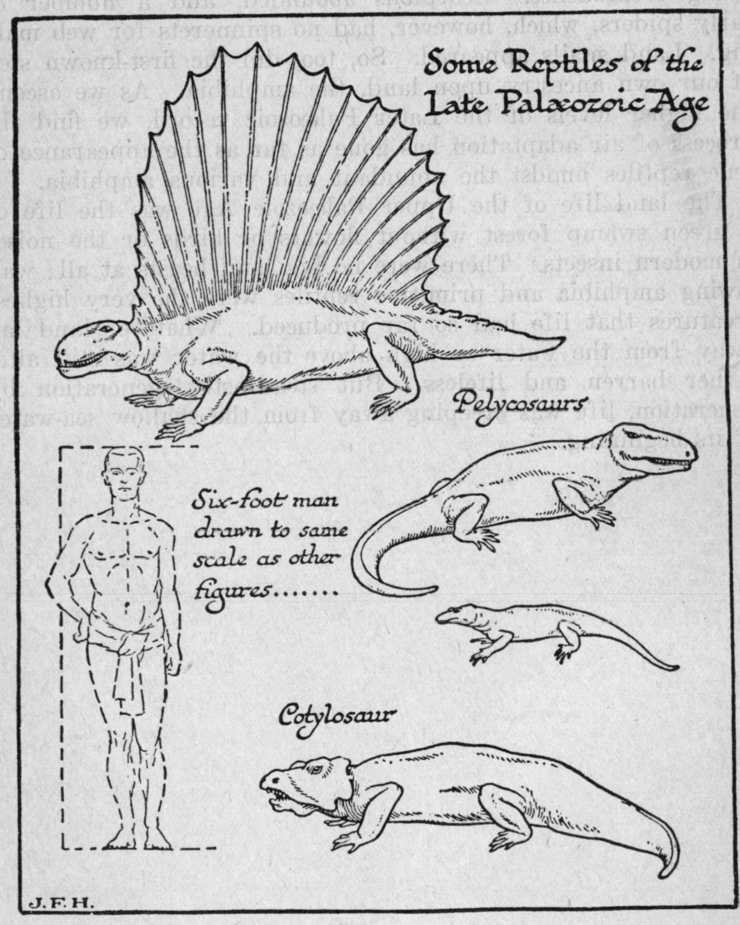

slime and fungoid growths that left few plain vestiges behind them. The abundant remains of these first swamp forests constitute the main coal measures of the world to-day.

Amidst this luxuriant primitive vegetation crawled and glided and flew the first insects. They were rigid-winged, four-winged creatures, often very big, some of them having wings measuring a foot in length. There were numerous dragon flies—one found in the Belgian coal-measures had a wing span of twenty-nine inches! There were also a great variety of flying cockroaches. Scorpions abounded, and a number of early spiders, which, however, had no spinnerets for web making. Land snails appeared. So, too, did the first-known step of our own ancestry upon land, the amphibia. As we ascend the higher levels of the Later Palæozoic record, we find the process of air adaptation has gone as far as the appearance of true reptiles amidst the abundant and various amphibia.

The land life of the Upper Palæozoic Age was the life of a green swamp forest without flowers or birds or the noises of modern insects. There were no big land beasts at all; wallowing amphibia and primitive reptiles were the very highest creatures that life had so far produced. Whatever land lay away from the water or high above the water was still altogether barren and lifeless. But steadfastly, generation by generation, life was creeping away from the shallow sea-water of its beginning.

V

THE AGE OF REPTILES

§ 1. The Age of Lowland Life. § 2. Flying Dragons. § 3. The First Birds. § 4. An age of Hardship and Death. § 5. The first appearance of Fur and Feathers.

§ 1

WE know that for hundreds of thousands of years the wetness and warmth, the shallow lagoon conditions that made possible the vast accumulations of vegetable matter which, compressed and mummified,[1] are now coal, prevailed over most of the world. There were some cold intervals, it is true; but they did not last long enough to destroy the growths. Then that long age of luxuriant low-grade vegetation drew to its end, and for a time life on the earth seems to have undergone a period of world-wide bleakness.

We cannot discuss fully here the changes that have gone on and are going on in the climate of the earth. A great variety of causes, astronomical movements, changes in the sun and changes upon and within the earth, combine to produce a ceaseless fluctuation of the conditions under which life exists. As these conditions change, life, too, must change or perish.

When the story resumes again after this arrest at the end of the Palæozoic period we find life entering upon a fresh phase of richness and expansion. Vegetation has made great advances in the art of living out of water. While the Palæozoic plants of the coal measures probably grew with swamp water flowing over their roots, the Mesozoic flora from its very outset included palm-like cycads and low-grown conifers that were distinctly land plants growing on soil above the water level.

[1] Dr. Marie Stopes, *Monograph on the Constitution of Coal.*

The lower levels of the Mesozoic land were no doubt covered by great fern brakes and shrubby bush and a kind of jungle growth of trees. But there existed as yet no grass, no small flowering plants, no turf nor greensward. Probably the Mesozoic was not an age of very brightly coloured vegetation. It must have had a flora green in the wet season and brown and purple in the dry. There were no gay flowers, no bright autumn tints before the fall of the leaf, because there was as yet no fall of the leaf. And beyond the lower levels the world was still barren, still unclothed, still exposed without any mitigation to the wear and tear of the wind and rain.

When one speaks of conifers in the Mesozoic the reader must not think of the pines and firs that clothe the high mountain slopes of our time. He must think of low-growing evergreens. The mountains were still as bare and lifeless as ever. The only colour effects among the mountains were the colour effects of naked rock, such colours as make the landscape of Colorado so marvellous to-day.

Amidst this spreading vegetation of the lower plains the reptiles were increasing mightily in multitude and variety. They were now in many cases absolutely land animals. There are numerous anatomical points of distinction between a reptile and an amphibian; they held good between such reptiles and amphibians as prevailed in the carboniferous time of the Upper Palæozoic; but the fundamental difference between reptiles and amphibia which matters in this history is that the amphibian must go back to the water to lay its eggs, and that in the early stages of its life it must live in and under water. The reptile, on the other hand, has cut out all the tadpole stages from its life cycle, or, to be more exact, its tadpole stages are got through before the young leave the egg case. The reptile has come out of the water altogether. Some had gone back to it again, just as the hippopotamus and the otter among mammals have gone back, but that is a further extension of the story to which we cannot give much attention in this *Outline*.

In the Palæozoic period, as we have said, life had not spread beyond the swampy river valleys and the borders of sea lagoons and the like; but in the Mesozoic, life was growing ever more accustomed to the thinner medium of the air, was sweeping boldly up over the plains and towards the hill-sides. It is well for the student of human history and the human future to

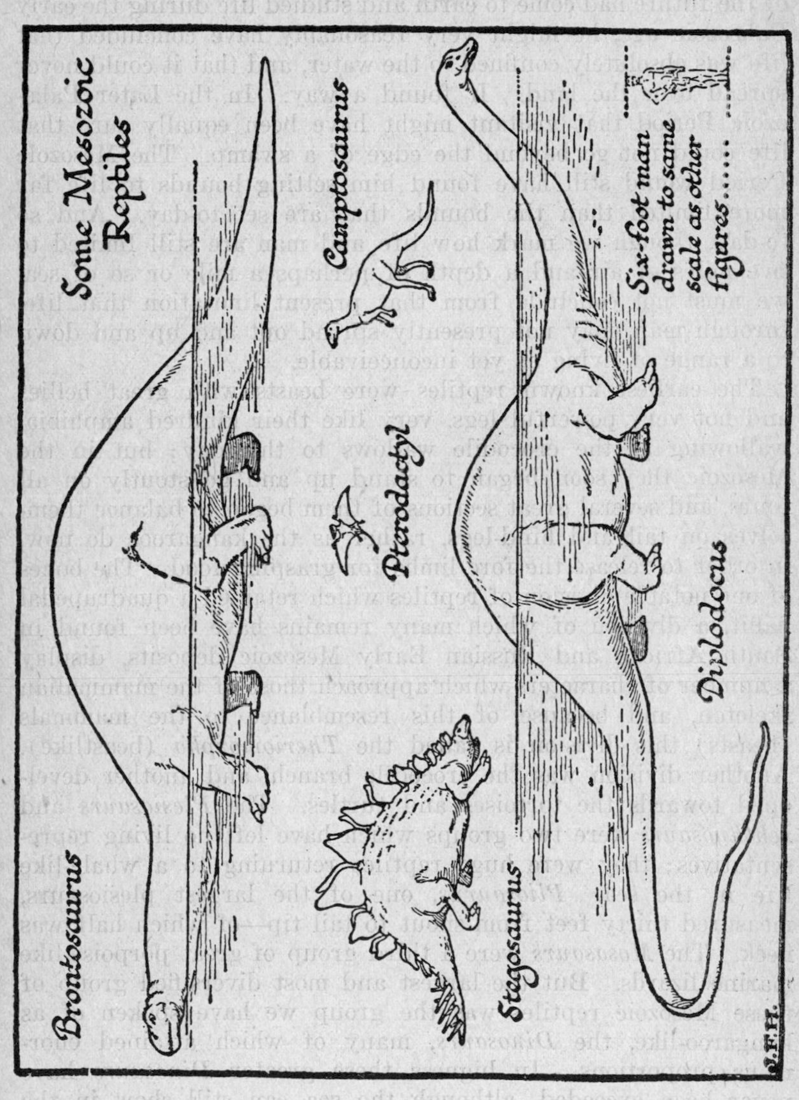
Some Mesozoic Reptiles
Camptosaurus
Pterodactyl
Brontosaurus
Stegosaurus
Diplodocus
Six-foot man drawn to same scale as other figures.....
J.F.H.

note that. If a disembodied intelligence with no knowledge of the future had come to earth and studied life during the early Palæozoic age, he might very reasonably have concluded that life was absolutely confined to the water, and that it could never spread over the land. It found a way. In the Later Palæozoic Period that visitant might have been equally sure that life could not go beyond the edge of a swamp. The Mesozoic Period would still have found him setting bounds to life far more limited than the bounds that are set to-day. And so to-day, though we mark how life and man are still limited to five miles of air and a depth of perhaps a mile or so of sea, we must not conclude from that present limitation that life, through man, may not presently spread out and up and down to a range of living as yet inconceivable.

The earliest known reptiles were beasts with great bellies and not very powerful legs, very like their kindred amphibia, wallowing as the crocodile wallows to this day; but in the Mesozoic they soon began to stand up and go stoutly on all fours, and several great sections of them began to balance themselves on tail and hind-legs, rather as the kangaroos do now, in order to release the fore limbs for grasping food. The bones of one notable division of reptiles which retained a quadrupedal habit, a division of which many remains have been found in South African and Russian Early Mesozoic deposits, display a number of characters which approach those of the mammalian skeleton, and because of this resemblance to the mammals (beasts) this division is called the *Theriomorpha* (beastlike). Another division was the crocodile branch, and another developed towards the tortoises and turtles. The *Plesiosaurs* and *Ichthyosaurs* were two groups which have left no living representatives; they were huge reptiles returning to a whale-like life in the sea. *Pliosaurus,* one of the largest plesiosaurs, measured thirty feet from snout to tail tip—of which half was neck. The *Mosasaurs* were a third group of great porpoise-like marine lizards. But the largest and most diversified group of these Mesozoic reptiles was the group we have spoken of as kangaroo-like, the *Dinosaurs,* many of which attained enormous proportions. In bigness these greater *Dinosaurs* have never been exceeded, although the sea can still show in the whales creatures as great. Some of these, and the largest among them, were herbivorous animals; they browsed on the rushy vegetation and among the ferns and bushes, or they stood up and grasped trees with their fore-legs while they devoured the foliage. Among the browsers, for example, were the *Diplodocus carnegii,* which measured eighty-four feet in length, and the *Atlantosaurus.* The *Gigantosaurus,* disinterred by a German expedition in 1912 from rocks in East Africa, was still more colossal. It measured well over a hundred feet! These greater monsters had legs, and they are usually figured as standing up on them; but it is very doubtful if they could have supported their weight in this way, out of water. Buoyed up by water or mud, they may have got along. Another noteworthy type we have figured is the *Triceratops.* There were also a number of great flesh-eaters who preyed upon these herbivores. Of these, *Tyrannosaurus* seems almost the last word in "frightfulness" among living things. Some species of this genus measured forty feet from snout to tail. Apparently it carried this vast body kangaroo fashion on its tail and hindlegs. Probably it reared itself up. Some authorities even suppose that it leapt through the air. If so, it possessed muscles of a quite miraculous quality. A leaping elephant would be a far less astounding idea. Much more probably it waded half submerged in pursuit of the herbivorous river saurians.

§ 2

One special development of the dinosaurian type of reptile was a light, hopping, climbing group of creatures which developed a bat-like web between the fifth finger and the side of the body, which was used in gliding from tree to tree after the fashion of the flying squirrels. These bat-lizards were the *Pterodactyls.* They are often described as *flying* reptiles, and pictures are drawn of Mesozoic scenery in which they are seen soaring and swooping about. But their breastbone has no keel such as the breastbone of a bird has for the attachment of muscles strong enough for long sustained flying. They must have flitted about like bats. They must have had a grotesque resemblance to heraldic dragons, and they played the part of bat-like birds in the Mesozoic jungles. But bird-like though they were, they were not birds nor the ancestors of birds. The structure of their wings was altogether different from that of birds. The structure of their wings was that of a hand with one long finger and a web; the wing of a bird is like an arm with feathers projecting from its hind edge. And these Pterodactyls had no feathers.

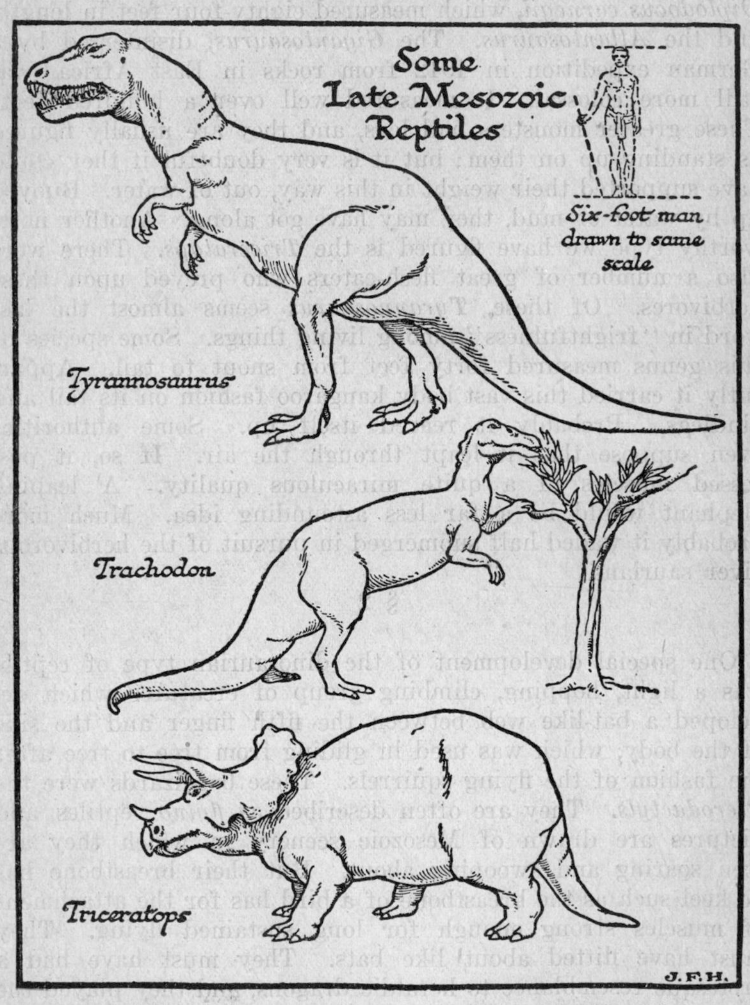

§ 3

Far less prevalent at this time were certain other truly bird-like creatures, of which the earlier sorts also hopped and clambered and the later sorts skimmed and flew. These were at first—by all the standards of classification—Reptiles. They developed into true birds as they developed wings and as their

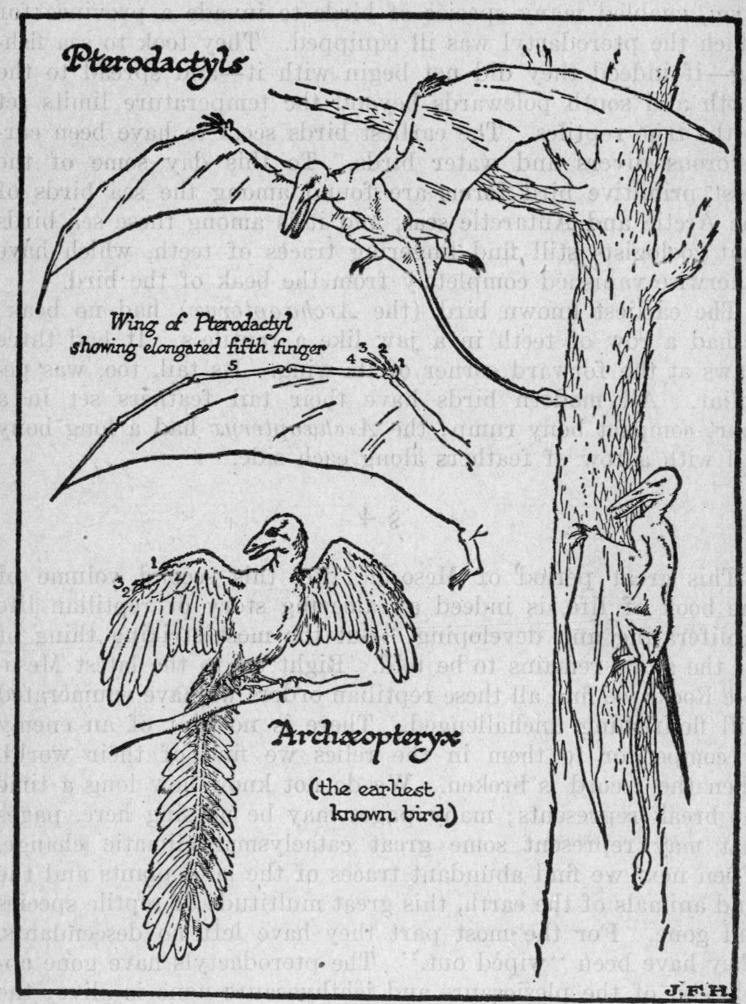

reptilian scales became long and complicated, fronds rather than scales, and so at last, by much spreading and splitting, feathers. Feathers are the distinctive covering of birds, and they give a power of resisting heat and cold far greater than that of any other integumentary covering except perhaps the thickest fur. At a very early stage this novel covering of feathers, this new heat-proof contrivance that life had chanced upon, enabled many species of birds to invade a province for which the pterodactyl was ill equipped. They took to sea fishing—if indeed they did not begin with it—and spread to the north and south polewards beyond the temperature limits set to the true reptiles. The earliest birds seem to have been carnivorous divers and water birds. To this day some of the most primitive bird forms are found among the sea birds of the Arctic and Antarctic seas, and it is among these sea birds that zoologists still find lingering traces of teeth, which have otherwise vanished completely from the beak of the bird.

The earliest known bird (the *Archæopteryx*) had no beak; it had a row of teeth in a jaw like a reptile's. It had three claws at the forward corner of its wing. Its tail, too, was peculiar. All modern birds have their tail feathers set in a short compact bony rump; the *Archæopteryx* had a long bony tail with a row of feathers along each side.

§ 4

This great period of Mesozoic life, this second volume of the book of life, is indeed an amazing story of reptilian life proliferating and developing. But the most striking thing of all the story remains to be told. Right up to the latest Mesozoic Rocks we find all these reptilian orders we have enumerated still flourishing unchallenged. There is no hint of an enemy or competitor to them in the relics we find of their world. Then the record is broken. We do not know how long a time the break represents; many pages may be missing here, pages that may represent some great cataclysmal climatic change. When next we find abundant traces of the land plants and the land animals of the earth, this great multitude of reptile species had gone. For the most part they have left no descendants. They have been "wiped out." The pterodactyls have gone absolutely, of the plesiosaurs and ichthyosaurs none is alive; the mosasaurs have gone; of the lizards a few remain, the monitors of the Dutch East Indies are the largest; all the multitude and diversity of the dinosaurs have vanished. Only the crocodiles and the turtles and tortoises carry on in any quantity into

Cainozoic times. The place of all these types in the picture that the Cainozoic fossils presently unfold to us is taken by other animals not closely related to the Mesozoic reptiles and certainly not descended from any of their ruling types. A new kind of life is in possession of the world.

This apparently abrupt ending up of the reptiles is, beyond all question, the most striking revolution in the whole history of the earth before the coming of mankind. It is probably connected with the close of a vast period of equable warm conditions and the onset of a new austerer age, in which the winters were bitterer and the summers brief but hot. The Mesozoic life, animal and vegetable alike, was adapted to warm conditions and capable of little resistance to cold. The new life, on the other hand, was before all things capable of resisting great changes of temperature.

Whatever it was that led to the extinction of the Mesozoic reptiles, it was probably some very far-reaching change indeed, for the life of the seas did at the same time undergo a similar catastrophic alteration. The crescendo and ending of the Reptiles on land was paralleled by the crescendo and ending of the Ammonites, a division of creatures like squids with coiled shells which swarmed in those ancient seas. All through the rocky record of this Mesozoic period there is a vast multitude and variety of these coiled shells; there are hundreds of species, and towards the end of the Mesozoic period they increased in diversity and produced exaggerated types. When the record resumes these, too, have gone. So far as the reptiles are concerned, people may perhaps be inclined to argue that they were exterminated because the Mammals that replaced them, competed with them, and were more fitted to survive; but nothing of the sort can be true of the Ammonites, because to this day their place has not been taken. Simply they are gone. Unknown conditions made it possible for them to live in the Mesozoic seas, and then some unknown change made life impossible for them. No genus of Ammonite survives to-day of all that vast variety, but there still exists one isolated genus very closely related to the Ammonites, the Pearly Nautilus. It is found, it is to be noted, in the warm waters of the Indian and Pacific oceans.

And as for the Mammals competing with and ousting the less fit reptiles, a struggle of which people talk at times, there is not a scrap of evidence of any such direct competition. To judge by the Record of the Rocks as we know it to-day, there is much more reason for believing that first the reptiles in some inexplicable way perished, and then that later on, after a very hard time for all life upon the earth, the mammals, as conditions became more genial again, developed and spread to fill the vacant world.

§ 5

Were there mammals in the Mesozoic period?

This is a question not yet to be answered precisely. Patiently and steadily the geologists gather fresh evidence and reason out completer conclusions. At any time some new deposit may reveal fossils that will illuminate this question. Certainly either mammals, or the ancestors of the mammals, must have lived throughout the Mesozoic period. In the very opening chapter of the Mesozoic volume of the Record there were those Theriomorphous Reptiles to which we have already alluded, and in the later Mesozoic a number of small jawbones are found, entirely mammalian in character. But there is not a scrap, not a bone, to suggest that there lived any Mesozoic Mammal which could look a dinosaur in the face. The Mesozoic mammals or mammal-like reptiles—for we do not know clearly which they were—seem to have been all obscure little beasts of the size of mice and rats, more like a downtrodden order of reptiles than a distinct class; probably they still laid eggs and were developing only slowly their distinctive covering of hair. They lived away from big waters, and perhaps in the desolate uplands, as marmots do now; probably they lived there beyond the pursuit of the carnivorous dinosaurs. Some perhaps went on all fours, some chiefly went on their hind-legs and clambered with their fore limbs. They became fossils only so occasionally that chance has not yet revealed a single complete skeleton in the whole vast record of the Mesozoic rocks by which to check these guesses.

These little Theriomorphs, these ancestral mammals, developed hair. Hairs, like feathers, are long and elaborately specialized scales. Hair is perhaps the clue to the salvation of the early mammals. Leading lives upon the margin of existence, away from the marshes and the warmth, they developed an outer covering only second in its warmth-holding (or heat-resisting) powers to the down and feathers of the Arctic sea-birds. And so they held out through the age of hardship be-

tween the Mesozoic and Cainozoic ages, to which most of the true reptiles succumbed.

All the main characteristics of this flora and sea and land fauna that came to an end with the end of the Mesozoic age were such as were adapted to an equable climate and to shallow and swampy regions. But in the case of their Cainozoic successors, both hair and feathers gave *a power of resistance to variable temperatures* such as no reptile possessed, and with it they gave a range far greater than any animal had hitherto attained.

The range of life of the Lower Palæozoic Period was confined to warm water.

The range of life of the Upper Palæozoic Period was confined to warm water or to warm swamps and wet ground.

The range of life of the Mesozoic Period as we know it was confined to water and fairly low-lying valley regions under equable conditions.

Meanwhile in each of these periods there were types involuntarily extending the range of life beyond the limits prevailing in that period; and when ages of extreme conditions prevailed, it was these marginal types which survived to inherit the depopulated world.

That perhaps is the most general statement we can make about the story of the geological record; it is a story of widening range. Classes, genera, and species of animals appear and disappear, but the range widens. It widens always. Life has never had so great a range as it has to-day. Life to-day, in the form of man, goes higher in the air than it has ever done before; man's geographical range is from pole to pole, he goes under the water in submarines, he sounds the cold, lifeless darkness of the deepest seas, he burrows into virgin levels of the rocks, and in thought and knowledge he pierces to the centre of the earth and reaches out to the uttermost star. Yet in all the relics of the Mesozoic time we find no certain memorials of his ancestry. His ancestors, like the ancestors of all the kindred mammals, must have been creatures so rare, so obscure, and so remote that they have left scarcely a trace amidst the abundant vestiges of the monsters that wallowed rejoicing in the steamy air and lush vegetation of the Mesozoic lagoons, or crawled or hopped or fluttered over the great river plains of that time.

VI

THE AGE OF MAMMALS

§ 1. A New Age of Life. § 2. Tradition Comes into the World. § 3. An Age of Brain Growth. § 4. The World Grows Hard Again.

§ 1

THE third great division of the geological record, the Cainozoic, opens with a world already physically very like the world we live in to-day. Probably the day was at first still perceptibly shorter, but the scenery had become very modern in its character. Climate was, of course, undergoing, age by age, its incessant and irregular variations; lands that are temperate to-day have passed, since the Cainozoic age began, through phases of great warmth, intense cold, and extreme dryness; but the landscape, if it altered, altered to nothing that cannot still be paralleled to-day in some part of the world or other. In the place of the cycads, sequoias, and strange conifers of the Mesozoic, the plant names that now appear in the lists of fossils include birch, beech, holly, tulip trees, ivy, sweet gum, bread-fruit trees. Flowers had developed concurrently with bees and butterflies. Palms were now very important. Such plants had already been in evidence in the later levels of the (American Cretaceous) Mesozoic, but now they dominated the scene altogether. Grass was becoming a great fact in the world. Certain grasses, too, had appeared in the later Mesozoic, but only with the Cainozoic period came grass plains and turf spreading wide over a world that was once barren stone.

The period opened with a long phase of considerable warmth; then the world cooled. And in the opening of this third part of the record, this Cainozoïc period, a gigantic crumpling of the earth's crust and an upheaval of mountain ranges was in progress. The Alps, the Andes, the Himalayas, are all Cainozoic mountain ranges; the background of an early Cainozoic scene to be typical should display an active volcano or so. It must have been an age of great earthquakes.

Geologists make certain main divisions of the Cainozoic period, and it will be convenient to name them here and to indicate their climate. First comes the *Eocene* (dawn of recent life), an age of exceptional warmth in the world's history, subdivided into an older and newer Eocene; then the *Oligocene* (but little of recent life), in which the climate was still equable. The *Miocene* (with living species still in a minority) was the great age of mountain building, and the general temperature was falling. In the *Pliocene* (more living than extinct species), climate was very much as its present phase; but with the *Pleistocene* (a great majority of living species) there set in a long period of extreme conditions—it was the Great Ice Age. Glaciers spread from the poles towards the equator, until England to the Thames was covered in ice. Thereafter to our own time came a period of partial recovery. We may be moving now towards a warmer phase. Half a million years hence this may be a much sunnier and pleasanter world to live in than it is to-day.

§ 2

In the forests and following the grass over the Eocene plains there appeared for the first time a variety and abundance of mammals. Before we proceed to any description of these mammals, it may be well to note in general terms what a mammal is.

From the appearance of the vertebrated animals in the Lower Palæozoic Age, when the fish first swarmed out into the sea, there has been a steady progressive development of vertebrated creatures. A fish is a vertebrated animal that breathes by gills and can live only in water. An amphibian may be described as a fish that has added to its gill-breathing the power of breathing air with its swimming-bladder in adult life, and that has also developed limbs with five toes to them in place of the fins of a fish. A tadpole is for a time a fish, it becomes a land creature as it develops. A reptile is a further stage in this detachment from water; it is an amphibian that is no longer amphibious; it passes through its tadpole stage—its fish stage that is—in an egg. From the beginning it must breathe in air; it can never breathe under water as a tadpole can do.

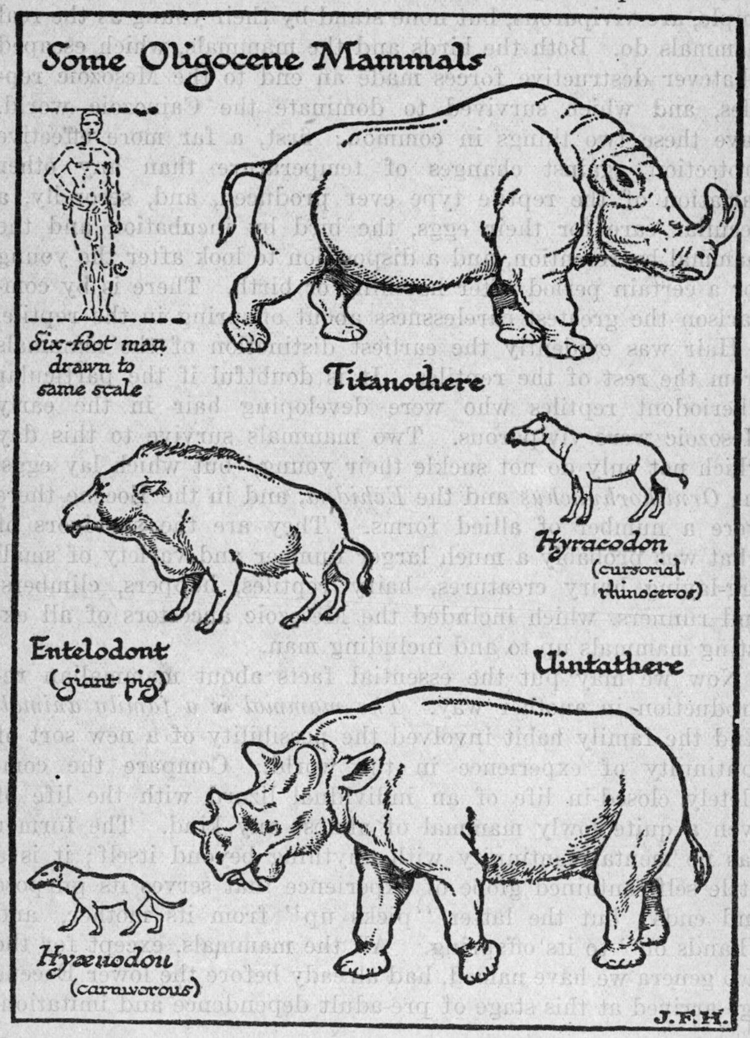

Now a modern mammal is really a sort of reptile that has developed a peculiarly effective protective covering, hair; and that also retains its eggs in the body until they hatch so that it brings forth living young (viviparous), and even after birth it cares for them and feeds them by its mammæ for a longer or shorter period. Some reptiles, some vipers for example, are viviparous, but none stand by their young as the real mammals do. Both the birds and the mammals, which escaped whatever destructive forces made an end to the Mesozoic reptiles, and which survived to dominate the Cainozoic world, have these two things in common; first, a far more effective protection against changes of temperature than any other variation of the reptile type ever produced, and, secondly, a peculiar care for their eggs, the bird by incubation and the mammal by retention, and a disposition to look after the young for a certain period after hatching or birth. There is by comparison the greatest carelessness about offspring in the reptile.

Hair was evidently the earliest distinction of the mammals from the rest of the reptiles. It is doubtful if the particular Theriodont reptiles who were developing hair in the early Mesozoic were viviparous. Two mammals survive to this day which not only do not suckle their young,[1] but which lay eggs, the *Ornithorhynchus* and the *Echidna,* and in the Eocene there were a number of allied forms. They are the survivors of what was probably a much larger number and variety of small egg-laying hairy creatures, hairy reptiles, hoppers, climbers, and runners, which included the Mesozoic ancestors of all existing mammals up to and including man.

Now we may put the essential facts about mammalian reproduction in another way. *The mammal is a family animal.* And the family habit involved the possibility of a new sort of continuity of experience in the world. Compare the completely closed-in life of an individual lizard with the life of even a quite lowly mammal of almost any kind. The former has no mental continuity with anything beyond itself; it is a little self-contained globe of experience that serves its purpose and ends; but the latter "picks up" from its mother, and "hands on" to its offspring. All the mammals, except for the two genera we have named, had already before the lower Eocene age arrived at this stage of pre-adult dependence and imitation.

1 They secrete a nutritive fluid on which the young feeds from glands scattered over the skin. But the glands are not gathered together into mammæ with nipples for suckling. The stuff oozes out, the mother lies on her back, and the young browse upon her moist skin.

They were all more or less imitative in youth and capable of a certain modicum of education; they all, as a part of their de-

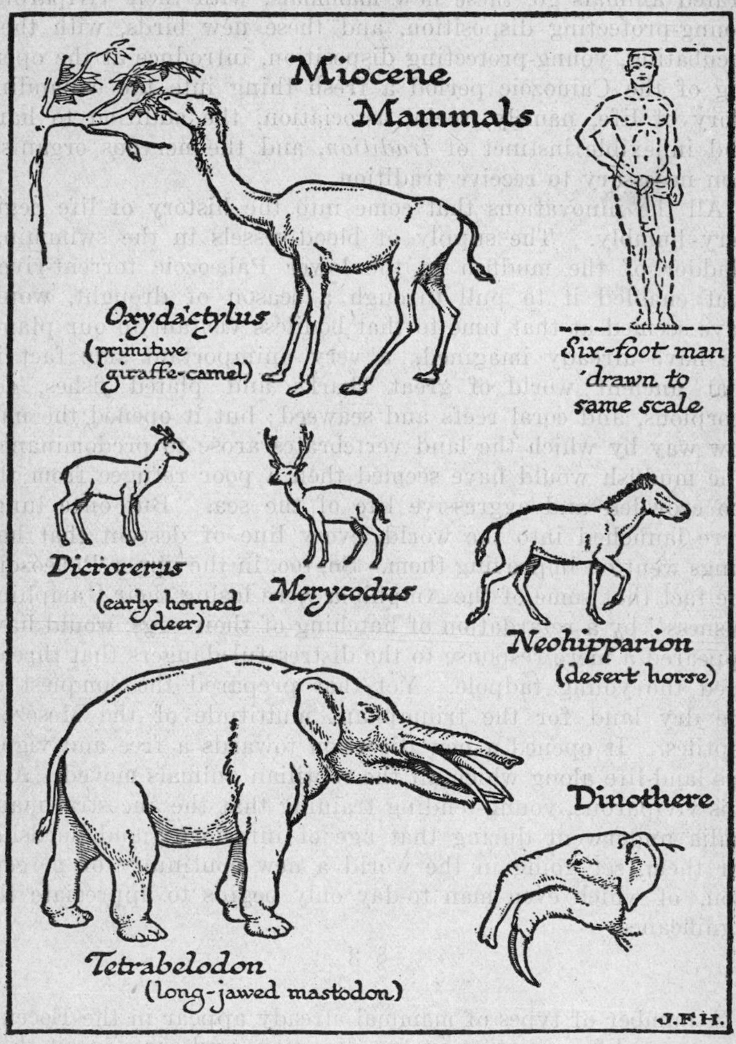

velopment, received a certain amount of care and example and even direction from their mother. This is as true of the hyæna and rhinoceros as it is of the dog or man; the difference of educability is enormous, but the fact of protection and educability in the young stage is undeniable. So far as the vertebrated animals go, these new mammals, with their viviparous, young-protecting disposition, and these new birds, with their incubating, young-protecting disposition, introduce at the opening of the Cainozoic period a fresh thing into the expanding story of life, namely, social association, the addition to hard and inflexible instinct of *tradition,* and the nervous organisation necessary to receive tradition.

All the innovations that come into the history of life begin very humbly. The supply of blood-vessels in the swimming-bladder of the mudfish in the lower Palæozoic torrent-river, that enabled it to pull through a season of drought, would have seemed at that time to that bodiless visitant to our planet we have already imagined, a very unimportant side fact in that ancient world of great sharks and plated fishes, sea scorpions, and coral reefs and seaweed; but it opened the narrow way by which the land vertebrates arose to predominance. The mudfish would have seemed then a poor refugee from the too crowded and aggressive life of the sea. But once lungs were launched into the world, every line of descent that had lungs went on improving them. So, too, in the upper Palæozoic, the fact that some of the Amphibia were losing their "amphibiousness" by a retardation of hatching of their eggs, would have appeared a mere response to the distressful dangers that threatened the young tadpole. Yet that prepared the conquest of the dry land for the triumphant multitude of the Mesozoic reptiles. It opened a new direction towards a free and vigorous land-life along which all the reptilian animals moved. And this viviparous, young-tending training that the ancestral mammalia underwent during that age of inferiority and hardship for them, set going in the world a new continuity of perception, of which even man to-day only begins to appreciate the significance.

§ 3

A number of types of mammal already appear in the Eocene. Some are differentiating in one direction, and some in another, some are perfecting themselves as herbivorous quadrupeds, some leap and climb among the trees, some turn back to the water to swim, but all types are unconsciously exploiting and developing the brain which is the instrument of this new power of acquisition and educability. In the Eocene rocks are found small early predecessors of the horse (Eohippus), tiny camels, pigs, early tapirs, early hedgehogs, monkeys and lemurs, opossums and carnivores. Now, all these were more or less ancestral to living forms, and all have brains relatively much smaller than their living representatives. There is, for instance, an early rhinoceros-like beast, *Titanotherium,* with a brain not one tenth the size of that of the existing rhinoceros. The latter is by no means a perfect type of the attentive and submissive student, but even so it is ten times more observant and teachable than its predecessor. This sort of thing is true of all the orders and families that survive until to-day. All the Cainozoic mammals were doing this one thing in common under the urgency of a common necessity; they were all growing brain. It was a parallel advance. In the same order or family to-day, the brain is usually from six to ten times what it was in the Eocene ancestor.

The Eocene period displayed a series of herbivorous brutes of which no representative survives to-day. Such were the Uintatheres and the Titanotheres. They were ousted by more specialized graminivorous forms as grass spread over the world. In pursuit of such beasts came great swarms of primitive dogs, some as big as bears, and the first cats, one in particular (*Smilodon*), a small fierce-looking creature with big knife-like canines, the first sabre-toothed tiger, which was to develop into greater things. American deposits in the Miocene display a great variety of camels, giraffe camels with long necks, gazelle camels, llamas, and true camels. North America, throughout most of the Cainozoic period, appears to have been in open and easy continuation with Asia, and when at last the glaciers of the Great Ice Age, and then the Bering Strait, came to separate the two great continental regions, the last camels were left in the old world and the llamas in the new.

In the Eocene the first ancestors of the elephants appear in northern Africa as snouted creatures; the elephant's trunk dawned on the world in the Miocene.

One group of creatures is of peculiar interest in a history that is mainly to be the story of mankind. We find fossils in the Eocene of monkeys and lemurs, but of one particular creature we have as yet not a single bone. It must have been a creature half ape, half monkey; it clambered about the trees and ran, and probably ran well, on its hind-legs upon the ground. It was small-brained by our present standards, but it had clever hands with which it handled fruits and beat nuts upon the rocks and caught up sticks and stones to smite its fellows. Spite of the lack of material evidence, the facts of biological science almost compel us to believe that such a creature existed, the common ancestor of the anthropoid apes and the two species of men we will describe in the next chapter.

§ 4

Through millions of simian generations the spinning world circled about the sun; slowly its orbit, which may have been nearly circular during the equable days of the early Eocene, was drawn by the attraction of the circling outer planets into a more elliptical form. Its axis of rotation, which had always heeled over to the plane of its orbit, as the mast of a yacht under sail heels over to the level of the water, heeled over by imperceptible degrees a little more and a little more. And each year its summer point shifted a little further from perihelion round its path. These were small changes to happen to a one-inch ball, circling at a distance of 330 yards from a flaming sun nine feet across, in the course of a few million years. They were changes an immortal astronomer in Neptune, watching the earth from age to age, would have found almost imperceptible. But from the point of view of the surviving mammalian life of the Miocene, they mattered profoundly. Age by age the winters grew on the whole colder and harder and a few hours longer relatively to the summers in a thousand years; age by age the summers grew briefer. On an average the winter snow lay a little later in the spring in each century, and the glaciers in the northern mountains gained an inch this year, receded half an inch next, came on again a few inches. . . .

The Record of the Rocks tells of the increasing chill. The Pliocene was a temperate time, and many of the warmth-loving plants and animals had gone. Then, rather less deliberately, some feet or some inches every year, the ice came on.

An arctic fauna, musk ox, woolly mammoth, woolly rhinoceros, lemming, ushers in the Pleistocene. Over North America, and Europe and Asia alike, the ice advanced. For thousands of years it advanced, and then for thousands of years it receded, to advance again. Europe down to the Baltic shores, Britain down to the Thames, North America down to New England, and more centrally as far south as Ohio, lay for ages under the glaciers. Enormous volumes of water were withdrawn from the ocean and locked up in those stupendous ice caps so as to cause a world-wide change in the relative levels of land and sea. Vast areas were exposed that are now again sea bottom.

The world to-day is still coming slowly out of the last of four great waves of cold. It is not growing warmer steadily. There have been fluctuations. Remains of bog oaks, for example, which grew two or three thousand years ago, are found in Scotland at latitudes in which not even a stunted oak will grow at the present time. And it is amidst this crescendo and diminuendo of frost and snow that we first recognize forms that are like the forms of men. The Age of Mammals culminated in ice and hardship and man.

VII

THE ANCESTRY OF MAN

§ 1. *Man Descended from a Walking Ape.* § 2. *First Traces of Man-like Creatures.* § 3. *The Heidelberg Sub-Man.* § 4. *The Piltdown Sub-Man.* § 5. *The Riddle of the Piltdown Remains.*

§ 1

THE origin of man is still very obscure. It is commonly asserted that he is "descended" from some man-like ape such as the chimpanzee, the orang-utang, or the gorilla, but that of course is as reasonable as saying that I am "descended" from some Hottentot or Esquimau as young or younger than myself. Others, alive to this objection, say that man is descended from the common ancestor of the chimpanzee, the orang-utang, and the gorilla. Some "anthropologists" have even indulged in a speculation whether mankind may not have a double or treble origin; the negro being descended from a gorilla-like ancestor, the Chinese from a chimpanzee-like ancestor, and so on. These are very fanciful ideas, to be mentioned only to be dismissed. It was formerly assumed that the human ancestor was "probably arboreal," but the current idea among those who are qualified to form an opinion seems to be that he was a "ground ape," and that the existing apes have developed in the arboreal direction.

Of course if one puts the skeleton of a man and the skeleton of a gorilla side by side, their general resemblance is so great that it is easy to jump to the conclusion that the former is derived from such a type as the latter by a process of brain growth and general refinement. But if one examines closely into one or two differences, the gap widens. Particular stress has recently been laid upon the tread of the foot. Man walks

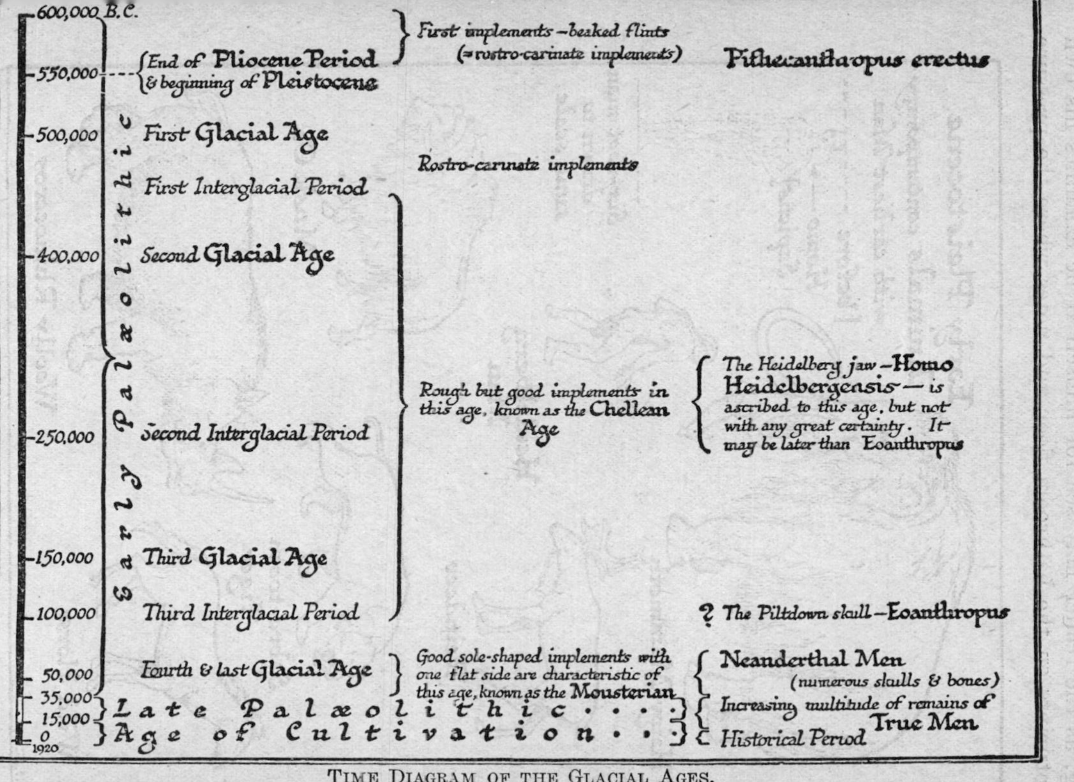

TIME DIAGRAM OF THE GLACIAL AGES.

The reader should compare this diagram carefully with our first time diagram, Chapter II, § 2, p. 11. That diagram, if it were on the same scale as this one, would be between 41 and 410 feet long. The position of the Eoanthropus is very uncertain; it may be as early as the Pliocene.

on his toe and his heel; his great toe is his chief lever in walking, as the reader may see for himself if he examines his own footprints on the bathroom floor and notes where the pressure

falls as the footprints become fainter. His great toe is the king of his toes.

Among all the apes and monkeys, the only group that have

their great toes developed on anything like the same fashion as man are some of the lemurs. The baboon walks on a flat foot and all his toes, using his middle toe as his chief throw-off, much as the bear does. And the three great apes all walk on the outer side of the foot in a very different manner from the walking of man.

The great apes are forest dwellers; their walking even now is incidental; they are at their happiest among trees. They have very distinctive methods of climbing; they swing by the arms much more than the monkeys do, and do not, like the latter, take off with a spring from the feet. They have a specially developed climbing style of their own. But man walks so well and runs so swiftly as to suggest a very long ancestry upon the ground. Also, he does not climb well now; he climbs with caution and hesitation. His ancestors may have been running creatures for long ages. Moreover, it is to be noted that he does not swim naturally; he has to learn to swim, and that seems to point to a long-standing separation from rivers and lakes and the sea. Almost certainly that ancestor was a smaller and slighter creature than its human descendants. Conceivably the human ancestor at the opening of the Cainozoic period was a running ape living chiefly on the ground, hiding among rocks rather than trees. It could still climb trees well and hold things between its great toe and its second toe (as the Japanese can to this day), but it was already coming down to the ground

POSSIBLE APPEARANCE OF THE SUB-MAN *Pithecanthropus*.
The face, jaws, and teeth are mere guess-work (*see* text). The creature may have been much less human-looking than this.

again from a still remoter, a Mesozoic arboreal ancestry. It is quite understandable that such a creature would very rarely die in water in such circumstances as to leave bones to become fossilized.

It must always be borne in mind that among its many other imperfections the Geological Record necessarily contains abundant traces only of water or marsh creatures or of creatures easily and frequently drowned. The same reasons that make any traces of the ancestors of the mammals rare and relatively unprocurable in the Mesozoic rocks, probably make the traces of possible human ancestors rare and relatively unprocurable in the Cainozoic rocks. Such knowledge as we have of the earliest men, for example, is almost entirely got from a few caves, into which they went and in which they left their traces. Until the hard Pleistocene times they lived and died in the open, and their bodies were consumed or decayed altogether.

But it is well to bear in mind also that the record of the rocks has still to be thoroughly examined. It has been studied only for a few generations, and by only a few men in each generation. Most men have been too busy making war, making profits out of their neighbours, toiling at work that machinery could do for them in a tenth of the time, or simply playing about, to give any attention to these more interesting things. There may be, there probably are, thousands of deposits still untouched containing countless fragments and vestiges of man and his progenitors. In Asia particularly, in India or the East Indies, there may be hidden the most illuminating clues. What we know to-day of early men is the merest scrap of what will presently be known.

The apes and monkeys already appear to have been differentiated at the beginning of the Cainozoic Age, and there are a number of Oligocene and Miocene apes whose relations to one another and to the human line have still to be made out. Among these we may mention *Dryopithecus* of the Miocene Age, with a very human-looking jaw. In the Siwalik Hills of northern India remains of some very interesting apes have been found, of which *Sivapithecus* and *Palæopithecus* were possibly related closely to the human ancestor. Possibly these animals already used implements. Charles Darwin represents baboons as opening nuts by breaking them with stones, using stakes to prise up rocks in the hunt for insects, and striking blows with sticks and stones. The chimpanzee makes itself a sort of tree hut by intertwining branches. Stones apparently chipped for use have been found in strata of Oligocene Age at Boncelles in Belgium. Possibly the implement-using disposition was already present in the Mesozoic ancestry from which we are descended.

§ 2

Among the earliest evidences of some creature, either human or at least more manlike than any living ape upon earth, are a number of flints and stones very roughly chipped and shaped so as to be held in the hand. These were probably used as hand-axes. These early implements ("Eoliths") are often so crude and simple that there was for a long time a controversy whether they were to be regarded as natural or artificial productions. The date of the earliest of them is put by geologists as Pliocene—that is to say, *before the First Glacial Age.* They occur also throughout the First Interglacial period. We know of no bones or other remains in Europe or America of the quasi-human beings of half a million years ago, who made and used these implements. They used them to hammer with, perhaps they used them to fight with, and perhaps they used bits of wood for similar purposes.[1]

But at Trinil, in Java, in strata which are said to correspond either to the later Pliocene or to the American and European First Ice Age, there have been found some scattered bones of a creature, such as the makers of these early implements may have been. The top of a skull, some teeth, and a thigh-bone have been found. The skull shows a brain-case about half-way in size between that of the chimpanzee and man, but the thigh-bone is that of a creature as well adapted to standing and running as a man, and as free, therefore, to use its hands. The creature was not a man, nor was it an arboreal ape like the chimpanzee. It was a walking ape. It has been named by naturalists *Pithecanthropus erectus* (the walking ape-man). We cannot say that it is a direct human ancestor, but we may guess that the creatures who scattered these first stone tools

[1] Some writers suppose that a Wood and Shell Age preceded the earliest Stone Age. South Sea Islanders, Negroes, and Bushmen still make use of wood and the sharp-edged shells of land and water molluscs as implements.

over the world must have been closely similar and kindred, and that our ancestor was a beast of like kind. This little trayful of bony fragments from Trinil is, at present, apart from stone implements, the oldest relic of early humanity, or of the close blood relations of early humanity, that is known.

While these early men or "sub-men" were running about Europe four or five hundred thousand years ago, there were mammoths, rhinoceroses, a huge hippopotamus, a giant beaver, and a bison and wild cattle in their world. There were also wild horses, and the sabre-toothed tiger still abounded. There are no traces of lions or true tigers at that time in Europe, but there were bears, otters, wolves, and a wild boar. It may be that the early sub-man sometimes played jackal to the sabre-toothed tiger, and finished up the bodies on which the latter had gorged itself.

§ 3

After this first glimpse of something at least sub-human in the record of geology, there is not another fragment of human or man-like bone yet known from that record for an interval of hundreds of thousands of years. It is not until we reach deposits which are stated to be of the Second Interglacial period, 200,000 years later, 200,000 or 250,000 years ago, that another little scrap of bone comes to hand. Then we find a jaw-bone.

This jaw-bone was found in a sand-pit near Heidelberg, at a depth of eighty feet from the surface, and it is not the jaw-bone of a man as we understand man, but it is man-like in every respect, except that it has absolutely no trace of a chin; it is more massive than a man's, and its narrowness behind could not, it is thought, have given the tongue sufficient play for articulate speech. It is not an ape's jaw-bone; the teeth are human. The owner of this jaw-bone has been variously named *Homo Heidelbergensis* and *Palæoanthropus Heidelbergensis,* according to the estimate formed of his humanity or sub-humanity by various authorities. He lived in a world not remotely unlike the world of the still earlier sub-man of the first implements; the deposits in which it is found show that there were elephants, horses, rhinoceroses, bison, a moose, and so forth with it in the world, but the sabre-toothed tiger was declining and the lion was spreading over Europe. The implements of this period (known as the Chellean period) are a very considerable advance upon those of the Pliocene Age. They are well made but *very much bigger* than any truly human implements. The Heidelberg man may have had a very big body and large fore limbs. He may have been a woolly, strange-looking creature.

§ 4

We must turn over the Record for, it may be, another 100,000 years for the next remains of anything human or sub-human. Then in a deposit ascribed to the Third Interglacial period, which may have begun 100,000 years ago and lasted 50,000 years, the smashed pieces of a whole skull turn up. The deposit is a gravel which may have been derived from the washing out of still earlier gravel strata, and this skull fragment may be in reality as old as the First Glacial Period. The bony remains discovered at Piltdown in Sussex display a creature still ascending only very gradually from the sub-human.

The first scraps of this skull were found in an excavation for road gravel in Sussex. Bit by bit other fragments of this skull were hunted out from the quarry heaps until most of it could be pieced together. It is a thick skull, thicker than that of any living race of men, and it has a brain capacity intermediate between that of Pithecanthropus and man. This creature has been named *Eoanthropus,* the dawn man. In the same gravel-pits were found teeth of rhinoceros, hippopotamus, and the leg-bone of a deer with marks upon it that may be cuts. A curious bat-shaped instrument of elephant bone has also been found.

There was moreover a jaw-bone among these scattered remains, which was at first assumed naturally enough to belong to *Eoanthropus,* but which it was afterwards suggested was probably that of a chimpanzee. It is extraordinarily like that of a chimpanzee, but Dr. Keith, one of the greatest authorities in these questions, assigns it, after an exhaustive analysis in his *Antiquity of Man* (1915), to the skull with which it is found. It is, as a jaw-bone, far less human in character than the jaw of the much more ancient *Homo Heidelbergensis,* but the teeth are in some respects more like those of living men.

Dr. Keith, swayed by the jaw-bone, does not think that *Eoanthropus,* in spite of its name, is a creature in the direct ancestry of man. Much less is it an intermediate form between the Heidelberg man and the Neanderthal man we shall presently describe. It was only related to the true ancestor of man as the orang is related to the chimpanzee. It was one of a number of sub-human running apes of more than ape-like intelligence, and if it was not on the line royal, it was at any rate a very close collateral.

After this glimpse of a skull, the Record for very many centuries gives nothing but flint implements, which improve steadily in quality. A very characteristic form is shaped like a sole, with one flat side stricken off at one blow and the other side worked. The archæologists, as the Record continues, are presently able to distinguish scrapers, borers, knives, darts, throwing stones, and the like. Progress is now more rapid; in a few centuries the shape of the hand-axe shows distinct and recognizable improvements. And then comes quite a number of remains. The Fourth Glacial Age is rising towards its maximum. Man is taking to caves and leaving vestiges there; at Krapina in Croatia, at Neanderthal near Düsseldorf, at Spy, human remains have been found, skulls and bones of a creature that is certainly a man. Somewhen about 50,000 years ago, if not earlier, appeared *Homo Neanderthalensis* (also called *Homo antiquus* and *Homo primigenius*), a quite passable human being. His thumb was not quite equal in flexibility and usefulness to a human thumb, he stooped forward and could not hold his head erect, as all living men do, he was chinless and perhaps incapable of speech, there were curious differences about the enamel and the roots of his teeth from those of all living men, he was very thick-set, he was, indeed, not quite of the human species; but there is no dispute about his attribution to the genus *Homo*. He was certainly not descended from Eoanthropus, but his jaw-bone is so like the Heidelberg jaw-bone, as to make it possible that the clumsier and heavier *Homo Heidelbergensis*, a thousand centuries before him, was of his blood and race.

VIII

THE NEANDERTHAL MEN, AN EXTINCT RACE

(The Early Palæolithic Age[1])

§ 1. *The World 50,000 Years Ago.* § 2. *The Daily Life of the First Men.* § 3. *The Last Palæolithic Men.*

§ 1

IN the time of the Third Interglacial period the outline of Europe and Western Asia was very different from what it is to-day. Vast areas to the west and north-west which are now under the Atlantic waters were then dry land; the Irish Sea and the North Sea were river valleys. Over these northern areas there spread and receded and spread again a great ice cap such as covers central Greenland to-day (see Map on p. 56). This vast ice cap, which covered both polar regions of the earth, withdrew huge masses of water from the ocean, and the sea-level consequently fell, exposing great areas of land that are now submerged again. The Mediterranean area was probably a great valley below the general sea-level, containing two inland seas cut off from the general ocean. The climate of this Mediterranean basin was perhaps cold temperate, and the region of the Sahara to the south was not then a desert of baked rock and blown sand, but a well-watered and fertile country. Between the ice sheets to the north and the Alps and Mediterranean valley to the south stretched a bleak wilderness

[1] Three phases of human history before the knowledge and use of metals are often distinguished. First there is the so-called Eolithic Age (dawn of stone implements), then the Palæolithic Age (old stone implements), and finally an age in which the implements are skilfully made and frequently well finished and polished (Neolithic Age). The Palæolithic Period is further divided into an earlier (sub-human) and a later (fully human) period. We shall comment on these divisions later.

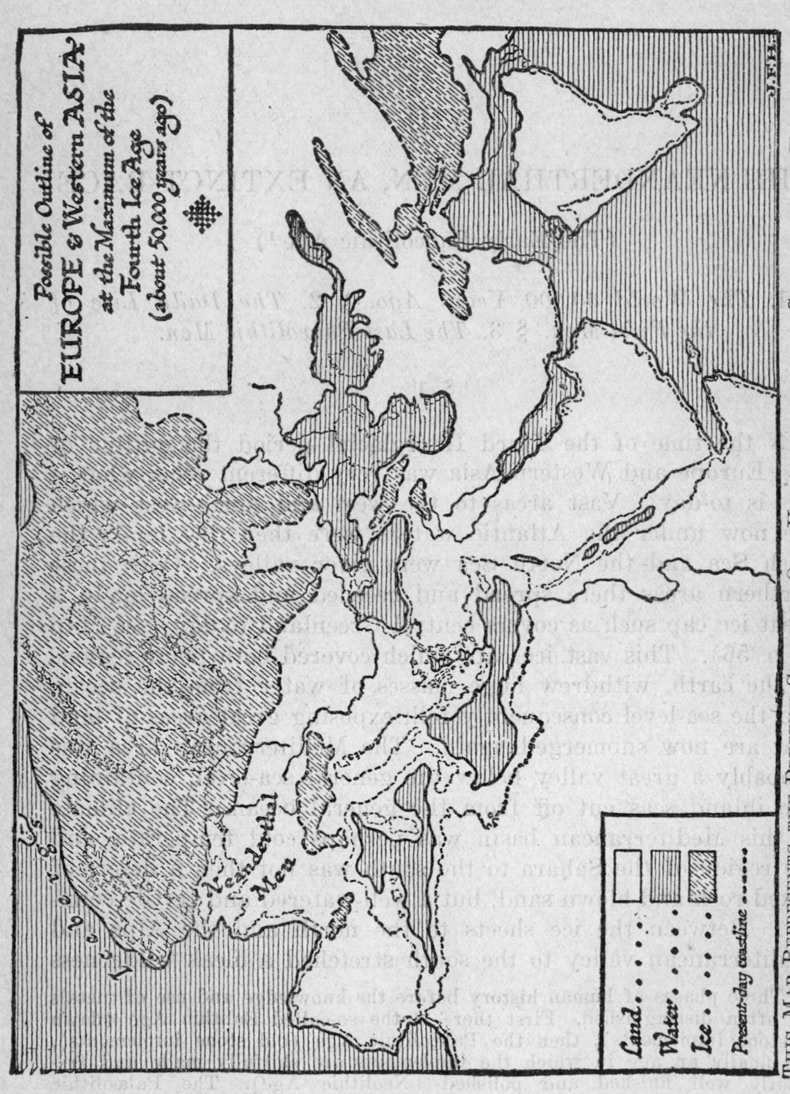

THIS MAP REPRESENTS THE PRESENT STATE OF OUR KNOWLEDGE OF THE GEOGRAPHY OF EUROPE AND WESTERN ASIA AT A PERIOD WHICH WE GUESS TO BE ABOUT 50,000 YEARS AGO, THE NEANDERTHALER AGE. Much of this map is of course speculative, but its broad outlines must be fairly like those of the world in which men first became men.

whose climate changed from harshness to a mild kindliness and then hardened again for the Fourth Glacial Age.

Across this wilderness, which is now the great plain of Europe, wandered a various fauna. At first there were hippopotami, rhinoceroses, mammoths, and elephants. The sabre-toothed tiger was diminishing towards extinction. Then, as the air chilled, the hippopotamus, and then other warmth-loving creatures, ceased to come so far north, and the sabre-toothed tiger disappeared altogether. The woolly mammoth, the woolly rhinoceros, the musk ox, the bison, the aurochs, and the reindeer became prevalent, and the temperate vegetation gave place to plants of a more arctic type. The glaciers spread southward to the maximum of the Fourth Glacial Age (about 50,000 years ago), and then receded again. In the earlier phase, the Third Interglacial period, a certain number of small family groups of men (*Homo Neanderthalensis*) and probably of sub-men (*Eoanthropus*) wandered over the land, leaving nothing but their flint implements to witness to their presence. They probably used a multitude and variety of wooden implements also; they had probably learnt much about the shapes of objects and the use of different shapes from wood, knowledge which they afterwards applied to stone; but none of this wooden material has survived; we can only speculate about its forms and uses. As the weather hardened to its maximum of severity, the Neanderthal men, already it would seem acquainted with the use of fire, began to seek shelter under rock ledges and in caves —and so leave remains behind them. Hitherto they had been accustomed to squat in the open about the fire, and near their water supply. But they were sufficiently intelligent to adapt themselves to the new and harder conditions. (As for the sub-men, they seem to have succumbed to the stresses of this Fourth Glacial Age altogether. At any rate, the rudest type of Palæolithic implements presently disappears.)

Not merely man was taking to the caves. This period also had a cave lion, a cave bear, and a cave hyæna. These creatures had to be driven out of the caves and kept out of the caves in which these early men wanted to squat and hide; and no doubt fire was an effective method of eviction and protection. Probably early men did not go deeply into the caves, because they had no means of lighting their recesses. They got in far enough to be out of the weather, and stored wood and food in odd corners. Perhaps they barricaded the cave mouths. Their only available light for going deeply into the caverns would be torches.

What did these Neanderthal men hunt? Their only possible weapons for killing such giant creatures as the mammoth or the cave bear, or even the reindeer, were spears of wood, wooden clubs, and those big pieces of flint they left behind them, the "Chellean" and "Mousterian" implements;[1] and probably their usual quarry was smaller game. But they did certainly eat the flesh of the big beasts when they had a chance, and perhaps they followed them when sick or when wounded by combats, or took advantage of them when they were bogged or in trouble with ice or water. (The Labrador Indians still kill the caribou with spears at awkward river crossings.) At Dewlish, in Dorset, an artificial trench has been found which is supposed to have been a Palæolithic trap for elephants.[2] We know that the Neanderthalers partly ate their kill where it fell; but they brought back the big marrow bones to the cave to crack and eat at leisure, because few ribs and vertebræ are found in the caves, but great quantities of cracked and split long bones. They used skins to wrap about them, and the women probably dressed the skins.

We know also that they were right-handed like modern men, because the left side of the brain (which serves the right side of the body) is bigger than the right. But while the back parts of the brain which deal with sight and touch and the energy of the body are well developed, the front parts, which are con-

[1] From Chelles and Le Moustier in France.
[2] Osmond Fisher, quoted in Wright's *Quaternary Ice Age*.

nected with thought and speech, are comparatively small. It was as big a brain as ours, but different. This species of *Homo* had certainly a very different mentality from ours; its individuals were not merely simpler and lower than we are, they were on another line. It may be they did not speak at all, or very sparingly. They had nothing that we should call a language.

§ 2

In Worthington Smith's *Man the Primeval Savage* there is a very vividly written description of early Palæolithic life, from which much of the following account is borrowed. In the original, Mr. Worthington Smith assumes a more extensive social life, a larger community, and a more definite division of labour among its members than is altogether justifiable in the face of such subsequent writings as J. J. Atkinson's memorable essay on Primal Law.[1] For the little tribe Mr. Worthington Smith described, there has been substituted, therefore, a family group under the leadership of one Old Man, and the suggestions of Mr. Atkinson as to the behaviour of the Old Man have been worked into the sketch.

Mr. Worthington Smith describes a squatting-place near a stream, because primitive man, having no pots or other vessels, must needs have kept close to a water supply, and with some chalk cliffs adjacent from which flints could be got to work. The air was bleak, and the fire was of great importance, because fires once out were not easily relit in those days. When not required to blaze it was probably banked down with ashes. The most probable way in which fires were started was by hacking a bit of iron pyrites with a flint amidst dry dead leaves; concretions of iron pyrites and flints are found together in England where the gault and chalk approach each other.[2] The little group of people would be squatting about amidst a litter of fern, moss, and such-like dry material. Some of the women and children would need to be continually gathering fuel to keep up the fires. It would be a tradition that had grown up.

1 *Social Origins,* by Andrew Lang, and *Primal Law,* by J. J. Atkinson. (Longmans, 1903.)

2 This first origin of fire was suggested by Sir John Lubbock (*Prehistoric Times*), and Ludwig Hopf, in *The Human Species,* says that "Flints and pieces of pyrites are found in close proximity in palæolithic settlements near the remains of mammoths."

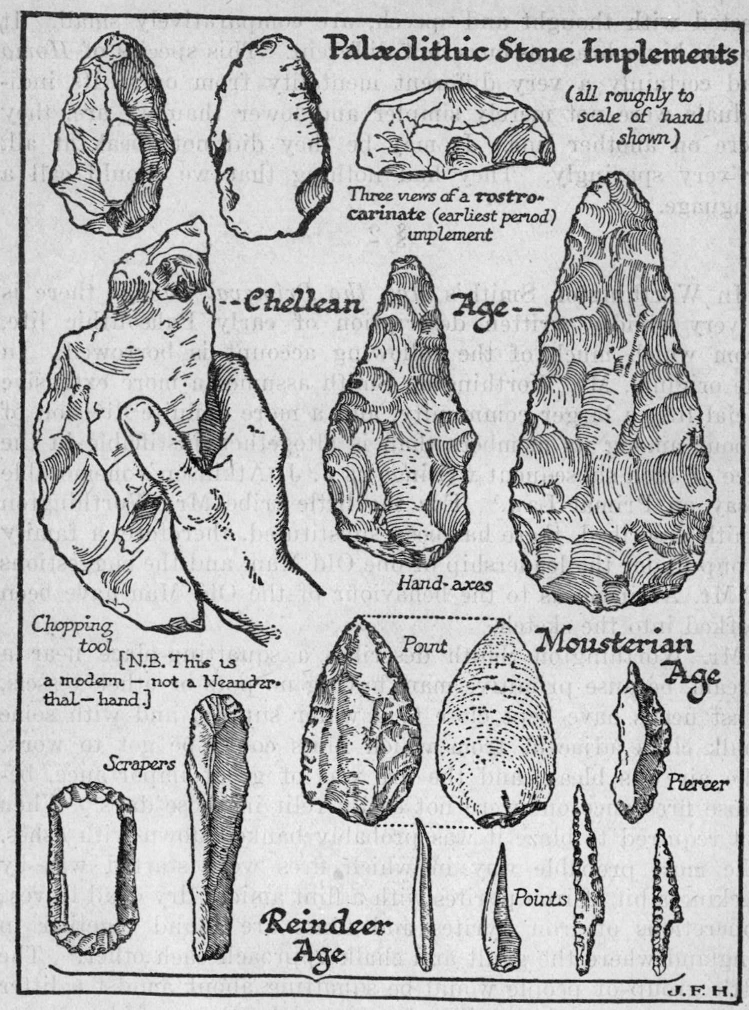

EARLY STONE IMPLEMENTS.

The Mousterian Age implements, and all above it, are those of Neanderthal men or, possibly in the case of the rostro-carinates, of sub-men. The lower row (Reindeer Age) are the work of true men. The student should compare this diagram with the time diagram attached to Chapter VII, § 1, and he should note the relatively *large size* of the pre-human implements.

The young would imitate their elders in this task. Perhaps there would be rude wind shelters of boughs on one side of the encampment.

The Old Man, the father and master of the group, would perhaps be engaged in hammering flints beside the fire. The children would imitate him and learn to use the sharpened fragments. Probably some of the women would hunt good flints; they would fish them out of the chalk with sticks and bring them to the squatting-place.

There would be skins about. It seems probable that at a very early time primitive men took to using skins. Probably they were wrapped about the children, and used to lie upon when the ground was damp and cold. A woman would perhaps be preparing a skin. The inside of the skin would be well scraped free of superfluous flesh with trimmed flints, and then strained and pulled and pegged out flat on the grass, and dried in the rays of the sun.

Away from the fire other members of the family group prowl in search of food, but at night they all gather closely round the fire and build it up, for it is their protection against the wandering bear and such-like beasts of prey. The Old Man is the only fully adult male in the little group. There are women, boys and girls, but so soon as the boys are big enough to rouse the Old Man's jealousy, he will fall foul of them and either drive them off or kill them. Some girls may perhaps go off with these exiles, or two or three of these youths may keep together for a time, wandering until they come upon some other group, from which they may try to steal a mate. Then they would probably fall out among themselves. Some day, when he is forty years old perhaps or even older, and his teeth are worn down and his energy abating, some younger male will stand up to the Old Man and kill him and reign in his stead. There is probably short shrift for the old at the squatting-place. So soon as they grow weak and bad-tempered, trouble and death come upon them.

What did they eat at the squatting-place?

"Primeval man is commonly described as a hunter of the great hairy mammoth, of the bear, and the lion, but it is in the highest degree improbable that the human savage ever hunted animals much larger than the hare, the rabbit, and the rat. Man was probably the hunted rather than the hunter.

"The primeval savage was both herbivorous and carnivorous. He had for food hazel-nuts, beech-nuts, sweet chestnuts, earth-nuts, and acorns. He had crab-apples, wild pears, wild cherries, wild gooseberries, bullaces, sorbs, sloes, blackberries, yewberries, hips and haws, watercress, fungi, the larger and softer leaf-buds, Nostoc (the vegetable substance called 'fallen stars' by countryfolk), the fleshy, juicy, asparagus-like rhizomes or sub-terranean stems of the *Labiatæ* and like plants, as well as other delicacies of the vegetable kingdom. He had birds' eggs, young birds, and the honey and honeycomb of wild bees. He had newts, snails, and frogs—the two latter delicacies are still highly esteemed in Normandy and Brittany. He had fish, dead and alive, and fresh-water mussels; he could easily catch fish with his hands and paddle and dive for and trap them. By the seaside he would have fish, mollusca, and seaweed. He would have many of the larger birds and smaller mammals, which he could easily secure by throwing stones and sticks, or by setting simple snares. He would have the snake, the slow worm, and the crayfish. He would have various grubs and insects, the large larvæ of beetles and various caterpillars. The taste for caterpillars still survives in China, where they are sold in dried bundles in the markets. A chief and highly nourishing object of food would doubtlessly be bones smashed up into a stiff and gritty paste.

While the waters were held up in the Polar Ice Caps, the sea-level was low enough to enable Palæolithic Man to reach Tasmania.

"A fact of great importance is this—primeval man would not be particular about having his flesh food over-fresh. He would constantly find it in a dead state, and, if semi-putrid, he would relish it none the less—the taste for high or half-putrid game still survives. If driven by hunger and hard pressed, he would perhaps sometimes eat his weaker companions or unhealthy children who happened to be feeble or unsightly or burthensome. The larger animals in a weak and dying state would no doubt be much sought for; when these were not forthcoming, dead and half-rotten examples would be made to suffice. An unpleasant odour would not be objected to; it is not objected to now in many continental hotels.

"The savages sat huddled close together round their fire, with fruits, bones, and half-putrid flesh. We can imagine the old man and his women twitching the skin of their shoulders, brows, and muzzles as they were annoyed or bitten by flies or other insects. We can imagine the large human nostrils, indicative of keen scent, giving rapidly repeated sniffs at the foul meat before it was consumed; the bad odour of the meat, and the various other disgusting odours belonging to a haunt of savages, being not in the least disapproved.

"Man at that time was not a *degraded* animal, for he had never been higher; he was therefore an exalted animal, and, low as we esteem him now, he yet represented the highest stage of development of the animal kingdom of his time."

That is at least an acceptable sketch of a Neanderthal squatting-place. But before extinction overtook them, even the Neanderthalers learnt much and went far.

Whatever the older Palæolithic men did with their dead, there is reason to suppose that the later *Homo Neanderthalensis* buried some individuals at least with respect and ceremony. One of the best-known Neanderthal skeletons is that of a youth who apparently had been deliberately interred. He had been placed in a sleeping posture, head on the right fore-arm. The head lay on a number of flint fragments carefully piled together "pillow fashion." A big hand-axe lay near his head, and around him were numerous charred and split ox bones, as though there had been a feast or an offering.

To this appearance of burial during the later Neanderthal age we shall return when we are considering the ideas that were inside the heads of primitive men.

This sort of men may have wandered, squatted about their fires, and died in Europe for a period extending over 100,000 years, if we assume, that is, that the Heidelberg jaw-bone belongs to a member of the species, a period so vast that all the subsequent history of our race becomes a thing of yesterday. Along its own line this species of men was accumulating a dim tradition, and working out its limited possibilities. Its thick skull imprisoned its brain, and to the end it was low-browed and brutish.

IX

THE LATER POSTGLACIAL PALÆOLITHIC MEN, THE FIRST TRUE MEN

(Later Palæolithic Age)

§ 1. *The Coming of Men Like Ourselves.* § 2. *Hunters Give Place to Herdsmen.* § 3. *No Sub-Men in America.*

§ 1

THE Neanderthal type of man prevailed in Europe at least for tens of thousands of years. For ages that make all history seem a thing of yesterday, these nearly human creatures prevailed. If the Heidelberg jaw was that of a Neanderthaler, and if there is no error in the estimate of the age of that jaw, then the Neanderthal Race lasted out for more than 200,000 years! Finally, between 40,000 and 25,000 years ago, as the Fourth Glacial Age softened towards more temperate conditions (see Map on p. 68), a different human type came upon the scene, and, it would seem, exterminated *Homo Neanderthalensis*.[1] This new type was probably developed in South Asia or North Africa, or in lands now sub-

[1] The opinion that the Neanderthal race (*Homo Neanderthalensis*) is an extinct species which did not interbreed with the true men (*Homo sapiens*) is held by Professor Osborn, and it is the view to which the writer inclines and to which he has pointed in the treatment of this section; but it is only fair to the reader to note that many writers do not share this view. They write and speak of living ''Neanderthalers'' in contemporary populations. One observer has written in the past of such types in the west of Ireland; another has observed them in Greece. These so-called ''living Neanderthalers'' have neither the peculiarities of neck, thumb, nor teeth that distinguish the Neanderthal race of pre-men. The cheek teeth of true men, for instance, have what we call fangs, long fangs; the Neanderthaler's cheek tooth is a *more complicated and specialized* cheek tooth, a long tooth with short fangs, and his canine teeth were *less* marked, *less* like dog-teeth, than ours. Nothing could show more clearly that he was on a different line of development. We must remember that so far only western Europe has been properly explored for Palæolithic

merged in the Mediterranean basin, and, as more remains are collected and evidence accumulates, men will learn more of their early stages. At present we can only guess where and how, through the slow ages, parallel with the Neanderthal cousin, these first *true men* arose out of some more ape-like progenitor. For hundreds of centuries they were acquiring skill of hand and limb, and power and bulk of brain, in that still unknown environment. They were already far above the Neanderthal level of achievement and intelligence, when first they come into our ken, and they had already split into two or more very distinctive races.

These newcomers did not migrate into Europe in the strict sense of the word, but rather, as century by century the climate ameliorated, they followed the food and plants to which they were accustomed, as those spread into the new realms that opened to them. The ice was receding, vegetation was increasing, big game of all sorts was becoming more abundant. Steppe-like conditions, conditions of pasture and shrub, were bringing with them vast herds of wild horse. Ethnologists (students of race) class these new human races in one same species as ourselves, and with all human races subsequent to them, under one

remains, and that practically all we know of the Neanderthal species comes from that area (see Map, p. 56). No doubt the ancestor of *Homo sapiens* (which species includes the Tasmanians) was a very similar and parallel creature to *Homo neanderthalensis.* And we are not so far from that ancestor as to have eliminated not indeed ''Neanderthal,'' but ''Neanderthaloid'' types. The existence of such types no more proves that the Neanderthal species, the makers of the Chellean and Mousterian implements, interbred with *Homo sapiens* in the European area than do monkey-faced people testify to an interbreeding with monkeys; or people with faces like horses, that there is an equine strain in our population.

common specific name of *Homo sapiens.* They had quite human brain-cases and hands. Their teeth and their necks were anatomically as ours are.

We know of two distinct sorts of skeletal remains in this period, the first of these known as the Cro-Magnon race, and the second the Grimaldi race; but the great bulk of the human traces and appliances we find are either without human bones or with insufficient bones for us to define their associated physical type. There may have been many more distinct races than these two. There may have been intermediate types. In the grotto of Cro-Magnon it was that complete skeletons of one main type of these Newer Palæolithic men, these true men, were first found, and so it is that they are spoken of as Cro-Magnards.

These Cro-Magnards were a tall people with very broad faces, prominent noses, and, all things considered, astonishingly big brains. The brain capacity of the woman in the Cro-Magnon cave exceeded that of the average male to-day. Her head had been smashed by a heavy blow. There were also in the same cave with her the complete skeleton of an older man, nearly six feet high, the fragments of a child's skeleton, and the skeletons of two young men. There were also flint implements and perforated sea-shells, used no doubt as ornaments. Such is one sample of the earliest true men. But at the Grimaldi cave, near Mentone, were discovered two skeletons also of the later Palæolithic Period, but of a widely contrasted type, with negroid characteristics that point rather to the negroid type. There can be no doubt that we have to deal in this period with at least two, and probably more, highly divergent races of true men. They may have overlapped in time, or Cro-Magnards may have followed the Grimaldi race, and either or both may have been contemporary with the late Neanderthal men. Various authorities have very strong opinions upon these points, but they are, at most, opinions.

The appearance of these truly human postglacial Palæolithic peoples was certainly an enormous leap forward in the history of mankind. Both of these main races had a human fore-brain, a human hand, an intelligence very like our own. They dispossessed *Homo Neanderthalensis* from his caverns and his stone quarries. And they agreed with modern ethnologists, it would seem, in regarding him as a different species. Unlike

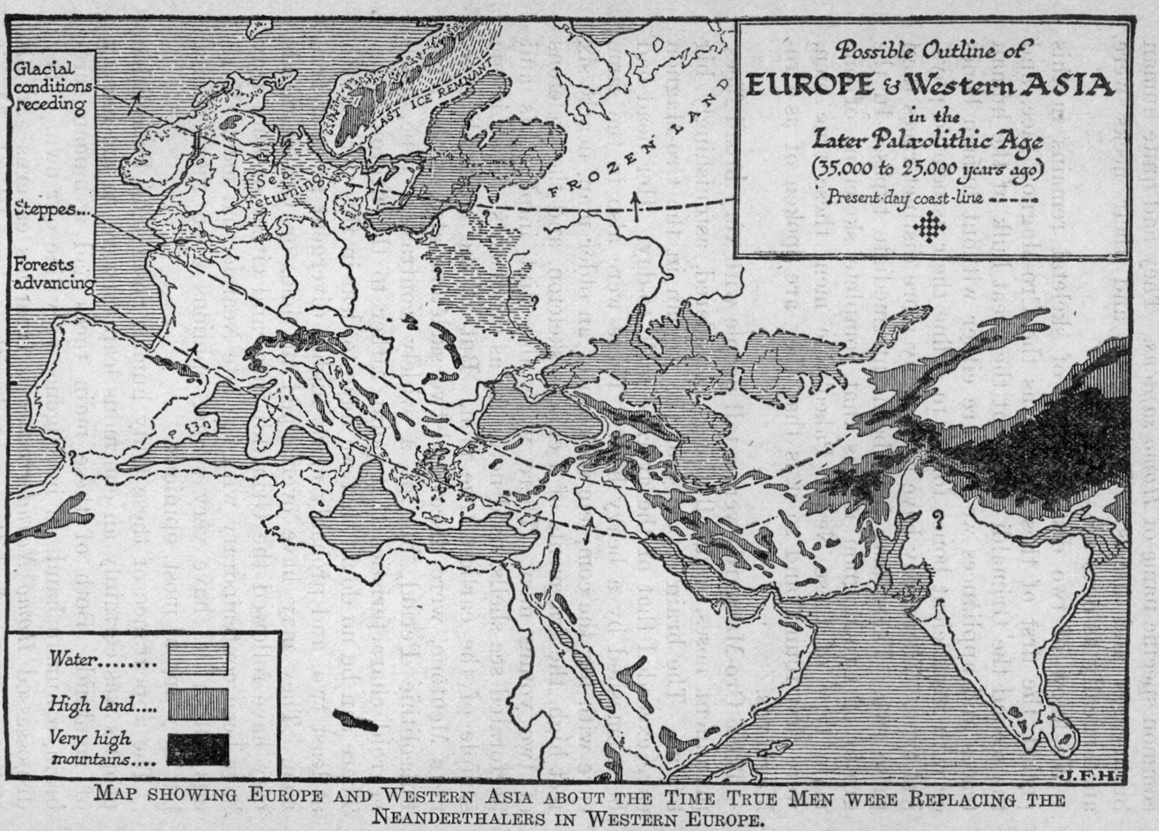

MAP SHOWING EUROPE AND WESTERN ASIA ABOUT THE TIME TRUE MEN WERE REPLACING THE NEANDERTHALERS IN WESTERN EUROPE.

most savage conquerors, who take the women of the defeated side for their own and interbreed with them, it would seem that the true men would have nothing to do with the Neanderthal

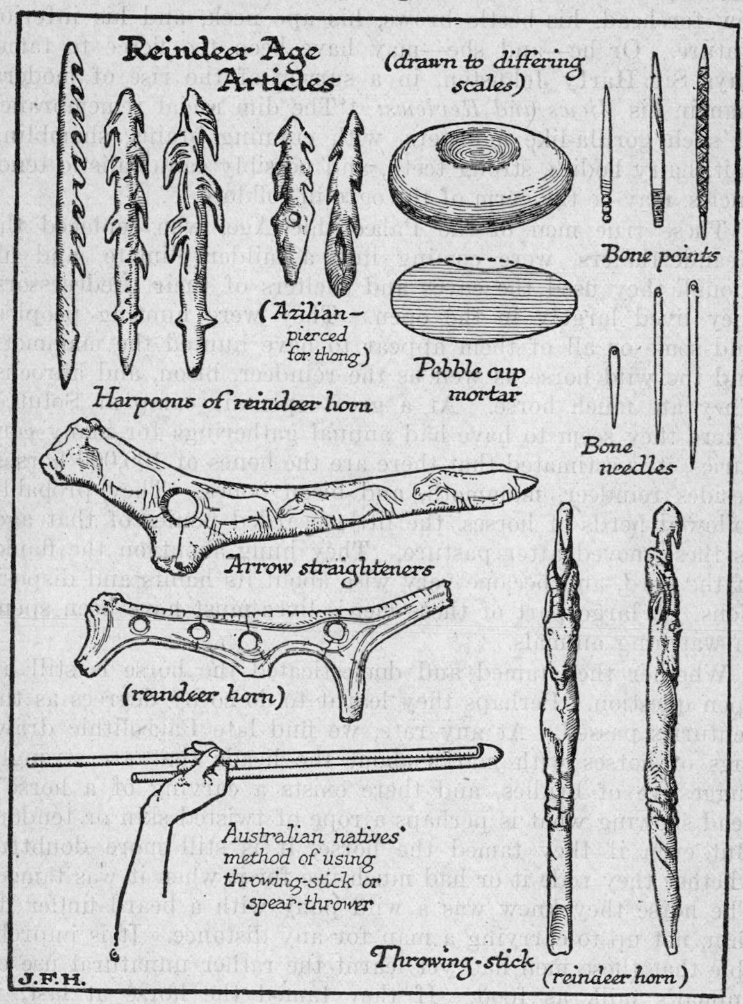

race, women or men. There is no trace of any intermixture between the races, in spite of the fact that the newcomers, being also flint users, were establishing themselves in the very same spots that their predecessors had occupied. We know nothing of the appearance of the Neanderthal man, but this absence of intermixture seems to suggest an extreme hairiness, an ugliness, or a repulsive strangeness in his appearance over and above his low forehead, his beetle brows, his ape neck, and his inferior stature. Or he—and she—may have been too fierce to tame. Says Sir Harry Johnston, in a survey of the rise of modern man in his *Views and Reviews:* "The dim racial remembrance of such gorilla-like monsters, with cunning brains, shambling gait, hairy bodies, strong teeth, and possibly cannibalistic tendencies, may be the germ of the ogre in folklore. . . ."

These true men of the Palæolithic Age, who replaced the Neanderthalers, were coming into a milder climate, and although they used the caves and shelters of their predecessors, they lived largely in the open. They were hunting peoples, and some or all of them appear to have hunted the mammoth and the wild horse as well as the reindeer, bison, and aurochs. They ate much horse. At a great open-air camp at Solutré, where they seem to have had annual gatherings for many centuries, it is estimated that there are the bones of 100,000 horses, besides reindeer, mammoth, and bison bones. They probably followed herds of horses, the little bearded ponies of that age, as these moved after pasture. They hung about on the flanks of the herd, and became very wise about its habits and dispositions. A large part of these men's lives must have been spent in watching animals.

Whether they tamed and domesticated the horse is still an open question. Perhaps they learnt to do so by degrees as the centuries passed. At any rate, we find late Palæolithic drawings of horses with marks about the heads that are strongly suggestive of bridles, and there exists a carving of a horse's head showing what is perhaps a rope of twisted skin or tendon. But even if they tamed the horse, it is still more doubtful whether they rode it or had much use for it when it was tamed. The horse they knew was a wild pony with a beard under its chin, not up to carrying a man for any distance. It is improbable that these men had yet learnt the rather unnatural use of animal's milk as food. If they tamed the horse at last, it was the only animal they seem to have tamed. They had no dogs, and they had little to do with any sort of domesticated sheep or cattle.

It greatly aids us to realize their common humanity that

these earliest true men could draw. Both races, it would seem, drew astonishingly well. They were by all standards savages, but they were artistic savages. They drew better than any of their successors down to the beginnings of history. They drew and painted on the cliffs and cave walls that they had wrested from the Neanderthal men. And the surviving drawings come to the ethnologist, puzzling over bones and scraps, with the effect of a plain message shining through guesswork and darkness. They drew on bones and antlers; they carved little figures.

These later Palæolithic people not only drew remarkably well for our information, and with an increasing skill as the centuries passed, but they have also left us other information about their lives in their graves. They buried. They buried their dead, often with ornaments, weapons, and food; they used a lot of colour in the burial, and evidently painted the body. From that one may infer that they painted their bodies during life. Paint was a big fact in their lives. They were inveterate painters; they used black, brown, red, yellow, and white pigments, and the pigments they used endure to this day in the caves of France and Spain. Of all modern races, none have shown so pictorial a disposition; the nearest approach to it has been among the American Indians.

These drawings and paintings of the later Palæolithic people went on through a long period of time, and present wide fluctuations in artistic merit. We give here some early sketches, from which we learn of the interest taken by these early men in the bison, horse, ibex, cave bear, and reindeer. In its early stages the drawing is often primitive like the drawing of clever children; quadrupeds are usually drawn with one hind-leg and one fore-leg, as children draw them to this day. The legs on the other side were too much for the artist's technique. Possibly the first drawings began as children's drawings begin, out of idle scratchings. The savage scratched with a flint on a smooth rock surface, and was reminded of some line or gesture. But their solid carvings are at least as old as their first pictures. The earlier drawings betray a complete incapacity to group animals. As the centuries progressed, more skilful artists appeared. The representation of beasts became at last astonishingly vivid and like. But even at the crest of their artistic time they still drew in profile as children do; perspective and the fore-shortening needed for back and front views were too much for them.[1] They rarely drew themselves. The vast majority of their drawings represent animals. The mammoth and the horse are among the commonest themes. Some of the people, whether Grimaldi people or Cro-Magnon people, also made little ivory and soapstone statuettes, and among these are some very fat female figures. These latter suggest the physique of Grimaldi rather than of Cro-Magnon artists. They are like

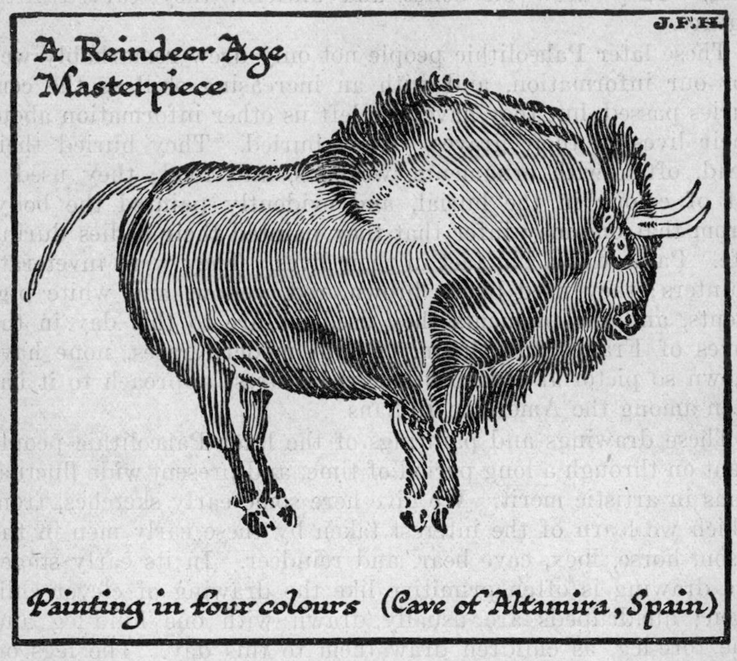

A Reindeer Age Masterpiece

Painting in four colours (Cave of Altamira, Spain)

Bushmen women. The human sculpture of the earlier times inclined to caricature, and generally such human figures as they represent are far below the animal studies in vigour and veracity.

Later on there was more grace and less coarseness in the human representations. One little ivory head discovered is that of a girl with an elaborate coiffure. These people at a later stage also scratched and engraved designs on ivory and bone. Some of the most interesting groups of figures are

[1] R. I. Pocock.

carved very curiously round bone, and especially round rods of deer bone, so that it is impossible to see the entire design

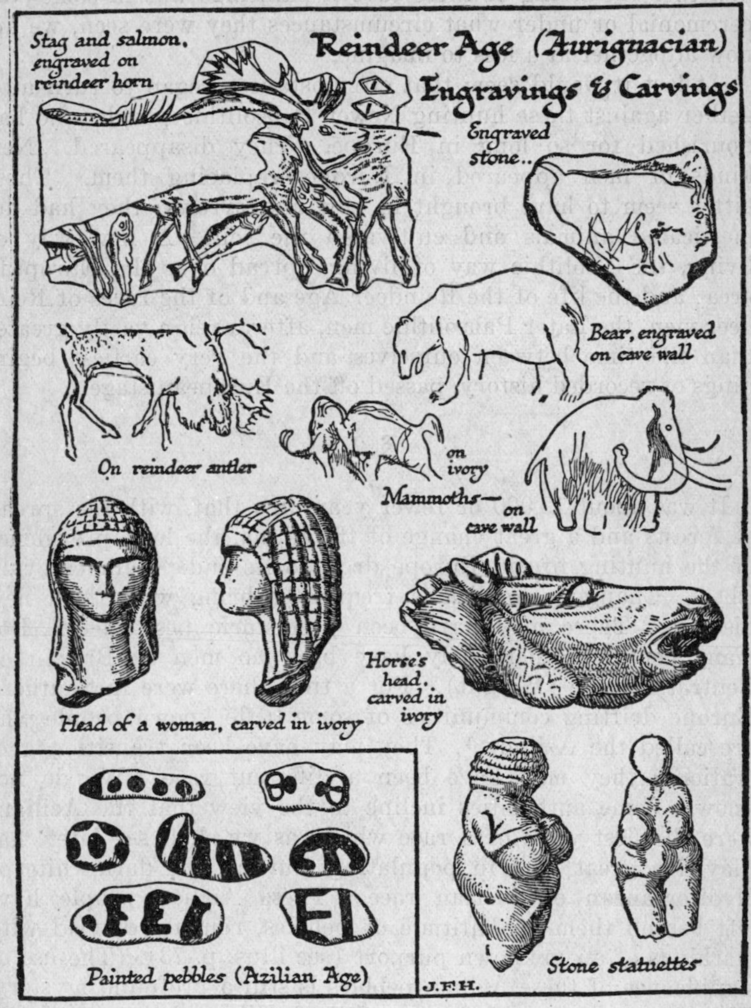

altogether. Figures have also been found modelled in clay, although no Palæolithic people made any use of pottery.

Many of the paintings are found in the depths of unlit caves. They are often difficult of access. The artists must have employed lamps to do their work, and shallow soapstone lamps in which fat could have been burnt have been found. Whether the seeing of these cavern paintings was in some way ceremonial or under what circumstances they were seen, we are now altogether at a loss to imagine.

At last it would seem that circumstances began to turn altogether against these hunting Newer Palæolithic people who had flourished for so long in Europe. They disappeared. New kinds of men appeared in Europe, replacing them. These latter seem to have brought in bow and arrows; they had domesticated animals and cultivated the soil. A new way of living, the Neolithic way of living, spread over the European area; and the life of the Reindeer Age and of the races of Reindeer men, the Later Palæolithic men, after a reign vastly greater than the time between ourselves and the very earliest beginnings of recorded history, passed off the European stage.

§ 2

It was about 12,000 or fewer years ago that, with the spread of forests and a great change of the fauna, the long prevalence of the hunting life in Europe drew to its end. Reindeer vanished. Changing conditions frequently bring with them new diseases. There may have been prehistoric pestilences. For many centuries there may have been no men in Britain or Central Europe (Wright). For a time there were in Southern Europe drifting communities of some little known people who are called the Azilians.[1] They may have been transition generations; they may have been a different race. We do not know. Some authorities incline to the view that the Azilians were the first wave of a race which, as we shall see later, has played a great part in populating Europe, the dark-white or Mediterranean or Iberian race. These Azilian people have left behind them a multitude of pebbles, roughly daubed with markings of an unknown purport (see illus. p. 73). The use or significance of these Azilian pebbles is still a profound mystery. Was this some sort of token writing? Were they counters in some game? Did the Azilians play with these pebbles or tell a story with them, as imaginative children will do with bits of

[1] From the cave of Mas d'Azil.

wood and stone nowadays? At present we are unable to cope with any of these questions.

We will not deal here with the other various peoples who left their scanty traces in the world during the close of the New Palæolithic period, the spread of the forests where formerly there had been steppes, and the wane of the hunters, some 10,000 or 12,000 years ago. We will go on to describe the new sort of human community that was now spreading over the northern hemisphere, whose appearance marks what is called the *Neolithic Age.* The map of the world was assuming something like its present outlines, the landscape and the flora and fauna were taking on their existing characteristics. The prevailing animals in the spreading woods of Europe were the royal stag, the great ox, and the bison; the mammoth and the musk ox had gone. The great ox, or aurochs, is now extinct, but it survived in the German forests up to the time of the Roman Empire. It was never domesticated.[1] It stood eleven feet high at the shoulder, as high as an elephant. There were still lions in the Balkan peninsula, and they remained there until about 1,000 or 1,200 B.C. The lions of Würtemberg and South Germany in those days were twice the size of the modern lion. South Russia and Central Asia were thickly wooded then, and there were elephants in Mesopotamia and Syria, and a fauna in Algeria that was tropical African in character.

Hitherto men in Europe had never gone farther north than the Baltic Sea or the British Isles, but now the Scandinavian peninsula and perhaps Great Russia were becoming possible regions for human occupation. There are no Palæolithic remains in Sweden or Norway. Man, when he entered these countries, was apparently already at the Neolithic stage of social development.

§ 3

Nor is there any convincing evidence of man in America before the end of the Pleistocene.[2] The same relaxation of the

[1] But our domestic cattle are derived from some form of aurochs—probably from some lesser Central Asiatic variety.—H. H. J.

[2] "The various finds of human remains in North America for which the geological antiquity has been claimed have been thus briefly passed under review. In every instance where enough of the bones is preserved for comparison, the evidence bears witness against the geological antiquity of the remains and for their close affinity to or identity with the modern

climate that permitted the retreat of the reindeer hunters into Russia and Siberia, as the Neolithic tribes advanced, may have allowed them to wander across the land that is now cut by Bering Strait, and so reach the American continent. They spread thence southward, age by age. When they reached South America, they found the giant sloth (the *Megatherium*), the glyptodon, and many other extinct creatures, still flourishing. The glyptodon was a monstrous South American armadillo, and a human skeleton has been found by Roth buried beneath its huge tortoise-like shell.[1]

All the human remains in America, even the earliest, it is to be noted, are of an Amer-Indian character. In America there does not seem to have been any preceding races of submen. Man was fully man when he entered America. The old world was the nursery of the sub-races of mankind.

Indian." (Smithsonian Institute, Bureau of American Ethnology, Bulletin 33. Dr. Hrdlicka.)

But J. Deniker quotes evidence to show that eoliths and early palæoliths have been found in America. See his compact but full summary of the evidence and views for and against in his *Races of Man*, pp. 510, 511.

[1] "Questioned by some authorities," says J. Deniker in *The Races of Man*.

X

NEOLITHIC MAN IN EUROPE

§ 1. *The Age of Cultivation Begins.* § 2. *Where Did the Neolithic Culture Arise?* § 3. *Everyday Neolithic Life.* § 4. *Primitive Trade.* § 5. *The Flooding of the Mediterranean Valley.*

§ 1

THE Neolithic phase of human affairs began in Europe about 10,000 or 12,000 years ago. But probably men had reached the Neolithic stage elsewhere some thousands of years earlier. Neolithic men came slowly into Europe from the south or south-east as the reindeer and the open steppes gave way to forest and modern European conditions.

The Neolithic stage in culture is characterized by: (1) the presence of polished stone implements, and in particular the stone *axe,* which was perforated so as to be the more effectually fastened to a wooden handle, and which was probably used rather for working wood than in conflict. There are also abundant arrow-heads. The fact that some implements are polished does not preclude the presence of great quantities of implements of unpolished stone. But there are differences in the make between even the unpolished tools of the Neolithic and of the Palæolithic Period. (2) The beginning of a sort of agriculture, and the use of plants and seeds. But at first there are abundant evidences that hunting was still of great importance in the Neolithic Age. Neolithic man did not at first sit down to his agriculture. He took snatch crops. He settled later. (3) Pottery and proper cooking. The horse is no longer eaten. (4) Domesticated animals. The dog appears very early. The Neolithic man had domesticated cattle, sheep, goats, and pigs.

He was a huntsman turned herdsman of the herds he once hunted. (5) Plaiting and weaving.

These Neolithic people probably "migrated" into Europe, in the same way that the Reindeer Men had migrated before them; that is to say, generation by generation and century by century, as the climate changed, they spread after their accustomed food. They were not "nomads." Nomadism, like civilization, had still to be developed. At present we are quite unable to estimate how far the Neolithic peoples were new-comers and how far their arts were developed or acquired by the descendants of some of the hunters and fishers of the Later Palæolithic Age.

Whatever our conclusions in that matter, this much we may say with certainty; there is no great break, no further sweeping away of one kind of man and replacement by another kind between the appearance of the Neolithic way of living and our own time. There are invasions, conquests, extensive emigrations and intermixtures, but the races as a whole carry on and continue to adapt themselves to the areas into which they began to settle in the opening of the Neolithic Age. The Neolithic men of Europe were white men ancestral to the modern Europeans. They may have been of a darker complexion than many of their descendants; of that we cannot speak with certainty. But there is no real break in culture from their time onward until we reach the age of coal, steam, and power-driven machinery that began in the eighteenth century.

After a long time gold, the first known of the metals, appears among the bone ornaments with jet and amber. Irish Neolithic remains are particularly rich in gold. Then, perhaps 6,000 or 7,000 years ago in Europe, Neolithic people began to use copper in certain centres, making out of it implements of much the same pattern as their stone ones. They cast the copper in moulds made to the shape of the stone implements. Possibly they first found native copper and hammered it into shape.[1] Later—we will not venture upon figures—men had found out how to get copper from its ore. Perhaps, as Lord Avebury suggested, they discovered the secret of smelting by the chance putting of lumps of copper ore among the ordinary stones with which they built the fire pits they used for cooking. In China,

[1] Native copper is still found to-day in Italy, Hungary, Cornwall, and many other places.

Hungary, Cornwall, and elsewhere copper ore and tinstone occur in the same veins; it is a very common association, and so, rather through dirtiness than skill, the ancient smelters, it

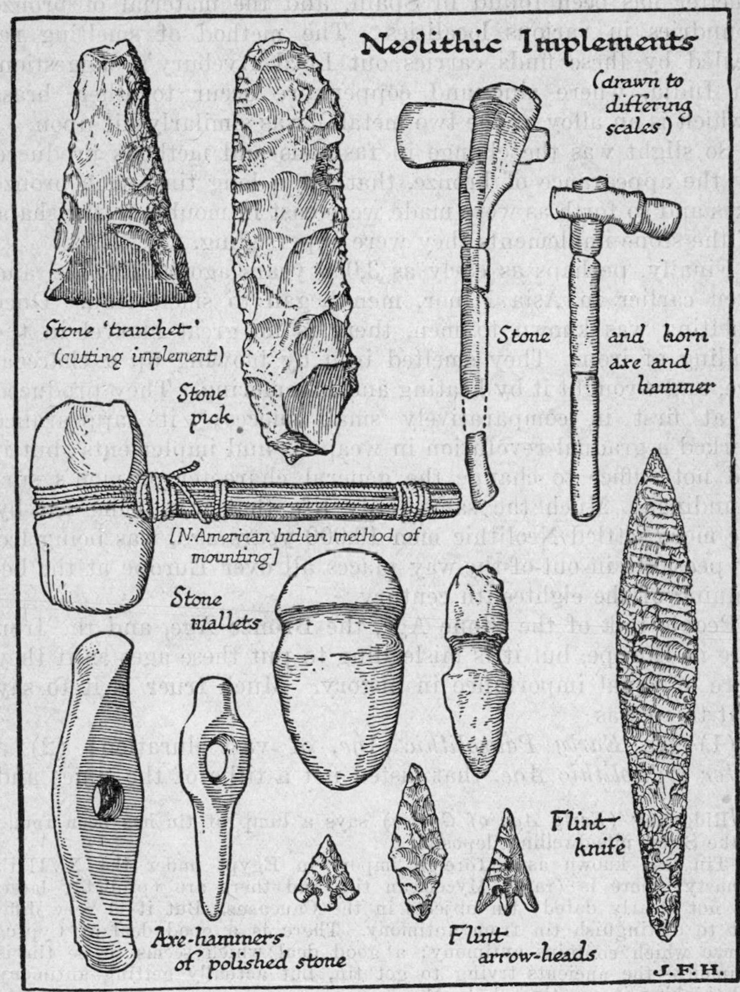

may be, hit upon the harder and better bronze, which is an alloy of copper and tin. Bronze is not only harder than copper, but the mixture of tin and copper is more fusible and easier to reduce. The so-called "pure-copper" implements usually contain a small proportion of tin, and there are no tin implements known, nor very much evidence to show that early men knew of tin as a separate metal.[1] [2] The plant of a prehistoric copper smelter has been found in Spain, and the material of bronze foundries in various localities. The method of smelting revealed by these finds carries out Lord Avebury's suggestion. In India, where zinc and copper ore occur together, brass (which is an alloy of the two metals) was similarly hit upon.

So slight was the change in fashions and methods produced by the appearance of bronze, that for a long time such bronze axes and so forth as were made were cast in moulds to the shape of the stone implements they were superseding.

Finally, perhaps as early as 3,000 years ago in Europe, and even earlier in Asia Minor, men began to smelt iron. Once smelting was known to men, there is no great marvel in the finding of iron. They smelted iron by blowing up a charcoal fire, and wrought it by heating and hammering. They produced it at first in comparatively small pieces;[3] its appearance worked a gradual revolution in weapons and implements; but it did not suffice to change the general character of men's surroundings. Much the same daily life that was being led by the more settled Neolithic men 10,000 years ago, was being led by peasants in out-of-the-way places all over Europe at the beginning of the eighteenth century.

People talk of the Stone Age, the Bronze Age, and the Iron Age in Europe, but it is misleading to put these ages as if they were of equal importance in history. Much truer is it to say that there was:

(1) An *Early Palæolithic Age,* of vast duration; (2) a *Later Palæolithic Age,* that lasted not a tithe of the time; and

[1] Ridgeway (*Early Age of Greece*) says a lump of tin has been found in the Swiss pile-dwelling deposits.

[2] Tin was known as a foreign import in Egypt under the XVIIIth Dynasty; there is (rare) Mycenæan tin, and there are (probably later, but not clearly dated) tin objects in the Caucasus. But it is very difficult to distinguish tin from antimony. There is a good deal of Cyprus bronze which contains antimony; a good deal which seems to be tin is antimony—the ancients trying to get tin, but actually getting antimony and thinking it was tin.—J. L. M.

[3] In connection with iron, note the distinction of ornamental and useful iron. Ornamental iron, a rarity, perhaps meteoric, as jewellery or magical stuff, occurs in east Europe sporadically in the time of the XVIIIth Dynasty. This must be distinguished from the copious useful iron which appears in Greece much later from the North.—J. L. M.

(3) the *Age of Cultivation,* the age of the white men in Europe, which began 10,000 or at most 12,000 years ago, of which the Neolithic Period was the beginning, and which is still going on.

§ 2

We do not know yet the region in which the ancestors of the brownish Neolithic peoples worked their way up from the Palæolithic stage of human development. Probably it was somewhere about south-western Asia, or in some region now submerged beneath the Mediterranean Sea or the Indian Ocean, that, while the Neanderthal men still lived their hard lives in the bleak climate of a glaciated Europe, the ancestors of the white men developed the rude arts of *their* Later Palæolithic period. But they do not seem to have developed the artistic skill of their more northerly kindred, the European Later Palæolithic races. And through the hundred centuries or so while Reindeer men were living under comparatively unprogressive conditions upon the steppes of France, Germany, and Spain, these more favoured and progressive people to the south were mastering agriculture, learning to develop their appliances, taming the dog, domesticating cattle, and, as the climate to the north mitigated and the equatorial climate grew more tropical, spreading northward. All these early chapters of our story have yet to be disinterred. They will probably be found in Asia Minor, Persia, Arabia, India, or north Africa, or they lie beneath the Mediterranean waters. Twelve thousand years ago, or thereabouts—we are still too early for anything but the roughest chronology—Neolithic peoples were scattered all over Europe, north Africa, and Asia. They were peoples at about the level of many of the Polynesian islanders of the last century, and they were the most advanced peoples in the world.

§ 3

It will be of interest here to give a brief account of the life of the European Neolithic people before the appearance of metals. We get our light upon that life from various sources. They scattered their refuse about, and in some places (*e.g.* on the Danish coast) it accumulated in great heaps, known as the kitchen-middens. They buried some of their people, but not the common herd, with great care and distinction, and made huge heaps of earth over their sepulchres; these heaps are the barrows or dolmens which contribute a feature to the European, Indian, and American scenery in many districts to this day. In connection with these mounds, or independently of them, they set up great stones (megaliths), either singly or in groups, of which Stonehenge in Wiltshire and Carnac in Brittany are among the best-known examples. In various places their villages are still traceable.

One fruitful source of knowledge about Neolithic life comes from Switzerland, and was first revealed by the very dry winter of 1854, when the water level of one of the lakes, sinking to an unheard-of lowness, revealed the foundations of prehistoric

Pottery from Lake Dwellings

pile dwellings of the Neolithic and early Bronze Ages, built out over the water after the fashion of similar homes that exist to-day in Celebes and elsewhere. Not only were the timbers of those ancient platforms preserved, but a great multitude of wooden, bone, stone, and earthenware utensils and ornaments, remains of food and the like, were found in the peaty accumulations below them. Even pieces of net and garments have been recovered. Similar lake dwellings existed in Scotland, Ireland, and elsewhere—there are well-known remains at Glastonbury in Somersetshire; in Ireland lake dwellings were inhabited from prehistoric times up to the days when O'Neil of Tyrone was fighting against the English before the plantation of Scotch colonists to replace the Irish in Ulster in the reign of James I of England. These lake villages had considerable defensive value, and there was a sanitary advantage in living over flowing water.

Probably these Neolithic Swiss pile dwellings did not shelter the largest communities that existed in those days. They were the homes of small patriarchal groups. Elsewhere upon fertile plains and in more open country there were probably already much larger assemblies of homes than in those mountain valleys. There are traces of such a large community of families in Wiltshire in England, for example; the remains of the stone circle of Avebury near Silbury mound were once the "finest megalithic ruin in Europe." It consisted of two circles of stones surrounded by a large circle and a ditch, and covering altogether twenty-eight and a half acres. From it two avenues of stones, each a mile and a half long, ran west and south on either side of Silbury Hill. Silbury Hill is the largest prehistoric artificial mound in England. The dimensions of this centre of a faith and a social life now forgotten altogether by men indicate the concerted efforts and interests of a very large number of people, widely scattered though they may have been over the west and south and centre of England. Possibly they assembled at some particular season of the year in a primitive sort of fair. The whole community "lent a hand" in building the mounds and hauling the stones. The Swiss pile dwellers, on the contrary, seem to have lived in practically self-contained villages.

These lake-village people were considerably more advanced in methods and knowledge, and probably much later in time than the early Neolithic people who accumulated the shell mounds, known as kitchen-middens, on the Danish and Scotch coasts. These kitchen-midden folk may have been as early as 10,000 B.C. or earlier; the lake dwellings were probably occupied continuously from 5,000 or 4,000 B.C. down almost to historic times. Those early kitchen-midden people were among the most barbaric of Neolithic peoples, their stone axes were rough, and they had no domesticated animal except the dog. The lake dwellers, on the other hand, had, in addition to the dog, which was of a medium-sized breed, oxen, goats, and sheep. Later on, as they were approaching the Bronze Age, they got swine. The remains of cattle and goats prevail n their débris, and, having regard to the climate and country about them, it seems probable that these beasts were sheltered in the buildings upon the piles in winter, and that fodder was stored for them. Probably the beasts lived in the same houses with the people, as the men and beasts do now in Swiss chalets. The people in the houses possibly milked the cows and goats, and milk perhaps played as important a part in their economy as it does in that of the mountain Swiss of to-day. But of that we are not sure at present. Milk is not a natural food for adults; it must have seemed queer stuff to take at first; and it may have been only after much breeding that a continuous supply of milk was secured from cows and goats. Some people think that the use of milk, cheese, butter, and other milk products came later into human life when men became nomadic. The writer is, however, disposed to give the Neolithic men credit for having discovered milking. The milk, if they did use it (and, no doubt, in that case sour curdled milk also, but not well-made cheese and butter), they must have kept in earthenware pots, for they had pottery, though it was roughly hand-made pottery and not the shapely product of the potter's wheel. They eked out this food supply by hunting. They killed and ate red deer and roe deer, bison and wild boar. And they ate the fox, a rather high-flavoured meat, and not what any one would eat in a world of plenty. Oddly enough, they do not seem to have eaten the hare, although it was available as food. They are supposed to have avoided eating it, as some savages are said to avoid eating it to this day, because they feared that the flesh of so timid a creature might make them, by a sort of infection, cowardly.[1]

Of their agricultural methods we know very little. No ploughs and no hoes have been found. They were of wood and have perished. Neolithic men cultivated and ate wheat, barley, and millet, but they knew nothing of oats or rye. Their grain they roasted, ground between stones and stored in pots, to be eaten when needed. And they made exceedingly solid and heavy bread, because round flat slabs of it have been got out of these deposits. Apparently they had no yeast. If they had no yeast, then they had no fermented drink. One sort of barley that they had is the sort that was cultivated by the ancient Greeks, Romans, and Egyptians, and they also had an Egyptian variety of wheat, showing that their ancestors had brought or derived this cultivation from the south-east. The centre of diffusion of wheat was somewhere in the eastern Mediterranean region. A

[1] Caesar *de Bello Gallico* says the Britons tabooed hare, fowl, and goose.—G. Wh.

wild form is still found in the neighbourhood of Mt. Hermon (see Footnote to Chap. XIV, § 1). When the lake dwellers sowed their little patches of wheat in Switzerland, they were already following the immemorial practice of mankind. The seed must have been brought age by age from that distant centre of diffusion. In the ancestral lands of the south-east men had already been sowing wheat perhaps for thousands of years.[1] Those lake dwellers also ate peas, and crab-apples—the only apples that then existed in the world. Cultivation and selection had not yet produced the apple of to-day.

They dressed chiefly in skins, but they also made a rough cloth of flax. Fragments of that flaxen cloth have been discovered. Their nets were made of flax; they had as yet no knowledge of hemp and hempen rope. With the coming of bronze, their pins and ornaments increased in number. There is reason to believe they set great store upon their hair, wearing it in large shocks with pins of bone and afterwards of metal. To judge from the absence of realistic carvings or engravings or paintings, they either did not decorate their garments or decorated them with plaids, spots, interlacing designs, or similar conventional ornament. Before the coming of bronze there is no evidence of stools or tables; the Neolithic people probably squatted on their clay floors. There were no cats in these lake dwellings; no mice or rats had yet adapted themselves to human dwellings; the cluck of the hen was not as yet added to the sounds of human life, nor the domestic egg to its diet.[2]

The chief tool and weapon of Neolithic man was his axe; his next the bow and arrow. His arrow-heads were of flint,

1 All Old World peoples who had entered upon the Neolithic stage grew and ate wheat, but the American Indians must have developed agriculture independently in America after their separation from the Old World populations. They never had wheat. Their cultivation was maize, Indian corn, a New World grain.

2 Poultry and hens' eggs were late additions to the human cuisine, in spite of the large part they now play in our dietary. The hen is not mentioned in the Old Testament (but note the allusion to an egg, Job vi, 6) nor by Homer. Up to about 1,500 B.C. the only fowls in the world were jungle denizens in India and Burmah. The crowing of jungle cocks is noted by Glasfurd in his admirable accounts of tiger shooting as the invariable preliminary of dawn in the Indian jungle. Probably poultry were first domesticated in Burmah. They got to China, according to the records, only about 1,100 B.C. They reached Greece via Persia before the time of Socrates. In the New Testament the crowing of the cock reproaches Peter for his desertion of the Master.

beautifully made, and he lashed them tightly to their shafts. Probably he prepared the ground for his sowing with a pole, or a pole upon which he had stuck a stag's horn. Fish he hooked or harpooned. These implements no doubt stood about in the interior of the house, from the walls of which hung his fowling-nets. On the floor, which was of clay or trodden cow-dung (after the fashion of hut floors in India to-day), stood pots and jars and woven baskets containing grain, milk, and such-like food. Some of the pots and pans hung by rope loops to the walls. At one end of the room, and helping to keep it warm in winter by their animal heat, stabled the beasts. The

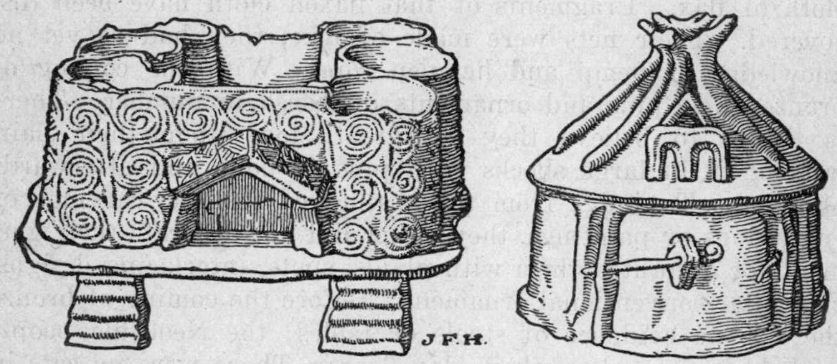

Hut urns, the first probably representing a lake-dwelling... After Lubbock.

children took the cows and goats out to graze, and brought them in at night before the wolves and bears came prowling.

Since Neolithic man had the bow, he probably also had stringed instruments, for the rhythmic twanging of a bow-string seems almost inevitably to lead to that. He also had earthenware drums across which skins were stretched; perhaps also he made drums by stretching skins over hollow tree stems.[1] We do not know when man began to sing, but evidently he was making music, and since he had words, songs were no doubt being made. To begin with, perhaps, he just let his voice loose as one may hear Italian peasants now behind their ploughs singing songs without words. After dark in the winter he sat in his house and talked and sang and made implements by

[1] Later Palæolithic bone whistles are known. One may guess that reed pipes were an early invention.

touch rather than sight. His lighting must have been poor, and chiefly firelight, but there was probably always some fire in the village, summer or winter. Fire was too troublesome to make for men to be willing to let it out readily. Sometimes a great disaster happened to those pile villages, the fire got free, and they were burnt out. The Swiss deposits contain clear evidence of such catastrophes.

All this we gather from the remains of the Swiss pile dwellings, and such was the character of the human life that spread over Europe, coming from the south and from the east with the forests as, 10,000 or 12,000 years ago, the reindeer and the Reindeer men passed away. It is evident that we have here a way of life already separated by a great gap of thousands of years of invention from its original Palæolithic stage. The steps by which it rose from that condition we can only guess at. From being a hunter hovering upon the outskirts of flocks and herds of wild cattle and sheep, and from being a co-hunter with the dog, man by insensible degrees may have developed a sense of proprietorship in the beasts and struck up a friendship with his canine competitor. He learnt to turn the cattle when they wandered too far; he brought his better brain to bear to guide them to fresh pasture. He hemmed the beasts into valleys and enclosures where he could be sure to find them again. He fed them when they starved, and so slowly he tamed them. Perhaps his agriculture began with the storage of fodder. He reaped, no doubt, before he sowed. The Palæolithic ancestor away in that unknown land of origin to the south-east first supplemented the precarious meat supply of the hunter by eating roots and fruits and wild grains. Man storing graminiferous grasses for his cattle might easily come to beat out the grain for himself.

§ 4

All these early beginnings must have taken place far back in time, and in regions of the world that have still to be effectively explored by the archæologists. They were probably going on in Asia or Africa, in what is now the bed of the Mediterranean, or in the region of the Indian Ocean, while the Reindeer man was developing his art in Europe. The Neolithic men who drifted over Europe and Western Asia 12,000 or 10,000 years ago were long past these beginnings; they were already close, a few thousand years, to the dawn of written tradition and the remembered history of mankind. Without any very great shock or break, bronze came at last into human life, giving a great advantage in warfare to those tribes who first obtained it. Written history had already begun before weapons of iron came into Europe to supersede bronze.

Already in those days a sort of primitive trade had sprung up. Bronze and bronze weapons, and such rare and hard stones as jade, gold because of its plastic and ornamental possibilities, and skins and flax-net and cloth, were being swapped and stolen and passed from hand to hand over great stretches of country. Salt also was probably being traded. On a meat dietary men can live without salt, but grain-consuming people need it just as herbivorous animals need it. Hopf says that bitter tribal wars have been carried on by the desert tribes of the Soudan in recent years for possession of the salt deposits between Fezzan and Murzuk. To begin with, barter, blackmail, tribute, and robbery by violence passed into each other by insensible degrees. Men got what they wanted by such means as they could.

§ 5

So far we have been telling of a history without events, a history of ages and periods and stages in development. But before we conclude this portion of the human story, we must record what was probably an event of primary importance and at first perhaps of tragic importance to developing mankind, and that was the breaking in of the Atlantic waters to the great Mediterranean valley.

The reader must keep in mind that we are endeavouring to give him plain statements that he can take hold of comfortably. But both in the matter of our time charts and the three maps we have given of prehistoric geography there is necessarily much speculative matter. We have dated the last Glacial Age and the appearance of the true men as about 40,000 or 35,000 years ago. Please bear that "about" in mind. The truth may be 60,000 or 20,000. But it is no good saying "a very long time" or "ages" ago, because then the reader will not know whether we mean centuries or millions of years. And similarly in these maps we give, they represent not the truth, but something like the truth. The outline of the land was "some such outline."

There were such seas and such land masses. But both Mr. Horrabin, who has drawn these maps, and I, who have incited him to do so, have preferred to err on the timid side. We are not geologists enough to launch out into original research in these matters, and so we have stuck to the 40-fathom line and the recent deposits as our guides for our postglacial map and for the map of 12,000 to 10,000 B.C. But in one matter we have gone beyond these guides. It is practically certain that at the end of the last Glacial Age the Mediterranean was a couple of land-locked sea basins, not connected—or only connected by a torrential overflow river. The eastern basin was the fresher; it was fed by the Nile, the "Adriatic" river, the "Red-Sea" river, and perhaps by a river that poured down amidst the mountains that are now the Greek Archipelago from the very much bigger Sea of Central Asia that then existed. Almost certainly human beings, and possibly even Neolithic men, wandered over that now lost Mediterranean valley.

The reasons for believing this are very good and plain. To this day the Mediterranean is a sea of evaporation. The rivers that flow into it do not make up for the evaporation from its surface. There is a constant current of water pouring into the Mediterranean from the Atlantic, and another current streaming in from the Bosporus and Black Sea. For the Black Sea gets more water than it needs from the big rivers that flow into it; it is an overflowing sea, while the Mediterranean is a thirsty sea. From which it must be plain that when the Mediterranean was cut off both from the Atlantic Ocean and the Black Sea it must have been a shrinking sea with its waters sinking to a much lower level than those of the ocean outside. This is the case of the Caspian Sea to-day. Still more so is it the case with the Dead Sea.

But if this reasoning is sound, then where to-day roll the blue waters of the Mediterranean there must once have been great areas of land, and land with a very agreeable climate. This was probably the case during the last Glacial Age, and we do not know how near it was to our time when the change occurred that brought back the ocean waters into the Mediterranean basin. Certainly there must have been Grimaldi people, and perhaps even Azilian and Neolithic people going about in the valleys and forests of these regions that are now submerged. The Neolithic Dark Whites, the people of the Mediterranean race, may have gone far towards the beginnings of settlement and civilization in that great lost Mediterranean valley.

Mr. W. B. Wright[1] gives us some very stimulating suggestions here. He suggests that in the Mediterranean basin there were two lakes, "one a fresh-water lake, in the eastern depression, which drained into the other in the western depression. It is interesting to think what must have happened when the ocean level rose once more as a result of the dissipation of the ice-sheets, and its waters began to pour over into the Mediterranean area. The inflow, small at first, must have ultimately increased to enormous dimensions, as the channel was slowly lowered by erosion and the ocean level slowly rose. If there were any unconsolidated materials on the sill of the Strait, the result must have been a genuine debacle, and if we consider the length of time which even an enormous torrent would take to fill such a basin as that of the Mediterranean, we must conclude that this result was likely to have been attained in any case. Now, this may seem all the wildest speculation, but it is not entirely so, for if we examine a submarine contour map of the Straits of Gibraltar, we find there is an enormous valley running up from the Mediterranean deep, right through the Straits, and trenching some distance out on to the Atlantic shelf. This valley or gorge is probably the work of the inflowing waters of the ocean at the termination of the period of interior drainage."

This refilling of the Mediterranean, which by the rough chronology we are employing in this book may have happened somewhen between 30,000 and 10,000 B.C., must have been one of the greatest single events in the pre-history of our race. If the later date is the truer, then, as the reader will see plainly enough after reading the next two chapters, the crude beginnings of civilization, the first lake dwellings and the first cultivation, were probably round that eastern Levantine Lake into which there flowed not only the Nile, but the two great rivers that are now the Adriatic and the Red Sea. Suddenly the ocean waters began to break through over the westward hills and to pour in upon these primitive peoples—the lake that had been their home and friend became their enemy; its waters rose and never abated; their settlements were submerged; the waters pursued them in their flight. Day by day and year by

[1] *The Quaternary Ice Age.*

year the waters spread up the valleys and drove mankind before them. Many must have been surrounded and caught by the continually rising salt flood. It knew no check; it came faster and faster; it rose over the tree-tops, over the hills, until it had filled the whole basin of the present Mediterranean and until it lapped the mountain cliffs of Arabia and Africa. Far away, long before the dawn of history, this catastrophe occurred.

XI

EARLY THOUGHT

§ 1. *Primitive Philosophy.* § 2. *The Old Man in Religion.* § 3. *Fear and Hope in Religion.* § 4. *Stars and Seasons.* § 5. *Story-telling and Myth-making.* § 6. *Complex Origins of Religion.*

§ 1

BEFORE we go on to tell how 6,000 or 7,000 years ago men began to gather into the first towns and to develop something more than the loose-knit tribes that had hitherto been their highest political association, something must be said about the things that were going on inside these brains of which we have traced the growth and development through a period of 500,000 years from the ape-man stage.

What was man thinking about himself and about the world in those remote days?

At first he thought very little about anything but immediate things. At first he was busy thinking such things as: "Here is a bear; what shall I do?" Or "There is a squirrel; how can I get it?" Until language had developed to some extent there could have been little thinking beyond the range of actual experience, for language is the instrument of thought as book-keeping is the instrument of business. It records and fixes and enables thought to get on to more and more complex ideas. It is the hand of the mind to hold and keep. Primordial man, before he could talk, probably saw very vividly, mimicked very cleverly, gestured, laughed, danced, and lived, without much speculation about whence he came or why he lived. He feared the dark, no doubt, and thunderstorms and big animals and queer things and whatever he dreamt about, and no doubt he did things to propitiate what he feared or to change his luck and please the imaginary powers in rock and beast and river. He made no clear distinction between animate and inanimate things; if a stick hurt him, he kicked it; if the river foamed and flooded, he thought it was hostile. His thought was probably very much at the level of a bright little contemporary boy of four or five. He had the same subtle unreasonableness of transition and the same limitations. But since he had little or no speech he would do little to pass on the fancies that came to him, and develop any tradition or concerted acts about them.

The drawings even of Late Palæolithic man do not suggest that he paid any attention to sun or moon or stars or trees. He was preoccupied only with animals and men. Probably he took day and night, sun and stars, trees and mountains, as being in the nature of things—as a child takes its meal times and its nursery staircase for granted. So far as we can judge, he drew no fantasies, no ghosts or anything of that sort. The Reindeer men's drawings are fearless familiar things, with no hint about them of any religious or occult feelings. There is scarcely anything that we can suppose to be a religious or mystical symbol at all in his productions. No doubt he had a certain amount of what is called *fetishism* in his life; he did things we should now think unreasonable to produce desired ends, for that is all fetishism amounts to; it is only incorrect science based on guess-work or false analogy, and entirely different in its nature from religion. No doubt he was excited by his dreams, and his dreams mixed up at times in his mind with his waking impressions and puzzled him. Since he buried his dead, and since even the later Neanderthal men seem to have buried their dead, and apparently with food and weapons, it has been argued that he had a belief in a future life. But it is just as reasonable to suppose that early men buried their dead with food and weapons because they doubted if they were dead, which is not the same thing as believing them to have immortal spirits, and that their belief in their continuing vitality was reinforced by dreams of the departed. They may have ascribed a sort of were-wolf existence to the dead, and wished to propitiate them. The Reindeer man, we feel, was too intelligent and too like ourselves not to have had some speech, but quite probably it was not very serviceable for anything beyond direct statement or matter-of-fact narrative. He lived in a larger community than the Neanderthaler, but how large we do not know. Except when game is swarming, hunting communities must not keep together in large bodies or they will starve. The Indians who depend upon the caribou in Labrador must be living under circumstances rather like those of the Reindeer men. They scatter in small family groups, as the caribou scatter in search of food; but when the deer collect for the seasonal migration, the Indians also collect. That is the time for trade and feasts and marriages. The simplest American Indian is 10,000 years more sophisticated than the Reindeer man, but probably that sort of gathering and dispersal was also the way of Reindeer men. At Solutré in France there are traces of a great camping and feasting place. There was no doubt an exchange of news there, but one may doubt if there was anything like an exchange of ideas. One sees no scope in such a life for theology or philosophy or superstition or speculation. Fears, yes; but unsystematic fears; fancies and freaks of the imagination, but personal and transitory freaks and fancies.

Perhaps there was a certain power of suggestion in these encouters. A fear really felt needs few words for its transmission; a value set upon something may be very simply conveyed.

In these questions of primitive thought and religion, we must remember that the lowly and savage peoples of to-day probably throw very little light on the mental state of men before the days of fully developed language. Primordial man could have had little or no tradition before the development of speech. All savage and primitive peoples of to-day, on the contrary, are soaked in tradition—the tradition of thousands of generations. They may have weapons like their remote ancestors and methods like them, but what were slight and shallow impressions on the minds of their predecessors are now deep and intricate grooves worn throughout the intervening centuries generation by generation.

§ 2

Certain very fundamental things there may have been in men's minds long before the coming of speech. Chief among these must have been fear of the Old Man of the tribe. The young of the primitive squatting-place grew up under that fear. Objects associated with him were probably forbidden. Every one was forbidden to touch his spear or to sit in his place, just as to-day little boys must not touch father's pipe or sit in his chair. He was probably the master of all the women. The youths of the little community had to remember that. The idea of *something forbidden,* the idea of things being, as it is called, *tabu,* not to be touched, not to be looked at, may thus have got well into the human mind at a very early stage indeed. J. J. Atkinson, in his *Primal Law,* an ingenious analysis of these primitive tabus which are found among savage peoples all over the world, the tabus that separate brother and sister, the tabus that make a man run and hide from his step-mother, traces them to such a fundamental cause as this. Only by respecting this primal law could the young male hope to escape the Old Man's wrath. And the Old Man must have been an actor in many a primordial nightmare. A disposition to propitiate him even after he was dead is quite understandable. One was not sure that he *was* dead. He might only be asleep or shamming. Long after an Old Man was dead, when there was nothing to represent him but a mound and a megalith, the women would convey to their children how awful and wonderful he was. And being still a terror to his own little tribe, it was easy to go on to hoping that he would be a terror to other and hostile people. In his life he had fought for his tribe, even if he had bullied it. Why not when he was dead? One sees that the Old Man idea was an idea very natural to the primitive mind and capable of great development. And opposed to the Old Man, more human and kindlier, was the Mother, who helped and sheltered and advised. The psycho-analysis of Freud and Jung has done much to help us to realize how great a part Father fear and Mother love still play in the adaptation of the human mind to social needs. They have made an exhaustive study of childish and youthful dreams and imaginations, a study which has done much to help in the imaginative reconstruction of the soul of primitive man. It was, as it were, the soul of a powerful child. He saw the universe in terms of the family herd. His fear of, his abjection before, the Old Man mingled with his fear of the dangerous animals about him. But the women goddesses were kindlier and more subtle. They helped, they protected, they gratified and consoled. Yet at the same time there was something about them less comprehensible than the direct brutality of the Old Man, a greater mystery. So that the Woman also had her vestiture of fear for him.

§ 3

Another idea probably arose early out of the mysterious visitation of infectious diseases, and that was the idea of uncleanness and of being accurst. From that, too, there may have come an idea of avoiding particular places and persons, and persons in particular phases of health. Here was the root of another set of tabus. Then man, from the very dawn of his mental life, may have had a feeling of the sinister about places and things. Animals who dread traps, have that feeling. A tiger will abandon its usual jungle route at the sight of a few threads of cotton.[1] Like most young animals, young human beings are easily made fearful of this or that by their nurses and seniors. Here is another set of ideas, ideas of repulsion and avoidance, that sprang up almost inevitably in men.

As soon as speech began to develop, it must have got to work upon such fundamental feelings and begun to systematize them, and keep them in mind. By talking together men would reinforce each other's fears, and establish a common tradition of tabus of things forbidden and of things unclean. With the idea of uncleanness would come ideas of cleansing and of removing a curse. The cleansing would be conducted through the advice and with the aid of wise old men or wise old women, and in such cleansing would lie the germ of the earliest priestcraft and witchcraft.

Speech from the first would be a powerful supplement to the merely imitative education and to the education of cuffs and blows conducted by a speechless parent. Mothers would tell their young and scold their young. As speech developed, men would find they had experiences and persuasions that gave them or seemed to give them power. They would make secrets of these things. There is a double streak in the human mind, a streak of cunning secretiveness and a streak perhaps of later origin that makes us all anxious to tell and astonish and impress each other. Many people make secrets in order to have secrets to tell. These secrets of early men they would convey to younger, more impressionable people, more or less honestly and impressively in some process of initiation. Moreover, the pedagogic spirit overflows in the human mind; most people like "telling other people not to." Extensive arbitrary prohibitions for the boys,

[1] Glasfurd's *Rifle and Romance in the Indian Jungle*, 1915.

for the girls, for the women, also probably came very early into human history.

Then the idea of the sinister has for its correlative the idea of the propitious, and from that to the idea of making things propitious by ceremonies is an easy step.

§ 4

Out of such ideas and a jumble of kindred ones grew the first quasi-religious elements in human life. With every development of speech it became possible to intensify and develop the tradition of tabus and restraints and ceremonies. There is not a savage or barbaric race to-day that is not held in a net of such tradition. And with the coming of the primitive herdsman there would be a considerable broadening out of all this sort of practice. Things hitherto unheeded would be found of importance in human affairs. Neolithic man was nomadic in a different spirit from the mere daylight drift after food of the primordial hunter. He was a herdsman upon whose mind a sense of direction and the lie of the land had been forced. He watched his flock by night as well as by day. The sun by day and presently the stars by night helped to guide his migrations; he began to find after many ages that the stars are steadier guides than the sun. He would begin to note particular stars and star groups, and to distinguish any individual thing was, for primitive man, to believe it individualized and personal. He would begin to think of the chief stars as persons, very shining and dignified and trustworthy persons looking at him like bright eyes in the night. His primitive tillage strengthened his sense of the seasons. Particular stars ruled his heavens when seedtime was due. Up to a certain point, a mountain peak or what not, a bright star moved, night after night. It stopped there, and then night after night receded. Surely this was a sign, a silent, marvellous warning to the wise. The beginnings of agriculture, we must remember, were in the sub-tropical zone, or even nearer the equator, where stars of the first magnitude shine with a splendour unknown in more temperate latitudes.

And Neolithic man was counting, and falling under the spell of numbers. There are savage languages that have no word for any number above five. Some peoples cannot go above two. But Neolithic man in the lands of his origin in Asia and Africa even more than in Europe was already counting his accumulating possessions. He was beginning to use tallies, and wondering at the triangularity of three and the squareness of four, and why some quantities like twelve were easy to divide in all sorts of ways, and others, like thirteen, impossible. Twelve became a noble, generous, and familiar number to him, and thirteen rather an outcast and disreputable one.

A Carved Statue ("Menhir") of the Neolithic Period—a Contrast to the Freedom and Vigour of Palæolithic Art.

Probably man began reckoning time by the clock of the full and new moons. Moonlight is an important thing to herdsmen who no longer merely hunt their herds, but watch and guard them. Moonlight, too, was, perhaps, his time for love-making, as indeed it may have been for primordial man and the ground ape ancestor before him. But from the phases of the moon, as his tillage increased, man's attitude would go on to the greater cycle of the seasons. Primordial man probably only drifted before the winter as the days grew cold. Neolithic man knew surely that the winter would come, and stored his fodder and presently his grain. He had to fix a seedtime, a propitious seedtime, or his sowing was a failure. The earliest recorded reckoning is by moons and by generations of men. The former seems to be the case in the Book of Genesis, where, if one reads the great ages of the patriarchs who lived before the flood as lunar months instead of years, Methusaleh and the others are reduced to a credible length of life. But with agriculture began the difficult task of squaring the lunar month with the solar year; a task which has left its scars on our calendar to-day. Easter shifts uneasily from year to year, to the great discomfort of holiday-makers; it is now inconveniently early and now late in the season because of this ancient reference of time to the moon.

And when men began to move with set intention from place to place with their animal and other possessions, then they would begin to develop the idea of other places in which they were not, and to think of what might be in those other places. And in any valley where they lingered for a time, they would, remembering how they got there, ask, "How did this or that other thing get here?" They would begin to wonder what was beyond the mountains, and where the sun went when it set, and what was above the clouds.

§ 5

The capacity for telling things increased with their vocabulary. The simple individual fancies, the unsystematic fetish tricks and fundamental tabus of Palæolithic man began to be handed on and made into a more consistent system. Men began to tell stories about themselves, about the tribe, about its tabus and why they had to be, about the world and the why for the world. A tribal mind came into existence, a tradition. Palæolithic man was certainly more of a free individualist, more of an artist, as well as more of a savage than Neolithic man. Neolithic man was coming under prescription; he could be trained from his youth and told to do things and not to do things; he was not so free to form independent ideas of his own about things. He had thoughts given to him; he was under a new power of suggestion. And to have more words and to attend more to words is not simply to increase mental power; words themselves are powerful things and dangerous things. Palæolithic man's words, perhaps, were chiefly just names. He used them for what they were. But Neolithic man was thinking about these words, he was thinking about a number of things with a great deal of verbal confusion, and getting to some odd conclusions. In speech he had woven a net to bind his race together, but also it was a net about his feet. Man was binding himself into new and larger and more efficient combinations indeed, but at a price. One of the most notable things about the Neolithic Age is the total absence of that free, direct artistic impulse which was the supreme quality of later Palæolithic man. We find much industry, much skill, polished implements, pottery with conventional designs, co-operation upon all sorts of things, but no evidence of personal creativeness.[1] Self-suppression is beginning for men. Man has entered upon the long and tortuous and difficult path towards a life for the common good, with all its sacrifice of personal impulse, which he is still treading to-day.

Certain things appear in the mythology of mankind again and again. Neolithic man was enormously impressed by serpents—and he no longer took the sun for granted. Nearly everywhere that Neolithic culture went, there went a disposition to associate the sun and the serpent in decoration and worship. This primitive serpent worship spread ultimately far beyond the regions where the snake is of serious practical importance in human life.

§ 6

With the beginnings of agriculture a fresh set of ideas arose in men's minds. We have already indicated how easily and naturally men may have come to associate the idea of sowing with a burial. Sir J. G. Frazer has pursued the development of this association in the human mind, linking up with it the conception of special sacrificial persons who are killed at seed-time, the conception of a specially purified class of people to kill these sacrifices, the first priests, and the conception of a *sacrament,* a ceremonial feast in which the tribe eats portions of the body of the victim in order to share in the sacrificial benefits.

Out of all these factors, out of the Old Man traditon, out of the emotions that surround Women for men and Men for

[1] Ludwig Hopf, in *The Human Species,* calls the later Palæolithic art "masculine" and the Neolithic "feminine." The pottery was made by women, he says, and that accounts for it. But the arrow-heads were made by men, and there was nothing to prevent Neolithic men from taking scraps of bone or slabs of rock and carving them—had they dared. We suggest they did not dare to do so.

women, out of the desire to escape infection and uncleanness, out of the desire for power and success through magic, out of the sacrificial tradition of seedtime, and out of a number of like

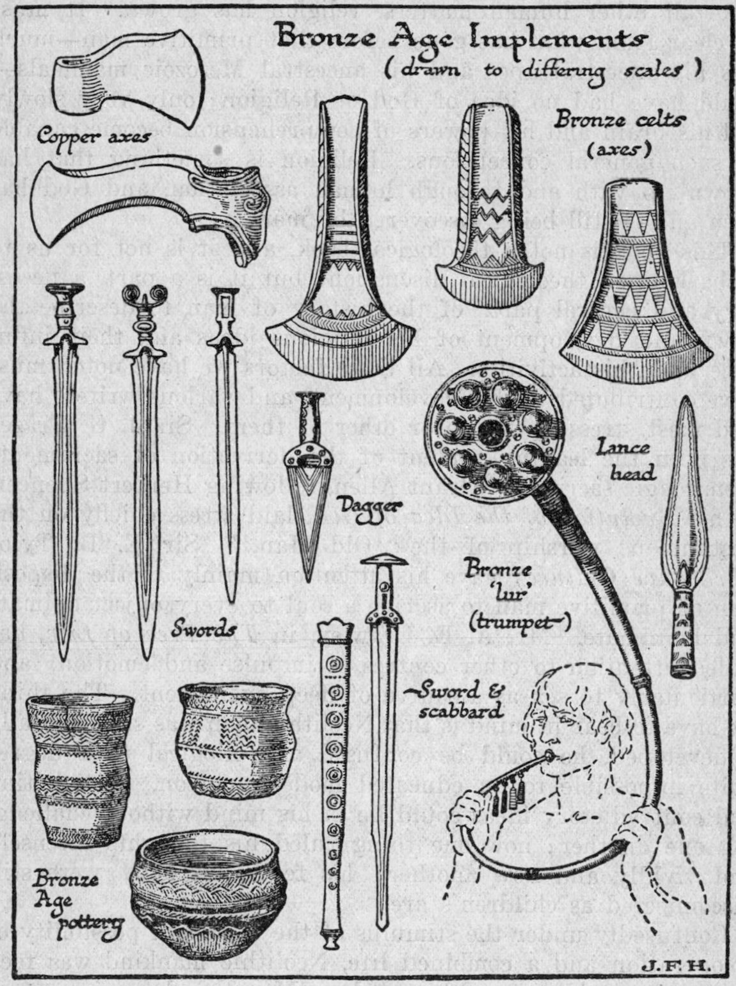

beliefs and mental experiments and misconceptions, a complex something was growing up in the lives of men which was beginning to bind them together mentally and emotionally in a common life and action. This something we may call *religion*

(Lat. *religare,* to bind[1]). It was not a simple or logical something, it was a tangle of ideas about commanding beings and spirits, about gods, about all sorts of "musts" and "must-nots." Like all other human matters, religion has grown. It must be clear from what has gone before that primitive man—much less his ancestral apes and his ancestral Mesozoic mammals—could have had no idea of God or Religion; only very slowly did his brain and his powers of comprehension become capable of such general conceptions. Religion is something that has grown up with and through human association, and God has been and is still being discovered by man.

This book is not a theological book, and it is not for us to embark upon theological discussion; but it is a part, a necessary and central part, of the history of man to describe the dawn and development of his religious ideas and their influence upon his activities. All these factors we have noted must have contributed to this development, and various writers have laid most stress upon one or other of them. Sir J. G. Frazer has been the leading student of the derivation of sacraments from magic sacrifices. Grant Allen, following Herbert Spencer, in his *Evolution of the Idea of God,* laid stress chiefly on the posthumous worship of the "Old Man." Sir E. B. Tylor (*Primitive Culture*) gave his attention mainly to the disposition of primitive man to ascribe a soul to every object animate and inanimate. Mr. A. E. Crawley, in *The Tree of Life,* has called attention to other centres of impulse and emotion, and particularly to sex as a source of deep excitement. The thing we have to bear in mind is that Neolithic man was still mentally undeveloped, he could be confused and illogical to a degree quite impossible to an educated modern person. Conflicting and contradictory ideas could lie in his mind without challenging one another; now one thing ruled his thoughts intensely and vividly and now another; his fears, his acts, were still disconnected as children's are.

Confusedly under the stimulus of the need and possibility of co-operation and a combined life, Neolithic mankind was feeling out for guidance and knowledge. Men were becoming aware that personally they needed protection and direction, cleansing

[1] But Cicero says relegere, "*to read over,*" and the "binding" by those who accept *religare* is often written of as being merely the binding of a vow.

from impurity, power beyond their own strength. Confusedly in response to that demand, bold men, wise men, shrewd and cunning men were arising to become magicians, priests, chiefs,

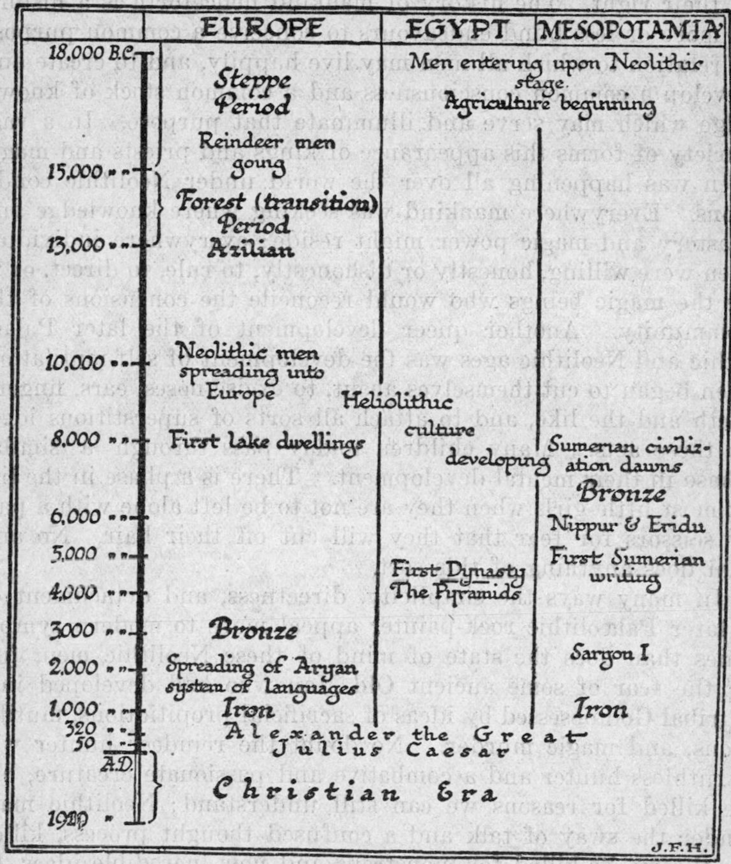

Time Diagram Showing the General Duration of the Neolithic Period in which Early Thought Developed.

By this scale, the diagram on p. 47 of the period since the earliest subhuman traces would be 12 feet long, and the diagram of geological time (ch. ii, § 2) somewhere between 1,500 feet and three miles.

and kings. They are not to be thought of as cheats or usurpers of power, nor the rest of mankind as their dupes. All men are mixed in their motives; a hundred things move men to seek ascendancy over other men, but not all such motives are base or bad. The magicians usually believed more or less in their own magic, the priests in their ceremonies, the chiefs in their right. The history of mankind henceforth is a history of more or less blind endeavours to conceive a common purpose in relation to which all men may live happily, and to create and develop a common consciousness and a common stock of knowledge which may serve and illuminate that purpose. In a vast variety of forms this appearance of kings and priests and magic men was happening all over the world under Neolithic conditions. Everywhere mankind was seeking where knowledge and mastery and magic power might reside; everywhere individual men were willing, honestly or dishonestly, to rule, to direct, or to be the magic beings who would reconcile the confusions of the community. Another queer development of the later Palæolithic and Neolithic ages was the development of self-mutilation. Men began to cut themselves about, to excise noses, ears, fingers, teeth and the like, and to attach all sorts of superstitious ideas to these acts. Many children to-day pass through a similar phase in their mental development. There is a phase in the life of most little girls when they are not to be left alone with a pair of scissors for fear that they will cut off their hair. No animal does anything of this sort.

In many ways the simplicity, directness, and detachment of a later Palæolithic rock-painter appeal more to modern sympathies than does the state of mind of these Neolithic men, full of the fear of some ancient Old Man who had developed into a tribal God obsessed by ideas of sacrificial propitiations, mutilations, and magic murder. No doubt the reindeer hunter was a ruthless hunter and a combative and passionate creature, but he killed for reasons we can still understand; Neolithic man, under the sway of talk and a confused thought process, killed on theory, he killed for monstrous and now incredible ideas, he killed those he loved through fear and under direction. Those Neolithic men not only made human sacrifices at seedtime; there is every reason to suppose they sacrificed wives and slaves at the burial of their chieftains; they killed men, women, and children whenever they were under adversity and thought the gods were athirst. They practised infanticide. All these things passed on into the Bronze Age.

Hitherto a social consciousness had been asleep and not even dreaming in human history. Before it awakened it produced nightmares.

Away beyond the dawn of history, 3,000 or 4,000 years ago, one thinks of the Wiltshire uplands in the twilight of a midsummer day's morning. The torches pale in the growing light. One has a dim apprehension of a procession through the avenue of stone, of priests, perhaps fantastically dressed with skins and horns and horrible painted masks—not the robed and bearded dignitaries our artists represent the Druids to have been—of chiefs in skins adorned with necklaces of teeth and bearing spears and axes, their great heads of hair held up with pins of bone, of women in skins or flaxen robes, of a great peering crowd of shock-headed men and naked children. They have assembled from many distant places; the ground between the avenues and Silbury Hill is dotted with their encampments. A certain festive cheerfulness prevails. And amidst the throng march the appointed human victims, submissive, helpless, staring towards the distant smoking altar at which they are to die—that the harvests may be good and the tribe increase. . . . To that had life progressed 3,000 or 4,000 years ago from its starting-place in the slime of the tidal beaches.

XII

THE RACES OF MANKIND

§ 1. *Is Mankind Still Differentiating?* § 2. *The Main Races of Mankind.* § 3. *The Brunet Peoples.*

§ 1

IT is necessary now to discuss plainly what is meant by a phrase, used often very carelessly, "The Races of Mankind."

It must be evident from what has already been explained in Chapter III that man, so widely spread and subjected therefore to great differences of climate, consuming very different food in different regions, attacked by different enemies, must always have been undergoing considerable local modification and differentiation. Man, like every other species of living thing, has constantly been tending to differentiate into several species; wherever a body of men has been cut off, in islands or oceans or by deserts or mountains, from the rest of humanity, it must have begun very soon to develop special characteristics, specially adapted to the local conditions. But, on the other hand, man is usually a wandering and enterprising animal for whom there exists few insurmountable barriers. Men imitate men, fight and conquer them, interbreed, one people with another. Concurrently for thousands of years there have been two sets of forces at work, one tending to separate men into a multitude of local varieties, and another to remix and blend these varieties together before a separate series has been established.

These two sets of forces may have fluctuated in this relative effect in the past. Palæolithic man, for instance, may have been more of a wanderer, he may have drifted about over a much greater area, than later Neolithic man; he was less fixed to any sort of home or lair, he was tied by fewer possessions. Being a hunter, he was obliged to follow the migrations of his ordinary quarry. A few bad seasons may have shifted him hundreds of miles. He may therefore have mixed very widely and developed few varieties over the greater part of the world.

The appearance of agriculture tended to tie those communities of mankind that took it up to the region in which it was most conveniently carried on, and so to favour differentiation. Mixing or differentiation is not dependent upon a higher or lower stage of civilization; many savage tribes wander now for hundreds of miles; many English villagers in the eighteenth century, on the other hand, had never been more than eight or ten miles from their villages, neither they nor their fathers nor grandfathers before them. Hunting peoples often have enormous range. The Labrador country, for instance, is inhabited by a few thousand Indians, who follow the one great herd of caribou as it wanders yearly north and then south again in pursuit of food. This mere handful of people covers a territory as large as France. Nomad peoples also range very widely. Some Kalmuck tribes are said to travel nearly a thousand miles between summer and winter pasture.

It carries out this suggestion, that Palæolithic man ranged widely and was distributed thinly indeed but uniformly, throughout the world, that the Palæolithic remains we find are everywhere astonishingly uniform. To quote Sir John Evans, "The implements in distant lands are so identical in form and character with the British specimens that they might have been manufactured by the same hands. . . . On the banks of the Nile, many hundreds of feet above its present level, implements of the European types have been discovered; while in Somaliland, in an ancient river-valley at a great elevation above the sea, Sir H. W. Seton-Karr has collected a large number of implements formed of flint and quartzite, which, judging from their form and character, might have been dug out of the drift-deposits of the Somme and the Seine, the Thames or the ancient Solent."

Phases of spreading and intermixture have probably alternated with phases of settlement and specilization in the history of mankind. But up to a few hundred years ago it is probable that since the days of the Palæolithic Age at least mankind has on the whole been differentiating. The species has differentiated in that period into a very great number of varieties, many of which have reblended with others, which have spread and undergone further differentiation or become extinct. Wherever there has been a strongly marked local difference of conditions and a check upon intermixture, there one is almost obliged to assume a variety of mankind must have appeared. Of such local varieties there must have been a great multitude.

In one remote corner of the world, Tasmania, a little cut-off population of people remained in the early Palæolithic stage until the discovery of that island by the Dutch in 1642. They are now, unhappily, extinct. The last Tasmanian died in 1877. They may have been cut off from the rest of mankind for 15,000 or 20,000 or 25,000 years.

But among the numerous obstacles and interruptions to intermixture there have been certain main barriers, such as the Atlantic Ocean, the highlands, once higher, and the now vanished seas of Central Asia and the like, which have cut off great groups of varieties from other great groups of varieties over long periods of time. These separated groups of varieties developed very early certain broad resemblances and differences. Most of the varieties of men in eastern Asia and America, but not all, have now this in common, that they have yellowish buff skins, straight black hair, and often high cheek-bones. Most of the native peoples of Africa south of the Sahara, but not all, have black or blackish skins, flat noses, thick lips, and frizzy hair. In north and western Europe a great number of peoples have fair hair, blue eyes, and ruddy complexions; and about the Mediterranean there is a prevalence of white-skinned peoples with dark eyes and black hair. The black hair of many of these dark whites is straight, but never so strong and waveless as the hair of the yellow peoples. It is straighter in the east than in the west. In southern India we find brownish and darker peoples with straight black hair, and these as we pass eastward give place to more distinctly yellow peoples. In scattered islands and in Papua and New Guinea we find another series of black and brownish peoples of a more lowly type with frizzy hair.

But it must be borne in mind that these are very loose-fitting generalizations. Some of the areas and isolated pockets of mankind in the Asiatic area may have been under conditions more like those in the European area; some of the African areas are of a more Asiatic and less distinctively African type. We find a wavy-haired, fairish, hairy-skinned race, the Ainu, in Japan. They are more like the Europeans in their facial type than the surrounding yellow Japanese. They may be a drifted patch of the whites or they may be a quite distinct people. We find primitive black people in the Andaman Islands far away from Australia and far away from Africa. There is a streak of very negroid blood traceable in south Persia and some parts of India. These are the "Asiatic" negroids. There

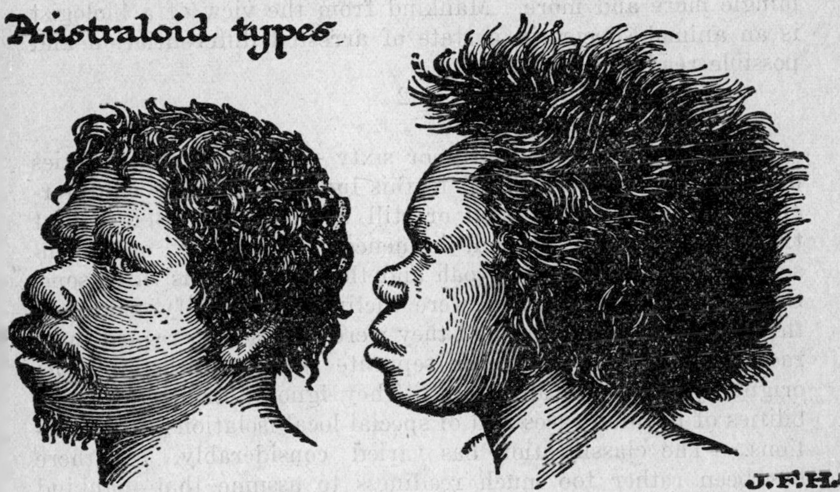

is little or no proof that all black people, the Australians, the Asiatic negroids, and the negroes, derive from one origin, but only that they have lived for vast periods under similar conditions. We must not assume that human beings in the eastern Asiatic area were all differentiating in one direction and all the human beings in Africa in another. There were great currents of tendency, it is true, but there were also backwaters, eddies, admixtures, readmixtures, and leakages from one main area to the other. A coloured map of the world to show the races would not present just four great areas of colour; it would have to be dabbed over with a multitude of tints and intermediate shades, simple here, mixed and overlapping there.

In the early Neolithic Period in Europe—it may be 10,000 or 12,000 years ago or so—man was differentiating all over the world, and he had already differentiated into a number of varieties, but he has never differentiated into different *species*. A "species," we must remember, in biological language is distinguished from a "variety" by the fact that varieties can interbreed, while species either do not do so or produce offspring which, like mules, are sterile. All mankind can interbreed freely, can learn to understand the same speech, can adapt itself to co-operation. And in the present age, man is probably no longer undergoing differentiation at all. Readmixture is now a far stronger force than differentiation. Men mingle more and more. Mankind from the view of a biologist is an animal species in a state of arrested differentiation and possible readmixture.

§ 2

It is only in the last fifty or sixty years that the varieties of men came to be regarded in this light, as a tangle of differentiations recently arrested or still in progress. Before that time students of mankind, influenced, consciously or unconsciously, by the story of Noah and the Ark and his three sons, Shem, Ham, and Japhet, were inclined to classify men into three or four great races and they were disposed to regard these races as having always been separate things, descended from originally separate ancestors. They ignored the great possibilities of blended races and of special local isolations and variations. The classification has varied considerably, but there has been rather too much readiness to assume that mankind *must* be completely divisible into three or four main groups. Ethnologists (students of race) have fallen into grievous disputes about a multitude of minor peoples, as to whether they were of this or that primary race or "mixed," or strayed early forms, or what not. But all races are more or less mixed. There are, no doubt, four main groups, but each is a miscellany, and there are little groups that will not go into any of the four main divisions.

Subject to these reservations, when it is clearly understood that when we speak of these main divisions we mean not simple and pure races, but groups of races, then they have a certain convenience in discussion. Over the European and Mediterranean area and western Asia there are, and have been for many thousand years, white peoples, usually called the CAUCASIANS, subdivided into two or three subdivisions, the northern blonds or Nordic race, an alleged intermediate race about which many authorities are doubtful, the so-called Alpine race, and the southern dark whites, the Mediterranean or Iberian race; over eastern Asia and America a second group of races prevails, the MONGOLIANS, generally with yellow skins, straight black hair, and sturdy bodies; over Africa the NEGROES, and in the region of Australia and New Guinea the black, primitive AUSTRALOIDS. These are convenient terms, provided the student bears in mind that they are are not exactly defined terms. They represent only the common characteristics of certain main groups of races; they leave out a number of little peoples who belong properly to none of these divisions, and they disregard the perpetual mixing where the main groups overlap.

§ 3

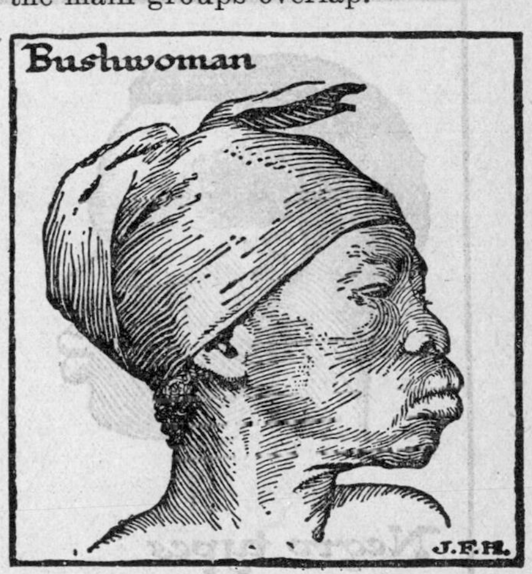

The Mediterranean or Iberian division of the Caucasian racc had a wider range in early times, and was a less specialized and distinctive type than the Nordic. It is very hard to define its southward boundaries from the Negro, or to mark off its early traces in Central Asia from those of early Mongolians. Wilfred Scawen Blunt[1] says that Huxley "had long suspected a common origin of the Egyptians and the Dravidians of India, perhaps a long belt of brown-skinned men from India to Spain in very early days."

It is possible that this "belt" of Huxley's of dark-white and brown-skinned men, this race of brunet-brown folk, ultimately spread even farther than India; that they reached to the shores of the Pacific, and that they were everywhere the original possessors of the Neolithic culture and the beginners of what we call civilization. It is possible that these Brunet peoples are so to speak the *basic* peoples of our modern world. The Nordic and the Mongolian peoples may have been but north-western and north-eastern branches from this more funda-

[1] *My Diaries,* under date of July 25, 1894.

mental stem. Or the Nordic race may have been a branch, while the Mongolian, like the Negro, may have been another equal and distinct stem with which the brunet-browns met and mingled in South China. Or the Nordic peoples also may have developed separately from a palæolithic stage.

At some period in human history (see Elliot Smith's *Migrations of Early Culture*) there seems to have been a special type of Neolithic culture widely distributed in the world which had a group of features so curious and so unlikely to have been independently developed in different regions of the earth,

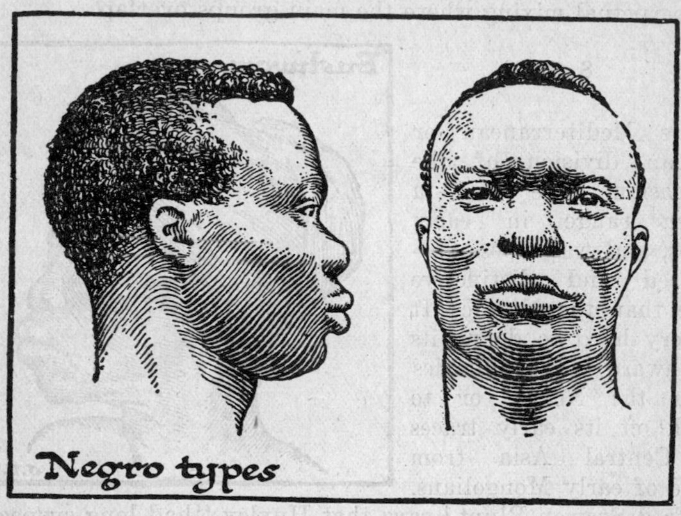

Negro types

as to compel us to believe that it was in effect one culture. It reached through all the regions inhabited by the brunet Mediterranean race, and beyond through India, Further India, up the Pacific coast of China, and it spread at last across the Pacific and to Mexico and Peru. It was a coastal culture not reaching deeply inland.

This peculiar development of the Neolithic culture, which Elliot Smith called the *heliolithic* [1] culture, included many or all of the following odd practices: (1) circumcision, (2) the very queer custom of sending the *father* to bed when a child

[1] "Sunstone" culture because of the sun worship and the megaliths. This is not a very happily chosen term. It suggests a division equivalent to palæolithic (old stone) and neolithic (new stone), whereas it is a subdivision of the neolithic culture.

is born, known as the *couvade,* (3) the practice of massage, (4) the making of mummies, (5) megalithic monuments[1] (*e.g.* Stonehenge), (6) artificial deformation of the heads of the

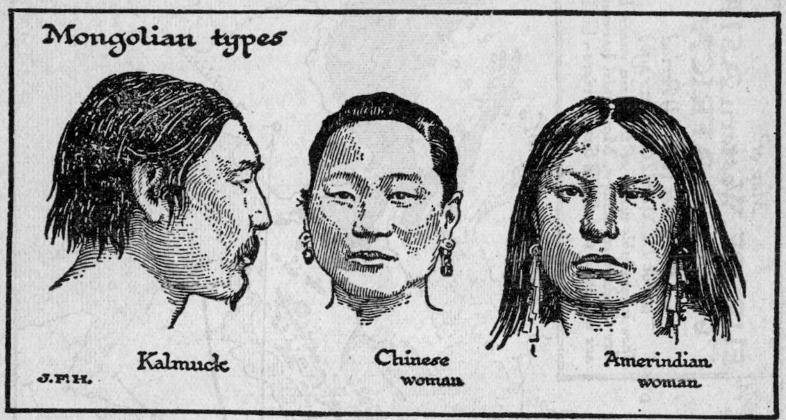

young by bandages, (7) tattooing, (8) religious association of the sun and the serpent, and (9) the use of the symbol known as the swastika (see figure) for good luck. This odd little

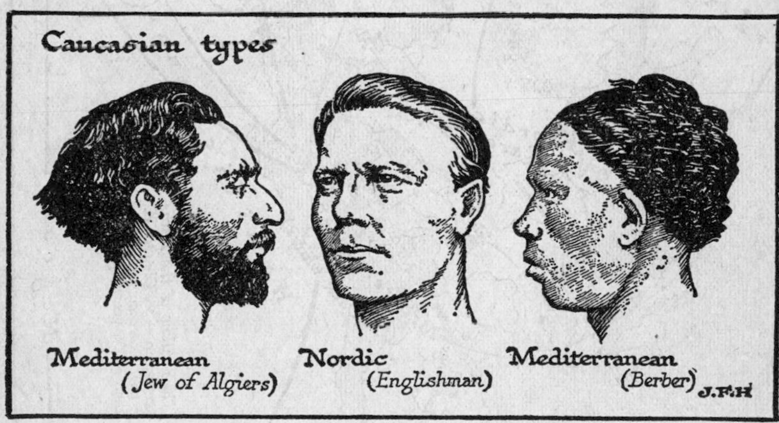

symbol spins gaily round the world; it seems incredible that men would have invented and made a pet of it twice over.

Elliot Smith traces these associated practices in a sort of

[1] Megalithic monuments have been made quite recently by primitive Indian peoples.

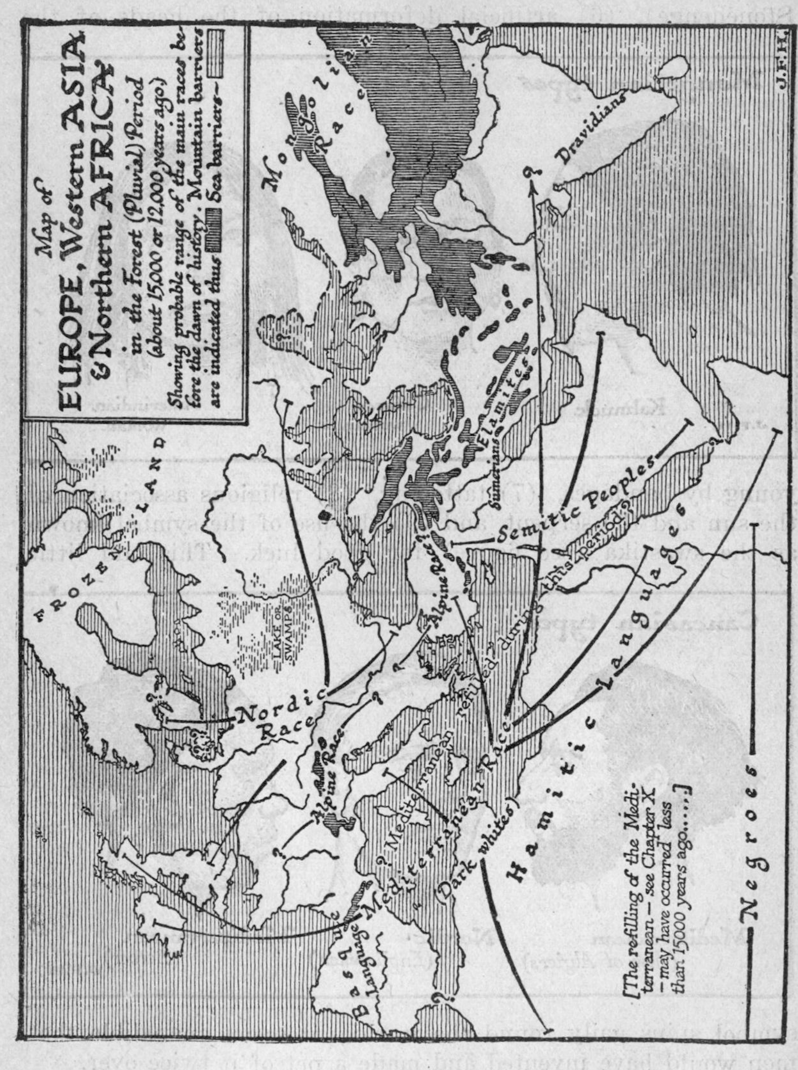
Map of
EUROPE, Western ASIA & Northern AFRICA
in the Forest (Pluvial) Period
(about 15,000 or 12,000 years ago)
Showing probable range of the main races before the dawn of history. Mountain barriers are indicated thus
Sea barriers
FROZEN LAND
LAKE OR SWAMPS
Nordic Race
Alpine Race
Alpine Race?
Mongolian Race
Dravidians
Elamites
Sumerians
Semitic Peoples
Semitic Peoples during this period?
Mediterranean refilled during this period?
Mediterranean Race
Dark whites
Basque Language
Hamitic Languages
Negroes
[The refilling of the Mediterranean—see Chapter X—may have occurred less than 15000 years ago.....]
J.F.H.

constellation all over this great Mediterranean-India Ocean-Pacific area. Where one occurs, most of the others occur. They link Brittany with Borneo and Peru. But this constellation of practices does not crop up in the primitive homes of Nordic or Mongolian peoples, nor does it extend southward much beyond equatorial Africa.

For thousands of years, from 15,000 to 1,000 B.C., such a heliolithic Neolithic culture and its brownish possessors may have been oozing round the world through the warmer regions of the world, drifting by canoes often across wide stretches of sea. It was then the highest culture in the world; it sustained the largest, most highly developed communities. And its region of origin may have been, as Elliot Smith suggests, the Mediterranean and North African region. It migrated slowly age by age. It must have been spreading up the Pacific Coast and across the island stepping-stones to America, long after it had passed on into other developments in its areas of origin. Many of the peoples of the East Indies, Melanesia and Polynesia were still in this heliolithic stage of development when they were discovered by European navigators in the eighteenth century. The first civilizations in Egypt and the Euphrates-Tigris valley probably developed directly out of this widespread culture. We will discuss later whether the Chinese civilization had a different origin. The Semitic nomads of the Arabian desert seem also to have had a heliolithic stage.

The Swastika

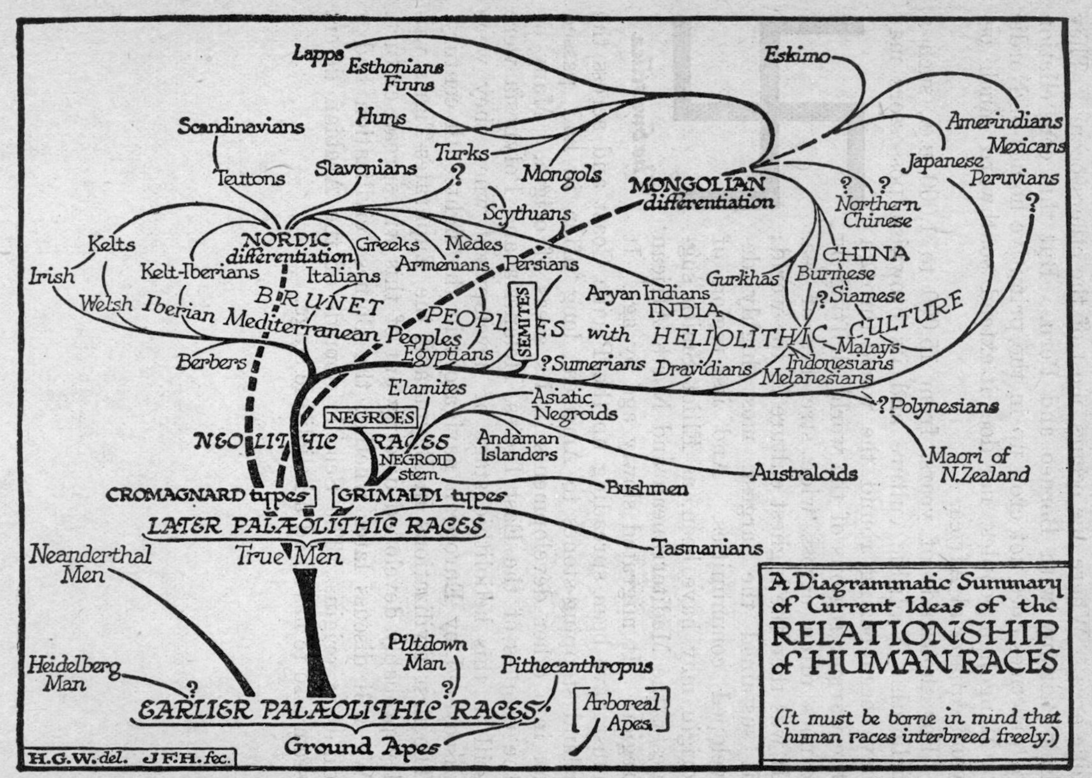
A Diagrammatic Summary of Current Ideas of the RELATIONSHIP of HUMAN RACES
(It must be borne in mind that human races interbreed freely.)
Eskimo
Amerindians
Mexicans
Peruvians
Japanese
Northern Chinese
CHINA
Burmese
Siamese
Malays
Indonesians
Melanesians
Polynesians
Maori of N. Zealand
Australoids
Tasmanians
Bushmen
MONGOLIAN differentiation
Gurkhas
Aryan Indians
INDIA
HELIOLITHIC CULTURE
Dravidians
Sumerians
Asiatic Negroids
Andaman Islanders
Lapps
Esthonians
Finns
Huns
Turks
Mongols
Scythians
Persians
SEMITES
Medes
Armenians
Slavonians
Greeks
Italians
Scandinavians
Teutons
NORDIC differentiation
BRUNET PEOPLES
Mediterranean Peoples
Egyptians
Elamites
NEGROES
NEGROID stem
Kelts
Kelt-Iberians
Iberian
Irish
Welsh
Berbers
NEOLITHIC RACES
CROMAGNARD types
GRIMALDI types
LATER PALÆOLITHIC RACES
True Men
Neanderthal Men
Piltdown Man
Pithecanthropus
Arboreal Apes
EARLIER PALÆOLITHIC RACES
Heidelberg Man
Ground Apes
H.G.W. del. J.F.H. fec.

XIII

THE LANGUAGES OF MANKIND

§ 1. *No One Primitive Language.* § 2. *The Aryan Languages.* § 3. *The Semitic Languages.* § 4. *The Hamitic Languages.* § 5. *The Ural-Altaic Languages.* § 6. *The Chinese Languages.* § 7. *Other Language Groups.* § 8. *A Possible Primitive Language Group.* § 9. *Some Isolated Languages.*

§ 1

IT is improbable that there was ever such a thing as a common human language. We know nothing of the language of Palæolithic man; we do not even know whether Palæolithic man talked freely.

We know that Palæolithic man had a keen sense of form and attitude, because of his drawings; and it has been suggested that he communicated his ideas very largely by gesture. Probably such words as the earlier men used were mainly cries of alarm or passion or names for concrete things, and in many cases they were probably imitative sounds made by or associated with the things named.[1]

The first languages were probably small collections of such words; they consisted of interjections and nouns. Probably the nouns were said in different intonations to convey different meanings. If Palæolithic man had a word for "horse" or "bear," he probably showed by tone or gesture whether he meant "bear is coming," "bear is going," "bear is to be hunted," "dead bear," "bear has been here," "bear did this," and so on. Only very slowly did the human mind develop methods of indicating action and relationship in a formal manner.

[1] Sir Arthur Evans suggests that in America sign-language arose before speech, because the sign-language is common to all Indians in North America, whereas the languages are different. See his *Anthropology and the Classics.*—G. M.

Modern languages contain many thousands of words, but the earlier languages could have consisted only of a few hundred. It is said that even modern European peasants can get along with something less than a thousand words, and it is quite conceivable that so late as the Early Neolithic Period that was the limit of the available vocabulary. Probably men did not indulge in those days in conversation or description. For narrative purposes they danced and acted rather than told. They had no method of counting beyond a method of indicating two by a dual number, and some way of expressing many. The growth of speech was at first a very slow process indeed, and grammatical forms and the expression of abstract ideas may have come very late in human history, perhaps only 400 or 500 generations ago.

§ 2

The students of languages (philologists) tell us that they are unable to trace with certainty any common features in all the languages of mankind. They cannot even find any elements common to all the Caucasian languages. They find over great areas groups of languages which have similar root words and similar ways of expressing the same idea, but then they find in other areas languages which appear to be dissimilar down to their fundamental structure, which express action and relation by entirely dissimilar devices, and have an altogether different grammatical scheme. One great group of languages, for example, now covers nearly all Europe and stretches out to India; it includes English, French, German, Spanish, Italian, Greek, Russian, Armenian, Persian, and various Indian tongues. It is called the Indo-European or ARYAN family. The same fundamental roots, the same grammatical ideas, are traceable through all this family. Compare, for example, English *father, mother,* German *vater, mutter,* Latin *pater, mater,* Greek *pater, meter,* French *père, mère,* Armenian *hair, mair,* Sanscrit *pitar, matar,* etc., etc. In a similar manner the Aryan languages ring the changes on a great number of fundamental words, *f* in the Germanic languages becoming *p* in Latin, and so on. They follow a law of variation called Grimm's Law. These languages are not different things, they are variations of one thing. The people who use these languages think in the same way.

At one time in the remote past, in the Neolithic Age, that is to say 6,000 years or more ago, there may have been one simple original speech from which all these Aryan languages have differentiated. Somewhere between Central Europe and Western Asia there must have wandered a number of tribes sufficiently intermingled to develop and use one tongue. It is convenient here to call them the Aryan peoples. Sir H. H. Johnston has called them "Aryan Russians." They belonged mostly to the Caucasian group of races and to the blond and northern subdivision of the group, to the Nordic race that is.

Here one must sound a note of warning. There was a time when the philologists were disposed to confuse languages and races, and to suppose that people who once all spoke the same tongue must be all of the same blood. That, however, is not the case, as the reader will understand if he will think of the negroes of the United States who now all speak English, or of the Irish, who—except for purposes of political demonstration—no longer speak the old Erse language but English, or of the Cornish people, who have lost their ancient Keltic speech. But what a common language does do, is to show that a common intercourse has existed, and the possibility of intermixture; and if it does not point to a common origin, it points at least to a common future.

But even this original Aryan language, which was a spoken speech perhaps 4,000 or 3,000 B.C., was by no means a *primordial* language or the language of a savage race. Its earliest speakers were in or past the Neolithic stage of civilization. It had grammatical forms and verbal devices of some complexity. The vanished methods of expression of the later Palæolithic peoples, of the Azilians, or of the early Neolithic kitchen-midden people for instance, were probably much cruder than the most elementary form of Aryan.

Probably the Aryan group of languages became distinct in a wide region of which the Danube, Dnieper, Don, and Volga were the main rivers, a region that extended eastward beyond the Ural mountains north of the Caspian Sea. The area over which the Aryan speakers roamed probably did not for a long time reach to the Atlantic or to the south of the Black Sea beyond Asia Minor. There was no effectual separation of Europe from Asia then at the Bosporus. The Danube flowed eastward to a great sea that extended across the Volga region of south-eastern Russia right into Turkestan, and included the Black, Caspian, and Aral Seas of to-day. Perhaps it sent out arms to the Arctic Ocean. It must have been a pretty effective barrier between the Aryan speakers and the people in north-eastern Asia. South of this sea stretched a continuous shore from the Balkans to Afghanistan. North-west of it a region of swamps and lagoons reached to the Baltic.

§ 3

Next to Aryan, philologists distinguish another group of languages which seem to have been made quite separately from the Aryan languages, the Semitic. Hebrew and Arabic are kindred, but they seem to have even a different set of root words from the Aryan tongues; they express their ideas of relationship in a different way; the fundamental ideas of their grammars are generally different. They were in all probability made by human communities quite out of touch with the Aryans, separately and independently. Hebrew, Arabic, Abyssinian, ancient Assyrian, ancient Phœnician, and a number of associated tongues are put together, therefore, as being derived from a second primary language, which is called the SEMITIC. In the very beginnings of recorded history we find Aryan-speaking peoples and Semitic-speaking peoples carrying on the liveliest intercourse of war and trade round and about the eastern end of the Mediterranean, but the fundamental differences of the primary Aryan and primary Semitic languages oblige us to believe that in early Neolithic times, before the historical period, there must for thousands of years have been an almost complete separation of the Aryan-speaking and the Semitic-speaking peoples. The latter seem to have lived either in south Arabia or in north-east Africa. In the opening centuries of the Neolithic Age the original Aryan speakers and the original Semitic speakers were probably living, so to speak, in different worlds with a minimum of intercourse. Racially, it would seem, they had a remote common origin; both Aryan speakers and Semites are classed as Caucasians; but while the original Aryan speakers seem to have been of Nordic race, the original Semites were rather of the Mediterranean type.

§ 4

Philologists speak with less unanimity of a third group of languages, the HAMITIC, which some declare to be distinct from, and others allied to, the Semitic. The weight of opinion inclines now towards the idea of some primordial connection of these two groups. The Hamitic group is certainly a much wider and more various language group than the Semitic or the Aryan, and the Semitic tongues are more of a family, have more of a common likeness, than the Aryan. The Semitic languages may have arisen as some specialized proto-Hamitic group, just as the birds arose from a special group of reptiles (Chap. IV). It is a tempting speculation, but one for which there is really no basis of justifying fact, to suppose that the rude primordial ancestor group of the Aryan tongues branched off from the proto-Hamitic speech forms at some still earlier date than the separation and specialization of Semitic. The Hamitic speakers to-day, like the Semitic speakers, are mainly of the Mediterranean Caucasian race. Among the Hamitic languages are the ancient Egyptian and Coptic, the Berber languages (of the mountain people of North Africa, the Masked Tuaregs, and other such peoples), and what are called the Ethiopic group of African languages in eastern Africa, including the speech of the Gallas and the Somalis. The general grouping of these various tongues suggests that they originated over some great area to the west, as the primitive Semitic may have arisen to the east, of the Red Sea divide. That divide was probably much more effective in Pleistocene times; the sea extended across to the west of the Isthmus of Suez, and a great part of lower Egypt was under water. Long before the dawn of history, however, Asia and Africa had joined at Suez, and these two language systems were in contact in that region. And if Asia and Africa were separated then at Suez, they may, on the other hand, have been joined by way of Arabia and Abyssinia.

These Hamitic languages may have radiated from a centre on the African coast of the Mediterranean, and they may have extended over the then existing land connections very widely into western Europe.

All these three great groups of languages, it may be noted, the Aryan, Semitic, and Hamitic, have one feature in common

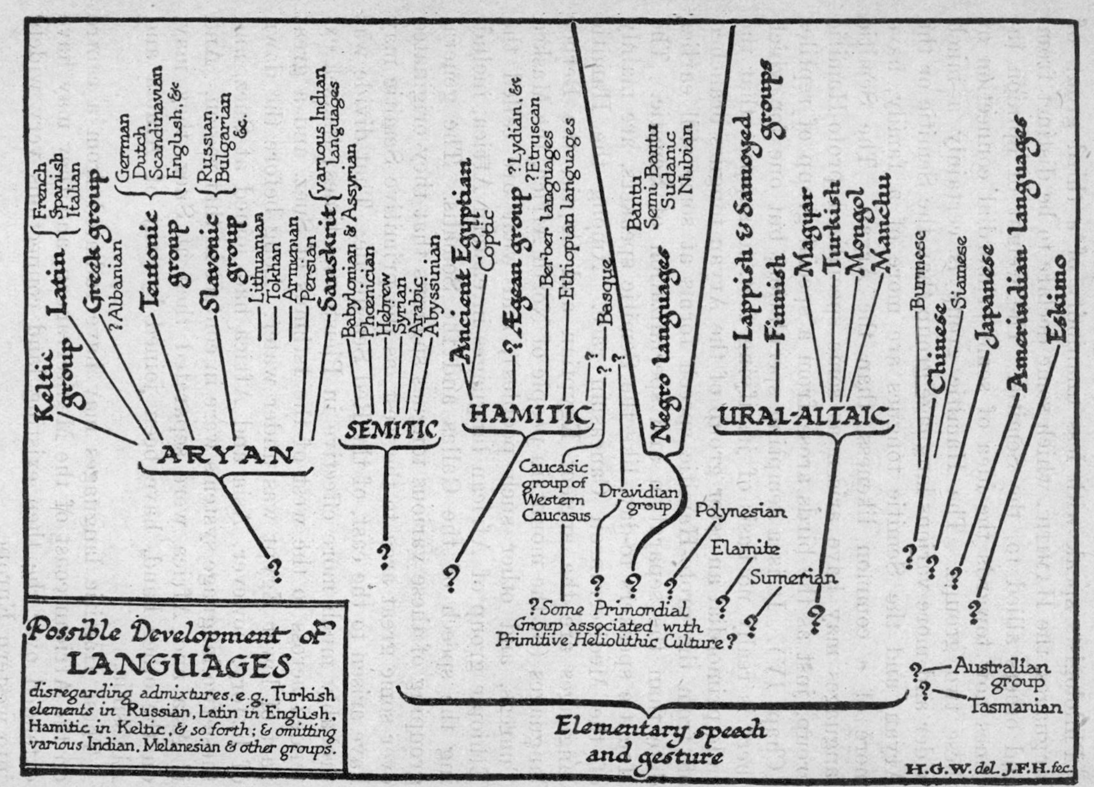
Possible Development of LANGUAGES
disregarding admixtures, e.g., Turkish elements in Russian, Latin in English, Hamitic in Keltic, & so forth; & omitting various Indian, Melanesian & other groups.
ARYAN
Keltic group
Latin
French
Spanish
Italian
Greek group
?Albanian
Teutonic group
German
Dutch
Scandinavian
English, &c
Slavonic group
Russian
Bulgarian &c.
Lithuanian
Tokhan
Armenian
Persian
Sanskrit
various Indian languages
SEMITIC
Babylonian & Assyrian
Phoenician
Hebrew
Syrian
Arabic
Abyssinian
HAMITIC
Ancient Egyptian
Coptic
?Ægean group
?Lydian, &c
?Etruscan
Berber languages
Ethiopian languages
Basque
Caucasic group of Western Caucasus
Dravidian group
Negro languages
Bantu
Semi Bantu
Sudanic
Nubian
Polynesian
Elamite
Sumerian
URAL-ALTAIC
Lappish & Samoyed groups
Finnish
Magyar
Turkish
Mongol
Manchu
Burmese
Chinese
Siamese
Japanese
Amerindian languages
Eskimo
?Some Primordial Group associated with Primitive Heliolithic Culture?
Australian group
Tasmanian
Elementary speech and gesture
H.G.W. del. J.F.H. fec.

which they do not share with any other language, and that is grammatical gender; but whether that has much weight as evidence of a remote common origin of Aryan, Semitic, and Hamitic, is a question for the philologist rather than for the general student. It does not affect the clear evidence of a very long and very ancient prehistoric separation of the speakers of these three diverse groups of tongues.

The bulk of the Semitic and Hamitic-speaking peoples are put by ethnologists with the Aryans among the Caucasian group of races. They are "white." The Semitic and Nordic "races" have a much more distinctive physiognomy; they seem, like their characteristic languages, to be more marked and specialized than the Hamitic-speaking peoples.

§ 5

Across to the north-east of the Aryan and Semitic areas there must once have spread a further distinct language system which is now represented by a group of languages known as the TURANIAN, or URAL-ALTAIC group. This includes the Lappish of Lapland and the Samoyed speech of Siberia, the Finnish language, Magyar, Turkish or Tartar, Manchu and Mongol; it has not as a group been so exhaustively studied by European philologists, and there is insufficient evidence yet whether it does or does not include the Korean and Japanese languages. H. B. Hulbert has issued a comparative grammar of Korean and certain of the Dravidian languages of India to demonstrate the close affinity he finds between them.

§ 6

A fifth region of language formation was south-eastern Asia, where there still prevails a group of languages consisting of monosyllables without any inflections, in which the tone used in uttering a word determines its meaning. This may be called the Chinese or MONOSYLLABIC group, and it includes Chinese, Burmese, Siamese, and Tibetan. The difference between any of these Chinese tongues and the more western languages is profound. In the Pekinese form of Chinese there are only about 420 primary monosyllables, and consequently each of these has to do duty for a great number of things, and the different meanings are indicated either by the context or by saying the word in a distinctive tone. The relations of these words to each other are expressed by quite different methods from the Aryan methods; Chinese grammar is a thing different in nature from English grammar; it is a separate and different invention. Many writers declare there is no Chinese grammar at all, and that is true if we mean by grammar anything in the European sense of inflections and concords. Consequently any such thing as a literal translation from Chinese into English is an impossibility. The very method of the thought is different.[1] Their philosophy remains still largely a sealed book to the European on this account and vice versa, because of the different nature of the expressions.

§ 7

In addition, the following other great language families are distinguished by the philologist. All the American-Indian languages, which vary widely among themselves, are separable from any Old World group. Here we may lump them together not so much as a family as a miscellany. There is one great group of languages in Africa, from a little way north of the equator to its southern extremity, the BANTU, and in addition a complex of other languages across the centre of the continent about which we will not trouble here. There are also two probably separate groups, the DRAVIDIAN in South India, and the MALAY-POLYNESIAN stretched over Polynesia, and also now including Indian tongues.

Now it seems reasonable to conclude from these fundamental differences that about the time when men were beginning to form rather larger communities than the family tribe, when they were beginning to tell each other long stories and argue and exchange ideas, human beings were distributed about the

[1] The four characters indicating "Affairs, query, imperative, old," placed in that order, for example, represent "Why walk in the ancient ways?" The Chinaman gives the bare cores of his meaning; the Englishman gets to it by a bold metaphor. He may be talking of conservatism in cooking or in book-binding, but he will say: "Why walk in the ancient ways?" Mr. Arthur Waley, in the interesting essay on Chinese thought and poetry which precedes his book, *170 Chinese Poems* (Constable, 1918), makes it clear how in these fields Chinese thought is kept practical and restricted by the limitations upon metaphor the contracted structure of Chinese imposes.

world in a number of areas which communicated very little with each other. They were separated by oceans, seas, thick forests, deserts or mountains from one another. There may have been in that remote time, it may be 15,000 years ago or more, Aryan, Semitic, Hamitic, Turanian, American and Chinese-speaking tribes and families, wandering over their several areas of hunting and pasture, all at very much the same stage of culture, and each developing its linguistic instrument in its own way. Probably each of these original tribes was not more numerous altogether than the Indians in Hudson Bay Territory to-day. Systematic agriculture was barely beginning then, and until agriculture made a denser population possible men may have been almost as rare as the great apes have always been. If agriculture was becoming at all important in human life at that time, and if population was anywhere denser, it was probably in the Mediterranean region and possibly in areas now submerged.

In addition to these Neolithic tribes, there must have been various still more primitive forest folks in Africa and in India. Central Africa, from the Upper Nile, was then a vast forest, impenetrable to ordinary human life, a forest of which the Congo forests of to-day are the last shrunken remains.

Possibly the spread of men of a race higher than primitive Australoids into the East Indies,[1] and the development of the languages of the Malay-Polynesian type came later in time than the origination of these other language groups.

The language divisions of the philologist do tally, it is manifest, in a broad sort of way with the main race classes of the ethnologist, and they carry out the same idea of age-long separations between great divisions of mankind. In the Glacial Age, ice, or at least a climate too severe for the free spreading of peoples, extended from the north pole into Central Europe and across Russia and Siberia to the great tablelands of Central Asia. After the last Glacial Age, this cold north mitigated its severities very slowly, and was for long without any other population than the wandering hunters who spread eastward and across Bering Strait. North and Central Europe and Asia did not become sufficiently temperate for agriculture until quite recent times, times that is within the limit of 12,000 or possibly

[1] The Polynesians appear to be a later eastward extension of the dark whites or brown peoples.

even 10,000 years, and a dense forest period intervened between the age of the hunter and the agricultural clearings.

This forest period was also a very wet period. It has been called the Pluvial or Lacustrine Age, the rain or pond period. It has to be remembered that the outlines of the land of the world have changed greatly even in the last hundred centuries. Across European Russia, from the Baltic to the Caspian Sea, as the ice receded there certainly spread much water and many impassable swamps; the Caspian Sea and the Sea of Aral and parts of the Desert of Turkestan, are the vestiges of a great extent of sea that reached far up to the Volga valley and sent an arm westward to join the Black Sea. Mountain barriers much higher than they are now, and the arm of the sea that is now the region of the Indus, completed the separation of the early Nordic races from the Mongolians and the Dravidians, and made the broad racial differentiation of those groups possible.

Again the blown-sand Desert of Sahara—it is not a dried-up sea, but a wind desert, and was once fertile and rich in life—becoming more and more dry and sandy, cut the Caucasians off from the sparse primitive Negro population in the central forest region of Africa.

The Persian Gulf extended very far to the north of its present head, and combined with the Syrian desert to cut off the Semitic peoples from the eastern areas, while on the other hand the south of Arabia, much more fertile than it is to-day, may have reached across what is now the Gulf of Aden towards Abyssinia and Somaliland. The Mediterranean and Red Sea may even have been fertile valleys containing a string of fresh-water lakes during the Pluvial Age. The Himalayas and the higher and vaster massif of Central Asia and the northward extension of the Bay of Bengal up to the present Ganges valley divided off the Dravidians from the Mongolians, the canoe was the chief link between Dravidian and Southern Mongol, and the Gobi system of seas and lakes which presently became the Gobi desert, and the great system of mountain chains which follow one another across Asia from the centre to the north-east, split the Mongolian races into the Chinese and the Ural-Altaic language groups.

Bering Strait, when this came into existence, before or after the Pluvial Period, isolated the Amerindians.

We are not suggesting here, be it noted, that these ancient separations were absolute separations, but that they were effectual enough at least to prevent any great intermixture of blood or any great intermixture of speech in those days of man's social beginnings. There was, nevertheless, some amount of meeting and exchange even then, some drift of knowledge that spread the crude patterns and use of various implements, and the seeds of a primitive agriculture about the world.

§ 8

The fundamental tongues of these nine main language groups we have noted were not by any means all the human speech beginnings of the Neolithic Age. They are the latest languages, the survivors, which have ousted their more primitive predecessors. There may have been other, and possibly many other, ineffective centres of speech which were afterwards overrun by the speakers of still surviving tongues, and of elementary languages which faded out. We find strange little patches of speech still in the world which do not seem to be connected with any other language about them. Sometimes, however, an exhaustive inquiry seems to affiliate these disconnected patches, seems to open out to us tantalizing glimpses of some simpler, wider, and more fundamental and universal form of human speech. One language group that has been keenly discussed is the Basque group of dialects. The Basques live now on the north and south slopes of the Pyrenees; they number perhaps 600,000 altogether in Europe, and to this day they are a very sturdy and independent-spirited people. Their language, as it exists to-day, is a fully developed one. But it is developed upon lines absolutely different from those of the Aryan languages about it. Basque newspapers have been published in the Argentine and in the United States to supply groups of prosperous emigrants. The earliest "French" settlers in Canada were Basque, and Basque names are frequent among the French Canadians to this day. Ancient remains point to a much wider distribution of the Basque speech and people over Spain. For a long time this Basque language was a profound perplexity to scholars, and its structural character led to the suggestion that it might be related to some Amerindian tongue. A. H. Keane, in *Man, Past and Present*, assembles reasons for linking it—though remotely—with the Berber language of North Africa, and through the Berber with the general body of Hamitic languages, but this relationship is questioned by other philologists. They find Basque more akin to certain similarly stranded vestiges of speech found in the Caucasian Mountains, and they are disposed to regard it as a last surviving member, much changed and specialized, of a once very widely extended group of pre-Hamitic languages, otherwise extinct, spoken chiefly by peoples of that brunet Mediterranean race which once occupied most of western and southern Europe and western Asia, and which may have been very closely related to the Dravidians of India and the peoples with a heliolithic culture who spread eastward, thence through the East Indies to Polynesia and beyond.

Racial types......From Egyptian tomb-paintings. (After Champollion.)

It is quite possible that over western and southern Europe language groups extended eight or ten thousand years ago that have completely vanished before Aryan tongues. Later on we shall note, in passing, the possibility of three lost language groups represented by (1) Ancient Cretan, Lydian, and the like (though these may have belonged, says Sir H. H. Johnston, to the "Basque—Caucasian —Dravidian [!] group"), (2) Sumerian, and (3) Elamite. The suggestion has been made—it is a mere guess—that ancient Sumerian may have been a linking language between the early Basque-Caucasian and early Mongolian groups. If this is true, then we have in this "Basque-Caucasian-Dravidian-Sumerian-proto-Mongolian" group a still more ancient and more ancestral system of speech than the fundamental Hamitic. We have something more like the linguistic "missing link," more like an ancestral language than anything else we can imagine at the present time. It may have been related to the Aryan and Semitic and Hamitic languages much as the primitive lizards of later Palæozoic times were related to the mammals, birds, and dinosaurs respectively.

§ 9

The Hottentot language is said to have affinities with the Hamitic tongues, from which it is separated by the whole breadth of Bantu-speaking Central Africa. A Hottentot-like language with Bushman affinities is still spoken in equatorial East Africa, and this strengthens the idea that the whole of East Africa was once Hamitic-speaking. The Bantu languages and peoples spread, in comparatively recent times, from some centre of origin in West Central Africa and cut off the Hottentots from the other Hamitic peoples. But it is at least equally probable that the Hottentot is a separate language group.

Among other remote and isolated little patches of language are the Papuan speech of New Guinea and the native Australian. The now extinct Tasmanian language is but little known. What we do know of it is in support of what we have guessed about the comparative speechlessness of Palæolithic man.

We may quote a passage from Hutchinson's *Living Races of Mankind* upon this matter:—

"The language of the natives is irretrievably lost, only imperfect indications of its structure and a small proportion of its words having been preserved. In the absence of sibilants and some other features, their dialects resembled the Australian, but were of ruder, of less developed structure, and so imperfect that, according to Joseph. Milligan, our best authority on the subject, they observed no settled order or arrangement of words in the construction of their sentences, but conveyed in a supplementary fashion by tone, manner, and gesture those modifications of meaning which we express by mood, tense, number, etc. Abstract terms were rare; for every variety of gum-tree or wattle-tree there was a name, but no word for 'tree' in general, nor for qualities such as hard, soft, warm, cold, long, short, round, etc. Anything hard was 'like a stone,' anything round 'like the moon,' and so on, usually suiting the action to the word and confirming by some sign the meaning to be understood."

XIV

THE FIRST CIVILIZATIONS

§ 1

IT was out of the so-called heliolithic culture we have described in Chapter XII that the first beginnings of anything that we can call a civilization arose. It is still doubtful whether we are to consider Mesopotamia or Egypt the earlier scene of the two parallel beginnings of settled communities living in towns. By 4,000 B.C., in both these regions of the earth, such communities existed, and had been going on for a very considerable time. The excavations of the American expedition at Nippur have unearthed evidence of a city community existing there at least as early as 5,000 B.C., and probably as early as 6,000 B.C., an earlier date than anything we know of in Egypt. The late Mr. Aaron Aaronson found a real wild wheat upon the slopes of Mt. Hermon, and it must be that somewhere in that part of the world its cultivation began. It may be that from the western end of the Mediterranean, possibly in some region now submerged, as a centre that the cultivation of wheat spread over the entire eastern hemisphere. But cultivation is not civilization; the growing of wheat had spread from the Atlantic to the Pacific coast with the distribution of the Neolithic culture by perhaps 15,000 or 10,000 B.C., before the beginnings of civilization. Civilization is something more than the occasional seasonal growing of wheat. It is the settlement of men upon an area continuously cultivated and possessed, who live in buildings continuously inhabited with a common rule and a common city or citadel. For a long time civilization may quite possibly have developed in Mesopotamia without any relations with the parallel beginnings in Egypt. The two settlements may have been quite independent, arising separately out of the widely diffused Heliolithic Neolithic culture. Or they may have had a common origin in the region of the Mediterranean, the Red Sea, and southern Arabia.

The first condition necessary to a real settling down of Neolithic men, as distinguished from a mere temporary settlement among abundant food, was of course a trustworthy all-the-year-round supply of water, fodder for the animals, food for themselves, and building material for their homes. There had to be everything they could need at any season, and no want that would tempt them to wander further. This was a possible state of affairs, no doubt, in many European and Asiatic valleys; and in many such valleys, as in the case of the Swiss lake dwellings, men settled from a very early date indeed; but nowhere, of any countries now known to us, were these favourable conditions found upon such a scale, and nowhere did they hold good so surely year in and year out as in Egypt and in the country between the upper waters of the Euphrates and Tigris and the Persian Gulf.[1] Here was a constant water supply under enduring sunlight; trustworthy harvests year by year; in Mesopotamia wheat yielded, says Herodotus, two hundredfold to the sower; Pliny says that it was cut twice and afterwards yielded good fodder for sheep; there were abundant palms and many sorts of fruits; and as for building material, in Egypt there was clay and easily worked stone, and in Mesopotamia a clay that becomes a brick in the sunshine. In such countries men would cease to wander and settle down almost unawares; they would multiply and discover themselves numerous and by their numbers safe from any casual assailant. They multiplied, producing a denser human population than the earth had ever known before; their houses became more substantial, wild beasts

[1] We shall use "Mesopotamia" here loosely for the Euphrates-Tigris country generally. Strictly, of course, as its name indicates, Mesopotamia (mid-rivers) means only the country *between* those two great rivers. That country in the fork was probably very marshy and unhealthy in early times (Sayce), until it was drained by man, and the early cities grew up west of the Euphrates and east of the Tigris. Probably these rivers then flowed separately into the Persian Gulf.

were exterminated over great areas, the security of life increased so that ordinary men went about in the towns and fields without encumbering themselves with weapons, and among themselves, at least, they became peaceful peoples. Men took root as man had never taken root before.

Map of The CRADLE of WESTERN CIVILIZATION 6,000 to 4,000 B.C.

But in the less fertile and more seasonal lands outside these favoured areas, in the forests of Europe, the Arabian deserts, and the seasonal pastures of Central Asia, there developed on the other hand a thinner, more active population of peoples, the primitive nomadic peoples. In contrast with the settled folk, the agriculturists, these nomads lived freely and dangerously.

They were in comparison lean and hungry men. Their herding was still blended with hunting; they fought constantly for their pastures against hostile families. The discoveries in the elaboration of implements and the use of metals made by the settled peoples spread to them and improved their weapons. They followed the settled folk from Neolithic phase to Bronze phase. It is possible that in the case of iron, the first users were nomadic. They became more warlike with better arms, and more capable of rapid movements with the improvement of their transport. One must not think of a nomadic stage as a predecessor of a settled stage in human affairs. To begin with, man was a slow drifter, following food. Then one sort of men began to settle down, and another sort became more distinctly nomadic. The settled sort began to rely more and more upon grain for food; the nomad began to make a greater use of milk for food. He bred his cows for milk. The two ways of life specialized in opposite directions. It was inevitable that nomad folk and the settled folk should clash, that the nomads should seem hard barbarians to the settled peoples, and the settled peoples soft and effeminate and very good plunder to the nomad peoples. Along the fringes of the developing civilizations there must have been a constant raiding and bickering between hardy nomad tribes and mountain tribes and the more numerous and less warlike peoples in the towns and villages.

For the most part this was a mere raiding of the borders. The settled folk had the weight of numbers on their side; the herdsmen might raid and loot, but they could not stay. That sort of mutual friction might go on for many generations. But ever and again we find some leader or some tribe amidst the disorder of free and independent nomads, powerful enough to force a sort of unity upon its kindred tribes, and then woe betide the nearest civilization. Down pour the united nomads on the unwarlike, unarmed plains, and there ensues a war of conquest. Instead of carrying off the booty, the conquerors settle down on the conquered land, which becomes all booty for them; the villagers and townsmen are reduced to servitude and tribute-paying, they become hewers of wood and drawers of water, and the leaders of the nomads become kings and princes, masters and aristocrats. They, too, settle down, they learn many of the arts and refinements of the conquered, they cease to be lean and hungry, but for many generations they retain traces of their old nomadic habits, they hunt and indulge in open-air sports, they drive and race chariots, they regard work, especially agricultural work, as the lot of an inferior race and class.

This in a thousand variations has been one of the main stories in history for the last seventy centuries or more. In the first history that we can clearly decipher we find already in all the civilized regions a distinction between a non-working ruler class and the working mass of the population. And we find, too, that after some generations, the aristocrat, having settled down, begins to respect the arts and refinements and lawabidingness of settlement, and to lose something of his original hardihood. He intermarries, he patches up a sort of toleration between conqueror and conquered; he exchanges religious ideas and learns the lessons upon which soil and climate insist. He becomes a part of the civilization he has captured. And as he does so, events gather towards a fresh invasion by the free adventurers of the outer world.

§ 2A

This alternation of settlement, conquest, refinement, fresh conquest, refinement, is particularly to be noted in the region of the Euphrates and Tigris, which lay open in every direction to great areas which are not arid enough to be complete deserts, but which were not fertile enough to support civilized populations. Perhaps the earliest people to form real cities in this part of the world, or indeed in any part of the world, were a people of mysterious origin called the Sumerians. They were probably brunets of Iberian or Dravidian affinities. They used a kind of writing which they scratched upon clay, and their language has been deciphered.[1] It was a language more like the unclassified Caucasic language groups than any others that now exist. These languages may be connected with Basque, and may represent what was once a widespread primitive language group extending from Spain and western Europe to eastern India, and reach-

[1] Excavations conducted at Eridu by Capt. R. Campbell Thompson during the recent war have revealed an early Neolithic agricultural stage, before the invention of writing or the use of bronze beneath the earliest Sumerian foundations. The crops were cut by sickles of earthenware. Capt. Thompson thinks that these pre-Sumerian people were not of Sumerian race, but proto-Elamites. Entirely similar Neolithic remains have been found at Susa, once the chief city of Elam.

ing southwards to Central Africa. These people shaved their heads and wore simple tunic-like garments of wool. They settled first on the lower courses of the great river and not very far from the Persian Gulf, which in those days ran up for a hundred and thirty miles[1] and more beyond its present head. They fertilized their fields by letting water run through irrigation trenches, and they gradually became very skilful hydraulic engineers; they had cattle, asses, sheep, and goats, but no horses; their collections of mud huts grew into towns, and their religion raised up tower-like temple buildings.

Clay, dried in the sun, was a very great fact in the lives of these people. This lower country of the Euphrates-Tigris val-

A very early Sumerian stone carving showing Sumerian warriors in phalanx

leys had little or no stone. They built of brick, they made pottery and earthenware images, and they drew and presently wrote upon thin tile-like cakes of clay. They do not seem to have had paper or to have used parchment. Their books and memoranda, even their letters, were potsherds.

At Nippur they built a great tower of brick to their chief god, El-lil (Enlil), the memory of which is supposed to be preserved in the story of the Tower of Babel. They seem to have been divided up into city states, which warred among themselves and maintained for many centuries their military capacity. Their soldiers carried long spears and shields, and fought in close formation. Sumerians conquered Sumerians. Sumeria remained unconquered by any stranger race for a very

[1] Sayce, in *Babylonian and Assyrian Life,* estimates that in 6,500 B.C. Eridu was on the sea-coast.

long period of time indeed. They developed their civilization, their writing, and their shipping, through a period that may be twice as long as the whole period from the Christian era to the present time.

The first of all known empires was that founded by the high priest of the god of the Sumerian city of Erech. It reached, says an inscription at Nippur, from the Lower (Persian Gulf) to the Upper (Mediterranean or Red?) Sea. Among the mud heaps of the Euphrates-Tigris valley the record of that vast period of history, that first half of the Age of Cultivation, is buried. There flourished the first temples and the first priest-rulers that we know of among mankind.

§ 2B

Upon the western edge of this country appeared nomadic tribes of Semitic-speaking peoples who traded, raided, and fought with the Sumerians for many generations. Then arose at last a great leader among these Semites, Sargon (2,750 B.C.), who united them, and not only conquered the Sumerians, but extended his rule from beyond the Persian Gulf on the east to the Mediterranean on the west. His own people were called the Akkadians and his empire is called the Sumerian Akkadian empire. It endured for over two hundred years.

But though the Semites conquered and gave a king to the Sumerian cities, it was the Sumerian civilization which prevailed over the simpler Semitic culture. The newcomers learnt the Sumerian writing (the "cuneiform" writing) and the Sumerian language; they set up no Semitic writing of their own. The Sumerian language became for these barbarians the language of knowledge and power, as Latin was the language of knowledge and power among the barbaric peoples of the middle ages in Europe. This Sumerian learning had a very great vitality. It was destined to survive through a long series of conquests and changes that now began in the valley of the two rivers.

§ 2C

As the people of the Sumerian Akkadian empire lost their political and military vigour, fresh inundations of a warlike people began from the east, the Elamites,[1] while from the west came the Semitic Amorites, pinching the Sumerian Akkadian empire between them. The Amorites settled in what was at first a small up-river town, named Babylon; and after a hundred years of warfare became masters of all Mesopotamia under a great king, Hammurabi (2,100 B.C.), who founded the first Babylonian empire.

Again came peace and security and a decline in aggressive prowess, and in another hundred years fresh nomads from the east were invading Babylonia, bringing with them the horse and the war chariot, and setting up their own king in Babylon. . . .

§ 2D

Higher up the Tigris, above the clay lands and with easy supplies of workable stone, a Semitic people, the Assyrians, while the Sumerians were still unconquered by the Semites, were settling about a number of cities of which Assur and Nineveh were the chief. Their peculiar physiognomy, the long nose and thick lips, was very like that of the commoner type of Polish Jew to-day. They wore great beards and ringletted long hair, tall caps and long robes. They were constantly engaged in mutual raiding with the Hittites to the west; they were conquered by Sargon I and became free again; a certain Tushratta, King of Mitanni, to the north-west, captured and held their capital, Nineveh, for a time; they intrigued with Egypt against Babylon and were in the pay of Egypt; they developed the military art to a very high pitch, and became mighty raiders and exacters of tribute; and at last, adopting the horse and the war chariot, they settled accounts for a time with the Hittites, and then, under Tiglath Pileser I, conquered Babylon for themselves (about 1,100 B.C.). But their hold on the lower, older, and more civilized land was not secure, and Nineveh, the stone city, as distinguished from Babylon, the brick city, remained their capital. For many centuries power swayed between Nineveh and Babylon, and sometimes it was an Assyrian and sometimes a Babylonian who claimed to be "king of the world."

1 Of unknown language and race, "neither Sumerians nor Semites," says Sayce. Their central city was Susa. Their archæology is still largely an unworked mine. They are believed by some, says Sir H. H. Johnston, to have been negroid in type. There is a strong negroid strain in the modern people of Elam.

For four centuries Assyria was restrained from expansion towards Egypt by a fresh northward thrust and settlement of another group of Semitic peoples, the Arameans, whose chief city was Damascus, and whose descendants are the Syrians of to-day. (There is, we may note, no connection whatever between the words Assyrian and Syrian. It is an accidental similarity.) Across these Syrians the Assyrian kings fought for power and expansion south-westward. In 745 B.C. arose another Tiglath Pileser, Tiglath Pileser III, the Tiglath Pileser of the Bible.[1] He not only directed the transfer of the Israelites to Media (the "Lost Ten Tribes" whose ultimate fate has exercised so many curious minds) but he conquered and ruled Babylon, so founding what historians know as the New Assyrian Empire. His son, Shalmaneser IV,[2] died during the siege of Samaria, and was succeeded by a usurper, who, no doubt to flatter Babylonian susceptibilities, took the ancient Akkadian Sumerian name of Sargon, Sargon II. He seems to have armed the Assyrian forces for the first time with iron weapons. It was probably Sargon II who actually carried out the deportation of the Ten Tribes.

Assyrian warrior
(Bas-relief from the palace of Sargon II)

Such shiftings about of population became a very distinctive part of the political methods of the Assyrian new empire. Whole nations who were difficult to control in their native country would be shifted *en masse* to unaccustomed regions and amidst strange neighbours, where their only hope of survival would lie in obedience to the supreme power.

Sargon's son, Sennacherib, led the Assyrian hosts to the borders of Egypt. There Sennacherib's army was smitten by

[1] II. Kings, xv. 29, and xvi. 7 *et seq.* [2] II. Kings xvii. 3.

a pestilence, a disaster described in the nineteenth chapter of the Second Book of Kings.

"And it came to pass that night, that the angel of the Lord went out, and smote in the camp of the Assyrians an hundred fourscore and five thousand: and when they arose early in the morning, behold, they were all dead corpses. So Sennacherib king of Assyria departed, and went and returned, and dwelt at Nineveh."[1]

Sennacherib's grandson, Assurbanipal (called by the Greeks Sardanapalus), did succeed in conquering and for a time holding lower Egypt.

§ 2E

The Assyrian empire lasted only a hundred and fifty years after Sargon II. Fresh nomadic Semites coming from the south-east, the Chaldeans, assisted by two Aryan-speaking peoples from the north, the Medes and Persians, combined against it, and took Nineveh in 606 B.C.

The Chaldean Empire, with its capital at Babylon (Second Babylonian Empire), lasted under Nebuchadnezzar the Great (Nebuchadnezzar II) and his successors until 539 B.C., when it collapsed before the attack of Cyrus, the founder of the Persian power. . . .

So the story goes on. In 330 B.C., as we shall tell later in some detail, a Greek conqueror, Alexander the Great, is looking on the murdered body of the last of the Persian rulers.

The story of the Tigris and Euphrates civilizations, of which we have given as yet only the bare outline, is a story of conquest following after conquest, and each conquest replaces old rulers and ruling classes by new; races like the Sumerian and the Elamite are swallowed up, their languages vanish, they interbreed and are lost, the Assyrian melts away into Chaldean and Syrian, the Hittites become Aryanized and lose distinction, the Semites who swallowed up the Sumerians give place to Aryan rulers, Medes and Persians appear in the place of the Elamites, the Aryan Persian language dominates the empire until the Aryan Greek ousts it from official life. Meanwhile

[1] To be murdered by his sons.

the plough does its work year by year, the harvests are gathered, the builders build as they are told, the tradesmen work and acquire fresh devices; the knowledge of writing spreads, novel things, the horse and wheeled vehicles and iron, are introduced and become part of the permanent inheritance of mankind; the volume of trade upon sea and desert increases, men's ideas widen, and knowledge grows. There are set-backs, massacres, pestilence; but the story is, on the whole, one of enlargement. For four thousand years this new thing, civilization, which had set its root into the soil of the two rivers, grew as a tree grows; now losing a limb, now stripped by a storm, but always growing and resuming its growth. After four thousand years the warriors and conquerors were still going to and fro over this growing thing they did not understand, but men had now (330 B.C.) got iron, horses, writing and computation, money, a greater variety of foods and textiles, a wider knowledge of their world.

The time that elapsed between the empire of Sargon I and the conquest of Babylon by Alexander the Great was as long, be it noted, at the least estimate, as the time from Alexander the Great to the present day. And before the time of Sargon, men had been settled in the Sumerian land, living in towns, worshipping in temples, following an orderly Neolithic agricultural life in an organized community for at least as long again. "Eridu, Lagash, Ur, Uruk, Larsa, have already an immemorial past when first they appear in history."[1]

One of the most difficult things for both the writer and student of history is to sustain the sense of these time-intervals and prevent these ages becoming shortened by perspective in his imagination. Half the duration of human civilization and the keys to all its chief institutions are to be found *before* Sargon I. Moreover, the reader cannot too often compare the scale of the dates in these latter fuller pages of man's history with the succession of countless generations to which the time diagrams given on pages 11 and 47, bear witness.

§ 3

Parallel with the ancient beginnings of civilization in Sumeria, a parallel process was going on in Egypt. It is still

[1] Winckler (Craig), *History of Babylonia and Assyria.*

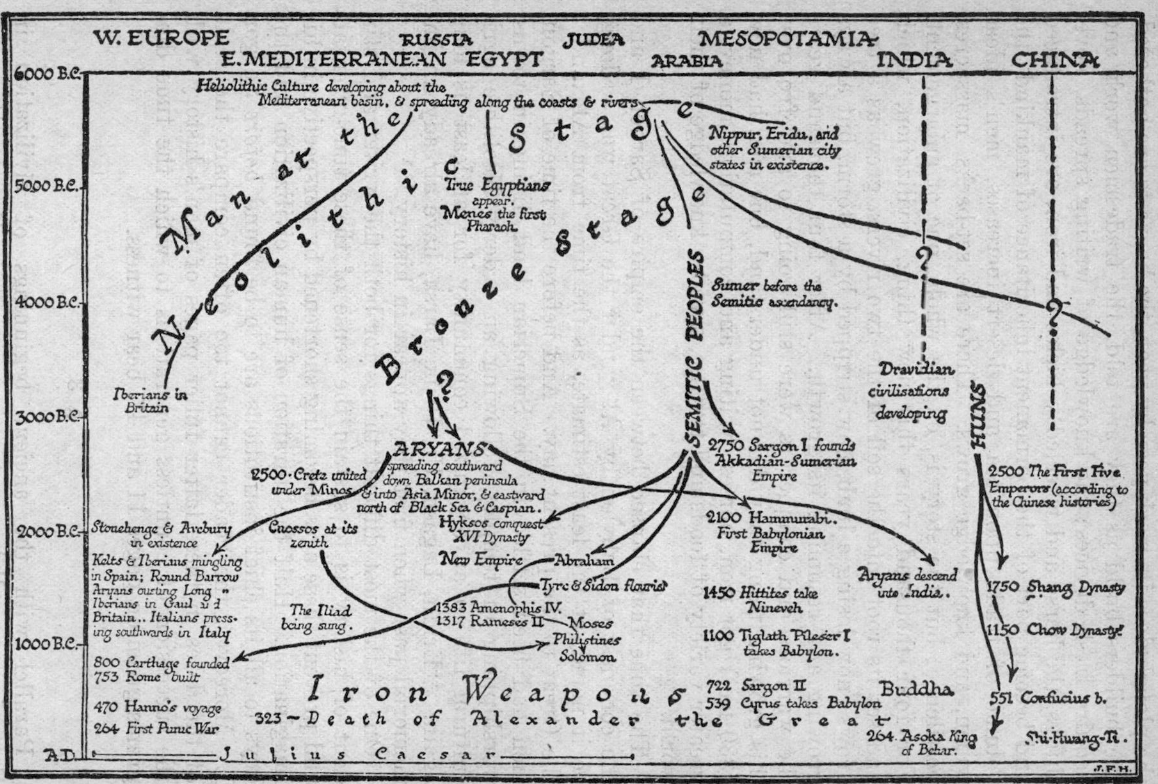
W. EUROPE
E. MEDITERRANEAN
RUSSIA
EGYPT
JUDEA
ARABIA
MESOPOTAMIA
INDIA
CHINA
6000 B.C.
5000 B.C.
4000 B.C.
3000 B.C.
2000 B.C.
1000 B.C.
A.D.
Heliolithic Culture developing about the Mediterranean basin, & spreading along the coasts & rivers
Man at the Neolithic Stage
Bronze Stage
Iron Weapons
Nippur, Eridu, and other Sumerian city states in existence.
True Egyptians appear. Menes the first Pharaoh.
Sumer before the Semitic ascendancy.
Iberians in Britain
Dravidian civilisations developing
SEMITIC PEOPLES
HUNS
ARYANS spreading southward down Balkan peninsula & into Asia Minor, & eastward north of Black Sea & Caspian.
2500 · Crete united under Minos
Cnossos at its zenith
Stonehenge & Avebury in existence
Kelts & Iberians mingling in Spain; Round Barrow Aryans ousting Long Iberians in Gaul and Britain.. Italians pressing southwards in Italy
2750 Sargon I founds Akkadian-Sumerian Empire
2100 Hammurabi. First Babylonian Empire
Hyksos conquest XVI Dynasty
New Empire
Abraham
Tyre & Sidon flourish
1383 Amenophis IV.
1317 Rameses II
Moses
Philistines
Solomon
The Iliad being sung.
1450 Hittites take Nineveh
1100 Tiglath Pileser I takes Babylon.
Aryans descend into India.
2500 The First Five Emperors (according to the Chinese histories)
1750 Shang Dynasty
1150 Chow Dynasty
800 Carthage founded
753 Rome built
722 Sargon II
539 Cyrus takes Babylon
Buddha
551 Confucius b.
470 Hanno's voyage
264 First Punic War
323 – Death of Alexander the Great
264 Asoka King of Behar.
Shi-Huang-Ti.
Julius Caesar
J.F.H.

a matter of discussion which was the most ancient of these two beginnings, or how far they had a common origin or derived one from the other.

The story of the Nile valley from the dawn of its traceable history until the time of Alexander the Great is not very dissimilar from that of Babylonia; but while Babylonia lay open on every side to invasion, Egypt was protected by desert to the west and by desert and sea to the east, while to the south she had only negro peoples. Consequently her history is less broken by the invasions of strange races than is the history of Assyria and Babylon, and until towards the eighth century B.C., when she fell under an Ethiopian dynasty, whenever a conqueror did come into her story, he came in from Asia by way of the Isthmus of Suez.

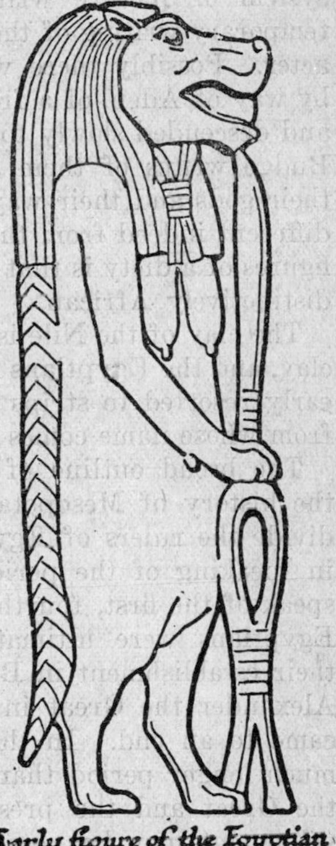

Early figure of the Egyptian hippopotamus goddess

The Stone Age remains in Egypt are of very uncertain date; there are Palæolithic and then Neolithic remains. It is not certain whether the Neolithic pastoral people who left those remains were the direct ancestors of the later Egyptians. In many respects they differed entirely from their successors. They buried their dead, but before they buried them they cut up the bodies and apparently ate portions of the flesh. They seem to have done this out of a feeling of reverence for the departed; the dead were "eaten with honour" according to the phrase of Mr. Flinders Petrie. It may have been that the survivors hoped to retain thereby some vestige of the strength and virtue that had died. Traces of similar savage customs have been found in the long barrows that were scattered over western Europe before the spreading of the Aryan peoples, and they have pervaded negro Africa, where they are only dying out at the present time.

About 5,000 B.C., or earlier, the traces of these primitive peoples cease, and the true Egyptians appear on the scene. The former people were hut builders and at a comparatively low stage of Neolithic culture, the latter were already a civilized Neolithic people; they used brick and wood buildings instead of their predecessors' hovels, and they were working stone. Very soon they passed into the Bronze Age. They possessed a system of picture writing almost as developed as the contemporary writing of the Sumerians, but quite different in character. Possibly there was an irruption from southern Arabia by way of Aden, of a fresh people, who came into upper Egypt and descended slowly towards the delta of the Nile. Dr. Wallis Budge writes of them as "conquerors from the East." But their gods and their ways, like their picture writing, were very different indeed from the Sumerian. One of the earliest known figures of a diety is that of a hippopotamus goddess, and so very distinctively African.

The clay of the Nile is not so fine and plastic as the Sumerian clay, and the Egyptians made no use of it for writing. But they early resorted to strips of the papyrus reed fastened together, from whose name comes our word "paper."

The broad outline of the history of Egypt is simpler than the history of Mesopotamia. It has long been the custom to divide the rulers of Egypt into a succession of Dynasties, and in speaking of the periods of Egyptian history it is usual to speak of the first, fourth, fourteenth, and so on, Dynasty. The Egyptians were ultimately conquered by the Persians after their establishment in Babylon, and when finally Egypt fell to Alexander the Great in 332 B.C., it was Dynasty XXXI that came to an end. In that long history of over 4,000 years, a much longer period than that between the career of Alexander the Great and the present day, certain broad phases of development may be noted here. There was a phase known as the "old kingdom," which culminated in the IVth Dynasty; this Dynasty marks a period of wealth and splendour, and its monarchs were obsessed by such a passion for making monuments for themselves as no men have ever before or since had a chance to display and gratify. It was Cheops [1] and Chephren and Mycerinus of this IVth Dynasty who raised the vast piles of the great and the second and the third pyramids at Gizeh.

[1] 3,733 B.C., Wallis Budge.

These unmeaning sepulchral piles, of an almost incredible vastness,[1] erected in an age when engineering science had scarcely begun, exhausted the resources of Egypt through three long reigns, and left her wasted as if by a war.

The story of Egypt from the IVth to the XVth Dynasty is a story of conflicts between alternative capitals and competing religions, of separations into several kingdoms and reunions. It is, so to speak, an internal history. Here we can name only one of that long series of Pharaohs, Pepi II, who reigned ninety years, the longest reign in history, and left a great abundance of inscriptions and buildings. At last there happened to Egypt what happened so frequently to the civilizations of Mesopotamia. Egypt was conquered by nomadic Semites, who founded a "shepherd" dynasty, the Hyksos (XVIth), which was finally expelled by native Egyptians. This invasion probably happened while that first Babylonian Empire which Hammurabi founded was flourishing, but the exact correspondences of dates between early Egypt and Babylonia are still very doubtful. Only after a long period of servitude did a popular uprising expel these foreigners again.

After the war of liberation (*circa* 1,600 B.C.) there followed a period of great prosperity in Egypt, *the New Empire*. Egypt became a great and united military state, and pushed her expeditions at last as far as the Euphrates, and so the age-long struggle between the Egyptian and Babylonian-Assyrian power began.

For a time Egypt was the ascendant power. Thothmes III[2]

[1] The great pyramid is 450 feet high and its side 700 feet long. It is calculated (says Wallis Budge) to weigh 4,883,000 tons. All this stone was lugged into place chiefly by human muscle.

[2] There are variants to these names, and to most Egyptian names, for few self-respecting Egyptologists will tolerate the spelling of their colleagues. One may find, for instance, Thethmosis, Thoutmosis, Tahutmes, Thutmose, or Tethmosis; Amunothph, Amenhotep or Amenothes. A pleasing variation is to break up the name, as, for instance, Amen Hetep. This particular little constellation of variants is given here not only because it is amusing, but because it is desirable that the reader should know such variations exist. For most names the rule of this book has been to follow whatever usage has established itself in English literature, regardless of the possible contemporary pronunciation. Amenophis, for example, has been so written in English books for two centuries. It came into the language by indirect routes, but it is now as fairly established as is Damascus as the English name of a Syrian town. Nevertheless, there are limits to this classicism. The writer, after some vacillation, has abandoned Oliver Goldsmith and Dr. Johnson in the case of "Peisistratus" and "Keltic," which were formerly spelt "Pisistratus" and "Celtic."

and Amenophis III (XVIIIth Dynasty) ruled from Ethiopia to the Euphrates in the fifteenth century B.C. For various reasons these names stand out with unusual distinctness in the Egyptian record. They were great builders, and left many monuments and inscriptions. Amenophis III founded Luxor, and added greatly to Karnak. At Tel-el-Amarna a mass of letters has been found, the royal correspondence with Babylonian and Hittite and other monarchs, including that Tushratta who took Nineveh, throwing a flood of light upon the political and social affairs of this particular age. Of Amenophis IV we shall have more to tell later, but of one, the most extraordinary and able of Egyptian monarchs, Queen Hatasu, we have no space to tell. She is represented upon her monuments in masculine garb, and with a long beard as a symbol of wisdom.

Thereafter there was a brief Syrian conquest of Egypt, a series of changing dynasties, among which we may note the XIXth, which included Rameses II, a great builder of temples, who reigned seventy-seven years (about 1,317 to 1,250 B.C.), and who is supposed by some to have been the Pharaoh of Moses, and the XXIInd, which included Shishak, who plundered Solomon's temple (*circa* 930 B.C.). An Ethiopian conqueror from the Upper Nile founded the XXVth Dynasty, a foreign dynasty, which went down (670 B.C.) before the new Assyrian Empire created by Tiglath Pileser III, Sargon II, and Sennacherib, of which we have already made mention.

The days of any Egyptian predominance over foreign nations were drawing to an end. For a time under Psammetichus I of the XXVIth Dynasty (664-610 B.C.) native rule was restored, and Necho II recovered for a time the old Egyptian possessions in Syria up to the Euphrates while the Medes and Chaldeans were attacking Nineveh. From those gains Necho II was routed out again after the fall of Nineveh and the Assyrians by Nebuchadnezzar II, the great Chaldean king, the Nebuchadnezzar of the Bible. The Jews, who had been the allies of Necho II, were taken into captivity by Nebuchadnezzar to Babylon.

When, in the sixth century B.C., Chaldea fell to the Persians, Egypt followed suit, a rebellion later made Egypt independent once more for sixty years, and in 332 B.C. she welcomed Alexander the Great as her conqueror, to be ruled thereafter by foreigners, first by Greeks, then by Romans, then in succession by Arabs, Turks, and British, until the present day.

Such briefly is the history of Egypt from its beginnings; a history first of isolation and then of increasing entanglement with the affairs of other nations, as increasing facilities of communication drew the peoples of the world into closer and closer interaction.

§ 4

The history we need to tell here of India is simpler even than this brief record of Egypt. The Dravidian peoples in the Ganges valley developed upon parallel lines to the Sumerian and Egyptian societies. But it is doubtful if they ever got to so high a stage of social development; they have left few monuments, and they never achieved any form of writing.

Somewhere about the time of Hammurabi or later, a branch of the Aryan-speaking people who then occupied North Persia and Afghanistan pushed down the north-west passes into India. They conquered their way until they prevailed over all the darker populations of North India, and spared their rule or influence over the whole peninsula. They never achieved any unity in India; their history is a history of warring kings and republics.

The Persian empire, in the days of its expansion after the capture of Babylon, pushed its boundaries beyond the Indus, and later Alexander the Great marched as far as the border of the desert that separates the Punjab from the Ganges valley. But with this bare statement we will for a time leave the history of India.

§ 5

Meanwhile, as this triple system of White Man civilization developed in India and in the lands about the meeting-places of Asia, Africa, and Europe, another and quite distinct civilization was developing and spreading out from the then fertile but now dry and desolate valley of the Tarim and from the slopes of the Kuen-lun mountains in two directions down the course of the Hwang-ho, and later into the valley of the Yang-tse-kiang. We know practically nothing as yet of the archæology of China, we do not know anything of the Stone Age in that part of the world, and at present our ideas of this early civilization are derived from the still very imperfectly explored Chinese literature. It has evidently been from the first and throughout a Mongolian civilization. Until after the time of Alexander the Great there are few traces of any Aryan or Semitic, much less of Hamitic influence. All such influences were still in another world, separated by mountains, deserts, and wild nomadic tribes until that time. The Chinese seem to have made their civilization spontaneously and unassisted. Some recent writers suppose indeed a connection with ancient Sumeria. Of course both China and Sumeria arose on the basis of the almost world-wide early Neolithic culture, but the Tarim valley and the lower Euphrates are separated by such vast obstacles of mountain and desert as to forbid the idea of any migration or interchange of peoples who had once settled down. Perhaps the movement from the north met another movement of culture coming from the south.

Though the civilization of China is wholly Mongolian (as we have defined Mongolian), it does not follow that the northern roots are the only ones from which it grew. If it grew first in the Tarim valley, then unlike all other civilizations (including the Mexican and Peruvian) it did not grow out of the heliolithic culture. We Europeans know very little as yet of the ethnology and pre-history of southern China. There the Chinese mingle with such kindred peoples as the Siamese and Burmese, and seem to bridge over towards the darker Dravidian peoples and towards the Malays. It is quite clear from the Chinese records that there were southern as well as northern beginnings of a civilization, and that the Chinese civilization that comes into history 2,000 years B.C. is the result of a long process of conflicts, minglings and interchanges between a southern and a northern culture of which the southern may have been the earlier and more highly developed. The southern Chinese perhaps played the rôle towards the northern Chinese that the Hamites or Sumerians played to the Aryan and Semitic peoples in the west, or that the settled Dravidians played towards the Aryans in India. They may have been the first agriculturists and the first temple builders. But so little is known as yet of this attractive chapter in pre-history, that we cannot dwell upon it further here.

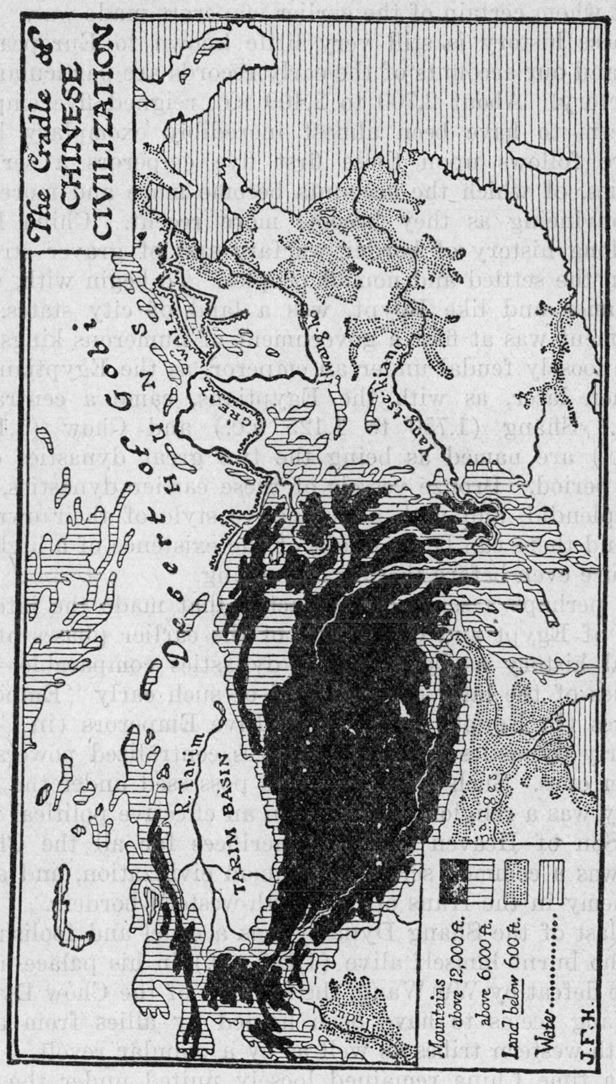
The Cradle of
CHINESE
CIVILIZATION
Desert of Gobi
HUNS
GREAT WALL
Hwang-ho
Yang-tse-Kiang
R. Tarim
TARIM BASIN
Ganges
Indus
Mountains above 12,000 ft.
above 6,000 ft.
Land below 600 ft.
Water
J.F.H.

The chief foreigners mentioned in the early annals of China were a Ural-Altaic people on the north-east frontier, the Huns, against whom certain of the earlier emperors made war.

Chinese history is still very little known to European students, and our accounts of the early records are particularly unsatisfactory. About 2,700 to 2,400 B.C. reigned five emperors, who seem to have been almost incredibly exemplary beings. There follows upon these first five emperors a series of dynasties, of which the accounts become more and more exact and convincing as they become more recent. China has to tell a long history of border warfare and of graver struggles between the settled and nomad peoples. To begin with, China, like Sumer and like Egypt, was a land of city states. The government was at first a government of numerous kings; they became loosely feudal under an emperor, as the Egyptians did; and then later, as with the Egyptians, came a centralizing empire. Shang (1,750 to 1,125 B.C.) and Chow (1,125 to 250 B.C.) are named as being the two great dynasties of the feudal period. Bronze vessels of these earlier dynasties, beautiful, splendid, and with a distinctive style of their own, still exist, and there can be no doubt of the existence of a high state of culture even before the days of Shang.

It is perhaps a sense of symmetry that made the later historians of Egypt and China talk of the earlier phases of their national history as being under dynasties comparable to the dynasties of the later empires, and of such early "Emperors" as Menes (in Egypt) or the First Five Emperors (in China). The early dynasties exercised far less centralized powers than the later ones. Such unity as China possessed under the Shang Dynasty was a religious rather than an effective political union. The "Son of Heaven" offered sacrifices for all the Chinese. There was a common script, a common civilization, and a common enemy in the Huns of the north-western borders.

The last of the Shang Dynasty was a cruel and foolish monarch who burnt himself alive (1,125 B.C.) in his palace after a decisive defeat by Wu Wang, the founder of the Chow Dynasty. Wu Wang seems to have been helped by allies from among the south-western tribes as well as by a popular revolt.

For a time China remained loosely united under the Chow emperors, as loosely united as was Christendom under the popes in the Middle Ages; the Chow emperors had become the traditional high priests of the land in the place of the Shang Dynasty and claimed a sort of overlordship in Chinese affairs, but gradually the loose ties of usage and sentiment that held the empire together lost their hold upon men's minds. Hunnish peoples to the north and west took on the Chinese civilization without acquiring a sense of its unity. Feudal princes began to regard themselves as independent. Mr. Liang-Chi-Chao,[1] one of the Chinese representatives at the Paris Conference of 1919, states that between the eighth and fourth centuries B.C. "there were in the Hwang-ho and Yang-tse valleys no less than five or six thousand small states with about a dozen powerful states dominating over them." The land was subjected to perpetual warfare ("Age of Confusion"). In the sixth century B.C. the great powers in conflict were Ts'i and Ts'in, which were northern Hwang-ho states, and Ch'u, which was a vigorous, aggressive power in the Yang-tse valley. A confederation against Ch'u laid the foundation for a league that kept the peace for a hundred years; the league subdued and incorporated Ch'u and made a general treaty of disarmament. It became the foundation of a new pacific empire.

The knowledge of iron entered China at some unknown date, but iron weapons began to be commonly used only about 500 B.C., that is to say two or three hundred years or more after this had became customary in Assyria, Egypt, and Europe. Iron was probably introduced from the north into China by the Huns.

The last rulers of the Chow Dynasty were ousted by the kings of Ts'in, the latter seized upon the sacred sacrificial bronze tripods, and so were able to take over the imperial duty of offering sacrifices to Heaven. In this manner was the Ts'in Dynasty established. It ruled with far more vigour and effect than any previous family. The reign of Shi Hwang-ti (meaning "first universal emperor") of this dynasty is usually taken to mark the end of feudal and divided China. He seems to have played the unifying rôle in the east that Alexander the Great might have played in the west, but he lived longer, and the unity he made (or restored) was comparatively permanent, while the empire of Alexander the Great fell to pieces, as we shall tell, at his death. Shi Hwang-ti, among other feats in the

[1] *China and the League of Nations*, a pamphlet by Mr. Liang-Chi-Chao. (*Pekin Leader* Office.)

direction of common effort, organized the building of the Great Wall of China against the Huns. A civil war followed close upon his reign, and ended in the establishment of the Han Dynasty. Under this Han Dynasty the empire grew greatly beyond its original two river valleys, the Huns were effectively restrained, and the Chinese penetrated westward until they began to learn at last of civilized races and civilizations other than their own.

By 100 B.C. the Chinese had heard of India, their power had spread across Tibet and into Western Turkestan, and they were trading by camel caravans with Persia and the western world. So much for the present must suffice for our account of China. We shall return to the distinctive characters of its civilization later.

§ 6

And in these thousands of years during which man was making his way step by step from the barbarism of the heliolithic culture to civilization at these old-world centres, what was happening in the rest of the world? To the north of these centres, from the Rhine to the Pacific, the Nordic and Mongolian peoples, as we have told, were also learning the use of metals; but while the civilizations were settling down these men of the great plains were becoming migratory and developing from a slow wandering life towards a complete seasonal nomadism. To the south of the civilized zone, in central and southern Africa, the negro was making a slower progress, and that, it would seem, under the stimulus of invasion by whiter tribes from the Mediterranean regions, bringing with them in succession cultivation and the use of metals. These white men came to the black by two routes: across the Sahara to the west as Berbers and Tuaregs and the like, to mix with the negro and create such quasi-white races as the Fulas; and also by way of the Nile, where the Baganda (= Gandafolk) of Uganda, for example, may possibly be of remote white origin. The African forests were denser then, and spread eastward and northward from the Upper Nile.

The islands of the East Indies, three thousand years ago, were probably still only inhabited here and there by stranded patches of Palæolithic Australoids, who had wandered thither in those immemorial ages when there was a nearly complete land bridge by way of the East Indies to Australia. The islands of Oceania were uninhabited. The spreading of the heliolithic peoples by sea-going canoes into the islands of the Pacific came much later in the history of man, at earliest a thousand years B.C. Still later did they reach Madagascar. The beauty of New Zealand also was as yet wasted upon mankind; its highest living creatures were a great ostrich-like bird, the moa, now extinct, and the little kiwi which has feathers like coarse hair and the merest rudiments of wings.

In North America a group of Mongoloid tribes were now cut off altogether from the old world. They were spreading slowly southward, hunting the innumerable bison of the plains. They had still to learn for themselves the secrets of a separate agriculture based on maize, and in South America to tame the llama to their service, and so build up in Mexico and Peru two civilizations roughly parallel in their nature to that of Sumer, but different in many respects, and later by six or seven thousand years.

When men reached the southern extremity of America, the *Megatherium,* the giant sloth, and the *Glyptodon,* the giant armadillo, were still living.

There is a considerable imaginative appeal in the obscure story of the early American civilizations. It was largely a separate development. Somewhen at last the southward drift of the Amerindians must have met and mingled with the eastward, canoe-borne drift of the heliolithic culture. But it was the heliolithic culture still at a very lowly stage and probably before the use of metals. It has to be noted as evidence of this canoe-borne origin of American culture, that elephant-headed figures are found in Central American drawings. American metallurgy may have arisen independently of the old-world use of metal, or it may have been brought by these elephant carvers. These American peoples got to the use of bronze and copper, but not to the use of iron; they had gold and silver; and their stonework, their pottery, weaving, and dyeing were carried to a very high level. In all these things the American product resembles the old-world product *generally,* but always it has characteristics that are distinctive. The American civilizations had picture-writing of a primitive sort, but it never developed even to the pitch of the earliest Egyptian hieroglyphics. In Yucatan only was there a kind of script, the Maya writing, but it was used simply for keeping a calendar. In Peru the beginnings of writing were superseded by a curious and complicated method of keeping records by means of knots tied upon strings of various colours and shapes. It is said that even laws and orders could be conveyed by this code. These string bundles were called *quipus,* but though *quipus* are still to be found in collections, the art of reading them is altogether lost. The Chinese histories, Mr. L. Y. Chen informs us, state that a similar method of record by knots was used in China before the invention of writing there. The Peruvians also got to making maps and the use of counting-frames. "But with all this there was no means of handing on knowledge and experience from one generation to another, nor was anything done to fix and summarize these intellectual possessions, which are the basis of literature and science."[1]

When the Spaniards came to America, the Mexicans knew nothing of the Peruvians nor the Peruvians of the Mexicans. Intercourse there was none. Whatever links had ever existed were lost and forgotten. The Mexicans had never heard of the potato which was a principal article of Peruvian diet. In 5,000 B.C. the Sumerians and Egyptians probably knew as little of one another. America was 6,000 years behind the Old World.

[1] F. Ratzel, *History of Mankind.*

XV

SEA PEOPLES AND TRADING PEOPLES

§ 1

THE first boats were made very early indeed in the Neolithic stage of culture by riverside and lakeside peoples. They were no more than trees and floating wood, used to assist the imperfect natural swimming powers of men. Then came the hollowing out of the trees, and then, with the development of tools and a primitive carpentry, the building of boats. Men in Egypt and Mesopotamia also developed a primitive type of basketwork boat, caulked with bitumen. Such was the "ark of bulrushes" in which Moses was hidden by his mother. A kindred sort of vessel grew up by the use of skins and hides expanded upon a wicker framework. To this day cow-hide wicker boats (coracles) are used upon the west coast of Ireland where there is plenty of cattle and a poverty of big trees. They are also still used on the Euphrates, and on the Towy in South Wales. Inflated skins may have preceded the coracle, and are still used on the Euphrates and upper Ganges. In the valleys of the great rivers, boats must early have become an important means of communication; and it seems natural to suppose that it was from the mouths of the great rivers that man, already in a reasonably seaworthy vessel, first ventured out upon what must have seemed to him then the trackless and homeless sea.

No doubt he ventured at first as a fisherman, having learnt the elements of seacraft in creeks and lagoons. Men may have navigated boats upon the Levantine lake before the refilling of the Mediterranean by the Atlantic waters. The canoe was an integral part of the heliolithic culture, it drifted with the culture upon the warm waters of the earth from the Mediterranean to (at last) America. There were not only canoes, but Sumerian boats and ships upon the Euphrates and Tigris, when these rivers in 7,000 B.C. fell by separate mouths into the Persian Gulf. The Sumerian city of Eridu, which stood at the head of the Persian Gulf (from which it is now separated by a hundred and thirty miles of alluvium [1]), had ships upon the sea then. We also find evidence of a fully developed sea life six thousand years ago at the eastern end of the Mediterranean, and possibly at that time there were already canoes on the seas among the islands of the nearer East Indies. There are predynastic Neolithic Egyptian representations of Nile ships of a fair size, capable of carrying elephants.[2]

Very soon the seafaring men must have realized the peculiar freedom and opportunities the ship gave them. They could get away to islands; no chief nor king could pursue a boat or ship with any certainty; every captain was a king. The seamen would find it easy to make nests upon islands and in strong positions on the mainland. There they could harbour, there they could carry on a certain agriculture and fishery; but their specialty and their main business was, of course, the expedition across the sea. That was not usually a trading expedition; it was much more frequently a piratical raid. From what we know of mankind, we are bound to conclude that the first sailors plundered when they could, and traded when they had to.

Because it developed in the comparatively warm and tranquil waters of the eastern Mediterranean, the Red Sea, the Persian Gulf, and the western horn of the Indian Ocean, the shipping of the ancient world retained throughout certain characteristics that make it differ very widely from the ocean-going sailing shipping, with its vast spread of canvas, of the last four hundred years. "The Mediterranean," says Mr. Torr,[3] "is a sea where a vessel with sails may lie becalmed for days together, while a vessel with oars would easily be traversing the smooth waters, with coasts and islands everywhere at hand to give her shelter in case of storm. In that sea, therefore, oars became the characteristic instruments of navigation, and the arrangement of oars the chief problem in shipbuilding. And

[1] Sayce.
[2] Mosso, *The Dawn of Mediterranean Civilization.*— R. L. C.
[3] Cecil Torr, *Ancient Ships.*

so long as the Mediterranean nations dominated Western Europe, vessels of the southern type were built upon the northern coasts, though there generally was wind enough here for sails and too much wave for oars. . . . The art of rowing can first be discerned upon the Nile. Boats with oars are represented in the earliest pictorial monuments of Egypt, dating from about 2,500 B.C.; and although some crews are paddling with their faces towards the bow, others are rowing with their faces towards the stern. The paddling is certainly the older practice, for the hieroglyph *chen* depicts two arms grasping an oar in the attitude of paddling, and the hieroglyphs were invented in the earliest ages. And that practice may really have ceased before 2,500 B.C., despite the testimony of monuments of that date; for in monuments dating from about 1,250 B.C., crews are represented unmistakably rowing with their faces towards the stern and yet grasping their oars in the attitude of paddling, so that even then Egyptian artists mechanically followed the turn of the hieroglyph to which their hands were accustomed. In these reliefs there are twenty rowers on the boats on the Nile, and thirty on the ships on the Red Sea; but in the earliest reliefs the number varies considerably, and seems dependent on the amount of space at the sculptor's disposal."

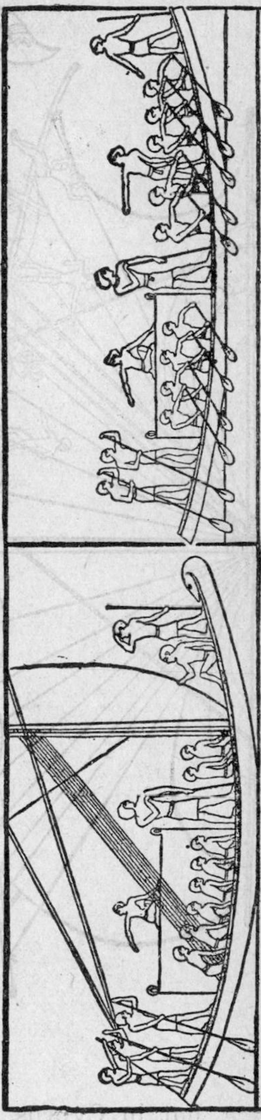

Boats on the Nile, about 2500 B.C.

[*From Torr's "Ancient Ships"*]

The Aryan peoples came late to the sea. The earliest ships on the sea were either Sumerian or Hamitic; the Semitic peoples followed close upon these pioneers. Along the eastern end of the Mediterranean, the Phœnicians, a Semitic people, set up a string of independent harbour towns of which Acre,

Tyre, and Sidon were the chief; and later they pushed their voyages westward and founded Carthage and Utica in North Africa. Possibly Phœnician keels were already in the Mediterranean by 2,000 B.C. Both Tyre and Sidon were originally on islands, and so easily defensible against a land raid. But before we go on to the marine exploits of this great sea-going race, we must note a very remarkable and curious nest of early sea people whose remains have been discovered in Crete.

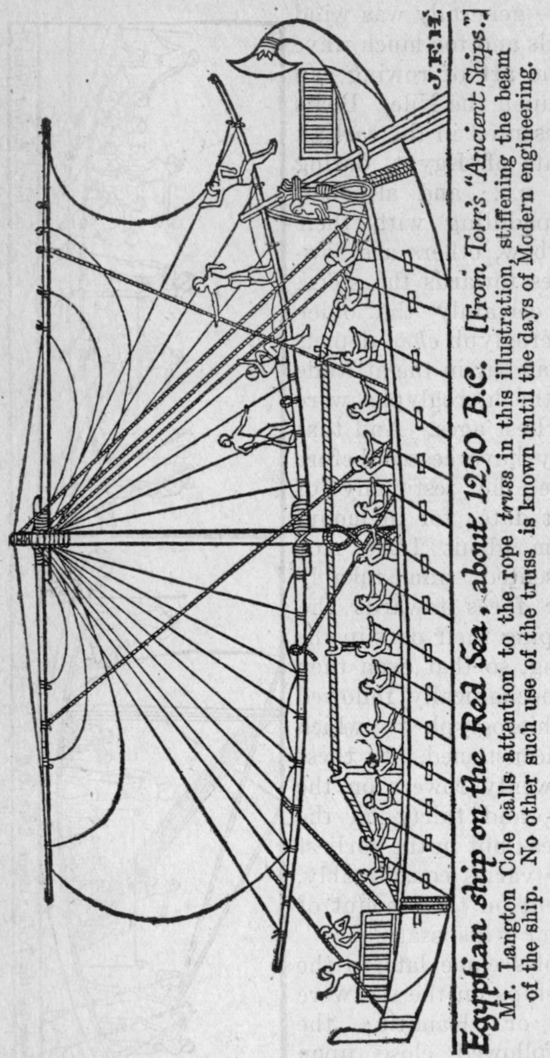

Egyptian ship on the Red Sea, about 1250 B.C. [*From Torr's "Ancient Ships."*]

Mr. Langton Cole calls attention to the rope *truss* in this illustration, stiffening the beam of the ship. No other such use of the truss is known until the days of Modern engineering.

§ 2

These early Cretans were of a race akin to the Iberians of Spain and Western Europe and the dark whites of Asia Minor and North Africa, and their language is unknown. This race lived not only in Crete, but in Cyprus, Greece, Asia Minor, Sicily, and South Italy. It was a civilized people for long ages before the fair Nordic Greeks spread southward through Macedonia. At

Cnossos, in Crete, there have been found the most astonishing ruins and remains, and Cnossos, therefore, is apt to overshadow the rest of these settlements in people's imaginations, but it is well to bear in mind that though Cnossos was no doubt a chief city of this Ægean civilization, these "Ægeans" had in the fullness of their time many cities and a wide range. Possibly, all that we know of them now are but the vestiges of the far more extensive heliolithic Neolithic civilization which is now submerged under the waters of the Mediterranean.

At Cnossos there are Neolithic remains as old or older than any of the pre-dynastic remains of Egypt. The Bronze Age began in Crete as soon as it did in Egypt, and there have been vases found by Flinders Petrie in Egypt and referred by him to the Ist Dynasty, which he declared to be importations from Crete. Stone vessels have been found in Crete of forms characteristic of the IVth (pyramid-building) Dynasty, and there can be no doubt that there was a vigorous trade between Crete and Egypt in the time of the XIIth Dynasty. This continued until about 1,000 B.C. It is clear that this island civilization arising upon the soil of Crete is at least as old as the Egyptian, and that it was already launched upon the sea as early as 4,000 B.C.

The great days of Crete were not so early as this. It was only about 2,500 B.C. that the island appears to have been unified under one ruler. Then began an age of peace and prosperity unexampled in the history of the ancient world. Secure from invasion, living in a delightful climate, trading with every civilized community in the world, the Cretans were free to develop all the arts and amenities of life. This Cnossos was not so much a town as the vast palace of the king and his people. It was not even fortified. The kings, it would seem, were called Minos always, as the kings of Egypt were all called Pharaoh; the king of Cnossos figures in the early legends of the Greeks as King Minos, who lived in the Labyrinth and kept there a horrible monster, half man, half bull, the Minotaur, to feed which he levied a tribute of youths and maidens from the Athenians. Those stories are a part of Greek literature, and have always been known, but it is only in the last few decades that the excavations at Cnossos have revealed how close these legends were to the reality. The Cretan labyrinth was a building as stately, complex, and luxurious as any in the ancient world. Among other details we find water-pipes, bathrooms, and the like conveniences, such as have hitherto been regarded as the latest refinements of modern life. The pottery, the textile manufactures, the sculpture and painting of these people, their gem and ivory work, their metal and inlaid work, is as admirable as any that mankind has produced. They were much given to festivals and shows, and, in particular, they were addicted to bull-fights and gymnastic entertainments. Their female costume became astonishingly "modern" in style; their women wore corsets and flounced dresses. They had a system of writing which has not yet been deciphered.

It is the custom nowadays to make a sort of wonder of these achievements of the Cretans, as though they were a people of incredible artistic ability living in the dawn of civilization. But their great time was long past that dawn; as late as 2,000 B.C. It took them many centuries to reach their best in art and skill, and their art and luxury are by no means so great a wonder if we reflect that for 3,000 years they were immune from invasion, that for a thousand years they were at peace. Century after century their artizans could perfect their skill, and their men and women refine upon refinement. Wherever men of almost any race have been comparatively safe in this fashion for such a length of time, they have developed much artistic beauty. Given the opportunity, all races are artistic. Greek legend has it that it was in Crete that Dædalus attempted to make the first flying machine. Dædalus (= cunning artificer) was a sort of personified summary of mechanical

skill. It is curious to speculate what germ of fact lies behind him and those waxen wings that, according to the legend, melted and plunged his son Icarus in the sea.

There came at last a change in the condition of the lives of these Cretans, for other peoples, the Greeks and the Phœnicians, were also coming out with powerful fleets upon the seas. We do not know what led to the disaster nor who inflicted it; but somewhen about 1,400 B.C. Cnossos was sacked and burnt, and though the Cretan life struggled on there rather lamely for another four centuries, there came at last a final blow about 1,000 B.C. (that is to say, in the days of the Assyrian ascendancy in the East). The palace at Cnossos was destroyed, and never rebuilt nor reinhabited. Possibly this was done by the ships of those new-comers into the Mediterranean, the barbaric Greeks, a group of Aryan-speaking tribes from the north, who may have wiped out Cnossos as they wiped out the city of Troy. The legend of Theseus tells of such a raid. He entered the Labyrinth (which may have been the Cnossos Palace) by the aid of Ariadne, the daughter of Minos, and slew the Minotaur.

J.F.H. from photos. by
Britis School at Athens

Faience figure from Cnossos..... A votary of the Snake Goddess.....

The *Iliad* makes it clear that destruction came upon Troy because the Trojans stole Greek women. Modern writers, with modern ideas in their heads, have tried to make out that the Greeks assailed Troy in order to secure a trade route or some such fine-spun commercial advantage. If so, the authors of the *Iliad* hid the motives of their characters very skilfully. It would be about as reasonable to say that the Homeric Greeks went to war with the Trojans in order to be well ahead with a station on the Berlin to Bagdad railway. The Homeric Greeks were a healthy barbaric Aryan people, with very poor ideas about trade and "trade routes"; they went to war with the Trojans because they were thoroughly annoyed about this stealing of women. It is fairly clear from the Minos legend and from the evidence of the Cnossos remains, that the Cretans kidnapped or stole youths and maidens to be slaves, bull-fighters, athletes, and perhaps sacrifices. They traded fairly with the Egyptians, but it may be they did not realize the gathering strength of the Greek barbarians; they "traded" violently with them, and so brought sword and flame upon themselves.

Another great sea people were the Phœnicians. They were great seamen because they were great traders. Their colony of Carthage (founded before 800 B.C. by Tyre) became at last greater than any of the older Phœnician cities, but already before 1,500 B.C. both Sidon and Tyre had settlements upon the African coast. Carthage was comparatively inaccessible to the Assyrian and Babylonian hosts, and, profiting greatly by the long siege of Tyre by Nebuchadnezzar II, became the greatest maritime power the world had hitherto seen. She claimed the Western Mediterranean as her own, and seized every ship she could catch west of Sardinia. Roman writers accuse her of great cruelties. She fought the Greeks for Sicily, and later (in the second century B.C.) she fought the Romans. Alexander the Great formed plans for her conquest; but he died, as we shall tell later, before he could carry them out.

§ 3

At her zenith Carthage probably had the hitherto unheard-of population of a million. This population was largely industrial, and her woven goods were universally famous. As well as a coasting trade, she had a considerable land trade with Central Africa,[1] and she sold negro slaves, ivory, metals, precious stones and the like, to all the Mediterranean people; she worked Spanish copper mines, and her ships went out into

[1] There were no domesticated camels in Africa until after the Persian conquest of Egypt. This must have greatly restricted the desert routes. (See Bunbury, *History of Ancient Geography,* note to Chap. VIII.) But the Sahara desert of 3,000 or 2,000 years ago was less parched and sterile than it is to-day. From rock engravings we may deduce the theory that the desert was crossed from oasis to oasis by riding oxen and by

the Atlantic and coasted along Portugal and France northward as far as the Cassiterides (the Scilly Isles, or Cornwall, in England) to get tin. About 520 B.C. a certain Hanno made a voyage that is still one of the most notable in the world. This Hanno, if we may trust the *Periplus of Hanno,* the Greek translation of his account which still survives, followed the African coast southward from the Straits of Gibraltar as far as the confines of Liberia. He had sixty big ships, and his main task was to found or reinforce certain Carthaginian stations upon the Morocco coast. Then he pushed southward. He founded a settlement in the Rio de Oro (on Kerne or Herne Island), and sailed on past the Senegal River. The voyagers passed on for seven days beyond the Gambia, and landed at last upon some island. This they left in a panic, because, although the day was silent with the silence of the tropical forests, at night they heard the sound of flutes, drums, and gongs, and the sky was red with the blaze of the bush fires. The coast country for the rest of the voyage was one blaze of fire, from the burning of the bush. Streams of fire ran down the hills into the sea, and at length a blaze arose so loftily that it touched the skies. Three days further brought them to an island containing a lake (?Sherbro Island). In this lake was another island (?Macaulay Island), and on this were wild, hairy men and women, "whom the interpreters called gorilla." The Carthaginians, having caught some of the females of these "gorillas"—they were probably chimpanzees—turned back and eventually deposited the skins of their captives—who had proved impossibly violent guests to entertain on board ship—in the Temple of Juno.

A still more wonderful Phœnician sea voyage, long doubted, but now supported by some archæological evidence, is related by Herodotus, who declares that the Pharaoh Necho of the XXVIth Dynasty commissioned some Phœnicians to attempt the circumnavigation of Africa, and that starting from the Gulf of Suez southward, they did finally come back through

ox-carts: perhaps, also, on horses and asses. The camel as a beast of transport was seemingly not introduced into North Africa till the Arab invasions of the seventh century A.D. The fossil remains of camels are found in Algeria, and wild camels may have lingered in the wastes of the Sahara and Somaliland till the domesticated camel was introduced. The Nubian wild ass also seems to have extended its range to the Sahara.—H. H. J.

the Mediterranean to the Nile delta. They took nearly three years to complete their voyage. Each year they landed, and sowed and harvested a crop of wheat before going on.

§ 4

The great trading cities of the Phœnicians are the most striking of the early manifestations of the peculiar and characteristic gift of the Semitic peoples to mankind, trade and exchange.[1] While the Semitic Phœnician peoples were spreading themselves upon the seas, another kindred Semitic people, the Arameans, whose occupation of Damascus we have already noted, were developing the caravan routes of the Arabian and Persian deserts, and becoming the chief trading people of Western Asia. The Semitic peoples, earlier civilized than the Aryan, have always shown, and still show to-day, a far greater sense of quality and quantity in marketable goods than the latter; it is to their need of account-keeping that the development of alphabetical writing is to be ascribed, and it is to them that most of the great advances in computation are due. Our modern numerals are Arabic; our arithmetic and algebra are essentially Semitic sciences.

The Semitic peoples, we may point out here, are to this day *counting peoples* strong in their sense of equivalents and reparation. The moral teaching of the Hebrews was saturated by such ideas. "With what measure ye mete, the same shall be meted unto you." Other races and peoples have imagined diverse and fitful and marvellous gods, but it was the trading Semites who first began to think of God as a Righteous Dealer, whose promises were kept, who failed not the humblest creditor, and called to account every spurious act.

The trade that was going on in the ancient world before the sixth or seventh century B.C. was almost entirely a barter trade. There was little or no credit or coined money. The ordinary standard of value with the early Aryans was cattle, as it still is with the Zulus and Kaffirs to-day. In the *Iliad*, the respective values of two shields are stated in head of cattle, and the Roman word for moneys, *pecunia*, is derived from

[1] There was Sumerian trade organized round the temples before the Semites got into Babylonia. See Hall and King, *Archaeological Discoveries in Western Asia*.—E. B.

pecus, cattle. Cattle as money had this advantage; it did not need to be carried from one owner to another, and if it needed attention and food, at any rate it bred. But it was inconvenient for ship or caravan transit. Many other substances have at various times been found convenient as a standard; tobacco was once legal tender in the colonial days in North America, and in West Africa fines are paid and bargains made in bottles of trade gin. The early Asiatic trade included metals; and weighed lumps of metal, since they were in general demand and were convenient for hoarding and storage, costing nothing for fodder and needing small houseroom, soon asserted their superiority over cattle and sheep. Iron, which seems to have been first reduced from its ores by the Hittites, was, to begin with, a rare and much-desired substance.[1] It is stated by Aristotle to have supplied the first currency. In the collection of letters found at Tel-el-Amarna, addressed to and from Amenophis III (already mentioned) and his successor Amenophis IV, one from a Hittite king promises iron as an extremely valuable gift. Gold, then as now, was the most precious, and therefore most portable, security. In early Egypt silver was almost as rare as gold until after the XVIIIth Dynasty. Later the general standard of value in the Eastern world became silver, measured by weight.

To begin with, metals were handed about in ingots and weighed at each transaction. Then they were stamped to indicate their fineness and guarantee their purity. The first recorded coins were minted about 600 B.C. in Lydia, a gold-producing country in the west of Asia Minor. The first-known gold coins were minted in Lydia by Crœsus, whose name has become a proverb for wealth; he was conquered, as we shall tell later, by that same Cyrus the Persian who took Babylon in 539 B.C. But very probably coined money had been used in Babylonia before that time. The "sealed shekel," a stamped piece of silver, came very near to being a coin. The promise to pay so much silver or gold on "leather" (= parchment) with the seal of some established firm is probably as old or older than coinage. The Carthaginians used such "leather money." We know very little of the way in which small traffic was conducted. Common people, who in those ancient times were in

[1] Iron bars of fixed weight were used for coin in Britain. Cæsar, *De Bello Gallico.*—G. Wh.

dependent positions, seem to have had no money at all; they did their business by barter. Early Egyptian paintings show this going on.[1]

§ 5

When one realizes the absence of small money or of any conveniently portable means of exchange in the pre-Alexandrian world, one perceives how impossible was private travel in those days.[2] The first "inns"—no doubt a sort of caravanserai—are commonly said to have come into existence in Lydia in the third or fourth century B.C. That, however, is too late a date. They are certainly older than that. There is good evidence of them at least as early as the sixth century. Æschylus twice mentions inns. His word is "all-receiver," or "all-receiving house."[3] Private travellers must have been fairly common in the Greek world, including its colonies, by this time. But such private travel was a comparatively new thing then. The early historians Hecatæus and Herodotus travelled widely. "I suspect," says Professor Gilbert Murray, "that this sort of travel 'for Historie' or 'for discovery' was rather a Greek invention. Solon is supposed to have practised it; and even Lycurgus." . . . The earlier travellers were traders travelling in a caravan or in a shipload, and carrying their goods and their minas and shekels of metal or gems or bales of fine stuff with them, or government officials travelling with letters of introduction and a proper retinue. Possibly there were a few mendicants, and, in some restricted regions, religious pilgrims.

That earlier world before 600 B.C. was one in which a lonely "stranger" was a rare and suspected and endangered being. He might suffer horrible cruelties, for there was little law to protect such as he. Few individuals strayed therefore. One

[1] The earliest coinage of the west coast of Asia Minor was in electrum, a mixture of gold and silver, and there is an interesting controversy as to whether the first issues were stamped by cities, temples, or private bankers.—P. G.

[2] Small change was in existence before the time of Alexander. The Athenians had a range of exceedingly small silver coins running almost down to the size of a pinhead which were generally carried in the mouth; a character in Aristophanes was suddenly assaulted, and swallowed his change in consequence.—P. G.

[3] There is an inn-keeper in Aristophanes, but it may be inferred from the circumstance that she is represented as letting lodgings in hell, that the early inn left much to be desired.—P. G.

lived and died attached and tied to some patriarchal tribe, if one was a nomad, or to some great household if one was civilized or to one of the big temple establishments which we will presently discuss. Or one was a herded slave. One knew nothing, except for a few monstrous legends, of the rest of the world in which one lived. We know more to-day, indeed, of the world of 600 B.C. than any single living being knew at that time. We map it out, see it as a whole in relation to past and future. We begin to learn precisely what was going on at the same time in Egypt and Spain and Media and India and China. We can share in imagination, not only the wonder of Hanno's sailors, but of the men who lit the warning beacons on the shore. We know that those "mountains flaming to the sky" were only the customary burning of the dry grass at that season of the year. Year by year, more and more rapidly, our common knowledge increases. In the years to come men will understand still more of those lives in the past, until perhaps they will understand them altogether.

XVI

WRITING

§ 1. *Picture-Writing.* § 2. *Syllable-Writing.* § 3. *Alphabet-Writing.* § 4. *The Place of Writing in Human Life.*

§ 1

IN the four preceding chapters (XII to XV) we have sketched in broad outline the development of the chief human communities from the primitive beginnings of the heliolithic culture to the great historical kingdoms and empires in the sixth century B.C. We must now study a little more closely the general process of social change, the growth of human ideas, and the elaboration of human relationships that was going on during these ages between 10,000 B.C. and 500 B.C. What we have done so far is to draw the map and name the chief kings and empires, to define the relations in time and space of Babylonia, Assyria, Egypt, Phœnicia, Cnossos, and the like; we come now to the real business of history, which is to get down below these outer forms to the thoughts and lives of individual men.

By far the most important thing that was going on during those fifty or sixty centuries of social development was the invention of writing and its gradual progress to importance in human affairs. It was a new instrument for the human mind, an enormous enlargement of its range of action, a new means of continuity. We have seen how in later Palæolithic and early Neolithic times the elaboration of articulate speech gave men a mental handhold for consecutive thought, and a vast enlargement of their powers of co-operation. For a time this new acquirement seems to have overshadowed their earlier achievement of drawing, and possibly it checked the use of gesture. But drawing presently reappeared again, for record, for signs, for the joy of drawing. Before real writing came picture-writing, such as is still practised by the Amerindians, the Bushmen, and savage and barbaric people in all parts of the world. It is essentially a drawing of things and acts, helped out by heraldic indications of proper names, and by strokes and dots to represent days and distances and such-like quantitative ideas.

Quite kindred to such picture-writing is the pictograph that one finds still in use to-day in international railway time-tables upon the continent of Europe, where a little black sign of a cup indicates a stand-up buffet for light refreshments; a crossed knife and fork, a restaurant; a little steamboat, a transfer to a steamboat; and a postilion's horn, a diligence. Similar signs are used in the well-known Michelin guides for automobilists in Europe, to show a postoffice (envelope) or a telephone (telephone receiver). The quality of hotels is shown by an inn with one, two, three, or four gables, and so forth. Similarly, the roads of Europe are marked with wayside signs representing a gate, to indicate a level crossing ahead, a sinuous bend for a dangerous curve, and the like. From such pictographic signs to the first elements of Chinese writing is not a very long stretch.

In Chinese writing there are still traceable a number of pictographs. Most are now difficult to recognize. A mouth was originally written as a mouth-shaped hole, and is now, for convenience of brushwork, squared; a child, originally a recognizable little manikin, is now a hasty wriggle and a cross; the sun, originally a large circle with a dot in the centre, has been converted, for the sake of convenience of combination, into a crossed oblong, which is easier to make with a brush. By combining these pictographs, a second order of ideas is expressed. For example, the pictograph for mouth combined with pictograph for vapour expressed "words."[1]

From such combinations one passes to what are called *ideograms:* the sign for "words" and the sign for "tongue" combine to make "speech"; the sign for "roof" and the sign for "pig" make "home"—for in the early domestic economy of China the pig was as important as it used to be in Ireland. But, as we have already noted earlier, the Chinese language consists of a comparatively few elementary monosyllabic sounds, which are all used in a great variety of meanings, and the Chinese soon discovered that a number of these *pictographs* and *ideographs* could be used also to express other ideas, not so conveniently

[1] See the *Encyclopaedia Brit.*, Article *China*, p. 218.

pictured, but having the same sound. Characters so used are called *phonograms*. For example, the sound *fang* meant not only "boat," but "a place," "spinning," "fragrant," "inquire," and several other meanings according to the context. But while a boat is easy to draw, most of the other meanings are undrawable. How can one draw "fragant" or "inquire"? The Chinese, therefore, took the same sign for all these meanings of "fang" but added to each of them another distinctive sign, the *determinative*, to show what sort of *fang* was intended. A "place" was indicated by the same sign as for "boat" (*fang*) and the determinative sign for "earth"; "spinning" by the sign for *fang* and the sign for "silk"; "inquire" by the sign for *fang*, and the sign for "words," and so on.

One may perhaps make this development of pictographs, ideograms, and phonograms a little clearer by taking an analogous case in English. Suppose we were making up a sort of picture-writing in English, then it would be very natural to use a square with a slanting line to suggest a lid, for the word and thing *box*. That would be a pictograph. But now suppose we had a round sign for money, and suppose we put this sign inside the box sign, that would do for "cash-box" or "treasury." That would be an ideogram. But the word "box" is used for other things than boxes. There is the box shrub which gives us boxwood. It would be hard to draw a recognizable box-tree distinct from other trees, but it is quite easy to put our sign "box," and add our sign for shrub as a determinative to determine that it is that sort of box and not a common box that we want to express. And then there is "box," the verb, meaning to fight with fists. Here, again, we need a determinative; we might add the two crossed swords, a sign which is used very often upon maps to denote a battle. A box at a theatre needs yet another determinative, and so we go on, through a long series of phonograms.

Now it is manifest that here in the Chinese writing is a very peculiar and complex system of sign-writing. A very great number of characters have to be learnt and the mind habituated to their use. The power it possesses to carry ideas and discussion is still ungauged by western standards, but we may doubt whether with this instrument it will ever be possible to establish such a wide, common mentality as the simpler and swifter alphabets of the western civilizations permit. In China it created a special reading-class, the mandarins, who were also the ruling and official class. Their necessary concentration upon words and classical forms, rather than upon ideas and realities, seems, in spite of her comparative peacefulness and the very high individual intellectual quality of her people, to have greatly hampered the social and economic development of China. Probably it is the complexity of her speech and writing, more than any other imaginable cause, that has made China to-day politically, socially, and individually a vast pool of backward people rather than the foremost power in the whole world.[1]

Specimens of American Indian picture-writing (after Schoolcraft.)

No. 1, painted on a rock on the shore of Lake Superior, records an expedition across the lake, in which five canoes took part. The upright strokes in each indicate the number of the crew, and the bird represents a chief, "The Kingfisher." The three circles (suns) under the arch (of heaven) indicate that the voyage lasted three days, and the tortoise, a symbol of land, denotes a safe arrival. No. 2 is a petition sent to the United States Congress by a group of Indian tribes, asking for fishing rights in certain small lakes. The tribes are represented by their totems, martens, bear, manfish, and catfish, led by the crane. Lines running from the heart and eye of each animal to the heart and eye of the crane denote that they are all of one mind; and a line runs from the eye of the crane to the lakes, shown in the crude little "map" in the lower left-hand corner.

§ 2

But while the Chinese mind thus made for itself an instrument which

[1] The writer's friend, Mr. L. Y. Chen, thinks that this is only partially true. He thinks that the emperors insisted upon a minute and rigorous study of the set classics in order to check intellectual innovation. This was especially the case with the Ming emperors, the first of whom, when reorganizing the examination system on a narrower basis, said definitely, "This will bring all the intellectuals of the world into my trap." The Five Classics and the Four Books have imprisoned the mind of China.

is probably too elaborate in structure, too laborious in use, and too inflexible in its form to meet the modern need for simple, swift, exact, and lucid communications, the growing civilizations of the west were working out the problem of a written record upon rather different and, on the whole, more advantageous lines. They did not seek to improve their script to make it swift and easy, but circumstances conspired to make it so. The Sumerian picture writing, which had to be done upon clay and with little styles, which made curved marks with difficulty and inaccurately, rapidly degenerated by a conventionalized dabbing down of wedged-shaped marks (cuneiform = wedge-shaped) into almost unrecognizable hints of the shapes intended. It helped the Sumerians greatly to learn to write, that they had to draw so badly. They got very soon to the Chinese pictographs, ideographs, and phonograms, and beyond them.

Most people know a sort of puzzle called a rebus. It is a way of representing words by pictures, not of the things the words represent, but by the pictures of other things having a similar sound. For example, two gates and a head is a rebus for Gateshead; a little streamlet (beck), a crowned monarch, and a ham, Beckingham. The Sumerian language was a language well adapted to this sort of representation. It was apparently a language of often quite vast polysyllables, made up of very distinct inalterable syllables; and many of the syllables taken separately were the names of concrete things. So that this cuneiform writing developed very readily into a syllabic way of writing, in which each sign conveys a syllable just as each act in a charade conveys a syllable. When presently the Semites conquered Sumeria, they adapted the syllabic system to their own speech, and so this writing became entirely a sign-for-a-sound writing. It was so used by the Assyrians and by the Chaldeans. But it was not a letter-writing, it was a syllable-writing. This cuneiform script prevailed for long ages over Assyria, Babylonia, and the Near East generally; there are vestiges of it in some of the letters of our alphabet to-day.

§ 3

But, meanwhile, in Egypt and upon the Mediterranean coast yet another system of writing grew up. Its beginnings are probably to be found in the priestly picture-writing (hieroglyphics) of the Egyptians, which also in the usual way became partly a sound-sign system. As we see it on the Egyptian monuments, the hieroglyphic writing consists of decorative but stiff and elaborate forms, but for such purpose as letter-writing and the keeping of recipes and the like, the Egyptian priests used a much simplified and flowing form of these characters, the *hieratic script.* Side by side with this hieratic script rose another, probably also derivative from the hieroglyphs, a script now lost to use, which was taken over by various non-Egyptian peoples in the Mediterranean, the Phœnicians, Libyans, Lydians, Cretans, and Celt-Iberians, and used for business purposes. Possibly a few letters were borrowed from the later cuneiform. In the hands of these foreigners this writing was, so to speak, cut off from its roots; it lost all but a few traces of its early pictorial character. It ceased to be pictographic or ideographic; it became simply a pure sound-sign system, an *alphabet.*

There were a number of such alphabets in the Mediterranean differing widely from each other. It may be noted that the Phœnician alphabet (and perhaps others) omitted vowels. Possibly they pronounced their consonants very hard and had rather indeterminate vowels, as is said to be still the case with tribes of South Arabia. Quite probably, too, the Phœnicians used their alphabet at first not so much for writing as for single initial letters in their business accounts and tallies. One of these Mediterranean alphabets reached the Greeks, long after the time of the *Iliad,* who presently set to work to make it express the clear and beautiful sounds of their own highly developed Aryan speech. It consisted at first of consonants, and the Greeks added the vowels. They began to write for record, to help and fix their bardic tradition. . . .

§ 4

So it was by a series of very natural steps that writing grew out of the life of man. At first and for long ages it was the interest and the secret of only a few people in a special class, a mere accessory to the record of pictures. But there were certain very manifest advantages, quite apart from the increased expressiveness of mood and qualification, to be gained by making writing a little less plain than straightforward pictures, and in conventionalizing and codifying it. One of these was that so messages might be sent understandable by the sender and receiver, but not plain to the uninitiated. Another was that so one might put down various matters and help one's memory and the memory of one's friends, without giving away too much to the common herd. Among some of the earliest Egyptian writings, for example, are medical recipes and magic formulæ. Accounts, letters, recipes, name lists, itineraries; these were the earliest of written documents. Then, as the art of writing and reading spread, came that odd desire, that pathetic desire so common among human beings, to astonish some strange and remote person by writing down something striking, some secret one knew, some strange thought, or even one's name, so that long after one had gone one's way, it might strike upon the sight and mind of another reader. Even in Sumeria men scratched on walls, and all that remains to us of the ancient world, its rocks, its buildings, is plastered thickly with the names and the boasting of those foremost among human advertisers, its kings. Perhaps half the early inscriptions in that ancient world are of this nature, if, that is, we group with the name-writing and boasting the epitaphs, which were probably in many cases pre-arranged by the deceased.

For long the desire for crude self-assertion of the name-scrawling sort and the love of secret understandings kept writing within a narrow scope; but that other, more truly social desire in men, the desire to *tell,* was also at work. The profounder possibilities of writing, the possibilities of a vast extension and definition and settlement of knowledge and tradition, only grew apparent after long ages. But it will be interesting at this point and in this connection to recapitulate certain elemental facts about life, upon which we laid stress in our earlier chapters, because they illuminate not only the huge value of writing in the whole field of man's history, but also the rôle it is likely to play in his future.

1. Life had at first, it must be remembered, only a discontinuous repetition of consciousness, as the old died and the young were born.

Such a creature as a reptile has in its brain a capacity for experience, but when the individual dies, its experience dies with it. Most of its motives are purely instinctive, and all the mental life that it has is the result of heredity (birth inheritance).

2. But ordinary mammals have added to pure instinct *tradition,* a tradition of experience imparted by the imitated example of the mother, and in the case of such mentally developed animals as dogs, cats, or apes, by a sort of mute precept also. For example, the mother cat chastises her young for misbehaviour. So do mother apes and baboons.

3. Primitive man added to his powers of transmitting experience, representative art and speech. Pictorial and sculptured record and *verbal tradition* began.

Verbal tradition was developed to its highest possibility by the bards. They did much to make language what it is to the world to-day.

4. With the invention of writing, which developed out of pictorial record, human tradition was able to become fuller and much more exact. Verbal tradition, which had hitherto changed from age to age, began to be fixed. Men separated by hundreds of miles could now communicate their thoughts. An increasing number of human beings began to share a common written knowledge and a common sense of a past and a future. Human thinking became a larger operation in which hundreds of minds in different places and in different ages could react upon one another; it became a process constantly more continuous and sustained. . . .

5. For hundreds of generations the full power of writing was not revealed to the world, because for a long time the idea of multiplying writings by taking prints of a first copy did not become effective. The only way of multiplying writings was by copying one copy at a time, and this made books costly and rare. Moreover, the tendency to keep things secret, to make a cult and mystery of them, and so to gain an advantage over the generality of men, has always been very strong in men's minds. It is only nowadays that the great masses of mankind are learning to read, and reaching out towards the treasures of knowledge and thought already stored in books.

Nevertheless, from the first writings onward a new sort of tradition, an enduring and immortal tradition, began in the minds of men. Life, through mankind, grew thereafter more and more distinctly conscious of itself and its world. It is a thin streak of intellectual growth we trace in history, at first in a world of tumultuous ignorance and forgetfulness; it is like a mere line of light coming through the chink of an opening door into a darkened room; but slowly it widens, it grows. At last came a time in the history of Europe when the door, at the push of the printer, began to open more rapidly. Knowledge flared up, and as it flared it ceased to be the privilege of a favoured minority. For us now that door swings wider, and the light behind grows brighter. Misty it is still, glowing through clouds of dust and reek.

The door is not half open; the light is but a light new lit. Our world to-day is only in the beginning of knowledge.

XVII

GODS AND STARS, PRIESTS AND KINGS

§ 1. *The Priest Comes into History.* § 2. *Priests and the Stars.* § 3. *Priests and the Dawn of Learning.* § 4. *King against Priest.* § 5. *How Bel-Marduk Struggled against the Kings.* § 6. *The God-Kings of Egypt.* § 7. *Shi Hwang-ti Destroys the Books.*

§ 1

WHEN we direct our attention to these new accumulations of human beings that were beginning in Egypt and Mesopotamia, we find that one of the most conspicuous and constant objects in all these cities is a temple or a group of temples. In some cases there arises beside it in these regions a royal palace, but as often the temple towers over the palace. This presence of the temple is equally true of the Phœnician cities and of the Greek and Roman as they arise. The palace of Cnossos, with its signs of comfort and pleasure-seeking, and the kindred cities of the Ægean peoples, include religious shrines, but in Crete there are also temples standing apart from the palatial city-households. All over the ancient civilized world we find them; wherever primitive civilization set its foot in Africa, Europe, or western Asia, a temple arose, and where the civilization is most ancient, in Egypt and in Sumer, there the temple is most in evidence. When Hanno reached what he thought was the most westerly point of Africa, he set up a temple to Hercules. The beginnings of civilization and the appearance of temples is simultaneous in history. The two things belong together. The beginning of cities is the temple stage of history.

In all these temples there was a shrine; dominating the shrine there was commonly a great figure usually of some monstrous half-animal form, before which stood an altar for sacrifices. In the Greek and Roman temples however the image was generally that of a divinity in human form. This figure was either regarded as the god or as the image or symbol of the god, for whose worship the temple existed. And connected with the temple there were a number, and often a considerable number, of priests or priestesses, and temple servants, generally wearing a distinctive costume and forming an important part of the city population. They belonged to no household; they made up a new kind of household of their own. They were a caste and a class apart, attracting intelligent recruits from the general population.

The primary duty of this priesthood was concerned with the worship of and the sacrifices to the god of the temple. And these things were done, not at any time, but at particular times and seasons. There had come into the life of man with his herding and agriculture a sense of a difference between the parts of the year and of a difference between day and day. Men were beginning to work—and to need days of rest. The temple, by its festivals, kept count. The temple in the ancient city was like the clock and calendar upon a writing-desk.

But it was a centre of other functions. It was in the early temples that the records and tallies of events were kept and that writing began. And there was knowledge there. The people went to the temple not only *en masse* for festivals, but individually for help. The early priests were also doctors and magicians. In the earliest temples we already find those little offerings for some private and particular end, which are still made in the chapels of Catholic churches to-day, *ex votos,* little models of hearts relieved and limbs restored, acknowledgment of prayers answered and accepted vows.

It is clear that here we have that comparatively unimportant element in the life of the early nomad, the medicine-man, the shrine-keeper, and the memorist, developed, with the development of the community and as a part of the development of the community from barbarism to civilized settlement, into something of very much greater importance. And it is equally evident that those primitive fears of (and hopes of help from) strange beings, the desire to propitiate unknown forces, the primitive desire for cleansing and the primitive craving for power and knowledge have all contributed to crystallize out this new social fact of the temple.

The temple was accumulated by complex necessities, it grew from many roots and needs, and the god or goddess that domi-

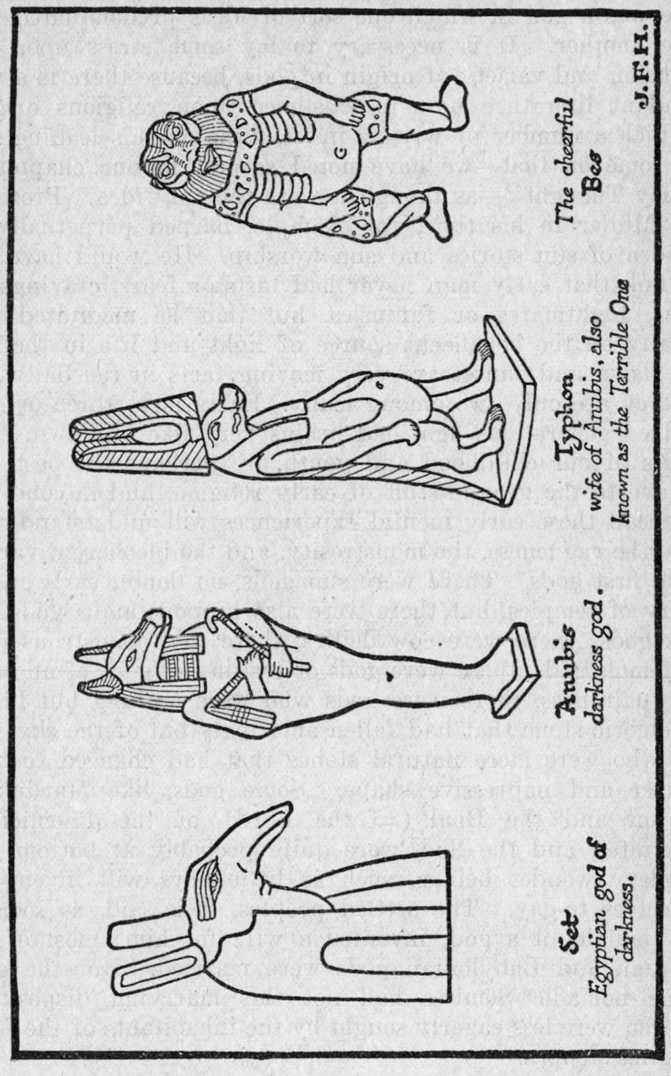

Set
Egyptian god of darkness.

Anubis
darkness god.

Typhon
wife of Anubis, also known as the Terrible One

The cheerful
Bes

nated the temple was the creation of many imaginations and made up of all sorts of impulses, ideas, and half ideas. Here there was a god in which one sort of ideas predominated, and there another. It is necessary to lay some stress upon this confusion and variety of origin in gods, because there is a very abundant literature now in existence upon religious origins, in which a number of writers insist, some on this leading idea and some on that—we have noted several in our chapter on "Early Thought"—as though it were the only idea. Professor Max Müller in his time, for example, harped perpetually on the idea of sun stories and sun worship. He would have had us think that early man never had lusts or fears, cravings for power, nightmares or fantasies, but that he meditated perpetually on the beneficent source of light and life in the sky. Now dawn and sunset are very moving facts in the daily life, but they are only two among many. Early men, three or four hundred generations ago, had brains very like our own. The fancies of our childhood and youth are perhaps the best clue we have to the ground-stuff of early religion, and anyone who can recall those early mental experiences will understand very easily the vagueness, the monstrosity, and the incoherent variety of the first gods. There were sun gods, no doubt, early in the history of temples, but there were also hippopotamus gods and hawk gods; there were cow deities, there were monstrous male and female gods, there were gods of terror and gods of an adorable quaintness, there were gods who were nothing but lumps of meteoric stone that had fallen amazingly out of the sky, and gods who were mere natural stones that had chanced to have a queer and impressive shape. Some gods, like Marduk of Babylon and the Baal (= the Lord) of the Phœnicians, Canaanites, and the like, were quite probably at bottom just legendary wonder beings, such as little boys will invent for themselves to-day. The settled peoples, it is said, as soon as they thought of a god, invented a wife for him; most of the Egyptian and Babylonian gods were married. But the gods of the nomadic Semites had not this marrying disposition. Children were less eagerly sought by the inhabitants of the food-grudging steppes.

Even more natural than to provide a wife for a god is to give him a house to live in to which offerings can be brought. Of this house the knowing man, the magician, would naturally become the custodian. A certain seclusion, a certain aloofness, would add greatly to the prestige of the god. The steps by which the early temple and the early priesthood developed so soon as an agricultural population settled and increased are all quite natural and understandable, up to the stage of the long temple with the image, shrine and altar at one end and the long nave in which the worshippers stood. And this temple, because it had records and secrets, because it was a centre of power, advice, and instruction, because it sought and attracted imaginative and clever people for its service, naturally became a kind of brain in the growing community. The attitude of the common people who tilled the fields and herded the beasts towards the temple would remain simple and credulous. There, rarely seen and so imaginatively enhanced, lived the god whose approval gave prosperity, whose anger meant misfortune; he could be propitiated by little presents and the help of his servants could be obtained. He was wonderful, and of such power and knowledge that it did not do to be disrespectful to him even in one's thoughts. Within the priesthood, however, a certain amount of thinking went on at a rather higher level than that.

§ 2

We may note here a very interesting fact about the chief temples of Egypt and, so far as we know—because the ruins are not so distinct—of Babylonia, and that is that they were "oriented"—that is to say, that the same sort of temple was built so that the shrine and entrance always faced in the same direction. In Babylonian temples this was most often due east, facing the sunrise on March 21st and September 21st, the equinoxes; and it is to be noted that it was at the spring equinox that the Euphrates and Tigris came down in flood. The Pyramids of Gizeh are also oriented east and west, and the Sphinx faces due east, but very many of the Egyptian temples to the south of the delta of the Nile do not point due east, but to the point where the sun rises at the longest day—and in Egypt the inundation comes close to that date. Others, however, pointed nearly northward, and others again pointed to the rising of the star Sirius or to the rising-point of other conspicuous stars. The fact of orientation links up with the

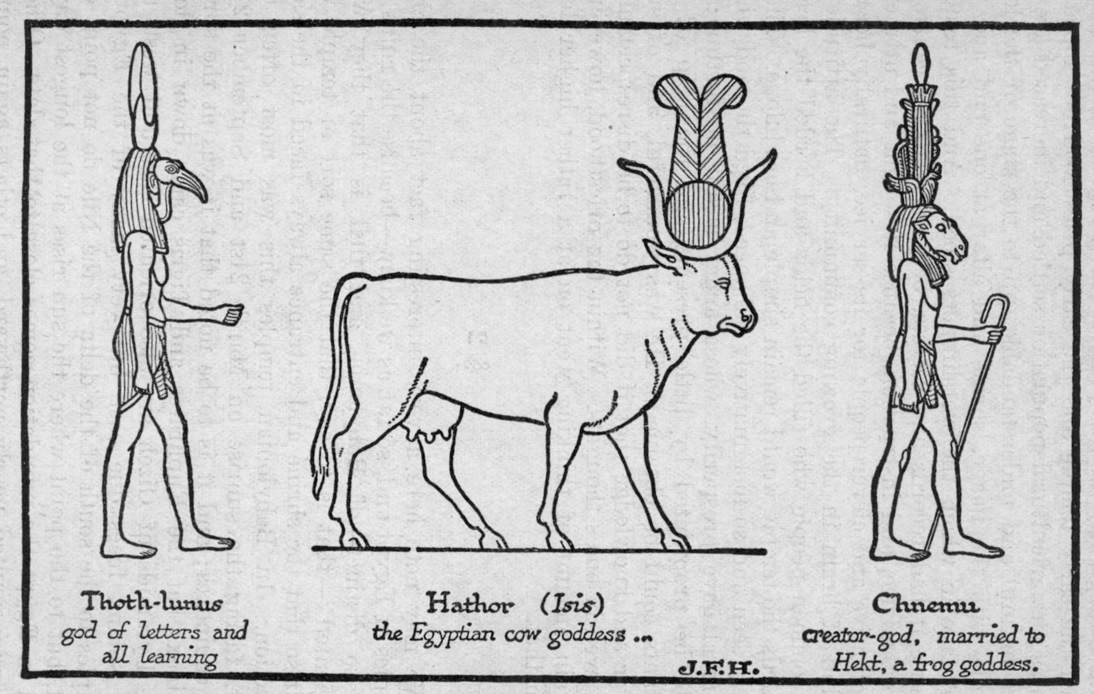
Thoth-lunus
god of letters and
all learning
Hathor (Isis)
the Egyptian cow goddess ...
J.F.H.
Chnemu
creator-god, married to
Hekt, a frog goddess.

fact that there early arose a close association between various gods and the sun and various fixed stars. Whatever the mass of people outside were thinking, the priests of the temples were beginning to link the movements of those heavenly bodies with the power in the shrine. They were thinking about the gods they served and thinking new meanings into them. They were brooding upon the mystery of the stars. It was very natural for them to suppose that these shining bodies, so irregularly distributed and circling so solemnly and silently, must be charged with portents to mankind.

Among other things, this orientation of the temples served to fix and help the great annual festival of the New Year. On one morning in the year, and one morning alone, in a temple oriented to the rising-place of the sun at Midsummer Day, the sun's first rays would smite down through the gloom of the temple and the long alley of the temple pillars, and light up the god above the altar and irradiate him with glory. The narrow, darkened structure of the ancient temples seems to be deliberately planned for such an effect. No doubt the people were gathered in the darkness before the dawn; in the darkness there was chanting and perhaps the offering of sacrifices; the god alone stood mute and invisible. Prayers and invocations would be made. Then upon the eyes of the worshippers, sensitized by the darkness, as the sun rose behind them, the god would suddenly shine.

So, at least, one explanation of orientation is found by such students of orientation as Sir Norman Lockyer.[1] Not only is orientation apparent in most of the temples of Egypt, Assyria, Babylonia, and the east, it is found in the Greek temples; Stonehenge is oriented to the midsummer sunrise, and so are most of the megalithic circles of Europe; the Altar of Heaven in Peking is oriented to midwinter. In the days of the Chinese Empire, up to a few years ago one of the most important of all the duties of the Emperor of China was to sacrifice and pray in this temple upon midwinter's day for a propitious year.

The Egyptian priests had mapped out the stars into the constellations, and divided up the zodiac into twelve signs by 3,000 B.C. . . .

[1] In his *Dawn of Astronomy.*

§ 3

This clear evidence of astronomical inquiry and of a development of astronomical ideas is the most obvious, but only the most obvious evidence of the very considerable intellectual activities that went on within the temple precincts in ancient times. There is a curious disposition among many modern writers to deprecate priesthoods and to speak of priests as though they had always been impostors and tricksters, preying upon the simplicity of mankind. But, indeed, they were for long the only writing class, the only reading public, the only learned and the only thinkers; they were all the professional classes of the time. You could have no intellectual life at all, you could not get access to literature or any knowledge except through the priesthood. The temples were not only observatories and libraries and clinics, they were museums and treasure-houses. The original *Periplus* of Hanno hung in one temple in Carthage, skins of his "gorillas" were hung and treasured in another. Whatever there was of abiding worth in the life of the community sheltered there. Herodotus, the early Greek historian (484-425 B.C.), collected most of his material from the priests of the countries in which he travelled, and it is evident they met him generously and put their very considerable resources completely at his disposal. Outside the temples the world was still a world of blankly illiterate and unspeculative human beings, living from day to day entirely for themselves. Moreover, there is little evidence that the commonalty felt cheated by the priests, or had anything but trust and affection for the early priesthoods. Even the great conquerors of later times were anxious to keep themselves upon the right side of the priests of the nations and cities whose obedience they desired, because of the immense popular influence of these priests.

No doubt there were great differences between temple and temple and cult and cult in the spirit and quality of the priesthood. Some probably were cruel, some vicious and greedy, many dull and doctrinaire, stupid with tradition, but it has to be kept in mind that there were distinct limits to the degeneracy or inefficiency of a priesthood. It had to keep its grip upon the general mind. It could not go beyond what people would stand—either towards the darkness or towards the light. Its authority rested, in the end, on the persuasion that its activities were propitious.

§ 4

The earliest civilized governments were essentially priestly governments. It was not kings and captains who first set men to the plough and a settled life. It was the ideas of the gods and plenty, working with the acquiescence of common men. The early rulers of Sumer we know were all priests, kings only because they were chief priests. And priestly government had its own weaknesses as well as its peculiar deep-rooted strength. The power of a priesthood is a power over their own people alone. It is a subjugation through mysterious fears and hopes. The priesthood can gather its people together for war, but its traditionalism and all its methods unfit it for military control. Against the enemy without, a priest-led people is feeble.

Moreover, a priest is a man vowed, trained, and consecrated, a man belonging to a special corps, and necessarily with an intense *esprit de corps*. He has given up his life to his temple and his god. This is a very excellent thing for the internal vigour of his own priesthood, his own temple. He lives or dies for the honour of his particular god. But in the next town or village is another temple with another god. It is his constant preoccupation to keep his people from that god. Religious cults and priesthoods are sectarian by nature; they will convert, they will overcome, but they will never coalesce. Our first perceptions of events in Sumer, in the dim uncertain light before history began, is of priests and gods in conflict; until the Sumerians were conquered by the Semites they were never united; and the same incurable conflict of priesthoods scars all the temple ruins of Egypt. It was impossible that it could have been otherwise, having regard to the elements out of which religion arose.

It was out of those two main weaknesses of all priesthoods, namely, the incapacity for efficient military leadership and their inevitable jealousy of all other religious cults, that the power of secular kingship arose. The foreign enemy either prevailed and set up a king over the people, or the priesthoods who would not give way to each other set up a common fighting captain, who retained more or less power in peace time. This secular king developed a group of officials about him and began, in relation to military organization, to take a share in the priestly administration of the people's affairs. So, growing out of priestcraft and beside the priest, the king, the protagonist of the priest, appears upon the stage of human history, and a very large amount of the subsequent experiences of mankind is only to be understood as an elaboration, complication, and

An Assyrian King & his Chief Minister

distortion of the struggle, unconscious or deliberate, between these two systems of human control, the temple and the palace. And it was in the original centres of civilization that this antagonism was most completely developed. The barbaric Aryan peoples, who became ultimately the masters of all the ancient civilizations of the Orient and of the western world, never passed through a phase of temple rule on their way to civilization; they came to civilization late; they found that drama already half-played. They took over the ideas of both temple and kingship, when those ideas were already elaborately developed, from the more civilized Hamitic or Semitic people they conquered.

Th greater importance of the gods and the priests in the earlier history of the Mesopotamian civilization is very apparent, but gradually the palace won its way until it was at last in a position to struggle definitely for the supreme power. At first, in the story, the palace is ignorant and friendless in the face of the temple; the priests alone read, the priests alone know the people are afraid of them. But in the dissensions of the various cults comes the opportunity of the palace. From other cities, from among captives, from defeated or suppressed religious cults, the palace gets men who also can read and who can do magic things.[1] The court also becomes a centre of writing and record; the king thinks for himself and becomes politic. Traders and foreigners drift to the court, and if the king has not the full records and the finished scholarship of the priests, he has a wider and fresher first-hand knowledge of many things. The priest comes into the temple when he is very young; he passes many years as a neophyte; the path of learning the clumsy letters of primitive times is slow and toilsome; he becomes erudite and prejudiced rather than a man of the world. Some of the more active-minded young priests may even cast envious eyes at the king's service. There are many complications and variations in this ages-long drama of the struggle going on beneath the outward conflicts of priest and king, between the made man and the born man, between learning and originality, between established knowledge and settled usage on the one hand, and creative will and imagination on the other. It is not always, as we shall find later, the priest who is the conservative and unimaginative antagonist. Sometimes a king struggles against narrow and obstructive priesthoods; sometimes priesthoods uphold the standards of civilization against savage, egotistical, or reactionary kings.

[1] Cp. Moses and the Egyptian Magicians.

One or two outstanding facts and incidents of the early stages of this fundamental struggle in political affairs are all that we can note here between 4,000 B.C. and the days of Alexander.

§ 5

In the early days of Sumeria and Akkadia the city-kings were priests and medicine-men rather than kings, and it was only when foreign conquerors sought to establish their hold in relation to existing institutions that the distinction of priest and king became definite. But the god of the priests remained as the real overlord of the land and of priest and king alike. He was the universal landlord; the wealth and authority of his temples and establishments outshone those of the king. Especially was this the case within the city walls. Hammurabi, the founder of the first Babylonian empire, is one of the earlier monarchs whom we find taking a firm grip upon the affairs of the community. He does it with the utmost politeness to the gods. In an inscription recording his irrigation work in Sumeria and Akkadia, he begins: "When Anu and Bel entrusted me with the rule of Sumer and Akkad——." We possess a code of laws made by this same Hammurabi—it is the earliest known code of law—and at the head of this code we see the figure of Hammurabi receiving the law from its nominal promulgator, the god Shamash.

An act of great political importance in the conquest of any city was the carrying off of its god to become a subordinate in the temple of its conqueror. This was far more important than the subjugation of king by king. Merodach, the Babylonian Jupiter, was carried off by the Elamites, and Babylon did not feel independent until its return. But sometimes a conqueror was afraid of the god he had conquered. In the collection of letters addressed to Amenophis III and IV at Tel-el-Amarna in Egypt, to which allusion has already been made, is one from a certain king, Tushratta, King of Mitanni, who has conquered Assyria and taken the statue of the goddess Ishtar. Apparently he has sent this statue into Egypt, partly to acknowledge the overlordship of Amenophis, but partly because he fears her anger. (Winckler.) In the Bible is related (Sam. i. v. 1) how the Ark of the Covenant of the God of the Hebrews was carried off by the Philistines, as a token of conquest, into the temple of the fish god, Dagon, at Ashdod, and how Dagon fell down and was broken, and how the people of Ashdod were smitten with disease. In the latter story particularly, the gods and priests fill the scene; there is no king in evidence at all.

Right through the history of the Babylonian and Assyrian empires no monarch seems to have felt his tenure of power secure in Babylon until he had "taken the hand of Bel"—that is to say, that he had been adopted by the priesthood of "Bel" as the god's son and representative. As our knowledge of Assyrian and Babylonian history grows clearer, it becomes plainer that the politics of that world, the revolutions, usurpations, changes of dynasty, intrigues with foreign powers, turned largely upon issues between the great wealthy priesthoods and the growing but still inadequate power of the monarchy. The king relied on his army, and this was usually a mercenary army of foreigners, speedily mutinous if there was no pay or plunder, and easily bribed. We have already noted the name of Sennacherib, the son of Sargon II, among the monarchs of the Assyrian empire. Sennacherib was involved in a violent quarrel with the priesthood of Babylon; he never "took the hand of Bel"; and finally struck at that power by destroying altogether the holy part of the city of Babylon (691 B.C.) and removing the statue of Bel-Marduk to Assyria. He was assassinated by one of his sons, and his successor, Esar-haddon (his son, but not the son who was his assassin), found it expedient to restore Bel-Marduk and rebuild his temple, and make his peace with the god.

Assurbanipal (Greek, Sardanapalus), the son of this Esar-haddon, is a particularly interesting figure from this point of view of the relationship of priesthood and king. His father's reconciliation with the priests of Bel-Marduk went so far that Sardanapalus was given a Babylonian instead of a military Assyrian education. He became a great collector of the clay documents of the past, and his library, which has been unearthed, is now the most precious source of historical material in the world. But for all his learning he kept his grip on the Assyrian army; he made a temporary conquest of Egypt, suppressed a rebellion in Babylon, and carried out a number of successful expeditions. As we have already told in Chapter XIV, he was almost the last of the Assyrian monarchs. The

Aryan tribes, who knew more of war than of priestcraft, and particularly the Scythians, the Medes and Persians, had long been pressing upon Assyria from the north and north-east. The Medes and Persians formed an alliance with the nomadic Semitic Chaldeans of the south for the joint undoing of Assyria. Nineveh, the Assyrian capital, fell to these Aryans in 606 B.C.

Sixty-seven years after the taking of Nineveh by the Aryans which left Babylonia to the Semitic Chaldeans, the last monarch of the Chaldean Empire (the Second Babylonian Empire), Nabonidus, the father of Belshazzar, was overthrown by Cyrus, the Persian. This Nabonidus, again, was a highly educated monarch, who brought far too much intelligence and imagination and not enough of the short range wisdom of this world to affairs of state. He conducted antiquarian researches, and to his researches it is that we owe the date of 3,750 B.C., assigned to Sargon I and still accepted by many authorities. He was proud of this determination, and left inscriptions to record it. It is clear he was a religious innovator; he built and rearranged temples and attempted to centralize religion in Babylon by bringing a number of local gods to the temple of Bel-Marduk. No doubt he realized the weakness and disunion of his empire due to these conflicting cults, and had some conception of unification in his mind.

CHEPHREN

Events were marching too rapidly for any such development. His innovation had manifestly raised the suspicion and hostility of the priesthood of Bel. They sided with the Persians.

"The soldiers of Cyrus entered Babylon without fighting." Nabonidus was taken prisoner, and Persian sentinels were set at the gates of the temple of Bel, "where the services continued without intermission."

Cyrus did, in fact, set up the Persian Empire in Babylon with the blessing of Bel-Marduk. He gratified the conservative instincts of the priests by packing off the local gods back to their ancestral temples. He also restored the Jews to Jerusalem.[1] These were merely matters of immediate policy to him. But in bringing in the irreligious Aryans, the ancient priesthood was paying too highly for the continuation of its temple services. It would have been wiser to have dealt with the innovations of Nabonidus, that earnest heretic, to have listened to his ideas, and to have met the needs of a changing world. Cyrus entered Babylon 539 B.C.; by 521 B.C. Babylon was in insurrection again, and in 520 B.C. another Persian monarch, Darius, was pulling down her walls. Within two hundred years the life had altogether gone out of those venerable rituals of Bel-Marduk, and the temple of Bel-Marduk was being used by builders as a quarry.

§ 6

The story of priest and king in Egypt is similar to, but by no means parallel with, that of Babylonia. The kings of Sumeria and Assyria were priests who had become kings; they were secularized priests. The Pharaoh of Egypt does not appear to have followed precisely that line. Already in the very oldest records the Pharaoh has a power, and importance exceeding that of any priest. He is, in fact, a god, and more than either priest or king. We do not know how he got to that position. No monarch of Sumeria or Babylonia or Assyria could have induced his people to do for him what the great pyramid-building Pharaohs of the IVth Dynasty made their people do in those vast erections. The earlier Pharaohs were not improbably regarded as incarnations of the dominant god. The falcon god Horus sits behind the head of the great statue of Chephren. So late a monarch as Rameses III (XIXth Dynasty) is represented upon his sarcophagus (now at Cam-

[1] See the last two verses of the Second Book of Chronicles, and Ezra, ch. i.

bridge) bearing the distinctive symbols of the three great gods of the Egyptian system. He carries the two sceptres of Osiris, the god of Day and Resurrection; upon his head are the horns of the cow goddess Hathor, and also the sun ball and feathers of Ammon Ra. He is not merely wearing the symbols of these gods as a devout Babylonian might wear the symbols of Bel-Marduk; he *is* these three gods in one.

Rameses III as Osiris—between the goddesses Nephthys and Isis...

Relief on the cover of the sarcophagus (at Cambridge). After Sharpe.

Inscription (round the edges of cover) as far as decipherable:—

"Osiris, King of Upper and Lower Egypt, lord of the two countries . . . son of the Sun, beloved of the gods, lord of diadems, Rameses, prince of Heliopolis, triumphant! Thou art in the condition of a god, thou shalt arise as Usr, there is no enemy to thee, I give to thee triumph among them. . . ." BUDGE, *Catalogue, Egyptian Collection, Fitzwilliam Museum, Cambridge.*

We find also a number of sculptures and paintings to enforce the idea that the Pharaohs were the actual sons of gods. The divine fathering anl birth of Amenophis III, for instance (of the XVIIIth Dynasty), is displayed in extraordinary detail in a series of sculptures at Luxor. Moreover, it was held that the Pharaohs, being of so divine a strain, could not marry common clay, and consequently they were accustomed to marry blood relations within the degrees of consanguinity now prohibited, even marrying their sisters.

The struggle between palace and temple came into Egyptian history, therefore, at a different angle from that at which it came into Babylonia. Nevertheless, it came in. Professor Maspero (in his *New Light on Ancient Egypt*) gives a very interesting account of the struggle of Amenophis IV with the priesthoods, and particularly with priests of the great god, Ammon Ra, Lord of Karnak. The mother of Amenophis IV was not of the race of Pharaoh; it would seem that his father, Amenophis III, made a love match with a subject, a beautiful Syrian named Tii, and Professor Maspero finds in the possible opposition to and annoyance of this queen by the priests of Ammon Ra the beginnings of the quarrel. She may, he thinks, have inspired her son with a fanatical hatred of Ammon Ra. But Amenophis IV may have had a wider view. Like the Babylonian Nabonidus, who lived a thousand years later, he may have had in mind the problem of moral unity in his empire. We have already noted that Amenophis III ruled from Ethiopia to the Euphrates, and that the store of letters to himself and his son found at Tel-Amarna show a very wide range of interest and influence. At any rate, Amenophis IV set himself to close all the Egyptian and Syrian temples, to put an end to all sectarian worship throughout his dominions, and to establish everywhere the worship of one god, Aton, the solar disk. He left his capital, Thebes, which was even more the city of Ammon Ra than later Babylon was the city of Bel-Marduk, and set up his capital at Tel-Amarna; he altered his name from "Amenophis," which consecrated him to Ammon (Amen) to "Akhnaton," the Sun's Glory; and he held his own against all the priesthoods of his empire for eighteen years and died a Pharaoh.

Opinions upon Amenophis IV, or Akhnaton, differ very widely. There are those who regard him as the creature of his mother's hatred of Ammon and the uxorious spouse of a beautiful wife. Certainly he loved his wife very passionately; he showed her great honour—Egypt honoured women, and was ruled at different times by several queens—and he was sculptured in one instance with his wife seated upon his knees, and in another in the act of kissing her in a chariot; but men who live under the sway of their womenkind do not sustain great empires in the face of the bitter hostility of the most influential organized bodies in their realm. Others write of him as a "gloomy fanatic." Matrimonial bliss is rare in the cases of gloomy fanatics. It is much more reasonable to regard him as the Pharaoh who refused to be a god. It is not simply his religious policy and his frank display of natural affection that seem to mark a strong and very original personality. His æsthetic ideas were his own. He refused to have his portrait conventionalized into the customary smooth beauty of the Pharaoh god, and his face looks out at us across an interval of thirty-four centuries, a man amidst ranks of divine insipidities.

Akhnaton (Amenophis IV)
[based on the cast at Cairo, & the reliefs in the Berlin Museum.]

A reign of eighteen years was not long enough for the revolution he contemplated, and his son-in-law who succeeded him went back to Thebes and made his peace with Ammon Ra.

To the very end of the story the divinity of kings haunted the Egyptian mind, and infected the thoughts of intellectually healthier races. When Alexander the Great reached Babylon, the prestige of Bel-Marduk was already far gone in decay, but in Egypt, Ammon Ra was still god enough to make a snob of the conquering Grecian. The priests of Ammon Ra, about the time of the XVIIIth or XIXth Dynasty (*circa* 1,400 B.C.), had set up in an oasis of the desert a temple and oracle. Here was an image of the god which could speak, move its head, and accept or reject scrolls of inquiry. This oracle was still flourishing in 332 B.C. The young master of the world, it is related, made a special journey to visit it; he came into the sanctuary, and the image advanced out of the darkness at the back to meet him. There was an impressive exchange of salutations. Some such formula as this must have been used (says Professor Maspero): "Come, son of my loins, who loves me so that I give thee the royalty of Ra and the royalty of Horus! I give thee valiance, I give thee to hold all countries and all religions under thy feet; I give thee to strike all the peoples united together with thy arm!"

So it was that the priests of Egypt conquered their conqueror, and an Aryan monarch first became a god.

§ 7

The struggle of priest and king in China cannot be discussed here at any length. It was different again, as in Egypt it was different from Babylonia, but we find the same effort on the part of the ruler to break up tradition because it divides up the people. The Chinese Emperor, the "Son of Heaven," was himself a high-priest, and his chief duty was sacrificial; in the more disorderly phases of Chinese history he ceases to rule and continues only to sacrifice. The literary class was detached from the priestly class at an early date. It became a bureaucratic body serving the local kings and rulers. That is a fundamental difference between the history of China and any Western history. While Alexander was overrunning Western Asia, China, under the last priest-emperors of the Chow Dynasty, was sinking into a state of great disorder. Each province clung to its separate nationality and traditions, and the Huns spread from province to province. The King of T'sin (who lived about eighty years after Alexander the Great), impressed by the mischief tradition was doing in the land, resolved to destroy the entire Chinese literature, and his son, Shi Hwang-ti, the "first universal Emperor," made a strenuous attempt to seek out and destroy all the existing classics. They vanished while he ruled, and he ruled without tradition, and welded China into a unity that endured for some centuries; but when he had passed, the hidden books crept out again. China remained united, though not under his descendants, but after a civil war under a fresh dynasty, the Han Dynasty (206 B.C.). The first Han monarch did not sustain this campaign of Shi Hwang-ti against the *literati*, and his successor made his peace with them and restored the texts of the classics.

XVIII

SERFS, SLAVES, SOCIAL CLASSES, AND FREE INDIVIDUALS

§ 1. *The Common Man in Ancient Times.* § 2. *The Earliest Slaves.* § 3. *The First "Independent" Persons.* § 4. *Social Classes Three Thousand Years Ago.* § 5. *Classes Hardening into Castes.* § 6. *Caste in India.* § 7. *The System of the Mandarins.* § 8. *A Summary of Five Thousand Years.*

§ 1

WE have been sketching in the last four chapters the growth of civilized states out of the primitive Neolithic agriculture that began in Mesopotamia perhaps 15,000 years ago. It was at first horticulture rather than agriculture; it was done with the hoe before the plough, and at first it was quite supplementary to the sheep, goat, and cattle tending that made the "living" of the family tribe. We have traced the broad outlines of the development in regions of exceptional fruitfulness of the first settled village communities into more populous towns and cities, and the growth of the village shrine and the village medicine-man into the city temple and the city priesthood. We have noted the beginnings of organized war, first as a flickering between villages, and then as a more disciplined struggle between the priest-king and god of one city and those of another. Our story has passed on rapidly from the first indications of conquest and empire in Sumer, 6,000 or 7,000 B.C., to the spectacle of great empires growing up, with roads and armies, with inscriptions and written documents, with educated priesthoods and kings and rulers sustained by a tradition already ancient. We have traced in broad outline the appearance and conflicts and replacements of these empires of the great rivers. We have directed attention, in particular, to the evidence of a development of still wider political ideas as we find it betrayed by the actions and utterances of such men as Nabonidus and Amenophis IV. It has been an outline of the accumulations of human experience for ten or fifteen thousand years, a vast space of time in comparison with all subsequent history, but a brief period when we measure it against the succession of endless generations that intervenes between us and the first rude flint-using human creatures of the Pleistocene dawn. But for these last four chapters we have been writing almost entirely not about mankind generally, but only about the men who thought, the men who could draw and read and write, the men who were altering their world. Beneath their activities what was the life of the mute multitude?

The life of the common man was, of course, affected and changed by these things, just as the lives of the domestic animals and the face of the cultivated country were changed; but for the most part it was a change suffered and not a change in which the common man upon the land had any voice or will. Reading and writing were not yet for the likes of him. He went on cultivating his patch, loving his wife and children, beating his dog and tending his beasts, grumbling at hard times, fearing the magic of the priests and the power of the gods, desiring little more except to be left alone by the powers above him. So he was in 10,000 B.C.; so he was, unchanged in nature and outlook, in the time of Alexander the Great; so over the greater part of the world he remains to-day. He got rather better tools, better seeds, better methods, a slightly sounder house, he sold his produce in a more organized market as civilization progressed. A certain freedom and a certain equality passed out of human life when men ceased to wander. Men paid in liberty for safety, shelter, and regular meals. By imperceptible degrees the common man found the patch he cultivated was not his own; it belonged to the god; and he had to pay a fraction of his produce to the god. Or the god had given it to the king, who exacted his rent and tax. Or the king had given it to an official, who was the lord of the common man. And sometimes the god or the king or the noble had work to be done, and then the common man had to leave his patch and work for his master.

How far the patch he cultivated was his own was never very clear to him. In ancient Assyria the land seems to have been held as a sort of freehold and the occupier paid taxes; in Babylonia the land was the god's, and he permitted the cultivator to work thereon. In Egypt the temples or Pharaoh-the-god or the nobles under Pharaoh were the owners and rent receivers. But the cultivator was not a slave; he was a peasant, and only bound to the land in so far that there was nothing else for him to do but cultivate, and nowhere else for him to go. He lived in a village or town, and went out to his work. The village, to begin with, was often merely a big household of related people under a patriarch headman, the early town a group of householders under its elders. There was no process of enslavement as civilization grew, but the headman and leaderly men grew in power and authority, and the common men did not keep pace with them, and fell into a tradition of dependence and subordination.

On the whole, the common men were probably well content to live under lord or king or god and obey their bidding. It was safer. It was easier. All animals—and man is no exception—begin life as dependents. Most men never shake themselves loose from the desire for leading and protection.[1]

§ 2

The earlier wars did not involve remote or prolonged campaigns, and they were waged by levies of the common people. But war brought in a new source of possessions, plunder, and a new social factor, the captive. In the earlier, simpler days of war, the captive man was kept only to be tortured or sacrificed to the victorious god; the captive women and children were assimilated into the tribe. But later many captives were spared to be slaves because they had exceptional gifts or peculiar arts. It would be the kings and captains who would take these slaves at first, and it would speedily become apparent to them that these men were much more their own than were the peasant cultivators and common men of their own race. The slave could be commanded to do all sorts of things for his master that the quasi-free common man would not do so willingly because of his attachment to his own patch of cultivation. From a very early period the artificer was often a household slave, and the

[1] There were literary expressions of social discontent in Egypt before 2,000 B.C. See "Social Forces and Religion" in Breasted's *Religion and Thought in Ancient Egypt* for some of the earliest complaints of the common man under the ancient civilizations.

manufacture of trade goods, pottery, textiles, metal ware, and so forth, such as went on vigorously in the household city of the Minos of Cnossos, was probably a slave industry from the beginning. Sayce, in his *Babylonians and Assyrians,* quotes Babylonian agreements for the teaching of trades to slaves, and dealing with the exploitation of slave products. Slaves produced slave children, enslavement in discharge of debts added to the slave population; it is probable that as the cities grew larger, a larger part of the new population consisted of these slave artificers and slave servants in the large households. They were by no means abject slaves; in later Babylon their lives and property were protected by elaborate laws. Nor were

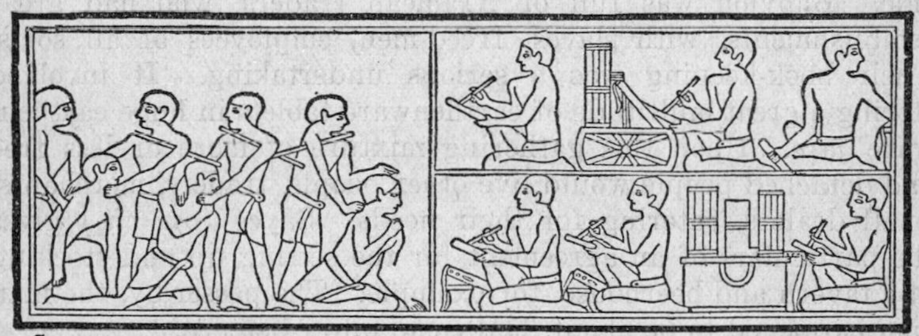

Egyptian peasants seized for non-payment of taxes... (Pyramid Age)

they all outlanders. Parents might sell their children into slavery, and brothers their orphan sisters. Free men who had no means of livelihood would even sell themselves into slavery. And slavery was the fate of the insolvent debtor. Craft apprenticeship, again, was a sort of fixed-term slavery. Out of the slave population, by a converse process, arose the freed-man and freed-woman, who worked for wages and had still more definite individual rights. Since in Babylon slaves could themselves own property, many slaves saved up and bought themselves. Probably the town slave was often better off and practically as free as the cultivator of the soil, and as the rural population increased, its sons and daughters came to mix with and swell the growing ranks of artificers, some bound, some free.

As the extent and complexity of government increased, the number of households multiplied. Under the king's household grew up the households of his great ministers and officials, under the temple grew up the personal households of temple functionaries; it is not difficult to realize how houses and patches of land would become more and more distinctly the property of the occupiers, and more and more definitely alienated from the original owner-god. The earlier empires in Egypt and China both passed into a feudal stage, in which families, originally official, became for a time independent noble families. In the later stages of Babylonian civilization we find an increasing propertied class of people appearing in the social structure, neither slaves nor peasants nor priests nor officials, but widows and descendants of such people, or successful traders and the like, and all *masterless* folk. Traders came in from the outside. Babylon was full of Aramean traders, who had great establishments, with slaves, freed-men, employees of all sorts. Their book-keeping was a serious undertaking. It involved storing a great multitude of earthenware tablets in huge earthenware jars. Upon this gathering mixture of more or less free and detached people would live other people, traders, merchants, small dealers, catering for their needs. Sayce (*op. cit.*) gives the particulars of an agreement for the setting up and stocking of a tavern and beerhouse, for example. The passer-by, the man who happened to be about, had come into existence.

But another and far less kindly sort of slavery also arose in the old civilization, and that was gang slavery. If it did not figure very largely in the cities, it was very much in evidence elsewhere. The king was, to begin with, the chief *entrepreneur*. He made the canals and organized the irrigation (*e.g.* Hammurabi's enterprises noted in the previous chapter). He exploited mines. He seems (at Cnossos, *e.g.*) to have organized manufactures for export. The Pharaohs of the 1st Dynasty were already working the copper and turquoise mines in the peninsula of Sinai. For many such purposes gangs of captives were cheaper and far more controllable than levies of the king's own people. From an early period, too, captives may have tugged the oars of the galleys, though Torr (*Ancient Ships*) notes that up to the age of Pericles (450 B.C.) the free Athenians were not above this task. And the monarch also found slaves convenient for his military expeditions. They were uprooted men; they did not fret to go home, because they had no homes to go to. The Pharaohs hunted slaves in Nubia, in order to have black troops for their Syrian expeditions. Closely allied to such slave troops were the mercenary barbaric troops the monarchs caught into their service, not by positive compulsion, but by the bribes of food and plunder and under the pressure of need. As the old civilization developed, these mercenary armies replaced the national levies of the old order more and more, and servile gang labour became a more and more important and significant factor in the economic system. From mines and canal and wall building, the servile gang spread into culti-

Brawl among boatmen... (From tomb of Ptah-hetep — —Pyramid Age).

vation. Notables and temples adopted the gang-slave system for their works. Plantation gangs began to oust the patch cultivation of the labourer-serf in the case of some staple products. . . .

§ 3

So, in a few paragraphs, we trace the development of the simple social structure of the early Sumerian cities to the complex city crowds, the multitude of individuals varying in race, tradition, education, and function, varying in wealth, freedom, authority, and usefulness, in the great cities of the last thousand years B.C. The most notable thing of all is the gradual increase amidst this heterogeneous multitude of what we may call *free individuals,* detached persons who are neither priests, nor kings, nor officials, nor serfs, nor slaves, who are under no great pressure to work, who have time to read and inquire. They appear side by side with the development of social security and private property. Coined money and monetary reckoning developed. The operations of the Arameans and such-like Semitic trading people led to the organization of credit and monetary security. In the earlier days almost the only property, except a few movables, consisted of rights in land and in houses; later, one could deposit and lend securities, could go away and return to find one's property faithfully held and secure. Towards the middle of the period of the Persian Empire there lived one free individual, Herodotus, who has a great interest for us because he was among the first writers of critical and intelligent history, as distinguished from a more priestly or court chronicle. It is worth while to glance here very briefly at the circumstances of his life. Later on we shall quote from his history.

We have already noted the conquest of Babylonia by the Aryan Persians under Cyrus in 539 B.C. We have noted, further, that the Persian Empire spread into Egypt, where its hold was precarious; and it extended also over Asia Minor. Herodotus was born about 484 B.C. in a Greek city of Asia Minor, Halicarnassus, which was under the overlordship of the Persians, and directly under the rule of a political boss or tyrant. There is no sign that he was obliged either to work for a living or spend very much time in the administration of his property. We do not know the particulars of his affairs, but it is clear that in this minor Greek city, under foreign rule, he was able to obtain and read and study manuscripts of nearly everything that had been written in the Greek language before his time. He travelled, so far as one can gather, with freedom and comfort about the Greek archipelagoes; he stayed wherever he wanted to stay, and he seems to have found comfortable accommodation; he went to Babylon and to Susa, the new capital the Persians had set up in Babylonia to the east of the Tigris; he toured along the coast of the Black Sea, and accumulated a considerable amount of knowledge about the Scythians, the Aryan people who were then distributed over South Russia; he went to the south of Italy, explored the antiquities of Tyre, coasted Palestine, landed at Gaza, and made a long stay in Egypt. He went about Egypt looking at temples and monuments and gathering information. We know not only from him, but from other evidence, that in those days the older temples and the pyramids (which were already nearly three thousand years old) were visited by strings of tourists, a special sort of priests acting as guides. The inscriptions the sightseers scribbled upon the walls remain to this day, and many of them have been deciphered and published.

As his knowledge accumulated, he conceived the idea of writ-

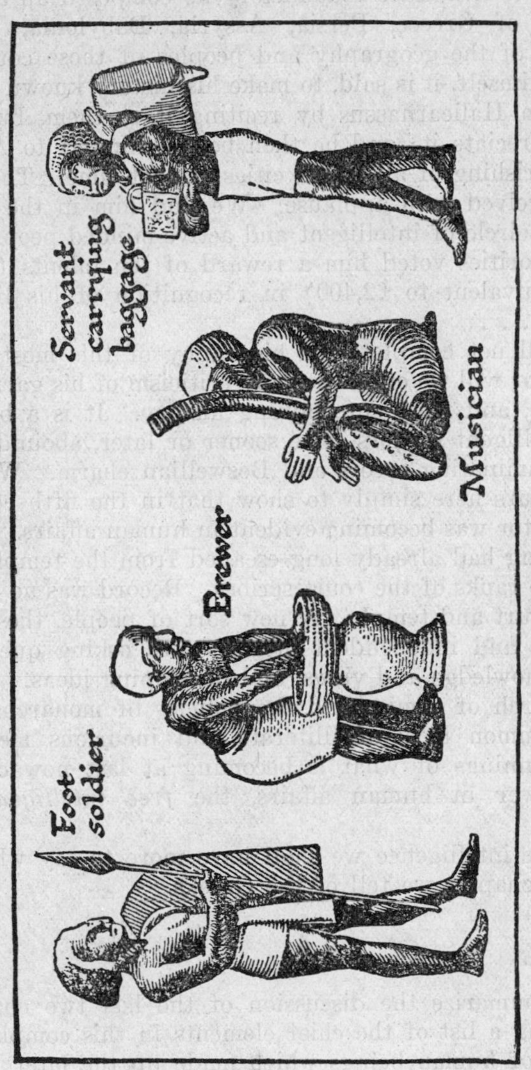

STATUETTES FROM MIDDLE-CLASS EGYPTIAN TOMBS SHOWING LOW-CLASS SOCIAL TYPES IN THE ANCIENT COMMUNITIES ing a great history of the attempts of Persia to subdue Greece. But in order to introduce that history he composed an account of the past of Greece, Persia, Assyria, Babylonia, Egypt, Scythia, and of the geography and peoples of those countries. He then set himself, it is said, to make his history known among his friends in Halicarnassus by reciting it to them, but they failed to appreciate it; and he then betook himself to Athens, the most flourishing of all Greek cities at that time. There his work was received with applause. We find him in the centre of a brilliant circle of intelligent and active-minded people, and the city authorities voted him a reward of ten talents (a sum of money equivalent to £2,400) in recognition of his literary achievement. . . .

But we will not complete the biography of this most interesting man, nor will we enter into any criticism of his garrulous, marvel-telling, and most entertaining history. It is a book to which all intelligent readers come sooner or later, abounding as it does in illuminating errors and Boswellian charm. We give these particulars here simply to show that in the fifth century B.C. a new factor was becoming evident in human affairs. Reading and writing had already long escaped from the temple precincts and the ranks of the court scribes. Record was no longer confined to court and temple. A new sort of people, these people of leisure and independent means, were asking questions, exchanging knowledge and views, and developing ideas. So beneath the march of armies and the policies of monarchs, and above the common lives of illiterate and incurious men, we note the beginnings of what is becoming at last nowadays a dominant power in human affairs, the *free intelligence of mankind.*

Of that free intelligence we shall have more to say when in a subsequent chapter we tell of the Greeks.

§ 4

We may summarize the discussion of the last two chapters here by making a list of the chief elements in this complicated accumulation of human beings which made up the later Babylonian and Egyptian civilizations of from two thousand five hundred to three thousand years ago. These elements grew up and became distinct one from another in the great river valleys of the world in the course of five or six thousand years. They developed mental dispositions and traditions and attitudes of thought one to another. The civilization in which we live to-day is simply carrying on and still further developing and working out and rearranging these relationships. This is the world from which we inherit. It is only by the attentive study of their origins that we can detach ourselves from the prejudices and immediate ideas of the particular class to which we may belong, and begin to understand the social and political questions of our own time.

(1) First, then, came the priesthood, *the temple system*, which was the nucleus and the guiding intelligence about which the primitive civilizations grew. It was still in these later days a great power in the world, the chief repository of knowledge and tradition, an influence over the lives of every one, and a binding force to hold the community together. But it was no longer all-powerful, because its nature made it conservative and inadaptable. It no longer monopolized knowledge nor initiated fresh ideas. Learning had already leaked out to other less pledged and controlled people, who thought for themselves. About the temple system were grouped its priests and priestesses, its scribes, its physicians, its magicians, its lay brethren, treasurers, managers, directors, and the like. It owned great properties and often hoarded huge treasures.

(2) Over against the priesthood, and originally arising out of it, was the *court system*, headed by a king or a "king of kings," who was in later Assyria and Babylonia a sort of captain and lay controller of affairs, and in Egypt a god-man, who had released himself from the control of his priests. About the monarch were accumulated his scribes, counsellors, record keepers, agents, captains, and guards. Many of his officials, particularly his provincial officials, had great subordinate establishments, and were constantly tending to become independent. The nobility of the old river valley civilizations arose out of the court system. It was, therefore, a different thing in its origins from the nobility of the early Aryans, which was a republican nobility of elders and leading men.

(3) At the base of the social pyramid was the large and most necessary class in the community, *the tillers of the soil*. Their status varied from age to age and in different lands; they were

free peasants paying taxes, or serfs of the god, or serfs or tenants of king or noble, or of a private owner, paying him a rent; in most cases tax or rent was paid in produce. In the states of the river valleys they were high cultivators, cultivating comparatively small holdings; they lived together for safety in villages, and had a common interest in maintaining their irrigation channels and a sense of community in their village life. The cultivation of the soil is an exacting occupation; the seasons and the harvest sunsets will not wait for men; children can be utilized at an early age, and so the cultivator class is generally a poorly educated, close-toiling class, superstitious by reason of ignorance and the uncertainty of the seasons, ill-informed and easily put upon. It is capable at times of great passive resistance, but it has no purpose in its round but crops and crops, to keep out of debt and hoard against bad times. So it has remained to our own days over the greater part of Europe and Asia.

(4) Differing widely in origin and quality from the tillers of the soil was *the artisan class.* At first, this was probably in part a town-slave class, in part it consisted of peasants who had specialized upon a craft. But in developing an art and mystery of its own, a technique that had to be learnt before it could be practised, each sort of craft probably developed a certain independence and a certain sense of community of its own. The artisans were able to get together and discuss their affairs more readily than the toilers on the land, and they were able to form guilds to restrict output, maintain rates of pay, and protect their common interest.

(5) As the power of the Babylonian rulers spread out beyond the original areas of good husbandry into grazing regions and less fertile districts, a class of *herdsmen* came into existence. In the case of Babylonia these were nomadic Semites, the Bedouin, like the Bedouin of to-day. They probably grazed their flocks over great areas much as the sheep ranchers of California do. They were paid and esteemed much more highly than the husbandmen.

(6) The first *merchants* in the world were shipowners like the people of Tyre and Cnossos, or nomads who carried and traded goods as they wandered between one area of primitive civilization and another. In the Babylonian and Assyrian world the traders were predominantly the Semitic Arameans,

the ancestors of the modern Syrians. They became a distinct factor in the life of the community; they formed great households of their own. Usury developed largely in the last thousand years B.C. Traders needed accommodations; cultivators wished to anticipate their crops. Sayce (*op. cit.*) gives an account of the Babylonian banking-house of Egibi, which lasted through several generations and outlived the Chaldean Empire.

(7) A class of *small retailers,* one must suppose, came into existence with the complication of society during the later days of the first empires, but it was not probably of any great importance.

(8) A growing class of *independent property owners.*

(9) As the amenities of life increased, there grew up in the court, temples, and prosperous private houses a class of *domestic servants,* slaves or freed slaves, or young peasants taken into the household.

(10) *Gang workers.*—These were prisoners of war or debt slaves, or impressed or deported men.

(11) *Mercenary soldiers.*—These were also often captives or impressed men. Sometimes they were enlisted from friendly foreign populations in which the military spirit still prevailed.

(12) *Seamen.*

In modern political and economic discussions we are apt to talk rather glibly of "labour." Much has been made of the *solidarity of labour* and its sense of community. It is well to note that in these first civilizations, what we speak of as "labour" is represented by five distinct classes dissimilar in origin, traditions, and outlook—namely, classes 3, 4, 5, 9, 10, and the oar-tugging part of 12. The "solidarity of labour" is, we shall find when we come to study the mechanical revolution of the nineteenth century A.D., a new idea and a new possibility in human affairs.

§ 5

Let us, before we leave this discussion of the social classes that were developing in these first civilizations, devote a little attention to their fixity. How far did they stand aloof from each other, and how far did they intermingle? So far as the classes we have counted as 9, 10, 11, and 12 go, the servants, the gang labourers and slaves, the gang soldiers, and to a lesser extent the sailors, or at any rate the galley rowers among the sailors, they were largely recruited classes, they did not readily and easily form homes, they were not distinctly breeding classes; they were probably replenished generation after generation by captives, by the failures of other classes, and especially from the failures of the class of small retailers, and by persuasion and impressment from among the cultivators. But so far as the sailors go, we have to distinguish between the mere rower and the navigating and shipowning seaman of such ports as Tyre and Sidon. The shipowners pass, no doubt, by insensible gradations into the mercantile class, but the navigators must have made a peculiar community in the great seaports, having homes there and handing on the secrets of seacraft to their sons. The eighth class we have distinguished was certainly a precarious class, continually increased by the accession of the heirs and dependents, the widows and retired members of the wealthy and powerful, and continually diminished by the deaths or speculative losses of these people and the dispersal of their properties. The priests and priestesses, too, so far as all this world west of India went, were not a very reproductive class; many priesthoods were celibate, and that class, too, may also be counted as a recruited class. Nor are servants, as a rule, reproductive. They live in the households of other people; they do not have households and rear large families of their own. This leaves us as the really vital classes of the ancient civilized community:

(*a*) The royal and aristocratic class, officials, military officers, and the like;
(*b*) The mercantile class;
(*c*) The town artisans;
(*d*) The cultivators of the soil; and
(*e*) The herdsmen.

Each of these classes reared its own children in its own fashion, and so naturally kept itself more or less continuously distinct from the others. General education was not organized in those ancient states, education was mainly a household matter (as it is still in many parts of India to-day), and so it was natural and necessary for the sons to follow in the footsteps of their father and to marry women accustomed to their own sort of household. Except during times of great political disturbance, therefore, there would be a natural and continuous separation of classes; which would not, however, prevent exceptional individuals from intermarrying or passing from one class to another. Poor aristocrats would marry rich members of the mercantile class; ambitious herdsmen, artisans, or sailors would become rich merchants. So far as one can gather, that was the general state of affairs in both Egypt and Babylonia. The idea was formerly entertained that in Egypt there was a fixity of classes, but this appears to be a misconception due to a misreading of Herodotus. The only exclusive class in Egypt which did not intermarry was, as in England to-day, the semi-divine royal family.

At various points in the social system there were probably developments of exclusiveness, an actual barring out of interlopers. Artisans of particular crafts possessing secrets, for example, have among all races and in all ages tended to develop guild organizations restricting the practice of their craft and the marriage of members outside their guild. Conquering people have also, and especially when there were marked physical differences of race, been disposed to keep themselves aloof from the conquered peoples, and have developed an aristocratic exclusiveness. Such organizations of restriction upon free intercourse have come and gone in great variety in the history of all long-standing civilizations. The natural boundaries of function were always there, but sometimes they have been drawn sharply and laid stress upon, and sometimes they have been made little of. There has been a general tendency among the Aryan peoples to distinguish noble (patrician) from common (plebeian) families; the traces of it are evident throughout the literature and life of Europe to-day, and it has received a picturesque enforcement in the "science" of heraldry. This tradition is still active even in democratic America. Germany, the most methodical of European countries, had in the Middle Ages a very clear conception of the fixity of such distinctions. Below the princes (who themselves constituted an exclusive class which did not marry beneath itself) there were the:

(*a*) Knights, the military and official caste, with heraldic coats-of-arms;

(*b* and *c*) The Bürgerstand, the merchants, shipping people, and artisans; and

(*d*) The Bauernstand, the cultivating serfs or peasants.

Mediæval Germany went as far as any of the Western heirs

of the first great civilizations towards a fixation of classes. The idea is far less congenial both to the English-speaking people and to the French and Italians, who, by a sort of instinct, favour a free movement from class to class. Such exclusive ideas began at first among, and were promoted chiefly by, the upper classes, but it is a natural response and a natural Nemesis to such ideas that the mass of the excluded should presently range themselves in antagonism to their superiors. It was in Germany, as we shall see in the concluding chapters of this story, that the conception of a natural and necessary conflict, "the class war," between the miscellaneous multitudes of the disinherited ("the class-conscious proletariat" of the Marxist) and the rulers and merchants first arose. It was an idea more acceptable to the German mind than to the British or French. . . . But before we come to that conflict, we must traverse a long history of many centuries.

§ 6

If now we turn eastward from this main development of civilization in the world between Central Asia and the Atlantic, to the social development of India in the 2,000 years next before the Christian era, we find certain broad and very interesting differences. The first of these is that we find such a fixity of classes in process of establishment as no other part of the world can present. This fixity of classes is known to Europeans as the institution of *caste;*[1] its origins are still in complete obscurity, but it was certainly well rooted in the Ganges valley before the days of Alexander the Great. It is a complicated horizontal division of the social structure into classes or castes, the members of which may neither eat nor intermarry with persons of a lower caste under penalty of becoming outcasts, and who may also "lose caste" for various ceremonial negligences and defilements. By losing caste a man does not sink to a lower caste; he becomes outcast. The various subdivisions of caste are very complex; many are practically trade organizations. Each caste has its local organization which maintains discipline, distributes various charities, looks after its own poor, protects the common interests of its members, and

[1] From *casta,* a word of Portuguese origin; the Indian word is *varna,* colour.

examines the credentials of new-comers from other districts. (There is little to check the pretensions of a travelling Hindu to be of a higher caste than is legitimately his.) Originally, the four main castes seem to have been:

The Brahmins—the priests and teachers;

The Kshatriyas—the warriors;

The Vaisyas—herdsmen, merchants, moneylenders, and land-owners;

The Sudras;

And, outside the castes, the Pariahs.

But these primary divisions have long been complicated by subdivision into a multitude of minor castes, all exclusive, each holding its members to one definite way of living and one group of associates. In Bengal the Kshatriyas and Vaisyas have largely disappeared. But this is too intricate a question for us to deal with here in any detail.

Next to this extraordinary fission and complication of the social body we have to note that the Brahmins, the priests and teachers of the Indian world, unlike so many Western priest-hoods, are a reproductive and exclusive class, taking no recruits from any other social stratum.

Whatever may have been the original incentive to this extensive fixation of class in India, there can be little doubt of the rôle played by the Brahmins as the custodians of tradition and the only teachers of the people in sustaining it. By some it is supposed that the first three of the four original castes, known also as the "twice born," were the descendants of the Vedic Aryan conquerors of India, who established these hard-and-fast separations to prevent racial mixing with the conquered Sudras and Pariahs. The Sudras are represented as a previous wave of northern conquerors, and the Pariahs are the original Dravidian inhabitants of India. But these speculations are not universally accepted, and it is, perhaps, rather the case that the uniform conditions of life in the Ganges valley throughout long centuries served to stereotype a difference of classes that have never had the same steadfastness of definition under the more various and variable conditions of the greater world to the west.

However caste arose, there can be no doubt of its extraordinary hold upon the Indian mind. In the sixth century B.C. arose Gautama, the great teacher of Buddhism, proclaiming,

"As the four streams that flow into the Ganges lose their names as soon as they mingle their waters in the holy river, so all who believe in Buddha cease to be Brahmins, Kshatriyas, Vaisyas, and Sudras." His teaching prevailed in India for some centuries; it spread over China, Tibet, Japan, Burmah, Ceylon, Turkestan, Manchuria; it is to-day the religion of a large fraction of the human race, but it was finally defeated and driven out of Indian life by the vitality and persistence of the Brahmins and of their caste ideas.

§ 7

In China we find a social system travelling along yet another, and only a very roughly parallel line to that followed by the Indian and Western civilizations. The Chinese civilization even more than the Hindu is organized for peace, and the warrior plays a small part in its social scheme. As in the Indian civilization, the leading class is an intellectual one; less priestly than the Brahmin and more official. But unlike the Brahmins, the mandarins, who are the literate men of China, are not a caste; one is not a mandarin by birth, but by education; they are drawn by education and examination from all classes of the community, and the son of a mandarin has no prescriptive right to succeed his father.[1] As a consequence of these differences, while the Brahmins of India are, as a class, ignorant even of their own sacred books, mentally slack, and full of a pretentious assurance, the Chinese mandarin has the energy that comes from hard mental work. But since his education so far has been almost entirely a scholarly study of the classical Chinese literature, his influence has been entirely conservative. Before the days of Alexander the Great, China had already formed itself and set its feet in the way in which it was still walking in the year 1,000 A.D. Invaders and dynasties had come and gone, but the routine of life of the yellow civilization remained unchanged.

The traditional Chinese social system recognized four main classes below the priest-emperor.

[1] In the time of Confucius classes were much more fixed than later. Under the Han dynasty the competitive examination system was not yet established. Scholars were recommended for appointments by local dignitaries, etc.—L. Y. C.

(*a*) The literary class, which was equivalent partly to the officials of the Western world and partly to its teachers and clerics. In the time of Confucius its education included archery and horsemanship. Rites and music, history and mathematics completed the "Six Accomplishments."

(*b*) The cultivators of the land.

(*c*) The artisans.

(*d*) The mercantile class.

But since from the earliest times it has been the Chinese way to divide the landed possessions of a man among all his sons, there has never been in Chinese history any class of great landowners, renting their land to tenants, such as most other countries have displayed. The Chinese land has always been cut up into small holdings, which are chiefly freeholds, and cultivated intensively. There are landlords in China who own one or a few farms and rent them to tenants, but there are no great, permanent estates. When a patch of land, by repeated division, is too small to sustain a man, it is sold to some prospering neighbour, and the former owner drifts to one of the great towns of China to join the mass of wage-earning workers there. In China, for many centuries, there have been these masses of town population with scarcely any property at all, men neither serfs nor slaves, but held to their daily work by their utter impecuniousness. From such masses it is that the soldiers needed by the Chinese Government are recruited, and also such gang labour as has been needed for the making of canals, the building of walls, and the like has been drawn. The war captive and the slave class play a smaller part in Chinese history than in any more westerly record of these ages before the Christian era.

One fact, we may note, is common to all these three stories of developing social structure and that is the immense power exercised by the educated class in the early stages before the crowd or the commonalty began to read and, consequently, to think for itself. In India, by reason of their exclusiveness, the Brahmins, the educated class, retain their influence to this day; over the masses of China, along entirely different lines and because of the complexities of the written language, the mandarinate has prevailed. The diversity of race and tradition in the more various and eventful world of the West has delayed, and perhaps arrested for ever, any parallel organization of the specially intellectual elements of society into a class ascendancy. In the Western world, as we have already noted, education early "slopped over," and soaked away out of the control of any special class; it escaped from the limitation of castes and priesthoods and traditions into the general life of the community. Writing and reading had been simplified down to a point when it was no longer possible to make a cult and mystery of them. It may be due to the peculiar elaboration and difficulty of the Chinese characters, rather than to any racial difference, that the same thing did not happen to the same extent in China.

§ 8

In these last six chapters we have traced in outline the whole process by which, in the course of 5,000 or 6,000 years—that is to say, in something between 150 and 200 generations—mankind passed from the stage of early Neolithic husbandry, in which the primitive skin-clad family tribe reaped and stored in their rude mud huts the wild-growing fodder and grain-bearing grasses with sickles of stone, to the days of the fourth century B.C., when all round the shores of the Mediterranean and up the Nile, and across Asia to India, and again over the great alluvial areas of China, spread the fields of human cultivation and busy cities, great temples, and the coming and going of human commerce. Galleys and lateen-sailed ships entered and left crowded harbours, and made their careful way from headland to headland and from headland to island, keeping always close to the land. Phœnician shipping under Egyptian owners was making its way into the East Indies and perhaps even further into the Pacific. Across the deserts of Africa and Arabia and through Turkestan toiled the caravans with their remote trade; silk was already coming from China, ivory from Central Africa, and tin from Britain to the centres of this new life in the world. Men had learnt to weave fine linen[1] and delicate fabrics of coloured wool; they could bleach and dye; they had iron as well as copper, bronze, silver, and gold; they had made the most beautiful pottery and porcelain; there was hardly a variety of precious stone in the world that they had not found and cut and polished; they could read and write; divert the course of rivers, pile pyramids, and make walls a

[1] Damascus was already making Damask, and "Damascening" steel.

thousand miles long. The fifty or sixty centuries in which all this had to be achieved may seem a long time in comparison with the threescore and ten years of a single human life, but it is utterly inconsiderable in comparison with the stretches of geological time. Measuring backward from these Alexandrian cities to the days of the first stone implements, the *rostro-carinate* implements of the Pliocene Age, gives us an extent of time fully a hundred times as long.

We have tried in this account, and with the help of maps and figures and time charts, to give a just idea of the order and shape of these fifty or sixty centuries. Our business is with that outline. We have named but a few names of individuals; though henceforth the personal names must increase in number. But the content of this outline that we have drawn here in a few diagrams and charts cannot but touch the imagination. If only we could look closelier, we should see through all these sixty centuries a procession of lives more and more akin in their fashion to our own. We have shown how the naked Palæolithic savage gave place to the Neolithic cultivator, a type of man still to be found in the backward places of the world. We have given an illustration of Sumerian soldiers copied from a carved stone that was set up long before the days when the Semitic Sargon I conquered the land. Day by day some busy brownish man carved those figures, and, no doubt, whistled as he carved. In those days the plain of the Egyptian delta was crowded with gangs of swarthy workmen unloading the stone that had come down the Nile to add a fresh course to the current pyramid. One might paint a thousand scenes from those ages: of some hawker merchant in Egypt spreading his stock of Babylonish garments before the eyes of some pretty, rich lady; of a miscellaneous crowd swarming between the pylons to some temple festival at Thebes; of an excited, dark-eyed audience of Cretans like the Spaniards of to-day, watching a bull-fight, with the bull-fighters in trousers and tightly girded, exactly like any contemporary bull-fighter; of children learning their cuneiform signs—at Nippur the clay exercise tiles of a school have been found; of a woman with a sick husband at home slipping into some great temple in Carthage to make a vow for his recovery. Or perhaps it is a wild Greek, skin-clad and armed with a bronze axe, standing motionless on some Illyrian mountain crest, struck with amazement at his first vision of a many-oared Cretan galley crawling like a great insect across the amethystine mirror of the Adriatic Sea. He went home to tell his folk a strange story of a monster, Briareus with his hundred arms. Of millions of such stitches in each of these 200 generations is the fabric of this history woven. But unless they mark the presence of a primary seam or join, we cannot pause now to examine any of these stitches.

XIX

THE HEBREW SCRIPTURES AND THE PROPHETS

§ 1. *The Place of the Israelites in History.* § 2. *Saul, David, and Solomon.* § 3. *The Jews a People of Mixed Origin.* § 4. *The Importance of the Hebrew Prophets.*

§ 1

WE are now in a position to place in their proper relationship to this general outline of human history the Israelites, and the most remarkable collection of ancient documents in the world, that collection which is known to all Christian peoples as the Old Testament. We find in these documents the most interesting and valuable lights upon the development of civilization, and the clearest indications of a new spirit that was coming into human affairs during the struggles of Egypt and Assyria for predominance in the world of men.

All the books that constitute the Old Testament were certainly in existence, and in very much their present form, at latest by the year 100 B.C. Most of them were probably recognized as sacred writings in the time of Alexander the Great (330 B.C.). They were the sacred literature of a people, the Jews, who, except for a small remnant of common people, had recently been deported to Babylonia from their own country in 587 B.C. by Nebuchadnezzar II, the Chaldean. They had returned to their city, Jerusalem, and had rebuilt their temple there under the auspices of Cyrus, that Persian conqueror who, we have already noted, in 539 B.C. overthrew Nabonidus, the last of the Chaldean rulers in Babylon. The Babylonian Captivity had lasted about fifty years, and many authorities are of opinion that there was a considerable admixture during that period both of race and ideas with the Babylonians.

The position of the land of Judea and of Jerusalem, its

capital, is a peculiar one. The country is a band-shaped strip between the Mediterranean to the west and the desert beyond the Jordan to the east; through it lies the natural high-road between the Hittites, Syria, Assyria, and Babylonia to the north and Egypt to the south. It was a country predestined, therefore, to a stormy history. Across it Egypt, and whatever power was ascendant in the north, fought for empire; against its people they fought for a trade route. It had itself neither the area, the agricultural possibilities, nor the mineral wealth to be important. The story of its people that these scriptures have preserved runs like a commentary to the greater history of the two systems of civilization to the north and south and of the sea peoples to the west.

These scriptures consist of a number of different elements. The first five books, the *Pentateuch,* were early regarded with peculiar respect. They begin in the form of a universal history with a double account of the Creation of the world and mankind, of the early life of the race, and of a great Flood by which, except for certain favoured individuals, mankind was destroyed. This flood story is very widely distributed in ancient traditions; it may be a memory of that flooding of the Mediterranean valley which occurred in the Neolithic age of mankind. Excavations have revealed Babylonian versions of both the Creation story and the Flood story of prior date to the restoration of the Jews, and it is therefore argued by Biblical critics that these opening chapters were acquired by the Jews during their captivity. They constitute the first ten chapters of Genesis.

There follows a history of the fathers and founders of the Hebrew nation, Abraham, Isaac, and Jacob. They are presented as patriarchal Bedouin chiefs, living the life of nomadic shepherds in the country between Babylonia and Egypt. The existing Biblical account is said by the critics to be made up out of several pre-existing versions; but whatever its origins, the story, as we have it to-day, is full of colour and vitality. What is called Palestine to-day was at that time the land of Canaan inhabited by a Semitic people called the Canaanites, closely related to the Phœnicians who founded Tyre and Sidon, and to the Amorites who took Babylon and, under Hammurabi, founded the first Babylonian Empire. The Canaanites were a settled folk in the days—which were perhaps contemporary with the

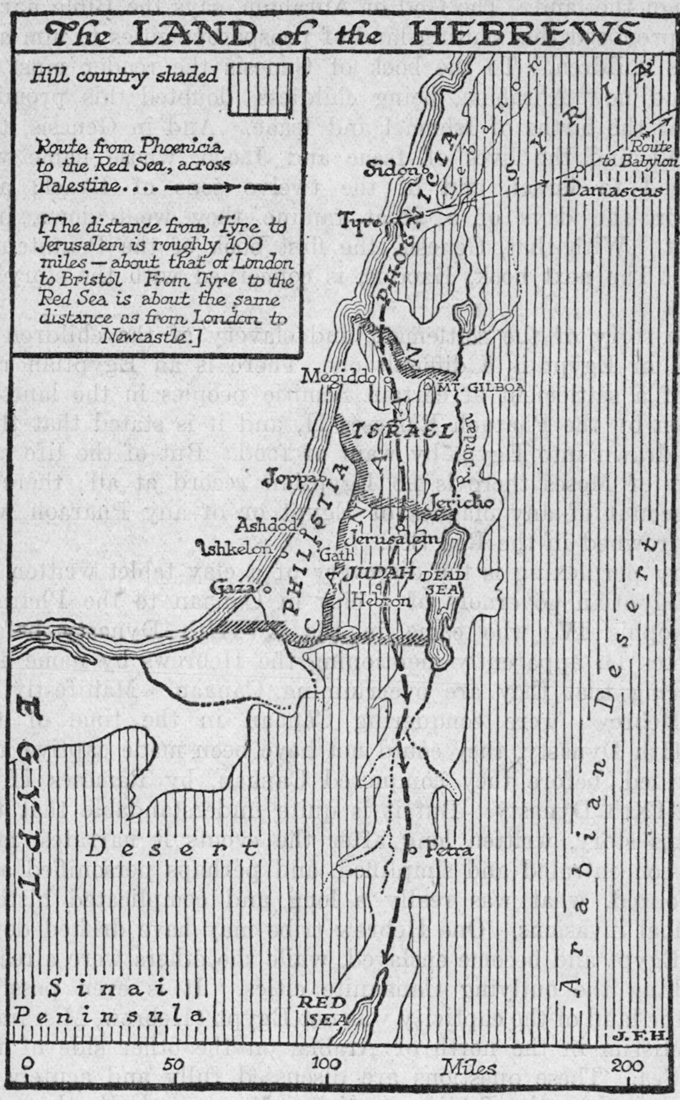
The LAND of the HEBREWS
Hill country shaded
Route from Phoenicia to the Red Sea, across Palestine....
[The distance from Tyre to Jerusalem is roughly 100 miles—about that of London to Bristol. From Tyre to the Red Sea is about the same distance as from London to Newcastle.]
Lebanon
SYRIA
Route to Babylon
Sidon
Damascus
Tyre
PHOENICIA
CANAAN
Megiddo
MT. GILBOA
R. Jordan
ISRAEL
Joppa
Jericho
Ashdod
Jerusalem
Ashkelon
PHILISTIA
Gath
JUDAH
DEAD SEA
Gaza
Hebron
EGYPT
Desert
Arabian Desert
Petra
Sinai Peninsula
RED SEA
J.F.H.
0
50
100
Miles
200

days of Hammurabi—when Abraham's flocks and herds passed through the land. The God of Abraham, says the Bible narrative, promised this smiling land of prosperous cities to him and to his children. To the book of Genesis the reader must go to read how Abraham, being childless, doubted this promise, and of the births of Ishmael and Isaac. And in Genesis, too, he will find the lives of Isaac and Jacob, whose name was changed to Israel, and of the twelve sons of Israel; and how in the days of a great famine they went down into Egypt. With that, Genesis, the first book of the Pentateuch, ends. The next book, Exodus, is concerned with the story of Moses.

The story of the settlement and slavery of the children of Israel in Egypt is a difficult one. There is an Egyptian record of a settlement of certain Semitic peoples in the land of Goshen by the Pharaoh Rameses II, and it is stated that they were drawn into Egypt by want of food. But of the life and career of Moses there is no Egyptian record at all; there is no account of any plagues of Egypt or of any Pharaoh who was drowned in the Red Sea.

Very perplexing is the discovery of a clay tablet written by the Egyptian governors of a city in Canaan to the Pharaoh Amenophis IV, who came in the XVIIIth Dynasty before Rameses II, apparently mentioning the Hebrews by name and declaring that they are overrunning Canaan. Manifestly, if the Hebrews were conquering Canaan in the time of the XVIIIth Dynasty, they could not have been made captive and oppressed, before they conquered Canaan, by Rameses II of the XIXth Dynasty. But it is quite understandable that the Exodus story, written long after the events it narrates, may have concentrated and simplified, and perhaps personified and symbolized, what was really a long and complicated history of tribal invasions. One Hebrew tribe may have drifted down into Egypt and become enslaved, while the others were already attacking the outlying Canaanite cities. It is even possible that the land of the captivity was not Egypt (Hebrew, Misraim) but Misrim in the north of Arabia, on the other side of the Red Sea. These questions are discussed fully and acutely in the *Encyclopædia Biblica* (articles *Moses* and *Exodus*), to which the curious reader must be referred.

[1] See also G. B. Gray, *A Critical Introduction to the Old Testament.*

Two other books of the Pentateuch, Deuteronomy and Leviticus, are concerned with the Law and the priestly rules. The book of Numbers takes up the wanderings of the Israelites in the desert and their invasion of Canaan.

Whatever the true particulars of the Hebrew invasion of Canaan may be, there can be no doubt that the country they invaded had changed very greatly since the days of the legendary promise, made centuries before, to Abraham. Then it seems to have been largely a Semitic land, with many prosperous trading cities. But great waves of strange peoples had washed along this coast. We have already told how the dark Iberian or Mediterranean peoples of Italy and Greece, the peoples of that Ægean civilization which culminated at Cnossos, were being assailed by the southward movement of Aryan-speaking races, such as the Italians and Greeks, and how Cnossos was sacked about 1,400 B.C., and destroyed altogether about 1,000 B.C. It is now evident that the people of these Ægean seaports were crossing the sea in search of securer land nests. They invaded the Egyptian delta and the African coast to the west, they formed alliances with the Hittites and other Aryan or Aryanized races. This happened after the time of Rameses II, in the time of Rameses III. Egyptian monuments record great sea fights, and also a march of these peo-le along the coast of Palestine towards Egypt. Their trans-ort was in the ox-carts characteristic of the Aryan tribes, and is clear that these Cretans were acting in alliance with some arly Aryan invaders. No connected narrative of these conflicts hat went on between 1,300 B.C. and 1,000 B.C. has yet been ade out, but it is evident from the Bible narrative, that when e Hebrews under Joshua pursued their slow subjugation of e promised land, they came against a new people, the Phil-tines, unknown to Abraham,[1] who were settling along the ast in a series of cities of which Gaza, Gath, Ashdod, Ascalon, d Joppa became the chief, who were really, like the Hebrews, w-comers, and probably chiefly these Cretans from the sea and om the north. The invasion, therefore, that began as an at-ck upon the Canaanites, speedily became a long and not very ccessful struggle for the coveted and promised land with ese much more formidable new-comers, the Philistines.

[1] This may seem to contradict Genesis xx. 15, and xxi. and xxvi. various ses, but compare with this the *Encyclopaedia Biblica* article *Philistines.*

It cannot be said that the promised land was ever completely in the grasp of the Hebrews. Following after the Pentateuch in the Bible come the books of Joshua, Judges, Ruth (a digression), Samuel I and II, and Kings I and II, with Chronicles repeating with variation much of the matter of Samuel II and Kings; there is a growing flavour of reality in most of this latter history, and in these books we find the Philistines steadfastly in possession of the fertile lowlands of the south, and the Canaanites and Phœnicians holding out against the Israelites in the north. The first triumphs of Joshua are not repeated. The book of Judges is a melancholy catalogue of failures. The people lose heart. They desert the worship of their own god Jehovah, and worship Baal and Ashtaroth (=Bel and Ishtar). They mixed their race with the Philistines, with the Hittites, and so forth, and became, as they have always subsequently been, a racially mixed people. Under a series of wise men and heroes they wage a generally unsuccessful and never very united warfare against their enemies. In succession they are conquered by the Moabites, the Canaanites, the Midianites, and the Philistines. The story of these conflicts, of Gideon and of Samson and the other heroes who now and then cast a gleam of hope upon the distress of Israel, is told in the book of Judges. In the first book of Samuel is told the story of their great disaster at Ebenezer in the days when Eli wa judge.

This was a real pitched battle in which the Israelites los 30,000 (!) men. They had previously suffered a reverse an lost 4,000 men, and then they brought out their most sacre symbol, the Ark of the Covenant of God.

"And when the ark of the covenant of the Lord came int the camp, all Israel shouted with a great shout, so that th earth rang again. And when the Philistines heard the nois of the shout, they said, 'What meaneth the noise of this gre shout in the camp of the Hebrews?' And they understood th the ark of the Lord was come into the camp. And the Ph istines were afraid, for they said, 'God is come into the cam And they said, 'Woe unto us! for there hath not been such thing heretofore. Woe unto us! who shall deliver us out the hand of these mighty Gods? these are the Gods that smo the Egyptians with all the plagues in the wilderness. strong, and quit yourselves like men, O ye Philistines, that be not servants unto the Hebrews, as they have been to you: quit yourselves like men, and fight.'

"And the Philistines fought, and Israel was smitten, and they fled every man into his tent: and there was a very great slaughter for there fell of Israel thirty thousand footmen. And the ark of God was taken; and the two sons of Eli, Hophni and Phinehas, were slain.

"And there ran a man of Benjamin out of the army, and came to Shiloh the same day, with his clothes rent, and with earth upon his head. And when he came, lo, Eli sat upon a seat by the wayside watching: for his heart trembled for the ark of God. And when the man came into the city, and told it, all the city cried out. And when Eli heard the noise of the crying, he said, 'What meaneth the noise of this tumult?' And the man came in hastily, and told Eli. Now Eli was ninety and eight years old; and his eyes were dim that he could not see. And the man said unto Eli, 'I am he that came out of the army, and I fled to-day out of the army.' And he said, 'What is there done, my son?' And the messenger answered and said, 'Israel is fled before the Philistines, and there hath been also a great slaughter among the people, and thy two sons also, Hophni and Phinehas, are dead, and the ark of God is taken.' And it came to pass, when he made mention of the ark of God, that Eli fell from off the seat backward, by the side of the gate, and his neck brake, and he died: for he was an old man, and heavy. And he had judged Israel orty years.

"And his daughter in law, Phinehas' wife, was with child, ear to be delivered: and when she heard the tidings that the rk of God was taken, and that her father in law and her usband were dead, she bowed herself and travailed: for her ains came upon her. And about the time of her death the omen that stood by her said unto her, 'Fear not, for thou ast borne a son.' But she answered not, neither did she regard . And she named the child I-chabod,[1] saying, 'The glory departed from Israel': because the ark of God was taken, id because of her father in law and her husband." (I. Sam., ap. iv.)

The successor of Eli and the last of the judges was Samuel, d at the end of his rule came an event in the history of

[1] That is, where is the glory?

Israel which paralleled and was suggested by the experience of the greater nations around. A king arose. We are told in vivid language the plain issue between the more ancient rule of priestcraft and the newer fashion in human affairs. It is impossible to avoid a second quotation.

"Then all the elders of Israel gathered themselves together, and came to Samuel unto Ramah, and said unto him: 'Behold, thou art old, and thy sons walk not in thy ways: now make us a king to judge us like all the nations.'

"But the thing displeased Samuel, when they said, 'Give us a king to judge us.' And Samuel prayed unto the Lord And the Lord said unto Samuel, 'Hearken unto the voice o the people in all that they say unto thee: for they have no rejected thee, but they have rejected me, that I should not reig over them. According to all the works which they have don since the day that I brought them up out of Egypt even unt this day, wherewith they have forsaken me, and serve othe gods, so do they also unto thee. Now, therefore, hearken unt their voice: howbeit yet protest solemnly unto them, and she them the manner of the king that shall reign over them.'

"And Samuel told all the words of the Lord unto the peopl that asked of him a king. And he said, 'This will be the ma ner of the king that shall reign over you: He will take you sons, and appoint them for himself, for his chariots, and to be h horsemen; and some shall run before his chariots. And he wi appoint him captains over thousands, and captains over fiftie and will set them to clear his ground, and to reap his harves and to make his instruments of war, and instruments of h chariots. And he will take your daughters to be confectione and to be cooks, and to be bakers. And he will take your fiel and your vineyards, and your oliveyards, even the best of the and give them to his servants. And he will take the tenth your seed, and of your vineyards, and give to his officers, a to his servants. And he will take your menservants, and yo maidservants, and your goodliest young men, and your ass and put them to his work. He will take the tenth of yo sheep: and ye shall be his servants. And ye shall cry out that day because of your king which ye shall have chosen yo and the Lord will not hear you in that day.'

"Nevertheless, the people refused to obey the voice of Samu and they said, 'Nay; but we will have a king over us; that also may be like all the nations; and that our king may judge us, and go out before us, and fight our battles.' " (I. Sam., chap. viii.)

§ 2

But the nature and position of their land was against the Hebrews, and their first king Saul was no more successful than their judges. The long intrigues of the adventurer David against Saul are told in the rest of the first book of Samuel, and the end of Saul was utter defeat upon Mount Gilboa. His army was overwhelmed by the Philistine archers.

"And it came to pass on the morrow, when the Philistines came to strip the slain, that they found Saul and his three sons fallen in Mount Gilboa. And they cut off his head, and stripped off his armour, and sent into the land of the Philistines round about, to publish it in the house of their idols, and among the people. And they put his armour in the house of Ashtaroth; and they fastened his body to the wall of Beth-shan." (I. Sam., chap. xxxi.)

David (990 B.C. roughly) was more politic and successful than his predecessor, and he seems to have placed himself under the protection of Hiram, King of Tyre. This Phœnician alliance sustained him, and was the essential element in the greatness of his son Solomon. His story, with its constant assassinations and executions, reads rather like the history of some savage chief than of a civilized monarch. It is told with great vividness in the second book of Samuel.

The first book of Kings begins with the reign of King Solomon (960 B.C. roughly). The most interesting thing in that story, from the point of view of the general historian, is the relationship of Solomon to the national religion and the priesthood, and his dealings with the tabernacle, the priest Zadok, and the prophet Nathan.

The opening of Solomon's reign is as bloody as his father's. The last recorded speech of David arranges for the murder of Shimei; his last recorded word is "blood." "But his hoar head bring thou down to the grave with blood," he says, pointing out that though old Shimei is protected by a vow David had made to the Lord so long as David lives, there is nothing to bind Solomon in that matter. Solomon proceeds to murder his brother, who has sought the throne but quailed and made submission. He then deals freely with his brother's party. The weak hold of religion upon the racially and mentally confused Hebrews at that time is shown by the ease with which he replaces the hostile chief priest by his own adherent Zadok, and still more strikingly by the murder of Joab by Benaiah, Solomon's chief ruffian, in the tabernacle, while the victim is claiming sanctuary and holding to the very horns of Jehovah's altar. Then Solomon sets to work, in what was for that time a thoroughly modern spirit, to recast the religion of his people. He continues the alliance with Hiram, King of Sidon, who uses Solomon's kingdom as a high road by which to reach and build shipping upon the Red Sea, and a hitherto unheard of wealth accumulates in Jerusalem as a result of this partnership. Gang labour appears in Israel; Solomon sends relays of men to cut cedarwood in Lebanon under Hiram, and organizes a service of porters through the land. (There is much in all this to remind the reader of the relations of some Central African chief to a European trading concern.) Solomon then builds a palace for himself, and a temple not nearly as big for Jehovah. Hitherto, the Ark of the Covenant, the divine symbol of these ancient Hebrews, had abode in a large tent, which had been shifted from one high place to another, and sacrifices had been offered to the God of Israel upon a number of different high places. Now the ark is brought into the golden splendours of the inner chamber of a temple of cedar-sheathed stone, and put between two great winged figures of gilded olivewood, and sacrifices are henceforth to be made only upon the altar before it.

This centralizing innovation will remind the reader of both Akhnaton and Nabonidus. Such things as this are done successfully only when the prestige and tradition and learning of the priestly order has sunken to a very low level.

"And he appointed, according to the order of David his father, the courses of the priests to their service, and the Levites to their charges, to praise and minister before the priests, as the duty of every day required; the porters also by their courses at every gate; for so had David the man of God commanded. And they departed not from the commandment of the king unto the priest and Levites concerning any matter, or concerning the treasures."

Neither Solomon's establishment of the worship of Jehovah

in Jerusalem upon this new footing, nor his vision of and conversation with his God at the opening of his reign, stood in the way of his developing a sort of theological flirtatiousness in his declining years. He married widely, if only for reasons of state and splendour, and he entertained his numerous wives by sacrificing to their national deities, to the Sidonian goddess Ashtaroth (Ishtar), to Chemosh (a Moabitish god), to Moloch, and so forth. The Bible account of Solomon does, in fact, show us a king and a confused people, both superstitious and mentally unstable, in no way more religious than any other people of the surrounding world.

A point of considerable interest in the story of Solomon, because it marks a phase in Egyption affairs, is his marriage to a daughter of Pharaoh. This must have been one of the Pharaohs of the XXIst Dynasty. In the great days of Amenophis III, as the Tel-el-Amarna letters witness, Pharaoh could condescend to receive a Babylonian princess into his harem, but he refused absolutely to grant so divine a creature as an Egyptian princess in marriage to the Babylonian monarch. It points to the steady decline of Egyptian prestige that now, three centuries later, such a petty monarch as Solomon could wed on equal terms with an Egyptian princess. There was, however, a revival with the next Egyptian dynasty (XXII); and the Pharaoh Shishak, the founder, taking advantage of the cleavage between Israel and Judah, which had been developing through the reigns of both David and Solomon, took Jerusalem and looted the all-to-brief splendours both of the new temple and of the king's house.

Shishak seems also to have subjugated Philistia. From this time onward it is to be noted that the Philistines fade in importance. They had already lost their Cretan language and adopted that of the Semites they had conquered, and although their cities remain more or less independent, they merge gradually into the general Semitic life of Palestine.

There is evidence that the original rude but convincing narrative of Solomon's rule, of his various murders, of his association with Hiram, of his palace and temple building, and the extravagances that weakened and finally tore his kingdom in twain, has been subjected to extensive interpolations and expansions by a later writer, anxious to exaggerate his prosperity and glorify his wisdom. It is not the place here to deal with the criticism of Bible origins, but it is a matter of ordinary common sense rather than of scholarship to note the manifest reality and veracity of the main substance of the account of David and Solomon, an account explaining sometimes and justifying sometimes, but nevertheless relating facts, even the harshest facts, as only a contemporary or almost contemporary writer, convinced that they cannot be concealed, would relate them, and then to remark the sudden lapse into adulation when the inserted passages occur. It is a striking tribute to the power of the written assertion over realities in men's minds that this Bible narrative has imposed, not only upon the Christian but upon the Moslem world, the belief that King Solomon was not only one of the most magnificent, but one of the wisest of men. Yet the first book of Kings tells in detail his utmost splendours, and beside the beauty and wonder of the buildings and organizations of such great monarchs as Thotmes III or Rameses II or half a dozen other Pharaohs, or of Sargon II or Sardanapalus or Nebuchadnezzar the Great, they are trivial. His temple measured internally was twenty cubits broad, about 35 feet[1]—that is, the breadth of a small villa residence—and sixty cubits, say 100 feet, long. And as for his wisdom and statescraft, one need go no further than the Bible to see that Solomon was a mere helper in the wide-reaching schemes of the trader-king Hiram, and his kingdom a pawn between Phœnicia and Egypt. His importance was due largely to the temporary enfeeblement of Egypt, which encouraged the ambition of the Phœnician and made it necessary to propitiate the holder of the key to an alternate trade route to the East. To his own people Solomon was a wasteful and oppressive monarch, and already before his death his kingdom was splitting, visibly to all men.

With the reign of King Solomon the brief glory of the Hebrews ends; the northern and richer section of his kingdom, long oppressed by taxation to sustain his splendours, breaks off from Jerusalem to become the separate kingdom of Israel, and this split ruptures that linking connection between Sidon and the Red Sea by which Solomon's gleam of wealth was possible. There is no more wealth in Hebrew history. Jerusalem remains the capital of one tribe, the tribe of Judah, the capital

[1] Estimates of the cubit vary. The greatest is 44 inches. This would extend the width to seventy-odd feet.

of a land of barren hills, cut off by Philistia from the sea and surrounded by enemies.

The tale of wars, of religious conflicts, of usurpations, assassinations, and of fratricidal murders to secure the throne goes on for three centuries. It is a tale frankly barbaric. Israel wars with Judah and the neighbouring states; forms alliances first with one and then with the other. The power of Aramean Syria burns like a baleful star over the affairs of the Hebrews, and then there rises behind it the great and growing power of the last Assyrian empire. For three centuries the life of the Hebrews was like the life of a man who insists upon living in the middle of a busy thoroughfare, and is consequently being run over constantly by omnibuses and motor-lorries.

"Pul" (apparently the same person as Tiglath Pileser III) is, according to the Bible narrative, the first Assyrian monarch to appear upon the Hebrew horizon, and Menahem buys him off with a thousand talents of silver (738 B.C.). But the power of Assyria is heading straight for the now aged and decadent land of Egypt, and the line of attack lies through Judea; Tiglath Pileser III returns and Shalmaneser follows in his steps, the King of Israel intrigues for help with Egypt, that "broken reed," and in 721 B.C., as we have already noted, his kingdom is swept off into captivity and utterly lost to history. The same fate hung over Judah, but for a little while it was averted. The fate of Sennacherib's army in the reign of King Hezekiah (701 B.C.), and how he was murdered by his sons (II. Kings xix. 37), we have already mentioned. The subsequent subjugation of Egypt by Assyria finds no mention in Holy Writ, but it is clear that before the reign of Sennacherib, King Hezekiah had carried on a diplomatic correspondence with Babylon (700 B.C.), which was in revolt against Sargon II of Assyria. There followed the conquest of Egypt by Esarhaddon, and then for a time Assyria was occupied with her own troubles; the Scythians and Medes and Persians were pressing her on the north, and Babylon was in insurrection. As we have already noted, Egypt, relieved for a time from Assyrian pressure, entered upon a phase of revival, first under Psammetichus and then under Necho II.

Again the little country in between made mistakes in its alliances. But on neither side was there safety. Josiah opposed Necho, and was slain at the battle of Megiddo (608 B.C.).

The king of Judah became an Egyptian tributary. Then when Necho, after pushing as far as the Euphrates, fell before Nebuchadnezzar II, Judah fell with him (604 B.C.). Nebuchadnezzar, after a trial of three puppet kings, carried off the greater part of the people into captivity in Babylon (586 B.C.), and the rest, after a rising and a massacre of Babylonian officials, took refuge from the vengeance of Chaldea in Egypt.

"And all the vessels of the house of God, great and small, and the treasures of the house of the Lord, and the treasures of the king, and of his princes; all these he brought to Babylon. And they burnt the house of God and brake down the wall of Jerusalem, and burnt all the palaces thereof with fire, and destroyed all the goodly vessels thereof. And them that had escaped from the sword carried he away to Babylon; where they were servants to him and his sons until the reign of the kingdom of Persia." (II. Chron. xxxvi. 18, 19, 20.)

So the four centuries of Hebrew kingship comes to an end. From first to last it was a mere incident in the larger and greater history of Egypt, Syria, Assyria, and Phœnicia. But out of it there were now to arise moral and intellectual consequences of primary importance to all mankind.

§ 3

The Jews who returned, after an interval of more than two generations, to Jerusalem from Babylonia in the time of Cyrus were a very different people from the warring Baal worshippers and Jehovah worshippers, the sacrificers in the high places and sacrificers at Jerusalem of the kingdoms of Israel and Judah. The plain fact of the Bible narrative is that the Jews went to Babylon barbarians and came back civilized. They went a confused and divided multitude, with no national self-consciousness; they came back with an intense and exclusive national spirit. They went with no common literature generally known to them, for it was only about forty years before the captivity that King Josiah is said to have discovered "a book of the law" in the temple (II. Kings xxii), and, besides that, there is not a hint in the record of any reading of books; and they returned with most of their material for the Old Testament. It is manifest that, relieved of their bickering and murderous kings, restrained from politics and in the intellectually stimulating atmosphere of that Babylonian world, the Jewish mind made a great step forward during the Captivity.

It was an age of historical inquiry and learning in Babylonia. The Babylonian influences that had made Sardanapalus collect a great library of ancient writings in Nineveh were still at work. We have already told how Nabonidus was so preoccupied with antiquarian research as to neglect the defence of his kingdom against Cyrus. Everything, therefore, contributed to set the exiled Jews inquiring into their own history, and they found an inspiring leader in the prophet Ezekiel. From such hidden and forgotten records as they had with them, genealogies, contemporary histories of David, Solomon, and their other kings, legends and traditions, they made out and amplified their own story, and told it to Babylon and themselves. The story of the Creation and the Flood, much of the story of Moses, much of Samson, were probably incorporated from Babylonian sources.[1] When the Jews returned to Jerusalem, only the Pentateuch had been put together into one book, but the grouping of the rest of the historical books was bound to follow.

The rest of their literature remained for some centuries as separate books, to which a very variable amount of respect was paid. Some of the later books are frankly post-captivity compositions. Over all this literature where thrown certain leading ideas. There was an idea, which even these books themselves gainsay in detail, that all the people were pure-blooded children of Abraham; there was next an idea of a promise made by Jehovah to Abraham that he would exalt the Jewish race above all other races; and, thirdly, there was the belief first of all that Jehovah was the greatest and most powerful of tribal gods, and then that he was a god above all other gods, and at last that he was the only true god. The Jews became convinced at last, as a people, that they were the chosen people of the one God of all the earth.

And arising very naturally out of these three ideas, was a fourth, the idea of a coming leader, a saviour, a Messiah who would realize the long-postponed promises of Jehovah.

This welding together of the Jews into one tradition-cemented people in the course of the "seventy years" is the first instance

[1] But one version of the Creation story and the Eden story, though originally from Babylon, seem to have been known to the Hebrews before the exile.—G. W. B.

in history of the new power of the written word in human affairs. It was a mental consolidation that did much more than unite the people who returned to Jerusalem. This idea of belonging to a chosen race predestined to pre-eminence was a very attractive one. It possessed also those Jews who remained in Babylonia. Its literature reached the Jews now established in Egypt. It affected the mixed people who had been placed in Samaria, the old capital of the kings of Israel when the ten tribes were deported to Media. It inspired a great number of Babylonians and the like to claim Abraham as their father, and thrust their company upon the returning Jews. Ammonites and Boabites became adherents. The book of Nehemiah is full of the distress occasioned by this invasion of the privileges of the chosen. The Jews were already a people dispersed in many lands and cities, when their minds and hopes were unified and they became an exclusive people. But at first their exclusiveness is merely to preserve soundness of doctrine and worship, warned by such lamentable lapses as those of King Solomon. To genuine proselytes of whatever race, Judaism long held out welcoming arms.

To Phœnicians after the falls of Tyre and Carthage, conversion to Judaism must have been particularly easy and attractive. Their language was closely akin to Hebrew. It is possible that the great majority of African and Spanish Jews are really of Phœnician origin. There were also great Arabian accessions. In South Russia, as we shall note later, there were even Mongolian Jews.

§ 4

The historical books from Genesis to Nehemiah, upon which the idea of the promise to the chosen people had been imposed later, were no doubt the backbone of Jewish mental unity, but they by no means complete the Hebrew literature from which finally the Bible was made up. Of such books as Job, said to be an imitation of Greek tragedy, the Song of Solomon, the Psalms, Proverbs, and others, there is no time to write in this *Outline,* but it is necessary to deal with the books known as "the Prophets" with some fullness. For those books are almost the earliest and certainly the best evidence of the appearance of a new kind of leading in human affairs.

These prophets are not a new class in the community; they are of the most various origins—Ezekiel was of the priestly caste and of priestly sympathies, and Amos was a shepherd; but they have this in common, that they bring into life a religious force outside the sacrifices and formalities of priesthood and temple. The earlier prophets seem most like the earlier priests, they are oracular, they give advice and foretell events; it is quite possible that at first, in the days when there were many high places in the land and religious ideas were comparatively unsettled, there was no great distinction between priest and prophet. The prophets danced, it would seem, somewhat after the Dervish fashion, and uttered oracles. Generally they wore a distinctive mantle of rough goatskin. They kept up the nomadic tradition as against the "new ways" of the settlement. But after the building of the temple and the organization of the priesthood the prophetic type remains over and outside the formal religious scheme. They were probably always more or less of an annoyance to the priests. They became informal advisers upon public affairs, denouncers of sin and strange practices, "self-constituted," as we should say, having no sanction but an inner light. "Now the word of the Lord came unto"—so and so; that is the formula.

In the latter and most troubled days of the kingdom of Judah, as Egypt, North Arabia, Assyria, and then Babylonia closed like a vice upon the land, these prophets became very significant and powerful. Their appeal was to anxious and fearful minds, and at first their exhortation was chiefly towards repentance, the pulling down of this or that high place, the restoration of worship in Jerusalem, or the like. But through some of the prophecies there runs already a note like the note of what we call nowadays a "social reformer." The rich are "grinding the faces of the poor"; the luxurious are consuming the children's bread; influential and wealthy people make friends with and imitate the splendours and vices of foreigners, and sacrifice the common people to these new fashions; and this is hateful to Jehovah, who will certainly punish the land.

But with the broadening of ideas that came with the Captivity, the tenor of prophecy broadens and changes. The jealous pettiness that disfigures the earlier tribal ideas of God gives place to a new idea of a god of universal righteousness. It is clear that the increasing influence of prophets was not confined to the Jewish people; it was something that was going on in those days all over the Semitic world. The breaking down of nations and kingdoms to form the great and changing empires of that age, the smashing up of cults and priesthoods, the mutual discrediting of temple by temple in their rivalries and disputes —all these influences were releasing men's minds to a freer and wider religious outlook. The temples had accumulated great stores of golden vessels and lost their hold upon the imaginations of men. It is difficult to estimate whether, amidst these constant wars, life had become more uncertain and unhappy than it had ever been before, but there can be no doubt that men had become more conscious of its miseries and insecurities. Except for the weak and the women, there remained little comfort or assurance in the sacrifices, ritual, and formal devotions of the temples. Such was the world to which the later prophets of Israel began to talk of the One God, and of a Promise that some day the world should come to peace and unity and happiness. This great God that men were now discovering lived in a temple "not made with hands, eternal in the heavens." There can be little doubt of a great body of such thought and utterance in Babylonia, Egypt, and throughout the Semitic east. The prophetic books of the Bible can be but specimens of the prophesyings of that time. . . .

We have already drawn attention to the gradual escape of writing and knowledge from their original limitation to the priesthood and the temple precincts, from the shell in which they were first developed and cherished. We have taken Herodotus as an interesting specimen of what we have called the free intelligence of mankind. Now here we are dealing with a similar overflow of moral ideas into the general community. The Hebrew prophets, and the steady expansion of their ideas towards one God in all the world, is a parallel development of the free conscience of mankind. From this time onward there runs through human thought, now weakly and obscurely, now gathering power, the idea of one rule in the world, and of a promise and possibility of an active and splendid peace and happiness in human affairs. From being a temple religion of the old type, the Jewish religion becomes, to a large extent, a prophetic and creative religion of a new type. Prophet succeeds prophet. Later on, as we shall tell, there was born a prophet of unprecedented power, Jesus, whose followers founded the great universal religion of Christianity. Still later Muhammad, another prophet, appears in Arabia and founds Islam. In spite of very distinctive features of their own, these two teachers do in a manner arise out of and in succession to these Jewish prophets. It is not the place of the historian to discuss the truth and falsity of religion, but it is his business to record the appearance of great constructive ideas. Two thousand four hundred years ago, and six or seven or eight thousand years after the walls of the first Sumerian cities arose, the ideas of the moral unity of mankind and of a world peace had come into the world.[1]

[1] Fletcher H. Swift's *Education in Ancient Israel from Earliest Times to* A.D. 70 is an interesting account of the way in which the Jewish religion, because it was a literature-sustained religion, led to the first efforts to provide elementary education for *all* the children in the community.

XX

THE ARYAN-SPEAKING PEOPLES IN PRE-HISTORIC TIMES

§ 1. *The Spreading of the Aryan-Speakers.* § 2. *Primitive Aryan Life.* § 3. *Early Aryan Daily Life.*

§ 1

WE have spoken of the Aryan language as probably arising in the region of the Danube and South Russia and spreading from that region of origin. We say "probably," because it is by no means certainly proved that that was the centre; there have been vast discussions upon this point and wide divergences of opinion. We give the prevalent view. It was originally the language of a group of peoples of the Nordic race. As it spread widely, Aryan began to differentiate into a number of subordinate languages. To the west and south it encountered the Basque language, which was then widely spread in Spain, and also possibly various other Mediterranean languages.

Before the spreading of the Aryans from their lands of origin southward and westward, the Iberian race was distributed over Great Britain, Ireland, France, Spain, north Africa, south Italy, and, in a more civilized state, Greece and Asia Minor. It was closely related to the Egyptian. To judge by its European vestiges it was a rather small human type, generally with an oval face and a long head. It buried its chiefs and important people in megalithic chambers—*i.e.* made of big stones—covered over by great mounds of earth; and these mounds of earth, being much longer than they are broad, are spoken of as the long barrows. These people sheltered at times in caves, and also buried some of their dead therein; and from the traces of charred, broken, and cut human bones, including the bones of children, it is inferred that they were cannibals.

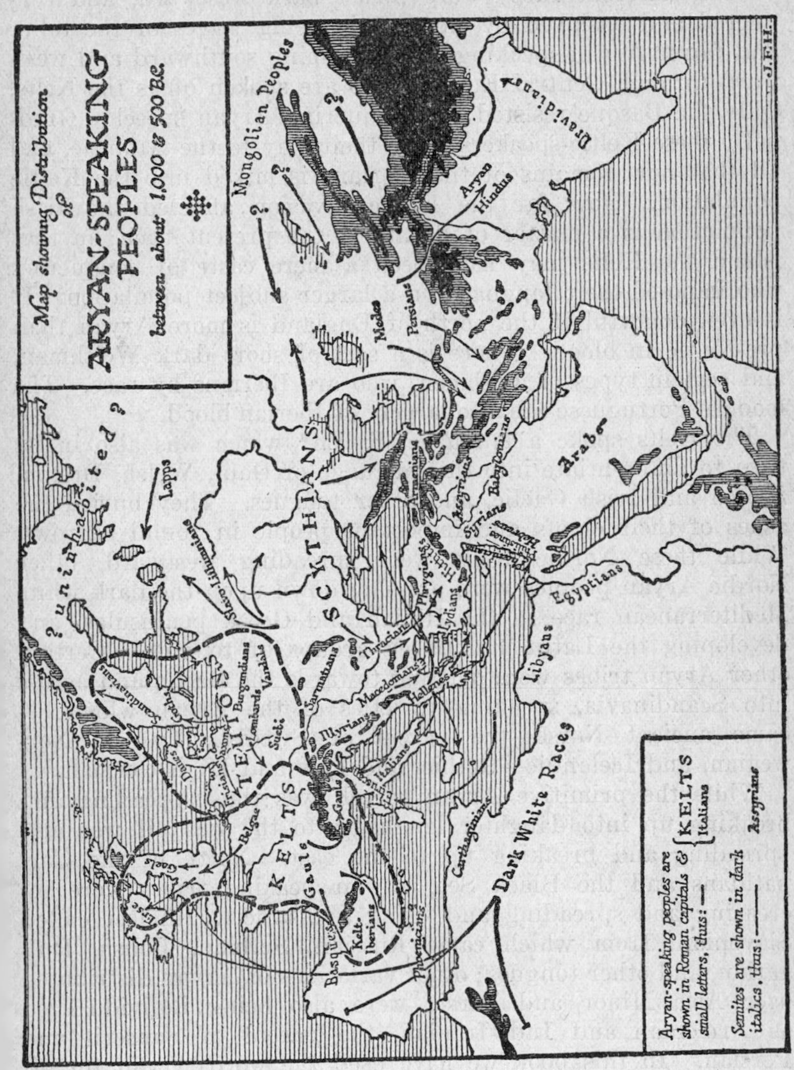
Map showing Distribution of
ARYAN-SPEAKING PEOPLES
between about 1,000 & 500 B.C.
Mongolian Peoples
Dravidians
Aryan Hindus
Persians
Medes
SCYTHIANS
Arabs
Babylonians
Assyrians
Syrians
Armenians
Hittites
Phrygians
Lydians
Thracians
Egyptians
Libyans
Hellenes
Macedonians
Illyrians
Sarmatians
Slavo-Lithuanians
Lapps
uninhabited?
TEUTONS
Scandinavians
Goths
Danes
Frisians
Burgundians
Lombards
Vandals
Suevi
KELTS
Gauls
Gaels
Erse
Belgae
Basques
Kelt-Iberians
Phoenicians
Carthaginians
Italians
Dark White Races
Aryan-speaking peoples are shown in Roman capitals & small letters, thus:— KELTS Italians
Semites are shown in dark italics, thus:— Assyrians
J.F.H.

These short dark Iberian tribes (and the Basques also if they were a different race) were thrust back westward, and conquered and enslaved by slowly advancing waves of the taller and fairer Aryan-speaking people, coming southward and westward through Central Europe, who are spoken of as the Kelts. Only the Basque resisted the conquering Aryan speech. Gradually these Keltic-speakers made their way to the Atlantic, and all that now remains of the Iberians is mixed into the Keltic population. How far the Keltic invasion affected the Irish population is a matter of debate at the present time; in that island the Kelts may have been a mere caste of conquerors who imposed their language on a larger subject population. It is even doubtful if the north of England is more Aryan than pre-Keltic in blood. There is a sort of short dark Welshman, and certain types of Irishmen, who are Iberians by race. The modern Portuguese are also largely of Iberian blood.

The Kelts spoke a language, Keltic,[1] which was also in its turn to differentiate into the language of Gaul, Welsh, Breton, Scotch and Irish Gaelic, and other tongues. They buried the ashes of their chiefs and important people in round barrows. While these Nordic Kelts were spreading westward, other Nordic Aryan peoples were pressing down upon the dark white Mediterranean race in the Italian and Greek peninsulas, and developing the Latin and Greek groups of tongues. Certain other Aryan tribes were drifting towards the Baltic and across into Scandinavia, speaking varieties of the Aryan which became ancient Norse—the parent of Swedish, Danish, Norwegian, and Icelandic—Gothic, and Low and High German.

While the primitive Aryan speech was thus spreading and breaking up into daughter languages to the west, it was also spreading and breaking up to the east. North of the Carpathians and the Black Sea, Aryan-speaking tribes were increasing and spreading and using a distinctive dialect called Slavonian, from which came Russian, Serbian, Polish, Bulgarian, and other tongues; other variations of Aryan distributed over Asia Minor and Persia were also being individualized as Armenian and Indo-Iranian, the parent of Sanscrit and Persian. In this book we have used the word Aryan for all

[1] "The Keltic group of languages, of which it has been said that they combined an Aryan vocabulary with a Berber (or Iberian) grammar."—Sir Henry Johnston.

this family of languages, but the term Indo-European is sometimes used for the entire family, and "Aryan" itself restricted in a narrower sense to the Indo-Iranian speech. This Indo-Iranian speech was destined to split later into a number of languages, including Persian and Sanscrit, the latter being the language of certain tribes of fair-complexioned Aryan speakers who pushed eastward into India somewhen between 3,000 and 1,000 B.C. and conquered dark Dravidian peoples who were then in possession of that land.

From their original range of wandering, other Aryan tribes spread to the north as well as to the south of the Black Sea, and ultimately, as these seas shrank and made way for them, to the north and east of the Caspian, and so began to come into conflict with and mix also with Mongolian peoples of the Ural-Altaic linguistic group the horse-keeping people of the grassy steppes of Central Asia. From these Mongolian races the Aryans seem to have acquired the use of the horse for riding and warfare. There were three or four prehistoric varieties or sub-species of horse in Europe and Asia, but it was the steppe or semi-desert lands that first gave horses of a build adapted to other than food uses.[1] All these peoples, it must be understood, shifted their ground rapidly, a succession of bad seasons might drive them many hundreds of miles, and it is only in a very rough and provisional manner that their "beats" can now be indicated. Every summer they went north, every winter they swung south again. This annual swing covered sometimes hundreds of miles. On our maps, for the sake of simplicity, we represent the shifting of nomadic peoples by a straight line; but really they moved in annual swings, as the broom of a servant who is sweeping out a passage swishes from side to side as she advances. Spreading round the north of the Black Sea, and probably to the north of the Caspian, from the range of the original Teutonic tribes of Central and North-central Europe to the Iranian peoples who became the Medes and Persians and (Aryan) Hindus, were the grazing lands of a confusion of tribes, about whom it is truer to be vague than precise, such as the Cimmerians, the Sarmatians, and those Scythians who, together with the Medes and Persians, came into effective contact with the Assyrian Empire by 1,000 B.C. or earlier.

[1] Roger Pocock's *Horses* is a good and readable book on these questions.

East and south of the Black Sea, between the Danube and the Medes and Persians, and to the north of the Semitic and Mediterranean peoples of the sea-coasts and peninsulas, ranged another series of equally ill-defined Aryan tribes, moving easily from place to place and intermixing freely—to the great confusion of historians. They seem, for instance, to have broken up and assimilated the Hittite civilization, which was probably pre-Aryan in its origin. These latter Aryans were, perhaps, not so far advanced along the nomadic line as the Scythians of the great plains.

§ 2

What sort of life did these prehistoric Aryans lead, these Nordic Aryans who were the chief ancestors of most Europeans and most white Americans and European colonists of to-day, as well as of the Armenians,[1] Persians, and high-caste Hindus?

In answering that question in addition to the dug-up remains and vestiges upon which we have had to rely in the case of the predecessors of the Aryans, we have a new source of knowledge. We have language. By careful study of the Aryan languages it has been found possible to deduce a number of conclusions about the life of these Aryan peoples 5,000 or 4,000 years ago. All these languages have a common resemblance, as each, as we have already explained, rings the changes upon a number of common roots. When we find the same root word running through all or most of these tongues, it seems reasonable to conclude that the thing that root word signifies must have been known to the common ancestors. Of course, if they have *exactly the same word* in their languages, this may not be the case; it may be the new name of a new thing or of a new idea that has spread over the world quite recently. "Gas," for instance, is a word that was made by Van Helmont, a Dutch chemist, about 1625, and has spread into most civilized tongues, and "tobacco" again is an American-Indian word which followed the introduction of smoking almost everywhere. But if the same word turns up in a number of languages, and *if it follows the characteristic modifications of each language,* we may feel sure that it has been in that language, and a part of that language, since the beginning, suffering the same changes

[1] But these may have been an originally Semitic people who learnt an Aryan speech.

with the rest of it. We know, for example, that the words for waggon and wheel run in this fashion through the Aryan tongues, and so we are able to conclude that the primitive Aryans, the more purely Nordic Aryans, had waggons, though it would seem from the absence of any common roots for spokes, rim, or axle that their wheels were not wheelwright's wheels with spokes, but made of the trunks of trees shaped out with an axe between the ends.

These primitive waggons were drawn by oxen. The early Aryans did not ride or drive horses; they had very little to do with horses. The Reindeer men were a horse-people, but the Neolithic Aryans were a cow-people. They ate beef, not horse; and after many ages they began this use of draught cattle. They reckoned wealth by cows. They wandered, following pasture, and "trekking" their goods, as the South African Boers do, in ox-wagons, though of course their waggons were much clumsier than any to be found in the world to-day. They probably ranged over very wide areas. They were migratory, but not in the strict sense of the word "nomadic"; they moved in a slower, clumsier fashion than did the later, more specialized nomadic peoples. They were forest and parkland people without horses. They were developing a migratory life out of the more settled "forest clearing" life of the earlier Neolithic period. Changes of climate which were replacing forest by pasture, and the accidental burning of forests by fire, may have assisted this development.

We have already described the sort of home the primitive Aryan occupied and his household life, so far as the remains of the Swiss pile dwellings enable us to describe these things. Mostly his houses were of too flimsy a sort, probably of wattle and mud, to have survived, and possibly he left them and trekked on for very slight reasons. The Aryan peoples burnt their dead, a custom they still preserve in India, but their predecessors, the long-barrow people, the Iberians, buried their dead in a sitting position. In some ancient Aryan burial mounds (round barrows) the urns containing the ashes of the departed are shaped like houses, and these represent rounded huts with thatched roofs. (*See* Fig., page 86.)

The grazing of the primitive Aryan was far more important to him than his agriculture. At first he cultivated with a rough wooden hoe; then, after he had found out the use of cattle for draught purposes, he began real ploughing with oxen, using at first a suitably bent tree bough as his plough. His first cultivation before that came about must have been rather in the form of garden patches near the house buildings than of fields. Most of the land his tribe occupied was common land on which the cattle grazed together.

He never used stone for building house walls until upon the very verge of history. He used stone for hearths (*e.g.* at Glastonbury), and sometimes stone sub-structures. He did, however, make a sort of stone house in the centre of the great mounds in which he buried the ashes of his illustrious dead. He may have learnt this custom from his Iberian neighbours and predecessors. It was these dark whites of the heliolithic culture, and not the primitive Aryans, who were responsible for such temples as Stonehenge or Carnac in Brittany.

These Aryans were congregated not in cities but in districts of pasturage, as clans and tribal communities. They formed loose leagues of mutual help under chosen leaders, they had centres where they could come together with their cattle in times of danger, and they made camps with walls of earth and palisades, many of which are still to be traced in the history-worn contours of the European scenery. The leaders under whom men fought in war were often the same men as the sacrificial purifiers who were their early priests.

The knowledge of bronze spread late in Europe. The Nordic European had been making his slow advances age by age for 7,000 or 8,000 years before the metals came. By that time his social life had developed so that there were men of various occupations and men and women of different ranks in the community. There were men who worked wood and leather, potters and carvers. The women span and wove and embroidered. There were chiefs and families that were distinguished as leaderly and noble. The Aryan tribesman varied the monotony of his herding and wandering, he consecrated undertakings and celebrated triumphs, held funeral assemblies, and distinguished the traditional seasons of the year, by *feasts*. His meats we have already glanced at; he was an eager user of intoxicating drinks. He made these of honey, of barley, and, as the Aryan-speaking tribes spread southward, of the grape. And he got merry and drunken. Whether he first used yeast to make his bread light or to ferment his drink we do not know.

At his feasts there were individuals with a gift for "playing the fool," who did so no doubt to win the laughter of their friends, but there was also another sort of men, of great importance in their time, and still more important to the historian, certain singers of songs and stories, the bards or rhapsodists. These *bards* existed among all the Aryan-speaking peoples; they were a consequence of and a further factor in that development of spoken language which was the chief of all the human advances made in Neolithic times. They chanted or recited stories of the past, or stories of the living chief and his people; they told other stories that they invented; they memorized jokes and catches. They found and seized upon and improved the rhythms, rhymes, alliterations, and such-like possibilities latent in language; they probably did much to elaborate and fix grammatical forms. They were the first great artists of the ear, as the later Aurignacian rock painters were the first great artists of the eye and hand. No doubt they used much gesture; probably they learnt appropriate gestures when they learnt their songs; but the order and sweetness and power of language was their primary concern.

And they mark a new step forward in the power and range of the human mind. They sustained and developed in men's minds a sense of a greater something than themselves, the tribe, and of a life that extended back into the past. They not only recalled old hatreds and battles, they recalled old alliances and a common inheritance. The feats of dead heroes lived again. The Aryans began to live in thought before they were born and after they were dead.

Like most human things, this bardic tradition grew first slowly and then more rapidly. By the time bronze was coming into Europe there was not an Aryan people that had not a profession and training of bards. In their hands language became as beautiful as it is ever likely to be. These bards were living books, man-histories, guardians and makers of a new and more powerful tradition in human life. Every Aryan people had its long poetical records thus handed down, its sagas (Teutonic), its epics (Greek), its vedas (Old Sanscrit). The earliest Aryan people were essentially a people of the voice. The recitation seems to have predominated even in those ceremonial and dramatic dances and that "dressing-up" which among most human races have also served for the transmission of tradition.

At that time there was no writing, and when first the art of writing crept into Europe, as we shall tell later, it must have seemed far too slow, clumsy, and lifeless a method of record for men to trouble very much about writing down these glowing and beautiful treasures of the memory. Writing was at first kept for accounts and matters of fact. The bards and rhapsodists flourished for long after the introduction of writing. They survived, indeed, in Europe as the minstrels into the Middle Ages.

Unhappily their tradition had not the fixity of a written record. They amended and reconstructed, they had their fashions and their phases of negligence. Accordingly we have now only the very much altered and revised vestiges of that spoken literature of prehistoric times. One of the most interesting and informing of these prehistoric compositions of the Aryans survives in the Greek *Iliad.* An early form of *Iliad* was probably recited by 1,000 B.C., but it was not written down until perhaps 700 or 600 B.C. Many men must have had to do with it as authors and improvers, but later Greek tradition attributed it to a blind bard named Homer, to whom also is ascribed the *Odyssey,* a composition of a very different spirit and outlook. It is possible that many of the Aryan bards were blind men. According to Professor J. L. Myres their bards were blinded to prevent their straying from the tribe. Mr. L. Lloyd has seen in Rhodesia the musician of a troupe of native dancers who had been blinded by his chief for this very reason. The Slavs called all bards *sliepac,* which was also their word for a blind man. The original recited version of the *Iliad* was older than that of the *Odyssey.* "The *Iliad* as a complete poem is older than the *Odyssey,* though the material of the *Odyssey,* being largely undatable folk-lore, is older than any of the historical material in the *Iliad.*" Both epics were probably written over and rewritten at a later date, in much the same manner that Lord Tennyson, the poet laureate of Queen Victoria, in his *Idylls of the King,* wrote over the *Morte d'Arthur* (which was itself a writing over by Sir Thomas Malory, *circ.* 1450, of pre-existing legends), making the speeches and sentiments and the characters more in accordance with those of his own time. But the events of the *Iliad* and the *Odyssey,* the way of living they describe, the spirit of the acts recorded, belong to the closing centuries of the prehistoric age.

These sagas, epics, and vedas do supply, in addition to archæology and philology, a third source of information about those vanished times.

Here, for example, is the concluding passage of the *Iliad,* describing very exactly the making of a prehistoric barrow. (We have taken here Chapman's rhymed translation, correcting certain words with the help of the prose version of Lang, Leaf, and Myers.)

"... Thus oxen, mules, in waggons straight they put,
Went forth, and an unmeasur'd pile of sylvan matter cut;
Nine days employ'd in carriage, but when the tenth morn shin'd
On wretched mortals, then they brought the bravest of his kind
Forth to be burned. Troy swam in tears. Upon the pile's most height
They laid the body, and gave fire. All day it burn'd, all night.
But when th' elev'nth morn let on earth her rosy fingers shine,
The people flock'd about the pile, and first with gleaming wine
Quench'd all the flames. His brothers then, and friends, the snowy bones
Gather'd into an urn of gold, still pouring out their moans.
Then wrapt they in soft purple veils the rich urn, digg'd a pit,
Grav'd it, built up the grave with stones, and quickly piled on it
A barrow, ...
... The barrow heap'd once, all the town
In Jove-nurs'd Priam's Court partook a sumptuous fun'ral feast,
And so horse-taming Hector's rites gave up his soul to rest."

There remains also an old English saga, *Beowulf,* made long before the English had crossed from Germany into England, which winds up with a similar burial. The preparation of a pyre is first described. It is hung round with shields and coats of mail. The body is brought and the pyre fired, and then for ten days the warriors built a mighty mound to be seen afar by the traveller on sea or land. *Beowulf,* which is at least a thousand years later than the *Iliad,* is also interesting because one of the main adventures in it is the looting of the treasures of a barrow already ancient in those days.

§ 3

The Greek epics reveal the early Greeks with no knowledge of iron, without writing, and before any Greek-founded cities existed in the land into which they had evidently come quite recently as conquerors. They were spreading southward from the Aryan region of origin. They seem to have been a fair people, new-comers in Greece, new-comers to a land that had been held hitherto by the Mediterranean or Iberian peoples.

Let us, at the risk of a slight repetition, be perfectly clear upon one point. The *Iliad* does not give us the primitive neolithic life of that Aryan region of origin; it gives us that life already well on the move towards a new state of affairs. The primitive neolithic way of living, with its tame and domesticated animals, its pottery and cooking, and its transitory patches of rude cultivation, we have already sketched. Between 15,000 and 6,000 B.C. the neolithic way of living had spread with the forests and abundant vegetation of the Pluvial Period, over the greater part of the old world, from the Niger to the Hwang-ho and from Ireland to the south of India. Now, as the climate of great portions of the earth was swinging towards drier and more open conditions again, the earlier, simpler, neolithic life was developing along two divergent directions. One was leading to a more wandering life, towards at last a constantly migratory life between summer and winter pasture, which is called NOMADISM; the other, in certain sunlit river valleys, was towards a water-treasuring life of irrigation, in which men gathered into the first towns and made the first CIVILIZATION. We have already described the first civilizations and their liability to recurrent conquests by nomadic peoples. We have already noted that for many thousands of years there has been an almost rhythmic recurrence of conquest of the civilizations by the nomads. Here we have to note that the Greeks, as the *Iliad* presents them, are neither simple neolithic nomads, innocent of civilization, nor are

Combat between Menelaus & Hector (in the Iliad)

From a platter ascribed to the end of the seventh century in the British Museum. This is probably the earliest known vase bearing a Greek inscription. Greek writing was just beginning. Note the Swastika.

they civilized men. They are nomads in an excited state, because they have just come upon civilization, and regard it as an opportunity for war and loot.

These early Greeks of the *Iliad* are sturdy fighters, but without discipline—their battles are a confusion of single combats. They have horses, but no cavalry; they use the horse, which is a comparatively recent addition to Aryan resources, to drag a rude fighting chariot into battle. The horse is still novel enough to be something of a terror in itself. For ordinary draught purposes, as in the quotation from the *Iliad* we have just made, oxen were employed.

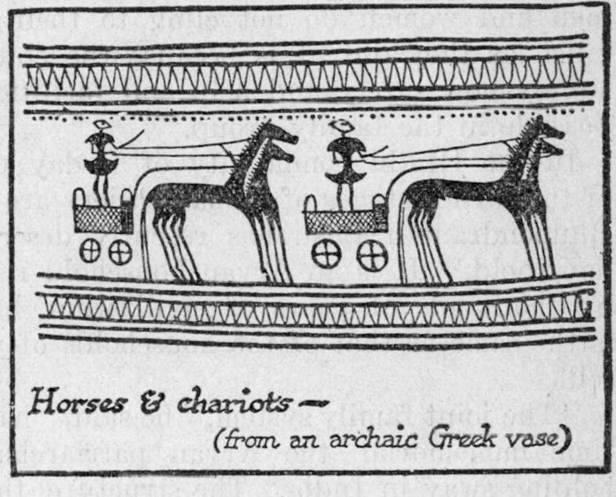

Horses & chariots—
(from an archaic Greek vase)

The only priests of these Aryans are the keepers of shrines and sacred places. There are chiefs, who are heads of families and who also perform sacrifices, but there does not seem to be much mystery or sacramental feeling in their religion. When the Greeks go to war, these heads and elders meet in council and appoint a king, whose powers are very loosely defined. There are no laws, but only customs; and no exact standards of conduct.

The social life of the early Greeks centred about the households of these leading men. There were no doubt huts for herds and the like, and outlying farm buildings; but the hall of the chief was a comprehensive centre, to which everyone went to feast, to hear the bards, to take part in games and exercises. The primitive craftsmen were gathered there. About it were cowsheds and stabling and such-like offices. Unimportant people slept about anywhere as retainers did in the mediæval castles and as people still do in Indian households. Except for quite personal possessions, there was still an air of patriarchal communism about the tribe. The tribe, or the chief as the head of the tribe, owned the grazing lands; forest and rivers were the wild.

The Aryan social organization seems, and indeed all early

communities seem, to have been without the little separate households that make up the mass of the population in western Europe or America to-day. The tribe was a big family; the nation a group of tribal families; a household often contained hundreds of people. Human society began, just as herds and droves begin among animals, by the family delaying its breaking up. Nowadays the lions in East Africa are apparently becoming social animals in this way, by the young keeping with the mother after they are fully grown, and hunting in a group. Hitherto the lion has been much more of a solitary beast. If men and women do not cling to their families nowadays as much as they did, it is because the state and the community supply now safety and help and facilities that were once only possible in the family group.

In the Hindu community of to-day these great households of the earlier stages of human society are still to be found. Mr. Bhupendranath Basu has recently described a typical Hindu household.[1] It is an Aryan household refined and made gentle by thousands of years of civilization, but its social structure is the same as that of the households of which the Aryan epics tell.

"The joint family system," he said, "has descended to us from time immemorial, the Aryan patriarchal system of old still holding sway in India. The structure, though ancient, remains full of life. The joint family is a co-operative corporation, in which men and women have a well-defined place. At the head of the corporation is the senior member of the family, generally the eldest male member, but in his absence the senior female member often assumes control." (Cp. Penelope in the *Odyssey.*)

"All able-bodied members must contribute their labour and earnings, whether of personal skill or agriculture and trade, to the common stock; weaker members, widows, orphans, and destitute relations, all must be maintained and supported; sons, nephews, brothers, cousins, all must be treated equally, for any undue preference is apt to break up the family. We have no word for cousins—they are either brothers or sisters, and we do not know what are cousins two degrees removed. The children of a first cousin are your nephews and nieces, just the same

[1] *Some Aspects of Hindu Life in India.* Paper read to the Royal Society of Arts, Nov. 28, 1918.

as the children of your brothers and sisters. A man can no more marry a cousin, however removed, than he can marry his own sister, except in certain parts of Madras, where a man may marry his maternal uncle's daughter. The family affections, the family ties, are always very strong, and therefore the maintenance of an equal standard among so many members is not so difficult as it may appear at first sight. Moreover, life is very simple. Until recently shoes were not in general use at home, but sandals without any leather fastenings. I have known of a well-to-do middle-class family of several brothers and cousins who had two or three pairs of leather shoes between them, these shoes being only used when they had occasion to go out, and the same practice is still followed in the case of the more expensive garments, like shawls, which last for generations, and with their age are treated with loving care, as having been used by ancestors of revered memory.

"The joint family remains together sometimes for several generations, until it becomes too unwieldy, when it breaks up into smaller families, and you thus see whole villages peopled by members of the same clan. I have said that the family is a co-operative society, and it may be likened to a small state, and is kept in its place by strong discipline based on love and obedience. You see nearly every day the younger members coming to the head of the family and taking the dust of his feet as a token of benediction; whenever they go on an enterprise, they take his leave and carry his blessing. . . . There are many bonds which bind the family together—the bonds of sympathy, of common pleasures, of common sorrows; when a death occurs, all the members go into mourning; when there is a birth or a wedding, the whole family rejoices. Then above all is the family deity, some image of Vishnu, the preserver; his place is in a separate room, generally known as the room of God, or in well-to-do families in a temple attached to the house, where the family performs its daily worship. There is a sense of personal attachment between this image of the deity and the family, for the image generally comes down from past generations, often miraculously acquired by a pious ancestor at some remote time. . . . With the household gods is intimately associated the family priest. . . . The Hindu priest is a part of the family life of his flock, between whom and himself the tie has existed for many generations. The priest is not generally a man of much learning; he knows, however, the traditions of his faith. . . . He is not a very heavy burden, for he is satisfied with little—a few handfuls of rice, a few home-grown bananas or vegetables, a little unrefined sugar made in the village, and sometimes a few pieces of copper are all that is needed. . . . A picture of our family life would be incomplete without the household servants. A female servant is known as the 'jhi,' or daughter, in Bengal—she is like the daughter of the house; she calls the master and the mistress father and mother, and the young men and women of the family brothers and sisters. She participates in the life of the family; she goes to the holy places along with her mistress, for she could not go alone, and generally she spends her life with the family of her adoption; her children are looked after by the family. The treatment of men servants is very similar. These servants, men and women, are generally people of the humbler castes, but a sense of personal attachment grows up between them and the members of the family, and as they get on in years they are affectionately called by the younger members elder brothers, uncles, aunts, etc. . . . In a well-to-do house there is always a resident teacher, who instructs the children of the family as well as other boys of the village; there is no expensive school building, but room is found in some veranda or shed in the courtyard for the children and their teacher, and into this school low-caste boys are freely admitted. These indigenous schools were not of a very high order, but they supplied an agency of instruction for the masses which was probably not available in many other countries. . . .

"With Hindu life is bound up its traditional duty of hospitality. It is the duty of a householder to offer a meal to any stranger who may come before midday and ask for one; the mistress of the house does not sit down to her meal until every member is fed, and, as sometimes her food is all that is left, she does not take her meal until well after midday lest a hungry stranger should come and claim one." . . .

We have been tempted to quote Mr. Basu at some length, because here we do get to something like a living understanding of the type of household which has prevailed in human communities since Neolithic days, which still prevails to-day in

India, China, and the Far East, but which in the west is rapidly giving ground before a state and municipal organization of education and a large-scale industrialism within which an amount of individual detachment and freedom is possible, such as these great households never knew. . . .

But let us return now to the history preserved for us in the Aryan epics.

The Sanscrit epics tell a very similar story to that underlying the *Iliad*, the story of a fair, beef-eating people—only later did they become vegetarians—coming down from Persia into the plain of North India and conquering their way slowly towards the Indus. From the Indus they spread over India, but as they spread they acquired much from the dark Dravidians they conquered, and they seem to have lost their bardic tradition. The vedas, says Mr. Basu, were transmitted chiefly in the households by the women. . . .

The oral literature of the Keltic peoples who pressed westward has not been preserved so completely as that of the Greeks or Indians; it was written down many centuries later, and so, like the barbaric, primitive English *Beowulf*, has lost any clear evidence of a period of migration into the lands of an antecedent people. If the pre-Aryans figure in it at all, it is as the fairy folk of the Irish stories. Ireland, most cut off of all the Keltic-speaking communities, retained to the latest date its primitive life; and the *Táin*, the Irish *Iliad*, describes a cattle-keeping life in which war chariots are still used, and war dogs also, and the heads of the slain are carried off slung round the horses' necks. The *Táin* is the story of a cattle raid. Here, too, the same social order appears as in the *Iliad;* the chiefs sit and feast in great halls, they build halls for themselves, there is singing and story-telling by the bards, and drinking and intoxication. Priests are not very much in evidence, but there is a sort of medicine-man who deals in spells and prophecy.

XXI

THE GREEKS AND THE PERSIANS

§ 1

THE Greeks appear in the dim light before the dawn of history (say, 1,500 B.C.) as one of the wandering imperfectly nomadic Aryan peoples who were gradually extending the range of their pasturage southward into the Balkan peninsula and coming into conflict and mixing with that preceding Ægean civilization of which Cnossos was the crown.

In the Homeric poems these Greek tribes speak one common language, and a common tradition upheld by the epic poems keeps them together in a loose unity; they call their various tribes by a common name, *Hellenes.* They probably came in successive waves. Three main variations of the ancient Greek speech are distinguished: the Ionic, the Æolic, and the Doric. There was a great variety of dialects. The Ionians seem to have preceded the other Greeks, and to have mixed very intimately with the civilized peoples they overwhelmed. Racially the people of such cities as Athens and Miletus may have been less Nordic than Mediterranean. The Doric apparently constituted the last most powerful and least civilized wave of the migration. These Hellenic tribes conquered and largely destroyed the Ægean civilization that had preceded their arrival; upon its ashes they built up a civilization of their own. They took to the sea and crossed by way of the islands to Asia Minor; and, sailing through the Dardanelles and Bosphorus, spread their settlements along the south, and presently along the north borders of the Black Sea. They spread also over the south of Italy, which was called at last Magna Græcia, and round the

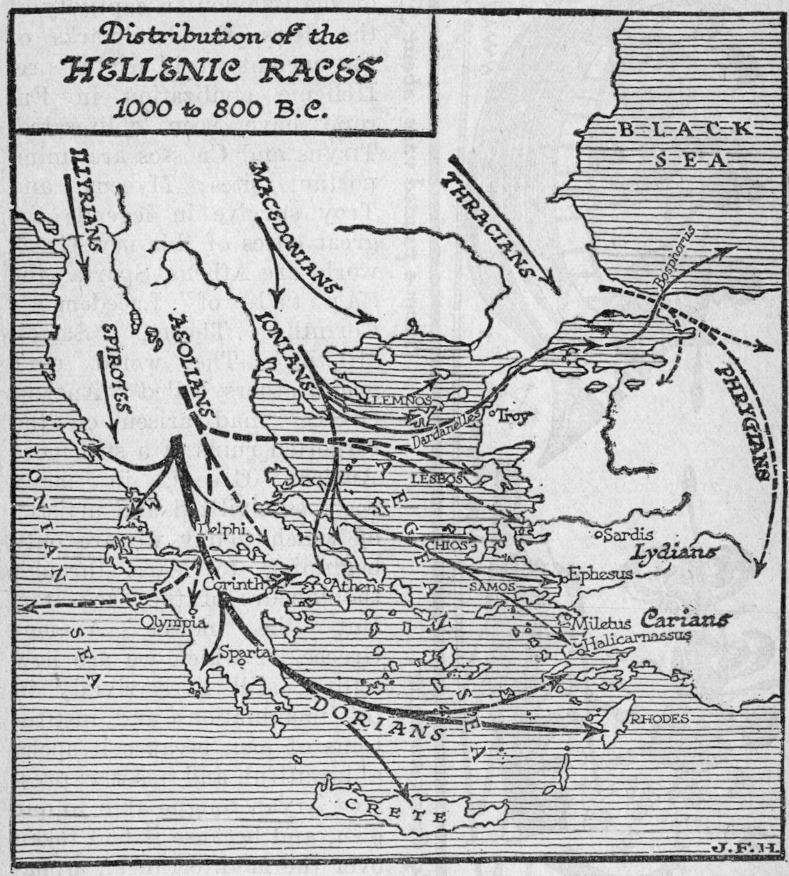

northern coast of the Mediterranean. They founded the town of Marseilles on the site of an earlier Phœnician colony. They began settlements in Sicily in rivalry with the Carthaginians as early as 735 B.C.

In the rear of the Greeks proper came the kindred Macedonians and Thracians; on their left wing, the Phrygians crossed by the Bosphorus into Asia Minor.

We find all this distribution of the Greeks effected before the

An early Greek sea-fight. From a painted vase, about 550 B.C.

beginnings of written history. By the seventh century B.C.—that is to say, by the time of the Babylonian captivity of the Jews—the landmarks of the ancient world of the pre-Hellenic civilization in Europe have been obliterated. Tiryns and Cnossos are unimportant sites; Mycenæ and Troy survive in legend; the great cities of this new Greek world are Athens, Sparta (the capital of Lacedemon), Corinth, Thebes, Samos, Miletus. The world our grandfathers called "Ancient Greece" had arisen on the forgotten ruins of a still more Ancient Greece, in many ways as civilized and artistic, of which to-day we are only beginning to learn through the labours of the excavator. But the newer Ancient Greece, of which we are now telling, still lives vividly in the imaginations and institutions of men because it spoke a beautiful and most expressive Aryan tongue akin to our own, and because it had taken over the Mediterranean alphabet and perfected it by the addition of vowels, so that reading and writing were now easy arts to learn and practise, and great numbers of people could master them and make a record for later ages.[1]

[1] Vowels were less necessary for the expression of a Semitic language. In the early Semitic alphabets only A, I, and U were provided with symbols, but for such a language as Greek, in which many of the inflectional endings are vowels, a variety of vowel signs was indispensable.

§ 2

Now this Greek civilization that we find growing up in South Italy and Greece and Asia Minor in the seventh century B.C., is a civilization differing in many important respects from the two great civilized systems whose growths we have already traced, that of the Nile and that of the Two Rivers of Mesopotamia. These civilizations grew through long ages where they are found; they grew slowly about a temple life out of a primitive agriculture; priest-kings and god-kings consolidated such early city states into empires. But the barbaric Greek herdsmen raiders came southward into a world whose civilization was already an old story. Shipping and agriculture, walled cities and writing were already there. The Greeks did not grow a civilization of their own; they wrecked one and put another together upon and out of the ruins.

To this we must ascribe the fact that there is no temple-state stage, no stage of priest-kings, in the Greek record. The Greeks got at once to the city organization that in the east had grown round the temple. They took over the association of temple and city; the idea was ready-made for them. What impressed them most about the city was probably its wall. It is doubtful if they took to city life and citizenship straight away. At first they lived in open villages outside the ruins of the cities they had destroyed, but there stood the model for them, a continual suggestion. They thought first of a city as a safe place in a time of strife, and of the temple uncritically as a proper feature of the city. They came into this inheritance of a previous civilization with the ideas and traditions of the woodlands still strong in their minds. The heroic social system of the *Iliad* took possession of the land, and adapted itself to the new conditions. As history goes on the Greeks became more religious and superstitious as the faiths of the conquered welled up from below.

We have already said that the social structure of the primitive Aryans was a two-class system of nobles and commoners, the classes not very sharply marked off from each other, and led in warfare by a king who was simply the head of one of the noble families, *primus inter pares,* a leader among his equals. With the conquest of the aboriginal population and with the building of towns there was added to this simple social arrangement of two classes a lower stratum of farm-workers and skilled and unskilled workers, who were for the most part slaves. But all the Greek communities were not of this "conquest" type. Some were "refugee" cities representing smashed communities, and in these the aboriginal substratum would be missing.

In many of the former cases the survivors of the earlier population formed a subject class, slaves of the state as a whole, as, for instance, the Helots in Sparta. The nobles and commoners became landlords and gentlemen farmers; it was they who directed the shipbuilding and engaged in trade. But some of the poorer free citizens followed mechanic arts, and, as we have already noted, would even pull an oar in a galley for pay. Such priests as there were in this Greek world were either the guardians of shrines and temples or sacrificial functionaries; Aristotle, in his *Politics,* makes them a mere subdivision of his official class. The citizen served as warrior in youth, ruler in his maturity, priest in his old age. The priestly *class,* in comparison with the equivalent class in Egypt and Babylonia, was small and insignificant. The gods of the Greeks proper, the gods of the heroic Greeks, were, as we have already noted, glorified human beings, and they were treated without very much fear or awe; but beneath these gods of the conquering freemen lurked other gods of the subjugated peoples, who found their furtive followers among slaves and women. The original Aryan gods were not expected to work miracles or control men's lives. But Greece, like most of the Eastern world in the thousand years B.C., was much addicted to consulting *oracles* or soothsayers. Delphi was particularly famous for its oracle. "When the Oldest Men in the tribe could not tell you the right thing to do," says Gilbert Murray, "you went to the blessed dead. All oracles were at the tombs of Heroes. They told you what was 'Themis,' what was the right thing to do, or, as religious people would put it now, what was the Will of the God."

The priests and priestesses of these temples were not united into one class, nor did they exercise any power as a class. It was the nobles and free commoners, two classes which, in some cases, merged into one common body of citizens, who constituted the Greek state. In many cases, especially in great city states, the population of slaves and unenfranchised strangers greatly outnumbered the citizens. But for them the state existed only by courtesy; it existed legally for the select body of citizens alone. It might or might not tolerate the outsider and the slave, but they had no legal voice in their treatment —any more than if it had been a despotism.

This is a social structure differing widely from that of the Eastern monarchies. The exclusive importance of the Greek citizen reminds one a little of the exclusive importance of the children of Israel in the later Jewish state, but there is no equivalent on the Greek side to the prophets and priests, nor to the idea of an overruling Jehovah.

Another contrast between the Greek states and any of the human communities to which we have hitherto given attention

Rowers in an Athenian warship, about 400 B.C. (Fragment of relief found on the Acropolis)

is their continuous and incurable division. The civilizations of Egypt, Sumeria, China, and no doubt North India, all began in a number of independent city states, each one a city with a few miles of dependent agricultural villages and cultivation around it, but out of this phase they passed by a process of coalescence into kingdoms and empires. But to the very end of their independent history the Greeks did not coalesce. Commonly, this is ascribed to the geographical conditions under which they lived. Greece is a country cut up into a multitude of valleys by mountain masses and arms of the sea that render intercommunication difficult; so difficult that few cities were able to hold many of the others in subjection for any length of time. Moreover, many Greek cities were on islands and scattered along remote coasts. To the end the largest city states of Greece remained smaller than many English counties; and some had an area of only a few square miles. Athens, one of the largest of the Greek cities, at the climax of its power had a population of perhaps a third of a million. Few other Greek cities exceeded 50,000. Of this, half or more were slaves and strangers, and two-thirds of the free body women and children.

§ 3

The government of these city states varied very widely in its nature. As they settled down after their conquests the Greeks retained for a time the rule of their kings, but these kingdoms drifted back more and more to the rule of the aristocratic class. In Sparta (Lacedemon) kings were still distinguished in the sixth century B.C. The Lacedemonians had a curious system of a double kingship; two kings, drawn from different royal families, ruled together. But most of the Greek city states had become aristocratic republics long before the sixth century. There is, however, a tendency towards slackness and inefficiency in most families that rule by hereditary right; sooner or later they decline; and as the Greeks got out upon the seas and set up colonies and commerce extended, new rich families arose to jostle the old and bring new personalities into power. These *nouveaux riches* became members of an expanded ruling class, a mode of government known as oligarchy—in opposition to aristocracy—though, strictly, the term oligarchy (= government by the few) should of course include hereditary aristocracy as a special case.

In many cities persons of exceptional energy, taking advantage of some social conflict or class grievance, secured a more or less irregular power in the state. This combination of personality and opportunity has occurred in the United States of America, for example, where men exercising various kinds of informal power are called *bosses*. In Greece they were called *tyrants*. But the tyrant was rather more than a boss; he was recognized as a monarch, and claimed the authority of a monarch. The modern boss, on the other hand, shelters behind legal forms which he has "got hold of" and uses for his own ends. Tyrants were distinguished from kings, who claimed some sort of right, some family priority, for example, to rule. They were supported, perhaps, by the poorer class with a grievance; Peisistratus, for example, who was tyrant of

Athens, with two intervals of exile, between 560 and 527 B.C., was supported by the poverty-struck Athenian hillmen. Sometimes, as in Greek Sicily, the tyrant stood for the rich against the poor. When, later on, the Persians began to subjugate the Greek cities of Asia Minor, they set up pro-Persian tyrants.

Aristotle, the great philosophical teacher, who was born under the hereditary Macedonian monarchy, and who was for some years tutor to the king's son, distinguishes in his *Politics* between kings who ruled by an admitted and inherent right, such as the King of Macedonia, whom he served, and tyrants who ruled without the consent of the governed. As a matter of fact, it is hard to conceive of a tyrant ruling without the consent of many, and the active participation of a substantial number of his subjects; and the devotion and unselfishness of your "true kings" has been known to rouse resentment and questioning. Aristotle was also able to say that while the king ruled for the good of the state, the tyrant ruled for his own good. Upon this point, as in his ability to regard slavery as a natural thing and to consider women unfit for freedom and political rights, Aristotle was in harmony with the trend of events about him.

A third form of government that prevailed increasingly in Greece in the sixth, fifth, and fourth centuries B.C., was known as *democracy*. As the modern world nowadays is constantly talking of democracy, and as the modern idea of democracy is something widely different from the democracy of the Greek city states, it will be well to be very explicit upon the meaning of democracy in Greece. Democracy then was government by the commonalty, the Demos; it was government by the whole body of the citizens, by the many as distinguished from the few. But let the modern reader mark that word "citizen." The slave was excluded, the freedman was excluded, the stranger; even the Greek born in the city, whose father had come eight or ten miles from the city beyond the headland, was excluded. The earlier democracies (but not all) demanded a property qualification from the citizen, and property in those days was land; this was subsequently relaxed, but the modern reader will grasp that here was something very different from modern democracy. At the end of the fifth century B.C. this property qualification had been abolished in Athens, for example; but Pericles, a great Athenian statesman of whom we shall have more to tell later, had established a law (451 B.C.) restricting citizenship to those who could establish Athenian descent on both sides. Thus, in the Greek democracies quite as much as in the oligarchies, the citizens formed *a closed corporation,* ruling sometimes, as in the case of Athens in its great days, a big population of serfs, slaves, and "outlanders." A modern politician used to the idea, the entirely new and different idea, that democracy in its perfected form means that every adult man and woman shall have a voice in the government, would, if suddenly spirited back to the extremist Greek democracy, regard it as a kind of oligarchy. The only real difference between a Greek "oligarchy" and a Greek democracy was that in the former the poorer and less important citizens had no voice in the government, and in the latter every citizen had. Aristotle, in his *Politics,* betrays very clearly the practical outcome of this difference. Taxation set lightly on the rich in the oligarchies; the democracies, on the other hand, taxed the rich, and generally paid the impecunious citizen a maintenance allowance and special fees. In Athens fees were paid to citizens even for attending the general assembly. But the generality of people outside the happy order of citizens worked and did what they were told, and if one desired the protection of the law, one sought a citizen to plead for one. For only the citizen had any standing in the law courts. The modern idea, that any one in the state should be a citizen, would have shocked the privileged democrats of Athens profoundly.

One obvious result of this monopolization of the state by the class of citizens was that the patriotism of these privileged people took an intense and narrow form. They would form alliances, but never coalesce with other city states. That would have obliterated every advantage by which they lived. The narrow geographical limits of these Greek states added to the intensity of their feeling. A man's love for his country was reinforced by his love for his native town, his religion, and his home; for these were all one. Of course the slaves did not share in these feelings, and in the oligarchic states very often the excluded class got over its dislike of foreigners in its greater dislike of the class at home which oppressed it. But in the main, patriotism in the Greek was a personal passion of an inspiring and dangerous intensity. Like rejected love, it was apt to turn into something very like hatred. The Greek exile resembled the French or Russian *émigré* in being ready to treat his beloved country pretty roughly in order to save her from the devils in human form who had taken possession of her and turned *him* out.

In the fifth century B.C. Athens formed a system of relationships with a number of other Greek city states which is often spoken of by historians as the Athenian Empire. But all the other city states retained their own governments. One "new fact" added by the Athenian Empire was the complete and effective suppression of piracy; another was the institution of a sort of international law. The law indeed was Athenian law; but actions could now be brought and justice administered between citizens of the different states of the League, which of course had not been possible before. The Athenian Empire had really developed out of a league of mutual defence against Persia; its seat had originally been in the island of Delos, and the allies had contributed to a common treasure at Delos; the treasure of Delos was carried off to Athens because it was exposed to a possible Persian raid. Then one city after another offered a monetary contribution instead of military service, with the result that in the end Athens was doing almost all the work and receiving almost all the money. She was supported by one or two of the larger islands. The "League" in this way became gradually an "Empire," but the citizens of the allied states remained, except where there were special treaties of intermarriage and the like, practically foreigners to one another. And it was chiefly the poorer citizens of Athens who sustained this empire by their most vigorous and incessant personal service. Every citizen was liable to military service at home or abroad between the ages of eighteen and sixty, sometimes on purely Athenian affairs and sometimes in defence of the cities of the Empire whose citizens had bought themselves off. There was probably no single man over twenty-five in the Athenian Assembly who had not served in several campaigns in different parts of the Mediterranean or Black Sea, and who did not expect to serve again. Modern imperialism is denounced by its opponents as the exploitation of the world by the rich; Athenian imperialism was the exploitation of the world by the poorer citizens of Athens.

Another difference from modern conditions, due to the small size of the Greek city states, was that in a democracy every citizen had the right to attend and speak and vote in the popular assembly. For most cities this meant a gathering of only a few hundred people; the greatest had no more than some thousands of citizens. Nothing of this sort is possible in a modern "democracy" with, perhaps, several million voters. The modern "citizen's" voice in public affairs is limited to the right to vote for one or other of the party candidates put before him. He, or she, is then supposed to have "assented" to the resultant government. Aristotle, who would have enjoyed the electoral methods of our modern democracies keenly, points out very subtly how the outlying farmer class of citizens in a democracy can be virtually disenfranchised by calling the popular assembly too frequently for their regular attendance. In the later Greek democracies (fifth century) the appointment of public officials, except in the case of officers requiring very special knowledge, was by casting lots. This was supposed to protect the general corporation of privileged citizens from the continued predominance of rich, influential, and conspicuously able men.

Some democracies (Athens and Miletus, *e.g.*) had an institution called the ostracism,[1] by which in times of crisis and conflict the decision was made whether some citizen should go into exile for ten years. This may strike a modern reader as an envious institution, but that was not its essential quality. It was, says Gilbert Murray, a way of arriving at a decision in a case when political feeling was so divided as to threaten a deadlock. There were in the Greek democracies parties and party leaders, but no regular government in office and no regular opposition. There was no way, therefore, of carrying out a policy, although it might be the popular policy, if a strong leader or a strong group stood out against it. But by the ostracism, the least popular or the least trusted of the chief leaders in the divided community was made to retire for a period without loss of honour or property. Professor Murray suggests that a Greek democracy, if it had found itself in such a position of deadlock as the British Empire did upon the question of Home Rule for Ireland in 1914, would have probably first ostracized Sir Edward Carson, and then proceeded to carry out the provisions of the Home Rule Bill.

This institution of the ostracism has immortalized one ob-

[1] From *ostrakon*, a tile; the voter wrote the name on a tile or shell.

scure and rather illiterate member of the democracy of Athens. A certain Aristides had gained a great reputation in the law court for his righteous dealing. He fell into a dispute with Themistocles upon a question of naval policy; Aristides was for the army, Themistocles was a "strong navy" man, and a deadlock was threatened. There was resort to an ostracism to decide between them. Plutarch relates that as Aristides walked through the streets while the voting was in progress, he was accosted by a strange citizen from the agricultural environs unaccustomed to the art of writing, and requested to write his own name on the proffered potsherd.

"But why?" he asked. "Has Aristides ever injured you?"

"No," said the citizen. "No. Never have I set eyes on him. But, oh! I am so *bored* by hearing him called Aristides the Just."

Whereupon, says Plutarch, without further parley Aristides wrote as the man desired. . . .

When one understands the true meaning of these Greek constitutions, and in particular the limitation of all power, whether in the democracies or the oligarchies, to a locally privileged class, one realizes how impossible was any effective union of the hundreds of Greek cities scattered about the Mediterranean region, or even of any effective co-operation between them for a common end. Each city was in the hands of a few or a few hundred men, to whom its separateness meant everything that was worth having in life. Only conquest from the outside could unite the Greeks, and until Greece was conquered they had no political unity. When at last they were conquered, they were conquered so completely that their unity ceased to be of any importance even to themselves; it was a unity of subjugation.

Yet there was always a certain tradition of unity between all the Greeks, based on a common language and script, on the common possession of the heroic epics, and on the continuous intercourse that the maritime position of the states made possible. And in addition, there were certain religious bonds of a unifying kind. Certain shrines, the shrines of the god Apollo in the island of Delos and at Delphi, for example, were sustained not by single states, but by leagues of states or Amphictyonies (= League of neighbours), which in such instances as the Delphic amphictyony became very wide-reaching unions. The league protected the shrine and the safety of pilgrims, kept up the roads leading thereunto, secured peace at the time of special festivals, upheld certain rules to mitigate the usages of war among its members, and—the Delian league especially—suppressed piracy. A still more important link of Hellenic union was the Olympian games that were held every four years at Olympia. Foot races, boxing, wrestling, javelin throwing, quoit throwing, jumping, and chariot and horse racing were the chief sports, and a record of victors and distinguished visitors was kept. From the year 776 B.C. onward[1] these games were held regularly for over a thousand years, and they did much to maintain that sense of a common Greek life (pan-Hellenic) transcending the narrow politics of the city states.

Such links of sentiment and association were of little avail against the intense "separatism" of the Greek political institutions. From the History of Herodotus the student will be able to gather a sense of the intensity and persistence of the feuds that kept the Greek world in a state of chronic warfare. In the old days (say, to the sixth century B.C.) fairly large families prevailed in Greece, and something of the old Aryan great household system (see Chap. XX), with its strong clan feeling and its capacity for maintaining an enduring feud, still remained. The history of Athens circles for many years about the feud of two great families, the Alcmæonidæ and the Peisistratidæ; the latter equally an aristocratic family, but founding its power on the support of the poorer class of the populace and the exploitation of their grievances. Later on, in the sixth and fifth centuries, a limitation of births and a shrinkage of families to two or three members—a process Aristotle notes without perceiving its cause—led to the disappearance of the old aristocratic clans, and the later wars were due rather to trade disputes and grievances caused and stirred up by individual adventurers than to family vendettas.

It is easy to understand, in view of this intense separatism of the Greeks, how readily the Ionians of Asia and of the islands fell first under the domination of the kingdom of Lydia, and then under that of the Persians when Cyrus overthrew Crœsus, the king of Lydia. They rebelled only to be reconquered. Then came the turn of European Greece. It is a matter of astonishment, the Greeks themselves were astonished,

[1] 776 B.C. is the year of the First Olympiad, a valuable starting-point in Greek chronology.

to find that Greece itself did not fall under the dominion of the Persians, these barbaric Aryan masters of the ancient civilizations of Western Asia. But before we tell of this struggle we must give some attention to these Asiatics against whom they were pitted; and particularly to these Medes and Persians who, by 538 B.C., were already in possession of the ancient civilizations of Assyria, Babylonia and about to subjugate Egypt.

§ 4

We have had occasion to mention the kingdom of Lydia, and it may be well to give a short note here upon the Lydians before proceeding with our story. The original population of the larger part of Asia Minor may perhaps have been akin to the original population of Greece and Crete. If so, it was of "Mediterranean" race. Or it may have been another branch of those still more generalized and fundamental darkish peoples from whom arose the Mediterranean race to the west and the Dravidians to the east. Remains of the same sort of art that distinguishes Cnossos and Mycenæ are to be found scattered over Asia Minor. But just as the Nordic Greeks poured southward into Greece to conquer and mix with the aborigines, so did other and kindred Nordic tribes pour over the Bosphorus into Asia Minor. Over some areas these Aryan peoples prevailed altogether, and became the bulk of the inhabitants and retained their Aryan speech. Such were the Phrygians, a people whose language was almost as close to that of the Greeks as the Macedonian. But over other areas the Aryans did not so prevail. In Lydia the original race and their language held their own. The Lydians were a non-Aryan people speaking a non-Aryan speech, of which at the present time only a few words are known. Their capital city was Sardis.

Their religion was also non-Aryan. They worshipped a Great Mother goddess. The Phrygians also, though retaining their Greek-like language, became infected with mysterious religion, and much of the mystical religion and secret ceremonial that pervaded Athens at a later date was Phrygian (when not Thracian) in origin.

At first the Lydians held the western sea-coast of Asia Minor, but they were driven back from it by the establishment of Ionian Greeks coming by the sea and founding cities. Later on, however, these Ionian Greek cities were brought into subjection by the Lydian kings.

The history of this country is not clearly known, and were it known it would scarcely be of sufficient importance to be related in this historical outline, but in the eighth century B.C. one monarch, named Gyges, becomes noteworthy. The country under his rule was subjected to another Aryan invasion; certain nomadic tribes called the Cimmerians came pouring across Asia Minor, and they were driven back with difficulty by Gyges and his son and grandson. Sardis was twice taken and burnt by these barbarians. And it is on record that Gyges paid tribute to Sardanapalus, which serves to link him up with our general ideas of the history of Assyria, Israel, and Egypt. Later Gyges rebelled against Assyria, and sent troops to help Psammetichus I to liberate Egypt from its brief servitude to the Assyrians.

It was Alyattes, the grandson of Gyges, who made Lydia into a considerable power. He reigned for seven years, and he reduced most of the Ionian cities of Asia Minor to subjection. The country became the centre of a great trade between Asia and Europe; it had always been productive and rich in gold, and now the Lydian monarch was reputed the richest in Asia. There was a great coming and going between the Black and Mediterranean Seas, and between the East and West. We have already noted that Lydia was reputed to be the first country in the world to produce coined money, and to provide the convenience of inns for travellers and traders. The Lydian dynasty seems to have been a trading dynasty of the type of Minos in Crete, with a banking and financial development. . . . So much we may note of Lydia by way of preface to the next section.

§ 5

Now while one series of Aryan-speaking invaders had developed along the lines we have described in Greece, Magna Græcia, and around the shores of the Black Sea, another series of Aryan-speaking peoples, whose originally Nordic blood was perhaps already mixed with a Mongolian element, were settling and spreading to the north and east of the Assyrian and Babylonian empires. We have already spoken of the arc-like dispersion of the Nordic Aryan peoples to the north of the Black and Caspian Seas; it was probably by this route that the Arvanspeaking races gradually came down into what is now the Persian country, and spread, on the one hand, eastward to India (? 2,000 to 1,000 B.C.), and on the other, increased and multiplied in the Persian uplands until they were strong enough to assail first Assyria (650 B.C.) and then Babylon (538 B.C.).

There is much that is not yet clear about the changes of climate that have been going on in Europe and Asia during the last 10,000 years. The ice of the last glacial age receded gradually, and gave way to a long period of steppe or prairie-like conditions over the great plain of Europe. About 12,000 or 10,000 years ago, as it is reckoned now, this state of affairs was giving place to forest conditions. We have already noted how, as a consequence of these changes, the Solutrian horse hunters gave place to Magdalenian fishers and forest deer hunters; and these, again, to the Neolithic herdsmen and agriculturists. For some thousands of years the European climate seems to have been warmer than it is to-day. A great sea spread from the coast of the Balkan peninsula far into Central Asia and extended northward into Central Russia, and the shrinkage of that sea and the consequent hardening of the climate of South Russia and Central Asia was going on contemporaneously with the development of the first civilizations in the river valleys. Many facts seem to point to a more genial climate in Europe and Western Asia, and still more strongly to a greater luxuriance of plant and vegetable life, 4,000 to 3,000 years ago, than we find to-day. There were forests then in South Russia and in the country which is now Western Turkestan, where now steppes and deserts prevail. On the other hand, between 1,500 and 2,000 years ago, the Aral-Caspian region was probably drier and those seas smaller than they are at the present time.

We may note in this connection that Thotmes III (say, the fifteenth century B.C.), in his expedition beyond the Euphrates, hunted a herd of 120 elephants in that region. Again, an Ægean dagger from Mycenæ, dating about 2,000 B.C., shows a lion-hunt in progress. The hunters carry big shields and spears, and stand in rows one behind the other. The first man spears the lion, and when the wounded beast leaps at him, drops flat under the protection of his big shield, leaving the next man to repeat his stroke, and so on, until the lion is speared to death. This method of hunting is practised by the Masai to-day, and could only have been worked out by a people in a land where lions were abundant. But abundant lions imply abundant game, and that again means abundant vegetation. About 2,000 B.C. the hardening of the climate in the central parts of the Old World, to which we have already referred, which put an end to elephants and lions in Asia Minor and Greece,[1] was turning the faces of the nomadic Aryan peoples southward towards the fields and forests of the more settled and civilized nations.

These Aryan peoples come down from the East Caspian regions into history about the time that Mycenæ and Troy and Cnossos are falling to the Greeks. It is difficult to disentangle the different tribes and races that appear under a multitude of names in the records and inscriptions that record their first appearance, but, fortunately, these distinctions are not needed in an elementary outline such as this present history. A people called the Cimmerians appear in the districts of Lake Urumiya and Van, and shortly after Aryans have spread from Armenia to Elam. In the ninth century B.C., a people called the Medes, very closely related to the Persians to the east of them, appear in the Assyrian inscriptions. Tiglath Pileser III and Sargon II, names already familiar in this story, profess to have made them pay tribute. They are spoken of in the inscriptions as the "dangerous Medes." They are as yet a tribal people, not united under one king.

About the ninth century B.C. Elam and the Elamites, whose capital was Susa, a people which possessed a tradition and civilization at least as old as the Sumerian, suddenly vanish from history. We do not know what happened. They seem to have been overrun and the population absorbed by the conquerors. Susa is in the hands of the Persians.

A fourth people, related to these Aryan tribes, who appear at this time in the narrative of Herodotus, are the "Scythians." For a while the monarchs of Assyria play off these various kindred peoples, the Cimmerians, the Medes, the Persians, and

[1] It is, at least, doubtful whether any change of climate expelled either lion or elephant from southeast Europe and Asia Minor; the cause of their gradual disappearance was—I think—nothing but Man, increasingly well armed for the chase. Lions lingered in the Balkan peninsula till about the fourth century B.C., if not later. Elephants had perhaps disappeared from western Asia by the eighth century B.C. The lion (much bigger than the existing form) stayed on in southern Germany till the Neolithic period. The panther inhabited Greece, southern Italy, and southern Spain likewise till the beginning of the historical period (say 1,000 B.C.).—H. H. J.

the Scythians, against each other. Assyrian princesses (a daughter of Esarhaddon, *e.g.*) are married to Scythian chiefs. Nebuchadnezzar the Great, on the other hand, marries a daughter of Cyaxares, who has become king of all the Medes. The Aryan Scythians are for the Semitic Assyrians; the Aryan Medes for the Semitic Babylonians. It was this Cyaxares who took Nineveh, the Assyrian capital, in 606 B.C., and so released Babylon from the Assyrian yoke to establish, under Chaldean rule, the Second Babylonian Empire. The Scythian allies of Assyria drop out of the story after this. They go on living their own life away to the north without much interference with the peoples to the south. A glance at the map of this period shows how, for two-thirds of a century, the Second Babylonian Empire lay like a lamb within the embrace of the Median lion.

Into the internal struggles of the Medes and Persians, that ended at last in the accession of Cyrus "the Persian" to the throne of Cyaxares in 550 B.C., we will not enter. In that year Cyrus was ruling over an empire that reached from the boundaries of Lydia to Persia and perhaps to India. Nabonidus, the last of the Babylonian rulers, was, as we have already told, digging up old records and building temples in Babylonia.

J.F.H.

Scythians... as portrayed by a Greek artist....

One of the Few Existing Representations of the Ancient Scythians. From a Greek Electrum Vase.

§ 6

But one monarch in the world was alive to the threat of the new power that lay in the hands of Cyrus. This was Crœsus, the Lydian king. His son had been killed in a very tragic manner, which Herodotus relates, but which we will not describe here. Says Herodotus:

"For two years then, Crœsus remained quiet in great mourning, because he was deprived of his son; but after this period of time, the overthrowing of the rule of the son of Cyaxares

by Cyrus, and the growing greatness of the Persians, caused Crœsus to cease from his mourning, and led him to a care of cutting short the power of the Persians if by any means he might, while yet it was in growth and before they should have become great."

He then made trial of the various oracles.

"To the Lydians who were to carry these gifts to the temples Crœsus gave charge that they should ask the Oracles this question: whether Crœsus should march against the Persians, and, if so, whether he should join with himself any army of men as his friends. And when the Lydians had arrived at the places to which they had been sent and had dedicated the votive offerings, they inquired of the Oracles, and said: 'Crœsus, king of the Lydians and of other nations, considering that these are the only true Oracles among men, presents to you gifts such as your revelations deserve, and asks you again now whether he shall march against the Persians, and, if so, whether he shall join with himself any army of men as allies.' They inquired thus, and the answers of both the Oracles agreed in one, declaring to Crœsus that if he should march against the Persians he should destroy a great empire. . . . So when the answers were brought back and Crœsus heard them, he was delighted with the Oracles, and expecting that he would certainly destroy the kingdom of Cyrus, he sent again to Pytho, and presented to the men of Delphi, having ascertained the number of them, two staters of gold for each man: and in return for this the Delphians gave to Crœsus and to the Lydians precedence in consulting the Oracle and freedom from all payments, and the right to front seats at the games, with this privilege also for all time, that any one of them who wished should be allowed to become a citizen of Delphi."

So Crœsus made a defensive alliance both with the Lacedemonians and the Egyptians. And Herodotus continues, "while Crœsus was preparing to march against the Persians, one of the Lydians, who even before this time was thought to be a wise man, but in consequence of this opinion got a very great name for wisdom among the Lydians, advised Crœsus as follows: 'O king, thou art preparing to march against men who wear breeches of leather, and the rest of their clothing is of leather also; and they eat food not such as they desire, but such as they can obtain, dwelling in a land which is rugged; and, moreover, they make no use of wine but drink water; and no figs have they for desert, nor any other good thing. On the one hand, if thou shalt overcome them, what wilt thou take away from them, seeing they have nothing? and, on the other hand, if thou shalt be overcome, consider how many good things thou wilt lose; for once having tasted our good things, they will cling to them fast, and it will not be possible to drive them away. I, for my own part, feel gratitude to the gods that they do not put it into the minds of the Persians to march against the Lydians.' Thus he spoke not persuading Crœsus; for it is true indeed that the Persians before they subdued the Lydians had no luxury nor any good thing."

Crœsus and Cyrus fought an indecisive battle at Pteria, from which Crœsus retreated. Cyrus followed him up, and he gave battle outside his capital town of Sardis. The chief strength of the Lydians lay in their cavalry; they were excellent, if undisciplined, horsemen, and fought with long spears.

"Cyrus, when he saw the Lydians being arrayed for battle, fearing their horsemen, did on the suggestion of Harpagos, a Mede, as follows: All the camels which were in the train of his army carrying provisions and baggage he gathered together and he took off their burdens and set men upon them provided with the equipment of cavalry; and, having thus furnished them, forth he appointed them to go in front of the rest of the army towards the horsemen of Crœsus; and after the camel-troop he ordered the infantry to follow; and behind the infantry he placed his whole force of cavalry. Then, when all his men had been placed in their several positions, he charged them to spare none of the other Lydians, slaying all who might come in their way, but Crœsus himself they were not to slay, not even if he should make resistance when he was being captured. Such was his charge: and he set the camels opposite the horsemen for this reason—because the horse has a fear of the camel and cannot endure either to see his form or to scent his smell: for this reason then the trick had been devised, in order that the cavalry of Crœsus might be useless, that very force wherewith the Lydian king was expecting most to shine. And as they were coming together to the battle, so soon as the horses scented the camels and saw them, they turned away back, and the hopes of Crœsus were at once brought to nought."

In fourteen days Sardis was stormed and Crœsus taken prisoner. . . .

"So the Persians having taken him brought him into the presence of Cyrus; and he piled up a great pyre and caused Crœsus to go up upon it bound it fetters, and along with him twice seven sons of Lydians, whether it was that he meant to dedicate this offering as first-fruits of his victory to some god, or whether he desired to fulfil a vow, or else had heard that Crœsus was a god-fearing man, and so caused him go up on the pyre because he wished to know if any one of the divine powers would save him, so that he should not be burnt alive. He, they say, did this; but to Crœsus as he stood upon the pyre there came, although he was in such evil case, a memory of the saying of Solon, how he had said with divine inspiration that no one of the living might be called happy. And when this thought came into his mind, they say that he sighed deeply and groaned aloud, having been for long silent, and three times he uttered the name of Solon. Hearing this, Cyrus bade the interpreters ask Crœsus who was this person on whom he called; and they came near and asked. And Crœsus for a time, it is said, kept silence when he was asked this, but afterwards, being pressed, he said: 'One whom more than much wealth I should have desired to have speech with all monarchs.' Then, since his words were of doubtful import, they asked again of that which he said; and as they were urgent with him and gave him no peace, he told how once Solon, an Athenian, had come and having inspected all his wealth had made light of it, with such and such words; and how all had turned out for him according as Solon had said, not speaking at all especially with a view to Crœsus himself, but with a view to the whole human race, and especially those who seem to themselves to be happy men. And while Crœsus related these things, already the pyre was lighted and the edges of it round about were burning. Then they say that Cyrus, hearing from the interpreters what Crœsus had said, changed his purpose and considered that he himself also was but a man, and that he was delivering another man, who had been not inferior to himself in felicity, alive to the fire; and, moreover, he feared the requital, and reflected that there was nothing of that which men possessed which was secure; therefore, they say, he ordered them to extinguish as quickly as possible the fire that was burning, and to bring down Crœsus and those who were with him from the pyre; and they, using endeavours, were not able now to get the mastery of the flames. Then it is related by the Lydians that Crœsus, having learned how Cyrus had changed his mind, and seeing that every one was trying to put out the fire, but that they were no longer able to check it, cried aloud, entreating Apollo that if any gift had ever been given by him which was acceptable to the god, he would come to his aid and rescue him from the evil which was now upon him. So he with tears entreated the god, and suddenly, they say, after clear sky and calm weather clouds gathered and a storm burst, and it rained with a very violent shower, and the pyre was extinguished.

"Then Cyrus, having perceived that Crœsus was a lover of the gods and a good man, caused him to be brought down from the pyre and asked him as follows: 'Crœsus, tell me who of all men was it who persuaded thee to march upon my land and so to become an enemy to me instead of a friend?' And he said: 'O king, I did this to thy felicity and to my own misfortune, and the causer of this was the god of the Hellenes, who incited me to march with my army. For no one is so senseless as to choose of his own will war rather than peace, since in peace the sons bury their fathers, but in war the fathers bury their sons. But it was pleasing, I suppose, to the divine powers that these things should come to pass thus.'"

So Crœsus became a councillor of Cyrus, and lived in Babylon. When Lydia was subdued, Cyrus turned his attention to Nabonidus in Babylon. He defeated the Babylonian army, under Belshazzar, outside Babylon, and then laid siege to the town. He entered the town (538 B.C.), probably as we have already suggested, with the connivance of the priests of Bel.

§ 7

Cyrus was succeeded by his son Cambyses, who took an army into Egypt (525 B.C.). There was a battle in the delta, in which Greek mercenaries fought on both sides. Herodotus declares that he saw the bones of the slain still lying on the field fifty or sixty years later, and comments on the comparative thinness of the Persian skulls. After this battle Cambyses took Memphis and most of Egypt.

In Egypt, we are told, Cambyses went mad. He took great liberties with the Egyptian temples, and remained at Memphis "opening ancient tombs and examining the dead bodies." He had already murdered both Crœsus, ex-king of Lydia, and his own brother Smerdis before coming to Egypt, and he died in Syria on the way back to Susa of an accidental wound, leaving no heirs to succeed him. He was presently succeeded by Darius the Mede (521 B.C.), the son of Hystaspes, one of the chief councillors of Cyrus.

The empire of Darius I was larger than any one of the preceding empires whose growth we have traced. It included all Asia Minor and Syria, that is to say, the ancient Lydian and Hittite empires, all the old Assyrian and Babylonian empires, Egypt, the Caucasus and Caspian regions, Media, Persia, and it extended, perhaps, into India to the Indus. The nomadic Arabians alone of all the peoples of what is nowadays called the Near East, did not pay tribute to the satraps (provincial governors) of Darius. The organization of this great empire seems to have been on a much higher level of efficiency than any of its precursors. Great arterial roads joined province to province, and there was a system of royal posts;[1] at stated intervals post horses stood always ready to carry the government messenger, or the traveller if he had a government permit, on to the next stage of his journey. Apart from this imperial right-of-way and the payment of tribute, the local governments possessed a very considerable amount of local freedom. They were restrained from internecine conflict, which was all to their own good. And at first the Greek cities of the mainland of Asia paid the tribute and shared in this Persian Peace.

Darius was first incited to attack the Greeks in Europe by a homesick Greek physician at his court, who wanted at any cost to be back in Greece. Darius had already made plans for an expedition into Europe, aiming not at Greece, but to the northward of Greece, across the Bosphorus and Danube. He wanted to strike at South Russia, which he believed to be the home country of the Scythian nomads who threatened him on his northern and north-eastern frontiers. But he lent an attentive ear to the tempter, and sent agents into Greece.

This great expedition of Darius opens out our view in this history. It lifts a curtain upon the Balkan country behind Greece about which we have said nothing hitherto; it carries us to and over the Danube. The nucleus of his army marched from Susa, gathering up contingents as they made their way to the Bosphorus. Here Greek allies (Ionian Greeks from Asia) had made a bridge of boats, and the army crossed over while the Greek allies sailed on in their ships to the Danube, and, two days' sail up from its mouth, landed to make another floating bridge. Meanwhile, Darius and his host advanced along the coast of what is now Bulgaria, but which was then called

[1] But a thousand years earlier the Hittites seem to have had paved highroads running across their country.

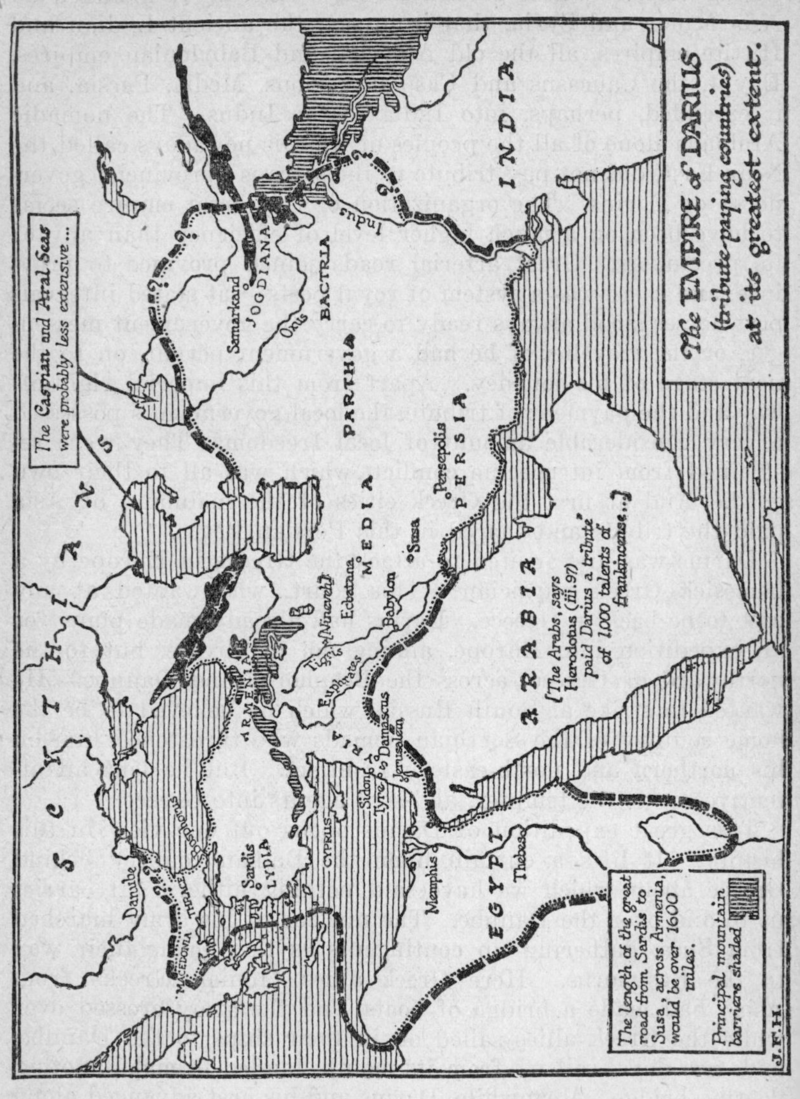
The EMPIRE of DARIUS
(tribute-paying countries)
at its greatest extent.
The Caspian and Aral Seas
were probably less extensive ...
The length of the great
road from Sardis to
Susa, across Armenia,
would be over 1600
miles.
Principal mountain
barriers shaded
[The Arabs, says
Herodotus (iii.97)
paid Darius a tribute
of 1,000 talents of
frankincense...]
SCYTHIANS
Danube
MACEDONIA
THRACE
Bosphorus
Sardis
LYDIA
ARMENIA
CYPRUS
Sidon
Tyre
SYRIA
Damascus
Jerusalem
Memphis
EGYPT
Thebes
ARABIA
Euphrates
Tigris
[Nineveh]
Ecbatana
MEDIA
Babylon
Susa
Persepolis
PERSIA
PARTHIA
BACTRIA
Samarkand
SOGDIANA
Oxus
Indus
INDIA
J.F.H.

Thrace. They crossed the Danube, and prepared to give battle to the Scythian army and take the cities of the Scythians.

But the Scythians had no cities, and they evaded a battle, and the war degenerated into a tedious and hopeless pursuit of more mobile enemies. Wells were stopped up and pastures destroyed by the nomads. The Scythian horsemen hung upon the skirts of the great army, which consisted mostly of foot soldiers, picking off stragglers and preventing foraging; and they did their best to persuade the Ionian Greeks, who had made and were guarding the bridge across the Danube, to break up the bridge, and so ensure the destruction of Darius. So long as Darius continued to advance, however, the loyalty of his Greek allies remained unshaken.

But privation, fatigue, and sickness hindered and crippled the Persian army; Darius lost many stragglers and consumed his supplies, and at last the melancholy conviction dawned upon him that a retreat across the Danube was necessary to save him from complete exhaustion and defeat.

In order to get a start in his retreat he sacrificed his sick and wounded. He had these men informed that he was about to attack the Scythians at nightfall, and under this pretence stole out of the camp with the pick of his troops and made off southward, leaving the camp fires burning and the usual noises and movements of the camp behind him. Next day the men left in the camp realized the trick their monarch had played upon them, and surrendered themselves to the mercy of the Scythians; but Darius had got his start, and was able to reach the bridge of boats before his pursuers came upon him. They were more mobile than his troops, but they missed their quarry in the darkness. At the river the retreating Persians "were brought to an extremity of fear," for they found the bridge partially broken down and its northern end destroyed.

At this point a voice echoes down the centuries to us. We see a group of dismayed Persians standing about the Great King upon the bank of the streaming river; we see the masses of halted troops, hungry and war-worn; a trail of battered transport stretches away towards the horizon, upon which at any time the advance guards of the pursuers may appear. There is not much noise in spite of the multitude, but rather an inquiring silence. Standing out like a pier from the further side of the great stream are the remains of the bridge of boats, an enigma. . . . We cannot discern whether there are men over there or not. The shipping of the Ionian Greeks seems still to be drawn up on the further shore, but it is all very far away.

"Now there was with Darius an Egyptian who had a voice louder than that of any other man on earth, and this man Darius ordered to take his stand upon the bank of the Ister (Danube) and to call Histiæus of Miletus."

This worthy—a day is to come, as we shall presently tell, when his decapitated head will be sent to Darius as Susa—appears approaching slowly across the waters in a boat.

There is a parley, and we gather that it is "all right."

The explanation Histiæus has to make is a complicated one. Some Scythians have been and have gone again. Scouts, perhaps, these were. It would seem there had been a discussion between the Scythians and the Greeks. The Scythians wanted the bridge broken down; they would then, they said, undertake to finish up the Persian army and make an end of Darius and his empire, and the Ionian Greeks of Asia could then free their cities again. Miltiades, the Athenian, was for accepting this proposal. But Histiæus had been more subtle. He would prefer, he said, to see the Persians completely destroyed before definitely abandoning their cause. Would the Scythians go back and destroy the Persians to make sure of them while the Greeks on their part destroyed the bridge? Anyhow, whichever side the Greeks took finally, it was clear to him that it would be wise to destroy the northern end of the bridge, because otherwise the Scythians might rush it. Indeed, even as they parleyed the Greeks set to work to demolish the end that linked them to the Scythians as quickly as possible. In accordance with the suggestions of Histiæus the Scythians rode off in search of the Persians, and so left the Greeks safe in either event. If Darius escaped, they could be on his side; if he were destroyed, there was nothing of which the Scythians could complain.

Histiæus did not put it quite in that fashion to Darius. He had at least kept the shipping and most of the bridge. He represented himself as the loyal friend of Persia, and Darius was not disposed to be too critical. The Ionian ships came over. With a sense of immense relief the remnant of the wasted Persians were presently looking back at the steely flood of the Danube streaming wide between themselves and their pursuers. . . .

The pleasure and interest had gone out of the European expedition for Darius. He returned to Susa, leaving an army in Thrace, under a trusted general Megabazus. This Megabazus set himself to the subjugation of Thrace, and among other states which submitted reluctantly to Darius was a kingdom, which thus comes into our history for the first time, the kingdom of Macedonia, a country inhabited by a people so closely allied to the Greeks that one of its princes had already been allowed to compete and take a prize in the Olympian games.

Darius was disposed to reward Histiæus by allowing him to build a city for himself in Thrace, but Megabazus had a different opinion of the trustworthiness of Histiæus, and prevailed upon the king to take him to Susa, and, under the title of councillor, to keep him a prisoner there. Histiæus was at first flattered by this court position, and then realized its true meaning. The Persian court bored him, and he grew homesick for Miletus. He set himself to make mischief, and was able to stir up a revolt against the Persians among the Ionian Greeks on the mainland. The twistings and turnings of the story, which included the burning of Sardis by the Ionians and the defeat of a Greek fleet at the battle of Ladé (495 B.C.), are too complicated to follow here. It is a dark and intricate story of treacheries, cruelties, and hate, in which the death of the wily Histiæus shines almost cheerfully. The Persian governor of Sardis, through which town he was being taken on his way back to Susa as a prisoner, having much the same opinion of him as Megabazus had, and knowing his ability to humbug Darius, killed him there and then, and sent on the head only to his master.

Cyprus and the Greek islands were dragged into this contest that Histiæus had stirred up, and at last Athens. Darius realized the error he had made in turning to the right and not to the left when he had crossed the Bosphorus, and he now set himself to the conquest of all Greece. He began with the islands. Tyre and Sidon were subject to Persia, and ships of the Phœnician and of the Ionian Greeks provided the Persians with a fleet by means of which one Greek island after another was subjugated.

§ 8

The first attack upon Greece proper was made in 490 B.C. It was a sea attack upon Athens, with a force long and carefully prepared for the task, the fleet being provided with specially

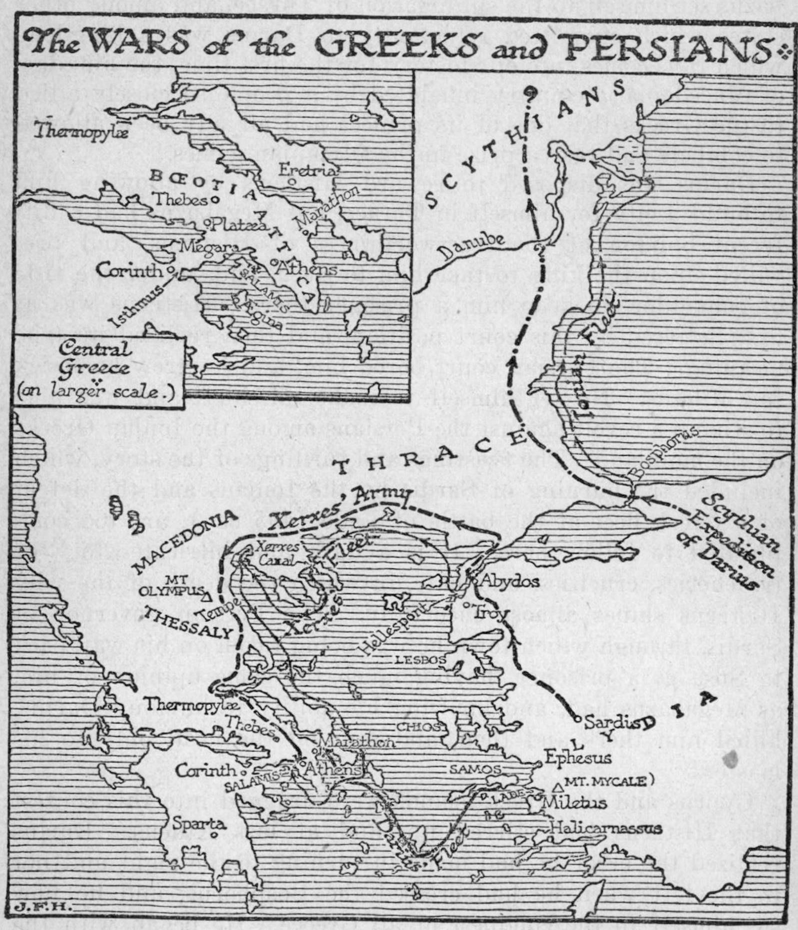

built transports for the conveyance of horses. This expedition made a landing near Marathon in Attica. The Persians were guided into Marathon by a renegade Greek, Hippias, the son of Peisistratus, who had been tyrant of Athens. If Athens fell, then Hippias was to be its tyrant, under the protection of the Persians. Meanwhile, so urgent was the sense of a crisis in the affairs of Hellas, that a man, a herald and runner, went from Athens to Sparta, forgetful of all feuds, to say: "Lacedemonians, the Athenians make request of you to come to their help, and not to allow a city most anciently established among the Hellenes to fall into slavery by the means of Barbarians; for even now Eretria has been enslaved and Hellas has become the weaker by a city of renown." This man, Pheidippides, did the distance from Athens to Sparta, nearly a hundred miles as the crow flies, and much more if we allow for the contours and the windings of the way, in something under eight and forty hours.

But before the Spartans could arrive on the scene the battle was joined. The Athenians charged the enemy. They fought —"in a memorable fashion: for they were the first of all the Hellenes about whom we know who went to attack the enemy at a run, and they were the first also who endured to face the Median garments and the men who wore them, whereas up to this time the very name of the Medes was to the Hellenes a terror to hear."

The Persian wings gave before this impetuous attack, but the centre held. The Athenians, however, were cool as well as vigorous; they let the wings run and closed in on the flanks of the centre, whereupon the main body of the Persians fled to their ships. Seven vessels fell into the hands of the Athenians; the rest got away, and, after a futile attempt to sail round to Athens and seize the city before the army returned thither, the fleet made a retreat to Asia. Let Herodotus close the story with a paragraph that still further enlightens us upon the tremendous prestige of the Medes at this time:

"Of the Lacedemonians there came to Athens two thousand after the full moon, making great haste to be in time, so that they arrived in Attica on the third day after leaving Sparta: and though they had come too late for the battle, yet they desired to behold the Medes; and accordingly they went on to Marathon and looked at the bodies of the slain: then afterwards they departed home, commending the Athenians and the work which they had done."

§ 9

So Greece, unified for a while by fear, gained her first victory over Persia. The news came to Darius simultaneously with the news of a rebellion in Egypt, and he died while still undecided in which direction to turn. His son and successor, Xerxes, turned first to Egypt and set up a Persian satrap there; then for four years he prepared a second attack upon Greece. Says Herodotus, who was, one must remember, a patriotic Greek, approaching now to the climax of his History:

"For what nation did Xerxes not lead out of Asia against Hellas? and what water was not exhausted, being drunk by his host, except only the great rivers? For some supplied ships, and others were appointed to serve in the land army; to some it was appointed to furnish cavalry, and to others vessels to carry horses, while they served in the expedition themselves also; others were ordered to furnish ships of war for the bridges, and others again ships with provisions."

Monument of Athenian foot soldier, found near Marathon.

Xerxes passed into Europe, not as Darius did at the half-mile crossing of the Bosphorus, but at the Hellespont (= the Dardanelles). In his account of the assembling of the great army, and its march from Sardis to the Hellespont, the poet in Herodotus takes possession of the historian. The great host passes in splendour by Troy, and Xerxes, who although a Persian and a Barbarian, seems to have had the advantages of a classical education, turns aside, says our historian, to visit the citadel of Priam. The Hellespont was bridged at Abydos, and upon a hill was set a marble throne from which Xerxes surveyed the whole array of his forces.

"And seeing all the Hellespont covered over with the ships and all the shores and the plains of Abydos full of men, then Xerxes pronounced himself a happy man, and after that he fell to weeping. Artabanus, his uncle, therefore perceiving him—the same who at first boldly declared his opinion advising Xerxes not to march against Hellas—this man, I say, having observed Xerxes wept, asked as follows: 'O king, how far different from one another are the things which thou hast done now and a short while before now! for having pronounced thyself a happy man, thou art now shedding tears.' He said: 'Yea, for after I had reckoned up, it came into my mind to feel pity at the thought how brief was the whole life of man, seeing that of these multitudes not one will be alive when a hundred years have gone by.'"

This may not be exact history, but it is great poetry. It is as splendid as anything in *The Dynasts*.

The Persian fleet, coasting from headland to headland, accompanied this land multitude during its march southward; but a violent storm did the fleet great damage and 400 ships were lost, including much corn transport. At first the united Hellenes marched out to meet the invaders at the Vale of Tempe near Mount Olympus, but afterwards retreated through Thessaly, and chose at last to await the advancing Persians at a place called Thermopylæ, where at that time—2,300 years have altered these things greatly—there was a great cliff on the landward side and the sea to the east, with a track scarcely wide enough for a chariot between. The great advantage to the Greeks of this position at Thermopylæ was that it prevented the use of either cavalry or chariots, and narrowed the battle front so as to minimize their numerical inequality. And there the Persians joined battle with them one summer day in the year 480 B.C.

For three days the Greeks held this great army, and did them much damage with small loss to themselves, and then on the third day a detachment of Persians appeared upon the rear of the Greeks, having learnt of a way over the mountains from a peasant. There were hasty discussions among the Greeks; some were for withdrawing, some for holding out. The leader of the whole force, Leonidas, was for staying; and with him he would keep, he said, 300 Spartans. The rest of the Greek army could, meanwhile, make good its retreat to the next defensible pass. The Thespian contingent of 700, however, refused to fall back. They preferred to stay and die with the Spartans. Also a contingent of 400 Thebans remained. As Thebes afterwards joined the Persians, there is a story that these Thebans were detained by force against their will, which seems on military as well as historical grounds improbable. These 1,400 stayed, and were, after a conflict of heroic quality, slain to a man. Two Spartans happened to be away, sick with ophthalmia. When they heard the news, one was too ill to move; the other made his helot guide him to the battle, and there struck blindly until he was killed. The other, Aristodemus, was taken away with the retreating troops, and returned to Sparta, where he was not actually punished for his conduct, but was known as Tresas, "the man who retreated." It was enough to distinguish him from all other Spartans, and he got himself killed at the Battle of Platæa a year later, performing prodigies of reckless courage. . . . For a whole day this little band had held the pass, assailed in front and rear by the whole force of the Persians. They had covered the retreat of the main Greek army, they had inflicted great losses on the invaders, and they had raised the prestige of the Greek warrior over that of the Mede higher even than the victory of Marathon had done.

The Persian cavalry and transport filtered slowly through the narrow passage of Thermopylæ, and marched on towards Athens, while a series of naval encounters went on at sea. The Hellenic fleet retreated before the advance of the Persian shipping, which suffered seriously through its comparative ignorance of the intricate coasts and of the tricks of the local weather. Weight of numbers carried the Persian army forward to Athens; now that Thermopylæ was lost, there was no line of defence nearer than the Isthmus of Corinth, and this meant the abandonment of all the intervening territory, including Athens. The population had either to fly or submit to the Persians. Thebes with all Bœotia submitted, and was pressed into the Persian army, except one town, Platæa, whose inhabitants fled to Athens. The turn of Athens came next, and great efforts were made to persuade her to make terms; but, instead, the whole population determined to abandon everything and take to the shipping. The women and non-combatants were carried to Salamis and various adjacent islands. Only a few people too old to move and a few dissentients remained in the town, which was occupied by the Persians and burnt. The sacred objects, statues, etc., which were burnt at this time, were afterwards buried in the Acropolis by the returning Athenians, and have been dug up in our own day with the marks of burning visible upon them. Xerxes sent off a mounted messenger to Susa with the news, and he invited the sons of Peisistratus, whom he had brought back with him, to enter upon their inheritance and sacrifice after the Athenian manner upon the Acropolis.

Meanwhile, the Hellenic confederate fleet had come round to Salamis, and in the council of war there were bitter differences of opinion. Corinth and the states behind the Isthmus wanted the fleet to fall back to that position, abandoning the cities of Megara and Ægina. Themistocles insisted with all his force on fighting in the narrows of Salamis. The majority was steadily in favour of retreat, when there suddenly arrived the news that retreat was cut off. The Persians had sailed round Salamis and held the sea on the other side. This news was brought by that Aristides the Just, of whose ostracism we have already told; his sanity and eloquence did much to help Themistocles to hearten the hesitating commanders. These two men had formerly been bitter antagonists; but, with a generosity rare in those days, they forgot their differences before the common danger. At dawn the Greek ships pulled out to battle.

The fleet before them was a fleet more composite and less united than their own. But it was about three times as great. On one wing were the Phœnicians, on the other Ionian Greeks from Asia and the Islands. Some of the latter fought stoutly; others remembered that they, too, were Greeks. The Greek ships, on the other hand, were mostly manned by freemen fighting for their homes. Throughout the early hours the battle raged confusedly. Then it became evident to Xerxes, watching the combat, that his fleet was attempting flight. The flight became disaster.

Xerxes had taken his seat to watch the battle. He saw his

galleys rammed by the sharp prows of other galleys; his fighting-men shot down; his ships boarded. Much of the sea-fighting in those days was done by ramming; the big galleys bore down their opponents by superior weight of impact, or sheared off their oars and so destroyed their manœuvring power and left them helpless. Presently, Xerxes saw that some of his broken

Soldiers of the Persian body-guard (*From frieze in the audience hall of Darius at Susa.*)

ships were surrendering. In the water he could see the heads of Greeks swimming to land; but "of the Barbarians the greater number perished in the sea, not knowing how to swim." The clumsy attempt of the hard-pressed first line of the Persian fleet to put about led to indescribable confusion. Some were rammed by the rear ships of their own side. This ancient shipping was poor, unseaworthy stuff by any modern standards. The west wind was blowing and many of the broken ships of Xerxes were now drifting away out of his sight to be wrecked on the coast beyond. Others were being towed towards Salamis by the Greeks. Others, less injured and still in fighting trim, were making for the beaches close beneath him that would bring them under the protection of his army. Scattered over the further sea, beyond the headlands, remote and vague, were ships in flight and Greek ships in pursuit. Slowly, incident by incident, the disaster had unfolded under his eyes. We can imagine something of the coming and going of messengers, the issuing of futile orders, the changes of plan, throughout the day. In the morning Xerxes had come out provided with tables to mark the most successful of his commanders for reward. In the gold of the sunset he beheld the sea power of Persia utterly scattered, sunken and destroyed, and the Greek fleet over against

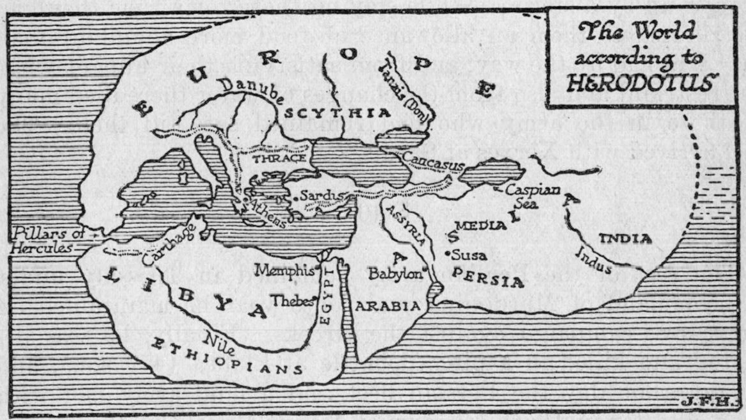

Salamis unbroken and triumphant, ordering its ranks, as if still incredulous of victory.

The Persian army remained as if in indecision for some days close to the scene of this sea fight, and then began to retreat to Thessaly, where it was proposed to winter and resume the campaign. But Xerxes, like Darius I before him, had conceived a disgust for European campaigns. He was afraid of the destruction of the bridge of boats. With part of the army he went on to the Hellespont, leaving the main force in Thessaly under a general, Mardonius. Of his own retreat the historian relates:

"Whithersoever they came on the march and to whatever nation they seized the crops of that people and used them for provisions; and if they found no crops, then they took the grass which was growing up from the earth, and stripped off the bark from the trees and plucked down the leaves and devoured them; alike of the cultivated trees and of those growing wild; and they left nothing behind them: thus they did by reason of famine. Then plague too seized upon the army and dysentery, which destroyed them by the way, and some of them also who were sick the king left behind, laying charge upon the cities where at the time he chanced to be in his march, to take care of them and support them; of these he left some in Thessaly, and some at Siris in Paionia, and some in Macedonia. . . . When, passing on from Thrace they came to the passage, they crossed over the Hellespont in haste to Abydos by means of the ships, for they did not find the floating bridges still stretched across, but broken up by a storm. While staying there for a time they had distributed to them an allowance of food more abundant than they had had by the way, and from satisfying their hunger without restraint and also from the changes of water there died many of those in the army who had remained safe till then. The rest arrived with Xerxes at Sardis."

§ 10

The rest of the Persian army remained in Thessaly under the command of Mardonius, and for a year he maintained an aggressive campaign against the Greeks. Finally, he was defeated and killed in a pitched battle at Platæa (479 B.C.), and on the same day the Persian fleet and a land army met with joint disaster under the shadow of Mount Mycale on the Asiatic mainland, between Ephesus and Miletus. The Persian ships, being in fear of the Greeks, had been drawn up on shore and a wall built about them; but the Greeks disembarked and stormed this enclosure. They then sailed to the Hellespont to destroy what was left of the bridge of boats, so that later the Persian fugitives, retreating from Platæa, had to cross by shipping at the Bosphorus, and did so with difficulty.

Encouraged by these disasters of the imperial power, says Herodotus, the Ionian cities in Asia began for a second time to revolt against the Persians.

With this the ninth book of the *History of Herodotus* comes to an end. He was born about 484 B.C., so that at the time of the battle of Platæa he was a child of five years old. Much of the substance of his story was gathered by him from actors in, and eye-witnesses of, the great events he relates. The war still dragged on for a long time; the Greeks supported a rebellion against Persian rule in Egypt, and tried unsuccessfully to take Cyprus; it did not end until about 449 B.C. Then the Greek coasts of Asia Minor and the Greek cities in the Black Sea remained generally free, but Cyprus and Egypt continued under Persian rule. Herodotus, who had been born a Persian subject in the Ionian city of Halicarnassus, was five and thirty years old by that time, and he must have taken an early opportunity after this peace of visiting Babylon and Persia. He probably went to Athens, with his History ready to recite, about 438 B.C.

The idea of a great union of Greece for aggression against Persia was not altogether strange to Herodotus. Some of his readers suspect him of writing to enforce it. It was certainly in the air at that time. He describes Aristagoras, the son-in-law of Histiæus, as showing the Spartans "a tablet of bronze on which was engraved a map of the whole earth with all the seas and rivers." He makes Aristagoras say: "These Barbarians are not valiant in fight. You, on the other hand, have now attained to the utmost skill in war. They fight with bows and arrows and a short spear: they go into battle wearing trousers and having caps on their heads. You have perfected your weapons and discipline. They are easily to be conquered. Not all the other nations of the world have what they possess; gold, silver, bronze, embroidered garments, beasts and slaves; *all this you might have for yourselves, if you so desired.*"

It was a hundred years before these suggestions bore fruit.

Xerxes was murdered in his palace about 465 B.C., and thereafter Persia made no further attempts at conquest in Europe. We have no such knowledge of the things that were happening in the empire of the Great King as we have of the occurrences in the little states of Central Greece. Greece had suddenly begun to produce literature, and put itself upon record as no other nation had ever done hitherto. After 479 B.C. (Platæa) the spirit seems to have gone out of the government of the Medes and Persians. The empire of the Great King enters upon a period of decay. An Artaxerxes, a second Xerxes, a second Darius, pass across the stage; there are rebellions in Egypt and Syria; the Medes rebel; a second Artaxerxes and a second Cyrus, his brother, fight for the throne. This history is even as the history of Babylonia, Assyria, and Egypt in the older times. It is autocracy reverting to its normal state of palace crime, blood-stained magnificence, and moral squalor. But the last-named struggle produced a Greek masterpiece, for this second Cyrus collected an army of Greek mercenaries and marched into Babylonia, and was there killed at the moment of victory over Artaxerxes II. Thereupon, the Ten Thousand Greeks, left with no one to employ them, made a retreat to the coast again (401 B.C.), and this retreat was immortalized in a book, one of the first of personal war books, the *Anabasis,* by their leader Xenophon.

Murders, revolts, chastisements, disasters, cunning alliances, and base betrayals, and no Herodotus to record them. Such is the texture of Persian history. An Artaxerxes III, covered with blood, flourishes dimly for a time. "Artaxerxes III is said to have been murdered by Bagoas, who places Arses, the youngest of the king's sons, on the throne only to slay him in turn when he seemed to be contemplating independent action."[1] So it goes on.

Athens, prospering for a time after the Persian repulse, was smitten by the plague in which Pericles, its greatest ruler, died (428 B.C.). But, as a noteworthy fact amidst these confusions, the Ten Thousand of Xenophon were scattering now among the Greek cities, repeating from their own experience the declaration of Aristagoras that the Persian empire was a rich confusion which it would be very easy for resolute men to conquer.

[1] Winckler, in Helmolt's *Universal History.*

XXII

GREEK THOUGHT IN RELATION TO HUMAN SOCIETY

§ 1. *The Athens of Pericles.* § 2. *Socrates.* § 3. *Plato and the Academy.* § 4. *Aristotle and the Lyceum.* § 5. *Philosophy becomes Unworldly.* § 6. *The Quality and Limitations of Greek Thought.*

§ 1

GREEK history for the next forty years after Platæa and Mycale is a story of comparative peace and tranquillity. There were wars, but they were not intense wars. For a little while in Athens, for a section of the prosperous, there was leisure and opportunity. And by a combination of accidents and through the character of a small group of people, this leisure and opportunity produced the most memorable results. Much beautiful literature was produced; the plastic arts flourished, and the foundations of modern science, already laid by the earlier philosophers of the Ionian Greek cities, were consolidated. Then, after an interlude of fifty odd years, the long-smouldering hostility between Athens and Sparta broke out into a fierce and exhausting war, which sapped at last the vitality of this creative movement.

This war is known in history as the Peloponnesian War; it went on for nearly thirty years, and wasted all the power of Greece. At first Athens was in the ascendant, then Sparta. Then arose Thebes, a city not fifty miles from Athens, to overshadow Sparta. Once more Athens flared into importance as the head of a confederation. It is a story of narrow rivalries and inexplicable hatreds that would have vanished long ago out of the memories of men, were it not that it is recorded and reflected in a great literature.

Through all this time Persia appears and reappears as the ally first of this league and then of that. About the middle of the fourth century B.C., Greece becomes aware of a new influence in its affairs, that of Philip, King of Macedonia. Macedonia does, indeed, arise in the background of this incurably divided Greece, as the Medes and Persians arose behind the Chaldean Empire. A time comes when the Greek mind turns round, so to speak, from its disputes, and stares in one united dismay at the Macedonian.

Planless and murderous squabbles are still planless and murderous squabbles even though Thucydides tells the story, even though the great beginnings of a new civilization are wrecked by their disorders; and in this general outline we can give no space at all to the particulars of these internecine feuds, to the fights and flights that sent first this Greek city and then that up to the sky in flames. Upon a one-foot globe Greece becomes a speck almost too small to recognize; and in a short history of mankind, all this century and more of dissension between the days of Salamis and Platæa and the rise of King Philip shrinks to a little, almost inaudible clash of disputation, to a mere note upon the swift passing of opportunity for nations as for men.

But what does not shrink into insignificance, because it has entered into the intellectual process of all subsequent nations, because it is inseparably a part of our mental foundation, is the literature that Greece produced during such patches and gleams of tranquillity and security as these times afforded her.

Says Professor Gilbert Murray:[1]

"Their outer political history, indeed, like that of all other nations, is filled with war and diplomacy, with cruelty and deceit. It is the inner history, the history of thought and feeling and character, that is so grand. They had some difficulties to contend with which are now almost out of our path. They had practically no experience, but were doing everything for the first time; they were utterly weak in material resources, and their emotions, their '*desires and fears and rages,*' were probably wilder and fiercer than ours. Yet they produced the Athens of Pericles and of Plato."

This remarkable culmination of the long-gathering creative power of the Greek mind, which for three and twenty centuries has been to men of intelligence a guiding and inspiring beacon out of the past, flared up after the battles of Marathon and

[1] *Ancient Greek Literature,* by Gilbert Murray (Heinemann, 1911).

Salamis had made Athens free and fearless, and, without any great excesses of power, predominant in her world. It was the work of a quite small group of men. A number of her citizens lived for the better part of a generation under conditions which, in all ages, have disposed men to produce good and beautiful work; they were secure, they were free, and they had pride; and they were without that temptation of apparent and unchallenged power which disposes all of us to inflict wrongs upon our fellow men. When political life narrowed down again to the waste and crimes of a fratricidal war with Sparta, there was so broad and well-fed a flame of intellectual activity burning that it lasted through all the windy distresses of this war and beyond the brief lifetime of Alexander the Great, for a period altogether of more than a hundred years after the wars began.

Flushed with victory and the sense of freedom fairly won, the people of Athens did for a time rise towards nobility. Under the guidance of a great demagogue, Pericles, the chief official of the Athenian general assembly, and a politician statesman rather of the calibre of Gladstone or Lincoln in modern history, they were set to the task of rebuilding their city and expanding their commerce. For a time they were capable of following a generous leader generously, and Fate gave them a generous leader. In Pericles there was mingled in the strangest fashion political ability with a real living passion for deep and high and beautiful things. He kept in power for over thirty years. He was a man of extraordinary vigour and liberality of mind. He stamped these qualities upon his time. As Winckler has remarked, the Athenian democracy had for a time "the face of Pericles." He was sustained by what was probably a very great and noble friendship. There was a woman of unusual education, Aspasia, from Miletus, whom he could not marry because of the law that restricted the citizenship of Athens to the home-born, but who was in effect his wife. She played a large part in gathering about him men of unusual gifts. All the great writers of the time knew her, and several have praised her wisdom. Plutarch, it is true, accuses her of instigating a troublesome and dangerous but finally successful war against Samos, but, as he himself shows later, this was necessitated by the naval hostility of the Samians, which threatened the overseas trade of Athens, upon which all the prosperity of the republic depended.

Men's ambitions are apt to reflect the standards of their intimates. Pericles was content, at any rate, to serve as a leader in Athens rather than to dominate as a tyrant. Alliances were formed under his guidance, new colonies and trading stations were established from Italy to the Black Sea; and the treasures of the league at Delos were brought to Athens. Convinced of his security from Persia, Pericles spent the war hoard of the allies upon the beautification of his city. This was an unrighteous thing to do by our modern standards, but it was not a base or greedy thing to do. Athens had accomplished the work of the Delian League, and is not the labourer worthy of his hire? This sequestration made a time of exceptional opportunity for architects and artists. The Parthenon of Athens, whose ruins are still a thing of beauty, was but the crown set upon the clustering glories of the Athens Pericles rebuilt. Such sculptures as those of Phidias, Myron, and Polyclitus that still survive, witness to the artistic quality of the time.

The reader must bear in mind that illuminating remark of Winckler's, which says that this renascent Athens bore for a time the face of Pericles. It was the peculiar genius of this man and of his atmosphere that let loose the genius of men about him, and attracted men of great intellectual vigour to Athens. Athens wore his face for a time as one wears a mask, and then became restless and desired to put him aside. There was very little that was great and generous about the common Athenian. We have told of the spirit of one sample voter for the ostracism of Aristides, and Lloyd (in his *Age of Pericles*) declares that the Athenians would not suffer the name of Miltiades to be mentioned in connection with the battle of Marathon. The sturdy self-respect of the common voters revolted presently against the beautiful buildings rising about them; against the favours shown to such sculptors as Phidias over popular worthies in the same line of business; against the donations made to a mere foreigner like Herodotus of Halicarnassus; against the insulting preference of Pericles for the company and conversation of a Milesian woman. The public life of Pericles was conspicuously orderly, and that presently set the man in the street thinking that his private life must be very corrupt. One gathers that Pericles was "superior" in his demeanour; he betrayed at times a contempt for the citizens he served.

"Pericles acquired not only an elevation of sentiment, and a loftiness and purity of style far removed from the low expression of the vulgar, but likewise a gravity of countenance which relaxed not into laughter, a firm and even tone of voice, an easy deportment, and a decency of dress which no vehemence of speaking ever put into disorder. These things, and others of a like nature, excited admiration in all that saw him. Such was his conduct, when a vile and abandoned fellow loaded him a whole day with reproaches and abuse; he bore it with patience and silence, and continued in public for the despatch of some urgent affairs. In the evening he walked softly home, this impudent wretch following, and insulting him all the way with the most scurrilous language. And as it was dark when he came to his own door, he ordered one of his servants to take a torch and light the man home. The poet Ion, however, says he was proud and supercilious in conversation, and that there was a great deal of vanity and contempt of others mixed with his dignity of manner. . . . He appeared not in the streets except when he went to the forum or the senate house. He declined the invitations of his friends, and all social entertainments and recreations; insomuch that in the whole time of his administration, which was a considerable length, he never went to sup with any of his friends but once, which was at the marriage of his nephew Euryptolemus, and he stayed there only until the ceremony of libation was ended. He considered that the freedom of entertainments takes away all distinction of office, and that dignity is but little consistent with familiarity. . . ."[1]

There was as yet no gutter journalism to tell the world of the vileness of the conspicuous and successful; but the common man, a little out of conceit with himself, found much consolation in the art of comedy, which flourished exceedingly. The writers of comedy satisfied that almost universal craving for the depreciation of those whose apparent excellence offends our self-love. They threw dirt steadily and industriously at Pericles and his friends. Pericles was portrayed in a helmet; a helmet became him, and it is to be feared he knew as much. This led to much joy and mirth over the pleasant suggestion

[1] *Plutarch.*

of a frightfully distorted head, an onion head. The "goings on" of Aspasia were of course a fruitful vineyard for the inventions of the street. . . .

Dreaming souls, weary of the vulgarities of our time, have desired to be transferred to the sublime Age of Pericles. But, plumped down into that Athens, they would have found themselves in very much the atmosphere of the lower sort of contemporary music-hall, very much in the vein of our popular newspapers; the same hot blast of braying libel, foul imputation, greedy "patriotism," and general baseness would have blown upon them, the "modern note" would have pursued them. As the memories of Platæa and Salamis faded and the new buildings grew familiar, Pericles and the pride of Athens became more and more offensive to the homely humour of the crowd. He was never ostracized—his prestige with the quieter citizens saved him from that; but he was attacked with increasing boldness and steadfastness. He lived and died a poor man; he was perhaps the most honest of demagogues; but this did not save him from an abortive prosecution for peculation. Defeated in that, his enemies resorted to a more devious method; they began to lop away his friends.

Athene of the Parthenon.

Religious intolerance and moral accusations are the natural weapons of the envious against the leaders of men. His friend Damon was ostracized. Phidias was attacked for impiety. On the shield of the great statue of the goddess Athene, Phidias had dared to put, among the combatants in a fight between Greeks and Amazons, portraits of Pericles and himself. Phidias died in prison. Anaxagoras, a stranger welcomed to Athens by Pericles—when there were plenty of honest fellows already there quite willing to satisfy any reasonable curiosities—was saying the strangest things about the sun and stars, and hinting not obscurely that there were no gods, but only one animating spirit (*nous*) in the world.[1] The comedy writers suddenly found they had deep religious feelings that could be profoundly and even dangerously shocked, and Anaxagoras fled the threat of a prosecution. Then came the turn of Aspasia. Athens seemed bent upon deporting her, and Pericles was torn between the woman who was the soul of his life and the ungracious city he had saved, defended, and made more beautiful and unforgettable than any other city in history. He stood up to defend Aspasia, he was seized by a storm of very human emotion, and as he spoke he wept—a gleeful thing for the rabble. His tears saved Aspasia for a time.

The Athenians were content to humiliate Pericles, but he had served them so long that they were indisposed to do without him. He had been their leader now for a third of a century.

In 431 B.C. came the war with Sparta. Plutarch accuses Pericles of bringing it on, because he felt his popularity waned so fast that a war was needed to make him indispensable.

"And as he himself was become obnoxious to the people upon Phidias's account, and was afraid of being called in question for it, he urged on the war, which as yet was uncertain, and blew up that flame which till then was stifled and suppressed. By this means he hoped to obviate the accusations that threatened him, and to mitigate the rage of envy, because such was his dignity and power, that in all important affairs, and in every great danger, the republic could place its confidence in him alone."

But the war was a slow and dangerous war, and the Athenian people were impatient. A certain Cleon arose, ambitious to oust Pericles from his leadership. There was a great clamour for a swift ending of the war. Cleon set out to be "the man who won the war." The popular poets got to work in this fashion:

> "Thou king of satyrs . . . why boast thy prowess,
> Yet shudder at the sound of sharpened swords,
> Spite of the flaming Cleon?"

An expedition under the leadership of Pericles was unsuccessful, and Cleon seized the opportunity for a prosecution.

[1] For an account of his views, see Burnet's *Early Greek Philosophy*. Gomperz' *Greek Thinkers* is also a good book for this section.

Pericles was suspended from his command and fined. The story goes that his oldest son—this was not the son of Aspasia, but of a former wife—turned against him, and pursued him with vile and incredible accusations. This young man was carried off by the plague. Then the sister of Pericles died, and then his last legitimate son. When, after the fashion of the time, he put the funeral garlands on the boy he wept aloud. Presently he himself took the contagion and died (428 B.C.).

The salient facts of this brief summary will serve to show how discordant Pericles was with much of the life of his city. This intellectual and artistic outbreak in Athens was no doubt favoured by the conditions of the time, but it was also due in part to the appearance of some very unusual men. It was not a general movement; it was the movement of a small group of people exceptionally placed and gifted.

§ 2

Another leading figure in this Athenian movement, a figure still more out of harmony with the life around him, and quite as much an original source and stimulant of the enduring greatness of his age, was a man called Socrates, a son of a stonemason. He was born about sixteen years later than Herodotus, and he was beginning to be heard of about the time when Pericles died. He himself wrote nothing, but it was his custom to talk in public places. There was in those days a great searching for wisdom going on; there was a various multitude of teachers called sophists who reasoned upon truth, beauty, and right living, and instructed the developing curiosities and imaginations of youth. This was so because there were no great priestly schools in Greece. And into these discussions this man came, a clumsy and slovenly figure, barefooted, gathering about him a band of admirers and disciples.

His method was profoundly sceptical; he believed that the only possible virtue was true knowledge; he would tolerate no belief, no hope that could not pass the ultimate acid test. For himself this meant virtue, but for many of his weaker followers it meant the loss of beliefs and moral habits that would have restrained their impulses. These weaklings became self-excusing, self-indulging scoundrels. Among his young associates were Plato, who afterwards immortalized his method in a series of philosophical dialogues, and founded the philosophical school of the Academy, which lasted nine hundred years, Xenophon, of the Ten Thousand, who described his death, and Isocrates, one of the wisest of Greek political thinkers; but there were also Critias, who, when Athens was utterly defeated by Sparta, was leader among the Thirty Tyrants appointed by the Spartans to keep the crushed city under;[1] Charmides, who was killed beside Critias when the Thirty were overthrown; and Alcibiades, a brilliant and complex traitor, who did much to lead Athens into the disastrous expedition against Syracuse which destroyed her strength, who betrayed her to the Spartans, and who was at last assassinated while on his way to the Persian court to contrive mischief against Greece. These latter pupils were not the only young men of promise whose vulgar faith and patriotism Socrates destroyed, to leave nothing in its place. His most inveterate enemy was a certain Anytus, whose son, a devoted disciple of Socrates, had become a hopeless drunkard. Through Anytus it was that Socrates was at last prosecuted for "corrupting" the youth of Athens, and condemned to death by drinking a poisonous draught made from hemlock (399 B.C.).

His death is described with great beauty in the dialogue of Plato called by the name of *Phædo*.

§ 3

Plato was born 427 B.C., and he lived for eighty years.

In mental temperament Plato was of an altogether different

[1] "But it was not only against the lives, properties, and liberties of Athenian citizens that the Thirty made war. They were not less solicitous to extinguish the intellectual force and education of the city, a project so perfectly in harmony both with the sentiment and practice of Sparta, that they counted on the support of their foreign allies. Among the ordinances which they promulgated was one, expressly forbidding any one 'to teach the art of words.' The edict of the Thirty was, in fact, a general suppression of the higher class of teachers or professors, above the rank of the elementary (teacher of letters or) grammatist. If such an edict could have been maintained in force for a generation, combined with the other mandates of the Thirty—the city out of which Sophocles and Euripides had just died, and in which Plato and Isocrates were in vigorous age, would have been degraded to the intellectual level of the meanest community in Greece. It was not uncommon for a Grecian despot to suppress all those assemblies wherein youths came together for the purpose of common training, either intellectual or gymnastic, as well as the public banquets and clubs or associations, as being dangerous to his authority, tending to elevation of courage, and to a consciousness of political rights among the citizens."—Grote's *History of Greece*.

type from Socrates. He was a most artistic and delicate writer, and Socrates could write nothing consecutive. He cared for beautiful things and Socrates despised them. He was supremely concerned with the ordering of public affairs and the scheming of happier human relationships, while Socrates, heedless of heat and cold and the opinion of his fellow creatures, concentrated his mind upon a serene disillusionment. Life, said Socrates, was deception; only the Soul lived. Plato had a very great affection for this rugged old teacher, he found his method of the utmost value in disentangling and cleaning up opinions, and he made him the central figure of his immortal dialogues; but his own thoughts and disposition turned him altogether away from the sceptical attitude. In many of the dialogues the voice is the voice of Socrates, but the thought is the thought of Plato.

Plato was living in a time of doubt and questioning about all human relationships. In the great days of Pericles, before 450 B.C., there seems to have been a complete satisfaction in Athens with social and political institutions. Then there seemed no reason for questioning. Men felt free; the community prospered; one suffered chiefly from jealousy. The History of Herodotus displays little or no dissatisfaction with Athenian political institutions.

But Plato, who was born about the time Herodotus died, and who grew up in the atmosphere of a disastrous war and great social distress and confusion, was from the first face to face with human discord and the misfit of human institutions. To that challenge his mind responded. One of his earlier works and his latest are bold and penetrating discussions of the possible betterment of social relations. Socrates had taught him to take nothing for granted, not even the common relations of husband and wife or parent and child. His *Republic*, the first of all Utopian books, is a young man's dream of a city in which human life is arranged according to a novel and a better plan; his last unfinished work, the *Laws*, is a discussion of the regulation of another such Utopia. There is much in Plato at which we cannot even glance here, but it is a landmark in this history, it is a new thing in the development of mankind, this appearance of the idea of wilfully and completely recasting human conditions. So far mankind has been living by tradition under the fear of the gods. Here is a man who says boldly to our race, and as if it were a quite reasonable and natural thing to say, "Take hold of your lives. Most of these things that distress you, you can avoid; most of these things that dominate you, you can overthrow. You can do as you will with them."

One other thing besides the conflicts of the time perhaps stimulated the mind of Plato in this direction. In the days of Pericles Athens had founded many settlements overseas, and the setting up of these settlements had familiarized men with the idea that a community need not grow, it could also be made.

Closely associated with Plato was a younger man, who later also maintained a school in Athens and lived to an even greater age. This was Isocrates. He was what we should call a publicist, a writer rather than an orator, and his peculiar work was to develop the idea of Herodotus, the idea of a unification of Greece against the Persian Empire, as a remedy for the baseness and confusion of her politics and the waste and destruction of her internecine wars. His political horizon was in some respects broader than Plato's, and in his later years he looked towards monarchy, and particularly towards the Macedonian monarchy of Philip, as a more unifying and broadening method of government than city democracy. The same drift to monarchist ideas had occurred in the case of that Xenophon whose *Anabasis* we have already mentioned. In his old age Xenophon wrote the *Cyropædia,* a "vindication both theoretically and practically of absolute monarchy as shown in the organization of the Persian Empire."[1]

§ 4

Plato taught in the Academy. To him in his old age came a certain good-looking youngster from Stagira in Macedonia, Aristotle, who was the son of the Macedonian king's physician, and a man with a very different type of mind from that of the great Athenian. He was naturally sceptical of the imaginative will, and with a great respect for and comprehension of established fact. Later on, after Plato was dead, he set up a school at the Lyceum in Athens and taught, criticizing Plato and Socrates with a certain hardness. When he taught, the shadow of Alexander the Great lay across the freedom of

[1] Mahaffy.

Greece, and he favoured slavery and constitutional kings. He had previously been the tutor of Alexander for several years at the court of Philip of Macedon. Intelligent men were losing heart in those days, their faith in the power of men to make their own conditions of life was fading. There were no more Utopias. The rush of events was manifestly too powerful for such organized effort as was then practicable between men of fine intelligence. It was possible to think of recasting human society when human society was a little city of a few thousand citizens, but what was happening about them was something cataclysmal; it was the political recasting of the whole known world, of the affairs of what even then must have amounted to something between fifty and a hundred million people. It was recasting upon a scale no human mind was yet equipped to grasp. It drove thought back upon the idea of a vast and implacable Fate. It made men snatch at whatever looked stable and unifying. Monarchy, for instance, for all its manifest vices, was a conceivable government for millions; it had, to a certain extent, *worked;* it imposed a ruling will where it would seem that a collective will was impossible. This change of the general intellectual mood harmonized with Aristotle's natural respect for existing fact. If, on the one hand, it made him approve of monarchy and slavery and the subjection of women as reasonable institutions, on the other hand it made him eager to understand fact and to get some orderly knowledge of these realities of nature and human nature that were now so manifestly triumphant over the creative dreams of the preceding generation. He is terribly sane and luminous, and terribly wanting in self-sacrificial enthusiasm. He questions Plato when Plato would exile poets from his Utopia, for poetry is a power; he directs his energy along a line diametrically opposed to Socrates' depreciation of Anaxagoras. He anticipates Bacon and the modern scientific movement in his realization of the importance of ordered knowledge. He set himself to the task of gathering together and setting down knowledge. He was the first natural historian. Other men before him had speculated about the nature of things, but he, with every young man he could win over to the task, set himself to classify and compare things. Plato says in effect: "Let us take hold of life and remodel it"; this soberer successor: "Let us first know more of life and meanwhile serve the king."

It was not so much a contradiction as an immense qualification of the master.

The peculiar relation of Aristotle to Alexander the Great enabled him to procure means for his work such as were not available again for scientific inquiry for long ages. He could command hundreds of talents (a talent = about £240) for his expenses. At one time he had at his disposal a thousand men scattered throughout Asia and Greece, collecting matter for his natural history. They were, of course, very untrained observers, collectors of stories rather than observers; but nothing of the kind had ever been attempted, had even been thought of, so far as we know, before his time. Political as well as natural science began. The students of the Lyceum under his direction made an analysis of 158 political constitutions. . . .

This was the first gleam of organized science in the world. The early death of Alexander and the breaking up of his empire almost before it had begun, put an end to endowments on this scale for 2,000 years. Only in Egypt at the Alexandria Museum did any scientific research continue, and that only for a few generations. Of that we will presently tell. Fifty years after Aristotle's death the Lyceum had already dwindled to insignificance.

§ 5

The general drift of thought in the concluding years of the fourth century B.C. was not with Aristotle, nor towards the laborious and necessary accumulation of ordered knowledge. It is possible that without his endowments from the king he would have made but a small figure in intellectual history. Through them he was able to give his splendid intelligence substance and effect. The ordinary man prefers easy ways so long as they may be followed, and is almost wilfully heedless whether they end at last in a cul-de-sac. Finding the stream of events too powerful to control at once, the generality of philosophical teachers drifted in those days from the scheming of model cities and the planning of new ways of living into the elaboration of beautiful and consoling systems of evasion.

Perhaps that is putting things coarsely and unjustly. But let Professor Gilbert Murray speak upon this matter.[1]

[1] *Ancient Greek Literature.*

"The Cynics cared only for virtue and the relation of the soul to God; the world and its learning and its honours were as dross to them. The Stoics and Epicureans, so far apart at first sight were very similar in their ultimate aim. What they really cared about was ethics—the practical question how a man should order his life. Both, indeed, gave themselves to some science—the Epicureans to physics, the Stoics to logic and rhetoric—but only as a means to an end. The Stoic tried to win men's hearts and convictions by sheer subtlety of abstract argument and dazzling sublimity of thought and expression. The Epicurean was determined to make Humanity go its way without cringing to capricious gods and without sacrificing Free-Will. He condensed his gospel into four maxims: "God is not to be feared; Death cannot be felt; the Good can be won: all that we dread can be borne and conquered.""

And meanwhile the stream of events flowed on, with a reciprocal indifference to philosophy.

§ 6

If the Greek classics are to be read with any benefit by modern men, they must be read as the work of men like ourselves. Regard must be had to their traditions, their opportunities, and their limitations. There is a disposition to exaggeration in all human admiration; most of our classical texts are very much mangled, and all were originally the work of human beings in difficulties, living in a time of such darkness and narrowness of outlook as makes our own age by comparison a period of dazzling illumination. What we shall lose in reverence by this familiar treatment, we shall gain in sympathy for that group of troubled, uncertain, and very modern minds. The Athenian writers were, indeed, the first of modern men. They were discussing questions that we still discuss; they began to struggle with the great problems that confront us to-day. Their writings are our dawn.[1]

[1] Jung in his *Psychology of the Unconscious* is very good in his Chapter I on the differences between ancient (pre-Athenian) thought and modern thought. The former he calls Undirected Thinking, the latter Directed Thinking. The former was a thinking in images, akin to dreaming; the latter a thinking in words. Science is an organization of directed thinking. The Antique spirit (before the Greek thinkers *i.e.*) created not science but mythology. The ancient human world was a world of subjective fantasies like the world of children and uneducated young people to-day,

They began an inquiry, and they arrived at no solutions. We cannot pretend to-day that we have arrived at solutions to most of the questions they asked. The mind of the Hebrews, as we have already shown, awoke suddenly to the endless miseries and disorders of life, saw that these miseries and disorders were largely due to the lawless acts of men, and concluded that salvation could come only through subduing ourselves to the service of the one God who rules heaven and earth. The Greek, rising to the same perception, was not prepared with the same idea of a patriarchal deity; he lived in a world in which there was not God but the gods; if perhaps he felt that the gods themselves were limited, then he thought of Fate behind them, cold and impersonal. So he put his problem in the form of an inquiry as to what was right living, without any definite correlation of the right-living man with the will of God. . . . To us, looking at the matter from a standpoint purely historical, the common problem can now be presented in a form that, for the purposes of history, covers both the Hebrew and Greek way of putting it. We have seen our kind rising out of the unconsciousness of animals to a continuing racial self-consciousness, realizing the unhappiness of its wild diversity of aims, realizing the inevitable tragedy of individual self-seeking, and feeling its way blindly towards some linking and subordinating idea to save it from the pains and accidents of mere individuality. The gods, the god-king, the idea of the tribe, the idea of the city; here are ideas that have claimed and held for a time the devotion of men, ideas in which they have a little lost their individual selfishness and escaped to the realization of a more enduring life. Yet, as our wars and disasters prove, none of these greater ideas have yet been great enough. The gods have failed to protect, the tribe has proved itself vile and cruel, the city ostracized one's best and truest friends, the god-king made a beast of himself. . . .

As we read over the speculative literature of this great period

and like the world of savages and dreams. Infantile thought and dreams re a re-echo of prehistoric and savage methods of thinking. Myths, ays Jung, are the mass dreams of peoples, and dreams the myths of individuals. We have already directed the reader's attention to the resemblance of the early gods of civilization to the fantasies of children. The work of hard and disciplined thinking by means of carefully analyzed vords and statements which was begun by the Greek thinkers and reumed by the scholastic philosophers of whom we shall tell in the middle ges, was a necessary preliminary to the development of modern science.

of the Greeks, we realize three barriers set about the Greek mind, from which it rarely escaped, but from which we now perhaps are beginning to escape.

The first of these limitations was the obsession of the Greek mind by the idea of the city as the ultimate state. In a world in which empire had followed empire, each greater than its predecessor, in a world through which men and ideas drove ever more loosely and freely, in a world visibly unifying even then, the Greeks, because of their peculiar physical and political circumstances, were still dreaming impossibly of a compact little city state, impervious to outer influences, valiantly secure against the whole world. Plato's estimate of the number of citizens in a perfect state varied between 1,000 (the *Republic*) and 5,040 (the *Laws*) citizens.[1] This state was to go to war and hold its own against other cities of the same size. And this was not a couple of generations after the hosts of Xerxes had crossed the Hellespont!

Perhaps these Greeks thought the day of world empires had passed for ever, whereas it was only beginning. At the utmost their minds reached out to alliances and leagues. There must have been men at the court of Artaxerxes thinking far away beyond these little ideas of the rocky creek, the island, and the mountain-encircled valley. But the need for unification against the greater powers that moved outside the Greek-speaking world, the Greek mind disregarded wilfully. These outsiders were barbarians, not to be needlessly thought about; they were barred out now from Greece for ever. One took Persian money; everybody took Persian money; what did it matter? Or one enlisted for a time in their armies (as Xenophon did) and hoped for his luck with a rich prisoner. Athens took sides in Egyptian affairs, and carried on minor wars with Persia, but there was no conception of a common policy or a common future for Greece. . . . Until at last a voice in Athens began to shout "Macedonia!" to clamour like a watch-dog, "Macedonia!" This was the voice of the orator and demagogue, Demosthenes, hurling warnings and threats and denunciations at King Philip

[1] "For the proper administration of justice and for the distribution of authority it is necessary that the citizens be acquainted with each other's characters, so that, where this cannot be, much mischief ensues, both in the use of authority and in the administration of justice; for it is not just to decide arbitrarily, as must be the case with excessive population." Aristotle: *Politics.*

of Macedon, who had learnt his politics not only from Plato and Aristotle, but also from Isocrates and Xenophon, and from Babylon and Susa, and who was preparing quietly, ably, and steadfastly to dominate all Greece, and through Greece to conquer the known world. . . .

There was a second thing that cramped the Greek mind, the institution of domestic slavery. Slavery was implicit in Greek life; men could conceive of neither comfort nor dignity without it. But slavery shuts off one's sympathy not only from a class of one's fellow subjects; it puts the slave-owner into a class and organization against all stranger men. One is of an elect tribe. Plato, carried by his clear reason and the noble sanity of his spirit beyond the things of the present, would have abolished slavery; much popular feeling and the New Comedy were against it; the Stoics and Epicureans, many of whom were slaves, condemned it as unnatural, but finding it too strong to upset, decided that it did not affect the soul and might be ignored. With the wise there was no bound or free. To the matter-of-fact Aristotle, and probably to most practical men, its abolition was inconceivable. So they declared that there were in the world men "naturally slaves." . . .

Finally, the thought of the Greeks was hampered by a want of knowledge that is almost inconceivable to us to-day. They had no knowledge of the past of mankind at all; at best they had a few shrewd guesses. They had no knowledge of geography beyond the range of the Mediterranean basin and the frontiers of Persia. We know far more to-day of what was going on in Susa, Persepolis, Babylon, and Memphis in the time of Pericles than he did. Their astronomical ideas were still in the state of rudimentary speculations. Anaxagoras, greatly daring, thought the sun and moon were vast globes, so vast that the sun was probably "as big as all the Peloponnesus." Their ideas in physics and chemistry were the results of profound cogitation; it is wonderful that they did guess at atomic structure. One has to remember their extraordinary poverty in the matter of experimental apparatus. They had coloured glass for ornament, but no white glass; no accurate means of measuring the minor intervals of time, no really efficient numerical notation, no very accurate scales, no rudiments of telescope or microscope. A modern scientific man dumped down in the Athens of Pericles would have found the utmost difficulty in demonstrating the elements of his knowledge, however crudely, to the men he would have found there. He would have had to rig up the simplest apparatus under every disadvantage, while Socrates pointed out the absurdity of seeking Truth with pieces of wood and string and metal such as small boys use for fishing. And our professor of science would also have been in constant danger of a prosecution for impiety.

Our world to-day draws upon relatively immense accumulations of knowledge of fact. In the age of Pericles scarcely the first stone of our comparatively tremendous cairn of things recorded and proved had been put in place. When we reflect upon this difference, then it ceases to be remarkable that the Greeks, with all their aptitude for political speculation, were blind to the insecurities of their civilization from without and from within, to the necessity for effective unification, to the swift rush of events that was to end for long ages these first brief freedoms of the human mind.

It is not in the results it achieved, but in the attempts it made, that the true value for us of this group of Greek talkers and writers lies. It is not that they answered questions, but that they dared to ask them. Never before had man challenged his world and the way of life to which he found his birth had brought him. Never had he said before that he could alter his conditions. Tradition and a seeming necessity had held him to life as he had found it grown up about his tribe since time immemorial. Hitherto he had taken the world as children still take the homes and habits in which they have been reared.

So in the fifth and fourth centuries B.C. we perceive, most plainly in Judea and in Athens, but by no means confined to those centres, the beginnings of a moral and an intellectual process in mankind, an appeal to righteousness and an appeal to the truth from the passions and confusions and immediate appearances of existence. It is like the dawn of the sense of responsibility in a youth, who suddenly discovers that life is neither easy nor aimless. Mankind is growing up. The rest of history for three and twenty centuries is threaded with the spreading out and development and interaction and the clearer and more effective statement of these main leading ideas. Slowly more and more men apprehend the reality of human brotherhood, the needlessness of wars and cruelties and oppression, the possibilities of a common purpose for the whole of our kind. In every generation thereafter there is the evidence of men seeking for that better order to which they feel our world must come. But everywhere and wherever in any man the great constructive ideas have taken hold, the hot greeds, the jealousies, the suspicions and impatience that are in the nature of every one of us, war against the struggle towards greater and broader purposes. The last twenty-three centuries of history are like the efforts of some impulsive, hasty immortal to think clearly and live rightly. Blunder follows blunder; promising beginnings end in grotesque disappointments; streams of living water are poisoned by the cup that conveys them to the thirsty lips of mankind. But the hope of men rises again at last after every disaster. . . .

We pass on now to the story of one futile commencement, one glorious shattered beginning of human unity. There was in Alexander the Great knowledge and imagination, power and opportunity, folly, egotism, detestable vulgarity, and an immense promise broken by the accident of his early death while men were still dazzled by its immensity.

XXIII

THE CAREER OF ALEXANDER THE GREAT

§ 1

THE true hero of the story of Alexander is not so much Alexander as his father Philip. The author of a piece does not shine in the limelight as the actor does, and it was Philip who planned much of the greatness that his son achieved, who laid the foundations and forged the tools, who had indeed already begun the Persian expedition at the time of his death. Philip, beyond doubting, was one of the greatest monarchs the world has ever seen; he was a man of the utmost intelligence and ability, and his range of ideas was vastly beyond the scope of his time. He made Aristotle his friend; he must have discussed with him those schemes for the organization of real knowledge which the philosopher was to realize later through Alexander's endowments. Philip, so far as we can judge, seems to have been Aristotle's "Prince"; to him Aristotle turned as men turn only to those whom they admire and trust. To Philip also Isocrates appealed as the great leader who should unify and ennoble the chaotic public life of Greece.

In many books it is stated that Philip was a man of incredible cynicism and of uncontrolled lusts. It is true that at feasts, like all the Macedonians of his time, he was a hard drinker and sometimes drunken—it was probably considered unamiable not to drink excessively at feasts; but of the other accusations there is no real proof, and for evidence we have only the railings of such antagonists as Demosthenes, the Athenian demagogue and orator, a man of reckless rhetoric.

The quotation of a phrase or so will serve to show to what the patriotic anger of Demosthenes could bring him. In one of the *Philippics,* as his denunciations of Philip are called, he gives vent in this style:

"Philip—a man who not only is no Greek, and no way akin to the Greeks, but is not even a barbarian from a respectable country—no, a pestilent fellow of Macedon, a country from which we never get even a decent slave." And so on and so on. We know, as a matter of fact, that the Macedonians were an Aryan people very closely akin to the Greeks, and that Philip was probably the best educated man of his time. This was the spirit in which the adverse accounts of Philip were written.

Philip of Macedon

When Philip became king of Macedonia in 359 B.C., his country was a little country without a seaport or industries or any considerable city. It had a peasant population, Greek almost in language and ready to be Greek in sympathies, but more purely Nordic in blood than any people to the south of it. Philip made this little barbaric state into a great one; he created the most efficient military organization the world had so far seen, and he had brought most of Greece into one confederacy under his leadership at the time of his death. And his extraordinary quality, his power of thinking out beyond the current ideas of his time, is shown not so much in those matters as in the care with which he had his son trained to carry on the policy he had created. He is one of the few monarchs in history who cared for his successor. Alexander was, as few other monarchs have ever been, a specially educated king; he was educated for empire. Aristotle was but one of the several able tutors his father chose for him. Philip confided his policy to him, and entrusted him wth commands and authority by the time he was sixteen. He commanded the cavalry at Chæronea under his father's eye. He was nursed into power —generously and unsuspiciously.

To any one who reads his life with care it is evident that Alexander started with an equipment of training and ideas of unprecedented value. As he got beyond the wisdom of his upbringing he began to blunder and misbehave—sometimes with a dreadful folly. The defects of his character had triumphed over his upbringing long before he died.

Philip was a king after the old pattern, a leader-king, first among his peers, of the ancient Nordic Aryan type. The army he found in Macedonia consisted of a general foot levy and a noble equestrian order called the "companions." The people were farmers and hunters and somewhat drunken in their habits, but ready for discipline and good fighting stuff. And if the people were homely, the government was intelligent and alert. For some generations the court language had been Attic (= Athenian) Greek, and the court had been sufficiently civilized to shelter and entertain such great figures as Euripides, who died there in 406 B.C., and Zeuxis the artist. Moreover, Philip, before his accession, had spent some years as a hostage in Greece. He had had as good an education as Greece could give at that time. He was, therefore, quite familiar with what we may call the idea of Isocrates—the idea of a great union of the Greek states in Europe to dominate the Eastern world; and he knew, too, how incapable was the Athenian democracy, because of its constitution and tradition, of taking the opportunity that lay before it. For it was an opportunity that would have to be shared. To the Athenians or the Spartans it would mean letting in a "lot of foreigners" to the advantages of citizenship. It would mean lowering themselves to the level of equality and fellowship with Macedonians—a people from whom "*we*" do not get "even a decent slave."

There was no way to secure unanimity among the Greeks for the contemplated enterprise except by some revolutionary political action. It was no love of peace that kept the Greeks from such an adventure; it was their political divisions. The resources of the several states were exhausted in a series of internecine wars—wars arising out of the merest excuses and fanned by oratorical wind. The ploughing of certain sacred lands near Delphi by the Phocians was, for example, the pretext for a sanguinary Sacred War.

Philip's first years of kingship were devoted to the discipline of his army. Hitherto most of the main battle fighting in the

world had been done by footmen in formation. In the very ancient Sumerian battle-pieces we see spearmen in close order forming the main battle, just as they did in the Zulu armies of the nineteenth century; the Greek troops of Philip's time were still fighting in that same style; the Theban phalanx was a mass of infantry holding spears, the hinder ranks thrusting their longer spears between the front-line men. Such a formation went through anything less disciplined that opposed it.

Mounted archers could, of course, inflict considerable losses on such a mass of men, and accordingly, as the horse came into warfare, horsemen appeared on either side as an accessory to this main battle. The reader must remember that the horse did not come into very effective use in western war until the rise of the Assyrians, and then at first only as a chariot horse. The chariots drove full tilt at the infantry mass and tried to break it. Unless its discipline was very solid they succeeded. The Homeric fighting is chariot fighting. It is not until the last thousand years B.C. that we begin to find mounted soldiers, as distinct from charioteers, playing a part in warfare. At first they appear to have fought in a scattered fashion, each man doing his personal feats. So the Lydians fought against Cyrus. It was Philip who seems to have created charging cavalry. He caused his "companions" to drill for a massed charge. And also he strengthened his phalanx by giving the rear men longer spears than had been used hitherto, and so deepening its mass. The Macedonian phalanx was merely a more solid version of the Theban phalanx. None of these massed infantry formations was flexible enough to stand a flank or rear attack. They had very slight manœuvring power. Both Philip's and his son's victories followed, therefore, with variations, one general scheme of co-operation between these two arms. The phalanx advanced in the centre and held the enemy's main body; on one wing or the other the cavalry charges swept away the enemy cavalry, and then swooped round upon the flank and rear of the enemy phalanx, the front of which the Macedonian phalanx was already smiting. The enemy main battle then broke and was massacred. As Alexander's military experience grew, he also added a use of catapults in the field, big stone-throwing affairs, to break up the enemy infantry. Before his time catapults had been used in sieges, but never in battles. He invented "artillery preparation."

With the weapon of his new army in his hand, Philip first turned his attention to the north of Macedonia. He carried expeditions into Illyria and as far as the Danube; he also spread his power along the coast as far as the Hellespont. He secured possession of a port, Amphipolis, and certain gold mines adjacent. After several Thracian expeditions he turned southward in good earnest. He took up the cause of the Delphic amphictyony against those sacrilegious Phocians, and so appeared as the champion of Hellenic religion.

There was a strong party of Greeks, it must be understood, a Pan-Hellenic party, in favour of the Greek headship of Philip. The chief writer of this Pan-Hellenic movement was Isocrates. Athens, on the other hand, was the head and front of the opposition to Philip, and Athens was in open sympathy with Persia, even sending emissaries to the Great King to warn him of the danger to him of a united Greece. The comings and goings of twelve years cannot be related here. In 338 B.C. the long struggle between division and pan-Hellenism came to a decisive issue, and at the battle of Chæronea Philip inflicted a crushing defeat upon Athens and her allies. He gave Athens peace upon astonishingly generous terms; he displayed himself steadfastly resolved to propitiate and favour that implacable city; and in 338 B.C. a congress of Greek states recognized him as captain-general for the war against Persia.

He was now a man of forty-seven. It seemed as though the world lay at his feet. He had made his little country into the leading state in a great Græco-Macedonian confederacy. That unification was to be the prelude to a still greater one, the unification of the Western world with the Persian empire into one world state of all known peoples. Who can doubt he had that dream? The writings of Isocrates convince us that he had it. Who can deny that he might have realized it? He had a reasonable hope of living for perhaps another quarter century of activity. In 336 B.C. his advanced guard crossed into Asia. . . .

But he never followed with his main force. He was assassinated.

§ 2

It is necessary now to tell something of the domestic life of King Philip. The lives of both Philip and his son were pervaded by the personality of a restless and evil woman, Olympias, the mother of Alexander.

She was the daughter of the king of Epirus, a country to the west of Macedonia, and, like Macedonia, a semi-Greek land. She met Philip, or was thrown in his way, at some religious gathering in Samothrace. Plutarch declares the marriage was a love-match, and there seems to be at least this much in the charges against Philip that, like many energetic and imaginative men, he was prone to impatient love impulses. He married her when he was already a king, and Alexander was born to him three years later.

It was not long before Olympias and Philip were bitterly estranged. She was jealous of him, but there was another and graver source of trouble in her passion for religious mysteries. We have already noted that beneath the fine and restrained Nordic religion of the Greeks the land abounded with religious cults of a darker and more ancient kind, aboriginal cults with secret initiations, orgiastic celebrations, and often with cruel and obscene rites. These religions of the shadows, these practices of the women and peasants and slaves, gave Greece her Orphic, Dionysic, and Demeter cults; they have lurked in the tradition of Europe down almost to our own times. The witchcraft of the Middle Ages, with its resort to the blood of babes, scraps of executed criminals, incantations and magic circles, seems to have been little else than the lingering vestiges of these solemnities of the dark whites. In these matters Olympias was an expert and an enthusiast, and Plutarch mentions that she achieved considerable celebrity by use of tame serpents in these pious exercises. The snakes invaded her domestic apartments, and history is not clear whether Philip found in them matter for exasperation or religious awe. These occupations of his wife must have been a serious inconvenience to Philip, for the Macedonian people were still in that sturdy stage of social development in which neither enthusiastic religiosity nor uncontrollable wives are admired.

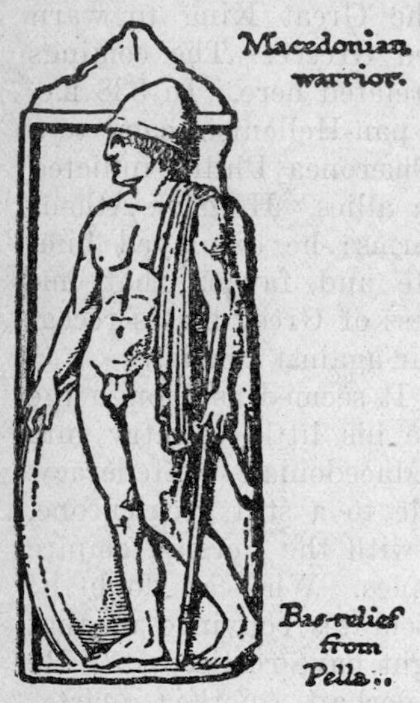
Macedonian warrior. Bas-relief from Pella.

The evidence of a bitter hostility between mother and father peeps out in many little things in the histories. She was evidently jealous of Philip's conquests; she hated his fame. There are many signs that Olympias did her best to set her son against his father and attach him wholly to herself. A story survives (in Plutarch's *Life*) that "whenever news was brought of Philip's victories, the capture of a city or the winning of some great battle, he never seemed greatly rejoiced to hear it; on the contrary he used to say to his play-fellows: 'Father will get everything in advance, boys; he won't leave any great task for me to share with you.' " . . .

It is not a natural thing for a boy to envy his father in this fashion without some inspiration. That sentence sounds like an echo.

We have already pointed out how manifest it is that Philip planned the succession of Alexander, and how eager he was to thrust fame and power into the boy's hands. He was thinking of the political structure he was building—but the mother was thinking of the glory and pride of that wonderful lady, Olympias. She masked her hatred of her husband under the cloak of a mother's solicitude for her son's future. When in 337 B.C. Philip, after the fashion of kings in those days, married a second wife who was a native Macedonian, Cleopatra, "of whom he was passionately enamoured," Olympias made much trouble.

Plutarch tells of a pitiful scene that occurred at Philip's marriage to Cleopatra. There was much drinking of wine at the banquet, and Attalus, the father of the bride, being "intoxicated with liquor," betrayed the general hostility to Olympias and Epirus by saying he hoped there would be a child by the marriage to give them a truly Macedonian heir. Whereupon Alexander, taut for such an insult, cried out, "What then am I?" and hurled his cup at Attalus. Philip, enraged, stood up and, says Plutarch, drew his sword, only to stumble and fall. Alexander, blind with rage and jealousy, taunted and insulted his father.

"Macedonians," he said. "See there the general who would go from Europe to Asia! Why! he cannot get from one table to another!"

How that scene lives still, the sprawl, the flushed faces, the angry voice of the boy! Next day Alexander departed with his mother—and Philip did nothing to restrain them. Olympias went home to Epirus; Alexander departed to Illyria. Thence Philip persuaded him to return.

Fresh trouble arose. Alexander had a brother of weak intellect, Aridæus, whom the Persian governor of Caria sought as a son-in-law. "Alexander's friends and his mother now infused notions into him again, though perfectly groundless, that by so noble a match, and the support consequent upon it, Philip designed the crown for Aridæus. Alexander, in the uneasiness these suspicions gave him, sent one Thessalus, a player, into Caria, to desire the grandee to pass by Aridæus, who was of spurious birth, and deficient in point of understanding, and to take the lawful heir to the crown into his alliance. Pixodarus was infinitely more pleased with this proposal. But Philip no sooner had intelligence of it, than he went to Alexander's apartment, taking along with him Philotas, the son of Parmenio, one of his most intimate friends and companions, and, in his presence, reproached him with his degeneracy and meanness of spirit, in thinking of being son-in-law to a man of Caria, one of the slaves of a barbarian king. At the same time he wrote to the Corinthians, insisting that they should send Thessalus to him in chains. Harpalus and Niarchus, Phrygius and Ptolemy, some of the other companions of the prince, he banished. But Alexander afterwards recalled them, and treated them with great distinction."

There is something very touching in this story of the father pleading with the son he manifestly loved, and baffled by the web of mean suggestion which had been spun about the boy's imagination.

It was at the marriage of his daughter to her uncle, the king of Epirus and the brother of Olympias, that Philip was stabbed. He was walking in a procession into the theatre unarmed, in a white robe, and he was cut down by one of his bodyguard. The murderer had a horse waiting, and would have got away, but the foot of his horse caught in a wild vine and he was thrown from the saddle by the stumble and slain by his pursuers. . . .

So at the age of twenty Alexander was at the end of his anxiety about the succession, and established king in Macedonia.

Olympias then reappeared in Macedonia, a woman proudly vindicated. It is said that she insisted upon paying the same funeral honours to the memory of the murderer as to Philip.

In Greece there were great rejoicings over this auspicious

event, and Demosthenes, when he had the news, although it was but seven days after the death of his own daughter, went into the public assembly at Athens in gay attire wearing a chaplet.

Whatever Olympias may have done about her husband's assassin, history does not doubt about her treatment of her supplanter, Cleopatra. So soon as Alexander was out of the way —and a revolt of the hillmen in the north called at once for his attention—Cleopatra's newly born child was killed in its mother's arms, and Cleopatra—no doubt after a little taunting —was then strangled. These excesses of womanly feeling are said to have shocked Alexander, but they did not prevent him from leaving his mother in a position of considerable authority in Macedonia. She wrote letters to him upon religious and political questions, and he showed a dutiful disposition in sending her always a large share of the plunder he made.

§ 3

There stories have to be told because history cannot be understood without them. Here was the great world of men between India and the Adriatic ready for union, ready as it had never been before for a unifying control. Here was the wide order of the Persian empire with its roads, its posts, its general peace and prosperity, ripe for the fertilizing influence of the Greek mind. And these stories display the quality of the human beings to whom those great opportunities came. Here was this Philip who was a very great and noble man, and yet he was drunken, he could keep no order in his household. Here was Alexander in many ways gifted above any man of his time, and he was vain, suspicious, and passionate, with a mind set awry by his mother.

We are beginning to understand something of what the world might be, something of what our race might become, were it not for our still raw humanity. It is barely a matter of seventy generations between ourselves and Alexander; and between ourselves and the savage hunters, our ancestors, who charred their food in the embers or ate it raw, intervene some four or five hundred generations. There is not much scope for the modification of a species in four or five hundred generations. Make men and women only sufficiently jealous or fearful or drunken or angry, and the hot red eyes of the cave men will glare out at us to-day. We have writing and teaching, science and power; we have tamed the beasts and schooled the lightning; but we are still only shambling towards the light. We have tamed and bred the beasts, but we have still to tame and breed ourselves.

From the very beginning of his reign the deeds of Alexander showed how well he had assimilated his father's plans, and how great were his own abilities. A map of the known world is needed to show the course of his life. At first, after receiving assurances from Greece that he was to be captain-general of the Grecian forces, he marched through Thrace to the Danube; he crossed the river and burnt a village, the second great monarch to raid the Scythian country beyond the Danube; then recrossed it and marched westward and so came down by Illyria. By that time the city of Thebes was in rebellion, and his next blow was at Greece. Thebes—unsupported of course by Athens—was taken and looted; it was treated with extravagant violence; all its buildings, except the temple and the house of the poet Pindar, were razed, and thirty thousand people sold into slavery. Greece was stunned, and Alexander was free to go on with the Persian campaign.

This destruction of Thebes betrayed a streak of violence in the new master of human destinies. It was too heavy a blow to have dealt. It was a barbaric thing to do. If the spirit of rebellion was killed, so also was the spirit of help. The Greek states remained inert thereafter, neither troublesome nor helpful. They would not support Alexander with their shipping, a thing which was to prove a very grave embarrassment to him.

There is a story told by Plutarch about this Theban massacre, as if it redounded to the credit of Alexander, but indeed it shows only how his saner and his crazy sides were in conflict. It tells of a Macedonian officer and a Theban lady. This officer was among the looters, and he entered this woman's house, inflicted unspeakable insults and injuries upon her, and at last demanded whether she had gold or silver hidden. She told him all her treasures had been put into the well, conducted him thither, and, as he stooped to peer down, pushed him suddenly in and killed him by throwing great stones upon him. Some allied soldiers came upon this scene and took her forthwith to Alexander for judgment.

She defied him. Already the extravagant impulse that had ordered the massacre was upon the wane, and he not only spared her, but had her family and property and freedom restored to her. This Plutarch makes out to be a generosity, but the issue is more complicated than that. It was Alexander who was outraging and plundering and enslaving all Thebes. That poor crumpled Macedonian brute in the well had been doing only what he had been told he had full liberty to do. Is a commander first to give cruel orders, and then to forgive and reward those who slay his instruments? This gleam of remorse at the instance of one woman who was not perhaps wanting in tragic dignity and beauty, is a poor set-off to the murder of a great city.

Mixed with the craziness of Olympias in Alexander was the sanity of Philip and the teachings of Aristotle. This Theban business certainly troubled the mind of Alexander. Whenever afterwards he encountered Thebans, he tried to show them special favour. Thebes, to his credit, haunted him.

Yet the memory of Thebes did not save three other great cities from similar brain storms; Tyre he destroyed, and Gaza, and a city in India, in the storming of which he was knocked down in fair fight and wounded; and of the latter place not a soul, not a child, was spared. He must have been badly frightened to have taken so evil a revenge.

At the outset of the war the Persians had this supreme advantage, they were practically masters of the sea. The ships of the Athenians and their allies sulked unhelpfully. Alexander, to get at Asia, had to go round by the Hellespont; and if he pushed far into the Persian empire, he ran the risk of being cut off completely from his base. His first task, therefore, was to cripple the enemy at sea, and this he could only do by marching along the coast of Asia Minor and capturing port after port until the Persian sea bases were destroyed. If the Persians had avoided battle and hung upon his lengthening line of communications they could probably have destroyed him, but this they did not do. A Persian army not very much greater than his own gave battle on the banks of the Granicus (334 B.C.) and was destroyed. This left him free to take Sardis, Ephesus, Miletus, and after a fierce struggle, Halicarnassus. Meanwhile the Persian fleet was on his right flank and between him and Greece, threatening much but accomplishing nothing.

In 333 B.C., pursuing this attack upon the sea bases, he marched along the coast as far as the head of the gulf now called the Gulf of Alexandretta. A huge Persian army, under the great king Darius III, was inland of his line of march, separated from the coast by mountains, and Alexander went right beyond this enemy force before he or the Persians realized their proximity. Scouting was evidently very badly done by Greek and Persian alike. The Persian army was a vast, ill-organized assembly of soldiers, transport, camp followers, and so forth. Darius, for instance, was accompanied by his harem, and there was a great multitude of harem slaves, musicians, dancers, and cooks. Many of the leading officers had brought their families to witness the hunting down of the Macedonian invaders. The troops had been levied from every province in the empire; they had no tradition or principle of combined action. Seized by the idea of cutting off Alexander from Greece, Darius moved this multitude over the mountains to the sea; he had the luck to get through the passes without opposition, and he encamped on the plain of Issus between the mountains and the shore. And there Alexander, who had turned back to fight, struck him. The cavalry charge and the phalanx smashed this great brittle host as a stone smashes a bottle. It was routed. Darius escaped from his war chariot—that out-of-date instrument—and fled on horseback, leaving even his harem in the hands of Alexander.

All the accounts of Alexander after this battle show him at his best. He was restrained and magnanimous. He treated the Persian princesses with the utmost civility. And he kept his head; he held steadfastly to his plan. He let Darius escape, unpursued, into Syria, and he continued his march upon the naval bases of the Persians—that is to say, upon the Phœnician ports of Tyre and Sidon.

Sidon surrendered to him; Tyre resisted.

Here, if anywhere, we have the evidence of great military ability on the part of Alexander. His army was his father's creation, but Philip had never shone in the siege of cities. When Alexander was a boy of sixteen, he had seen his father repulsed by the fortified city of Byzantium upon the Bosphorus. Now he was face to face with an inviolate city which had stood

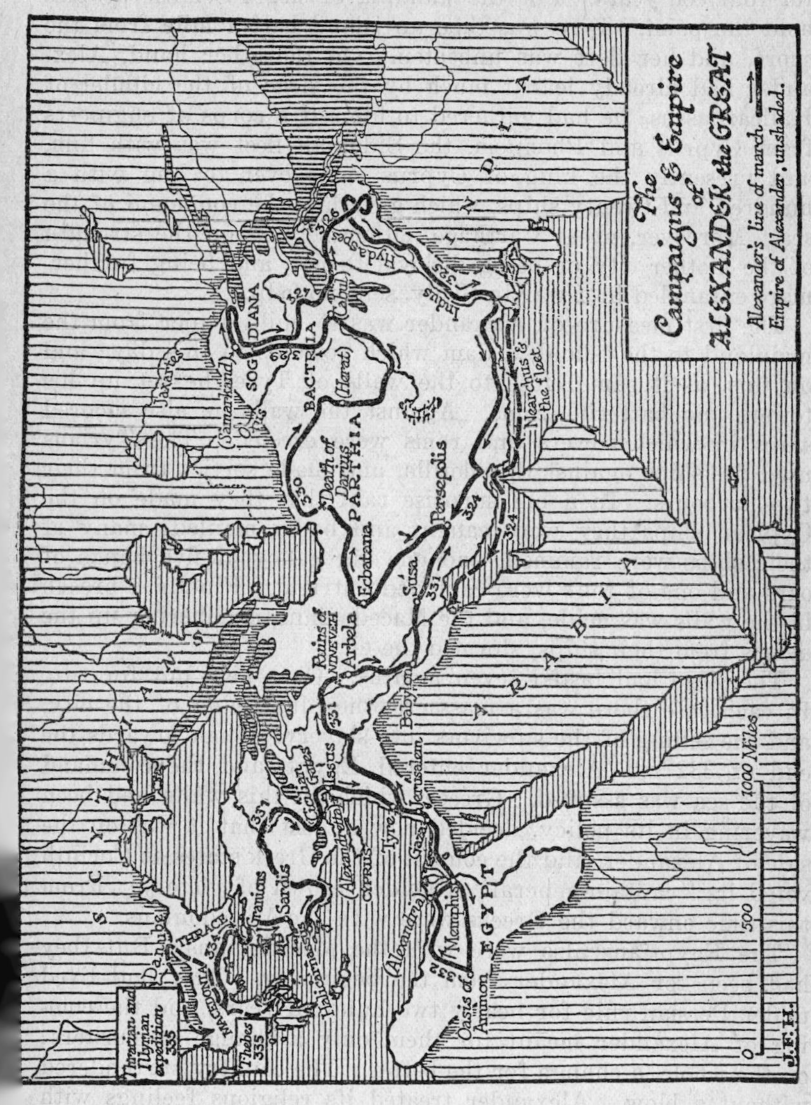
The Campaigns & Empire of ALEXANDER the GREAT
Alexander's line of march
Empire of Alexander, unshaded.
S C Y T H I A N S
I N D I A
A R A B I A
EGYPT
PARTHIA
BACTRIA
SOGDIANA
THRACE
MACEDONIA
Danube
Jaxartes
(Samarkand)
(Herat)
(Cabul)
Hydaspes
Indus
Nearchus & the fleet
Persepolis
Susa
Ecbatana
Death of Darius
Arbela
Ruins of NINEVEH
Babylon
Jerusalem
Tyre
Gaza
Memphis
(Alexandria)
Oasis of Ammon
Issus
Cilician Gates
(Alexandretta)
CYPRUS
Sardis
Granicus
Halicarnassus
Thracian and Illyrian expedition 335
Thebes 335
334
332
331
330
329
327
326
325
324
0 500 1000 Miles
J.F.H.

siege after siege, which had resisted Nebuchadnezzar the Great for fourteen years. For the standing of sieges Semitic peoples hold the palm. Tyre was then an island half a mile from the shore, and her fleet was unbeaten. On the other hand, Alexander had already learnt much by the siege of the citadel of Halicarnassus; he had gathered to himself a corps of engineers from Cyprus and Phœnicia, the Sidonian fleet was with him, and presently the king of Cyprus came over to him with a hundred and twenty ships, which gave him the command of the sea. Moreover, great Carthage, either relying on the strength of the mother city or being disloyal to her, and being furthermore entangled in a war in Sicily, sent no help.

The first measure of Alexander was to build a pier from the mainland to the island, a dam which remains to this day; and on this, as it came close to the walls of Tyre, he set up his towers and battering-rams. Against the walls he also moored ships in which towers and rams were erected. The Tyrians used fire-ships against this flotilla, and made sorties from their two harbours. In a big surprise raid that they made on the Cyprian ships they were caught and badly mauled; many of their ships were rammed, and one big galley of five banks of oars and one of four were captured outright. Finally a breach in the walls was made, and the Macedonians, clambering up the debris from their ships, stormed the city.

The siege had lasted seven months. Gaza held out for two. In each case there was a massacre, the plundering of the city, and the selling of the survivors into slavery. Then towards the end of 332 B.C. Alexander entered Egypt, and the command of the sea was assured. Greece, which all this while had been wavering in its policy, decided now at last that it was on the side of Alexander, and the council of the Greek states at Corinth voted its "captain-general" a golden crown of victory. From this time onward the Greeks were with the Macedonians.

The Egyptians also were with the Macedonians. But they had been for Alexander from the beginning. They had lived under Persian rule for nearly two hundred years, and the coming of Alexander meant for them only a change of masters; on the whole, a change for the better. The country surrendered without a blow. Alexander treated its religious feelings with extreme respect. He unwrapped no mummies as Cambyses had done; he took no liberties with Apis, the sacred bull of

Memphis. Here, in great temples and upon a vast scale, Alexander found the evidences of a religiosity, mysterious and irrational, to remind him of the secrets and mysteries that had entertained his mother and impressed his childhood. During his four months in Egypt he flirted with religious emotions.

He was still a very young man, we must remember, divided against himself. The strong sanity he inherited from his father had made him a great soldier; the teaching of Aristotle had given him something of the scientific outlook upon the world. He had destroyed Tyre; in Egypt, at one of the mouths of the Nile, he now founded a new city, Alexandria, to replace that ancient centre of trade. To the north of Tyre, near Issus, he founded a second port, Alexandretta. Both of these cities flourish to this day, and for a time Alexandria was perhaps the greatest city in the world. The sites, therefore, must have been wisely chosen. But also Alexander had the unstable emotional imaginativeness of his mother, and side by side with such creative work he indulged in religious adventures. The gods of Egypt took possession of his mind. He travelled four hundred miles to the remote oasis of the oracle of Ammon. He wanted to settle certain doubts about his true parentage. His mother had inflamed his mind by hints and vague speeches of some deep mystery about his parentage. Was so ordinary a human being as Philip of Macedon really his father?

For nearly four hundred years Egypt had been a country politically contemptible, overrun now by Ethiopians, now by Assyrians, now by Babylonians, now by Persians. As the indignities of the present became more and more disagreeable to contemplate, the past and the other world became more splendid to Egyptian eyes. It is from the festering humiliations of peoples that arrogant religious propagandas spring. To the triumphant the downtrodden can say, "It is naught in the sight of the true gods." So the son of Philip of Macedon, the master-general of Greece, was made to feel a small person amidst the gigantic temples. And he had an abnormal share of youth's normal ambition to impress everybody. How gratifying then for him to discover presently that he was no mere successful mortal, not one of these modern vulgar Greekish folk, but ancient and divine, the son of a god, the Pharaoh god, son of Ammon Ra!

Already in a previous chapter we have given a description of that encounter in the desert temple.

Not altogether was the young man convinced. He had his moments of conviction; he had his saner phases when the thing was almost a jest. In the presence of Macedonians and Greeks he doubted if he was divine. When it thundered loudly, the ribald Aristarchus could ask him: "Won't *you* do something of the sort, oh Son of Zeus?" But the crazy notion was, nevertheless, present henceforth in his brain, ready to be inflamed by wine or flattery.

Next spring (331 B.C.) he returned to Tyre, and marched thence round towards Assyria, leaving the Syrian desert on his right. Near the ruins of forgotten Nineveh he found a great Persian army, that had been gathering since the battle of Issus, awaiting him. It was another huge medley of contingents, and it relied for its chief force upon that now antiquated weapon, the war chariot. Of these Darius had a force of two hundred, and each chariot had scythes attached to its wheels and to the pole and body of the chariot. There seem to have been four horses to each chariot, and it will be obvious that if one of those horses was wounded by javelin or arrow, that chariot was held up. The outer horses acted chiefly as buffers for the inner wheel horses; they were hitched to the chariot by a single outside trace which could be easily cut away, but the loss of one of the wheel horses completely incapacitated the whole affair. Against broken footmen or a crowd of individualist fighters such vehicles might be formidable; but Darius began the battle by flinging them against the cavalry and light infantry. Few reached their objective, and those that did were readily disposed of. There was some manœuvring for position. The well-drilled Macedonians moved obliquely across the Persian front, keeping good order; the Persians, following this movement to the flank, opened gaps in their array. Then suddenly the disciplined Macedonian cavalry charged at one of these torn places and smote the centre of the Persian host. The infantry followed close upon their charge. The centre and left of the Persians crumpled up. For a while the light cavalry on the Persian right gained ground against Alexander's left, only to be cut to pieces by the cavalry from Thessaly, which by this time had become almost as good as its Macedonian model. The Persian forces ceased to resemble an army. They dissolved into a vast multitude of fugitives streaming under great dust clouds and without a single rally across the hot plain towards Arbela. Through the dust and the flying crowd rode the victors, slaying and slaying until darkness stayed the slaughter. Darius led the retreat.

Such was the battle of Arbela. It was fought on October the 1st, 331 B.C. We know its date so exactly, because it is recorded that, eleven days before it began, the soothsayers on both sides had been greatly exercised by an eclipse of the moon.

Darius fled to the north into the country of the Medes. Alexander marched on to Babylon. The ancient city of Hammurabi (who had reigned seventeen hundred years before) and of Nebuchadnezzar the Great and of Nabonidus was still, unlike Nineveh, a prosperous and important centre. Like the Egyptians, the Babylonians were not greatly concerned at a change of rule to Macedonian from Persian. The temple of Bel-Marduk was in ruins, a quarry for building material, but the tradition of the Chaldean priests still lingered, and Alexander promised to restore the building.

Thence he marched on to Susa, once the chief city of the vanished and forgotten Elamites, and now the Persian capital.

He went on to Persepolis, where, as the climax of a drunken carouse, he burnt down the great palace of the king of kings. This he afterwards declared was the revenge of Greece for the burning of Athens by Xerxes.

§ 4

And now begins a new phase in the story of Alexander. For the next seven years he wandered with an army chiefly of Macedonians in the north and east of what was then the known world. At first it was a pursuit of Darius. Afterwards it became——? Was it a systematic survey of a world he meant to consolidate into one great order, or was it a wild-goose chase? His own soldiers, his own intimates, thought the latter, and at last stayed his career beyond the Indus. On the map it looks very like a wild-goose chase; it seems to aim at nothing in particular and to get nowhere.

The pursuit of Darius III soon came to a pitiful end. After the battle of Arbela his own generals seem to have revolted against his weakness and incompetence; they made him a prisoner, and took him with them in spite of his desire to throw himself upon the generosity of his conqueror. Bessus, the satrap of Bactria, they made their leader. There was at last a hot and exciting chase of the flying caravan which conveyed the captive king of kings. At dawn, after an all-night pursuit, it was sighted far ahead. The flight became a headlong bolt. Baggage, women, everything was abandoned by Bessus and his captains; and one other impediment also they left behind. By the side of a pool of water far away from the road a Macedonian trooper presently found a deserted mule-cart with its mules still in the traces. In this cart lay Darius, stabbed in a score of places and bleeding to death. He had refused to go on with Bessus, refused to mount the horse that was brought to him. So his captains had run him through with their spears and left him. . . . He asked his captors for water. What else he may have said we do not know. The historians have seen fit to fabricate a quite impossible last dying speech for him. Probably he said very little. . . .

When, a little after sunrise, Alexander came up, Darius was already dead. . . .

To the historian of the world the wanderings of Alexander have an interest of their own quite apart from the light they throw upon his character. Just as the campaign of Darius I lifted the curtain behind Greece and Macedonia, and showed us something of the silent background to the north of the audible and recorded history of the early civilizations, so now Alexander's campaigns take us into regions about which there had hitherto been no trustworthy record made.

We discover they were not desert regions, but full of a gathering life of their own.

He marched to the shores of the Caspian, thence he travelled eastward across what is now called Western Turkestan. He founded a city that is now known as Herat; whence he went northward by Cabul and by what is now Samarkand, right up into the mountains of Central Turkestan. He returned southward, and came down into India by the Khyber Pass. He fought a great battle on the Upper Indus against a very tall and chivalrous king, Porus, in which the Macedonian infantry encountered an array of elephants and defeated them. Possibly he would have pushed eastward across the deserts to the Ganges valley, but his troops refused to go further. Possibly, had they not done so, then or later he would have gone on until he vanished eastward out of history. But he was forced to turn about. He built a fleet and descended to the mouth of the Indus. There he divided his forces. The main army he took along the desolate coast back to the Persian Gulf, and on the way it suffered dreadfully and lost many men through thirst. The fleet followed him by sea, and rejoined him at the entrance to the Persian Gulf. In the course of this six-year tour he fought battles, received the submission of many strange peoples, and founded cities. He saw the dead body of Darius in June, 330 B.C.; he returned to Susa in 324 B.C. He found the empire in disorder: the provincial satraps raising armies of their own, Bactria and Media in insurrection, and Olympias making government impossible in Macedonia. Harpalus, the royal treasurer, had bolted with all that was portable of the royal treasure, and was making his way, bribing as he went, towards Greece. Some of the Harpalus money is said to have reached Demosthenes.

But before we deal with the closing chapter of the story of Alexander, let us say a word or so about these northern regions into which he wandered. It is evident that from the Danube region right across South Russia, right across the country to the north of the Caspian, right across the country to the east of the Caspian, as far as the mountain masses of the Pamir Plateau and eastward into the Tarim basin of Eastern Turkestan, there spread then a series of similar barbaric tribes and peoples all at about the same stage of culture, and for the most part Aryan in their language and possibly Nordic in their race. They had few cities, mostly they were nomadic; at times they settled temporarily to cultivate the land. They were certainly already mingling in Central Asia with Mongolian tribes, but the Mongolian tribes were not then prevalent there.

An immense process of drying up and elevation has been going on in these parts of the world during the last ten thousand years. Ten thousand years ago there was probably a continuous water barrier between the basin of the Obi and the Aral-Caspian sea. As this had dried up and the marshy land had become steppe-like country, Nordic nomads from the west and Mongolian nomads from the east had met and mixed, and the riding horse had come back into the western world. It is evident this great stretch of country was becoming a region of accumulation for these barbaric peoples. They were very loosely attached to the lands they occupied. They lived in tents and wagons rather than houses. A brief cycle of plentiful and healthy years, or a cessation of tribal warfare under some strong ruler, would lead to considerable increases of population; then two or three hard years would suffice to send the tribes wandering again in search of food.

From before the dawn of recorded history this region of human accumulation between the Danube and China had been, as it were, intermittently *raining* out tribes southward and westward. It was like a cloud bank behind the settled landscape that accumulated and then precipitated invaders. We have noted how the Keltic peoples drizzled westward, how the Italians, the Greeks, and their Epirote, Macedonian, and Phrygian kindred came south. We have noted, too, the Cimmerian drive from the east, like a sudden driving shower of barbarians across Asia Minor, the southward coming of the Scythians and Medes and Persians, and the Aryan descent into India. About a century before Alexander there had been a fresh Aryan invasion of Italy by Keltic people, the Gauls, who had settled in the valley of the Po. Those various races came down out of their northern obscurity into the light of history; and meanwhile beyond that light the reservoir accumulated for fresh discharges. Alexander's march in Central Asia brings now into our history names that are fresh to us; the Parthians, a race of mounted bowmen who were destined to play an important rôle in history a century or so later, and the Bactrians who lived in the sandy native land of the camel. Everywhere he seems to have met Aryan-speaking peoples. The Mongolian barbarians to the north-eastward were still unsuspected, no one imagined there was yet another great cloud bank of population beyond the Scythians and their kind, in the north of China, that was presently also to begin a drift westward and southward, mixing as it came with the Nordic Scythians and every other people of kindred habits that it encountered. As yet only China knew of the Huns; there were no Turks in Western Turkestan or anywhere else then, no Tartars in the world.

This glimpse of the state of affairs in Turkestan in the fourth century B.C. is one of the most interesting aspects of the wanderings of Alexander; another is his raid through the Punjab. From the point of view of the teller of the human story it is provocative that he did not go on into the Ganges country, and that consequently we have no independent accounts by Greek writers of the life in ancient Bengal. But there is a considerable literature in various Indian languages dealing with Indian history and social life that still needs to be made accessible to European readers.

§ 5

Alexander had been in undisputed possession of the Persian empire for six years. He was now thirty-one. In those six years he had created very little. He had retained most of the organization of the Persian provinces, appointing fresh satraps or retaining the former ones; the roads, the ports, the organization of the empire was still as Cyrus, his greater predecessor, had left them; in Egypt he had merely replaced old provincial governors by new ones; in India he had defeated Porus, and then left him in power much as he found him, except that Porus was now called a satrap by the Greeks. Alexander had, it is true, planned out a number of towns, and some of them were to grow into great towns; seventeen Alexandrias he founded altogether;[1] but he had destroyed Tyre, and with Tyre the security of the sea routes which had hitherto been the chief westward outlet for Mesopotamia. Historians say that he Hellenized the east. But Babylonia and Egypt swarmed with Greeks before his time; he was not the cause, he was a part of the Hellenization. For a time the whole world, from the Adriatic to the Indus, was under one ruler; so far he had realized the dreams of Isocrates and Philip his father. But how far was he making this a permanent and enduring union? How far as yet was it anything more than a dazzling but transitory flourish of his own magnificent self?

He was making no great roads, setting up no sure sea communications. It is idle to accuse him of leaving education alone, because the idea that empires must be cemented by education was still foreign to human thought. But he was forming no group of statesmen about him; he was thinking of no successor; he was creating no tradition—nothing more than a personal legend. The idea that the world would have to go on after

[1] Mahaffy. Their names have undergone various changes—*e.g.*, Candahar (Iskender) and Secunderabad.

Alexander, engaged in any other employment than the discussion of his magnificence, seems to have been outside his mental range. He was still young, it is true, but well before Philip was one and thirty he had been thinking of the education of Alexander.

Was Alexander a statesman at all?

Some students of his career assure us that he was; that now at Susa he planned a mighty world empire, seeing it not simply as a Macedonian conquest of the world, but as a melting together of racial traditions. He did one thing, at any rate, that gives colour to this idea; he held a great marriage feast, in which he and ninety of his generals and friends were married to Persian brides. He himself married a daughter of Darius, though already he possessed an Asiatic wife in Roxana, the daughter of the king of Samarkand. This wholesale wedding was made a very splendid festival, and at the same time all of his Macedonian soldiers, to the number of several thousands, who had married Asiatic brides, were given wedding gifts. This has been called the Marriage of Europe and Asia; the two continents were to be joined, wrote Plutarch, "in lawful wedlock and by community of offspring." And next he began to train recruits from Persia and the north, Parthians, Bactrians, and the like, in the distinctive disciplines of the phalanx and the cavalry. Was that also to assimilate Europe and Asia, or was it to make himself independent of his Macedonians? They thought the latter, at any rate, and mutinied, and it was with some difficulty that he brought them to a penitent mood and induced them to take part in a common feast with the Persians. The historians have made a long and eloquent speech for him on this occasion, but the gist of it was that he bade his Macedonians begone, and gave no sign of how he proposed they should get home out of Persia. After three days of dismay they submitted to him and begged his forgiveness.

Here is the matter for a very pretty discussion. Was Alexander really planning a racial fusion or had he just fallen in love with the pomp and divinity of an Oriental monarch, and wished to get rid of these Europeans to whom he was only a king-leader? The writers of his own time, and those who lived near to his time, lean very much to the latter alternative. They insist upon his immense vanity. They relate how he began to wear the robes and tiara of a Persian monarch. "At first only before the barbarians and privately, but afterwards he came to wear it in public when he sat for the dispatch of business." And presently he demanded Oriental prostrations from his friends.

One thing seems to support the suggestion of great personal vanity in Alexander. His portrait was painted and sculptured frequently, and always he is represented as a beautiful youth, with wonderful locks flowing backward from a broad forehead. Previously most men had worn beards. But Alexander, enamoured of his own youthful loveliness, would not part with it; he remained a sham boy at thirty-two; he shaved his face, and so set a fashion in Greece and Italy that lasted many centuries.

Alexander the Great
(silver coin of Lysimachus, 321-281 B.C.)

The stories of violence and vanity in his closing years cluster thick upon his memory. He listened to tittle-tattle about Philotas, the son of Parmenio, one of his most trusted and faithful generals. Philotas, it was said, had boasted to some woman he was making love to that Alexander was a mere boy; that, but for such men as his father and himself, there would have been no conquest of Persia, and the like. Such assertions had a certain element of truth in them. The woman was brought to Alexander, who listened to her treacheries. Presently Philotas was accused of conspiracy, and, upon very insufficient evidence, tortured and executed. Then Alexander thought of Parmenio, whose other two sons had died for him in battle. He sent swift messengers to assassinate the old man before he could hear of his son's death! Now Parmenio had been one of the most trusted of Philip's generals; it was Parmenio who had led the Macedonian armies into Asia before the murder of Philip. There can be little doubt of the substantial truth of this story, nor about the execution of Callisthenes, the nephew of Aristotle, who refused Alexander divine honours, and "went about with as much pride as if he had demolished a tyranny, while the young men followed him as the only freeman among thousands." Mixed with such incidents we have the very illuminating story of the drunken quarrel in which he killed Clitus. The monarch and his company had been drinking hard, and the drink had made the talk loud and free. There was much flattery of the "young god," much detraction of Philip, at which Alexander had smiled with satisfaction.[1] This drunken self-complacency was more than the Macedonians could stand; it roused Clitus, his foster-brother, to a frenzy. Clitus reproached Alexander with his Median costume and praised Philip, there was a loud quarrel, and, to end it, Clitus was hustled out of the room by his friends. He was, however, in the obstinate phase of drunkenness, and he returned by another entrance. He was heard outside quoting Euripides "in a bold and disrespectful tone":

> "Are these your customs? Is it thus that Greece
> Rewards her combatants? Shall one man claim
> The trophies won by thousands?"

Whereupon Alexander snatched a spear from one of his guards and ran Clitus through the body as he lifted the curtain to come in. . . .

One is forced to believe that this was the real atmosphere of the young conqueror's life. Then the story of his frantic and cruel display of grief for Hephæstion can scarcely be all invention. If it is true, or in any part true, it displays a mind ill-balanced and altogether wrapped up in personal things, to whom empire was no more than opportunity for egoistic display, and all the resources of the world, stuff for freaks of that sort of "generosity" which robs a thousand people to extort the admiration of one astounded recipient.

Hephæstion, being ill, was put upon a strict diet, but in the absence of his physician at the theatre he ate a roasted fowl and drank a flagon of iced wine, in consequence of which he died.

[1] D. G. Hogarth.

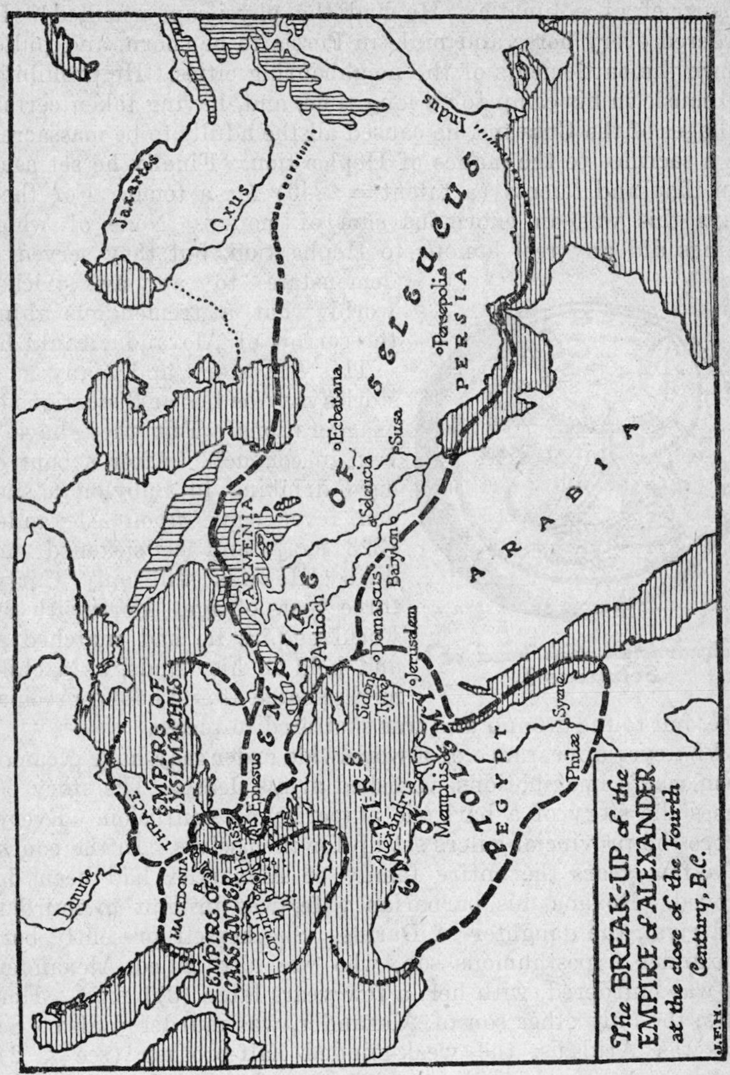

The BREAK-UP of the EMPIRE of ALEXANDER at the close of the Fourth Century, B.C.

Thereupon Alexander decided upon a display of grief. It was the grief of a lunatic. He had the physician crucified! He ordered every horse and mule in Persia to be shorn, and pulled down the battlements of the neighbouring cities. He prohibited all music in his camp for a long time, and, having taken certain villages of the Cusæans, he caused all the adults to be massacred, as a sacrifice to the manes of Hephæstion. Finally he set aside ten thousand talents (a talent = £240) for a tomb. For those days this was an enormous sum of money. None of which things did any real honour to Hephæstion, but they served to demonstate to an awe-stricken world what a tremendous thing the sorrow of Alexander could be.

Tetradrachm with head of Seleucus I.

This last story and many such stories may be lies or distortions or exaggerations. But they have a vein in common. After a bout of hard drinking in Babylon a sudden fever came upon Alexander (323 B.C.), and he sickened and died. He was still only thirty-three years of age. Forthwith the world empire he had snatched at and held in his hands, as a child might snatch at and hold a precious vase, fell to the ground and was shattered to pieces.

Whatever appearance of a worldwide order may have gleamed upon men's imaginations, vanished at his death. The story becomes the story of a barbaric autocracy in confusion. Everywhere the provincial rulers set up for themselves. In the course of a few years the entire family of Alexander had been destroyed. Roxana, his barbarian wife, was prompt to murder, as a rival, the daughter of Darius. She herself presently bore Alexander a posthumous son, who was also called Alexander. He was murdered, with her, a few years later (311 B.C.). Hercules, the only other son of Alexander, was murdered also. So, too, was Aridæus, the weak-minded half-brother (see § 2). Plutarch gives a last glimpse of Olympias during a brief interval of power in Macedonia, accusing first this person and then that of poisoning her wonderful son. Many she killed in her fury. The bodies of some of his circle who had died after his death she caused to be dug up, but we do not know if any fresh light was shed upon his death by these disinterments. Finally Olympias was killed in Macedonia by the friends of those she had slain.

§ 6

From this welter of crime there presently emerged three leading figures. Much of the old Persian empire, as far as the Indus eastward and almost to Lydia in the west, was held by one general Seleucus, who founded a dynasty, the Seleucid Dynasty; Macedonia fell to another Macedonian general, Antigonus; a third Macedonian, Ptolemy, secured Egypt, and making Alexandria his chief city, established a sufficient naval ascendancy to keep also Cyprus and most of the coast of Phœnicia and Asia Minor. The Ptolemaic and Seleucid empires lasted for a considerable time; the forms of government in Asia Minor and the Balkans were more unstable. Two maps will help the reader to a sense of the kaleidoscopic nature of the political boundaries of the third century B.C. Antigonus was defeated and killed at the battle of Ipsus (301), leaving Lysimachus, the governor of Thrace, and Cassander, of Macedonia and Greece, as equally transitory successors. Minor governors carved out smaller states. Meanwhile the barbarians swung down into the broken-up and enfeebled world of civilization from the west and from the east. From the west came the Gauls, a people closely related to the Kelts. They raided down through Macedonia and Greece to Delphi, and (227 B.C.) two sections of them crossed the Bosphorus into Asia Minor, being first employed as mercenaries and then setting up for themselves as independent plunderers; and after raiding almost to the Taurus, they settled in the old Phrygian land, holding the people about them to tribute. (These Gauls of Phrygia became the Galatians of St. Paul's Epistle.) Armenia and the southern shores of the Black Sea became a confusion of changing rulers. Kings with Hellenistic ideas appeared in Cappadocia, in Pontus (the south shore of the Black Sea), in Bithynia, and in Pergamum. From the east the Scythians and the Parthians and Bactrians also drove southward. . . . For a time there were Greek-ruled Bactrian states becoming more and more Orientalized; in the second century B.C. Greek adventurers from

Bactria raided down into North India and founded short-lived kingdoms there, the last eastward fling of the Greek; then gradually barbarism fell again like a curtain between the Western civilizations and India.

§ 7

Amidst all these shattered fragments of the burst bubble of Hellenic empire one small state stands out and demands at least a brief section to itself, the kingdom of Pergamum. We hear first of this town as an independent centre during the struggle that ended in the battle of Ipsus. While the tide of the Gaulish invasion swirled and formed to and fro about Asia Minor between the years 277 and 241, Pergamum for a time paid them tribute, but she retained her general independence, and at last, under Attalus I, refused her tribute and defeated them in two decisive battles. For more than a century thereafter (until 133 B.C.) Pergamum remained free, and was perhaps during that period the most highly civilized state in the world. On the hill of the Acropolis was reared a rich group of buildings, palaces, temples, a museum, and a library, rivals of those of Alexandria of which we shall presently tell, and almost the first in the world. Under the princes of Pergamum, Greek art blossomed afresh, and the reliefs of the altar of the temple of Zeus and the statues of the fighting and dying Gauls which were made there, are among the great artistic treasures of mankind.

In a little while, as we shall tell later, the influence of a new power began to be felt in the Eastern Mediterranean, the power of the Roman republic, friendly to Greece and to Greek civilization; and in this power the Hellenic communities of Pergamum and Rhodes found a natural and useful ally and supporter against the Galatians and against the Orientalized Seleucid empire. We shall relate how at last the Roman power came into Asia, how it defeated the Seleucid empire at the battle of Magnesia (190 B.C.), and drove it out of Asia Minor and beyond the Taurus mountains, and how finally in 133 B.C. Attalus III, the last king of Pergamum, bowing to his sense of an inevitable destiny, made the Roman republic the heir to his kingdom, which became then the Roman province of "Asia."

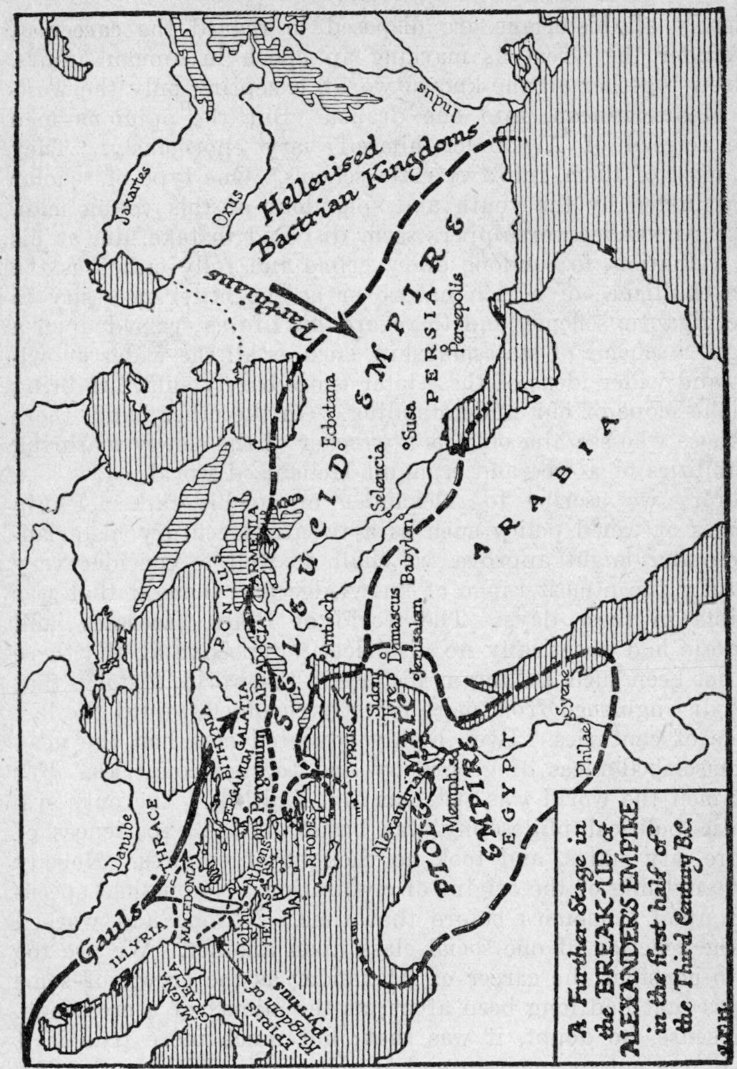

A Further Stage in the BREAK-UP of ALEXANDER'S EMPIRE in the first half of the Third Century B.C.

§ 8

Nearly all historians are disposed to regard the career of Alexander the Great as marking an epoch in human affairs. It drew together all the known world, excepting only the western Mediterranean, into one drama. But the opinions men have formed of Alexander himself vary enormously. They fall, most of them, into two main schools. One type of scholar is fascinated by the youth and splendour of this young man. These Alexander-worshippers seem disposed to take him at his own valuation, to condone every crime and folly either as the mere ebullience of a rich nature or as the bitter necessity to some gigantic scheme, and to regard his life as framed upon a design, a scheme of statesmanship, such as all the wider knowledge and wider ideas of these later times barely suffice to bring into the scope of our understanding. On the other hand, there are those who see him only as a wrecker of the slowly maturing possibilities of a free and tranquil Hellenized world.

Before we ascribe to Alexander or to his father Philip schemes of world policy such as a twentieth-century historian-philosopher might approve, we shall do well to consider very carefully the utmost range of knowledge and thought that was possible in those days. The world of Plato, Isocrates, and Aristotle had practically no historical perspective at all; there had not been such a thing as history in the world, history, that is, as distinguished from mere priestly chronicles, until the last couple of centuries. Even highly educated men had the most circumscribed ideas of geography and foreign countries. For most men the world was still flat and limitless. The only systematic political philosophy was based on the experiences of minute city states, and took no thought of empires. Nobody knew anything of the origins of civilization. No one had speculated upon economics before that time. No one had worked out the reaction of one social class upon another. We are too apt to consider the career of Alexander as the crown of some process that had long been afoot; as the climax of a crescendo. In a sense, no doubt, it was that; but much more true is it that it was not so much an end as a beginning; it was the first revelation to the human imagination of the oneness of human affairs. The utmost reach of the thought of Greece before his time was of a Persian empire Hellenized, a predominance in the world of Macedonians and Greeks. But before Alexander was dead, and much more after he was dead and there had been time to think him over, the conception of a world law and organization was a practicable and assimilable idea for the minds of men.

For some generations Alexander the Great was for mankind the symbol and embodiment of world order and world dominion. He became a fabulous being. His head, adorned with the divine symbols of the demi-god Hercules or the god Ammon Ra, appears on the coins of such among his successors as could claim to be his heirs. Then the idea of world dominion was taken up by another great people, a people who for some centuries exhibited considerable political genius, the Romans; and the figure of another conspicuous adventurer, Cæsar, eclipsed for the western half of the old world the figure of Alexander.

So by the beginning of the third century B.C. we find already arisen in the Western civilization of the old world three of the great structural ideas that rule the mind of contemporary mankind. We have already traced the escape of writing and knowledge from the secrets and mysteries and initiations of the old-world priesthoods, and the development of the idea of a universal knowledge, of a universally understandable and communicable history and philosophy. We have taken the figures of Herodotus and Aristotle as typical exponents of this first great idea, the idea of *science*—using the word science in its widest and properest sense, to include history and signify a clear vision of man in relation to the things about him. We have traced also the generalization of religion among the Babylonians, Jews, and other Semitic peoples, from the dark worship in temples and consecrated places of some local or tribal god to the open service of *one universal God of Righteousness,* whose temple is the whole world. And now we have traced also the first germination of the idea of *a world polity.* The rest of the history of mankind is very largely the history of those three ideas of science, of a universal righteousness, and of a human commonweal, spreading out from the minds of the rare and exceptional persons and peoples in which they first originated, into the general consciousness of the race, and giving first a new colour, then a new spirit, and then a new direction to human affairs.

XXIV

SCIENCE AND RELIGION AT ALEXANDRIA

§ 1. *The Science of Alexandria.* § 2. *Philosophy of Alexandria.* § 3. *Alexandria as a Factory of Religions.*

§ 1

ONE of the most prosperous fragments of the brief world empire of Alexander the Great was Egypt, which fell to the share of the Ptolemy whose name we have already noted as one of the associates of Alexander whom King Philip had banished. The country was at a secure distance from plundering Gaul or Parthian, and the destruction of Tyre and the Phœnician navy, and the creation of Alexandria gave Egypt a temporary naval ascendancy in the Eastern Mediterranean. Alexandria grew to proportions that rivalled Carthage; eastward she had an overseas trade through the Red Sea with Arabia and India; and westward her traffic competed with the Carthaginian. In the Macedonian and Greek governors of the Ptolemies, the Egyptians found a government more sympathetic and tolerable than any they had ever known since they ceased to be a self-governing empire. Indeed it is rather that Egypt conquered and annexed the Ptolemies politically, than that the Macedonians ruled Egypt.

There was a return to Egyptian political ideas, rather than any attempt to Hellenize the government of the country. Ptolemy became Pharaoh, the god-king, and his administration continued the ancient tradition of Pepi, Thotmes, Rameses, and Necho. Alexandria, however, for her town affairs, and subject to the divine overlordship of Pharaoh, had a constitution of the Greek city type. And the language of the court and administration was Attic Greek. Greek became so much the general language of educated people in Egypt that the Jewish community there found it necessary to translate their Bible into the Greek language, many men of their own people being no longer able to understand Hebrew. Attic Greek for some centuries before and after Christ was the language of all educated men from the Adriatic to the Persian Gulf.

Of all Alexander's group of young men, Ptolemy seems to have done most to carry out those ideas of a systematic organization of knowledge with which Aristotle had no doubt familiarized the court of Philip of Macedon. Ptolemy was a man of very extraordinary intellectual gifts, at once creative and modest, with a certain understandable cynicism towards the strain of Olympias in the mind of Alexander. His contemporary history of Alexander's campaigns has perished; but it was a source to which all the surviving accounts are deeply indebted.

The Museum he set up in Alexandria was in effect the first university in the world. As its name implies, it was dedicated to the service of the Muses, which was also the case with the Peripatetic school at Athens. It was, however, a religious body only in form, in order to meet the legal difficulties of endowment in a world that had never foreseen such a thing as a secular intellectual process. It was essentially a college of learned men engaged chiefly in research and record, but also to a certain extent in teaching. At the outset, and for two or three generations, the Museum at Alexandria presented such a scientific constellation as even Athens at its best could not rival. Particularly sound and good was the mathematical and geographical work. The names of Euclid, familiar to every schoolboy, Eratosthenes, who measured the size of the earth and came within fifty miles of the true diameter, Apollonius, who wrote on conic sections, stand out. Hipparchus made the first attempt to catalogue and map the stars with a view to checking any changes that might be occurring in the heavens. Hero devised the first steam engine. Archimedes came to Alexandria to study, and remained a frequent correspondent of the Museum. The medical school of Alexandria was equally famous. For the first time in the world's history a standard of professional knowledge was set up. Herophilus, the greatest of the Alexandrian anatomists, is said to have conducted vivisections upon condemned criminals. Other teachers, in opposition to Herophilus, condemned the study of anatomy and developed the science of drugs. But this scientific blaze at Alexandria did not endure altogether for more than a century. The organization of the Museum was not planned to ensure its mental continuity. It was a "royal" college; its professors and fellows (as we may call them) were appointed and paid by Pharaoh. "The republican character of the private corporations called the schools or academies at Athens was far more stable and independent." Royal patronage was all very well so long as Pharaoh was Ptolemy I, or Ptolemy II, but the strain degenerated, and the long tradition of Egyptian priestcraft presently swallowed up the Ptolemies—and destroyed the Aristotelian mentality of the Museum altogether. The Museum had not existed for a hundred years before its scientific energy was extinct.

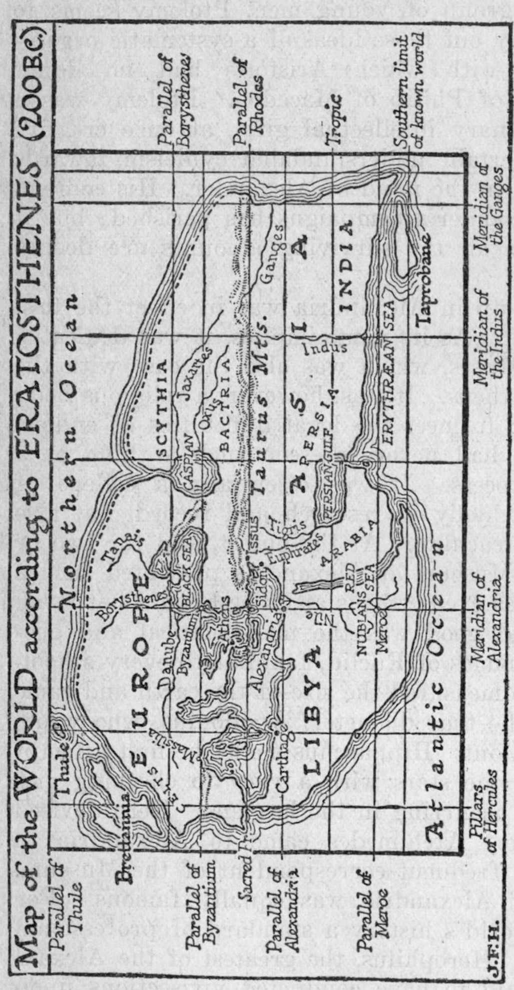

Map of the WORLD according to ERATOSTHENES (200 B.C.)

Side by side with the Museum, Ptolemy I created a more enduring monument to himself in the great library. This was a combination of state library and state publishing upon a scale hitherto unheard of. It was to be altogether encyclopædic. If any stranger brought an unknown book to Egypt, he had to have it copied for the collection, and a considerable staff of copyists was engaged continually in making duplicates of all the more popular and necessary works. The library, like a university press, had an outward trade. It was a book-selling affair. Under Callimachus, the head of the library during the time of Ptolemy II and III, the arrangement and cataloguing of the accumulations was systematically undertaken. In those days, it must be remembered, books were not in pages, but rolled like the music-rolls of the modern piano-player, and in order to refer to any particular passage, a reader had to roll back or roll forward very tediously, a process which wore out books and readers together. One thinks at once of a simple and obvious little machine by which such a roll could have been quickly wound to and fro for reference, but nothing of the sort seems to have been used. Every time a roll was read it was handled by two perspiring hands. It was to minimize the waste of time and trouble that Callimachus broke up long works, such as the History of Herodotus, into "books" or volumes, as we should call them, each upon a separate roll. The library of Alexandria drew a far vaster crowd of students than the teachers of the Museum. The lodging and catering for these visitors from all parts of the world became a considerable business interest for the Alexandrian population.

It is curious to note how slowly the mechanism of the intellectual life improves. Contrast the ordinary library facilities of a middle-class English home, such as the present writer is now working in, with the inconveniences and deficiencies of the equipment of an Alexandrian writer, and one realizes the enormous waste of time, physical exertion, and attention that went on through all the centuries during which that library flourished. Before the present writer lie half a dozen books, and there are good indices to three of them. He can pick up any one of these six books, refer quickly to a statement, verify a quotation, and go on writing. Contrast with that the tedious unfolding of a rolled manuscript. Close at hand are two encyclopædias, a dictionary, an atlas of the world, a biographical dictionary, and other books of reference. They have no marginal indices, it is true; but that perhaps is asking for too much at present. There were no such resources in the world in 300 B.C. Alexandria had still to produce the first grammar and the first dictionary. This present book is being written in manuscript; it is then taken by a typist and typewritten very accurately. It can then, with the utmost convenience, be read over, corrected amply, rearranged freely, retyped, and recorrected. The Alexandrian author had to dictate or recopy every word he wrote. Before he could turn back to what he had written previously, he had to dry his last words by waving them in the air or pouring sand over them; he had not even blotting-

paper. Whatever an author wrote had to be recopied again and again before it could reach any considerable circle of readers, and every copyist introduced some new error. Whenever a need for maps or diagrams arose, there were fresh difficulties. Such a science as anatomy, for example, depending as it does upon accurate drawing, must have been enormously hampered by the natural limitations of the copyist. The transmission of geographical fact again must have been almost incredibly tedious. No doubt a day will come when a private library and writing-desk of the year A.D. 1919 will seem quaintly clumsy and difficult; but, measured by the standards of Alexandria, they are astonishingly quick, efficient, and economical of nervous and mental energy.

No attempt seems to have been made at Alexandria to print anything at all. That strikes one at first as a very remarkable fact. The world was crying out for books, and not simply for books. There was an urgent public need for notices, proclamations, and the like. Yet there is nothing in the history of the Western civilizations that one can call printing until the fifteenth century A.D. It is not as though printing was a recondite art or dependent upon any precedent and preliminary discoveries. Printing is the most obvious of dodges. In principle it has always been known. As we have already stated, there is ground for supposing that the Palæolithic men of the Magdalenian period may have printed designs on their leather garments. The "seals" of ancient Sumeria again were printing devices. Coins are print. Illiterate persons in all ages have used wooden or metal stamps for their signatures; William I, the Norman Conqueror of England, for example, used such a stamp with ink to sign documents. In China the classics were being printed by the second century A.D. Yet either because of a complex of small difficulties about ink or papyrus or the form of books, or because of some protective resistance on the part of the owners of the slave copyists, or because the script was too swift and easy to set men thinking how to write it still more easily, as the Chinese character or the Gothic letters did, or because of a gap in the social system between men of thought and knowledge and men of technical skill, printing was not used —not even used for the exact reproduction of illustrations.

The chief reason for this failure to develop printing systematically lies, no doubt, in the fact that there was no abundant supply of printable material of a uniform texture and convenient form. The supply of papyrus was strictly limited, strip had to be fastened to strip, and there was no standard size of sheet. Paper had yet to come from China to release the mind of Europe. Had there been presses, they would have had to stand idle while the papyrus rolls were slowly made. But this explanation does not account for the failure to use block printing in the case of illustrations and diagrams.

These limitations enable us to understand why it was that

Alexandria could at once achieve the most extraordinary intellectual triumphs—for such a feat as that of Eratosthenes, for instance, having regard to his poverty of apparatus, is sufficient to put him on a level with Newton or Pasteur—and yet have little or no effect upon the course of politics or the lives and thoughts of people round about her. Her Museum and library were a centre of light, but it was light in a dark lantern hidden from the general world. There were no means of carrying its results even to sympathetic men abroad except by tedious letter-writing. There was no possibility of communicating what was known there to the general body of men. Students had to come at great cost to themselves to this crowded centre because there was no other way of gathering even scraps of knowledge. At Athens and Alexandria there were bookstalls where manuscript note-books of variable quality could be bought at reasonable prices, but any extension of education to larger classes and other centres would have produced at once a restrictive shortage of papyrus. Education did not reach into the masses at all; to become more than superficially educated one had to abandon the ordinary life of the times and come for long years to live a hovering existence in the neighbourhood of ill-equipped and overworked sages. Learning was not indeed so complete a withdrawal from ordinary life as initiation into a priesthood, but it was still something in that nature.

And very speedily that feeling of freedom, that openness and directness of statement which is the vital air of the true intellectual life, faded out of Alexandria. From the first the patronage even of Ptolemy I set a limit to political discussion. Presently the dissensions of the schools let in the superstitions and prejudices of the city mob to scholastic affairs.

Wisdom passed away from Alexandria and left pedantry behind. For the use of books was substituted the worship of books. Very speedily the learned became a specialized queer class with unpleasant characteristics of its own. The Museum had not existed for half a dozen generations before Alexandria was familiar with a new type of human being; shy, eccentric, unpractical, incapable of essentials, strangely fierce upon trivialities of literary detail, as bitterly jealous of the colleague within as of the unlearned without, the bent Scholarly Man. He was as intolerant as a priest, though he had no altar; as obscurantist as a magician, though he had no cave. For him no method of copying was sufficiently tedious and no rare book sufficiently inaccessible. He was a sort of by-product of the intellectual process of mankind. For many precious generations the new-lit fires of the human intelligence were to be seriously banked down by this by-product.

Right thinking is necessarily an open process, and the only science and history of full value to men consist of what is generally and clearly known; this is surely a platitude, but we have still to discover how to preserve our centres of philosophy and research from the caking and darkening accumulations of narrow and dingy-spirited specialists. We have still to ensure that a man of learning shall be none the less a man of affairs, and that all that can be thought and known is kept plainly, honestly, and easily available to the ordinary men and women who are the substance of mankind.

§ 2

At first the mental activities of Alexandria centred upon the Museum, and were mainly scientific. Philosophy, which in a more vigorous age had been a doctrine of power over self and the material world, without abandoning these pretensions, became in reality a doctrine of secret consolation. The stimulant changed into an opiate. The philosopher let the world, as the vulgar say, *rip*, the world of which he was a part, and consoled himself by saying in very beautiful and elaborate forms that the world was illusion and that there was in him something quintessential and sublime, outside and above the world. Athens, politically insignificant, but still a great and crowded mart throughout the fourth century, decaying almost imperceptibly so far as outer seeming went, and treated with a strange respect that was half contempt by all the warring powers and adventurers of the world, was the fitting centre of such philosophical teaching. It was quite a couple of centuries before the schools of Alexandria became as important in philosophical discussion.

§ 3

If Alexandria was late to develop a distinctive philosophy, she was early prominent as a great factory and exchange of religious ideas.

The Museum and Library represented only one of the three sides of the triple city of Alexandria. They represented the Aristotelian, the Hellenic, and Macedonian element. But Ptolemy I had brought together two other factors to this strange centre. First there was a great number of Jews, brought partly from Palestine, but largely also from those settlements in Egypt which had never returned to Jerusalem; these latter were the Jews of the Diaspora or Dispersion, a race of Jews who, as we have already noted in Chapter XIX, had not shared the Babylonian Captivity, but who were nevertheless in possession of the Bible and in close correspondence with their co-religionists throughout the world. These Jews populated so great a quarter of Alexandria that the town became the largest Jewish city in the world, with far more Jews in it than there were in Jerusalem. We have already noted that they had found it necessary to translate their scriptures into Greek. And, finally, there was a great population of native Egyptians, also for the most part speaking Greek, but with the superstitious temperament of the dark whites and with the vast tradition of forty centuries of temple religion and temple sacrifices at the back of their minds. In Alexandria three types of mind and spirit met, the three main types of the white race, the clear-headed criticism of the Aryan Greek, the moral fervour and monotheism of the Semitic Jew, and the deep Mediterranean tradition of mysteries and sacrifices that we have already seen at work in the secret cults and occult practices of Greece, ideas which in Hamitic Egypt ruled proudly in great temples in the open light of day.

These three were the permanent elements of the Alexandrian blend. But in the seaport and markets mingled men of every known race, comparing their religious ideas and customs. It is even related that in the third century B.C. Buddhist missionaries came from the court of King Asoka in India. Aristotle remarks in his *Politics* that the religious beliefs of men are apt to borrow their form from political institutions, "men assimilate the lives no less than the bodily forms of the gods to their own," and this age of Greek-speaking great empires under autocratic monarchs was bearing hardly upon those merely local celebrities, the old tribal and city deities. Men were requiring deities with an outlook at least as wide as the empires, and except where the interests of powerful priesthoods stood in the way, a curious process of assimilation of gods was going on. Men found that though there were many gods, they were all very much alike. Where there had been many gods, men came to think there must be really only one god under a diversity of names. He had been everywhere—under an alias. The Roman Jupiter, the Greek Zeus, the Egyptian Ammon, the putative father of Alexander and the old antagonist of Amenophis IV the Babylonian Bel-Marduk, were all sufficiently similar to be identified.

> "Father of all in every age, in every clime adored
> By saint, by savage and by sage, Jehovah, Jove or Lord."

Where there were distinct differences, the difficulty was met by saying that these were different *aspects* of the same god. Bel-Marduk, however, was now a very decadent god indeed, who hardly survived as a pseudonym; Assur, Dagon, and the like, poor old gods of fallen nations, had long since passed out of memory, and did not come into the amalgamation. Osiris, a god popular with the Egyptian commonalty, was already identified with Apis, the sacred bull in the temple of Memphis, and somewhat confused with Ammon. Under the name of Serapis he became the great god of Hellenic Alexandria. He was Jupiter-Serapis. The Egyptian cow goddess, Hathor or Isis, was also represented now in human guise as the wife of Osiris, to whom she bore the infant Horus, who grew up to be Osiris again. These bald statements sound strange, no doubt, to a modern mind, but these identifications and mixing up of one god with another are very illustrative of the struggle the quickening human intelligence was making to cling still to religion and its emotional bonds and fellowship, while making its gods more reasonable and universal.

Isis and Horus

This fusing of one god with another is called *theocrasia,* and nowhere was it more vigorously going on than in Alexandria.

Only two peoples resisted it in this period: the Jews, who already had their faith in the One God of Heaven and Earth, Jehovah, and the Persians who had a monotheistic sun worship.

Serapis

It was Ptolemy I who set up not only the Museum in Alexandria, but the Serapeum, devoted to the worship of a trinity of god which represented the result of a process of theocrasia applied more particularly to the gods of Greece and Egypt.

This trinity consisted of the god Serapis (= Osiris + Apis), the goddess Isis (= Hathor, the cow-moon goddess), and the child-god Horus. In one way or another almost every other god was identified with one or other of these three aspects of the one God, even the sun god Mithras of the Persians. And they were each other; they were three, but they were also one. They were worshipped with great fervour, and the jangling of a peculiar instrument, the *sistrum,* a frame set with bells and used rather after the fashion of the tambourine in the proceedings of the modern Salvation Army, was a distinctive accessory to the ceremonies. And now for the first time we find the idea of immortality becoming the central idea of a religion that extended beyond Egypt. Neither the early Aryans nor the early Semites seem to have troubled very much about immortality, it has affected the Mongolian mind very little, but the continuation of the individual life after death had been from the earliest times an intense preoccupation of the Egyptians. It played now a large part in the worship of Serapis. In the devotional literature of his cult he is spoken of as "the saviour and leader of souls, leading souls to the light and receiving them again." It is stated that "he raises the dead, he shows forth the longed-for light of the sun to those who see, whose holy tombs contain multitudes of sacred books"; and again, "we never can escape him, he will save us, after death we shall still be the care of his providence."[1]

The ceremonial burning of candles and the offering of ex-votos, that is to say of small models of parts of the human body in need of succour, was a part of the worship of the Serapeum. Isis attracted many devotees, who vowed their lives to her. Her images stood in the temple, crowned as the Queen of Heaven and bearing the infant Horus in her arms. The candles flared and guttered before her, and the wax ex-votos hung about the shrine. The novice was put through a long and careful preparation, he took vows of celibacy, and when he was initiated his head was shaved and he was clad in a linen garment. . . .

In this worship of Serapis, which spread very widely throughout the civilized world in the third and second centuries B.C., we see the most remarkable anticipations of usages and forms of expression that were destined to dominate the European world throughout the Christian era. The essential idea, the living spirit, of Christianity was, as we shall presently show, a new thing in the history of the mind and will of man; but the garments of ritual and symbol and formula that Christianity has worn, and still in many countries wears to this day, were certainly woven in the cult and temples of Jupiter, Serapis, and Isis that spread now from Alexandria throughout the civilized world in the age of theocrasia in the second and first centuries before Christ.

[1] Legge, *Forerunners and Rivals of Christianity.*

XXV

THE RISE AND SPREAD OF BUDDHISM

§ 1. *The Story of Gautama.* § 2. *Teaching and Legend in Conflict.* § 3. *The Gospel of Gautama Buddha.* § 4. *Buddhism and Asoka.*[1] § 5. *Two Great Chinese Teachers.* § 6. *The Corruptions of Buddhism.* § 7. *The Present Range of Buddhism.*

§ 1

IT is interesting to turn from the mental and moral activities of Athens and Alexandria, and the growth of human ideas in the Mediterranean world, to the almost entirely separate intellectual life of India. Here was a civilization which from the first seems to have grown up upon its own roots and with a character of its own. It was cut off from the civilizations to the west and to the east by vast mountain barriers and desert regions. The Aryan tribes who had come down into the peninsula soon lost touch with their kindred to the west and north, and developed upon lines of their own. This was more particularly the case with those who had passed on into the Ganges country and beyond. They found a civilization already scattered over India, the Dravidian civilization. This had arisen independently, just as the Sumerian, Cretan, and Egyptian civilizations seem to have arisen, out of that widespread development of the neolithic culture, the heliolithic culture, whose characteristics we have already described. They revived and changed this Dravidian civilization much as the Greeks did the Ægean or the Semites the Sumerian.

These Indian Aryans were living under different conditions from those that prevailed to the north-west. They were living in a warmer climate, in which a diet of beef and fermented liquor was destructive; they were forced, therefore, to a generally vegetarian dietary, and the prolific soil, almost unasked, gave them all the food they needed. There was no further

[1] Pronounced Ashoka.

reason for them to wander; the crops and seasons were trustworthy. They wanted little clothing or housing. They wanted so little that trade was undeveloped. There was still land for every one who desired to cultivate a patch—and a little patch sufficed. Their political life was simple and comparatively secure; no great conquering powers had arisen as yet in India, and her natural barriers sufficed to stop the early imperialisms to the west of her and to the east. Thousands of comparatively pacific little village republics and chieftainships were spread over the land. There was no sea life, there were no pirate raiders, no strange traders. One might write a history of India coming down to four hundred years ago and hardly mention the sea.

The history of India for many centuries had been happier, less fierce, and more dreamlike than any other history. The noblemen, the rajahs, hunted; life was largely made up of love stories. Here and there a maharajah arose amidst the rajahs and built a city, caught and tamed many elephants, slew many tigers, and left a tradition of his splendour and his wonderful processions.

It was somewhen between 500 and 600 B.C., when Crœsus was flourishing in Lydia and Cyrus was preparing to snatch Babylon from Nabonidus, that the founder of Buddhism was born in India. He was born in a small republican tribal community in the north of Bengal under the Himalayas, in what is now overgrown jungle country on the borders of Nepal. The little state was ruled by a family, the Sakya clan, of which this man, Siddhattha Gautama, was a member. Siddhattha was his personal name, like Caius or John; Gautama, or Gôtama, his family name, like Cæsar or Smith; Sakya his clan name, like Julius. The institution of caste was not yet fully established in India, and the Brahmins, though they were privileged and influential, had not yet struggled to the head of the system; but there were already strongly marked class distinctions and a practically impermeable partition between the noble Aryans and the darker common people. Gautama belonged to the former race. His teaching, we may note, was called the Aryan Path, the Aryan Truth.

It is only within the last half-century that the increasing study of the Pali language, in which most of the original sources were written, has given the world a real knowledge of the life and actual thought of Gautama. Previously his story was overlaid by monstrous accumulations of legend, and his teaching violently misconceived. But now we have a very human and understandable account of him.

He was a good-looking, capable young man of fortune, and until he was twenty-nine he lived the ordinary aristocratic life of his time. It was not a very satisfying life intellectually. There was no literature except the oral tradition of the Vedas, and that was chiefly monopolized by the Brahmins; there was even less knowledge. The world was bound by the snowy Himalayas to the north and spread indefinitely to the south. The city of Benares, which had a king, was about a hundred miles away. The chief amusements were hunting and lovemaking. All the good that life seemed to offer, Gautama enjoyed. He was married at nineteen to a beautiful cousin. For some years they remained childless. He hunted and played and went about in his sunny world of gardens and groves and irrigated rice-fields. And it was amidst this life that a great discontent fell upon him. It was the unhappiness of a fine brain that seeks employment. He lived amidst plenty and beauty, he passed from gratification to gratification, and his soul was not satisfied. It was as if he heard the destinies of the race calling to him. He felt that the existence he was leading was not the reality of life, but a holiday—a holiday that had gone on too long.

While he was in this mood he saw four things that served to point his thoughts. He was driving on some excursion of pleasure, when he came upon a man dreadfully broken down by age. The poor bent, enfeebled creature struck his imagination. "Such is the way of life," said Channa, his charioteer, and "to that we must all come." While this was yet in his mind he chanced upon a man suffering horribly from some loathsome disease. "Such is the way of life," said Channa. The third vision was of an unburied body, swollen, eyeless, mauled by passing birds and beasts and altogether terrible. "That is the way of life," said Channa.

The sense of disease and mortality, the insecurity and the unsatisfactoriness of all happiness, descended upon the mind of Gautama. And then he and Channa saw one of those wandering ascetics who already existed in great numbers in India. These men lived under severe rules, spending much time in meditation and in religious discussion. For many men before Gautama in that land of uneventful sunshine had found life distressing and mysterious. These ascetics were all supposed to be seeking some deeper reality in life, and a passionate desire to do likewise took possession of Gautama.

He was meditating upon this project, says the story, when the news was brought to him that his wife had been delivered of his first-born son. "This is another tie to break," said Gautama.

He returned to the village amidst the rejoicings of his fellow clansmen. There was a great feast and a Nautch dance to celebrate the birth of this new tie, and in the night Gautama awoke in a great agony of spirit, "like a man who is told that his house is on fire." In the ante-room the dancing girls were lying in strips of darkness and moonlight. He called Channa, and told him to prepare his horse. Then he went softly to the threshold of his wife's chamber, and saw her by the light of a little oil lamp, sleeping sweetly, surrounded by flowers, with his infant son in her arm. He felt a great craving to take up the child in one first and last embrace before he departed, but the fear of waking his wife prevented him, and at last he turned away and went out into the bright Indian moonshine to Channa waiting with the horses, and mounted and stole away.

As he rode through the night with Channa, it seemed to him that Mara, the Tempter of Mankind, filled the sky and disputed with him. "Return," said Mara, "and be a king, and I will make you the greatest of kings. Go on, and you will fail. Never will I cease to dog your footsteps. Lust or malice or anger will betray you at last in some unwary moment; sooner or later you will be mine."

Very far they rode that night, and in the morning he stopped outside the lands of his clan, and dismounted beside a sandy river. There he cut off his flowing locks with his sword, removed all his ornaments, and sent them and his horse and sword back to his house by Channa. Then going on he presently met a ragged man and exchanged clothes with him, and so having divested himself of all worldly entanglements, he was free to pursue his search after wisdom. He made his way southward to a resort of hermits and teachers in a hilly spur running into Bengal northward from the Vindhya Mountains, close to the town of Rajgir. There a number of wise men lived in a warren

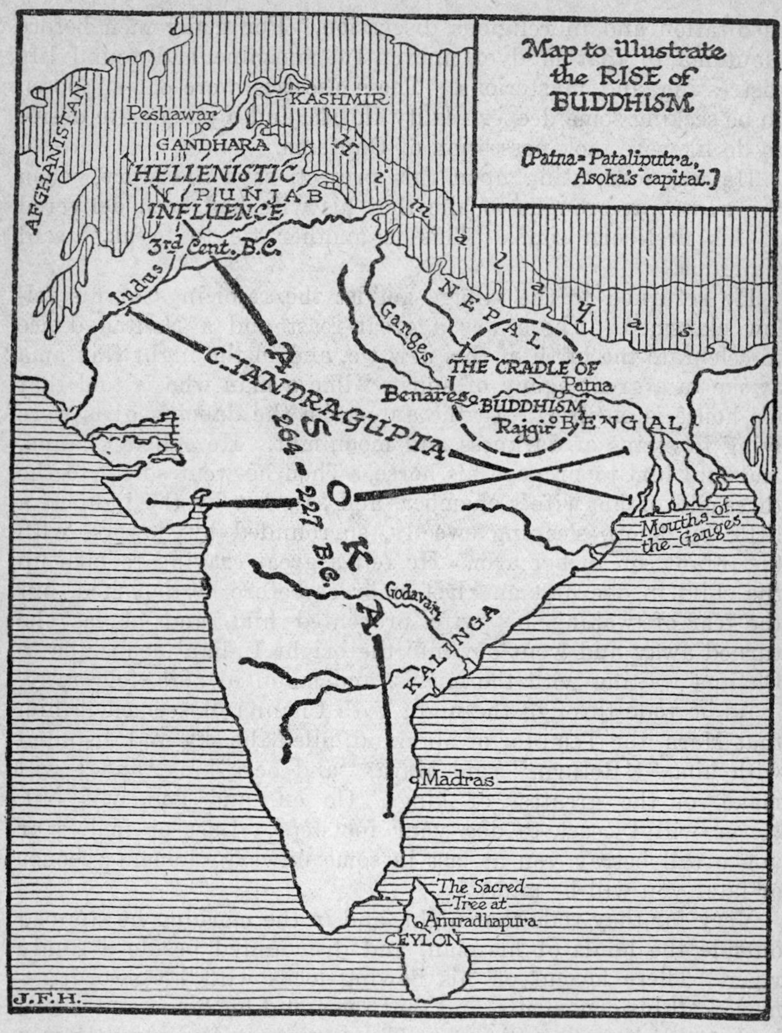

of caves, going into the town for their simple supplies and imparting their knowledge by word of mouth to such as cared to come to them.

This instruction must have been very much in the style of the Socratic discussions that were going on in Athens a couple of centuries later. Gautama became versed in all the metaphysics of his age. But his acute intelligence was dissatisfied with the solutions offered him.

The Indian mind has always been disposed to believe that power and knowledge may be obtained by extreme asceticism, by fasting, sleeplessness, and self-torment, and these ideas Gautama now put to the test. He betook himself with five disciple companions to the jungle in a gorge in the Vindhya Mountains, and there he gave himself up to fasting and terrible penances. His fame spread, "like the sound of a great bell hung in the canopy of the skies."[1] But it brought him no sense of truth achieved. One day he was walking up and down, trying to think in spite of his enfeebled state. Suddenly he staggered and fell unconscious. When he recovered, the preposterousness of these semi-magic ways of attempting wisdom was plain to him.

He amazed and horrified his five companions by demanding ordinary food and refusing to continue his self-mortifications. He had realized that whatever truth a man may reach is reached best by a nourished brain in a healthy body. Such a conception was absolutely foreign to the ideas of the land and age. His disciples deserted him, and went off in a melancholy state to Benares. The boom of the great bell ceased. Gautama the wonderful had fallen.

For a time Gautama wandered alone, the loneliest figure in history, battling for light.

When the mind grapples with a great and intricate problem, it makes its advances, it secures its positions step by step, with but little realization of the gains it has made, until suddenly, with an effect of abrupt illumination, it realizes its victory. So it would seem it happened to Gautama. He had seated himself under a great tree by the side of a river to eat, when this sense of clear vision came to him. It seemed to him that he saw life plain. He is said to have sat all day and all night in profound thought, and then he rose up to impart his vision to the world.

§ 2

Such is the plain story of Gautama as we gather it from a comparison of early writings. But common men must have their cheap marvels and wonders.

[1] The *Burmese Chronicle*, quoted by Rhys Davids.

It is nothing to them that this little planet should at last produce upon its surface a man thinking of the past and the future and the essential nature of existence. And so we must have this sort of thing by some worthy Pali scribe, making the most of it:

"When the conflict began between the Saviour of the World and the Prince of Evil a thousand appalling meteors fell. . . . Rivers flowed back towards their sources; peaks and lofty mountains where countless trees had grown for ages rolled crumbling to the earth . . . the sun enveloped itself in awful darkness, and a host of headless spirits filled the air."[1]

Of which phenomena history has preserved no authentication. Instead we have only the figure of a lonely man walking towards Benares.

Extraordinary attention has been given to the tree under which Guatama had this sense of mental clarity. It was a tree of the fig genus, and from the first it was treated with peculiar veneration. It was called the Bo Tree. It has long since perished, but close at hand lives another great tree which may be its descendant, and in Ceylon there grows to this day a tree, the oldest historical tree in the world, which we know certainly to have been planted as a cutting from the Bo Tree in the year 245 B.C. From that time to this it has been carefully tended and watered; its great branches are supported by pillars, and the earth has been terraced up about it so that it has been able to put out fresh roots continually. It helps us to realize the shortness of all human history to see so many generations spanned by the endurance of one single tree. Gautama's disciples unhappily have cared more for the preservation of his tree than of his thought, which from the first they misconceived and distorted.

At Benares Gautama sought out his five pupils, who were still leading the ascetic life. There is an account of their hesitation to receive him when they saw him approaching. He was a backslider. But there was some power of personality in him that prevailed over their coldness, and he made them listen to his new convictions. For five days the discussion was carried on. When he had at last convinced them that he was now enlightened, they hailed him as the Buddha. There was already in those days a belief in India that at long intervals Wisdom

[1] The *Madhurattha Vilasini,* quoted by Rhys Davids.

returned to the earth and was revealed to mankind through a chosen person known as the Buddha. According to Indian belief there have been many such Buddhas; Gautama Buddha is only the latest one of a series. But it is doubtful if he himself accepted that title or recognized that theory. In his discourses he never called himself the Buddha.

He and his recovered disciples then formed a sort of Academy in the Deer Park at Benares. They made themselves huts, and accumulated other followers to the number of threescore or more. In the rainy season they remained in discourse at this settlement, and during the dry weather they dispersed about the country, each giving his version of the new teachings. All their teaching was done, it would seem, by word of mouth. There was probably no writing yet in India at all. We must remember that in the time of Buddha it is doubtful if even the *Iliad* had been committed to writing. Probably the Mediterranean alphabet, which is the basis of most Indian scripts, had not yet reached India. The master, therefore, worked out and composed pithy and brief verses, aphorisms, and lists of "points," and these were expanded in the discourse of his disciples. It greatly helped them to have these points and aphorisms numbered. The modern mind is apt to be impatient of the tendency of Indian thought to a numerical statement of things, the Eightfold Path, the Four Truths, and so on, but this enumeration was a mnemonic necessity in an undocumented world.

§ 3

The fundamental teaching of Gautama, as it is now being made plain to us by the study of original sources, is clear and simple and in the closest harmony with modern ideas. It is beyond all dispute the achievement of one of the most penetrating intelligences the world has ever known.

We have what are almost certainly the authentic heads of his discourse to the five disciples which embodies his essential doctrine. All the miseries and discontents of life he traces to insatiable selfishness. Suffering, he teaches, is due to the craving individuality, to the torment of greedy desire. Until a man has overcome every sort of personal craving his life is trouble and his end sorrow. There are three principal forms the craving of life takes, and all are evil. The first is the desire to gratify the senses, sensuousness. The second is the desire for personal immortality. The third is the desire for prosperity, worldliness. All these must be overcome—that is to say, a man must no longer be living for himself—before life can become serene. But when they are indeed overcome and no longer rule a man's life, when the first personal pronoun has vanished from his private thoughts, then he has reached the higher wisdom, Nirvana, serenity of soul. For Nirvana does not mean, as many people wrongly believe, extinction, but the extinction of the futile personal aims that necessarily make life base or pitiful or dreadful.

Now here, surely we have the completest analysis of the problem of the soul's peace. Every religion that is worth the name, every philosophy, warns us to lose ourselves in something greater than ourselves. "Whosoever would save his life, shall lose it;" there is exactly the same lesson.

The teaching of history, as we are unfolding it in this book, is strictly in accordance with this teaching of Buddha. There is, as we are seeing, no social order, no security, no peace or happiness, no righteous leadership or kingship, unless men lose themselves in something greater than themselves. The study of biological progress again reveals exactly the same process—the merger of the narrow globe of the individual experience in a wider being (compare what has been said in Chaps. XI and XVI). To forget oneself in greater interests is to escape from a prison.

The self-abnegation must be complete. From the point of view of Gautama, that dread of death, that greed for an endless continuation of his mean little individual life which drove the Egyptian and those who learnt from him with propitiations and charms into the temples, was as mortal and ugly and evil a thing as lust or avarice or hate. The religion of Gautama is flatly opposite to the "immortality" religions. And his teaching is set like flint against asceticism, as a mere attempt to win personal power by personal pains.

But when we come to the rule of life, the Aryan Path, by which we are to escape from the threefold base cravings that dishonour human life, then the teaching is not so clear. It is not so clear for one very manifest reason, Gautama had no knowledge nor vision of history; he had no clear sense of the vast and many-sided adventure of life opening out in space and time. His mind was confined within the ideas of his age and people, and their minds were shaped into notions of perpetual recurrence, of world following world and of Buddha following Buddha, a stagnant circling of the universe. The idea of mankind as a great Brotherhood pursuing an endless destiny under the God of Righteousness, the idea that was already dawning upon the Semitic consciousness in Babylon at this time, did not exist in his world. Yet his account of the Eightfold Path is, nevertheless, within these limitations, profoundly wise.

Let us briefly recapitulate the eight elements of the Aryan Path. First, Right Views; Gautama placed the stern examination of views and ideas, the insistence upon *truth* as the first research of his followers. There was to be no clinging to tawdry superstitions. He condemned, for instance, the prevalent belief in the transmigration of souls. In a well-known early Buddhist dialogue there is a destructive analysis of the idea of an enduring individual soul. Next to Right Views came Right Aspirations; because nature abhors a vacuum, and since base cravings are to be expelled, other desires must be encouraged—love for the service of others, desire to do and secure justice and the like. Primitive and uncorrupted Buddhism aimed not at the destruction of desire, but at the change of desire. Devotion to science and art, or to the betterment of things manifestly falls into harmony with the Buddhistic Right Aspirations, provided such aims are free from jealousy or the craving for fame. Right Speech, Right Conduct, and Right Livelihood, need no expansion here. Sixthly in this list came Right Effort, for Gautama had no toleration for good intentions and slovenly application; the disciple had to keep a keenly critical eye upon his activities. The seventh element of the path, Right Mindfulness, is the constant guard against a lapse into personal feeling or glory for whatever is done or not done. And, finally, comes Right Rapture, which seems to be aimed against the pointless ecstacies of the devout, such witless gloryings, for instance, as those that went to the jingle of the Alexandrian sistrum.

We will not discuss here the Buddhistic doctrine of *Karma*, because it belongs to a world of thought that is passing away. The good or evil of every life was supposed to determine the happiness or misery of some subsequent life, that was in some inexplicable way identified with its predecessor. Nowadays we realize that a life goes on in its consequences for ever, but we find no necessity to suppose that any particular life resumes again. The Indian mind was full of the idea of cyclic recurrence; everything was supposed to come round again. This is a very natural supposition for men to make; so things seem to be until we analyze them. Modern science has made clear to us that there is no such exact recurrence as we are apt to suppose; every day is by an infinitesimal quantity a little longer than the day before; no generation repeats the previous generation precisely; history never repeats itself; change, we realize now, is inexhaustible; all things are eternally new. But these differences between our general ideas and those Buddha must have possessed need not in any way prevent us from appreciating the unprecedented wisdom, the goodness, and the greatness of this plan of an emancipated life as Gautama laid it down somewhen in the sixth century before Christ.

And if he failed in theory to gather together all the wills of the converted into the one multifarious activity of our race, battling against death and deadness in time and space, he did in practice direct his own life and that of all his immediate disciples into one progressive adventure, which was to preach and spread the doctrine and methods of Nirvana or soul-serenity throughout our fevered world. For them at least his teaching was complete and full. But all men cannot preach or teach; doctrine is but one of many of the functions of life that are fundamentally righteous. To the modern mind it seems at least equally acceptable that a man may, though perhaps against greater difficulties, cultivate the soil, rule a city, make roads, build houses, construct engines, or seek and spread knowledge, in perfect self-forgetfulness and serenity. As much was inherent in Gautama's teaching, but the stress was certainly laid upon the teaching itself, and upon withdrawal from rather than upon the ennoblement of the ordinary affairs of men.

In certain other respects this primitive Buddhism differed from any of the religions we have hitherto considered. It was primarily a religion of conduct, not a religion of observances and sacrifices. It had no temples, and since it had no sacrifices, it had no sacred order of priests. Nor had it any theology. It neither asserted nor denied the reality of the innumerable and often grotesque gods who were worshipped in India at that time. It passed them by.

§ 4

From the very first this new teaching was misconceived. One corruption was perhaps inherent in its teaching. Because the world of men had as yet no sense of the continuous progressive effort of life, it was very easy to slip from the idea of renouncing self to the idea of renouncing active life. As Gautama's own experiences had shown, it is easier to flee from this world than from self. His early disciples were strenuous thinkers and teachers, but the lapse into mere monastic seclusion was a very easy one, particularly easy in the climate of India, where an extreme simplicity of living is convenient and attractive, and exertion more laborious than anywhere else in the world.

And it was early the fate of Gautama, as it has been the fate of most religious founders since his days, to be made into a wonder by his less intelligent disciples in their efforts to impress the outer world. We have already noted how one devout follower could not but believe that the moment of the master's mental irradiation must necessarily have been marked by an epileptic fit of the elements. This is one small sample of the vast accumulation of vulgar marvels that presently sprang up about the memory of Gautama.

There can be no doubt that for the great multitude of human beings then as now the mere idea of an emancipation from self is a very difficult one to grasp. It is probable that even among the teachers Buddha was sending out from Benares there were many who did not grasp it and still less were able to convey it to their hearers. Their teaching quite naturally took on the aspect of salvation not from oneself—that idea was beyond them—but from misfortunes and sufferings here and hereafter. In the existing superstitions of the people, and especially in the idea of the transmigration of the soul after death, though this idea was contrary to the Master's own teaching, they found stuff of fear they could work upon. They urged virtue upon the people lest they should live again in degraded or miserable forms, or fall into some one of the innumerable hells of torment with which the Brahminical teachers had already familiarized their minds. They represented Buddha as the saviour from almost unlimited torment.

There seems to be no limit to the lies that honest but stupid disciples will tell for the glory of their master and for what they regard as the success of their propaganda. Men who would scorn to tell a lie in everyday life will become unscrupulous cheats and liars when they have given themselves up to propagandist work; it is one of the perplexing absurdities of our human nature. Such honest souls, for most of them were indubitably honest, were presently telling their hearers of the miracles that attended the Buddha's birth—they no longer called him Gautama, because that was too familiar a name—of his youthful feats of strength, of the marvels of his everyday life, winding up with a sort of illumination of his body at the moment of death. Of course it was impossible to believe that Buddha was the son of a mortal father. He was miraculously conceived through his mother dreaming of a beautiful white elephant! Previously he had himself been a marvellous elephant with six tusks; he had generously given them all to a needy hunter—and even helped him to saw them off. And so on.

Hariti (painting from Chinese Turkestan, 6th Cent.y A.D.)

[after Foucher]

Moreover, a theology grew up about Buddha. He was discovered to be a god. He was one of a series of divine beings, the Buddhas. There was an undying "Spirit of all the Buddhas"; there was a great series of Buddhas past and Buddhas (or Buddisatvas) yet to come. But we cannot go further into these complications of Asiatic theology. "Under the overpowering influence of these sickly imaginations the moral teachings of Gautama have been almost hid from view. The theories grew and flourished; each new step, each new hypothesis, demanded another; until the whole sky was filled with forgeries of the brain, and the nobler and simpler lessons of the founder of the religion were smothered beneath the glittering mass of metaphysical subtleties.''[1]

In the third century B.C. Buddhism was gaining wealth and power, and the little groups of simple huts in which the teachers of the Order gathered in the rainy season were giving place to substantial monastic buildings. To this period belong the beginnings of Buddhistic art. Now if we remember how recent was the adventure of Alexander, that all the Punjab was still under Seleucid rule, that all India abounded with Greek adventurers, and that there was still quite open communication by sea and land with Alexandria, it is no great wonder to find that this early Buddhist art was strongly Greek in character, and that the new Alexandrian cult of Serapis and Isis was extraordinarily influential in its development.

The kingdom of Gandhara on the north-west frontier near Peshawar, which flourished in the third century B.C., was a typical meeting-place of the Hellenic and Indian worlds. Here are to be found the earliest Buddhist sculptures, and interwoven with them are figures which are recognizably the figures of Serapis and Isis and Horus already worked into the legendary net that gathered about Buddha. No doubt the Greek artists who came to Gandhara were loth to relinquish a familiar theme. But Isis, we are told, is no longer Isis but Hariti, a pestilence goddess whom Buddha converted and made benevolent. Foucher traces Isis from this centre into China, but here other influences were also at work, and the story becomes too complex for us to disentangle in this *Outline*.[2] China had a Taoist deity, the Holy Mother, the Queen of Heaven, who took on the name (originally a male name) of Kuan-yin and who came to resemble the Isis figure very closely. The Isis figures, we feel, must have influenced the treatment of Kuan-yin. Like Isis she was also Queen of the Seas, Stella Maris. In Japan she was called Kwannon. There seems to have been a constant exchange of the outer forms of religion between east and west. We read in Huc's Travels how perplexing he and his fellow

[1] Rhys Davids, *Buddhism.*
[2] See R. F. Johnston, *Buddhist China.*—L. C. B.

missionary found this possession of a common tradition of worship. "The cross," he says, "the mitre, the dalmatica, the cope, which the Grand Lamas wear on their journeys, or when they are performing some ceremony out of the temple; the service with double choirs, the psalmody, the exorcisms, the censer, suspended from five chains, which you can open or close at pleasure; the benedictions given by the Lamas by extending the right hand over the heads of the faithful; the chaplet, ecclesiastical celibacy, spiritual retirement, the worship of the saints, the fasts, the processions, the litanies, the holy water, all these are analogies between the Buddhists and ourselves."[1]

The cult and doctrine of Gautama, gathering corruptions and variations from Brahminism and Hellenism alike, was spread throughout India by an increasing multitude of teachers in the fourth and third centuries B.C. For some generations at least it retained much of the moral beauty and something of the simplicity of the opening phase. Many people who have no intellectual grasp upon the meaning of self-abnegation and disinterestedness have nevertheless the ability to appreciate a splendour in the reality of these qualities. Early Buddhism was certainly producing noble lives, and it is not only through reason that the latent response to nobility is aroused in our minds. It spread rather in spite of than because of the concessions that it made to vulgar imaginations. It spread because many of the early Buddhists were sweet and gentle, helpful and noble and admirable people, who compelled belief in their sustaining faith.

Quite early in its career Buddhism came into conflict with the growing pretensions of the Brahmins. As we have already noted, this priestly caste was still only struggling to dominate Indian life in the days of Gautama. They had already great advantages. They had the monopoly of tradition and religious sacrifices. But their power was being challenged by the development of kingship, for the men who became clan leaders and kings were usually not of the Brahminical caste.

Kingship received an impetus from the Persian and Greek invasions of the Punjab. We have already noted the name of King Porus whom, in spite of his elephants, Alexander defeated and turned into a satrap. There came also to the Greek camp upon the Indus a certain adventurer named Chandra-

[1] Huc's *Travels in Tartary, Thibet, and China.*

gupta Maurya, whom the Greeks called Sandracottus, with a scheme for conquering the Ganges country. The scheme was not welcome to the Macedonians, who were in revolt against marching any further into India, and he had to fly the camp. He wandered among the tribes upon the north-west frontier, secured their support, and after Alexander had departed, overran the Punjab, ousting the Macedonian representatives. He then conquered the Ganges country (321 B.C.), waged a successful war (303 B.C.) against Seleucus (Seleucus I) when the latter attempted to recover the Punjab, and consolidated a great empire reaching across all the plain of northern India from the western to the eastern sea. And this King Chandragupta came into much the same conflict with the growing power of the Brahmins, into the conflict between crown and priesthood, that we have already noted as happening in Babylonia and Egypt and China. He saw in the spreading doctrine of Buddhism an ally against the growth of priestcraft and caste. He supported and endowed the Buddhistic Order, and encouraged its teachings.

He was succeeded by his son, who conquered Madras and was in turn succeeded by Asoka (264 to 227 B.C.), one of the great monarchs of history, whose dominions extended from Afghanistan to Madras. He is the only military monarch on record who abandoned warfare after victory. He had invaded Kalinga (255 B.C.), a country along the east coast of Madras, perhaps with some intention of completing the conquest of the tip of the Indian peninsula. The expedition was successful, but he was disgusted by what he saw of the cruelties and horrors of war. He declared, in certain inscriptions that still exist, that he would no longer seek conquest by war, but by religion, and the rest of his life was devoted to the spreading of Buddhism throughout the world.

He seems to have ruled his vast empire in peace and with great ability. He was no mere religious fanatic. But in the year of his one and only war he joined the Buddhist community as a layman, and some years later he became a full member of the Order, and devoted himself to the attainment of Nirvana by the Eightfold Path. How entirely compatible that way of living then was with the most useful and beneficent activities his life shows. Right Aspiration, Right Effort, and Right Liveli-

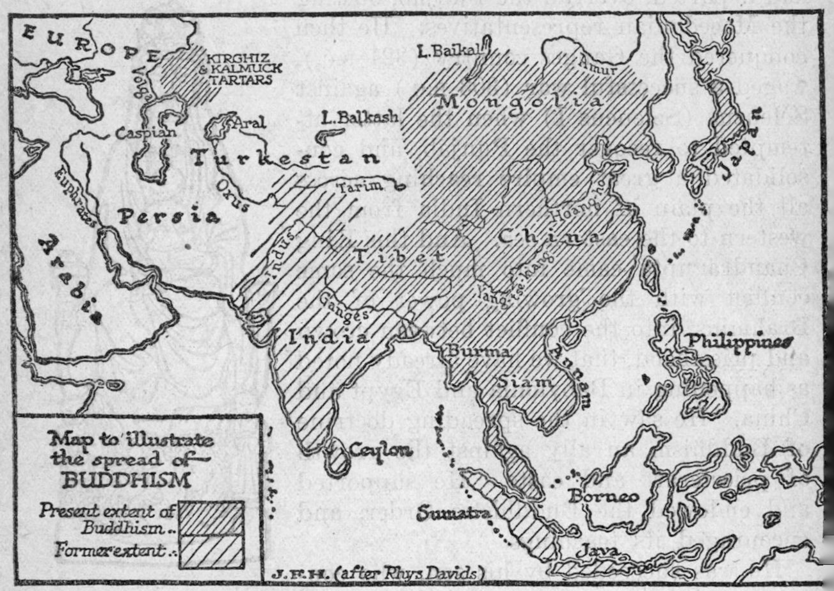

hood distinguished his career. He organized a great digging of wells in India, and the planting of trees for shade. He appointed officers for the supervision of charitable works. He founded hospitals and public gardens. He had gardens made for the growing of medicinal herbs. Had he had an Aristotle to inspire him, he would no doubt have endowed scientific research upon a great scale. He created a ministry for the care of the aborigines and subject races. He made provision for the education of women. He made, he was the first monarch to make, an attempt to educate his people into a common view of the ends and way of life. He made vast benefactions to the Buddhist teaching orders, and tried to stimulate them to a better study of their own literature. All over the land he set up long inscriptions rehearsing the teaching of Gautama, and it is the simple and human teaching and not the preposterous accretions. Thirty-five of his inscriptions survive to this day. Moreover, he sent missionaries to spread the noble and reasonable teaching of his master throughout the world, to Kashmir, to Ceylon, to the Seleucids, and the Ptolemies. It was one of these missions which carried that cutting of the Bo Tree, of which we have already told, to Ceylon.

For eight and twenty years Asoka worked sanely for the real needs of men. Amidst the tens of thousands of names of monarchs that crowd the columns of history, their majesties and graciousnesses and serenities and royal highnesses and the like, the name of Asoka shines, and shines almost alone, a star. From the Volga to Japan his name is still honoured. China, Tibet, and even India, though it has left his doctrine, preserve the tradition of his greatness. More living men cherish his memory to-day than have ever heard the names of Constantine or Charlemagne.

§ 5

It is thought that the vast benefactions of Asoka finally corrupted Buddhism by attracting to its Order great numbers of mercenary and insincere adherents, but there can be no doubt that its rapid extension throughout Asia was very largely due to his stimulus.

It made its way into Central Asia through Afghanistan and Turkestan, and so reached China. Buddhist teaching had spread widely in China before 200 B.C. Buddhism found there a popular and prevalent religion, Taoism, a development of very ancient and primitive magic and occult practices. It was reorganized as a distinctive cult by Chang Daoling in the days of the Han dynasty. Tao means the Way, which corresponds closely with the idea of the Aryan Path. The two religions spread side by side and underwent similar changes, so that nowadays their outward practice is very similar. Buddhism also encountered Confucianism, which was even less theological and even more a code of personal conduct. And finally it encountered the teachings of Lao Tse, "anarchist, evolutionist, pacifist and moral philosopher,"[1] which were not so much a

[1] S. N. Fu.

religion as a philosophical rule of life. The teachings of this Lao Tse were later to become incorporated with the Taoist religion by Chen Tuan, the founder of modern Taoism.

Confucius, the founder of Confucianism, like the great southern teacher Lao Tse and Gautama, lived also in the sixth century B.C. His life has some interesting parallelisms with that of some of the more political of the Greek philosophers of the fifth and fourth. The sixth century B.C. falls into the period assigned by Chinese historians to the Chow Dynasty, but in those days the rule of that dynasty had become little more than nominal; the emperor conducted the traditional sacrifices of the Son of Heaven, and received a certain formal respect. Even his nominal empire was not a sixth part of the China of to-day. In Chapter XIV we have already glanced at the state of affairs in China at this time; practically China was a multitude of warring states open to the northern barbarians. Confucius was a subject in one of those states, Lu; he was of aristocratic birth, but poor; and, after occupying various official positions, he set up a sort of Academy in Lu for the discovery and imparting of Wisdom. And we also find Confucius travelling from state to state in China, seeking a prince who would make him his counsellor and become the centre of a reformed world. Plato, two centuries later, in exactly the same spirit, went as adviser to the tyrant Dionysius of Syracuse, and we have already noted the attitudes of Aristotle and Isocrates towards Philip of Macedonia.

The teaching of Confucius centred upon the idea of a noble life which he embodied in a standard or ideal, the Aristocratic Man. This phrase is often translated into English as the Superior Person, but as "superior" and "person," like "respectable" and "genteel," have long become semi-humorous terms of abuse, this rendering is not fair to Confucianism. He did present to his time the ideal of a devoted public man. The public side was very important to him. He was far more of a constructive political thinker than Gautama or Lao Tse. His mind was full of the condition of China, and he sought to call the Aristocratic Man into existence very largely in order to produce the noble state. One of his sayings may be quoted here: "It is impossible to withdraw from the world, and associate with birds and beasts that have no affinity with us. With whom should I associate but with suffering men? The disorder that prevails is what requires my efforts. If right principles ruled through the kingdom, there would be no necessity for me to change its state."

The political basis of his teaching seems to be characteristic of Chinese moral ideas; there is a much directer reference to the State than is the case with most Indian and European moral and religious doctrine. For a time he was appointed magistrate in Chung-tu, a city of the dukedom of Lu, and here he sought to regulate life to an extraordinary extent, to subdue every relationship and action indeed to the rule of an elaborate etiquette. "Ceremonial in every detail, such as we are wont to see only in the courts of rulers and the households of high dignitaries, became obligatory on the people at large, and all matters of daily life were subject to rigid rule. Even the food which the different classes of people might eat was regulated; males and females were kept apart in the streets; even the thickness of coffins and the shape and situation of graves were made the subject of regulations.[1]

This is all, as people say, very Chinese. No other people have ever approached moral order and social stability through the channel of manners. Yet in China, at any rate, the methods of Confucius have had an enormous effect, and no nation in the world to-day has such a universal tradition of decorum and self-restraint.

Later on the influence of Confucius over his duke was undermined, and he withdrew again into private life. His last days were saddened by the deaths of some of his most promising disciples. "No intelligent ruler," he said, "arises to take me as his master, and my time has come to die." . . .

But he died to live. Says Hirth, "There can be no doubt that Confucius has had a greater influence on the development of the Chinese national character than many emperors taken together. He is, therefore, one of the essential figures to be considered in connection with any history of China. That he could influence his nation to such a degree was, it appears to me, due more to the peculiarity of the nation than to that of his own personality. Had he lived in any other part of the world, his name would perhaps be forgotten. As we have seen, he had

[1] Hirth's *The Ancient History of China*.

Siva
Brahma
Vishnu
J.F.H.

formed his character and his personal views on man's life from a careful study of documents closely connected with the moral philosophy cultivated by former generations. What he preached to his contemporaries was, therefore, not all new to them; but, having himself, in the study of old records, heard the dim voice of the sages of the past, he became, as it were, the megaphone phonograph through which were expressed to the nation those views which he had derived from the early development of the nation itself. . . . The great influence of Confucius's personality on national life in China was due not only to his writings and his teachings as recorded by others, but also to his doings. His personal character, as described by his disciples and in the accounts of later writers, some of which may be entirely legendary, has become the pattern for millons of those who are bent on imitating the outward manners of a great man. . . . Whatever he did in public was regulated to the minutest detail by ceremony. This was no invention of his own, since ceremonial life had been cultivated many centuries before Confucius; but his authority and example did much to perpetuate what he considered desirable social practices."

The Chinese speak of Buddhism and the doctrines of Lao Tse and Confucius as the Three Teachings. Together they constitute the basis and point of departure of all later Chinese thought. Their thorough study is a necessary preliminary to the establishment of any real intellectual and moral community between the great people of the East and the Western world.

There are certain things to be remarked in common of all these three teachers, of whom Gautama was indisputably the greatest and profoundest, whose doctrines to this day dominate the thought of the great majority of human beings; there are certain features in which their teaching contrasts with the thoughts and feelings that were soon to take possession of the Western world. Primarily they are personal and tolerant doctrines; they are doctrines of a Way, of a Path, of a Nobility, and not doctrines of a church or a general rule. And they offer nothing either for or against the existence and worship of the current gods. The Athenian philosophers, it is to be noted, had just the same theological detachment! Socrates was quite willing to bow politely or sacrifice formally to almost any divinity,—reserving his private thoughts. This attitude is flatly antagonistic to the state of mind that was growing up in the Jewish communities of Judea, Egypt, and Babylonia, in which the thought of the one God was first and foremost. Neither Gautama nor Lao Tse nor Confucius had any inkling of this idea of a *jealous* God, a God who would have "none other gods," a God of terrible Truth, who would not tolerate any lurking belief in magic, witchcraft, or old customs, or any sacrificing to the god-king or any trifling with the stern unity of things.

§ 6

The intolerance of the Jewish mind did keep its essential faith clear and clean. The theological disregard of the great Eastern teachers, neither assenting nor denying, did on the other hand permit elaborations of explanation and accumulations of ritual from the very beginning. Except for Gautama's insistence upon Right Views, which was easily disregarded, there was no *self-cleansing* element in either Buddhism, Taoism, or Confucianism. There was no effective prohibition of superstitious practices, spirit raising, incantations, prostrations, and supplementary worships. At an early stage a process of encrustation began, and continued. The new faiths caught almost every disease of the corrupt religions they sought to replace; they took over the idols and the temples, the altars and the censers.

Tibet to-day is a Buddhistic country, yet Gautama, could he return to earth, might go from end to end of Tibet seeking his own teaching in vain. He would find that most ancient type of human ruler, a god-king, enthroned, the Dalai Lama, the "living Buddha." At Lhassa he would find a huge temple filled with priests, abbots, and lamas—he whose only buildings were huts and who made no priests—and above a high altar he would behold a huge golden idol, which he would learn was called "Gautama Buddha"! He would hear services intoned before this divinity, and certain precepts, which would be dimly familiar to him, murmured as responses. Bells, incense, prostrations, would play their part in these amazing proceedings. At one point in the service a bell would be rung and a mirror lifted up, while the whole congregation, in an access of reverence, bowed lower. . . .

About this Buddhist countryside he would discover a number of curious little mechanisms, little wind-wheels and water-

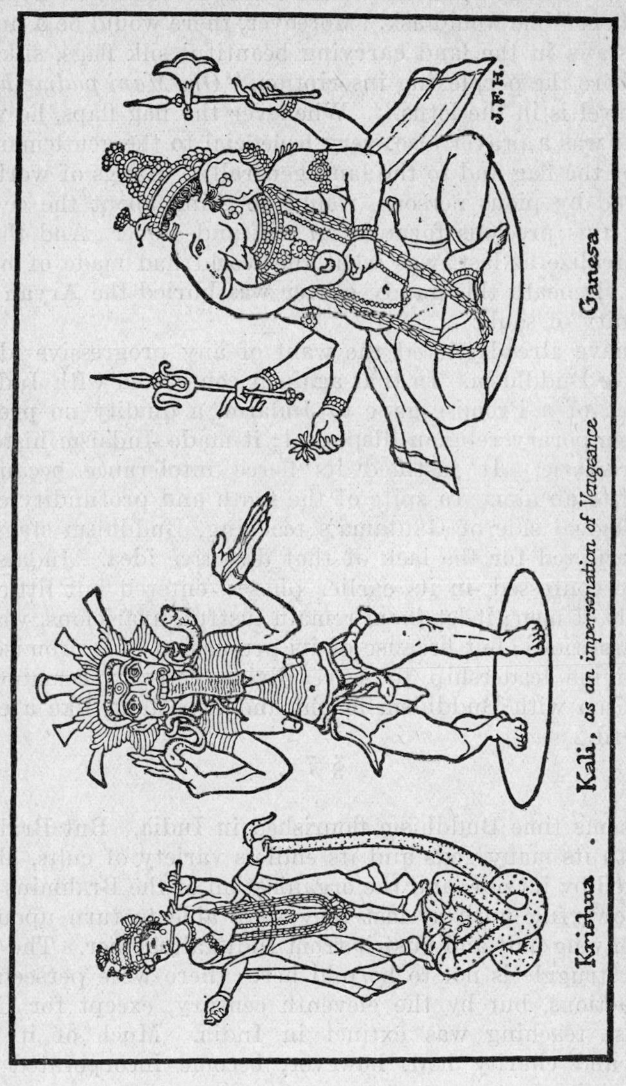

Krishna . Kali, *as an impersonation of Vengeance* Ganesa

wheels spinning, on which brief prayers were inscribed. Every time these things spin, he would learn, it counts as a prayer. "To whom?" he would ask. Moreover, there would be a number of flagstaffs in the land carrying beautiful silk flags, silk flags which bore the perplexing inscription, "*Om Mani padme hum,*" "the jewel is in the lotus." Whenever the flag flaps, he would learn, it was a prayer also, very beneficial to the gentleman who paid for the flag and to the land generally. Gangs of workmen, employed by pious persons, would be going about the country cutting this precious formula on cliff and stone. And this, he would realize at last, was what the world had made of his religion! Beneath this gaudy glitter was buried the Aryan Way to serenity of soul.

We have already noted the want of any progressive idea in primitive Buddhism. In that again it contrasted with Judaism. The idea of a Promise gave to Judaism a quality no previous or contemporary religion displayed; it made Judaism historical and dramatic. It justified its fierce intolerance because it pointed to an aim. In spite of the truth and profundity of the psychological side of Gautama's teaching, Buddhism stagnated and corrupted for the lack of that directive idea. Judaism, it must be confessed, in its earlier phases, entered but little into the souls of men; it let them remain lustful, avaricious, worldly or superstitious; but because of its persuasion of a promise and of a divine leadership to serve divine ends, it remained in comparison with Buddhism bright and expectant, like a cared-for sword.

§ 7

For some time Buddhism flourished in India. But Brahminism, with its many gods and its endless variety of cults, always flourished by its side, and the organization of the Brahmins grew more powerful, until at last they were able to turn upon this caste-denying cult and oust it from India altogether. The story of that struggle is not to be told here; there were persecutions and reactions, but by the eleventh century, except for Orissa Buddhist teaching was extinct in India. Much of its gentleness and charity had, however, become incorporated with Brahminism.

Over great areas of the world, as our map has shown, it still survives; and it is quite possible that in contact with western science, and inspired by the spirit of history, the original teaching of Gautama, revived and purified, may yet play a large part in the direction of human destiny.

But with the loss of India the Aryan Way ceased to rule the lives of any Aryan peoples. It is curious to note that while the one great Aryan religion is now almost exclusively confined to Mongolian peoples, the Aryans themselves are under the sway of two religions, Christianity and Islam, which are, as we shall see, essentially Semitic. And both Buddhism and Christianity wear garments of ritual and formula that seem to be derived through Hellenistic channels from that land of temples and priestcraft, Egypt, and from the more primitive and fundamental mentality of the brown Hamitic peoples.

XXVI

THE TWO WESTERN REPUBLICS

§ 1

IT is now necessary to take up the history of the two great republics of the Western Mediterranean, Rome and Carthage, and to tell how Rome succeeded in maintaining for some centuries an empire even greater than that achieved by the conquests of Alexander. But this new empire was, as we shall try to make clear, a political structure differing very profoundly in its nature from any of the great Oriental empires that had preceded it. Great changes in the texture of human society and in the conditions of social interrelations had been going on for some centuries. The flexibility and transferability of money was becoming a power and, like all powers in inexpert hands, a danger in human affairs. It was altering the relations of rich men to the state and to their poorer fellow citizens. This new empire, the Roman empire, unlike all the preceding empires, was not the creation of a great conqueror. No Sargon, no Thotmes, no Nebuchadnezzar, no Cyrus nor Alexander nor Chandragupta, was its fountain head. It was made by a republic. It grew by a kind of necessity through new concentrating and unifying forces that were steadily gathering power in human affairs.

But first it is necessary to give some idea of the state of affairs in Italy in the centuries immediately preceding the appearance of Rome in the world's story.

Before 1200 B.C., that is to say before the rise of the Assyrian empire, the siege of Troy, and the final destruction of Cnossos, but after the time of Amenophis IV, Italy, like Spain, was probably still inhabited mainly by dark white people of the more fundamental Iberian or Mediterranean race. This aboriginal population was probably a thin and backward one. But already in Italy, as in Greece, the Aryans were coming southward. By 1000 B.C. immigrants from the north had settled over most of the north and centre of Italy, and, as in Greece, they had intermarried with their darker predecessors

and established a group of Aryan languages, the Italian group, more akin to the Keltic (Gaelic) than to any other, of which the most interesting from the historical point of view was that spoken by the Latin tribes in the plains south and east of the river Tiber. Meanwhile the Greeks had been settling down in Greece, and now they were taking to the sea and crossing over to South Italy and Sicily and establishing themselves there. Subsequently they established colonies along the French Riviera and founded Marseilles upon the site of an older Phœnician colony. Another interesting people also had come into Italy by sea. These were a brownish sturdy people, to judge from the pictures they have left of themselves; very probably they were a tribe of those Ægean "dark whites" who were being driven out of Greece and Asia Minor and the islands in between by the Greeks. We have already told the tale of Cnossos (Chapter XV) and of the settlement of the kindred Philistines in Palestine (Chapter XIX, § 1). These Etruscans, as they were

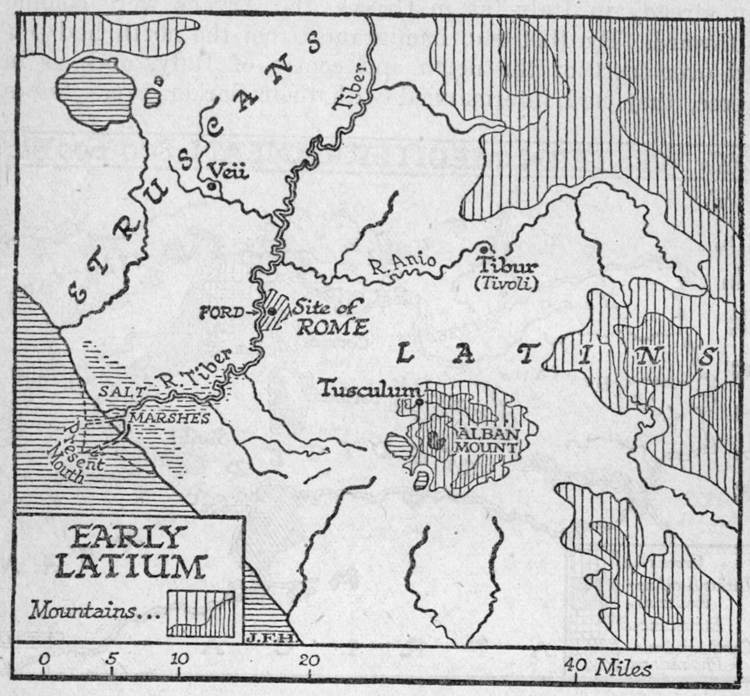

called in Italy, were known even in ancient times to be of Asiatic origin, and it is tempting, but probably unjustifiable, to connect this tradition with the Æneid, the sham epic of the Latin poet Virgil, in which the Latin civilization is ascribed to Trojan immigrants from Asia Minor. (But the Trojans themselves were probably an Aryan people allied to the Phrygians.) These Etruscan people conquered most of Italy north of the Tiber from the Aryan tribes who were scattered over that country. Probably the Etruscans ruled over a subjugated Italian population, so reversing the state of affairs in Greece, in which the Aryans were uppermost.

Our map, which may be taken to represent roughly the state of affairs about 750 B.C., also shows the establishments of the Phœnician traders, of which Carthage was the chief, along the shores of Africa and Spain.

Of all the peoples actually in Italy, the Etruscans were by far the most civilized. They built sturdy fortresses of the Mycænean type of architecture; they had a metal industry; they used imported Greek pottery of a very fine type. The Latin tribes on the other side of the Tiber were by comparison barbaric.

The Latins were still a rude farming people. The centre of their worship was a temple to the tribal god Jupiter, upon the Alban Mount. There they gathered for their chief festivals very much after the fashion of the early tribal gathering we have already imagined at Avebury. This gathering place was not a town. It was a high place of assembly. There was no population permanently there. There were, however, twelve townships in the Latin league. At one point upon the Tiber there was a ford, and here there was a trade between Latins and Etruscans. At this ford Rome had its beginnings. Traders assembled there, and refugees from the twelve towns found an asylum and occupation at this trading centre. Upon the seven hills near the ford a number of settlements sprang up, which finally amalgamated into one city.

Most people have heard the story of the two brothers Romulus and Remus, who founded Rome, and the legend of how they were exposed as infants and sheltered and suckled by a wolf. Little value is now attached to this tale by modern historians. The date 753 B.C. is given for the founding of Rome, but there are Etruscan tombs beneath the Roman Forum of a much earlier date than that, and the so-called tomb of Romulus bears an indecipherable Etruscan inscription.

The peninsula of Italy was not then the smiling land of vineyards and olive orchards it has since become. It was still a rough country of marsh and forest, in which the farmers grazed their cattle and made their clearings. Rome, on the boundary between Latin and Etruscan, was not in a very strong position for defence. At first there were perhaps Latin kings in Rome, then it would seem the city fell into the hands of Etruscan rulers whose tyrannous conduct led at last to their expulsion, and Rome became a Latin-speaking republic. The Etruscan kings were expelled from Rome in the sixth century B.C., while the successors of Nebuchadnezzar were ruling by the sufferance of the Medes in Babylon, while Confucius was seeking a king to reform the disorders of China, and while Gautama was teaching the Aryan Way to his disciples at Benares.

Etruscan painting of a Ceremonial Burning of the Dead

Of the struggle between the Romans and the Etruscans we cannot tell in any detail here. The Etruscans were the better armed, the more civilized, and the more numerous, and it would probably have gone hard with the Romans if they had had to fight them alone. But two disasters happened to the Etruscans which so weakened them that the Romans were able at last to master them altogether. The first of these was a war with the Greeks of Syracuse in Sicily which destroyed the Etruscan fleet (474 B.C.), and the second was a great raid of the Gauls from the north into Italy. These latter people swarmed into North Italy and occupied the valley of the Po towards the end of the fifth century B.C., as a couple of centuries later their kindred were to swarm down into Greece and Asia Minor and settle in Galatia. The Etruscans were thus caught between hammer and anvil, and after a long and intermittent war the Romans were able to capture Veii, an Etruscan fortress, a few miles from Rome, which had hitherto been a great threat and annoyance to them.

It is to this period of struggle against the Etruscan monarchs, the Tarquins, that Macaulay's *Lays of Ancient Rome,* familiar to every schoolboy, refer.

But the invasion of the Gauls was one of those convulsions of the nations that leave nothing as it has been before. They carried their raiding right down the Italian peninsula, devastating all Etruria. They took and sacked Rome (390 B.C.). According to Roman legends—on which doubt is thrown—the citadel on the Capitol held out, and this also the Gauls would have taken by surprise at night, if certain geese had not been awakened by their stealthy movements and set up such a cackling as to arouse the garrison. After that the Gauls, who were ill-equipped for siege operations, and perhaps suffering from disease in their camp, were bought off, and departed to the northward again, and, though they made subsequent raids, they never again reached Rome.

The leader of the Gauls who sacked Rome was named Brennus. It is related of him that as the gold of the ransom was being weighed, there was some dispute about the justice of the counterpoise, whereupon he flung his sword into the scale, saying, "*Vœ victus!*" ("Woe to the vanquished!")—a phrase that has haunted the discussions of all subsequent ransoms and indemnities down to the present time.

For half a century after this experience Rome was engaged in a series of wars to establish herself at the head of the Latin tribes. For the burning of the chief city seems to have stimulated rather than crippled her energies. However much she had suffered, most of her neighbours seem to have suffered more. By 290 B.C. Rome was the mistress city of all Central Italy from the Arno to south of Naples. She had conquered the Etruscans altogether, and her boundaries marched with those of the Gauls to the north and with the regions of Italy under Greek dominion (Magna Græcia) to the south. Along the Gaulish boundary she had planted garrisons and colonial cities, and no doubt it was because of that line of defence that the raiding enterprises of the Gauls were deflected eastward into the Balkans.

After what we have already told of the history of Greece and the constitutions of her cities, it will not surprise the reader to learn that the Greeks of Sicily and Italy were divided up into a number of separate city governments, of which Syracuse and Tarentum (the modern Taranto) were the chief, and that they had no common rule of direction or policy. But now, alarmed at the spread of the Roman power, they looked across the Adriatic for help, and found it in the ambitions of Pyrrhus, the king of Epirus. Between the Romans and Pyrrhus these Greeks of Magna Græcia were very much in the same position that Greece proper had been in, between the Macedonians and the Persians half a century before.

The reader will remember that Epirus, the part of Greece

that is closest to the heel of Italy, was the native land of Olympias, the mother of Alexander. In the kaleidoscopic changes of the map that followed the death of Alexander, Epirus was sometimes swamped by Macedonia, sometimes independent. This Pyrrhus was a kinsman of Alexander the Great, and a monarch of ability and enterprise, and he seems to have planned a career of conquest in Italy and Sicily. He commanded an admirable army, against which the comparatively inexpert Roman levies could at first do little. His army included all the established military devices of the time, an infantry phalanx, Thessalian cavalry, and twenty fighting elephants from the east. He routed the Romans at Heraclea (280 B.C.), and, pressing after them, defeated them again at Ausculum (279 B.C.) in their own territory. Then, instead of pursuing the Romans further, he made a truce with them, turned his attention to the subjugation of Sicily, and so brought the sea power of Carthage into alliance against him. For Carthage could not afford to have a strong power established so close to her as Sicily. Rome in those days seemed to the Carthaginians a far less serious threat than the possibility of another Alexander the Great ruling Sicily. A Carthaginian fleet appeared off the mouth of the Tiber, therefore, to encourage or induce the

Romans to renew the struggle, and Rome and Carthage were definitely allied against the invader.

This interposition of Carthage was fatal to Pyrrhus. Without any decisive battle his power wilted, and, after a disastrous repulse in an attack upon the Roman camp of Beneventum, he had to retire to Epirus (275 B.C.).

It is recorded that when Pyrrhus left Sicily, he said he left it to be the battleground of Rome and Carthage. He was killed three years later in a battle in the streets of Argos. The war against Pyrrhus was won by the Carthaginian fleet, and Rome reaped a full half of the harvest of victory. Sicily fell completely to Carthage, and Rome came down to the toe and heel of Italy, and looked across the Straits of Messina at her new rival. In eleven years' time (264 B.C.) the prophecy of Pyrrhus was fulfilled, and the first war with Carthage, the first of the three Punic[1] Wars, had begun.

§ 2

But we write "Rome" and the "Romans," and we have still to explain what manner of people these were who were playing a rôle of conquest that had hitherto been played only by able and aggressive monarchs.

Their state was, in the fifth century B.C., a republic of the Aryan type very similar to a Greek aristocratic republic. The earliest accounts of the social life of Rome give us a picture of a very primitive Aryan community. "In the second half of the fifth century before Christ, Rome was still an aristocratic community of free peasants, occupying an area of nearly 400 square miles, with a population certainly not exceeding 150,000, almost entirely dispersed over the country-side and divided into seventeen districts or rural tribes. Most of the families had a small holding and a cottage of their own, where father and sons lived and worked together, growing corn for the most part, with here and there a strip of vine or olive. Their few head of cattle were kept at pasture on the neighbouring common land; their clothes and simple implements of husbandry they made for themselves at home. Only at rare intervals and on special

[1] Latin *Poeni* = Carthaginians. *Punicus* (*adj.*) = Carthaginian, *i.e.* Phœnician.

occasions would they make their way into the fortified town, which was the centre at once of their religion and their government. Here were the temples of the gods, the houses of the wealthy, and the shops of the artisans and traders, where corn, oil, or wine could be bartered in small quantities for salt or rough tools and weapons of iron."[1]

ROMAN COIN STRUCK TO COMMEMORATE THE VICTORY OVER PYRRHUS AND HIS ELEPHANTS.

This community followed the usual tradition of a division into aristocratic and common citizens, who were called in Rome patricians and plebeians. These were the citizens; the slave or outlander had no more part in the state than he had in Greece. But the constitution differed from any Greek constitution in the fact that a great part of the ruling power was gathered into the hands of a body called the Senate, which was neither purely a body of hereditary members nor directly an elected and representative one. It was a nominated one, and in the earlier period it was nominated solely from among the patricians. It existed before the expulsion of the kings, and in the time of the kings it was the king who nominated the senators. But after the expulsion of the kings (510 B.C.), the supreme government was vested in the hands of two elected rulers, the *consuls;* and it was the consuls who took over the business of appointing senators. In the early days of the Republic only patricians were eligible as consuls or senators, and the share of the plebeians in the government consisted merely in a right to vote for the consuls and other public officials. Even for that purpose their votes did not have the same value as those of their patrician fellow citizens. But their votes had at any rate sufficient weight to induce many of the patrician candidates to profess a more or less sincere concern for plebeian grievances. In the early phases of the Roman state, moreover, the plebeians were not only excluded from public office, but from intermarriage with the patrician class. The administration was evidently primarily a patrician affair.

[1] Ferrero. *The Greatness and Decline of Rome.*

The early phase of Roman affairs was therefore an aristocracy of a very pronounced type, and the internal history of Rome for the two centuries and a half between the expulsion of the last Etruscan king, Tarquin the Proud, and the beginning of the first Punic War (264 B.C.), was very largely a struggle for mastery between those two orders, the patricians and the plebeians. It was, in fact, closely parallel with the struggle of aristocracy and democracy in the city states of Greece, and, as in the case of Greece, there were whole classes in the community, slaves, freed slaves, unpropertied free men, outlanders, and the like, who were entirely outside and beneath the struggle. We have already noted the essential difference of Greek democracy and what is called democracy in the world to-day. Another misused word is the Roman term *proletariat* which in modern jargon means all the unpropertied people in a modern state. In Rome the *proletarii* were a voting division of fully qualified citizens whose property was less than 10,000 copper asses (=£275). They were an enrolled class; their value to the state consisted in their raising families of citizens (proles = offspring), and from their ranks were drawn the colonists who went to form new Latin cities or to garrison important points. But the proletarii were quite distinct in origin from slaves or freedmen or the miscellaneous driftage of a town slum, and it is a great pity that modern political discussion should be confused by an inaccurate use of a term which has no exact modern equivalent and which expresses nothing real in modern social classification.

The mass of the details of this struggle between patricians and plebeians we can afford to ignore in this outline. It was a struggle which showed the Romans to be a people of a curiously shrewd character, never forcing things to a destructive crisis, but being within the limits of their discretion grasping hard dealers. The patricians made a mean use of their political advantages to grow rich through the national conquests at the expense not only of the defeated enemy, but of the poorer plebeian, whose farm had been neglected and who had fallen into debt during his military service. The plebeians were ousted from any share in the conquered lands, which the patricians divided up among themselves. The introduction of money probably increased the facilities of the usurer and the difficulties of the borrowing debtor.

Three sorts of pressure won the plebeians a greater share in the government of the country and the good things that were coming to Rome as she grew powerful. The first of these (1) was the general strike of plebeians. Twice they actually marched right out of Rome, threatening to make a new city higher up the Tiber, and twice this threat proved conclusive. The second method of pressure (2) was the threat of a tyranny. Just as in Attica (the little state of which Athens was the capital), Peisistratus raised himself to power on the support of the poorer districts, so there was to be found in most periods of plebeian discontent some ambitious man ready to figure as a leader and wrest power from the Senate. For a long time the Roman patricians were clever enough to beat every such potential tyrant by giving in to a certain extent to the plebeians. And finally (3) there were patricians big-minded and far-seeing enough to insist upon the need of reconciliation with the plebeians.

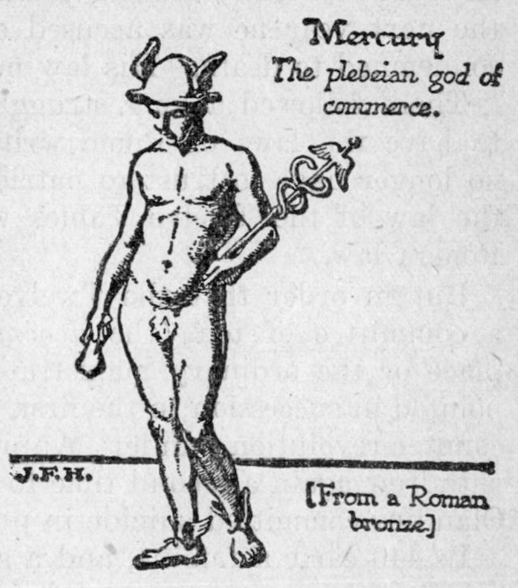

Mercury
The plebeian god of commerce.
[From a Roman bronze.]

Thus in 509 B.C., Valerius Poplicola (3), the consul, enacted that whenever the life or rights of any citizen were at stake, there should be an appeal from the magistrates to the general assembly. This Lex Valeria was "the Habeas Corpus of Rome," and it freed the Roman plebeians from the worst dangers of class vindictiveness in the law courts.

In 494 B.C. occurred a strike (1). "After the Latin war the pressure of debt had become excessive, and the plebeians saw with indignation their friends, who had often served the state bravely in the legions, thrown into chains and reduced to slavery at the demand of patrician creditors. War was raging against the Volscians; but the legionaries, on their victorious return, refused any longer to obey the consuls, and marched, though without any disorder, to the Sacred Mount beyond the Anio (up the Tiber). There they prepared to found a new city, since the rights of citizens were denied to them in the old one. The patricians were compelled to give way, and the plebeians, returning to Rome from the "First Secession," received the privilege of having officers of their own, tribunes and ædiles."[1]

In 486 B.C. arose Spurius Cassius (2), a consul who carried an Agrarian Law securing public land for the plebeians. But the next year he was accused of aiming at royal power, and condemned to death. His law never came into operation.

There followed a long struggle on the part of the plebeians to have the laws of Rome written down, so that they would no longer have to trust to patrician memories. In 451-450 B.C. the law of the Twelve Tables was published, the basis of all Roman law.

But in order that the Twelve Tables should be formulated, a committee of ten (the *decemvirate*) was appointed in the place of the ordinary magistrates. A second decemvirate, appointed in succession to the first, attempted a sort of aristocratic counter-revolution under Appius Claudius. The plebeians withdrew again a second time to the Sacred Mount, and Appius Claudius committed suicide in prison.

In 440 came a famine, and a second attempt to found a popular tyranny upon the popular wrongs, by Spurius Mælius, a wealthy plebeian, which ended in his assassination.

After the sack of Rome by the Gauls (390 B.C.), Marcus Manlius, who had been in command of the Capitol when the geese had saved it, came forward as a popular leader. The plebeians were suffering severely from the after-war usury and profiteering of the patricians, and were incurring heavy debts in rebuilding and restocking their farms. Manlius spent his fortune in releasing debtors. He was accused by the patricians of tyrannous intentions, condemned, and suffered the fate of condemned traitors in Rome, being flung from the Tarpeian Rock, the precipitous edge of that same Capitoline Hill he had defended.

In 376 B.C., Licinius, who was one of the ten tribunes for the people, began a long struggle with the patricians by making certain proposals called the Licinian Rogations, that there should be a limit to the amount of public land taken by any single citizen, so leaving some for everybody, that outstanding

[1] J. Wells, *Short History of Rome to the Death of Augustus.*

debts should be forgiven without interest upon the repayment of the principal, and that henceforth one at least of the two consuls should be a plebeian. This precipitated a ten-year struggle. The plebeian power to stop business by the veto of their representatives, the tribunes, was fully exercised. In cases of national extremity it was the custom to set all other magistrates aside and appoint one leader, the Dictator. Rome had done such a thing during times of military necessity before, but now the patricians set up a Dictator in a time of profound peace, with the idea of crushing Licinius altogether. They appointed Camillus, who had besieged and taken Veii from the Etruscans. But Camillus was a wiser man than his supporters; he brought about a compromise between the two orders in which most of the demands of the plebeians were conceded (366 B.C.), dedicated a temple to Concord, and resigned his power.

Thereafter the struggle between the orders abated. It abated because, among other influences, the social differences between patricians and plebeians were diminishing. Trade was coming to Rome with increasing political power, and many plebeians were growing rich and many patricians becoming relatively poor. Intermarriage had been rendered possible by a change in the law, and social intermixture was going on. While the rich plebeians were becoming, if not aristocratic, at least oligarchic in habits and sympathy, new classes were springing up in Rome with fresh interests and no political standing. Particularly abundant were the freedmen, slaves set free, for the most part artisans, but some of them traders, who were growing wealthy. And the Senate, no longer a purely patrician body—since various official positions were now open to plebeians, and such plebeian officials became senators—was becoming now an assembly of all the wealthy, able, energetic, and influential men in the state. The Roman power was expanding, and as it expanded these old class oppositions of the early Latin community were becoming unmeaning. They were being replaced by new associations and new antagonisms. Rich men of all origins were being drawn together into a common interest against the communistic ideas of the poor.

In 390 B.C. Rome was a miserable little city on the borders of Etruria, being sacked by the Gauls; in 275 B.C. she was ruling and unifying all Italy, from the Arno to the Straits of Messina. The compromise of Camillus (367 B.C.) had put an end to internal dissensions, and left her energies free for expansion. And the same queer combination of sagacity and aggressive selfishness that had distinguished the war of her orders at home and enabled her population to worry out a balance of power without any catastrophe, marks her policy abroad. She understood the value of allies; she could assimilate; abroad as at home she could in those days at least "give and take" with a certain fairness and sanity. There lay the peculiar power of Rome. By that it was she succeeded where Athens, for example, had conspicuously failed.

The Athenian democracy suffered much from that narrowness of "patriotism," which is the ruin of all nations. Athens was disliked and envied by her own empire because she dominated it in a spirit of civic egotism; her disasters were not felt and shared as disasters by her subject-cities. The shrewder, nobler Roman senators of the great years of Rome, before the first Punic War overstrained her moral strength and began her degeneration, were not only willing in the last resort to share their privileges with the mass of their own people, but eager to incorporate their sturdiest antagonists upon terms of equality with themselves. They extended their citizenship cautiously but steadily. Some cities became Roman, with even a voting share in the government. Others had self-government and the right to trade or marry in Rome, without full Roman citizenship. Garrisons of full citizens were set up at strategic points, and colonies with variable privileges established amidst the purely conquered peoples. The need to keep communications open in this great and growing mass of citizenship was evident from the first. Printing and paper were not yet available for intercourse, but a system of high roads followed the Latin speech and the Roman rule. The first of these, the Appian Way, ran from Rome ultimately into the heel of Italy. It was begun by the censor Appius Claudius (who must not be confused with the decemvir Appius Claudius of a century earlier) in 312 B.C.

According to a census made in 265 B.C., there were already in the Roman dominions, that is to say in Italy south of the Arno, 300,000 citizens. They all had a common interest in the welfare of the state; they were all touched a little with the diffused kingship of the republic. This was, we have to note, an absolutely new thing in the history of mankind. All considerable states and kingdoms and empires hitherto had been communities by mere obedience to some head, some monarch, upon whose moods and character the public welfare was helplessly dependent. No republic had hitherto succeeded in being anything more than a city state. The so-called Athenian "empire" was simply a city state directing its allies and its subjugated cities. In a few decades the Roman republic was destined to extend its citizenship into the valley of the Po, to assimilate the kindred Gauls, replacing their language by Latin, and to set up a Latin city, Aquileia, at the very head of the Adriatic Sea. In 89 B.C. all free inhabitants of Italy became Roman citizens; in 212 A.D. the citizenship was extended to all free men in the empire.

This extraordinary political growth was manifestly the precursor of all modern states of the western type. It is as interesting to the political student, therefore, as a carboniferous amphibian or an *archæopteryx* to the student of zoological development. It is the primitive type of the now dominant order. Its experiences throw light upon all subsequent political history.

One natural result of this growth of a democracy of hundreds of thousands of citizens scattered over the greater part of Italy was the growth in power of the Senate. There had been in the development of the Roman constitution a variety of forms of the popular assembly, the plebeian assembly, the assembly by tribes, the assembly by centuries, and the like, into which variety we cannot enter here with any fullness; but the idea was established that with the popular assembly lay the power of initiating laws. It is to be noted that there was a sort of parallel government in this system. The assembly by tribes or by centuries was an assembly of the *whole citizen body,* patrician and plebeian together; the assembly of the plebeians was of course an assembly only of the plebeian class. Each assembly had its own officials; the former, the consuls, etc.; the latter, the tribunes. While Rome was a little state, twenty miles square, it was possible to assemble something like a representative gathering of the people, but it will be manifest that with the means of communication existing in Italy at that time, it was now impossible for the great bulk of the citizens even to keep themselves informed of what was going on at Rome, much less to take any effective part in political life there. Aristotle in his *Politics* had already pointed out the virtual disenfranchisement of voters who lived out of the city and were preoccupied with agricultural pursuits, and this sort of disenfranchisement by mechanical difficulties applied to the vast majority of Roman citizens. With the growth of Rome an unanticipated weakness crept into political life through these causes, and the popular assembly became more and more a gathering of political hacks and the city riffraff, and less and less a representation of the ordinary worthy citizens. The popular assembly came nearest to power and dignity in the fourth century B.C. From that period it steadily declined in influence, and the new Senate, which was no longer a patrician body, with a homogeneous and on the whole a noble tradition, but a body of rich men, ex-magistrates, powerful officials, bold adventurers and the like, pervaded by a strong disposition to return to the idea of hereditary qualification, became for three centuries the ruling power in the Roman world.

There are two devices since known to the world which might have enabled the popular government of Rome to go on developing beyond its climax in the days of Appius Claudius the Censor, at the close of the fourth century B.C., but neither of them occurred to the Roman mind. The first of these devices was a proper use of print. In our account of early Alexandria we have already remarked upon the strange fact that printed books did not come into the world in the fourth or third century B. C. This account of Roman affairs forces us to repeat that remark. To the modern mind it is clear that a widespread popular government demands, as a necessary condition for health, a steady supply of correct information upon public affairs to all the citizens and a maintenance of interest. The popular governments in the modern states that have sprung up on either side of the Atlantic during the last two centuries have been possible only through the more or less honest and thorough ventilation of public affairs through the press. But in Italy the only way in which the government at Rome could communicate with any body of its citizens elsewhere was by sending a herald, and with the individual citizen it could hold no communication by any means at all.

The second device, for which the English are chiefly responsible in the history of mankind, which the Romans never used, was the almost equally obvious one of representative government. For the old Popular Assembly (in its threefold form) it would have been possible to have substituted a gathering of delegates. Later on in history, the English did, as the state grew, realize this necessity. Certain men, the Knights of the Shire, were called up to Westminster to speak and vote for local feeling, and were more or less formally elected for that end. The Roman situation seems to a modern mind to have called aloud for such a modification. It was never made.

The method of assembling the *comitia tributa* (one of the three main forms of the Popular Assembly) was by the proclamation of a herald, who was necessarily inaudible to most of Italy, seventeen days before the date of the gathering. The augurs, the priests of divination whom Rome had inherited from the Etruscans, examined the entrails of sacrificial beasts on the night before the actual assembly, and if they thought fit to say that these gory portents were unfavourable, the *comitia tributa* dispersed. But if the augurs reported that the livers were propitious, there was a great blowing of horns from the Capitol and from the walls of the city, and the assembly went on. It was held in the open air, either in the little Forum beneath the Capitol or in a still smaller recess opening out of the Forum, or in the military exercising ground, the Campus Martius, now the most crowded part of modern Rome, but then an open space. Business began at dawn with prayer. There were no seats, and this probably helped to reconcile the citizen to the rule that everything ended at sunset.

After the opening prayer came a discussion of the measures to be considered by the assembly, and the proposals before the meeting were read out. Is it not astonishing that there were no printed copies distributed? If any copies were handed about, they must have been in manuscript, and each copy must have been liable to errors and deliberate falsification. No questions seem to have been allowed, but private individuals might address the gathering with the permission of the presiding magistrate.

The multitude then proceeded to go into enclosures like cattle-pens according to their tribes, and each tribe voted upon the measure under consideration. The decision was then taken not by the majority of the citizens, but by the majority of tribes, and it was announced by the heralds.

The Popular Assembly by centuries, *comitia centuriata,* was very similar in its character, except that instead of thirty-five tribes there were, in the third century B.C., 373 centuries, and there was a sacrifice as well as prayer to begin with. The centuries, originally military (like the "hundreds" of primitive English local government), had long since lost any connection with the number one hundred. Some contained only a few people; some very many. There were eighteen centuries of knights (equites), who were originally men in a position to maintain a horse and serve in the cavalry, though later the Roman knighthood, like knighthood in England, became a vulgar distinction of no military, mental, or moral significance. (These equites became a very important class as Rome traded and grew rich; for a time they were the real moving class in the community. There was as little chivalry left among them at last as there is in the "honours list" knights of England of to-day. The senators from about 200 B.C. were excluded from trade. The equites became, therefore, the great business men, *negotiatores,* and as *publicani* they farmed the taxes.) There were, in addition, eighty (!) centuries of wealthy men (worth over 100,000 asses), twenty-two of men worth over 75,000 asses, and so on. There were two centuries each of mechanics and musicians, and the *proletarii* made up one century. The decision in the *comitia centuriata* was by the majority of centuries.

Is it any wonder that with the growth of the Roman state and the complication of its business, power shifted back from such a Popular Assembly to the Senate, which was a comparatively compact body varying between three hundred as a minimum, and, at the utmost, nine hundred members (to which it was raised by Cæsar), men who had to do with affairs and big business, who knew each other more or less, and had a tradition of government and policy? The power of nominating and calling up the senators vested in the Republic first with the consuls, and when, some time after, "censors" were created, and many of the powers of the consuls had been transferred to them, they were also given this power. Appius Claudius, one of the first of the censors to exercise it, enrolled freedmen in the tribes and called sons of freedmen to the Senate. But this was a shocking arrangement to the conservative instincts of the time; the consuls would not recognize his Senate, and the next censors (304 B.C.) set aside his invitations. His attempt, however, serves to show how far the Senate had progressed from its original condition as a purely patrician body. Like the contemporary British House of Lords, it had become a gathering of big business men, energetic politicians, successful adventurers, great landowners, and the like; its patrician dignity was a picturesque sham; but, unlike the British House of Lords, it was unchecked legally by anything but the inefficient Popular Assembly we have already described, and by the tribunes elected by the plebeian assembly. Its legal control over the consuls and proconsuls was not great; it had little executive power; but in its prestige and experience lay its strength and influence. The interests of its members were naturally antagonistic to the interests of the general body of citizens, but for some generations that great mass of ordinary men was impotent to express its dissent from the proceedings of this oligarchy. Direct popular government of a state larger than a city state had already failed therefore in Italy, because as yet there was no public education, no press, and no representative system; it had failed through these mere mechanical difficulties, before the first Punic War. But its appearance is of enormous interest, as the first appearance of a set of problems with which the whole political intelligence of the world wrestles at the present time.

The Senate met usually in a Senate House in the Forum, but on special occasions it would be called to meet in this or that temple; and when it had to deal with foreign ambassadors or its own generals (who were not allowed to enter the city while in command of troops), it assembled in the Campus Martius outside the walls.

§ 3

It has been necessary to deal rather fully with the political structure of the Roman republic because of its immense importance to this day. The constitution of Carthage need not detain us long.

Italy under Rome was a republican country; Carthage was that much older thing, a republican city. She had an "empire," as Athens had an "empire," of tributary states which did not love her, and she had a great and naturally disloyal industrial slave population.

In the city there were two elected "kings," as Aristotle calls them, the *suffetes,* who were really equivalent to the Roman censors; their Semitic name was the same as that used for the Jewish *judges.* There was an impotent public assembly and a senate of leading personages; but two committees of this senate, nominally elected, but elected by easily controlled methods, the Hundred and Four and the Thirty, really constituted a close oligarchy of the richest and most influential men. They told as little as they could to their allies and fellow citizens, and consulted them as little as possible. They pursued schemes in which the welfare of Carthage was no doubt subordinated to the advantage of their own group. They were hostile to new men or novel measures, and confident that a sea ascendancy that had lasted two centuries must be in the very nature of things.

Carthaginian coins.

§ 4

It would be interesting, and not altogether idle, to speculate what might have happened to mankind if Rome and Carthage could have settled their differences and made a permanent alliance in the Western world. If Alexander the Great had lived, he might have come westward and driven these two powers into such a fusion of interests. But that would not have suited the private schemes and splendours of the Carthaginian oligarchy, and the new Senate of greater Rome was now growing fond of the taste of plunder and casting covetous eyes across the Straits of Messina upon the Carthaginian possessions in Sicily. They were covetous, but they were afraid of the Carthaginian sea-power. Roman popular "patriotism," however, was also jealous and fearful of these Carthaginians, and less inclined to count the cost of a conflict. The alliance Pyrrhus had forced upon Rome and Carthage held good for eleven years, but Rome was ripe for what is called in modern political jargon an "offensive defensive" war. The occasion arose in 264 B.C.

At that time Sicily was not completely in Carthaginian hands. The eastward end was still under the power of the Greek king of Syracuse, Hiero, a successor of that Dionysius to whom Plato had gone as resident court philosopher. A band of mercenaries who had been in the service of Syracuse seized upon Messina (289 B.C.), and raided the trade of Syracuse so that at last Hiero was forced to take measures to suppress them (270 B.C.). Thereupon Carthage, which was also vitally concerned in the suppression of piracy, came to his aid, and put in a Carthaginian garrison at Messina. This was an altogether justifiable proceeding. Now that Tyre had been destroyed, the only capable guardian of sea law in the Mediterranean was Carthage, and the suppression of piracy was her task by habit and tradition.

The pirates of Messina appealed to Rome, and the accumulating jealousy and fear of Carthage decided the Roman people to help them. An expedition was dispatched to Messina under the consul Appius Claudius (the third Appius Claudius we have had to mention in this history).

So began the first of the most wasteful and disastrous series of wars that has ever darkened the history of mankind. But this is how one historian, soaked with the fantastic political ideas of our times, is pleased to write of this evil expedition. "The Romans knew they were entering on war with Carthage; but the political instincts of the people were right, for a Carthaginian garrison on the Sicilian Straits would have been a dangerous menace to the peace of Italy." So they protected the peace of Italy from this "menace" by a war that lasted nearly a quarter of a century. They wrecked their own slowly acquired political *moral* in the process.

The Romans captured Messina, and Hiero deserted from the Carthaginians to the Romans. Then for some time the struggle centred upon the town Agrigentum. This the Romans besieged, and a period of trench warfare ensued. Both sides suffered greatly from plague and irregular supplies; the Romans lost 30,000 men; but in the end (261 B.C.) the Carthaginians evacuated the place and retired to their fortified towns on the western coast of the island of which Lilybæum was the chief. These they could supply easily from the African mainland, and, as long as their sea ascendancy held, they could exhaust any Roman effort against them.

And now a new and very extraordinary phase of the war began. The Romans came out upon the sea, and to the astonishment of the Carthaginians and themselves defeated the Carthaginian fleet. Since the days of Salamis there had been a considerable development of naval architecture. Then the ruling type of battleship was a trireme, a galley with three banks (rows) of oars; now the leading Carthaginian battleship was a quinquereme, a much bigger galley with five banks of oars, which could ram or shear the oars of any feebler vessel. The Romans had come into the war with no such shipping. Now they set to work to build quinqueremes, being helped, it is said, in their designing by one of these Carthaginian vessels coming ashore. In two months they built a hundred quinqueremes and thirty triremes. But they had no skilled navigators, no experienced oarsmen, and these deficiencies they remedied partly with the assistance of their Greek allies and partly by the invention of new tactics. Instead of relying upon ramming or breaking the oars of the adversary, which demanded more seamanship than they possessed, they decided to board the enemy, and they constructed a sort of long draw-bridge on their ships, held up to a mast by a pulley and with grappling-hooks and spikes at the end. They also loaded their galleys with soldiers. Then as the Carthaginian rammed or swept alongside, this *corvus,* as it was called, could be let down and the boarders could swarm aboard him.

Simple as this device was, it proved a complete success. It changed the course of the war and the fate of the world. The small amount of invention needed to counteract the *corvus* was not apparently within the compass of the Carthaginian rulers. At the battle of Mylæ (260 B.C.) the Romans gained their first naval victory and captured or destroyed fifty vessels.

At the great battle of Ecnomus (256 B.C.), "probably the greatest naval engagement of antiquity,"[1] in which seven or eight hundred big ships were engaged, the Carthaginians showed that they had learnt nothing from their former disaster. According to rule they outmanœuvred and defeated the Romans, but the *corvus* again defeated them. The Romans sank thirty vessels and captured sixty-four.

Thereafter the war continued with violent fluctuations of fortune, but with a continuous demonstration of the greater energy, solidarity, and initiative of the Romans. After Ecnomus the Romans invaded Africa by sea, and sent an insufficiently supported army, which after many successes and the capture of Tunis (within ten miles of Carthage) was completely defeated. They lost their sea ascendancy through a storm, and regained it by building a second fleet of two hundred and twenty ships within three months. They captured Palermo, and defeated a great Carthaginian army there (251 B.C.), capturing one hundred and four elephants, and making such a triumphal procession into Rome as that city had never seen before. They made an unsuccessful siege of Lilybæum, the chief surviving Carthaginian stronghold in Sicily. They lost their second fleet in a great naval battle at Drepanum (249 B.C.), losing one hundred and eighty out of two hundred and ten vessels; and a third fleet of one hundred and twenty battleships and eight hundred transports was lost in the same year partly in battle and partly in a storm.

For seven years a sort of war went on between the nearly exhausted combatants, a war of raids and feeble sieges, during which the Carthaginians had the best of it at sea. Then by a last supreme effort Rome launched a fourth fleet of two hundred keels, and defeated the last strength of the Carthaginians at the battle of the Ægatian Isles (241 B.C.), after which Carthage (240 B.C.) sued for peace.

By the terms of this peace, all Sicily, except for the dominions of Hiero of Syracuse, became an "estate" of the Roman people. There was no such process of assimilation as had been practised in Italy; Sicily became a conquered province, paying tribute and yielding profit like the provinces of the older empires. And, in addition, Carthage paid a war indemnity of 3,200 talents (= £788,000).

[1] J. Wells, *op. cit.*

§ 5

For twenty-two years there was peace between Rome and Carthage. It was peace without prosperity. Both combatants were suffering from the want and disorganization that follow naturally and necessarily upon all great wars. The territories of Carthage seethed with violent disorder; the returning soldiers could not get their pay, and mutinied and looted; the land went uncultivated. We read of horrible cruelties in the suppression of these troubles by Hamilcar, the Carthaginian general; of men being crucified by the thousand. Sardinia and Corsica revolted. The "peace of Italy" was scarcely happier. The Gauls rose and marched south; they were defeated, and 40,000 of them killed at Telamon. It is manifest that Italy was incomplete until it reached the Alps. Roman colonies were planted in the valley of the Po, and the great northward artery, the Via Flaminia, was begun. But it shows the moral and intellectual degradation of this post-war period that when the Gauls were threatening Rome, human sacrifices were proposed and carried out. The old Carthaginian sea law was broken up—it may have been selfish and monopolistic, but it was at least orderly—the Adriatic swarmed with Illyrian pirates, and as the result of a quarrel arising out of this state of affairs, Illyria, after two wars, had to be annexed as a second "province." By sending expeditions to annex Sardinia and Corsica, which were Carthaginian provinces in revolt, the Romans prepared the way for the Second Punic War.

Roman As (bronze, 4th Cent. B.C. Half size)

The First Punic War had tested and demonstrated the relative strength of Rome and Carthage. With a little more wisdom on either side, with a little more magnanimity on the part of Rome, there need never have been a renewal of the struggle. But Rome was an ungracious conqueror. She seized Corsica and Sardinia on no just grounds, she increased the indemnity by 1,200 talents, she set a limit, the Ebro, to Carthaginian developments in Spain. There was a strong party in Carthage, led by Hanno, for the propitiation of Rome; but it was natural that many Carthaginians should come to regard their national adversary with a despairing hatred.

Hatred is one of the passions that can master a life, and there is a type of temperament very prone to it, ready to see life in terms of vindictive melodrama, ready to find stimulus and satisfaction in frightful demonstrations of "justice" and revenge. The fears and jealousies of the squatting-place and the cave still bear their dark blossoms in our lives; we are not four hundred generations yet from the old Stone Age. Great wars, as all Europe knows, give this "hating" temperament the utmost scope, and the greed and pride and cruelty that the First Punic War had released were now producing a rich crop of anti-foreign monomania. The outstanding figure upon the side of Carthage was a great general and administrator, Hamilcar Barca, who now set himself to circumvent and shatter Rome. He was the father-in-law of Hasdrubal and the father of a boy Hannibal, destined to be the most dreaded enemy that ever scared the Roman Senate. The most obvious course before Carthage was the reconstruction of its fleet and naval administration, and the recovery of sea power, but this, it would seem, Hamilcar could not effect. As an alternative he resolved to organize Spain as the base of a land attack upon Italy. He went to Spain as governor in 236 B.C., and Hannibal related afterwards that his father then—he was a boy of eleven—made him vow deathless hostility to the Roman power.

This quasi-insane concentration of the gifts and lives of the Barca family upon revenge is but one instance of the narrowing and embitterment of life that the stresses and universal sense of insecurity of this great struggle produced in the minds of men. A quarter of a century of war had left the whole western world miserable and harsh. While the eleven-year-old Hannibal was taking his vow of undying hatred, there was running about a farmhouse of Tusculum a small but probably very disagreeable child of two named Marcus Porcius Cato. This boy lived to be eighty-five years old, and his ruling passion seems to have been hatred for any human happiness but his own. He was a good soldier, and had a successful political career. He held a command in Spain, and distinguished himself by his cruelties. He posed as a champion of religion and public morality, and under this convenient cloak carried on a lifelong war against everything that was young, gracious, or pleasant. Whoever roused his jealousy incurred his moral disapproval. He was energetic in the support and administration of all laws against dress, against the personal adornment of women, against entertainments and free discussion. He was so fortunate as to be made censor, which gave him great power over the private lives of public people. He was thus able to ruin public opponents through private scandals. He expelled Manlius from the Senate for giving his wife a kiss in the daytime in the sight of their daughter. He persecuted Greek literature, about which, until late in life, he was totally ignorant. Then he read and admired Demosthenes. He wrote in Latin upon agriculture and the ancient and lost virtues of Rome. From these writings much light is thrown upon his qualities. One of his maxims was that when a slave was not sleeping he should be working. Another was that old oxen and slaves should be sold off. He left the war horse that had carried him through his Spanish campaigns behind him when he returned to Italy in order to save freight. He hated other people's gardens, and cut off the supply of water for garden use in Rome. After entertaining company, when dinner was over he would go out to correct any negligence in the service with a leather thong. He admired his own virtues very greatly, and insisted upon them in his writings. There was a battle at Thermopylæ against Antiochus the Great, of which he wrote, "those who saw him charging the enemy, routing and pursuing them, declared that Cato owed less to the people of Rome, than the people of Rome owed to Cato."[1] In his old age Cato became lascivious and misconducted himself with a woman slave. Finally, when his son protested against this disorder of their joint household, he married a young wife, the daughter of his secretary, who was not in a position to refuse his offer. (What became of the woman slave is not told. Probably he sold her.) This compendium of all the old Roman virtues died at an advanced age, respected and feared. Almost his last public act was to urge on the Third Punic War and the final destruction of Carthage. He had gone to Carthage as a

[1] Plutarch, *Life of Cato.*

commissioner to settle certain differences between Carthage and Numidia, and he had been shocked and horrified to find some evidences of prosperity and even of happiness in that country.

From the time of that visit onward Cato concluded every speech he made in the Senate by croaking out *"Delenda est Carthago"* ("Carthage must be destroyed").

Such was the type of man that rose to prominence in Rome during the Punic struggle, such was the protagonist of Hannibal and the Carthaginian *revanche,* and by him and by Hannibal we may judge the tone and quality of the age.

The two great western powers, and Rome perhaps more than Carthage, were strained mentally and morally by the stresses of the First War. The evil side of life was uppermost. The history of the Second and Third Punic Wars (219 to 201 and 149 to 146 B.C.), it is plain, is not the history of perfectly sane peoples. It is nonsense for historians to write of the "political instincts" of the Romans or Carthaginians. Quite other instincts were loose. The red eyes of the ancestral ape had come back into the world. It was a time when reasonable men were howled down or murdered; the true spirit of the age is shown in the eager examination for signs and portents of the still quivering livers of those human victims who were sacrificed in Rome during the panic before the battle of Telamon. The western world was indeed black with homicidal monomania. Two great peoples, both very necessary to the world's development, fell foul of one another, and at last Rome succeeded in murdering Carthage.

§ 6

We can only tell very briefly here of the particulars of the Second and Third Punic Wars. We have told how Hamilcar began to organize Spain, and how the Romans forbade him to cross the Ebro. He died in 228 B.C., and was followed by his son-in-law Hasdrubal, who was assassinated in 221 B.C. and succeeded by Hannibal, who was now twenty-six. The actual war was precipitated by the Romans making a breach of their own regulations, and interfering with affairs south of the Ebro. Whereupon Hannibal marched straight through the south of Gaul, and crossed the Alps (218 B.C.) into Italy.

The history of the next fifteen years is the story of the most brilliant and futile raid in history. For fifteen years Hannibal held out in Italy, victorious and unconquered. The Roman generals were no match for the Carthaginian, and whenever they met him they were beaten. But one Roman general, P. Cornelius Scipio, had the strategic sense to take a course that robbed all Hannibal's victories of fruit. At the outbreak of the war he had been sent by sea to Marseilles to intercept Hannibal; he arrived three days late, and, instead of pursuing him, he sent on the army into Spain to cut up Hannibal's supplies and reinforcements. Throughout all the subsequent war there remained this Roman army of Spain between Hannibal and his base. He was left "in the air," incapable of conducting sieges or establishing conquests.

Whenever he met the Romans in open fight he beat them. He gained two great victories in North Italy, and won over the Gauls to his side. He pressed south into Etruria, and ambushed, surrounded, and completely destroyed a Roman army at Lake Trasimene. In 216 B.C. he was assailed by a vastly superior Roman force under Varro at Cannæ, and destroyed it utterly. Fifty thousand men are said to have been killed and ten thousand prisoners taken. He was, however, unable to push on and capture Rome because he had no siege equipment.

But Cannæ produced other fruits. A large part of Southern Italy came over to Hannibal, including Capua, the city next in size to Rome, and the Macedonians allied themselves with him. Moreover, Hiero of Syracuse, the faithful ally of Rome, was now dead, and his successor Hieronymus turned over to the Carthaginians. The Romans carried on the war, however, with great toughness and resolution; they refused to treat with Hannibal after Cannæ, they pressed a slow but finally successful blockade and siege of Capua, and a Roman army set itself to reduce Syracuse. The siege of Syracuse is chiefly memorable for the brilliant inventions of the philosopher Archimedes, which long held the Romans at bay. We have already named this Archimedes as one of the pupils and correspondents of the school of the Alexandrian Museum. He was killed in the final storm of the town. Tarentum (209 B.C.), Hannibal's chief port and means of supply from Carthage, at last followed Syracuse (212 B.C.) and Capua (211 B.C.), and his communications became irregular.

Spain also was wrested bit by bit from the Carthaginian grip. When at last reinforcements for Hannibal under his brother Hasdrubal (not to be confused with his brother-in-law of the same name who was assassinated) struggled through into Italy, they were destroyed at the battle of the Metaurus (207 B.C.), and the first news that came to Hannibal of the disaster was the hacked-off head of his brother thrown into his camp.

Thereafter Hannibal was blockaded into Calabria, the heel of Italy. He had no forces for further operations of any magnitude, and he returned at last to Carthage in time to command the Carthaginians in the last battle of the war.

This last battle, the battle of Zama (202 B.C.), was fought close to Carthage.

It was the first defeat Hannibal experienced and so it is well to give a little attention to the personality of his conqueror, Scipio Africanus the Elder, who stands out in history as a very fine gentleman indeed, a great soldier and a generous man. We have already mentioned a certain P. Cornelius Scipio who struck at Hannibal's base in Spain; this was his son; until after Zama this son bore the same name of P. Cornelius Scipio, and then the surname of Africanus was given him. (The younger Scipio Africanus, Scipio Africanus Minor, who was later to end the Third Punic War, was the adopted son of the son of this first Scipio Africanus the Elder.) Scipio Africanus was everything that aroused the distrust, hatred, and opposition of old-fashioned Romans of the school of Cato. He was young, he was happy and able, he spent money freely, he was well versed in Greek literature, and inclined rather to Phrygian novelties in religion than to the sterner divinities of Rome. And he did not believe in the extreme discretion that then ruled Roman strategy.

After the early defeats of the Second Punic War, Roman military operations were dominated by the personality of a general, Fabius, who raised the necessity of avoiding battle with Hannibal into a kind of sacred principle. For ten years "Fabian tactics" prevailed in Italy. The Romans blockaded, cut up convoys, attacked stragglers, and ran away whenever Hannibal appeared. No doubt it was wise for a time after their first defeats to do this sort of thing, but the business of the stronger power, and Rome was the stronger power throughout the Second Punic War, is not to tolerate an interminable war, but to repair losses, discover able generals, train better armies, and destroy the enemy power. Decision is one of the duties of strength.

To such men as young Scipio, the sly, ineffective artfulness of Fabianism, which was causing both Italy and Carthage to bleed slowly to death, was detestable. He clamoured for an attack upon Carthage itself.

"But Fabius, on this occasion, filled the city with alarms, as if the commonwealth was going to be brought into the most extreme danger by a rash and indiscreet young man; in short, he scrupled not to do or say anything he thought likely to dissuade his countrymen from embracing the proposal. With the Senate he carried his point. But the people believed that his opposition to Scipio proceeded either from envy of his success, or from a secret fear that if this young hero should perform some signal exploit, put an end to the war, or even remove it out of Italy, his own slow proceedings through the course of so many years might be imputed to indolence or timidity. . . . He applied to Crassus, the colleague of Scipio, and endeavoured to persuade him not to yield that province to Scipio, but, if he thought it proper to conduct the war in that manner, to go himself against Carthage. Nay, he even hindered the raising of money for that expedition, so that Scipio was obliged to find the supplies as he could. . . . He endeavoured to prevent the young men who offered to go as volunteers from giving in their names, and loudly declared, both in the Senate and Forum, 'That Scipio did not only himself avoid Hannibal, but intended to carry away with him the remaining strength of Italy, persuading the young men to abandon their parents, their wives, and native city, while an unsubdued and potent enemy was still at their doors.' With these assertions he so terrified the people, that they allowed Scipio to take with him only the legions that were in Sicily, and three hundred of those men who had served him with so much fidelity in Spain. . . . After Scipio was gone over into Africa, an account was soon brought to Rome of his glorious and wonderful achievements. This account was followed by rich spoils, which confirmed it. A Numidian king was taken prisoner; two camps were burned and destroyed; and in them a vast number of men, arms, and horses; and the Carthaginians sent orders to Hannibal to quit his fruitless hopes in Italy, and return home to defend his own country. Whilst every tongue was applauding these exploits of Scipio, Fabius proposed that his successor should be appointed, without any shadow of reason for it, except what this well-known maxim implies: viz., 'That it is dangerous to trust affairs of such importance to the fortune of one man, because it is not likely that he will be always successful.' . . . Nay, even when Hannibal embarked his army and quitted Italy, Fabius ceased not to disturb the general joy and to damp the spirits of Rome, for he took the liberty to affirm, 'That the commonwealth was now come to her last and worst trial; that she had the most reason to dread the efforts of Hannibal when he should arrive in Africa, and attack her sons under the walls of Carthage; that Scipio would have to do with an army yet warm with the blood of so many Roman generals, dictators, and consuls.' The city was alarmed with these declamations, and though the war was removed into Africa, the danger seemed to approach nearer Rome than ever."

Before the battle of Zama there were a brief truce and negotiations, which broke down through the fault of the Carthaginians. As with the battle of Arbela, so the exact day of the battle of Zama can be fixed by an eclipse, which in this case occurred during the fighting. The Romans had been joined by the Numidians, the hinterland people of Carthage, under their king Massinissa, and this gave them—for the first time in any battle against Hannibal—a great superiority of cavalry. Hannibal's cavalry wings were driven off, while at the same time the sounder discipline of Scipio's infantry enabled them to open lanes for the charge of the Carthaginian war elephants without being thrown into confusion. Hannibal attempted to extend his infantry line to envelop the Roman infantry mass, but while at Cannæ all the advantage of training and therefore of manœuvring power had been on his side, and he had been able to surround and massacre a crowd of infantry, he now found against him an infantry line better than his own. His own line broke as it extended, the Roman legion charged home, and the day was lost. The Roman cavalry came back from the pursuit of Hannibal's horse to turn what was already a defeat into a disastrous rout.

Carthage submitted without any further struggle. The terms were severe, but they left it possible for her to hope for an honourable future. She had to abandon Spain to Rome, to give up all her war fleet except ten vessels, to pay 10,000 talents (£2,400,000), and, what was the most difficult condition of all, to agree not to wage war without the permission of Rome. Finally a condition was added that Hannibal, as the great enemy of Rome, should be surrendered. But he saved his countrymen from this humiliation by flying to Asia.

These were exorbitant conditions, with which Rome should have been content. But there are nations so cowardly that they dare not merely conquer their enemies; they must *mak siccar* and destroy them. The generation of Romans that saw greatness and virtue in a man like Cato the Censor, necessarily made their country a mean ally and a cowardly victor.

§ 7

The history of Rome for the fifty-six years that elapsed between the battle of Zama and the last act of the tragedy, the Third Punic War, tells of a hard ungracious expansion of power abroad and of a slow destruction, by the usury and greed of the rich, of the free agricultural population at home.

The spirit of the nation had become harsh and base; there was no further extension of citizenship, no more generous attempts at the assimilation of congenial foreign populations. Spain was administered badly and settled slowly and with great difficulty. Complicated interventions led to the reduction of Illyria and Macedonia to the position of tribute-paying provinces; Rome, it was evident, was going to "tax the foreigner" now and release her home population from taxation. After 168 B.C. the old land tax was no longer levied in Italy, and the only revenue derived from Italy was from the state domains and through a tax on imports from overseas. The revenues from the province of "Asia" defrayed the expenses of the Roman state. At home men of the Cato type were acquiring farms by loans and foreclosure, often the farms of men impoverished by war service; they were driving the free citizens off their land, and running their farms with the pitilessly driven slave labour that was made cheap and abundant. Such men regarded alien populations abroad merely as unimported slaves. Sicily was handed over to the greedy enterprise of tax-farmers. Corn could be grown there by rich men using slaves, and imported very profitably into Rome, and so the home land could be turned over to cattle and sheep feeding. Consequently a drift of the uprooted Italian population to the towns, and particularly to Rome, began.

Of the first conflicts of the spreading power of Rome with the Seleucids, and how she formed an alliance with Egypt, we can tell little here, nor of the tortuous fluctuations of the Greek cities under the shadow of her advance until they fell into actual subjugation. A map must suffice to show the extension of her empire at this time.

The general grim baseness of the age was not without its protesting voices. We have already told how the wasting disease of the Second Punic War, a disease of the state which was producing avaricious rich men exactly as diseases of the body will sometimes produce great pustules, was ended by the vigour of Scipio Africanus. When it had seemed doubtful whether the Senate would let him go as the Roman general, he had threatened an appeal to the people. Thereafter he was a marked man for the senatorial gang, who were steadily changing Italy from a land of free cultivators to a land of slave-worked cattle ranches; they attempted to ruin him before ever he reached Africa; they gave him forces insufficient, as they hoped, for victory; and after the war they barred him strictly from office. Interest and his natural malice alike prompted Cato to attack him.

Scipio Africanus the Elder seems to have been of a generous and impatient temperament, and indisposed to exploit the popular discontent with current tendencies and his own very great popularity to his own advantage. He went as subordinate to his brother Lucius Scipio, when the latter commanded the first Roman army to pass into Asia. At Magnesia in Lydia a great composite army under Antiochus III, the Seleucid monarch, suffered the fate (190 B.C.) of the very similar Persian armies of a hundred and forty years before. This victory drew down upon Lucius Scipio the hostility of the Senate, and he was accused of misappropriating moneys received from Antiochus. This filled Africanus with honest rage. As Lucius stood up in the Senate with his accounts in his hands ready for the badgering of his accusers, Africanus snatched the documents from him, tore them up, and flung the fragments down. His brother, he said, had paid into the treasury 200,000 sestertia

The EXTENT of the ROMAN POWER & its ALLIANCES about 150 B.C.
[i.e., on the eve of the Third Punic War.]
GAUL
Rhine
ALPS
Rhone
CISALPINE GAUL
SPAIN
Ebro
Tagus
CORSICA
Rome
SARDINIA
SICILY
Cannae
DALMATIA
Danube
MACEDONIA
THRACE
GREECE
EPIRUS
NUMIDIA
Carthage
BITHYNIA
PONTUS
GALATIA
PERGAMUM
Magnesia
RHODES
CRETE
CYPRUS
CAUCASUS
CASPIAN
ARMENIA
TAURUS MTS.
PARTHIANS
Antioch
SELEUCID EMPIRE
Seleucia
SYRIA
Alexandria
Jerusalem
Memphis
PTOLEMAIC EMPIRE
Philae
ARABIA
AFRICA
Roman power....
Ptolemaic Empire..
Other Allies of Rome
J.F.H.

(=£2,000,000). Was he now to be pestered and tripped up upon this or that item? When, later on, Lucius was prosecuted and condemned, Africanus rescued him by force. Being impeached, he reminded the people that the day was the anniversary of the battle of Zama, and defied the authorities amidst the plaudits of the crowd.

The Roman people seem to have liked and supported Scipio Africanus, and, after an interval of two thousand years, men must like him still. He was able to throw torn paper in the face of the Senate, and when Lucius was attacked again, one of the tribunes of the people interposed his veto and quashed the proceedings. But Scipio Africanus lacked that harder alloy which makes men great democratic leaders. He was no Cæsar. He had none of the qualities that subdue a man to the base necessities of political life. After these events he retired in disgust from Rome to his estates, and there he died in the year 183 B.C.

In the same year died Hannibal. He poisoned himself in despair. The steadfast fear of the Roman Senate had hunted him from court to court. In spite of the indignant protests of Scipio, Rome in the peace negotiations had demanded his surrender from Carthage, and she continued to make this demand of every power that sheltered him. When peace was made with Antiochus III, this was one of the conditions. He was run to earth at last in Bithynia; the king of Bithynia detained him in order to send him to Rome, but he had long carried the poison he needed in a ring, and by this he died.

It adds to the honour of the name of Scipio that it was another Scipio, Scipio Nasica, who parodied Cato's *Delenda est Carthago* by ending all his speeches in the Senate with "Carthage must stand." He had the wisdom to see that the existence and stimulus of Carthage contributed to the general prosperity of Rome.

Yet it was the second Scipio Africanus, grandson by adoption of Scipio Africanus the Elder, who took and destroyed Carthage. The sole offence of the Carthaginians, which brought about the third and last Punic War, was that they continued to trade and prosper. Their trade was not a trade that competed with that of Rome; when Carthage was destroyed, much of her trade died with her, and North Africa entered upon a phase of economic retrogression; but her prosperity aroused that passion of envy which was evidently more powerful even than avarice in the "old Roman" type. The rich Equestrian order resented any wealth in the world but its own. Rome provoked the war by encouraging the Numidians to encroach upon Carthage until the Carthaginians were goaded to fight in despair. Rome then pounced upon Carthage, and declared she had broken the treaty! She had made war without permission.

The Carthaginians sent the hostages Rome demanded, they surrendered their arms, they prepared to surrender territory. But submission only increased the arrogance of Rome and the pitiless greed of the rich Equestrian order which swayed her counsels. She now demanded that Carthage should be abandoned, and the population removed to a spot at least ten miles from the sea. This demand they made to a population that subsisted almost entirely by overseas trade!

This preposterous order roused the Carthaginians to despair. They recalled their exiles and prepared for resistance. The military efficiency of the Romans had been steadily declining through a half-century of narrow-minded and base-spirited government, and the first attacks upon the town in 149 B.C. almost ended in disaster. Young Scipio, during these operations, distinguished himself in a minor capacity. The next year was also a year of failure for the incompetents of the Senate. That august body then passed from a bullying mood to one of extreme panic. The Roman populace was even more seriously scared. Young Scipio, chiefly on account of his name, although he was under the proper age, and in other respects not qualified for the office, was made consul, and bundled off to Africa to save his precious country.

There followed the most obstinate and dreadful of sieges. Scipio built a mole across the harbour, and cut off all supplies by land or sea. The Carthaginians suffered horribly from famine; but they held out until the town was stormed. The street fighting lasted for six days, and when at last the citadel capitulated, there were fifty thousand Carthaginians left alive out of an estimated population of half a million. These survivors went into slavery, the whole city was burnt, the ruins were ploughed to express final destruction, and a curse was invoked with great solemnities upon anyone who might attempt to rebuild it.

In the same year (146 B.C.) the Roman Senate and Equestrians also *murdered* another great city that seemed to limit their trade monopolies, Corinth. They had a justification, for Corinth had been in arms against them, but it was an inadequate justification.

§ 8

We must note here, in a brief section, a change in the military system of Rome, after the Second Punic War, that was of enormous importance in her later development. Up to that period the Roman armies had been levies of free citizens. Fighting power and voting power were closely connected; the public assembly by centuries followed the paraphernalia of a military mobilization, and marched, headed by the Equestrian centuries, to the Campus Martius. The system was very like that of the Boers before the last war in South Africa. The ordinary Roman citizen, like the ordinary Boer, was a farmer; at the summons of his country he went "on commando." The Boers were, indeed, in many respects, the last survivors of Aryanism. They fought extraordinarily well, but at the back of their minds was an anxious desire to go back to their farms. For prolonged operations, such as the siege of Veii, the Romans reinforced and relieved their troops in relays; the Boers did much the same at the siege of Ladysmith.

The necessity for subjugating Spain after the Second Punic War involved a need for armies of a different type. Spain was too far off for periodic reliefs, and the war demanded a more thorough training than was possible with these on and off soldiers. Accordingly men were enlisted for longer terms and *paid.* So the paid soldier first appeared in Roman affairs. And to pay was added booty. Cato distributed silver treasure among his command in Spain; and it is also on record that he attacked Scipio Africanus for distributing booty among his troops in Sicily. The introduction of military pay led on to a professional army, and this, a century later, to the disarmament of the ordinary Roman citizen, who was now drifting in an impoverished state into Rome and the larger towns. The great wars had been won, the foundations of the empire had been well and truly laid by the embattled farmers of Rome before 200 B.C. In the process the embattled farmers of Rome had already largely disappeared. The change that began after the Second Punic War was completed towards the close of the century in the reorganization of the army by Marius, as we will tell in its place. After his time we shall begin to write of "the army," and then of "the legions," and we shall find we are dealing with a new kind of army altogether, no longer held together in the solidarity of a common citizenship. As that tie fails, the legions discover another in *esprit de corps,* in their common difference from and their common interest against the general community. They begin to develop a warmer interest in their personal leaders, who secure them pay and plunder. Before the Punic Wars it was the tendency of ambitious men in Rome to court the plebeians; after that time they began to court the legions.

§ 9

The history of the Roman Republic thus far, is in many respects much more modern in flavour, especially to the American or Western European reader, than anything that has preceded it. For the first time we have something like a self-governing "nation," something larger than a mere city state, seeking to control its own destinies. For the first time we have a wide countryside under one conception of law. We get in the Senate and the popular assembly a conflict of groups and personalities, an argumentative process of control, far more stable and enduring than any autocracy can be, and far more flexible and adaptable than any priesthood. For the first time also we encounter social conflicts comparable to our own. Money has superseded barter, and financial capital has become fluid and free; not perhaps so fluid and free as it is to-day, but much more so than it had ever been before. The Punic Wars were wars of peoples, such as were no other wars we have yet recorded. Indubitably the broad lines of our present world, the main ideas, the chief oppositions, were appearing in those days.

But, as we have already pointed out, certain of the elementary facilities and some of the current political ideas of our time were still wanting in the Rome of the Punic Wars. There were no newspapers,[1] and there was practically no use of elected representatives in the popular assemblies. And another deficiency, very understandable to us nowadays, but quite beyond the scope of anyone then, was the absence of any general elementary political education at all. The plebeians of Rome had shown some glimmering of the idea that without knowledge votes cannot make men free, when they had insisted upon the publication of the law of the Twelve Tables; but they had never been able, it was beyond the possibilities of the time, to imagine any further extension of knowledge to the bulk of the people. It is only nowadays that men are beginning to understand fully the political significance of the maxim that "knowledge is power." Two British Trade Unions, for example, have recently set up a Labour College to meet the special needs of able working-men in history, political and social science, and the like. But education in republican Rome was the freak of the individual parent, and the privilege of wealth and leisure. It was mainly in the hands of Greeks, who were in many cases slaves. There was a thin small stream of very fine learning and very fine thinking up to the first century of the monarchy, let Lucretius and Cicero witness, but it did not spread into the mass of the people. The ordinary Roman was not only blankly ignorant of the history of mankind, but also of the conditions of foreign peoples; he had no knowledge of economic laws nor or social possibilities. Even his own interests he did not clearly understand.

Of course, in the little city states of Greece and in that early Roman state of four hundred square miles, men acquired by talk and observation a sufficient knowledge for the ordinary duties of citizenship, but by the beginning of the Punic Wars the business was already too big and complicated for illiterate men. Yet nobody seems to have observed the gap that was

[1] Julius Cæsar (60 B.C.) caused the proceedings of the Senate to be published by having them written up upon bulletin boards, *in albo* (upon the white). It had been the custom to publish the annual edict of the prætor in this fashion. There were professional letter-writers who sent news by special courier to rich country correspondents, and these would copy down the stuff upon the Album (white board). Cicero, while he was governor in Cilicia, got the current news from such a professional correspondent. He complains in one letter that it was not what he wanted; the expert was too full of the chariot races and other sporting intelligence, and failed to give any view of the political situation. Obviously this news-letter system was available only for public men in prosperous circumstances.

opening between the citizen and his state, and so there is no record at all of any attempt to enlarge the citizen by instruction to meet his enlarged duties. From the second century B.C. and onward everyone is remarking upon the ignorance of the common citizen and his lack of political wisdom, everything is suffering from the lack of political solidarity due to this ignorance, but no one goes on to what we should now consider the inevitable corollary, no one proposes to destroy the ignorance complained of. There existed no means whatever for the instruction of the masses of the people in a common political and social ideal. It was only with the development of the great propagandist religions in the Roman world, of which Christianity was the chief and the survivor, that the possibility of such a systematic instruction of great masses of people became apparent in the world. That very great political genius, the Emperor Constantine the Great, six centuries later, was the first to apprehend and to attempt to use this possibility for the preservation and the mental and moral knitting-together of the world community over which he ruled.

But it is not only in these deficiencies of news and of education and of the expedient of representative government that this political system of Rome differed from our own. True, it was far more like a modern civilized state than any other state we have considered hitherto, but in some matters it was strangely primordial and "sub-civilized." Every now and then the reader of Roman history, reading it in terms of debates and measures, policies and campaigns, capital and labour, comes upon something that gives him much the same shock he would feel if he went down to an unknown caller in his house and extended his hand to meet the misshapen hairy paw of *Homo Neanderthalensis* and looked up to see a chinless, bestial face. We have noted the occurrence of human sacrifice in the third century B.C., and much that we learn of the religion of republican Rome carries us far back beyond the days of decent gods, to the age of shamanism and magic. We talk of a legislative gathering, and the mind flies to Westminster; but how should we feel if we went to see the beginning of a session of the House of Lords, and discovered the Lord Chancellor, with bloody fingers, portentously fiddling about among the entrails of a newly killed sheep? The mind would recoil from Westminster to the customs of Benin. And the slavery of

Rome was a savage slavery, altogether viler than the slavery of Babylon. We have had a glimpse of the virtuous Cato among his slaves in the second century B.C. Moreover, in the third century B.C., when King Asoka was ruling India in light and gentleness, the Romans were reviving an Etruscan sport, the setting on of slaves to fight for their lives. One is reminded of West Africa again in the origin of this amusement; it grew out of the prehistoric custom of a massacre of captives at the

Gladiators (from a wall-painting at Pompeii)

burial of a chief. There was a religious touch about this sport; the slaves with hooks, who dragged the dead bodies out of the arena, wore masks to represent the infernal ferryman-god, Charon. In 264 B.C., the very year in which Asoka began to reign and the First Punic War began, the first recorded gladiatorial combat took place in the forum at Rome, to celebrate the funeral of a member of the old Roman family of Brutus. This was a modest display of three couples, but soon gladiators were fighting by the hundred. The taste for these combats grew rapidly, and the wars supplied an abundance of captives. The old Roman moralists, who were so severe upon kissing and women's ornaments and Greek philosophy, had nothing but good to say for this new development. So long as pain was inflicted, Roman morality, it would seem, was satisfied.

If Republican Rome was the first of modern self-governing national communities, she was certainly the "Neanderthal" form of them.

In the course of the next two or three centuries the gladiatorial shows of Rome grew to immense proportions. To begin with, while wars were frequent, the gladiators were prisoners of war. They came with their characteristic national weapons, tattooed Britons, Moors, Scythians, negros, and the like, and there was perhaps some military value in these exhibitions. Then criminals of the lower classes condemned to death were also used. The ancient world did not understand that a criminal condemned to death still has rights, and at any rate the use of a criminal as a gladiator was not so bad as his use as "material" for the vivisectors of the Museum at Alexandria. But as the profits of this sort of show business grew and the demand for victims increased, ordinary slaves were sold to the trainers of gladiators, and any slave who had aroused his owner's spite might find himself in an establishment for letting out gladiators. And dissipated young men who had squandered their property, and lads of spirit would go voluntarily into the trade for a stated time, trusting to their prowess to survive. As the business developed, a new use was found for gladiators as armed retainers; rich men would buy a band, and employ it as a bodyguard or hire it out for profit at the shows. The festivities of a show began with a ceremonial procession (*pompa*) and a sham fight (*prœlusio*). The real fighting was heralded by trumpets. Gladiators who objected to fight for any reason were driven on by whips and hot irons. A wounded man would sometimes call for pity by holding up his forefinger. The spectators would then either wave their handkerchiefs in token of mercy, or condemn him to death by holding out their clenched fists with the thumbs down.[1] The slain and nearly dead were dragged out to a particular place, the *spoliarium*, where they were stripped of their arms and possessions, and those who had not already expired were killed.

This organization of murder as a sport and show serves to measure the great gap in moral standards between the Roman community and our own. No doubt cruelties and outrages upon human dignity as monstrous as this still go on in the world, but they do not go on in the name of the law and without a single dissentient voice. For it is true that until the time of Seneca (first century A.D.) there is no record of any plain protest against his business. The conscience of mankind was

[1] Authorities differ here. Mayor says thumbs up (to the breast) meant death and thumbs down meant "Lower that sword." The popular persuasion is that thumbs down meant death.

weaker and less intelligent then than now. Presently a new power was to come into the human conscience through the spread of Christianity. The spirit of Jesus in Christianity became the great antagonist in the later Roman state of these cruel shows and of slavery, and, as Christianity spread, these two evil things dwindled and disappeared.[1]

[1] "A little more needs to be said on this matter. The Greeks cited gladiatorial shows as a reason for regarding the Romans as *Barbaroi*, and there were riots when some Roman proconsul tried to introduce them in Corinth. Among Romans, the better people evidently disliked them, but as a sort of shyness prevented them from frankly denouncing them as cruel. For instance, Cicero, when he had to attend the Circus, took his tablets and his secretary with him, and didn't look. He expresses particular disgust at the killing of an elephant; and somebody in Tacitus (Drusus, Ann. 1. 76) was unpopular because he was too fond of gladiatorial bloodshed—'*quamquam vili sanguine nimis gaudens*' ('rejoicing too much in blood, worthless blood though it was'). The games were unhesitatingly condemned by Greek philosophy, and at different times two Cynics and one Christian gave their lives in the arena, protesting against them, before they were abolished.

"I do not think Christianity had any such relation to slavery as is here stated. St. Paul's action in sending back a slave to his master, and his injunction, 'Slaves, obey your masters,' were regularly quoted on the pro-slavery side, down to the nineteenth century; on the other hand, both the popular philosophies and the Mystery religions were against slavery in their whole tendency, and Christianity of course in time became the chief representative of these movements. Probably the best test is the number of slaves who occupied posts of honour in the religious and philosophic systems, like Epictetus, for instance, or the many slaves who hold offices in the Mithraic Inscriptions. I do not happen to know if any slaves were made Christian bishops, but by analogy I should think it likely that some were. In all the Mystery religions, as soon as you entered the community, and had communion with God, earthly distinctions shrivelled away."—G. M.

XXVII

FROM TIBERIUS GRACCHUS TO THE GOD EMPEROR IN ROME

§ 1. *The Science of Thwarting the Common Man.* § 2. *Finance in the Roman State.* § 3. *The Last Years of Republican Politics.* § 4. *The Era of the Adventurer Generals.* § 5. *The End of the Republic.* § 6. *The Coming of the Princeps.* § 7. *Why the Roman Republic Failed.*

§ 1

WE have already twice likened the self-governing community of Rome to a "Neanderthal" variety of the modern "democratic" civilized state, and we shall recur again to this comparison. In form the two things, the first great primitive essay and its later relations, are extraordinarily similar; in spirit they differ very profoundly. Roman political and social life, and particularly Roman political and social life in the century between the fall of Carthage and the rise of Cæsar and Cæsarism, has a very marked general resemblance to the political and social life in such countries as the United States of America or the British Empire to-day. The resemblance is intensified by the common use, with a certain inaccuracy in every case, of such terms as "senate," "democracy," "poletariat," and the like. But everything in the Roman state was earlier, cruder, and clumsier; the injustices were more glaring, the conflicts harsher. There was comparatively little knowledge and few general ideas. Aristotle's scientific works were only beginning to be read in Rome in the first century B.C.; Ferrero,[1] it is true, makes Cæsar familiar with the Politics of Aristotle, and ascribes to him the dream of making a "Periclean Rome," but in doing so, Ferrero seems to be indulging in one of those lapses into picturesque romanc-

[1] *Greatness and Decline of Rome,* **bk. i. ch. xi.**

ing which are at once the joy and the snare of all historical writers.

Attention has already been drawn to the profound difference between Roman and modern conditions due to the absence of a press, of any popular education or of the representative idea in the popular assembly. Our world to-day is still far from solving the problem of representation and from producing a public assembly which will really summarize, crystallize, and express the thought and will of the community; our elections are still largely an ingenious mockery of the common voter who finds himself helpless in the face of party organizations which reduce his free choice of a representative to the less unpalatable of two political hacks, but, even so, his vote, in comparison with the vote of an ordinary honest Roman citizen, is an effective instrument. Too many of our histories dealing with this period of Roman history write of "the popular party," and of the votes of the people and so forth, as though such things were as much working realities as they are to-day. But the senators and politicians of Rome saw to it that such things never did exist as clean and wholesome realities. These modern phrases are very misleading unless they are carefully qualified.

We have already described the gatherings of the popular comitia; but that clumsy assembly in sheep pens does not convey the full extent to which the gerrymandering of popular representation could be carried in Rome. Whenever there was a new enfranchisement of citizens in Italy, there would be the most elaborate trickery and counter-trickery to enrol the new voters into as few or as many of the thirty old "tribes" as possible, or to put them into as few as possible new tribes. Since the vote was taken by tribes, it is obvious that however great the number of new additions made, if they were all got together into one tribe, their opinion would only count for one tribal vote, and similarly if they were crowded into just a few tribes, old or new. On the other hand, if they were put into too many tribes their effect in any particular tribe might be inconsiderable. Here was the sort of work to fascinate every smart knave in politics. The *comitia tributa* could be *worked* at times so as to vote right counter to the general feeling of the people. And as we have already noted, the great mass of voters in Italy were also disenfranchised by distance. About the middle period of the Carthaginian wars there were upwards of 300,000 Roman citizens; about 100 B.C. there were more than 900,000, but in effect the voting of the popular assembly was confined to a few score thousand resident in and near Rome, and mostly men of a base type. And the Roman voters were "organized" to an extent that makes the Tammany machine of New York seem artless and honest. They belonged to clubs, *collegia sodalicia,* having usually some elegant religious pretensions; and the rising politician working his way to office went first to the usurers and then with the borrowed money to these clubs. If the outside voters were moved enough by any question to swarm into the city, it was always possible to put off the voting by declaring the omens unfavourable. If they came in unarmed, they could be intimidated; if they brought in arms, then the cry was raised that there was a plot to overthrow the republic, and a massacre would be organized.

There can be no doubt that all Italy, all the empire was festering with discomfort, anxiety, and discontent in the century after the destruction of Carthage; a few men were growing very rich, and the majority of people found themselves entangled in an inexplicable net of uncertain prices, jumpy markets, and debts; but yet there was no way at all of stating and clearing up the general dissatisfaction. There is no record of a single attempt to make the popular assembly a straightforward and workable public organ. Beneath the superficial appearances of public affairs struggled a mute giant of public opinion and public will, who sometimes made some great political effort a rush to vote or such like, and sometimes broke into actual violence. So long as there was no actual violence, the Senate and the financiers kept on in their own disastrous way. Only when they were badly frightened would governing cliques or parties desist from some nefarious policy and heed the common good. The real method of popular expression in Italy in those days was not the *comitia tributa,* but the strike and insurrection, the righteous and necessary methods of all cheated or suppressed peoples. We have seen in our own days in Great Britain a decline in the prestige of parliamentary government and a drift towards unconstitutional methods on the part of the masses through exactly the same cause, through the incurable disposition of politicians to gerrymander the electoral machine until the community is driven to explosion.

For insurrectionary purposes a discontented population needs a leader, and the political history of the concluding century of Roman republicanism is a history of insurrectionary leaders and counter-revolutionary leaders. Most of the former are manifestly unscrupulous adventurers who try to utilize the public necessity and unhappiness for their own advancement. Many of the historians of this period betray a disposition to take sides, and are either aristocratic in tone or fiercely democratic; but, indeed, neither side in these complex and intricate disputes has a record of high aims or clean hands. The Senate and the rich Equestrians were vulgar and greedy spirits, hostile and contemptuous towards the poor mob; and the populace was ignorant, unstable, and at least equally greedy. The Scipios in all this record shine by comparison, a group of gentlemen. To the motives of one or the other figures of the time, to Tiberius Gracchus, for example, we may perhaps extend the benefit of the doubt. But for the rest, they do but demonstrate how clever and cunning men may be, how subtle in contention, how brilliant in pretence, and how utterly wanting in wisdom or grace of spirit. "A shambling, hairy, brutish, but probably very cunning creature with a big brain *behind;*" so someone, I think it was Sir Harry Johnston, has described *Homo Neanderthalensis.*

To this day we must still use similar terms to describe the soul of the politician. The statesman has still to oust the politician from his lairs and weapon heaps. History has still to become a record of human dignity.

§ 2

Another respect in which the Roman system was a crude anticipation of our own, and different from any preceding political system we have considered, was that it was a cash and credit-using system. Money had been in the world as yet for only a few centuries. But its use had been growing; it was providing a fluid medium for trade and enterprise, and changing economic conditions profoundly. In republican Rome, the financier and the "money" interest began to play a part recognizably similar to their rôles to-day.

We have already noted—in our account of Herodotus—that a first effect of money was to give freedom of movement and leisure to a number of people who could not otherwise have enjoyed these privileges. And that is the peculiar value of money to mankind. Instead of a worker or helper being paid in kind and in such a way that he is tied as much in his enjoyment as in his labour, money leaves him free to do as he pleases amidst a wide choice of purchasable aids, eases, and indulgences. He may eat his money or drink it or give it to a temple or spend it in learning something or save it against some unforeseen occasion. That is the good of money, the freedom of its universal convertibility. But the freedom money gives the poor man is nothing to the freedom money has given the rich man. With money rich men ceased to be tied to lands, houses, stores, flocks and herds. They could change the nature and locality of their possessions with an unheard-of freedom. In the third and second century B.C., this release, this untethering of wealth, began to tell upon the general economic life of the Roman and Hellenized world. People began to buy land and the like not for use, but to sell again at a profit; people borrowed to buy, speculation developed. No doubt there were bankers in the Babylon of 1000 B.C., but they lent in a far more limited and solid way, bars of metal and stocks of goods. That earlier world was a world of barter and payment in kind, and it went slowly—and much more staidly and stably—for that reason. In that state the vast realm of China has remained almost down to the present time.

The big cities before Rome were trading and manufacturing cities. Such were Corinth and Carthage and Syracuse. But Rome never produced a very considerable industrial population, and her warehouses never rivalled those of Alexandria. The little port of Ostia was always big enough for her needs. Rome was a political and financial capital, and in the latter respect, at least, she was a new sort of city. She imported profits and tribute, and very little went out from her in return. The wharves of Ostia were chiefly busy unloading corn from Sicily and Africa and loot from all the world.

After the fall of Carthage the Roman imagination went wild with the hitherto unknown possibilities of finance. Money, like most other inventions, had "happened" to mankind, and men had still to develop—to-day they have still to perfect—the science and morality of money. One sees the thing "catching on" in the recorded life and the writings of Cato the Censor.

In his early days he was bitterly virtuous against usury; in his later he was devising ingenious schemes for safe usury.

In this curiously interesting century of Roman history we find man after man asking, "What has happened to Rome?" Various answers are made—a decline in religion, a decline from the virtues of the Roman forefathers, Greek "intellectual poison," and the like. We who can look at the problem with a large perspective, can see that what had happened to Rome was "money"—the new freedoms and chances and opportunities that money opened out. Money floated the Romans off the firm ground, everyone was getting hold of money, the majority by the simple expedient of running into debt; the eastward expansion of the empire was very largely a hunt for treasure in strong rooms and temples to keep pace with the hunger of the new need. The Equestrian order, in particular, became the money power. Everyone was developing property. Farmers were giving up corn and cattle, borrowing money, buying slaves, and starting the more intensive cultivation of oil and wine. Money was young in human experience and wild, nobody had it under control. It fluctuated greatly. It was now abundant and now scarce. Men made sly and crude schemes to corner it, to hoard it, to send up prices by releasing hoarded metals. A small body of very shrewd men was growing immensely rich. Many patricians were growing poor and irritated and unscrupulous. Among the middle sort of peoples there was much hope, much adventure, and much more disappointment. The growing mass of the expropriated was permeated by that vague, baffled, and hopeless sense of being inexplicably bested, which is the preparatory condition for all great revolutionary movements.

§ 3

The first conspicuous leader to appeal to the gathering revolutionary feeling in Italy was Tiberius Gracchus. He looks more like an honest man than any other figure in this period of history, unless it be Scipio Africanus the Elder. At first Tiberius Gracchus was a moderate reformer of a rather reactionary type. He wished to restore the yeoman class to property, very largely because he believed that class to be the backbone of the army, and his military experience in Spain before and after the destruction of Carthage had impressed upon him the declining efficiency of the legions. He was what we should call nowadays a "Back-to-the-land" man. He did not understand and few people understand to-day, how much easier it is to shift population from the land into the towns, than to return it to the laborious and simple routines of agricultural life. He wanted to revive the Licinian laws, which had been established when Camillus built his temple of Concord nearly two centuries and a half before (see Chap. xxvi, § 2), so far as they broke up great estates and restrained slave labour.

These Licinian Laws had repeatedly been revived and repeatedly lapsed to a dead letter again. It was only when the big proprietors in the Senate opposed this proposal that Tiberius Gracchus turned to the people and began a furious agitation for popular government. He created a commission to inquire into the title of all landowners. In the midst of his activities occurred one of the most extraordinary incidents in history. Attalus, the king of the rich country of Pergamum in Asia Minor, died (133 B.C.), and left his kingdom to the Roman people.

It is difficult for us to understand the motives of this bequest. Pergamum was a country allied to Rome, and so moderately secure from aggression; and the natural consequence of such a will was to provoke a violent scramble among the senatorial gangs and a dispute between them and the people for the spoils of the new acquisition. Practically Attalus handed over his country to be looted. There were of course many Italian business people established in the country and a strong party of native rich men in close relations with Rome. To them, no doubt, a coalescence with the Roman system would have been acceptable. Josephus bears witness to such a desire for annexation among the rich men of Syria, a desire running counter to the wishes of both king and people. This Pergamum bequest, astonishing in itself, had the still more astonishing result of producing imitations in other quarters. In 96 B.C. Ptolemy Apion bequeathed Cyrenaica, in North Africa, to the Roman people; in 81 B.C. Alexander II, King of Egypt, followed suit with Egypt, a legacy too big for the courage if not for the appetite of the Senators, and they declined it; in 74 B.C. Nicomedes, King of Bithynia, demised Bithynia. Of these latter testamentary freaks we will say no more here. But it will be manifest how great an opportunity was given Tiberius Gracchus by the bequest of Attalus, of accusing the rich of greed and of proposing to decree the treasures of Attalus to the commonalty. He proposed to use this new wealth to provide seed, stock, and agricultural implements for the resettlement of the land.

His movement was speedily entangled in the complexities of the Roman electoral system—without a simple and straightforward electoral method, all popular movements in all ages necessarily become entangled and maddened in constitutional intricacies, and almost as necessarily lead to bloodshed. It was needed, if his work was to go on, that Tiberius Gracchus should continue to be tribune, and it was illegal for him to be tribune twice in succession. He overstepped the bounds of legality, and stood for the tribuneship a second time; the peasants who came in from the countryside to vote for him came in armed; the cry that he was aiming at a tyranny, the cry that had long ago destroyed Mælius and Manlius, was raised in the Senate, the friends of "law and order" went to the Capitol in state, accompanied by a rabble of dependents armed with staves and bludgeons; there was a conflict, or rather a massacre of the revolutionaries, in which nearly three hundred people were killed, and Tiberius Gracchus was beaten to death with the fragments of a broken bench by two Senators.

Thereupon the Senators attempted a sort of counter-revolution, and proscribed many of the followers of Tiberius Gracchus; but the state of public opinion was so sullen and threatening that this movement was dropped and Scipio Nasica, who was implicated in the death of Tiberius, though he occupied the position of pontifex maximus and should have remained in Rome for the public sacrifices which were the duties of that official, went abroad to avoid trouble.

The uneasiness of Italy next roused Scipio Africanus the Younger to propose the enfranchisement of all Italy. But he died suddenly before he could carry the proposal into effect.

Then followed the ambiguous career of Caius Gracchus, the brother of Tiberius, who followed some tortuous "policy" that still exercises the mind of historians. He increased the burthens of taxation laid upon the provinces, it is supposed with the idea of setting the modern financiers (the Equites) against the senatorial landowners. He gave the former the newly bequeathed taxes of Asia to farm, and, what is worse, he gave them control of the special courts set up to prevent extortion. He started enormous public works and particularly the construction of new roads, and he is accused of making a political use of the contracts. He revived the proposal to enfranchise Italy. He increased the distribution of subsidized cheap corn to the Roman citizens. . . . Here we cannot attempt to disentangle his schemes, much less to judge him. But that his policy was offensive to the groups that controlled the Senate there can be no doubt whatever. He was massacred by the champions of "law and order," with about three thousands of his followers, in the streets of Rome in 121 B.C. His decapitated head was carried to the Senate on the point of a pike.

(A reward of its weight in gold, says Plutarch, had been offered for this trophy: and its captor, acting in the true spirit of a champion of "big business," filled the brain-case with lead on its way to the scales.)

In spite of these prompt firm measures the Senate was not to enjoy the benefits of peace and the advantages of a control of the imperial resources for long. Within ten years the people were in revolt again.

In 118 B.C. the throne of Numidia, the semi-barbaric kingdom that had arisen in North Africa upon the ruins of the civilized Carthaginian power, was seized by a certain able Jugurtha, who had served with the Roman armies in Spain, and had a knowledge of the Roman character. He provoked the military intervention of Rome. But the Romans found that their military power, under a Senate of financiers and landlords, was very different from what it had been even in the days of the younger Scipio Africanus. "Jugurtha bought over the Commissioners sent out to watch him, the Senators charged with their prosecution, and the generals in command against him."[1] There is a mistaken Roman proverb: *"pecunia non olet"* (money does not stink), for the money of Jugurtha stank even in Rome. There was an angry agitation; and a capable soldier of lowly origin, Marius, was carried to the consulship (107 B.C.) on the wave of popular indignation. Marius made no attempt on the model of the Gracchi to restore the backbone of the army by rehabilitating the yeoman class. He was a professional soldier with a high standard of efficiency and a

[1] Ferrero.

disposition to take short cuts. He simply raised troops from among the poor, whether countrymen or townsmen, paid them well, disciplined them thoroughly, and (106 B.C.) ended the seven years' war with Jugurtha by bringing that chieftain in chains to Rome. It did not occur to anybody that incidentally Marius had also created a professional army with no interest to hold it together but its pay. He then held on to the consulship more or less illegally for several years, and in 102 and 101 B.C. repelled a threatening move of the Germans (who thus appear in our history for the first time), who were raiding through Gaul towards Italy. He gained two victories; one on Italian soil. He was hailed as the saviour of his country, a second Camillus (100 B.C.).

The social tensions of the time mocked that comparison with Camillus. The Senate benefited by the greater energy in foreign affairs and the increased military efficiency that Marius had introduced, but the sullen, shapeless discontent of the mass of the people was still seeking some effective outlet. The rich grew richer and the poor poorer. It was impossible to stifle the consequences of that process for ever by political trickery. The Italian people were still unenfranchised. Two extreme democratic leaders, Saturninus and Glaucia, were assassinated, but that familiar senatorial remedy failed to assuage the populace on this occasion. In 92 B.C. an aristocratic official, Rutilius Rufus, who had tried to restrain the exactions of the financiers in Asia Minor, was condemned on a charge of corruption so manifestly trumped up that it deceived no one; and in 91 B.C., Livius Drusus, a newly elected tribune of the people, who was making capital out of the trial of Rutilius Rufus, was assassinated. He had proposed a general enfranchisement of the Italians, and he had foreshadowed not only another land law, but a general abolition of debts. Yet for all this vigour on the part of the senatorial usurers, landgrabbers, and forestallers, the hungry and the anxious were still insurgent. The murder of Drusus was the last drop in the popular cup; Italy blazed into a desperate insurrection.

There followed two years of bitter civil war, the Social War. It was a war between the idea of a united Italy and the idea of the rule of the Roman Senate. It was not a "social" war in the modern sense, but a war between Rome and her Italian allies (allies = Socii). "Roman generals, trained in the traditions of colonial warfare, marched ruthlessly up and down Italy, burning farms, sacking towns, and carrying off men, women, and children, to sell them in the open market or work them in gangs upon their estates."[1] Marius and an aristocratic general, Sulla, who had been with him in Africa and who was his bitter rival, both commanded on the side of Rome. But though the insurgents experienced defeats and looting, neither of these generals brought the war to an end. It was ended in a manner (89 B.C.) by the practical surrender of the Roman Senate to the idea of reform. The spirit was taken out of the insurrection by the concession of their demands "in principle"; and then as soon as the rebels had dispersed, the usual cheating of the new voters, by such methods as we have explained in § 1 of this chapter, was resumed.

By the next year (88 B.C.) the old round had begun again. It was mixed up with the personal intrigues of Marius and Sulla against each other; but the struggle had taken on another complexion through the army reforms of Marius, which had created a new type of legionary, a landless professional soldier with no interest in life but pay and plunder, and with no feeling of loyalty except to a successful general. A popular tribune, Sulpicius, was bringing forward some new laws affecting debt, and the consuls were dodging the storm by declaring a suspension of public business. Then came the usual resort to violence, and the followers of Sulpicius drove the consuls from the forum. But here it is that the new forces which the new army had made possible came into play. King Mithridates of Pontus, the Helenized king of the southern shores of the Black Sea east of Bithynia, was pressing Rome into war. One of the proposed laws of Sulpicius was that Marius should command the armies sent against this Mithridates. Whereupon Sulla marched the army he had commanded throughout the Social War to Rome, Marius and Sulpicius fled, and a new age, an age of military pronunciamentos, began.

Of how Sulla had himself made commander against Mithridates and departed, and of how legions friendly to Marius then seized power, how Marius returned to Italy and enjoyed a thorough massacre of his political opponents and died, sated, of fever, we cannot tell in any detail. But one measure during the Marian reign of terror did much to relieve the social

[1] Ferrero.

tension, and that was the abolition of three-quarters of all outstanding debts. Nor can we tell here how Sulla made a discreditable peace with Mithridates (who had massacred a hundred thousand Italians in Asia Minor) in order to bring his legions back to Rome, defeat the Marians at the battle of the Colline Gate of Rome, and reverse the arrangements of Marius. Sulla restored law and order by the proscription and execution of over five thousand people. He desolated large parts of Italy, restored the Senate to power, repealed many of the recent laws, though he was unable to restore the cancelled burden of debt, and then, feeling bored by politics and having amassed great riches, he retired with an air of dignity into private life, gave himself up to abominable vices, and so presently died, eaten up with some disgusting disease produced by debauchery.[1]

§ 4

Political life in Italy was not so much tranquillized as stunned by the massacres and confiscations of Marius and Sulla. The scale upon which this history is planned will not permit us to tell here of the great adventurers who, relying more and more on the support of the legions, presently began to scheme and intrigue again for dictatorial power in Rome. In 73 B.C. all Italy was terrified by a rising of the slaves, and particularly of the gladiators, led by a gladiator from Thessaly, Spartacus. He and seventy others had fled out from a gladiatorial "farm" at Capua. Similar risings had already occurred in Sicily. The forces under Spartacus necessarily became a miscellaneous band drawn from east and west, without any common idea except the idea of dispersing and getting home; nevertheless, he held out in southern Italy for two years, using the then apparently extinct crater of Vesuvius for a time as a natural fortress. The Italians, for all their love of gladiatorial display, failed to appreciate this conversion of the whole country into an arena, this bringing of the gladiatorial sword to the door, and when at last Spartacus was overthrown, their terror changed to frantic cruelty, six thousand of his captured followers were

[1] Plutarch. To which, however, G. M. adds the following note: "It is generally believed that Sulla died through bursting a blood-vessel in a fit of temper. The story of abominable vices seems to be only the regular slander of the Roman mob against anyone who did not live in public."

crucified—long miles of nailed and drooping victims—along the Appian Way.

Here we cannot deal at any length with Lucullus, who invaded Pontus and fought Mithridates, and brought the cultivated cherry-tree to Europe; nor can we tell how ingeniously Pompey the Great stole the triumph and most of the prestige Lucullus had won in Armenia beyond Pontus. Lucullus, like Sulla, retired into an opulent private life, but with more elegance and with a more gracious end. We cannot relate in any detail how Julius Cæsar accumulated reputation in the west, by conquering Gaul, defeating the German tribes upon the Rhine, and pushing a punitive raid across the Straits of Dover into Britain. More and more important grow the legions; less and less significant are the Senate and the assemblies of Rome. But there is a certain grim humour about the story of Crassus that we cannot altogether neglect.

This Crassus was a great money-lender and forestaller. He was a typical man of the new Equestrian type, the social equivalent of a modern munition profiteer. He first grew rich by buying up the property of those proscribed by Sulla. His earliest exploits in the field were against Spartacus, whom finally he crushed by great payments and exertions after a prolonged and expensive campaign. He then, as the outcome of complicated bargains, secured the command in the east and prepared to emulate the glories of Lucullus, who had pushed east from Pergamum and Bithynia into Pontus, and of Pompey, who had completed the looting of Armenia.

His experiences serve to demonstrate the gross ignorance with which the Romans were conducting their affairs at that time. He crossed the Euphrates, expecting to find in Persia another Hellenized kingdom like Pontus. But, as we have already intimated, the great reservoirs of nomadic peoples that stretched round from the Danube across Russia into Central Asia, had been raining back into the lands between the Caspian Sea and the Indus that Alexander had conquered for Hellenism. Crassus found himself against the "Scythian" again; against mobile tribes of horsemen led by a monarch in Median costume.[1] The particular variety of "Scythian" he encountered was called the Parthian. It is possible that in the Parthians a Mongolian (Turanian) element was now mingled with the Aryan

[1] Plutarch.

strain; but the campaign of Crassus beyond the Euphrates is curiously like the campaign of Darius beyond the Danube; there is the same heavy thrusting of an infantry force against elusive light horsemen. But Crassus was less quick than Darius to realize the need of withdrawal, and the Parthians were better bowmen than the Scythians Darius met. They seem to have had some sort of noisy projectile of unusual strength and force, something different from an ordinary arrow.[1] The campaign culminated in that two days' massacre of the hot, thirsty, hungry, and weary Roman legions which is known as the battle of Carrhæ (53 B.C.). They toiled through the sand, charging an enemy who always evaded their charge and rode round them and shot them to pieces. Twenty thousand of them were killed, and ten thousand marched on eastward as prisoners into slavery in Iran.

What became of Crassus is not clearly known. There is a story, probably invented for our moral benefit and suggested by his usuries, that he fell alive into the hands of the Parthians and was killed by having molten gold poured down his throat.

But this disaster has a very great significance indeed to our general history of mankind. It serves to remind us that from the Rhine to the Euphrates, all along to the north of the Alps and Danube and Black Sea, stretched one continuous cloud of nomadic and semi-nomadic peoples, whom the statescraft of imperial Rome was never able to pacify and civilize, nor her military science subdue. We have already called attention to a map showing how the Second Babylonian Empire, the Chaldean Empire, lay like a lamb in the embrace of the Median power. In exactly the same way the Roman Empire lay like a lamb in the embrace of this great crescent of outer barbarians. Not only was Rome never able to thrust back or assimilate that superincumbent crescent, but she was never able to organize the Mediterranean Sea into a secure and

[1] The bow was probably the composite bow, so-called because it is made of several plates (five or so) of horn, like the springs of a carriage: it discharges a high-speed arrow with a twang. This was the bow the Mongols used. This short composite bow (it was not a long bow) was quite old in human experience. It was the bow of Odysseus; the Assyrians had it in a modified form. It went out in Greece, but it survived as the Mongol bow. It was quite short, very stiff to pull, with a flat trajectory, a remarkable range, and a great noise (cp. Homer's reference to the twang of the bow). It went out in the Mediterranean because the climate was not good for it, and because there were insufficient animals to supply the horn.—J. L. M.

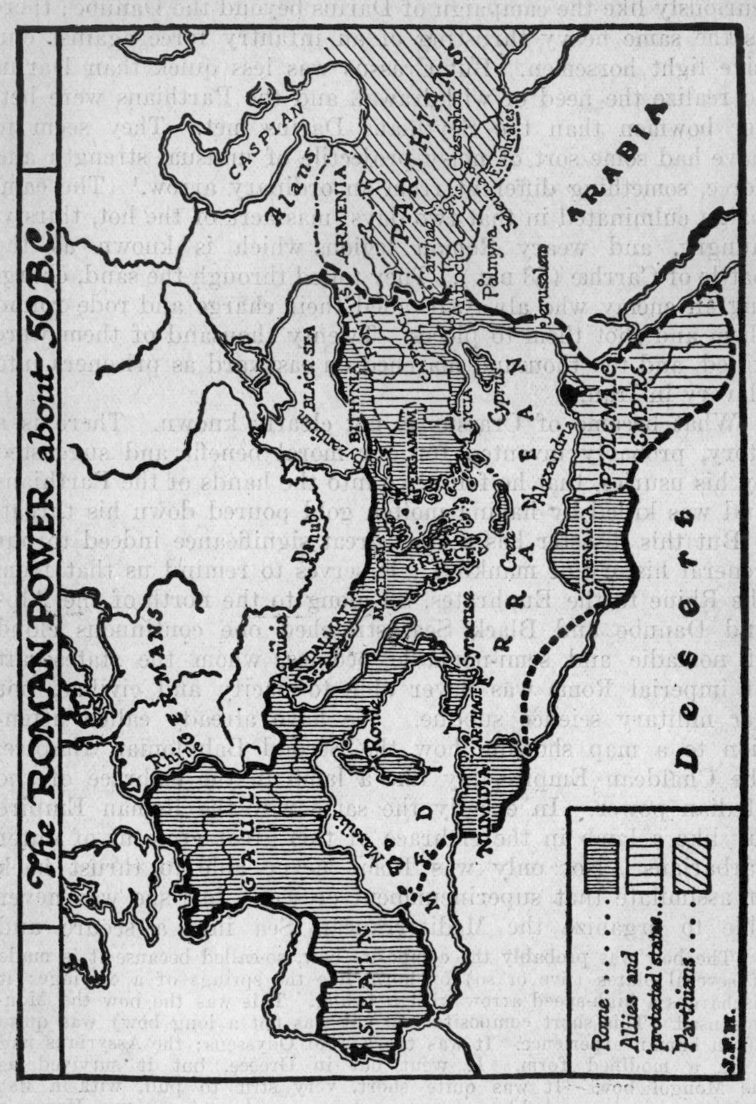
The ROMAN POWER about 50 B.C.
CASPIAN
Alans
ARMENIA
PARTHIANS
ARABIA
Ctesiphon
Euphrates
Tigris
Seleucia
Carrhae
Antioch
Palmyra
Jerusalem
PONTUS
CAPPADOCIA
BLACK SEA
BITHYNIA
Byzantium
PERGAMUM
LYCIA
Cyprus
PTOLEMAIC EMPIRE
Alexandria
Crete
GREECE
MACEDONIA
Danube
DALMATIA
Aquileia
Syracuse
CYRENAICA
GERMANS
Rhine
Rome
CARTHAGE
NUMIDIA
Massilia
GAUL
SPAIN
MEDITERRANEAN
Deserts
Rome
Allies and 'protected' states
Parthians
J.F.H.

orderly system of communication between one part of her empire and another. Quite unknown as yet to Rome, the Mongolian tribes from North-eastern Asia, the Huns and their kin, walled back and driven out from China by the Tsi and Han dynasties, were drifting and pressing westward, mixing with the Parthians, the Scythians, the Teutons and the like, or driving them before them.

Never at any time did the Romans succeed in pushing their empire beyond Mesopotamia, and upon Mesopotamia their hold was never very secure. Before the close of the republic that power of assimilation which had been the secret of their success was giving way to "patriotic" exclusiveness and "patriotic" greed. Rome plundered and destroyed Asia Minor and Babylonia, which were the necessary basis for an eastward extension to India, just as she had destroyed and looted Carthage and so had no foothold for extension into Africa, and just as she had destroyed Corinth and so cut herself off from an easy way into the heart of Greece. Western European writers, impressed by the fact that later on Rome Romanized and civilized Gaul and South Britain and restored the scene of her earlier devastations in Spain to prosperity, are apt to ignore that over far greater areas to the south and east her influence was to weaken and so restore to barbarism the far wider conquests of Hellenic civilization.

§ 5

But among the politicians of Italy in the first century B.C. there were no maps of Germany and Russia, Africa and Central Asia, and no sufficient intelligence to study them had they existed. Rome never developed the fine curiosities that sent Hanno and the sailors of Pharaoh Necho down the coasts of Africa. When, in the first century B.C., the emissaries of the Han dynasty reached the eastern shores of the Caspian Sea, they found only stories of a civilization that had receded. The memory of Alexander still lived in these lands, but of Rome men only knew that Pompey had come to the western shores of the Caspian and gone away again, and that Crassus had been destroyed. Rome was pre-occupied at home. What mental energy remained over in the Roman citizen from the attempt to grow personally rich and keep personally safe was intent upon the strategems and strokes and counter-strokes of the various adventurers who were now manifestly grappling for the supreme power.

It is the custom of historians to treat these struggles with extreme respect. In particular the figure of Julius Cæsar is set up as if it were a star of supreme brightness and importance in the history of mankind. Yet a dispassionate consideration of the known facts fails altogether to justify this demigod theory of Cæsar. Not even that precipitate wrecker of splendid possibilities, Alexander the Great, has been so magnified and dressed up for the admiration of careless and uncritical readers. There is a type of scholar who, to be plain, sits and *invents* marvellous world policies for the more conspicuous figures in history with the merest scraps of justification or with no justification at all. We are told that Alexander planned the conquest of Carthage and Rome and the complete subjugation of India and that only his death shattered these schemes. What we know for certain is that he conquered the Persian Empire, and never went far beyond its boundaries; and that when he was supposed to be making these vast and noble plans, he was in fact indulging in such monstrous antics as his mourning for his favourite Hephæstion, and as his main occupation he was drinking himself to death. So, too, Julius Cæsar is credited with the intention of doing just that one not impossible thing which would have secured the Roman Empire from its ultimate collapse—namely, the systematic conquest and civilization of Europe as far as the Baltic and the Dnieper. He was to have marched upon Germany, says Plutarch, through Parthia and Scythia, round the north of the Caspian and Black Seas. Yet the fact we have to reconcile with this wise and magnificent project is that at the crest of his power, Cæsar, already a bald, middle-aged man, past the graces and hot impulses of youthful love, spent the better part of a year in Egypt, feasting and entertaining himself in amorous pleasantries with the Egyptian queen, Cleopatra. And afterwards he brought her with him to Rome, where her influence over him was bitterly resented. Such complications with a woman mark the elderly sensualist or sentimentalist—he was fifty-four at the commencement of the *affaire*—rather than the master-ruler of men.

On the side of the superman idea of Cæsar, we have to count a bust in the Naples Museum. It represents a fine and intellectual face, very noble in its expression, and we can couple with that the story that his head, even at birth, was unusually large and finely formed. But there is really no satisfying evidence that this well-known bust does represent Cæsar, and it is hard to reconcile its austere serenity with the reputation for violent impulse and disorderliness that clung to him. Other busts of a quite different man are also, with more probability, ascribed to him.

There can be little doubt that he was a dissolute and extravagant young man—the scandals cluster thick about his sojourn in Bithynia, whither he fled from Sulla; he was the associate of the reprobate Clodius and the conspirator Catiline, and there is nothing in his political career to suggest any aim higher or remoter than his own advancement to power, and all the personal glory and indulgence that power makes possible. We will not attempt to tell here of the turns and devices of his career. Although he was of an old patrician family, he came into politics as the brilliant darling of the people. He spent great sums and incurred heavy debts to provide public festivals on the most lavish scale. He opposed the tradition of Sulla, and cherished the memory of Marius, who was his uncle by marriage. For a time he worked in conjunction with Crassus and Pompey, but after the death of Crassus he and Pompey came into conflict. By 49 B.C. he and Pompey, with their legions, he from the west and Pompey from the east, were fighting openly for predominance in the Roman state. He had broken the law by bringing his legions across the Rubicon, which was the boundary between his command and Italy proper. At the battle of Pharsalos in Thessaly (48 B.C.), Pompey was routed, and, fleeing to Egypt, was murdered, leaving Cæsar more master of the Roman world than ever Sulla had been.

He was then created dictator for ten years in 46 B.C., and early in 45 B.C. he was made dictator for life. This was monarchy; if not hereditary monarchy, it was at least electoral life monarchy. It was unlimited opportunity to do his best for the world. And by the spirit and quality of his use of this dictatorial power during these four years we are bound to judge him. A certain reorganization of local administration he effected, and he seems to have taken up what was a fairly obvious necessity of the times, a project for the restoration of the two murdered seaports of Corinth and Carthage, whose destruction had wrecked the sea-life of the Mediterranean. But much more evident was the influence of Cleopatra and Egypt upon his mind. Like Alexander before him, his head seems to have been turned by the king-god tradition, assisted no doubt in his case by the adulation of that charming hereditary goddess, Cleopatra. We find evidence of exactly that same conflict upon the score of divine pretensions, between him and his personal friends, that we have already recorded in the case of Alexander. So far as the Hellenized east was concerned, the paying of divine honours to rulers was a familiar idea; but it was still repulsive to the lingering Aryanism of Rome.

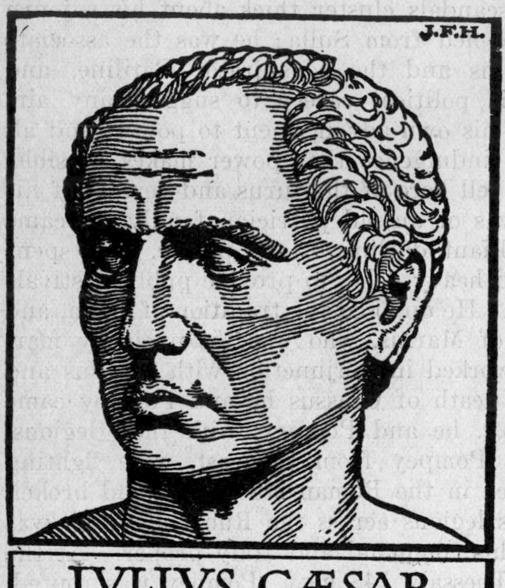

JVLIVS CÆSAR
(from the Naples bust)

Antony, who had been his second in command at Pharsalos, was one of the chief of his flatterers. Plutarch describes a scene at the public games in which Antony tried to force a crown upon Cæsar, which, Cæsar, after a little coyness and in face of the manifested displeasure of the crowd, refused. But he had adopted the ivory sceptre and throne, which were the traditional insignia of the ancient kings of Rome. His image was carried amidst that of the gods in the opening *pompa* of the arena, and his statue was set up in a temple with an inscription, "To the Unconquerable God!" Priests even were appointed for his godhead. These things are not the symptoms of great-mindedness, but of a common man's megalomania. Cæsar's record of vulgar scheming for the tawdriest mockeries of personal worship is a silly and shameful record; it is incompatible with the idea that he was a wise and wonderful superman setting the world to rights.

Finally (44 B.C.) he was assassinated by a group of his own friends and supporters, to whom these divine aspirations had become intolerable. He was beset in the Senate, and stabbed in three and twenty places, dying at the foot of the statue of his fallen rival Pompey the Great. The scene marks the complete demoralization of the old Roman governing body. Brutus, the ringleader of the murderers, would have addressed the senators, but, confronted by this crisis, they were scuttling off in every direction. For the best part of a day Rome did not know what to make of this event; the murderers marched about with their bloody weapons through an undecided city, with no one gainsaying them and only a few joining them; then public opinion turned against them, some of their houses were attacked, and they had to hide and fly for their lives.

§ 6

But the trend of things was overwhelmingly towards monarchy. For thirteen years more the struggle of personalities went on. One single man is to be noted as inspired by broad ideas and an ambition not entirely egoistic, Cicero. He was a man of modest origin, whose eloquence and literary power had won him a prominent place in the Senate. He was a little tainted by the abusive tradition of Demosthenes, nevertheless he stands out, a noble and pathetically ineffective figure, pleading with the now utterly degenerate, base, and cowardly Senate for the high ideals of the Republic. He was a writer of great care and distinction, and the orations and private letters he has left us make him one of the most real and living figures of this period to the modern reader. He was proscribed and killed in 43 B.C., the year after the murder of Julius Cæsar, and his head and hands were nailed up in the Roman forum. Octavian, who became at last the monarch of Rome, seems to have made an effort to save Cicero; that murder was certainly not his crime.

Here we cannot trace out the tangle of alliances and betrayals that ended in the ascendancy of this Octavian, the adopted heir of Julius Cæsar. The fate of the chief figures is interwoven with that of Cleopatra.

After the death of Cæsar, she set herself to capture the emotions and vanity of Antony, a much younger man than Cæsar, with whom she was probably already acquainted. For a time Octavian and Antony and a third figure, Lepidus, divided the Roman world just as Cæsar and Pompey had divided it before their final conflict. Octavian took the hardier west, and consolidated his power; Antony had the more gorgeous east—and Cleopatra. To Lepidus fell that picked bone, Carthaginian Africa. He seems to have been a good man of good traditions, set upon the restoration of Carthage rather than upon wealth or personal vanities. The mind of Antony succumbed to those same ancient ideas of divine kingship that had already proved too much for the mental equilibrium of Julius Cæsar. In the company of Cleopatra he gave himself up to love, amusements, and a dream of sensuous glory, until Octavian felt that the time was ripe to end these two Egyptian divinities.

In 32 B.C. Octavian induced the Senate to depose Antony from the command of the east, and proceeded to attack him. A great naval battle at Actium (31 B.C.) was decided by the unexpected desertion of Cleopatra with sixty ships in the midst of the fight. It is quite impossible for us to decide now whether this was due to premeditated treachery or to the sudden whim of a charming woman. The departure of these ships threw the fleet of Antony into hopeless confusion, which was increased by the headlong flight of this model lover in pursuit. He went off in a swift galley after her without informing his commanders. He left his followers to fight and die as they thought fit, and for a time they were incredulous that he had gone. The subsequent encounter of the two lovers and their reconciliation is a matter of ironical speculation on the part of Plutarch.

Octavian's net closed slowly round his rival. It is not improbable that there was some sort of understanding between Octavian and Cleopatra, as perhaps in the time of Julius Cæsar there may have been between the queen and Antony. Antony gave way to much mournful posturing, varied by love scenes, during this last stage of his little drama. For a time he posed as an imitator of the cynic Timon, as one who had lost all faith in mankind, though one may think that his deserted sailors at Actium had better reason for such an attitude. Finally he found himself and Cleopatra besieged by Octavian in

Alexandria. There were some sallies and minor successes, and Antony was loud with challenges to Octavian to decide the matter by personal combat. Being led to believe that Cleopatra had committed suicide, this star of romance stabbed himself, but so ineffectually as to die lingeringly, and he was carried off to expire in her presence (30 B.C.).

Plutarch's account of Antony, which was derived very largely from witnesses who had seen and known him, describes him as of heroic mould. He is compared to the demigod Hercules, from whom indeed he claimed descent, and also to the Indian Bacchus. There is a disgusting but illuminating description of a scene in the Senate when he attempted to speak while drunk, and was overtaken by one of the least dignified concomitants of intoxication.

For a little while Cleopatra still clung to life, and perhaps to the hope that she might reduce Octavian to the same divine rôle that had already been played by Julius Cæsar and Antony. She had an interview with Octavian, in which she presented herself as beauty in distress and very lightly clad. But when it became manifest that Octavian lacked the godlike spark, and that his care for her comfort and welfare was dictated chiefly by his desire to exhibit her in a triumphal procession through the streets of Rome, she also committed suicide. An asp was smuggled to her past the Roman sentries, concealed in a basket of figs, and by its fangs she died.

Octavian seems to have been almost entirely free from the divine aspirations of Julius Cæsar and Antony. He was neither God nor romantic hero; he was a man. He was a man of far greater breadth and capacity than any other player in this last act of the Republican drama in Rome. All things considered, he was perhaps the best thing that could have happened to Rome at that time. He "voluntarily resigned the extraordinary powers which he had held since 43, and, to quote his own words, 'handed over the republic to the control of the senate and the people of Rome.' The old constitutional machinery was once more set in motion; the senate, assembly, and magistrates resumed their functions, and Octavian himself was hailed as the 'restorer of the commonwealth and the champion of freedom.' It was not so easy to determine what relation he himself, the actual master of the Roman world, should occupy towards this revived republic. His abdication, in any real sense of the word, would have simply thrown everything back into confusion. The interests of peace and order required that he should retain at least the substantial part of his authority; and this object was in fact accomplished, and the rule of the emperors founded in a manner which has no parallel in history. Any revival of the kingly title was out of the question, and Octavian himself expressly refused the dictatorship. Nor was any new office created or any new official title invented for his benefit. But by senate and people he was invested according to the old constitutional forms with certain powers, as many citizens had been before him, and so took his place by the side of the lawfully appointed magistrates of the republic; only, to mark his pre-eminent dignity, as the first of them all, the senate decreed that he should take as an additional cognomen that of 'Augustus,' while in common parlance he was henceforth styled Princeps, a simple title of courtesy, familiar to republican usage and conveying no other idea than that of a recognized primacy and precedence over his fellow-citizens. The ideal sketched by Cicero in his *De Republica,* of a constitutional president of a free republic, was apparently realized; but it was only in appearance. For in fact the special prerogatives conferred upon Octavian gave him back in substance the autocratic authority he had resigned, and as between the restored republic and its new *princeps* the balance of power was overwhelmingly on the side of the latter."[1]

§ 7

In this manner it was that Roman republicanism ended in a *princeps* or ruling prince, and the first great experiment in a self-governing community on a scale larger than that of tribe or city, collapsed and failed.

The essence of its failure was that it could not sustain unity. In its early stages its citizens, both patrician and plebeian, had a certain tradition of justice and good faith, and of the loyalty of all citizens to the law, and of the goodness of the law for all citizens; it clung to this idea of the importance of the law and of law-abidingness nearly into the first century B.C. But the unforeseen invention and development of money, the temptations and disruptions of imperial expansion, the entanglement of

[1] H. S. Jones in *The Encyclopaedia Britannica,* article "Rome."

electoral methods, weakened and swamped this tradition by presenting old issues in new disguises under which the judgment did not recognize them, and by enabling men to be loyal to the professions of citizenship and disloyal to its spirit. The bond of the Roman people had always been a moral rather than a religious bond; their religion was sacrificial and superstitious; it embodied no such great ideas of a divine leader and of a sacred mission as Judaism was developing. As the idea of citizenship failed and faded before the new occasions, there remained no inner, that is to say no real, unity in the system at all. Every man tended more and more to do what was right in his own eyes.

Under such conditions there was no choice between chaos and a return to monarchy, to the acceptance of some chosen individual as the one unifying will in the state. Of course in that return there is always hidden the expectation that the monarch will become as it were magic, will cease to be merely a petty human being, and will think and feel as something greater and more noble, as indeed a state personage; and of course monarchy invariably fails to satisfy that expectation. We shall glance at the extent of this failure in the brief review we shall presently make of the emperors of Rome. We shall find at last one of the more constructive of these emperors, Constantine the Great, conscious of his own inadequacy as a unifying power, turning to the faith, the organization, and teaching network of one of the new religious movements in the empire, to supply just that permeating and correlating factor in men's minds that was so manifestly wanting.

With Cæsar, the civilization of Europe and Western Asia went back to monarchy, and, through monarchy, assisted presently by organized Christianity, it sought to achieve peace, righteousness, happiness, and world order for close upon eighteen centuries. Then almost suddenly it began reverting to republicanism, first in one country and then in another, and, assisted by the new powers of printing and the press and of organized general education, and by the universalist religious ideas in which the world had been soaked for generations, it seems now to have resumed again the effort to create a republican world-state and a world-wide scheme of economic righteousness which the Romans had made so prematurely and in which they had so utterly and disastrously failed.

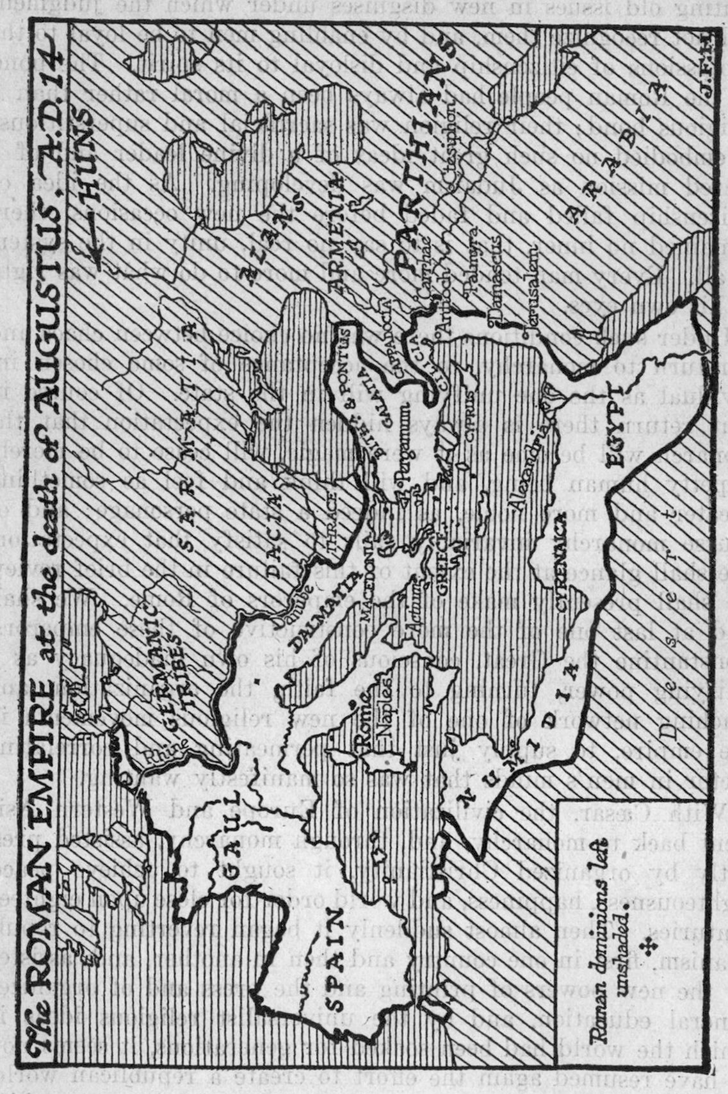
The ROMAN EMPIRE at the death of AUGUSTUS, A.D. 14
HUNS
SARMATIA
ALANS
ARMENIA
PARTHIANS
Ctesiphon
ARABIA
J.F.H.
GERMANIC TRIBES
Rhine
Danube
DACIA
THRACE
BITHYNIA & PONTUS
GALATIA
CAPPADOCIA
CILICIA
Carrhae
Antioch
Palmyra
Damascus
Jerusalem
Pergamum
CYPRUS
Alexandria
EGYPT
CYRENAICA
Desert
NUMIDIA
MACEDONIA
GREECE
Actium
DALMATIA
Rome
Naples
GAUL
SPAIN
Roman dominions left unshaded.

Certain conditions, we are now beginning to perceive, are absolutely necessary to such a creation; conditions which it is inconceivable that any pre-Christian Roman could have regarded as possible. We may still think the attainment of these conditions a vastly laborious and difficult and uncertain undertaking, but we understand that the attempt must be made because no other prospect before us gives even a promise of happiness or self-respect or preservation of our kind. The first of these conditions is that there should be a common political idea in the minds of all men, an idea of the state thought of as the personal possession of each individual and as the backbone fact of his scheme of duties. In the early days of Rome, when it was a little visible state, twenty miles square, such notions could be and were developed in children in their homes, and by what they saw and heard of the political lives of their fathers; but in a larger country such as Rome had already become before the war with Pyrrhus, there was a need of an organized teaching of the history, of the main laws, and of the general intentions of the state towards every one if this moral unity was to be maintained. But the need was never realized, and no attempt at any such teaching was ever made. At the time it could not have been made. It is inconceivable that it could have been made. The knowledge was not there, and there existed no class from which the needed teachers could be drawn and no conception of an organization for any such systematic moral and intellectual training as the teaching organization of Christianity, with its creeds and catechisms and sermons and confirmations, presently supplied.

Moreover, we know nowadays that even a universal education of this sort supplies only the basis for a healthy republican state. Next to education there must come abundant, prompt, and truthful information of what is going on in the state, and frank and free discussion of the issues of the time. Even nowadays these functions are performed only very imperfectly and badly by the press we have and by our publicists and politicians; but badly though it is done, the thing is done, and the fact that it is done at all argues that it may ultimately be done well. In the Roman state it was not even attempted. The Roman citizen got his political facts from rumour and the occasional orator. He stood wedged in the forum, imperfectly hearing a distant speaker. He probably misconceived every issue upon which he voted.

And of the monstrous ineffectiveness of the Roman voting system we have already written.

Unable to surmount or remove these obstacles to a sane and effective popular government, the political instincts of the Roman mind turned towards monarchy. But it was not monarchy of the later European type, not hereditary monarchy, which was now installed in Rome. The *princeps* was really like an American war-time president, but he was elected not for four years but for life, he was able to appoint senators instead of being restrained by an elected senate, and with a rabble popular meeting in the place of the house of representatives. He was also *pontifex maximus,* chief of the sacrificial priests, a function unknown at Washington; and in practice it became usual for him to designate and train his successor and to select for that honour a son or an adopted son or a near relation whom he could trust. The power of the *princeps* was in itself enormous to entrust to the hands of a single man without any adequate checks, but it was further enhanced by the tradition of monarch worship which had now spread out from Egypt over the entire Hellenized east, and which was coming to Rome in the head of every Oriental slave and immigrant. By natural and imperceptible degrees the idea of the god-emperor came to dominate the whole Romanized world.

Only one thing presently remained to remind the god-emperor that he was mortal, and that was the army. The god-emperor was never safe upon the Olympus of the Palatine Hill at Rome. He was only secure while he was the beloved captain of his legions. And as a consequence only the hardworking emperors who kept their legions active and in close touch with themselves had long reigns. The sword overhung the emperor and spurred him to incessant activity. If he left things to his generals, one of those generals presently replaced him. This spur was perhaps the redeeming feature of the Roman Imperial system. In the greater, compacter, and securer empire of China there was not the same need of legions, and so there was not the same swift end for lazy or dissipated or juvenile monarchs that overtook such types in Rome.

XXVIII

THE CÆSARS BETWEEN THE SEA AND THE GREAT PLAINS OF THE OLD WORLD

§ 1. *A Short Catalogue of Emperors.* § 2. *Roman Civilization at its Zenith.* § 3. *Limitations of the Roman Mind.* § 4. *The Stir of the Great Plains.* § 5. *The Western (true Roman) Empire Crumples Up.* § 6. *The Eastern (revived Hellenic) Empire.*

§ 1

WESTERN writers are apt, through their patriotic predispositions, to overestimate the organization, civilizing work, and security of the absolute monarchy that established itself in Rome after the accession of Augustus Cæsar. From it we derive the political traditions of Britain, France, Spain, Germany, and Italy, and these countries loom big in the perspectives of European writers. By the scale of a world history the Roman Empire ceases to seem so overwhelmingly important. It lasted about four centuries in all before it was completely shattered. The Byzantine Empire was no genuine continuation of it; it was a resumption of the Hellenic Empire of Alexander; it spoke Greek; its monarch had a Roman title no doubt, but so for that matter had the late Tsar of Bulgaria. During its four centuries of life the empire of Rome had phases of division and complete chaos; its prosperous years, if they are gathered together and added up, do not amount in all to a couple of centuries. Compared with the quiet steady expansion, the security, and the civilizing task of the contemporary Chinese Empire, or with Egypt between 4000 and 1000 B.C., or with Sumeria before the Semitic conquest, this amounts to a mere incident in history. The Persian Empire of Cyrus again, which reached from the Hellespont to the Indus, had as high a standard of civilization; and its homelands remained unconquered and fairly prosperous for over two hundred years.

Its predecessor, the Median Empire, had endured for half a century. After a brief submergence by Alexander the Great, it rose again as the Seleucid Empire, which endured for some centuries. The Seleucid dominion shrank at last to the west of the Euphrates, and became a part of the Roman Empire; but Persia, revived by the Parthians as a new Persian Empire, first under the Arsacids and then under the Sassanids, outlived the empire of Rome. The Sassanids repeatedly carried war into the Byzantine Empire, and held the line of the Euphrates steadfastly. In 616 A.D. under Chosroes II, they were holding Damascus, Jerusalem, and Egypt, and threatening the Hellespont. But there has been no tradition to keep alive the glories of the Sassanids. The reputation of Rome has flourished through the prosperity of her heirs. The tradition of Rome is greater than its reality.

History distinguishes two chief groups of Roman emperors who were great administrators. The first of these groups began with:—

Augustus Cæsar (27 B.C. to 14 A.D.), the Octavian of the previous section, who worked hard at the reorganization of the provincial governments and at financial reform. He established a certain tradition of lawfulness and honesty in the bureaucracy, and he restrained the more monstrous corruptions and tyrannies by giving the provincial citizen the right to appeal to Cæsar. But he fixed the European boundaries of the empire along the Rhine and Danube, so leaving Germany, which is the necessary backbone of a safe and prosperous Europe, to barbarism; and he made a similar limitation in the east at the Euphrates, leaving Armenia independent, to be a constant bone of contention with the Arsacids and Sassanids. It is doubtful whether he considered that he was fixing the final boundaries of the empire along these lines, or whether he thought it desirable to consolidate for some years before any further attempts at expansion.

Tiberius (14 to 37 A.D.) is also described as a capable ruler, but he became intensely unpopular in Rome, and it would seem that he was addicted to gross and abominable vices. But his indulgence in these and his personal tyrannies and cruelties did not interfere with the general prosperity of the empire. It is difficult to judge him; nearly all our sources of information are manifestly hostile to him.

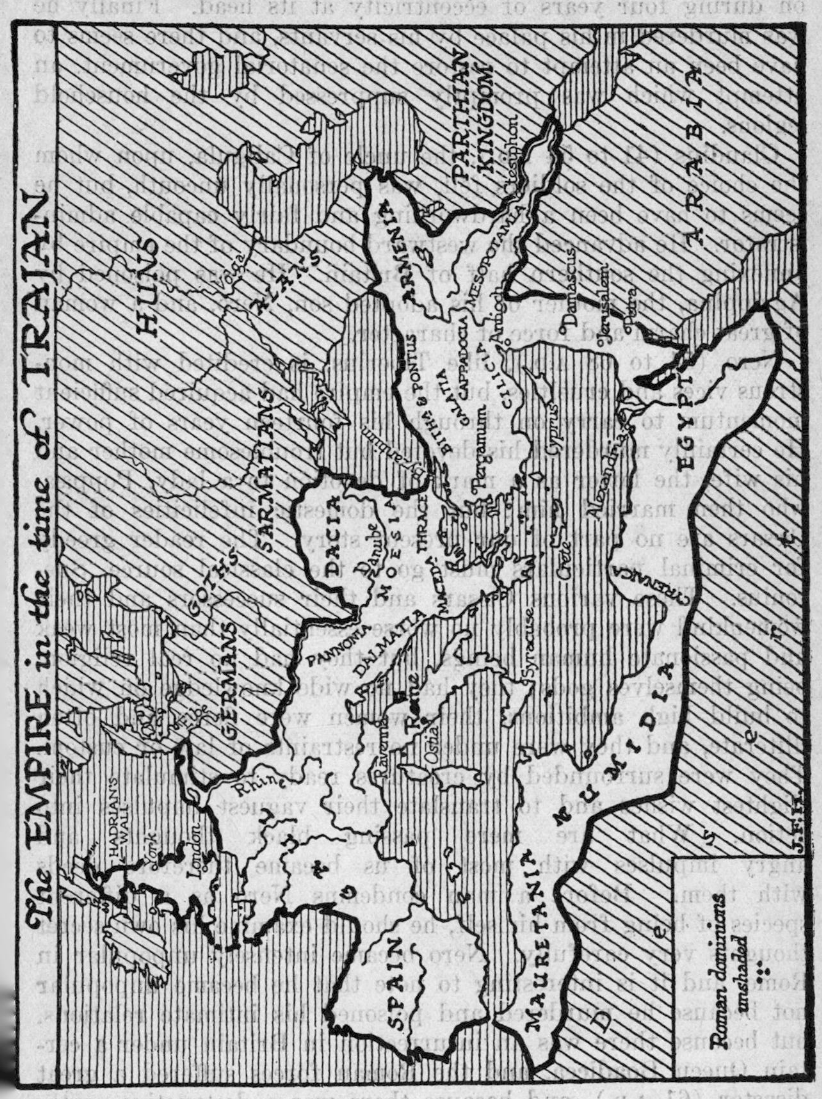
The EMPIRE in the time of TRAJAN
HUNS
ALANS
Volga
SARMATIANS
GOTHS
GERMANS
Elbe
Rhine
HADRIAN'S WALL
York
London
GAUL
SPAIN
PARTHIAN KINGDOM
Ctesiphon
ARMENIA
MESOPOTAMIA
ARABIA
Damascus
Jerusalem
Petra
Antioch
CAPPADOCIA
GALATIA
BITHA & PONTUS
CILICIA
Cyprus
Pergamum
Byzantium
DACIA
Danube
MOESIA
THRACE
MACEDA
PANNONIA
DALMATIA
Ravenna
Rome
Ostia
Syracuse
Crete
Alexandria
EGYPT
CYRENAICA
NUMIDIA
MAURETANIA
D e s e r t
Roman dominions unshaded
J.F.H.

Caligula (37 to 41 A.D.) was insane, but the empire carried on during four years of eccentricity at its head. Finally he was murdered in his palace by his servants, and there seems to have been an attempt to restore the senatorial government, an attempt which was promptly suppressed by the household legions.

Claudius (41 to 54 A.D.), the uncle of Caligula, upon whom the choice of the soldiers fell, was personally uncouth, but he seems to have been a hardworking and fairly capable administrator. He advanced the westward boundary of the empire by annexing the southern half of Britain. He was poisoned by Agrippina, the mother of his adopted son, Nero, and a woman of great charm and force of character.

Nero (54 to 68 A.D.), like Tiberius, is credited with monstrous vices and cruelties, but the empire had acquired sufficient momentum to carry on through his fourteen years of power. He certainly murdered his devoted but troublesome mother and his wife, the latter as a mark of devotion to a lady, Poppæa, who then married him; but the domestic infelicities of the Cæsars are no part of our present story. The reader greedy for criminal particulars must go to the classical source, Suetonius. These various Cæsars and their successors and their womenkind were probably no worse essentially than most weak and passionate human beings, but they had no real religion, being themselves gods; they had no wide knowledge on which to build high ambitions, their women were fierce and often illiterate, and they were under no restraints of law or custom. They were surrounded by creatures ready to stimulate their slightest wishes and to translate their vaguest impulses into action. What are mere passing black thoughts and angry impulses with most of us became therefore deeds with them. Before a man condemns Nero as a different species of being from himself, he should examine his own secret thoughts very carefully. Nero became intensely unpopular in Rome, and it is interesting to note that he became unpopular not because he murdered and poisoned his intimate relations, but because there was an insurrection in Britain under a certain Queen Boadicea, and the Roman forces suffered a great disaster (61 A.D.), and because there was a destructive earthquake in Southern Italy. The Roman population, true to its Etruscan streak, never religious and always superstitious, did not mind a wicked Cæsar, but it did object strongly to an unpropitious one. The Spanish legions rose in insurrection under an elderly general of seventy-three, Galba, whom they acclaimed emperor. He advanced upon Rome carried in a litter. Nero, hopeless of support, committed suicide (68 A.D.).

Galba, however, was only one of a group of would-be emperors. The generals in command of the Rhine legions, the Palatine troops, and the eastern armies, each attempted to seize power. Rome saw four emperors in a year, Galba, Otho, Vitellus, and Vespasian; the fourth, Vespasian (69-79 A.D.), from the eastern command, had the firmest grip, and held and kept the prize. But with Nero the line of Cæsars born or adopted ended. Cæsar ceased to be the family name of the Roman emperors and became a title, Divus Cæsar, the Cæsar god. The monarchy took a step forward towards orientalism by an increased insistence upon the worship of the ruler.

Vespasian (69 to 79 A.D.) and his sons Titus (79 A.D.) and Domitian (81 A.D.) constitute, as it were, a second dynasty, the Flavian; then after the assassination of Domitian came a group of emperors related to one another not by blood, but by adoption, the adoptive emperors. Nerva (96 A.D.) was the first of this line, and Trajan (98 A.D.) the second. They were followed by the indefatigable Hadrian (117 A.D.), Antoninus Pius (138 A.D.), and Marcus Aurelius (161 to 180 A.D.). Under both the Flavians and the Antonines the boundaries of the empire crept forward again. North Britain was annexed in 84 A.D., the angle of the Rhine and Danube was filled in, and what is now Transylvania was made into a new province, Dacia. Trajan also invaded Parthia and annexed Armenia, Assyria, and Mesopotamia. Under his rule the empire reached its maximum extent. Hadrian, his successor, was of a cautious and retractile disposition. He abandoned these new eastern conquests of Trajan's, and he also abandoned North Britain. He adopted the Chinese idea of the limiting wall against barbarism, an excellent idea so long as the pressure of population on the imperial side of the wall is greater than the pressure from without, but worthless otherwise. He built Hadrian's wall across Britain, and a palisade between the Rhine and the Danube. The full tide of Roman expansion was past, and in the reign of his successor the North

European frontier was already actively on the defensive against the aggression of Teutonic and Slavic tribes.

Marcus Aurelius Antoninus is one of those figures in history about which men differ widely and intensely. To some critics he seems to have been a priggish person; he dabbled in religions, and took a pleasure in conducting priestly ceremonies in priestly garments—a disposition offensive to common men—and they resent his alleged failure to restrain the wickedness of his wife Faustina. The stories of his domestic infelicity, however, rest on no very good foundations, though certainly his son Commodus was a startling person for a good home to produce. On the other hand, he was unquestionably a devoted and industrious emperor, holding social order together through a series of disastrous years of vile weather, great floods, failing harvests and famine, barbaric raids and revolts, and at last a terrible universal pestilence. Says F. W. Farrar, quoted in the *Encyclopædia Britannica,* "He regarded himself as being, in fact, the servant of all. The registry of the citizens, the suppression of litigation, the elevation of public morals, the care of minors, the retrenchment of public expenses, the limitation of gladiatorial games and shows, the care of roads, the restoration of senatorial privileges, the appointment of none but worthy magistrates, even the regulation of street traffic, these and numberless other duties so completely absorbed his attention that, in spite of indifferent health, they often kept him at severe labour from early morning till long after midnight. His position, indeed, often necessitated his presence at games and shows; but on these occasions he occupied himself either in reading, or being read to, or in writing notes. He was one of those who held that nothing should be done hastily, and that few crimes were worse than waste of time."

But it is not by these industries that he is now remembered. He was one of the greatest exponents of the Stoical philosophy, and in his *Meditations,* jotted down in camp and court, he has put so much of a human soul on record as to raise up for himself in each generation a fresh series of friends and admirers.

With the death of Marcus Aurelius this phase of unity and comparatively good government came to an end, and his son Commodus inaugurated an age of disorder. Practically the empire had been at peace within itself for two hundred years.

Now for a hundred years the student of Roman history must master the various criminology of a number of inadequate emperors, while the frontier crumbled and receded under barbarian pressure. One or two names only seem to be the names of able men: such were Septimius Severus, Aurelian, and Probus. Septimius Severus was a Carthaginian, and his sister was never able to master Latin. She conducted her Roman household in the Punic language, which must have made Cato the elder turn in his grave. The rest of the emperors of this period were chiefly adventurers too unimportant to the general scheme of things for us to note. At times there were separate emperors ruling in different parts of the distracted empire. From our present point of view the Emperor Decius, who was defeated and killed during a great raid of the Goths into Thrace in 251 A.D., and the Emperor Valerian, who, together with the great city of Antioch, was captured by the Sassanid Shah of Persia in 260 A.D., are worthy of notice because they mark the insecurity of the whole Roman system, and the character of the outer pressure upon it. So, too, is Claudius, "the Conqueror of the Goths," because he gained a great victory over these people at Nish in Serbia (270 A.D.), and because he died, like Pericles, of the plague.

Through all these centuries intermittent pestilences were playing a part in weakening races and altering social conditions, a part that has still to be properly worked out by historians. There was, for instance, a great plague throughout the empire between the years 164 and 180 A.D. in the reign of the Emperor Marcus Aurelius. It probably did much to disorganize social life and prepare the way for the troubles that followed the accession of Commodus. This same pestilence devastated China, as we shall note in § 4 of this chapter. Considerable fluctuations of climate had also been going on in the first and second centuries, producing stresses and shiftings of population, whose force historians have still to appraise. But before we go on to tell of the irruptions of the barbarians and the attempts of such later emperors as Diocletian (284 A.D.) and Constantine the Great (312 A.D.) to hold together the heaving and splitting vessel of the state, we must describe something of the conditions of human life in the Roman Empire during its two centuries of prosperity.

§ 2

The impatient reader of history may be disposed to count the two centuries of order between 27 B.C. and 180 A.D. as among the wasted opportunities of mankind. It was an age of spending rather than of creation, an age of architecture and trade in which the rich grew richer and the poor poorer and the soul and spirit of man decayed. Looked at superficially, as a man might have looked at it from an aeroplane a couple of thousand feet in the air, there was a considerable flourish of prosperity. Everywhere, from York to Cyrene and from Lisbon to Antioch, he would have noted large and well-built cities, with temples, theatres, amphitheatres, markets, and the like; thousands of such cities, supplied by great aqueducts and served by splendid high roads, whose stately remains astonish us to this day. He would have noted an abundant cultivation, and have soared too high to discover that this cultivation was the grudging work of slaves. Upon the Mediterranean and the Red Sea a considerable traffic would be visible; and the sight of two ships alongside each other would not at that altitude reveal the fact that one was a pirate and plundering the other.

And even if the observer came down to a closer scrutiny, there would still be much accumulated improvement to note. There had been a softening of manners and a general refinement since the days of Julius Cæsar. With this there had been a real increase of humane feeling. During the period of the Antonines, laws for the protection of slaves from extreme cruelty came into existence, and it was no longer permissible to sell them to the gladiatorial schools. Not only were the cities outwardly more splendidly built, but within the homes of the wealthy there had been great advances in the art of decoration. The gross feasting, animal indulgence, and vulgar display of the earlier days of Roman prosperity were now tempered by a certain refinement. Dress had become richer, finer, and more beautiful. There was a great trade in silk with remote China, for the mulberry-tree and the silkworm had not yet begun to move west. By the time silk had ended its long and varied journey to Rome it was worth its weight in gold. Yet it was used abundantly, and there was a steady flow of the precious metals eastward in exchange. There had been very considerable advances in gastronomy and the arts of entertainment. Petronius describes a feast given by a wealthy man under the early Cæsars, a remarkable succession of courses, some delicious, some amazing, exceeding anything that even the splendours and imagination of modern New York could produce; and the festival was varied by music and by displays of tight-rope dancing, juggling, Homeric recitations, and the like. There was a considerable amount of what we may describe as "rich men's culture" throughout the empire. Books were far more plentiful than they had been before the time of the Cæsars. Men prided themselves upon their libraries, even when the cares and responsibilities of property made them too busy to give their literary treasures much more than a passing examination. The knowledge of Greek spread eastward and of Latin westward, and if the prominent men of this or that British or Gallic city lacked any profound Greek culture themselves, they could always turn to some slave or other, whose learning had been guaranteed of the highest quality by the slave-dealer, to supply the deficiency.

The generation of Cato had despised Greeks and the Greek language, but now all that was changed. The prestige of Greek learning of an approved and settled type was as high in the Rome of Antoninus Pius as it was in the Oxford and Cambridge of Victorian England. The Greek scholar received the same mixture of unintelligent deference and practical contempt. There was a very considerable amount of Greek scholarship, and of written criticism and commentary. Indeed there was so great an admiration for Greek letters as almost completely to destroy the Greek spirit; and the recorded observations of Aristotle were valued so highly as to preclude any attempt to imitate his organization of further inquiry. It is noteworthy that while Aristotle in the original Greek fell like seed upon stony soil in the Roman world, he was, in Syrian and Arabic translations, immensely stimulating to the Arabic civilization of a thousand years later. Nor were the æsthetic claims of Latin neglected in this heyday of Greek erudition. As Greece had her epics and so forth, the Romans felt that they, too, must have their epics. The age of Augustus was an age of imitative literature. Virgil in the *Æneid* set himself modestly but resolutely, and with an elegant sort of successfulness, to parallel the *Odyssey* and *Iliad*.

All this wide-spread culture of the wealthy householder is to the credit of the early Roman Empire, and Gibbon makes the most of it in the sunny review of the age of the Antonines with which he opens his *Decline and Fall of the Roman Empire.* His design for that great work demanded a prelude of splendour and tranquillity. But he was far too shrewd and subtle not to qualify his apparent approval of the conditions he describes. "Under the Roman Empire," he writes, "the labour of an industrious and ingenious people was variously but incessantly employed in the service of the rich. In their dress, their table, their houses, and their furniture, the favourites of fortune united every refinement of convenience, of elegance, and of splendour, whatever could soothe their pride, or gratify their sensuality. Such refinements, under the odious name of luxury, have been severely arraigned by the moralists of every age; and it might perhaps be more conducive to the virtue, as well as happiness, of mankind, if all possessed the necessaries, and none the superfluities of life. But in the present imperfect condition of society, luxury, though it may proceed from vice or folly, seems to be the only means that can correct the unequal distribution of property. The diligent mechanic and the skilful artist, who have obtained no share in the division of the earth, receive a voluntary tax from the possessors of land; and the latter are prompted, by a sense of interest, to improve those estates, with whose produce they may purchase additional pleasure. This operation, the particular effects of which are felt in every society, acted with much more diffuse energy in the Roman world. The provinces would soon have been exhausted of their wealth, if the manufactures and commerce of luxury had not insensibly restored to the industrious subjects the sums which were exacted from them by the arms and authority of Rome." And so on, with a sting of satire in every fold of the florid description.

If we look a little more widely than a hovering aeroplane can do at the movement of races upon the earth, or a little more closely than an inspection of streets, amphitheatres, and banquets goes, into the souls and thoughts of men, we shall find that this impressive display of material prosperity is merely the shining garment of a polity blind to things without and things within, and blind to the future. If, for instance, we compare the two centuries of Roman ascendancy and opportunity, the first and second centuries A.D., with the two centuries of Greek and Hellenic life beginning about 466 B.C. with the supremacy of Pericles in Athens, we are amazed by—we cannot call it an inferiority, it is a complete absence of science. The incuriousness of the Roman rich and the Roman rulers was more massive and monumental even than their architecture.

In one field of knowledge particularly we might have expected the Romans to have been alert and enterprising, and that was geography. Their political interests demanded a steadfast inquiry into the state of affairs beyond their frontiers, and yet that inquiry was never made. There is practically no literature of Roman travel beyond the imperial limits, no such keen and curious accounts as Herodotus gives of the Scythians, the Africans, and the like. There is nothing in Latin to compare with the early descriptions of India and Siberia that are to be found in Chinese. The Roman legions went at one time into Scotland, yet there remains no really intelligent account of Picts or Scots, much less any glance at the seas beyond. Such explorations as those of Hanno or Pharaoh Necho seem to have been altogether beyond the scope of the Roman imagination. It is probable that after the destruction of Carthage the amount of shipping that went out into the Atlantic through the Straits of Gibraltar fell to inconsiderable proportions. Still more impossible in this world of vulgar wealth, enslaved intelligence, and bureaucratic rule was any further development of the astronomy and physiography of Alexandria. The Romans do not seem even to have inquired what manner of men wove the silk and prepared the spices or collected the amber and the pearls that came into their markets. Yet the channels of inquiry were open and easy; pathways led in every direction to the most convenient "jumping-off places" for explorers it is possible to imagine.

"The most remote countries of the ancient world were ransacked to supply the pomp and delicacy of Rome. The forests of Scythia afforded some valuable furs. Amber was brought overland from the shores of the Baltic to the Danube, and the barbarians were astonished at the price which they received in exchange for so useless a commodity. There was a considerable demand for Babylonian carpets and other manufactures of the East; but the most important branch of foreign trade was carried on with Arabia and India. Every year, about the time of the summer solstice, a fleet of a hundred and twenty vessels sailed from Myos-hormos, a port of Egypt on the Red Sea. By the periodical assistance of the monsoons, they traversed the ocean in about forty days. The coast of Malabar, or the island of Ceylon, was the usual term of their navigation, and it was in those markets that the merchants from the more remote countries of Asia expected their arrival. The return of the fleet to Egypt was fixed to the months of December or January, and as soon as their rich cargo had been transported, on the backs of camels, from the Red Sea to the Nile, and had descended that river as far as Alexandria, it was poured, without delay, into the capital of the empire."[1]

Yet Rome was content to feast, exact, grow rich, and watch its gladiatorial shows without the slightest attempt to learn anything of India, China, Persia or Scythia, Buddha or Zoroaster, or about the Huns, the Negroes, the people of Scandinavia, or the secrets of the western sea.

When we realize the uninspiring quality of the social atmosphere which made this indifference possible, we are able to account for the failure of Rome during its age of opportunity to develop any physical or chemical science, and as a consequence to gain any increased control over matter. Most of the physicians in Rome were Greeks and many of them slaves—for the Roman wealthy did not even understand that a bought mind is a spoilt mind. Yet this was not due to any want of natural genius among the Roman people; it was due entirely to their social and economic conditions. From the Middle Ages to the present day Italy has produced a great number of brilliant scientific men. And one of the most shrewd and inspired of scientific writers was an Italian, Lucretius, who lived between the time of Marius and Julius Cæsar (about 100 B.C. to about 55 B.C.). This amazing man was of the quality of Leonardo da Vinci (also an Italian) or Newton. He wrote a long Latin poem about the processes of Nature, *De Rerum Naturia,* in which he guessed with astonishing insight about the constitution of matter and about the early history of mankind. Osborn in his *Old Stone Age* quotes with admiration long passages from Lucretius about primitive man, so good and true are they to-day. But this was an individual display, a seed that bore no fruit. Roman science was still-born into a suffocating atmosphere of vile wealth and military oppression. The true figure to represent

[1] Gibbon.

the classical Roman attitude to science is not Lucretius, but that Roman soldier who hacked Archimedes to death at the storming of Syracuse.

And if physical and biological science wilted and died on the stony soil of Roman prosperity, political and social science never had a chance to germinate. Political discussion would have been treason to the emperor, social or economic inquiry would have threatened the rich. So Rome, until disaster fell upon her, never examined into her own social health, never questioned the ultimate value of her hard officialism. Consequently, there was no one who realized the gravity of her failure to develop any intellectual imagination to hold her empire together, any general education in common ideas that would make men fight and work for the empire as men will fight and work for a dear possession. But the rulers of the Roman Empire did not want their citizens to fight for anything in any spirit at all. The rich had eaten the heart out of their general population, and they were content with the meal they had made. The legions were filled with Germans, Britons, Numidians, and the like; and until the very end the wealthy Romans thought they could go on buying barbarians to defend them against the enemy without and the rebel poor within. How little was done in education by the Romans is shown by an account of what was done. Says Mr. H. Stuart Jones, "Julius Cæsar bestowed Roman citizenship on 'teachers of the liberal arts'; Vespasian endowed professorships of Greek and Latin oratory at Rome; and later emperors, especially Antoninus Pius, extended the same benefits to the provinces. Local enterprise and munificence were also devoted to the cause of education; we learn from the correspondence of the younger Pliny that public schools were founded in the towns of Northern Italy. But though there was a wide diffusion of knowledge under the empire, there was no true intellectual progress. Augustus, it is true, gathered about him the most brilliant writers of his time, and the debut of the new monarchy coincided with the Golden Age of Roman literature; but this was of brief duration, and the beginnings of the Christian era saw the triumph of Classicism and the first steps in the decline which awaits all literary movements which look to the past rather than the future."

There is a diagnosis of the intellectual decadence of the age in a treatise upon the sublime by a Greek writer who wrote somewhen in the second, third, or fourth century A.D., and who may possibly have been Longinus Philologus, which states very distinctly one manifest factor in the mental sickness of the Roman world. He is cited by Gibbon: "The sublime Longinus, who, in somewhat a later period and in the court of a Syrian queen, Zenobia, preserved the spirit of ancient Athens, observes and laments the degeneracy of his contemporaries, which debased their sentiments, enervated their courage, and depressed their talents. 'In the same manner,' says he, 'as some children always remain pigmies, whose infant limbs have been too closely confined, thus our tender minds, fettered by the prejudices and habits of a just servitude, are unable to expand themselves or to attain that well-proportioned greatness which we admire in the ancients, who, living under a popular government, wrote with all the same freedom as they acted.' "

But this critic grasped only one aspect of the restraints upon mental activity. The leading-strings that kept the Roman mind in a permanent state of infantilism constituted a double servitude; they were economic as well as political. The account Gibbon gives of the life and activities of a certain Herodes Atticus, who lived in the time of Hadrian, shows just how little was the share of the ordinary citizen in the outward magnificence of the time. This Atticus had an immense fortune, and he amused himself by huge architectural benefactions to various cities. Athens was given a racecourse, and a theatre of cedar, curiously carved, was set up there to the memory of his wife; a theatre was built at Corinth, a racecourse was given to Delphi, baths to Thermopylæ, an aqueduct to Canusium, and so on and so on. One is struck by the spectacle of a world of slaves and common people who were not consulted and over whose heads, without any participation on their part, this rich man indulged in his displays of "taste." Numerous inscriptions in Greece and Asia still preserve the name of Herodes Atticus, "patron and benefactor," who ranged about the empire as though it was his private garden, commemorating himself by these embellishments. He did not confine himself to splendid buildings. He was also a philosopher, though none of his wisdom has survived. He had a large villa near Athens, and there philosophers were welcome guests so long as they convinced their patron of the soundness of their pretensions, received his discourses with respect, and did not offend him by insolent controversy.

The world, it is evident, was not progressing during these two centuries of Roman prosperity. But was it happy in its stagnation? There are signs of a very unmistakable sort that the great mass of human beings in the empire, a mass numbering something between a hundred and a hundred and fifty millions, was not happy, was probably very acutely miserable, beneath its outward magnificence. True there were no great wars and conquests within the empire, little of famine or fire or sword to afflict mankind; but, on the other hand, there was a terrible restraint by government, and still more by the property of the rich, upon the free activities of nearly everyone. Life for the great majority who were neither rich nor official, nor the womankind and the parasites of the rich and official, must have been laborious, tedious, and lacking in interest and freedom to a degree that a modern mind can scarcely imagine.

Three things in particular may be cited to sustain the opinion that this period was a period of widespread unhappiness. The first of these is the extraordinary apathy of the population to political events. They saw one upstart pretender to empire succeed another with complete indifference. Such things did not seem to matter to them; hope had gone. When presently the barbarians poured into the empire, there was nothing but the legions to face them. There was no popular uprising against them at all. Everywhere the barbarians must have been outnumbered if only the people had resisted. But the people did not resist. It is manifest that to the bulk of its inhabitants the Roman Empire did not seem to be a thing worth fighting for. To the slaves and common people the barbarian probably seemed to promise more freedom and less indignity than the pompous rule of the imperial official and grinding employment by the rich. The looting and burning of palaces and an occasional massacre did not shock the folk of the Roman underworld as it shocked the wealthy and cultured people to whom we owe such accounts as we have of the breaking down of the imperial system. Great numbers of slaves and common people probably joined the barbarians, who knew little of racial or patriotic prejudices, and were openhanded to any promising recruit. No doubt in many cases the population found that the barbarian was a worse infliction even than the tax-gatherer and the slave-driver. But that discovery came too late for resistance or the restoration of the old order.

And as a second symptom that points to the same conclusion that life was hardly worth living for the poor and the slaves and the majority of people during the age of the Antonines, we must reckon the steady depopulation of the empire. People refused to have children. They did so, we suggest, because their homes were not safe from oppression, because in the case of slaves there was no security that the husband and wife would not be separated, because there was no pride nor reasonable hope in children any more. In modern states the great breeding-ground has always been the agricultural countryside where there is a more or less secure peasantry; but under the Roman Empire the peasant and the small cultivator was either a worried debtor, or he was held in a network of restraints that made him a spiritless serf, or he had been ousted altogether by the gang production of slaves.

A third indication that this outwardly flourishing period was one of deep unhappiness and mental distress for vast multitudes, is to be found in the spread of new religious movements throughout the population. We have seen how in the case of the little country of Judea a whole nation may be infected by the persuasion that life is unsatisfactory and *wrong*, and that something is needed to set it right. The mind of the Jews, as we know, had crystallized about the idea of the Promise of the One True God and the coming of a Saviour or Messiah. Rather different ideas from these were spreading through the Roman Empire. They were but varying answers to one universal question: "What must we do for salvation?" A frequent and natural consequence of disgust with life as it is, is to throw the imagination forward to an after-life, which is to redeem all the miseries and injustices of this one. The belief in such compensation is a great opiate for present miseries. Egyptian religion had long been saturated wth anticipations of immortality, and we have seen how central was that idea of the cult of Serapis and Isis at Alexandria. The ancient mysteries of Demeter and Orpheus, the mysteries of the Mediterranean race, revived and made a sort of *theocrasia* with these new cults.

A second great religious movement was Mithraism, a development of Zoroastrianism, a religion of very ancient Aryan origin, traceable back to the Indo-Iranian people before they split into Persians and Hindus. We cannot here examine its mysteries in any detail.[1] Mithras was a god of light, a Sun of Righteousness, and in the shrines of the cult he was always represented as slaying a sacred bull whose blood was the seed of life. Suffice it that, complicated with many added ingredients, this worship of Mithras came into the Roman Empire about the time of Pompey the Great, and began to spread very widely under the Cæsars and Antonines. Like the Isis religion, it promised immortality. Its followers were mainly slaves, soldiers, and distressed people. In its methods of worship, in the burning of candles before the altar and so forth, it had a certain superficial resemblance to the later developments of the ritual of the third great religious movement in the Roman world, Christianity.

Christianity also was a doctrine of immortality and salvation, and it, too, spread at first chiefly among the lowly and unhappy. Christianity has been denounced by modern writers as a "slave religion." It was. It took the slaves and the downtrodden, and it gave them hope and restored their self-respect, so that they stood up for righteousness like men and faced persecution and torment. But of the origins and quality of Christianity we will tell more fully in a later chapter.

§ 3

We have already shown reason for our statement that the Roman imperial system was a very unsound political growth indeed. It is absurd to write of its statecraft; it had none. At its best it had a bureaucratic administration which kept the peace of the world for a time and failed altogether to secure it.

Let us note here the main factors in its failure.

The clue to all its failure lies in the absence of any free mental activity and any organization for the increase, development, and application of knowledge. It respected wealth and it despised science. It gave government to the rich, and imagined that wise men could be bought and bargained for in the slave markets when they were needed. It was, therefore, a colossally ignorant and unimaginative empire. It foresaw nothing.

It had no strategic foresight, because it was blankly ignorant

[1] See Legge, *Forerunners and Rivals of Christianity.*

of geography and ethnology. It knew nothing of the conditions of Russia, Central Asia, and the East. It was content to keep the Rhine and Danube as its boundaries, and to make no effort to Romanize Germany. But we need only look at the map of Europe and Asia showing the Roman Empire to see that a willing and incorporated Germany was absolutely essential to the life and security of Western Europe. Excluded, Germany became a wedge that needed only the impact of the Hunnish hammer to split up the whole system.

Moreover, this neglect to push the boundaries northward to the Baltic left that sea and the North Sea as a region of experiment and training and instruction in seamanship for the Northmen of Scandinavia, Denmark, and the Frisian coast. But Rome went on its way quite stupidly, oblivious to the growth of a newer and more powerful piracy in the north.

The same unimaginative quality made the Romans leave the seaways of the Mediterranean undeveloped. When presently the barbarians pressed down to the warm water, we read of no swift transport of armies from Spain or Africa or Asia to the rescue of Italy and the Adriatic coasts. Instead, we see the Vandals becoming masters of the western Mediterranean without so much as a naval battle.

The Romans had been held at the Euphrates by an array of mounted archers. It was clear that as the legion was organized it was useless in wide open country, and it should have been equally clear that sooner or later the mounted nomads of east Germany, south Russia or Parthia were bound to try conclusions with the empire. But the Romans, two hundred years after Cæsar's time, were still marching about, the same drilled and clanking cohorts they had always been, easily ridden round and shot to pieces. The empire had learnt nothing even from Carrhæ.

The incapacity of the Roman imperialism for novelty in methods of transport again is amazing. It was patent that their power and unity depended upon the swift movement of troops and supplies from one part of the empire to another. The republic made magnificent roads; the empire never improved upon them. Four hundred years before the Antonines, Hero of Alexandria had made the first steam-engine. Beautiful records of such beginnings of science were among the neglected treasures of the rich men's libraries throughout the imperial domains. They were seed lying on stony ground. The armies and couriers of Marcus Aurelius drudged along the roads exactly as the armies of Scipio Africanus had done three centuries before them.

The Roman writers were always lamenting the effeminacy of the age. It was their favourite cant. They recognized that the free men of the forest and steppes and desert were harder and more desperate fighters than their citizens, but the natural corollary of developing the industrial power of their accumulations of population to make a countervailing equipment never entered their heads. Instead they took the barbarians into their legions, taught them the arts of war, marched them about the empire, and returned them, with their lesson well learnt, to their own people.

In view of these obvious negligences, it is no wonder that the Romans disregarded that more subtle thing, the soul of the empire, altogether, and made no effort to teach or train or win its common people into any conscious participation with its life. Such teaching or training would indeed have run counter to all the ideas of the rich men and the imperial officials. They had made a tool of religion; science, literature, and education they had entrusted to the care of slaves, who were bred and trained and sold like dogs or horses; ignorant, pompous, and base, the Roman adventurers of finance and property who created the empire, lorded it with a sense of the utmost security while their destruction gathered without the empire and within.

By the second and third centuries A.D. the overtaxed and overstrained imperial machine was already staggering towards its downfall.

§ 4

And now it is necessary, if we are to understand clearly the true situation of the Roman Empire, to turn our eyes to the world beyond its northern and eastern borders, the world of the plains, that stretches, with scarcely a break, from Holland across Germany and Russia to the mountains of Central Asia and Mongolia, and to give a little attention to the parallel empire in China that was now consolidating and developing a far tougher and more enduring moral and intellectual unity than the Romans ever achieved.

"It is the practice," says Mr. E. H. Parker, "even amongst our most highly educated men in Europe, to deliver sonorous sentences about being 'masters of the world,' 'bringing all nations of the earth under her sway,' and so on, when in reality only some corner of the Mediterranean is involved, or some ephemeral sally into Persia and Gaul. Cyrus and Alexander, Darius and Xerxes, Cæsar and Pompey, all made very interesting excursions, but they were certainly not on a larger scale or charged with greater human interest than the campaigns which were going on at the other end of Asia. Western civilization possessed much in art and science for which China never cared, but, on the other hand, the Chinese developed a historical and critical literature, a courtesy of demeanour, a luxury of clothing, and an administrative system of which Europe might have been proud. In one word, the history of the Far East is quite as interesting as that of the Far West. It only requires to be able to read it. When we brush away contemptuously from our notice the tremendous events which took place on the plains of Tartary, we must not blame the Chinese too much for declining to interest themselves in the doings of what to them appear insignificant states dotted round the Mediterranean and Caspian, which, at this time, was practically all the world of which we knew in Europe."[1]

We have already mentioned (in Chap. XIV and elsewhere) the name of Shi Hwang-ti, who consolidated an empire much smaller, indeed, than the present limits of China, but still very great and populous, spreading from the valleys of the Hwang-ho and the Yang-tse. He became king of Ch'in in 246 B.C. and emperor in 220 B.C., and he reigned until 210 B.C., and during this third of a century he effected much the same work of consolidation that Augustus Cæsar carried out in Rome two centuries later. At his death there was dynastic trouble for four years, and then (206 B.C.) a fresh dynasty, the Han, established itself and ruled for two hundred and twenty-nine years. The opening quarter century of the Christian era was troubled by a usurper; then what is called the Later Han Dynasty recovered power and ruled for another century and a half until China, in the time of the Antonines, was so devastated by an eleven-year pestilence as to fall into disorder. This same pestilence, we may note, also helped to produce a

[1] E. H. Parker, *A Thousand Years of the Tartars.*

Map of
ASIA (with EUROPE)
to illustrate the general conditions of life during the Historical Period
The Northern Forest Belt
The Homelands of the Nomads
The Semitic Zone
Mountains and highlands shaded vertically
Tundra, and ice regions
Forest
Steppe: lands of seasonal pasture (nomadic life
Lands of cultivation, irrigation, woodland or pasture
Desert

century of confusion in the Western world (see § 1). But altogether until this happened, for more than four hundred years Central China was generally at peace, and on the whole well governed, a cycle of strength and prosperity unparalleled by anything in the experience of the Western world.

Only the first of the Han monarchs continued the policy of Shi Hwang-ti against the *literati*. His successor restored the classics, for the old separatist tradition was broken, and in the uniformity of learning throughout the empire lay, he saw, the cement of Chinese unity. While the Roman world was still blind to the need of any universal mental organization, the Han emperors were setting up a uniform system of education and of literary degrees throughout China that has maintained the intellectual solidarity of that great and always expanding country into modern times. The bureaucrats of Rome were of the most miscellaneous origins and traditions; the bureaucrats of China were, and are still, made in the same mould, all members of one tradition. Since the Han days China has experienced great vicissitudes of political fortune, but they have never changed her fundamental character; she has been divided, but she has always recovered her unity; she has been conquered, and she has always absorbed and assimilated her conquerors.

But from our present point of view, the most important consequences of this consolidation of China under Shi Hwang-ti and the Hans was in its reaction upon the unsettled tribes of the northern and western border of China. Throughout the disordered centuries before the time of Shi Hwang-ti, the Hiung-nu or Huns had occupied Mongolia and large portions of Northern China, and had raided freely into China and interfered freely in Chinese politics. The new power and organization of the Chinese civilization began to change this state of affairs for good and all.

We have already, in our first account of Chinese beginnings, noted the existence of these Huns. It is necessary now to explain briefly who and what they were. Even in using this word Hun as a general equivalent for the Hiung-nu, we step on to controversial ground. In our accounts of the development of the Western world we have had occasion to name the Scythians, and to explain the difficulty of distinguishing clearly between Cimmerians, Sarmatians, Medes, Persians, Parthians, Goths, and other more or less nomadic, more or less Aryan peoples who drifted to and fro in a great arc between the Danube and Central Asia. While sections of the Aryans were moving south and acquiring and developing civilization, these other Aryan peoples were developing mobility and nomadism; they were learning the life of the tent, the wagon, and the herd. They were learning also to use milk as a food basis, and were probably becoming less agricultural, less disposed to take even snatch crops, than they had been. Their development was being aided by a slow change in climate that was replacing the swamps and forests and parklands of South Russia and Central Asia by steppes, by wide grazing lands that is, which favoured a healthy, unsettled life, and necessitated an annual movement between summer and winter pasture. These peoples had only the lowest political forms; they split up, they mingled together; the various races had identical social habits; and so it is that the difficulty, the impossibility of sharp distinctions between them arises. Now the case of the Mongolian races to the north and north-west of the Chinese civilization is very parallel. There can be little doubt that the Hiung-nu, the Huns, and the later people called the Mongols, were all very much the same people, and that the Turks and Tartars presently branched off from this same drifting Mongolian population. Kalmucks and Buriats are later developments of the same strain. Here we shall favour the use of the word "Hun" as a sort of general term for these tribes, just as we have been free and wide in our use of "Scythian" in the West.

The consolidation of China was a very serious matter for these Hunnish peoples. Hitherto their overflow of population had gone adventuring southward into the disorders of divided China as water goes into a sponge. Now they found a wall built against them, a firm government, and disciplined armies cutting them off from the grass plains. And though the wall held them back, it did not hold back the Chinese. They were increasing and multiplying through these centuries of peace, and as they increased and multiplied, they spread steadily with house and plough wherever the soil permitted. They spread westward into Tibet and northward and north-westwardly, perhaps to the edge of the Gobi desert. They spread into the homes and pasturing and hunting-grounds of the Hunnish nomads, exactly as the white people of the United States spread westward into the hunting-grounds of the Red Indians. And in spite of raid and massacre, they were just as invincible because they had the pressure of numbers and a strong avenging government behind them. Even without the latter support the cultivating civilization of China has enormous powers of permeation and extension. It has spread slowly and continuously for three thousand years. It is spreading in Manchuria and Siberia to-day. It roots deeply where it spreads.

Partly the Huns were civilized and assimilated by the Chinese. The more northerly Huns were checked and their superabundant energies were turned westward. The southern Huns were merged into the imperial population.

If the reader will examine the map of Central Asia, he will see that very great mountain barriers separate the Southern, Western, and Eastern peoples of Asia. (But he should be wary of forming his ideas from a map upon Mercator's projection, which enormously exaggerates the areas and distances of Northern Asia and Siberia.) He will find that from the central mountain masses three great mountain systems radiate eastward; the Himalayas going south-eastward, south of Tibet, the Kuen Lun eastward, north of Tibet, and the Thien Shan north-eastward to join the Altai mountains. Further to the north is the great plain, still steadily thawing and drying. Between the Thien Shan and the Kuen Lun is an area, the Tarim Basin (= roughly Eastern Turkestan), of rivers that never reach the sea, but end in swamps and intermittent lakes. This basin was much more fertile in the past than it is now. The mountain barrier to the west of this Tarim Basin is high, but not forbidding; there are many practicable routes downward into Western Turkestan, and it is possible to travel either along the northern foothills of the Kuen Lun or by the Tarim valley westward from China to Kashgar (where the roads converge), and so over the mountains to Kokand, Samarkand, and Bokhara. Here then is the natural meeting-place in history of Aryan and Mongolian. Here or round by the sea.

We have already noted how Alexander the Great came to one side of the barrier in 329 B.C. High among the mountains of Turkestan a lake preserves his name. Indeed, so living is the tradition of his great raid, that almost any stone ruin in Central Asia is still ascribed to "Iskander." After this brief glimpse, the light of history upon this region fades again, and when it becomes bright once more it is on the eastern and not upon the western side. Far away to the east Shi Hwang-ti had routed the Huns and walled them out of China proper. A portion of these people remained in the north of China, a remnant which was destined to amalgamate with Chinese life under the Hans, but a considerable section had turned westward and (second and first centuries B.C.) driven before them a kindred people called the Yueh-Chi, driving them from the eastern to the western extremity of the Kuen Lun, and at last right over the barrier into the once Aryan region of Western Turkestan.[1] These Yueh-Chi conquered the slightly Hellenized kingdom of Bactria, and mixed with Aryan people there. Later on these Yueh-Chi became, or were merged with Aryan elements into, a people called the Indo-Scythians, who went on down the Khyber Pass and conquered northern portions of India as far as Benares (100-150 A.D.), wiping out the last vestiges of Hellenic rule in India. This big splash over of the Mongolian races westward was probably not the first of such splashes, but it is the first recorded splash. In the rear of the Yueh-Chi were the Huns, and in the rear of the Huns and turning them now northward was the vigorous Han Dynasty of China. In the reign of the greatest of the Han monarchs, Wu-Ti (140-86 B.C.), the Huns had been driven northward out of the whole of Eastern Turkestan or subjugated, the Tarim Basin swarmed with Chinese settlers, and caravans were going over westward with silk and lacquer and jade to trade for the gold and silver of Armenia and Rome.

The splash over of the Yueh-Chi is recorded, but it is fairly evident that much westward movement of sections of the Hunnish peoples is not recorded. From 200 B.C. to 200 A.D. the Chinese Empire maintained a hard, resolute, advancing front towards nomadism, and the surplus of the nomads drifted steadily west. There was no such settling down behind a final frontier on the part of the Chinese as we see in the case of the Romans at the Rhine and Danube. The drift of the nomads before this Chinese thrust, century by century, turned southward at first towards Bactria. The Parthians of the first century B.C. probably mingled Scythian and Mongolian elements. The "singing arrows" that destroyed the army of Crassus came,

[1] Even in Eastern Turkestan there are still strong evidences of Nordic blood in the physiognomy of the people. Ella and Percy Sykes, *Through Deserts and Oases of Central Asia.*

it would seem, originally from the Altai and the Thien Shan. After the first century B.C. the line of greater attraction and least resistance lay for a time towards the north of the Caspian. In a century or so all the country known as Western Turkestan was "Mongolized," and so it remains to this day. A second great thrust by China began about 75 A.D., and accelerated the westward drift of the nomads. In 102, Pan Chau, a Chinese general, was sending explorers from his advanced camp upon the Caspian (or, as some authorities say, the Persian Gulf) to learn particulars of the Roman power. But their reports decided him not to proceed.

By the first century A.D. nomadic Mongolian peoples were in evidence upon the eastern boundaries of Europe, already greatly mixed with Nordic nomads and with uprooted Nordic elements from the Caspian-Pamir region. There were Hunnish peoples established between the Caspian Sea and the Urals. West of them were the Alans, probably also a Mongolian people with Nordic elements; they had fought against Pompey the Great when he was in Armenia in 65 B.C. These were as yet the furthest westward peoples of the new Mongolian advance, and they made no further westward push until the fourth century A.D. To the north-west the Finns, a Mongolian people, had long been established as far west as the Baltic.

West of the Huns, beyond the Don, there were purely Nordic tribes, the Goths. These Goths had spread south-eastward from their region of origin in Scandinavia. They were a Teutonic people, and we have already marked them crossing the Baltic in the map we have given of the earlier distribution of the Aryan-speaking people. These Goths continued to move south-eastward across Russia, using the rivers and never forgetting their Baltic watercraft. No doubt they assimilated much Scythian population as they spread down to the Black Sea. In the first century A.D. they were in two main divisions, the Ostrogoths, the east Goths, who were between the Don and the Dnieper, and the Visigoths, or west Goths, west of the Dnieper. During the first century there was quiescence over the great plains, but population was accumulating and the tribes were fermenting. The second and third centuries seem to have been a phase of comparatively moist seasons and abundant grass. Presently in the fourth and fifth centuries the weather

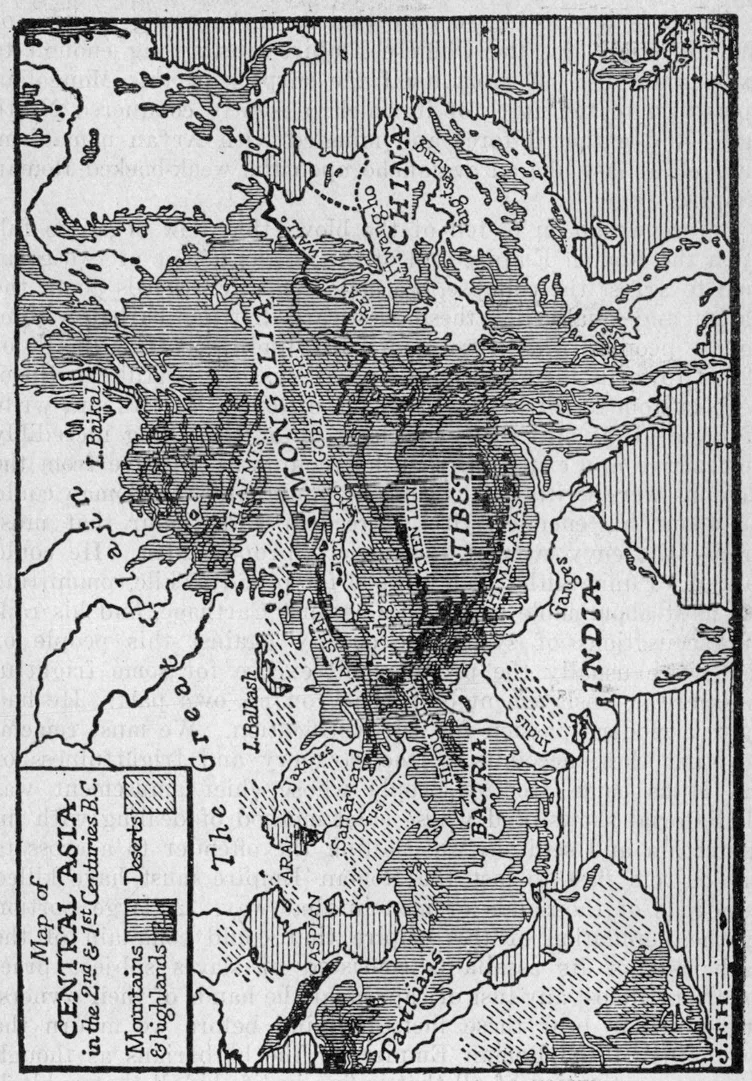
Map of
CENTRAL ASIA
in the 2nd & 1st Centuries B.C.
Mountains & highlands
Deserts
The Great Plain
L. Baikal
ALTAI MTS.
MONGOLIA
GOBI DESERT
GREAT WALL
Hwang-ho
CHINA
Yang-tse-kiang
L. Balkash
TIAN SHAN
Tarim
Lob Nor
Kashgar
KUEN LUN
TIBET
HIMALAYAS
Ganges
INDIA
Indus
HINDU KUSH
BACTRIA
Oxus
Samarkand
Jaxartes
ARAL
CASPIAN
Parthians
J.F.H.

grew drier and the grass became scanty and the nomads stirred afresh.

But it is interesting to note that in the opening century of the Christian era, the Chinese Empire was strong enough to expel and push off from itself the surplus of this Mongolian nomadism to the north of it which presently conquered North India and gathered force and mingled with Aryan nomadism, and fell at last like an avalanche upon the weak-backed Roman Empire.

Before we go on to tell of the blows that now began to fall upon the Roman Empire and of the efforts of one or two great men to arrest the collapse, we may say a few words about the habits and quality of these westward-drifting barbaric Mongolian peoples who were now spreading from the limits of China towards the Black and Baltic Seas. It is still the European custom to follow the lead of the Roman writers and write of these Huns and their associates as of something incredibly destructive and cruel. But such accounts as we have from the Romans were written in periods of panic, and the Roman could lie about his enemies with a freedom and vigour that must arouse the envy even of the modern propagandist. He could talk of "Punic faith" as a byword for perfidy while committing the most abominable treacheries against Carthage, and his railing accusations of systematic cruelty against this people or that were usually the prelude and excuse for some frightful massacre or enslavement or robbery on his own part. He had quite a modern passion for self-justification. We must remember that these accounts of the savagery and frightfulness of the Huns came from a people whose chief amusement was gladiatorial shows, and whose chief method of dealing with insurrection and sedition was nailing the offender to a cross to die. From first to last the Roman Empire must have killed hundreds of thousands of men in that way. A large portion of the population of this empire that could complain of the barbarism of its assailants consisted of slaves subject practically to almost any lust or caprice at the hands of their owners. It is well to bear these facts in mind before we mourn the swamping of the Roman Empire by the barbarians as though it was an extinction of all that is fine in life by all that is black and ugly.

These facts seem to be that the Hunnish peoples were the eastern equivalent of the primitive Aryans, and that, in spite of their profound racial and linguistic differences, they mixed with the nomadic and semi-nomadic residuum of the Aryan-speaking races north of the Danube and Persia very easily and successfully. Instead of killing, they enlisted and intermarried with the peoples they invaded. They had that necessary gift for all peoples destined to political predominance, tolerant assimilation. They came rather later in time, and their nomadic life was more highly developed than that of the primitive Aryans. The primitive Aryans were a forest and ox-wagon people who took to the horse later. The Hunnish peoples had grown up with the horse. Somewhen about 1200 or 1000 years B.C. they began to ride the horse. The bit, the saddle, the stirrup, these are not primitive things, but they are necessary if man and horse are to keep going for long stretches. It is well to bear in mind how modern a thing is riding. Altogether man has not been in the saddle for much more than three thousand years.[1] We have already noted the gradual appearance of the war-chariot, the mounted man, and finally of disciplined cavalry in this history. It was from the Mongolian regions of Asia that these things came. To this day men in Central Asia go rather in the saddle than on their proper feet. Says Ratzel,[2] "Strong, long-necked horses are found in enormous numbers on the steppes. For Mongols and Turcomans riding is not a luxury; even the Mongol shepherds tend their flocks on horseback. Children are taught to ride in early youth; and the boy of three years old often takes his first riding-lesson on a safe child's saddle and makes quick progress."

It is impossible to suppose that the Huns and the Alans could have differed very widely in character from the present nomads of the steppe regions, and nearly all observers are agreed in describing these latter as open and pleasant people. They are thoroughly honest and free-spirited. "The character of the herdsmen of Central Asia," says Ratzel,[3] "when unadulterated, is ponderous eloquence, frankness, rough good-nature, pride, but also indolence, irritability, and a tendency to vindictiveness. Their faces show a considerable share of frankness

1 See Roger Pocock, *Horses*, a very interesting and picturesque little book.
2 *The History of Mankind*, book v., C.
3 *Ibid.*

combined with amusing naïveté. . . . Their courage is rather a sudden blaze of pugnacity than cold boldness. Religious fanaticism they have none. Hospitality is universal.'' This is not an entirely disagreeable picture. Their personal bearing, he says further, is quieter and more dignified than that of the townsmen of Turkestan and Persia. Add to this that the nomadic life prevents any great class inequalities or any extensive development of slavery.

Of course these peoples out of Asia were totally illiterate and artistically undeveloped. But we must not suppose, on that account, that they were primitive barbarians, and that their state of life was at the level from which the agricultural civilization had long ago arisen. It was not. They, too, had developed, but they had developed along a different line, a line with less intellectual complication, more personal dignity perhaps, and certainly with a more intimate contact with wind and sky.

§ 5

The first serious irruptions of the German tribes into the Roman Empire began in the third century with the decay of the central power. We will not entangle the reader here with the vexed and intricate question of the names, identity, and inter-relationships of the various Germanic tribes. Historians find great difficulties in keeping them distinct, and these difficulties are enhanced by the fact that they themselves took little care to keep themselves distinct. We find in 236 A.D. a people called the Franks breaking bounds upon the Lower Rhine, and another, the Alamanni, pouring into Alsace. A much more serious push southward was that of the Goths. We have already noted the presence of these people in South Russia, and their division by the Dnieper into Western and Eastern Goths. They had become a maritime people again upon the Black Sea—probably their traditional migration from Sweden was along the waterways, for it is still possible to row a boat, with only a few quite practicable portages, from the Baltic right across Russia to either the Black or Caspian Sea—and they had wrested the command of the eastern seas from the control of Rome. They were presently raiding the shores of Greece. They also crossed the Danube in a great land raid in 247, and defeated and killed the Emperor Decius in what is now Serbia. The province of Dacia vanished from Roman history. In 270 they were defeated at Nish in Serbia by Claudius, and in 276 they were raiding Pontus. It is characteristic of the invertebrate nature of the empire that the legions of Gaul found that the most effective method of dealing with the Franks and the Alamanni at this time was by setting up a separate emperor in Gaul and doing the job by themselves.

Then for a while the barbarians were held, and the Emperor Probus in 276 forced the Franks and the Alamanni back over the Rhine. But it is significant of the general atmosphere of insecurity created by these raids that Aurelian (270-275) fortified Rome, which had been an open and secure city for all the earlier years of the empire.

In 321 A.D. the Goths were again over the Danube, plundering what is now Serbia and Bulgaria. They were driven back by Constantine the Great, of whom we shall have more to tell in the next chapter. About the end of his reign (337 A.D.) the Vandals, a people closely kindred to the Goths, being pressed by them, obtained permission to cross the Danube into Pannonia, which is now that part of Hungary west of the river.

But by the middle of the fourth century the Hunnish people to the east were becoming aggressive again. They had long subjugated the Alani, and now they made the Ostrogoths, the east Goths, tributary. The Visigoths (or west Goths) followed the example of the Vandals, and made arrangements to cross the Danube into Roman territory. There was some dispute upon the terms of this settlement, and the Visigoths, growing fierce, assumed the offensive, and at Adrianople defeated the Emperor Valens, who was killed in this battle. They were then allowed to settle in what is now Bulgaria, and their army became nominally a Roman army, though they retained their own chiefs, the foremost of whom was Alaric. It exhibits the complete "barbarization" of the Roman empire that had already occurred, that the chief opponent of Alaric the Goth, Stilicho, was a Pannonian Vandal. The legions in Gaul were under the command of a Frank, and the Emperor Theodosius I (emp. 379-395) was a Spaniard chiefly supported by Gothic auxiliaries.

The empire was now splitting finally into an eastern (Greek-speaking) and a western (Latin-speaking) half. Theodosius the Great was succeeded by his sons Arcadius at Constantinople and Honorius at Ravenna. Alaric made a puppet of the eastern monarch and Stilicho of the western. Huns now first appear within the empire as auxiliary troops enlisted under Stilicho. In this struggle of East and West, the frontier—if we can still speak of a frontier between the unauthorized barbarian without and the barbarian in employment within—gave way. Fresh Vandals, more Goths, Alans, Suevi, marched freely westward, living upon the country. Amidst this confusion occurred a crowning event. Alaric the Goth marched down Italy, and after a short siege captured Rome (410).

By 425 or so, the Vandals (whom originally we noted in East Germany) and a portion of the Alani (whom we first mentioned in South-east Russia) had traversed Gaul and the Pyrenees, and had amalgamated and settled in the south of Spain. There were Huns in possession of Pannonia and Goths in Dalmatia. Into Bohemia and Moravia came and settled a Slavic people, the Czechs (451). In Portugal and north of the Vandals in Spain were Visigoths and Suevi. Gaul was divided among Visigoths, Franks, and Burgundians. Britain was being invaded by Low German tribes, the Jutes, Angles and Saxons, before whom the Keltic British of the south-west were flying across the sea to what is now Brittany in France. The usual date given for this invasion is 449, but it was probably earlier.[1] And as the result of intrigues between two imperial politicians, the Vandals of the south of Spain, under their king Genseric, embarked *en masse* for North Africa (429), became masters of Carthage (439), secured the mastery of the sea, raided, captured, and pillaged Rome (455), crossed into Sicily, and set up a kingdom in West Sicily, which endured there for a hundred years (up to 534). At the time of its greatest extent (477) this Vandal kingdom included also Corsica, Sardinia, and the Balearic Isles, as well as much of North Africa.

About this Vandal kingdom facts and figures are given that show very clearly the true nature of these barbarian irruptions. They were not really the conquest and replacement of one people or race by another; what happened was something very different: it was a social revolution started and masked by a

[1] E. B.

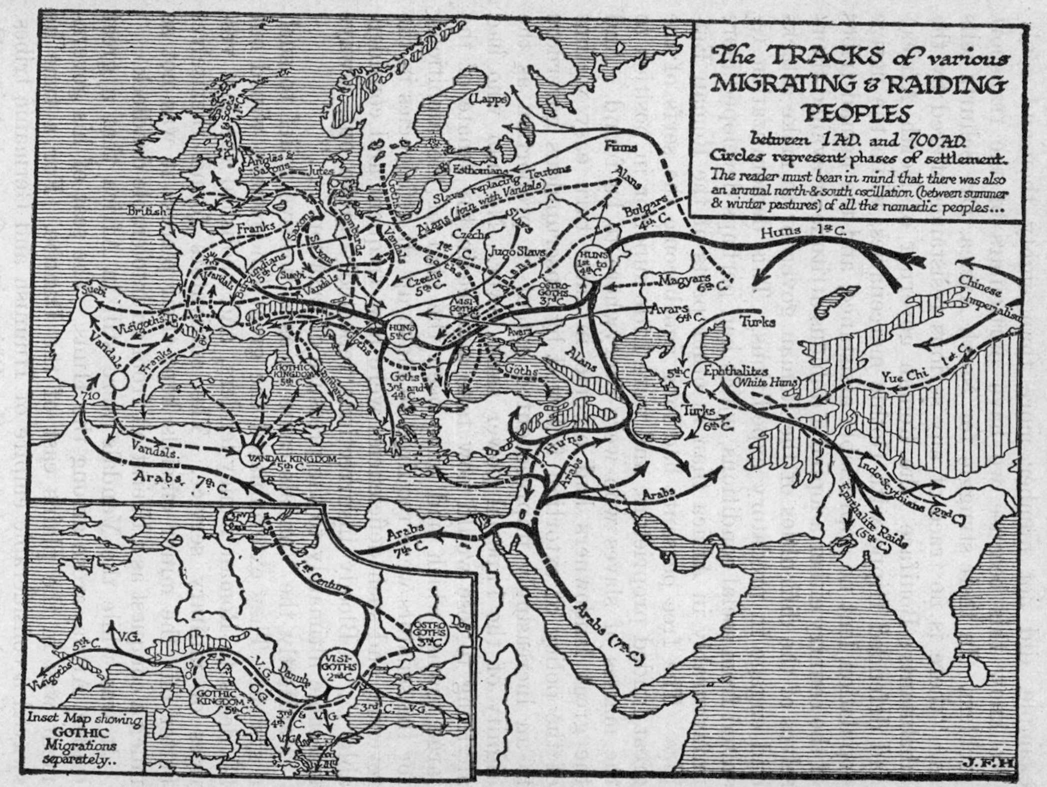
The TRACKS of various
MIGRATING & RAIDING
PEOPLES
between 1 A.D. and 700 A.D.
Circles represent phases of settlement.
The reader must bear in mind that there was also an annual north-&-south oscillation (between summer & winter pastures) of all the nomadic peoples...
Huns 1st C.
Chinese Imperialism
1st C.
Yue Chi
Indo-Scythians (2nd C.)
Ephthalite Raids (5th C.)
Ephthalites (White Huns)
5th C.
Turks
Turks 6th C.
Magyars 6th C.
Avars 6th C.
Bulgars 4th C.
Huns 1st to 4th C.
Ostro-Goths 3rd C.
Alans
Finns
(Lapps)
Esthonians
Slavs replacing Teutons
Alans (join with Vandals)
Czech
Jugo Slavs
Czechs 5th C.
Huns 5th C.
Goths 3rd and 4th C.
Goths
Huns
Arabs
Arabs (7th C.)
Arabs 7th C.
Vandal Kingdom 5th C.
Vandals.
Gothic Kingdom 5th C.
Lombards
Saxons
Vandals
Suebi
Burgundians 5th C.
Franks
British
Angles & Saxons
Jutes
Picts & Scots
Visigoths
Vandals
710
Inset Map showing
GOTHIC
Migrations
separately..
1st Century
Ostro-Goths 3rd C.
Visi-Goths 2nd C.
Don
Danube
V.G.
O.G.
5th C.
3rd C.
Gothic Kingdom 5th C.
J.F.H.

superficial foreign conquest. The whole Vandal nation, men, women, and children, that came from Spain to Africa, for example, did not number more than eighty thousand souls. We know this because we have particulars of the transport problem. In their struggle for North Africa, Dr. Schurtz tells us,[1] "there is no trace of any serious resistance offered by the inhabitants; Boniface (the Roman governor of North Africa) had defended Hippo with Gothic mercenaries, while the native population lent no appreciable assistance, and the nomad tribes of the country either adopted a dubious attitude or availed themselves of the difficulties of the Roman governor to make attacks and engage in predatory expeditions. This demoralization resulted from social conditions, which had perhaps developed more unfavourably in Africa than in other parts of the Roman Empire. The free peasants had long ago become the serfs of the great landed proprietors, and were little superior in position to the masses of slaves who were everywhere to be found. And the great landowners had become in their turn easy victims of the policy of extortion followed by unscrupulous governors to an increasingly unprecedented extent in proportion as the dignity of the imperial power sank lower. No man who had anything to lose would now take a place in the senate of the large towns, which had once been the goal of the ambitious, for the senators were required to make up all deficiencies in the revenue, and such deficiencies were now frequent and considerable. . . . Bloody insurrections repeatedly broke out, always traceable ultimately to the pressure of taxation. . . ."

Manifestly the Vandals came in as a positive relief to such a system. They exterminated the great landowners, wiped out all debts to Roman money-lenders, and abolished the last vestiges of military service. The cultivators found themselves better off; the minor officials kept their places; it was not so much a conquest as a liberation from an intolerable deadlock.

It was while the Vandals were still in Africa that a great leader, Attila, arose among the Huns. The seat of his government was in the plains east of the Danube. For a time he swayed a considerable empire of Hunnish and Germanic tribes, and his rule stretched from the Rhine into Central Asia. He negotiated on equal terms with the Chinese emperor. He bullied Ravenna and Constantinople for ten years. Honoria,

[1] In Helmolt's *History of the World.*

the grand-daughter of Theodosius II, Emperor of the Eastern empire, one of those passionate young ladies who cause so much trouble in the world, having been put under restraint because of a love affair with a court chamberlain, sent her ring to Attila and called upon him to be her husband and deliverer. He was also urged to attack the Eastern empire by Genseric the Vandal, who was faced by an alliance of the Western and Eastern emperors. He raided southward to the very walls of Constantinople, completely destroying, says Gibbon, seventy cities in his progress, and forcing upon the emperor an onerous peace, which apparently did not involve the liberation of Honoria to her hero.

At this distance of time we are unable to guess at the motives for this omission. Attila continued to speak of her as his affianced bride, and to use the relationship as a pretext for aggressions. In the subsequent negotiations a certain Priscus accompanied an embassy to the camp of the Hunnish monarch, and the fragments that still survive of the narrative he wrote give us a glimpse of the camp and way of living of the great conqueror.

The embassy was itself a curiously constituted body. Its head was Maximin, an honest diplomatist who went in good faith. Quite unknown to him and, at the time, to Priscus, Vigilius, the interpreter of the expedition, had also a secret mission from the court of Theodosius which was to secure by bribery the assassination of Attila. The little expedition went by way of Nish; it crossed the Danube in canoes, dug out of a single tree, and it was fed by contributions from the villages on the route. Differences in dietary soon attracted the attention of the envoys. Priscus mentions mead in the place of wine, millet for corn, and a drink either distilled[1] or brewed from barley. The journey through Hungary will remind the reader in many of its incidents of the journeys of travellers in Central Africa during the Victorian period. The travellers were politely offered temporary wives.

Attila's capital was rather a vast camp and village than a town. There was only one building of stone, a bath constructed on the Roman model. The mass of the people were in huts and tents; Attila and his leading men lived in timber palaces in great stockaded enclosures with their numerous wives and min-

[1] Gibbon.

isters about them. There was a vast display of loot, but Attila himself affected a nomadic simplicity; he was served in wooden cups and platters, and never touched bread. He worked hard, kept open court before the gate of his palace, and was commonly in the saddle. The primitive custom of both Aryans and Mongols of holding great feasts in hall still held good, and there was much hard drinking. Priscus describes how bards chanted before Attila. They "recited the verses which they had composed, to celebrate his valour and his victories. A profound silence prevailed in the hall, and the attention of the guests was captivated by the vocal harmony, which revived and perpetuated the memory of their own exploits; a martial ardour flashed from the eyes of the warriors, who were impatient for battle; and the tears of the old men expressed their generous despair, that they could no longer partake the danger and glory of the field. This entertainment, which might be considered as a school of military virtue, was succeeded by a farce that debased the dignity of human nature. A Moorish and Scythian buffoon successively excited the mirth of the rude spectators by their deformed figures, ridiculous dress, antic gestures, absurd speeches, and the strange, unintelligible confusion of the Latin, the Gothic, and the Hunnish languages, and the hall resounded with loud and licentious peals of laughter. In the midst of this intemperate riot, Attila alone, without change of countenance, maintained his steadfast and inflexible gravity."[1]

Although Attila was aware, through the confession of the proposed assassin, of the secret work of Vigilius, he allowed this embassy to return in safety, with presents of numerous horses and the like, to Constantinople. Then he despatched an ambassador to Theodosius II to give that monarch, as people say, a piece of his mind. "Theodosius," said the envoy, "is the son of an illustrious and respectable parent; Attila, likewise, is descended from a noble race; and *he* has supported, by his actions the dignity which he inherited from his father Munzuk. But Theodosius has forfeited his parental honours, and, by consenting to pay tribute, has degraded himself to the condition of a slave. It is therefore just that he should reverence the man whom fortune and merit have placed above him; instead of attempting, like a wicked slave, clandestinely to conspire against his master."

[1] Gibbon.

This straightforward bullying was met by abject submission. The emperor sued for pardon, and paid a great ransom.

In 451 Attila declared war on the western empire. He invaded Gaul. So far as the imperial forces were concerned, he had things all his own way, and he sacked most of the towns of France as far south as Orleans. Then the Franks and Visigoths and the imperial forces united against him, and a great and obstinate battle at Chalons (451), in which over 150,000 men were killed on both sides, ended in his repulse and saved Europe from a Mongolian overlord. This disaster by no means exhausted Attila's resources. He turned his attention southward, and overran North Italy. He burnt Aquileia and Padua, and looted Milan, but he made peace at the entreaty of Pope Leo I. He died in 453. . . .

Hereafter the Huns, so far as that name goes in Europe, the Huns of Attila, disappeared out of history. They dissolve into the surrounding populations. They were probably already much mixed, and rather Aryan than Mongolian. They did not become, as one might suppose, the inhabitants of Hungary, though they have probably left many descendants there. About a hundred years after came another Hunnish or mixed people, the Avars, out of the east into Hungary, but these were driven out eastward again by Charlemagne in 791-5. The Magyars, the modern Hungarians, came westward later. They were a Turko-Finnish people. The Magyar is a language belonging to the Finno-Ugrian division of the Ural-Altaic tongues. The Magyars were on the Volga about 550. They settled in Hungary about 900. . . . But we are getting too far on in our story, and we must return to Rome.

In 493 Theodoric, a Goth, became King of Rome, but already for seventeen years there had been no Roman emperor. So it was in utter social decay and collapse that the great slave-holding "world-ascendancy" of the God-Cæsars and the rich men of Rome can to an end.

§ 6

But though throughout the whole of Western Europe and North Africa the Roman imperial system had collapsed, though credit had vanished, luxury production had ceased and money was hidden, though creditors were going unpaid and slaves masterless, the tradition of the Cæsars was still being carried on in Constantinople. We have already had occasion to mention as two outstanding figures among the late Cæsars, Diocletian (284) and Constantine the Great (312), and it was to the latter of these that the world owes the setting up of a fresh imperial centre at Constantinople. Very early during the imperial period the unsuitability of the position of Rome as a world capital, due to the Roman failure to use the sea, was felt.

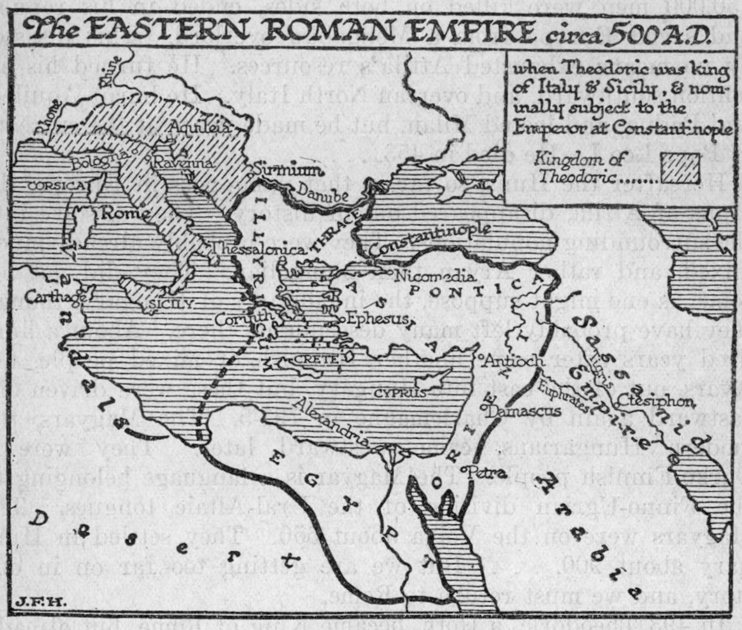

The destruction of Carthage and Corinth had killed the shipping of the main Mediterranean sea-routes. For a people who did not use the sea properly, having the administrative centre at Rome meant that every legion, every draft of officials, every order, had to travel northward for half the length of Italy before it could turn east or west. Consequently nearly all the more capable emperors set up their headquarters at some subordinate centre in a more convenient position. Sirmium (on the River Save), Milan, Lyons, and Nicomedia (in Bithynia) were among such supplementary capitals. For a time under Diocletian, Durazzo was the imperial capital. Ravenna, near the head of the Adriatic, was the capital of the last Roman emperors in the time of Alaric and Stilicho.

It was Constantine the Great who determined upon the permanent transfer of the centre of imperial power to the Bosphorus. We have already noted the existence of the city of Byzantium, which Constantine chose to develop into his new capital. It played a part in the story of the intricate Histiæus (Chap. xxi, § 4); it repulsed Philip of Macedon (Chap. xxiii, § 3). If the reader will examine its position, he will see that in the hands of a line of capable emperors, and as the centre of a people with some solidarity and spirit and seacraft (neither of which things were vouchsafed to it), it was extraordinarily well placed. Its galleys could have penetrated up the rivers to the heart of Russia and outflanked every barbarian advance. It commanded practicable trade routes to the east, and it was within a reasonable striking distance of Mesopotamia, Egypt, Greece, and all the more prosperous and civilized regions of the world at that period. And even under the rule of a series of inept monarchs and under demoralized social conditions, the remains of the Roman Empire centring at Constantinople held out for nearly a thousand years.

It was the manifest intention of Constantine the Great that Constantinople should be the centre of an undivided empire. But having regard to the methods of travel and transport available at the time, the geographical conditions of Europe and Western Asia do not point to any one necessary centre of government. If Rome faced westward instead of eastward, and so failed to reach out beyond the Euphrates, Constantinople on the other hand was hopelessly remote from Gaul. The enfeebled Mediterranean civilization, after a certain struggle for Italy, did in fact let go of the west altogether and concentrated upon what were practically the central vestiges, the stump, of the empire of Alexander. The Greek language resumed its sway, which had never been very seriously undermined by the official use of Latin. This "Eastern" or Byzantine empire is generally spoken of as if it were a continuation of the Roman tradition. It is really far more like a resumption of Alexander's.

The Latin language had not the intellectual vigour behind it, it had not the literature and the science, to make it a necessity to intelligent men and so to maintain an ascendancy over the Greek. For no language, whatever officialdom may do,

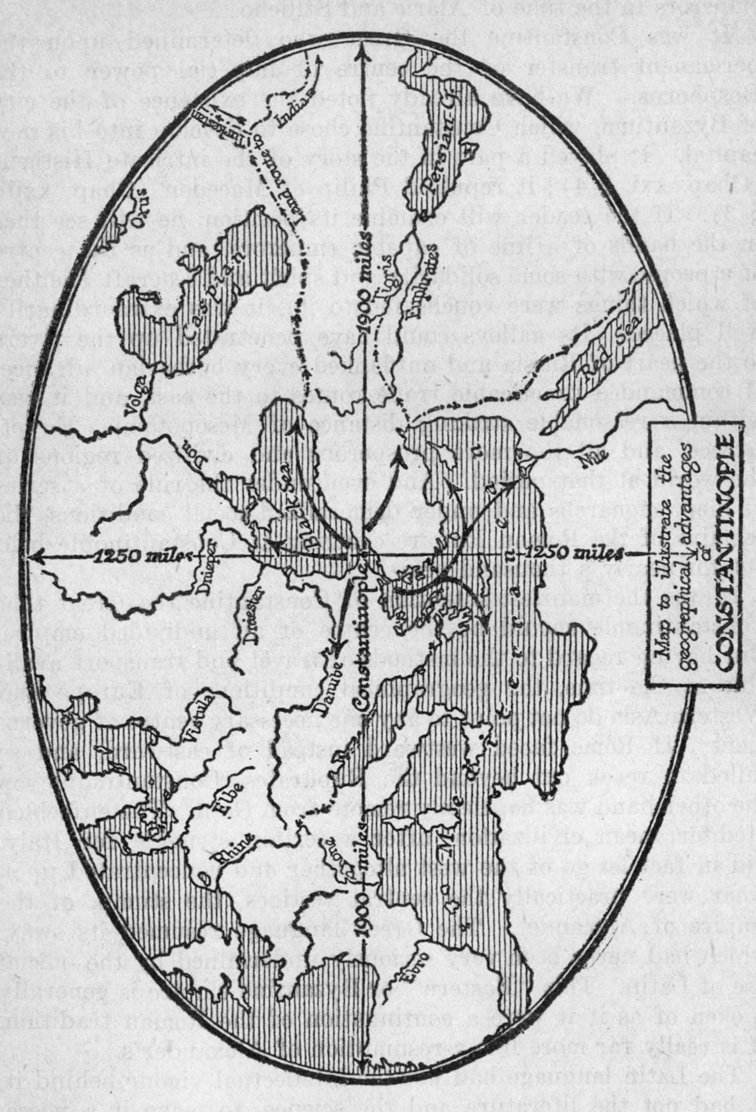
Map to illustrate the geographical advantages of CONSTANTINOPLE
1900 miles
1250 miles
1250 miles
1900 miles
Constantinople
Black Sea
Caspian
Persian G.
Red Sea
Nile
Tigris
Euphrates
Indus
Oxus
Volga
Don
Dnieper
Dniester
Danube
Vistula
Elbe
Rhine
Rhone
Ebro
Land route to India
Mediterranean

can impose itself in competition with another that can offer the advantages of a great literature or encyclopædic information. Aggressive languages must bring gifts, and the gifts of Greek were incomparably greater than the gifts of Latin. The Eastern empire was from the beginnings of its separation Greek-speaking, and a continuation, though a degenerate continuation, of the Hellenic tradition. Its intellectual centre was no longer in Greece, but Alexandria. Its mentality was no longer the mentality of free-minded plain-speaking citizens, of the Stagirite Aristotle and the Greek Plato; its mentality was the mentality of the pedants and of men politically impotent; its philosophy was a pompous evasion of real things, and its scientific impulse was dead. Nevertheless, it was Hellenic and not Latin. The Roman had come, and he had gone again. Indeed he had gone very extensively from the west also. By the sixth century A.D. the populations of Europe and North Africa had been stirred up like sediment. When presently in the seventh and eighth centuries the sediment begins to settle down again and populations begin to take on a definite localized character, the Roman is only to be found by name in the region about Rome. Over large parts of his Western empire we find changed and changing modifications of his Latin speech; in Gaul, where the Frank is learning a Gallic form of Latin and evolving French in the process; in Italy, where, under the influence of Teutonic invaders, the Lombards and Goths, Latin is being modified into various Italian dialects; in Spain and Portugal, where it is becoming Spanish and Portuguese. The fundamental Latinity of the languages in these regions serves to remind us of the numerical unimportance of the various Frankish, Vandal, Avar, Gothic, and the like German-speaking invaders, and serves to justify our statement that what happened to the Western empire was not so much conquest and the replacement of one population by another as a political and social revolution. The district of Valais in South Switzerland also retained a fundamentally Latin speech and so did the Canton Grisons; and, what is more curious and interesting, is that in Dacia and Mœsia Inferior, large parts of which to the north of the Danube became the modern Rumania (= Romania), although these regions were added late to the empire and lost soon, the Latin speech also remained.

In Britain Latin was practically wiped out by the conquering

Anglo-Saxons, from among whose various dialects the root stock of English presently grew.

But while the smashing of the Roman social and political structure was thus complete, while in the east it was thrown off by the older and stronger Hellenic tradition, and while in the west it was broken up into fragments that began to take on a new and separate life of their own, there was one thing that did not perish, but grew, and that was the tradition of the world empire of Rome and of the supremacy of the Cæsars. When the reality was destroyed, the legend had freedom to expand. Removed from the possibility of verification, the idea of a serene and splendid Roman world-supremacy grew up in the imagination of mankind, and still holds it to this day.

Ever since the time of Alexander, human thought has been haunted by the possible political unity of the race. All the sturdy chiefs and leaders and kings of the barbarians, who raided through the prostrate but vast disorder of the decayed empire, were capable of conceiving of some mighty king of kings greater than themselves and giving a real law for all men, and they were ready to believe that elsewhere in space and time, and capable of returning presently to resume his supremacy, Cæsar had been such a king of kings. Far above their own titles, therefore, they esteemed and envied the title of Cæsar. The international history of Europe from this time henceforth is largely the story of kings and adventurers setting up to be Cæsar and Imperator (Emperor). We shall tell of some of them in their places. So universal did this "Cæsaring" become, that the Great War of 1914-18 mowed down no fewer than four Cæsars, the German Kaiser (= Cæsar), the Austrian Kaiser, the Tsar (= Cæsar) of Russia, and that fantastic figure, the Tsar of Bulgaria. The French "Imperator" (Napoleon III) had already fallen in 1871. There is now (1920) no one left in the world to carry on the Imperial title or the tradition of Divus Cæsar except the Turkish Sultan and the British monarch. The former commemorates his lordship over Constantinople as Kaisar-i-Roum; the latter is called the Cæsar of India (a country no real Cæsar ever looked upon), Kaisar-i-Hind.

XXIX

THE BEGINNINGS, THE RISE, AND THE DIVISIONS OF CHRISTIANITY

§ 1. *Judea at the Christian Era.* § 2. *The Teachings of Jesus of Nazareth.* § 3. *The New Universal Religions.* § 4. *The Crucifixion of Jesus of Nazareth.* § 5. *Doctrines Added to the Teachings of Jesus.* § 6. *The Struggles and Persecutions of Christianity.* § 7. *Constantine the Great.* § 8. *The Establishment of Official Christianity.* § 9. *The Map of Europe, A. D. 500.* § 10. *The Salvation of Learning by Christianity.*

§ 1

BEFORE we can understand the qualities of Christianity, which must now play a large part in our history, and which opened men's eyes to fresh aspects of the possibility of a unified world, we must go back some centuries and tell of the condition of affairs in Palestine and Syria, in which countries Christianity arose. We have already told the main facts about the origin of the Jewish nation and tradition, about the Diaspora, about the fundamentally scattered nature of Jewry even from the beginning, and the gradual development of the idea of one just God ruling the earth and bound by a special promise to preserve and bring to honour the Jewish people. The Jewish idea was and is a curious combination of theological breadth and an intense racial patriotism. The Jews looked for a special saviour, a Messiah, who was to redeem mankind by the agreeable process of restoring the fabulous glories of David and Solomon, and bringing the whole world at last under the benevolent but firm Jewish heel. As the political power of the Semitic peoples declined, as Carthage followed Tyre into the darkness and Spain became a Roman province, this dream grew and spread. There can be little doubt that the scattered Phœnicians in Spain and Africa and throughout the

Mediterranean, speaking as they did a language closely akin to Hebrew and being deprived of their authentic political rights, became proselytes to Judaism. For phases of vigorous proselytism alternated with phases of exclusive jealousy in Jewish history. On one occasion the Idumeans, being conquered, were all forcibly made Jews.[1] There were Arab tribes who were Jews in the time of Muhammad, and a Turkish people who were mainly Jews in South Russia in the ninth century. Judaism is indeed the reconstructed political ideal of many shattered peoples—mainly Semitic. It is to the Phœnician contingent and to Aramean accessions in Babylon that the financial and commercial tradition of the Jews is to be ascribed. But as a result of these coalescences and assimilations, almost everywhere in the towns throughout the Roman Empire, and far beyond it in the east, Jewish communities traded and flourished, and were kept in touch through the Bible, and through a religious and educational organization. The main part of Jewry never was in Judea and had never come out of Judea.

Manifestly this intercommunicating series of Judaized communities had very great financial and political facilities. They could assemble resources, they could stir up, they could allay. They were neither so abundant nor so civilized as the still more widely diffused Greeks, but they had a tradition of greater solidarity. Greek was hostile to Greek; Jew stood by Jew. Wherever a Jew went, he found men of like mind and like tradition with himself. He could get shelter, food, loans, and legal help. And by reason of this solidarity rulers had everywhere to take account of this people as a help, as a source of loans, or as a source of trouble. So it is that the Jews have persisted as a people while Hellenism has become a universal light for mankind.

We cannot tell here in any detail the history of that smaller part of Jewry that lived in Judea. These Jews had returned to their old position of danger; again they were seeking peace in, so to speak, the middle of a highway. In the old time they had been between Syria and Assyria to the north and Egypt to the south; now they had the Seleucids to the north and the Ptolemys to the south, and when the Seleucids went, then down came the Roman power upon them. The independence of Judea was always a qualified and precarious thing. The reader

[1] Josephus.

must go to the *Antiquities* and the *Wars of the Jews* of Flavius Josephus, a copious, tedious, and maddeningly patriotic writer, to learn of the succession of their rulers, of their high-priest monarchs, and of the Maccabæans, the Herods and the like. These rulers were for the most part of the ordinary eastern type, cunning, treacherous, and blood-stained. Thrice Jerusalem was taken and twice the temple was destroyed. It was the support of the far more powerful Diaspora that prevented the little country from being wiped out altogether, until 70 A.D., when Titus, the adopted son and successor of the Emperor Vespasian, after a siege that ranks in bitterness and horror with that of Tyre and Carthage, took Jerusalem and destroyed city and temple altogether. He did this in an attempt to destroy Jewry, but indeed he made Jewry stronger by destroying its one sensitive and vulnerable point.

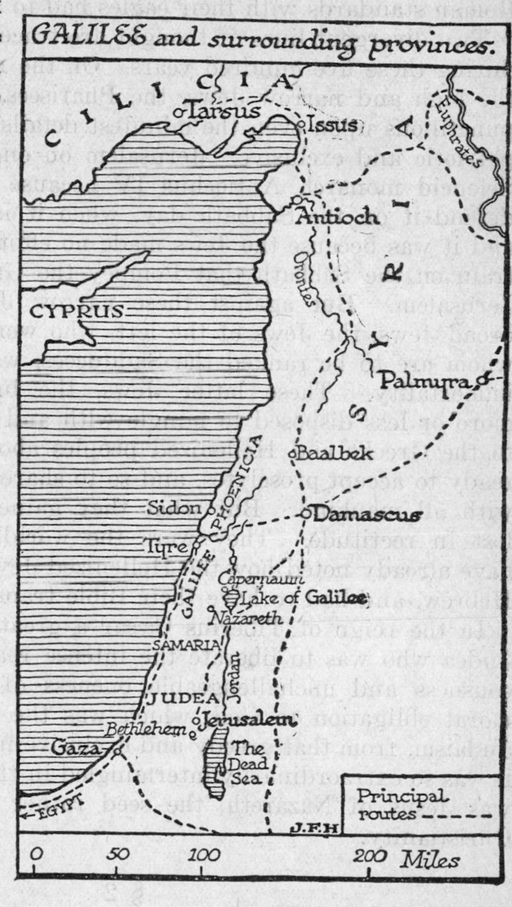

Throughout a history of five centuries of war and civil commotion between the return from captivity and the destruction of Jerusalem, certain constant features of the Jew persisted. He remained obstinately monotheistic; he would have none other gods but the one true God. In Rome, as in Jerusalem, he stood out manfully against the worship of any god-Cæsar. And to the best of his ability he held to his covenants with his God. No graven images could enter Jerusalem; even the Roman standards with their eagles had to stay outside.

Two divergent lines of thought are traceable in Jewish affairs during these five hundred years. On the right, so to speak, are the high and narrow Jews, the Pharisees, very orthodox, very punctilious upon even the minutest details of the law, intensely patriotic and exclusive. Jerusalem on one occasion fell to the Seleucid monarch Antiochus IV because the Jews would not defend it on the Sabbath day, when it is forbidden to work; and it was because the Jews made no effort to destroy his siege train on the Sabbath that Pompey the Great was able to take Jerusalem. But against these narrow Jews were pitted the broad Jews, the Jews of the left, who were Hellenizers, among whom are to be ranked the Sadducees, who did not believe in immortality. These latter Jews, the broad Jews, were all more or less disposed to mingle with and assimilate themselves to the Greeks and Hellenized peoples about them. They were ready to accept proselytes, and so to share God and his promise with all mankind. But what they gained in generosity they lost in rectitude. They were the worldlings of Judea. We have already noted how the Hellenized Jews of Egypt loss their Hebrew, and had to have their Bible translated into Greek.

In the reign of Tiberius Cæsar a great teacher arose out of Judea who was to liberate the intense realization of the righteousness and unchallengeable oneness of God, and of man's moral obligation to God, which was the strength of orthodox Judaism, from that greedy and exclusive narrowness with which it was so extraordinarily intermingled in the Jewish mind. This was Jesus of Nazareth, the seed rather than the founder of Christianity.

§ 2

The audience to which this book will first be presented will be largely an audience of Christians, with perhaps a sprinkling of Jewish readers, and the former at least will regard Jesus of Nazareth as being much more than a human teacher, and his appearance in the world not as a natural event in history, but as something of a supernatural sort interrupting and changing that steady development of life towards a common consciousness and a common will, which we have hitherto been tracing in this book. But these persuasions, dominant as they are in Europe and America, are nevertheless not the persuasions of all men or of the great majority of mankind, and we are writing this outline of the story of life with as complete an avoidance of controversial matter as may be. We are trying to write as if this book was to be read as much by Hindus or Moslems or Buddhists as by Americans and Western Europeans. We shall therefore hold closely to the apparent facts, and avoid, without any disputation or denial, the theological interpretations that have been imposed upon them. We shall tell what men have believed about Jesus of Nazareth, but him we shall treat as being what he appeared to be, a man, just as a painter must needs paint him as a man. The documents that testify to his acts and teachings we shall treat as ordinary human documents. If the light of divinity shine through our recital, we will neither help nor hinder it. This is what we have already done in the case of Buddha, and what we shall do later with Muhammad. About Jesus we have to write not theology but history, and our concern is not with the spiritual and theological significance of his life, but with its effects upon the political and every-day life of men.

Almost our only sources of information about the personality of Jesus are derived from the four gospels, all of which were certainly in existence a few decades after his death, and from allusions to his life in the letters (epistles) of the early Christian propagandists. The first three gospels, the gospels of Matthew, Mark, and Luke, many suppose to be derived from some earlier documents; the gospel of St. John has more idiosyncrasy and is coloured by theology of a strongly Hellenic type. Critics are disposed to regard the gospel of St. Mark as being the most trustworthy account of the personality and actual words of Jesus. But all four agree in giving us a picture of a very definite personality; they carry the same conviction of reality that the early accounts of Buddha do. In spite of miraculous and incredible additions, one is obliged to say, "Here was a man. This part of the tale could not have been invented."

But just as the personality of Gautama Buddha has been distorted and obscured by the stiff squatting figure, the gilded idol of later Buddhism, so one feels that the lean and strenuous personality of Jesus is much wronged by the unreality and conventionality that a mistaken reverence has imposed upon his figure in modern Christian art. Jesus was a penniless teacher, who wandered about the dusty sun-lit country of Judea, living upon casual gifts of food; yet he is always represented clean, combed, and sleek, in spotless raiment, erect, and with something motionless about him as though he was gliding through the air. This alone has made him unreal and incredible to many people who cannot distinguish the core of the story from the ornamental and unwise additions of the unintelligently devout.

And it may be that the early parts of the gospels are accretions of the same nature. The miraculous circumstances of the birth of Jesus, the great star that brought wise men from the east to worship at his manger cradle, the massacre of the male infant children in the region of Bethlehem by Herod as a consequence of these portents, and the flight into Egypt, are all supposed to be such accretionary matter by many authorities. At the best they are events unnecessary to the teaching, and they rob it of much of the strength and power it possesses when we strip it of such accompaniment. So, too, do the discrepant genealogies given by Matthew and Luke, in which there is an endeavour to trace the direct descent of Joseph, his father, from King David, as though it was any honour to Jesus or to anyone to have such a man as an ancestor. The insertion of these genealogies is the more peculiar and unreasonable, because, according to the legend, Jesus was not the son of Joseph at all, but miraculously conceived.

We are left, if we do strip this record of these difficult accessories, with the figure of a being, very human, very earnest and passionate, capable of swift anger, and teaching a new and simple and profound doctrine—namely, the universal loving Fatherhood of God and the coming of the Kingdom of Heaven. He was clearly a person—to use a common phrase—of intense personal magnetism. He attracted followers and filled them with love and courage. Weak and ailing people were heartened and healed by his presence. Yet he was probably of a delicate physique, because of the swiftness with which he died under the pains of crucifixion. There is a tradition that he fainted when, according to the custom, he was made to bear his cross to the place of execution. When he first appeared as a teacher he was a man of about thirty. He went about the country for some time spreading his doctrine, and then he came to Jerusalem and was accused of trying to set up a strange kingdom in Judea; he was tried upon this charge, and crucified together with two thieves. Long before these two were dead, his sufferings were over.

Now it is a matter of fact that in the gospels all that body of theological assertion which constitutes Christianity finds little support. There is, as the reader may see for himself, no clear and emphatic assertion in these books of the doctrines which Christian teachers of all denominations find generally necessary to salvation. Except for one or two passages in St. John's Gospel it is difficult to get any words actually ascribed to Jesus in which he claimed to be the Jewish Messiah (rendered in Greek by "the Christ") and still more difficult is it to find any claim to be a part of the godhead, or any passage in which he explained the doctrine of the Atonement or urged any sacrifices or sacraments (that is to say, priestly offices) upon his followers. We shall see presently how later on all Christendom was torn by disputes about the Trinity. There is no evidence that the apostles of Jesus ever heard of the Trinity—at any rate from him. The observance of the Jewish Sabbath, again, tranferred to the Mithraic Sun-day, is an important feature of many Christian cults; but Jesus deliberately broke the Sabbath, and said that it was made for man and not man for the Sabbath. Nor did he say a word about the worship of his mother Mary, in the guise of Isis, the Queen of Heaven. All that is most characteristically Christian in worship and usage, he ignored. Sceptical writers have had the temerity to deny that Jesus can be called a Christian at all. For light upon these extraordinary gaps in his teaching, each reader must go to his own religious guides. Here we are bound to mention these gaps on account of the difficulties and controversies that arose out of them, and we are equally bound not to enlarge upon them.

As remarkable is the enormous prominence given by Jesus to the teaching of what he called the Kingdom of Heaven, and its comparative insignificance in the procedure and teaching of most of the Christian churches.

This doctrine of the Kingdom of Heaven, which was the main teaching of Jesus, and which plays so small a part in the Christian creeds, is certainly one of the most revolutionary doctrines that ever stirred and changed human thought. It is small wonder if the world of that time failed to grasp its full significance, and recoiled in dismay from even a half apprehension of its tremendous challenges to the established habits and institutions of mankind. It is small wonder if the hesitating convert and disciple presently went back to the old familiar ideas of temple and altar, of fierce deity and propitiatory observance, of consecrated priest and magic blessing, and—these things being attended to—reverted then to the dear old habitual life of hates and profits and competition and pride. For the doctrine of the Kingdom of Heaven, as Jesus seems to have preached it, was no less than a bold and uncompromising demand for a complete change and cleansing of the life of our struggling race, an utter cleansing, without and within. To the gospels the reader must go for all that is preserved of this tremendous teaching; here we are only concerned with the jar of its impact upon established ideas.

The Jews were persuaded that God, the one God of the whole world, was a righteous god, but they also thought of him as a trading god who had made a bargain with their Father Abraham about them, a very good bargain indeed for them, to bring them at last to predominance in the earth. With dismay and anger they heard Jesus sweeping away their dear securities. God, he taught, was no bargainer; there were no chosen people and no favourites in the Kingdom of Heaven. God was the loving father of all life, as incapable of showing favour as the universal sun. And all men were brothers—sinners alike and beloved sons alike—of this divine father. In the parable of the Good Samaritan Jesus cast scorn upon that natural tendency we all obey, to glorify our own people and to minimize the righteousness of other creeds and other races. In the parable of the labourers he thrust aside the obstinate claim of the Jews to have a sort of first mortgage upon God. All whom God takes into the kingdom, he taught, God serves alike; there is no distinction in his treatment, because there is no measure to his bounty. From all, moreover, as the parable of the buried talent witnesses, and as the incident of the widow's mite enforces, he demands the utmost. There are no privileges, no rebates, and no excuses in the Kingdom of Heaven.

But it was not only the intense tribal patriotism of the Jews that Jesus outraged. They were a people of intense family loyalty, and he would have swept away all the narrow and restrictive family affections in the great flood of the love of God. The whole Kingdom of Heaven was to be the family of his followers. We are told that, "While he yet talked to the people, behold, his mother and his brethren stood without, desiring to speak with him. Then one said unto him, Behold, thy mother and thy brethren stand without, desiring to speak with thee. But he answered and said unto him that told him, Who is my mother? and who are my brethren? And he stretched forth his hand towards his disciples, and said, Behold my mother and my brethren! For whosoever shall do the will of my Father which is in heaven, the same is my brother, and sister, and mother."[1]

And not only did Jesus strike at patriotism and the bonds of family loyalty in the name of God's universal fatherhood and the brotherhood of all mankind, but it is clear that his teaching condemned all the gradations of the economic system, all private wealth, and personal advantages. All men belonged to the kingdom; all their possessions belonged to the kingdom; the righteous life for all men, the only righteous life, was the service of God's will with all that we had, with all that we were. Again and again he denounced private riches and the reservation of any private life.

"And when he was gone forth into the way, there came one running, and kneeled to him, and asked him, Good Master, what shall I do that I may inherit eternal life? And Jesus said unto him, Why callest thou me good? there is none good but one, that is, God. Thou knowest the commandments, Do not commit adultery, Do not kill, Do not steal, Do not bear false witness, Defraud not, Honour thy father and mother. And he answered and said unto him, Master, all these things have I observed from my youth. Then Jesus beholding him loved him, and said unto him, One thing thou lackest: go thy way, sell whatsoever thou hast, and give to the poor, and thou shalt have treasure in heaven: and come, take up the cross, and follow me. And he was sad at that saying, and went away grieved: for he had great possessions.

"And Jesus looked round about, and saith unto his disciples, How hardly shall they that have riches enter into the kingdom

[1] Matt. xii. 46-50.

of God! And the disciples were astonished at his words. But Jesus answered again, and saith unto them, Children, how hard is it for them that trust in riches to enter into the kingdom of God! It is easier for a camel to go through the eye of a needle, than for a rich man to enter into the kingdom of God."[1]

Moreover, in his tremendous prophecy of this kingdom which was to make all men one together in God, Jesus had small patience for the bargaining righteousness of formal religion. Another large part of his recorded utterances is aimed against the meticulous observance of the rules of the pious career. "Then came together unto him the Pharisees, and certain of the scribes, which came from Jerusalem. And when they saw some of his disciples eat bread with defiled, that is to say, with unwashen, hands, they found fault. For the Pharisees, and all the Jews, except they wash their hands oft, eat not, holding the tradition of the elders. And when they come from the market, except they wash, they eat not. And many other things there be, which they have received to hold, as the washing of cups, and pots, brazen vessels, and of tables. Then the Pharisees and scribes asked him, Why walk not thy disciples according to the tradition of the elders, but eat bread with unwashen hands? He answered and said unto them, Well hath Isaiah prophesied of you hypocrites, as it is written,

"This people honoureth me with their lips,
"But their heart is far from me.
"Howbeit in vain do they worship me,
"Teaching for doctrines the commandments of men.

"For laying aside the commandment of God, ye hold the tradition of men, as the washing of pots and cups: and many other such things ye do. And he said unto them, Full well ye reject the commandment of God, that ye may keep your own tradition."[2]

So, too, we may note a score of places in which he flouted that darling virtue of the formalist, the observance of the Sabbath.

It was not merely a moral and a social revolution that Jesus proclaimed; it is clear from a score of indications that his teaching had a political bent of the plainest sort. It is true that he said his kingdom was not of this world, that it was in the hearts of men and not upon a throne; but it is equally clear

[1] Mark x. 17-25. [2] Mark vii. 1-9.

that wherever and in what measure his kingdom was set up in the hearts of men, the outer world would be in that measure revolutionized and made new.

Whatever else the deafness and blindness of his hearers may have missed in his utterances, it is plain that they did not miss his resolve to revolutionize the world. Some of the questions that were brought to Jesus and the answers he gave enable us to guess at the drift of much of his unrecorded teaching. The directness of his political attack is manifest by such an incident as that of the coin—

"And they send unto him certain of the Pharisees and of the Herodians, to catch him in his words. And when they were come, they say unto him, Master, we know that thou art true, and carest for no man: for thou regardest not the person of men, but teachest the way of God in truth: Is it lawful to give tribute to Cæsar, or not? Shall we give, or shall we not give? But he, knowing their hypocrisy, said unto them, Why tempt ye me? bring me a penny, that I may see it. And they brought it. And he saith unto them, Whose is this image and superscription? And they said unto him, Cæsar's. And Jesus answering said unto them, Render to Cæsar the things that are Cæsar's, and to God the things that are God's"[1]—which in view of all else that he had taught, left very little of a man or his possessions for Cæsar.

The whole tenor of the opposition to him and the circumstances of his trial and execution show clearly that to his contemporaries he seemed to propose plainly and did propose plainly to change and fuse and enlarge all human life. But even his disciples did not grasp the profound and comprehensive significance of that proposal. They were ridden by the old Jewish dream of a king, a Messiah to overthrow the Hellenized Herods and the Roman overlord, and restore the fabled glories of David. They disregarded the substance of his teaching, plain and direct though it was; evidently they thought it was merely his mysterious and singular way of setting about the adventure that would at last put him on the throne of Jerusalem. They thought he was just another king among the endless succession of kings, but of a quasi-magic kind, and making quasi-magic profession of an impossible virtue.

"And James and John, the sons of Zebedee, come unto him,

[1] Mark xii. 13-17.

saying Master, we would that thou shouldest do for us whatsoever we shall desire. And he said unto them, What would ye that I should do for you? They said unto him, Grant unto us that we may sit, one on thy right hand, and the other on thy left hand, in thy glory. But Jesus said unto them, Ye know not what ye ask: can ye drink of the cup that I drink of? and be baptized with the baptism that I am baptized with? And they said unto him, We can. And Jesus said unto them, Ye shall indeed drink of the cup that I drink of; and with the baptism that I am baptized withal shall ye be baptized: but to sit on my right hand and on my left hand is not mine to give; but it shall be given to them for whom it is prepared. And when the ten heard it, they began to be much displeased with James and John. But Jesus called them to him, and saith unto them, Ye know that they which are accounted to rule over the Gentiles exercise lordship over them; and their great ones exercise authority upon them. But so shall it not be among you: but whosoever will be great among you, shall be your minister: and whosoever of you will be the chiefest, shall be servant of all. For even the Son of Man came not to be ministered unto, but to minister, and to give his life a ransom for many."[1]

This was cold comfort for those who looked for a due reward for their services and hardships in his train. They could not believe this hard doctrine of a kingdom of service which was its own exceeding great reward. Even after his death upon the cross, they could still, after their first dismay, revert to the belief that he was nevertheless in the vein of the ancient world of pomps and privileges, that presently by some amazing miracle he would become undead again and return, and set up his throne with much splendour and graciousness in Jerusalem. They thought his life was a stratagem and his death a trick.

He was too great for his disciples. And in view of what he plainly said, is it any wonder that all who were rich and prosperous felt a horror of strange things, a swimming of their world at his teaching? Perhaps the priests and the rulers and the rich men understood him better than his followers. He was dragging out all the little private reservations they had made from social service into the light of a universal religious life.

[1] Mark x. 35-45.

He was like some terrible moral huntsman digging mankind out of the snug burrows in which they had lived hitherto. In the white blaze of this kingdom of his there was to be no property, no privilege, no pride and precedence; no motive indeed and no reward but love. It is any wonder that men were dazzled and blinded and cried out against him? Even his disciples cried out when he would not spare them the light. Is it any wonder that the priests realized that between this man and themselves there was no choice but that he or priestcraft should perish? Is it any wonder that the Roman soldiers, confronted and amazed by something soaring over their comprehension and threatening all their disciplines, should take refuge in wild laughter, and crown him with thorns and robe him in purple and make a mock Cæsar of him? For to take him seriously was to enter upon a strange and alarming life, to abandon habits, to control instincts and impulses, to essay an incredible happiness. . . .

Is it any wonder that to this day this Galilean is too much for our small hearts?

§ 3

Yet be it noted that while there was much in the real teachings of Jesus that a rich man or a priest or a trader or an imperial official or any ordinary respectable citizen could not accept without the most revolutionary changes in his way of living, yet there was nothing that a follower of the actual teaching of Gautama Sakya might not receive very readily, nothing to prevent a primitive Buddhist from being also a Nazarene, and nothing to prevent a personal disciple of Jesus from accepting all the recorded teachings of Buddha.

Again consider the tone of this extract from the writings of a Chinaman, Mo Ti, who lived somewhen in the fourth century B.C., when the doctrines of Confucius and Lao Tse prevailed in China, before the advent of Buddhism to that country, and note how "Nazarene" it is.

"The mutual attacks of state on state; the mutual usurpations of family on family; the mutual robberies of man on man; the want of kindness on the part of the sovereign and of loyalty on the part of the minister; the want of tenderness and filial duty between father and son—these, and such as these, are the things injurious to the empire. All this has arisen from want of mutual love. If but that one virtue could be made universal, the princes loving one another would have no battle-fields; the chiefs of families would attempt no usurpations; men would commit no robberies; rulers and ministers would be gracious and loyal; fathers and sons would be kind and filial; brothers would be harmonious and easily reconciled. Men in general loving one another, the strong would not make prey of the weak; the many would not plunder the few, the rich would not insult the poor, the noble would not be insolent to the mean; and the deceitful would not impose upon the simple."[1]

This is extraordinarily like the teaching of Jesus of Nazareth cast into political terms. The thoughts of Mo Ti came close to the Kingdom of Heaven.

This essential identity is the most important historical aspect of these great world religions. They were in their beginnings quite unlike the priest, altar, and temple cults, those cults for the worship of definite finite gods that played so great and so essential a part in the earlier stages of man's development between 15,000 B.C. and 600 B.C. These new world religions, from 600 B.C. onward, were essentially religions of the heart and of the universal sky. They swept away all those various and limited gods that had served the turn of human needs since the first communities were welded together by fear and hope. And presently when we come to Islam we shall find that for a third time the same fundamental new doctrine of the need of a universal devotion of all men to one Will reappears. Warned by the experiences of Christianity, Muhammad was very emphatic in insisting that he himself was merely a man and so saved his teaching from much corruption and misrepresentation.

We speak of these great religions of mankind which arose between the Persian conquest of Babylon and the break-up of the Roman empire as rivals; but it is their defects, their accumulations and excrescences, their differences of language and phrase, that cause the rivalry; and it is not to one overcoming the other or to any new variant replacing them that we must look, but to the white truth in each being burnt free from its dross, and becoming manifestly the same truth—namely, that

[1] Hirth, *The Ancient History of China*, Chap. viii.

the hearts of men, and therewith all the lives and institutions of men, must be subdued to one common Will, ruling them all.[1]

And though much has been written foolishly about the antagonism of science and religion, there is indeed no such antagonism. What all these world religions declare by inspiration and insight, history as it grows clearer and science as its range extends display, as a reasonable and demonstrable fact, that men form one universal brotherhood, that they spring from one common origin, that their individual lives, their nations and races, interbreed and blend and go on to merge again at last in one common human destiny upon this little planet amidst the stars. And the psychologist can now stand beside the preacher and assure us that there is no reasoned peace of heart, no balance and no safety in the soul, until a man in losing his life has found it, and has schooled and disciplined his interests and will beyond greeds, rivalries, fears, instincts, and narrow affections. The history of our race and personal religious experience run so closely parallel as to seem to a modern observer almost the same thing; both tell of a being at first scattered and blind and utterly confused, feeling its way slowly to the serenity and salvation of an ordered and coherent purpose. That, in the simplest, is the outline of history; whether one have a religious purpose or disavow a religious purpose altogether, the lines of the outline remain the same.

§ 4

In the year 30 A.D., while Tiberius, the second emperor, was Emperor of Rome and Pontius Pilate was procurator of Judea, a little while before the Feast of the Passover, Jesus of Nazareth came into Jerusalem. Probably he came then for the first time. Hitherto he had been preaching chiefly in Galilee, and for the most part round and about the town of Capernaum. In Capernaum he had preached in the synagogue.

His entry into Jerusalem was a pacific triumph. He had gathered a great following in Galilee—he had sometimes to preach from a boat upon the Lake of Galilee, because of the pressure of the crowd upon the shore—and his fame had spread

1 "St. Paul understood what most Christians never realize, namely, that the Gospel of Christ is not *a* religion, but religion itself in its most universal and deepest significance."—Dean Inge in *Outspoken Essays*.

before him to the capital. Great crowds came out to greet him. It is clear they did not understand the drift of his teaching, and that they shared the general persuasion that by some magic of righteousness he was going to overthrow the established order. He rode into the city upon the foal of an ass that had been borrowed by his disciples. The crowd accompanied him with cries of triumph and shouts of "Hosanna," a word of rejoicing.

He went to the temple. Its outer courts were cumbered with the tables of money-changers and with the stalls of those who sold doves to be liberated by pious visitors to the temple. These traders upon religion he and his followers cast out, overturning the tables. It was almost his only act of positive rule.

Then for a week he taught in Jerusalem, surrounded by a crowd of followers who made his arrest by the authorities difficult. Then officialdom gathered itself together against this astonishing intruder. One of his disciples, Judas, dismayed and disappointed at the apparent ineffectiveness of this capture of Jerusalem, went to the Jewish priests to give them his advice and help in the arrest of Jesus. For this service he was rewarded with thirty pieces of silver. The high priest and the Jews generally had many reasons for dismay at this gentle insurrection that was filling the streets with excited crowds; for example, the Romans might misunderstand it or use it as an occasion to do some mischief to the whole Jewish people. Accordingly the high priest Caiaphas, in his anxiety to show his loyalty to the Roman overlord, was the leader in the proceedings against this unarmed Messiah, and the priests and the orthodox mob of Jerusalem the chief accusers of Jesus.

How he was arrested in the garden of Gethsemane, how he was tried and sentenced by Pontius Pilate, the Roman procurator, how he was scourged and mocked by the Roman soldiers and crucified upon the hill called Golgotha, is told with unsurpassable simplicity and dignity in the gospels.

The revolution collapsed utterly. The disciples of Jesus with one accord deserted him, and Peter, being taxed as one of them, said, "I know not the man." This was not the end they had anticipated in their great coming to Jerusalem. His last hours of aching pain and thirst upon the cross were watched only by a few women and near friends. Towards the end of the long day of suffering this abandoned leader roused himself to one supreme effort, cried out with a loud voice, "My God! my

God! why hast thou forsaken me?" and, leaving these words to echo down the ages, a perpetual riddle to the faithful, died.

It was inevitable that simple believers should have tried to enhance the stark terrors of this tragedy by foolish stories of physical disturbances similar to those which had been invented to emphasize the conversion of Gautama. We are told that a great darkness fell upon the earth, and that the veil of the temple was rent in twain; but if indeed these things occurred, they produced not the slightest effect upon the minds of people in Jerusalem at that time. It is difficult to believe nowadays that the order of nature indulged in any such meaningless comments. Far more tremendous is it to suppose a world apparently indifferent to those three crosses in the red evening twilight, and to the little group of perplexed and desolated watchers. The darkness closed upon the hill; the distant city set about its preparations for the Passover; scarcely anyone but that knot of mourners on the way to their homes troubled whether Jesus of Nazareth was still dying or already dead. . . .

The souls of the disciples were plunged for a time into utter darkness. Then presently came a whisper among them and stories, rather discrepant stories, that the body of Jesus was not in the tomb in which it had been placed, and that first one and then another had seen him alive. Soon they were consoling themselves with the conviction that he had risen from the dead, that he had shown himself to many, and had ascended visibly into heaven. Witnesses were found to declare that they had positively seen him go up, visibly in his body. He had gone through the blue—to God. Soon they had convinced themselves that he would presently come again, in power and glory, to judge all mankind. In a little while, they said, he would come back to them; and in these bright revivals of their old-time dream of an assertive and temporal splendour they forgot the greater measure, the giant measure, he had given them of the Kingdom of God.

§ 5

The story of the early beginnings of Christianity is the story of the struggle between the real teachings and spirit of Jesus of Nazareth and the limitations, amplifications, and misunderstandings of the very inferior men who had loved and followed him from Galilee, and who were now the bearers and custodians of his message to mankind. The gospels and the Acts of the Apostles present a patched and uneven record, but there can be little question that on the whole it is a quite honest record of those early days.

The early Nazarenes, as the followers of Jesus were called, present from the first a spectacle of a great confusion between these two strands, his teaching on the one hand, and the glosses and interpretations of the disciples on the other. They continued for a time his disciplines of the complete subjugation of self; they had their goods in common, they had no bond but love. Nevertheless, they built their faith upon the stories that were told of his resurrection and magical ascension, and the promised return. Few of them understood that the renunciation of self is its own reward, that it is itself the Kingdom of Heaven; they regarded it as a sacrifice that entitled them to the compensation of power and dominion when presently the second coming occurred. They had now all identified Jesus with the promised Christ, the Messiah so long expected by the Jewish people. They found out prophecies of the crucifixion in the prophets—the Gospel of Matthew is particularly insistent upon these prophecies. Revived by these hopes, enforced by the sweet and pure lives of many of the believers, the Nazarene doctrine began to spread very rapidly in Judea and Syria.

And presently there arose a second great teacher, whom many modern authorities regard as the real founder of Christianity, Saul of Tarsus, or Paul. Saul apparently was his Jewish and Paul his Roman name; he was a Roman citizen, and a man of much wider education and a much narrower intellectuality than Jesus seems to have been. By birth he was probably a Jew, though some Jewish writers deny this; he had certainly studied under Jewish teachers. But he was well versed in the Hellenic theologies of Alexandria, and his language was Greek. Some classical scholars profess to find his Greek unsatisfactory; he did not use the Greek of Athens, but the Greek of Alexandria; but he used it with power and freedom.[1] He was a religious theorist and teacher long before he heard of Jesus of Nazareth,

[1] Paul's Greek is very good. He is affected by the philosophical jargon of the Hellenistic schools and by that of Stoicism. But his mastery of sublime language is amazing.—G. M.

and he appears in the New Testament narrative at first as the bitter critic and antagonist of the Nazarenes.

The present writer has been unable to find any discussion of the religious ideas of Paul before he became a follower of Jesus. They must have been a basis, if only a basis of departure, for his new views, and their phraseology certainly supplied the colour of his new doctrines. We are almost equally in the dark as to the teachings of Gamaliel, who is named as the Jewish teacher at whose feet he sat. Nor do we know what Gentile teachings had reached him. It is highly probable that he had been influenced by Mithraism. He uses phrases curiously like Mithraistic phrases. What will be clear to anyone who reads his various Epistles, side by side with the Gospels, is that his mind was saturated by an idea which does not appear at all prominently in the reported sayings and teachings of Jesus, the idea of a sacrificial person, who is offered up to God as an atonement for sin. What Jesus preached was a new birth of the human soul; what Paul preached was the ancient religion of priest and altar and propitiatory bloodshed. Jesus was to him the Easter lamb, that traditional human victim without spot or blemish who haunts all the religions of the dark white peoples. Paul came to the Nazarenes with overwhelming force because he came to them with this completely satisfactory explanation of the disaster of the crucifixion. It was a brilliant elucidation of what had been utterly perplexing.

Paul had never seen Jesus. His knowledge of Jesus and his teaching must have been derived from the hearsay of the original disciples. It is clear that he apprehended much of the spirit of Jesus and his doctrine of a new birth, but he built this into a theological system, a very subtle and ingenious system, whose appeal to this day is chiefly intellectual. And it is clear that the faith of the Nazarenes, which he found as a doctrine of motive and a way of living, he made into a doctrine of *belief*. He found the Nazarenes with a spirit and hope, and he left them Christians with the beginning of a creed.

But we must refer the reader to the Acts of the Apostles and the Pauline Epistles for an account of Paul's mission and teaching. He was a man of enormous energy, and he taught at Jerusalem, Antioch, Athens, Corinth, Ephesus, and Rome.

Possibly he went into Spain. The manner of his death is not certainly known, but it is said that he was killed in Rome during the reign of Nero. A great fire had burnt a large part of Rome, and the new sect was accused of causing this. The rapid spread of Christian teaching certainly owes more to Paul than to any other single man. Within two decades of the crucifixion this new religion was already attracting the attention of the Roman rulers in several provinces. If it had acquired a theology in the hands of St. Paul, it still retained much of the revolutionary and elementary quality of the teachings of Jesus. It had become somewhat more tolerant of private property; it would accept wealthy adherents without insisting upon the communization of their riches, and St. Paul has condoned the institution of slavery ("Slaves, be obedient to your masters"), but it still set its face like flint against certain fundamental institutions of the Roman world. It would not tolerate the godhead of Cæsar; not even by a mute gesture at the altar would the Christians consent to worship the Emperor, though their lives were at stake in the matter. It denounced the gladiatorial shows. Unarmed, but possessing enormous powers of passive resistance, Christianity thus appeared at the outset plainly as rebellion, striking at the political if not at the economic essentials of the imperial system. The first evidences of Christianity in non-Christian literature we find when perplexed Roman officials began to write to one another and exchange views upon the strange problem presented by this infectious rebellion of otherwise harmless people.

Much of the history of the Christians in the first two centuries of the Christian era is very obscure. They spread far and wide throughout the world, but we know very little of their ideas or their ceremonies and methods during that time. As yet they had no settled creeds, and there can be little doubt that there were wide local variations in their beliefs and disciplines during this formless period. But whatever their local differences, everywhere they seem to have carried much of the spirit of Jesus; and though everywhere they aroused bitter enmity and active counter-propaganda, the very charges made against them witness to the general goodness of their lives.

During this indefinite time a considerable amount of a sort of theocrasia seems to have gone on between the Christian cult and the almost equally popular and widely diffused Mithraic cult, and the cult of Serapis-Isis-Horus. From the former it would seem the Christians adopted Sun-day as their chief day of worship instead of the Jewish Sabbath, the abundant use of candles in religious ceremonies, the legend of the adoration by the shepherds, and probably also those ideas and phrases, so distinctive of certain sects to this day, about being "washed in the blood" of Christ, and of Christ being a blood sacrifice. For we have to remember that a death by crucifixion is hardly a more bloody death than hanging; to speak of Jesus shedding his blood for mankind is really a most inaccurate expression. Even when we remember that he was scourged, that he wore a crown of thorns, and that his side was pierced by a spear, we are still far from a "fountain filled with blood." But Mithraism centred upon some now forgotten mysteries about Mithras sacrificing a sacred and benevolent bull; all the Mithraic shrines seem to have contained a figure of Mithras killing this bull, which bleeds copiously from a wound in its side, and from this blood a new life sprang. The Mithraist votary actually bathed in the blood of the sacrificial bull, and was "born again" thereby. At his initiation he went beneath a scaffolding on which the bull was killed, and the blood ran down on him.

The contributions of the Alexandrine cult to Christian thought and practices were even more considerable. In the personality of Horus, who was at once the son of Serapis and identical with Serapis, it was natural for the Christians to find an illuminating analogue in their struggles with the Pauline mysteries. From that to the identification of Mary with Isis, and her elevation to a rank quasi-divine—in spite of the saying of Jesus about his mother and his brothers that we have already quoted—was also a very natural step. Natural, too, was it for Christianity to adopt, almost insensibly, the practical methods of the popular religions of the time. Its priests took on the head-shaving and the characteristic garments of the Egyptian priests, because that sort of thing seemed to be the right way of distinguishing a priest. One accretion followed another. Almost insensibly the originally revolutionary teaching was buried under these customary acquisitions. We have already tried to imagine Gautama Buddha returning to Tibet, and his amazement at the worship of his own image in Lhassa. We will but suggest the parallel amazement of some earnest Nazarene who had known and followed his dusty and travel-worn Master through the dry sunlight of Galilee, restored suddenly to this world and visiting, let us say, a mass in St. Peter's at Rome, at learning that the consecrated wafer upon the altar was none other than his crucified teacher.

Religion in a world community is not many things but one thing, and it was inevitable that all the living religious faiths in the world at the time, and all the philosophy and religious thought that came into contact with Christianity, should come to an account with Christianity and exchange phrases and ideas. The hopes of the early Nazarenes had identified Jesus with the Christ; the brilliant mind of Paul had surrounded his career with mystical significance. Jesus had called men and women to a giant undertaking, to the renunciation of self, to the new birth into the kingdom of love. The line of least resistance for the flagging convert was to intellectualize himself away from this plain doctrine, this stark proposition, into complicated theories and ceremonies—that would leave his essential self alone. How much easier is it to sprinkle oneself with blood than to purge oneself from malice and competition; to eat bread and drink wine and pretend one had absorbed divinity, to give candles rather than the heart, to shave the head and retain the scheming privacy of the brain inside it! The world was full of such evasive philosophy and theological stuff in the opening centuries of the Christian era. It is not for us here to enlarge upon the distinctive features of Neoplatonism, Gnosticism, Philonism, and the like teachings which abounded in the Alexandrian world. But it was all one world with that in which the early Christians were living. The writings of such men as Origen, Plotinus, and Augustine witness to the inevitable give and take of the time.

Jesus called himself the Son of God and also the Son of Man; but he laid little stress on who he was or what he was, and much upon the teachings of the Kingdom. In declaring that he was more than a man and divine, Paul and his other followers, whether they were right or wrong, opened up a vast field of argument. Was Jesus God? Or had God created him? Was he identical with God or separate from God? It is not the function of the historian to answer such questions, but he is bound to note them, and to note how unavoidable they were, because of the immense influence they have had upon the whole subsequent life of western mankind. By the fourth century of the Christian Era we find all the Christian communities so agitated and exasperated by tortuous and elusive arguments about the nature of God as to be largely negligent of the simpler teachings of charity, service, and brotherhood that Jesus had inculcated.

The chief views that the historian notices are those of the Arians, the Sabellians, and the Trinitarians. The Arians followed Arius, who taught that Christ was less than God; the Sabellians taught that he was a mode or aspect of God; God was Creator, Saviour, and Comforter just as one man may be father, trustee, and guest; the Trinitarians, of whom Athanasius was the great leader, taught that the Father, the Son, and the Holy Ghost were three distinct Persons, but one God. The reader is referred to the Athanasian Creed[1] for the exact expression of the latter mystery, and for the alarming consequences to him of any failure to grasp and believe it. To Gibbon he must go for a derisive statement of these controversies. The present writer can deal with them neither with awe nor derision; they seem to him, he must confess, a disastrous ebullition of the human mind entirely inconsistent with the plain account of Jesus preserved for us in the gospels. Orthodoxy became a test not only for Christian office, but for Christian trade and help. A small point of doctrine might mean affluence or beggary to a man. It is difficult to read the surviving literature of the time without a strong sense of the dogmatism, the spites, rivalries, and pedantries of the men who tore Christianity to pieces for the sake of these theological refinements. Most of the Trinitarian disputants—for it is chiefly Trinitarian documents that survive—accuse their antagonists, probably with truth, of mean and secondary motives, but they do so in a manner that betrays their own base spirit very clearly. Arius, for example, is accused of adopting heretical opinions because he was not appointed Bishop of Alexandria. Riots and excommunications and banishments punctuated these controversies, and finally came official persecutions. These fine differences about the constitution of the Deity interwove with politics and international disputes. Men who quarrelled over business affairs, wives who wished to annoy their husbands, developed antagonistic views upon this exalted theme. Most of the barbarian invaders of the empire were Arians; probably because

[1] In any English prayer book of the Episcopalian Church. The Athanasian Creed embodies the view of Athanasius, but probably was not composed by him.

their simple minds found the Trinitarian position incomprehensible.

It is easy for the sceptic to mock at these disputes. But even if we think that these attempts to say exactly how God was related to himself were presumptuous and intellectually monstrous, nevertheless we are bound to recognize that beneath these preposterous refinements of impossible dogmas there lay often a real passion for truth—even if it was truth ill conceived. Both sides produced genuine martyrs. And the zeal of these controversies, though it is a base and often malicious zeal, did at any rate make the Christian sects very energetically propagandist and educational. Moreover, because the history of the Christian body in the fourth and fifth centuries is largely a record of these unhappy disputes, that must not blind us to the fact that the spirit of Jesus did live and ennoble many lives among the Christians. The text of the gospels, though it was probably tampered with during this period, was not destroyed, and Jesus of Nazareth, in his own manifest inimitable greatness, still taught through that text. Nor did these unhappy quarrels prevent Christianity from maintaining a united front against gladiatorial shows and against the degrading worship of idols and of the god-Cæsar.

§ 6

So far as it challenged the divinity of Cæsar and the characteristic institutions of the empire, Christianity is to be regarded as a rebellious and disintegrating movement, and so it was regarded by most of the emperors before Constantine the Great. It encountered considerable hostility, and at last systematic attempts to suppress it. Decius was the first emperor to organize an official persecution, and the great era of the martyrs was in the time of Diocletian (303 and following years). The persecution of Diocletian was indeed the crowning struggle of the old idea of the god-emperor against the already great and powerful organization that denied his divinity. Diocletian had reoganized the monarchy upon lines of extreme absolutism; he had abolished the last vestiges of republican institutions; he was the first emperor to surround himself completely with the awe-inspiring etiquette of an eastern monarch. He was forced by the logic of his assumptions to attempt the complete eradication of a system that flatly denied them. The test in the persecution was that the Christian was required to offer sacrifice to the emperor.

"Though Diocletian, still averse to the effusion of blood, had moderated the fury of Galerius, who proposed that everyone refusing to offer sacrifice should immediately be burnt alive, the penalties inflicted on the obstinacy of the Christians might be deemed sufficiently rigorous and effectual. It was enacted that their churches, in all the provinces of the empire, should be demolished to their foundations; and the punishment of death was denounced against all who should presume to hold any secret assemblies for the purpose of religious worship. The philosophers, who now assumed the unworthy office of directing the blind zeal of persecution, and diligently studied the nature and genius of the Christian religion; and as they were not ignorant that the speculative doctrines of the faith were supposed to be contained in the writings of the prophets, of the evangelists, and of the apostles, they most probably suggested the order that the bishops and presbyters should deliver all their sacred books into the hands of the magistrates, who were commanded, under the severest penalties, to burn them in a public and solemn manner. By the same edict, the property of the church was at once confiscated; and the several parts of which it might consist were either sold to the highest bidder, united to the imperial domain, bestowed on the cities or corporations, or granted to the solicitations of rapacious courtiers. After taking such effectual measures to abolish the worship, and to dissolve the government of the Christians, it was thought necessary to subject to the most intolerable hardships the condition of those perverse individuals who should still reject the religion of nature, of Rome, and of their ancestors. Persons of a liberal birth were declared incapable of holding any honours or employments; slaves were for ever deprived of the hopes of freedom; and the whole body of the Christians were put out of the protection of the law. The judges were authorized to hear and to determine every action that was brought against a Christian; but the Christians were not permitted to complain of any injury which they themselves had suffered; and those unfortunate sectaries were exposed to the severity, while they were excluded from the benefits, of public justice. . . . This edict was scarcely exhibited to the public view, in the most conspicuous place in Nicomedia, before it was torn down by the hands of a Christian, who expressed at the same time, by the bitterest of invectives, his contempt as well as abhorrence for such impious and tyrannical governors. His offence, according to the mildest laws, amounted to treason, and deserved death, and if it be true that he was a person of rank and education, those circumstances could serve only to aggravate his guilt. He was burnt, or rather roasted, by a slow fire; and his executioners, zealous to revenge the personal insult which had been offered to the emperors, exhausted every refinement of cruelty without being able to subdue his patience, or to alter the steady and insulting smile which in his dying agonies he still preserved in his countenance."[1]

So with the death of this unnamed martyr the great persecution opened. But, as Gibbon points out, our information as to its severity is of very doubtful value. He estimates the total of victims as about two thousand, and contrasts this with the known multitudes of Christians martyred by their fellow-Christians during the period of the Reformation. Gibbon was strongly prejudiced against Christianity, and here he seems disposed to minimize the fortitude and sufferings of the Christians. In many provinces, no doubt, there must have been a great reluctance to enforce the edict. But there was a hunt for the copies of Holy Writ, and in many places a systematic destruction of Christian churches. There were tortures and executions, as well as a great crowding of the gaols with Christian presbyters and bishops. We have to remember that the Christian community was now a very considerable element of the population, and that an influential proportion of the officials charged with the execution of the edict were themselves of the proscribed faith. Galerius, who was in control of the eastern provinces, was among the most vigorous of the persecutors, but in the end, on his death bed (371), he realized the futility of his attacks upon this huge community, and granted toleration in an edict, the gist of which Gibbon translates as follows:—

"Among the important cares which have occupied our mind for the utility and preservation of the empire, it was our intention to correct and re-establish all things according to the ancient laws and public discipline of the Romans. We were particularly desirous of reclaiming into the way of reason and nature

[1] Gibbon, *The Decline and Fall of the Roman Empire*, chap. xvi.

the deluded Christians who had renounced the religion and ceremonies instituted by their fathers; and presumptuously despising the practice of antiquity, had invented extravagant laws and opinions according to the dictates of their fancy, and had collected a various society from the different provinces of our empire. The edicts which we have published to enforce the worship of the gods having exposed many of the Christians to danger and distress, many having suffered death, and many more who still persist in their impious folly, being left destitute of any public exercise of religion, we are disposed to extend to those unhappy men the effects of our wonted clemency. We permit them, therefore, freely to profess their private opinions and to assemble in their conventicles without fear or molestation, provided always that they preserve a due respect to the established laws and government. By another rescript we shall signify our intentions to the judges and magistrates; and we hope that our indulgence will engage the Christians to offer up their prayers to the deity whom they adore, for our safety and prosperity, for their own, and for that of the republic."

In a few years Constantine the Great was reigning, first as associated emperor (312) and then as the sole ruler (324), and the severer trials of Christianity were over. If Christianity was a rebellious and destructive force towards a pagan Rome, it was a unifying and organizing force within its own communion. This fact the genius of Constantine grasped. The spirit of Jesus, for all the doctrinal dissensions that prevailed, made a great freemasonry throughout and even beyond the limits of the empire. The faith was spreading among the barbarians beyond the border; it had extended into Persia and Central Asia. It provided the only hope of moral solidarity he could discern in the great welter of narrow views and self-seeking over which he had to rule. It, and it alone, had the facilities for organizing *will,* for the need of which the empire was falling to pieces like a piece of rotten cloth. In 312 Constantine had to fight for Rome and his position against Maxentius. He put the Christian monogram upon the shields and banners of his troops and claimed that the God of the Christians had fought for him in his complete victory at the battle of the Milvian Bridge just outside Rome. By this act he renounced all those pretensions to divinity that the vanity of Alexander the Great had first brought into the western world, and with the applause and enthusiastic support of the Christians he established himself as a monarch more absolute even than Diocletian.

In a few years' time Christianity had become the official religion of the empire, and in A.D. 337 Constantine upon his death-bed was baptized as a Christian.

§ 7

The figure of Constantine the Great is at least as cardinal in history as that of Alexander the Great or Augustus Cæsar. We know very little of his personality or of his private life; no Plutarch, no Suetonius, has preserved any intimate and living details about him. Abuse we have of him from his enemies, and much obviously fulsome panegyric to set against it; but none of these writers give us a living character of him; he is a party symbol for them, a partisan flag. It is stated by the hostile Zosimus that, like Sargon I, he was of illegitimate birth; his father was a distinguished general and his mother, Helena, an innkeeper's daughter of Nish in Serbia. Gibbon, however, is of opinion that there was a valid marriage. In any case it was a lowly marriage, and the personal genius of Constantine prevailed against serious disadvantages. He was comparatively illiterate, he knew little or no Greek. It appears to be true that he banished his eldest son Crispus, and caused him to be executed at the instigation of the young man's stepmother, Fausta; and it is also recorded that he was afterwards convinced of the innocence of Crispus, and caused Fausta to be executed—according to one account by being boiled to death in her bath, and according to another by being exposed naked to wild beasts on a desolate mountain—while there is also very satisfactory documentary evidence that she survived him. If she was executed, the fact remains that her three sons, together with two nephews, became the appointed heirs of Constantine. Clearly there is nothing solid to be got from this libellous tangle, and such soufflé as is possible with these scanty materials is to be found admirably done by Gibbon (chap. xviii.). Gibbon, because of his anti-Christian animus, is hostile to Constantine; but he admits that he was temperate and chaste. He accuses him of prodigality because of his great public buildings, and of being vain and dissolute (!)

because in his old age he wore a wig—Gibbon wore his own hair tied with a becoming black bow—and a diadem and magnificent robes. But all the later emperors after Diocletian wore diadems and magnificent robes.

Yet if the personality of Constantine the Great remains phantom-like, if the particulars of his domestic life reveal nothing but a vague tragedy, we can still guess at much that was in his mind. It must, in the closing years of his life, have been a very lonely mind. He was more of an autocrat than any previous emperor had been—that is to say, he had less counsel and help. No class of public-spirited and trustworthy men remained; no senate nor council shared and developed his schemes. How much he apprehended the geographical weakness of the empire, how far he saw the complete disaster that was now so near, we can only guess. He made his real capital at Nicomedia in Bithynia; Constantinople across the Bosphorus was still being built when he died. Like Diocletian, he seems to have realized the broken-backed outline of his dominions, and to have concentrated his attention on foreign affairs and more particularly on the affairs of Hungary, South Russia, and the Black Sea. He reorganized all the official machinery of the empire; he gave it a new constitution and sought to establish a dynasty. He was a restless remaker of things; the social confusion he tried to fix by assisting in the development of a caste system. This was following up the work of his great predecessor, Diocletian. He tried to make a caste of the peasants and small cultivators, and to restrict them from moving from their holdings. In fact he sought to make them serfs. The supply of slave labour had fallen off because the empire was no longer an invading but an invaded power; he turned to serfdom as the remedy. His creative efforts necessitated unprecedentedly heavy taxation. All these things point to a lonely and forcible mind. It is in his manifest understanding of the need of some unifying moral force if the empire was to hold together that his claim to originality lies.

It was only after he had turned to Christianity that he seems to have realized the fierce dissensions of the theologians. He made a great effort to reconcile these differences in order to have one uniform and harmonious teaching in the community, and at his initiative a general council of the Church was held at Nicæa, a town near Nicomedia and over against Constantinople, in 325. Eusebius gives a curious account of this strange gathering, over which the Emperor, although he was not yet a baptized Christian, presided. It was not his first council of the Church, for he had already (in 313) presided over a council at Arles. He sat in the midst of the council of Nicæa upon a golden throne, and as he had little Greek, we must suppose he was reduced to watching the countenances and gestures of the debaters, and listening to their intonations. The council was a stormy one. When old Arius rose to speak, one Nicholas of Myra struck him in the face, and afterwards many ran out, thrusting their fingers into their ears in affected horror at the old man's heresies. One is tempted to imagine the great Emperor, deeply anxious for the soul of his empire, firmly resolved to end these divisions, bending towards his interpreters to ask them the meaning of the uproar.

The views that prevailed at Nicæa are embodied in the Nicene Creed, a strictly Trinitarian statement, and the Emperor sustained the Trinitarian position. But afterwards, when Athanasius bore too hardly upon the Arians, he had him banished from Alexandria; and when the church at Alexandria would have excommunicated Arius, he obliged it to readmit him to communion.

§ 8

This date 325 A.D. is a very convenient date in our history. It is the date of the first complete general ("œcumenical") council of the entire Christian world. (That at Arles we have mentioned had been a gathering of only the western half.) It marks the definite entry upon the stage of human affairs of the Christian church and of Christianity as it is generally understood in the world to-day. It marks the exact definition of Christian teaching by the Nicene Creed.

It is necessary that we should recall the reader's attention to the profound differences between this fully developed Christianity of Nicæa and the teaching of Jesus of Nazareth. All Christians hold that the latter is completely contained in the former, but that is a question outside our province. What is clearly apparent is that the teaching of Jesus of Nazareth was a *prophetic teaching* of the new type that began with the Hebrew prophets. It was not priestly, it had no consecrated temple and no altar. It had no rites and ceremonies. Its sacrifice was "a broken and a contrite heart." Its only organization was an organization of preachers, and its chief function was the sermon. But the fully fledged Christianity of the fourth century, though it preserved as its nucleus the teachings of Jesus in the gospels, was mainly a *priestly religion* of a type already familiar to the world for thousands of years. The centre of its elaborate ritual was an altar, and the essential act of worship the sacrifice, by a consecrated priest, of the mass. And it had a rapidly developing organization of deacons, priests, and bishops.

But if Christianity had taken on an extraordinary outward resemblance to the cults of Serapis, Ammon, or Bel-Marduk, we must remember that even its priestcraft had certain novel features. Nowhere did it possess any quasi-divine image of God. There was no head temple containing the god, because God was everywhere. There was no holy of holies. Its widespread altars were all addressed to the unseen universal Trinity. Even in its most archaic aspects there was in Christianity something new.

A very important thing for us to note is the rôle played by the Emperor in the fixation of Christianity. Not only was the council of Nicæa assembled by Constantine the Great, but all the great councils, the two at Constantinople (381 and 553), Ephesus (431), and Chalcedon (451), were called together by the imperial power. And it is very manifest that in much of the history of Christianity at this time the spirit of Constantine the Great is as evident as, or more evident than, the spirit of Jesus. He was, we have said, a pure autocrat. The last vestiges of Roman republicanism had vanished in the days of Aurelian and Diocletian. To the best of his lights he was trying to remake the crazy empire while there was yet time, and he worked without any councillors, any public opinion, or any sense of the need of such aids and checks. The idea of stamping out all controversy and division, stamping out all thought, by imposing one dogmatic creed upon all believers, is an altogether autocratic idea, it is the idea of the single-handed man who feels that to work at all he must be free from opposition and criticism. The history of the Church under his influence becomes now therefore a history of the violent struggles that were bound to follow upon his sudden and rough summons to unanimity. From him the Church acquired the disposition to be authoritative and unquestioned, to develop a centralized organization and run parallel to the empire.

A second great autocrat who presently contributed to the stamping upon Catholic Christianity of a distinctly authoritative character was Theodosius I, Theodosius the Great (379-395). He forbade the unorthodox to hold meetings, handed over all churches to the Trinitarians, and overthrew the heathen temples, throughout the empire, and in 390 he caused the great statue of Serapis at Alexandria to be destroyed. There was to be no rivalry, no qualification to the rigid unity of the Church.

Here we cannot tell of the vast internal troubles of the Church, its indigestions of heresy; of Arians and Paulicians, of Gnostics and Manicheans. Had it been less authoritative and more tolerant of intellectual variety, it might perhaps have been a still more powerful body than it became. But, in spite of all these disorders, it did for some time maintain a conception of human unity more intimate and far wider than was ever achieved before. By the fifth century Christendom was already becoming greater, sturdier, and more enduring than any empire had ever been, because it was something not merely imposed upon men, but interwoven with the texture of their minds. It reached out far beyond the utmost limits of the empire, into Armenia, Persia, Abyssinia, Ireland, Germany, India, and Turkestan. "Though made up of widely scattered congregations, it was thought of as one body of Christ, one people of God. This ideal unity found expression in many ways. Intercommunication between the various Christian communities was very active. Christians upon a journey were always sure of a warm welcome and hospitable entertainment from their fellow-disciples. Messengers and letters were sent freely from one church to another. Missionaries and evangelists went continually from place to place. Documents of various kinds, including gospels and apostolic epistles, circulated widely. Thus in various ways the feeling of unity found expression, and the development of widely separated parts of Christendom conformed more or less closely to a common type."[1]

Christendom retained at least the formal tradition of this general unity of spirit until 1054, when the Latin-speaking Western church and the main and original Greek-speaking

[1] *Encyclopaedia Britannica,* art. "Church History," p. 336.

church, the "Orthodox" church, severed themselves from one another, ostensibly upon the question of adding two words to the creed. The older creed had declared that the "Holy Ghost proceeded from the Father." The Latins wanted to add, and did add "*Filioque*" (= and from the son), and placed the Greeks out of their communion because they would not follow this lead. But already as early as the fifth century the Christians in Eastern Syria, Persia, Central Asia—there were churches at Merv, Herat, and Samarkand—and India had detached themselves on a similar score. These extremely interesting Asiatic Christians are known in history as the Nestorian Church, and their influence extended in China. The Egyptian and Abyssinian churches also detached themselves very early upon similarly inexplicable points. Long before this formal separation of the Latin and Greek-speaking halves of the main church, however, there was a practical separation following upon the breaking up of the empire. Their conditions diverged from the first. While the Greek-speaking Eastern Empire held together and the emperor at Constantinople remained dominant in the Church, the Latin half of the empire, as we have already told, collapsed, and left the Church free of any such imperial control. Moreover, while ecclesiastical authority in the empire of Constantinople was divided between the high-bishops, or patriarchs, of Constantinople, Antioch, Alexandria, and Jerusalem, authority in the West was concentrated in the Patriarch, or Pope, of Rome. The Bishop of Rome had always been recognized as first among the patriarchs, and all these things conspired to justify exceptional pretensions upon his part to a quasi-imperial authority. With the final fall of the Western Empire, he took over the ancient title of *pontifex maximus* which the emperors had held, and so became the supreme sacrificial priest of the Roman tradition. Over the Christians of the West his supremacy was fully recognized, but from the beginning it had to be urged with discretion within the dominions of the Eastern emperor and the jurisdictions of the other four patriarchs.

Ideas of worldly rule by the Church were already prevalent in the fourth century. St. Augustine, a citizen of Hippo in North Africa, who wrote between 354 and 430, gave expression to the developing political ideas of the Church in his book *The City of God*. *The City of God* leads the mind very directly towards the possibility of making the world into a theological and organized Kingdom of Heaven. The city, as Augustine puts it, is "a spiritual society of the predestined faithful," but the step from that to a political application was not a very wide one. The Church was to be the ruler of the world over all nations, the divinely led ruling power over a great league of terrestrial states. In later years these ideas developed into a definite political theory and policy. As the barbarian races settled and became Christian, the Pope began to claim an overlordship of their kings. In a few centuries the Pope had become in theory, and to a certain extent in practice, the high priest, censor, judge, and divine monarch of Christendom; his influence extended in the west far beyond the utmost range of the old empire, to Ireland, Norway and Sweden, and over all Germany. For more than a thousand years this idea of the unity of Christendom, of Christendom as a sort of vast Amphictyony, whose members even in war time were restrained from many extremities by the idea of a common brotherhood and a common loyalty to the Church, dominated Europe. The history of Europe from the fifth century onward to the fifteenth is very largely the history of the failure of this great idea of a divine world government to realize itself in practice.

§ 9

We have already given an account in the previous chapter of the chief irruptions of the barbarian races. We may now, with the help of a map, make a brief review of the political divisions of Europe at the close of the fifth century. No vestige of the Western Empire, the original Roman Empire, remained as a distinct and separate political division. Politically it was completely broken up. Over many parts of Europe a sort of legendary overlordship of the Hellenic Eastern Empire as *the* Empire held its place in men's minds. The emperor at Constantinople was, in theory at least, still emperor. In Britain, the quite barbaric Teutonic Angles, Saxons and Jutes had conquered the eastern half of England; in the west of the island the Britons still held out, but were gradually being forced back into Wales and Cornwall. The Anglo-Saxons seem to have been among the most ruthless and effective of barbarian conquerors, for, wherever they prevailed, their language completely replaced the Keltic or Latin speech—it is not certain which—used by the British. These Anglo-Saxons were as yet not Christianized. Most of Gaul, Holland, and the Rhineland was under the fairly vigorous, Christianized, and much more civilized kingdom of the Franks. But the Rhone valley was under the separate kingdom of the Burgundians. Spain and some of the south of France were under the rule of the Visigoths, but the Suevi were in possession of the north-west corner of the peninsula. Of the Vandal kingdom in Africa we have already written; and Italy, still in its population and habits Roman, came under the rule of the Ostrogoths. There was no emperor left in Rome; Theodoric I ruled there as the first of a line of Gothic kings, and his rule extended across the Alps into Pannonia and down the Adriatic to Dalmatia and Serbia. To the east of the Gothic kingdom the emperors of Constantinople ruled definitely. The Bulgars were still at this time a Mongolian tribe of horse-riding nomads in the region of the Volga; the Aryan Serbs had recently come southward to the shores of the Black Sea into the original home of the Visigoths; the Turko-Finnish Magyars were not yet in Europe. The Lombards were as yet north of the Danube.

The sixth century was marked by a phase of vigour on the part of the Eastern Empire under the Emperor Justinian (527-565). The Vandal kingdom was recovered in 534; the Goths were expelled from Italy in 553. So soon as Justinian was dead (565), the Lombards descended into Italy and settled in Lombardy, but they left Ravenna, Rome, Southern Italy, and North Africa under the rule of the Eastern Empire.

Such was the political condition of the world in which the idea of Christendom developed. The daily life of that time was going on at a very low level indeed physically, intellectually, and morally. It is frequently said that Europe in the sixth and seventh centuries relapsed into barbarism, but that does not express the reality of the case. It is far more correct to say that the civilization of the Roman empire had passed into a phase of extreme demoralization. Barbarism is a social order of an elementary type, orderly within its limits; but the state of Europe beneath its political fragmentation was a social disorder. Its *morale* was not that of a kraal, but that of a slum. In a savage kraal a savage knows that he belongs to a community, and lives and acts accordingly; in a slum, the individual neither knows of nor acts in relation to any greater being.

Only very slowly and weakly did Christianity restore that lost sense of community and teach men to rally about the idea of Christendom. The social and economic structure of the Roman Empire was in ruins. That civilization had been a civilization of wealth and political power sustained by the limitation and slavery of the great mass of mankind. It had presented a spectacle of outward splendour and luxurious refinement, but beneath that brave outward show were cruelty, stupidity, and stagnation. It had to break down, it had to be removed before anything better could replace it.

We have already called attention to its intellectual deadness. For three centuries it had produced neither science nor literature of any importance. It is only where men are to be found neither too rich and powerful to be tempted into extravagant indulgences nor too poor and limited to care for anything beyond the daily need that those disinterested curiosities and serene impulses can have play that give sane philosophy and science and great art to the world, and the plutocracy of Rome had made such a class impossible. When men and women are unlimited and unrestrained, the evidence of history shows clearly that they are all liable to become monsters of self-indulgence; when, on the other hand, they are driven and unhappy, then their impulse is towards immoderate tragical resorts, towards wild revolts or towards the austerities and intensities of religion.

It is not perhaps true to say that the world became miserable in these "dark ages" to which we have now come; much nearer the truth is it to say that the violent and vulgar fraud of Roman imperialism, that world of politicians, adventurers, landowners and financiers, collapsed into a sea of misery that was already there. Our histories of these times are very imperfect: there were few places where men could write, and little encouragement to write at all; no one was sure even of the safety of his manuscript or the possibility of its being read. But we know enough to tell that this age was an age not merely of war and robbery, but of famine and pestilence. No effective sanitary organization had yet come into the world, and the migrations of the time must have destroyed whatever hygienic balance had been established. Attila's ravages in North Italy were checked by an outbreak of fever in 452. There was a great epidemic of bubonic plague towards the end of the reign of Justinian (565) which did much to weaken the defence of Italy against the Lombards. In 543 ten thousand

people had died in one day in Constantinople. (Gibbon says "each day.") Plague was raging in Rome in 590. The seventh century was also a plague-striken century. The Englishman Bede, one of the few writers of the time, records pestilences in England in 664, 672, 678, and 683, no fewer than four in twenty years! Gibbon couples the Justinian epidemic with the great comet of 531, and with the very frequent and serious earthquakes of that reign. "Many cities of the east were left vacant, and in several districts of Italy the harvest and the vintage withered on the ground." He alleges "a visible decrease of the human species which has never been made good in some of the fairest countries of the globe." To many in those dark days it seemed that all learning and all that made life seemly and desirable was perishing.

How far the common lot was unhappier under these conditions of squalor and insecurity than it had been under the grinding order of the imperial system it is impossible to say. There was possibly much local variation, the rule of violent bullies here and a good-tempered freedom there, famine this year and plenty the next. If robbers abounded, tax-gatherers and creditors had disappeared. Such kings as those of the Frankish and Gothic kingdoms were really phantom rulers to most of their so-called subjects; the life of each district went on at a low level, with little trade or travel. Greater or lesser areas of countryside would be dominated by some able person, claiming with more or less justice the title of lord or count or duke from the tradition of the later empire or from the king. Such local nobles would assemble bands of retainers and build themselves strongholds. Often they adapted pre-existing buildings. The Colosseum at Rome, for example, the arena of many great gladiatorial shows, was converted into a fortress, and so was the amphitheatre at Arles. So also was the great tomb of Hadrian at Rome. In the decaying and now insanitary towns and cities shrunken bodies of artisans would hold together and serve the needs of the cultivating villages about them by their industry, placing themselves under the protection of some adjacent noble.

§ 10

A very important share in the social recrystallization that went on in the sixth and seventh centuries after the breakdown and fusion of the fourth and fifth was taken by the Christian monastic orders that were now arising in the Western world.

Monasteries had existed in the world before Christianity. During the period of social unhappiness among the Jews before the time of Jesus of Nazareth, there was a sect of Essenes who lived apart in communities vowed to austere lives of solitude, purity, and self-denial. Buddhism, too, had developed its communities of men who withdrew from the general effort and commerce of the world to lead lives of austerity and contemplation. Indeed, the story of Buddha as we have told it, shows that such ideas must have prevailed in India long before his time, and that at last he repudiated them. Quite early in the history of Christianity there arose a similar movement away from the competition and heat and stress of the daily life of men. In Egypt, particularly, great numbers of men and women went out into the desert and there lived solitary lives of prayer and contemplation, living in absolute poverty in caves or under rocks, and subsisting on the chance alms of those whom their holiness impressed. Such lives would signify little to the historian, they are indeed of their very nature lives withdrawn from history, were it not for the turn this monastic tendency presently took among the more energetic and practical Europeans.

One of the central figures in the story of the development of monasticism in Europe is St. Benedict, who lived between 480 and 544. He was born at Spoleto in Italy, and he was a young man of good family and ability. The shadow of the times fell upon him, and, like Buddha, he took to the religious life and at first set no limit to his austerities. Fifty miles from Rome is Subiaco, and there at the end of a gorge of the Anio, beneath a jungle growth of weeds and bushes, rose a deserted palace built by the Emperor Nero, overlooking an artificial lake that had been made in those days of departed prosperity by damming back the waters of the river. Here, with a hair shirt as his chief possession, Benedict took up his quarters in a cave in the high southward-looking cliff that overhangs the stream, in so inaccessible a position that his food had to be lowered to him on a cord by a faithful admirer. Three years he lived here, and his fame spread as Buddha's did nearly a thousand years before under similar circumstances.

As in the case of Buddha, the story of Benedict has been overlaid by foolish and credulous disciples with a mass of silly stories of miracles and manifestations. But presently we find him, no longer engaged in self-torment, but controlling a group of twelve monasteries, and the resort of a great number of people. Youths are brought to him to be educated, and the whole character of his life has changed.

From Subiaco he moved further southward to Monte Cassino, half-way between Rome and Naples, a lonely and beautiful mountain, in the midst of a great circle of majestic heights.

Here, it is interesting to note that in the sixth century A.D. he found a temple of Apollo and a sacred grove and the countryside still worshipping at this shrine. His first labours had to be missionary labours, and it was with difficulty that he persuaded the simple pagans to demolish their temple and cut down their grove. The establishment upon Monte Cassino became a famous and powerful centre within the lifetime of its founder. Mixed up with the imbecile inventions of marvel-loving monks about demons exorcised, disciples walking on the water, and dead children restored to life, we can still detect something of the real spirit of Benedict. Particularly significant are the stories that represent him as discouraging extreme mortification. He sent a damping message to a solitary who had invented a new degree in saintliness by chaining himself to a rock in a narrow cave. "Break thy chain," said Benedict, "for the true servant of God is chained not to rocks by iron, but to righteousness by Christ."

And next to the discouragement of solitary self-torture it is Benedict's distinction that he insisted upon hard work. Through the legends shines the clear indication of the trouble made by his patrician students and disciples who found themselves obliged to toil instead of leading lives of leisurely austerity under the ministrations of the lower class brethren. A third remarkable thing about Benedict was his political influence. He set himself to reconcile Goths and Italians, and it is clear that Totila, his Gothic king, came to him for counsel and was greatly influenced by him. When Totila retook Naples from the Greeks, the Goths protected the women from insult and treated even the captured soldiers with humanity. When Belisarius, Justinian's general, had taken the same place ten years previously, he had celebrated his triumph by a general massacre.

Now the monastic organization of Benedict was a very great beginning in the western world. One of his prominent followers was Pope Gregory the Great (540-604), the first monk to become pope (590); he was one of the most capable and energetic of the popes, sending successful missions to the unconverted, and particularly to the Anglo-Saxons. He ruled in Rome like an independent king, organizing armies, making treaties. To his influence is due the imposition of the Benedictine rule upon nearly the whole of Latin monasticism.

Closely associated with these two names in the development

of a civilizing monasticism out of the merely egotistic mortifications of the early recluses is that of Cassiodorus (490-585). He was evidently much senior to Pope Gregory, and younger by ten years than Benedict, and, like these two, he belonged to a patrician family, a Syrian family settled in Italy. He had a considerable official career under the Gothic kings; and when, between 545 and 553, the overthrow of those kings and the great pestilence paved the way for the new barbaric rule of the Lombards, he took refuge in a monastic career. He founded a monastery upon his private estates, and set the monks he gathered to work in quite the Benedictine fashion, though whether his monks actually followed the Benedictine rule that was being formulated about the same time from Monte Cassino we do not know. But there can be no question of his influence upon the development of this great working, teaching, and studying order. It is evident that he was profoundly impressed by the universal decay of education and the possible loss of all learning and of the ancient literature by the world; and from the first he directed his brethren to the task of preserving and restoring these things. He collected ancient MSS. and caused them to be copied. He made sundials, water clocks, and similar apparatus, a little last gleam of experimental science in the gathering darkness. He wrote a history of the Gothic kings, and, what is more significant of his sense of the needs of the time, he produced a series of school books on the liberal arts and a grammar. Probably his influence was even greater than that of St. Benedict in making monasticism into a powerful instrument for the restoration of social order in the Western world.

The spread of monasteries of the Benedictine order or type in the seventh and eighth centuries was very considerable. Everywhere we find them as centres of light, restoring, maintaining, and raising the standard of cultivation, preserving some sort of elementary education, spreading useful arts, multiplying and storing books, and keeping before the eyes of the world the spectacle and example of a social backbone. For eight centuries thenceforth the European monastic system remained a system of patches and fibres of enlightenment in what might otherwise have been a wholly chaotic world. Closely associated with the Benedictine monasteries were the schools that grew presently into the mediæval universities. The schools of the Roman world had been altogether swept away in the general social breakdown. There was a time when very few priests in Britain or Gaul could read the gospel or their service books. Only gradually was teaching restored to the world. But when it was restored, it came back not as the duty work of a learned slave, but as the religious service of a special class of devoted men.

In the east also there was a breach of educational continuity, but there the cause was not so much social disorder as religious intolerance, and the break was by no means so complete. Justinian closed and dispersed the schools of Athens (529), but he did this very largely in order to destroy a rival to the new school he was setting up in Constantinople, which was more directly under imperial control. Since the new Latin learning of the developing western universities had no text-books and literature of its own, it had, in spite of its strong theological bias to the contrary, to depend very largely upon the Latin classics and the Latin translations of the Greek literature. It was obliged to preserve far more of that splendid literature than it had a mind to do.

XXX

SEVEN CENTURIES IN ASIA (CIRCA 50 B.C. TO A.D. 650)

§ 1. *Justinian the Great.* § 2. *The Sassanid Empire in Persia.* § 3. *The Decay of Syria under the Sassanids.* § 4. *The First Message from Islam.* § 5. *Zoroaster and Mani.* § 6. *Hunnish Peoples in Central Asia and India.* § 7. *The Great Age of China.* § 8. *Intellectual Fetters of China.* § 9. *The Travels of Yuan Chwang.*

§ 1

IN the preceding two chapters we have concentrated our attention chiefly on the collapse in the comparatively short space of four centuries of the political and social order of the western part of the great Roman Empire of Cæsar and Trajan. We have dwelt upon the completeness of that collapse. To any intelligent and public-spirited mind living in the time and under the circumstances of St. Benedict or Cassiodorus, it must have seemed, indeed, as if the light of civilization was waning and near extinction. But with the longer views a study of universal history gives us, we can view those centuries of shadow as a phase, and probably a necessary phase, in the onward march of social and political ideas and understandings. And if, during that time, a dark sense of calamity rested upon Western Europe, we must remember that over large portions of the world there was no retrogression.

With their Western prepossessions European writers are much too prone to underrate the tenacity of the Eastern empire that centred upon Constantinople. This empire embodied a tradition much more ancient than that of Rome. If the reader will look at the map we have given of its extent in the sixth century, and if he will reflect that its official language had then become Greek, he will realize that what we are dealing with here is only nominally a branch of the Roman Empire; it is really the Hellenic Empire of which Herodotus dreamt and which Alexander the Great founded. True it called itself Roman and its people "Romans," and to this day modern Greek is called "Romaic." True also that Constantine the Great knew no Greek and that Justinian's accent was bad. These superficialities of name and form cannot alter the fact that the empire was in reality Hellenic, with a past of six centuries at the time of Constantine the Great, and that while the real Roman Empire crumpled up completely in four centuries, this Hellenic "Roman Empire" held out for more than eleven—from 312, the beginning of the reign of Constantine the Great, to 1453, when Constantinople fell to the Ottoman Turks.

And while we have had to tell of something like a complete social collapse in the west, there were no such equivalent breakdowns in the east. Towns and cities flourished, the countryside was well cultivated, trade went on. For many centuries Constantinople was the greatest and richest city in the world. We will not trouble ourselves here with the names and follies, the crimes and intrigues, of its tale of emperors. As with most monarchs of great states, they did not guide their empire; they were carried by it. We have already dealt at some length with Constantine the Great (312-337), we have mentioned Theodosius the Great (379-395), who for a little while reunited the empire, and Justinian I (527-565). Presently we shall tell something of Heraclius (610-641). Justinian, like Constantine, may have had Slav blood in his veins. He was a man of great ambition and great organizing power, and he had the good fortune to be married to a woman of equal or greater ability, the Empress Theodora, who had in her youth been an actress of doubtful reputation. But his ambitious attempts to restore the ancient greatness of the empire probably overtaxed its resources. As we have told, he reconquered the African province from the Vandals and most of Italy from the Goths. He also recovered the South of Spain. He built the great and beautiful church of Sancta Sophia in Constantinople, founded a university, and codified the law.[1] But against this we must set his closing of the schools

[1] Great importance is attached to this task by historians, including one of the editors of this history. We are told that the essential contribution

of Athens. Meanwhile a great plague swept the world, and at his death this renewed and expanded empire of his collapsed like a pricked bladder. The greater part of his Italian conquests was lost to the Lombards. Italy was indeed at that time almost a desert; the Lombard historians assert they came into an empty country. The Avars and Slavs struck down from the Danube country towards the Adriatic, Slav populations establishing themselves in what is now Serbia, Croatia, and Dalmatia, to become the Yugo-Slavs of to-day. Moreover, a great and exhausting struggle began with the Sassanid Empire in Persia.

But before we say anything of this struggle, in which the Persians thrice came near to taking Constantinople, and which was decided by a great Persian defeat at Nineveh (627), it is necessary to sketch very briefly the history of Persia from the Parthian days.

§ 2

We have already drawn a comparison between the brief four centuries of Roman imperialism and the obstinate vitality of the imperialism of the Euphrates-Tigris country. We have glanced very transitorily at the Hellenized Bactrian and Seleucid monarchies that flourished in the eastern half of Alexander's area of conquest for three centuries, and told how the Parthians came down into Mesopotamia in the last century B.C. We have described the battle of Carrhæ and the end of Crassus. Thereafter for two centuries and a half the Parthian dynasty of the Arsacids ruled in the east and the Roman in the west, with Armenia and Syria between them, and the boundaries shifted east and west as either side grew stronger.

of Rome to the inheritance of mankind is the idea of society founded on *law*, and that this exploit of Justinian was the crown of the gift. The writer is ill-equipped to estimate the peculiar value of Roman legalism to mankind. Existing law seems to him to be based upon a confused foundation of conventions, arbitrary assumptions, and working fictions about human relationship, and to be a very impracticable and antiquated system indeed; he is persuaded that a time will come when the whole theory and practice of law will be recast in the light of a well-developed science of social psychology in accordance with a scientific conception of human society as one developing organization and in definite relationship to a system of moral and intellectual education. He contemplates the law and lawyers of today with a temperamental lack of appreciation. This may have made him negligent of Justinian and unjust to Rome as a whole.

We have marked the utmost eastward extension of the Roman Empire under Trajan (see map to Chap. XXVIII, § 3), and we have noted that about the same time the Indo-Scythians (Chap. XXVIII, § 4) poured down into India.

In 227 occurred a revolution, and the Arsacid dynasty gave way to a more vigorous line, the Sassanid, a national Persian line under Ardashir I. In one respect the empire of Ardashir I presented a curious parallelism with that of Constantine the Great a hundred years later. Ardashir attempted to consolidate it by insisting upon religious unity, and adopted as the state religion the old Persian faith of Zoroaster, of which we shall have more to say later.

This new Sassanid Empire immediately became aggressive, and under Sapor I, the son and successor of Ardashir, took Antioch. We have already noted how the Emperor Valerian was defeated (260) and taken prisoner. But as Sapor was retiring from a victorious march into Asia Minor, he was fallen upon and defeated by Odenathus, the Arab king of a great desert-trading centre, Palmyra.

For a brief time under Odenathus, and then under his widow Zenobia, Palmyra was a considerable state, wedged between the two empires. Then it fell to the Emperor Aurelian, who carried off Zenobia in chains to grace his triumph at Rome (272).

We will not attempt to trace the fluctuating fortunes of the Sassanids during the next three centuries. Throughout that time war between Persia and the empire of Constantinople wasted Asia Minor like a fever. Christianity spread widely and was persecuted, for after the Christianization of Rome the Persian monarch remained the only god-monarch on earth, and he saw in Christianity merely the propaganda of his Byzantine rival. Constantinople became the protector of the Christians and Persia of the Zoroastrians; in a treaty of 422, the one empire agreed to tolerate Zoroastrianism and the other Christianity. In 483, the Christians of the east split off from the Orthodox church and became the Nestorian church; which, as we have already noted, spread its missionaries far and wide throughout Central and Eastern Asia. This separation from Europe, since it freed the Christian bishops of the east from the rule of the Byzantine patriarchs, and so lifted from the Nestorian church the suspicion of political disloyalty, led to a complete toleration of Christianity in Persia. With Chosroes I (531-579) came a last period of Sassanid vigour. He was the contemporary and parallel of Justinian. He reformed taxation, restored the orthodox Zoroastrianism, extended his power into Southern Arabia (Yemen), which he rescued from the rule of Abyssinian Christians, pushed his northern frontier into Western Turkestan, and carried on a series of wars with Justinian. His reputation as an enlightened ruler stood so high, that when Justinian closed the schools of Athens, the last Greek philosophers betook themselves to his court. They sought in him the philosopher king—that mirage which, as we have noted, Confucius and Plato had sought in their day. The philosophers found the atmosphere of orthodox Zoroastrianism even less to their taste than orthodox Christianity, and in 549 Chosroes had the kindness to insert a clause in an armistice with Justinian, permitting their return to Greece, and ensuring that they should not be molested for their pagan philosophy or their transitory pro-Persian behaviour.

It is in connection with Chosroes that we hear now of a new Hunnish people in Central Asia, the Turks, who are, we learn, first in alliance with him and then with Constantinople.

Chosroes II (590-628), the grandson of Chosroes I, experienced extraordinary fluctuations of fortune. At the outset of his career he achieved astonishing successes against the empire of Constantinople. Three times (in 608, 615, and 627) his armies reached Chalcedon, which is over against Constantinople; he took Antioch, Damascus, and Jerusalem (614), and from Jerusalem he carried off a cross, said to be the true cross on which Jesus was crucified, to his capital Ctesiphon. (But some of this or some other true cross had already got to Rome. It had been brought from Jerusalem, it was said, by the "Empress Helena," the idealized and canonized mother of Constantine, a story for which Gibbon displayed small respect.[1]) In 619, Chosroes II conquered that facile country, Egypt. This career of conquest was at last arrested by the Emperor Heraclius (610), who set about restoring the ruined military power of Constantinople. For some time Heraclius avoided a great battle while he gathered his forces. He took the field in good earnest in 623. The Persians experienced a series of defeats culminating in the battle of Nineveh (627); but neither

[1] *The Decline and Fall of the Roman Empire,* chap. xxiii.

side had the strength for the complete defeat of the other. At the end of the struggle there was still an undefeated Persian army upon the Bosphorus, although there were victorious Byzantine forces in Mesopotamia. In 628 Chosroes II was deposed and murdered by his son. An indecisive peace was concluded between the two exhausted empires a year or so later, restoring their old boundaries; and the true cross was sent back to Heraclius, who replaced it in Jerusalem with much pomp and ceremony.

§ 3

So we give briefly the leading events in the history of the Persian as of the Byzantine Empire. What is more interesting for us and less easy to give are the changes that went on in the lives of the general population of those great empires during that time. The present writer can find little of a definite character about the great pestilences that we know swept the world in the second and sixth centuries of this era. Certainly they depleted population, and probably they disorganized social order in these regions just as much as we know they did in the Roman and Chinese empires.

The late Sir Mark Sykes, whose untimely death in Paris during the influenza epidemic of 1919 was an irreparable loss to Great Britain, wrote in *The Caliph's Last Heritage* a vivid review of the general life of Nearer Asia during the period we are considering. In the opening centuries of the present era, he says: "The direction of military administration and imperial finance became entirely divorced in men's minds from practical government; and notwithstanding the vilest tyranny of sots, drunkards, tyrants, lunatics, savages, and abandoned women, who from time to time held the reins of government, Mesopotamia, Babylonia, and Syria contained enormous populations, huge canals and dykes were kept in repair, and commerce and architecture flourished, in spite of a perpetual procession of hostile armies and a continual changing of the nationality of the governor. Each peasant's interest was centred in his ruling town; each citizen's interest was in the progress and prosperity of his city; and the advent of an enemy's army may have sometimes been looked on even with satisfaction, if his victory was assured and the payment of his contracts a matter of certainty.

"A raid from the north,[1] on the other hand, must have been a matter for dread. Then the villagers had need to take refuge behind the walls of the cities, from whence they could descry the smoke which told of the wreck and damage caused by the nomads. So long, however, as the canals were not destroyed (and, indeed, they were built with such solidity and

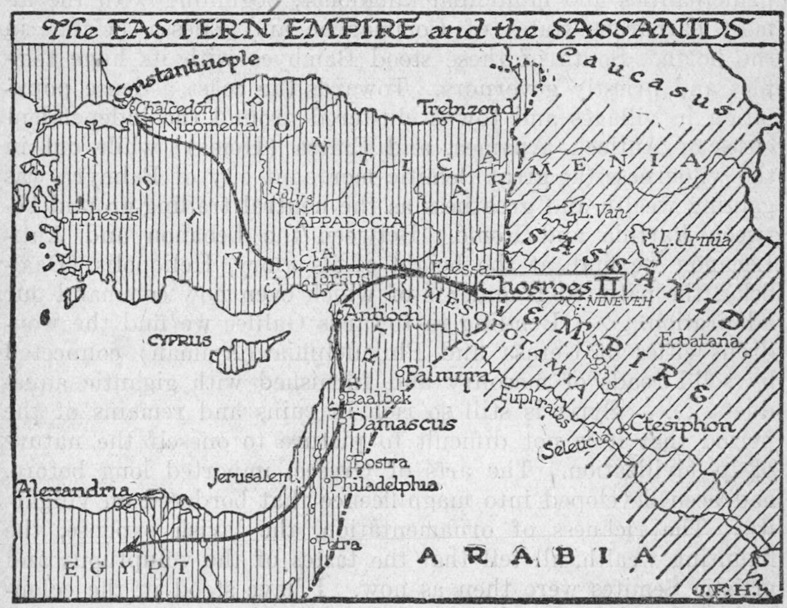

caution that their safety was assured), no irreparable damage could be effected. . . .

"In Armenia and Pontus the condition of life was quite otherwise. These were mountain districts, containing fierce tribes headed by powerful native nobility under recognized ruling kings, while in the valleys and plains the peaceful cultivator provided the necessary economic resources. . . . Cilicia and Cappadocia were now thoroughly subject to Greek influence, and contained numerous wealthy and highly civilized towns, besides possessing a considerable merchant marine. Passing from Cilicia to the Hellespont, the whole Mediterranean coast was crowded with wealthy cities and Greek col-

[1] Turanians from Turkestan or Avars from the Caucasus.

onies, entirely cosmopolitan in thought and speech, with those municipal and local ambitions which seem natural to the Grecian character. The Grecian Zone extended from Caria to the Bosphorus, and followed the coast as far as Sinope on the Black Sea, where it gradually faded away.

"Syria was broken up into a curious quilt-like pattern of principalities and municipal kingdoms; beginning with the almost barbarous states of Commagene and Edessa (Urfa) in the north. South of these stood Bambyce with its huge temples and priestly governors. Towards the coast a dense population in villages and towns clustered around the independent cities of Antioch, Apamea, and Emesa (Homs); while out in the wilderness the great Semitic merchant city of Palmyra was gaining wealth and greatness as the neutral trading-ground between Parthia and Rome. Between the Lebanon and Anti-Lebanon we find, at the height of its glory, Heliopolis (Baalbek), the battered fragments of which even now command our admiration. . . . Bending in towards Galilee we find the wondrous cities of Gerasa and Philadelphia (Amman) connected by solid roads of masonry and furnished with gigantic aqueducts. . . . Syria is still so rich in ruins and remains of the period that it is not difficult to picture to oneself the nature of its civilization. The arts of Greece, imported long before, had been developed into magnificence that bordered on vulgarity. The richness of ornamentation, the lavish expense, the flaunting wealth, all tell that the tastes of the voluptuous and artistic Semites were then as now. I have stood in the colonnades of Palmyra and I have dined in the Hotel Cecil, and, save that the latter is built of iron, daubed with sham wood, sham stucco, sham gold, sham velvet, and sham stone, the effect is identical. In Syria there were slaves in sufficient quantity to make real buildings, but the artistic spirit is as debased as anything made by machinery. Over against the cities the village folk must have dwelt pretty much as they do now, in houses of mud and dry stone wall; while out in the distant pastures the Bedouin tended their flocks in freedom under the rule of the Nabatean kings of their own race, or performed the office of guardians and agents of the great trading caravans.

"Beyond the herdsmen lay the parching deserts, which acted as the impenetrable barrier and defence of the Parthian Empire behind the Euphrates, where stood the great cities of

Ctesiphon, Seleucia, Hatra, Nisibin, Harran, and hundreds more whose very names are forgotten. These great townships subsisted on the enormous cereal wealth of Mesopotamia, watered as it then was by canals, whose makers' names were even then already lost in the mists of antiquity. Babylon and Nineveh had passed away; the successors of Persia and Macedon had given place to Parthia; but the people and the culti-

vation were the same as when Cyrus the Conqueror had first subdued the land. The language of many of the towns was Greek, and the cultured citizens of Seleucia might criticize the philosophies and tragedies of Athens; but the millions of the agricultural population knew possibly no more of these things than does many an Essex peasant of to-day know of what passes in the metropolis."

Compare with this the state of affairs at the end of the seventh century.

"Syria was now an impoverished and stricken land, and her

great cities, though still populated, must have been encumbered with ruins which the public funds were not sufficient to remove. Damascus and Jerusalem themselves had not recovered from the effects of long and terrible sieges; Amman and Gerash had declined into wretched villages under the sway and lordship of the Bedouin. The Hauran, perhaps, still showed signs of the prosperity for which it had been noted in the days of Trajan; but the wretched buildings and rude inscriptions of this date all point to a sad and depressing decline. Out in the desert, Palmyra stood empty and desolate save for a garrison in the castle. On the coasts and in the Lebanon a shadow of the former business and wealth was still to be seen; but in the north, ruin, desolation, and abandonment must have been the common state of the country, which had been raided with unfailing regularity for one hundred years and had been held by an enemy for fifteen. Agriculture must have declined, and the population notably decreased through the plagues and distresses from which it had suffered.

"Cappadocia had insensibly sunk into barbarism; and the great basilicas and cities, which the rude countrymen could neither repair nor restore, had been leveled with the ground. The Anatolian peninsula had been ploughed and harrowed by the Persian armies; the great cities had been plundered and sacked."

§ 4

It was while Heraclius was engaged in restoring order in this already desolated Syria after the death of Chosroes II and before the final peace with Persia, that a strange message was brought to him. The bearer had ridden over to the imperial outpost at Bostra in the wilderness south of Damascus. The letter was in Arabic, the obscure Semitic language of the nomadic peoples of the southern desert; and probably only an interpretation reached him—presumably with deprecatory notes by the interpreter.

It was an odd, florid challenge from someone who called himself "Muhammad, the Prophet of God." This Muhammad, it appeared, called upon Heraclius to acknowledge the one true God and to serve him. Nothing else was definite in the document.

There is no record of the reception of this missive, and

presumably it went unanswered. The emperor probably shrugged his shoulders, and was faintly amused at the incident.

But at Ctesiphon they knew more about this Muhammad. He was said to be a tiresome false prophet, who had incited Yemen, the rich province of Southern Arabia, to rebel against the King of Kings. Kavadh was much occupied with affairs. He had deposed and murdered his father Chosroes II, and he was attempting to reorganize the Persian military forces. To him also came a message identical with that sent to Heraclius. The thing angered them. He tore up the letter, flung the fragments at the envoy, and bade him begone.

When this was told to the sender far away in the squalid little town of Medina, he was very angry. "Even so, O Lord!" he cried; "rend Thou his kingdom from him." (A.D. 628.)

§ 5

But before we go on to tell of the rise of Islam in the world, it will be well to complete our survey of the condition of Asia in the dawn of the seventh century. And a word or so is due to religious developments in the Persian community during the Sassanid period.

From the days of Cyrus onward Zoroastrianism had prevailed over the ancient gods of Nineveh and Babylon. Zoroaster (the Greek spelling of the Iranian "Zarathustra"), like Buddha, was an Aryan. We know nothing of the age in which he lived; some authorities make him as early as 1000 B.C., others make him contemporary with Buddha or Confucius; and as little do we know of his place of birth or his exact nationality. His teachings are preserved to us in the Zend Avesta, but here, since they no longer play any great part in the world's affairs, we cannot deal with them in any detail. The opposition of a good god, Ormuzd, the god of light, truth, frankness, and the sun, and a bad god, Ahriman, god of secrecy, cunning, diplomacy, darkness, and night, formed a very central part of his religion. As we find it in history, it is already surrounded by a ceremonial and sacerdotal system; it has no images, but it has priests, temples, and altars, on which burn a sacred fire and at which sacrificial ceremonies are performed. Among other distinctive features is its prohibition of either the burning or the burial of the dead. The Parsees of India, the last surviving Zoroastrians, still lay their dead out within certain open towers, the Towers of Silence, to which the vultures come.

Under the Sassanid kings from Ardashir onward (227), this religion was the official religion; its head was the second person in the state next to the king, and the king in quite the ancient fashion was supposed to be divine or semi-divine and upon terms of peculiar intimacy with Ormuzd.

But the religious fermentation of the world did not leave the supremacy of Zoroastrianism undisputed in the Persian Empire. Not only was there a great eastward diffusion of Christianity, to which we have already given notice, but new sects arose in Persia, incorporating the novel ideas of the time. One early variant or branch of Zoroastrianism, Mithraism, we have already named. It had spread into Europe by the first century B.C., after the eastern campaigns of Pompey the Great. It became enormously popular with the soldiers and common people, and, until the time of Constantine the Great, continued to be a serious rival to Christianity. Indeed, one of his successors, the Emperor Julian (361-363), known in Christian history as "Julian the Apostate," made a belated attempt to substitute it for the accepted faith. Mithras was a god of light, "proceeding" from Ormuzd and miraculously born, in much the same way that the third person in the Christian Trinity proceeds from the first. Of this branch of the Zoroastrian stem we need say no more. In the third century A.D., however, another religion, Manichæism, arose, which deserves some notice now.

Mani, the founder of Manichæism, was born the son of a good family of Ecbatana, the old Median capital (A.D. 216). He was educated at Ctesiphon. His father was some sort of religious sectary, and he was brought up in an atmosphere of religious discussion. There came to him that persuasion that he at last had the complete light, which is the moving power of all religious initiators. He was impelled to proclaim his doctrine. In A.D. 242, at the accession of Sapor I, the second Sassanid monarch, he began his teaching.

It is characteristic of the way in which men's minds were moving in those days that his teaching included a sort of theocrasia. He was not, he declared, proclaiming anything new. The great religious founders before him had all been right: Moses, Zoroaster, Buddha, Jesus Christ—all had been true prophets, but to him it was appointed to clarify and crown their imperfect and confused teaching. This he did in Zoroastrian language. He explains the perplexities and contradictions of life as a conflict of light and darkness, Ormuzd was God and Ahriman Satan. But how man was created, how he fell from light into darkness, how he is being disentangled and redeemed from the darkness, and of the part played by Jesus in this strange mixture of religions we cannot explain here even if we would. Our interest with the system is historical and not theological.

But of the utmost historical interest is the fact that Mani not only went about Iran preaching these new and to him these finally satisfying ideas of his, but into Turkestan, into India, and over the passes into China. This freedom of travel is to be noted. It is interesting also because it brings before us the fact that Turkestan was no longer a country of dangerous nomads, but a country in which cities were flourishing and men had the education and leisure for theological argument. The ideas of Mani spread eastward and westward with great rapidity, and they were a most fruitful rootstock of heresies throughout the entire Christian world for nearly a thousand years.

Somewhen about A.D. 270 Mani came back to Ctesiphon and made many converts. This brought him into conflict with the official religion and the priesthood. In 277 the reigning monarch had him crucified and his body, for some unknown reason, flayed, and there began a fierce persecution of his adherents. Nevertheless, Manichæism held its own in Persia with Nestorian Christianity and orthodox Zoroastrianism (Mazdaism) for some centuries.

§ 6

It becomes fairly evident that in the fifth and sixth centuries A.D. not merely Persia, but the regions that are now Turkestan and Afghanistan were far more advanced in civilization than were the French and English of that time. The obscurity of the history of these regions has been lifted in the last two decades, and a very considerable literature written in languages of the Turkish group has been discovered. These extant manuscripts date from the seventh century onward. The alphabet is an adaptation of the Syrian, introduced by Manichæan missionaries, and many of the MSS. discovered—parchments have been found in windows in the place of glass—are as beautifully written as any Benedictine production. Mixed up with a very extensive Manichæan literature are translations of the Christian scriptures and Buddhistic writings. Much of this early Turkish material still awaits examination.

Everything points to the conclusion that those centuries, which were centuries of disaster and retrogression in Europe, were comparatively an age of progress in Middle Asia eastward into China.

A steady westward drift to the north of the Caspian of Hunnish peoples, who were now called Tartars and Turks, was still going on in the sixth century, but it must be thought of as an overflow rather than as a migration of whole peoples. The world from the Danube to the Chinese frontiers was still largely a nomadic world, with towns and cities growing up upon the chief trade routes. We need not tell in any detail here of the constant clash of the Turkish peoples of Western Turkestan with the Persians to the south of them, the age-long bickering of Turanian and Iranian. We hear nothing of any great northward marches of the Persians, but there were great and memorable raids to the south both by the Turanians to the east and the Alans to the west of the Caspian before the big series of movements of the third and fourth century westward that carried the Alans and Huns into the heart of Europe. There was a nomadic drift to the east of Persia and southward through Afghanistan towards India, as well as this drift to the north-west. These streams of nomads flowed by Persia on either side. We have already mentioned the Yue-Chi (Chap. xxviii, § 4), who finally descended into India as the Indo-Scythians in the second century. A backward, still nomadic section of these Yue-Chi remained in Central Asia, and became numerous upon the steppes of Turkestan, as the Ephthalites or White Huns. After being a nuisance and a danger to the Persians for three centuries, they finally began raiding into India in the footsteps of their kinsmen about the year 470, about a quarter of a century after the death of Attila. They did not migrate into India; they went to and fro, looting in India and returning with their loot to their own country, just as later the Huns established themselves in the great plain of the Danube and raided all Europe.

The history of India during these seven centuries we are now reviewing is punctuated by these two invasions of the Yue-Chi, the Indo-Scythians who, as we have said, wiped out the last traces of Hellenic rule, and the Ephthalites. Before the former of these, the Indo-Scythians, a wave of uprooted populations, the Sakas, had been pushed; so that altogether India experienced three waves of barbaric invasion, about A.D. 100, about A.D. 120, and about A.D. 470. But only the second of these invasions was a permanent conquest and settlement. The Indo-Scythians made their headquarters on the North-west Frontier and set up a dynasty, the Kushan dynasty, which ruled most of North India as far east as Benares.

An Ephthalite Coin.....

The chief among these Kushan monarchs was Kanishka (date unknown), who added to North India Kashgar, Yarkand, and Khotan. Like Asoka, he was a great and vigorous promoter of Buddhism, and these conquests, this great empire of the North-west Frontier, must have brought India into close and frequent relations with China and Tibet.

We will not trouble to record here the divisions and coalescences of power in India, nor the dynasties that followed the Kushans, because these things signify very little to us from our present point of view. Sometimes all India was a patchwork quilt of states; sometimes such empires as that of the Guptas prevailed over great areas. These things made little difference in the ideas, the religion, and the ordinary way of life of the Indian peoples. Brahminism held its own against Buddhism, and the two religions prospered side by side. The mass of the population was living then very much as it lives to-day; dressing, cultivating, and building its houses in much the same fashion.

The irruption of the Ephthalites is memorable not so much because of its permanent effects as because of the atrocities perpetrated by the invaders. These Ephthalites very closely resembled the Huns of Attila in thir barbarism; they merely raided, they produced no such dynasty as the Kushan monarchy; and their chiefs retained their headquarters in Western Turkestan. Mihiragula, their most capable leader, has been called the Attila of India. One of his favourite amusements, we are told, was the expensive one of rolling elephants down precipitous places in order to watch their sufferings. His abominations roused his Indian tributary princes to revolt, and he was overthrown (528). But the final ending of the Ephthalite raids into India was effected not by Indians, but by the destruction of their central establishment of the Ephthalites on the Oxus (565) by the growing power of the Turks, working in alliance with the Persians. After this break-up, the Ephthalites dissolved very rapidly and completely into the surrounding populations, much as the European Huns did after the death of Attila a hundred years earlier. Nomads without central grazing lands must disperse; nothing else is possible. Some of the chief Rajput clans of to-day in Rajputana in North India are descended, it is said, from these White Huns.

§ 7

These seven centuries which saw the beginning and the end of the emperors in Rome and the complete breakdown and recasting of the social, economic, political, and religious life of Western Europe, saw also very profound changes in the Chinese world. It is too commonly assumed by both Chinese, Japanese, and European historians, that the Han dynasty, under which we find China at the beginning of this period, and the Tang dynasty, with which it closed, were analogous ascendancies controlling a practically similar empire, and that the four centuries of division that elapsed between the end of the Han dynasty (220) and the beginning of the Tang period (619) were centuries of disturbance rather than essential change. The divisions of China are supposed to be merely political and territorial; and, deceived by the fact that at the close as at the commencement of these four centuries, China occupied much the same wide extent of Asia, and was still recognizably China, still with a common culture, a common script, and a common body of ideas, they ignore the very fundamental breaking down and reconstruction that went on, and the many parallelisms to the European experience that China displayed.

It is true that the social collapse was never so complete in the Chinese as in the European world. There remained throughout the whole period considerable areas in which the elaboration of the arts of life could go on. There was no such complete deterioration in cleanliness, decoration, artistic and literary production as we have to record in the West, and no such abandonment of any search for grace and pleasure. We note, for instance, that "tea" appeared in the world, and its use spread throughout China. China began to drink tea in the sixth century A.D. And there were Chinese poets to write delightfully about the effects of the first cup and the second cup and the third cup, and so on. China continued to produce beautiful paintings long after the fall of the Han rule. In the second, third, and fourth centuries some of the most lovely landscapes were painted that have ever been done by men. A considerable production of beautiful vases and carvings also continued. Fine building and decoration went on. Printing from wood blocks began about the same time as tea-drinking, and with the seventh century came a remarkable revival of poetry.

Certain differences between the great empires of the East and West were all in favour of the stability of the former. China had no general coinage. The cash and credit system of the Western world, at once efficient and dangerous, had not strained her economic life. Not that the monetary idea was unknown. For small transactions the various provinces were using perforated zinc and brass "cash," but for larger there was nothing but stamped ingots of silver. This great empire was still carrying on most of its business on a basis of barter like that which prevailed in Babylon in the days of the Aramean merchants. And so it continued to do to the dawn of the twentieth century.

We have seen how under the Roman republic economic and social order was destroyed by the too great fluidity of property that money brought about. Money became abstract, and lost touch with the real values it was supposed to represent. Individuals and communities got preposterously into debt, and the world was saddled by a class of rich men who were creditors, men who did not handle and administer any real wealth, but who had the power to call up money. No such development of "finance" occurred in China. Wealth in China remained real and visible. And China had no need for any Licinian law, nor for a Tiberius Gracchus. The idea of property in China did not extend far beyond tangible things. There was no

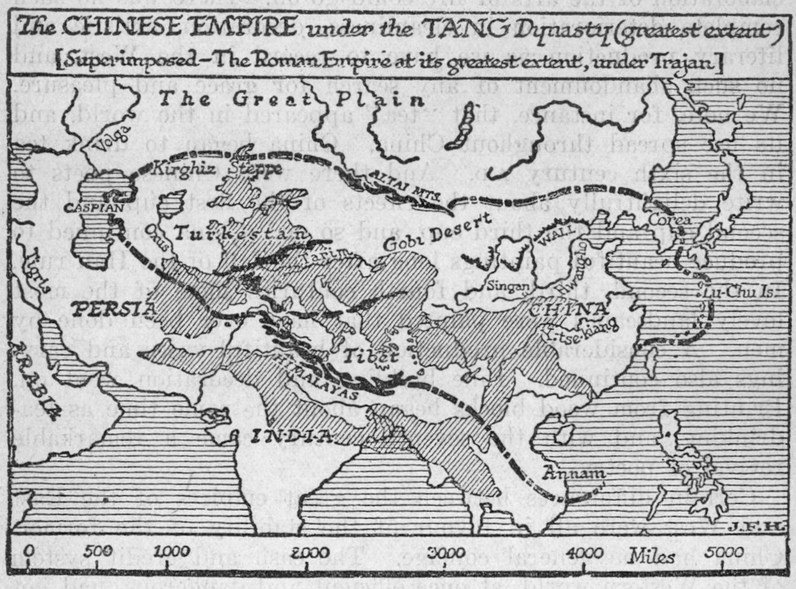

"labour" slavery, no gang servitude.[1] The occupier and user of the land was in most instances practically the owner of it, subject to a land tax. There was a certain amount of small scale landlordism, but no great estates. Landless men worked for wages paid mostly in kind—as they were in ancient Babylon.

These things made for stability and the geographical form of China for unity; nevertheless, the vigour of the Han dynasty declined, and when at last at the close of the second century A.D. the world catastrophe of the great pestilence struck

[1] There were girl slaves who did domestic work and women who were bought and sold.—J. J. L. D.

the system, the same pestilence that inaugurated a century of confusion in the Roman empire, the dynasty fell like a rotten tree before a gale. And the same tendency to break up into a number of warring states, and the same eruption of barbaric rulers, was displayed in East and West alike. In China, as in the Western empire, faith had decayed. Mr. Fu ascribes much of the political nervelessness of China in this period to Epicureanism, arising, he thinks, out of the sceptical individualism of Lao Tse. This phase of division is known as the "Three Kingdom Period." The fourth century saw a dynasty of more or less civilized Huns established as rulers in the province of Shen-si. This Hunnish kingdom included not merely the north of China, but great areas of Siberia; its dynasty absorbed the Chinese civilization, and its influence carried Chinese trade and knowledge to the Arctic circle. Mr. Fu compares this Siberian monarchy to the empire of Charlemagne in Europe; it was the barbarian becoming "Chinized" as Charlemagne was a barbarian becoming Romanized. Out of a fusion of these Siberian with native north Chinese elements arose the Suy dynasty, which conquered the south. This Suy dynasty marks the beginning of a renascence of China. Under a Suy monarch the Lu-chu isles were annexed to China, and there was a phase of great literary activity. The number of volumes at this time in the imperial library was increased, we are told, to 54,000. The dawn of the seventh century saw the beginning of the great Tang dynasty, which was to endure for three centuries.

The renascence of China that began with Suy and culminated in Tang was, Mr. Fu insists, a real new birth. "The spirit," he writes, "was a new one; it marked the Tang civilization with entirely distinctive features. Four main factors had been brought together and fused: (1) Chinese liberal culture; (2) Chinese classicism; (3) Indian Buddhism; and (4) Northern bravery. A new China had come into being. The provincial system, the central administration, and the military organization of the Tang dynasty were quite different from those of their predecessors. The arts had been much influenced and revivified by Indian and Central Asiatic influences. The literature was no mere continuation of the old; it was a new production. The religious and philosophical schools of Buddhism were fresh features. It was a period of substantial change.

"It may be interesting to compare this making of China with the fate of the Roman Empire in her later days. As the Roman world was divided into the eastern and western halves, so was the Chinese world into the southern and the northern. The barbarians in the case of Rome and in the case of China made similar invasions. They established dominions of a similar sort. Charlemagne's empire corresponded to that of the Siberian dynasty (Later Wei), the temporary recovery of the Western empire by Justinian corresponded to the temporary recovery of the north by Liu Yu. The Byzantine line corresponded to the southern dynasties. But from this point the two worlds diverged. China recovered her unity; Europe has still to do so."

The dominions of the emperor, Tai-tsung (627), the second Tang monarch, extended southward into Annam and westward to the Caspian sea. His southern frontier in that direction marched with that of Persia. His northern ran along the Altai from the Kirghis steppe, north of the desert of Gobi. But it did not include Corea, which was conquered and made tributary by his son. This Tang dynasty civilized and incorporated into the Chinese race the whole of the southward population, and just as the Chinese of the north call themselves the "men of Han," so the Chinese of the south call themselves the "men of Tang." The law was codified, the literary examination system was revised, and a complete and accurate edition of all the Chinese classics was produced. To the court of Tai-tsung came an embassy from Byzantium, and, what is more significant, from Persia came a company of Nestorian missionaries (635). These latter Tai-tsung received with great respect; he heard them state the chief articles of their creed, and ordered the Christian scriptures to be translated into Chinese for his further examination. In 638 he announced that he found the new religion entirely satisfactory, and that it might be preached within the empire. He also allowed the building of a church and the foundation of a monastery.

A still more remarkable embassy also came to the court of Tai-tsung in the year 628, five years earlier than the Nestorians. This was a party of Arabs, who came by sea to Canton in a trading vessel from Yanbu, the port of Medina in Arabia. (Incidentally it is interesting to know that there were such vessels engaged in an east and west trade at this time.) These Arabs had been sent by that Muhammad we have already mentioned, who styled himself "The Prophet of God," and the message they brought to Tai-tsung was probably identical with the summons which was sent in the same year to the Byzantine emperor Heraclius and to Kavadh in Ctesiphon. But the Chinese monarch neither neglected the message as Heraclius did, nor insulted the envoys after the fashion of the parricide Kavadh. He received them well, expressed great interest in their theological views, and assisted them, it is said, to build a mosque for the Arab traders in Canton—a mosque which survives to this day. It is one of the oldest mosques in the world.

§ 8

The urbanity, the culture, and the power of China under the early Tang rulers are in so vivid a contrast with the decay, disorder, and divisions of the Western world, as at once to raise some of the most interesting questions in the history of civilization. Why did not China keep this great lead she had won by her rapid return to unity and order? Why does she not to this day dominate the world culturally and politically?

For a long time she certainly did keep ahead. It is only a thousand years later, in the sixteenth and seventeenth centuries, with the discovery of America, the spread of printed books and education in the West, and the dawn of modern scientific discovery, that we can say with confidence that the Western world began to pull ahead of China. Under the Tang rule, her greatest period, and then again under the artistic but rather decadent Sung dynasty (960-1279), and again during the period of the cultured Mings (1358-1644), China presented a spectacle of prosperity, happiness, and artistic activity far in front of any contemporary state. And seeing that she achieved so much, why did she not achieve more? Chinese shipping was upon the seas, and there was a considerable overseas trade during that time.[1] Why did the Chinese never discover Amer-

[1] It is doubtful if the Chinese knew of the mariner's compass. Hirth, *Ancient History of China,* p. 126 sqq., comes to the conclusion, after a careful examination of all data, that, although it is probable something like the compass was known in high antiquity, the knowledge of it was lost for a long time afterwards, until, in the Middle Ages, it reappears as an instrument in the hands of geomancers (people who selected favour-

ica or Australia? There was much isolated observation, ingenuity, and invention. The Chinese knew of gunpowder in the sixth century, they used coal and gas heating centuries before these things were used in Europe; their bridge-building, their hydraulic engineering was admirable; the knowledge of materials shown in their enamel and lacquer ware is very great. Why did they never organize the system of record and co-operation in inquiry that has given the world modern science? And why, in spite of their general training in good manners and self-restraint, did intellectual education never soak down into the general mass of the population? Why are the masses of China to-day, and why have they always been, in spite of an exceptionally high level of natural intelligence, illiterate?

It is customary to meet such questions with rather platitudinous answers. We are told that the Chinaman is the most conservative of human beings, that, in contrast with the European races, his mind is twisted round towards the past, that he is the willing slave of etiquette and precedent to a degree inconceivable to Western minds. He is represented as having a mentality so distinct that one might almost expect to find a difference in brain structure to explain it. The appeals of Confucius to the wisdom of the ancients are always quoted to clinch this suggestion.

If, however, we examine this generalization more closely, it dissolves into thin air. The superior intellectual initiative, the liberal enterprise, the experimental disposition that is supposed to characterize the Western mind, is manifest in the history of that mind only during certain phases and under exceptional circumstances. For the rest, the Western world displays itself as traditional and conservative as China. And, on the other hand, the Chinese mind has, under conditions of stimulus, shown itself quite as inventive and versatile as the European, and the very kindred Japanese mind even more so. For, take the case of the Greeks, the whole swing of their mental vigour falls into the period between the sixth century B.C. and the decay

able sites for graves, etc.). The earliest unmistakable mention of its use as a guide to mariners occurs in a work of the 12th century and refers to its use on foreign ships trading between China and Sumatra. Hirth is rather inclined to assume that Arab travellers may have seen it in the hands of Chinese geomancers and applied its use to navigation, so that it was afterwards brought back by them to China as the "mariner's compass."—J. J. L. D.

of the Alexandrian Museum under the later Ptolemies in the second century B.C. There were Greeks before that time and Greeks since, but a history of a thousand years of the Byzantine Empire showed the Hellenic world at least as intellectually stagnant as China. Then we have already drawn attention to the comparatively sterility of the Italian mind during the Roman period and its abundant fertility since the Renaissance of learning. The English mind again had a phase of brightness in the seventh and eighth centuries, and it did not shine again until the fifteenth. Again, the mind of the Arabs, as we shall presently tell, blazed out like a star for half a dozen generations after the appearance of Islam, having never achieved anything of importance before or since. On the other hand, there was always a great deal of scattered inventiveness in China, and the progress of Chinese art witnesses to new movements and vigorous innovations. We exaggerate the reverence of the Chinese for their fathers; parricide was a far commoner crime among the Chinese emperors than it was even among the rulers of Persia. Moreover, there have been several liberalizing movements in China, several recorded struggles against the "ancient ways."

It has already been suggested that phases of real intellectual progress in any community seem to be connected with the existence of a detached class of men, sufficiently free not to be obliged to toil or worry exhaustively about mundane needs, and not rich and powerful enough to be tempted into extravagances of lust, display, or cruelty. They must have a sense of security, but not a conceit of superiority. This class, we have further insinuated, must be able to talk freely and communicate easily. It must not be watched for heresy or persecuted for any ideas it may express. Such a happy state of affairs certainly prevailed in Greece during its best days. A class of intelligent, free gentlefolk is indeed evident in history whenever there is a record of bold philosophy or effective scientific advances.

In the days of T'ang and Sung and Ming there must have been an abundance of pleasantly circumstanced people in China of just the class that supplied most of the young men of the Academy at Athens, or the bright intelligences of Renaissance Italy, or the members of the London Royal Society, that mother society of modern science; and yet China did not produce in these periods of opportunity any such large beginnings of recorded and analyzed fact.

If we reject the idea that there is some profound racial difference between China and the West which makes the Chinese by nature conservative and the West by nature progressive, then we are forced to look for the operating cause of this difference in progressiveness in some other direction. Many people are disposed to find that operating cause which has, in spite of her original advantages, retarded China so greatly during the last four or five centuries, in the imprisonment of the Chinese mind in a script and in an idiom of thought so elaborate and so difficult that the mental energy of the country has been largely consumed in acquiring it. This view deserves examination.

We have already given an account in Chap. xvi of the peculiarities of Chinese writing and of the Chinese language. The Japanese writing is derived from the Chinese, and consists of a more rapidly written system of forms. A great number of these forms are ideograms taken over from the Chinese and used exactly as the Chinese ideograms are used, but also a number of signs are used to express syllables; there is a Japanese syllabary after the fashion of the Sumerian syllabary we have described in Chap. xvi. The Japanese writing remains a clumsy system, as clumsy as cuneiform, though not so clumsy as Chinese; and there has been a movement in Japan to adopt a Western alphabet. Korea long ago went a step farther and developed a true alphabet from the same Chinese origins. With these exceptions all the great writing systems now in use in the world are based on the Mediterranean alphabets, and are beyond comparison more easily learnt and mastered than the Chinese. This means that while other peoples learn merely a comparatively simple and straightforward method of setting down the language with which they are familiar, the Chinaman has to master a great multitude of complex word signs and word groups. He must not simply learn the signs, but the established grouping of those signs to represent various meanings. He must familiarize himself, therefore, with a number of exemplary classical works. Consequently in China, while you will find great numbers of people who know the significance of certain frequent and familiar characters, you discover only a few whose knowledge is sufficiently extensive to grasp the meaning of a newspaper paragraph, and still fewer who can read any subtlety of intention or fine shades of meaning. In a lesser degree this is true also of Japan. No doubt European readers, especially of such word-rich languages as English or Russian, vary greatly among themselves in regard to the extent of books they can understand and how far they understand them; their power varies according to their vocabularies; but the corresponding levels of understanding among the Chinese represent a far greater expenditure of time and labour upon their attainment. A mandarin's education in China is, mainly, learning to read.

And it may be that the consequent preoccupation of the educated class during its most susceptible years upon the Chinese classics gave it a bias in favour of this traditional learning upon which it had spent so much time and energy. Few men who have toiled to build up any system of knowledge in their minds will willingly scrap it in favour of something strange and new; this disposition is as characteristic of the West as of the East; it is shown as markedly by the scholars of the British and American universities as by any Chinese mandarins, and the British at the present time, in spite of the great and manifest advantages in popular education and national propaganda the change would give them, refuse to make any move from their present barbaric orthography towards a phonetic alphabet and spelling. The peculiarities of the Chinese script, and the educational system arising out of that script, must have acted age after age as an invincible filter that favoured the plastic and scholarly mind as against the restive and originating type, and kept the latter out of positions of influence and authority. There is much that is plausible in this explanation.

There have been several attempts to simplify the Chinese writing and to adopt an alphabetical system. In the early days of Buddhism in China, when there was a considerable amount of translation from Sanscrit, Indian influences came near to achieving this end; two Chinese alphabets were indeed invented, and each had some little use. But what hindered the general adoption of these, and what stands in the way of any phonetic system of Chinese writing to-day, is this, that while the literary script and phraseology is the same from one end of China to the other, the spoken language of the common people, both in pronunciation and in its familiar idioms, varies so widely that men from one province may be incomprehensible to men from another. There is, however, a "standard Chinese," a rather bookish spoken idiom, which is generally understood by educated people; and it is upon the possibility of applying an alphabetical system of writing to this standard Chinese that the hopes of modern educational reformers in China are based at the present time. For fresh attempts are now being made to release the Chinese mind from this ancient entanglement.

A Chinese alphabet has been formed; it is taught in the common schools, and newspapers and pamphlets are issued in it. And the rigid examination system that killed all intellectual initiatives has been destroyed. There has also been a considerable simplification in the direction of introducing spoken idioms into written Chinese. This makes for ease and lucidity; even in the old characters such Chinese is more easily read and written, and it is far better adapted than classical Chinese to the needs of modern literary expression.

The very success and early prosperity and general contentment of China in the past must have worked to justify in that land all the natural self-complacency and conservatism of mankind. No animal will change when its conditions are "good enough" for present survival. And in this matter man is still an animal. Until the nineteenth century, for more than two thousand years, there was little in the history of China that could cause any serious doubts in the mind of a Chinaman of the general superiority of his own civilization to that of the rest of the world, and there was no reason apparent therefore for any alteration. China produced a profusion of beautiful art, some delightful poetry, astonishing cookery, and thousands of millions of glowingly pleasant lives generation after generation. Her ships followed her marvellous inland waterways, and put to sea but rarely, and then only to India or Borneo as their utmost adventure.[1] (Until the sixteenth century we must remember European seamen never sailed out into the Atlantic Ocean. The Norse discovery of America, the Phœnician circumnavigation of Africa, were exceptional feats.) And these things were attained without any such general boredom, servitude, indignity, and misery as underlay the rule of the rich in the Roman Empire. There was much poverty, much discontent, but it was not massed poverty, it was not a necessary

[1] But Mr. Vogan tells me that rock carvings of a distinctively Chinese character have been found in New Zealand and New Caledonia.

popular discontent. For a thousand years the Chinese system, though it creaked and swayed at times, seemed proof against decay. Dynastic changes there were, rebellions, phases of disorder, famines, pestilences; two great invasions that set foreign dynasties upon the throne of the Son of Heaven, but no such shock as to revolutionize the order of the daily round. The emperors and dynasties might come and go; the mandarins, the examinations, the classics, and the traditions and habitual life remained. China's civilization had already reached its culmination in the seventh century A.D., its crowning period was the Tang period, and though it continued to spread slowly and steadily into Annam, into Cambodia, into Siam, into Tibet, into Nepal, Korea, Mongolia, and Manchuria, there is henceforth little more than such geographical progress to record of it in this history for a thousand years.

§ 9

In the year 629, the year after the arrival of Muhammad's envoys at Canton and thirty odd years after the landing of Pope Gregory's missionaries in England, a certain learned and devout Buddhist named Yuan Chwang started out from Sian-fu, Tai-tsung's capital, upon a great journey to India. He was away sixteen years, he returned in 645, and he wrote an account of his travels which is treasured as a Chinese classic. One or two points about his experiences are to be noted here because they contribute to our general review of the state of the world in the seventh century A.D.

Yuan Chwang was as eager for marvels and as credulous as Herodotus, and without the latter writer's fine sense of history; he could never pass a monument or ruin without learning some fabulous story about it; Chinese ideas of the dignity of literature perhaps prevented him from telling us much detail of how he travelled, who were his attendants, how he was lodged, or what he ate and how he paid his expenses—details precious to the historian; nevertheless, he gives us a series of illuminating flashes upon China, Central Asia, and India in the period now under consideration.

His journey was an enormous one. He went and came back by way of the Pamirs. He went by the northern route, crossing the desert of Gobi, passing along the southern slopes of the

Thien Shan, skirting the great deep blue lake of Issik Kul, and so to Tashkend and Samarkand, and then more or less in the footsteps of Alexander the Great southward to the Khyber Pass and Peshawar. He returned by the southern route, crossing the Pamirs from Afghanistan to Kashgar, and so along the line of retreat the Yue-Chi had followed in the reverse direction seven centuries before, and by Yarkand, along the slopes of the Kuen Lun to rejoin his former route near the desert end of

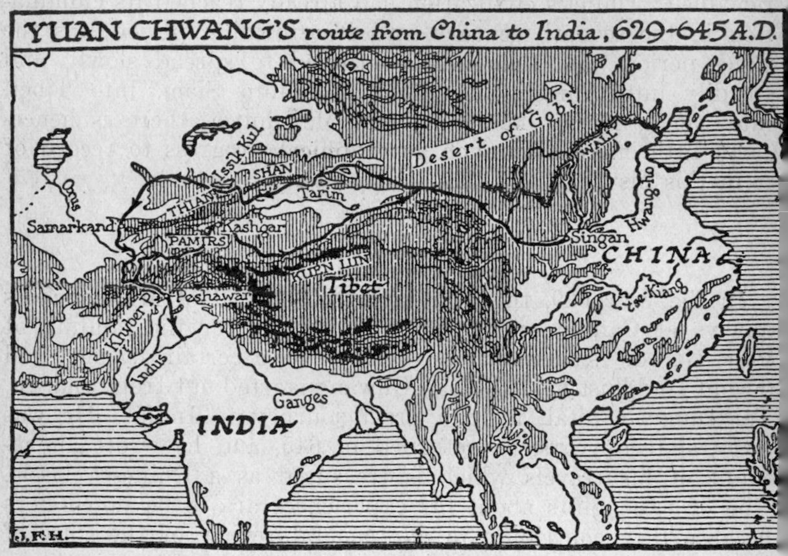

the Great Wall. Each route involved some hard mountaineering. His journeyings in India are untraceable; he was there fourteen years, and he went all over the peninsula from Nepal to Ceylon.

At that time there was an imperial edict forbidding foreign travel, so that Yuan Chwang started from Sian-fu like an escaping criminal. There was a pursuit to prevent him carrying out his project. How he bought a lean red-coloured horse that knew the desert paths from a strange grey-beard, how he dodged a frontier guard-house with the help of a "foreign person" who made him a bridge of brushwood lower down the river, how he crossed the desert guided by the bones of men and cattle, how he saw a mirage, and how twice he narrowly escaped being shot by arrows when he was getting water near the watch-towers on the desert track, the reader will find in the *Life*. He lost his way in the desert of Gobi, and for four nights and five days he had no water; when he was in the mountains among the glaciers, twelve of his party were frozen to death. All this is in the *Life;* he tells little of it in his own account of his travels.

He shows us the Turks, this new development of the Hun tradition, in possession not only of what is now Turkestan, but all along the northern route. He mentions many cities and considerable cultivation. He is entertained by various rulers, allies of or more or less nominally tributaries to China, and among others by the Khan of the Turks, a magnificent person in green satin, with his long hair tied with silk.

"The gold embroidery of this grand tent shone with a dazzling splendour; the ministers of the presence in attendance sat on mats in long rows on either side all dressed in magnificent brocade robes, while the rest of the retinue on duty stood behind. You saw that although it was a case of a frontier ruler, yet there was an air of distinction and elegance. The Khan came out from his tent about thirty paces to meet Yuan Chwang, who, after a courteous greeting, entered the tent. . . . After a short interval envoys from China and Kao-chang were admitted and presented their despatches and credentials, which the Khan perused. He was much elated, and caused the envoys to be seated; then he ordered wine and music for himself and them and grape-syrup for the pilgrim. Hereupon all pledged each other, and the filling and draining of the winecups made a din and bustle, while the mingled music of various instruments rose loud: although the airs were the popular strains of foreigners, yet they pleased the senses and exhilarated the mental faculties. After a little, piles of roasted beef and mutton were served for the others, and lawful food, such as cakes, milk, candy, honey, and grapes, for the pilgrim. After the entertainment, grape-syrup was again served and the Khan invited Yuan Chwang to improve the occasion, whereupon the pilgrim expounded the doctrines of the 'ten virtues,' compassion for animal life, and the paramitas and emancipation. The Khan, raising his hands, bowed, and gladly believed and accepted the teaching."

Yuan Chwang's account of Samarkand is of a large and prosperous city, "a great commercial entrepôt, the country about it very fertile, abounding in trees and flowers and yielding many fine horses. Its inhabitants were skilful craftsmen, smart and energetic." At that time we must remember there was hardly such a thing as a town in Anglo-Saxon England.

As his narrative approached his experiences in India, however, the pious and learned pilgrim in Yuan Chwang got the better of the traveller, and the book becomes congested with monstrous stories of incredible miracles. Nevertheless, we get an impression of houses, clothing, and the like, closely resembling those of the India of to-day. Then, as now, the kaleidoscopic variety of an Indian crowd contrasted with the blue uniformity of the multitude in China. In the time of Buddha it is doubtful if there were reading and writing in India; now reading and writing were quite common accomplishments. Yuan Chwang gives an interesting account of a great Buddhist university at Nalanda, where ruins have quite recently been discovered and excavated. Nalanda and Taxilla seem to have been considerable educational centres as early as the opening of the schools of Athens. The caste system Yuan Chwang found fully established in spite of Buddha, and the Brahmins were now altogether in the ascendant. He names the four main castes we have mentioned in Chap. xviii., § 4 (*q.v.*), but his account of their functions is rather different. The Sudras, he says, were the tillers of the soil. Indian writers say that their function was to wait upon the three "twice born" castes above them.

But, as we have already intimated, Yuan Chwang's account of Indian realities is swamped by his accumulation of legends and pious inventions. For these he had come, and in these he rejoiced. The rest, as we shall see, was a task that had been set him. The faith of Buddha which in the days of Asoka, and even so late as Kaniska, was still pure enough to be a noble inspiration, we now discover absolutely lost in a wilderness of preposterous rubbish, a philosophy of endless Buddhas, tales of manifestations and marvels like a Christmas pantomime, immaculate conceptions by six-tusked elephants, charitable princes giving themselves up to be eaten by starving tigresses, temples built over a sacred nail-paring, and the like. We cannot give such stories here; if the reader likes that sort of thing, he must go to the publications of the Royal Asiatic Society or the India Society, where he will find a delirium of such imaginations. And in competition with this Buddhism, intellectually undermined as it now was and smothered in gilded decoration, Brahminism was everywhere gaining ground again, as Yuan Chwang notes with regret.

Side by side with these evidences of a vast intellectual decay in India we may note the repeated appearance in Yuan Chwang's narrative of ruined and deserted cities. Much of the country was still suffering from the ravages of the Ephthalites and the consequent disorders. Again and again we find such passages as this: "He went north-east through a great forest, the road being a narrow, dangerous path, with wild buffalo and wild elephants, and robbers and hunters always in wait to kill travellers, and emerging from the forest he reached the country of Kou-shih-na-ka-lo (Kúsinagara). The city walls were in ruins, and the towns and villages were deserted. The brick foundations of the 'old city' (that is, the city which had been the capital) were above ten *li* in circuit; there were very few inhabitants, the interior of the city being a wild waste." This ruin was, however, by no means universal; there is at least as much mention of crowded cities and villages and busy cultivations.

The *Life* tells of many hardships upon the return journey: he fell among robbers; the great elephant that was carrying the bulk of his possessions was drowned; he had much difficulty in getting fresh transport. Here we cannot deal with these adventures.

The return of Yuan Chwang to Sian-fu, the Chinese capital, was, we gather, a triumph. Advance couriers must have told of his coming. There was a public holiday; the streets were decorated by gay banners and made glad with music. He was escorted into the city with great pomp and ceremony. Twenty horses were needed to carry the spoils of his travels; he had brought with him hundreds of Buddhist books written in Sanscrit, and made of trimmed leaves of palm and birch bark strung together in layers; he had many images great and small of Buddha, in gold, silver, crystal, and sandal-wood; he had holy pictures, and no fewer than one hundred and fifty well authenticated true relics of Buddha. Yuan Chwang was presented to the emperor, who treated him as a personal friend, took him into the palace, and questioned him day by day about the wonders of these strange lands in which he had stayed so long.

But while the emperor asked about India, the pilgrim was disposed only to talk about Buddhism.

The subsequent history of Yuan Chwang contains two incidents that throw light upon the mental workings of this great monarch, Tai-tsung, who was probably quite as much a Moslem as he was a Christian or a Buddhist. The trouble about all religious specialists is that they know too much about their own religion and how it differs from others; the advantage, or disadvantage, of such creative statesmen as Tai-tsung and Constantine the Great is that they know comparatively little of such matters. Evidently the fundamental good of all these religions seemed to Tai-tsung to be much the same fundamental good. So it was natural to him to propose that Yuan Chwang should now give up the religious life and come into his foreign office, a proposal that Yuan Chwang would not entertain for a moment. The emperor then insisted at least upon a written account of the travels, and so got this classic we treasure. And finally Tai-tsung proposed to this highly saturated Buddhist that he should now use his knowledge of Sanscrit in translating the works of the great Chinese teacher, Lao Tse, so as to make them available for Indian readers. It seemed, no doubt, to the emperor a fair return and a useful service to the fundamental good that lies beneath all religions. On the whole, he thought Lao Tse might very well rank with or even a little above Buddha, and therefore that if his work was put before the Brahmins, they would receive it gladly. In much the same spirit Constantine the Great had done his utmost to make Arius and Athanasius settle down amicably together. But naturally enough this suggestion was repulsed by Yuan Chwang. He retired to a monastery and spent the rest of his years translating as much as he could of the Buddhist literature he had brought with him into elegant Chinese writing.

XXXI

MUHAMMAD AND ISLAM

§ 1. *Arabia Before Muhammad.* § 2. *Life of Muhammad to the Hegira.* § 3. *Muhammad Becomes a Fighting Prophet.* § 4. *The Teachings of Islam.* § 5. *The Caliphs Abu Bekr and Omar.* § 6. *The Great Days of the Omayyads.* § 7. *The Decay of Islam Under the Abbasids.* § 8. *The Intellectual Life of Arab Islam.*

§ 1

WE have already described how in A.D. 628 the courts of Heraclius, of Kavadh, and of Tai-tsung were visited by Arab envoys sent from a certain Muhammad, "The Prophet of God," at the small trading town of Medina in Arabia. We must tell now who this prophet was who had arisen among the nomads and traders of the Arabian desert.

From time immemorial Arabia, except for the fertile strip of the Yemen to the south, had been a land of nomads, the headquarters and land of origin of the Semitic peoples. From Arabia at various times waves of these nomads had drifted north, east, and west into the early civilizations of Egypt, the Mediterranean coast, and Mesopotamia. We have noted in this history how the Sumerians were swamped and overcome by such Semitic waves, how the Semitic Phœnicians and Canaanites established themselves along the eastern shores of the Mediterranean, how the Babylonians and Assyrians were settled Semitic peoples, how the Hyksos conquered Egypt, how the Arameans established themselves in Syria with Damascus as their capital, and how the Hebrews partially conquered their "Promised Land." At some unknown date the Chaldeans drifted in from Eastern Arabia and settled in the old southern Sumerian lands. With each invasion first this and then that section of the Semitic peoples comes into history. But each of such swarmings still leaves a tribal nucleus behind to supply fresh invasions in the future.

The history of the more highly organized empires of the horse and iron period, the empires of roads and writing, shows Arabia thrust like a wedge between Egypt, Palestine, and the Euphrates-Tigris country, and still a reservoir of nomadic tribes who raid and trade and exact tribute for the immunity and protection of caravans. There are temporary and flimsy subjugations. Egypt, Persia, Macedonia, Rome, Syria, Constantinople, and again Persia claim some unreal suzerainty in turn over Arabia, profess some unsubstantial protection. Under Trajan there was a Roman province of "Arabia," which included the then fertile region of the Hauran and extended as far as Petra. Now and then some Arab chief and his trading city rises to temporary splendour. Such was that Odenathus of Palmyra, whose brief career we have noted and another such transitory desert city whose ruins still astonish the traveller was Baalbek.

After the destruction of Palmyra, the desert Arabs began to be spoken of in the Roman and Persian records as Saracens.

In the time of Chosroes II, Persia claimed a certain ascendancy over Arabia, and maintained officials and tax collectors in the Yemen. Before that time the Yemen had been under the rule of the Abyssinian Christians for some years, and before that for seven centuries it had had native princes professing, be it noted, the Jewish faith.

Until the opening of the seventh century A.D. there were no signs of any unwonted or dangerous energy in the Arabian deserts. The life of the country was going on as it had gone on for long generations. Wherever there were fertile patches, wherever, that is, there was a spring or a well, a scanty agricultural population subsisted, living in walled towns because of the Bedouin who wandered with their sheep, cattle, and horses over the desert. Upon the main caravan routes the chief towns rose to a certain second-rate prosperity, and foremost among them were Medina and Mecca. In the beginning of the seventh century Medina was a town of about 15,000 inhabitants all told; Mecca may have had twenty or twenty-five thousand. Medina was a comparatively well-watered town, and possessed abundant date groves; its inhabitants were Yemenites, from the fertile land to the south. Mecca was a town of a different character, built about a spring of water with a bitter taste, and inhabited by recently settled Bedouin.

Mecca was not merely nor primarily a trading centre; it was a place of pilgrimage. Among the Arab tribes there had long existed a sort of Amphictyony centering upon Mecca and certain other sanctuaries; there were months of truce to war and

blood feuds, and customs of protection and hospitality for the pilgrim. In addition there had grown up an Olympic element in these gatherings; the Arabs were discovering possibilities of beauty in their language, and there were recitations of war poetry and love songs. The sheiks of the tribes, under a "king of the poets," sat in judgment and awarded prizes; the prize songs were sung through all Arabia.

The Kaaba, the sanctuary at Mecca, was of very ancient date. It was a small square temple of black stones, which had for its corner-stone a meteorite. This meteorite was regarded as a god, and all the little tribal gods of Arabia were under his protection. The permanent inhabitants of Mecca were a tribe of Bedouin who had seized this temple and constituted themselves its guardians. To them there came in the months of truce a great incourse of people, who marched about the Kaaba ceremonially, bowed themselves, and kissed the stone, and also engaged in trade and poetical recitations. The Meccans profited much from these visitors.

All of this is very reminiscent of the religious and political state of affairs in Greece fourteen centuries earlier. But the paganism of these more primitive Arabs was already being assailed from several directions. There had been a great proselytizing of Arabs during the period of the Meccabæans and Herods in Judea; and, as we have already noted, the Yemen had been in succession under the rule of Jews (Arab proselytes to Judaism, *i.e.*), Christians, and Zoroastrians. It is evident that there must have been plenty of religious discussion during the pilgrimage fairs at Mecca and the like centres. Naturally enough Mecca was a stronghold of the old pagan cult which gave it its importance and prosperity; Medina, on the other hand, had Jewish proclivities, and there were Jewish settlements near by. It was inevitable that Mecca and Medina should be in a state of rivalry and bickering feud.

§ 2

It was in Mecca about the year A.D. 570 that Muhammad, the founder of Islam, was born. He was born in considerable poverty, and even by the standards of the desert he was uneducated; it is doubtful if he ever learnt to write. He was for some years a shepherd's boy; then he became the servant of a certain Kadija, the widow of a rich merchant. Probably he had to look after her camels or help in her trading operations; and he is said to have travelled with caravans to the Yemen and to Syria. He does not seem to have been a very useful trader, but he had the good fortune to find favour in the lady's eyes, and she married him, to the great annoyance of her family. He was then only twenty-five years old. It is uncertain if his wife was much older, though tradition declares she was forty. After the marriage he probably made no more long journeys. There were several children, one of whom was named Abd Manif—

that is to say, the servant of the Meccan god Manif, which demonstrates that at that time Muhammad had made no religious discoveries.

Until he was forty he did indeed live a particularly undistinguished life in Mecca, as the husband of a prosperous wife. There may be some ground for the supposition that he became partner in a business in agricultural produce. To anyone visiting Mecca about A.D. 600 he would probably have seemed something of a loafer, a rather shy, good-looking individual, sitting about and listening to talk, a poor poet, and an altogether second-rate man.

About his internal life we can only speculate. Imaginative writers have supposed that he had great spiritual struggles, that he went out into the desert in agonies of doubt and divine desire. "In the silence of the desert night, in the bright heat of noontide desert day, he, as do all men, had known and felt himself alone yet not in solitude, for the desert is of God, and in the desert no man may deny him."[1] Maybe that was so, but there is no evidence of any such desert trips. Yet he was certainly thinking deeply of the things about him. Possibly he had seen Christian churches in Syria; almost certainly he knew much of the Jews and their religion, and he heard their scorn for this black stone of the Kaaba that ruled over the three hundred odd tribal gods of Arabia. He saw the pilgrimage crowds, and noted the threads of insincerity and superstition in the paganism of the town. It oppressed his mind. The Jews had perhaps converted him to a belief in the One True God, without his knowing what had happened to him.

At last he could keep these feelings to himself no longer. When he was forty he began to talk about the reality of God, at first apparently only to his wife and a few intimates. He produced certain verses, which he declared had been revealed to him by an angel. They involved an assertion of the unity of God and some acceptable generalizations about righteousness. He also insisted upon a future life, the fear of hell for the negligent and evil, and the reservation of paradise for the believer in the One God. Except for his claim to be a new prophet, there does not seem to have been anything very new about these doctrines at the time, but this was seditious teaching for Mecca, which partly subsisted upon its polytheistic cult,

[1] Mark Sykes.

and which was therefore holding on to idols when all the rest of the world was giving them up. Like Mani, Muhammad claimed that the prophets before him, and especially Jesus and Abraham, had been divine teachers, but that he crowned and completed their teaching. Buddhism, however, he did not name, probably because he had never heard of Buddha. Desert Arabia was in a theological backwater.

For some years the new religion was the secret of a small group of simple people, Kadija, the Prophet's wife, Ali, an adopted son, Zeid, a slave, and Abu Bekr, a friend and admirer. For some years it was an obscure sect in a few households of Mecca, a mere scowl and muttering at idolatry, so obscure and unimportant that the leading men of the town did not trouble about it in the least. Then it gathered strength. Muhammad began to preach more openly, to teach the doctrine of a future life, and to threaten idolaters and unbelievers with hell fire. He seems to have preached with considerable effect. It appeared to many that he was aiming at a sort of dictatorship in Mecca, and drawing many susceptible and discontented people to his side; and an attempt was made to discourage and suppress the new movement.

Mecca was a place of pilgrimage and a sanctuary; no blood could be shed within its walls; nevertheless, things were made extremely disagreeable for the followers of the new teacher. Boycott and confiscation were used against them. Some were driven to take refuge in Christian Abyssinia. But the Prophet himself went unscathed because he was well connected, and his opponents did not want to begin a blood feud. We cannot follow the fluctuations of the struggle here, but it is necessary to note one perplexing incident in the new Prophet's career, which, says Sir Mark Sykes, "proves him to have been an Arab of the Arabs." After all his insistence upon the oneness of God, he wavered. He came into the courtyard of the Kaaba, and declared that the gods and goddesses of Mecca might, after all, be real, might be a species of saints with a power of intercession.

His recantation was received with enthusiasm, but he had no sooner made it than he repented, and his repentance shows that he had indeed the fear of God in him. His lapse from honesty proves him honest. He did all he could to repair the evil he had done. He said that the devil had possessed his tongue, and denounced idolatry again with renewed vigour. The struggle against the antiquated deities, after a brief interval of peace, was renewed again more grimly, and with no further hope of reconciliation.

For a time the old interests had the upper hand. At the end of ten years of prophesying, Muhammad found himself a man of fifty, and altogether unsuccessful in Mecca. Kadija, his first wife, was dead, and several of his chief supporters had also recently died. He sought a refuge at the neighbouring town of Tayf, but Tayf drove him out with stones and abuse. Then, when the world looked darkest to him, opportunity opened before him. He found he had been weighed and approved in an unexpected quarter. The city of Medina was much torn by internal dissension, and many of its people, during the time of pilgrimage to Mecca, had been attracted by Muhammad's teaching. Probably the numerous Jews in Medina had shaken the ancient idolatry of the people. An invitation was sent to him to come and rule in the name of his God in Medina.

He did not go at once. He parleyed for two years, sending a disciple to preach in Medina and destroy the idols there. Then he began sending such followers as he had in Mecca to Medina to await his coming there; he did not want to trust himself to unknown adherents in a strange city. This exodus of the faithful continued, until at last only he and Abu Bekr remained.

In spite of the character of Mecca as a sanctuary, he was very nearly murdered there. The elders of the town evidently knew of what was going on in Medina, and they realized the danger to them if this seditious prophet presently found himself master of a town on their main caravan route to Syria. Custom must bow to imperative necessity, they thought; and they decided that, blood feud or no blood feud, Muhammad must die. They arranged that he should be murdered in his bed; and in order to share the guilt of this breach of sanctuary they appointed a committee to do this, representing every family in the city except Muhammad's own. But Muhammad had already prepared his flight; and when in the night they rushed into his room, they found Ali, his adopted son, sleeping, or feigning sleep, on his bed.

The flight (the Hegira) was an adventurous one, the pursuit being pressed hard. Expert desert trackers sought for the spoor to the north of the town, but Muhammad and Abu Bekr had gone south to certain caves where camels and provisions were hidden, and thence he made a great detour to Medina. There he and his faithful companion arrived, and were received with great enthusiasm on September 20, 622. It was the end of his probation and the beginning of his power.

§ 3

Until the Hegira, until he was fifty-one, the character of the founder of Islam is a matter of speculation and dispute. Thereafter he is in the light. We discover a man of great imaginative power but tortuous in the Arab fashion, and with most of the virtues and defects of the Bedouin.

The opening of his reign was "very Bedouin." The rule of the One God of all the earth, as it was interpreted by Muhammad, began with a series of raids—which for more than a year were invariably unsuccessful—upon the caravans of Mecca. Then came a grave scandal, the breaking of the ancient customary truce of the Arab Amphictyony in the sacred month of Rahab. A party of Moslems, in this season of profound peace, treacherously attacked a small caravan and killed a man. It was their only success, and they did it by the order of the Prophet.

Presently came a battle. A force of seven hundred men had come out from Mecca to convoy home another caravan, and they encountered a large raiding party of three hundred. There was a fight, the battle of Badr, and the Meccans got the worst of it. They lost about fifty or sixty killed and as many wounded. Muhammad returned in triumph to Medina, and was inspired by Allah and this success to order the assassination of a number of his opponents among the Jews in the town who had treated his prophetic claims with a disagreeable levity.

But Mecca resolved to avenge Badr, and at the battle of Uhud, near Medina, inflicted an indecisive defeat upon the Prophet's followers. Muhammad was knocked down and nearly killed, and there was much running away among his followers. The Meccans, however, did not push their advantage and enter Medina.

For some time all the energies of the Prophet were concentrated upon rallying his followers, who were evidently much dispirited. The Koran records the chastened feelings of those days. "The *suras* of the Koran," says Sir Mark Sykes, "which are attributed to this period, excel nearly all the others in their majesty and sublime confidence." Here, for the judgment of the reader, is an example of these majestic utterances, from the recent orthodox translation by the Maulvi Muhammad Ali.[1]

"Oh, you who believe! If you obey those who disbelieve, they will turn you back upon your heels, so you will turn back losers.

"Nay! Allah is your Patron, and He is the best of the helpers.

"We will cast terror into the hearts of those who disbelieve, because they set up with Allah that for which He has sent down no authority, and their abode is the fire; and evil is the abode of the unjust.

"And certainly Allah made good to you his promise, when you slew them by His permission, until when you became weak-hearted and disputed about the affair and disobeyed after He had shown you that which you loved; of you were some who desired this world, and of you were some who desired the hereafter; then He turned you away from them that He might try you; and He has certainly pardoned you, and Allah is Gracious to the believers.

"When you ran off precipitately, and did not wait for any-one, and the Apostle was calling you from your rear, so He gave you another sorrow instead of your sorrow, so that you might not grieve at what had escaped you, nor at what befell you; and Allah is aware of what you do.

"Then after sorrow he sent down security upon you, a calm coming upon a party of you, and there was another party whom their own souls had rendered anxious; they entertained about Allah thoughts of ignorance quite unjustly, saying: We have no hand in this affair. Say, surely the affair is wholly in the hands of Allah. They conceal within their souls what they would not reveal to you. They say: Had we any hand in the affair, we would not have been slain here. Say: had you remained in your houses, those for whom slaughter was ordained would certainly have gone forth to the places where they would be slain, and that Allah might test what was in your breasts and that He might purge what was in your hearts; and Allah knows what is in the breasts.

[1] Published by the *Islamic Review*.

"As for those of you who turned back on the day when the two armies met, only the devil sought to cause them to make a slip on account of some deeds they had done, and certainly Allah has pardoned them; surely Allah is Forgiving, Forbearing."

Inconclusive hostilities continued for some years, and at last Mecca made a crowning effort to stamp out for good and all the growing power of Medina. A mixed force of no fewer than 10,000 men was scraped together, an enormous force for the time and country. It was, of course, an entirely undisciplined force of footmen, horsemen, and camel riders, and it was prepared for nothing but the usual desert scrimmage. Bows, spears, and swords were its only weapons. When at last it arrived amid a vast cloud of dust in sight of the hovels and houses of Medina, instead of a smaller force of the same kind drawn up for battle, as it had expected, it found a new and entirely disconcerting phenomenon, a trench and a wall. Assisted by a Persian convert, Muhammad had entrenched himself in Medina!

This trench struck the Bedouin miscellany as one of the most unsportsmanlike things that had ever been known in the history of the world. They rode about the place. They shouted their opinion of the whole business to the besieged. They discharged a few arrows, and at last encamped to argue about this amazing outrage. They could arrive at no decision. Muhammad would not come out; the rains began to fall, the tents of the allies got wet and the cooking difficult, views became divergent and tempers gave way, and at last this great host dwindled again into its constituent parts without ever having given battle (627). The bands dispersed north, east, and south, became clouds of dust, and ceased to matter. Near Medina was a castle of Jews, against whom Muhammad was already incensed because of their disrespect for his theology. They had shown a disposition to side with the probable victor in this last struggle, and Muhammad now fell upon them, slew all the men, nine hundred of them, and enslaved the women and children. Possibly many of their late allies were among the bidders for these slaves. Never again after this quaint failure did Mecca make an effective rally against Muhammad, and one by one its leading men came over to his side.

We need not follow the windings of the truce and the treaty that finally extended the rule of the Prophet to Mecca. The gist of the agreement was that the faithful should turn towards Mecca when they prayed instead of turning towards Jerusalem, as they had hitherto done, and that Mecca should be the pilgrimage centre of the new faith. So long as the pilgrimage continued, the men of Mecca, it would seem, did not care very much whether the crowd assembled in the name of one god or many. Muhammad was getting more and more hopeless of any extensive conversion of the Jews and Christians, and he was ceasing to press his idea that all these faiths really worshipped the same One God. Allah was becoming more and more his own special God, tethered now by this treaty to the meteoric stone of the Kaaba, and less and less the father of all mankind. Already the Prophet had betrayed a disposition to make a deal with Mecca, and at last it was effected. The lordship of Mecca was well worth the concession. Of comings and goings and a final conflict we need not tell. In 629 Muhammad came to the town as its master. The image of Manif, the god after whom he had once named his son, was smashed under his feet as he entered the Kaaba.

Thereafter his power extended, there were battles, treacheries, massacres; but on the whole he prevailed, until he was master of all Arabia; and when he was master of all Arabia in 632, at the age of sixty-two, he died.

Throughout the concluding eleven years of his life after the Hegira, there is little to distinguish the general conduct of Muhammad from that of any other welder of peoples into a monarchy. The chief difference is his use of a religion of his own creation as his cement. He was diplomatic, treacherous, ruthless, or compromising as the occasion required and as any other Arab king might have been in his place; and there was singularly little spirituality in his kingship. Nor was his domestic life during his time of power and freedom one of exceptional edification. Until the death of Kadija, when he was fifty, he seems to have been the honest husband of one wife; but then, as many men do in their declining years, he developed a disagreeably strong interest in women.

He married two wives after the death of Kadija, one being the young Ayesha, who became and remained his favourite and most influential partner; and subsequently a number of other women, wives and concubines, were added to his establishment. This led to much trouble and confusion, and in spite of many special and very helpful revelations on the part of Allah, these complications still require much explanation and argument from the faithful. There was, for example, a scandal about Ayesha; she was left behind on one occasion when the howdah and the camel went on, while she was looking for her necklace among the bushes; and so Allah had to intervene with some heat and denounce her slanderers. Allah also had to speak very plainly about the general craving among this household of women for "this world's life and its ornature" and for "finery." Then there was much discussion because the Prophet first married his young cousin Zainib to his adopted son Zaid, and afterwards, "when Zaid had accomplished his want of her," the Prophet took her and married her—but, as the inspired book makes clear, only in order to show the difference between an adopted and a real son. "We gave her to you as a wife, so that there should be no difficulty for the believers in respect of the wives of their adopted sons, when they have accomplished their want of them, and Allah's command shall be performed." Yet surely a simple statement in the Koran should have sufficed without this excessively practical demonstration. There was, moreover, a mutiny in the harem on account of the undue favours shown by the Prophet to an Egyptian concubine who had borne him a boy, a boy for whom he had a great affection, since none of Kadija's sons had survived. These domestic troubles mingle inextricably with our impression of the Prophet's personality. One of his wives was a Jewess, Safiyya, whom he had married on the evening of the battle in which her husband had been captured and executed. He viewed the captured women at the end of the day, and she found favour in his eyes and was taken to his tent.

These are salient facts in these last eleven years of Muhammad's career. Because he, too, founded a great religion, there are those who write of this evidently lustful and rather shifty leader as though he were a man to put beside Jesus of Nazareth or Gautama or Mani. But it is surely manifest that he was a being of a commoner clay; he was vain, egotistical, tyrannous, and a self-deceiver; and it would throw all our history out of proportion if, out of an insincere deference to the possible Moslem reader, we were to present him in any other light.

Yet, unless we balance it, this insistence upon his vanity, egotism, self-deception, and hot desire does not complete the justice of the case. We must not swing across from the repudiation of the extravagant pretensions of the faithful to an equally extravagant condemnation. Can a man who has no good qualities hold a friend? Because those who knew Muhammad best believed in him most. Kadija for all her days believed in him—but she may have been a fond woman. Abu Bekr is a better witness, and he never wavered in his devotion. Abu Bekr believed in the Prophet, and it is very hard for anyone who reads the history of these times not to believe in Abu Bekr. Ali again risked his life for the Prophet in his darkest days. Muhammad was no impostor, at any rate, though at times his vanity made him behave as though Allah was at his beck and call, and as if his thoughts were necessarily God's thoughts. And if his bloodstained passion with Safiyya amazes and disgusts our modern minds, his love for little Ibrahim, the son of Mary the Egyptian, and his passionate grief when the child died, reinstate him in the fellowship of all those who have known love and loss.

He smoothed the earth over the little grave with his own hands. "This eases the afflicted heart," he said. "Though it neither profits nor injures the dead, yet it is a comfort to the living."

§ 4

But the personal quality of Muhammad is one thing and the quality of Islam, the religion he founded, is quite another. Muhammad was not pitted against Jesus or Mani, and his relative stature is only a very secondary question for us; it is Islam which was pitted against the corrupted Christianity of the seventh century and against the decaying tradition of the Zoroastrian Magi with which the historian has the greater concern. And whether it was through its Prophet or whether it was in spite of its Prophet, and through certain accidents in its origin and certain qualities of the desert from which it sprang, there can be no denying that Islam possesses many fine and noble attributes. It is not always through sublime persons that great things come into human life. It is the folly of the simple disciple which demands miraculous frippery on the majesty of truth and immaculate conceptions for righteousness.

A year before his death, at the end of the tenth year of the Hegira, Muhammad made his last pilgrimage from Medina to Mecca. He made then a great sermon to his people of which the tradition is as follows. There are, of course, disputes as to the authenticity of the words, but there can be no dispute that the world of Islam, a world still of three hundred million people, receives them to this day as its rule of life, and to a great extent observes it. The reader will note that the first paragraph sweeps away all plunder and blood feuds among the followers of Islam. The last makes the believing Negro the equal of the Caliph. They may not be sublime words, as certain utterances of Jesus of Nazareth are sublime; but they established in the world a great tradition of dignified fair dealing, they breathe a spirit of generosity, and they are human and workable. They created a society more free from widespread cruelty and social oppression than any society had ever been in the world before.

"Ye people: Hearken to my words; for I know not whether, after this year, I shall ever be amongst you here again. Your lives and property are sacred and inviolable amongst one another until the end of time.

"The Lord hath ordained to every man the share of his inheritance; a testament is not lawful to the prejudice of heirs.

"The child belongeth to the parent; and the violator of wedlock shall be stoned.

"Whoever claimeth falsely another for his father, or another for his master, the curse of God and the angels and of all mankind shall rest upon him.

"Ye people! Ye have rights demandable of your wives, and they have rights demandable of you. Upon them it is incumbent not to violate their conjugal faith nor commit any act of open impropriety; which things if they do, ye have authority to shut them up in separate apartments and to beat them with stripes, yet not severely. But if they refrain therefrom, clothe them and feed them suitably. And treat your women well, for they are with you as captives and prisoners; they have not power over anything as regards themselves. And ye have verily taken them on the security of God, and have made their persons lawful unto you by the words of God.

"And your slaves, see that ye feed them with such food as ye eat yourselves, and clothe them with the stuff ye wear. And if they commit a fault which ye are not inclined to forgive, then sell them, for they are the servants of the Lord, and are not to be tormented.

"Ye people! hearken to my speech and comprehend the same. Know that every Moslem is the brother of every other Moslem. All of you are on the same equality."

This insistence upon kindliness and consideration in the daily life is one of the main virtues of Islam, but it is not the only one. Equally important is the uncompromising monotheism, void of any Jewish exclusiveness, which is sustained by the Koran. Islam from the outset was fairly proof against the theological elaborations that have perplexed and divided Christianity and smothered the spirit of Jesus. And its third source of strength has been in the meticulous prescription of methods of prayer and worship, and its clear statement of the limited and conventional significance of the importance ascribed to Mecca. All sacrifice was barred to the faithful; no loophole was left for the sacrificial priest of the old dispensation to come back into the new faith. It was not simply a new faith, a purely prophetic religion, as the religion of Jesus was in the time of Jesus, or the religion of Gautama in the lifetime of Gautama, but it was so stated as to remain so. Islam to this day has learned doctors, teachers, and preachers; but it has no priests.

It was full of the spirit of kindliness, generosity, and brotherhood; it was a simple and understandable religion; it was instinct with the chivalrous sentiment of the desert; and it made its appeal straight to the commonest instincts in the composition of ordinary men. Against it were pitted Judaism, which had made a racial hoard of God; Christianity talking and preaching endlessly now of trinities, doctrines, and heresies no ordinary man could make head or tail of; and Mazdaism, the cult of the Zoroastrian Magi, who had inspired the crucifixion of Mani. The bulk of the people to whom the challenge of Islam came did not trouble very much whether Muhammad was lustful or not, or whether he had done some shifty and questionable things; what appealed to them was that this God, Allah, he preached, was by the test of the conscience in their hearts a God of righteousness, and that the honest acceptance of his doctrine and method opened the door wide in a world of uncertainty, treachery, and intolerable divisions to a great and increasing brotherhood of trustworthy men on earth, and to a paradise not of perpetual exercises in praise and worship, in which saints, priests, and anointed kings were still to have the upper places, but of equal fellowship and simple and understandable delights such as their souls craved for. Without any ambiguous symbolism, without any darkening of altars or chanting of priests, Muhammad had brought home those attractive doctrines to the hearts of mankind.

§ 5

The true embodiment of the spirit of Islam was not Muhammad, but his close friend and supporter, Abu Bekr. There can be little doubt that if Muhammad was the mind and imagination of primitive Islam, Abu Bekr was its conscience and its will. Throughout their life together it was Muhammad who said the thing, but it was Abu Bekr who believed the thing. When Muhammad wavered, Abu Bekr sustained him. Abu Bekr was a man without doubts, his beliefs cut down to acts cleanly as a sharp knife cuts. We may feel sure that Abu Bekr would never have temporized about the minor gods of Mecca, or needed inspirations from Allah to explain his private life. When in the eleventh year of the Hegira (632) the Prophet sickened of a fever and died, it was Abu Bekr who succeeded him as Caliph and leader of the people (Kalifa = Successor), and it was the unflinching confidence of Abu Bekr in the righteousness of Allah which prevented a split between Medina and Mecca, which stamped down a widespread insurrection of the Bedouin against taxation for the common cause, and carried out a great plundering raid into Syria that the dead Prophet had projected. And then Abu Bekr, with that faith which moves mountains, set himself simply and sanely to organize the subjugation of the whole world to Allah—with little armies of 3,000 or 4,000 Arabs—according to those letters the Prophet had written from Medina in 628 to all the monarchs of the world.

And the attempt came near to succeeding. Had there been in Islam a score of men, younger men to carry on his work, of Abu Bekr's quality, it would certainly have succeeded. It came near to succeeding because Arabia was now a centre of faith and will, and because nowhere else in the world until China was reached, unless it was upon the steppes of Russia or Turkestan, was there another community of free-spirited men with any power of belief in their rulers and leaders. The head of the Byzantine Empire, Heraclius, the conqueror of Chosroes II, was past his prime and suffering from dropsy, and his empire was exhausted by the long Persian war. Nor

had he at any time displayed such exceptional ability as the new occasion demanded. The motley of people under his rule knew little of him and cared less. Persia was at the lowest depths of monarchist degradation, the parricide Kavadh II had died after a reign of a few months, and a series of dynastic intrigues and romantic murders enlivened the palace but weakened the country. The war between Persia and the Byzantine Empire was only formally concluded about the time of the beginning of Abu Bekr's rule. Both sides had made great use of Arab auxiliaries; over Syria a number of towns and settlements of Christianized Arabs were scattered who professed a baseless loyalty to Constantinople; the Persian marches between Mesopotamia and the desert were under the control of an Arab tributary prince, whose capital was at Hira. Arab influence was strong in such cities as Damascus, where Christian Arab gentlemen would read and recite the latest poetry from the desert competitors. There was thus a great amount of easily assimilable material ready at hand for Islam.

And the military campaigns that now began were among the most brilliant in the world's history. Arabia had suddenly become a garden of fine men. The name of Khalid stands out as the brightest star in a constellation of able and devoted Moslem generals. Whenever he commanded he was victorious, and when the jealousy of the second Caliph, Omar, degraded him unjustly and inexcusably,[1] he made no ado, but served Allah cheerfully and well as a subordinate to those over whom he had ruled. We cannot trace the story of this warfare here; the Arab armies struck simultaneously at Byzantine Syria and the Persian frontier city of Hira, and everywhere they offered a choice of three alternatives: either pay tribute, or confess the true God and join us, or die. They encountered armies, large and disciplined but spiritless armies, and defeated them. And nowhere was there such a thing as a popular resistance. The people of the populous irrigation lands of Mesopotamia cared not a jot whether they paid taxes to Byzantium or Persepolis or to Medina; and of the two, Arabs or Persian court, the Arabs, the Arabs of the great years, were manifestly the cleaner people, more just and more merciful. The Christian Arabs joined the invaders very readily and so did many Jews. Just as in the west, so now in the east, an invasion became a social revolution. But here it was also a religious revolution with a new and distinctive mental vitality.

It was Khalid who fought the decisive battle (634) with the army of Heraclius upon the banks of the Yarmuk, a tributary of the Jordan. The legions, as ever, were without proper

[1] But Schurtz, in Helmolt's *History of the World*, says that the private life of the gallant Khalid was a scandal to the faithful. He committed adultery, a serious offence in a world of polygamy.

cavalry; for seven centuries the ghost of old Crassus had haunted the east in vain; the imperial armies relied upon Christian Arab auxiliaries, and these deserted to the Moslems as the armies joined issue. A great parade of priests, sacred banners, pictures, and holy relics was made by the Byzantine host, and it was further sustained by the chanting of monks. But there was no magic in the relics and little conviction about the chanting. On the Arab side of the emirs and sheiks harangued the troops, and after the ancient Arab fashion the shrill voices of women in the rear encouraged their men. The Moslem ranks were full of believers before whom shone victory or paradise. The battle was never in doubt after the defection of the irregular cavalry. An attempt to retreat dissolved into a rout and became a massacre. The Byzantine army had fought with its back to the river, which was presently choked with its dead.

Thereafter Heraclius slowly relinquished all Syria, which he had so lately won back from the Persians, to his new antagonists. Damascus soon fell, and a year later the Moslems entered Antioch. For a time they had to abandon it again to a last effort from Constantinople, but they re-entered it for good under Khalid.

Meanwhile on the eastern front, after a swift initial success which gave them Hira, the Persian resistance stiffened. The dynastic struggle had ended at last in the coming of a king of kings, and a general of ability had been found in Rustam. He gave battle at Kadessia (637). His army was just such another composite host as Darius had led into Thrace or Alexander defeated at Issus; it was a medley of levies. He had thirty-three war elephants, and he sat on a golden throne upon a raised platform behind the Persian ranks, surveying the battle, which throne will remind the reader of Herodotus, the Hellespont, and Salamis more than a thousand years before. The battle lasted three days; each day the Arabs attacked and the Persian host held its ground until nightfall called a truce. On the third day the Arabs received reinforcements, and towards the evening the Persians attempted to bring the struggle to an end by a charge of elephants. At first the huge beasts carried all before them; then one was wounded painfully and became uncontrollable, rushing up and down between the armies. Its panic affected the others, and for a time both armies remained dumbfounded in the red light of sunset, watching the frantic efforts of these grey, squealing monsters to escape from the tormenting masses of armed men that hemmed them in. It was by the merest chance that at last they broke through the Persian and not through the Arab array, and that it was the Arabs who were able to charge home upon the resulting confusion. The twilight darkened to night, but this time the armies did not separate. All through the night the Arabs smote in the name of Allah, and pressed upon the shattered and retreating Persians. Dawn broke upon the vestiges of Rustam's army in flight far beyond the litter of the battlefield. Its path was marked by scattered weapons and war material, abandoned transport, and the dead and dying. The platform and the golden throne were broken down, and Rustam lay dead among a heap of dead men. . . .

Already in 634 Abu Bekr had died and given place to Omar, the Prophet's brother-in-law, as Caliph; and it was under Omar (634-643) that the main conquests of the Moslems occurred. The Byzantine Empire was pushed out of Syria altogether. But at the Taurus Mountains the Moslem thrust was held. Armenia was overrun, all Mesopotamia was conquered and Persia beyond the rivers. Egypt passed almost passively from Greek to Arab; in a few years the Semitic race, in the name of God and His Prophet, had recovered nearly all the dominions it had lost to the Aryan Persians a thousand years before. Jerusalem fell early, making a treaty without standing siege, and so the True Cross which had been carried off by the Persians a dozen years before, and elaborately restored by Heraclius, passed once more out of the rule of Christians. But it was still in Christian hands; the Christians were to be tolerated, paying only a poll tax; and all the churches and all the relics were left in their possession.

Jerusalem made a peculiar condition for its surrender. The city would give itself only to the Caliph Omar in person. Hitherto he had been in Medina organizing armies and controlling the general campaign. He came to Jerusalem (638), and the manner of his coming shows how swiftly the vigour and simplicity of the first Moslem onset was being sapped by success. He came the six-hundred-mile journey with only one attendant; he was mounted on a camel, and a bag of barley, another of dates, a water-skin, and a wooden platter were his provision for the journey. He was met outside the city by his chief

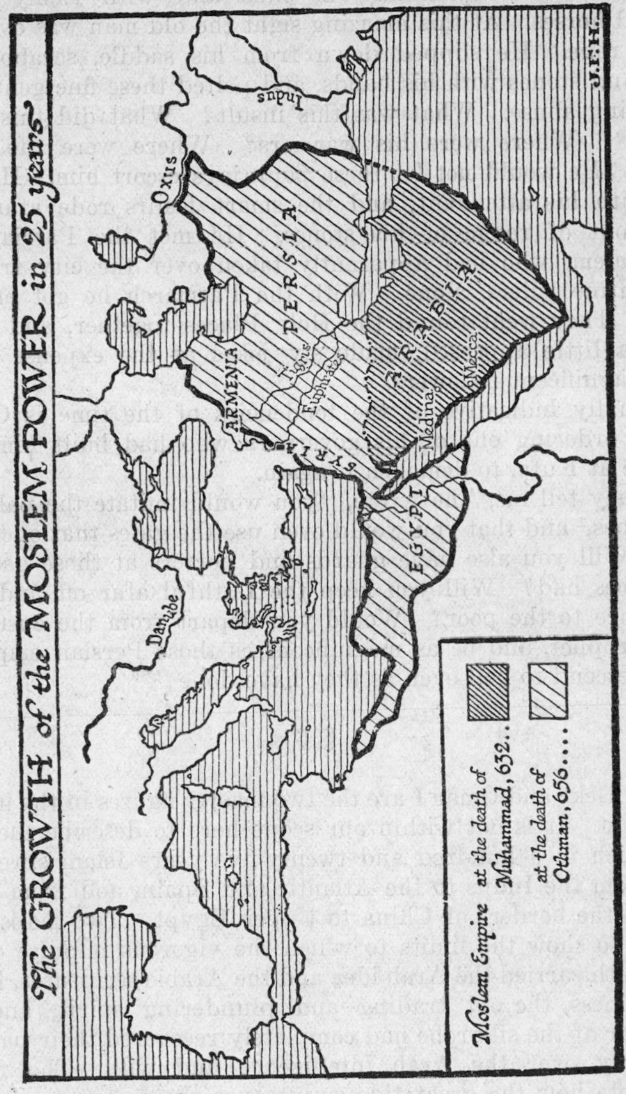
The GROWTH of the MOSLEM POWER in 25 years
Oxus
Indus
PERSIA
ARMENIA
Tigris
Euphrates
SYRIA
ARABIA
Medina
Mecca
EGYPT
Danube
J.F.H.
Moslem Empire
at the death of Muhammad, 632...
at the death of Othman, 656.....

captains, robed splendidly in silks and with richly caparisoned horses. At this amazing sight the old man was overcome with rage. He slipped down from his saddle, scrabbled up dirt and stones with his hands, and pelted these fine gentlemen, shouting abuse. What was this insult? What did this finery mean? Where were his warriors? Where were the desert men? He would not let these popinjays escort him. He went on with his attendant, and the smart Emirs rode afar off—well out of range of his stones. He met the Patriarch of Jerusalem, who had apparently taken over the city from its Byzantine rulers, alone. With the Patriarch he got on very well. They went round the Holy Places together, and Omar, now a little appeased, made sly jokes at the expense of his too magnificent followers.

Equally indicative of the tendencies of the time is Omar's letter ordering one of his governors who had built himself a palace at Kufa, to demolish it again.

"They tell me," he wrote, "you would imitate the palace of Chosroes,[1] and that you would even use the gates that once were his. Will you also have guards and porters at those gates, as Chosroes had? Will you keep the faithful afar off and deny audience to the poor? Would you depart from the custom of our Prophet, and be as magnificent as those Persian emperors, and descend to hell even as they have done?"[2]

§ 6

Abu Bekr and Omar I are the two master figures in the history of Islam. It is not within our scope here to describe the wars by which in a hundred and twenty-five years Islam spread itself from the Indus to the Atlantic and Spain, and from Kashgar on the borders of China to Upper Egypt. Two maps must suffice to show the limits to which the vigorous impulse of the new faith carried the Arab idea and the Arabic scriptures, before worldliness, the old trading and plundering spirit, and the glamour of the silk robe had completely recovered their paralyzing sway over the Arab intelligence and will. The reader will note how the great tide swept over the footsteps of Yuan Chwang, and how easily in Africa the easy conquests of the

1 At Ctesiphon.
2 Paraphrased from Schurtz in Helmolt's *History of the World.*

Vandals were repeated in the reverse direction. And if the reader entertains any delusions about a fine civilization, either Persian, Roman, Hellenic, or Egyptian, being submerged by this flood, the sooner he dismisses such ideas the better. Islam prevailed because it was the best social and political order the times could offer. It prevailed because everywhere it found politically apathetic peoples, robbed, oppressed, bullied, uneducated, and unorganized, and it found selfish and unsound governments out of touch with any people at all. It was the broadest, freshest, and cleanest political idea that had yet come into actual activity in the world, and it offered better terms than any other to the mass of mankind. The capitalistic and slave-holding system of the Roman Empire and the literature and culture and social tradition of Europe had altogether decayed and broken down before Islam arose; it was only when mankind lost faith in the sincerity of its representatives that Islam, too, began to decay.

The larger part of its energy spent itself in conquering and assimilating Persia and Turkestan; its most vigorous thrusts were northwardly from Persia and westwardly through Egypt. Had it concentrated its first vigour upon the Byzantine Empire, there can be little doubt that by the eighth century it would have taken Constantinople and come through into Europe as easily as it reached the Pamirs. The Caliph Muawiya, it is true, besieged the capital for seven years (672 to 678), and Suleiman in 717 and 718; but the pressure was not sustained, and for three or four centuries longer the Byzantine Empire remained the crazy bulwark of Europe. In the newly Christianized or still pagan Avars, Bulgars, Serbs, Slavs, and Saxons, Islam would certainly have found as ready converts as it did in the Turks of Central Asia. And though, instead of insisting upon Constantinople, it first came round into Europe by the circuitous route of Africa and Spain, it was only in France, at the end of a vast line of communications from Arabia, that it encountered a power sufficiently vigorous to arrest its advance.

From the outset the Bedouin aristocrats of Mecca dominated the new empire. Abu Bekr, the first Caliph, was in an informal shouting way elected at Medina, and so were Omar I and Othman, the third Caliph, but all three were Meccans of good family. They were not men of Medina. And though Abu

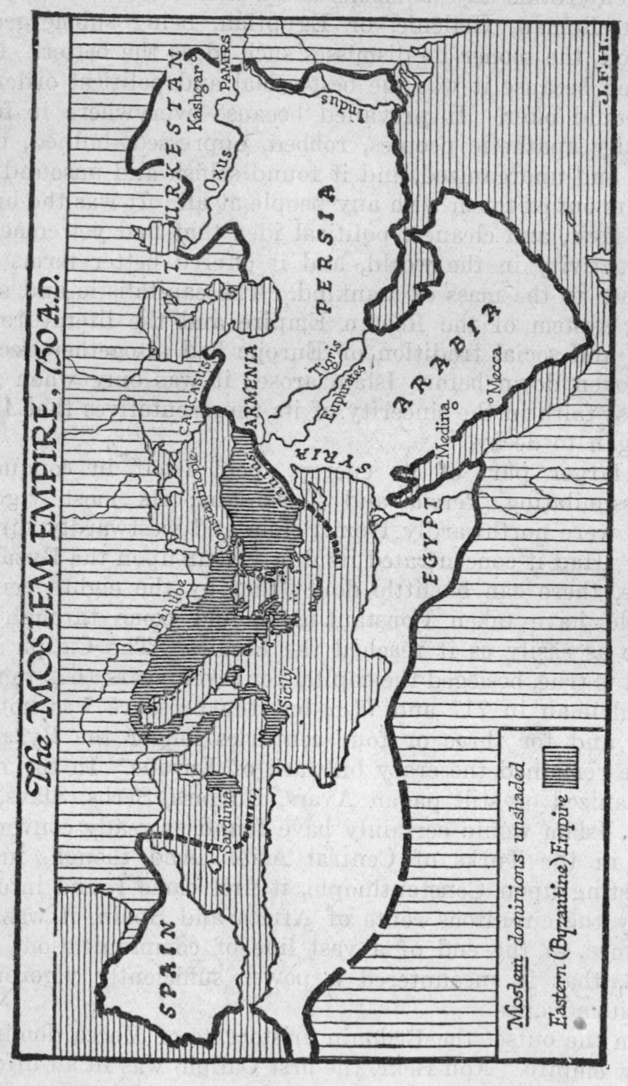

The MOSLEM EMPIRE, 750 A.D.

Bekr and Omar were men of stark simplicity and righteousness Othman was of a baser quality, a man quite in the vein of those silk robes, to whom conquest was not conquest for Allah but for Arabia, and especially for Mecca in Arabia, and more particularly for himself and for the Meccans and for his family, the Omayyads. He was a worthy man, who stood out for his country and his town and his "people." He was no early convert as his two predecessors had been; he had joined the Prophet for reasons of policy in fair give and take. With his accession the Caliph ceases to be a strange man of fire and wonder, and becomes an Oriental monarch like many Oriental monarchs before and since, a fairly good monarch by Eastern standards as yet, but nothing more.

The rule and death of Othman brought out the consequences of Muhammad's weaknesses as clearly as the lives of Abu Bekr and Omar had witnessed to the divine fire in his teaching. Muhammad had been politic at times when Abu Bekr would have been firm, and the new element of aristocratic greediness that came in with Othman was one fruit of those politic moments. And the legacy of that carelessly compiled harem of the Prophet, the family complications and jealousies which had lurked in the background of Moslem affairs during the rule of the first two Caliphs, was now coming out into the light of day. Alī, who was the nephew, the adopted son, and the son-in-law of the Prophet—he was the husband of the Prophet's daughter Fatima—he had considered himself the rightful Caliph. His claims formed an undertow to the resentment of Medina and of the rival families of Mecca against the advancement of the Omayyads. But Ayesha, the favourite wife of the Prophet, had always been jealous of Fatima and hostile to Ali. She supported Othman. . . . The splendid opening of the story of Islam collapses suddenly into this squalid dispute and bickering of heirs and widows.

In 656 Othman, an old man of eighty, was stoned in the streets of Medina by a mob, chased to his house, and murdered; and Ali became at last Caliph, only to be murdered in his turn (661). In one of the battles in this civil war, Ayesha, now a gallant, mischievous old lady, distinguished herself by leading a charge, mounted on a camel. She was taken prisoner and treated well.

While the armies of Islam were advancing triumphantly to

the conquest of the world, this sickness of civil war smote at its head. What was the rule of Allah in the world to Ayesha when she could score off the detested Fatima, and what heed were the Omayyads and the partisans of Ali likely to take of the unity of mankind when they had a good hot feud of this sort to entertain them, with the caliphate as a prize? The world of Islam was rent in twain by the spites, greeds, and partisan silliness of a handful of men and women in Medina. That quarrel still lives. To this day one main division of the Moslems, the Shiites, maintain the hereditary right of Ali to be Caliph *as an article of faith!* They prevail in Persia and India. But an equally important section, the Sunnites, with whom it is difficult for a disinterested observer not to agree, deny this peculiar addendum to Muhammad's simple creed. So far as we can gather at this length of time, Ali was an entirely commonplace individual.

To watch this schism creeping across the brave beginnings of Islam is like watching a case of softening of the brain. To the copious literature of the subject we must refer the reader who wishes to learn how Hasan, the son of Ali, was poisoned by his wife, and how Husein, his brother, was killed. We do but name them here because they still afford a large section of mankind scope for sentimental partisanship and mutual annoyance. They are the two chief Shiite martyrs. Amidst the coming and going of their conflicts the old Kaaba at Mecca was burnt down, and naturally there began endless disputation whether it should be rebuilt in exactly its ancient form or on a much larger scale.

In this and the preceding sections we have seen once more the inevitable struggle of this newest and latest unifying impulse in the world's affairs against the everyday worldliness of mankind, and we have seen also how from the first the complicated household of Muhammad was like an evil legacy to the new faith. But as this history now degenerates into the normal crimes and intrigues of an Oriental dynasty, the student of history will realize a third fundamental weakness in the world reforms of Muhammad. He was an illiterate Arab, ignorant of history, totally ignorant of all the political experiences of Rome and Greece, and almost as ignorant of the real history of Judea; and he left his followers with no scheme for a stable government embodying and concentrating the general will of the faithful, and no effective form to express the very real spirit of democracy (using the word in its modern sense) that pervades the essential teaching of Islam. His own rule was unlimited autocracy, and autocratic Islam has remained. Politically Islam was not an advance, but a retrogression from the traditional freedoms and customary laws of the desert. The breach of the pilgrims' truce that led to the battle of Badr is the blackest mark against early Islam. Nominally Allah is its chief ruler—but practically its master has always been whatever man was vigorous and unscrupulous enough to snatch and hold the Caliphate—and, subject to revolts and assassinations, its final law has been that man's will.

For a time, after the death of Ali, the Omayyad family was in the ascendant, and for nearly a century they gave rulers to Islam.

The Arab historians are so occupied with the dynastic squabbles and crimes of the time, that it is difficult to trace the external history of the period. We find Moslem shipping upon the seas defeating the Byzantine fleet in a great sea fight off the coast of Lycia (A.D. 655), but how the Moslems acquired this victorious fleet thus early we do not clearly know. It was probably chiefly Egyptian. For some years Islam certainly controlled the eastern Mediterranean, and in 662 and again in 672, during the reign of Muawiya (662-680), the first great Omayyad Caliph, made two sea attacks upon Constantinople. They had to be sea attacks because Islam, so long as it was under Arab rule, never surmounted the barrier of the Taurus Mountains. During the same period the Moslems were also pressing their conquests further and further into Central Asia. While Islam was already decaying at its centre, it was yet making great hosts of new adherents and awakening a new spirit among the hitherto divided and aimless Turkish peoples. Medina was no longer a possible centre for its vast enterprises in Asia, Africa, and the Mediterranean, and so Damascus became the usual capital of the Omayyad Caliphs.

Chief among these, as for a time the clouds of dynastic intrigue clear, are Abdal Malik (685-705) and Walid I (705-715), under whom the Omayyad line rose to the climax of its successes. The western boundary was carried to the Pyrenees, while to the east the domains of the Caliph marched with China.

The son of Walid, Suleiman (715), carried out a second series of Moslem attacks upon Constantinople which his father had planned and proposed. As with the Caliph Muawiya half a century before, the approach was by sea—for Asia Minor, as we have just noted, was still unconquered—and the shipping was drawn chiefly from Egypt. The emperor, a usurper, Leo the Isaurian, displayed extraordinary skill and obstinacy in the defence; he burnt most of the Moslem shipping in a brilliant sortie, cut up the troops they had landed upon the Asiatic side of the Bosphorus, and after a campaign in Europe of two years (717-718), a winter of unexampled severity completed their defeat.

From this point onward the glory of the Omayyad line decays. The first tremendous impulse of Islam was now spent. There was no further expansion and a manifest decline in religious zeal. Islam had made millions of converts, and had digested those millions very imperfectly. Cities, nations, whole sects and races, Arab pagans, Jews, Christians, Manichæans, Zoroastrians, Turanian pagans had been swallowed up into this new vast empire of Muhammad's successors. It has hitherto been the common characteristic of all the great unifying religious initiators of the world, the common oversight, that they have accepted the moral and theological ideals to which the first appeal was made, as though they were universal ideals. Muhammad's appeal, for example, was to the traditional chivalry and underlying monotheistic feelings of the intelligent Arabs of his time. These things were latent in the mind and conscience of Mecca and Medina; he did but call them forth. Then, as the new teaching spread and stereotyped itself, it had to work on a continually more uncongenial basis, it had to grow in soil that distorted and perverted it. Its sole text-book was the Koran. To minds untuned to the melodies of Arabic, this book seemed to be, as it seems to many European minds to-day, a mixture of fine-spirited rhetoric with—to put it plainly—formless and unintelligent gabble. Countless converts missed the real thing in it altogether. To that we must ascribe the readiness of the Persian and Indian sections of the faith to join the Shiite schism upon a quarrel that they could at least understand and feel. And to the same attempt to square the new stuff with old prepossessions was due such extravagant theology as presently disputed whether the

Koran was and always had been co-existent with God.[1] We should be stupefied by the preposterousness of this idea if we did not recognize in it at once the well-meaning attempt of some learned Christian convert to Islamize his belief that "In the beginning was the Word, and the Word was with God, and the Word was God."[2]

None of the great unifying religious initiators of the world hitherto seems to have been accompanied by any understanding of the vast educational task, the vast work of lucid and varied exposition and intellectual organization involved in its propositions. They all present the same history of a rapid spreading, like a little water poured over a great area, and then of a superficiality and corruption.

In a little while we hear stories of an Omayyad Caliph, Walid II (743-744), who mocked at the Koran, ate pork, drank wine, and did not pray. Those stories may have been true or they may have been circulated for political reasons. There began a puritan reaction in Mecca and Medina against the levity and luxury of Damascus. Another great Arab family, the Abbas family, the Abbasids, a thoroughly wicked line, had long been scheming for power, and was making capital out of the general discontent. The feud of the Omayyads and the Abbasids was older than Islam; it had been going on before Muhammad was born. These Abbasids took up the tradition of the Shiite "martyrs," Ali and his sons Hasan and Husein, and identified themselves with it. The banner of the Omayyads was white; the Abbasid adopted a black banner, black in mourning for Hasan and Husein, black because black is more impressive than any colour; moreover, the Abbasids declared that all the Caliphs after Ali were usurpers. In 749 they accomplished a carefully prepared revolution, and the last of the Omayyad Caliphs was hunted down and slain in Egypt. Abul Abbas was the first of the Abbasid Caliphs, and he began his reign by collecting into one prison every living male of the Omayyad line upon whom he could lay hands and causing them all to be massacred. Their bodies, it is said, were heaped together, a leathern carpet was spread over them, and on this gruesome table Abul Abbas and his councillors feasted. Moreover, the tombs of the Omayyad Caliphs were rifled, and their bones burnt and scattered to the four winds of heaven. So the

[1] Mark Sykes. [2] St. John's Gospel, chap. i. 1.

grievances of Ali were avenged at last, and the Omayyad line passed out of history.

There was, it is interesting to note, a rising on behalf of the Omayyads in Khorasan which was assisted by the Chinese Emperor.

§ 7

But the descendants of Ali were not destined to share in this triumph for long. The Abbasids were adventurers and rulers of an older school than Islam. Now that the tradition of Ali had served its purpose, the next proceeding of the new Caliph was to hunt down and slaughter the surviving members of his family, the descendants of Ali and Fatima.

Clearly the old traditions of Sassanid Persia and of Persia before the Greeks were returning to the world. With the accession of the Abbasids the control of the sea departed from the Caliph, and with it went Spain and North Africa, in which, under an Omayyad survivor in the former case, independent Moslem states now arose. The centre of gravity of Islam shifted across the desert from Damascus to Mesopotamia. Mansur, the successor of Abul Abbas, built himself a new capital at Bagdad near the ruins of Ctesiphon, the former Sassanid capital. Turks and Persians as well as Arabs became Emirs, and the army was reorganized upon Sassanid lines. Medina and Mecca were now only of importance as pilgrimage centres, to which the faithful turned to pray. But because it was a fine language, and because it was the language of the Koran, Arabic continued to spread until presently it had replaced Greek and become the language of educated men throughout the whole Moslem world.

Of the Abbasid monarchs after Abul Abbas we need tell little here. A bickering war went on year by year in Asia Minor in which neither Byzantium nor Bagdad made any permanent gains, though once or twice the Moslems raided as far as the Bosphorus. A false prophet Mokanna, who said he was God, had a brief but troublesome career. There were plots, there were insurrections; they lie flat and colourless now in the histories like dead flowers in an old book. One other Abbasid Caliph only need be named, and that quite as much for his legendary as for his real importance, Haroun-al-Raschid (786-809). He was not only the Caliph of an outwardly prosperous empire in the world of reality, but he was also the Caliph of an undying empire in the deathless world of fiction, he was the Haroun-al-Raschid of the *Arabian Nights.*

Sir Mark Sykes [1] gives an account of the reality of his empire from which we will quote certain passages. He says: "The Imperial Court was polished, luxurious, and unlimitedly wealthy; the capital, Bagdad, a gigantic mercantile city surrounding a huge administrative fortress, wherein every department of state had a properly regulated and well-ordered public office; where schools and colleges abounded; whither philosophers, students, doctors, poets, and theologians flocked from all parts of the civilized globe. . . . The provincial capitals were embellished with vast public buildings, and linked together by an effective and rapid service of posts and caravans; the frontiers were secure and well garrisoned, the army loyal, efficient, and brave; the governors and ministers honest and forbearing. The empire stretched with equal strength and unimpaired control from the Cilician gates to Aden, and from Egypt to Central Asia. Christians, Pagans, Jews, as well as Moslems, were employed in the government service. Usurpers, rebellious generals, and false prophets seemed to have vanished from the Moslem dominions. Traffic and wealth had taken the place of revolution and famine. . . . Pestilence and disease were met by Imperial hospitals and government physicians. . . . In government business the rough-and-ready methods of Arabian administration had given place to a complicated system of Divans, initiated partly from the Roman, but chiefly taken from the Persian system of government. Posts, Finance, Privy Seal, Crown Lands, Justice, and Military affairs were each administered by separate bureaux in the hands of ministers and officials; an army of clerks, scribes, writers, and accountants swarmed into these offices and gradually swept the whole power of the government into their own hands by separating the Commander of the Faithful from any direct intercourse with his subjects. The Imperial Palace and the entourage were equally based on Roman and Persian precedents. Eunuchs, closely veiled 'harems' of women, guards, spies, go-betweens, jesters, poets, and dwarfs clustered around the person of the Commander of the Faithful, each, in his degree, endeavouring to gain the royal favour and indirectly distracting the

[1] *The Caliph's Last Heritage.*

royal mind from affairs of business and state. Meanwhile the mercantile trade of the East poured gold into Bagdad, and supplemented the other enormous stream of money derived from the contributions of plunder and loot despatched to the capital by the commanders of the victorious raiding forces which harried Asia Minor, India, and Turkestan. The seemingly unending supply of Turkish slaves and Byzantine specie added to the richness of the revenues of Irak, and, combined with the vast commercial traffic of which Bagdad was the centre, produced a large and powerful moneyed class, composed of the sons of generals, officials, landed proprietors, royal favourites, merchants, and the like, who encouraged the arts, literature, philosophy, and poetry as the mood took them, building palaces for themselves, vying with each other in the luxury of their entertainments, suborning poets to sound their praises, dabbling in philosophy, supporting various schools of thought, endowing charities, and, in fact, behaving as the wealthy have always behaved in all ages.

"I have said that the Abbasid Empire in the days of Haroun-al-Raschid was weak and feeble to a degree, and perhaps the reader will consider this a foolish proposition when he takes into consideration that I have described the Empire as orderly, the administration definite and settled, the army efficient, and wealth abundant. The reason I make the suggestion is that the Abbasid Empire had lost touch with everything original and vital in Islam, and was constructed entirely by the reunion of the fragments of the empires Islam had destroyed. There was nothing in the empire which appealed to the higher instincts of the leaders of the people; the holy war had degenerated into a systematic acquisition of plunder. The Caliph had become a luxurious Emperor or King of Kings; the administration had changed from a patriarchal system to a bureaucracy. The wealthier classes were rapidly losing all faith in the religion of the state; speculative philosophy and high living were taking the place of Koranic orthodoxy and Arabian simplicity. The solitary bond which could have held the empire together, the sternness and plainness of the Moslem faith, was completely neglected by both the Caliph and his advisers. . . . Haroun-al-Raschid himself was a winebibber, and his palace was decorated with graven images of birds and beasts and men. . . .

"For a moment we stand amazed at the greatness of the Abbasid dominion; then suddenly we realize that it is but as a fair husk enclosing the dust and ashes of dead civilizations.''

Haroun-al-Raschid died in 809. At his death his great empire fell immediately into civil war and confusion, and the next great event of unusual importance in this region of the world comes two hundred years later when the Turks, under the chiefs of the great family of the Seljuks, poured southward out of Turkestan, and not only conquered the empire of Bagdad, but Asia Minor also. Coming from the north-east as they did, they were able to outflank the great barrier of the Taurus Mountains, which had hitherto held back the Moslems. They were still much the same people as those of whom Yuan Chwang gave us a glimpse four hundred years earlier, but now they were Moslems, and Moslems of the primitive type, men whom Abu Bekr would have welcomed to Islam. They caused a great revival of vigour in Islam, and they turned the minds of the Moslem world once more in the direction of a religious war against Christendom. For there had been a sort of truce between these two great religions after the cessation of the Moslem advance and the decline of the Omayyads. Such warfare as had gone on between Christianity and Islam had been rather border-bickering than sustained war. It became only a bitter fanatical struggle again in the eleventh century.

§ 8

But before we go on to tell of the Turks and the Crusaders, the great wars that began between Christendom and Islam, and which have left a quite insane intolerance between these great systems right down to the present time, it is necessary to give a little more attention to the intellectual life of the Arabic-speaking world which was now spreading more and more widely over the regions which Hellenism had once dominated. For some generations before Muhammad, the Arab mind had been, as it were, smouldering, it had been producing poetry and much religious discussion; under the stimulus of the national and racial successes it presently blazed out with a brilliance second only to that of the Greeks during their best period. From a new angle and with a fresh vigour it took up that systematic development of positive knowledge which the Greeks had begun and relinquished. It revived the human pursuit of science. If the Greek was the father, then the Arab was the foster-father of the scientific method of dealing with reality, that is to say, by absolute frankness, the utmost simplicity of statement and explanation, exact record, and exhaustive criticism. Through the Arabs it was and not by the Latin route that the modern world received that gift of light and power.

Their conquests brought the Arabs into contact with the Greek literary tradition, not at first directly, but through the Syrian translations of the Greek writers. The Nestorian Christians, the Christians to the east of orthodoxy, seem to have been much more intelligent and active-minded than the court theologians of Byzantium, and at a much higher level of general education than the Latin-speaking Christians of the west. They had been tolerated during the latter days of the Sassanids, and they were tolerated by Islam until the ascendancy of the Turks in the eleventh century. They had preserved much of the Hellenic medical science, and had even added to it. In the Omayyad times most of the physicians in the Caliph's dominions were Nestorians, and no doubt many learned Nestorians professed Islam without any serious compunction or any great change in their work and thoughts. They had preserved much of Aristotle both in Greek and in Syrian translations. They had a considerable mathematical literature. Their equipment makes the contemporary resources of St. Benedict or Cassiodorus seem very pitiful. To these Nestorian teachers came the fresh Arab mind out of the desert, keen and curious, and learnt much and improved upon its teaching.

But the Nestorians were not the only teachers available for the Arabs. Throughout all the rich cities of the east the kindred Jews were scattered with their own distinctive literature and tradition, and the Arab and the Jewish mind reacted upon one another to a common benefit. The Arab was informed and the Jew sharpened to a keener edge. The Jews have never been pedants in the matter of their language; we have already noted that a thousand years before Islam they spoke Greek in Hellenized Alexandria, and now all over this new Moslem world they were speaking and writing Arabic. Some of the greatest of Jewish literature was written in Arabic, the religious writings of Maimonides, for example. Indeed, it is difficult to say in the case of this Arabic culture where the Jew ends and the Arab begins, so important and essential were its Jewish factors.

Moreover, there was a third source of inspiration, more particularly in mathematical science, to which at present it is difficult to do justice—India. There can be little doubt that the Arab mind during its best period was in effective contact with Sanscrit literature and with Indian ideas, and that it derived much from this source.

The distinctive activities of the Arab mind were already manifest under the Omayyads, though it was during the Abbasid time that it made its best display. History is the beginning and core of all sound philosophy and all great literature, and the first Arab writers of distinction were historians, biographers, and quasi-historical poets. Romantic fiction and the short story followed as a reading public developed, willing to be amused. And as reading ceased to be a special accomplishment, and became necessary to every man of affairs and to every youth of breeding, came the systematic growth of an educational system and an educational literature. By the ninth and tenth centuries there are not only grammars, but great lexicons, and a mass of philological learning in Islam.

And a century or so in advance of the west, there grew up in the Moslem world at a number of centres, at Basra, at Kufa, at Bagdad and Cairo, and at Cordoba, out of what were at first religious schools dependent upon mosques, a series of great universities. The light of these universities shone far beyond the Moslem world, and drew students to them from east and west. At Cordoba in particular there were great numbers of Christian students, and the influence of Arab philosophy coming by way of Spain upon the universities of Paris, Oxford, and North Italy and upon Western European thought generally, was very considerable indeed. The name of Averroes (Ibn-rushd) of Cordoba (1126-1198) stands out as that of the culminating influence of Arab philosophy upon European thought. He developed the teachings of Aristotle upon lines that made a sharp division between religious and scientific truth, and so prepared the way for the liberation of scientific research from the theological dogmatism that restrained it both under Christianity and under Islam. Another great name is that of Avicenna (Ibnsinā), the Prince of Physicians (980-1037), who was born at the other end of the Arabic world at Bokhara, and who travelled in Khorasan. . . . The book-copying industry flourished at Alexandria, Damascus, Cairo, and Bagdad, and about the year 970 there were twenty-seven free schools open in Cordoba for the education of the poor.

"In mathematics," says Thatcher and Schwill,[1] "the Arabs built on the foundations of the Greek mathematicians. The origin of the so-called Arabic numerals is obscure. Under Theodoric the Great, Boethius made use of certain signs which were in part very like the nine digits which we now use. One of the pupils of Gerbert also used signs which were still more like ours, but the zero was unkown till the twelfth century, when it was invented by an Arab mathematician named Muhammad-Ibn-Musa, who also was the first to use the decimal notation, and who gave the digits the value of position. In geometry the Arabs did not add much to Euclid, but algebra is practically their creation; also they developed spherical trigonometry, invented the sine, tangent, and cotangent. In physics they invented the pendulum, and produced work on optics. They made progress in the science of astronomy. They built several observatories, and constructed many astronomical instruments which are still in use. They calculated the angle of the ecliptic and the precession of the equinoxes. Their knowledge of astronomy was undoubtedly considerable.

"In medicine they made great advances over the work of the Greeks. They studied physiology and hygiene, and their *materia medica* was practically the same as ours to-day. Many of their methods of treatment are still in use among us. Their surgeons understood the use of anæsthetics, and performed some of the most difficult operations known. At the time when in Europe the practice of medicine was forbidden by the Church, which expected cures to be effected by religious rites performed by the clergy, the Arabs had a real science of medicine. In chemistry they made a good beginning. They discovered many new substances, such as alcohol,[2] potash, nitrate of silver, corrosive sublimate, and nitric and sulphuric acid. . . . In manufactures they outdid the world in variety and beauty of design and perfection of workmanship. They worked in all the

[1] *A General History of Europe.*

[2] Alcohol as "spirits of wine" was known to Pliny (79 A.D.). The student of the history of science should consult Campbell Brown's *History of Chemistry* and check these statements in the text.

metals—gold, silver, copper, bronze, iron, and steel. In textile fabrics they have never been surpassed. They made glass and pottery of the finest quality. They knew the secrets of dyeing, and they manufactured paper. They had many processes of dressing leather, and their work was famous throughout Europe. They made tinctures, essences, and syrups. They made sugar from the cane, and grew many fine kinds of wine. They practised farming in a scientific way, and had good systems of irrigation. They knew the value of fertilizers, and adapted their crops to the quality of the ground. They excelled in horticulture, knowing how to graft and how to produce new varieties of fruit and flowers. They introduced into the west many trees and plants from the east, and wrote scientific treatises on farming."

One item in this account must be underlined here because of its importance in the intellectual life of mankind, the manufacture of paper. This the Arabs seem to have learnt from the Chinese by way of Central Asia. The Europeans acquired it from the Arabs. Until that time books had to be written upon parchment or papyrus, and after the Arab conquest of Egypt Europe was cut off from the papyrus supply. Until paper became abundant, the art of printing was of little use, and newspapers and popular education by means of books was impossible. This was probably a much more important factor in the relative backwardness of Europe during the dark ages than historians seem disposed to admit. . . .

And all this mental life went on in the Moslem world in spite of a very considerable amount of political disorder. From first to last the Arabs never grappled with the problem, the still unsolved problem, of the stable progressive state; everywhere their form of government was absolutist and subject to the convulsions, changes, intrigues, and murders that have always characterized the extremer forms of monarchy. But for some centuries, beneath the crimes and rivalries of courts and camps, the spirit of Islam did preserve a certain general decency and restraint in life; the Byzantine Empire was impotent to shatter this civilization, and the Turkish danger in the north-east gathered strength only very slowly. Until the Turk fell upon it, the intellectual life of Islam continued. Perhaps it secretly flattered itself that it would always be able to go on in spite of the thread of violence and unreason in its political direction.

Hitherto in all countries that has been the characteristic attitude of science and literature. The intellectual man has been loth to come to grips with the forcible man. He has generally been something of a courtier and time-server. Possibly he has never yet been quite sure of himself. Hitherto men of reason and knowledge have never had the assurance and courage of the religious fanatic. But there can be little doubt that they have accumulated settled convictions and gathered confidence during the last few centuries; they have slowly found a means to power through the development of popular education and popular literature, and to-day they are far more disposed to say things plainly and to claim a dominating voice in the organization of human affairs than they have ever been before in the world's history.

XXXII

CHRISTENDOM AND THE CRUSADES

§ 1. *The Western World at its Lowest Ebb.* § 2. *The Feudal System.* § 3. *The Frankish Kingdom of the Merovingians.* § 4. *The Christianization of the Western Barbarians.* § 5. *Charlemagne becomes Emperor of the West.* § 6. *The Personality of Charlemagne.* § 7. *The French and the Germans become Distinct.* § 8. *The Normans, the Saracens, the Hungarians and the Seljuk Turks.* § 9. *How Constantinople Appealed to Rome.* § 10. *The Crusades.* § 11. *The Crusades a Test of Christianity.* § 12. *The Emperor Frederick II.* § 13. *Defects and Limitations of the Papacy.* § 14. *A List of Leading Popes.*

§ 1

LET us turn again now from this intellectual renascence in the cradle of the ancient civilizations to the affairs of the Western world. We have described the complete :conomic, social, and political break-up of the Roman imperial ystem in the west, the confusion and darkness that followed in he sixth and seventh centuries, and the struggles of such men s Cassiodorus to keep alight the flame of human learning amidst hese windy confusions. For a time it would be idle to write f states and rulers. Smaller or greater adventurers seized castle or a countryside and ruled an uncertain area. The ritish Islands, for instance, were split up amidst a multitude f rulers; numerous Keltic chiefs in Ireland and Scotland nd Wales and Cornwall fought and prevailed over and sucumbed to each other; the English invaders were also divided ıto a number of fluctuating "kingdoms," Kent, Wessex, Essex, ussex, Mercia, Northumbria, and East Anglia, which were onstantly at war with one another. So it was over most of ıe Western world. Here a bishop would be the monarch, as regory the Great was in Rome; here a town or a group of towns would be under the rule of the duke or prince of this or that. Amidst the vast ruins of the city of Rome half-independent families of quasi-noble adventurers and their retainers maintained themselves. The Pope kept a sort of general predominance there, but he was sometimes more than balanced by a "Duke of Rome." The great arena of the Colosseum had been made into a privately-owned castle, and so, too, had the vast circular tomb of the Emperor Hadrian; and the adventurers who had possession of these strongholds and their partisans waylaid each other and fought and bickered in the ruinous streets of the once imperial city. The tomb of Hadrian was known after the days of Gregory the Great as the Castle of St. Angelo, the Castle of the Holy Angel, because when he was crossing the bridge over the Tiber on his way to St. Peter's to pray against the great pestilence which was devastating the city, he had had a vision of a great angel standing over the dark mass of the mausoleum and sheathing a sword, and he had known then that his prayers would be answered. This Castle of St. Angelo played a very important part in Roman affairs during this age of disorder.

Spain was in much the same state of political fragmentation as Italy or France or Britain; and in Spain the old feud of Carthaginian and Roman was still continued in the bitter hostility of their descendants and heirs, the Jew and the Christian. So that when the power of the Caliph had swept along the North African coast to the Straits of Gibraltar, it found in the Spanish Jews ready helpers in its invasion of Europe. A Moslem army of Arabs and of Berbers, the nomadic Hamitic people of the African desert and mountain hinterland who had been converted to Islam, crossed and defeated the West Goths in a great battle in 711. In a few years the whole country was in their possession.

In 720 Islam had reached the Pyrenees, and had pushed round their eastern end into France; and for a time it seemed that the faith was likely to subjugate Gaul as easily as it had subjugated the Spanish peninsula. But presently it struck against something hard, a new kingdom of the Franks, which had been consolidating itself for some two centuries in the Rhineland and North France.

Of this Frankish kingdom, the precursor of France and Germany, which formed the western bulwark of Europe agains the faith of Muhammad, as the Byzantine empire behind the Taurus Mountains formed the eastern, we shall now have much to tell; but first we must give some account of the new system of social groupings out of which it arose.

§ 2

It is necessary that the reader should have a definite idea of the social condition of western Europe in the eighth century. It was not a barbarism. Eastern Europe was still barbaric and savage; things had progressed but little beyond the state of affairs described by Gibbon in his account of the mission of Priscus to Attila (see p. 485). But western Europe was a shattered civilization, without law, without administration, with roads destroyed and education disorganized, but still with great numbers of people with civilized ideas and habits and traditions. It was a time of confusion, of brigandage, of crimes unpunished and universal insecurity. It is very interesting to trace how, out of the universal mêlée, the beginnings of a new order appeared. In a modern breakdown there would probably be the formation of local vigilance societies, which would combine and restore a police administration and a roughly democratic rule. But in the broken-down western empire of the sixth, seventh, and eighth centuries, men's ideas turned rather to leaders than to committees, and the centres about which affairs crystallized were here barbaric chiefs, here a vigorous bishop or some surviving claimant to a Roman official position, here a long-recognized landowner or man of ancient family, and here again some vigorous usurper of power. No solitary man was safe. So men were forced to link themselves with others, preferably people stronger than themselves. The lonely man chose the most powerful and active person in his district and became *his* man. The freeman or the weak lordling of a petty territory linked himself to some more powerful lord. The protection of that lord (or the danger of his hostility) became more considerable with every such accession. So very rapidly there went on a process of political crystallization in the confused and lawless sea into which the Western Empire had liquefied. These natural associations and alliances of protector and subordinates grew very rapidly into a system, *the feudal system,* traces of which are still to be found in the social structure of every European community west of Russia.

This process speedily took on technical forms and laws of its own. In such a country as Gaul it was already well in progress in the days of insecurity *before* the barbarian tribes broke into the empire as conquerors. The Franks when they came into Gaul brought with them an institution, which we have already noted in the case of the Macedonians, and which was probably of very wide distribution among the Nordic people, the gathering about the chief or war king of a body of young men of good family, the companions or *comitatus*, his counts or captains. It was natural in the case of invading peoples that the relations of a weak lord to a strong lord should take on the relations of a count to his king, and that a conquering chief should divide seized and confiscated estates among his companions. From the side of the decaying empire there came to feudalism the idea of the grouping for mutual protection of men and estates; from the Teutonic side came the notions of knightly association, devotion, and personal service. The former was the economic side of the institution, the latter the chivalrous.

The analogy of the aggregation of feudal groupings with crystallization is a very close one. As the historian watches the whirling and eddying confusion of the fourth and fifth centuries in Western Europe, he begins to perceive the appearance of these pyramidal growths of heads and subordinates and sub-subordinates, which jostle against one another, branch, dissolve again, or coalesce. "We use the term 'feudal system' for convenience sake, but with a degree of impropriety if it conveys the meaning 'systematic.' Feudalism in its most flourishing age was anything but systematic. It was confusion roughly organized. Great diversity prevailed everywhere, and we should not be surprised to find some different fact or custom in every lordship. Anglo-Norman feudalism attained in the eleventh and twelfth centuries a logical completeness and a uniformity of practice which, in the feudal age proper, can hardly be found elsewhere through so large a territory. . . .

"The foundation of the feudal relationship proper was the *fief*, which was usually land, but might be any desirable thing, as an office, a revenue in money or kind, the right to collect a toll, or operate a mill. In return for the fief, the man became the *vassal* of his lord; he knelt before him, and, with his hands between his lord's hands, promised him fealty and service. . . . The faithful performance of all the duties he had assumed in homage constituted the vassal's right and title to his fief. So long as they were fulfilled, he, and his heir after him, held the fief as his property, practically and in relation to all under-tenants as if he were the owner. In the ceremony of homage

and investiture, which is the creative contract of feudalism, the obligations assumed by the two parties were, as a rule, not specified in exact terms. They were determined by local custom. . . . In many points of detail the vassal's services differed widely in different parts of the feudal world. We may say, however, that they fall into two classes, general and specific. The general included all that might come under the idea of loyalty, seeking the lord's interests, keeping his secrets, betraying the plans of his enemies, protecting his family, etc. The specific services are capable of more definite statement, and they usually received exact definition in custom and sometimes in written documents. The most characteristic of these was the military service, which included appearance in the field on summons with a certain force, often armed in a specified way, and remaining a specified length of time. It often included also the duty of guarding the lord's castle, and of holding one's own castle subject to the plans of the lord for the defence of his fief. . . .

"Theoretically regarded, feudalism covered Europe with a network of these fiefs, rising in graded ranks one above the other from the smallest, the knight's fee, at the bottom, to the king at the top, who was the supreme landowner, or who held the kingdom from God. . . ."[1]

But this was the theory that was superimposed upon the established facts. The reality of feudalism was its voluntary co-operation.

"The feudal state was one in which, it has been said, private law had usurped the place of public law." But rather is it truer that public law had failed and vanished and private law had come in to fill the vacuum. Public duty had become private obligation.

§ 3

We have already mentioned various kingdoms of the barbarian tribes who set up a more or less flimsy dominion over this or that area amidst the debris of the empire, the kingdoms of the Suevi and West Goths in Spain, the East-Gothic kingdom in Italy, and the Italian Lombard kingdom which succeeded the Goths after Justinian had expelled the latter and after the great pestilence had devastated Italy. The Frankish kingdom was another such barbarian power which arose first in what is now Belgium, and which spread southward to the Loire, but it developed far more strength and solidarity than any of the others. It was the first real state to emerge from the universal wreckage. It became at last a wide and vigorous political reality, and from it are derived two great powers of modern Europe, France and the German Empire. Its founder was Clovis (481-511) who began as a small king in Belgium and ended with his southern frontiers nearly at the Pyrenees. He divided his kingdom among his four sons, but the Franks

[1] *Encyclopaedia Britannica*, article "Feudalism," by Professor G. B. Adams.

retained a tradition of unity in spite of this division, and for a time fraternal wars for a single control united rather than divided them. A more serious split arose, however, through the Latinization of the Western Franks, who occupied Romanized Gaul and who learnt to speak the corrupt Latin of the subject population, while the Franks of the Rhineland retained

their Low German speech. At a low level of civilization, differences in language cause very powerful political strains. For a hundred and fifty years the Frankish world was split in two, Neustria, the nucleus of France, speaking a Latinish speech, which became at last the French language we know, and Austrasia, the Rhineland, which remained German.[1]

[1] The Franks differed from the Swabians and South Germans, and came much nearer the Anglo-Saxons in that they spoke a "Low German" and not a "High German" dialect. Their language resembled plattdeutsch and Anglo-Saxon, and was the direct parent of Dutch and Flemish. In fact, the Franks where they were not Latinized became Flemings and

We will not tell here of the decay of the dynasty, the Merovingian dynasty, founded by Clovis; nor how in Austrasia a certain court official, the Mayor of the Palace, gradually became the king *de facto* and used the real king as a puppet. The position of Mayor of the Palace also became hereditary in the seventh century, and in 687 a certain Pepin of Heristhal, the Austrasian Mayor of the Palace, had conquered Neustria and reunited all the Franks. He was followed in 714 by his son, Charles Martel, who also bore no higher title than Mayor of the Palace. (His poor little Merovingian kings do not matter in the slightest degree to us here.) It was this Charles Martel who stopped the Moslems. They had pushed as far as Tours when he met them, and in a great battle between that place and Poitiers (732) utterly defeated them and broke their spirit. Thereafter the Pyrenees remained their utmost boundary; they came no further into Western Europe.

Charles Martel divided his power between two sons, but one resigned and went into a monastery, leaving his brother Pepin sole ruler. This Pepin it was who finally extinguished the descendants of Clovis. He sent to the Pope to ask who was the true king of the Franks, the man who held the power or the man who wore the crown; and the Pope, who was in need of a supporter, decided in favour of the Mayor of the Palace. So Pepin was chosen king at a gathering of the Frankish nobles in the Merovingian capital Soissons, and anointed and crowned. That was in 751. The Franco-Germany he united was consolidated by his son Charlemagne. It held together until the death of his grandson Louis (840), and then France and Germany broke away again—to the great injury of mankind. It was not a difference of race or temperament, it was a difference of language and tradition that split these Frankish peoples asunder.

That old separation of Neustria and Austrasia still works out in bitter consequences. In 1916 the ancient conflict of Neustria and Austrasia had broken out into war once more. In the August of that year the present writer visited Soissons and crossed the temporary wooden bridge that had been built by

"Dutchmen" of South Holland (North Holland is still Friesisch—*i.e.* Anglo-Saxon). The "French" which the Latinized Franks and Burgundians spoke in the seventh to the tenth centuries was remarkably like the Rumansch language of Switzerland, judging from the vestiges that remain in old documents.—H. H. J.

the English after the Battle of the Aisne from the main part of the town to the suburb of St. Médard. Canvas screens protected passengers upon the bridge from the observation of the German sharpshooters who were sniping from their trenches down the curve of the river. He went with his guides across a field and along by the wall of an orchard in which a German shell exploded as he passed. So he reached the battered buildings that stand upon the site of the ancient abbey of St. Médard, in which the last Merovingian was deposed and Pepin the Short was crowned in his stead. Beneath these ancient buildings there were great crypts, very useful as dug-outs—for the German advanced lines were not more than a couple of hundred yards away. The sturdy French soldier lads were cooking and resting in these shelters, and lying down to sleep among the stone coffins that had held the bones of their Merovingian kings.

§ 4

The populations over which Charles Martel and King Pepin ruled were at very different levels of civilization in different districts. To the west and south the bulk of the people consisted of Latinized and Christian Kelts; in the central regions these rulers had to deal with such more or less Christianized Germans as the Franks and Burgundians and Alemanni; to the north-east were still pagan Frisians and Saxons; to the east were the Bavarians, recently Christianized through the activities of St. Boniface; and to the east of them again pagan Slavs and Avars. The "Paganism" of the Germans and Slavs was very similar to the primitive religion of the Greeks; it was a manly religion in which temple, priest, and sacrifices played a small part, and its gods were like men, a kind of "school prefects" of more powerful beings who interfered impulsively and irregularly in human affairs. The Germans had a Jupiter in Odin, a Mars in Thor, a Venus in Freya, and so on. Throughout the seventh and eighth centuries a steady process of conversion to Christianity went on amidst these German and Slavonic tribes.

It will be interesting to English-speaking readers to note that the most zealous and successful missionaries among the Saxons and Frisians came from England. Christianity was twice planted in the British Isles. It was already there while

Britain was a part of the Roman Empire; a martyr, St. Alban, gave his name to the town of St. Albans, and nearly every visitor to Canterbury has also visited little old St. Martin's church, which was used during the Roman times. From Britain, as we have already said, Christianity spread beyond the imperial boundaries into Ireland—the chief missionary was St. Patrick—and there was a vigorous monastic movement with which are connected the names of St. Columba and the religious settlements of Iona. Then in the fifth and sixth centuries came the fierce and pagan English, and they cut off the early Church of Ireland from the main body of Christianity. In the seventh century Christian missionaries were converting the English, both in the north from Ireland and in the south from Rome. The Rome mission was sent by Pope Gregory the Great just at the close of the sixth century. The story goes that he saw English boys for sale in the Roman slave market, though it is a little difficult to understand how they got there. They were very fair and good-looking. In answer to his inquiries, he was told that they were Angles. "Not Angles, but Angels," said he, "had they but the gospel."

The mission worked through the seventh century. Before that century was over, most of the English were Christians; though Mercia, the central English kingdom, held out stoutly against the priests and for the ancient faith and ways. And there was a swift progress in learning upon the part of these new converts. The monasteries of the kingdom of Northumbria in the north of England became a centre of light and learning. Theodore of Tarsus was one of the earliest archbishops of Canterbury (669-690). "While Greek was utterly unknown in the west of Europe, it was mastered by some of the pupils of Theodore. The monasteries contained many monks who were excellent scholars. Most famous of all was Bede, known as the Venerable Bede (673-735), a monk of Jarrow (on Tyne). He had for his pupils the six hundred monks of that monastery, besides the many strangers who came to hear him. He gradually mastered all the learning of his day, and left at his death forty-five volumes of his writings, the most important of which are 'The Ecclesiastical History of the English' and his translation of the Gospel of John into English. His writings were widely known and used throughout Europe. He reckoned all dates from the birth of Christ, and through his works the use of Christian chronology became common in Europe. Owing to the large number of monasteries and monks

in Northumbria, that part of England was for a time far in advance of the south in civilization.''[1]

In the seventh and eighth centuries we find the English missionaries active upon the eastern frontiers of the Frankish

[1] *A General History of Europe,* Thatcher and Schwill.

kingdom. Chief among these was St. Boniface (680-755), who was born at Crediton, in Devonshire, who converted the Frisians, Thuringians, and Hessians, and who was martyred in Holland.

Both in England and on the Continent the ascendant rulers seized upon Christianity as a unifying force to cement their conquests. Christianity became a banner for aggressive chiefs —as it did in Uganda in Africa in the bloody days before that country was annexed to the British Empire. After Pepin, who died in 768, came two sons, Charles and another, who divided his kingdom; but the brother of Charles died in 771, and Charles then became sole king (771-814) of the growing realm of the Franks. This Charles is known in history as Charles the Great, or Charlemagne. As in the case of Alexander the Great and Julius Cæsar, posterity has enormously exaggerated his memory. He made his wars of aggression definitely religious wars. All the world of north-western Europe, which is now Great Britain, France, Germany, Denmark, and Norway and Sweden, was in the ninth century an arena of bitter conflict between the old faith and the new. Whole nations were converted to Christianity by the sword just as Islam in Arabia, Central Asia, and Africa had converted whole nations a century or so before.

With fire and sword Charlemagne preached the Gospel of the Cross to the Saxons, Bohemians, and as far as the Danube into what is now Hungary; he carried the same teaching down the Adriatic Coast through what is now Dalmatia, and drove the Moslems back from the Pyrenees as far as Barcelona.

Moreover, he it was who sheltered Egbert, an exile from Wessex, in England, and assisted him presently to establish himself as King in Wessex (802). Egbert subdued the Britons in Cornwall, as Charlemagne conquered the Britons of Brittany, and, by a series of wars, which he continued after the death of his Frankish patron, made himself at last the first King of all England (828).

But the attacks of Charlemagne upon the last strongholds of paganism provoked a vigorous reaction on the part of the unconverted. The Christianized English had retained very little of the seamanship that had brought them from the mainland, and the Franks had not yet become seamen. As the Christian propaganda of Charlemagne swept towards the shores of the

North and Baltic Seas, the pagans were driven to the sea. They retaliated for the Christian persecutions with plundering raids and expeditions against the northern coasts of France and

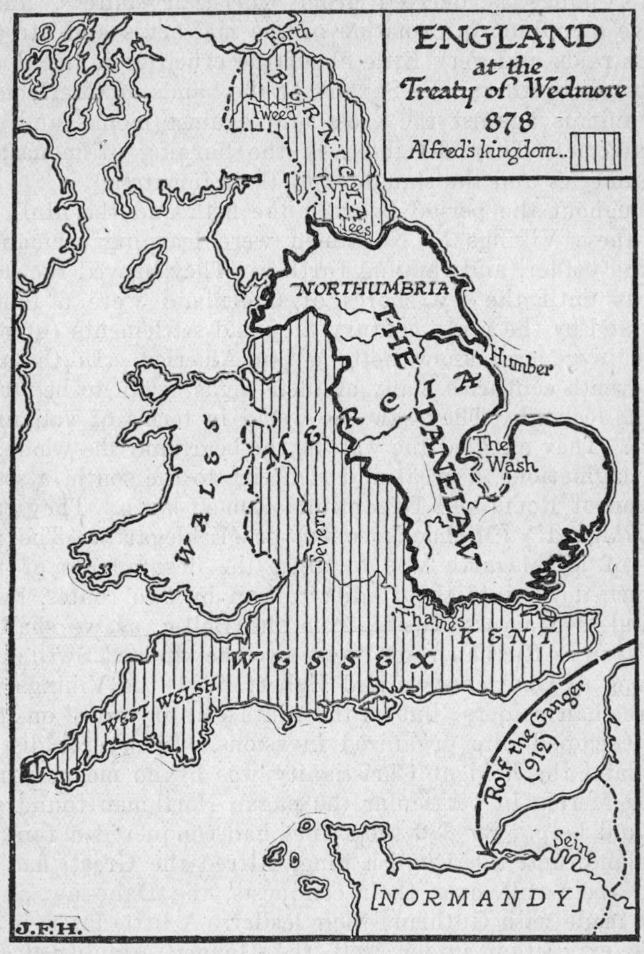

against Christian England. These pagan Saxons and English of the mainland and their kindred from Denmark and Norway are the Danes and Northmen of our national histories. They were also called Vikings,[1] which means "inlet-men," be-

[1] N.B.—Vik-ings, not Vi-kings, Vik = a fiord or inlet.

cause they came from the deep inlets of the Scandinavian coast. They came in long black galleys, making little use of sails. Most of our information about these wars and invasions of the Pagan Vikings is derived from Christian sources, and so we have abundant information of the massacres and atrocities of their raids and very little about the cruelties inflicted upon their pagan brethren, the Saxons, at the hands of Charlemagne. Their animus against the cross and against monks and nuns was extreme. They delighted in the burning of monasteries and nunneries and the slaughter of their inmates.

Throughout the period between the fifth and the ninth centuries these Vikings or Northmen were learning seamanship, becoming bolder, and ranging further. They braved the northern seas until the icy shores of Greenland were a familiar haunt, and by the ninth century they had settlements (of which Europe in general knew nothing) in America. In the tenth and eleventh centuries many of their sagas began to be written down in Iceland. They saw the world in terms of valiant adventure. They assailed the walrus, the bear, and the whale. In their imaginations, a great and rich city to the south, a sort of confusion of Rome and Byzantium, loomed large. They called it "Miklagard" (Michael's court) or Micklegarth. The magnetism of Micklegarth was to draw the descendants of these Northmen down into the Mediterranean by two routes, by the west and also across Russia from the Baltic, as we shall tell later. By the Russian route went also the kindred Swedes.

So long as Charlemagne and Egbert lived, the Vikings were no more than raiders; but as the ninth century wore on, these raids developed into organized invasions. In several districts of England the hold of Christianity was by no means firm as yet. In Mercia in particular the pagan Northmen found sympathy and help. By 886 the Danes had conquered a fair part of England, and the English king, Alfred the Great, had recognized their rule over their conquests, the Dane-law, in the pact he made with Guthrum their leader. A little later, in 912, another expedition under Rolf the Ganger established itself upon the coast of France in the region that was known henceforth as Normandy (= Northman-dy). But of how there was presently a fresh conquest of England by the Danes, and how finally the Duke of Normandy became King of England, we cannot tell at any length. There were very small racial and social differences between Angle, Saxon, Jute, Dane, or Norman; and though these changes loom large in the imaginations of the English, they are seen to be very slight rufflings indeed of the stream of history when we measure them by the standards of a greater world. The issue between Christianity and paganism vanished presently from the struggle. By the Treaty of Wedmore the Danes agreed to be baptized if they were assured of their conquests; and the descendants of Rolf in Normandy were not merely Christianized, but they learnt to speak French from the more civilized people about them, forgetting their own Norse tongue. Of much greater significance in the history of mankind are the relations of Charlemagne with his neighbours to the south and east, and to the imperial tradition.

§ 5

Through Charlemagne the tradition of the Roman Cæsar was revived in Europe. The Roman Empire was dead and decaying; the Byzantine Empire was far gone in decline; but the education and mentality of Europe had sunken to a level at which new creative political ideas were probably impossible. In all Europe there survived not a tithe of the speculative vigour that we find in the Athenian literature of the fifth century B.C. There was no power to postulate a new occasion or to conceive and organize a novel political method. Official Christianity had long overlaid and accustomed itself to ignore those strange teachings of Jesus of Nazareth from which it had arisen. The Roman Church, clinging tenaciously to its possession of the title of *pontifex maximus,* had long since abandoned its appointed task of achieving the Kingdom of Heaven. It was preoccupied with the revival of Roman ascendancy on earth, which it conceived of as its inheritance. It had become a political body, using the faith and needs of simple men to forward its schemes. Europe drifted towards a dreary imitation and revival of the misconceived failures of the past. For eleven centuries from Charlemagne onwards, "Emperors" and "Cæsars" of this line and that come and go in the history of Europe like fancies in a disordered mind. We shall have to tell of a great process of mental growth in Europe, of enlarged horizons and accumulating power, but it was a process that went on independently of, and in spite of, and the political forms

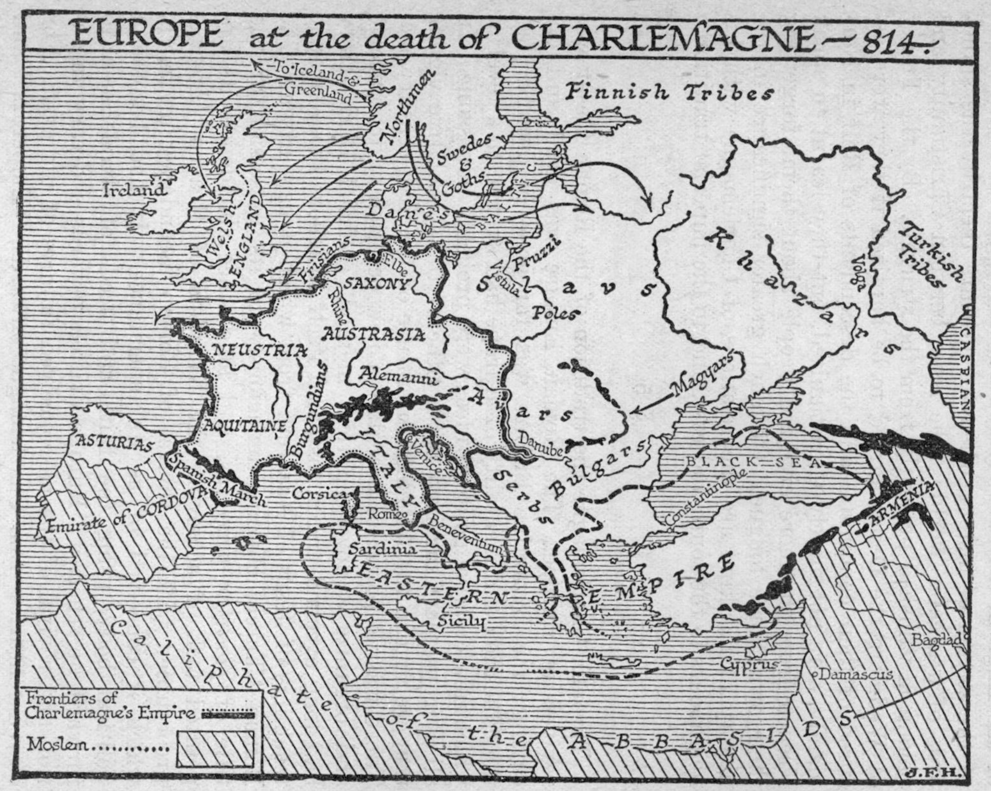

EUROPE at the death of CHARLEMAGNE—814.

of the time, until at last it shattered those forms altogether. Europe during those eleven centuries of the imitation Cæsars which began with Charlemagne, and which closed only in the monstrous bloodshed of 1914-1918, has been like a busy factory owned by a somnambulist, who is sometimes quite unimportant and sometimes disastrously in the way. Or rather than a somnambulist, let us say by a corpse that magically simulates a kind of life. The Roman Empire staggers, sprawls, is thrust off the stage, and reappears, and—if we may carry the image one step further—it is the Church of Rome which plays the part of the magician and keeps this corpse alive.

And throughout the whole period there is always a struggle going on for the control of the corpse between the spiritual and various temporal powers. We have already noted the spirit of St. Augustine's *City of God.* It was a book which we know Charlemagne read, or had read to him—for his literary accomplishments are rather questionable. He conceived of this Christian Empire as being ruled and maintained in its orthodoxy by some such great Cæsar as himself. He was to rule even the Pope. But at Rome the view taken of the revived empire differed a little from that. There the view taken was that the Christian Cæsar must be anointed and guided by the Pope—who would even have the power to excommunicate and depose him. Even in the time of Charlemagne this divergence of view was apparent. In the following centuries it became acute.

The idea of the revived Empire dawned only very gradually upon the mind of Charlemagne. At first he was simply the ruler of his father's kingdom of the Franks, and his powers were fully occupied in struggles with the Saxons and Bavarians, and with the Slavs to the east of them, with the Moslem in Spain, and with various insurrections in his own dominions. And as the result of a quarrel with the King of Lombardy, his father-in-law, he conquered Lombardy and North Italy. We have noted the establishment of the Lombards in North Italy about 570 after the great pestilence, and after the overthrow of the East Gothic kings by Justinian. These Lombards had always been a danger and a fear to the Popes, and there had been an alliance between Pope and Frankish King against them in the time of Pepin. Now Charlemagne completely subjugated Lombardy (774), sent his father-in-law to a monastery, and carried his conquests beyond the present north-eastern boundaries of Italy into Dalmatia in 776. In 781 he caused one of his sons, Pepin, who did not outlive him, to be crowned King of Italy in Rome.

There was a new Pope, Leo III, in 795, who seems from the first to have resolved to make Charlemagne emperor. Hitherto the court at Byzantium had possessed a certain indefinite authority over the Pope. Strong emperors like Justinian had bullied the Popes and obliged them to come to Constantinople; weak emperors had annoyed them ineffectively. The idea of a breach, both secular and religious, with Constantinople had long been entertained at the Lateran,[1] and in the Frankish power there seemed to be just the support that was necessary if Constantinople was to be defied. So at his accession Leo III sent the keys of the tomb of St. Peter and a banner to Charlemagne as the symbols of his sovereignty in Rome as King of Italy. Very soon the Pope had to appeal to the protection he had chosen. He was unpopular in Rome; he was attacked and ill-treated in the streets during a procession, and obliged to fly to Germany (799). Eginhard says his eyes were gouged out and his tongue cut off; he seems, however, to have had both eyes and tongue again a year later. Charlemagne brought him back and reinstated him (800).

Then occurred a very important scene. On Christmas Day, in the year 800, as Charles was rising from prayer in the Church of St. Peter, the Pope, who had everything in readiness, clapped a crown upon his head and hailed him Cæsar and Augustus. There was great popular applause. But Eginhard, the friend and biographer of Charlemagne, says that the new emperor was by no means pleased by this coup of Pope Leo's. If he had known this was to happen, he said, "he would not have entered the church, great festival though it was." No doubt he had been thinking and talking of making himself emperor, but he had evidently not intended that the Pope should make him emperor. He had some idea of marrying the Empress Irene, who at that time reigned in Constantinople, and so becoming monarch of both Eastern and Western Empires. He was now obliged to accept the title in the manner that Leo III had adopted as a gift from the Pope, and in a way that estranged Constantinople and secured the separation of Rome from the Byzantine Church.

1 The Lateran was the earlier palace of the Popes in Rome. Later they occupied the Vatican.

At first Byzantium was unwilling to recognize the imperial title of Charlemagne. But in 810 a great disaster fell upon the Byzantine Empire. The pagan Bulgarians, under their Prince Krum (802-814), defeated and destroyed the armies of the Emperor Nicephorus, whose skull became a drinking-cup for Krum. The greater part of the Balkan peninsula was conquered by these people. (The Bulgarian and the English nations thus became established as political unities almost simultaneously.) After this misfortune Byzantium was in no position to dispute this revival of the empire in the West, and in 812 Charlemagne was formally recognized by Byzantine envoys as Emperor and Augustus.

So the Empire of Rome, which had died at the hands of Odoacer in 476, rose again in 800 as the "Holy Roman Empire." While its physical strength lay north of the Alps, the centre of its idea was Rome. It was therefore from the beginning a divided thing of uncertain power, a claim and an argument rather than a necessary reality. The German sword was always clattering over the Alps into Italy, and missions and legates toiling over in the reverse direction. But the Germans could never hold Italy permanently, because they could not stand the malaria that the ruined, neglected, undrained country fostered. And in Rome, as well as in several other of the cities of Italy, there smouldered a more ancient tradition, the tradition of the aristocratic republic, hostile to both Emperor and Pope.

§ 6

In spite of the fact that we have a life of him written by his contemporary, Eginhard,[1] the character and personality of Charlemagne are difficult to visualize. Eginhard lacks vividness; he tells many particulars, but not the particulars that make a man live again in the record. Charlemagne, he says, was a tall man, with a rather feeble voice; and he had bright eyes and a long nose. "The top of his head was round," whatever that may mean, and his hair was "white." He had a thick, rather short neck, and "his belly too prominent." He wore a tunic with a silver border, and gartered hose. He had a blue cloak, and was always girt with his sword, hilt and belt being

[1] Eginhard's *Life of Karl the Great.* (Glaister.)

of gold and silver. He was evidently a man of great activity, one imagines him moving quickly, and his numerous love affairs did not interfere at all with his incessant military and political labours. He had numerous wives and mistresses. He took much exercise, was fond of pomp and religious ceremonies, and gave generously. He was a man of very miscellaneous activity and great intellectual enterprise, and with a self-confidence that is rather suggestive of William II, the ex-German Emperor, the last, perhaps for ever, of this series of imitation Cæsars in Europe which Charlemagne began.

The mental life that Eginhard records of him is interesting, because it not only gives glimpses of a curious character, but serves as a sample of the intellectuality of the time. He could read probably; at meals he "listened to music or reading," but we are told that he had not acquired the art of writing; "he used to keep his writing-book and tablets under his pillow, that when he had leisure he might practice his hand in forming letters, but he made little progress in an art begun too late in life." He had, however, a real respect for learning and a real desire for knowledge, and he did his utmost to attract men of learning to his court. Among others who came was Alcuin, a learned Englishman. All those learned men were, of course, clergymen, there being no other learned men, and naturally they gave a strongly clerical tinge to the information they imparted to their master. At his court, which was usually at Aix-la-Chapelle or Mayence, he maintained in the winter months a curious institution called his "school," in which he and his erudite associates affected to lay aside all thoughts of worldly position, assumed names taken from the classical writers or from Holy Writ, and discoursed upon theology and literature. Charlemagne himself was "David." He developed a considerable knowledge of theology, and it is to him that we must ascribe the addition of the word *filioque* to the Nicene Creed, an addition that finally split the Latin and Greek churches asunder. But it is more than doubtful if he had any such separation in mind. He wanted to add a word or so to the creed, just as the Emperor William II wanted to write operas and paint pictures,[1] and he took up what was originally a Spanish innovation.

[1] The addition was discreetly opposed by Leo III "In the correspondence between them the Pope assumes the liberality of a statesman and the prince descends to the prejudice and passions of a priest."—Gibbon, chap. lx.

Of his organization of his empire there is little to be said here. He was far too restless and busy to consider the quality of his successor or the condition of political stability, and the most noteworthy thing in this relationship is that he particularly schooled his son and successor, Louis the Pious (814-840), to take the crown from the altar and *crown himself*. But Louis the Pious was too pious to adhere to those instructions when the Pope made an objection.

The legislation of Charlemagne was greatly coloured by Bible reading; he knew his Bible well, as the times went; and it is characteristic of him that after he had been crowned emperor he required every male subject above the age of twelve to renew his oath of allegiance, and to undertake to be not simply a good subject, but a good Christian. To refuse baptism and to retract after baptism were crimes punishable by death. He did much to encourage architecture, and imported many Italian architects, chiefly from Ravenna, to whom we owe many of the pleasant Byzantine buildings that still at Worms and Cologne and elsewhere delight the tourist in the Rhineland. He founded a number of cathedrals and monastic schools, did much to encourage the study of classical Latin, and was a distinguished amateur of church music. The possibility of his talking Latin and understanding Greek is open to discussion; probably he talked French-Latin. Frankish, however, was his habitual tongue. He made a collection of old German songs and tales, but these were destroyed by his successor Louis the Pious on account of their paganism.

He corresponded with Haroun-al-Raschid, the Abbasid Caliph at Bagdad, who was not perhaps the less friendly to him on account of his vigorous handling of the Omayyad Arabs in Spain. Gibbon supposes that this "public correspondence was founded on vanity," and that "their remote situation left no room for a competition of interest." But with the Byzantine Empire between them in the East, and the independent caliphate of Spain in the West, and a common danger in the Turks of the great plains, they had three very excellent reasons for cordiality. Haroun-al-Raschid, says Gibbon, sent Charlemagne by his ambassadors a splendid tent, a water clock, an elephant, and the keys of the Holy Sepulchre. The last item suggests that Charlemagne was to some extent regarded by the Saracen monarch as the protector of the Christians and Christian properties in his dominions. Some historians declare explicitly that there was a treaty to that effect.

§ 7

The Empire of Charlemagne did not outlive his son and successor, Louis the Pious. It fell apart into its main constituents. The Latinized Keltic and Frankish population of Gaul begins now to be recognizable as France, though this France was broken up into a number of dukedoms and principalities, often with no more than a nominal unity; the German-speaking peoples between the Rhine and the Slavs to the east similarly begin to develop an even more fragmentary intimation of Germany. When at length a real emperor reappears in Western Europe (962), he is not a Frank, but a Saxon; the conquered in Germany have become the masters.

It is impossible here to trace the events of the ninth and tenth centuries in any detail, the alliances, the treacheries, the claims and acquisitions. Everywhere there was lawlessness, war, and a struggle for power. In 987 the nominal kingdom of France passed from the hands of the Carlovingians, the last descendants of Charlemagne, into the hands of Hugh Capet, who founded a new dynasty. Most of his alleged subordinates were in fact independent, and willing to make war on the king at the slightest provocation. The dominions of the Duke of Normandy, for example, were more extensive and more powerful than the patrimony of Hugh Capet. Almost the only unity of this France over which the king exercised a nominal authority lay in the common resolution of its great provinces to resist incorporation in any empire dominated either by a German ruler or by the Pope. Apart from the simple organization dictated by that common will, France was a mosaic of practically independent nobles. It was an era of castle-building and fortification, and what was called "private war" throughout all Europe.

The state of Rome in the tenth century is almost indescribable. The decay of the Empire of Charlemagne left the Pope without a protector, threatened by Byzantium and the Saracens (who had taken Sicily), and face to face with the unruly nobles of Rome. Among the most powerful of these were two women, Theodora and Marozia, mother and daughter [1] who in succes-

[1] Gibbon mentions a second Theodora, the sister of Marozia.

sion held the Castle of St. Angelo (§ 1), which Theophylact, the patrician husband of Theodora, had seized with most of the temporal power of the Pope; these two women were as bold, unscrupulous, and dissolute as any male prince of the time could have been, and they are abused by historians as though they were ten times worse. Marozia seized and imprisoned Pope John X (928), who speedily died under her care. She subsequently made her illegitimate son pope, under the title of John XI. After him her grandson, John XII, filled the chair of St. Peter. Gibbon's account of the manners and morals of John XII takes refuge at last beneath a veil of Latin footnotes. This Pope, John XII, was finally degraded by the new German Emperor Otto, who came over the Alps and down into Italy to be crowned in 962.[1]

This new line of Saxon emperors, which thus comes into prominence, sprang from a certain Henry the Fowler, who was elected King of Germany by an assembly of German nobles, princes, and prelates in 919. In 936 he was succeeded as King by his son, Otto I, surnamed the Great, who was also elected to be his successor at Aix-la-Chapelle, and who finally descended upon Rome at the invitation of John XII, to be crowned emperor in 962. His subsequent degradation of John was forced upon him by that pope's treachery. With his assumption of the imperial dignity, Otto I did not so much overcome Rome as restore the ancient tussle of Pope and Emperor for ascendancy to something like decency and dignity again. Otto I was followed by Otto II (973-983), and he again by a third Otto (983-1002).[2]

The struggle between the Emperor and the Pope for ascendancy over the Holy Roman Empire plays a large part in the

[1] This period is a tangled one. The authority is Gregorovius, *History of the City of Rome in the Middle Ages.* John X owed the tiara to his mistress, the elder Theodora, but he was "the foremost statesman of his age." He fell in 928 owing to Marozia. John XI became Pope in 931 (after two Popes had intervened in the period 928-931); he was Marozia's son, possibly by Pope Sergius III. John XII did not come at once after John XI, who died in 936; there were several Popes in between; and he became Pope in 955.—E. B.

[2] There were three dynasties of emperors in the early middle ages:
Saxon: Otto I (962) to Henry II, ending 1024.
Salian: Conrad II to Henry V, ending about 1125.
Hohenstaufen: Conrad III to Frederic II, ending in 1250.
The Hohenstaufens were Swabian in origin. Then came the Habsburgs with Rudolph I in 1273, who lasted until 1918.

history of the early Middle Ages, and we shall have presently to sketch its chief phases. Though the church never sank quite to the level of John XII again, nevertheless the story fluctuates through phases of great violence, confusion, and intrigue. Yet the outer history of Christendom is not the whole history of Christendom. That the Lateran was as cunning, foolish, and criminal as most other contemporary courts has to be recorded; but, if we are to keep due proportions in this history, it must not be unduly emphasized. We must remember that through all those ages, leaving profound consequences, but leaving no conspicuous records upon the historian's page, countless men and women were touched by that Spirit of Jesus which still lived and lives still at the core of Christianity, that they led lives that were on the whole gracious and helpful, and that they did unselfish and devoted deeds. Through those ages such lives cleared the air and made a better world possible. Just as in the Moslem world the Spirit of Islam generation by generation produced its crop of courage, integrity, and kindliness.

§ 8

While the Holy Roman Empire and the kingdoms of France and England were thus appearing amidst the extreme political fragmentation of the civilization of Western Europe, both that civilization and the Byzantine Empire were being subjected to a threefold attack: from the Saracen powers, from the Northmen, and, more slowly developed and most formidable of all, from a new westward thrust of the Turkish peoples through South Russia, and also by way of Armenia and the Empire of Bagdad from Central Asia.

After the overthrow of the Omayyads by the Abbasid dynasty, the strength of the Saracenic impulse against Europe diminished. Islam was no longer united. Spain was under a separate Omayyad Caliph, North Africa, though nominally subject to the Abbasids, was really independent, and presently (969) Egypt became a separate power with a Shiite Caliph of its own, a pretender claiming descent from Ali and Fatima (the Fatimite Caliphate). These Egyptian Fatimites, the green flag Moslems, were fanatics in comparison with the Abbasids, and did much to embitter the genial relations of Islam and Christianity. They took Jerusalem, and interfered

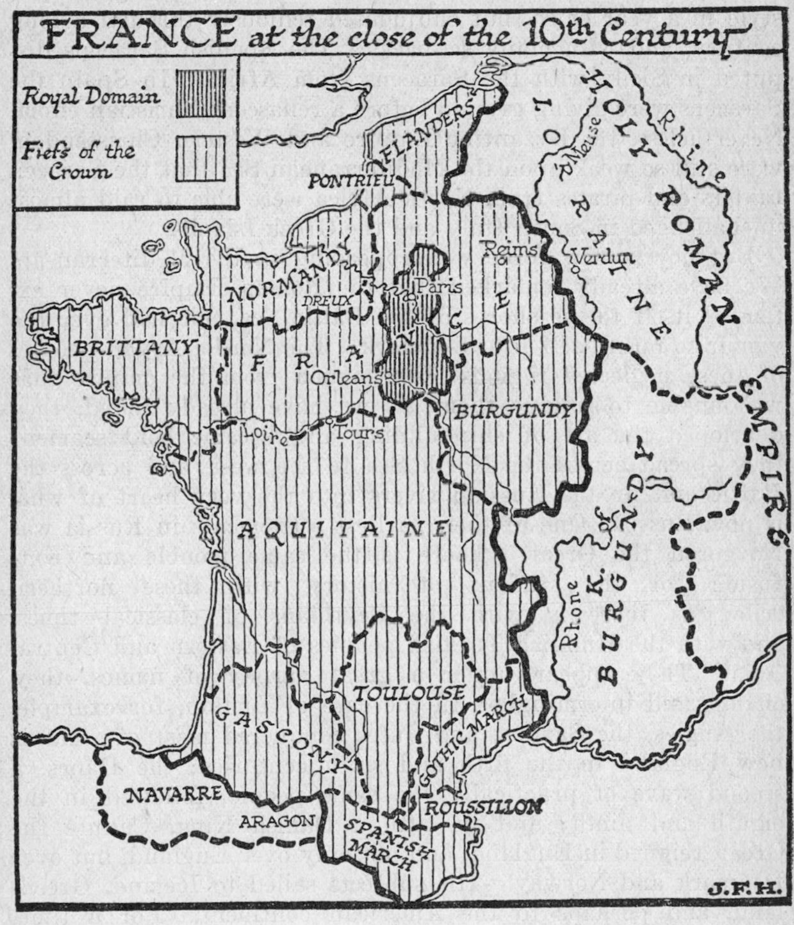
FRANCE at the close of the 10th Century
Royal Domain
Fiefs of the Crown
FLANDERS
PONTRIEU
NORMANDY
DREUX
Paris
Reims
Verdun
Meuse
Rhine
LORRAINE
HOLY ROMAN EMPIRE
BRITTANY
FRANCE
Orleans
Loire
Tours
BURGUNDY
K. of BURGUNDY
Rhone
AQUITAINE
TOULOUSE
GASCONY
GOTHIC MARCH
NAVARRE
ARAGON
SPANISH MARCH
ROUSSILLON
J.F.H.

with the Christian access to the Holy Sepulchre. On the other side of the shrunken Abbasid domain there was also a Shiite kingdom in Persia. The chief Saracen conquest in the ninth century was Sicily; but this was not overrun in the grand old style in a year or so, but subjugated tediously through a long century, and with many set-backs. The Spanish Saracens disputed in Sicily with the Saracens from Africa. In Spain the Saracens were giving ground before a renascent Christian effort. Nevertheless, the Byzantine Empire and Western Christendom were still so weak upon the Mediterranean Sea that the Saracen raiders and pirates from North Africa were able to raid almost unchallenged in South Italy and the Greek Islands.

But now a new force was appearing in the Mediterranean. We have already remarked that the Roman Empire never extended itself to the shores of the Baltic Sea, nor had ever the vigour to push itself into Denmark. The Nordic Aryan peoples of these neglected regions learnt much from the empire that was unable to subdue them; as we have already noted, they developed the art of shipbuilding and became bold seamen; they spread across the North Sea to the west, and across the Baltic and up the Russian rivers into the very heart of what is now Russia. One of their earliest settlements in Russia was Novgorod the Great. There is the same trouble and confusion for the student of history with these northern tribes as there is with the Scythians of classical times, and with the Hunnish Turkish peoples of Eastern and Central Asia. They appear under a great variety of names, they change and intermingle. In the case of Britain, for example, the Angles, the Saxons, and Jutes conquered most of what is now England in the fifth and sixth centuries; the Danes, a second wave of practically the same people, followed in the eighth and ninth; and in 1016 a Danish King, Canute the Great, reigned in England, and not only over England, but over Denmark and Norway. His subjects sailed to Iceland, Greenland, and perhaps to the American continent. For a time, under Canute and his sons, it seemed possible that a great confederation of the Northmen might have established itself. Then in 1066 a third wave of the same people flowed over England from the "Norman" state in France, where the Northmen had been settled since the days of Rolf the Ganger (912), and where they had learnt to speak French. William, Duke of

Normandy, became the William the Conqueror (1066) of English history. Practically, from the standpoint of universal history, all these peoples were the same people, waves of one Nordic stock. These waves were not only flowing westward, but eastward. Already we have mentioned a very interesting earlier movement of the same peoples under the name of Goths from Baltic to the Black Sea. We have traced the splitting of these Goths into the Ostrogoths and the Visigoths, and the adventurous wanderings that ended at last in the Ostrogoth kingdom in Italy and the Visigoth states in Spain. In the ninth century a second movement of the Northmen across Russia was going on at the same time that their establishments in England and their dukedom of Normandy were coming into existence. The population of South Scotland, England, East Ireland, Flanders, Normandy, and the Russias have more elements in common than we are accustomed to recognize. All are fundamentally Gothic and Nordic peoples. Even in their weights and measures the kinship of Russian and English is to be noted; both have the Norse inch and foot, and many early Norman churches in England are built on a scale that shows the use of the sajene (7 ft.) and quarter sajene, a Norse measure still used in Russia. These "Russian" Norsemen travelled in the summer-time, using the river routes that abounded in Russia; they carried their ships by portages from the northward-running rivers to those flowing southward. They appeared as pirates, raiders, and traders both upon the Caspian and the Black Sea. The Arabic chroniclers note their apparition upon the Caspian, and learnt to call them Russians. They raided Persia, and threatened Constantinople with a great fleet of small craft (in 865, 904, 941, and 1043).[1] One of these Northmen, Rurik (*circa* 850), established himself as the ruler of Novgorod and his successor, the duke Oleg, took Kief, and laid the foundations of modern Russia. The fighting qualities of the Russian Vikings were speedily appreciated at Constantinople; the Greeks called them Varangians, and an Imperial Varangian bodyguard was formed. After the conquest of England by the Normans (1066), a number of Danes and English were driven into exile and joined these Russian Varangians, apparently finding few obstacles to intercourse in their speech and habits.

[1] These dates are from Gibbon. Beazley gives 865, 904-7, 935, 944, 971-2. (*History of Russia,* Clarendon Press.)

Meanwhile the Normans from Normandy were also finding their way into the Mediterranean from the West. They came first as mercenaries, and later as independent invaders; and they came mainly, not, it is to be noted, by sea, but in scattered bands by land. They came through the Rhineland and Italy partly in the search for warlike employment and loot, partly as pilgrims. For the ninth and tenth centuries saw a great development of pilgrimage. These Normans, as they grew powerful, discovered themselves such rapacious and vigorous robbers that they forced the Eastern Emperor and the Pope into a feeble and ineffective alliance against them (1053). They defeated and captured and were pardoned by the Pope; they established themselves in Calabria and South Italy, conquered Sicily from the Saracens (1060-1090), and under Robert Guiscard, who had entered Italy as a pilgrim adventurer and began his career as a brigand in Calabria, threatened the Byzantine Empire itself (1081). His army, which contained a contingent of Sicilian Moslems, crossed from Brindisi to Epirus in the reverse direction to that in which Pyrrhus had crossed to attack the Roman Republic, thirteen centuries before (275 B.C.). He laid siege to the Byzantine stronghold of Durazzo.

Robert captured Durazzo (1082), but the pressure of affairs in Italy recalled him, and ultimately put an end to this first Norman attack upon the Empire of Byzantium, leaving the way open for the rule of a comparatively vigorous Comnenian dynasty (1081-1204). In Italy, amidst conflicts too complex for us to tell here, it fell to Robert Guiscard to besiege and sack Rome (1084); and Gibbon notes with quiet satisfaction the presence of that contingent of Sicilian Moslems amongst the looters. There were in the twelfth century three other Norman attacks upon the Eastern power, one by the son of Robert Guiscard, and the two others directly from Sicily by sea. . . .

But neither the Saracens nor the Normans pounded quite so heavily against the old empire at Byzantium or against the Holy Roman Empire, the vamped-up Roman Empire of the West, as did the double thrust from the Turanian centres in Central Asia, of which we must now tell. We have already noted the westward movement of the Avars, and the Turkish Magyars who followed in their track. From the days of Pepin

The EMPIRE of OTTO the GREAT
K. of DENMARK
Prussians
FRISIA
Dy. of SAXONY
Elbe
NORTH MARK
Dy. of POLAND
Vistula
Oder
EAST MARK
THURINGIA
MEISSEN MARK
Lower Duchies of LORRAINE Upper
Rhine
Duchies of FRANCONIA
Dy. of BOHEMIA
MORAVIA
K. of FRANCE
Paris
Seine
Dy. of SWABIA
Danube
Dy. of BAVARIA
EAST MARK (AUSTRIA)
Danube
K. of HUNGARY
Loire
K. of BURGUNDY
Rhone
Dy. of CARINTHIA
Drave
Save
K. of ITALY
LOMBARDY
Po
Venice
K. of CROATIA
SERBIA
ROMAGNA
TUSCANY
SPOLETO
STATE of the CHURCH
Rome
BENEVENTO
SALERNO
CORSICA
Moslem
SARDINIA
EASTERN EMPIRE
J.F.H.

I onward, the Frankish power and its successors in Germany were in conflict with these Eastern raiders along all the Eastern borderlands. Charlemagne held and punished them, and established some sort of overlordship as far east as the Carpathians; but amidst the enfeeblement that followed his death, these peoples, more or less blended now in the accounts under the name

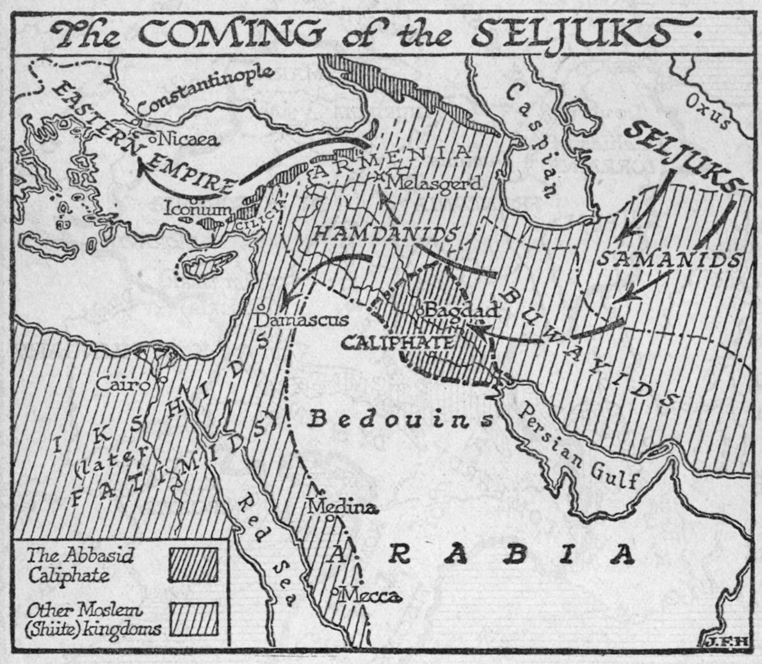

of Hungarians, led by the Magyars, re-established their complete freedom again, and raided yearly, often as far as the Rhine. They destroyed, Gibbon notes, the monastery of St. Gall in Switzerland, and the town of Bremen. Their great raiding period was between 900 and 950. Their biggest effort, through Germany right into France, thence over the Alps and home again by North Italy, was in 938-9.

Thrust southward by these disturbances, and by others to be presently noted, the Bulgarians established themselves under Krum, between the Danube and Constantinople. Originally a Turkish people, the Bulgarians, since their first appearance in the east of Russia, had become by repeated admixture almost entirely Slavonic in race and language. For some time after their establishment in Bulgaria they remained pagan. Their king, Boris (852-884), entertained Moslem envoys, and seems to have contemplated an adhesion to Islam, but finally he married a Byzantine princess, and handed himself and his people over to the Christian faith.

The Hungarians were drubbed into a certain respect for civilization by Henry the Fowler, the elected King of Germany, and Otto the First, the first Saxon emperor, in the tenth century. But they did not decide to adopt Christianity until about A.D. 1000. Though they were Christianized, they retained their own Turko-Finnic language (Magyar), and they retain it to this day.

Bulgarians and Hungarians do not, however, exhaust the catalogue of the peoples whose westward movements embodied the Turkish thrust across South Russia. Behind the Hungarians and Bulgarians thrust the Khazars, a Turkish people, with whom were mingled a very considerable proportion of Jews who had been expelled from Constantinople, and who had mixed with them and made many proselytes. To these Jewish Khazars are to be ascribed the great settlements of Jews in Poland and Russia.[1] Behind the Khazars again, and overrunning them, were the Petschenegs (or Patzinaks), a savage Turkish people who are first heard of in the ninth century, and who were destined to dissolve and vanish as the kindred Huns did five centuries before. And while the trend of all these peoples was westward, we have, when we are thinking of the present population of these South Russian regions, to remember also the coming and going of the Northmen between the Baltic and the Black Sea, who interwove with the Turkish migrants like warp and woof, and bear in mind also that there was a considerable Slavonic population, the heirs and descendants of Scythians, Sarmatians, and the like, already established in these restless, lawless, but fertile areas. All these races mixed with and reacted upon one another. The universal prevalence of Slavonic languages, except in Hungary, shows that the population remained predominantly Slav. And in what is now Rumania, for all the passage

[1] "A Turkish people whose leaders had adopted Judaism," says Harold Williams.

of peoples, and in spite of conquest after conquest, the tradition and inheritance of the Roman provinces of Dacia and Mœsia Inferior still kept a Latin speech and memory alive.

But this direct thrust of the Turkish peoples against Christendom to the north of the Black Sea was, in the end, not nearly so important as their indirect thrust south of it through the empire of the Caliph. We cannot deal here with the tribes and dissensions of the Turkish peoples of Turkestan, nor with the particular causes that brought to the fore the tribes under the rule of the Seljuk clan. In the eleventh century these Seljuk Turks broke with irresistible force not in one army, but in a group of armies, and under two brothers, into the decaying fragments of the Moslem Empire. For Islam had long ceased to be one empire. The orthodox Sunnite Abbasid rule had shrunken to what was once Babylonia; and even in Bagdad the Caliph was the mere creature of his Turkish palace guards. A sort of mayor of the palace, a Turk, was the real ruler. East of the Caliph, in Persia, and west of him in Palestine, Syria, and Egypt, were Shiite heretics. The Seljuk Turks were orthodox Sunnites; they now swept down upon and conquered the Shiite rulers and upstarts, and established themselves as the protectors of the Bagdad Caliph, taking over the temporal powers of the mayor of the palace. Very early they conquered Armenia from the Greeks, and then, breaking the bounds that had restrained the power of Islam for four centuries, they swept on to the conquest of Asia Minor, almost to the gates of Constantinople. The mountain barrier of Cilicia that had held the Moslem so long had been turned by the conquest of Armenia from the north-east. Under Alp Arslan, who had united all the Seljuk power in his own hands, the Turks utterly smashed the Byzantine army at the battle of Manzikert, or Melasgird (1071). The effect of this battle upon people's imaginations was very great. Islam, which had appeared far gone in decay, which had been divided religiously and politically, was suddenly discovered to have risen again, and it was the secure old Byzantine Empire that seemed on the brink of dissolution. The loss of Asia Minor was very swift. The Seljuks established themselves at Iconium (Konia), in what is now Anatolia. In a little while they were in possession of the fortress of Nicæa over against the capital.

§ 9

We have already told of the attack of the Normans upon the Byzantine Empire from the west, and of the battle of Durazzo (1081); and we have noted that Constantinople had still vivid memories of the Russia sea raids (1043). Bulgaria, it is true, had been tamed, but there was heavy and uncertain warfare going on with the Petschenegs. North and west, the emperor's hands were full. This swift advance of the Turks into country that had been so long securely Byzantine must have seemed like the approach of final disaster. The Eastern Emperor, Michael VII, under the pressure of these convergent dangers, took a step that probably seemed both to himself and to Rome of the utmost political significance. He appealed to the Pope, Gregory VII, for assistance. His appeal was repeated still more urgently by his successor, Alexius Comnenus, to Pope Urban II.

To the counsellors of Rome this must have presented itself as a supreme opportunity for the assertion of the headship of the Pope over the entire Christian world.

In this history we have traced the growth of this idea of a religious government of Christendom—and through Christendom of mankind—and we have shown how naturally and how necessarily, because of the tradition of world empire, it found a centre at Rome. The Pope of Rome was the only Western patriarch; he was the religious head of a vast region in which the ruling tongue was Latin; the other patriarchs of the Orthodox Church spoke Greek, and so were inaudible throughout his domains; and the word *filioque*, which had been added to the Latin creed, had split off the Byzantine Christians by one of those impalpable and elusive doctrinal points upon which there is no reconciliation. (The final rupture was in 1054.) The life of the Lateran changed in its quality with every occupant of the chair of St. Peter: sometimes papal Rome was a den of corruption and uncleanness, as it had been in the days of John XII; sometimes it was pervaded by the influence of widely thinking and nobly thinking men. But behind the Pope was the assembly of the cardinals, priests, and a great number of highly educated officials, who never, even in the darkest and wildest days, lost sight altogether of the very grand idea of a divine world dominion, of a peace of Christ throughout the earth that St. Augustine had expressed. Through all the

Middle Ages that idea was the guiding influence in Rome. For a time, perhaps, mean minds would prevail there, and in the affairs of the world Rome would play the part of a greedy, treacherous, and insanely cunning old woman; followed a phase of masculine and quite worldly astuteness perhaps, or a phase of exaltation. Came an interlude of fanaticism or pedantry, when all the pressure was upon exact doctrine. Or there was a moral collapse, and the Lateran became the throne of some sensuous or æsthetic autocrat, ready to sell every hope or honour the church could give for money to spend upon pleasure or display. Yet, on the whole, the papal ship kept its course, and came presently into the wind again.

In this period to which we have now come, the period of the eleventh century, we discover a Rome dominated by the personality of an exceptionally great statesmen, Hildebrand, who occupied various official positions under a succession of Popes, and finally became Pope himself under the name of Gregory VII (1073-1085). We find that under his influence, vice, sloth, and corruption have been swept out of the church, that the method of electing the Popes has been reformed, and that a great struggle has been waged with the Emperor upon the manifestly vital question of "investitures," the question whether Pope or temporal monarch should have the decisive voice in the appointment of the bishops in their domains. Vital that question was not only to the church, but to the monarchs, for in many countries more than a quarter of the land was clerical property. Hitherto the Roman clergy had been able to marry; but now, to detach them effectually from the world and to make them more completely the instruments of the church, celibacy was imposed upon all priests. . . .

Gregory VII had been prevented by his struggle over the investitures from any effectual answer to the first appeal from Byzantium; but he had left a worthy successor in Urban II (1087-1099); and when the letter of Alexius came to hand, Urban seized at once upon the opportunity it afforded for drawing together all the thoughts and forces of Western Europe into one passion and purpose. Thereby he might hope to end the private warfare that prevailed, and find a proper outlet for the immense energy of the Normans. He saw, too, an opportunity of thrusting the Byzantine power and Church aside, and extending the influence of the Latin Church over Syria, Palestine, and Egypt. The envoys of Alexius were heard at a church council, hastily summoned at Piazenza (= Placentia), and next year (1095) at Clermont, Urban held a second great council, in which all the slowly gathered strength of the Church was organized for a universal war propaganda against the Moslems. Private war, all war among Christians, was to cease until the infidel had been swept back and the site of the Holy Sepulchre was again in Christian hands.

The fervour of the response enables us to understand the great work of creative organization that had been done in Western Europe in the previous five centuries. In the beginning of the seventh century we saw Western Europe as a chaos of social and political fragments, with no common idea nor hope, a system shattered almost to a dust of self-seeking individuals. Now in the dawn of the eleventh century there is everywhere a common belief, a linking idea, to which men may devote themselves, and by which they can co-operate together in a universal enterprise. We realize that, in spite of much weakness and intellectual and moral unsoundness, to this extent the Christian Church has *worked*. We are able to measure the evil phases of tenth-century Rome, the scandals, the filthiness, the murders and violence, at their proper value by the scale of this fact. No doubt also all over Christendom there had been many lazy, evil, and foolish priests; but it is manifest that this task of teaching and co-ordination that had been accomplished could have been accomplished only through a great multitude of right-living priests and monks and nuns. A new and greater amphictyony, the amphictyony of Christendom, had come into the world, and it had been built by thousands of anonymous, faithful lives.

And this response to the appeal of Urban the Second was not confined only to what we should call educated people. It was not simply knights and princes who were willing to go upon this crusade. Side by side with the figure of Urban we must put the figure of Peter the Hermit, a type novel to Europe, albeit a little reminiscent of the Hebrew prophets. This man appeared preaching the crusade to the common people. He told a story—whether truthful or untruthful hardly matters in this connection—of his pilgrimage to Jerusalem, of the wanton destruction at the Holy Sepulchre by the Seljuk Turks, who took it in 1073, and of the exactions, brutalities, and deliberate cruelties practised upon the Christian pilgrims to the Holy Places. Barefooted, clad in a coarse garment, riding on an ass, and bearing a huge cross, this man travelled about France and Germany, and everywhere harangued vast crowds in church or street or market-place.

Here for the first time we discover Europe with an idea and a soul! Here is a universal response of indignation at the story of a remote wrong, a swift understanding of a common cause for rich and poor alike. You cannot imagine this thing happening in the Empire of Augustus Cæsar, or indeed in any previous state in the world's history. Something of the kind might perhaps have been possible in the far smaller world of Hellas, or in Arabia before Islam. But this movement affected nations, kingdoms, tongues, and peoples. It is clear that we are dealing with something new that has come into the world, a new clear connection of the common interest with the consciousness of the common man.

§ 10

From the very first this flaming enthusiasm was mixed with baser elements. There was the cold and calculated scheme of the free and ambitious Latin Church to subdue and replace the emperor-ruled Byzantine Church; there was the freebooting instinct of the Normans, who were tearing Italy to pieces, which turned readily enough to a new and richer world of plunder; and there was something in the multitude who now turned their faces east, something deeper than love in the human composition, namely, fear-born hate, that the impassioned appeals of the propagandists and the exaggeration of the horrors and cruelties of the infidel had fanned into flame. And there were still other forces; the intolerant Seljuks and the intolerant Fatimites lay now an impassable barrier across the eastward trade of Genoa and Venice that had hitherto flowed through Bagdad and Aleppo, or through Egypt. They must force open these closed channels, unless Constantinople and the Black Sea route were to monopolize Eastern trade altogether. Moreover, in 1094 and 1095 there had been a pestilence and famine from the Scheldt to Bohemia, and there was great social disorganization. "No wonder," says Mr. Ernest Barker, "that a stream of emigration set towards the East, such as would in modern times flow towards a newly discovered goldfield—a stream carrying in its turbid waters much refuse, tramps and bankrupts, camp-followers and hucksters, fugitive monks and escaped villeins, and marked by the same motley grouping, the same fever of

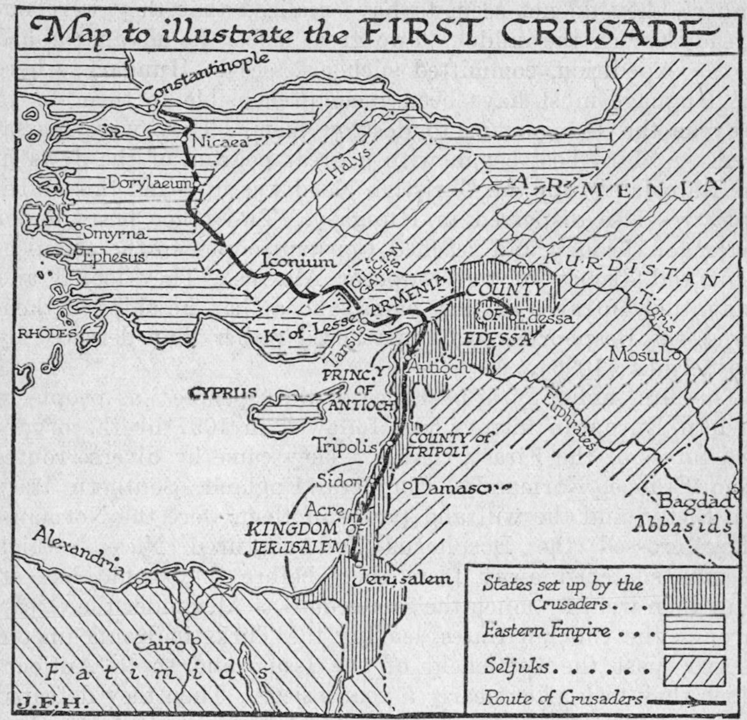

life, the same alternations of affluence and beggary, which mark the rush for a goldfield to-day."

But these were secondary contributory causes. The fact of predominant interest to the historian of mankind is this *will to crusade* suddenly revealed as a new mass possibility in human affairs.

The story of the crusades abounds in such romantic and picturesque detail that the writer of an Outline of History must ride his pen upon the curb through this alluring field. The first forces to move eastward were great crowds of undisciplined people rather than armies, and they sought to make their way by the valley of the Danube, and thence southward to Constantinople. This was the "people's crusade." Never before in the whole history of the world had there been such a spectacle as these masses of practically leaderless people moved by an idea. It was a very crude idea. When they got among foreigners, they do not seem to have realized that they were not already among the infidel. Two great mobs, the advance guard of the expedition, committed such excesses in Hungary, where the language must have been incomprehensible to them, as to provoke the Hungarians to destroy them. They were massacred. A third host began with a great pogrom of the Jews in the Rhineland—for the Christian blood was up—and this multitude was also dispersed in Hungary. Two other hosts under Peter got through and reached Constantinople, to the astonishment and dismay of the Emperor Alexius. They looted and committed outrages as they came, and at last he shipped them across the Bosphorus, to be massacred rather than defeated by the Seljuks (1096).

This first unhappy appearance of the "people" as people in modern European history was followed in 1097 by the organized forces of the First Crusade. They came by diverse routes from France, Normandy, Flanders, England, Southern Italy and Sicily, and the will and power of them were the Normans. They crossed the Bosphorus and captured Nicæa, which Alexius snatched away from them before they could loot it. They then went by much the same route as Alexander the Great, through the Cilician Gates, leaving the Turks in Konia unconquered, past the battlefield of the Issus, and so to Antioch, which they took after nearly a year's siege. Then they defeated a great relieving army from Mosul. A large part of the Crusaders remained in Antioch, a smaller force under Godfrey of Bouillon (in Belgium) went on to Jerusalem. "After a little more than a month's siege, the city was finally captured (July 15). The slaughter was terrible; the blood of the conquered ran down the streets, until men splashed in blood as they rode. At nightfall, 'sobbing for excess of joy,' the crusaders came to the Sepulchre from their treading of the winepress, and put their blood-stained hands together in prayer. So, on that day of July, the First Crusade came to an end."[1]

The authority of the Patriarch of Jerusalem was at once seized upon by the Latin clergy with the expedition, and the

[1] E. Barker, art. "Crusades," *Encyclopaedia Britannica.*

Orthodox Christians found themselves in rather a worse case under Latin rule than under the Turk. There were already Latin principalities established at Antioch and Edessa, and there began a struggle for ascendancy between these various courts and kings, and an unsuccessful attempt to make Jerusalem a property of the Pope. These are complications beyond our present scope.

Let us quote, however, a characteristic passage from Gibbon:—

"In a style less grave than that of history, I should perhaps compare the Emperor Alexius to the jackal, who is said to follow the steps and to devour the leavings of the lion. Whatever had been his fears and toils in the passage of the First Crusade, they were amply recompensed by the subsequent benefits which he derived from the exploits of the Franks. His dexterity and vigilance secured their first conquest of Nicæa, and from this threatening station the Turks were compelled to evacuate the neighbourhood of Constantinople. While the Crusaders, with blind valour, advanced into the midland countries of Asia, the crafty Greek improved the favourable occasion when the emirs of the sea coast were recalled to the standard of the Sultan. The Turks were driven from the isles of Rhodes and Chios; the cities of Ephesus and Smyrna, of Sardes, Philadelphia, and Laodicea were restored to the empire, which Alexius enlarged from the Hellespont to the banks of the Mæander and the rocky shores of Pamphylia. The churches resumed their splendour; the towns were rebuilt and fortified; and the desert country was peopled with colonies of Christians, who were gently removed from the more distant and dangerous frontier. In these paternal cares we may forgive Alexius, if we forget the deliverance of the holy sepulchre; but, by the Latins, he was stigmatized with the foul reproach of treason and desertion. They had sworn fidelity and obedience to his throne; but *he* had promised to assist their enterprise in person, or at least, with his troops and treasures; his base retreat dissolved their obligations; and the sword, which had been the instrument of their victory, was the pledge and title of their just independence. It does not appear that the emperor attempted to revive his obsolete claims over the kingdom of Jerusalem, but the borders of Cilicia and Syria were more recent in his possession and more accessible to his arms.

The great army of the Crusaders was annihilated or dispersed; the principality of Antioch was left without a head, by the surprise and captivity of Bohemond; his ransom had oppressed him with a heavy debt; and his Norman followers were insufficient to repel the hostilities of the Greeks and Turks. In this distress, Bohemond embraced a magnanimous resolution, of leaving the defence of Antioch to his kinsman, the faithful Tancred; of arming the West against the Byzantine Empire, and of executing the design which he inherited from the lessons and example of his father Guiscard. His embarkation was clandestine; and if we may credit a tale of the Princess Anna, he passed the hostile sea closely secreted in a coffin. (Anna Comnena adds, that to complete the imitation, he was shut up with a dead cock; and condescends to wonder how the barbarian could endure the confinement and putrefaction. This absurd tale is unknown to the Latins.) But his reception in France was dignified by the public applause and his marriage with the king's daughter; his return was glorious, since the bravest spirits of the age enlisted under his veteran command; and he repassed the Adriatic at the head of five thousand horse and forty thousand foot, assembled from the most remote climates of Europe. The strength of Durazzo and prudence of Alexius, the progress of famine and approach of winter, eluded his ambitious hopes; and the venal confederates were seduced from his standard. A treaty of peace suspended the fears of the Greeks."

We have dealt thus lengthily with the First Crusade, because it displays completely the quality of all these expeditions. The reality of the struggle between the Latin and the Byzantine system became more and more nakedly apparent. In 1101 came reinforcements, in which the fleet of the mercantile republics of Venice and Genoa played a prominent part, and the power of the kingdom of Jerusalem was extended. The year 1147 saw a Second Crusade, in which both the Emperor Conrad III and King Louis of France participated. It was a much more stately and far less successful and enthusiastic expedition than its predecessor. It had been provoked by the fall of Edessa to the Moslems in 1144. One large division of Germans, instead of going to the Holy Land, attacked and subjugated the still pagan Wends east of the Elbe. This, the Pope agreed, counted as crusading, and so did the capture of Lisbon, and the foundation of the Christian kingdom of Portugal by the Flemish and English contingents.

In 1169 a Kurdish adventurer, named Saladin, became ruler of Egypt, in which country the Shiite heresy had now fallen before a Sunnite revival. This Saladin reunited the efforts of Egypt and Bagdad, and preached a Jehad, a Holy War, a counter-crusade, of all the Moslems against the Christians. This Jehad excited almost as much feeling in Islam as the First Crusade had done in Christendom. It was now a case of crusader against crusader; and in 1187 Jerusalem was retaken. This provoked the Third Crusade (1189). This also was a grand affair, planned jointly by the Emperor Frederick I (known better as Frederick Barbarossa), the King of France, and the King of England (who at that time owned many of the fairest French provinces). The papacy played a secondary part in this expedition; it was in one of its phases of enfeeblement; and the crusade was the most courtly, chivalrous, and romantic of all. Religious bitterness was mitigated by the idea of knightly gallantry, which obsessed both Saladin and Richard I (1189-1199) of England (Cœur-de-Lion), and the lover of romance may very well turn to the romances about this period for its flavour. The crusade saved the principality of Antioch for a time, but failed to retake Jerusalem. The Christians, however, remained in possession of the sea-coast of Palestine.

By the time of the Third Crusade, the magic and wonder had gone out of these movements altogether. The common people had found them out. Men went, but only kings and nobles straggled back; and that often only after heavy taxation for a ransom. The idea of the crusades was cheapened by their too frequent and trivial use. Whenever the Pope quarrelled with anyone now, he called for a crusade, until the word ceased to mean anything but an attempt to give flavour to an unpalatable civil war. There was a crusade against the heretics in the south of France, one against John (King of England), one against the Emperor Frederick II. The Popes did not understand the necessity of dignity to the papacy. They had achieved a moral ascendancy in Christendom. Forthwith they began to fritter it away. They not only cheapened the idea of the crusades, but they made their tremendous power of excommunication, of putting people outside all the sacraments, hopes, and comforts of religion, ridiculous by using it in mere disputes of policy. Frederick II was not only crusaded against, but excommunicated—without visible injury. He was excommunicated again in 1239, and this sentence was renewed by Innocent IV in 1245.

The bulk of the Fourth Crusade never reached the Holy Land at all. It started from Venice (1202), captured Zara, encamped at Constantinople (1203), and finally, in 1204, stormed the city. It was frankly a combined attack on the Byzantine Empire. Venice took much of the coasts and islands of the empire, and a Latin, Baldwin of Flanders, was set up as emperor in Constantinople. The Latin and Greek Churches were declared to be reunited, and Latin emperors ruled as conquerors in Constantinople from 1204 to 1261.

In 1212 occurred a dreadful thing, a children's crusade. An excitement that could no longer affect sane adults was spread among the children in the south of France and in the Rhone valley. A crowd of many thousands of French boys marched to Marseilles; they were then lured on board ship by slave traders, who sold them into slavery in Egypt. The Rhineland children tramped into Italy, many perishing by the way, and there dispersed. Pope Innocent III made great capital out of this strange business. "The very children put us to shame," he said; and sought to whip up enthusiasm for a Fifth Crusade. This crusade aimed at the conquest of Egypt, because Jerusalem was now held by the Egyptian Sultan; its remnants returned in 1221, after an inglorious evacuation of its one capture, Damietta, with the Jerusalem vestiges of the True Cross as a sort of consolation concession on the part of the victor. We have already noted the earlier adventures of this venerable relic before the days of Muhammad when it was carried off by Chosroes II to Ctesiphon, and recovered by the Emperor Heraclius. Fragments of the True Cross, however, had always been in Rome at the church of S. Croce-in-Gerusalemme, since the days of the Empress Helena (the mother of Constantine the Great) to whom, says the legend, its hiding-place had been revealed in a vision during her pilgrimage to the Holy Land.[1]

[1] "The custody of the *True Cross,* which on Easter Sunday was solemnly exposed to the people, was entrusted to the Bishop of Jerusalem; and he alone might gratify the curious devotion of the pilgrims, by the gift of small pieces, which they encased in gold or gems, and carried away in triumph to their respective countries. But, as this gainful branch of com

The Sixth Crusade (1229) was a crusade bordering upon absurdity. The Emperor Frederick II had promised to go upon a crusade, and evaded his vow. He had made a false start and returned. He was probably bored by the mere idea of a crusade. But the vow had been part of the bargain by which he secured the support of Pope Innocent III in his election as emperor. He busied himself in reorganizing the government of his Sicilian kingdom, though he had given the Pope to understand that he would relinquish those possessions if he became emperor; and the Pope was anxious to stop this process of consolidation by sending him to the Holy Land. The Pope did not want Frederick II, or any German emperor at all in Italy, because he himself wished to rule Italy. As Frederick II remained evasive, Gregory IX excommunicated him, proclaimed a crusade against him, and invaded his dominions in Italy (1228). Whereupon the Emperor sailed with an army to the Holy Land. There he had a meeting with the Sultan of Egypt (the Emperor spoke six languages freely, including Arabic); and it would seem these two gentlemen, both of sceptical opinions, exchanged views of a congenial sort, discussed the Pope in a worldly spirit, debated the Mongolian rush westward, which threatened them both alike, and agreed finally to a commercial convention, and the surrender of a part of the kingdom of Jerusalem to Frederick. This indeed was a new sort of crusade, a crusade by private treaty. As this astonishing crusader had been excommunicated, he had to indulge in a purely secular coronation in Jerusalem, taking the crown from the altar with his own hand, in a church from which all the clergy had gone. Probably there was no one to show him the Holy Places; indeed these were presently all put under an interdict by the Patriarch of Jerusalem and locked up; manifestly the affair differed altogether in spirit from the red onslaught of the First Crusade. It had not even the kindly sociability of the Caliph Omar's visit six hundred years before. Frederick II rode out of Jerusalem almost alone, returned from this unromantic success to Italy, put his affairs there in order very rapidly, chased the papal armies out of his possessions, and obliged the Pope to give him absolution from

merce must soon have been annihilated, it was found convenient to suppose that the marvellous wood possessed a secret power of vegetation, and that its substance, though continually diminished, still remained entire and unimpaired.''—Gibbon.

his excommunication (1230). This Sixth Crusade was indeed not only the *reductio ad absurdum* of crusades, but of papal excommunications. Of this Frederick II we shall tell more in a later section, because he was very typical of certain new forces that were coming into European affairs.

The Christians lost Jerusalem again in 1244; it was taken from them very easily by the Sultan of Egypt when they attempted an intrigue against him. This provoked the Seventh Crusade, the Crusade of St. Louis, King of France (Louis IX), who was taken prisoner in Egypt and ransomed in 1250. Not until 1918, when it fell to a mixed force of French, British, and Indian troops, did Jerusalem slip once more from the Moslem grasp. . . .

One more crusade remains to be noted, an expedition to Tunis by this same Louis IX, who died of fever there.

§ 11

The essential interest of the crusades for the historian of mankind lies in the wave of emotion, of unifying feeling, that animated the first. Thereafter these expeditions became more and more an established process, and less and less vital events. The First Crusade was an occurrence like the discovery of America; the later ones were more and more like a trip across the Atlantic. In the eleventh century, the idea of the crusade must have been like a strange and wonderful light in the sky; in the thirteenth one can imagine honest burghers saying in tones of protest, "What! *another* crusade!" The experience of St. Louis in Egypt is not like a fresh experience for mankind; it is much more like a round of golf over some well-known links, a round that was dogged by misfortune. It is an insignificant series of events. The interest of life had shifted to other directions.

The beginning of the crusades displays all Europe saturated by a naïve Christianity, and ready to follow the leading of the Pope trustfully and simply. The scandals of the Lateran during its evil days, with which we are all so familiar now, were practically unknown outside Rome. And Gregory VII and Urban II had redeemed all that. But intellectually and morally their successors at the Lateran and the Vatican[1] were not equal to their opportunities. The strength of the papacy lay in the faith men had in it, and it used that faith so carelessly as to enfeeble it. Rome has always had too much of the shrewdness of the priest and too little of the power of the prophet. So that while the eleventh century was a century of ignorant and confiding men, the thirteenth was an age of knowing and disillusioned men. It was a far more civilized and profoundly sceptical world.

The bishops, priests, and the monastic institutions of Latin Christendom before the days of Gregory VII had been perhaps rather loosely linked together and very variable in quality; but it is clear that they were, as a rule, intensely intimate with the people among whom they found themselves, and with much of the spirit of Jesus still alive in them; they were trusted, and they had enormous power *within the conscience of their followers.* The church, in comparison with its later state, was more in the hands of local laymen and the local ruler; it lacked its later universality. The energetic bracing up of the church organization by Gregory VII, which was designed to increase the central power of Rome, broke many subtle filaments between priest and monastery on the one hand, and the countryside about them on the other. Men of faith and wisdom believe in growth and their fellow men; but priests, even such priests as Gregory VII, believe in the false "efficiency" of an imposed discipline. The squabble over investitures made every prince in Christendom suspicious of the bishops as agents of a foreign power; this suspicion filtered down to the parishes. The political enterprises of the papacy necessitated an increasing demand for money. Already in the thirteenth century it was being said everywhere that the priests were not good men, that they were always hunting for money.

In the days of ignorance there had been an extraordinary willingness to believe the Catholic priesthood good and wise. Relatively it was better and wiser in those days. Great powers beyond her spiritual functions had been entrusted to the church,

[1] The Popes inhabited the palace of the Lateran until 1305, when a French Pope set up the papal court at Avignon. When the Pope returned to Rome in 1377 the Lateran was almost in ruins, and the palace of the Vatican became the seat of the papal court. It was, among other advantages, much nearer to the papal stronghold, the Castle of St. Angelo.

and very extraordinary freedoms. Of this confidence the fullest advantage had been taken. In the Middle Ages the church had become a state within the state. It had its own law courts. Cases involving not merely priests, but monks, students, crusaders, widows, orphans, and the helpless, were reserved for the clerical courts; and whenever the rites or rules of the church were involved, there the church claimed jurisdiction over such matters as wills, marriage, oaths, and of course over heresy, sorcery, and blasphemy. There were numerous clerical prisons in which offenders might pine all their lives. The Pope was the supreme law-giver of Christendom, and his court at Rome the final and decisive court of appeal. And the church levied taxes; it had not only vast properties and a great income from fees, but it imposed a tax of a tenth, the tithe, upon its subjects. It did not call for this as a pious benefaction; it demanded it as a right. The clergy, on the other hand, were now claiming exemption from lay taxation.

This attempt to trade upon their peculiar prestige and evade their share in fiscal burdens was certainly one very considerable factor in the growing dissatisfaction with the clergy. Apart from any question of justice, it was impolitic. It made taxes seem ten times more burthensome to those who had to pay. It made everyone feel the immunities of the church. And a still more extravagant and unwise claim made by the church was the claim to the power of *dispensation*. The Pope might in many instances set aside the laws of the church in individual cases; he might allow cousins to marry, permit a man to have two wives, or release anyone from a vow. But to do such things is to admit that the laws affected are not based upon necessity and an inherent righteousness; that they are in fact restrictive and vexatious. The law-giver, of all beings, most owes the law allegiance. He of all men should behave as though the law compelled him. But it is the universal weakness of mankind that what we are given to administer we presently imagine we own.

§ 12

The Emperor Frederick II is a very convenient example of the sort of doubter and rebel the thirteenth century could produce. It may be interesting to tell a little of this intelligent and cynical man. He was the son of the German Emperor,

Henry VI, and grandson of Frederick Barbarossa, and his mother was the daughter of Roger I, the Norman King of Sicily. He inherited this kingdom in 1198, when he was four years old; his mother was his guardian for six months, and when she died, Pope Innocent III (1198 to 1216) became regent and guardian. He seems to have had an exceptionally good and remarkably mixed education, and his accomplishments earned him the flattering title of *Stupor mundi,* the amazement of the world. The result of getting an Arabic view of Christianity, and a Christian view of Islam, was to make him believe that all religions were impostures, a view held perhaps by many a stifled observer in the Age of Faith. But he talked about his views; his blasphemies and heresies are on record. Growing up under the arrogant rule of Innocent III, who never seems to have realized that his ward had come of age, he developed a slightly humorous evasiveness. It was the papal policy to prevent any fresh coalescence of the power of Germany and Italy, and it was equally Frederick's determination to get whatever he could. When presently opportunity offered him the imperial crown of Germany, he secured the Pope's support by agreeing, if he were elected, to relinquish his possessions in Sicily and South Italy, and to put down heresy in Germany. For Innocent III was one of the great persecuting Popes, an able, grasping, and aggressive man. (For a Pope, he was exceptionally young. He became Pope at thirty-seven.) It was Innocent who had preached a cruel crusade against the heretics in the south of France, a crusade that presently became a looting expedition beyond his control. So soon as Frederick was elected emperor (1211),[1] Innocent pressed for the performance of the vows and promises he had wrung from his dutiful ward. The clergy were to be free from lay jurisdiction and from taxation, and exemplary cruelties were to be practised upon the heretics. None of which things Frederick did. As we have already told, he would not even relinquish Sicily. He liked Sicily as a place of residence better than he liked Germany.

Innocent III died baffled in 1216, and his successor, Honorius III, effected nothing. Honorius was succeeded by Gregory IX (1227), who evidently came to the papal throne with a nervous resolution to master this perplexing young man. He excom-

[1] He was crowned emperor in 1220 by Honorius III, the successor of Innocent.

municated him at once for failing to start upon his crusade, which was now twelve years overdue; and he denounced his vices, heresies, and general offences in a public letter (1227). To this Frederick replied in a far abler document addressed to all the princes of Europe, a document of extreme importance in history, because it is the first clear statement of the issue between the pretensions of the Pope to be absolute ruler of all Christendom, and the claims of the secular rulers.[1] This conflict had always been smouldering; it had broken out here in one form, and there in another; but now Frederick put it in clear general terms upon which men could combine together.

Having delivered this blow, he departed upon the pacific crusade of which we have already told. In 1239, Gregory IX was excommunicating him for a second time, and renewing that warfare of public abuse in which the papacy had already suffered severely. The controversy was revived after Gregory IX was dead, when Innocent IV was Pope; and again a devastating letter, which men were bound to remember, was written by Frederick against the church. He denounced the pride and irreligion of the clergy, and ascribed all the corruptions of the time to their pride and wealth. He proposed to his fellow princes a general confiscation of church property—for the good of the church. It was a suggestion that never afterwards left the imagination of the European princes.

We will not go on to tell of his last years or of the disaster at Parma, due to his carelessness, which cast a shadow of failure over his end. The particular events of his life are far less significant than its general atmosphere. It is possible to piece together something of his court life in Sicily. He is described towards the end of his life as "red, bald, and short-sighted"; but his features were good and pleasing. He was luxurious in his way of living, and fond of beautiful things. He is described as licentious. But it is clear that his mind was not satisfied by religious scepticism, and that he was a man of very effectual curiosity and inquiry. He gathered Jewish and Moslem as well as Christian philosophers at his court, and he did much to irrigate the Italian mind with Saracenic influences. Through him Arabic numerals and algebra were introduced to Christian students, and among other philosophers at his court was Michael

[1] Some authorities deny his authorship of this letter.

Scott, who translated portions of Aristotle and the commentaries thereon of the great Arab philosopher Averroes (of Cordoba). In 1224 Frederick founded the University of Naples, and he enlarged and enriched the great medical school at Salerno University, the most ancient of universities. He also founded a zoological garden. He left a book on hawking, which shows him to have been an acute observer of the habits of birds, and he was one of the first Italians to write Italian verse. Italian poetry was indeed born at his court. He has been called by an able writer, "the first of the moderns," and the phrase expresses aptly the unprejudiced detachment of his intellectual side. His was an all-round originality. During a gold shortage he introduced and made a success of a coinage of stamped leather, bearing his promise to pay in gold, a sort of leather bank-note issue.[1]

In spite of the torrent of abuse and calumny in which Frederick was drenched, he left a profound impression upon the popular imagination. He is still remembered in South Italy almost as vividly as is Napoleon I by the peasants of France; he is the "Gran Federigo." And German scholars declare that, in spite of Frederick's manifest dislike for Germany, it is he, and not Frederick I, Frederick Barbarossa, to whom that German legend originally attached—that legend which represents a great monarch slumbering in a deep cavern, his beard grown round a stone table, against a day of awakening when the world will be restored by him from an extremity of disorder to peace. Afterwards, it seems, the story was transferred to the Crusader Barbarossa, the grandfather of Frederick II.

A difficult child was Frederick II for Mother Church, and he was only the precursor of many such difficult children. The princes and educated gentlemen throughout Europe read his letters and discussed them. The more enterprising university students found, marked, and digested the Arabic Aristotle he had made accessible to them in Latin. Salerno cast a baleful light upon Rome. All sorts of men must have been impressed by the futility of the excommunications and interdicts that were levelled at Frederick.

[1] Perhaps parchment rather than leather. Such promises on parchment were also used by the Carthaginians. Was Frederick's money an inheritance from an old tradition living on in Sicily since Carthaginian times?—E. B.

§ 13

We have said that Innocent III never seemed to realize that his ward, Frederick II, was growing up. It is equally true that the papacy never seemed to realize that Europe was growing up. It is impossible for an intelligent modern student of history not to sympathize with the underlying idea of the papal court, with the idea of one universal rule of righteousness keeping the peace of the earth, and not to recognize the many elements of nobility that entered into the Lateran policy. Sooner or later mankind must come to one universal peace, unless our race is to be destroyed by the increasing power of its own destructive inventions; and that universal peace must needs take the form of a government, that is to say a law-sustaining organization, in the best sense of the word religious; a government ruling men through the educated co-ordination of their minds in a common conception of human history and human destiny.

The papacy we must now recognize as the first clearly conscious attempt to provide such a government in the world. We cannot too earnestly examine its deficiencies and inadequacies, for every lesson we can draw from them is necessarily of the greatest value to us in forming our ideas of our own international relationships. We have tried to suggest the main factors in the breakdown of the Roman Republic, and it now behoves us to attempt a diagnosis of the failure of the Roman Church to secure and organize the good will of mankind.

The first thing that will strike the student is the intermittence of the efforts of the church to establish the world City of God. The policy of the church was not whole-heartedly and continuously set upon that end. It was only now and then that some fine personality or some group of fine personalities dominated it in that direction. The kingdom of God that Jesus of Nazareth had preached was overlaid, as we have explained, almost from the beginning by the doctrines and ceremonial traditions of an earlier age, and of an intellectually inferior type. Christianity almost from its commencement ceased to be purely prophetic and creative. It entangled itself with archaic traditions of human sacrifice, with Mithraic blood-cleansing, with priestcraft as ancient as human society, and with elaborate doctrines about the structure of the divinity. The gory forefinger of the Etruscan pontifex maximus emphasized the teachings of Jesus of Nazareth; the mental complexity of the Alexandrian Greek entangled them. In the inevitable jangle of these incompatibles the church had become dogmatic. In despair of other solutions to its intellectual discords it had resorted to arbitrary authority. Its priests and bishops were more and more men moulded to creeds and dogmas and set procedures; by the time they became cardinals or popes they were usually oldish men, habituated to a politic struggle for immediate ends and no longer capable of world-wide views. They no longer wanted to see the Kingdom of God established in the hearts of men—they had forgotten about that; they wanted to see the power of the church, which was their own power, dominating men. They were prepared to bargain even with the hates and fears and lusts in men's hearts to ensure that power. And it was just because many of them probably doubted secretly of the entire soundness of their vast and elaborate doctrinal fabric, that they would brook no discussion of it. They were intolerant of questions or dissent, not because they were sure of their faith, but because they were not. They wanted conformity for reasons of policy. By the thirteenth century the church was evidently already morbidly anxious about the gnawing doubts that might presently lay the whole structure of its pretensions in ruins. It had no serenity of soul. It was hunting everywhere for heretics as timid old ladies are said to look under beds and in cupboards for burglars before retiring for the night.

We have already mentioned the Persian Mani, who was crucified and flayed in the year 277. His way of representing the struggle between good and evil was as a struggle between a power of light which was, as it were, in rebellion against a power of darkness inherent in the universe. All these profound mysteries are necessarily represented by symbols and poetic expressions, and the ideas of Mani still find a response in many intellectual temperaments to-day. One may hear Manichæan doctrines from many Christian pulpits. But the orthodox Catholic symbol was a different one. These Manichæan ideas had spread very widely in Europe, and particularly in Bulgaria and the south of France. In the south of France the people who held them were called the Cathars or Albigenses. Their ideas jarred so little with the essentials of Christianity, that they believed themselves to be devout Christians. As a body they lived lives of conspicuous virtue and purity in a violent, undisciplined, and vicious age. But they questioned the doctrinal soundness of Rome and the orthodox interpretation of the Bible. They thought Jesus was a rebel against the cruelty of the God of the Old Testament, and not his harmonious son. Closely associated with the Albigenses were the Waldenses, the followers of a man called Waldo, who seems to have been quite soundly Catholic in his theology, but equally offensive to the church because he denounced the riches and luxury of the clergy. This was enough for the Lateran, and so we have the spectacle of Innocent III preaching a crusade against these unfortunate sectaries, and permitting the enlistment of every wandering scoundrel at loose ends to carry fire and sword and rape and every conceivable outrage among the most peaceful subjects of the King of France. The accounts of the cruelties and abominations of this crusade are far more terrible to read than any account of Christian martyrdoms by the pagans, and they have the added horror of being indisputably true.

This black and pitiless intolerance was an evil spirit to be mixed into the project of a rule of God on earth. This was a spirit entirely counter to that of Jesus of Nazareth. We do not hear of his smacking the faces or wringing the wrists of recalcitrant or unresponsive disciples. But the Popes during their centuries of power were always raging against the slightest reflection upon the intellectual sufficiency of the church.

And the intolerance of the church was not confined to religious matters. The shrewd, pompous, irascible, and rather malignant old men who manifestly constituted a dominant majority in the councils of the church resented any knowledge but their own knowledge, and distrusted any thought at all that they did not correct and control. They set themselves to restrain science, of which they were evidently jealous. Any mental activity but their own struck them as being insolent. Later on they were to have a great struggle upon the question of the earth's position in space, and whether it moved round the sun or not. This was really not the business of the church at all. She might very well have left to reason the things that are reason's, but she seems to have been impelled by an inner necessity to estrange the intellectual conscience in men.

Had this intolerance sprung from a real intensity of conviction it would have been bad enough, but it was accompanied by a scarcely disguised contempt for the intelligence and mental dignity of the common man that makes it far less acceptable to our modern judgments, and which no doubt made it far less acceptable to the free spirits of the time. We have told quite dispassionately the policy of the Roman church towards her troubled sister in the East. Many of the tools and expedients she used were abominable. In her treatment of her own people a streak of real cynicism is visible. She destroyed her prestige by disregarding her own teaching of righteousness. Of dispensations we have already spoken (§ 11). Her crowning folly in the sixteenth century was the sale of *indulgences,* whereby the sufferings of the soul in purgatory could be commuted for a money payment. But the spirit that led at last to this shameless and, as it proved, disastrous proceeding, was already very evident in the twelfth and thirteenth centuries.

Long before the seed of criticism that Frederick II had sown had germinated in men's minds and produced its inevitable crop of rebellion, there was apparent a strong feeling in Christendom that all was not well with the spiritual atmosphere. There began movements, movements that nowadays we should call "revivalist," within the church, that implied rather than uttered a criticism of the sufficiency of her existing methods and organization. Men sought fresh forms of righteous living outside the monasteries and priesthood. One notable figure is that of St. Francis of Assisi (1181-1226). We cannot tell here in any detail of how this pleasant young gentleman gave up all the amenities and ease of his life and went forth to seek God; the opening of the story is not unlike the early experiences of Gautama Buddha. He had a sudden conversion in the midst of a life of pleasure, and, taking a vow of extreme poverty, he gave himself up to an imitation of the life of Christ, and to the service of the sick and wretched, and more particularly to the service of the lepers, who then abounded in Italy. He was joined by great multitudes of disciples, and so the first Friars of the Franciscan Order came into existence. An order of women devotees was set up beside the original confraternity, and in addition great numbers of men and women were brought into less formal association. He preached, unmolested by the Moslems, be it noted, in Egypt and Palestine, though the Fifth Crusade was then in progress. His relations with the church are still a matter for discussion. His work had been sanctioned by Pope Innocent III, but while he was in the East there was a reconstitution of his order, intensifying its discipline and substituting authority for responsive impulse, and as a consequence of these changes he resigned its headship. To the end he clung passionately to the ideal of poverty, but he was hardly dead before the order was holding property through trustees and building a great church and monastery to his memory at Assisi. The disciplines of the order that were applied after his death to his immediate associates are scarcely to be distinguished from a persecution; several of the more conspicuous zealots for simplicity were scourged, others were imprisoned, one was killed while attempting to escape, and Brother Bernard, the "first disciple," passed a year in the woods and hills, hunted like a wild beast.

This struggle within the Franciscan Order is a very interesting one, because it foreshadows the great troubles that were coming to Christendom. All through the thirteenth century a section of the Franciscans were straining at the rule of the church, and in 1318 four of them were burnt alive at Marseilles as incorrigible heretics. There seems to have been little difference between the teaching and spirit of St. Francis and that of Waldo in the twelfth century, the founder of the murdered sect of Waldenses. Both were passionately enthusiastic for the spirit of Jesus of Nazareth. But while Waldo rebelled against the church, St. Francis did his best to be a good child of the church, and his comment on the spirit of official Christianity was only implicit. But both were instances of an outbreak of conscience against authority and the ordinary procedure of the church. And it is plain that in the second instance, as in the first, the church scented rebellion.

A very different character to St. Francis was the Spaniard St. Dominic (1170-1221), who was, of all things, orthodox. He had a passion for the argumentative conversion of heretics, and he was commissioned by Pope Innocent III to go and preach to the Albigenses. His work went on side by side with the fighting and massacres of the crusade; whom Dominic could not convert, Innocent's crusaders slew; yet his very activities and the recognition and encouragement of his order by the Pope witness to the rising tide of discussion, and to the persuasion even of the papacy that force was no remedy. In several respects the development of the Black Friars or Dominicans—

the Franciscans were the Grey Friars—shows the Roman church at the parting of the ways, committing itself more and more deeply to organized dogma, and so to a hopeless conflict with the quickening intelligence and courage of mankind. She whose one duty was to lead, chose to compel. The last discourse of St. Dominic to the heretics he had sought to convert is preserved to us. It is a signpost in history. It betrays the fatal exasperation of a man who has lost his faith in the power of truth because *his* truth has not prevailed. "For many years," he said, "I have exhorted you in vain, with gentleness, preaching, praying, and weeping. But according to the proverb of my country, 'where blessing can accomplish nothing, blows may avail.' We shall rouse against you princess and prelates, who, alas! will arm nations and kingdoms against this land . . . and thus blows will avail where blessings and gentleness have been powerless."[1]

The thirteenth century saw the development of a new institution in the church, the papal Inquisition. Before this time it had been customary for the Pope to make occasional inquests or inquiries into heresy in this region or that, but now Innocent III saw in the new order of the Dominicans a powerful instrument of suppression. The Inquisition was organized as a standing inquiry under their direction, and with fire and torment the church set itself, through this instrument, to assail and weaken the human conscience in which its sole hope of world dominion resided. Before the thirteenth century the penalty of death had been inflicted but rarely upon heretics and unbelievers. Now in a hundred market-places in Europe the dignitaries of the church watched the blackened bodies of its antagonists, for the most part poor and insignificant people, burn and sink pitifully, and their own great mission to mankind burn and sink with them into dust and ashes.

The beginnings of the Franciscans and the Dominicans were but two among many of the new forces that were arising in Christendom, either to help or shatter the church, as its own wisdom might decide. Those two orders the church did assimilate and use, though with a little violence in the case of the former. But other forces were more frankly disobedient and critical. A century and a half later came Wycliffe (1320-1384). He was a learned doctor at Oxford; for a time he was

[1] *Encyclopaedia Britannica,* art. "Dominic."

Master of Balliol; and he held various livings in the church. Quite late in his life he began a series of outspoken criticisms of the corruption of the clergy and the unwisdom of the church. He organized a number of poor priests, the Wycliffites, to spread his ideas throughout England; and in order that people should judge between the church and himself, he translated the Bible into English. He was a more learned and far abler man than either St. Francis or St. Dominic. He had supporters in high places and a great following among the people; and though Rome raged against him, and ordered his imprisonment, he died a free man, still administering the Sacraments as parish priest of Lutterworth. But the black and ancient spirit that was leading the Catholic church to its destruction would not let his bones rest in his grave. By a decree of the Council of Constance in 1415, his remains were ordered to be dug up and burnt, an order which was carried out at the command of Pope Martin V by Bishop Fleming in 1428. This desecration was not the act of some isolated fanatic; it was the official act of the church.

§ 14

The history of the papacy is confusing to the general reader because of the multitude and abundance of the Popes. They mostly began to reign as old men, and their reigns were short, averaging less than two years each. But certain of the Popes stand out and supply convenient handles for the student to grasp. Such were Gregory I (590-604) the Great, the first monkish Pope, the friend of Benedict, the sender of the English mission. Other noteworthy Popes are Leo III (795-816), who crowned Charlemagne, the scandalous Popes John XI (931-936) and John XII (955-963), which latter was deposed by the Emperor Otto I, and the great Hildebrand, who ended his days as Pope Gregory VII (1073-1085), and who did so much by establishing the celibacy of the clergy, and insisting upon the supremacy of the church over kings and princes, to centralize the power of the church in Rome. There was a great struggle between Hildebrand and the Emperor elect Henry IV upon the question of investitures. The emperor attempted to depose the pope; the pope excommunicated the emperor and released his subjects from their allegiance. The emperor was obliged to go in penitence to the pope at Canossa and to await forgiveness for three days and nights in the courtyard of the castle, clad in sackcloth and barefooted to the snow. The next Pope but one after Gregory VII was Urban II (1087-1099), the Pope of the First Crusade. The period from the time of Gregory VII onward for a century and a half, was the great period of ambition and effort for the church. There was a real sustained attempt to unite all Christendom under a purified and reorganized church.

The setting up of Latin kingdoms in Syria and the Holy Land, in religious communion with Rome, after the First Crusade, marked the opening stage of a conquest of Eastern Christianity by Rome that reached its climax during the Latin rule in Constantinople (1204-1261).

In 1176, at Venice, the Emperor Frederick Barbarossa (Frederick I) knelt to the Pope Alexander III, recognized his spiritual supremacy, and swore fealty to him. But after the death of Alexander III, in 1181, the peculiar weakness of the papacy, its liability to fall to old and enfeebled men, became manifest. Five Popes tottered to the Lateran to die within the space of ten years. Only with Innocent III (1198-1216) did another vigorous Pope take up the great policy of the City of God.

Under Innocent III, the guardian of that Emperor Frederick II, whose career we have already studied in §§ 10 and 12, and the five Popes who followed him, the Pope of Rome came nearer to being the monarch of a united Christendom than he had ever been before, and was ever to be again. The empire was weakened by internal dissensions, Constantinople was in Latin hands, from Bulgaria to Ireland and from Norway to Sicily and Jerusalem the Pope was supreme. Yet this supremacy was more apparent than real. For, as we have seen, while in the time of Urban the power of faith was strong in all Christian Europe, in the time of Innocent III the papacy had lost its hold upon the hearts of princes, and the faith and conscience of the common people was turning against a merely political and aggressive church.

The church in the thirteenth century was extending its legal power in the world, and losing its grip upon men's consciences. It was becoming less persuasive and more violent. No intelligent man can tell of this process, or read of this process of failure without very mingled feelings. The church had sheltered and formed a new Europe throughout the long ages of European darkness and chaos; it had been the matrix in which the new civilization had been cast. But this new-formed civilization was impelled to grow by its own inherent vitality, and the church lacked sufficient power of growth and accommodation. The time was fast approaching when this matrix was to be broken.

The first striking intimation of the decay of the living and sustaining forces of the papacy appeared when presently the Popes came into conflict with the growing power of the French king. During the lifetime of the Emperor Frederick II, Germany fell into disunion, and the French king began to play the rôle of guard, supporter, and rival to the Pope that had hitherto fallen to the Hohenstaufen emperors. A series of Popes pursued the policy of supporting the French monarchs. French princes were established in the kingdom of Sicily and Naples, with the support and approval of Rome, and the French kings saw before them the possibility of restoring and ruling the Empire of Charlemagne. When, however, the German interregnum after the death of Frederick II, the last of the Hohenstaufens, came to an end and Rudolf of Habsburg was elected first Habsburg Emperor (1273), the policy of the Lateran began to fluctuate between France and Germany, veering about with the sympathies of each successive Pope. In the East in 1261 the Greeks recaptured Constantinople from the Latin emperors, and the founder of the new Greek dynasty, Michael Palæologus, Michael VIII, after some unreal tentatives of reconciliation with the Pope, broke away from the Roman communion altogether, and with that, and the fall of the Latin kingdoms in Asia, the eastward ascendancy of the Popes came to an end.

In 1294 Boniface VIII became Pope. He was an Italian, hostile to the French, and full of a sense of the great traditions and mission of Rome. For a time he carried things with a high hand. In 1300 he held a jubilee, and a vast multitude of pilgrims assembled in Rome. "So great was the influx of money into the papal treasury, that two assistants were kept busy with rakes collecting the offerings that were deposited at the tomb of St. Peter."[1] But this festival was a delusive tri-

[1] J. H. Robinson.

umph. It is easier to raise a host of excursionists than a band of crusaders. Boniface came into conflict with the French king in 1302, and in 1303, as he was about to pronounce sentence of excommunication against that monarch, he was surprised and arrested in his own ancestral palace, at Anagni, by Guillaume de Nogaret. This agent from the French king forced an entrance into the palace, made his way into the bedroom of the frightened Pope—he was lying in bed with a cross in his hands —and heaped threats and insults upon him. The Pope was liberated a day or so later by the townspeople, and returned to Rome; but there he was seized upon and again made prisoner by the Orsini family, and in a few weeks' time the shocked and disillusioned old man died a prisoner in their hands.

The people of Anagni did resent the first outrage, and rose against Nogaret to liberate Boniface, but then Anagni was the Pope's native town. The important point to note is that the French king, in this rough treatment of the head of Christendom, was acting with the full approval of his people; he had summoned a council of the Three Estates of France (lords, church, and commons) and gained their consent before proceeding to extremities. Neither in Italy, Germany, nor England was there the slightest general manifestation of disapproval at this free handling of the sovereign pontiff. The idea of Christendom had decayed until its power over the minds of men had gone.

Throughout the fourteenth century the papacy did nothing to recover its moral sway. The next Pope elected, Clement V, was a Frenchman, the choice of King Philip of France. He never came to Rome. He set up his court in the town of Avignon, which then belonged not to France, but to the Papal See, though embedded in French territory, and there his successors remained until 1377, when Pope Gregory XI returned to the Vatican palace in Rome. But Gregory XI did not take the sympathies of the whole church with him. Many of the cardinals were of French origin, and their habits and associations were rooted deep at Avignon. When in 1378 Gregory XI died, and an Italian, Urban VI, was elected, these dissentient cardinals declared the election invalid, and elected another Pope, the anti-Pope, Clement VII. This split is called the Great Schism. The Popes remained in Rome, and all the anti-French powers, the Emperor, the King of England, Hungary,

Poland, and the North of Europe were loyal to them. The anti-Popes, on the other hand, continued in Avignon, and were supported by the King of France, his ally the King of Scotland, Spain, Portugal, and various German princes. Each Pope excommunicated and cursed the adherents of his rival, so that by one standard or another all Christendom was damned during this time (1378-1417). The lamentable effect of this split upon the solidarity of Christendom it is impossible to exaggerate. Is it any marvel that such men as Wycliffe began to teach men to think on their own account when the fountain of truth thus squirted against itself? In 1417 the Great Schism was healed at the Council of Constance, the same council that dug up and burnt Wycliffe's bones, and which, as we shall tell later, caused the burning of John Huss; at this council, Pope and anti-Pope resigned or were swept aside, and Martin V became the sole Pope of a formally reunited but spiritually very badly strained Christendom.

How later on the Council of Basle (1437) led to a fresh schism, and to further anti-Popes, we cannot relate here.

Such, briefly, is the story of the great centuries of papal ascendancy and papal decline. It is the story of the failure to achieve the very noble and splendid idea of a unified and religious world. We have pointed out in the previous section how greatly the inheritance of a complex dogmatic theology encumbered the church in this its ambitious adventure. It had too much theology, and not enough religion. But it may not be idle to point out here how much the individual insufficiency of the Popes also contributed to the collapse of its scheme and dignity. There was no such level of education in the world as to provide a succession of cardinals and popes with the breadth of knowledge and outlook needed for the task they had undertaken; they were not sufficiently educated for their task, and only a few, by sheer force of genius, transcended that defect. And, as we have already pointed out, they were, when at last they got to power, too old to use it. Before they could grasp the situation they had to control, most of them were dead. It would be interesting to speculate how far it would have tilted the balance in favour of the church if the cardinals had retired at fifty, and if no one could have been elected Pope after fifty-five. This would have lengthened the average reign of each Pope, and enormously increased the continuity of the policy of the church.

And it is perhaps possible that a more perfect system of selecting the cardinals, who were the electors and counsellors of the Pope, might have been devised. The rules and ways by which men reach power are of very great importance in human affairs. The psychology of the ruler is a science that has still to be properly studied. We have seen the Roman Republic wrecked, and here we see the church failing in its world mission very largely through ineffective electoral methods.

XXXIII

THE GREAT EMPIRE OF JENGIS KHAN AND HIS SUCCESSORS

(The Age of the Land Ways)

§ 1

WE have to tell now of the last and greatest of all the raids of nomadism upon the civilizations of the East and West. We have traced in this history the development side by side of these two ways of living, and we have pointed out that as the civilizations grew more extensive and better organized, the arms, the mobility, and the intelligence of the nomads also improved. The nomad was not simply an uncivilized man, he was a man specialized and specializing along his own line. From the very beginning of history the nomad and the settled people have been in reaction. We have told of the Semitic and Elamite raids upon Sumeria; we have seen the Western empire smashed by the nomads of the great plains and Persia conquered and Byzantium shaken by the nomads of Arabia. Whenever civilization seems to be choking amidst its weeds of wealth and debt and servitude, when its faiths seem rotting into cynicism and its powers of further growth are hopelessly entangled in effete formulæ, the nomad drives in like a plough to break up the festering stagnation and release the world to new beginnings. The Mongol aggression, which began with the thirteenth century, was the greatest, and so far it has been the last, of all these destructive reploughings of human association.

From entire obscurity the Mongols came very suddenly into history towards the close of the twelfth century. They appeared in the country to the north of China, in the land of origin of the Huns and Turks, and they were manifestly of the same strain as these peoples. They were gathered together under a chief, with whose name we will not tax the memory of the reader; under his son Jengis Khan their power grew with extraordinary swiftness.

The reader will already have an idea of the gradual breaking up of the original unity of Islam. In the beginning of the thirteenth century there were a number of separate and discordant Moslem states in Western Asia. There was Egypt (with Palestine and much of Syria) under the successors of Saladin, there was the Seljuk power in Asia Minor, there was still an Abbasid caliphate in Bagdad, and to the east of this again there had grown up a very considerable empire, the Kharismian empire, that of the Turkish princes from Khiva who had conquered a number of fragmentary Seljuk principalities and reigned from the Ganges valley to the Tigris. They had but an insecure hold on the Persian and Indian populations.

The state of the Chinese civilization was equally inviting to an enterprising invader. Our last glimpse of China in this history was in the seventh century during the opening years of the Tang dynasty, when that shrewd and able emperor Tai-tsung was weighing the respective merits of Nestorian Christianity, Islam, Buddhism, and the teachings of Lao Tse, and on the whole inclining to the opinion that Lao Tse was as good a teacher as any. We have described his reception of the traveller Yuan Chwang. Tai-tsung tolerated all religions, but several of his successors conducted a pitiless persecution of the Buddhist faith; it flourished in spite of these persecutions, and its monasteries played a somewhat analogous part in at first sustaining learning and afterwards retarding it, that the Christian monastic organization did in the West. By the tenth century the great Tang dynasty was in an extreme state of decay; the usual degenerative process through a series of voluptuaries and incapables had gone on, and China broke up again politically into a variable number of contending states, "The age of the Ten States," an age of confusion that lasted through the first

Map of
EUROPE and ASIA
about 1200 A.D.
K. of NORWAY
K. of SWEDEN
K. of ENGLAND
K. of DENMARK
Pr.ty or REP. of NOVGOROD
RUSSIA
PRUSSIA
LITHUANIA
POLAND
K. of LEON
K. of PORTUGAL
K. of CASTILE
NAVARRE
ARAGON
English domination
K. of FRANCE
THE EMPIRE
K. of HUNGARY
Pr.ty of KIEFF
Tartar peoples
SERBIA
BULGARIA
APULIA
SICILY
BYZANTINE EMPIRE
SELJUKS
CYPRUS
Successors of SALADIN
The Caliphate
ARABIA
Moslem Kingdoms
KHVAN (Kharismian) EMPIRE
Oldest Settlements of the Mongols
L. Baikal
Early power of JENGIS KHAN
Karakorum
MONGOLIA
KIN EMPIRE
HSIA EMPIRE
Uigurs
TIBET
SUNG EMPIRE
Dravidian kingdoms
J.F.H.

half of the tenth century. Then arose a dynasty, the Northern Sung (960-1127), which established a sort of unity, but which was in constant struggle with a number of Hunnish peoples from the north who were pressing down the eastern coast. For a time one of these peoples, the Khitan, prevailed. In the twelfth century these people had been subjugated and had given place to another Hunnish empire, the empire of the Kin, with its capital at Pekin and its southern boundary south of Hwang-ho. The Sung empire shrank before this Kin empire. In 1138 the capital was shifted from Nankin, which was now too close to the northern frontier, to the city of Han Chau on the coast. From 1127 onward to 1295, the Sung dynasty is known as the Southern Sung. To the north-west of its territories there was now the Tartar empire of the Hsia; to the north, the Kin empire, both states in which the Chinese population was under rulers in whom nomadic traditions were still strong. So that here on the east also the main masses of Asiatic mankind were under uncongenial rulers and ready to accept, if not to welcome, the arrival of a conqueror.

Northern India we have already noted was also a conquered country at the opening of the thirteenth century. It was at first a part of the Khivan empire, but in 1206 an adventurous ruler, Kutub, who had been a slave and who had risen as a slave to be governor of the Indian province, set up a separate Moslem state of Hindustan in Delhi. Brahminism had long since ousted Buddhism from India, but the converts to Islam were still but a small ruling minority in the land.

Such was the political state of Asia when Jengis Khan began to consolidate his power among the nomads in the country between Lakes Balkash and Baikal in the beginning of the thirteenth century.

§ 2

The career of conquest of Jengis Khan and his immediate successors astounded the world, and probably astounded no one more than these Mongol Khans themselves.

The Mongols were in the twelfth century a tribe subject to those Kin who had conquered North-east China. They were a horde of nomadic horsemen living in tents, and subsisting mainly upon mare's milk products and meat. Their occupations were pasturage and hunting, varied by war. They drifted northward as the snows melted for summer pasture, and southward to winter pasture after the custom of the steppes. Their military education began with a successful insurrection against the Kin. The empire of Kin had the resources of half China behind it, and in the struggle the Mongols learnt very much of the military science of the Chinese. By the end of the twelfth century they were already a fighting tribe of exceptional quality.

The opening years of the career of Jengis were spent in developing his military machine, in assimilating the Mongols and the associated tribes about them into one organized army. His first considerable extension of power was westward, when the Tartar Kirghis and the Uigurs (who were the Tartar people of the Tarim basin) were not so much conquered as induced to join his organization. He then attacked the Kin empire and took Pekin (1214). The Khitan people, who had been so recently subdued by the Kin, threw in their fortunes with his, and were of very great help to him. The settled Chinese population went on sowing and reaping and trading during this change of masters without lending its weight to either side.

We have already mentioned the very recent Kharismian empire of Turkestan, Persia, and North India. This empire extended eastward to Kashgar, and it must have seemed one of the most progressive and hopeful empires of the time. Jengis Khan, while still engaged in this war with the Kin empire, sent envoys to Kharismia. They were put to death, an almost incredible stupidity. The Kharismian government, to use the political jargon of to-day, had decided not to "recognize" Jengis Khan, and took this spirited course with him. Thereupon (1218) the great host of horsemen that Jengis Khan had consolidated and disciplined swept over the Pamirs and down into Turkestan. It was well armed, and probably it had some guns and gunpowder for siege work—for the Chinese were certainly using gunpowder at this time, and the Mongols learnt its use from them. Kashgar, Khokand, Bokhara fell and then Samarkand, the capital of the Kharismian empire. Thereafter nothing held the Mongols in the Kharismian territories. They swept westward to the Caspian, and southward as far as Lahore. To the north of the Caspian a Mongol army encountered a Russian force from Kieff. There was a series of

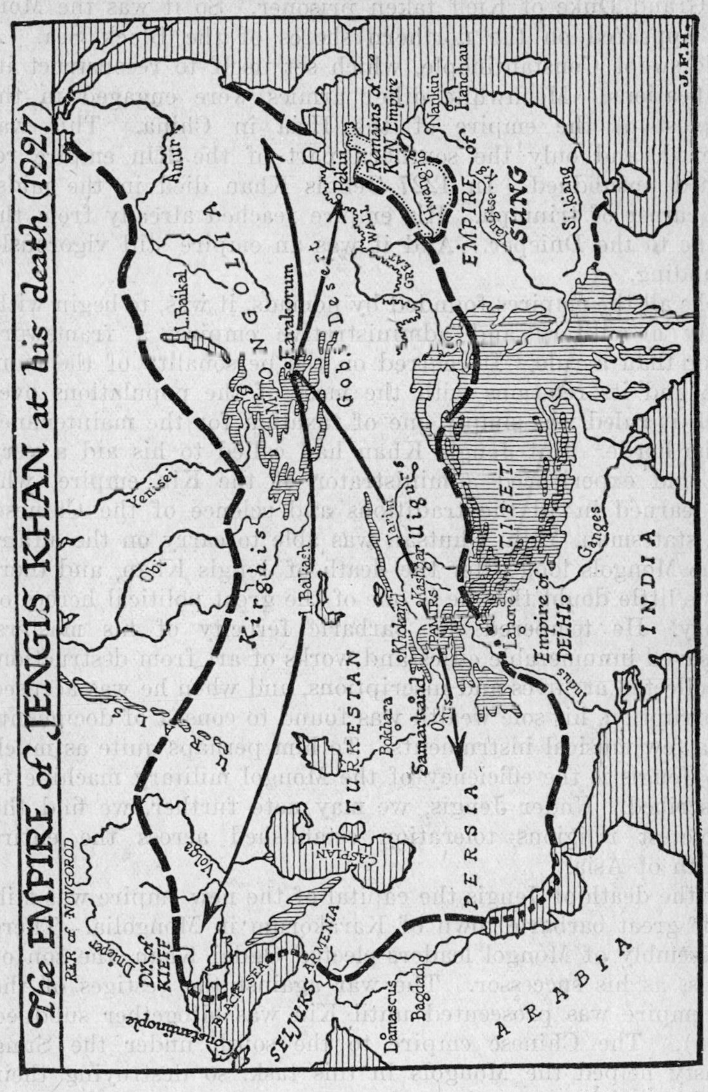
The EMPIRE of JENGIS KHAN at his death (1227)
RER of NOVGOROD
Dy. of KIEFF
Dnieper
Volga
Constantinople
BLACK SEA
ARMENIA
SELJUKS
Damascus
Bagdad
ARABIA
CASPIAN
PERSIA
TURKESTAN
Bokhara
Samarkand
Oxus
Khokand
Kashgar
PAMIRS
L. Balkash
Kirghis
Obi
Yenisei
L. Baikal
MONGOLIA
Karakorum
Gobi Desert
Uigurs
Tarim
TIBET
Lahore
Empire of DELHI
Indus
INDIA
Ganges
EMPIRE of SUNG
Hwang ho
GREAT WALL
Pekin
Remains of KIN Empire
Nankin
Hanchau
Amur
Si Kiang
J.F.H.

battles, in which the Russian armies were finally defeated and the Grand Duke of Kieff taken prisoner. So it was the Mongols appeared on the northern shores of the Black Sea. A panic swept Constantinople, which set itself to reconstruct its fortifications. Meanwhile other armies were engaged in the conquest of the empire of the Hsia in China. This was annexed, and only the southern part of the Kin empire remained unsubdued. In 1227 Jengis Khan died in the midst of a career of triumph. His empire reached already from the Pacific to the Dnieper. And it was an empire still vigorously expanding.

Like all the empires founded by nomads, it was, to begin with, purely a military and administrative empire, a framework rather than a rule. It centred on the personality of the monarch, and its relations with the mass of the populations over which it ruled was simply one of taxation for the maintenance of the horde. But Jengis Khan had called to his aid a very able and experienced administrator of the Kin empire, who was learned in all the traditions and science of the Chinese. This statesman, Yeliu Chutsai, was able to carry on the affairs of the Mongols long after the death of Jengis Khan, and there can be little doubt that he is one of the great political heroes of history. He tempered the barbaric ferocity of his masters, and saved innumerable cities and works of art from destruction. He collected archives and inscriptions, and when he was accused of corruption, his sole wealth was found to consist of documents and a few musical instruments. To him perhaps quite as much as to Jengis is the efficiency of the Mongol military machine to be ascribed. Under Jengis, we may note further, we find the completest religious toleration established across the entire breadth of Asia.

At the death of Jengis the capital of the new empire was still in the great barbaric town of Karakorum in Mongolia. There an assembly of Mongol leaders elected Ogdai Khan, the son of Jengis, as his successor. The war against the vestiges of the Kin empire was prosecuted until Kin was altogether subdued (1234). The Chinese empire to the south under the Sung dynasty helped the Mongols in this task, so destroying their own bulwark against the universal conquerors. The Mongol hosts then swept right across Asia to Russia (1235), an amazing march. Kieff was destroyed in 1240, and nearly all Russia became tributary to the Mongols. Poland was ravaged, and a mixed army of Poles and Germans was annihilated at the battle of Liegnitz in Lower Silesia in 1241. The Emperor Frederick II does not seem to have made any great efforts to stay the advancing tide.

"It is only recently," says Bury in his notes to Gibbon's *Decline and Fall of the Roman Empire,* "that European history has begun to understand that the successes of the Mongol army which overran Poland and occupied Hungary in the spring of A.D. 1241 were won by consummate strategy and were not due to a mere overwhelming superiority of numbers. But this fact has not yet become a matter of common knowledge; the vulgar opinion which represents the Tartars as a wild horde carrying all before them solely by their multitude, and galloping through Eastern Europe without a strategic plan, rushing at all obstacles and overcoming them by mere weight, still prevails. . . .

"It was wonderful how punctually and effectually the arrangements of the commander were carried out in operations extending from the Lower Vistula to Transylvania. Such a campaign was quite beyond the power of any European army of the time, and it was beyond the vision of any European commander. There was no general in Europe, from Frederick II downward, who was not a tyro in strategy compared to Subutai. It should also be noticed that the Mongols embarked upon the enterprise with full knowledge of the political situation of Hungary and the condition of Poland—they had taken care to inform themselves by a well-organized system of spies; on the other hand, the Hungarians and Christian powers, like childish barbarians, knew hardly anything about their enemies."

But though the Mongols were victorious at Liegnitz, they did not continue their drive westward. They were getting into woodlands and hilly country, which did not suit their tactics; and so they turned southward and prepared to settle in Hungary, massacring or assimilating the kindred Magyar, even as these had previously massacred and assimilated the mixed Scythians and Avars and Huns before them. From the Hungarian plain they would probably have made raids west and south as the Hungarians had done in the ninth century, the Avars in the seventh and eighth, and the Huns in the fifth. But in Asia the Mongols were fighting a stiff war of conquest against the Sung, and they were also raiding Persia and Asia Minor; Ogdai died suddenly, and in 1242 there was trouble about the succession, and recalled by this, the undefeated hosts of Mongols began to pour back across Hungary and Rumania towards the east.

To the great relief of Europe the dynastic troubles at Karakorum lasted for some years, and this vast new empire showed signs of splitting up. Mangu Khan became the Great Khan in 1251, and he nominated his brother Kublai Khan as Governor-General of China. Slowly but surely the entire Sung empire was subjugated, and as it was subjugated the eastern Mongols became more and more Chinese in their culture and methods. Tibet was invaded and devastated by Mangu, and Persia and Syria invaded in good earnest. Another brother of Mangu, Hulagu, was in command of this latter war. He turned his arms against the caliphate and captured Bagdad, in which city he perpetrated a massacre of the entire population. Bagdad was still the religious capital of Islam, and the Mongols had become bitterly hostile to the Moslems. This hostility exacerbated the natural discord of nomad and townsman. In 1259 Mangu died, and in 1260—for it took the best part of a year for the Mongol leaders to gather from the extremities of this vast empire, from Hungary and Syria and Scind and China—Kublai was elected Great Khan. He was already deeply interested in Chinese affairs; he made his capital Pekin instead of Karakorum, and Persia, Syria, and Asia Minor became virtually independent under his brother Hulagu, while the hordes of Mongols in Russia and Asia next to Russia, and various smaller Mongol groups in Turkestan became also practically separate. Kublai died in 1294, and with his death even the titular supremacy of the Great Khan disappeared.

At the death of Kublai there was a main Mongol empire, with Pekin as its capital, including all China and Mongolia; there was a second great Mongol empire, that of Kipchak in Russia; there was a third in Persia, that founded by Hulagu, the Ilkhan empire, to which the Seljuk Turks in Asia Minor were tributary; there was a Siberian state between Kipchak and Mongolia; and another separate state "Great Turkey" in Turkestan. It is particularly remarkable that India beyond the Punjab was never invaded by the Mongols during this period, and that an army under the Sultan of Egypt completely defeated Ketboga, Hulagu's general, in Palestine (1260), and stopped them from entering Africa. By 1260 the impulse of

Mongol conquest had already passed its zenith. Thereafter the Mongol story is one of division and decay.

The Mongol dynasty that Kublai Khan had founded in China, the Yuan dynasty, lasted from 1280 until 1368. Later on a recrudescence of Mongolian energy in Western Asia was destined to create a still more enduring monarchy in India.

§ 3

Now this story of Mongolian conquests is surely the most remarkable in all history. The conquests of Alexander the Great cannot compare with them in extent. And their effect in diffusing and broadening men's ideas, though such things are more difficult to estimate, is at least comparable to the spread of the Hellenic civilization which is associated with Alexander's adventure. For a time all Asia and Western Europe enjoyed an open intercourse; all the roads were temporarily open, and representatives of every nation appeared at the court of Karakorum. The barriers between Europe and Asia set up by the religious feud of Christianity and Islam were lowered. Great hopes were entertained by the papacy for the conversion of the Mongols to Christianity. Their only religion so far had been Shamanism, a primitive paganism. Envoys of the Pope, Buddhist priests from India, Parisian and Italian and Chinese artificers, Byzantine and Armenian merchants, mingled with Arab officials and Persian and Indian astronomers and mathematicians at the Mongol court. We hear too much in history of the campaigns and massacres of the Mongols, and not enough of their indubitable curiosity and zest for learning. Not perhaps as an originative people, but as transmitters of knowledge and method their influence upon the world's history has been enormous. And everything one can learn of the vague and romantic personalities of Jengis or Kublai tends to confirm the impression that these men were built upon a larger scale, and were at least as understanding and creative monarchs as either that flamboyant but egotistical figure Alexander the Great, or that raiser of political ghosts, that energetic but illiterate theologian, Charlemagne.

The missionary enterprises of the papacy in Mongolia ended in failure. Christianity was losing its persuasive power. The Mongols had no prejudice against Christianity; they evidently

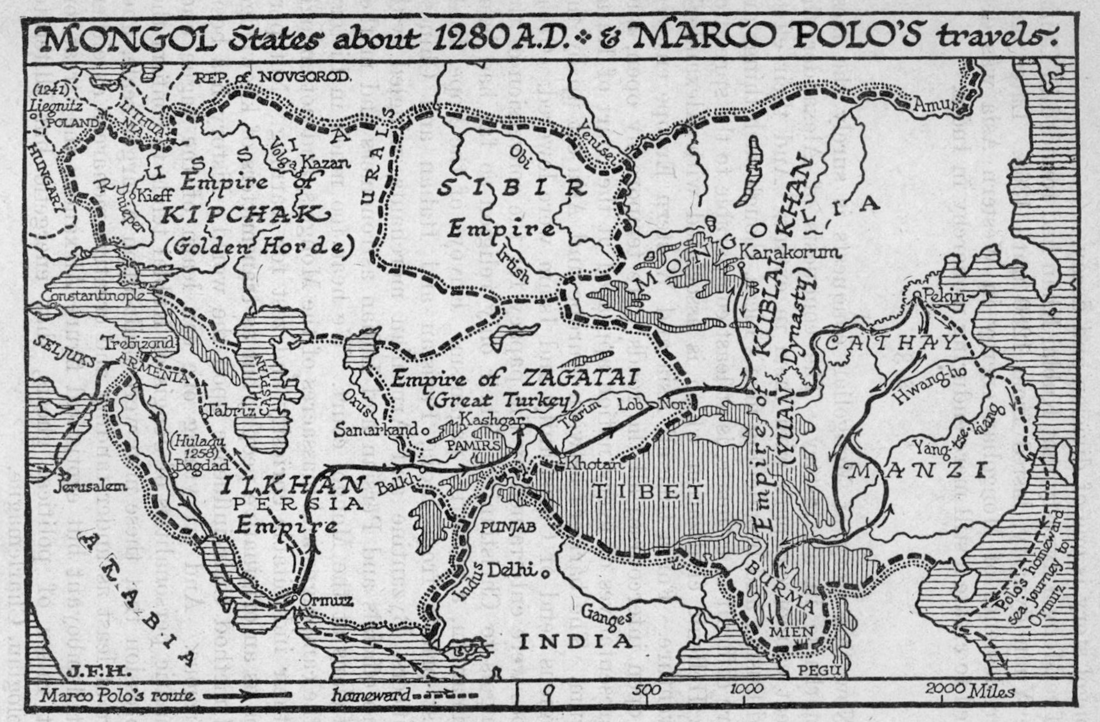
MONGOL States about 1280 A.D. ✣ & MARCO POLO'S travels.
REP. of NOVGOROD
(1241) Liegnitz
POLAND
LITHUANIA
HUNGARY
RUSSIA
Kieff
Dnieper
Volga
Kazan
Empire of KIPCHAK (Golden Horde)
URALS
Obi
Yenisei
Irtish
SIBIR Empire
Amur
MONGOLIA
Karakorum
KUBLAI KHAN
Empire of (YUAN) Dynasty
CATHAY
Pekin
Hwang-ho
Yang-tse-kiang
MANZI
Polo's homeward sea journey to Ormuz
Constantinople
Trebizond
SELJUKS
ARMENIA
CASPIAN
Tabriz
Empire of ZAGATAI (Great Turkey)
Oxus
Samarkand
Kashgar
PAMIRS
Tarim
Lob Nor
Khotan
TIBET
(Hulagu 1258)
Bagdad
Jerusalem
ILKHAN PERSIA Empire
Balkh
PUNJAB
Indus
Delhi
Ganges
INDIA
BURMA
MIEN
PEGU
Ormuz
ARABIA
J.F.H.
Marco Polo's route
homeward
0
500
1000
2000 Miles

preferred it at first to Islam; but the missions that came to them were manifestly using the power in the great teachings of Jesus to advance the vast claims of the Pope to world dominion. Christianity so vitiated was not good enough for the Mongol mind. To make the empire of the Mongols part of the kingdom of God might have appealed to them; but not to make it a fief of a group of French and Italian priests, whose claims were as gigantic as their powers and outlook were feeble, who were now the creatures of the Emperor of Germany, now the nominees of the King of France, and now the victims of their own petty spites and vanities. In 1269 Kublai Khan sent a mission to the Pope with the evident intention of finding some common mode of action with Western Christendom. He asked that a hundred men of learning and ability should be sent to his court to establish an understanding. His mission found the Western world popeless, and engaged in one of those disputes about the succession that are so frequent in the history of the papacy. For two years there was no pope at all. When at last a pope was appointed, he dispatched two Dominican friars to convert the greatest power in Asia to his rule! Those worthy men were appalled by the length and hardship of the journey before them, and found an early excuse for abandoning the expedition.

But this abortive mission was only one of a number of attempts to communicate, and always they were feeble and feeble-spirited attempts, with nothing of the conquering fire of the earlier Christian missions. Innocent IV had already sent some Dominicans to Karakorum, and St. Louis of France had also dispatched missionaries and relics by way of Persia; Mangu Khan had numerous Nestorian Christians at his court, and subsequent papal envoys actually reached Pekin. We hear of the appointment of various legates and bishops to the East, but many of these seem to have lost themselves and perhaps their lives before they reached China. There was a papal legate in Pekin in 1346, but he seems to have been a mere papal diplomatist. With the downfall of the Mongolian (Yuan) dynasty (1368), the dwindling opportunity of the Christian missions passed altogether. The house of Yuan was followed by that of Ming, a strongly nationalist Chinese dynasty, at first very hostile to all foreigners. There may have been a massacre of the Christian missions. Until the later days of the Mings (1644) little more is heard of Christianity, whether Nestorian or Catholic, in China. Then a fresh and rather more successful attempt to propagate Catholic Christianity in China was made by the Jesuits, but this second missionary wave reached China by the sea.

In the year 1298 a naval battle occurred between the Genoese and the Venetians, in which the latter were defeated. Among the 7,000 prisoners taken by the Genoese was a Venetian gentleman named Marco Polo, who had been a great traveller, and who was very generally believed by his neighbours to be given to exaggeration. He had taken part in that first mission to Kublai Khan, and had gone on when the two Dominicans turned back. While this Marco Polo was a prisoner in Genoa, he beguiled his tedium by talking of his travels to a certain writer named Rusticiano, who wrote them down. We will not enter here into the vexed question of the exact authenticity of Rusticiano's story—we do not certainly know in what language it was written—but there can be no doubt of the general truth of this remarkable narrative, which became enormously popular in the fourteenth and fifteenth centuries with all men of active intelligence. *The Travels of Marco Polo* is one of the great books of history. It opens this world of the thirteenth century, this century which saw the reign of Frederick II and the beginnings of the Inquisition, to our imaginations as no mere historian's chronicle can do. It led directly to the discovery of America.

It begins by telling of the journey of Marco's father, Nicolo Polo, and uncle, Maffeo Polo, to China. These two were Venetian merchants of standing, living in Constantinople, and somewhen about 1260 they went to the Crimea and thence to Kazan; from that place they journeyed to Bokhara, and at Bokhara they fell in with a party of envoys from Kublai Khan in China to his brother Hulagu in Persia. These envoys pressed them to come on to the Great Khan, who at that time had never seen men of the "Latin" peoples. They went on; and it is clear they made a very favourable impression upon Kublai, and interested him greatly in the civilization of Christendom. They were made the bearers of that request for a hundred teachers and learned men, "intelligent men acquainted with the Seven Arts, able to enter into controversy and able clearly to prove to idolators and other kinds of folk that the Law of Christ was best," to which we have just alluded. But when they returned Christendom was in a phase of confusion, and it was only after a delay of two years that they got their authorization to start for China again in the company of those two faint-hearted Dominicans. They took with them young Marco, and it is due to his presence and the boredom of his subsequent captivity at Genoa that this most interesting experience has been preserved to us.

The three Polos started by way of Palestine and not by the Crimea, as in the previous expedition. They had with them a gold tablet and other indications from the Great Khan that must have greatly facilitated their journey. The Great Khan had asked for some oil from the lamp that burns in the Holy Sepulchre at Jerusalem; and so thither they first went, and then by way of Cilicia into Armenia. They went thus far north because the Sultan of Egypt was raiding the Ilkhan domains at this time. Thence they came by way of Mesopotamia to Ormuz on the Persian Gulf, as if they contemplated a sea voyage. At Ormuz they met merchants from India. For some reason they did not take ship, but instead turned northward through the Persian deserts, and so by way of Balkh over the Pamir to Kashgar, and by way of Kotan and the Lob Nor (so following in the footsteps of Yuan Chwang) into the Hwangho valley and on to Pekin. Pekin, Polo calls "Cambaluc"; Northern China, "Cathay" (= Khitan); and Southern China of the former Sung dynasty, "Manzi." At Pekin was the Great Khan, and they were hospitably entertained. Marco particularly pleased Kublai; he was young and clever, and it is clear he had mastered the Tartar language very thoroughly. He was given an official position and sent on several missions, chiefly in South-west China. The tale he had to tell of vast stretches of smiling and prosperous country, "all the way excellent hostelries for travellers," and "fine vineyards, fields and gardens," of "many abbeys" of Buddhist monks, of manufactures of "cloth of silk and gold and many fine taffetas," a "constant succession of cities and boroughs," and so on, first roused the incredulity and then fired the imagination of all Europe. He told of Burmah, and of its great armies with hundreds of elephants, and how these animals were defeated by the Mongol bowmen, and also of the Mongol conquest of Pegu. He told of Japan, and greatly exaggerated the amount of gold in that country. And, still more wonderful, he told of Christians and Christian rulers in China, and of a certain "Prester John," John the Priest, who was the "king" of a Christian people. Those people he had not seen. Apparently they were a tribe of Nestorian Tartars in Mongolia. An understandable excitement probably made Rusticiano over-emphasize what must have seemed to him the greatest marvel of the whole story, and Prester John became one of the most stimulating legends of the fourteenth and fifteenth centuries. It encouraged European enterprise enormously to think that far away in China was a community of their co-religionists, presumably ready to welcome and assist them. For three years Marco ruled the city of Yang-chow as governor, and he probably impressed the Chinese inhabitants as being very little more of a foreigner than any Tartar would have been. He may also have been sent on a mission to India. Chinese records mention a certain Polo attached to the imperial council in 1277, a very valuable confirmation of the general truth of the Polo story.

The Polos had taken about three and a half years to get to China. They stayed there upwards of sixteen. Then they began to feel homesick. They were the protégés of Kublai, and possibly they felt that his favours roused a certain envy that might have disagreeable results after his death. They sought his permission to return. For a time he refused it, and then an opportunity occurred. Argon, the Ilkhan monarch of Persia, the grandson of Hulagu, Kublai's brother, had lost his Mongol wife, and on her deathbed had promised not to wed any other woman but a Mongol of her own tribe. He sent ambassadors to Pekin, and a suitable princess was selected, a girl of seventeen. To spare her the fatigues of the caravan route, it was decided to send her by sea with a suitable escort. The "Barons" in charge of her asked for the company of the Polos because these latter were experienced travellers and sage men, and the Polos snatched at this opportunity of getting homeward. The expedition sailed from some port on the east of South China; they stayed long in Sumatra and South India, and they reached Persia after a voyage of two years. They delivered the young lady safely to Argon's successor—for Argon was dead—and she married Argon's son. The Polos then went by Tabriz to Trebizond, sailed to Constantinople, and got back to Venice about 1295. It is related that the returned travellers, dressed in Tartar garb, were refused admission to their own house. It was some time before they could establish their identity. Many people who admitted that, were still inclined to look askance at them as shabby wanderers; and, in order to dispel such doubts, they gave a great feast, and when it was at its height they had their old padded suits brought to them, dismissed the servants, and then ripped open these garments, whereupon an incredible display of "rubies, sapphires, carbuncles, emeralds, and diamonds" poured out before the dazzled company. Even after this, Marco's accounts of the size and population of China were received with much furtive mockery. The wits nicknamed him *Il Milione,* because he was always talking of millions of people and millions of ducats.

Such was the story that raised eyebrows first in Venice and then throughout the Western world. The European literature, and especially the European romance of the fifteenth century, echoes with the names in Marco Polo's story, with Cathay and Cambaluc and the like.

§ 4

These travels of Marco Polo were only the beginning of a very considerable intercourse. That intercourse was to bring many revolutionary ideas and many revolutionary things to Europe, including a greatly extended use of paper and printing from blocks, the almost equally revolutionary use of gunpowder in warfare, and the mariner's compass which was to release the European shipping from navigation by coasting. The popular imagination has always been disposed to ascribe every such striking result to Marco Polo. He has become the type and symbol for all such interchanges. As a matter of fact, there is no evidence that he had any share in these three importations. There were many mute Marco Polos who never met their Rusticianos, and history has not preserved their names. Before we go on, however, to describe the great widening of the mental horizons of Europe that was now beginning, and to which this book of travels was to contribute very materially, it will be convenient first to note a curious side consequence of the great Mongol conquests, the appearance of the Ottoman Turks upon the Dardanelles, and next to state in general terms the breaking up and development of the several parts of the empire of Jengis Khan.

The Ottoman Turks were a little band of fugitives who fled south-westerly before the first invasion of Western Turkestan by Jengis. They made their long way from Central Asia, over deserts and mountains and through alien populations, seeking some new lands in which they might settle. "A small band of alien herdsmen," says Sir Mark Sykes, "wandering unchecked through crusades and counter-crusades, principalities, empires, and states. Where they camped, how they moved and preserved their flocks and herds, where they found pasture, how they made their peace with the various chiefs through whose territories they passed, are questions which one may well ask in wonder."

They found a resting-place at last and kindred and congenial neighbours on the table-lands of Asia Minor among the Seljuk Turks. Most of this country, the modern Anatolia, was now largely Turkish in speech and Moslem in religion, except that there was a considerable proportion of Greeks, Jews, and Armenians in the town populations. No doubt the various strains of Hittite, Phrygian, Trojan, Lydian, Ionian Greek, Cimmerian, Galatian, and Italian (from the Pergamus times) still flowed in the blood of the people, but they had long since forgotten these ancestral elements. They were indeed much the same blend of ancient Mediterranean dark whites, Nordic Aryans, Semites and Mongolians as were the inhabitants of the Balkan peninsula, but they believed themselves to be a pure Turanian race, and altogether superior to the Christians on the other side of the Bosphorus.

Gradually the Ottoman Turks became important, and at last dominant among the small principalities into which the Seljuk empire, the empire of "Roum," had fallen. Their relations with the dwindling empire of Constantinople remained for some centuries tolerantly hostile. They made no attack upon the Bosphorus, but they got a footing in Europe at the Dardanelles, and, using this route, the route of Xerxes and not the route of Darius, they pushed their way steadily into Macedonia, Epirus, Illyria, Yugo-Slavia, and Bulgaria. In the Serbs (Yugo-Slavs) and Bulgarians the Turks found people very like themselves in culture and, though neither side recognized it, probably very similar in racial admixture, with a little less of the dark Mediterranean and Mongolian strains than the Turks and a trifle more of the Nordic element. But these Balkan peoples were Christians, and bitterly divided among themselves. The Turks on the other hand spoke one language; they had a greater sense of unity, they had the Moslem habits of temperance and frugality, and they were on the whole better soldiers. They converted what they could of the conquered people to Islam; the

Christians they disarmed, and conferred upon them the monopoly of tax-paying. Gradually the Ottoman princes consolidated an empire that reached from the Taurus mountains in the east to Hungary and Rumania in the west. Adrianople became their chief city. They surrounded the shrunken empire of Constantinople on every side.

The Ottomans organized a standing military force, the Janissaries, rather on the lines of the Mamelukes who dominated Egypt. "These troops were formed of levies of Christian youths to the extent of one thousand per annum, who were affiliated to the Bektashi order of dervishes, and though at first not obliged to embrace Islam, were one and all strongly imbued with the mystic and fraternal ideas of the confraternity to which they were attached. Highly paid, well disciplined, a close and jealous secret society, the Janissaries provided the newly formed Ottoman state with a patriotic force of trained infantry soldiers, which, in an age of light cavalry and hired companies of mercenaries, was an invaluable asset. . . .

"The relations between the Ottoman Sultans and the Emperors has been singular in the annals of Moslem and Christian states. The Turks had been involved in the family and dynastic quarrels of the Imperial City, were bound by ties of blood to the ruling families, frequently supplied troops for the defence of Constantinople, and on occasion hired parts of its garrison to assist them in their various campaigns; the sons of the Emperors and Byzantine statesmen even accompanied the Turkish forces in the field, yet the Ottomans never ceased to annex Imperial territories and cities both in Asia and Thrace. This curious intercourse between the House of Osman and the Imperial government had a profound effect on both institutions; the Greeks grew more and more debased and demoralized by the shifts and tricks that their military weakness obliged them to adopt towards their neighbours, the Turks were corrupted by the alien atmosphere of intrigue and treachery which crept into their domestic life. Fratricide and parricide, the two crimes which most frequently stained the annals of the Imperial Palace, eventually formed a part of the policy of the Ottoman dynasty. One of the sons of Murad I embarked on an intrigue with Andronicus, the son of the Greek Emperor, to murder their respective fathers. . . .

"The Byzantine found it more easy to negotiate with the Ottoman Pasha than with the Pope. For years the Turks and Byzantines had intermarried, and hunted in couples in strange bypaths of diplomacy. The Ottoman had played the Bulgar and the Serb of Europe against the Emperor, just as the Emperor had played the Asiatic Amir against the Sultan; the Greek and Turkish Royal Princes had mutually agreed to hold each other's rivals as prisoners and hostages; in fact, Turk and Byzantine policy had so intertwined that it is difficult to say whether the Turks regarded the Greeks as their allies, enemies, or subjects,

or whether the Greeks looked upon the Turks as their tyrants, destroyers, or protectors. . . ."[1]

It was in 1453, under the Ottoman Sultan, Muhammad II, that Constantinople at last fell to the Moslems. He attacked it from the European side, and with a great power of artillery. The Greek Emperor was killed, and there was much looting and massacre. The great church of St, Sophia which Justinian the Great had built (532) was plundered of its treasures and turned at once into a mosque. This event sent a wave of

[1] Sir Mark Sykes, *The Caliphs' Last Heritage.*

excitement throughout Europe, and an attempt was made to organize a crusade, but the days of the crusades were past.

Says Sir Mark Sykes: "To the Turks the capture of Constantinople was a crowning mercy and yet a fatal blow. Constantinople had been the tutor and polisher of the Turks. So long as the Ottomans could draw science, learning, philosophy, art, and tolerance from a living fountain of civilization in the heart of their dominions, so long had the Ottomans not only brute force, but intellectual power. So long as the Ottoman Empire had in Constantinople a free port, a market, a centre of world finance, a pool of gold, an exchange, so long did the Ottomans never lack for money and financial support. Muhammad was a great statesman, the moment he entered Constantinople he endeavoured to stay the damage his ambition had done; he supported the patriarch, he conciliated the Greeks, he did all he could to continue Constantinople the city of the Emperors . . . but the fatal step had been taken, Constantinople as the city of the Sultans was Constantinople no more; the markets died away, the culture and civilization fled, the complex finance faded from sight; and the Turks had lost their governors and their support. On the other hand, the corruptions of Byzantium remained, the bureaucracy, the eunuchs, the palace guards, the spies, the bribers, go-betweens—all these the Ottomans took over, and all these survived in luxuriant life. The Turks, in taking Stambul, let slip a treasure and gained a pestilence. . . ."

Muhammad's ambition was not sated by the capture of Constantinople. He set his eyes also upon Rome. He captured and looted the Italian town of Otranto, and it is probable that a very vigorous and perhaps successful attempt to conquer Italy —for the peninsula was divided against itself—was averted only by his death (1481). His sons engaged in fratricidal strife. Under Bayezid II (1481-1512), his successor, war was carried into Poland, and most of Greece was conquered. Selim (1512-1520), the son of Bayezid, extended the Ottoman power over Armenia and conquered Egypt. In Egypt, the last Abbasid Caliph was living under the protection of the Mameluke Sultan —for the Fatamite caliphate was a thing of the past. Selim bought the title of Caliph from this last degenerate Abbasid, and acquired the sacred banner and other relics of the Prophet. So the Ottoman Sultan became also Caliph of all Islam. Selim was followed by Suleiman the Magnificent (1520-1566), who

The OTTOMAN EMPIRE at the death of Suleiman the Magnificent 1566 A.D.
GERMAN EMPIRE
Vienna
POLAND
HUNGARY
Venice
Moldavia
Danube
Wallachia
OTTOMAN EMPIRE
NAPLES
Naples
Otranto
Constantinople
Trebizond
ARMENIA
Lepanto
Crete (Venetian)
Cyprus
SYRIA
Bagdad
Damascus
Jerusalem
EGYPT
Cairo
J.F.H.

conquered Bagdad in the east and the greater part of Hungary in the west, and very nearly captured Vienna. His fleets also took Algiers, and inflicted a number of reverses upon the Venetians. In most of his warfare with the empire he was in alliance with the French. Under him the Ottoman power reached its zenith.

§ 5

Let us now very briefly run over the subsequent development of the main masses of the empire of the Great Khan. In no case did Christianity succeed in capturing the imagination of these Mongol states. Christianity was in a phase of moral and intellectual insolvency, without any collective faith, energy, or honour; we have told of the wretched brace of timid Dominicans which was the Pope's reply to the appeal of Kublai Khan, and we have noted the general failure of the overland missions of the thirteenth and fourteenth centuries. That apostolic passion that could win whole nations to the Kingdom of Heaven was dead in the church.

In 1305, as we have told, the Pope became the kept pontiff of the French king. All the craft and policy of the Popes of the thirteenth century to oust the Emperor from Italy had only served to let in the French to replace him. From 1305 to 1377 the Popes remained at Avignon; and such slight missionary effort as they made was merely a part of the strategy of Western European politics. In 1377 the Pope Gregory XI did indeed re-enter Rome and die there, but the French cardinals split off from the others at the election of his successor, and two Popes were elected, one at Avignon and one at Rome. This split, the Great Schism, lasted from 1378 to 1418. Each Pope cursed the other, and put all his supporters under an interdict. Such was the state of Christianity, and such were now the custodians of the teachings of Jesus of Nazareth. All Asia was white unto harvest, but there was no effort to reap it.

When at last the church was reunited and missionary energy returned with the foundation of the order of the Jesuits, the days of opportunity were over. The possibility of a world-wide moral unification of East and West through Christianity had passed away. The Mongols in China and Central Asia turned to Buddhism; in South Russia, Western Turkestan, and the Ilkhan Empire they embraced Islam.

§ 5A

In China the Mongols were already saturated with Chinese civilization by the time of Kublai. After 1280 the Chinese annals treat Kublai as a Chinese monarch, the founder of the Yuan dynasty (1280-1368). This Mongol dynasty was finally overthrown by a Chinese nationalist movement which set up the Ming dynasty (1368-1644), a cultivated and artistic line of emperors, ruling until a northern people, the Manchus, who were the same as the Kin whom Jengis had overthrown, conquered China and established a dynasty which gave way only to a native republican form of government in 1912.

It was the Manchus who obliged the Chinese to wear pigtails as a mark of submission. The pigtailed Chinaman is quite a recent figure in history. With the coming of the republic the wearing of the pigtail has ceased to be compulsory, and many Chinamen no longer wear it.

§ 5B

In the Pamirs, in much of Eastern and Western Turkestan, and to the north, the Mongols dropped back towards the tribal conditions from which they had been lifted by Jengis. It is possible to trace the dwindling succession of many of the small Khans who became independent during this period, almost down to the present time. The Kalmuks in the seventeenth and eighteenth centuries founded a considerable empire, but dynastic troubles broke it up before it had extended its power beyond Central Asia. The Chinese recovered Eastern Turkestan from them about 1757.

Tibet was more and more closely linked with China, and became the great home of Buddhism and Buddhist monasticism.

Over most of the area of Western Central Asia and Persia and Mesopotamia, the ancient distinction of nomad and settled population remains to this day. The townsmen despise and cheat the nomads, the nomads ill-treat and despise the townsfolk.

§ 5C

The Mongols of the great realm of Kipchak remained nomadic, and grazed their stock across the wide plains of South

Russia and Western Asia adjacent to Russia. They became not very devout Moslems, retaining many traces of their earlier barbaric Shamanism. Their chief Khan was the Khan of the Golden Horde. To the west, over large tracts of open country, and more particularly in what is now known as Ukrainia, the old Scythian population, Slavs with a Mongol admixture, reverted to a similar nomadic life. These Christian nomads, the Cossacks, formed a sort of frontier screen against the Tartars, and their free and adventurous life was so attractive to the peasants of Poland and Lithuania that severe laws had to be passed to prevent a vast migration from the plough-lands to the steppes. The serf-owning landlords of Poland regarded the Cossacks with considerable hostility on this account, and war was as frequent between the Polish chivalry and the Cossacks as it was between the latter and the Tartars.

In the empire of Kipchak, as in Turkestan almost up to the present time, while the nomads roamed over wide areas, a number of towns and cultivated regions sustained a settled population which usually paid tribute to the nomad Khan. In such towns as Kieff, Moscow, and the like, the pre-Mongol, Christian town life went on under Russian dukes or Tartar governors, who collected the tribute for the Khan of the Golden Horde. The Grand Duke of Moscow gained the confidence of the Khan, and gradually, under his authority, obtained an ascendancy over many of his fellow tributaries. In the fifteenth century, under its grand duke, Ivan III, Ivan the Great (1462-1505), Moscow threw off its Mongol allegiance and refused to pay tribute any longer (1480). The successors of Constantine no longer reigned in Constantinople, and Ivan took possession of the Byzantine double-headed eagle for his arms. He claimed to be the heir to Byzantium because of his marriage (1472) with Zoe Palæologus of the imperial line. This ambitious grand dukedom of Moscow assailed and subjugated the ancient Northman trading republic of Novgorod to the north, and so the foundations of the modern Russian Empire were laid and a link with the mercantile life of the Baltic established. Ivan III did not, however, carry his claim to be the heir of the Christian rulers of Constantinople to the extent of assuming the imperial title. This step was taken by his grandson, Ivan IV (Ivan the Terrible, because of his insane cruelties; 1533-1584). Although the ruler of Moscow thus came to be called Tsar (Cæsar), his tradition was in many respects Tartar rather than European; he was autocratic after the unlimited Asiatic pattern, and the form of Christianity he affected was the Eastern, court-ruled, "orthodox" form, which had reached Russia long before the Mongol conquest, by means of Bulgarian missionaries from Constantinople.

To the west of the domains of Kipchak, outside the range of Mongol rule, a second centre of Slav consolidation had been set up during the tenth and eleventh centuries in Poland. The Mongol wave had washed over Poland, but had never subjugated it. Poland was not "orthodox," but Roman Catholic in religion; it used the Latin alphabet instead of the strange Russian letters, and its monarch never assumed an absolute independence of the Emperor. Poland was in fact in its origins an outlying part of Christendom and of the Holy Empire; Russia never was anything of the sort.

§ 5D

The nature and development of the empire of the Ilkhans in Persia, Mesopotamia, and Syria is perhaps the most interesting of all the stories of these Mongol powers, because in this region nomadism really did attempt, and really did to a very considerable degree succeed in its attempt to stamp a settled civilized system out of existence. When Jengis Khan first invaded China, we are told that there was a serious discussion among the Mongol chiefs whether all the towns and settled populations should not be destroyed. To these simple practitioners of the open-air life the settled populations seemed corrupt, crowded, vicious, effeminate, dangerous, and incomprehensible; a detestable human efflorescence upon what would otherwise have been good pasture. They had no use whatever for the towns. The early Franks and the Anglo-Saxon conquerors of South Britain seem to have had much the same feeling towards townsmen. But it was only under Hulagu in Mesopotamia that these ideas seem to have been embodied in a deliberate policy. The Mongols here did not only burn and massacre; they destroyed the irrigation system that had endured for at least eight thousand years, and with that the mother civilization of all the Western world came to an end. Since the days of the priest-kings of

Sumeria there had been a continuous cultivation in these fertile regions, an accumulation of tradition, a great population, a succession of busy cities, Eridu, Nippur, Babylon, Nineveh, Ctesiphon, Bagdad. Now the fertility ceased. Mesopotamia became a land of ruins and desolation, through which great waters ran to waste, or overflowed their banks to make malarious swamps. Later on Mosul and Bagdad revived feebly as second-rate towns. . . .

But for the defeat and death of Hulagu's general Kitboga in Palestine (1260), the same fate might have overtaken Egypt. But Egypt was now a Turkish sultanate; it was dominated by a body of soldiers, the Mamelukes, whose ranks, like those of their imitators, the Janissaries of the Ottoman Empire, were recruited and kept vigorous by the purchase and training of boy slaves. A capable Sultan such men would obey; a weak or evil one they would replace. Under this ascendancy Egypt remained an independent power until 1517, when it fell to the Ottoman Turks.

The first destructive vigor of Hulagu's Mongols soon subsided, but in the fifteenth century a last tornado of nomadism arose in Western Turkestan under the leadership of a certain Timur the Lame, or Timurlane. He was descended in the female line from Jengis Khan. He established himself in Samarkand, and spread his authority over Kipchak (Turkestan to South Russia), Siberia, and southward as far as the Indus. He assumed the title of Great Khan in 1369. He was a nomad of the savage school, and he created an empire of desolation from North India to Syria. Pyramids of skulls were his particular architectural fancy; after the storming of Ispahan he made one of 70,000. His ambition was to restore the empire of Jengis Khan as he conceived it, a project in which he completely failed. He spread destruction far and wide; the Ottoman Turks—it was before the taking of Constantinople and their days of greatness—and Egypt paid him tribute; the Punjab he devastated; and Delhi surrendered to him. After Delhi had surrendered, however, he made a frightful massacre of its inhabitants. At the time of his death (1405) very little remained to witness to his power but a name of horror, ruins and desolated countries, and a shrunken and impoverished domain in Persia.

The dynasty founded by Timur in Persia was extinguished by another Turkoman horde fifty years later.

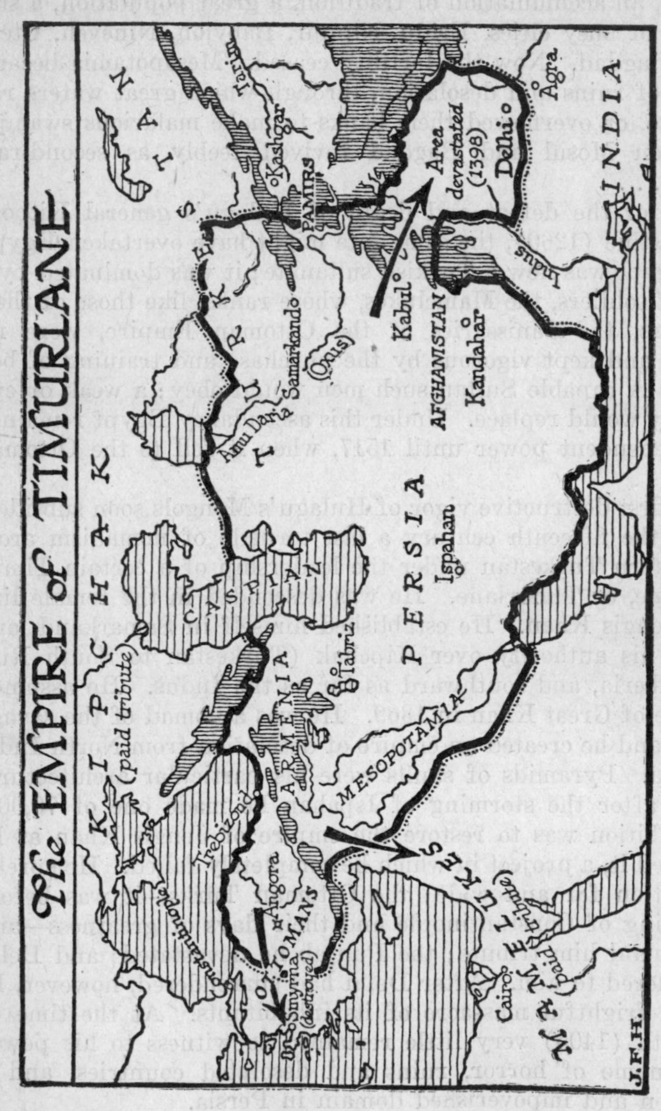
The EMPIRE of TIMURLANE
K I P C H A K
(paid tribute)
T U R K E S T A N
Tarim
Kashgar
PAMIRS
Amu Daria
Samarkando
(Oxus)
Kabul
AFGHANISTAN
Kandahar
Area devastated (1398)
Delhi
Agra
Indus
INDIA
PERSIA
Ispahan
CASPIAN
Tabriz
ARMENIA
MESOPOTAMIA
Trebizond
Constantinople
Angora
OTTOMANS
Smyrna (destroyed)
Cairo
MAMELUKES
(paid tribute)
J.F.H.

§ 5E

In 1505 a small Turkoman chieftain, Baber, a descendant of Timur and therefore of Jengis, was forced after some years of warfare and some temporary successes—for a time he held Samarkand—to fly with a few followers over the Hindu Kush to Afghanistan. There his band increased, and he made himself master of Cabul. He assembled an army, accumulated guns, and then laid claim to the Punjab, because Timur had conquered it a hundred and seven years before. He pushed his successes beyond the Punjab. India was in a state of division, and quite ready to welcome any capable invader who promised peace and order. After various fluctuations of fortune Baber met the Sultan of Delhi at Panipat (1525), ten miles north of that town, and though he had but 25,000 men, provided, however, with guns, against a thousand elephants and four times as many men—the numbers, by the by, are his own estimate—he gained a complete victory. He ceased to call himself King of Cabul, and assumed the title of Emperor of Hindustan. "This," he wrote, "is quite a different world from our countries." It was finer, more fertile, altogether richer. He conquered as far as Bengal, but his untimely death in 1530 checked the tide of Mongol conquest for a quarter of a century, and it was only after the accession of his grandson Akbar that it flowed again. Akbar subjugated all India as far as Berar, and his great-grandson Aurungzeb (1658-1707) was practically master of the entire peninsula. This great dynasty of Baber (1526-1530), Humayun (1530-1556), Akbar (1556-1605), Jehangir (1605-1628), Shah Jehan (1628-1658), and Aurungzeb (1658-1707), in which son succeeded father for six generations, this "Mogul (= Mongol) dynasty,"[1] marks the most splendid age that had hitherto drawn upon India. Akbar, next perhaps to Asoka, was one of the greatest of Indian monarchs, and one of the few royal figures that approach the stature of great men.

To Akbar it is necessary to give the same distinctive attention that we have shown to Charlemagne or Constantine the Great. He is one of the hinges of history. Much of his work of consolidation and organization in India survives to this day.

[1] "Mogul" is our rendering of the Arabic spelling Mughal, which itself was a corruption of Mongol, the Arabic alphabet having no symbol for *ng*.—H. H. J.

It was taken over and continued by the British when they became the successors of the Mogul emperors. The British monarch, indeed, now uses as his Indian title the title of the Mogul emperors, *Kaisar-i-Hind.* All the other great administrations of the descendants of Jengis Khan, in Russia, throughout Western and Central Asia and in China, have long since dissolved away and given place to other forms of government. Their governments were indeed little more than taxing governments; a system of revenue-collecting to feed the central establishment of the ruler, like the Golden Horde in South Russia or the imperial city at Karakorum or Pekin. The life and ideas of the people they left alone, careless how they lived—so long as they paid. So it was that after centuries of subjugation, a Christian Moscow and Kieff, a Shiite Persia, and a thoroughly Chinese China rose again from their Mongol submergence. But Akbar made a new India. He gave the princes and ruling classes of India some inklings at least of a common interest. If India is now anything more than a sort of rag-bag of incoherent states and races, a prey to every casual raider from the north, it is very largely due to him.

His distinctive quality was his openness of mind. He set himself to make every sort of able man in India, whatever his race or religion, available for the public work of Indian life. His instinct was the true statesman's instinct for synthesis. His empire was to be neither a Moslem nor a Mongol one, nor was it to be Rajput or Aryan, or Dravidian, or Hindu, or high or low caste; it was to be *Indian.* "During the years of his training he enjoyed many opportunities of noting the good qualities, the fidelity, the devotion, often the nobility of soul, of those Hindu princes, whom, because they were followers of Brahma, his Moslem courtiers devoted mentally to eternal torments. He noted that these men, and men who thought like them, constituted the vast majority of his subjects. He noted, further, of many of them, and those the most trustworthy, that though they had apparently much to gain from a worldly point of view by embracing the religion of the court, they held fast to their own. His reflective mind, therefore, was unwilling from the outset to accept the theory that because he, the conqueror, the ruler, happened to be born a Muhammadan, therefore Muhammadanism was true for all mankind. Gradually his thoughts found words in the utterance: 'Why should I claim to guide men before I myself am guided?' and, as he listened to other doctrines and other creeds, his honest doubts became confirmed, and, noting daily the bitter narrowness of sectarianism, no matter of what form of religion, he became more and more wedded to the principle of toleration for all."

"The son of a fugitive emperor," says Dr. Emil Schmit, "born in the desert, brought up in nominal confinement, he had known the bitter side of life from his youth up. Fortune had given him a powerful frame, which he trained to support the extremities of exertion. Physical exercise was with him a passion; he was devoted to the chase and especially to the fierce excitement of catching the wild horse or elephant or slaying the dangerous tiger. On one occasion, when it was necessary to persuade the Raja of Jodhpore to abandon his intention of forcing the widow of his deceased son to mount the funeral pyre, Akbar rode two hundred and twenty miles in two days. In battle he displayed the utmost bravery. He led his troops in person during the dangerous part of a campaign, leaving to his generals the lighter task of finishing the war. In every victory he displayed humanity to the conquered, and decisively opposed any exhibition of cruelty. Free from all those prejudices which separate society and create dissension, tolerant to men of other beliefs, impartial to men of other races, whether Hindu or Dravidian, he was a man obviously marked out to weld the conflicting elements of his kingdom into a strong and prosperous whole.

"In all seriousness he devoted himself to the work of peace. Moderate in all pleasures, needing but little sleep and accustomed to divide his time with the utmost accuracy, he found leisure to devote himself to science and art after the completion of his State duties. The famous personages and scholars who adorned the capital he had built for himself at Fatehpur-Sikri were at the same time his friends; every Thursday evening a circle of these was collected for intellectual conversation and philosophical discussion. His closest friends were two highly talented brothers, Faizi and Abul Fazl, the sons of a learned free-thinker. The elder of these was a famous scholar in Hindu literature; with his help, and under his direction, Akbar had the most important of the Sanskrit works translated into Persian. Fazl, on the other hand, who was an especially close friend of Akbar, was a general, a statesman, and an organizer, and to his activity Akbar's kingdom chiefly owed the solidarity of its internal organization."[1]

(Such was the quality of the circle that used to meet in the palaces of Fatehpur-Sikri, buildings which still stand in the Indian sunlight—but empty now and desolate. Fatehpur-Sikri, like the city of Ambar, is now a dead city. A few years ago the child of a British official was killed by a panther in one of its silent streets.)

All this that we have quoted reveals a pre-eminent monarch. But Akbar, like all men, great or petty, lived within the limitations of his period and its circle of ideas. And a Turkoman, ruling in India, was necessarily ignorant of much that Europe had been painfully learning for a thousand years. He knew nothing of the growth of a popular consciousness in Europe, and little or nothing of the wide educational possibilities that the church had been working out in the West. His upbringing in Islam and his native genius made it plain to him that a great nation in India could only be cemented by common ideas upon a religious basis, but the knowledge of how such a solidarity could be created and sustained by universal schools, cheap books, and a university system at once organized and free to think, to which the modern state is still feeling its way, was as impossible to him as a knowledge of steamboats or aeroplanes. The form of Islam he knew best was the narrow and fiercely intolerant form of the Turkish Sunnites. The Moslems were only a minority of the population. The problem he faced was indeed very parallel to the problem of Constantine the Great. But it had peculiar difficulties of its own. He never got beyond an attempt to adapt Islam to a wider appeal by substituting for "There is one God, and Muhammad is his prophet," the declaration, "There is one God, and the Emperor is his vicegerent." This he thought might form a common platform for every variety of faith in India, that kaleidoscope of religions. With this faith he associated a simple ritual borrowed from the Persian Zoroastrians (the Parsees) who still survived, and survive to-day, in India. This new state religion, however, died with him, because it had no roots in the minds of the people about him.

The essential factor in the organization of a living state, the world is coming to realize, is the organization of an educa-

[1] Dr. Schmit in Helmolt's *History of the World.*

tion. This Akbar never understood. And he had no class of men available who would suggest such an idea to him or help him to carry it out. The Moslem teachers in India were not so much teachers as conservators of an intense bigotry; they did not want a common mind in India, but only a common intolerance in Islam. The Brahmins, who had the monopoly of teaching among the Hindus, had all the conceit and slackness of hereditary privilege. Yet though Akbar made no general educational scheme for India, he set up a number of Moslem and Hindu schools. He knew less and he did more for India in these matters than the British who succeeded him. Some of the British viceroys have aped his magnificence, his costly tents and awnings, his palatial buildings and his elephants of state, but none have gone far enough beyond the political outlook of this mediæval Turkoman to attempt that popular education which is an absolute necessity to India before she can play her fitting part in the commonweal of mankind.

§ 5F

A curious side result of these later Mongol perturbations, those of the fourteenth century of which Timurlane was the head and centre, was the appearance of drifting batches of a strange refugee Eastern people in Europe, the Gipsies. They appeared somewhen about the end of the fourteenth and early fifteenth centuries in Greece, where they were believed to be Egyptians (hence Gipsy), a very general persuasion which they themselves accepted and disseminated. Their leaders, however, styled themselves "Counts of Asia Minor." They had probably been drifting about Western Asia for some centuries before the massacres of Timurlane drove them over the Hellespont. They may have been dislodged from their original homeland—as the Ottoman Turks were—by the great cataclysm of Jengis or even earlier. They had drifted about as the Ottoman Turks had drifted about, but with less good fortune. They spread slowly westward across Europe, strange fragments of nomadism in a world of plough and city, driven off their ancient habitat of the Bactrian steppes to harbour upon European commons and by hedgerows and in wild woodlands and neglected patches. The Germans called them "Hungarians" and "Tartars" the French, "Bohemians." They do not seem to have kept the true tradition of their origin, but they have a distinctive language which indicates their lost history; it contains many North Indian words, and is probably in its origin North Indian. There are also considerable Armenian and Persian elements in their speech. They are found in all European countries to-day; they are tinkers, pedlars, horse-dealers, showmen, fortune-tellers, and beggars. To many imaginative minds their wayside encampments, with their smoking fires, their rounded tents, their hobbled horses, and their brawl of sunburnt children, have a very strong appeal. Civilization is so new a thing in history, and has been for most of the time so very local a thing, that it has still to conquer and assimilate most of our instincts to its needs. In most of us, irked by its conventions and complexities, there stirs the nomad strain. We are but half-hearted home-keepers. The blood in our veins was brewed on the steppes as well as on the plough-lands.

XXXIV

THE RENASCENCE OF WESTERN CIVILIZATION[1]

(Land Ways Give Place to Sea Ways)

§ 1. *Christianity and Popular Education.* § 2. *Europe Begins to Think for Itself.* § 3. *The Great Plague and the Dawn of Communism.* § 4. *How Paper Liberated the Human Mind.* § 5. *Protestantism of the Princes and Protestantism of the Peoples.* § 6. *The Reawakening of Science.* § 7. *The New Growth of European Towns.* § 8. *America Comes into History.* § 9. *What Machiavelli Thought of the World.* § 10. *The Republic of Switzerland.* § 11A. *The Life of the Emperor Charles V.* § 11B. *Protestants if the Prince Wills It.* § 11C. *The Intellectual Undertow.*

§ 1

JUDGED by the map, the three centuries from the beginning of the thirteenth to the end of the fifteenth century were an age of recession for Christendom. These centuries were the Age of the Mongolian peoples. Nomadism from Central Asia dominated the known world. At the crest of this period there were rulers of Mongol or the kindred Turkish race and nomadic tradition in China, India, Persia, Egypt, North Africa, the Balkan peninsula, Hungary, and Russia. The Ottoman Turk had even taken to the sea, and fought the Venetian upon his own Mediterranean waters. In 1529 the Turks

[1] Renascence here means rebirth, and it is applied to the recovery of the entire Western world. It is not to be confused with the "Renaissance," an educational, literary, and artistic revival that went on in Italy and the Western world affected by Italy during the fourteenth and fifteenth centuries. The Renaissance was only a part of the Renascence of Europe. The Renaissance was a revival due to the exhumation of classical art and learning; it was but one factor in the very much larger and more complicated resurrection of European capacity and vigour, with which we are dealing in this chapter.

besieged Vienna, and were defeated rather by the weather than by the defenders. The Habsburg empire of Charles V paid the Sultan tribute. It was not until the battle of Lepanto in 1571, the battle in which Cervantes, the author of Don Quixote, lost his left arm, that Christendom, to use his words, "broke the pride of the Osmans and undeceived the world which had regarded the Turkish fleet as invincible." The sole region of Christian advance was Spain. A man of foresight surveying the world in the early sixteenth century might well have concluded that it was only a matter of a few generations before the whole world became Mongolian—and probably Moslem. Just as to-day most people seem to take it for granted that European rule and a sort of liberal Christianity are destined to spread over the whole world. Few people seem to realize how recent a thing is this European ascendancy. It was only as the fifteenth century drew to its close that any indications of the real vitality of Western Europe became clearly apparent.

Our history is now approaching our own times, and our study becomes more and more a study of the existing state of affairs. The European or Europeanized system in which the reader is living, is the same system that we see developing in the crumpled-up, Mongol-threatened Europe of the early fifteenth century. Its problems then were the embryonic form of the problems of to-day. It is impossible to discuss that time without discussing our own time. We become political in spite of ourselves. "Politics without history has no root," said Sir J. R. Seeley; "history without politics has no fruit."

Let us try, with as much detachment as we can achieve, to discover what the forces were that were dividing and holding back the energies of Europe during this tremendous outbreak of the Mongol peoples, and how we are to explain the accumulation of mental and physical energy that undoubtedly went on during this phase of apparent retrocession, and which broke out so impressively at its close.

Now, just as in the Mesozoic Age, while the great reptiles lorded it over the earth, there were developing in odd out-of-the-way corners those hairy mammals and feathered birds who were finally to supersede that tremendous fauna altogether by another far more versatile and capable, so in the limited territories of Western Europe of the Middle Ages, while the Mongolian monarchies dominated the world from the Danube to

EUROPE at the time of the FALL of CONSTANTINOPLE
Republic of Novgorod
Duchy of Moscow
KIPCHAK (Golden Horde)
Volga
Dy. of LITHUANIA
Dnieper
Knights
K. of SWEDEN
NORWAY
Kingdom of DENMARK
Teutonic
K. of POLAND
Vistula
Moldavia
Wallachia
K. of HUNGARY
Danube
OTTOMAN EMPIRE
Constantinople
Trebizond
(to Genoa)
MAMELUKES
Cyprus
Crete
(to Venice)
Albania
Bosnia
(to Genoa)
Rep. of Venice
K. of NAPLES
Sicily
Sardinia
THE EMPIRE
Austria
Switz'd
Elbe
Rhine
Flanders
Burgundy
K. of FRANCE
Aquitaine
K. of ENGLAND
K. of Scotland
Ireland
Navarre
K. of ARAGON
K. of CASTILE
Leon
K. of Portugal
Granada (Moslem)
Moorish Kingdoms
J.F.H.

the Pacific and from the Arctic seas to Madras and Morocco and the Nile, the fundamental lines of a new and harder and more efficient type of human community were being laid down. This type of community, which is still only in the phase of formation, which is still growing and experimental, we may perhaps speak of as the "modern state." This is, we must recognize, a vague expression, but we shall endeavour to get meaning into it as we proceed. We have noted the appearance of its main root ideas in the Greek republics and especially in Athens, in the great Roman republic, in Judaism, in Islam, and in the story of Western Catholicism. Essentially this modern state, as we see it growing under our eyes to-day, is a tentative combination of two apparently contradictory ideas, the idea of a *community of faith and obedience,* such as the earliest civilizations undoubtedly were, and the idea of a *community of will,* such as were the primitive political groupings of the Nordic and Hunnish peoples. For thousands of years the settled civilized peoples, who were originally in most cases dark-white Caucasians, or Dravidian or Southern Mongolian peoples, seem to have developed their ideas and habits along the line of worship and personal subjection, and the nomadic peoples theirs along the line of personal self-reliance and self-assertion. Naturally enough under the circumstances the nomadic peoples were always supplying the civilizations with fresh rulers and new aristocracies. That is the rhythm of all early history. It was only after thousands of years of cyclic changes between refreshment by nomadic conquest, civilization, decadence, and fresh conquest that the present process of a mutual blending of "civilized" and "free" tendencies into a new type of community, that now demands our attention and which is the substance of contemporary history, began.

We have traced in this history the slow development of larger and larger "civilized" human communities from the days of the primitive Palæolithic family tribe. We have seen how the advantages and necessities of cultivation, the fear of tribal gods, the ideas of the priest-king and the god-king, played their part in consolidating continually larger and more powerful societies in regions of maximum fertility. We have watched the interplay of priest, who was usually native, and monarch, who was usually a conqueror, in these early civilizations, the development of a written tradition and its escape from priestly control, and the appearance of novel forces, at first apparently incidental and secondary, which we have called the free intelligence and the free conscience of mankind. We have seen the rulers of the primitive civilizations of the river valleys widening their area and extending their sway, and simultaneously over the less fertile areas of the earth we have seen mere tribal savagery develop into a more and more united and politically competent nomadism. Steadily and divergently mankind pursued one or other of these two lines. For long ages all the civilizations grew and developed along monarchist lines, upon lines of absolute monarchy, and in every monarchy and dynasty we have watched, as if it were a necessary process, efficiency and energy give way to pomp, indolence, and decay, and finally succumb to some fresher lineage from the desert or the steppe. The story of the early cultivating civilizations and their temples and courts and cities bulks large in human history, but it is well to remember that the scene of that story was never more than a very small part of the land surface of the globe. Over the greater part of the earth until quite recently, until the last two thousand years, the hardier, less numerous tribal peoples of forest and parkland and the nomadic peoples of the seasonal grasslands maintained and developed their own ways of life.

The primitive civilizations were, we may say, "communities of obedience"; obedience to god-kings or kings under gods was their cement; the nomadic tendency on the other hand has always been towards a different type of association which we shall here call a "community of will." In a wandering, fighting community the individual must be at once self-reliant and disciplined. The chiefs of such communities must be chiefs who are followed, not masters who compel. This community of will is traceable throughout the entire history of mankind; everywhere we find the original disposition of all the nomads alike, Nordic, Semitic, or Mongolian, was individually more *willing* and more *erect* than that of the settled folk. The Nordic peoples came into Italy and Greece under leader kings; they did not bring any systematic temple cults with them, they found such things in the conquered lands and adapted as they adopted them. The Greeks and Latins lapsed very easily again into republics, and so did the Aryans in India. There was a tradition of election also in the early Frankish and German kingdoms, though the decision was usually taken between one or other members of a royal caste or family. The early Caliphs were elected, the Judges of Israel and the "kings" of Carthage and Tyre were elected, and so was the Great Khan of the Mongols until Kublai became a Chinese monarch. . . . Equally constant in the settled lands do we find the opposite idea, the idea of a non-elective divinity in kings and of their natural and inherent right to rule. . . . As our history has developed we have noted the appearance of new and complicating elements in the story of human societies; we have seen that nomad turned go-between, the trader, appear, and we have noted the growing importance of shipping in the world. It seems as inevitable that voyaging should make men free in their minds as that settlement within a narrow horizon should make men timid and servile. . . . But in spite of all such complications, the broad antagonism between the method of obedience and the method of will runs through history down into our own times. To this day their reconciliation is incomplete.

Civilization even in its most servile forms has always offered much that is enormously attractive, convenient, and congenial to mankind; but something restless and untamed in our race has striven continually to convert civilization from its original reliance upon unparticipating obedience into a community of participating wills. And to the lurking nomadism in our blood, and particularly in the blood of monarchs and aristocracies, we must ascribe also that incessant urgency towards a wider range that forces every state to extend its boundaries if it can, and to spread its interests to the ends of the earth. The power of nomadic restlessness that tends to bring all the earth under one rule, seems to be identical with the spirit that makes most of us chafe under direction and restraint, and seek to participate in whatever government we tolerate. And this natural, this temperamental struggle of mankind to reconcile civilization with freedom has been kept alive age after age by the military and political impotence of every "community of obedience" that has ever existed. Obedience, once men are broken to it, can be easily captured and transferred; witness the passive rôle of Egypt, Mesopotamia, and India, the original and typical lands of submission, the "cradles of civilization," as they have passed from one lordship to another. A servile civilization is a standing invitation to predatory free men. But on the other hand a "community of will" necessitates a fusion of intractable materials; it is a far harder community to bring about, and still more difficult to maintain. The story of Alexander the Great displays the community of will of the Macedonian captains gradually dissolving before his demand that they should worship him. The incident of the murder of Clitus is quite typical of the struggle between the free and the servile tradition that went on whenever a new conqueror from the open lands and the open air found himself installed in the palace of an ancient monarchy.

In the case of the Roman Republic, history tells of the first big community of will in the world's history, the first free community much larger than a city, and how it weakened with growth and spent itself upon success until at last it gave way to a monarchy of the ancient type, and decayed swiftly into one of the feeblest communities of servitude that ever collapsed before a handful of invaders. We have given some attention in this book to the factors in that decay, because they are of primary importance in human history. One of the most evident was the want of any wide organization of education to base the ordinary citizens' minds upon the idea of service and obligation to the republic, to keep them *willing*, that is; another was the absence of any medium of general information to keep their activities in harmony, to enable them to *will* as one body. The community of will is limited in size by the limitations set upon the possibilities of a community of knowledge. The concentration of property in a few hands and the replacement of free workers by slaves were rendered possible by the decay of public spirit and the confusion of the public intelligence that resulted from these limitations. There was, moreover, no efficient religious idea behind the Roman state; the dark Etruscan liver-peering cult of Rome was as little adapted to the political needs of a great community as the very similar Shamanism of the Mongols. It is in the fact that both Christianity and Islam, in their distinctive ways, did at least promise to supply, for the first time in human experience, this patent gap in the Roman republican system as well as in the nomadic system, to give a common moral education for a mass of people, and to supply them with a common history of the past and a common idea of a human purpose and destiny, that their enormous historical importance lies. Aristotle, as we have noted, had set a limit to the ideal community of a few thousand citizens, because he could not conceive how a larger multitude could be held together by a common idea. He had had no experience of any sort of education beyond the tutorial methods of his time. Greek education was almost purely *viva-voce* education; it could reach therefore only to a limited aristocracy. Both the Christian church and Islam demonstrated the unsoundness of Aristotle's limitation. We may think they did their task of education in their vast fields of opportunity crudely or badly, but the point of interest to us is that they did it at all. Both sustained almost world-wide propagandas of idea and inspiration. Both relied successfully upon the power of the written word to link great multitudes of diverse men together in common enterprises. By the eleventh century, as we have seen, the idea of Christendom had been imposed upon all the vast warring miscellany of the smashed and pulverized Western empire, and upon Europe far beyond its limits, as a uniting and inspiring idea. It had made a shallow but effective community of will over an unprecedented area and out of an unprecedented multitude of human beings. Only one other thing at all like this had ever happened to any great section of mankind before, and that was the idea of a community of good behaviour that the *literati* had spread throughout China.[1]

The Catholic Church provided what the Roman Republic had lacked, a system of popular teaching, a number of universities and methods of intellectual inter-communication. By this achievement it opened the way to the new possibilities of human government that now become apparent in this Outline, possibilities that are still being apprehended and worked out in the world in which we are living. Hitherto the government of states had been either authoritative, under some uncriticized and unchallenged combination of priest and monarch, or it had been a democracy, uneducated and uninformed, degenerating with any considerable increase of size, as Rome and Athens did, into a mere rule by mob and politician. But by the thirteenth century the first intimations had already dawned of an ideal of government which is still making its way to realization, the modern ideal, the ideal of a world-wide *educational government*, in which the ordinary man is neither the slave

[1] But the Jews were already holding their community together by systematic education at least as early as the beginning of the Christian era.

of an absolute monarch nor of a demagogue-ruled state, but an informed, inspired, and consulted part of his community. It is upon the word educational that stress must be laid, and upon the idea that information must precede consultation. It is in the practical realization of this idea that education is a collective function and not a private affair that one essential distinction of the "modern state" from any of its precursors lies. The modern citizen, men are coming to realize, must be informed first and then consulted. Before he can vote he must hear the evidence; before he can decide he must know. It is not by setting up polling booths, but by setting up schools and making literature and knowledge and news universally accessible that the way is opened from servitude and confusion to that willingly co-operative state which is the modern ideal. Votes in themselves are worthless things. Men had votes in Italy in the time of the Gracchi. Their votes did not help them. Until a man has education, a vote is a useless and dangerous thing for him to possess. The ideal community towards which we move is not a community of will simply; it is *a community of knowledge and will,* replacing *a community of faith and obedience.* Education is the adapter which will make the nomadic spirit of freedom and self-reliance compatible with the co-operations and wealth and security of civilization.

§ 2

But though it is certain that the Catholic Church, through its propagandas, its popular appeals, its schools and universities, opened up the prospect of the modern educational state in Europe, it is equally certain that the Catholic Church never intended to do anything of the sort. It did not send out knowledge with its blessing; it let it loose inadvertently. It was not the Roman Republic whose heir the Church esteemed itself, but the Roman Emperor. Its conception of education was not release, not an invitation to participate, but the subjugation of minds. Two of the greatest educators of the Middle Ages were indeed not churchmen at all, but monarchs and statesmen, Charlemagne and Alfred the Great of England, who made use of the church organization. But it was the church that had provided the organization. Church and monarchs in their mutual grapple for power were both calling to their aid the thoughts of the common man. In response to these conflicting appeals appeared the common man, the unofficial outside independent man, thinking for himself.

Already in the thirteenth century we have seen Pope Gregory IX and the Emperor Frederick II engaging in a violent public controversy. Already then there was a sense that a new arbitrator greater than pope or monarchy had come into the world, that there were readers and a public opinion. The exodus of the popes to Avignon, and the divisions and disorders of the Papacy during the fourteenth century, stimulated this free judgment upon authority throughout Europe enormously.

At first the current criticism upon the church concerned only moral and material things. The wealth and luxury of the higher clergy and the heavy papal taxation were the chief grounds of complaint. And the earlier attempts to restore Christian simplicity, the foundation of the Franciscans, for example, were not movements of separation, but movements of revival. Only later did a deeper and more distinctive criticism develop which attacked the central fact of the church's teaching and the justification of priestly importance; namely, the sacrifice of the mass.

We have sketched in broad outlines the early beginnings of Christianity, and we have shown how rapidly that difficult and austere conception of the Kingdom of God, which was the central idea of the teachings of Jesus of Nazareth, was overlaid by a revival of the ancient sacrificial idea, a doctrine more difficult indeed to grasp, but easier to reconcile with the habits and dispositions and acquiescences of everyday life in the Near East. We have noted how a sort of theocrasia went on between Christianity and Judaism and the cult of the Serapeum and Mithraism and other competing cults, by which the Mithraist Sunday, the Jewish idea of blood as a religious essential, the Alexandrian importance of the Mother of God, the shaven and fasting priest, self-tormenting asceticism, and many other matters of belief and ritual and practice, became grafted upon the developing religion. These adaptations, no doubt, made the new teaching much more understandable and acceptable in Egypt and Syria and the like. They were things in the way of thought of the dark-white Mediterranean race; they were congenial to that type. But as we have shown in our story of Muhammad, these acquisitions did not make Christianity more acceptable to the Arab nomads; to them these features made it disgusting. And so, too, the robed and shaven monk and nun and priest seem to have roused something like an instinctive hostility in the Nordic barbarians of the North and West. We have noted the peculiar bias of the early Anglo-Saxons and Northmen against the monks and nuns. They seem to have felt that the lives and habits of these devotees were queer and unnatural.

The clash between what we may call the "dark-white" factors and the newer elements in Christianity was no doubt intensified by Pope Gregory VII's imposition of celibacy upon the Catholic priests in the eleventh century. The East had known religious celibates for thousands of years; in the West they were regarded with scepticism and suspicion.

And now in the thirteenth and fourteenth centuries, as the lay mind of the Nordic peoples began to acquire learning, to read and write and express itself, and as it came into touch with the stimulating activities of the Arab mind, we find a much more formidable criticism of Catholicism beginning, an intellectual attack upon the priest as priest, and upon the ceremony of the mass as the central fact of the religious life, coupled with a demand for a return to the personal teachings of Jesus as recorded in the Gospels.

We have already mentioned the career of the Englishman Wycliffe (*c.* 1320-1384), and how he translated the Bible into English in order to set up a counter authority to that of the Pope. He denounced the doctrines of the church about the mass as disastrous error, and particularly the teaching that the consecrated bread eaten in that ceremony becomes in some magical way the actual body of Christ. We will not pursue the question of transubstantiation, as this process of the mystical change of the elements in the sacrament is called, into its intricacies. These are matters for the theological specialist. But it will be obvious that any doctrine, such as the Catholic doctrine, which makes the consecration of the elements in the sacrament a miraculous process performed by the priest, and only to be performed by the priest, and which makes the sacrament the central necessity of the religious system, enhances the importance of the priestly order enormously. On the other hand, the view, which was the typical "Protestant" view, that this sacrament is a mere eating of bread and drinking of wine as a personal remembrance of Jesus of Nazareth, does away at last with any particular need for a consecrated priest at all. Wycliffe himself did not go to this extremity; he was a priest, and he remained a priest to the end of his life, he held that God was spiritually if not substantially present in the consecrated bread, but his doctrine raised a question that carried men far beyond his positions. From the point of view of the historian, the struggle against Rome that Wycliffe opened became very speedily a struggle of what one may call rational or layman's religion making its appeal to the free intelligence and the free conscience in mankind, against authoritative, traditional, ceremonial, and priestly religion. The ultimate tendency of this complicated struggle was to strip Christianity as bare as Islam of every vestige of ancient priestcraft, to revert to the Bible documents as authority, and to recover, if possible, the primordial teachings of Jesus. Most of its issues are still undecided among Christians to this day.

Wycliffe's writings had nowhere more influence than in Bohemia. About 1396 a learned Czech, John Huss, delivered a series of lectures in the university of Prague based upon the doctrines of the great Oxford teacher. Huss became rector of the university, and his teachings roused the church to excommunicate him (1412). This was at the time of the Great Schism, just before the Council of Constance (1414-1418) gathered to discuss the scandalous disorder of the church. We have already told how the schism was ended by the election of Martin V. The council aspired to reunite Christendom completely. But the methods by which it sought this reunion jar with our modern consciences. Wycliffe's bones were condemned to be burnt. Huss was decoyed to Constance under promise of a safe conduct, and he was then put upon his trial for heresy. He was ordered to recant certain of his opinions. He replied that he could not recant until he was convinced of his error. He was told that it was his duty to recant if his superiors required it of him, whether he was convinced or not. He refused to accept this view. In spite of the Emperor's safe conduct, he was burnt alive (1415), a martyr not for any specific doctrine, but for the free intelligence and free conscience of mankind.

It would be impossible to put the issue between priest and anti-priest more clearly than it was put at this trial of John Huss, nor to demonstrate more completely the evil spirit in priestcraft. A colleague of Huss, Jerome of Prague, was burnt in the following year.

These outrages were followed by an insurrection of the Hussites in Bohemia (1419), the first of a series of religious wars that marked the breaking-up of Christendom. In 1420 the Pope, Martin V, issued a bull proclaiming a crusade "for the destruction of the Wycliffites, Hussites, and all other heretics in Bohemia," and attracted by this invitation the unemployed soldiers of fortune and all the drifting blackguardism of Europe converged upon that valiant country. They found in Bohemia, under its great leader Ziska, more hardship and less loot than crusaders were disposed to face. The Hussites were conducting their affairs upon extreme democratic lines, and the whole country was aflame with enthusiasm. The crusaders beleaguered Prague, but failed to take it, and they experienced a series of reverses that ended in their retreat from Bohemia. A second crusade (1421) was no more successful. Two other crusades failed. Then unhappily the Hussites fell into internal dissensions. Encouraged by this, a fifth crusade (1431) crossed the frontier under Frederick, Margrave of Brandenburg.

The army of these crusaders, according to the lowest estimates, consisted of 90,000 infantry and 40,000 horsemen. Attacking Bohemia from the west, they first laid siege to the town of Tachov, but failing to capture the strongly fortified city, they stormed the little town of Most, and here, as well as in the surrounding country, committed the most horrible atrocities on a population a large part of which was entirely innocent of any form of theology whatever. The crusaders, advancing by slow marches, penetrated further into Bohemia, till they reached the neighbourhood of the town of Domazlice (Tauss). "It was at three o'clock on August 14th, 1431, that the crusaders, who were encamped in the plain between Domazlice and Horsuv Tyn, received the news that the Hussites, under the leadership of Prokop the Great, were approaching. Though the Bohemians were still four miles off, the rattle of their war-wagons and the song, 'All ye warriors of God,' which their whole host was chanting, could already be heard." The enthusiasm of the crusaders evaporated with astounding rapidity. Lützow[1] describes how the papal representative and the Duke of Saxony ascended a convenient hill to inspect the battlefield. It was, they discov-

[1] Lützow's *Bohemia*.

ered, not going to be a battlefield. The German camp was in utter confusion. Horsemen were streaming off in every direction, and the clatter of empty wagons being driven off almost drowned the sound of that terrible singing. The crusaders were abandoning even their loot. Came a message from the Margrave of Brandenburg advising flight; there was no holding any of their troops. They were dangerous now only to their own side, and the papal representative spent an unpleasant night hiding from them in the forest. . . . So ended the Bohemian crusade.

In 1434 civil war again broke out among the Hussites, in which the extreme and most valiant section was defeated, and in 1436 an agreement was patched up between the Council of Basle and the moderate Hussites, in which the Bohemian church was allowed to retain certain distinctions from the general Catholic practice, which held good until the German Reformation in the sixteenth century.

§ 3

The split among the Hussites was largely due to the drift of the extremer section towards a primitive communism, which alarmed the wealthier and more influential Czech noblemen. Similar tendencies had already appeared among the English Wycliffites. They seem to follow naturally enough upon the doctrines of equal human brotherhood that emerge whenever there is an attempt to reach back to the fundamentals of Christianity.

The development of such ideas had been greatly stimulated by a stupendous misfortune that had swept the world and laid bare the foundations of society, a pestilence of unheard-of virulence. It was called the Black Death, and it came nearer to the extirpation of mankind than any other evil has ever done. It was far more deadly than the plague of Pericles, or the plague of Marcus Aurelius, or the plague waves of the time of Justinian and Gregory the Great that paved the way for the Lombards in Italy. It arose in South Russia or Central Asia, and came by way of the Crimea and a Genoese ship to Genoa and Western Europe. It passed by Armenia to Asia Minor, Egypt, and North Africa. It reached England in 1348. Two-thirds of the students at Oxford died, we are told; it is estimated that between a quarter and a half of the whole population of England perished at this time. Throughout all Europe there was as great a mortality. Hecker estimates the total as twenty-five million dead. It spread eastward to China, where, the Chinese records say, thirteen million people perished. In China the social disorganization led to a neglect of the river embankments, and as a consequence great floods devastated the crowded agricultural lands.[1]

Never was there so clear a warning to mankind to seek knowledge and cease from bickering, to unite against the dark powers of nature. All the massacres of Hulagu and Timurlane were as nothing to this. "Its ravages," says J. R. Green, "were fiercest in the greater towns, where filthy and undrained streets afforded a constant haunt to leprosy and fever. In the burial-ground which the piety of Sir Walter Manny purchased for the citizens of London, a spot whose site was afterwards marked by the Charter House, more than fifty thousand corpses are said to have been interred. Thousands of people perished at Norwich, while in Bristol the living were hardly able to bury the dead. But the Black Death fell on the villages almost as fiercely as on the towns. More than one-half of the priests of Yorkshire are known to have perished; in the diocese of Norwich two-thirds of the parishes changed their incumbents. The whole organization of labour was thrown out of gear. The scarcity of hands made it difficult for the minor tenants to perform the services due for their lands, and only a temporary abandonment of half the rent by the landowners induced the farmers to refrain from the abandonment of their farms. For a time cultivation became impossible. 'The sheep and cattle strayed through the fields and corn,' says a contemporary, 'and there were none left who could drive them.' "

It was from these distresses that the peasant wars of the fourteenth century sprang. There was a great shortage of labour and a great shortage of goods, and the rich abbots and monastic cultivators who owned so much of the land, and the nobles and rich merchants, were too ignorant of economic laws

[1] Dr. C. O. Stallybrass says that this plague reached China thirty or forty years after its first appearance in Europe. Ibn Batuta, the Arab traveller who was in China from 1342 to 1346, first met with it on his return to Damascus. The Black Death is the human form of a disease endemic among the jerboas and other small rodents in the districts round the head of the Caspian Sea.

to understand that they must not press upon the toilers in this time of general distress. They saw their property deteriorating,

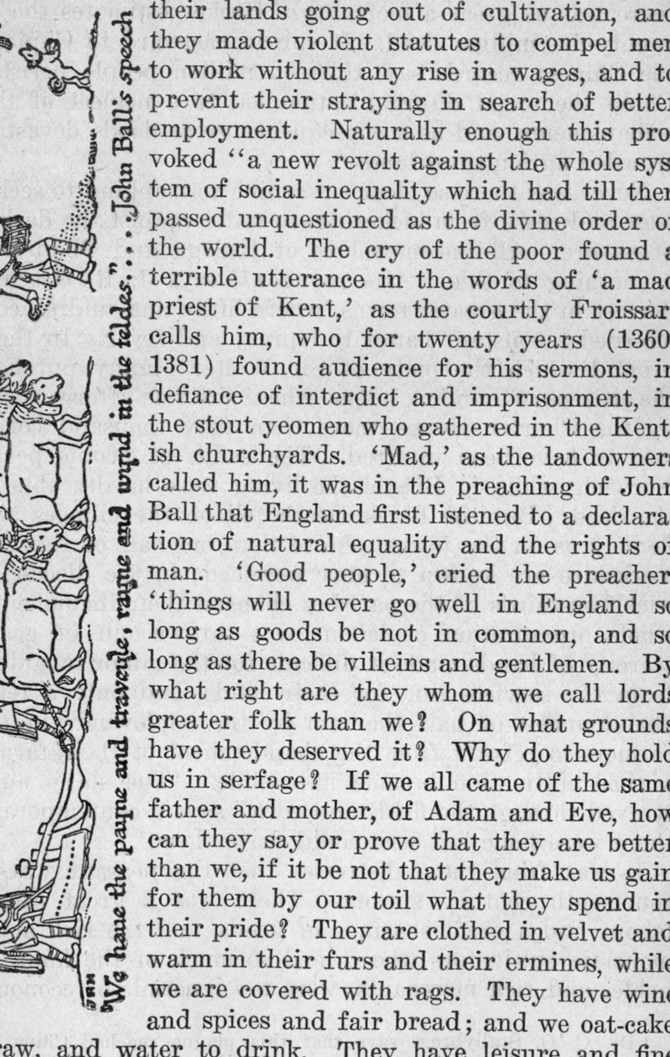

"We haue the payne and traveyle, rayne and wynd in the feldes." . . John Ball's speech

their lands going out of cultivation, and they made violent statutes to compel men to work without any rise in wages, and to prevent their straying in search of better employment. Naturally enough this provoked "a new revolt against the whole system of social inequality which had till then passed unquestioned as the divine order of the world. The cry of the poor found a terrible utterance in the words of 'a mad priest of Kent,' as the courtly Froissart calls him, who for twenty years (1360-1381) found audience for his sermons, in defiance of interdict and imprisonment, in the stout yeomen who gathered in the Kentish churchyards. 'Mad,' as the landowners called him, it was in the preaching of John Ball that England first listened to a declaration of natural equality and the rights of man. 'Good people,' cried the preacher, 'things will never go well in England so long as goods be not in common, and so long as there be villeins and gentlemen. By what right are they whom we call lords greater folk than we? On what grounds have they deserved it? Why do they hold us in serfage? If we all came of the same father and mother, of Adam and Eve, how can they say or prove that they are better than we, if it be not that they make us gain for them by our toil what they spend in their pride? They are clothed in velvet and warm in their furs and their ermines, while we are covered with rags. They have wine and spices and fair bread; and we oat-cake and straw, and water to drink. They have leisure and fine houses; we have pain and labour, the rain and the wind in the fields. And yet it is of us and of our toil that these men hold their state.' A spirit fatal to the whole system of the Middle

Ages breathed in the popular rhyme which condensed the levelling doctrine of John Ball: 'When Adam delved and Eve span, who was then the gentleman?' "[1]

Wat Tyler, the leader of the English insurgents, was assassinated by the Mayor of London in the presence of the young King Richard II (1381), and his movement collapsed. The communist side of the Hussite movement was a part of the same system of disturbance. A little earlier than the English outbreak had occurred the French "Jacquerie" (1358), in which the French peasants had risen, burnt châteaux, and devastated the countryside. A century later the same urgency was to sweep Germany into a series of bloody Peasant Wars. These began late in the fifteenth century. Economic and religious disturbance mingled in the case of Germany even more plainly than in England. One conspicuous phase of these German troubles was the Anabaptist outbreak. The sect of the Anabaptists appeared in Wittenberg in 1521 under three "prophets," and broke out into insurrection in 1525. Between 1532 and 1535 the insurgents held the town of Münster in Westphalia, and did their utmost to realize their ideas of a religious communism. They were besieged by the Bishop of Münster, and under the distresses of the siege a sort of insanity ran rife in the town; cannibalism is said to have occurred, and a certain John of Leyden seized power, proclaimed himself the successor of King David, and followed that monarch's evil example by practising polygamy. After the surrender of the city the victorious bishop had the Anabaptist leaders tortured very horribly and executed

[1] The seeds of conflict which grew up into the Peasants' Revolt of 1381 were sown upon ground which is strangely familiar to any writer in 1920. A European catastrophe had reduced production and consequently increased the earnings of workers and traders. Rural wages had risen by 48 per cent. in England, when an unwise executive endeavoured to enforce in the Ordinance and Statute of Labourers (1350-51) a return to the pre-plague wages and prices of 1346, and aimed a blow in the Statute of 1378 against labour combinations. The villeins were driven to desperation by the loss of their recent increase of comfort, and the outbreak came, as Froissart saw it from the angle of the Court, "all through the too great comfort of the commonalty." Other ingredients which entered into the outbreak were the resentment felt by the new working class at the restrictions imposed on its right to combine, the objection of the lower clergy to papal taxes, and a frank dislike of foreigners and landlords. There was no touch of Wycliffe's influence in the rising. It was at its feeblest in Leicestershire, and it murdered one of the only other Liberal churchmen in England.—P. G.

in the market-place, their mutilated bodies being hung in cages from a church tower to witness to all the world that decency and order were now restored in Münster. . . .

These upheavals of the common labouring men of the Westtern European countries in the fourteenth and fifteenth centuries were more serious and sustained than anything that had ever happened in history before. The nearest previous approach to them were certain communistic Muhammadan movements in Persia. There was a peasant revolt in Normandy about A.D. 1000, and there were revolts of peasants (Bagaudæ) in the later Roman Empire, but these were not nearly so formidable. They show a new spirit growing in human affairs, a spirit altogether different from the unquestioning apathy of the serfs and peasants in the original regions of civilization or from the anarchist hopelessness of the serf and slave labour of the Roman capitalists. All these early insurrections of the workers that we have mentioned were suppressed with much cruelty, but the movement itself was never completely stamped out. From that time to this there has been a spirit of revolt in the lower levels of the pyramid of civilization. There have been phases of insurrection, phases of repression, phases of compromise and comparative pacification; but from that time until this, the struggle has never wholly ceased. We shall see it flaring out during the French Revolution at the end of the eighteenth century, insurgent again in the middle and at the opening of the last quarter of the nineteenth century, and achieving vast proportions in the world of to-day. The socialist movement of the nineteenth century was only one version of that continuing revolt.

In many countries, in France and Germany and Russia, for example, this labour movement has assumed at times an attitude hostile to Christianity, but there can be little doubt that this steady and, on the whole, growing pressure of the common man in the West against a life of toil and subservience is closely associated with Christian teaching. The church and the Christian missionary may not have intended to spread equalitarian doctrines, but behind the church was the unquenchable personality of Jesus of Nazareth, and even in spite of himself the Christian preacher brought the seeds of freedom and responsibility with him, and sooner or later they shot up where he had been.

This steady and growing upheaval of "Labour," its development of a consciousness of itself as a class and of a definite claim upon the world at large, quite as much as the presence of schools and universities, quite as much as abundant printed books, and a developing and expanding process of scientific research, mark off our present type of civilization, the "modern civilization," from any pre-existing state of human society, and mark it, for all its incidental successes, as a thing unfinished and transitory. It is an embryo or it is something doomed to die. It may be able to solve this complex problem of co-ordinated toil and happiness, and so adjust itself to the needs of the human soul, or it may fail and end in a catastrophe as the Roman system did. It may be the opening phase of some more balanced and satisfying order of society, or it may be a system destined to disruption and replacement by some differently conceived method of human association. Like its predecessor, our present civilization may be no more than one of those crops farmers sow to improve their land by the fixation of nitrogen from the air; it may have grown only that, accumulating certain traditions, it may be ploughed into the soil again for better things to follow. Such questions as these are the practical realities of history, and in all that follows we shall find them becoming clearer and more important, until in our last chapter we shall end, as all our days and years end, with a recapitulation of our hopes and fears—and a note of interrogation.

§ 4

The development of free discussion in Europe during this age of fermentation was enormously stimulated by the appearance of printed books. It was the introduction of paper from the East that made practicable the long latent method of printing. It is still difficult to assign the honour of priority in the use of the simple expedient of printing for multiplying books. It is a trivial question that has been preposterously debated. Apparently the glory, such as it is, belongs to Holland. In Haarlem, one Coster was printing from movable type somewhen before 1446. Gutenberg was printing at Mainz about the same time. There were printers in Italy by 1465, and Caxton set up his press in Westminster in 1477. But long before this time there had been a partial use of printing. Manuscripts as early as the twelfth century display initial letters that may have been printed from wooden stamps.

Far more important is the question of the manufacture of paper. It is scarcely too much to say that paper made the revival of Europe possible. Paper originated in China, where its use probably goes back to the second century B.C. In 751 the Chinese made an attack upon the Arab Moslems in Samarkand; they were repulsed, and among the prisoners taken from them were some skilled paper-makers, from whom the art was learnt. Arabic paper manuscripts from the ninth century onward still exist. The manufacture entered Christendom either through Greece or by the capture of Moorish paper-mills during the Christian reconquest of Spain. But under the Christian Spanish the product deteriorated sadly. Good paper was not made in Christian Europe until near the end of the thirteenth century, and then it was Italy which led the world. Only by the fourteenth century did the manufacture reach Germany, and not until the end of that century was it abundant and cheap enough for the printing of books to be a practicable business proposition. Thereupon printing followed naturally and necessarily, and the intellectual life of the world entered upon a new and far more vigorous phase. It ceased to be a little trickle from mind to mind; it became a broad flood, in which thousands and presently scores and hundreds of thousands of minds participated.

One immediate result of this achievement of printing was the appearance of an abundance of Bibles in the world. Another was a cheapening of school-books. The knowledge of reading spread swiftly. There was not only a great increase of books in the world, but the books that were now made were plainer to read and so easier to understand. Instead of toiling at a crabbed text and then thinking over its significance, readers now could think unimpeded as they read. With this increase in the facility of reading, the reading public grew. The book ceased to be a highly decorated toy or a scholar's mystery. People began to write books to be read as well as looked at by ordinary people. With the fourteenth century the real history of the European literatures begins. We find a rapid replacement of local dialects by standard Italian, standard English, standard French, standard Spanish, and, later, standard German. These languages became literary languages in their several countries; they were tried over, polished by use, and made exact and vigorous. They became at last as capable of the burden of philosophical discussion as Greek or Latin.

§ 5

Here we devote a section to certain elementary statements about the movement in men's religious ideas during the fifteenth and sixteenth centuries. They are a necessary introduction to the political history of the seventeenth and eighteenth centuries that follows.

We have to distinguish clearly between two entirely different systems of opposition to the Catholic church. They intermingled very confusingly. The church was losing its hold upon the consciences of princes and rich and able people; it was also losing the faith and confidence of common people. The effect of its decline of spiritual power upon the former class was to make them resent its interference, its moral restrictions, its claims to overlordship, its claim to tax, and to dissolve allegiances. They ceased to respect its power and its property. This insubordination of princes and rulers was going on throughout the Middle Ages, but it was only when in the sixteenth century the church began to side openly with its old antagonist the Emperor, when it offered him its support and accepted his help in its campaign against heresy, that princes began to think seriously of breaking away from the Roman communion and setting up fragments of a church. And they would never have done so if they had not perceived that the hold of the church upon the masses of mankind had relaxed.

The revolt of the princes was essentially an irreligious revolt against the world-rule of the church. The Emperor Frederick II, with his epistles to his fellow princes, was its forerunner. The revolt of the people against the church, on the other hand, was as essentially religious. They objected not to the church's power, but to its weaknesses. They wanted a deeply righteous and fearless church to help them and organize them against the wickedness of powerful men. Their movements against the church, within it and without, were movements not for release from a religious control, but for a fuller and more abundant religious control. They did not want less religious control, but more—but they wanted to be assured that it was religious. They objected to the Pope not because he was the religious head of the world, but because he was not; because he was a wealthy earthly prince when he ought to have been their spiritual leader.

The contest in Europe from the fourteenth century onward therefore was a three-cornered contest. The princes wanted to use the popular forces against the Pope, but not to let those forces grow too powerful for their own power and glory. For a long time the church went from prince to prince for an ally without realizing that the lost ally it needed to recover was popular veneration.

Because of this triple aspect of the mental and moral conflicts that were going on in the fourteenth and fifteenth and sixteenth centuries, the series of ensuing changes, those changes that are known collectively in history as the Reformation, took on a threefold aspect. There was the Reformation according to the princes, who wanted to stop the flow of money to Rome and to seize the moral authority, the educational power, and the material possessions of the church within their dominions. There was the Reformation according to the people, who sought to make Christianity a power against unrighteousness, and particularly against the unrighteousness of the rich and powerful. And finally there was the Reformation within the church, of which St. Francis of Assisi was the precursor, which sought to restore the goodness of the church and, through its goodness, to restore its power.

The Reformation according to the princes took the form of a replacement of the Pope by the prince as the head of the religion and the controller of the consciences of his people. The princes had no idea and no intention of letting free the judgments of their subjects more particularly with the object-lessons of the Hussites and the Anabaptists before their eyes; they sought to establish national churches dependent upon the throne. As England, Scotland, Sweden, Norway, Denmark, North Germany, and Bohemia broke away from the Roman communion, the princes and other ministers showed the utmost solicitude to keep the movement well under control. Just as much reformation as would sever the link with Rome they permitted; anything beyond that, any dangerous break towards the primitive teachings of Jesus or the crude direct interpretation of the Bible, they resisted. The Established Church of England is one of the most typical and successful of the resulting compromises. It is still sacramental and sacerdotal; but its organization centres in the Court and the Lord Chancellor, and though subversive views may, and do, break out in the lower and less prosperous ranks of its priesthood, it is impossible for them to struggle up to any position of influence and authority.

The Reformation according to the common man was very different in spirit from the Princely Reformation. We have already told something of the popular attempts at Reformation in Bohemia and Germany. The wide spiritual upheavals of the time were at once more honest, more confused, more enduring, and less immediately successful than the reforms of the princes. Very few religious-spirited men had the daring to break away or the effrontery to confess that they had broken away from all authoritative teaching, and that they were now relying entirely upon their own minds and consciences. That required a very high intellectual courage. The general drift of the common man in this period in Europe was to set up his new acquisition, the Bible, as a counter authority to the church. This was particularly the case with the great leader of German Protestantism, Martin Luther (1483-1546). All over Germany, and indeed all over Western Europe, there were now men spelling over the black-letter pages of the newly translated and printed Bible, over the Book of Leviticus and the Song of Solomon and the Revelation of St. John the Divine —strange and perplexing books—quite as much as over the simple and inspiring record of Jesus in the Gospels. Naturally they produced strange views and grotesque interpretations. It is surprising that they were not stranger and grotesquer. But the human reason is an obstinate thing, and will criticize and select in spite of its own resolutions. The bulk of these new Bible students took what their consciences approved from the Bible and ignored its riddles and contradictions. All over Europe, wherever the new Protestant churches of the princes were set up, a living and very active residuum of Protestants remained who declined to have their religion made over for them in this fashion. These were the Nonconformists, a medley of sects, having nothing in common but their resistance to authoritative religion, whether of the Pope or the State.[1] Most, but not all of these Nonconformists held to the Bible as a divinely inspired and authoritative guide. This was a strategic rather

[1] But Noncomformity was stamped out in Germany. See § 11B of this chapter.

than an abiding position, and the modern drift of Nonconformity has been onward away from this original Bibliolatry towards a mitigated and sentimentalized recognition of the bare teachings of Jesus of Nazareth. Beyond the range of Nonconformity, beyond the range of professed Christianity at all, there is also now a great and growing mass of equalitarian belief and altruistic impulse in the modern civilizations, which certainly owes, as we have already asserted, its spirit to Christianity, which began to appear in Europe as the church lost its grip upon the general mind.

Let us say a word now of the third phase of the Reformation process, the Reformation within the church. This was already beginning in the twelfth and thirteenth centuries with the appearance of the Black and Grey Friars (Chap. xxxii, § 13). In the sixteenth century, and when it was most needed, came a fresh impetus of the same kind. This was the foundation of the Society of the Jesuits by Inigo Lopez de Recalde, better known to the world of to-day as St. Ignatius of Loyola.

Loyola

Ignatius began his career as a very tough and gallant young Spaniard. He was clever and dexterous and inspired by a passion for pluck, hardihood, and rather showy glory. His love affairs were free and picturesque. In 1521 the French took the town of Pampeluna in Spain from the Emperor Charles V, and Ignatius was one of the defenders. His legs were smashed by a cannon-ball, and he was taken prisoner. One leg was badly set and had to be broken again, and these painful and complex operations nearly cost him his life. He received the last sacraments. In the night, thereafter, he began to mend, and presently he was convalescent and facing the prospect of a life in which he would perhaps always be a cripple. His thoughts turned to the adventure of religion. Sometimes he would think of a certain great lady, and how, in spite of his broken state, he might yet win her admiration by some amazing deed; and sometimes he would think of being in some especial and personal way the Knight of Christ. In the midst of these confusions, one night as he lay awake, he tells us, a new great lady claimed his attention; he had a vision of the Blessed Virgin Mary carrying the Infant Christ in her arms. "Immediately a loathing seized him for the former deeds of his life." He resolved to give up all further thoughts of earthly women, and to lead a life of absolute chastity and devotion to the Mother of God. He projected great pilgrimages and a monastic life.

His final method of taking his vows marks him the countryman of Don Quixote. He had regained his strength, and he was riding out into the world rather aimlessly, a penniless soldier of fortune with little but his arms and the mule on which he rode, when he fell into company with a Moor. They went on together and talked, and presently disputed about religion. The Moor was the better educated man; he had the best of the argument, he said offensive things about the Virgin Mary that were difficult to answer, and he parted triumphantly from Ignatius. The young Knight of our Lady was boiling with shame and indignation. He hesitated whether he should go after the Moor and kill him or pursue the pilgrimage he had in mind. At a fork in the road he left things to his mule, which spared the Moor. He came to the Benedictine Abbey of Manresa near Montserrat, and here he imitated that peerless hero of the mediæval romance, Amadis de Gaul, and kept an all-night vigil before the Altar of the Blessed Virgin. He presented his mule to the abbey, he gave his worldly clothes to a beggar, he laid his sword and dagger upon the altar, and clothed himself in a rough sackcloth garment and hempen shoes. He then took himself to a neighbouring hospice and gave himself up to scourgings and austerities. For a whole week he fasted absolutely. Thence he went on a pilgrimage to the Holy Land.

For some years he wandered, consumed with the idea of founding a new order of religious knighthood, but not knowing clearly how to set about this enterprise. He became more and more aware of his own illiteracy, and the Inquisition, which was beginning to take an interest in his proceedings, forbade him to attempt to teach others until he had spent at least four years in study. So much cruelty and intolerance is laid at the door of the Inquisition that it is pleasant to record that in its handling of this heady, imaginative young enthusiast it showed itself both sympathetic and sane. It recognized his vigour and possible uses; it saw the dangers of his ignorance. He studied at Salamanca and Paris, among other places. He was ordained a priest in 1538, and a year later his long-dreamt-of order was founded under the military title of the "Company of Jesus." Like the Salvation Army of modern England, it made the most direct attempt to bring the generous tradition of military organization and discipline to the service of religion.

This Ignatius of Loyola who founded the order of Jesuits was a man of forty-seven; he was a very different man, much wiser and steadier, than the rather absurd young man who had aped Amadis de Gaul and kept vigil in the abbey of Manresa; and the missionary and educational organization he now created and placed at the disposal of the Pope was one of the most powerful instruments the church had ever handled. These men gave themselves freely and wholly to be used by the church. It was the Order of the Jesuits which carried Christianity to China again after the downfall of the Ming Dynasty, and Jesuits were the chief Christian missionaries in India and North America. To their civilizing work among the Indians in South America we shall presently allude. But their main achievement lay in raising the standard of Catholic education. Their schools became and remained for a long time the best schools in Christendom. Says Lord Verulam (= Sir Francis Bacon): "As for the pedagogic part . . . consult the schools of the Jesuits, for nothing better has been put in practice." They raised the level of intelligence, they quickened the conscience of all Catholic Europe, they stimulated Protestant Europe to competitive educational efforts. . . . Some day it may be we shall see a new order of Jesuits, vowed not to the service of the Pope, but to the service of mankind.

And concurrently with this great wave of educational effort, the tone and quality of the church was also greatly improved by the clarification of doctrine and the reforms in organization and discipline that were made by the Council of Trent. This council met intermittently either at Trent or Bologna between the years 1545 and 1563, and its work was at least as important as the energy of the Jesuits in arresting the crimes and blunders that were causing state after state to fall away from the Roman communion. The change wrought by the Reformation within the Church of Rome was as great as the change wrought in the Protestant churches that detached themselves from the mother body. There are henceforth no more open scandals or schisms to record. But if anything, there has been an intensification of doctrinal narrowness, and such phases of imaginative vigour as are represented by Gregory the Great, or by the group of Popes associated with Gregory VII and Urban II, or by the group that began with Innocent III, no longer enliven the sober and pedestrian narrative. The world war of 1914-1918 was a unique opportunity for the Papacy; the occasion was manifest for some clear strong voice proclaiming the universal obligation to righteousness, the brotherhood of men, the claims of human welfare over patriotic passion. No such moral lead was given. The Papacy seemed to be balancing its traditional reliance upon the faithful Habsburgs against its quarrel with republican France.

§ 6

The reader must not suppose that the destructive criticism of the Catholic Church and of Catholic Christianity, and the printing and study of the Bible, were the only or even the most important of the intellectual activities of the fourteenth and fifteenth centuries. That was merely the popular and most conspicuous aspect of the intellectual revival of the time. Behind this conspicuous and popular awakening to thought and discussion, other less immediately striking but ultimately more important mental developments were in progress. Of the trend of these developments we must now give some brief indications. They had begun long before books were printed, but it was printing that released them from obscurity.

We have already told something of the first appearance of the free intelligence, the spirit of inquiry and plain statement, in human affairs. One name is central in the record of that first attempt at systematic knowledge, the name of Aristotle. We have noted also the brief phase of scientific work at Alexandria. From that time onward the complicated economic and political and religious conflicts of Europe and Western Asia impeded further intellectual progress. These regions, as we have seen, fell for long ages under the sway of the Oriental type of monarchy and of Oriental religious traditions. Rome tried and abandoned a slave system of industry. The first great capitalistic system developed and fell into chaos through its own inherent rottenness. Europe relapsed into universal insecurity. The Semite rose against the Aryan, and replaced Hellenic civilization throughout Western Asia and Egypt by an Arabic culture. All Western Asia and half of Europe fell under Mongolian rule. It is only in the twelfth and thirteenth centuries that we find the Nordic intelligence struggling through again to expression.

We then find in the growing universities of Paris, Oxford, and Bologna an increasing amount of philosophical discussion going on. In form it is chiefly a discussion of logical questions. As the basis of this discussion we find part of the teachings of Aristotle, not the whole mass of writings he left behind him, but his logic only. Later on his work became better known through the Latin translations of the Arabic edition annotated by Averroes. Except for these translations of Aristotle, and they were abominably bad translations, very little of the Greek philosophical literature was read in Western Europe until the fifteenth century. The creative Plato—as distinguished from the scientific Aristotle—was almost unknown. Europe had the Greek criticism without the Greek impulse. Some neo-Platonic writers were known, but neo-Platonism had much the same relation to Plato that Christian Science has to Christ.

It has been the practice of recent writers to decry the philosophical discussion of the mediæval "schoolmen" as tedious and futile. It was nothing of the sort. It had to retain a severely technical form because the dignitaries of the church, ignorant and intolerant, were on the watch for heresy. It lacked the sweet clearness, therefore, of fearless thought. It often hinted what it dared not say. But it dealt with fundamentally important things, it was a long and necessary struggle to clear up and correct certain inherent defects of the human mind, and many people to-day blunder dangerously through their neglect of the issues the schoolmen discussed.

There is a natural tendency in the human mind to exaggerate the differences and resemblances upon which classification is based, to suppose that things called by different names are altogether different, and that things called by the same name are practically identical. This tendency to exaggerate classification produces a thousand evils and injustices. In the sphere of race or nationality, for example, a "European" will often treat an "Asiatic" almost as if he were a different animal, while he will be disposed to regard another "European" as necessarily as virtuous and charming as himself. He will, as a matter of course, take sides with Europeans against Asiatics. But, as the reader of this history must realize, there is no such difference as the opposition of these names implies. It is a phantom difference created by two names. . . .

The main mediæval controversy was between the "Realists" and the "Nominalists," and it is necessary to warn the reader that the word "Realist" in mediæval discussion has a meaning almost diametrically opposed to "Realist" as it is used in the jargon of modern criticism. The modern "Realist" is one who insists on materialist details; the mediæval "Realist" was far nearer what nowadays we should call an Idealist, and his contempt for incidental detail was profound. The Realists outdid the vulgar tendency to exaggerate the significance of class. They held that there was something in a name, in a common noun that is, that was essentially real. For example, they held there was a typical "European," an ideal European, who was far more real than any individual European. Every European was, as it were, a failure, a departure, a flawed specimen of this profounder reality. On the other hand the Nominalist held that the only realities in the case were the individual Europeans, that the name "European" was merely a name and nothing more than a name applied to all these instances.

Nothing is quite so difficult as the compression of philosophical controversies, which are by their nature voluminous and various and tinted by the mental colours of a variety of minds. With the difference of Realist and Nominalist stated baldly, as we have stated it here, the modern reader unaccustomed to philosophical discussion may be disposed to leap at once to the side of the Nominalist. But the matter is not so simple that it can be covered by one instance, and here we have purposely chosen an extreme instance. Names and classifications differ in their value and reality. While it is absurd to suppose that there can be much depth of class difference between men called Thomas and men called William, or that there is an ideal and quintessential Thomas or William, yet on the other hand there may be much profounder differences between a white man and a Hottentot, and still more between *Homo sapiens* and *Homo neanderthalensis*. While again the distinction between the class of pets and the class of useful animals is dependent upon very slight differences of habit and application, the difference of a cat and dog is so profound that the microscope can trace it in a drop of blood or a single hair. When this aspect of the question is considered, it becomes understandable how Nominalism had ultimately to abandon the idea that names were as insignificant as labels, and how, out of a revised and amended Nominalism, there grew up that systematic attempt to find the *true*—the most significant and fruitful—classification of things and substances which is called Scientific Research.

And it will be almost as evident that while the tendency of Realism, which is the natural tendency of every untutored mind, was towards dogma, harsh divisions, harsh judgments, and uncompromising attitudes, the tendency of earlier and later Nominalism was towards qualified statements, towards an examination of individual instances, and towards inquiry and experiment and scepticism.

So while in the market-place and the ways of the common life men were questioning the morals and righteousness of the clergy, the good faith and propriety of their celibacy, and the justice of papal taxation; while in theological circles their minds were set upon the question of transubstantiation, the question of the divinity or not of the bread and wine in the mass, in studies and lecture-rooms a wider-reaching criticism of the methods of ordinary Catholic teaching was in progress. We cannot attempt here to gauge the significance in this process of such names as Peter Abelard (1079-1142), Albertus Magnus (1193-1280), and Thomas Aquinas (1225-1274). These men sought to reconstruct Catholicism on a sounder system of reasoning. They turned towards Nominalism. Chief among their critics and successors were Duns Scotus (?-1308), an Oxford Franciscan and, to judge by his sedulous thought and deliberate subtleties, a Scotchman, and Occam, an Englishman (?-1347). Both these latter, like Averroes (see Chap. xxxi., § 8), made a definite distinction between theological and philosophical truth; they placed theology on a pinnacle, but they placed it where it could no longer obstruct research; Duns Scotus declared that it was impossible to prove by reasoning the existence of God or of the Trinity or the credibility of the

Act of Creation; Occam was still more insistent upon this separation—which manifestly released scientific inquiry from dogmatic control. A later generation, benefiting by the freedoms towards which these pioneers worked, and knowing not the sources of its freedom, had the ingratitude to use the name of Scotus as a term for stupidity, and so we have our English word "Dunce." Says Professor Pringle Pattison,[1] "Occam, who is still a Scholastic, gives us the Scholastic justification of the spirit which had already taken hold upon Roger Bacon, and which was to enter upon its rights in the fifteenth and sixteenth centuries."

Standing apart by himself because of his distinctive genius is this Roger Bacon (about 1210 to about 1293), who was also English. He was a Franciscan of Oxford, and a very typical Englishman indeed, irritable, hasty, honest, and shrewd. He was two centuries ahead of his world. Says H. O. Taylor of him[2]:

"The career of Bacon was an intellectual tragedy, conforming to the old principles of tragic art: that the hero's character shall be large and noble, but not flawless, inasmuch as the fatal consummation must issue from character, and not happen through chance. He died an old man, as in his youth, so in his age, a devotee of tangible knowledge. His pursuit of a knowledge which was not altogether learning had been obstructed by the Order of which he was an unhappy and rebellious member; quite as fatally his achievement was deformed from within by the principles which he accepted from his time. But he was responsible for his acceptance of current opinions; and as his views roused the distrust of his brother Friars, his intractable temper drew their hostility on his head. Persuasiveness and tact were needed by one who would impress such novel views as his upon his fellows, or, in the thirteenth century, escape persecution for their divulgence. Bacon attacked dead and living worthies, tactlessly, fatuously, and unfairly. Of his life scarcely anything is known, save from his allusions to himself and others; and these are insufficient for the construction of even a slight consecutive narrative. Born; studied at Oxford; went to Paris, studied, experimented; is at Oxford again, and a Franciscan; studies, teaches, becomes suspect to his

1 *Encyclopaedia Britannica,* article "Scholasticism."
2 *The Medieval Mind,* by Henry Osborn Taylor.

Order, is sent back to Paris, kept under surveillance, receives a letter from the Pope, writes, writes, writes—his three best-known works; is again in trouble, confined for many years, released, and dead, so very dead, body and fame alike, until partly unearthed after five centuries.''

The bulk of these ''three best-known works'' is a hotly phrased and sometimes quite abusive, but entirely just attack on the ignorance of the times, combined with a wealth of suggestions for the increase of knowledge. In his passionate insistence upon the need of experiment and of collecting knowledge, the spirit of Aristotle lives again in him. ''Experiment, experiment,'' that is the burthen of Roger Bacon. Yet of Aristotle himself Roger Bacon fell foul. He fell foul of him because men, instead of facing facts boldly, sat in rooms and pored over the bad Latin translations which were then all that was available of the master. ''If I had my way,'' he wrote, in his intemperate fashion, ''I should burn all the books of Aristotle, for the study of them can only lead to a loss of time, produce error, and increase ignorance,'' a sentiment that Aristotle would probably have echoed could he have returned to a world in which his works were not so much read as worshipped—and that, as Roger Bacon showed, in these most abominable translations.

Throughout his books, a little disguised by the necessity of seeming to square it all with orthodoxy for fear of the prison and worse, Roger Bacon shouted to mankind, ''Cease to be ruled by dogmas and authorities; *look at the world!*'' Four chief sources of ignorance he denounced; respect for authority, custom, the sense of the ignorant crowd, and the vain proud unteachableness of our dispositions. Overcome but these, and a world of power would open to men:—

''Machines for navigating are possible without rowers, so that great ships suited to river or ocean, guided by one man, may be borne with greater speed than if they were full of men. Likewise cars may be made so that without a draught animal they may be moved *cum impetu inæstimabili,* as we deem the scythed chariots to have been from which antiquity fought. And flying machines are possible, so that a man may sit in the middle turning some device by which artificial wings may beat the air in the manner of a flying bird.''

Occam, Roger Bacon, these are the early precursors of a great movement in Europe away from ''Realism'' towards reality.

For a time the older influences fought against the naturalism of the new Nominalists. In 1339 Occam's books were put under a ban and Nominalism solemnly condemned. As late as 1473 an attempt, belated and unsuccessful, was made to bind teachers of Paris by an oath to teach Realism. It was only in the sixteenth century with the printing of books and the increase of intelligence that the movement from absolutism towards experiment became massive, and that one investigator began to cooperate with another.

Throughout the thirteenth and fourteenth centuries experimenting with material things was on the increase, items of knowledge were being won by men, but there was no interrelated advance. The work was done in a detached, furtive, and inglorious manner. A tradition of isolated investigation came into Europe from the Arabs, and a considerable amount of private and secretive research was carried on by the alchemists, for whom modern writers are a little too apt with their contempt. These alchemists were in close touch with the glass and metal workers and with the herbalists and medicine-makers of the times; they pried into many secrets of nature, but they were obsessed by "practical" ideas; they sought not knowledge, but power; they wanted to find out how to manufacture gold from cheaper materials, how to make men immortal by the elixir of life, and such-like vulgar dreams. Incidentally in their researches they learnt much about poisons, dyes, metallurgy, and the like; they discovered various refractory substances, and worked their way towards clear glass and so to lenses and optical instruments; but as scientific men tell us continually, and as "practical" men still refuse to learn, it is only when knowledge is sought for her own sake that she gives rich and unexpected gifts in any abundance to her servants. The world of to-day is still much more disposed to spend money on technical research than on pure science. Half the men in our scientific laboratories still dream of patents and secret processes. We live to-day largely in the age of alchemists, for all our sneers at their memory. The "business man" of to-day still thinks of research as a sort of alchemy.

Closely associated with the alchemists were the astrologers, who were also a "practical" race. They studied the stars—to tell fortunes. They lacked that broader faith and understanding which induces men simply to study the stars.

Not until the fifteenth century did the ideas which Roger Bacon first expressed begin to produce their first-fruits in new knowledge and a widening outlook. Then suddenly, as the sixteenth century dawned, and as the world recovered from the storm of social trouble that had followed the pestilences of the fourteenth century, Western Europe broke out into a galaxy of names that outshine the utmost scientific reputations of the best age of Greece. Nearly every nation contributed, the reader will note, for science knows no nationality.

One of the earliest and most splendid in this constellation is the Florentine, Leonardo da Vinci (1452-1519), a man with an almost miraculous vision for reality. He was a naturalist, an anatomist, an engineer, as well as a very great artist. He was the first modern to realize the true nature of fossils,[1] he made note-books of observations that still amaze us, he was convinced of the practicability of mechanical flight. Another great name is that of Copernicus, a Pole (1473-1543), who made the first clear analysis of the movements of the heavenly bodies and showed that the earth moves round the sun. Tycho Brahe (1546-1601), a Dane working at the university of Prague, rejected this latter belief, but his observations of celestial movements were of the utmost value to his successors, and especially to the German, Kepler (1571-1630). Galileo Galilei (1564-1642) was the founder of the science of dynamics. Before his time it was believed that a weight a hundred times greater than another would fall a hundred times as fast. Galileo denied this. Instead of arguing about it like a scholar and a gentleman, he put it to the coarse test of experiment by dropping two unequal weights from an upper gallery of the leaning tower of Pisa—to the horror of all erudite men. He made what was almost the first telescope, and he developed the astronomical views of Copernicus; but the church, still struggling gallantly against the light, decided that to believe that the earth was smaller and inferior to the sun made man and Christianity of no account, and diminished the importance of the Pope; so Galileo, under threats of dire punishment, when he was an old man of sixty-nine, was made to recant this view and put the earth back in its place as the immovable centre of the universe. He knelt before ten cardinals in scarlet, an assembly august enough to overawe truth itself, while he

[1] *Cp.* Chap. II, § 1, towards the end.

amended the creation he had disarranged. The story has it that as he rose from his knees, after repeating his recantation, he muttered, "*Eppur si Muove*"—"it moves nevertheless."

Newton (1642-1727) was born in the year of Galileo's death. By his discovery of the law of gravitation he completed the clear vision of the starry universe that we have to-day. But Newton carries us into the eighteenth century. He carries us too far for the present chapter. Among the earlier names, that of Dr. Gilbert (1540-1603), of Colchester, is pre-eminent. Roger Bacon had preached experiment, Gilbert was one of the first to practise it. There can be little doubt that his work, which was chiefly upon magnetism, helped to form the ideas of Francis Bacon, Lord Verulam (1561-1626), Lord Chancellor to James I of England. This Francis Bacon has been called the "Father of Experimental Philosophy," but of his share in the development of scientific work far too much has been made.[1] He was, says Sir R. A. Gregory, "not the founder but the apostle" of the scientific method. His greatest service to science was a fantastic book, *The New Atlantis.* "In his *New Atlantis,* Francis Bacon planned in somewhat fanciful language a palace of invention, a great temple of science, where the pursuit of knowledge in all its branches was to be organized on principles of the highest efficiency."

From this Utopian dream arose the Royal Society of London, which received a Royal Charter from Charles II of England in 1662. The essential use and virtue of this society was and is *publication.* Its formation marks a definite step from isolated inquiry towards co-operative work, from the secret and solitary investigations of the alchemist to the frank report and open discussion which is the life of the modern scientific process. For the true scientific method is this: to trust no statements without verification, to test all things as rigorously as possible, to keep no secrets, to attempt no monopolies, to give out one's best modestly and plainly, serving no other end but knowledge.

The long-slumbering science of anatomy was revived by Harvey (1578-1657), who demonstrated the circulation of the blood. . . . Presently the Dutchman, Leeuwenhoek (1632-1723) brought the first crude microscope to bear upon the hidden minutiæ of life.

These are but some of the brightest stars amidst that in-

[1] See Gregory's *Discovery,* chap. vi.

creasing multitude of men who have from the fifteenth century to our own time, with more and more collective energy and vigour, lit up our vision of the universe, and increased our power over the conditions of our lives.

§ 7

We have dealt thus fully with the recrudescence of scientific studies in the Middle Ages because of its ultimate importance in human affairs. In the long run, Roger Bacon is of more significance to mankind than any monarch of his time. But the contemporary world, for the most part, knew nothing of this smouldering activity in studies and lecture-rooms and alchemists' laboratories that was presently to alter all the conditions of life. The church did indeed take notice of what was afoot, but only because of the disregard of her conclusive decisions. She had decided that the earth was the very centre of God's creation, and that the Pope was the divinely appointed ruler of the earth. Men's ideas on these essential points, she insisted, must not be disturbed by any contrary teaching. So soon, however, as she had compelled Galileo to say that the world did not move she was satisfied; she does not seem to have realized how ominous it was for her that, after all, the earth did move.

Very great social as well as intellectual developments were in progress in Western Europe throughout this period of the later Middle Ages. But the human mind apprehends events far more vividly than changes; and men for the most part, then as now, kept on in their own traditions in spite of the shifting scene about them.

In an outline such as this it is impossible to crowd in the clustering events of history that do not clearly show the main process of human development, however bright and picturesque they may be. We have to record the steady growth of towns and cities, the reviving power of trade and money, the gradual re-establishment of law and custom, the extension of security, the supersession of private warfare that went on in Western Europe in the period between the first crusade and the sixteenth century. Of much that looms large in our national histories we cannot tell anything. We have no space for the story of the repeated attempts of the English kings to conquer Scotland and set themselves up as kings of France, nor of how the Norman English established themselves insecurely in Ireland (twelfth century), and how Wales was linked to the English crown (1282). All through the Middle Ages the struggle of England with Scotland and France was in progress; there were times when it seemed that Scotland was finally subjugated and when the English king held far more land in France than its titular sovereign. In the English histories this struggle with France is too often represented as a single-handed and almost successful attempt to conquer France. In reality it was a joint enterprise undertaken in concert first with the Flemings and Bavarians and afterwards with the powerful French vassal state of Burgundy to conquer and divide the patrimony of Hugh Capet. Of the English rout by the Scotch at Bannockburn (1314), and of William Wallace, and Robert the Bruce, the Scottish national heroes, of the battles of Crecy (1346) and Poitiers (1356) and Agincourt (1415) in France, which shine like stars in the English imagination, little battles in which sturdy bowmen through some sunny hours made a great havoc among French knights in armour, of the Black Prince and Henry V of England, and of how a peasant girl, Joan of Arc, the Maid of Orleans, drove the English out of her country again (1429-1430), this history relates nothing. For every country has such cherished national events. They are the ornamental tapestry of history, and no part of the building. Rajputana or Poland, Russia, Spain, Persia, and China can all match or outdo the utmost romance of western Europe, with equally adventurous knights and equally valiant princesses and equally stout fights against the odds. Nor can we tell how Louis XI of France (1461-1483), the son of Joan of Arc's Charles VII, brought Burgundy to heel and laid the foundations of a centralized French monarchy. It signifies more than in the thirteenth and fourteenth centuries, gunpowder, that Mongol gift, came to Europe so that the kings (Louis XI included) and the law, relying upon the support of the growing towns, were able to batter down the castles of the half-independent robber knights and barons of the earlier Middle Ages and consolidate a more centralized power. The fighting nobles and knights of the barbaric period disappear slowly from history during these centuries; the Crusades consumed them, such dynastic wars as the English Wars of the Roses killed them off, the arrows from the English long-bow pierced them and stuck out a yard behind, infantry so armed swept them from the stricken field; they became reconciled to trade and changed their nature. They disappeared in everything but a titular sense from the west and south of Europe before they disappeared from Germany. The knight in Germany remained a professional fighting man into the sixteenth century.

Between the eleventh and the fifteenth centuries in western Europe, and particularly in France and England, there sprang up like flowers a multitude of very distinctive and beautiful buildings, cathedrals, abbeys, and the like, the Gothic architecture. This lovely efflorescence marks the appearance of a body of craftsmen closely linked in its beginnings to the church. In Italy and Spain, too, the world was beginning to build freely and beautifully again. At first it was the wealth of the church that provided most of these buildings; then kings and merchants also began to build.

From the twelfth century onward, with the increase of trade, there was a great revival of town life throughout Europe. Prominent among these towns were Venice, with its dependents Ragusa and Corfu, Genoa, Verona, Bologna, Pisa, Florence, Naples, Milan, Marseilles, Lisbon, Barcelona, Narbonne, Tours, Orleans, Bordeaux, Paris, Ghent, Bruges, Boulogne, London, Oxford, Cambridge, Southampton, Dover, Antwerp, Hamburg, Bremen, Cologne, Mayence, Nuremberg, Munich, Leipzig, Magdeburg, Breslau, Stettin, Dantzig, Königsberg, Riga, Pskof, Novgorod, Wisby, and Bergen.

"A West German town, between 1400 and 1500,[1] embodied all the achievements of progress at that time, although from a modern standpoint much seems wanting. . . . The streets were mostly narrow and irregularly built, the houses chiefly of wood, while almost every burgher kept his cattle in the house, and the herd of swine which was driven every morning by the town herdsman to the pasture-ground formed an inevitable part of city life.[2] In Frankfort-on-Main it was unlawful after 1481 to keep swine in the Altstadt, but in the Neustadt and in Sachsenhausen this custom remained as a matter of course. It was only in 1645, after a corresponding attempt in 1556 had failed, that the swine-pens in the inner town were pulled down at

[1] From Dr. Tille in Helmolt's *History of the World.*

[2] Charles Dickens in his *American Notes* mentions swine in Broadway, New York, in the middle nineteenth century.

Leipzig. The rich burghers, who occasionally took part in the great trading companies, were conspicuously wealthy landowners, and had extensive courtyards with large barns inside the town walls. The most opulent of them owned those splendid patrician houses which we still admire even to-day. But even in the older towns most houses of the fifteenth century have disappeared; only here and there a building with open timber-work and overhanging storeys, as in Bacharach or Miltenburg, reminds us of the style of architecture then customary in the houses of burghers. The great bulk of the inferior population, who lived on mendicancy, or got a livelihood by the exercise of the inferior industries, inhabited squalid hovels outside the town; the town wall was often the only support for these wretched buildings. The internal fittings of the houses, even amongst the wealthy population, were very defective according to modern ideas; the Gothic style was as little suitable for the petty details of objects of luxury as it was splendidly adapted for the building of churches and town halls. The influence of the Renaissance added much to the comfort of the house.

"The fourteenth and fifteenth centuries saw the building of numerous Gothic town churches and town halls throughout Europe which still in many cases serve their original purpose. The power and prosperity of the towns find their best expression in these and in fortifications, with their strong towers and gateways. Every picture of a town of the sixteenth or later centuries shows conspicuously these latter erections for the protection and honour of the town. The town did many things which in our time are done by the State. Social problems were taken up by town administration or the corresponding municipal organization. The regulation of trade was the concern of the guilds in agreement with the council, the care of the poor belonged to the church, while the council looked after the protection of the town walls and the very necessary fire brigades. The council, mindful of its social duties, superintended the filling of the municipal granaries, in order to have supplies in years of scarcity. Such store-houses were erected in almost every town during the fifteenth century. Tariffs of prices for the sale of all wares, high enough to enable every artisan to make a good livelihood, and to give the purchaser a guarantee for the quality of the wares, were maintained. The town was also the chief capitalist; as a seller of annuities on

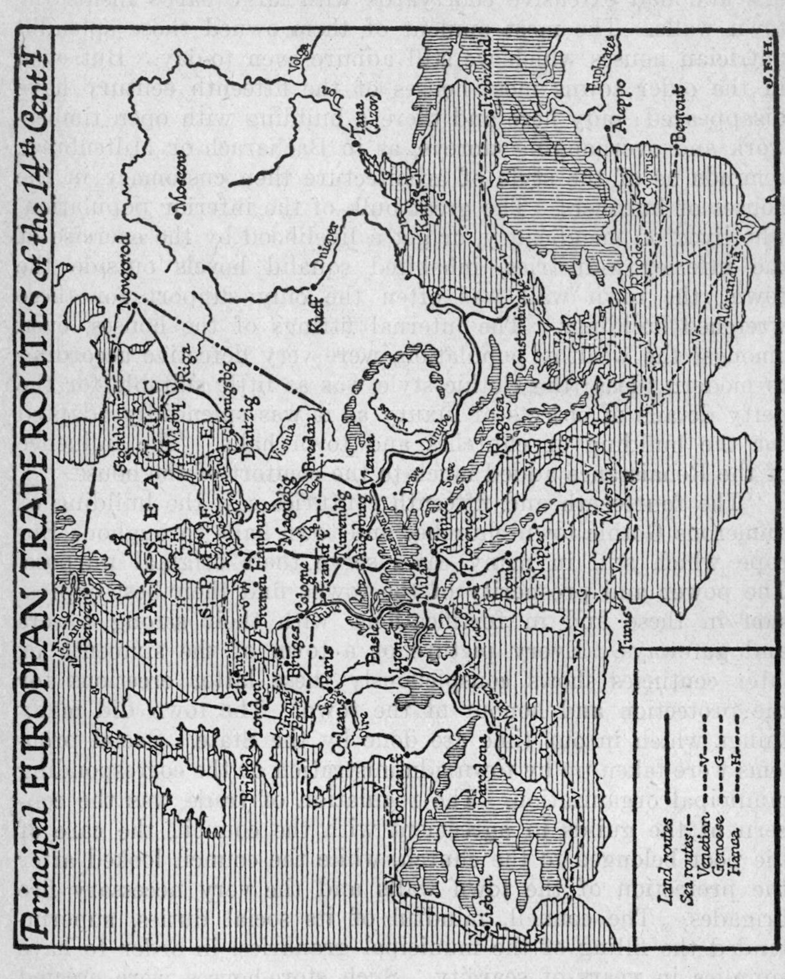
Principal EUROPEAN TRADE ROUTES of the 14th Centy
J.F.H.
Land routes
Sea routes:—
Venetian
Genoese
Hansa
Iceland
Bergen
Stockholm
Novgorod
Moscow
Wisby
Riga
Konigsbg
Dantzig
Kieff
Dnieper
Volga
Tana (Azov)
Kaffa
Trebizond
Euphrates
Aleppo
Beyrout
Cyprus
Rhodes
Alexandria
Constantinople
Danube
Ragusa
Messina
Naples
Rome
Florence
Venice
Milan
Vienna
Breslau
Vistula
Magdeburg
Hamburg
Bremen
Cologne
Nuremberg
Augsburg
Basle
Lyons
Paris
Bruges
London
Bristol
Orleans
Loire
Bordeaux
Barcelona
Lisbon
Tunis
Rhine
Elbe
Oder
Drave
Save
Theiss
H A N S E A T I C

lives and inheritances it was a banker and enjoyed unlimited credit. In return it obtained means for the construction of fortifications or for such occasions as the acquisition of sovereign rights from the hand of an impecunious prince."

For the most part these European towns were independent or quasi-independent aristocratic republics. Most admitted a vague overlordship on the part of the church, or of the emperor or of a king. Others were parts of kingdoms, or even the capitals of dukes or kings. In such cases their internal freedom was maintained by a royal or imperial charter. In England the Royal City of Westminster on the Thames stood cheek by jowl with the walled city of London, into which the King came only with ceremony and permission. The entirely free Venctian republic ruled an empire of dependent islands and trading ports, rather after the fashion of the Athenian republic. Genoa also stood alone. The Germanic towns of the Baltic and North Sea from Riga to Middelburg in Holland, Dortmund, and Cologne were loosely allied in a confederation, the confederation of the Hansa towns, under the leadership of Hamburg, Bremen, and Lubeck, a confederation which was still more loosely attached to the empire. This confederation, which included over seventy towns in all, and which had depôts in Novgorod, Bergen, London, and Bruges, did much to keep the northern seas clean of piracy, that curse of the Mediterranean and of the Eastern seas. The Eastern Empire throughout its last phase, from the Ottoman conquest of its European hinterland in the fourteenth and early fifteenth century until its fall in 1453, was practically only the trading town of Constantinople, a town state like Genoa or Venice, except that it was encumbered by a corrupt imperial court.

The fullest and most splendid developments of this city life of the later Middle Ages occurred in Italy. After the end of the Hohenstaufen line in the thirteenth century, the hold of the Holy Roman Empire upon North and Central Italy weakened, although, as we shall tell, German Emperors were still crowned as kings and emperors in Italy up to the time of Charles V (*circ.* 1530). There arose a number of quasi-independent city states to the north of Rome, the papal capital. South Italy and Sicily, however, remained under foreign dominion. Genoa and her rival, Venice, were the great trading seaports of this time; their noble palaces, their lordly paintings, still win our admiration. Milan, at the foot of the St. Gothard pass, revived to wealth and power. Inland was Florence, a trading and financial centre which, under the almost monarchical rule of the Medici family in the fifteenth century, enjoyed a second "Periclean age." But already before the time of these cultivated Medici "bosses," Florence had produced much beautiful art. Giotto's tower (Giotto, born 1266, died 1337) and the Duomo (by Brunellesco, born 1377, died 1446) already existed. Towards the end of the fourteenth century Florence became the centre of the rediscovery, restoration, and imitation of antique art (the "Renaissance" in its narrower sense). Artistic productions, unlike philosophical thought and scientific discovery, are the ornaments and expression rather than the creative substance of history, and here we cannot attempt to trace the development of the art of Filippo Lippi, Botticelli, Donatello (died 1466), Leonardo da Vinci (died 1519), Michelangelo (1475-1564), and Raphael (died 1520). Of the scientific speculation of Leonardo we have already had occasion to speak.

§ 8

In 1453, as we have related, Constantinople fell. Throughout the next century the Turkish pressure upon Europe was heavy and continuous. The boundary line between Mongol and Aryan, which had lain somewhere east of the Pamirs in the days of Pericles, had receded now to Hungary. Constantinople had long been a mere island of Christians in a Turk-ruled Balkan peninsula. Its fall did much to interrupt the trade with the East.

Of the two rival cities of the Mediterranean, Venice was generally on much better terms with the Turks than Genoa. Every intelligent Genoese sailor fretted at the trading monopoly of Venice, and tried to invent some way of getting through it or round it. And there were now new peoples taking to the sea trade, and disposed to look for new ways to the old markets because the ancient routes were closed to them. The Portuguese, for example, were developing an Atlantic coasting trade. The Atlantic was waking up again after a vast period of neglect that dated from the Roman murder of Carthage. It is rather a delicate matter to decide whether the western European was pushing out into the Atlantic or whether he was being pushed out into it by the Turk, who lorded it in the Mediterranean until the Battle of Lepanto (1571). The Venetian and Genoese ships were creeping round to Antwerp, and the Hansa town seamen were coming south and extending their range. And there were considerable developments of seamanship and shipbuilding in progress. The Mediterranean is a sea for galleys and coasting. But upon the Atlantic Ocean and the North Sea winds are more prevalent, seas run higher, the shore is often a danger rather than a refuge. The high seas called for the sailing ship, and in the fourteenth and fifteenth centuries it appears keeping its course by the compass and the stars.

By the thirteenth century the Hansa merchants were already sailing regularly from Bergen across the grey cold seas to the Northmen in Iceland. In Iceland men knew of Greenland, and adventurous voyagers had long ago found a further land beyond, Vinland, where the climate was pleasant and where men could settle if they chose to cut themselves off from the rest of human kind. This Vinland was either Nova Scotia or, what is more probable, New England.

All over Europe in the fifteenth century merchants and sailors were speculating about new ways to the East. The Portuguese, unaware that Pharaoh Necho had solved the problem ages ago, were asking whether it was not possible to go round to India by the coast of Africa. Their ships followed in the course that Hanno took to Cape Verde (1445). They put out to sea to the west and found the Canary Isles, Madeira, and the Azores.[1] That was a fairly long stride across the Atlantic. In 1486 a Portuguese, Diaz, reported that he had rounded the south of Africa. . . .

A certain Genoese, Christopher Columbus, began to think more and more of what is to us a very obvious and natural enterprise, but which strained the imagination of the fifteenth century to the utmost, a voyage due west across the Atlantic. At that time nobody knew of the existence of America as a separate continent. Columbus knew that the world was a sphere, but he underestimated its size; the travels of Marco Polo had given him an exaggerated idea of the extent of Asia,

[1] In these maritime adventures in the eastern Atlantic and the west African coast the Portuguese were preceded in the thirteenth, fourteenth, and early fifteenth centuries by Normans, Catalonians, and Genoese.

and he supposed therefore that Japan, with its reputation for a great wealth of gold, lay across the Atlantic in about the position of Mexico. He had made various voyages in the Atlantic; he had been to Iceland and perhaps heard of Vinland, which must have greatly encouraged these ideas of his, and this project of sailing into the sunset became the ruling purpose of his life. He was a penniless man, some accounts say he was a bankrupt, and his only way of securing a ship was to get someone to entrust him with a command. He went first to King John II of Portugal, who listened to him, made difficulties, and then arranged for an expedition to start without his knowledge, a purely Portuguese expedition. This highly diplomatic attempt to steal a march on an original man failed, as it deserved to fail; the crew became mutinous, the captain lost heart and returned (1483). Columbus then went to the Court of Spain.

At first he could get no ship and no powers. Spain was assailing Granada, the last foothold of the Moslems in western Europe. Most of Spain had been recovered by the Christians between the eleventh and the thirteenth century; then had come a pause; and now all Spain, united by the marriage of Ferdinand of Aragon and Isabella of Castile, was setting itself to the completion of the Christian conquest. Despairing of Spanish help, Columbus sent his brother Bartholomew to Henry VII of England, but the adventure did not attract that canny monarch. Finally in 1492 Granada fell, and then, helped by some merchants of the town of Palos, Columbus got his ships, three ships, of which only one, the *Santa Maria,* of 100 tons burthen, was decked. The two other were open boats of half that tonnage.

The little expedition—it numbered altogether eighty-eight men!—went south to the Canaries, and then stood out across the unknown seas, in beautiful weather and with a helpful wind.

The story of that momentous voyage of two months and nine days must be read in detail to be appreciated. The crew was full of doubts and fears; they might, they feared, sail on for ever. They were comforted by seeing some birds, and later on by finding a pole worked with tools, and a branch with strange berries. At ten o'clock, on the night of October 11th, 1492, Columbus saw a light ahead; the next morning land was sighted, and, while the day was still young, Columbus landed on the shores of the new world, richly apparelled and bearing the royal banner of Spain. . . .

Early in 1493 Columbus returned to Europe. He brought gold, cotton, strange beasts and birds, and two wild-eyed painted Indians to be baptized. He had not found Japan, it was thought, but India. The islands he had found were called therefore the West Indies. The same year he sailed again with a great expedition of seventeen ships and fifteen hundred men, with the express permission of the Pope to take possession of these new lands for the Spanish crown. . . .

We cannot tell of his experiences as Governor of this Spanish colony, nor how he was superseded and put in chains. In a little while a swarm of Spanish adventurers were exploring the new lands. But it is interesting to note that Columbus died ignorant of the fact that he had discovered a new continent. He believed to the day of his death that he had sailed round the world to Asia.

The news of his discoveries caused a great excitement throughout western Europe. It spurred the Portuguese to fresh attempts to reach India by the South African route. In 1497, Vasco da Gama sailed from Lisbon to Zanzibar, and thence, with an Arab pilot, he struck across the Indian Ocean to Calicut in India. In 1515 there were Portuguese ships in Java and the Moluccas. In 1519 a Portuguese sailor, Magellan, in the employment of the Spanish King, coasted to the south of South America, passed through the dark and forbidding "Strait of Magellan," and so came into the Pacific Ocean, which had already been sighted by Spanish explorers who had crossed the Isthmus of Panama.

Magellan's expedition continued across the Pacific Ocean westward. This was a far more heroic voyage than that of Columbus; for *eight and ninety days* Magellan sailed unflinchingly over that vast, empty ocean, sighting nothing but two little desert islands. The crews were rotten with scurvy; there was little water and that bad, and putrid biscuit to eat. Rats were hunted eagerly; cowhide was gnawed and sawdust devoured to stay the pangs of hunger. In this state the expedition reached the Ladrones. They discovered the Philippines, and here Magellan was killed in a fight with the natives. Several other captains were murdered. Five ships had started with Magellan in August 1519 and two hundred and eighty men;

in July 1522 the *Vittoria,* with a remnant of one and thirty men aboard, returned up the Atlantic to her anchorage near the Mole of Seville, in the river Guadalquivir—the first ship that ever circumnavigated this planet.

The English and French and Dutch and the sailors of the Hansa towns came rather later into this new adventure of exploration. They had not the same keen interest in the eastern trade. And when they did come in, their first efforts were directed to sailing round the north of America as Magellan had sailed round the south, and to sailing round the north of Asia as Vasco da Gama had sailed round the south of Africa. Both these enterprises were doomed to failure by the nature of things. Both in America and the East, Spain and Portugal had half a century's start of England and France and Holland. And Germany never started. The King of Spain was Emperor of Germany in those crucial years, and the Pope had given the monopoly of America to Spain, and not simply to Spain, but to the kingdom of Castile. This must have restrained both Germany and Holland at first from American adventures. The Hansa towns were quasi-independent; they had no monarch behind them to support them, and no unity among themselves for so big an enterprise as oceanic exploration. It was the misfortune of Germany, and perhaps of the world, that, as we will presently tell, a storm of warfare exhausted her when all the Western powers were going to this newly opened school of trade and administration upon the high seas.

Slowly throughout the sixteenth century the immense good fortune of Castile unfolded itself before the dazzled eyes of Europe. She had found a new world, abounding in gold and silver and wonderful possibilities of settlement. It was all hers, because the Pope had said so. The Court of Rome, in an access of magnificence, had divided this new world of strange lands which was now opening out to the European imagination, between the Spanish, who were to have everything west of a line 370 leagues west of the Cape Verde islands, and the Portuguese, to whom everything east of this line was given.

At first the only people encountered by the Spaniards in America were savages of a Mongoloid type. Many of these savages were cannibals. It is a misfortune for science that the first Europeans to reach America were these rather incurious Spaniards, without any scientific passion, thirsty for gold, and

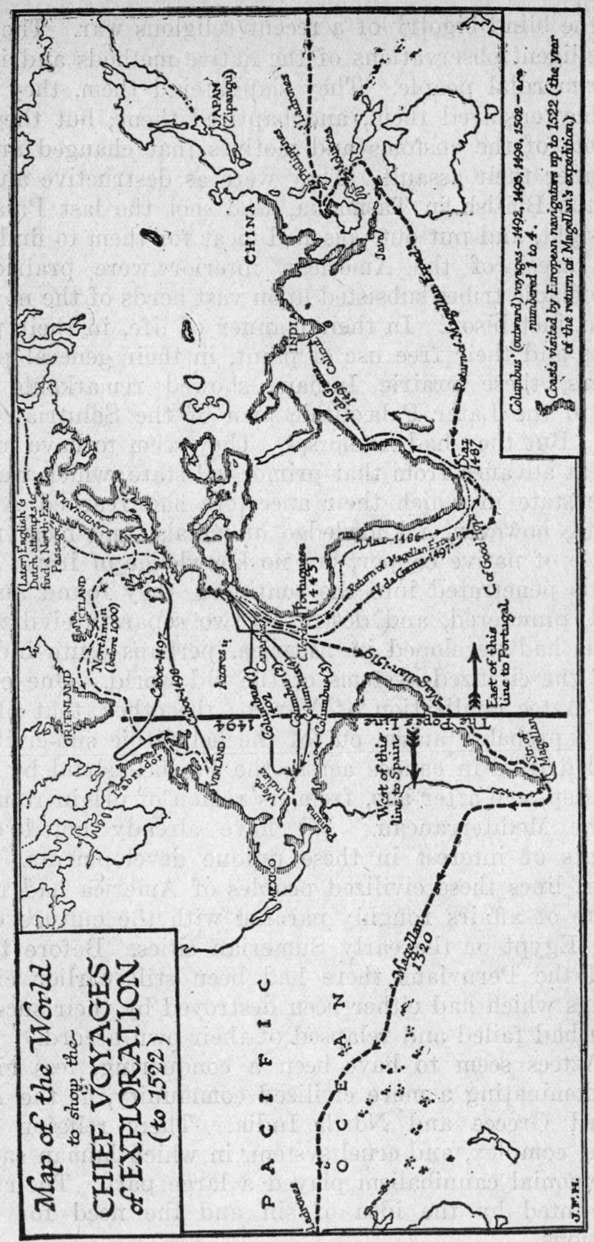
Map of the World
to show the
CHIEF VOYAGES
of EXPLORATION
(to 1522)
Columbus' (outward) voyages—1492, 1493, 1498, 1502—are numbered 1 to 4.
Coasts visited by European navigators up to 1522 (the year of the return of Magellan's expedition)
PACIFIC
OCEAN
CHINA
INDIA
JAPAN (Zipangu)
Ladrones
Philippines
Moluccas
Java
Calicut
V. da Gama 1498
Return of Magellan Exped.
Diaz 1487
C. of Good Hope
Diaz 1486
Return of Magellan Exped.
V. da Gama 1497
Portuguese 1445
C. Verde
Canaries
Azores
Magellan 1519
The Pope's Line
1494
East of this line to Portugal
West of this line to Spain
Str. of Magellan
Magellan 1520
Ladrones
Panama
MEXICO
West Indies
Columbus (1) 1492
Columbus (2)
Columbus (3)
Columbus (4)
VINLAND
Labrador
GREENLAND
Cabot 1497
Cabot 1498
Northmen (before 1000)
ICELAND
SCANDINAVIA
(Later) English & Dutch attempts to find a North-East Passage
J.F.H.

full of the blind bigotry of a recent religious war. They made few intelligent observations of the native methods and ideas of these primordial people. They slaughtered them, they robbed them, they enslaved them, and baptized them; but they made small note of the customs and motives that changed and vanished under their assault. They were as destructive and reckless as the British in Tasmania, who shot the last Palæolithic men at sight, and put out poisoned meat for them to find.

Great areas of the American interior were prairie land, whose nomadic tribes subsisted upon vast herds of the now practically extinct bison. In their manner of life, in their painted garments and their free use of paint, in their general physical characters, these prairie Indians showed remarkable resemblances to the Later Palæolithic men of the Solutrian age in Europe. But they had no horses. They seem to have made no very great advance from that primordial state, which was probably the state in which their ancestors had reached America. They had, however, a knowledge of metals, and most notably a free use of native copper, but no knowledge of iron. As the Spaniards penetrated into the continent, they found and they attacked, plundered, and destroyed two separate civilized systems that had developed in America, perhaps quite independently of the civilized systems of the old world. One of them was the Aztec civilization of Mexico; the other, that of Peru. They had probably arisen out of the heliolithic sub-civilization that had drifted in canoes across the Pacific, island by island, step by step, age after age, from its region of origin round and about the Mediterranean. We have already noted one or two points of interest in these unique developments. Along their own lines these civilized peoples of America had reached to a state of affairs roughly parallel with the culture of predynastic Egypt or the early Sumerian cities. Before the Aztecs and the Peruvians there had been still earlier civilized beginnings which had either been destroyed by their successors, or which had failed and relapsed of their own accord.

The Aztecs seem to have been a conquering, less civilized people, dominating a more civilized community, as the Aryans dominated Greece and North India. Their religion was a primitive, complex, and cruel system, in which human sacrifices and ceremonial cannibalism played a large part. Their minds were haunted by the idea of sin and the need for bloody propitiations.

The Aztec civilization was destroyed by an expedition under Cortez. He had eleven ships, four hundred Europeans, two hundred Indians, sixteen horses, and fourteen guns. But in Yucatan he picked up a stray Spaniard who had been a captive with the Indians for some years, and who had more or less learnt various Indian languages, and knew that the Aztec rule was deeply resented by many of its subjects. It was in alliance with these that Cortez advanced over the mountains into the valley of Mexico (1519). How he entered Mexico, how its monarch, Montezuma, was killed by his own people for favouring the Spaniards, how Cortez was besieged in Mexico, and escaped with the loss of his guns and horses, and how after a terrible retreat to the coast he was able to return and subjugate the whole land, is a romantic and picturesque story which we cannot even attempt to tell here. The population of Mexico to this day is largely of native blood, but Spanish has replaced the native languages, and such culture as exists is Catholic and Spanish.

The still more curious Peruvian state fell a victim to another adventurer, Pizarro. He sailed from the Isthmus of Panama in 1530, with an expedition of a hundred and sixty-eight Spaniards. Like Cortez in Mexico, he availed himself of the native dissensions to secure possession of the doomed state. Like Cortez, too, who had made a captive and tool of Montezuma, he seized the Inca of Peru by treachery, and attempted to rule in his name. Here again we cannot do justice to the tangle of subsequent events, the ill-planned insurrections of the natives, the arrival of Spanish reinforcements from Mexico, and the reduction of the state to a Spanish province. Nor can we tell much more of the swift spread of Spanish adventurers over the rest of America, outside the Portuguese reservation of Brazil. To begin with, each story is nearly always a story of adventurers and of cruelty and loot. The Spaniards ill-treated the natives, they quarrelled among themselves, the law and order of Spain were months and years away from them; it was only very slowly that the phase of violence and conquest passed into a phase of government and settlement. But long before there was much order in America, a steady stream of gold and silver began to flow across the Atlantic to the Spanish government and people.

After the first violent treasure hunt came plantation and the working of mines. With that arose the earliest labour difficulty in the new world. At first the Indians were enslaved with much brutality and injustice; but to the honour of the Spaniards this did not go uncriticized. The natives found champions, and

very valiant champions, in the Dominican Order and in a secular priest, Las Casas, who was for a time a planter and slave-owner in Cuba until his conscience smote him. An importation of negro slaves from West Africa also began quite early in the sixteenth century. After some retrogression, Mexico, Brazil, and Spanish South America began to develop into great slave-holding, wealth-producing lands. . . .

We cannot tell here, as we would like to do, of the fine civilizing work done in South America, and more especially among the natives, by the Franciscans, and presently by the Jesuits, who came into America in the latter half of the sixteenth century (after 1549). . . .

So it was that Spain rose to a temporary power and prominence in the world's affairs. It was a very sudden and very memorable rise. From the eleventh century this infertile and corrugated peninsula had been divided against itself, its Christian population had sustained a perpetual conflict with the Moors; then by what seems like an accident it achieved unity just in time to reap the first harvest of benefit from the discovery of America. Before that time Spain had always been a poor country; it is a poor country to-day, almost its only wealth lies in its mines. For a century, however, through its monopoly of the gold and silver of America, it dominated the world. The east and centre of Europe were still overshadowed by the Turk and Mongol; the discovery of America was itself a consequence of the Turkish conquests; very largely through the Mongolian inventions of compass and paper, and under the stimulus of travel in Asia and of the growing knowledge of eastern Asiatic wealth and civilization, came this astonishing blazing up of the mental, physical, and social energies of the "Atlantic fringe." For close in the wake of Portugal and Spain came France and England, and presently Holland, each in its turn taking up the rôle of expansion and empire overseas. The centre of interest for European history which once lay in the Levant shifts now from the Alps and the Mediterranean Sea to the Atlantic. For some centuries the Turkish Empire and Central Asia and China are relatively neglected by the limelight of the European historian. Nevertheless, these central regions of the world remain central, and their welfare and participation is necessary to the permanent peace of mankind.

§ 9

And now let us consider the political consequences of this vast release and expansion of European ideas in the fourteenth and fifteenth centuries with the new development of science, the exploration of the world, the great dissemination of knowledge through paper and printing, and the spread of a new craving for freedom and equality. How was it affecting the mentality of the courts and kings that directed the formal affairs of mankind? We have already shown how the hold of the Catholic church upon the consciences of men was weakening at this time. Only the Spaniards, fresh from a long and finally successful religious war against Islam, had any great enthusiasm left for the church. The Turkish conquests and the expansion of the known world robbed the Roman Empire of its former prestige of universality. The old mental and moral framework of Europe was breaking up. What was happening to the dukes, princes, and kings of the old dispensation during this age of change?

In England, as we shall tell later, very subtle and interesting tendencies were leading towards a new method in government, the method of parliament, that was to spread later on over nearly all the world. But of these tendencies the world at large was as yet practically unconscious in the sixteenth century.

Few monarchs have left us intimate diaries; to be a monarch and to be frank are incompatible feats; monarchy is itself necessarily a pose. The historian is obliged to speculate about the contents of the head that wears a crown as best he can. No doubt regal psychology has varied with the ages. We have, however, the writings of a very able man of this period who set himself to study and expound the arts of kingcraft as they were understood in the later fifteenth century. This was the celebrated Florentine, Niccolo Machiavelli (1469-1527). He was of good birth and reasonable fortune, and he had entered the public employment of the republic by the time he was twenty-five. For eighteen years he was in the Florentine diplomatic service; he was engaged upon a number of embassies, and in 1500 he was sent to France to deal with the French king. From 1502 to 1512 he was the right-hand man of the gonfalonier (the life president) of Florence, Soderini. Machiavelli reorganized the Florentine army, wrote speeches for the gonfalonier, was indeed the ruling intelligence in Florentine affairs. When Soderini, who had leant upon the French, was overthrown by the Medici family whom the Spanish supported, Machiavelli, though he tried to transfer his services to the victors, was tortured on the rack and expelled. He took up his quarters in a villa near San Casciano, twelve miles or so from Florence, and there entertained himself partly by collecting and writing salacious stories to a friend in Rome, and partly by writing books about Italian politics in which he could no longer play a part. Just as we owe Marco Polo's book of travels to his imprisonment, so we owe Machiavelli's *Prince,* his *Florentine History,* and *The Art of War* to his downfall and the boredom of San Casciano.

The enduring value of these books lies in the clear idea they give us of the quality and limitations of the ruling minds of this age. Their atmosphere was his atmosphere. If he brought an exceptionally keen intelligence to their business, that merely throws it into a brighter light.

His susceptible mind had been greatly impressed by the cunning, cruelty, audacity, and ambition of Cæsar Borgia, the Duke of Valentino, in whose camp he had spent some months as an envoy. In his *Prince* he idealized this dazzling person. Cæsar Borgia (1476-1507), the reader must understand, was the son of Pope Alexander VI, Rodrigo Borgia (1492-1503). The reader will perhaps be startled at the idea of a Pope having a son, but this, we must remember, was a pre-reformation Pope. The Papacy at this time was in a mood of moral relaxation, and though Alexander was, as a priest, pledged to live unmarried, this did not hinder him from living openly with a sort of unmarried wife, and devoting the resources of Christendom to the advancement of his family. Cæsar was a youth of spirit even for the times in which he lived; he had early caused his elder brother to be murdered, and also the husband of his sister, Lucrezia. He had indeed betrayed and murdered a number of people. With his father's assistance he had become duke of a wide area of Central Italy when Machiavelli visited him. He had shown little or no military ability, but considerable dexterity and administrative power. His magnificence was of the most temporary sort. When presently his father died, it collapsed like a pricked bladder. Its unsoundness was not evident to Machiavelli. Our chief interest in Cæsar Borgia is that he realized Machiavelli's highest ideals of a superb and successful prince.

Much has been written to show that Machiavelli had wide and noble intentions behind his political writings, but all such attempts to ennoble him will leave the sceptical reader, who insists on reading the lines instead of reading imaginary things between the lines of Machiavelli's work, cold towards him. This man manifestly had no belief in any righteousness at all, no belief in a God ruling over the world or in a God in men's hearts, no understanding of the power of conscience in men. Not for him were Utopian visions of world-wide human order, or attempts to realize the *City of God.* Such things he did not want. It seemed to him that to get power, to gratify one's desires and sensibilities and hates, to swagger triumphantly in the world, must be the crown of human desire. Only a prince could fully realize such a life. Some streak of timidity or his sense of the poorness of his personal claims had evidently made him abandon such dreams for himself; but at least he might hope to serve a prince, to live close to the glory, to share the plunder and the lust and the gratified malice. He might even make himself indispensable! He set himself, therefore, to become an "expert" in prince-craft. He assisted Soderini to fail. When he was racked and rejected by the Medicis, and had no further hopes of being even a successful court parasite, he wrote these handbooks of cunning to show what a clever servant some prince had lost. His ruling thought, his great contribution to political literature, was that the moral obligations upon ordinary men cannot bind princes.

There is a disposition to ascribe the virtue of patriotism to Machiavelli because he suggested that Italy, which was weak and divided—she had been invaded by the Turks and saved from conquest only by the death of the Sultan Muhammad, and she was being fought over by the French and Spanish as though she was something inanimate—might be united and strong; but he saw in that possibility only a great opportunity for a prince. And he advocated a national army only because he saw the Italian method of carrying on war by hiring bands of foreign mercenaries was a hopeless one. At any time such troops might go over to a better paymaster or decide to plunder the state they protected. He had been deeply impressed by the victories of the Swiss over the Milanese, but he never fathomed the secret of the free spirit that made those victories possible. The Florentine militia he created was a complete failure. He was a man born blind to the qualities that make peoples free and nations great.

Yet this morally blind man was living in a little world of morally blind men. It is clear that his style of thought was the style of thought of the court of his time. Behind the princes of the new states that had grown up out of the wreckage of the empire and the failure of the Church, there were everywhere chancellors and secretaries and trusted ministers of the Machiavellian type. Cromwell, for instance, the minister of Henry VIII of England after his breach with Rome, regarded Machiavelli's *Prince* as the quintessence of political wisdom.

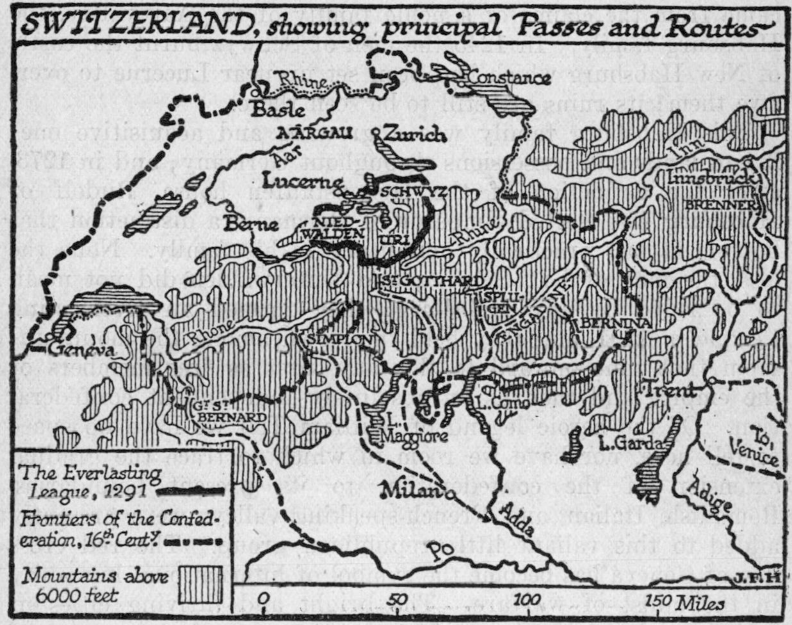

When the princes were themselves sufficiently clever they, too, were Machiavellian. They were scheming to outdo one another, to rob weaker contemporaries, to destroy rivals, so that they might for a brief interval swagger. They had little or no vision of any scheme of human destinies greater than this game they played against one another.

§ 10

It is interesting to note that this Swiss infantry which had so impressed Machiavelli was no part of the princely system of Europe. At the very centre of the European system there had arisen a little confederation of free states, the Swiss Confederation, which after some centuries of nominal adhesion to the Holy Roman Empire, became frankly republican in 1499. As early as the thirteenth century, the peasant farmers of three valleys round about the Lake of Lucerne took it into their heads that they would dispense with an overlord and manage their own affairs in their own fashion. Their chief trouble came from the claims of a noble family of the Aar valley, the Habsburg family. In 1245 the men of Schwyz burnt the castle of New Habsburg which had been set up near Lucerne to overawe them; its ruins are still to be seen there.

This Habsburg family was a growing and acquisitive one; it had lands and possessions throughout Germany; and in 1273, after the extinction of the Hohenstaufen house, Rudolf of Habsburg was elected Emperor of Germany, a distinction that became at last practically hereditary in his family. None the less, the men of Uri, Schwyz, and Unterwalden did not mean to be ruled by any Habsburg; they formed an Everlasting League in 1291, and they held their own among the mountains from that time onward to this day, first as free members of the empire and then as an absolutely independent confederation. Of the heroic legend of William Tell we have no space to tell here, nor have we room in which to trace the gradual extension of the confederation to its present boundaries. Romanish, Italian, and French-speaking valleys were presently added to this valiant little republican group. The red cross flag of Geneva has become the symbol of international humanity in the midst of warfare. The bright and thriving cities of Switzerland have been a refuge for free men from a score of tyrannies.

§ 11A

Most of the figures that stand out in history, do so through some exceptional personal quality, good or bad, that makes them more significant than their fellows. But there was born at Ghent in Belgium in 1500 a man of commonplace abilities and melancholy temperament, the son of a mentally defective mother who had been married for reasons of state, who was, through no fault of his own, to become the focus of the accumulating stresses of Europe. The historian must give him a quite unmerited and accidental prominence side by side with such marked individualities as Alexander and Charlemagne and Frederick II. This was the Emperor Charles V. For a time he had an air of being the greatest monarch in Europe since Charlemagne. Both he and his illusory greatness were the results of the matrimonial statecraft of his grandfather, the Emperor Maximilian I (born 1459, died 1519).

Some families have fought, others have intrigued their way to world power; the Habsburg married their way. Maximilian began his career with the inheritance of the Habsburgs, Austria, Styria, part of Alsace and other districts; he married—the lady's name scarcely matters to us—the Netherlands and Burgundy. Most of Burgundy slipped from him after his first wife's death, but the Netherlands he held. Then he tried unsuccessfully to marry Brittany. He became Emperor in succession to his father, Frederick III, in 1493, and married the duchy of Milan. Finally he married his son to the weak-minded daughter of Ferdinand and Isabella, the Ferdinand and Isabella of Columbus, who not only reigned over a freshly united Spain, and over Sardinia and the kingdom of the two Sicilies, but by virtue of the papal gifts to Castile, over all America west of Brazil. So it was that Charles, his grandson, inherited most of the American continent and between a third and a half of what the Turks had left of Europe. The father of Charles died in 1506, and Maximilian did his best to secure his grandson's election to the imperial throne.

Charles succeeded to the Netherlands in 1506; he became practically king of the Spanish dominions, his mother being imbecile, when his grandfather Ferdinand died in 1516; and his grandfather Maximilian dying in 1516, he was in 1520 elected Emperor at the still comparatively tender age of twenty.

His election as Emperor was opposed by the young and brilliant French King, Francis I, who had succeeded to the French throne in 1515 at the age of twenty-one. The candidature of Francis was supported by Leo X (1513), who also requires from us the epithet brilliant. It was indeed an age of brilliant monarchs. It was the age of Baber in India (1526-1530) and Suleiman in Turkey (1520). Both Leo and Francis dreaded the concentration of so much power in the hands of one man as the election of Charles threatened. The only other monarch who seemed to matter in Europe was Henry VIII,

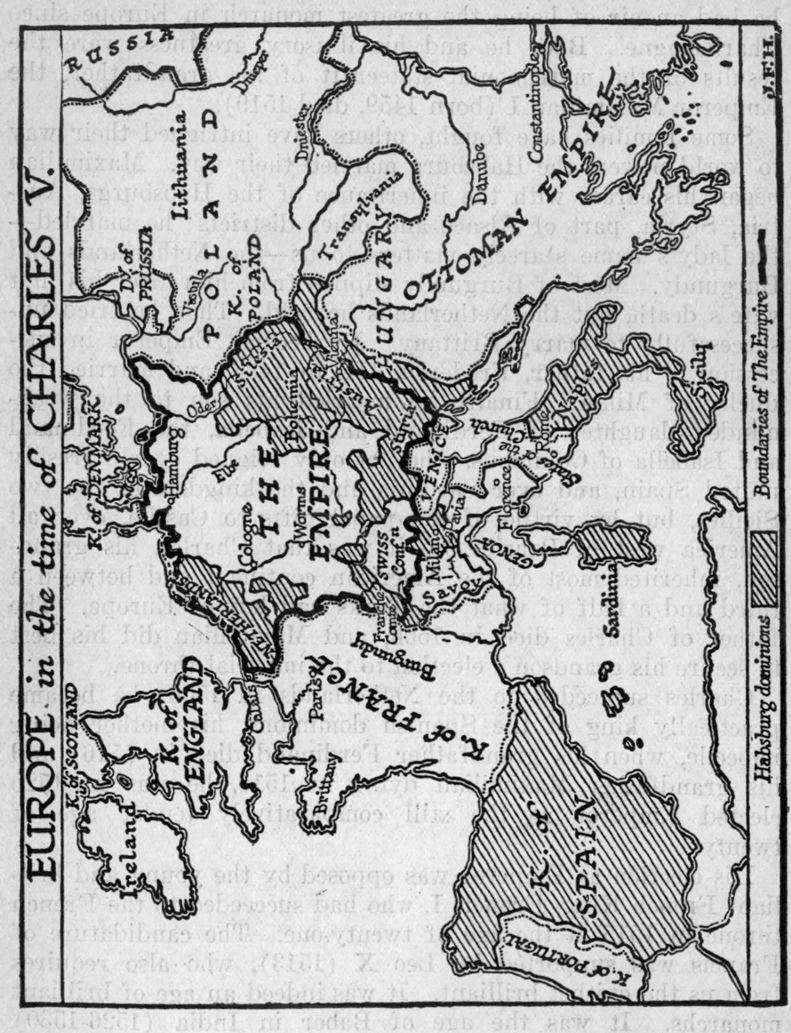
EUROPE in the time of CHARLES V.
RUSSIA
Dnieper
Lithuania
POLAND
D.y of PRUSSIA
Vistula
K. of POLAND
Dniester
Transylvania
HUNGARY
Danube
Constantinople
OTTOMAN EMPIRE
Silesia
Oder
Bohemia
Vienna
Austria
Styria
K. of DENMARK
Hamburg
Elbe
THE EMPIRE
Cologne
Worms
SWISS Conf.n
Milan
Pavia
VENICE
Florence
Rome
States of the Church
Naples
Sicily
GENOA
Savoy
Franche Comté
NETHERLANDS
Burgundy
K. of FRANCE
Paris
Calais
Brittany
K. of ENGLAND
K. of SCOTLAND
Ireland
Sardinia
K. of SPAIN
K. of PORTUGAL
Habsburg dominions
Boundaries of The Empire
J.F.H.

who had become King of England in 1509 at the age of eighteen. He also offered himself as a candidate for the empire, and the imaginative English reader may amuse himself by working out the possible consequences of such an election. There was much scope for diplomacy in this triangle of kings. Charles on his way from Spain to Germany visited England and secured the support of Henry against Francis by bribing his minister, Cardinal Wolsey. Henry also made a great parade of friendship with Francis, there was feasting, tournaments, and such-like antiquated gallantries in France, in a courtly picnic known to historians as the Field of the Cloth of Gold (1520). Knighthood was becoming a picturesque affectation in the sixteenth century. The Emperor Maximilian I is still called "the last of the knights" by German historians.

Luther
(after Cranach)

The election of Charles was secured, it is to be noted, by a vast amount of bribery. He had as his chief supporters and creditors the great German business house of the Fuggers. That large treatment of money and credit which we call finance, which had gone out of European political life with the collapse of the Roman Empire, was now coming back to power. This appearance of the Fuggers, whose houses and palaces outshone those of the emperors, marks the upward movement of forces that had begun two or three centuries earlier in Cahors in France and in Florence and other Italian towns. Money, public debts, and social unrest and discontent re-enter upon the miniature stage of this *Outline*. Charles V was not so much a Habsburg as a Fugger emperor.

For a time this fair, not very intelligent-looking young man with the thick upper lip and long, clumsy chin—features which still afflict his descendants—was largely a puppet in the hands of his ministers. Able servants after the order of Machiavelli guided him at first in the arts of kingship. Then in a slow but effectual way he began to assert himself. He was confronted at the very outset of his reign in Germany with the perplexing dissensions of Christendom. The revolt against the papal rule which had been going on since the days of Huss and Wycliffe had been recently exasperated by a new and unusually cynical selling of indulgences to raise money for the completion of St. Peter's at Rome. A monk named Luther, who had been consecrated as a priest, who had taken to reading the Bible, and who, while visiting Rome on the business of his order, had been much shocked by the levity and worldly splendour of the Papacy, had come forward against these papal expedients at Wittenberg (1517), offering disputation and propounding certain theses. An important controversy ensued. At first Luther carried on this controversy in Latin, but presently took to German, and speedily had the people in a ferment. Charles found this dispute raging when he came from Spain to Germany. He summoned an assembly or "diet" of the empire at Worms on the Rhine. To this, Luther, who had been asked to recant his views by Pope Leo X, and who had refused to do so, was summoned. He came, and, entirely in the spirit of Huss, refused to recant unless he was convinced of his error by logical argument or the authority of Scripture. But his protectors among the princes were too powerful for him to suffer the fate of John Huss.

Here was a perplexing situation for the young Emperor. There is reason to suppose that he was inclined at first to support Luther against the Pope. Leo X had opposed the election of Charles, and was friendly with his rival, Francis I. But Charles V was not a good Machiavellian, and he had acquired in Spain a considerable religious sincerity. He decided against Luther. Many of the German princes, and especially the Elector of Saxony, sided with the reformer. Luther went into hiding under the protection of the Saxon Elector, and Charles found himself in the presence of the opening rift that was to split Christendom into two contending camps.

Close upon these disturbances, and probably connected with them, came a widespread peasants' revolt throughout Germany. This outbreak frightened Luther very effectually. He was shocked by its excesses, and from that time forth the Reformation he advocated ceased to be a Reformation according to the people and became a Reformation according to the princes. He lost his confidence in that free judgment for which he had stood up so manfully.

Meanwhile Charles realized that his great empire was in very serious danger both from the west and from the east. On the west of him was his spirited rival, Francis I; to the east was the Turk in Hungary, in alliance with Francis and clamouring for certain arrears of tribute from the Austrian dominions. Charles had the money and army of Spain at his disposal, but it was extremely difficult to get any effective support in money from Germany. His grandfather had developed a German infantry on the Swiss model, very much upon the lines expounded in Machiavelli's *Art of War,* but these troops had to be paid and his imperial subsidies had to be supplemented by unsecured borrowings, which were finally to bring his supporters, the Fuggers, to ruin.

On the whole, Charles, in alliance with Henry VIII, was successful against Francis I and the Turk. Their chief battlefield was north Italy; the generalship was dull on both sides; their advances and retreats depended chiefly on the arrival of reinforcements. The German army invaded France, failed to take Marseilles, fell back into Italy, lost Milan, and was besieged in Pavia. Francis I made a long and unsuccessful siege of Pavia, was caught by fresh German forces, defeated, wounded, and taken prisoner. He sent back a message to his queen that all was "lost but honour," made a humiliating peace, and broke it as soon as he was liberated, so that even the salvage of honour was but temporary. Henry VIII and the Pope, in obedience to the rules of Machiavellian strategy, now went over to the side of France in order to prevent Charles becoming too powerful. The German troops in Milan, under the Constable of Bourbon, being unpaid, forced rather than followed their commander into a raid upon Rome. They stormed the city and pillaged it (1527). The Pope took refuge in the Castle of St. Angelo while the looting and slaughter went on. He bought off the German troops at last by the payment of four hundred thousand ducats. Ten years of such stupid and confused fighting impoverished all Europe and left the Emperor in possession of Milan. In 1530 he was crowned by the Pope—he was the last German Emperor to be crowned by the Pope—at Bologna. One thinks of the rather dull-looking blonde face, with its long lip and chin, bearing the solemn expression of one who endures a doubtful though probably honourable ceremony.

Meanwhile the Turks were making great headway in Hungary. They had defeated and killed the King of Hungary in 1526, they held Buda-Pesth, and in 1529, as we have already noted, Suleiman the Magnificent very nearly took Vienna. The Emperor was greatly concerned by these advances, and did his utmost to drive back the Turks, but he found the greatest difficulty in getting the German princes to unite even with this formidable enemy upon their very borders. Francis I remained implacable for a time, and there was a new French war; but in 1538 Charles won his rival over to a more friendly attitude by ravaging the south of France. Francis and Charles then formed an alliance against the Turk, but the Protestant princes, the German princes who were resolved to break away from Rome, had formed a league, the Schmalkaldic League (named after the little town of Schmalkalden in Hesse, at which its constitution was arranged), against the Emperor, and in the place of a great campaign to recover Hungary for Christendom Charles had to turn his mind to the gathering internal struggle in Germany. Of that struggle he saw only the opening war. It was a struggle, a sanguinary irrational bickering of princes for ascendancy, now flaming into war and destruction, now sinking back to intrigues and diplomacies; it was a snake's sack of Machiavellian policies, that was to go on writhing incurably right into the nineteenth century, and to waste and desolate Central Europe again and again.

Henry VIII.

The Emperor never seems to have grasped the true forces at work in these gathering troubles. He was for his time and station an exceptionally worthy man, and he seems to have taken the religious dissensions that were tearing Europe into warring fragments as genuine theological differences. He gathered diets and councils in futile attempts at reconciliation. Formulæ and confessions were tried over. The student of German history must struggle with the details of the Religious Peace of Nuremberg, the settlement at the diet of Ratisbon, the Interim of Augsburg, and the like. Here we do but mention them as details in the worried life of this culminating emperor. As a matter of fact, hardly one of the multifarious princes and rulers in Europe seems to have been acting in good faith. The wide-spread religious trouble of the world, the desire of the common people for truth and social righteousness, the spreading knowledge of the time, all those things were merely counters in the imaginations of princely diplomacy. Henry VIII of England, who had begun his career with a book written against heresy, and who had been rewarded by the Pope with the title of "Defender of the Faith," being anxious to divorce his first wife in favour of an animated young lady named Anne Boleyn,[1] and wishing also to turn against the Emperor in favour of Francis I and to loot the vast wealth of the church in England, joined the company of Protestant princes in 1530. Sweden, Denmark, and Norway had already gone over to the Protestant side.

The German religious war began in 1546, a few months after the death of Martin Luther. We need not trouble about the incidents of the campaign. The Protestant Saxon army was badly beaten at Lochau. By something very like a breach of faith Philip of Hesse, the Emperor's chief remaining antagonist, was caught and imprisoned, and the Turks were bought off by the payment of an annual tribute. In 1547, to the great relief of the Emperor, Francis I died. So by 1547 Charles

[1] But he had a better reason for doing this in the fact that there was no heir to the throne. The Wars of the Roses, a bitter dynastic war, were still very vivid in the minds of English people.—F. H. H.

got to a kind of settlement, and made his last efforts to effect peace where there was no peace. In 1552 all Germany was at war again, only a precipitate flight from Innsbruck saved Charles from capture, and in 1552, with the treaty of Passau, came another unstable equilibrium. Charles was now utterly weary of the cares and splendours of empire; he had never had a very sound constitution, he was naturally indolent, and he was suffering greatly from gout. He abdicated. He made over all his sovereign rights in Germany to his brother Ferdinand, and Spain and the Netherlands he resigned to his son Philip. He then retired to a monastery at Yuste, among the oak and chestnut forests in the hills to the north of the Tagus valley, and there he died in 1558.

Much has been written in a sentimental vein of this retirement, this renunciation of the world by this tired majestic Titan, world-weary, seeking in an austere solitude his peace with God. But his retreat was neither solitary nor austere; he had with him nearly a hundred and fifty attendants; his establishment had all the indulgences without the fatigues of a court, and Philip II was a dutiful son to whom his father's advice was a command. As for his austerities, let Prescott witness: "In the almost daily correspondence between Quixada, or Gaztelu, and the Secretary of State at Valladolid, there is scarcely a letter that does not turn more or less on the Emperor's eating or his illness. The one seems naturally to follow, like a running commentary, on the other. It is rare that such topics have formed the burden of communications with the department of state. It must have been no easy matter for the secretary to preserve his gravity in the perusal of despatches in which politics and gastronomy were so strangely mixed together. The courier from Valladolid to Lisbon was ordered to make a detour, so as to take Jarandilla in his route, and bring supplies for the royal table. On Thursdays he was to bring fish to serve for the *jour maigre* that was to follow. The trout in the neighbourhood Charles thought too small so others, of a larger size, were to be sent from Valladolid. Fish of every kind was to his taste, as, indeed, was anything that in its nature or habits at all approached to fish. Eels, frogs, oysters, occupied an important place in the royal bill of fare. Potted fish, especially anchovies, found great favour with him; and he regretted that he had not brought a better supply of these from the Low Countries. On an eel-pasty he particularly doted." . . .[1]

In 1554 Charles had obtained a bull from Pope Julius III granting him a dispensation from fasting, and allowing him to break his fast early in the morning even when he was to take the sacrament.

"That Charles was not altogether unmindful of his wearing apparel in Yuste, may be inferred from the fact that his wardrobe contained no less than sixteen robes of silk and velvet, lined with ermine, or eider down, or the soft hair of the Barbary goat. As to the furniture and upholstery of his apartments, how little reliance is to be placed on the reports so carelessly circulated about these may be gathered from a single glance at the inventory of his effects, prepared by Quixada and Gaztelu soon after their master's death. Among the items we find carpets from Turkey and Alcarez, canopies of velvet and other stuffs, hangings of fine black cloth, which since his mother's death he had always chosen for his own bedroom; while the remaining apartments were provided with no less than twenty-five suits of tapestry, from the looms of Flanders, richly embroidered with figures of animals and with landscapes." . . . "Among the different pieces of plate we find some of pure gold, and others especially noted for their curious workmanship; and as this was an age in which the art of working the precious metals was carried to the highest perfection, we cannot doubt that some of the finest specimens had come into the Emperor's possession. The whole amount of plate was estimated at between twelve and thirteen thousand ounces in weight." . . .[2]

Charles had never acquired the habit of reading, but he would be read aloud to at meals after the fashion of Charlemagne, and would make what one narrator describes as a "sweet and heavenly commentary." He also amused himself with technical toys, by listening to music or sermons, and by attending to the imperial business that still came drifting in to him. The death of the Empress, to whom he was greatly attached, had turned his mind towards religion, which in his case took a punctilious and ceremonial form; every Friday in Lent he scourged himself with the rest of the monks with such

1 Prescott's Appendix to Robertson's *History of Charles V.*
2 Prescott.

good will as to draw blood. These exercises and the gout released a bigotry in Charles that had been hitherto restrained by considerations of policy. The appearance of Protestant teaching close at hand in Valladolid roused him to fury. "Tell the grand inquisitor and his council from me to be at their posts, and to lay the axe at the root of the evil before it spreads further." . . . He expressed a doubt whether it would not be well, in so black an affair, to dispense with the ordinary course of justice, and to show no mercy; "lest the criminal, if pardoned, should have the opportunity of repeating his crime." He recommended, as an example, his own mode of proceeding in the Netherlands, "where all who remained obstinate in their errors were burned alive, and those who were admitted to penitence were beheaded."

Among the chief pleasures of the Catholic monarch between meals during this time of retirement were funeral services. He not only attended every actual funeral that was celebrated at Yuste, but he had services conducted for the absent dead, he held a funeral service in memory of his wife on the anniversary of her death, and finally he celebrated his own obsequies. "The chapel was hung with black, and the blaze of hundreds of wax-lights was scarcely sufficient to dispel the darkness. The brethren in their conventual dress, and all the Emperor's household clad in deep mourning, gathered round a huge catafalque, shrouded also in black, which had been raised in the centre of the chapel. The service for the burial of the dead was then performed; and, amidst the dismal wail of the monks, the prayers ascended for the departed spirit, that it might be received into the mansions of the blessed. The sorrowful attendants were melted to tears, as the image of their master's death was presented to their minds—or they were touched, it may be, with compassion by this pitiable display of weakness. Charles, muffled in a dark mantle, and bearing a lighted candle in his hand, mingled with his household, the spectator of his own obsequies; and the doleful ceremony was concluded by his placing the taper in the hands of the priest, in sign of his surrendering up his soul to the Almighty."

Other accounts make Charles wear a shroud and lie in the coffin, remaining there alone until the last mourner had left the chapel.

Within two months of this masquerade he was dead. And

the greatness of the Holy Roman Empire died with him. The Holy Roman Empire struggled on indeed to the days of Napoleon, but as an invalid and dying thing.

§ 11B

Ferdinand, the brother of Charles V, took over his abandoned work and met the German princes at the diet of Augsburg in 1555. Again there was an attempt to establish a religious peace. Nothing could better show the quality of that attempted settlement and the blindness of the princes and statesmen concerned in it, to the deeper and broader processes of the time, than the form that settlement took. The recognition of religious freedom was to apply to the states and not to individual citizens; *cujus regio ejus religio, "the confession of the subject was to be dependent on that of the territorial lord."*

§ 11C

We have given as much attention as we have done to the writings of Machiavelli and to the personality of Charles V because they throw a flood of light upon the antagonisms of the next period in our history. This present chapter has told the story of a vast expansion of human horizons and of a great increase and distribution of knowledge, we have seen the conscience of common men awakening and intimations of a new and profounder social justice spreading throughout the general body of the Western civilization. But this process of light and thought was leaving courts and the political life of the world untouched. There is little in Machiavelli that might not have been written by some clever secretary in the court of Chosroes I or Shi Hwang-ti—or even of Sargon I or Pepi. While the world in everything else was moving forward, in political ideas, in ideas about the relationship of state to state and of sovereign to citizen, it was standing still. Nay, it was falling back. For the great idea of the Catholic Church as the world city of God had been destroyed in men's minds by the church itself, and the dream of a world imperialism had, in the person of Charles V, been carried in effigy through Europe to limbo. Politically the world seemed falling back towards personal monarchy of the Assyrian or Macedonian pattern.

It is not that the newly awakened intellectual energies of western European men were too absorbed in theological restatement, in scientific investigations, in exploration and mercantile development, to give a thought to the claims and responsibilities of rulers. Not only were common men drawing ideas of a theocratic or republican or communistic character from the now accessible Bible, but the renewed study of the Greek classics was bringing the creative and fertilizing spirit of Plato to bear upon the Western mind. In England Sir Thomas More produced a quaint imitation of Plato's *Republic* in his *Utopia,* setting out a sort of autocratic communism. In Naples, a century later, a certain friar Campanella was equally bold in his *City of the Sun.* But such discussions were having no immediate effect upon political arrangements. Compared with the massiveness of the task, these books do indeed seem poetical and scholarly and flimsy. (Yet later on the *Utopia* was to bear fruit in the English Poor Laws.) The intellectual and moral development of the Western mind and this drift towards Machiavellian monarchy in Europe were for a time going on concurrently in the same world, but they were going on almost independently. The statesmen still schemed and manœuvred as if nothing grew but the power of wary and fortunate kings. It was only in the seventeenth and eighteenth centuries that these two streams of tendency, the stream of general ideas and the drift of traditional and egoistic monarchical diplomacy, interfered and came into conflict.

XXXV

PRINCES, PARLIAMENTS, AND POWERS

§ 1

IN the preceding chapter we have traced the beginnings of a new civilization, the civilization of the "modern" type which becomes at the present time world-wide. It is still a vast unformed thing, still only in the opening phases of growth and development to-day. We have seen the mediæval ideas of the Holy Roman Empire and of the Roman Church, as forms of universal law and order, fade in its dawn. They fade out, as if it were necessary in order that these ideas of one law and one order for all men should be redrawn on world-wide lines. And while in nearly every other field of human interest there was advance, the effacement of these general political ideas of the Church and Empire led back for a time in things political towards merely personal monarchy and monarchist nationalism of the Macedonian type. There came an interregnum, as it were, in the consolidation of human affairs, a phase of the type the Chinese annalists would call an "Age of Confusion." This interregnum has lasted as long as that between the fall of the Western Empire and the crowning of Charlemagne in Rome. We are living in it to-day. It may be drawing to its close; we cannot tell yet. The old leading ideas had broken down, a medley of new and untried projects and suggestions perplexed men's minds and actions, and meanwhile the world at large had to fall back for leadership upon the ancient tradition of an individual prince. There was no new way clearly apparent for men to follow, and the prince was there.

All over the world the close of the sixteenth century saw monarchy prevailing and tending towards absolutism. Germany and Italy were patchworks of autocratic princely dominions, Spain was practically autocratic, the throne had never been so powerful in England, and as the seventeenth century drew on, the French monarchy gradually became the greatest and most consolidated power in Europe. The phases and fluctuations of its ascent we cannot record here.

At every court there were groups of ministers and secretaries who played a Machiavellian game against their foreign rivals. Foreign policy is the natural employment of courts and monarchies. Foreign offices are, so to speak, the leading characters in all the histories of the seventeenth and eighteenth centuries. They kept Europe in a fever of wars. And wars were becoming expensive. Armies were no longer untrained levies, no longer assemblies of feudal knights who brought their own horses and weapons and retainers with them; they needed more and more artillery; they consisted of paid troops who insisted on their pay; they were professional and slow and elaborate, conducting long sieges, necessitating elaborate fortifications. War expenditure increased everywhere and called for more and more taxation. And here it was that these monarchies of the sixteenth and seventeenth centuries came into conflict with new and shapeless forces of freedom in the community. In practice the princes found they were not masters of their subjects' lives or property. They found an inconvenient resistance to the taxation that was necessary if their diplomatic aggressions and alliances were to continue. Finance became an unpleasant spectre in every council chamber. In theory the monarch owned his country. James I of England (1603) declared that "As it is atheism and blasphemy to dispute what God can do; so it is presumption and high contempt in a subject to dispute what a king can do, or say that a king cannot do this or that." In practice, however, he found, and his son Charles I (1625) was to find still more effectually, that there were in his dominions a great number of landlords and merchants, substantial and intelligent persons, who set a very definite limit to the calls and occasions of the monarch and his ministers. They were prepared to tolerate his rule if they themselves might also be monarchs of their lands and businesses and trades and what not. But not otherwise.

Everywhere in Europe there was a parallel development. Beneath the kings and princes there were these lesser monarchs, the private owners, noblemen, wealthy citizens and the like, who were now offering the sovereign prince much the same resistance that the kings and princes of Germany had offered the Emperor. They wanted to limit taxation so far as it pressed upon themselves, and to be free in their own houses and estates. And the spread of books and reading and intercommunication was enabling these smaller monarchs, these monarchs of ownership, to develop such a community of ideas and such a solidarity of resistance as had been possible at no previous stage in the world's history. Everywhere they were disposed to resist the prince, but it was not everywhere that they found the same faculties for an organized resistance. The economic circumstances and the political traditions of the Netherlands and England made those countries the first to bring this antagonism of monarchy and private ownership to an issue.

At first this seventeenth-century "public," this public of property owners, cared very little for foreign policy. They did not perceive at first how it affected them. They did not want to be bothered with it; it was, they conceded, the affairs of kings and princes. They made no attempt therefore to control foreign entanglements. But it was with the direct consequences of these entanglements that they quarrelled; they objected to heavy taxation, to interference with trade, to arbitrary imprisonment, and to the control of consciences by the monarch. It was upon these questions that they joined issue with the Crown.

§ 2

The breaking away of the Netherlands from absolutist monarchy was the beginning of a series of such conflicts throughout the sixteenth and seventeenth centuries. They varied very greatly in detail according to local and racial peculiarities, but essentially they were all rebellious against the idea of a predominating personal "prince" and his religious and political direction.

In the twelfth century all the lower Rhine country was divided up among a number of small rulers, and the population was a Low German one on a Celtic basis, mixed with subsequent Danish ingredients very similar to the English admixture. The south-eastern fringe of it spoke French dialects; the bulk, Frisian, Dutch, and other Low German languages. The Netherlands figured largely in the crusades. Godfrey of Bouillon, who took Jerusalem (First Crusade), was a Belgian; and the founder of the so-called Latin Dynasty of emperors in Constantinople (Fourth Crusade) was Baldwin of Flanders. (They were called Latin emperors because they were on the side of the Latin church.) In the thirteenth and fourteenth centuries considerable towns grew up in the Netherlands: Ghent, Bruges, Ypres, Utrecht, Leyden, Haarlem, and so forth; and these towns developed quasi-independent municipal governments and a class of educated townsmen. We will not trouble the reader with the dynastic accidents that linked the affairs of the Netherlands with Burgundy (Eastern France), and which finally made their overlordship the inheritance of the Emperor Charles V.

It was under Charles that the Protestant doctrines that now prevailed in Germany spread into the Netherlands. Charles persecuted with some vigour, but in 1556, as we have told, he handed over the task to his son Philip (Philip II). Philip's spirited foreign policy—he was carrying on a war with France—presently became a second source of trouble between himself and the Netherlandish noblemen and townsmen, because he had to come to them for supplies. The great nobles, led by William the Silent, Prince of Orange, and the Counts of Egmont and Horn, made themselves the heads of a popular objection to taxation from the objection to religious persecution. The great nobles were not at first Protestants. They became Protestants as the struggle grew in bitterness. The resistance, in which it is now impossible to disentangle the people were often bitterly Protestant.

Philip was resolved to rule both the property and consciences of his Netherlanders. He sent picked Spanish troops into the country, and he made governor-general a nobleman named Alva, one of those ruthless "strong" men who wreck governments and monarchies. For a time he ruled the land with a hand of iron, but the hand of iron begets a soul of iron in the body it grips, and in 1567 the Netherlands were in open revolt. Alva murdered, sacked, and massacred—in vain. Counts Egmont and Horn were executed. William the Silent became the great leader of the Dutch, a king *de facto*. For a long time, and with many complications, the struggle for liberty continued, and through it all it is noteworthy that the rebels continued to cling to the plea that Philip II was their king—if only he would be a reasonable and limited king. But the idea of limited monarchy was distasteful to the crowned heads of Europe at that time, and at last Philip drove the United Provinces, for which we now use the name of Holland, to the republican form of government. Holland, be it noted—not all the Netherlands; the southern Netherlands, Belgium as we now call that country, remained at the end of the struggle a Spanish possession and Catholic.

The siege of Alkmaar (1573), as Motley[1] describes it, may be taken as a sample of that long and hideous conflict between the little Dutch people and the still vast resources of Catholic Imperialism.

"'If I take Alkmaar,' Alva wrote to Philip, 'I am resolved not to leave a single creature alive; the knife shall be put to every throat.' . . .

"And now, with the dismantled and desolate Haarlem before their eyes, a prophetic phantom, perhaps, of their own imminent fate, did the handful of people shut up within Alkmaar prepare for the worst. Their main hope lay in the friendly sea. The vast sluices called the Zyp, through which the inundation of the whole northern province could be very soon effected, were but a few miles distant. By opening these gates, and by piercing a few dykes, the ocean might be made to fight for them. To obtain this result, however, the consent of the inhabitants was requisite, as the destruction of all the standing crops would be inevitable. The city was so closely invested, that it was a matter of life and death to venture forth, and it was difficult, therefore, to find an envoy for this hazardous mission. At last, a carpenter in the city, Peter Van der Mey by name, undertook the adventure. . . .

"Affairs soon approached a crisis within the beleaguered city.

[1] *Rise of the Dutch Republic.*

Daily skirmishes, without decisive results, had taken place outside the walls. At last, on the 18th of September, after a steady cannonade of nearly twelve hours, Don Frederick, at three in the afternoon, ordered an assault. Notwithstanding his seven months' experience at Haarlem, he still believed it certain that he should carry Alkmaar by storm. The attack took place at once upon the Frisian gate and upon the red tower on the opposite side. Two choice regiments, recently arrived from Lombardy, led the onset, rending the air with their shouts and confident of an easy victory. They were sustained by what seemed an overwhelming force of disciplined troops. Yet never, even in the recent history of Haarlem, had an attack been received by more dauntless breasts. Every living man was on the walls. The storming parties were assailed with cannon, with musketry, with pistols. Boiling water, pitch and oil, molten lead, and unslaked lime were poured upon them every moment. Hundreds of tarred and burning hoops were skilfully quoited around the necks of the soldiers, who struggled in vain to extricate themselves from these fiery ruffs, while as fast as any of the invaders planted foot upon the breach, they were confronted face to face with sword and dagger by the burghers, who hurled them headlong into the moat below.

"Thrice was the attack renewed with ever-increasing rage—thrice repulsed with unflinching fortitude. The storm continued four hours long. During all that period not one of the defenders left his post, till he dropped from it dead or wounded. . . . The trumpet of recall was sounded, and the Spaniards, utterly discomfited, retired from the walls, leaving at least one thousand dead in the trenches, while only thirteen burghers and twenty-four of the garrison lost their lives. . . . Ensign Solis, who had mounted the breach for an instant, and miraculously escaped with his life, after having been hurled from the battlements, reported that he had seen 'neither helmet nor harness' as he looked down into the city: only some plain-looking people, generally dressed like fishermen. Yet these plain-looking fishermen had defeated the veterans of Alva. . . .

"Meantime, as Governor Sonoy had opened many of the dykes, the land in the neighbourhood of the camp was becoming plashy, although as yet the threatened inundation had not taken place. The soldiers were already very uncomfortable and very refractory. The carpenter-envoy had not been idle. . . ."

He returned with despatches for the city. By accident or contrivance he lost these despatches as he made his way into the town, so that they fell into Alva's hands. They contained a definite promise from the Duke of Orange to flood the country so as to drown the whole Spanish army. Incidentally this would also have drowned most of the Dutch harvest and cattle. But Alva, when he had read these documents, did not wait for the opening of any more sluices. Presently the stout men of Alkmaar, cheering and jeering, watched the Spainards breaking camp. . . .

The form assumed by the government of liberated Holland was a patrician republic under the headship of the house of Orange. The States-General was far less representative of the whole body of citizens than was the English Parliament we shall next relate.

Though the worst of the struggle was over after Alkmaar, Holland was not effectively independent until 1609, and its independence was only fully and completely recognized by the treaty of Westphalia in 1648.

§ 3

The open struggle of the private property owner against the aggressions of the "Prince" begins in England far back in the twelfth century. The phase in this struggle that we have to study now is the phase that opened with the attempts of Henry VII and VIII and their successors, Edward VI, Mary and Elizabeth, to make the government of England a "personal monarchy" of the continental type. It became more acute when, by dynastic accidents, James, King of Scotland, became James I, King of both Scotland and England (1603), and began to talk in the manner we have already quoted of his "divine right" to do as he pleased. But never had the path of English monarchy been a smooth one. In all the monarchies of the Northmen and Germanic invaders of the empire there had been a tradition of a popular assembly of influential and representative men to preserve their general liberties, and in none was it more living than in England. France had her tradition of the assembly of the Three Estates, Spain her Cortes, but the English assembly was peculiar in two respects; that it had behind it a documentary declaration of certain elementary and universal rights, and that it contained elected "Knights of the Shire," as well as elected burghers from the towns. The French and Spanish assemblies had the latter, but not the former element.

These two features gave the English Parliament a peculiar strength in its struggle with the Throne. The document in question was *Magna Carta*, the Great Charter, a declaration which was forced from King John (1199-1216), the brother and successor of Richard Cœur de Lion (1189-99), after a revolt of the Barons in 1215. It rehearsed a number of fundamental rights that made England a legal and not a regal state. It rejected the power of the king to control the personal property and liberty of every sort of citizen—save with the consent of that man's equals.

The presence of the elected shire representatives in the English Parliament, the second peculiarity of the British situation, came about from very simple and apparently innocuous beginnings. From the shires, or county divisions, knights seem to have been summoned to the national council to testify to the taxable capacity of their districts. They were sent up by the minor gentry, freeholders and village elders of their districts as early as 1254, two knights from each shire. This idea inspired Simon de Montfort,[1] who was in rebellion against Henry III, the successor of John, to summon to the national council two knights from each shire and two citizens from each city or borough. Edward I, the successor to Henry III, continued this practice because it seemed a convenient way of getting into financial touch with the growing towns. At first there was considerable reluctance on the parts of the knights and townsmen to attend Parliament, but gradually the power they possessed of linking the redress of grievances with the granting of subsidies was realized. Quite early, if not from the first, these representatives of the general property owners in town and country, the Commons, sat and debated apart from the great Lords and Bishops. So there grew up in England a representative assembly, the Commons, beside an episcopal and patrician one, the Lords. There was no profound and fundamental difference between the personnel of the two assemblies; many of the knights of the shire were substantial men who

1 This is not the same Simon de Montfort as the leader of the crusades against the Albigenses, but his son.

might be as wealthy and influential as peers and also the sons and brothers of peers, but on the whole the Commons was the more plebeian assembly. From the first these two assemblies, and especially the Commons, displayed a disposition to claim the entire power of taxation in the land. Gradually they extended their purview of grievances to a criticism of all the affairs of the realm. We will not follow the fluctuations of the power and prestige of the English Parliament through the time of the Tudor monarchs (*i.e.*, Henry VII and VIII, Edward VI, Mary and Elizabeth), but it will be manifest from what has been said that when at last James Stuart made his open claim to autocracy, the English merchants, peers, and private gentlemen found themselves with a tried and honoured traditional means of resisting him such as no other people in Europe possessed.

Another peculiarity of the English political conflict was its comparative detachment from the great struggle between Catholic and Protestant that was now being waged all over Europe. There were, it is true, very distinct religious issues mixed up in the English struggle, but upon its main lines it was a political struggle of King against the Parliament embodying the class of private-property-owning citizens. Both Crown and people were formally reformed and Protestant. It is true that many people on the latter side were Protestants of a Bible-respecting, non-sacerdotal type, representing the reformation according to the peoples, and that the king was the nominal head of a special sacerdotal and sacramental church, the established Church of England, representing the reformation according to the princes, but this antagonism never completely obscured the essentials of the conflict.

The struggle of King and Parliament had already reached an acute phase before the death of James I (1625), but only in the reign of his son Charles I did it culminate in civil war. Charles did exactly what one might have expected a king to do in such a position, in view of the lack of Parliamentary control over foreign policy; he embroiled the country in a conflict with both Spain and France, and then came to the country for supplies in the hope that patriotic feeling would override the normal dislike to giving him money. When Parliament refused supplies, he demanded loans from various subjects, and attempted similar illegal exactions. This produced from Parliament in 1628 a very memorable document, the *Petition of Right*, citing the Great Charter and rehearsing the legal limitations upon the power of the English king, denying his right to levy charges upon, or to imprison, or punish anyone, or to quarter soldiers on the people, without due process of law. The Petition of Right stated the case of the English Parliament. The disposition to "state a case" has always been a very marked English characteristic. When President Wilson, during the Great War of 1914-18, prefaced each step in his policy by a "Note," he was walking in the most respectable traditions of the English. Charles dealt with this Parliament with a high hand, he dismissed it in 1629, and for eleven years he summoned no Parliament. He levied money illegally, but not enough for his purpose; and realizing that the church could be used as an instrument of obedience, he made Laud, an aggressive high churchman, very much of a priest and a very strong believer in "divine right," Archbishop of Canterbury, and so head of the Church of England.

In 1638 Charles tried to extend the half-Protestant, half-Catholic characteristics of the Church of England to his other kingdom of Scotland, where the secession from catholicism had been more complete, and where a non-sacerdotal, non-sacramental form of Christianity, Presbyterianism, had been established as the national church. The Scotch revolted, and the English levies Charles raised to fight them mutinied. Insolvency, at all times the natural result of a "spirited" foreign policy, was close at hand. Charles, without money or trustworthy troops, had to summon a Parliament at last in 1640. This Parliament, the Short Parliament, he dismissed in the same year; he tried a Council of Peers at York (1640), and then in the November of that year summoned his last Parliament.

This body, the Long Parliament, assembled in the mood for conflict. It seized Laud, the Archbishop of Canterbury, and charged him with treason. It published a "Grand Remonstrance," which was a long and full statement of its case against Charles. It provided by a bill for a meeting of Parliament at least once in three years, whether the King summoned it or no. It prosecuted the King's chief ministers who had helped him to reign for so long without Parliament, and in particular the Earl of Strafford. To save Strafford the King plotted for a sudden seizure of London by the army. This was discovered, and the Bill for Strafford's condemnation was hurried on in the midst of a vast popular excitement. Charles I, who was probably one of the meanest and most treacherous occupants the English throne has ever known, was frightened by the London crowds. Before Strafford could die by due legal process, it was necessary for the King to give his assent. Charles gave it—and Strafford was beheaded. Meanwhile the King was plotting and looking for help in strange quarters—from the Catholic Irish, from treasonable Scotchmen. Finally he resorted to a forcible-feeble display of violence. He went down to the Houses of Parliament to arrest five of his most active opponents. He entered the House of Commons and took the Speaker's chair. He was prepared with some bold speech about treason, but when he saw the places of his five antagonists vacant, he was baffled, confused, and spoke in broken sentences. He learnt that they had departed from his royal city of Westminster and taken refuge in the city of London (see Chap. XXXIV, § 7). London defied him. A week later the Five Members were escorted back in triumph to the Parliament House in Westminster by the Trained Bands of London, and the King, to avoid the noise and hostility of the occasion, left Whitehall for Windsor.

Both parties then prepared openly for war.

The King was the traditional head of the army, and the habit of obedience in soldiers is to the King. The Parliament had the greater resources. The King set up his standard at Nottingham on the eve of a dark and stormy August day in 1642. There followed a long and obstinate civil war, the King holding Oxford, the Parliament, London. Success swayed from side to side, but the King could never close on London nor Parliament take Oxford. Each antagonist was weakened by moderate adherents who "did not want to go too far." There emerged among the Parliamentary commanders a certain Oliver Cromwell, who had raised a small troop of horse and who rose to the position of general. Lord Warwick, his contemporary, describes him as a plain man, in a cloth suit "made by an ill country tailor." He was no mere fighting soldier, but a military organizer; he realized the inferior quality of many of the Parliamentary forces, and set himself to remedy it. The Cavaliers of the King had the picturesque tradition of chivalry and loyalty on their side; Parliament was something new and difficult—without any comparable traditions. "Your troops are most of them old decayed serving men and tapsters," said Cromwell. "Do you think that the spirits of such base and mean fellows will ever be able to encounter gentlemen that have honour and courage and resolution in them?" But there is something better and stronger than picturesque chivalry in the world, religious enthusiasm. He set himself to get together a "godly" regiment. They were to be earnest, sober-living men. Above all, they were to be men of strong convictions. He disregarded all social traditions, and drew his officers from every class. "I had rather have a plain, russet-coated captain *that knows what he fights for and loves what he knows,* than what you call a gentleman and is nothing else." England discovered a new force, the Ironsides, in its midst, in which footmen, draymen, and ships' captains held high command, side by side with men of family. They became the type on which the Parliament sought to reconstruct its entire army. The Ironsides were the backbone of this "New Model." From Marston Moor to Naseby these men swept the Cavaliers before them. The King was at last a captive in the hands of Parliament.

There were still attempts at settlement that would have left the King a sort of king, but Charles was a man doomed to tragic issues, incessantly scheming, "so false a man that he is not to be trusted." The English were drifting towards a situation new in the world's history, in which a monarch should be formally tried for treason to his people and condemned.

Most revolutions are precipitated, as this English one was, by the excesses of the ruler, and by attempts at strength and firmness beyond the compass of the law; and most revolutions swing by a kind of necessity towards an extremer conclusion than is warranted by the original quarrel. The English revolution was no exception. The English are by nature a compromising and even a vacillating people, and probably the great majority of them still wanted the King to be King and the people to be free, and all the lions and lambs to lie down together in peace and liberty. But the army of the New Model could not go back. There would have been scant mercy for these draymen and footmen who had ridden down the King's gentlemen if the King came back. When Parliament began to treat again with this regal trickster, the New Model intervened; Colonel Pride turned out eighty members from the House of Commons who favoured the King, and the illegal residue, the Rump Parliament, then put the King on trial.

But indeed the King was already doomed. The House of Lords rejected the ordinance for the trial, and the Rump then proclaimed "that the People are, under God, the original of all just power," and that "the Commons of England . . . have the supreme power in this nation," and—assuming that it was itself the Commons—proceeded with the trial. The King was condemned as a "tyrant, traitor, murderer, and enemy of his country." He was taken one January morning in 1649 to a scaffold erected outside the windows of his own banqueting-room at Whitehall. There he was beheaded. He died with piety and a certain noble self-pity—eight years after the execution of Strafford, and after six and a half years of a destructive civil war which had been caused almost entirely by his own lawlessness.

This was indeed a great and terrifying thing that Parliament had done. The like of it had never been heard of in the world before. Kings had killed each other times enough; parricide, fratricide, assassination, those are the privileged expedients of princes; but that a section of the people should rise up, try its king solemnly and deliberately for disloyalty, mischief, and treachery, and condemn and kill him, sent horror through every court in Europe. The Rump Parliament had gone beyond the ideas and conscience of its time. It was as if a committee of jungle deer had taken and killed a tiger—a crime against nature. The Tsar of Russia chased the English envoy from his court. France and Holland committed acts of open hostility. England, confused and conscience-stricken at her own sacrilege, stood isolated before the world.

But for a time the personal quality of Oliver Cromwell and the discipline and strength of the army he had created maintained England in the republican course she had taken. The Irish Catholics had made a massacre of the Protestant English in Ireland, and now Cromwell suppressed the Irish insurrection with great vigour. Except for certain friars at the storm of Drogheda, none but men with arms in their hands were killed by his troops; but the atrocities of the massacre were fresh in his mind, no quarter was given in battle, and so his memory still rankles in the minds of the Irish, who have a long memory for their own wrongs. After Ireland came Scotland, where Cromwell shattered a Royalist army at the Battle of Dunbar (1650). Then he turned his attention to Holland, which country had rashly seized upon the divisions among the English as an excuse for the injury of a trade rival. The Dutch were then the rulers of the sea, and the English fleet fought against odds; but after a series of obstinate sea fights the Dutch were driven from the British seas and the English took their place as the ascendant naval power. Dutch and French ships must dip their flags to them. An English fleet went into the Mediterranean—the first English naval force to enter those waters; it put right various grievances of the English shippers with Tuscany and Malta, and bombarded the pirate nest of Algiers and destroyed the pirate fleet—which in the lax days of Charles had been wont to come right up to the coasts of Cornwall and Devon to intercept ships and carry off slaves to Africa. The strong arm of England also intervened to protect the Protestants in the south of France, who were being hunted to death by the Duke of Savoy. France, Sweden, Denmark, all found it wiser to overcome their first distaste for regicide and allied themselves with England. Came a war with Spain, and the great English Admiral Blake destroyed the Spanish Plate Fleet at Teneriffe in an action of almost incredible daring. He engaged land batteries. He was the first man "that brought ships to contemn castles on the shore." (He died in 1657, and was buried in Westminster Abbey, but after the restoration of the monarchy his bones were dug out by the order of Charles II, and removed to St. Margaret's, Westminster.) Such was the figure that England cut in the eyes of the world during her brief republican days.

On September 3rd, 1658, Cromwell died in the midst of a great storm that did not fail to impress the superstitious. Once his strong hand lay still, England fell away from this premature attempt to realize a righteous commonweal of free men. In 1660 Charles II, the son of Charles the "Martyr," was welcomed back to England with all those manifestations of personal loyalty dear to the English heart, and the country relaxed from its military and naval efficiency as a sleeper might wake and stretch and yawn after too intense a dream. The Puritans were done with. "Merrie England" was herself again, and in

1667 the Dutch, once more masters of the sea, sailed up the Thames to Gravesend and burnt an English fleet in the Medway. "On the night when our ships were burnt by the Dutch," says Pepys, in his diary, "the King did sup with my Lady Castelmaine, and there they were all mad, hunting a poor moth." Charles, from the date of his return, 1660, took control of the foreign affairs of the state, and in 1670 concluded a secret treaty with Louis XIV of France by which he undertook to subordinate entirely English foreign policy to that of France for an annual pension of £100,000. Dunkirk, which Cromwell had taken, had already been sold back to France. The King was a great sportsman; he had the true English love for watching horse races, and the racing centre at Newmarket is perhaps his most characteristic monument.

While Charles lived, his easy humour enabled him to retain the British crown, but he did so by wariness and compromise, and when in 1685 he was succeeded by his brother James II, who was a devout Catholic, and too dull to recognize the hidden limitation of the monarchy in Britain, the old issue between Parliament and Crown became acute. James set himself to force his country into a religious reunion with Rome. In 1688 he was in flight to France. But this time the great lords and merchants and gentlemen were too circumspect to let this revolt against the King fling them into the hands of a second Pride or a second Cromwell. They had already called in another king, William, Prince of Orange, to replace James. The change was made rapidly. There was no civil war—except in Ireland—and no release of the deeper revolutionary forces of the country. Of William's claim to the throne, or rather of his wife Mary's claim, we cannot tell here, its interest is purely technical, nor how William III and Mary ruled, nor how, after the widower William had reigned alone for a time, the throne passed on to Mary's sister Anne (1702-14). Anne seems to have thought favourably of a restoration of the Stuart line, but the Lords and the Commons, who now dominated English affairs, preferred a less competent king. Some sort of claim could be made out for the Elector of Hanover, who became King of England as George I (1714-27). He was entirely German, he could speak no English, and he brought a swarm of German women and German attendants to the English court; a dullness, a tarnish, came over the intellectual life of the land with his coming, but this isolation of the court from English life was his conclusive recommendation to the great landowners and the commercial interests who chiefly brought him over. England entered upon a phase which Lord Beaconsfield has called the "Venetian oligarchy" stage; the supreme power resided in Parliament, dominated now by the Lords, for the art of bribery and a study of the methods of working elections carried to a high pitch by Sir Robert Walpole had robbed the House of Commons of its original freedom and vigour. By ingenious devices the parliamentary vote was restricted to a shrinking number of electors, old towns with little or no population would return one or two members (old Sarum had one non-resident voter, no population, and two members), while newer populous centres had no representation at all. And by insisting upon a high property qualification for members, the chance of the Commons speaking in common accents of vulgar needs was still more restricted. George I was followed by the very similar George II (1727-60), and it was only at his death that England had again a king who had been born in England, and one who could speak English fairly well, his grandson George III. On this monarch's attempt to recover some of the larger powers of monarchy we shall have something to say in a later section.

Such briefly is the story of the struggle in England during the seventeenth and eighteenth centuries between the three main factors in the problem of the "modern state"; between the crown, the private property owners, and that vague power, still blind and ignorant, the power of the quite common people. This latter factor appears as yet only at moments when the country is most deeply stirred; then it sinks back into the depths. But the end of the story, thus far, is a very complete triumph of the British private property owner over the dreams and schemes of Machiavellian absolutism. With the Hanoverian Dynasty, England became—as the *Times* recently styled her—a "crowned republic." She had worked out a new method of government, Parliamentary government, recalling in many ways the Senate and Popular Assembly of Rome, but more steadfast and efficient because of its use, however restricted, of the representative method. Her assembly at Westminster was to become the "Mother of Parliaments" throughout the world. Towards the crown the English Parliament has held and still holds much the relation of the mayor of the palace to the Merovingian kings. The king is conceived of as ceremonial and irresponsible, a living symbol of the royal and imperial system. But much power remains latent in the tradition and prestige of the crown, and the succession of the four Hanoverian Georges, William IV (1830), Victoria (1837), Edward VII (1901), and the present king, George V (1910), is of a quite different strain from the feeble and short-lived Merovingian monarchs. In the affairs of the church, the military and naval organizations, and the foreign office, these sovereigns have all in various degrees exercised an influence which is none the less important because it is indefinable.

§ 4

Upon no part of Europe did the collapse of the idea of a unified Christendom bring more disastrous consequences than to Germany. Naturally one would have supposed that the Emperor, being by origin a German, both in the case of the earlier lines and in the case of the Habsburgs, would have developed into the national monarch of a united German-speaking state. It was the accidental misfortune of Germany that her Emperors never remained German. Frederick II, the last Hohenstaufen, was, as we have seen, a half-Orientalized Sicilian; the Habsburgs, by marriage and inclination, became in the person of Charles V, first Burgundian and then Spanish in spirit. After the death of Charles V, his brother Ferdinand took Austria and the empire, and his son Philip II took Spain, the Netherlands, and South Italy; but the Austrian line, obstinately Catholic, holding its patrimony mostly on the eastern frontiers, deeply entangled therefore with Hungarian affairs and paying tribute, as Ferdinand and his two successors did, to the Turk, retained no grip upon the north Germans with their disposition towards Protestantism, their Baltic and westward affinities, and their ignorance of or indifference to the Turkish danger.

The sovereign princes, dukes, electors, prince bishops and the like, whose domains cut up the map of the Germany of the Middle Ages into a crazy patchwork, were really not the equivalents of the kings of England and France. They were rather on the level of the great land-owning dukes and peers of France and England. Until 1701 none of them had the title of "King."

Many of their dominions were less both in size and value than the larger estates of the British nobility. The German Diet was like the States-General or like a parliament without the presence of elected representatives. So that the great civil war in Germany that presently broke out, the Thirty Years' War

Central EUROPE after the Peace of Westphalia, 1648.

(1618-48) was in its essential nature much more closely akin to the civil war in England (1643-49) and to the war of the Fronde (1648-53), the league of feudal nobles against the Crown in France, than appears upon the surface. In all these cases the Crown was either Catholic or disposed to become Catholic, and the recalcitrant nobles found their individualistic disposition tending to a Protestant formula. But while in England and Holland the Protestant nobles and rich merchants ultimately triumphed and in France the success of the Crown was even more complete, in Germany neither was the Emperor strong enough, nor had the Protestant princes a sufficient unity and organization among themselves to secure a conclusive triumph. It ended there in a torn-up Germany. Moreover, the German issue was complicated by the fact that various non-German peoples, the Bohemians and the Swedes (who had a new Protestant monarchy which had arisen under Gustava Vasa as a direct result of the Reformation), were entangled in the struggle. Finally, the French monarchy, triumphant now over its own nobles, although it was Catholic, came in on the Protestant side with the evident intention of taking the place of the Habsburgs as the imperial line.

The prolongation of the war, and the fact that it was not fought along a determinate frontier, but all over an empire of patches, Protestant here, Catholic there, made it one of the most cruel and destructive that Europe had known since the days of the barbarian raids. Its peculiar mischief lay not in the fighting, but in the concomitants of the fighting. It came at a time when military tactics had developed to a point that rendered ordinary levies useless against trained professional infantry. Volley firing with muskets at a range of a few score yards had abolished the individualistic knight in armour, but the charge of disciplined masses of cavalry could still disperse any infantry that had not been drilled into a mechanical rigidity. The infantry with their muzzle-loading muskets could not keep up a steady enough fire to wither determined cavalry before it charged home. They had, therefore, to meet the shock standing or kneeling behind a bristling wall of pikes or bayonets. For this they needed great discipline and experience. Iron cannon were still of small size and not very abundant, and they did not play a decisive part as yet in warfare. They could "plough lanes" in infantry, but they could not easily smash and scatter it if it was sturdy and well drilled. War under these conditions was entirely in the hands of seasoned professional soldiers, and the question of their pay was as important a one to the generals of that time as the question of food or munitions. As the long struggle dragged on from phase to phase, and the financial distress of the land increased, the commanders of both sides were forced to fall back upon the looting of towns and villages, both for supply and to make up the arrears of their soldiers' pay.

The soldiers became, therefore, more and more mere brigands living on the country, and the Thirty Years' War set up a tradition of looting as a legitimate operation in warfare and of outrage as a soldier's privilege that has tainted the good name of Germany right down to the Great War of 1914. The earlier chapters of Defoe's *Memoirs of a Cavalier,* with its vivid description of the massacre and burning of Magdeburg, will give the reader a far better idea of the warfare of this time than any formal history. So harried was the land that the farmers ceased from cultivation, what snatch crops could be harvested were hidden away, and great crowds of starving women and children became camp followers of the armies, and supplied a thievish tail to the rougher plundering. At the close of the struggle all Germany was ruined and desolate. Central Europe did not fully recover from these robberies and devastations for a century.

Here we can but name Tilly and Wallenstein, the great plunder captains on the Habsburg side, and Gustavus Adolphus, the King of Sweden, the Lion of the North, the champion of the Protestants, whose dream was to make the Baltic Sea a "Swedish Lake." Gustavus Adolphus was killed in his decisive victory over Wallenstein at Lützen (1632), and Wallenstein was murdered in 1634. In 1648 the princes and diplomatists gathered amidst the havoc they had made to patch up the affairs of Central Europe at the Peace of Westphalia. By that peace the power of the Emperor was reduced to a shadow, and the acquisition of Alsace brought France up to the Rhine. And one German prince, the Hohenzollern Elector of Brandenburg, acquired so much territory as to become the greatest German power next to the Emperor, a power that presently (1701) became the kingdom of Prussia. The Treaty also recognized two long accomplished facts, the separation from the empire and the complete independence of both Holland and Switzerland.

§ 5

We have opened this chapter with the stories of two countries, the Netherlands and Britain, in which the resistance of the private citizen to this new type of monarchy, the Machiavellian monarchy, that was arising out of the moral collapse of Christendom, succeeded. But in France, Russia, in many parts of

Germany and of Italy—Saxony and Tuscany *e.g.*—personal monarchy was not so restrained and overthrown; it established itself indeed as the ruling European system during the seventeenth and eighteenth centuries. And even in Holland and Britain the monarchy was recovering power during the eighteenth century.

(In Poland conditions were peculiar, and they will be dealt with in a later section.)

In France there had been no Magna Carta, and there was not quite so definite and effective a tradition of parliamentary rule. There was the same opposition of interests between the crown on the one hand and the landlords and merchants on the other, but the latter had no recognized gathering-place, and no dignified method of unity. They formed oppositions to the crown, they made leagues of resistance—such was the "Fronde," which was struggling against the young King Louis XIV and his great minister Mazarin, while Charles I was fighting for his life in England—but ultimately (1652), after a civil war, they were conclusively defeated; and while in England after the establishment of the Hanoverians the House of Lords and their subservient Commons ruled the country, in France, on the contrary, after 1652, the court entirely dominated the aristocracy. Cardinal Mazarin was himself building upon a foundation that Cardinal Richelieu, the contemporary of King James I of England, had prepared for him. After the time of Mazarin we hear of no great French nobles unless they are at court as court servants and officials. They have been tamed—but at a price, the price of throwing the burthen of taxation upon the voiceless mass of the common people. From many taxes both the clergy and the nobility—everyone indeed who bore a title—were exempt. In the end this injustice became intolerable, but for a while the French monarchy flourished like the Psalmist's green bay tree. By the opening of the eighteenth century English writers are already calling attention to the misery of the French lower classes and the comparative prosperity, *at that time,* of the English poor.

On such terms of unrighteousness what we may call "Grand Monarchy" established itself in France. Louis XIV, styled the Grand Monarque, reigned for the unparalleled length of seventy-two years (1643-1715), and set a pattern for all the kings of Europe. At first he was guided by his Machiavellian minister, Cardinal Mazarin; after the death of the Cardinal he himself in his own proper person became the ideal "Prince." He was, within his limitations, an exceptionally capable king; his ambition was stronger than his baser passions, and he guided his country towards bankruptcy, through the complication of a spirited foreign policy, with an elaborate dignity that still extorts our admiration. His immediate desire was to consolidate and extend France to the Rhine and Pyrenees, and to absorb the Spanish Netherlands; his remoter view saw the French kings as the possible successors of Charlemagne in a recast Holy Roman Empire. He made bribery a state method almost more important than warfare. Charles II of England was in his pay, and so were most of the Polish nobility, presently to be described. His money, or rather the money of the tax-paying classes in France, went everywhere. But his prevailing occupation was splendour. His great palace at Versailles, with its salons, its corridors, its mirrors, its terraces and fountains and parks and prospects, was the envy and admiration of the world. He provoked a universal imitation. Every king and princelet in Europe was building his own Versailles as much beyond his means as his subjects and credits would permit. Everywhere the nobility rebuilt or extended their chateaux to the new pattern. A great industry of beautiful and elaborate fabrics and furnishings developed. The luxurious arts flourished everywhere; sculpture in alabaster, faience, gilt woodwork, metal work, stamped leather, much music, magnificent painting, beautiful printing and bindings, fine cookery, fine vintages. Amidst the mirrors and fine furniture went a strange race of "gentlemen" in vast powdered wigs, silks and laces, poised upon high red heels, supported by amazing canes; and still more wonderful "ladies," under towers of powdered hair and wearing vast expansions of silk and satin sustained on wire. Through it all postured the great Louis, the sun of his world, unaware of the meagre and sulky and bitter faces that watched him from those lower darknesses to which his sunshine did not penetrate.

We cannot give here at any length the story of the wars and doings of this monarch. In many ways Voltaire's *Siécle de Louis XIV* is still the best and most wholesome account. He created a French navy fit to face the English and Dutch; a very considerable achievement. But because his intelligence did not rise above the lure of that Fata Morgana, that crack in the political wits of Europe, the dream of a world-wide Holy Roman Empire, he drifted in his later years to the propitiation of the Papacy, which had hitherto been hostile to him. He set himself against those spirits of independence and disunion, the Protestant princes, and he made war against Protestantism in France. Great numbers of his most sober and valuable subjects were driven abroad by his religious persecutions, taking arts and industries with them. The English silk manufacture, for instance, was founded by French Protestants. Under his rule were carried out the "dragonnades," a peculiarly malignant and effectual form of persecution. Rough soldiers were quartered in the houses of the Protestants, and were free to disorder the life of their hosts and insult their womankind as they thought fit. Men yielded to that sort of pressure who would not have yielded to rack and fire. The education of the next generation of Protestants was broken up, and the parents had to give Catholic instruction or none. They gave it, no doubt, with a sneer and an intonation that destroyed all faith in it. While more tolerant countries became mainly sincerely Catholic or sincerely Protestant, the persecuting countries, like France and Spain and Italy, so destroyed honest Protestant teaching that these peoples became mainly Catholic believers or Catholic atheists, ready to break out into blank atheism when-

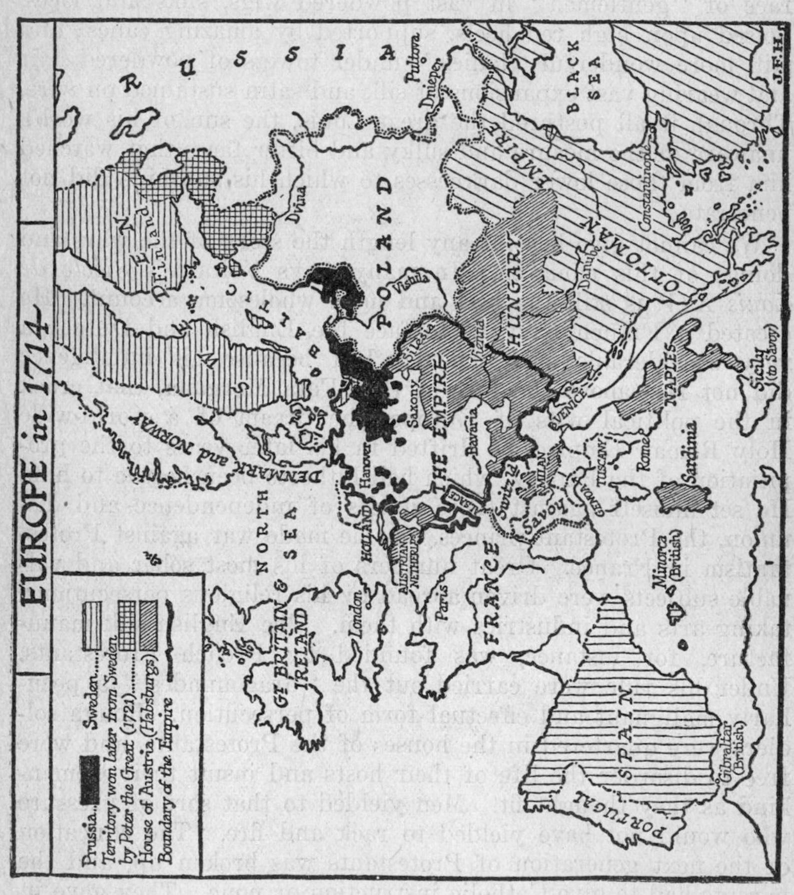
EUROPE in 1714
Prussia
Sweden
Territory won later from Sweden by Peter the Great (1721)
House of Austria (Habsburgs)
Boundary of the Empire
RUSSIA
POLAND
OTTOMAN EMPIRE
HUNGARY
BLACK SEA
Constantinople
Danube
Dnieper
Pultova
Dvina
Vistula
Silesia
Saxony
Vienna
Bavaria
THE EMPIRE
Hanover
HOLLAND
AUSTRIAN NETHERLANDS
DENMARK and NORWAY
SWEDEN
Finland
BALTIC SEA
NORTH SEA
GT BRITAIN & IRELAND
London
Paris
FRANCE
Switz'd
Savoy
MILAN
VENICE
GENOA
TUSCANY
Rome
NAPLES
Sardinia
Sicily (to Savoy)
Minorca (British)
SPAIN
PORTUGAL
Gibraltar (British)
J.F.H.

ever the opportunity offered. The next reign, that of Louis XV, was the age of that supreme mocker, Voltaire (1694-1778), an age in which everybody in French society conformed to the Roman church and hardly anyone believed in it.

It was part—and an excellent part—of the pose of Grand Monarchy to patronize literature and the sciences. Louis XIV set up an academy of sciences in rivalry with the English Royal Society of Charles II and the similar association at Florence. He decorated his court with poets, playwrights, philosophers, and scientific men. If the scientific process got little inspiration from this patronage, it did at any rate acquire resources for experiment and publication, and a certain prestige in the eyes of the vulgar.

Louis XV was the great-grandson of Louis XIV, and an incompetent imitator of his predecessor's magnificence. He posed as a king, but his ruling passion was that common obsession of our kind, the pursuit of women, tempered by a superstitious fear of hell. How such women as the Duchess of Châteauroux, Madame de Pompadour, and Madame du Barry dominated the pleasures of the king, and how wars and alliances were made, provinces devastated, thousands of people killed, because of the vanities and spites of these creatures, and how all the public life of France and Europe was tainted with intrigue and prostitution and imposture because of them, the reader must learn from the memoirs of the time. The spirited foreign policy went on steadily under Louis XV towards its final smash.

In 1774 this Louis, Louis the Well-Beloved, as his flatterers called him, died of smallpox, and was succeeded by his grandson, Louis XVI (1774-93), a dull, well-meaning man, an excellent shot, and an amateur locksmith of some ingenuity. Of how he came to follow Charles I to the scaffold we shall tell in a later section. Our present concern is with Grand Monarchy in the days of its glory.

Among the chief practitioners of Grand Monarchy outside France we may note first the Prussian kings, Frederick William I (1713-40), and his son and successor, Frederick II, Frederick the Great (1740-86). The story of the slow rise of the Hohenzollern family, which ruled the kingdom of Prussia, from inconspicuous beginnings is too tedious and unimportant for us to follow here. It is a story of luck and violence, of bold claims and sudden betrayals. It is told with great appreciation in Carlyle's *Frederick the Great.* By the eighteenth century the Prussian kingdom was important enough to threaten the empire; it had a strong, well-drilled army, and its king was an attentive and worthy student of Machiavelli. Frederick the Great perfected his Versailles at Potsdam. There the park of Sans Souci, with its fountains, avenues, statuary, aped its model; there also was the New Palace, a vast brick building erected at enormous expense, the Orangery in the Italian style, with a collection of pictures, a Marble Palace, and so on. Frederick carried culture to the pitch of authorship, and corresponded with and entertained Voltaire, to their mutual exasperation.

The Austrian dominions were kept too busy between the hammer of the French and the anvil of the Turks to develop the real Grand Monarch style until the reign of Maria Theresa (who, being a woman, did not bear the title of Empress) (1740-80). Joseph II, who was Emperor from 1765-92, succeeded to her palaces in 1780.

With Peter the Great (1682-1725) the empire of Muscovy broke away from her Tartar traditions and entered the sphere of French attraction. Peter shaved the Oriental beards of his nobles and introduced Western costume. These were but the outward and visible symbols of his westering tendencies. To release himself from the Asiatic feeling and traditions of Moscow, which, like Pekin, has a sacred inner city, the Kremlin, he built himself a new capital, Petrograd, upon the swamp of the Neva. And of course he built his Versailles, the Peterhof, about eighteen miles from this new Paris, employing a French architect and having a terrace, fountains, cascades, picture gallery, park, and all the recognized features. His more distinguished successors were Elizabeth (1741-62) and Catherine the Great, a German princess, who, after obtaining the crown in sound Oriental fashion through the murder of her husband, the legitimate Tsar, reverted to advanced Western ideals and ruled with great vigour from 1762 to 1796. She set up an academy, and corresponded with Voltaire. And she lived to witness the end of the system of Grand Monarchy in Europe and the execution of Louis XVI.

We cannot even catalogue here the minor Grand Monarchs of the time in Florence (Tuscany) and Savoy and Saxony and

Denmark and Sweden. Versailles, under a score of names, is starred in every volume of Bædeker, and the tourist gapes in their palaces. Nor can we deal with the war of the Spanish Succession. Spain, overstrained by the imperial enterprises of Charles V and Philip II, and enfeebled by a bigoted persecution of Protestants, Moslems, and Jews, was throughout the seventeenth and eighteenth centuries sinking down from her temporary importance in European affairs to the level of a secondary power again.

These European monarchs ruled their kingdoms as their noblemen ruled their estates: they plotted against one another, they were politic and far-seeing in an unreal fashion, they made wars, they spent the substance of Europe upon absurd "policies" of aggression and resistance. At last there burst upon them a great storm out of the depths. That storm, the First French Revolution, the indignation of the common man in Europe, took their system unawares. It was but the opening outbreak of a great cycle of political and social storms that still continue, that will perhaps continue until every vestige of nationalist monarchy has been swept out of the world and the skies clear again for the great peace of the federation of mankind.

§ 6

We have seen how the idea of a world-rule and a community of mankind first came into human affairs, and we have traced how the failure of the Christian churches to sustain and establish those conceptions of its founder, led to a moral collapse in political affairs and a reversion to egotism and want of faith. We have seen how Machiavellian monarchy set itself up against the spirit of brotherhood in Christendom, and how Machiavellian monarchy developed throughout a large part of Europe into the Grand Monarchies and Parliamentary Monarchies of the seventeenth and eighteenth centuries. But the mind and imagination of man is incessantly active, and beneath the sway of the grand monarchs, a complex of notions and traditions was being woven as a net is woven, to catch and entangle men's minds, the conception of international politics not as a matter of dealings between princes, but as a matter of dealings between a kind of immortal Beings, the Powers. The Princes came and went; a Louis XIV would be followed by a petticoat-hunting Louis XV, and he again by that dull-witted amateur locksmith, Louis XVI. Peter the Great gave place to a succession of empresses; the chief continuity of the Habsburgs after Charles V, either in Austria or Spain, was a continuity of thick lips, clumsy chins, and superstition; the amiable scoundrelism of a Charles II would make a mock of his own pretensions. But what remained much more steadfast were the secretariats of the foreign ministries and the ideas of people who wrote of state concerns. The ministers maintained a continuity of policy during the "off days" of their monarchs, and between one monarch and another.

So we find that the prince gradually became less important in men's minds than the "Power" of which he was the head. We begin to read less and less of the schemes and ambitions of King This or That, and more of the "Designs of France" or the "Ambitions of Prussia." In an age when religious faith was declining, we find men displaying a new and vivid belief in the reality of these personifications. These vast vague phantoms, the "Powers," crept insensibly into European political thought, until in the later eighteenth and in the nineteenth centuries they dominated it entirely. To this day they dominate it. European life remained nominally Christian, but to worship one God in spirit and in truth is to belong to one community with all one's fellow worshippers. In practical reality Europe does not do this, she has given herself up altogether to the worship of this strange state mythology. To these sovereign deities, to the unity of "Italy," to the hegemony of "Prussia," to the glory of "France," and the destinies of "Russia," she has sacrificed many generations of possible unity, peace, and prosperity and the lives of millions of men.

To regard a tribe or a state as a sort of personality is a very old disposition of the human mind. The Bible abounds in such personifications. Judah, Edom, Moab, Assyria, figure in the Hebrew Scriptures as if they were individuals; it is sometimes impossible to say whether the Hebrew writer is dealing with a person or with a nation. It is manifestly a primitive and natural tendency. But in the case of modern Europe it is a retrocession. Europe, under the idea of Christendom, had gone far towards unification. And while such tribal persons as "Israel" or "Tyre" did represent a certain community of blood, a certain uniformity of type, and a homogeneity of interest, the European powers which arose in the seventeenth and eighteenth centuries were entirely fictitious unities. Russia was in truth an assembly of the most incongruous elements, Cossacks, Tartars, Ukrainians, Muscovites, and, after the time of Peter, Esthonians and Lithuanians; the France of Louis XV comprehended German Alsace and freshly assimilated regions of Burgundy; it was a prison of suppressed Huguenots and a sweating-house for peasants. In "Britain," England carried on her back the Hanoverian dominions in Germany, Scotland, the profoundly alien Welsh and the hostile and Catholic Irish. Such powers as Sweden, Prussia, and still more so Poland and Austria, if we watch them in a series of historical maps, contract, expand, thrust out extensions, and wander over the map of Europe as amœbæ do under the microscope. . . .

If we consider the psychology of international relationship as we see it manifested in the world about us, and as it is shown by the development of the "Power" idea in modern Europe, we shall realize certain historically very important facts about the nature of man. Aristotle said that man is a political animal, but in our modern sense of the word politics, which now covers world-politics, he is nothing of the sort. He has still the instincts of the family tribe, and beyond that he has a disposition to attach himself and his family to something larger, to a tribe, a city, a nation, or a state. But that disposition, left to itself, is a vague and very uncritical disposition. If anything, he is inclined to fear and dislike criticism of this something larger that encloses his life and to which he has given himself, and to avoid such criticism. Perhaps he has a subconscious fear of the isolation that may ensue if the system is broken or discredited. He takes the *milieu* in which he finds himself for granted; he accepts his city or his government, just as he accepts the nose or the digestion which fortune has bestowed upon him. But men's loyalties, the sides they take in political things, are not innate, they are educational results. For most men their education in these matters is the silent, continuous education of things about them. Men find themselves a part of Merry England or Holy Russia; they grow up into these devotions; they accept them as a part of their nature.

It is only slowly that the world is beginning to realize how profoundly the tacit education of circumstances can be supplemented, modified, or corrected by positive teaching, by literature, discussion, and properly criticized experience. The real life of the ordinary man is his everyday life, his little circle of affections, fears, hungers, lusts, and imaginative impulses. It is only when his attention is directed to political affairs as something vitally affecting this personal circle, that he brings his reluctant mind to bear upon them. It is scarcely too much to say that the ordinary man thinks as little about political matters as he can, and stops thinking about them as soon as possible. It is still only very curious and exceptional minds, or minds that have by example or good education acquired the scientific habit of wanting to know *why,* or minds shocked and distressed by some public catastrophe and roused to wide apprehensions of danger, that will not accept governments and institutions, however preposterous, that do not directly annoy them, as satisfactory. The ordinary human being, until he is so aroused, will acquiesce in any collective activities that are going on in this world in which he finds himself, and any phrasing or symbolization that meets his vague need for something greater to which his personal affairs, his individual circle, can be anchored.

If we keep these manifest limitations of our nature in mind, it no longer becomes a mystery how, as the idea of Christianity as a world brotherhood of men sank into discredit because of its fatal entanglement with priestcraft and the Papacy on the one hand and with the authority of princes on the other, and the age of faith passed into our present age of doubt and disbelief, men shifted the reference of their lives from the kingdom of God and the brotherhood of mankind to these apparently more living realities, France and England, Holy Russia, Spain, Prussia, which were at least embodied in active courts, which maintained laws, exerted power through armies and navies, waved flags with a compelling solemnity, and were self-assertive and insatiably greedy in an entirely human and understandable fashion. Certainly such men as Cardinal Richelieu and Cardinal Mazarin thought of themselves as serving greater ends than their own or their monarch's; they served the quasi-divine France of their imaginations. And as certainly these habits of mind percolated down from them to their subordinates and to the general body of the population. In the thirteenth and fourteenth centuries the general population of Europe was religious and only vaguely patriotic; by the nineteenth it had become wholly patriotic. In a crowded English or French or German railway carriage of the later nineteenth century it would have aroused far less hostility to have jeered at God than to have jeered at one of those strange beings, England or France or Germany. To these things men's minds clung, and they clung to them because in all the world there appeared nothing else so satisfying to cling to. They were the real and living gods of Europe.

This idealization of governments and foreign offices, this mythology of "Powers" and their loves and hates and conflicts, has so obsessed the imaginations of Europe and Western Asia as to provide it with its "forms of thought." Nearly all the histories, nearly all the political literature of the last two centuries in Europe, have been written in its phraseology. Yet a time is coming when a clear-sighted generation will read with perplexity how in the community of western Europe, consisting everywhere of very slight variations of a common racial mixture of Nordic and Iberian peoples and immigrant Semitic and Mongolian elements, speaking nearly everywhere modifications of the same Aryan speech, having a common past in the Roman Empire, common religious forms, common social usages, and a common art and science, and intermarrying so freely that no one could tell with certainty the "nationality" of any of his great-grandchildren, men could be moved to the wildest excitement upon the question of the ascendancy of "France," the rise and unification of "Germany," the rival claims of "Russia" and "Greece" to possess Constantinople. These conflicts will seem then as reasonless and insane as those dead, now incomprehensible feuds of the "greens" and "blues" that once filled the streets of Byzantium with shouting and bloodshed.

Tremendously as these phantoms, the Powers, rule our minds and lives to-day, they are, as this history shows clearly, things only of the last few centuries, a mere hour, an incidental phase, in the vast deliberate history of our kind. They mark a phase of relapse, a backwater, as the rise of Machiavellian monarchy marks a backwater; they are part of the same eddy of faltering faith, in a process altogether greater and altogether different in its general tendency, the process of the moral and intellectual reunion of mankind. For a time men have relapsed upon these national or imperial gods of theirs; it is but for a time. The idea of the world state, the universal kingdom of righteousness of which every living soul shall be a citizen, was already in the world two thousand years ago never more to leave it. Men know that it is present even when they refuse to recognize it. In the writings and talk of men about international affairs today, in the current discussions of historians and political journalists, there is an effect of drunken men growing sober, and terribly afraid of growing sober. They still talk loudly of their "love" for France, of their "hatred" of Germany, of the "traditional ascendancy of Britain at sea," and so on and so on, like those who sing of their cups in spite of the steadfast onset of sobriety and a headache. These are dead gods they serve. By sea or land men want no Powers ascendant, but only law and service. That silent unavoidable challenge is in all our minds like dawn breaking slowly, shining between the shutters of a disordered room.

§ 7

The seventeenth century in Europe was the century of Louis XIV; he and French ascendancy and Versailles are the central motif of the story. The eighteenth century was equally the century of the "rise of Prussia as a great power," and the chief figure in the story is Frederick II, Frederick the Great. Interwoven with his history is the story of Poland.

The condition of affairs in Poland was peculiar. Unlike its three neighbours, Prussia, Russia, and the Austro-Hungarian monarchy of the Habsburgs, Poland had not developed a Grand Monarchy. Its system of government may be best described as republican with a king, an elected life-president. Each king was separately elected. It was in fact rather more republican than Britain, but its republicanism was more aristocratic in form. Poland had little trade and few manufactures; she was agricultural and still with great areas of grazing, forest, and waste; she was a poor country, and her landowners were poor aristocrats. The mass of her population was a downtrodden and savagely ignorant peasantry, and she also harboured great masses of very poor Jews. She had remained Catholic. She was, so to speak, a poor Catholic inland Britain, entirely surrounded by enemies instead of by the sea. She had no definite boundaries at all, neither sea nor mountain. And it added to her misfortunes that some of her elected kings had been brilliant and aggressive rulers. Eastward her power extended weakly into regions inhabited almost entirely by Russians; westward she overlapped a German subject population.

Because she had no great trade, she had no great towns to compare with those of western Europe, and no vigorous universities to hold her mind together. Her noble class lived on their estates, without much intellectual intercourse. They were patriotic, they had an aristocratic sense of freedom—which was entirely compatible with the systematic impoverishment of their serfs—but their patriotism and freedom were incapable of effective co-operation. While warfare was a matter of levies of men and horses, Poland was a comparatively strong power; but it was quite unable to keep pace with the development of military art that was making standing forces of professional soldiers the necessary weapon in warfare. Yet divided and disabled as she was, she could yet count some notable victories to her credit. The last Turkish attack upon Vienna (1683) was defeated by the Polish cavalry under King John Sobiesky, King John III. (This same Sobiesky, before he was elected king, had been in the pay of Louis XIV, and had also fought for the Swedes against his native country.) Needless to say, this weak aristocratic republic, with its recurrent royal elections, invited aggression from all three of its neighbours. "Foreign money," and every sort of exterior interference, came into the country at each election. And like the Greeks of old, every disgruntled Polish patriot flew off to some foreign enemy to wreak his indignation upon his ungrateful country.

Even when the King of Poland was elected, he had very little power because of the mutual jealousy of the nobles. Like the English peers, they preferred a foreigner, and for much the same reason, because he had no roots of power in the land; but, unlike the British, their own government had not the solidarity which the periodic assembling of Parliament in London, the "coming up to town," gave the British peers. In London there was "Society," a continuous intermingling of influential persons and ideas. Poland had no London and no "Society." So practically Poland had no central government at all. The King of Poland could not make war nor peace, levy a tax nor alter the law, without the consent of the Diet, and *any single member of the Diet had the power of putting a veto upon any proposal before it.* He had merely to rise and say,

"I disapprove," and the matter dropped. He could even carry his free veto, his *liberum veto,* further. He could object to the assembly of the Diet, and the Diet was thereby dissolved. Poland was not simply a crowned aristocratic republic like the British, it was a paralyzed crowned aristocratic republic.

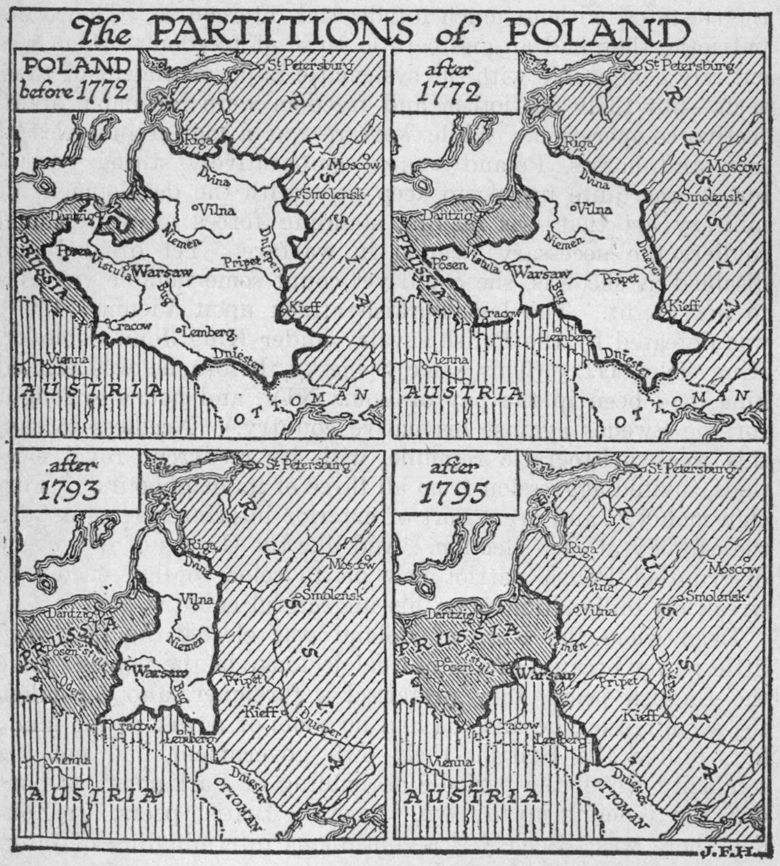

To Frederick the Great the existence of Poland was particularly provocative because of the way in which an arm of Poland reached out to the Baltic at Dantzig and separated his ancestral dominions in East Prussia from his territories within the empire. It was he who incited Catherine the Second of

Russia and Maria Theresa of Austria, whose respect he had earned by depriving her of Silesia, to a joint attack upon Poland.

Let four maps of Poland tell the tale.

After this first outrage of 1772 Poland underwent a great change of heart. Poland was indeed born as a nation on the eve of her dissolution. There was a hasty but very considerable development of education, literature, and art; historians and poets sprang up, and the impossible constitution that had made Poland impotent was swept aside. The free veto was abolished, the crown was made hereditary to save Poland from the foreign intrigues that attended every election, and a Parliament in imitation of the British was set up. There were, however, lovers of the old order in Poland who resented these necessary changes, and these obstructives were naturally supported by Prussia and Russia, who wanted no Polish revival. Came the second partition, and, after a fierce patriotic struggle that began in the region annexed by Prussia and found a leader and national hero in Kosciusko, the final obliteration of Poland from the map. So for a time ended this Parliamentary threat to Grand Monarchy in Eastern Europe. But the patriotism of the Poles grew stronger and clearer with suppression. For a hundred and twenty years Poland struggled like a submerged creature beneath the political and military net that held her down. She rose again in 1918, at the end of the Great War.

§ 8

We have given some account of the ascendancy of France in Europe, the swift decay of the sappy growth of Spanish power and its separation from Austria, and the rise of Prussia. So fas as Portugal, Spain, France, Britain, and Holland were concerned, their competition for ascendancy in Europe was extended and complicated by a struggle for dominion overseas.

The discovery of the huge continent of America, thinly inhabited, undeveloped, and admirably adapted for European settlement and exploitation, and simultaneous discovery of great areas of unworked country south of the torrid equatorial regions of Africa that had hitherto limited European knowledge, and the gradual realization of vast island regions in the Eastern seas, as yet untouched by Western civilization, was a presentation of opportunity to mankind unprecedented in all history. It was as if the peoples of Europe had come into some splendid legacy. Their world had suddenly quadrupled. There was more than enough for all; they had only to take these lands and continue to do well by them, and their crowded poverty would vanish like a dream. And they received this glorious legacy like ill-bred heirs; it meant no more to them than a fresh occasion for atrocious disputes. But what community of human beings has ever yet preferred creation to conspiracy? What nation in all our story has ever worked with another when, at any cost to itself, it could contrive to do that other an injury? The Powers of Europe began by a frantic "claiming" of the new realms. They went on to exhausting conflicts. Spain, who claimed first and most, and who was for a time "mistress" of two-thirds of America, made no better use of her possession than to bleed herself nearly to death therein.

We have told how the Papacy in its last assertion of world dominion, instead of maintaining the common duty of all Christendom to make a great common civilization in the new lands, divided the American continent between Spain and Portugal. This naturally roused the hostility of the excluded nations. The seamen of England showed no respect for either claim, and set themselves particularly against the Spanish; the Swedes turned their Protestantism to a similar account. The Hollanders, so soon as they had shaken off their Spanish masters, also set their sails westward to flout the Pope and share in the good things of the new world. His Most Catholic Majesty of France hesitated as little as any Protestant. All these powers were soon busy staking out claims in North America and the West Indies.

Neither the Danish kingdom (which at that time included Norway and Iceland) nor the Swedes secured very much in the scramble. The Danes annexed some of the West Indian islands. Sweden got nothing. Both Denmark and Sweden at this time were deep in the affairs of Germany. We have already named Gustavus Adolphus, the Protestant "Lion of the North," and mentioned his campaigns in Germany, Poland, and Russia. These Eastern European regions are great absorbents of energy, and the strength that might have given Sweden a large share in the new world reaped a barren harvest of glory in Europe.

Such small settlements as the Swedes made in America presently fell to the Dutch.

The Hollanders, too, with the French monarchy under Cardinal Richelieu and under Louis XIV eating its way across the Spanish Netherlands towards their frontier, had not the undistracted resources that Britain, behind her "silver streak" of sea, could put into overseas adventures.

Moreover, the absolutist efforts of James I and Charles I, and the restoration of Charles II, had the effect of driving out from England a great number of sturdy-minded, republican-spirited Protestants, men of substance and character, who set up in America, and particularly in New England, out of reach, as they supposed, of the king and his taxes. The *Mayflower* was only one of the pioneer vessels of a stream of emigrants. It was the luck of Britain that they remained, though dissentient in spirit, under the British flag. The Dutch never sent out settlers of the same quantity and quality, first because their Spanish rulers would not let them, and then because they had got possession of their own country. And though there was a great emigration of Protestant Huguenots from the dragonnades and persecution of Louis XIV, they had Holland and England close at hand as refuges, and their industry, skill, and sobriety went mainly to strengthen those countries, and particularly England. A few of them founded settlements in Carolina, but these did not remain French; they fell first to the Spanish and finally to the English.

The Dutch settlements, with the Swedish, also succumbed to Britain; Nieuw Amsterdam became British in 1674, and its name was changed to New York, as the reader may learn very cheerfully in Washington Irving's *Knickerbocker's History of New York*. The state of affairs in North America in 1750 is indicated very clearly by a map we have adapted from one in Robinson's *Medieval and Modern Times*. The British power was established along the east coast from Savannah to the St. Lawrence River, and Newfoundland and considerable northern areas, the Hudson Bay Company territories, had been acquired by treaty from the French. The British occupied Barbados (almost our oldest possession) in 1605, and acquired Jamaica, the Bahamas, and British Honduras from the Spaniards. But France was pursuing a very dangerous and alarming game, a game even more dangerous

and alarming on the map than in reality. She had made real settlements in Quebec and Montreal to the north and at New Orleans in the south, and her explorers and agents had pushed south and north, making treaties with the American Indians of the great plains and setting up claims—without setting up towns—right across the continent behind the British. But the realities of the case are not adequately represented in this way. The British colonies were being very solidly settled by a good class of pople; they already numbered a population of over a million; the French at that time hardly counted a tenth of that. They had a number of brilliant travellers and missionaries at work, but no substance of population behind them.

Many old maps of America in this period are still to be found, maps designed to scare and "rouse" the British to a sense of the "designs of France" in America. War broke out in 1754, and in 1759 the British and Colonial forces under General Wolfe took Quebec and completed the conquest of Canada in the next year. In 1763 Canada was finally ceded to Britain. (But the western part of the rather indefinite region of Louisiana in the south, named after Louis XIV, remained outside the British sphere. It was taken over by Spain; and in 1800 it was recovered by France. Finally, in 1803, it was bought from France by the United States government.) In this Canadian war the American colonists gained a considerable experience of the military art, and a knowledge of British military organization that was to be of great use to them a little later.

§ 9

It was not only in America that the French and British powers clashed. The condition of India at this time was one very interesting and attractive to European adventurers. The great Mongol Empire of Baber, Akbar, and Aurangzeb was now far gone in decay. What had happened to India was very parallel to what had happened to Germany. The Great Mogul at Delhi in India, like the Holy Roman Emperor in Germany, was still legally overlord, but after the death of Aurangzeb he exerted only a nominal authority except in the immediate neighborhood of his capital. In the south-west a Hindu people, the Mahrattas, had risen against Islam, restored Brahminism as the ruling religion, and for a time extended their power over the whole southern triangle of India. In Rajputana also the rule of Islam was replaced by Brahminism, and at Bhurtpur and Jaipur there ruled powerful Rajput princes. In Oudh there was a Shiite kingdom, with its capital at Lucknow, and

Bengal was also a separate (Moslem) kingdom. Away in the Punjab to the north had arisen a very interesting religious body, the Sikhs, proclaiming the universal rule of one God and assailing both the Hindu Vedas and the Moslem Koran. Originally a pacific sect, the Sikhs presently followed the example of Islam, and sought—at first very disastrously to themselves—to establish the kingdom of God by the sword. And into this confused and disordered India there presently (1738) came an invader from the north, Nadir Shah (1736-47), the Turcoman ruler of Persia, who swept down through the Kyber pass, broke every army that stood in his way, and captured and sacked Delhi, carrying off an enormous booty. He left the north of India so utterly broken, that in the next twenty years there were no less than six other successful plundering raids into North India from Afghanistan, which had become an independent state at the death of Nadir Shah. For a time Mahrattas fought with Afghans for the rule of North India; then the Mahratta power broke up into a series of principalities, Indore, Gwalior, Baroda, and others. . . .

This was the India into which the French and English were thrusting during the eighteenth century. A succession of other European powers had been struggling for a commercial and political footing in India and the east ever since Vasco da Gama had made his memorable voyage round the Cape to Calicut. The sea trade of India had previously been in the hands of the Red Sea Arabs, and the Portuguese won it from them in a series of sea fights. The Portuguese ships were the bigger, and carried a heavier armament. For a time the Portuguese held the Indian trade as their own, and Lisbon outshone Venice as a mart for oriental spices; the seventeenth century, however, saw the Dutch grasping at this monopoly. At the crest of their power the Dutch had settlements at the Cape of Good Hope, they held Mauritius, they had two establishments in Persia, twelve in India, six in Ceylon, and all over the East Indies they had dotted their fortified stations. But their selfish resolution to exclude traders of any other European nationality forced the Swedes, Danes, French, and English into hostile competition. The first effectual blows at their overseas monopoly were struck in European waters by the victories of Blake, the English republican admiral; and by the opening of the eighteenth century both the English and French were in vigorous competition with the Dutch for trade and privileges throughout India. At Madras, Bombay, and Calcutta the English established their headquarters; Pondicherry and Chandernagore were the chief French settlements.

At first all these European powers came merely as traders, and the only establishments they attempted were warehouses;

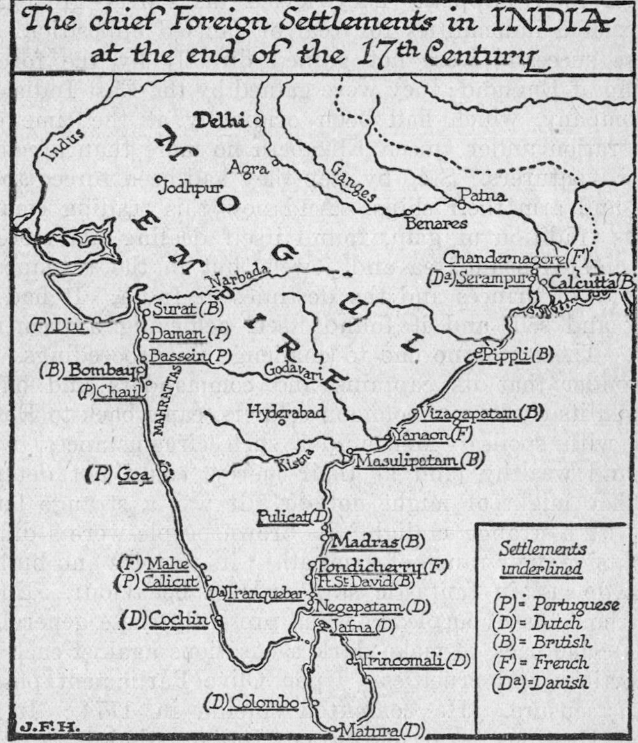

but the unsettled state of the country, and the unscrupulous methods of their rivals, made it natural for them to fortify and arm their settlements, and this armament made them attractive allies of the various warring princes who now divided India. And it was entirely in the spirit of the New European nationalist politics that when the French took one side, the British should take another. The great leader upon the English side was Robert Clive, who was born in 1725, and went to India in 1743. His chief antagonist was Dupleix. The story of this struggle throughout the first half of the eighteenth century is too long and intricate to be told here. By 1761 the British found themselves completely dominant in the Indian peninsula. At Plassey (1757) and at Buxar (1764) their armies gained striking and conclusive victories over the army of Bengal and the army of Oudh. The Great Mogul, nominally their overlord, became in effect their puppet. They levied taxes over great areas; they exacted indemnities for real or fancied opposition.

These successes were not gained directly by the forces of the King of England; they were gained by the East India Trading Company, which had been originally at the time of its incorporation under Queen Elizabeth no more than a company of sea adventurers. Step by step they had been forced to raise troops and arm their ships. And now this trading company, with its tradition of gain, found itself dealing not merely in spices and dyes and tea and jewels, but in the revenues and territories of princes and the destinies of India. It had come to buy and sell, and it found itself achieving a tremendous piracy. There was no one to challenge its proceedings. Is it any wonder that its captains and commanders and officials, nay, even its clerks and common soldiers, came back to England loaded with spoils? Men under such circumstances, with a great and wealthy land at their mercy, could not determine what they might or might not do. It was a strange land to them, with a strange sunlight; its brown people were a different race, outside their range of sympathy; its temples and buildings seemed to sustain fantastic standards of behaviour. Englishmen at home were perplexed when presently these generals and officials came back to make dark accusations against each other of extortions and cruelties. Upon Clive Parliament passed a vote of censure. He commited suicide in 1774. In 1788 Warren Hastings, a second great Indian administrator, was impeached and acquitted (1792). It was a strange and unprecedented situation in the world's history. The English Parliament found itself ruling over a London trading company, which in its turn was dominating an empire far greater and more populous than all the domains of the British crown. To the bulk of the English people India was a remote, fantastic, almost inaccessible land, to which adventurous poor young men went out, to return after many years very rich and very choleric old gentlemen. It was difficult for the English to conceive what the life of these countless brown millions in the eastern sunshine could be. Their imaginations declined the task. India remained romantically unreal. It was impossible for the English, therefore, to exert any effective supervision and control over the company's proceedings.

§ 10

And while the great peninsula of the south of Asia was thus falling under the dominion of the English sea traders, an equally remarkable reaction of Europe upon Asia was going on in the north. We have told in Chap. XXXIII, § 5c, how the Christian states of Russia recovered their independence from the Golden Horde, and how the Tsar of Moscow became master of the republic of Novgorod; and in § 5 of this chapter we have told of Peter the Great joining the circle of Grand Monarchs and, as it were, dragging Russia into Europe. The rise of this great central power of the old world, which is neither altogether of the East nor altogether of the West, is one of the utmost importance to our human destiny. We have also told in the same chapter of the appearance of a Christian steppe people, the Cossacks, who formed a barrier between the feudal agriculture of Poland and Hungary to the west and the Tartar to the east. The Cossacks were the wild east of Europe, and in many ways not unlike the wild west of the United States in the middle nineteenth century. All who had made Russia too hot to hold them, criminals as well as the persecuted innocent, rebellious serfs, religious sectaries, thieves, vagabonds, murderers, sought asylum in the southern steppes, and there made a fresh start and fought for life and freedom against Pole, Russian, and Tartar alike. Doubtless fugitives from the Tartars to the east also contributed to the Cossack mixture. Chief among these new nomad tribes were the Ukraine Cossacks on the Dnieper and the Don Cossacks on the Don. Slowly these border folk were incorporated in the Russian imperial service, much as the Highland clans of Scotland were converted into regiments by the British government. New lands were offered them in Asia. They became a weapon against the dwindling power of the Mongolian nomads, first in Turkestan and then across Siberia as far as the Amur.

The decay of Mongol energy in the seventeenth and eighteenth centuries is very difficult to explain. Within two or three centuries from the days of Jengis and Timurlane, central

Asia had relapsed from a period of world ascendancy to extreme political impotence. Changes of climate, unrecorded pestilences, infections of a malarial type, may have played their part in this recession—which may be only a temporary recession measured by the scale of universal history—of the Central Asian

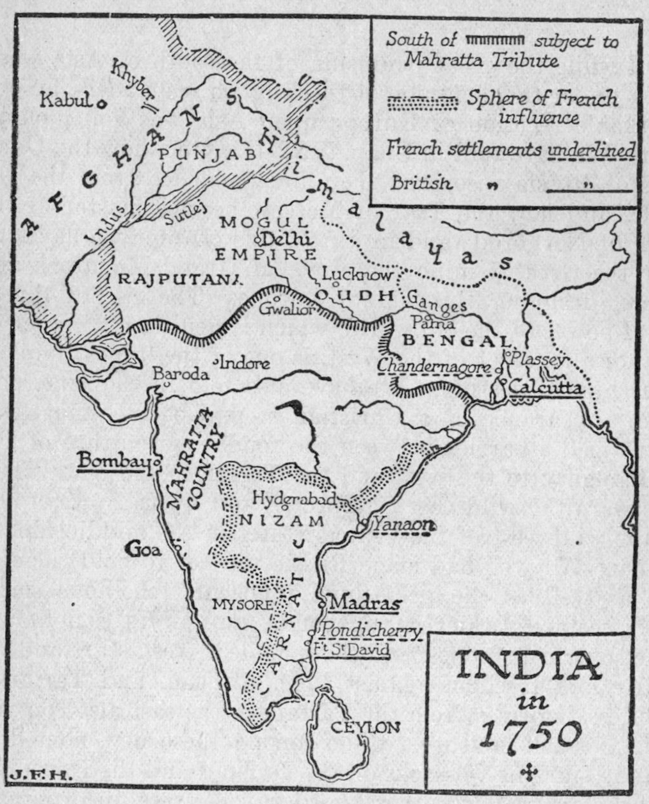

peoples. Some authorities think that the spread of Buddhist teaching from China also had a pacifying influence upon them. At any rate, by the sixteenth century the Mongol Tartar and Turkish peoples were no longer pressing outward, but were being invaded, subjugated, and pushed back both by Christian Russia in the west and by China in the east.

All through the seventeenth century the Cossacks were spreading eastward from European Russia, and settling wherever they found agricultural conditions. Cordons of forts and stations formed a moving frontier to these settlements to the south, where the Turkomans were still strong and active; to the north-east, however, Russia had no frontier until she reached right to the Pacific. . . .

At the same time China was in a phase of expansion. In 1644 the Ming Dynasty, in a state of artistic decay and greatly weakened by a Japanese invasion, fell to Manchu conquerors, a people apparently identical with the former Kin Dynasty, which had ruled at Pekin over North China until the days of Jengis. It was the Manchus who imposed the pigtail as a mark of political loyalty upon the Chinese population. They brought a new energy into Chinese affairs, and their northern interests led to a considerable northward expansion of the Chinese civilization and influence into Manchuria and Mongolia. So it was that by the middle of the eighteenth century the Russians and Chinese were in contact in Mongolia. At this period China ruled eastern Turkestan, Tibet, Nepal, Burmah, and Annam. . . .

We have mentioned a Japanese invasion of China (or rather of Korea). Except for this aggression upon China, Japan plays no part in our history before the nineteenth century. Like China under the Mings, Japan had set her face resolutely against the interference of foreigners in her affairs. She was a country leading her own civilized life, magically sealed against intruders. We have told little of her hitherto because there was little to tell. Her picturesque and romantic history stands apart from the general drama of human affairs. Her population was chiefly a Mongolian population, with some very interesting white people of a Nordic type, the Hairy Ainu, in the northern islands. Her civilization seems to have been derived almost entirely from Korea and China; her art is a special development of Chinese art, her writing an adaptation of the Chinese script.

§ 11

In the preceding ten sections we have been dealing with an age of division, of separated nationalities. We have already described this period of the seventeenth and eighteenth centuries as an interregnum in the progress of mankind towards a world-wide unity. Throughout this period there was no ruling unifying idea in men's minds. The impulse of the empire had failed until the Emperor was no more than one of a number of competing princes, and the dream of Christendom also was a fading dream. The developing "powers" jostled one another throughout the world; but for a time it seemed that they might jostle one another indefinitely without any great catastrophe to mankind. The great geographical discoveries of the sixteenth century had so enlarged human resources that, for all their divisions, for all the waste of their wars and policies, the people of Europe enjoyed a considerable and increasing prosperity. Central Europe recovered steadily from the devastation of the Thirty Years' War.

Looking back upon this period, which came to its climax in the eighteenth century, looking back, as we can begin to do nowadays, and seeing its events in relation to the centuries that came before it and to the great movements of the present time, we are able to realize how transitory and provisional were its political forms and how unstable its securities. Provisional it was as no other age has been provisional, an age of assimilation and recuperation, a political pause, a gathering up of the ideas of men and the resources of science for a wider human effort. But the contemporary mind did not see it in that light. The failure of the great creative ideas as they had been formulated in the Middle Ages had left human thought for a time destitute of the guidance of creative ideas; even educated and imaginative men saw the world undramatically; no longer as an interplay of effort and destiny, but as the scene in which a trite happiness was sought and the milder virtues were rewarded. It was not simply the contented and conservative-minded who, in a world of rapid changes, were under the sway of this assurance of an achieved fixity of human conditions. Even highly critical and insurgent intelligences, in default of any sustaining movements in the soul of the community, betrayed the same disposition. Political life, they felt, had ceased to be the urgent and tragic thing it had once been; it had become a polite comedy. The eighteenth was a century of comedy—which at the end grew dim. It is inconceivable that that world of the middle eighteenth century could have produced a Jesus of Nazareth, a Gautama, a Francis of Assisi, an Ignatius of Loyola. If one may imagine an eighteenth-century John Huss, it is impossible to imagine anyone with sufficient passion to burn him. Until the stirrings of conscience in Britain that developed into the Methodist revival began, we can detect scarcely a suspicion that there still remained great tasks in hand for our race to do, that enormous disturbances were close at hand, or that the path of man through space and time was dark with countless dangers, and must to the end remain a high and terrible enterprise.

We have quoted again and again in this history from Gibbon's *Decline and Fall of the Roman Empire.* Now we shall quote from it for the last time and bid it farewell, for we have come to the age in which it was written. Gibbon was born in 1737, and the last volume of his history was published in 1787, but the passage we shall quote was probably written in the year 1780. Gibbon was a young man of delicate health and fairly good fortune; he had a partial and interrupted education at Oxford, and then he completed his studies in Geneva; on the whole his outlook was French and cosmopolitan rather than British, and he was much under the intellectual influence of that great Frenchman who is best known under the name of Voltaire (François Marie Arouet de Voltaire, 1694-1778). Voltaire was an author of enormous industry; seventy volumes of him adorn the present writer's shelves, and another edition of Voltaire's works runs to ninety-four; he dealt largely with history and public affairs, and he corresponded with Catherine the Great of Russia, Frederick the Great of Prussia, Louis XV, and most of the prominent people of the time. Both Voltaire and Gibbon had the sense of history strong in them; both have set out very plainly and fully their visions of human life; and it is clear that to both of them the system in which they lived, the system of monarchy, of leisurely and privileged gentlefolks, of rather despised industrial and trading people and of downtrodden and negligible labourers and poor and common people, seemed the most stably established way of living that the world has ever seen. They postured a little as republicans, and sneered at the divine pretensions of monarchy; but the republicanism that appealed to Voltaire was the crowned republicanism of the Britain of those days, in which the king was simply the official head, the first and greatest of the gentlemen.

The ideal they sustained was the ideal of a polite and polished world in which men—men of quality, that is, for no others counted—would be ashamed to be cruel or gross or enthusiastic, in which the appointments of life would be spacious and elegant, and the fear of ridicule the potent auxiliary of the law in maintaining the decorum and harmonies of life. Voltaire had in him the possibility of a passionate hatred of injustice, and his interventions on behalf of persecuted or ill-used men are the high lights of his long and complicated life-story. And this being the mental disposition of Gibbon and Voltaire, and of the age in which they lived, it is natural that they should find the existence of religion in the world, and in particular the existence of Christianity, a perplexing and rather unaccountable phenomenon. The whole of that side of life seemed to them a kind of craziness in the human make-up. Gibbon's great history is essentially an attack upon Christianity as the operating cause of the decline and fall. He idealized the crude and gross plutocracy of Rome into a world of fine gentlemen upon the eighteenth-century model, and told how it fell before the Barbarian from without because of the decay through Christianity within. In our history here we have tried to set that story in a better light. To Voltaire official Christianity was *"l'infâme"*; something that limited people's lives, interfered with their thoughts, persecuted harmless dissentients. And indeed in that period of the interregnum there was very little life or light in either the orthodox Christianity of Rome or in the orthodox tame churches of Russia and of the Protestant princes. In an interregnum incommoded with an abundance of sleek parsons and sly priests it was hard to realize what fires had once blazed in the heart of Christianity, and what fires of political and religious passion might still blaze in the hearts of men.

At the end of his third volume Gibbon completed his account of the breaking up of the Western Empire. He then raised the question whether civilization might ever undergo again a similar collapse. This led him to review the existing state of affairs (1780) and to compare it with the state of affairs during the decline of imperial Rome. It will be very convenient to our general design to quote some passages from that comparison here, for nothing could better illustrate the state of mind of the liberal thinkers of Europe at the crest of the political interregnum of the age of the Great Powers, before the first intimations of those profound political and social forces of disintegration that have produced at length the dramatic interrogations of our own times.

"This awful revolution," wrote Gibbon of the Western collapse, "may be usefully applied to the useful instruction of the present age. It is the duty of a patriot to prefer and promote the exclusive interest and glory of his native country; but a philosopher may be permitted to enlarge his views, and to consider Europe as one great republic, whose various inhabitants have attained almost the same level of politeness and cultivation. The balance of power will continue to fluctuate, and the prosperity of our own or the neighbouring kingdoms may be alternately exalted or depressed; but these partial events cannot essentially injure our general state of happiness, the system of arts, and laws, and manners, which so advantageously distinguish, above the rest of mankind, the Europeans and their colonies. The savage nations of the globe are the common enemies of civilized society; and we may enquire with anxious curiosity whether Europe is still threatened with a repetition of those calamities which formerly oppressed the arms and institutions of Rome. Perhaps the same reflections will illustrate the fall of that mighty empire and explain the probable causes of our actual security.

"The Romans were ignorant of the extent of their danger, and the number of their enemies. Beyond the Rhine and Danube, the northern countries of Europe and Asia were filled with innumerable tribes of hunters and shepherds, poor, voracious, and turbulent; bold in arms, and impatient to ravish the fruits of industry. The Barbarian world was agitated by the rapid impulse of war; and the peace of Gaul or Italy was shaken by the distant revolutions of China. The Huns, who fled before a victorious enemy, directed their march towards the west; and the torrent was swelled by the gradual accession of captives and allies. The flying tribes who yielded to the Huns assumed in *their* turn the spirit of conquest; the endless column of barbarians pressed on the Roman Empire with accumulated weight and, if the foremost were destroyed, the vacant space was instantly replenished by new assailants. Such formidable emigrations can no longer issue from the North; and the long repose, which has been imputed to the decrease of population, is the happy consequence of the progress of arts and agriculture. Instead of some rude villages, thinly scattered among its woods and morasses, Germany now produces a list of two thousand three hundred walled towns; the Christian kingdoms of Denmark, Sweden, and Poland have been successively established; and the Hanse merchants, with the Teutonic knights, have extended their colonies along the cost of the Baltic, as far as the Gulf of Finland. From the Gulf of Finland to the Eastern Ocean, Russia now assumes the form of a powerful and civilized empire. The plough, the loom, and the forge are introduced on the banks of the Volga, the Oby, and the Lena; and the fiercest of the Tartar hordes have been taught to tremble and obey. . . .

"The Empire of Rome was firmly established by the singular and perfect coalition of its members. . . . But this union was purchased by the loss of national freedom and military spirit; and the servile provinces, destitute of life and motion, expected their safety from the mercenary troops and governors, who were directed by the orders of a distant court. The happiness of a hundred millions depended on the personal merit of one or two men, perhaps children, whose minds were corrupted by education, luxury, and despotic power. Europe is now divided into twelve powerful, though unequal kingdoms, three respectable commonwealths, and a variety of smaller, though independent, states; the chances of royal and ministerial talents are multiplied, at least with the number of its rulers; and a Julian[1] or Semiramis[2] may reign in the north, while Arcadius and Honorius[3] again slumber on the thrones of the House of Bourbon. The abuses of tyranny are restrained by the mutual influence of fear and shame; republics have acquired order and stability; monarchies have imbibed the principles of freedom, or, at least, of moderation; and some sense of honour and justice is introduced into the most defective constitutions by the general manners of the times. In peace, the progress of knowledge and industry is accelerated by the emulation of so many active rivals: in war, the European forces are exercised by temperate and undecisive contests. If a savage conqueror should issue from the deserts of Tartary, he must repeatedly vanquish the robust peasants of Russia, the numerous armies of Germany, the gallant nobles of France, and the intrepid freemen

[1] Frederick the Great of Prussia.
[2] Catherine the Great of Russia.
[3] Louis XVI of France and Charles III of Spain.

of Britain; who, perhaps, might confederate for their common defence. Should the victorious Barbarians carry slavery and desolation as far as the Atlantic Ocean, ten thousand vessels would transport beyond their pursuit the remains of civilized society; and Europe would revive and flourish in the American world which is already filled with her colonies and institutions.

"Cold, poverty, and a life of danger and fatigue fortify the strength and courage of Barbarians. In every age they have oppressed the polite and peaceful nations of China, India, and Persia, who neglected, and still neglect, to counterbalance these natural powers by the resources of military art. The warlike states of antiquity, Greece, Macedonia, and Rome, educated a race of soldiers; exercised their bodies, disciplined their courage, multiplied their forces by regular evolutions, and converted the iron which they possessed into strong and serviceable weapons. But this superiority insensibly declined with their laws and manners; and the feeble policy of Constantine and his successors armed and instructed, for the ruin of the empire, the rude valour of the Barbarian mercenaries. The military art has been changed by the invention of gunpowder; which enables man to command the two most powerful agents of nature, air and fire. Mathematics, chemistry, mechanics, architecture, have been applied to the service of war; and the adverse parties oppose to each other the most elaborate modes of attack and of defence. Historians may indignantly observe that the preparations of a siege would found and maintain a flourishing colony; yet we cannot be displeased that the subversion of a city should be a work of cost and difficulty, or that an industrious people should be protected by those arts, which survive and supply the decay of military virtue. Cannon and fortifications now form an impregnable barrier against the Tartar horse[1]; and Europe is secure from any future irruption of Barbarians; since, before they can conquer, they must cease to be barbarous. . . .

"Should these speculations be found doubtful or fallacious, there still remains a more humble source of comfort and hope. The discoveries of ancient and modern navigators, and the domestic history, or tradition, of the most enlightened nations, represent the *human savage,* naked both in mind and body, and

1 Gibbon forgets here that cannon and the fundamentals of modern military method came to Europe with the Mongols.

destitute of laws, of arts, of ideas, and almost of language. From this abject condition, perhaps the primitive and universal state of man, he has gradually arisen to command the animals, to fertilize the earth, to traverse the ocean, and to measure the heavens. His progress in the improvement and exercise of his mental and corporeal faculties has been irregular and various, infinitely slow in the beginning, and increasing by degrees with redoubled velocity; ages of laborious ascent have been followed by a moment of rapid downfall; and the several climates of the globe have felt the vicissitudes of light and darkness. Yet the experience of four thousand years should enlarge our hopes, and diminish our apprehensions; we cannot determine to what height the human species may aspire in their advances towards perfection; but it may safely be presumed that no people, unless the face of nature is changed, will relapse into their original barbarism.

"Since the first discovery of the arts, war, commerce, and religious zeal have diffused, among the savages of the Old and New World, those inestimable gifts, they have been successively propagated; they can never be lost. We may therefore acquiesce in the pleasing conclusion that every age of the world has increased, and still increases, the real wealth, the happiness, the knowledge, and perhaps the virtue, of the human race."

§ 12

One of the most interesting aspects of this story of Europe in the seventeenth and earlier eighteenth century during the phase of the Grand and Parliamentary Monarchies, is the comparative quiescence of the peasants and workers. The insurrectionary fires of the fourteenth and fifteenth and sixteenth centuries seem to have died down. The acute economic clashes of the earlier period had been mitigated by rough adjustments. The discovery of America had revolutionized and changed the scale of business and industry, had brought a vast volume of precious metal for money into Europe, had increased and varied employment. For a time life and work ceased to be intolerable to the masses of the poor. This did not, of course, prevent much individual misery and discontent; the poor we have always had with us, but this misery and discontent was divided and scattered. It became inaudible.

In the earlier period the common people had had an idea to crystallize upon, the idea of Christian communism. They had found an educated leadership in the dissentient priests and doctors of the Wycliffe type. As the movement for a revival in Christianity spent its force, as Lutheranism fell back for leadership from Jesus upon the Protestant Princes, this contact and reaction of the fresher minds of the educated class upon the illiterate mass was interrupted. However numerous a downtrodden class may be, and however extreme its miseries, it will never be able to make an effective protest until it achieves solidarity by the development of some common general idea. Educated men and men of ideas are more necessary to a popular political movement than any other political process. A monarchy learns by ruling, and an oligarchy of any type has the education of affairs; but the common man, the peasant or toiler, has no experience in large matters, and can exist politically only through the services, devotion, and guidance of educated men. The Reformation, the Reformation that succeeded, the Reformation that is of the Princes, by breaking up educational facilities, largely destroyed the poor scholar and priest class whose persuasion of the crowd had rendered the Reformation possible.

The Princes of the Protestant countries when they seized upon the national churches early apprehended the necessity of gripping the universities also. Their idea of education was the idea of capturing young clever people for the service of their betters. Beyond that they were disposed to regard education as a mischievous thing. The only way to an education, therefore, for a poor man was through patronage. Of course there was a parade of encouragement towards learning in all the Grand Monarchies, a setting up of Academies and Royal Societies, but these benefited only a small class of subservient scholars. The church also had learnt to distrust the educated poor man. In the great aristocratic "crowned republic" of Britain there was the same shrinkage of educational opportunity. "Both the ancient universities," says Hammond, in his account of the eighteenth century, "were the universities of the rich. There is a passage in Macaulay describing the state and pomp of Oxford at the end of the seventeenth century, 'when her Chancellor, the Venerable Duke of Ormonde, sat in his embroidered mantle on his throne under the painted ceiling of the Sheldonian theatre, surrounded by hundreds of graduates robed according to their rank, while the noblest youths of England were solemnly presented to him as candidates for academical honours.' The university was a power, not in the sense in which that could be said of a university like the old university of Paris, whose learning could make Popes tremble, but in the sense that the university was part of the recognized machinery of aristocracy. What was true of the universities was true of the public schools. Education in England was the nursery not of a society, but of an order; not of a state, but of a race of owner-rulers.'' The missionary spirit had departed from education throughout Europe. To that quite as much as to the amelioration of things by a diffused prosperity, this phase of quiescence among the lower classes is to be ascribed. They had lost brains and speech, and they were fed. The community was like a pithed animal in the hands of the governing class.[1]

Moreover, there had been considerable changes in the proportions of class to class. One of the most difficult things for the historian to trace is the relative amount of the total property of the community held at any time by any particular class in that community. These things fluctuate very rapidly. The peasant wars of Europe indicate a phase of comparatively concentrated property when large masses of people could feel themselves expropriated and at a common disadvantage, and so take mass action. This was the time of the rise and prosperity of the Fuggers and their like, a time of international finance. Then with the vast importation of silver and gold and commodities into Europe from America, there seems to have been a restoration of a more diffused state of wealth. The poor were just as miserable as ever, but there were perhaps not so many poor relatively, and they were broken up into a variety of types without any ideas in common. In Great Britain the agricultural life which had been dislocated by the confiscations of the Reformation had settled down again into a system of tenant farming under great landowners. Side by side with the large estates there was still, however, much common land

[1] ''Our present public school system is candidly based on training a dominant master class. But the uprising of the workers and modern conditions are rapidly making the dominant method unworkable. . . . The change in the aim of schools will transform all the organizations and methods of schools, and my belief is that this change will make the new era.''—F. W. Sanderson, Head Master of Oundle, in an address at Leeds, February 16th, 1920.

for pasturing the beasts of the poorer villagers, and much land cultivated in strips upon communal lines. The middling sort of man, and even the poorer sort of man upon the land, were leading an endurable existence in 1700. The standard of life, the idea, that is, of what is an endurable existence, was, however, rising during the opening phase of Grand Monarchy; after a time the process of the upward concentration of wealth seems to have been resumed, the larger landowners began to acquire and crowd out the poorer free cultivators, and the proportion of poor people and of people who felt they were leading impoverished lives increased again. The bigger men were unchallenged rulers of Great Britain, and they set themselves to enact laws, the Enclosure Acts, that practically confiscated the unenclosed and common lands, mainly for the benefit of the larger landowners. The smaller men sank to the level of wage workers upon the land over which they had once possessed rights of cultivation and pasture.

The peasant in France and upon the Continent generally was not so expropriated; his enemy was not the landlord, but the taxgatherer; he was squeezed on his land instead of being squeezed off it.

As the eighteenth century progressed, it is apparent in the literature of the time that what to do with "the poor" was again exercising men's thoughts. We find such active-minded English writers as Defoe (1659-1731) and Fielding (1707-54) deeply exercised by this problem. But as yet there is no such revival of the communistic and equalitarian ideas of primitive Christianity as distinguished the time of Wycliffe and John Huss. Protestantism in breaking up the universal church had for a time broken up the idea of universal human solidarity. Even if the universal church of the Middle Ages had failed altogether to realize that idea, it had at any rate been the symbol of that idea.

Defoe and Fielding were men of a livelier practical imagination than Gibbon, and they realized something of the economic processes that were afoot in their time. So did Oliver Goldsmith (1728-74); his *Deserted Village* (1770) is a pamphlet on enclosures disguised as a poem. But Gibbon's circumstances had never brought economic facts very vividly before his eyes, he saw the world as a struggle between barbarism and civilization, but he perceived nothing of that other struggle over which he floated, the mute, unconscious struggle of the commonalty against able, powerful, rich, and selfish men. He did not perceive the accumulation of stresses that were presently to strain and break up all the balance of his "twelve powerful, though unequal, kingdoms," his "three respectable commonwealths," and their rag, tag, and bobtail of independent minor princes, reigning dukes, and so forth. Even the civil war that had begun in the British colonies in America did not rouse him to the nearness of what we now call "Democracy."

From what we have been saying hitherto, the reader may suppose that the squeezing of the small farmer and the peasant off the land by the great landowners, the mere grabbing of commons and the concentration of property in the hands of a powerful privileged and greedy class, was all that was happening to the English land in the eighteenth century. So we do but state the worse side of the change. Concurrently with this change of ownership there was going on a great improvement in agriculture. There can be little doubt that the methods of cultivation pursued by the peasants, squatters, and small farmers were antiquated, wasteful, and comparatively unproductive, and that the larger private holdings and estates created by the Enclosure Acts were much more productive (one authority says twenty times more productive) than the old ways. The change was perhaps a necessary one and the evil of it was not that it was brought about, but that it was brought about so as to increase both wealth and the numbers of the poor. Its benefits were intercepted by the bigger private owners. The community was injured to the great profit of this class.

And here we come upon one of the chief problems of our lives at the present time, the problem of the deflection of the profits of progress. For two hundred years there has been, mainly under the influence of the spirit of science and enquiry, a steady improvement in the methods of production of almost everything that humanity requires. If our sense of community and our social science were equal to the tasks required of them, there can be little question that this great increment in production would have benefited the whole community, would have given everyone an amount of education, leisure, and freedom such as mankind had never dreamt of before. But though the common standard of living has risen, the rise has been on a scale disproportionately small. The rich have developed a freedom and luxury unknown in the world hitherto, and there has been an increase in the proportion of rich people and stagnantly prosperous and unproductive people in the community; but that also fails to account for the full benefit. There has been much sheer waste. Vast accumulations of material and energy have gone into warlike preparations and warfare. Much has been devoted to the futile efforts of unsuccessful business competition. Huge possibilities have remained undeveloped because of the opposition of owners, forestallers, and speculators to their economical exploitation. The good things that science and organization have been bringing within the reach of mankind have not been taken methodically and used to their utmost, but they have been scrambled for, snatched at, seized upon by gambling adventurers and employed upon selfish and vain ends. The eighteenth century in Europe, and more particularly in Great Britain and Poland, was the age of private ownership. "Private enterprise," which meant in practice that everyone was entitled to get everything he could out of the business of the community, reigned supreme. No sense of obligation to the state in business matters is to be found in the ordinary novels, plays, and such-like representative literature of the time. Everyone is out "to make his fortune," there is no recognition that it is wrong to be an unproductive parasite on the community, and still less that a financier or merchant or manufacturer can ever be overpaid for his services to mankind. This was the moral atmosphere of the time, and those lords and gentlemen who grabbed the people's commons, assumed possession of the mines under their lands, and crushed down the yeoman farmers and peasants to the status of pauper labourers, had no idea that they were living anything but highly meritorious lives.

Concurrently with this change in Great Britain from traditional patch agriculture and common pasture to large and more scientific agriculture, very great changes were going on in the manufacture of commodities. In these changes Great Britain was, in the eighteenth century, leading the world. Hitherto, throughout the whole course of history from the beginnings of civilization, manufactures, building, and industries generally had been in the hands of craftsmen and small masters who worked in their own houses. They had been organized in guilds, and were mostly their own employers. They formed an essential and permanent middle class. There were capitalists among them, who let out looms and the like, supplied material, and took the finished product, but they were not big capitalists. There had been no rich manufacturers. The rich men of the world before this time had been great landowners or money-lenders and money manipulators or merchants. But in the eighteenth century, workers in certain industries began to be collected together into factories in order to produce things in larger quantities through a systematic division of labour, and the employer, as distinguished from the master worker, began to be a person of importance. Moreover, mechanical invention was producing machines that simplified the manual work of production, and were capable of being driven by water power and presently by steam. In 1765 Watt's steam engine was constructed, a very important date in the history of industrialism.

The cotton industry was one of the first to pass into factory production (originally with water-driven machinery). The woollen industry followed. At the same time iron smelting, which had been restrained hitherto to small methods by the use of charcoal, resorted to coke made from coal, and the coal and iron industries also began to expand. The iron industry shifted from the wooded country of Sussex and Surrey to the coal districts. By 1800 this change-over of industry from a small scale business with small employers to a large scale production under big employers was well in progress. Everywhere there sprang up factories using first water, then steam power. It was a change of fundamental importance in human economy. From the dawn of history the manufacturer and craftsman had been, as we have said, a sort of middle-class townsman. The machine and the employer now superseded his skill, and he either became an employer of his fellows, and grew towards wealth and equality with the other rich classes, or he remained a worker and sank very rapidly to the level of a mere labourer. This great change in human affairs is known as the Industrial Revolution. Beginning in Great Britain, it spread during the nineteenth century throughout the world.

As the Industrial Revolution went on, a great gulf opened between employer and employed. In the past every manufacturing worker had the hope of becoming an independent master. Even the slave craftsmen of Babylon and Rome were protected by laws that enabled them to save and buy their freedom and to set up for themselves. But now a factory and its engines and machines became a vast and costly thing measured by the scale of the worker's pocket. Wealthy men had to come together to create an enterprise; credit and plant, that is to say, "Capital," were required. "Setting up for oneself" ceased to be a normal hope for an artisan. The worker was henceforth a worker from the cradle to the grave. Besides the landlords and merchants and the money-dealers who financed trading companies and lent their money to the merchants and the state, there arose now this new wealth of industrial capital —a new sort of power in the state.

Of the working out of these beginnings we shall tell later. The immediate effect of the industrial revolution upon the countries to which it came, was to cause a vast, distressful shifting and stirring of the mute, uneducated, leaderless, and now more and more propertyless common population. The small cultivators and peasants, ruined and dislodged by the Enclosure Acts, drifted towards the new manufacturing regions, and there they joined the families of the impoverished and degraded craftsmen in the factories. Great towns of squalid houses came into existence. Nobody seems to have noted clearly what was going on at the time. It is the keynote of "private enterprise" to mind one's own business, secure the utmost profit, and disregard any other consequences. Ugly great factories grew up, built as cheaply as possible, to hold as many machines and workers as possible. Around them gathered the streets of workers' homes, built at the cheapest rate, without space, without privacy, barely decent, and let at the utmost rent that could be exacted. These new industrial centres were at first without schools, without churches. . . .

The English gentleman of the closing decades of the eighteenth century read Gibbon's third volume and congratulated himself that there was henceforth no serious fear of the Barbarians, with this new barbarism growing up, with this metamorphosis of his countrymen into something dark and desperate, in full progress, within an easy walk perhaps of his door.

XXXVI

THE NEW DEMOCRATIC REPUBLICS OF AMERICA AND FRANCE

§ 1. *Inconveniences of the Great Power System.* § 2. *The Thirteen Colonies Before Their Revolt.* § 3. *Civil War Is Forced Upon the Colonies.* § 4. *The War of Independence.* § 5. *The Constitution of the United States.* § 6. *Primitive Features of the United States Constitution.* § 7. *Revolutionary Ideas in France.* § 8. *The Revolution of the Year 1789.* § 9. *The French "Crowned Republic" of '89–91.* § 10. *The Revolution of the Jacobins.* § 11. *The Jacobin Republic, 1792–94.* § 12. *The Directory.* § 13. *The Pause in Reconstruction and the Dawn of Modern Socialism.*

§ 1

WHEN Gibbon, nearly a century and a half ago, was congratulating the world of refined and educated people that the age of great political and social catastrophes was past, he was neglecting many signs which we—in the wisdom of accomplished facts—could have told him portended far heavier jolts and dislocations than any he foresaw. We have told how the struggle of the sixteenth and seventeenth-century princes for ascendancies and advantages developed into a more cunning and complicated struggle of foreign offices, masquerading as idealized "Great Powers," as the eighteenth century wore on. The intricate and pretentious art of diplomacy developed. The "Prince" ceased to be a single and secretive Machiavellian schemer, and became merely the crowned symbol of a Machiavellian scheme. Prussia, Russia, and Austria fell upon and divided Poland. France was baffled in profound schemes against Spain. Britain circumvented the "designs of France" in America and acquired Canada, and got the better of France in India. And then a remarkable thing occurred, a thing very shocking to European diplomacy. The British colonies in America flatly refused to have further part or lot in this game of "Great Powers." They objected that they had no voice and no great interest in these European schemes and conflicts, and they refused to bear any portion of the burthen of taxation these foreign policies entailed. "Taxation without representation is tyranny"; this was their dominant idea.

Of course this decision to separate did not flash out complete and finished from the American mind at the beginning of these troubles. In America in the eighteenth century, just as in England in the seventeenth, there was an entire willingness, indeed a desire on the part of ordinary men, to leave foreign affairs in the hands of the king and his ministers. But there was an equally strong desire on the part of ordinary men to be neither taxed nor interfered with in their ordinary pursuits. These are incompatible wishes. Common men cannot shirk world politics and at the same time enjoy private freedom; but it has taken them countless generations to learn this. The first impulse in the American revolt against the government in Great Britain was therefore simply a resentment against the taxation and interference that followed necessarily from "foreign policy" without any clear recognition of what was involved in that objection. It was only when the revolt was consummated that the people of the American colonies recognized at all clearly that they had repudiated the Great Power view of life. The sentence in which that repudiation was expressed was Washington's injunction to "avoid entangling alliances." For a full century the united colonies of Great Britain in North America, liberated and independent as the United States of America, stood apart altogether from the blood-stained intrigues and conflicts of the European foreign offices. Soon after (1810 to 1823) they were able to extend their principle of detachment to the rest of the continent, and to make all the New World "out of bounds" for the scheming expansionists of the old. When at length, in 1917, they were obliged to re-enter the arena of world politics, it was to bring the new spirit and new aims their aloofness had enabled them to develop into the tangle of international relationships. They were not, however, the first to stand aloof. Since the treaty of Westphalia (1648), the confederated states of Switzerland, in their mountain fastnesses, had sustained their right to exclusion from the schemes of kings and empires.

But since the North American peoples are now to play an increasingly important part in our history, it will be well to devote a little more attention than we have hitherto given to their development. We have already glanced at this story in § 8 of the preceding chapter. We will now tell a little more fully—though still in the barest outline—what these colonies were, whose recalcitrance was so disconcerting to the king and ministers of Great Britain in their diplomatic game against the rest of mankind.

§ 2

The extent of the British colonies in America in the early half of the eighteenth century is shown in the accompanying map. The darker shading represents the districts settled in 1700, the lighter the growth of the settlements up to 1760. It will be seen that the colonies were a mere fringe of population along the coast, spreading gradually inland and finding in the Alleghany and Blue Mountains a very serious barrier. Among the oldest of these settlements was the colony of Virginia, the name of which commemorates Queen Elizabeth, the Virgin Queen of England. The first expedition to found a colony in Virginia was made by Sir Walter Raleigh in 1584, but there was no permanent settlement at that time; and the real beginnings of Virginia date from the foundation of the Virginia Company in 1606 in the reign of James I (1603-25). The story of John Smith and the early founders of Virginia and of how the Indian "princess" Pocahontas married one of his gentlemen, is an English classic.[1] In growing tobacco the Virginians found the beginning of prosperity. At the same time that the Virginian Company was founded, the Plymouth Company obtained a charter for the settlement of the country to the north of Long Island Sound, to which the English laid claim. But it was only in 1620 that the northern region began to be settled, and that under fresh charters. The settlers of the northern region (New England), which became Connecticut, New Hampshire, Rhode Island, and Massachusetts, were men of a different stamp to the Virginia people. They were Protestants discontented with the Anglican Church compromise, and republican-spirited men hopeless of resistance to the Grand

[1] *John Smith's Travels.*

Monarchy of James I and Charles I. Their pioneer ship was the *Mayflower,* which founded New Plymouth in 1620. The dominant northern colony was Massachusetts. Differences in religious method and in ideas of toleration led to the separation of the three other Puritan colonies from Massachusetts. It illustrates the scale upon which things were done in those days that the whole state of New Hampshire was claimed as belonging to a certain Captain John Mason, and that he offered to sell it to the king (King Charles II in 1671) in exchange for the right to import 300 tons of French wine free of duty—an offer which was refused. The present state of Maine was bought by Massachusetts from its alleged owner for twelve hundred and fifty pounds.

In the Civil War that ended with the decapitation of Charles I the sympathies of New England were for the Parliament, and Virginia was Cavalier; but two hundred and fifty miles separated these settlements, and there were no serious hostilities. With the return of the monarchy in 1660, there was a vigorous development of British colonization in America. Charles II and his associates were greedy for gain, and the British crown had no wish to make any further experiments in illegal taxation at home. But the undefined relations of the colonies to the crown and the British government seemed to afford promise of financial adventure across the Atlantic. There was a rapid development of plantations and proprietary colonies. Lord Baltimore had already in 1632 set up a colony that was to be a home of religious freedom for Catholics under the attractive name of Maryland, to the north and east of Virginia; and now the Quaker Penn (whose father had rendered valuable services to Charles II) established himself to the north at Philadelphia and founded the colony of Pennsylvania. Its main boundary with Maryland and Virginia was delimited by two men, Mason and Dixon, whose "Mason and Dixon's Line" was destined to become a very important line indeed in the later affairs of the United States. Carolina, which was originally an unsuccessful French Protestant establishment, and which owed its name not to Charles (Carolus) II of England, but to Charles IX of France, had fallen into English hands and was settled at several points. Between Maryland and New England stretched a number of small Dutch and Swedish settlements, of which the chief town was New Amsterdam. These settlements were captured from the Dutch by the British in 1664, lost again in 1673, and restored by treaty when Holland and England made peace in 1674. Thereby the whole

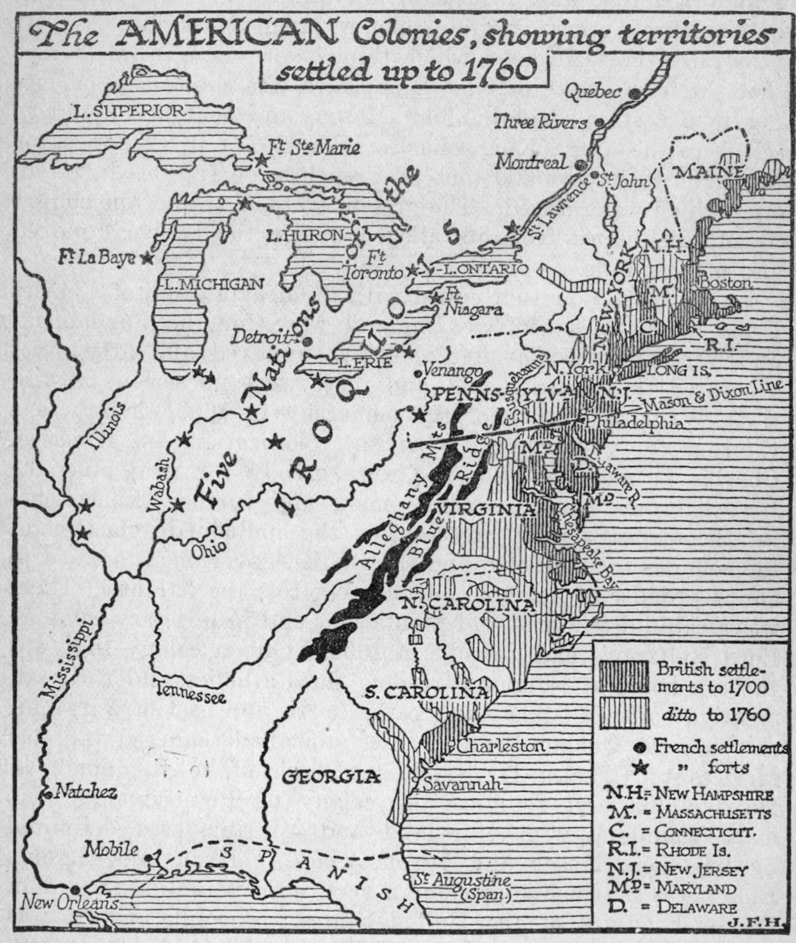

coast from Maine to Carolina became in some form or other a British possession. To the south the Spanish were established; their headquarters were at Fort St. Augustine in Florida, and in 1732 the town of Savannah was settled by a philanthropist Oglethorpe from England, who had taken pity on the miserable people imprisoned for debt in England, and rescued a number of them from prison to become the founders of a new colony, Georgia, which was to be a bulwark against the Spanish. So by the middle of the eighteenth century we have these settlements along the American coast-line: the New England group of Puritans and free Protestants, Maine (belonging to Massachusetts), New Hampshire, Connecticut, Rhode Island, and Massachusetts; the captured Dutch group, which was now divided up into New York (New Amsterdam rechristened), New Jersey, and Delaware (Swedish before it was Dutch, and in its earliest British phase attached to Pennsylvania); then came Catholic Maryland; Cavalier Virginia; Carolina (which was presently divided into North and South) and Oglethorpe's Georgia. Later on a number of Tyrolese Protestants took refuge in Georgia, and there was a considerable immigration of a good class of German cultivators into Pennsylvania.

Such were the miscellaneous origins of the citizens of the Thirteen Colonies. The possibility of their ever becoming closely united would have struck an impartial observer in 1760 as being very slight. Superadded to the initial differences of origin, fresh differences were created by climate. North of the Mason and Dixon line farming was practised mainly upon British or Central European lines by free white cultivators. The settled country of New England took on a likeness to the English countryside; considerable areas of Pennsylvania developed fields and farmhouses like those of South Germany. The distinctive conditions in the north had, socially, important effects. Masters and men had to labour together as backwoodsmen, and were equalized in the process. They did not start equally; many "servants" are mentioned in the roster of the *Mayflower*. But they rapidly became equal under colonial conditions; there was, for instance, a vast tract of land to be had for the taking, and the "servant" went off and took land like his master. The English class system disappeared. Under colonial conditions there arose equality "in the faculties both of body and mind," and an individual independence of judgment impatient of interference from England. But south of the Mason and Dixon line tobacco growing began, and the warmer climate encouraged the establishment of plantations with gang labour. Red Indian captives were tried, but found to be too homicidal; Cromwell sent Irish prisoners of war to

Virginia, which did much to reconcile the Royalist planters to republicanism; convicts were sent out, and there was a considerable trade in kidnapped children, who were "spirited away" to America to become apprentices or bond slaves. But the most convenient form of gang labour proved to be that of negro slaves. The first negro slaves were brought to Jamestown in Virginia by a Dutch ship as early as 1620. By 1700 negro slaves were scattered all over the states, but Virginia, Maryland, and the Carolinas were their chief regions of employment, and while the communities to the north were communities of not very rich and not very poor farming men, the south developed a type of large proprietor and a white community of overseers and professional men subsisting on slave labour. Slave labour was a necessity to the social and economic system that had grown up in the south; in the north the presence of slaves was unnecessary and in some respects inconvenient. Conscientious scruples about slavery were more free, therefore, to develop and flourish in the northern atmosphere. To this question of the revival of slavery in the world we must return when we come to consider the perplexities of American Democracy. Here we note it simply as an added factor in the heterogeneous mixture of the British Colonies.

But if the inhabitants of the Thirteen Colonies were miscellaneous in their origins and various in their habits and sympathies, they had three very strong antagonisms in common. They had a common interest against the Red Indians. For a time they shared a common dread of French conquest and dominion. And thirdly, they were all in conflict with the claims of the British crown and the commercial selfishness of the narrow oligarchy who dominated the British Parliament and British affairs.

So far as the first danger went, the Indians were a constant evil, but never more than a threat of disaster. They remained divided against themselves. Yet they had shown possibilities of combination upon a larger scale. The Five Nations of the Iroquois (see map, p. 830) was a very important league of tribes. But it never succeeded in playing off the French against the English to secure itself, and no Red Indian Jengis Khan ever arose among these nomads of the new world. The French aggression was a more serious threat. The French never made settlements in America on a scale to compete with the English, but their government set about the encirclement of the colonies and their subjugation in a terrifyingly systematic manner. The English in America were colonists; the French were explorers, adventurers, agents, missionaries, merchants, and soldiers. Only in Canada did they strike root. French statesmen sat over maps and dreamt dreams, and their dreams are to be seen in our map in the chain of forts creeping southward from the great lakes and northward up the Mississippi and Ohio rivers. The struggle of France and Britain was a world-wide struggle. It was decided in India, in Germany, and on the high seas. In the Peace of Paris (1763) the French gave England Canada, and relinquished Louisiana to the inert hands of declining Spain. It was the complete abandonment of America by France. The lifting of the French danger left the colonists unencumbered to face their third common antagonist—the crown and government of their mother land.

§ 3

We have noted in the previous chapter how the governing class of Great Britain steadily acquired the land and destroyed the liberty of the common people throughout the eighteenth century, and how greedily and blindly the new industrial revolution was brought about. We have noted also how the British Parliament, through the decay of the representative methods of the House of Commons, had become both in its upper and lower houses merely the instrument of government through the big landowners. Both these big property-holders and the crown were deeply interested in America; the former as private adventurers, the latter partly as representing the speculative exploitations of the Stuart kings, and partly as representing the state in search of funds for the expenses of foreign policy, and neither lords nor crown were disposed to regard the traders, planters, and common people of the colonies with any more consideration than they did the yeomen and small cultivators at home. At bottom the interests of the common man in Great Britain, Ireland, and America were the same. Each was being squeezed by the same system. But while in Britain oppressor and oppressed were closely tangled up in one intimate social system, in America the crown and the exploiter were far away, and men could get together and develop a sense of community against their common enemy.

Moreover, the American colonist had the important advantage of possessing a separate and legal organ of resistance to the British government in the assembly or legislature of his colony that was necessary for the management of local affairs. The common man in Britain, cheated out of his proper representation in the Commons, had no organ, no centre of expression and action for his discontents.

It will be evident to the reader, bearing in mind the variety of the colonies, that here was the possibility of an endless series of disputes, aggressions, and counter-aggressions. The story of the development of irritations between the colonies and Britain is a story far too intricate, subtle, and lengthy for the scheme of this Outline. Suffice it that the grievances fell under three main heads: attempts to secure for British adventurers or the British government the profits of the exploitation of new lands; systematic restrictions upon trade designed to keep the foreign trade of the colonies entirely in British hands, so that the colonial exports all went through Britain and only British-made goods were used in America; and finally attempts at taxation through the British Parliament as the supreme taxing authority of the empire. Under the pressure of this triple system of annoyances, the American colonists were forced to do a very considerable amount of hard political thinking. Such men as Patrick Henry and James Otis began to discuss the fundamental ideas of government and political association very much as they had been discussed in England in the great days of Cromwell's Commonweal. They began to deny both the divine origin of kingship and the supremacy of the British Parliament, and (James Otis, 1762) to say such things as:—

"God made all men naturally equal.

"Ideas of earthly superiority are educational, not innate.

"Kings were made for the good of the people, and not the people for them.

"No government has a right to make slaves of its subjects.

"Though most governments are *de facto* arbitrary, and consequently the curse and scandal of human nature, yet none are *de jure* arbitrary."

Some of which propositions reach far.

This ferment in the political ideas of the Americans was

started by English leaven. One very influential English writer was John Locke (1632-1704), whose *Two Treatises on Civil Government* may be taken, as much as any one single book can be taken in such cases, as the point of departure for modern democratic ideas. He was the son of a Cromwellian soldier, he was educated at Christ Church, Oxford, during the republican ascendancy, he spent some years in Holland in exile, and his writings form a bridge between the bold political thinking of those earlier republican days and the revolutionary movement both in America and France.

But men do not begin to act upon theories. It is always some real danger, some practical necessity, that produces action; and it is only after action has destroyed old relationships and produced a new and perplexing state of affairs that theory comes to its own. Then it is that theory is put to the test. The discord in interests and ideas between the colonists was brought to a fighting issue by the obstinate resolve of the British Parliament after the peace of 1763 to impose taxation upon the American colonies. Britain was at peace and flushed with successes; it seemed an admirable opportunity for settling accounts with these recalcitrant settlers. But the great British property-owners found a power beside their own, of much the same mind with them, but a little divergent in its ends—the reviving crown. King George III, who had begun his reign in 1760, was resolved to be much more of a king than his two German predecessors. He could speak English; he claimed to "glory in the name of Briton"—and indeed it is not a bad name for a man without a perceptible drop of English, Welsh, or Scotch blood in his veins. In the American colonies and the overseas possessions generally, with their indefinite charters or no charters at all, it seemed to him that the crown might claim authority and obtain resources and powers absolutely denied to it by the strong and jealous aristocracy in Britain. This inclined many of the Whig noblemen to a sympathy with the colonists that they might not otherwise have shown. They had no objection to the exploitation of the colonies in the interests of British "private enterprise," but they had very strong objections to the strengthening of the crown by that exploitation so as to make it presently independent of themselves.

The war that broke out was therefore in reality not a war between Britain and the colonists, it was a war between the British government and the colonists, with a body of Whig noblemen and a considerable amount of public feeling in England on the side of the latter. An early move after 1763 was an attempt to raise revenue for Britain in the colonies by requiring that newspapers and documents of various sorts should be stamped. This was stiffly resisted, the British crown was intimidated, and the Stamp Acts were repealed (1766). Their repeal was greeted by riotous rejoicings in London, more hearty even than those in the colonies.

But the Stamp Act affair was only one eddy in a turbulent stream flowing towards civil war. Upon a score of pretexts, and up and down the coast, the representatives of the British government were busy asserting their authority and making British government intolerable. The quartering of soldiers upon the colonists was a great nuisance. Rhode Island was particularly active in defying the trade restrictions; the Rhode Islanders were "free traders,"—that is to say, smugglers; a government schooner, the *Gaspee,* ran aground off Providence; she was surprised, boarded, and captured by armed men in boats, and burnt. In 1773, with a total disregard of the existing colonial tea trade, special advantages for the importation of tea into America were given by the British Parliament to the East India Company. It was resolved by the colonists to refuse and boycott this tea. When the tea importers at Boston showed themselves resolute to land their cargoes, a band of men disguised as Indians, in the presence of a great crowd of people, boarded the three tea ships and threw the tea overboard (December 16th, 1773).

All 1774 was occupied in the gathering up of resources on either side for the coming conflict. It was decided by the British Parliament in the spring of 1774 to punish Boston by closing her port. Her trade was to be destroyed unless she accepted that tea. It was a quite typical instance of that silly "firmness" which shatters empires. In order to enforce this measure, British troops were concentrated at Boston under General Gage. The colonists took counter-measures. The first colonial Congress met at Philadelphia in September, at which twelve colonies were represented: Massachusetts, Connecticut, New Hampshire, Rhode Island, New York, New Jersey, Pennsylvania, Maryland, Delaware, Virginia, and North and South Carolina. Georgia was not present. True to the best English traditions, the Congress documented its attitude by a "Declaration of Rights." Practically this Congress was an insurrectionary government, but no blow was struck until the spring of 1775. Then came the first shedding of blood.

Two of the American leaders, Hancock and Samuel Adams, had been marked down by the British Government for arrest and trial for treason; they were known to be at Lexington, about

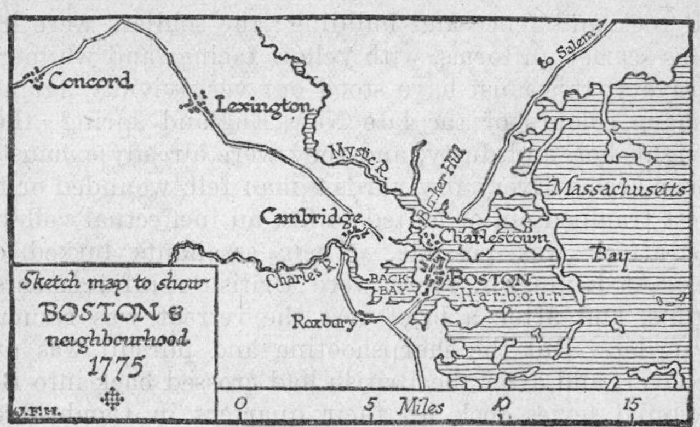

eleven miles from Boston; and in the night of April 18th, 1775, Gage set his forces in motion for their arrest.

That night was a momentous one in history. The movement of Gage's troops had been observed, signal lanterns were shown from a church tower in Boston, and two men, Dawes and Paul Revere, stole away in boats across the Back Bay to take horse and warn the countryside. The British were also ferried over the water, and as they marched through the night towards Lexington, the firing of signal cannon and the ringing of church bells went before them. As they entered Lexington at dawn, they saw a little company of men drawn up in military fashion. It seems that the British fired first. There was a single shot and then a volley, and the little handful decamped, apparently without any answering shots, leaving eight dead and nine wounded upon the village green.

The British then marched on to Concord, ten miles further, occupied the village, and stationed a party on the bridge at that place. The expedition had failed in its purpose of arresting Hancock and Adams, and the British commander seems to have been at a loss what to do next. Meanwhile the colonial levies were coming up from all directions, and presently the picket upon the bridge found itself subjected to an increasing fire from a gathering number of assailants firing from behind trees and fences. A retreat to Boston was decided upon. It was a disastrous retreat. The country had risen behind the British; all the morning the colonials had been gathering. Both sides of the road were now swarming with sharpshooters firing from behind rock and fence and building; the soldiers were in conspicuous scarlet uniforms, with yellow facings and white gaiters and cravats; this must have stood out very vividly against the cold sharp colours of the late New England spring; the day was bright, hot, and dusty, and they were already exhausted by a night march. Every few yards a man fell, wounded or killed. The rest tramped on, or halted to fire an ineffectual volley. No counter-attack was possible. Their assailants lurked everywhere. At Lexington there were British reinforcements and two guns, and after a brief rest the retreat was resumed in better order. But the sharpshooting and pursuit was pressed to the river, and after the British had crossed back into Boston, the colonial levies took up their quarters in Cambridge and prepared to blockade the city.

§ 4

So the war began. It was not a war that promised a conclusive end. The colonists had no one vulnerable capital; they were dispersed over a great country, with a limitless wilderness behind it, and so they had great powers of resistance. They had learnt their tactics largely from the Indians; they could fight well in open order, and harry and destroy troops in movement. But they had no disciplined army that could meet the British in a pitched battle, and little military equipment; and their levies grew impatient at a long campaign, and tended to go home to their farms. The British, on the other hand, had a well-drilled army, and their command of the sea gave them the power of shifting their attack up and down the long Atlantic seaboard. They were at peace with all the world. But the king was stupid and greedy to interfere in the conduct of affairs; the generals he favoured were stupid "strong men" or flighty men of birth and fashion; and the heart of England was not in the business. He trusted rather to being able to blockade, raid, and annoy the colonists into submission than to a conclusive conquest and occupation of the land. But the methods employed, and particularly the use of hired German troops, who still retained the cruel traditions of the Thirty Years' War, and of Indian auxiliaries, who harried the outlying settlers, did not so much weary the Americans of the war as of the British. The Congress, meeting for the second time in 1775, endorsed the actions of the New England colonists, and appointed George Washington the American commander-in-chief. In 1777, General Burgoyne, in an attempt to get down to New York from Canada, was defeated at Freeman's Farm on the Upper Hudson, and surrounded and obliged to capitulate at Saratoga with his whole army. This disaster encouraged the French and Spanish to come into the struggle on the side of the colonists. The French sent General Lafayette to the States to assist them with his advice, and their fleet did much to minimize the advantage of the British at sea. General Cornwallis was caught in the Yorktown peninsula in Virginia in 1781, and capitulated with his army. The British Government, now heavily engaged with France and Spain in Europe, was at the end of its resources.

At the outset of the war the colonists in general seem to have been as little disposed to repudiate monarchy and claim complete independence as were the Hollanders in the opening phase of Philip II's persecutions and follies. The separatists were called radicals; they were mostly extremely democratic, as we should say in England to-day, and their advanced views frightened many of the steadier and wealthier colonists, for whom class privileges and distinctions had considerable charm. But early in 1776 an able and persuasive Englishman, Thomas Paine, published a pamphlet at Philadelphia with the title of *Common Sense,* which had an enormous effect on public opinion. Its style was rhetorical by modern standards. "The blood of the slain, the weeping voice of Nature cries, ''Tis time to part,' " and so forth. But its effects were very great. It converted thousands to the necessity of separation. The turn-over of opinion, once it had begun, was rapid.

Only in the summer of 1776 did Congress take the irrevocable step of declaring for separation. "The Declaration of Independence," another of those exemplary documents which it has been the peculiar service of the English to produce for mankind, was drawn up by Thomas Jefferson; and after various amendments and modifications it was made the fundamental document of the United States of America. There were two noteworthy amendments to Jefferson's draft. He had denounced the slave trade fiercely, and blamed the home government for interfering with colonial attempts to end it. This was thrown out, and so, too, was a sentence about the British: "we must endeavour to forget our former love for them . . . we might have been a free and a great people together."

Towards the end of 1782, the preliminary articles of the treaty in which Britain recognized the complete independence of the United States were signed at Paris. The end of the war was proclaimed on April 19th, 1783, exactly eight years after Paul Revere's ride, and the retreat of Gage's men from Concord to Boston. The Treaty of Peace was finally signed at Paris in September.

§ 5

From the point of view of human history, the way in which the Thirteen States became independent is of far less importance than the fact that they did become independent. And with the establishment of their independence came a new sort of community into the world. It was like something coming out of an egg. It was a western European civilization that had broken free from the last traces of Empire and Christendom; it had not a vestige of monarchy left and no state religion. It had no dukes, princes, counts, nor any sort of title-bearers claiming to ascendancy or respect as a right. Even its unity was as yet a mere unity for defence and freedom. It was in these respects such a clean start in political organization as the world had not seen before. The absence of any binding religious tie is especially noteworthy. It had a number of forms of Christianity, its spirit was indubitably Christian; but as a state document of 1796 explicitly declared, "The government of the United States is not in any sense founded on the Christian religion."[1] The new community had in fact gone right down to the bare and stripped fundamentals of human associa-

[1] The Tripoli Treaty, see Channing, vol. iii, chap. xviii.

tion, and it was building up a new sort of society and a new sort of state upon those foundations.

Here were about four million people scattered over vast areas with very slow and difficult means of intercommunication, poor

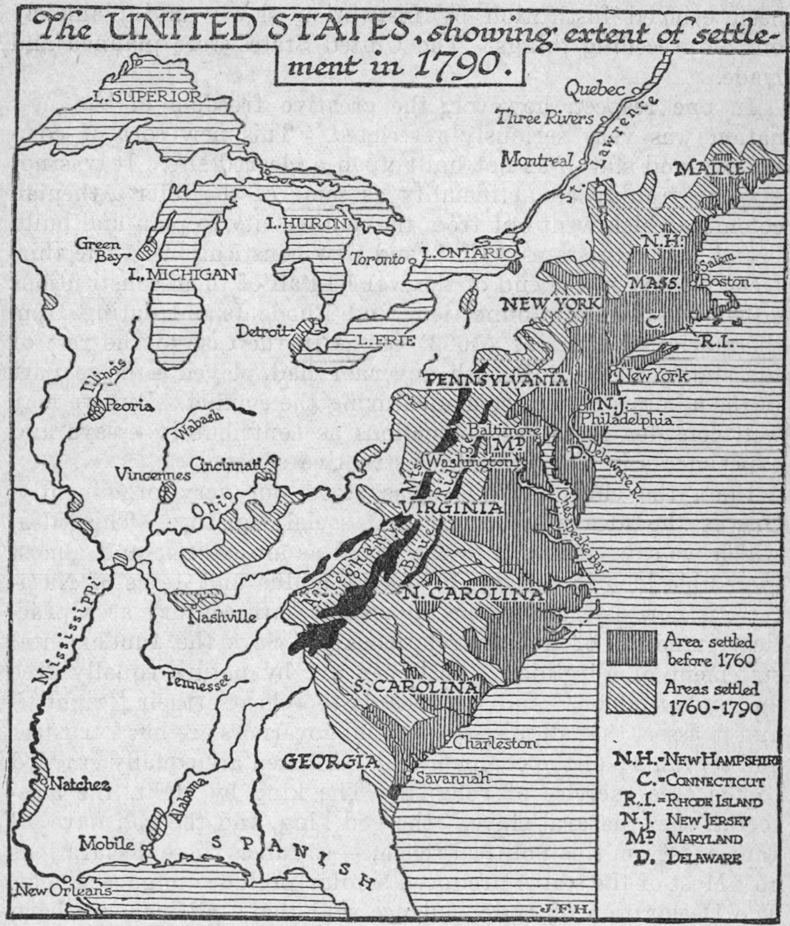

as yet, but with the potentiality of limitless wealth, setting out to do in reality on a huge scale such a feat of construction as the Athenian philosophers twenty-two centuries before had done in imagination and theory.

This situation marks a definite stage in the release of man from precedent and usage, and a definite step forward towards the conscious and deliberate reconstruction of his circumstances to suit his needs and aims. It was a new method becoming practical in human affairs. The modern states of Europe have been evolved institution by institution slowly and planlessly out of preceding things. The United States were planned and made.

In one respect, however, the creative freedom of the new nation was very seriously restricted. This new sort of community and state was not built upon a cleared site. It was not even so frankly an artificiality as some of the later Athenian colonies, which went out from the mother city to plan and build brand new city states with brand new constitutions. The thirteen colonies by the end of the war had all of them constitutions either like that of Connecticut and Rhode Island dating from their original charters (1662) or, as in the case of the rest of the states, where a British governor had played a large part in the administration, re-made during the conflict. But we may well consider these reconstructions as contributory essays and experiments in the general constructive effort.

Upon the effort certain ideas stood out very prominently. One is the idea of political and social equality. This idea, which we saw coming into the world as an extreme and almost incredible idea in the age between Buddha and Jesus of Nazareth, is now asserted in the later eighteenth century as a practical standard of human relationship. Says the fundamental statement of Virginia: "All men are by nature equally free and independent," and it proceeds to rehearse their "rights," and to assert that all magistrates and governors are but "trustees and servants" of the commonweal. All men are equally entitled to the free exercise of religion. The king by right, the aristocrat, the "natural slave," the god king, and the god have all vanished from this political scheme—so far as these declarations go. Most of the states produced similar preludes to government. The Declaration of Independence said that "all men are born equal." It is everywhere asserted in eighteenth-century terms that the new community is to be—to use the phraseology we have introduced in an earlier chapter—a community of will and not a community of obedience. But the thinkers of that time had a rather clumsier way of putting the thing they imagined a sort of individual choice of and assent to citizenship that never in fact occurred—the so-called Social Contract. The Massachusetts preamble, for instance, asserts that the state is a voluntary association, "by which the whole people covenants with each citizen and each citizen with the whole people that all shall be governed by certain laws for the common good."

Now it will be evident that most of these fundamental statements are very questionable statements. Men are not born equal, they are not born free; they are born a most various multitude enmeshed in an ancient and complex social net. Nor is any man invited to sign the social contract or, failing that, to depart into solitude. The statements, literally interpreted, are so manifestly false that it is impossible to believe that the men who made them intended them to be literally interpreted. They made them in order to express certain elusive but profoundly important ideas—ideas that after another century and a half of thinking the world is in a better position to express. Civilization, as this outline has shown, arose as a community of obedience, and was essentially a community of obedience. But generation after generation the spirit was abused by priests and rulers. There was a continual influx of masterful will from the forests, parklands, and steppes. The human spirit had at last rebelled altogether against the blind obediences of the common life; it was seeking—and at first it was seeking very clumsily—to achieve a new and better sort of civilization that should also be a community of will. To that end it was necessary that every man should be treated as the sovereign of himself; his standing was to be one of fellowship and not of servility. His real use, his real importance depended upon his individual quality.

The method by which these creators of political America sought to secure this community of will was an extremely simple and crude one. They gave what was for the time, and in view of American conditions, a very wide franchise. Conditions varied in the different states; the widest franchise was in Pennsylvania, where every adult male taxpayer voted, but, compared with Britain, all the United States were well within sight of manhood suffrage by the end of the eighteenth century. These makers of America also made efforts, considerable for their times, but puny by more modern standards, to secure a widely diffused common education. The information of the citizens as to what was going on at home and abroad, they left, apparently without any qualms of misgiving, to public meetings and the privately owned printing press.

The story of the various state constitutions, and of the constitution of the United States as a whole, is a very intricate one, and we can only deal with it here in the broadest way. The most noteworthy point in a modern view is the disregard of women as citizens. The American community was a simple, largely agricultural community, and most women were married; it seemed natural that they should be represented by their men folk. But New Jersey admitted a few women to vote on a property qualification. Another point of great interest is the almost universal decision to have two governing assemblies, confirming or checking each other, on the model of the Lords and Commons of Britain. Only Pennsylvania had a single representative chamber, and that was felt to be a very dangerous and ultra-democratic state of affairs. Apart from the argument that legislation should be slow as well as sure, it is difficult to establish any necessity for this "bi-cameral" arrangement. It seems to have been a fashion with constitution planners in the eighteenth century rather than a reasonable imperative. The British division was an old one; the Lords, the original parliament, was an assembly of "notables," the leading men of the kingdom; the House of Commons came in as a new factor, as the elected spokesmen of the burghers and the small landed men. It was a little too hastily assumed in the eighteenth century that the commonalty would be given to wild impulses and would need checking; opinion was for democracy, but for democracy with powerful brakes always on, whether it was going up hill or down. About all the upper houses there was therefore a flavour of selectness; they were elected on a more limited franchise. This idea of making an upper chamber which shall be a stronghold for the substantial man does not appeal to modern thinkers so strongly as it did to the men of the eighteenth century, but the bi-cameral idea in another form still has its advocates. They suggest that a community may with advantage consider its affairs from two points of view—through the eyes of a body elected to represent trades, industries, professions, public services, and the like, a body representing *function*, and through the eyes of a second body elected by localities to represent *communities*. For the mem-

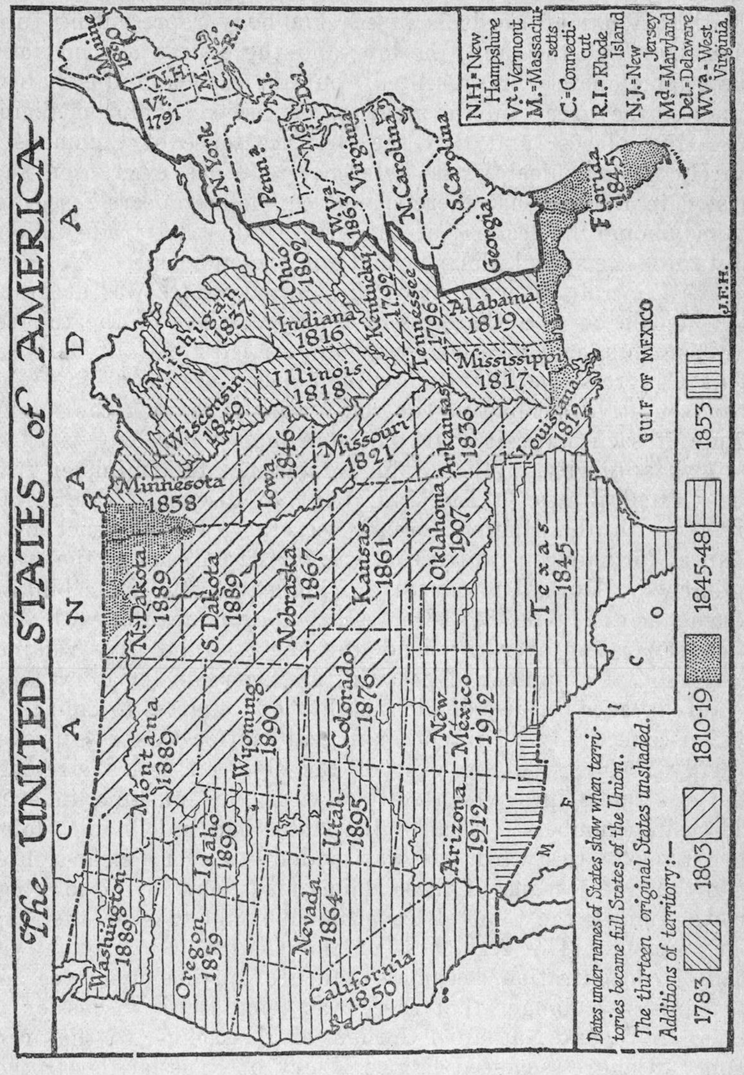
The UNITED STATES of AMERICA
C A N A D A
M E X I C O
GULF OF MEXICO
Washington 1889
Oregon 1859
California 1850
Idaho 1890
Nevada 1864
Montana 1889
Wyoming 1890
Utah 1895
Arizona 1912
N. Dakota 1889
S. Dakota 1889
Colorado 1876
New Mexico 1912
Nebraska 1867
Kansas 1861
Oklahoma 1907
Texas 1845
Minnesota 1858
Iowa 1846
Missouri 1821
Arkansas 1836
Louisiana 1812
Wisconsin 1849
Illinois 1818
Michigan 1837
Indiana 1816
Ohio 1802
Kentucky 1792
Tennessee 1796
Mississippi 1817
Alabama 1819
Florida 1845
Georgia
S. Carolina
N. Carolina
Virginia
W. Va. 1863
Penn.
N. York
N.J.
Md.
Del.
Vt. 1791
N.H.
M.
C.
R.I.
Maine 1820
N.H.=New Hampshire
Vt.=Vermont
M.=Massachusetts
C.=Connecticut
R.I.=Rhode Island
N.J.=New Jersey
Md.=Maryland
Del.=Delaware
W.Va.=West Virginia
Dates under names of States show when territories became full States of the Union.
The thirteen original States unshaded.
Additions of territory:—
1783
1803
1810-19
1845-48
1853
J.F.H.

bers of the former a man would vote by his calling, for the latter by his district of residence. They point out that the British House of Lords is in effect a body representing function, in which the land, the law, and the church are no doubt disproportionately represented, but in which industrialism, finance, the great public services, art, science, and medicine, also find places; and that the British House of Commons is purely geographical in its reference. It has even been suggested in Britain that there should be "labour peers," selected from among the leaders of the great industrial trade unions. But these are speculations beyond our present scope.

The Central Government of the United States was at first a very feeble body, a Congress of representatives of the thirteen governments, held together by certain Articles of Confederation. This Congress was little more than a conference of sovereign representatives; it had no control, for instance, over the foreign trade of each state, it could not coin money nor levy taxes by its own authority. When John Adams, the first minister from the United States to England, went to discuss a commercial treaty with the British foreign secretary, he was met by a request for thirteen representatives, one from each of the states concerned. He had to confess his inadequacy to make binding arrangements. The British presently began dealing with each state separately over the head of Congress, and they retained possession of a number of posts in the American territory about the great lakes because of the inability of Congress to hold these regions effectually. In another urgent matter Congress proved equally feeble. To the west of the thirteen states stretched limitless lands into which settlers were now pushing in ever-increasing numbers. Each of the states had indefinable claims to expansion westward. It was evident to every clear-sighted man that the jostling of these claims must lead in the long run to war, unless the Central Government could take on their apportionment. The feebleness of the Central Government, its lack of concentration, became so much of an inconvenience and so manifest a danger that there was some secret discussion of a monarchy, and Nathaniel Gorham of Massachusetts, the president of Congress, caused Prince Henry of Prussia, the brother of Frederick the Great, to be approached on the subject. Finally a constitutional convention was called in 1787 at Philadelphia, and there it was that the present constitution of the United

States was in its broad lines hammered out. A great change of spirit had gone on during the intervening years, a widespread realization of the need of unity.

When the Articles of Confederation were drawn up, men had thought of the people of Virginia, the people of Massachusetts, the people of Rhode Island, and the like; but now there appears a new conception, "the people of the United States." The new government, with the executive President, the senators, congressmen, and the Supreme Court, that was now created, was declared to be the government of "the people of the United States"; it was a synthesis and not a mere assembly. It said "we the people," and not "we the states," as Lee of Virginia bitterly complained. It was to be a "federal" and not a confederate government.

State by state the new constitution was ratified, and in the spring of 1788 the first congress upon the new lines assembled at New York, electing to its presidency George Washington, who had been the national commander-in-chief throughout the War of Independence. The constitution then underwent considerable revision, and Washington upon the Potomac was selected as the Federal capital.

§ 6

In an earlier chapter we have described the Roman republic, and its mixture of modern features with dark superstition and primordial savagery, as the Neanderthal anticipation of the modern democratic state. A time may come when people will regard the contrivances and machinery of the American constitution as the political equivalents of the implements and contrivances of Neolithic man. They have served their purpose well, and under their protection the people of the States have grown into one of the greatest, most powerful, and most civilized communities that the world has yet seen; but there is no reason in that for regarding the American constitution as a thing more final and inalterable than the pattern of street railway that overshadows many New York thoroughfares, or the excellent and homely type of house architecture that still prevails in Philadelphia. These things also have served a purpose well, they have their faults, and they can be improved. Our political contrivances, just as much as our domestic and mechanical contrivances, need to undergo constant revision as knowledge and understanding grow.

Since the American constitution was planned, our conception of history and our knowledge of collective psychology has undergone very considerable development. We are beginning to see many things in the problem of government to which the men of the eighteenth century were blind; and, courageous as their constructive disposition was in relation to whatever political creation had gone before, it fell far short of the boldness which we in these days realize to be needful if this great human problem of establishing a civilized community of will in the earth is to be solved. They took many things for granted that now we know need to be made the subject of the most exacting scientific study and the most careful adjustment. They thought it was only necessary to set up schools and colleges, with a grant of land for maintenance, and that they might then be left to themselves. But education is not a weed that will grow lustily in any soil, it is a necessary and delicate crop that may easily wilt and degenerate. We learn nowadays that the under-development of universities and educational machinery is like some under-development of the brain and nerves, which hampers the whole growth of the social body. By European standards, by the standard of any state that has existed hitherto, the level of the common education of America is high; but by the standard of what it might be, America is an uneducated country. And those fathers of America thought also that they had but to leave the press free, and everyone would live in the light. They did not realize that a free press could develop a sort of constitutional venality due to its relations with advertisers, and that large newspaper proprietors could become buccaneers of opinion and insensate wreckers of good beginnings. And, finally, the makers of America had no knowledge of the complexities of vote manipulation. The whole science of elections was beyond their ken, they knew nothing of the need of the transferable vote to prevent the "working" of elections by specialized organizations, and the crude and rigid methods they adopted left their political system the certain prey of the great party machines that have robbed American democracy of half its freedom and most of its political soul. Politics became a trade, and a very base trade; decent and able men, after the first great period, drifted out of politics and attended to "business," and what I have called elsewhere the "sense of the state"[1] declined. Private enterprise ruled in many matters of common concern, because political corruption made collective enterprise impossible.

Yet the defects of the great political system created by the Americans of the revolutionary period did not appear at once. For several generations the history of the United States was one of rapid expansion and of an amount of freedom, homely happiness, and energetic work unparalleled in the world's history. And the record of America for the whole last century and a half, in spite of many reversions towards inequality, in spite of much rawness and much blundering, is nevertheless as bright and honourable a story as that of any other contemporary people.

Benjamin Franklin

In this brief account of the creation of the United States of America we have been able to do little more than mention the names of some of the group of great men who made this new departure in human history. We have named casually or we have not even named such men as Tom Paine, Benjamin Franklin, Patrick Henry, Thomas Jefferson, the Adams cousins, Madison, Alexander Hamilton, and George Washington. It is hard to measure the men of one period of history with those in another. Some writers, even American writers, impressed by the artificial splendours of the European courts and by the tawdry and destructive exploits of a Frederick the Great or a Great Catherine, display a snobbish shame of something homespun about these makers of America. They feel that Benjamin Franklin at the court of Louis XVI, with his long hair, his plain clothes, and his pawky manner, was sadly lacking in aristocratic distinction. But stripped to their personalities, Louis XVI was hardly gifted enough or noble-minded enough to be Franklin's valet. If human greatness is a matter of scale

[1] Wells, *The Future in America.*

and glitter, then no doubt Alexander the Great is at the apex of human greatness. But is greatness that? Is not a great man rather one who, in a great position or amidst great opportunities—and great gifts are no more than great opportunities—serves God and his fellows with a humble heart? And quite a number of these Americans of the revolutionary time do seem to have displayed much disinterestedness and devotion. They were limited men, fallible men; Washington was, for example, a conspicuously indolent man; but on the whole they seemed to have cared more for the commonweal they were creating than for any personal end or personal vanity.

Washington

They were all limited men. They were limited in knowledge and outlook; they were limited by the limitations of the time. And there was no perfect man among them. They were, like all of us, men of mixed motives; good impulses arose in their minds, great ideas swept through them, and also they could be jealous, lazy, obstinate, greedy, vicious. If one were to write a true, full, and particular history of the making of the United States, it would have to be written with charity and high spirits as a splendid comedy. And in no other regard do we find the rich tortuous humanity of the American story so finely displayed as in regard to slavery. Slavery, having regard to the general question of labour, is the test of this new soul in the world's history, the American soul.

Slavery began very early in the European history of America, and no European people who went to America can be held altogether innocent in the matter. At a time when the German is still the moral whipping-boy of Europe, it is well to note that the German record is in this respect the best of all. Almost the first outspoken utterances against negro slavery came from German settlers in Pennsylvania. But the German settler was working with free labour upon a temperate countryside, well north of the plantation zone; he was not under serious temptation in this matter. American slavery began with the enslavement of Indians for gang work in mines and upon plantations, and it is curious to note that it was a very good and humane man indeed, Las Casas, who urged that negroes should be brought to America to relieve his tormented Indian protégés. The need for labour upon the plantations of the West Indies and the south was imperative. When the supply of Indian captives proved inadequate, the planters turned not only to the negro, but to the jails and poorhouses of Europe for a supply of toilers. The reader of Defoe's *Moll Flanders* will learn how the business of Virginian white slavery looked to an intelligent Englishman in the early eighteenth century. But the negro came very early. The year (1620) that saw the Pilgrim Fathers landing at Plymouth in New England, saw a Dutch sloop disembarking the first cargo of negroes at Jamestown in Virginia. Negro slavery was as old as New England; it had been an American institution for over a century and a half before the War of Independence. It was to struggle on for the better part of a century more.

But the conscience of thoughtful men in the colonies was never quite easy upon this score, and it was one of the accusations of Thomas Jefferson against the crown and lords of Great Britain that every attempt to ameliorate or restrain the slave trade on the part of the colonists had been checked by the great proprietary interests in the mother country.[1] With the moral and intellectual ferment of the revolution, the question of negro slavery came right into the foreground of the public conscience. The contrast and the challenge glared upon the mind. "All men are by nature free and equal," said the Virginia Bill of Rights, and outside in the sunshine, under the whip of the overseer, toiled the negro slave.

It witnesses to the great change in human ideas since the Roman Imperial system dissolved under the barbarian inrush, that there could be this heart-searching. Conditions of industry, production, and land tenure had long prevented any recrudescence of gang slavery; but now the cycle had come round again, and there were enormous immediate advantages to be reaped by the owning and ruling classes in the revival of that

[1] In 1776 Lord Dartmouth wrote that the colonists could not be allowed "to check or discourage a traffic so beneficent to the nation."

ancient institution in mines, upon plantations, and upon great public works. It was revived—but against great opposition. From the beginning of the revival there were protests, and they grew. The revival was counter to the new conscience of mankind. In some respects the new gang slavery was worse than anything in the ancient world. Peculiarly horrible was the provocation by the trade of slave wars and man hunts in Western Africa, and the cruelties of the long transatlantic voyage. The poor creatures were packed on the ships often with insufficient provision of food and water, without proper sanitation, without medicines. Many who could tolerate slavery upon the plantations found the slave trade too much for their moral digestions. Three European nations were chiefly concerned in this dark business, Britain, Spain, and Portugal, because they were the chief owners of the new lands in America. The comparative innocence of the other European powers is to be ascribed largely to their lesser temptations. They were similar communities; in parallel circumstances they would have behaved similarly.

Throughout the middle part of the eighteenth century there was an active agitation against negro slavery in Great Britain as well as in the States. It was estimated that in 1770 there were fifteen thousand slaves in Britain, mostly brought over by their owners from the West Indies and Virginia. In 1771 the issue came to a conclusive test in Britain before Lord Mansfield. A negro named James Somersett had been brought to England from Virginia by his owner. He ran away, was captured, and violently taken on a ship to be returned to Virginia. From the ship he was extracted by a writ of *habeas corpus*. Lord Mansfield declared that slavery was a condition unknown to English law, an "odious" condition, and Somersett walked out of the court a free man.

The Massachusetts constitution of 1780 had declared that "all men are born free and equal." A certain negro, Quaco, put this to the test in 1783, and in that year the soil of Massachusetts became like the soil of Britain, intolerant of slavery; to tread upon it was to become free. At that time no other state in the Union followed this example. At the census of 1790, Massachusetts, alone of all the states, returned "no slaves."

The state of opinion in Virginia is remarkable, because it brings to light the peculiar difficulties of the southern states.

The great Virginian statesmen, such as Washington and Jefferson, condemned the institution, yet because there was no other form of domestic service, Washington owned slaves. There was in Virginia a strong party in favour of emancipating slaves. But they demanded that the emancipated slaves should leave the state within a year or be outlawed! They were naturally alarmed at the possibility that a free barbaric black community, many of its members African-born and reeking with traditions of cannibalism and secret and dreadful religious rites, should arise beside them upon Virginian soil. When we consider that point of view, we can understand why it was that a large number of Virginians should be disposed to retain the mass of blacks in the country under control as slaves, while at the same time they were bitterly opposed to the slave trade and the importation of any fresh blood from Africa. The free blacks, one sees, might easily become a nuisance; indeed the free state of Massachusetts presently closed its borders to their entry. . . . The question of slavery, which in the ancient world was usually no more than a question of status between individuals racially akin, merged in America with the different and profounder question of relationship between two races at opposite extremes of the human species and of the most contrasted types of tradition and culture. If the black man had been white, there can be little doubt that negro slavery, like white servitude, would have vanished from the United States within a generation of the Declaration of Independence as a natural consequence of the statements in that declaration.

§ 7

We have told of the War of Independence in America as the first great break away from the system of European monarchies and foreign offices, as the repudiation by a new community of Machiavellian statescraft as the directive form of human affairs. Within a decade there came a second and much more portentous revolt against this strange game of Great Powers, this tangled interaction of courts and policies which obsessed Europe. But this time it was no breaking away at the outskirts. In France, the nest and home of Grand Monarchy, the heart and centre of Europe, came this second upheaval. And, unlike the American colonists, who simply repudiated a king, the French, following in the footsteps of the English revolution, beheaded one.

Like the British revolution and like the revolution in the United States, the French revolution can be traced back to the ambitious absurdities of the French monarchy. The schemes of aggrandisement, the aims and designs of the Grand Monarch, necessitated an expenditure upon war equipment throughout Europe out of all proportion to the taxable capacity of the age. And even the splendours of monarchy were enormously costly, measured by the productivity of the time. In France, just as in Britain and in America, the first resistance was made not to the monarch as such and to his foreign policy as such, nor with any clear recognition of these things as the roots of the trouble, but merely to the inconveniences and charges upon the individual life caused by them. The practical taxable capacity of France must have been relatively much less than that of England because of the various exemptions of the nobility and clergy. The burthen resting directly upon the common people was heavier. That made the upper classes the confederates of the court instead of the antagonists of the court as they were in England, and so prolonged the period of waste further; but when at last the bursting-point did come, the explosion was more violent and shattering.

During the years of the American War of Independence there were few signs of any impending explosion in France. There was much misery among the lower classes, much criticism and satire, much outspoken liberal thinking, but there was little to indicate that the thing as a whole, with all its customs, usages, and familiar discords, might not go on for an indefinite time. It was consuming beyond its powers of production, but as yet only the inarticulate classes were feeling the pinch. Gibbon, the historian, knew France well; Paris was as familiar to him as London; but there is no suspicion to be detected in the passage we have quoted that days of political and social dissolution were at hand. No doubt the world abounded in absurdities and injustices, yet nevertheless, from the point of view of a scholar and a gentleman, it was fairly comfortable, and it seemed fairly secure.

There was much liberal thought, speech, and sentiment in France at this time. Parallel with and a little later than John Locke in England, Montesquieu (1689-1755) in France, in the earlier half of the eighteenth century, had subjected social, political, and religious institutions to the same searching and fundamental analysis, especially in his *Esprit des Lois.* He had stripped the magical prestige from the absolutist monarchy in France. He shares with Locke the credit for clearing away many of the false ideas that had hitherto prevented deliberate and conscious attempts to reconstruct human society. It was not his fault if at first some extremely unsound and impermanent shanties were run up on the vacant site. The generation that followed him in the middle and later decades of the eighteenth century was boldly speculative upon the moral and intellectual clearings he had made. A group of brilliant writers, the "Encyclopædists," mostly rebel spirits from the excellent schools of the Jesuits, set themselves under the leadership of Diderot to scheme out, in a group of works, a new world (1766). The glory of the Encyclopædists, says Mallet, lay "in their hatred of things unjust, in their denunciation of the trade in slaves, of the inequalities of taxation, of the corruption of justice, of the wastefulness of wars, in their dreams of social progress, in their sympathy with the rising empire of industry which was beginning to transform the world." Their chief error seems to have been an indiscriminate hostility to religion. They believed that man was naturally just and politically competent, whereas his impulse to social service and self-forgetfulness is usually developed only through an education essentially religious, and sustained only in an atmosphere of honest co-operation. Unco-ordinated human initiatives lead to nothing but social chaos.

Side by side with the Encyclopædists were the Economists or Physiocrats, who were making bold and crude inquiries into the production and distribution of food and goods. Morally, the author of the *Code de la Nature,* denounced the institution of private property and proposed a communistic organization of society. He was the precursor of that large and various school of collectivist thinkers in the nineteenth century who are lumped together as Socialists.

Both the Encyclopædists and the various Economists and Physiocrats demanded a considerable amount of hard thinking in their disciples. An easier and more popular leader to follow was Rousseau (1712-78). He displayed a curious mingling of logical rigidity and sentimental enthusiasm. He preached the alluring doctrine that the primitive state of man was one of virtue and happiness, from which he had declined through the rather inexplicable activities of priests, kings, lawyers, and the like. Rousseau's intellectual influence was on the whole demoralizing. It struck not only at the existing social fabric, but at any social organization. When he wrote of the *Social Contract,* he seemed rather to excuse breaches of the covenant than to emphasize its necessity. Man is so far from perfect, that a writer who apparently sustained the thesis that the almost universal disposition, against which we all have to fortify ourselves, to repudiate debts, misbehave sexually, and evade the toil and expenses of education for ourselves and others, is not after all a delinquency, but a fine display of Natural Virtue, was bound to have a large following in every class that could read him. Rousseau's tremendous vogue did much to popularize a sentimental and declamatory method of dealing with social and political problems.

We have already remarked that hitherto no human community has begun to act upon theory. There must first be some breakdown and necessity for direction that lets theory into her own. Up to 1788 the republican and anarchist talk and writing of French thinkers must have seemed as ineffective and politically unimportant as the æsthetic socialism of William Morris at the end of the nineteenth century. There was the social and political system going on with an effect of invincible persistence, the king hunting and mending his clocks, the court and the world of fashion pursuing their pleasures, the financiers conceiving continually more enterprising extensions of credit, business blundering clumsily along its ancient routes, much incommoded by taxes and imposts, the peasants worrying, toiling, and suffering, full of a hopeless hatred of the nobleman's château. Men talked—and felt they were merely talking. Anything might be said, because nothing would ever happen.

§ 8

The first jar to this sense of the secure continuity of life in France came in 1787. Louis XVI (1774-92) was a dull, ill-educated monarch, and he had the misfortune to be married to a silly and extravagant woman, Marie Antoinette, the sister of the Austrian emperor. The question of her virtue is one of profound interest to a certain type of historical writer, but we need not discuss it here. She lived, as Paul Wiriath[1] puts it, "side by side, but not at the side" of her husband. She was rather heavy-featured, but not so plain as to prevent her posing as a beautiful, romantic, and haughty queen. When the exchequer was exhausted by the war in America (an enterprise to weaken England of the highest Machiavellian quality), when the whole country was uneasy with discontents, she set her influence to thwart the attempts at economy of the king's ministers, to encourage every sort of aristocratic extravagance, and to restore the church and the nobility to the position they had held in the great days of Louis XIV. Non-aristocratic officers were to be weeded from the army; the power of the church over private life was to be extended. She found in an upper-class official, Calonne, her ideal minister of finance. From 1783-87 this wonderful man produced money as if by magic—and as if by magic it disappeared again. Then in 1787 he collapsed. He had piled loan on loan, and now he declared that the monarchy, the Grand Monarchy that had ruled France since the days of Louis XIV, was bankrupt. No more money could be raised. There must be a gathering of the notables of the kingdom to consider the situation.

To the gathering of notables, a summoned assembly of leading men, Calonne propounded a scheme for a subsidy to be levied upon all landed property. This roused the aristocrats to a pitch of great indignation. They demanded the summoning of a body roughly equivalent to the British parliament, the States General, which had not met since 1610. Regardless of the organ of opinion they were creating for the discontents below them, excited only by the proposal that they should bear part of the weight of the financial burthens of the country, the French notables insisted. And in May, 1789, the States General met.

It was an assembly of the representatives of three orders, the nobles, the clergy, and the Third Estate, the commons. For the Third Estate the franchise was very wide, nearly every taxpayer of twenty-five having a vote. (The parish priests voted as clergy, the small noblesse as nobles.) The States General was a body without any tradition of procedure. Enquiries were sent to the antiquarians of the Academy of Inscriptions in that

[1] Article "France," *Encyclopaedia Britannica.*

matter. Its opening deliberations turned on the question whether it was to meet as one body or as three, each estate having an equal vote. Since the Clergy numbered 308, the Nobles 285, and the Deputies 621, the former arrangement would put the Commons in an absolute majority, the latter gave them one vote in three. Nor had the States General any meeting-place. Should it meet in Paris or in some provincial city? Versailles was chosen, "because of the hunting."

It is clear that the king and queen meant to treat this fuss about the national finance as a terrible bore, and to allow it to interfere with their social routine as little as possible. We find the meetings going on in salons that were not wanted, in orangeries and tennis-courts, and so forth.

The question whether the voting was to be by the estates or by head was clearly a vital one. It was wrangled over for six weeks. The Third Estate, taking a leaf from the book of the English House of Commons, then declared that it alone represented the nation, and that no taxation must be levied henceforth without its consent. Whereupon the king closed the hall in which it was sitting, and intimated that the deputies had better go home. Instead, the deputies met in a convenient tennis-court, and there took oath, the Oath of the Tennis Court, not to separate until they had established a constitution in France.

The king took a high line, and attempted to disperse the Third Estate by force. The soldiers refused to act. On that the king gave in with a dangerous suddenness, and accepted the principle that the Three Estates should all deliberate and vote together as one National Assembly. Meanwhile, apparently at the queen's instigation, foreign regiments in the French service, who could be trusted to act against the people, were brought up from the provinces under the Marshal de Broglie, and the king prepared to go back upon his concessions. Whereupon Paris and France revolted. Broglie hesitated to fire on the crowds. A provisional city government was set up in Paris and in most of the other large cities, and a new armed force, the National Guard, a force designed primarily and plainly to resist the forces of the crown, was brought into existence by these municipal bodies.

The revolt of July 1789 was really the effective French revolution. The grim-looking prison of the Bastille, very feebly defended, was stormed by the people of Paris, and the insurrection spread rapidly throughout France. In the east and north-west provinces many châteaux belonging to the nobility were burnt by the peasants, their title-deeds carefully destroyed, and the owners murdered or driven away. The insurrection spread throughout France. In a month the ancient and decayed system of the aristocratic order had collapsed. Many of the leading princes and courtiers of the queen's party fled abroad. The National Assembly found itself called upon to create a new political and social system for a new age.

§ 9

The French National Assembly was far less fortunate in the circumstances of its task than the American Congress. The latter had half a continent to itself, with no possible antagonist but the British Government. Its religious and educational organizations were various, collectively not very powerful, and on the whole friendly. King George was far away in England, and sinking slowly towards an imbecile condition. Nevertheless, it took the United States several years to hammer out a working constitution. The French, on the other hand, were surrounded by aggressive neighbours with Machiavellian ideas, they were encumbered by a king and court resolved to make mischief, and the church was one single great organization inextricably bound up with the ancient order. The queen was in close correspondence with the Count of Artois, the Duke of Bourbon, and the other exiled princes who were trying to induce Austria and Prussia to attack the new French nation. Moreover, France was already a bankrupt country, while the United States had limitless undeveloped resources; and the revolution, by altering the conditions of land tenure and marketing, had produced an economic disorganization that has no parallel in the case of America.

These were the unavoidable difficulties of the situation. But in addition the Assembly made difficulties for itself. There was no orderly procedure. The English House of Commons had had more than five centuries of experience in its work, and Mirabeau, one of the great leaders of the early Revolution, tried in vain to have the English rules adopted. But the feeling of the times was all in favour of outcries, dramatic interruptions, and such-like manifestations of Natural Virtue. And the disorder did not come merely from the assembly. There was a great gallery, much too great a gallery, for strangers; but who would restrain the free citizens from having a voice in the national control? This gallery swarmed with people eager for a "scene," ready to applaud or shout down the speakers below. The abler speakers were obliged to play to the gallery, and take a sentimental and sensational line. It was easy at a crisis to bring in a mob to kill debate.

So encumbered, the Assembly set about its constructive task. On the Fourth of August it achieved a great dramatic success. Led by several of the liberal nobles, it made a series of resolutions, abolishing serfdom, privileges, tax exemptions, tithes, and feudal courts. (In many parts of the country, however, these resolutions were not carried into effect until three or four years later.) Titles went with these other renunciations. Long before France was a republic it was an offence for a nobleman to sign his name with his title. For six weeks the Assembly devoted itself, with endless opportunities for rhetoric, to the formulation of a Declaration of the Rights of Man—on the lines of the Bills of Rights that were the English preliminaries to organized change. Meanwhile the court plotted for reaction, and the people felt that the court was plotting. The story is complicated here by the scoundrelly schemes of the king's cousin, Philip of Orleans, who hoped to use the discords of the time to replace Louis on the French throne. His gardens at the Palais Royal were thrown open to the public, and became a great centre of advanced discussion. His agents did much to intensify the popular suspicion of the king. And things were exacerbated by a shortage of provisions—for which the king's government was held guilty.

Presently the loyal Flanders regiment appeared at Versailles. The royal family was scheming to get farther away from Paris—in order to undo all that had been done, to restore tyranny and extravagance. Such constitutional monarchists as General Lafayette were seriously alarmed. And just at this time occurred an outbreak of popular indignation at the scarcity of food, that passed by an easy transition into indignation against the threat of royalist reaction. It was believed that there was an abundance of provisions at Versailles; that food was being kept there away from the people. The public mind had been much disturbed by reports, possibly by exaggerated reports, of a recent banquet at Versailles, hostile to the nation. Here are some extracts from Carlyle descriptive of that unfortunate feast.

"The Hall of the Opera is granted; the Salon d'Hercule shall be drawing-room. Not only the Officers of Flandre, but of the Swiss, of the Hundred Swiss; nay of the Versailles National Guard, such of them as have any loyalty, shall feast; it will be a Repast like few.

"And now suppose this Repast, the solid part of it, transacted; and the first bottle over. Suppose the customary loyal toasts drunk; the King's health, the Queen's with deafening vivats; that of the nation 'omitted,' or even 'rejected.' Suppose champagne flowing; with pot-valorous speech, with instrumental music; empty featherheads growing ever the noisier, in their own emptiness, in each other's noise. Her Majesty, who looks unusually sad to-night (His Majesty sitting dulled with the day's hunting), is told that the sight of it would cheer her. Behold! She enters there, issuing from her State-rooms, like the Moon from clouds, this fairest unhappy Queen of Hearts; royal Husband by her side, young Dauphin in her arms! She descends from the Boxes, amid splendour and acclaim; walks queen-like round the Tables; gracefully nodding; her looks full of sorrow, yet of gratitude and daring, with the hope of France on her mother-bosom! And now, the band striking up, *O Richard, O mon Roi, l'univers t'abandonne* (Oh Richard, O my king, the world is all forsaking thee), could man do other than rise to height of pity, of loyal valour? Could featherheaded young ensigns do other than, by white Bourbon Cockades, handed them from fair fingers; by waving of swords, drawn to pledge the Queen's health; by trampling of National Cockades; by scaling the Boxes, whence intrusive murmurs may come; by vociferation, sound, fury and distraction, within doors and without—testify what tempest-tost state of vacuity they are in? . . .

"A natural Repast; in ordinary times, a harmless one: now fatal. . . . Poor ill-advised Marie Antoinette; with a woman's vehemence, not with a sovereign's foresight! It was so natural, yet so unwise. Next day, in public speech of ceremony, her Majesty declares herself 'delighted with Thursday.'"

And here to set against this is Carlyle's picture of the mood of the people.

"In squalid garret, on Monday morning Maternity awakes, to hear children weeping for bread. Maternity must forth to the streets, to the herb-makers and bakers'-queues; meets there with hunger-stricken Maternity, sympathetic, exasperative. O we unhappy women! But, instead of bakers'-queues, why not to Aristocrats' palaces, the root of the matter? *Allons!* Let us assemble. To the Hôtel-de-Ville; to Versailles. . . ."

There was much shouting and coming and going in Paris before this latter idea realized itself. One Maillard appeared with organizing power, and assumed a certain leadership. There can be little doubt that the revolutionary leaders, and particularly General Lafayette, used and organized this outbreak to secure the king, before he could slip away—as Charles I did to Oxford—to begin a civil war. As the afternoon wore on, the procession started on its eleven mile tramp. . . .

Again we quote Carlyle:

"Maillard has halted his draggled Menads on the last hilltop; and now Versailles, and the Château of Versailles, and far and wide the inheritance of Royalty opens to the wondering eye. From far on the right, over Marly and Saint-Germain-en-Laye; round towards Rambouillet, on the left, beautiful all; softly embosomed; as if in sadness, in the dim moist weather! And near before us is Versailles, New and Old; with that broad frondent *Avenue de Versailles* between—stately frondent, broad, three hundred feet as men reckon, with its four rows of elms; and then the Château de Versailles, ending in royal parks and pleasances, gleaming lakelets, arbours, labyrinths, the *Ménagerie,* and Great and Little Trianon. High-towered dwellings, leafy pleasant places; where the gods of this lower world abide: whence, nevertheless, black care cannot be excluded; whither Menadic hunger is even now advancing, armed with pike-thyrsi!"

Rain fell as the evening closed.

"Behold the Esplanade, over all its spacious expanse, is covered with groups of squalid dripping women; of lank-haired male rascality, armed with axes, rusty pikes, old muskets, iron-shod clubs (*batons ferrés,* which end in knives or swordblades, a kind of extempore billhook); looking nothing but hungry revolt. The rain pours; Gardes-du-Corps so caracoling through the groups 'amid hisses'; irritating and agitating what is but dispersed here to reunite there. . . .

"Innumerable squalid women beleaguer the President and Deputation; insist on going with him: has not his Majesty himself, looking from the window, sent out to ask, What we wanted? 'Bread, and speech with the King,' that was the answer. Twelve women are clamourously added to the deputation; and march with it, across the Esplanade; through dissipated groups, caracoling bodyguards and the pouring rain."

"Bread and not too much talking!" Natural demands.

"One learns also that the royal Carriages are getting yoked, as if for Metz. Carriages, royal or not, have verily showed themselves at the back gates. They even produced, or quoted, a written order from our Versailles Municipality—which is a monarchic not a democratic one. However, Versailles patrols drove them in again; as the vigilant Lecointre had strictly charged them to do. . . .

"So sink the shadows of night, blustering, rainy; and all paths grow dark. Strangest night ever seen in these regions; perhaps since the Bartholomew Night, when Versailles, as Bassompierre writes of it, was a *chetif château.*

"O for the lyre of some Orpheus, to constrain, with touch of melodious strings, these mad masses into Order! For here all seems fallen asunder, in wide-yawning dislocation. The highest, as in down-rushing of a world, is come in contact with the lowest: the rascality of France beleaguering the royalty of France; 'iron-shod batons' lifted round the diadem, not to guard it! With denunciations of bloodthirsty anti-national body-guards, are heard dark growlings against a queenly name.

"The Court sits tremulous, powerless: varies with the varying temper of the Esplanade, with the varying colour of the rumours from Paris. Thick-coming rumours; now of peace, now of war. Necker and all the Ministers consult; with a blank issue. The Œil-de-Bœuf is one tempest of whispers: We will fly to Metz; we will not fly. The royal carriages again attempt egress—though for trial merely; they are again driven in by Lecointre's patrols."

But we must send the reader to Carlyle to learn of the coming of the National Guard in the night under General Lafayette himself, the bargaining between the Assembly and the King, the outbreak of fighting in the morning between the bodyguard and the hungry besiegers, and how the latter stormed into the palace and came near to a massacre of the royal family. Lafayette and his troops turned out in time to prevent that, and timely cartloads of loaves arrive from Paris for the crowd.

At last it was decided that the king should come to Paris.

"Processional marches not a few our world has seen; Roman triumphs and ovations, Cabiric cymbal-beatings, Royal progresses, Irish funerals; but this of the French Monarchy marching to its bed remained to be seen. Miles long, and of breadth losing itself in vagueness, for all the neighbouring country crowds to see. Slow: stagnating along, like shoreless Lake, yet with a noise like Niagara, like Babel and Bedlam. A splashing and a tramping; a hurrahing, uproaring, musket-volleying; the truest segment of Chaos seen in these latter Ages! Till slowly it disembogue itself, in the thickening dusk, into expectant Paris, through a double row of faces all the way from Passy to the Hôtel-de-Ville.

"Consider this: Vanguard of National troops; with trains of artillery; of pikemen and pikewomen, mounted on cannons, on carts, hackney-coaches, or on foot. . . . Loaves stuck on the points of bayonets, green boughs stuck in gun-barrels. Next, as main-march, 'fifty cart-loads of corn,' which have been lent, for peace, from the stores of Versailles. Behind which follow stragglers of the Garde-du-Corps; all humiliated, in Grenadier bonnets. Close on these comes the royal carriage; come royal carriages; for there are a hundred national deputies too, among whom sits Mirabeau—his remarks not given. Then finally, pell-mell, as rear-guard, Flandre, Swiss, Hundred Swiss, other bodyguards, brigands, whosoever cannot get before. Between and among all which masses flows without limit Saint-Antoine and the Menadic cohort. Menadic especially about the royal carriage. . . . Covered with tricolor; singing 'allusive songs'; pointing with one hand to the royal carriage, which the allusions hit, and pointing to the provision-wagons with the other hand, and these words: 'Courage, Friends! We shall not want bread now; we are bringing you the Baker, the Bakeress and Baker's boy.' . . .

"The wet day draggles the tricolor, but the joy is unextinguishable. Is not all well now? *'Ah Madame, notre bonne Reine,'* said some of these Strong-women some days hence, 'Ah, Madame, our good Queen, don't be a traitor any more and we will all love you!' . . ."

This was October the sixth, 1789. For nearly two years the royal family dwelt unmolested in the Tuileries. Had the court kept common faith with the people, the king might have died there, a king.

From 1789 to 1791 the early Revolution held its own; France was a limited monarchy, the king kept a diminished state in the Tuileries, and the National Assembly ruled a country at peace. The reader who will glance back to the maps of Poland we have given in the previous chapter will realize what occupied Russia, Prussia, and Austria at this time. While France experimented with a crowned republic in the west, the last division of the crowned republic of the east was in progress. France could wait.

When we consider its inexperience, the conditions under which it worked, and the complexities of its problems, one must concede that the Assembly did a very remarkable amount of constructive work. Much of that work was sound and still endures, much was experimental and has been undone. Some was disastrous. There was a clearing up of the penal code; torture, arbitrary imprisonment, and persecutions for heresy were abolished. The ancient provinces of France, Normandy, Burgundy, and the like gave place to eighty departments. Promotion to the highest ranks in the army was laid open to men of every class. An excellent and simple system of law courts was set up, but its value was much vitiated by having the judges appointed by popular election for short periods of time. This made the crowd a sort of final court of appeal, and the judges, like the members of the Assembly, were forced to play to the gallery. And the whole vast property of the church was seized and administered by the state; religious establishments not engaged in education or works of charity were broken up, and the salaries of the clergy made a charge upon the nation. This in itself was not a bad thing for the lower clergy in France, who were often scandalously underpaid in comparison with the richer dignitaries. But in addition the choice of priests and bishops was made elective, which struck at the very root idea of the Roman church, which centred everything upon the Pope, and in which all authority is from above downward. Practically the National Assembly wanted at one blow to make the church in France Protestant, in organization if not in doctrine. Everywhere there were disputes and conflicts between the state priests created by the National Assembly and the recalcitrant (non-juring) priests who were loyal to Rome. . . .

One curious thing the National Assembly did which greatly weakened its grip on affairs. It decreed that no member of the Assembly should be an executive minister. This was in imitation of the American constitution, where also ministers are separated from the legislature. The British method has been to have all ministers in the legislative body, ready to answer questions and account for their interpretation of the laws and their conduct of the nation's business. If the legislature represents the sovereign people, then it is surely necessary for the ministers to be in the closest touch with their sovereign. This severance of the legislature and executive in France caused misunderstandings and mistrust; the legislature lacked control and the executive lacked moral force. This led to such an ineffectiveness in the central government that in many districts at this time, communes and towns were to be found that were practically self-governing communities; they accepted or rejected the commands of Paris as they thought fit, declined the payment of taxes, and divided up the church lands according to their local appetites.

§ 10

It is quite possible that with the loyal support of the crown and a reasonable patriotism on the part of the nobility, the National Assembly, in spite of its noisy galleries, its Rousseauism, and its inexperience, might have blundered through to a stable form of parliamentary government for France. In Mirabeau it had a statesman with clear ideas of the needs of the time; he knew the strength and the defects of the British system, and apparently he had set himself to establish in France a parallel political organization upon a wider, more honest franchise. He had, it is true, indulged in a sort of Ruritanian flirtation with the queen, seen her secretly, pronounced her very solemnly the "only *man*" about the king, and made rather a fool of himself in that matter, but his schemes were drawn upon a much larger scale than the scale of the back stairs of the Tuileries. By his death in 1791 France certainly lost one of her most constructive statesmen, and the National Assembly its last chance of any co-operation with the king. When there is a court there is usually a conspiracy, and royalist schemes and royalist mischief-making were the last straw in the balance against the National Assembly. The royalists did not care for Mirabeau, they did not care for France; they wanted to be back in their lost paradise of privilege, haughtiness, and limitless expenditure, and it seemed to them that if only they could make the government of the National Assembly impossible, then by a sort of miracle the dry bones of the ancient régime would live again. They had no sense of the other possibility, the gulf of the republican extremists, that yawned at their feet.

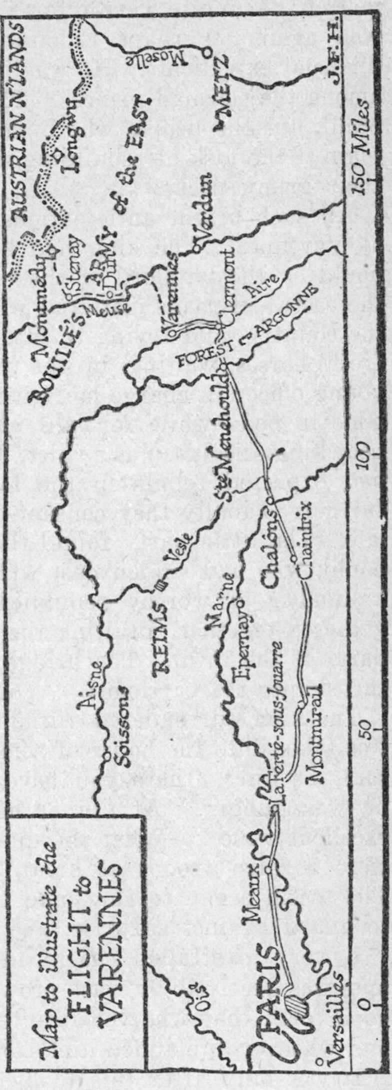

Map to illustrate the FLIGHT to VARENNES

One June night in 1791, between eleven o'clock and midnight, the king and queen and their two children slipped out of the Tuileries disguised, threaded their palpitating way through Paris, circled round from the north of the city to the east, and got at last into a travelling-carriage that was waiting upon the road to Chalons. They were flying to the army of the east. The army of the east was "loyal," that is to say, its general and officers at least were prepared to betray France to the king and court. Here was adventure at last after the queen's heart, and one can understand the pleasurable excitement of the little party as the miles lengthened between themselves and Paris. Away over the hills were reverence, deep bows, and the kissing of hands. Then back to Versailles. A little shooting of the mob in Paris—artillery, if need be. A few executions—but not of the sort of people who matter. A White Terror for a few months. Then all would be well again. Perhaps Calonne might return, too, with fresh financial expedients. He was busy just then gathering support among the German princes. There were a lot of châteaux to rebuild, but the people who burnt them down could hardly complain if the task of rebuilding them pressed rather heavily upon their grimy necks. . . .

All such bright anticipations were cruelly dashed that night at Varennes. The king had been recognized at Sainte Menehould by the landlord of the post house, and as the night fell, the eastward roads clattered with galloping messengers rousing the country, and trying to intercept the fugitives. There were fresh horses waiting in the upper village of Varennes—the young officer in charge had given the king up for the night and gone to bed—while for half an hour in the lower village the poor king, disguised as a valet, disputed with his postillions, who had expected reliefs in the lower village and refused to go further. Finally they consented to go on. They consented too late. The little party found the postmaster from Sainte Menehould, who had ridden past while the postillions wrangled, and a number of worthy republicans of Varennes whom he had gathered together, awaiting them at the bridge between the two parts of the town. The bridge was barricaded. Muskets were thrust into the carriage: "Your passports?"

The king surrendered without a struggle. The little party was taken into the house of some village functionary. "Well," said the king, "here you have me!" Also he remarked that he was hungry. At dinner he commended the wine, "quite excellent wine." What the queen said is not recorded. There were royalist troops at hand, but they attempted no rescue. The tocsin began to ring, and the village "illuminated itself," to guard against surprise. . . .

A very crestfallen coachload of royalty returned to Paris, and was received by vast crowds—*in silence*. The word had gone forth that whoever insulted the king should be thrashed, and whoever applauded him should be killed. . . .

It was only after this foolish exploit that the idea of a republic took hold of the French mind. Before this flight to Varennes there was no doubt much abstract republican sentiment, but there was scarcely any expressed disposition to abolish monarchy in France. Even in July, a month after the flight, a great meeting in the Champ de Mars, supporting a petition for the dethronement of the king, was dispersed by the authorities, and many people were killed. But such displays of firmness could not prevent the lesson of that flight soaking into men's minds. Just as in England in the days of Charles I, so now in France men realized that the king could not be trusted—he was dangerous. The Jacobins grew rapidly in strength. Their leaders, Robespierre, Danton, Marat, who had hitherto been figured as impossible extremists, began to dominate French affairs.

These Jacobins were the equivalents of the American radicals, men with untrammelled advanced ideas. Their strength lay in the fact that they were unencumbered and downright. They were poor men with nothing to lose. The party of moderation, of compromise with the relics of the old order, was led by such men of established position as General Lafayette, the general who had represented France in America, and Mirabeau, an aristocrat who was ready to model himself on the rich and influential aristocrats of England. But Robespierre was a needy but clever young lawyer from Arras, whose most precious possession was his faith in Rousseau; Danton was a scarcely more wealthy barrister in Paris, a big, gesticulating, rhetorical figure; Marat was an older man, a Swiss of very great scientific distinction, but equally unembarrassed by possessions. On Marat's scientific standing it is necessary to lay stress because there is a sort of fashion among English writers to misrepresent the leaders of great revolutionary movements as ignorant men. This gives a false view of the mental processes of revolution; and it is the task of the historian to correct it. Marat, we find, was conversant with English, Spanish, German, and Italian; he had spent several years in England, he was made an honorary M.D. of St. Andrew's, and had published some valuable contributions to medical science in English. Both Benjamin Franklin and Goethe were greatly interested in his work in physics. This is the man who is called by Carlyle "rabid dog," "atrocious," "squalid," and "Dog-leech"—this last by way of tribute to his science.

The revolution called Marat to politics, and his earliest contributions to the great discussion were fine and sane. There was a prevalent delusion in France that England was a land of liberty. His *Tableau des vices de la constitution d'Angleterre* showed the realities of the English position. His last years were maddened by an almost intolerable skin disease which he caught while hiding in the sewers of Paris to escape the consequences of his denunciation of the king as a traitor after the flight to Varennes. Only by sitting in a hot bath could he collect his mind to write. He had been treated hardly and suffered, and he became hard; nevertheless he stands out in history as a man of rare, unblemished honesty. His poverty seems particularly to have provoked the scorn of Carlyle.

"What a road he has travelled; and sits now, about half-past seven of the clock, stewing in slipper-bath; sore afflicted; ill of Revolution Fever. . . . Excessively sick and worn, poor man: with precisely elevenpence halfpenny of ready-money, in paper; with slipper-bath; strong three-footed stool for writing on, the while: and a squalid Washerwoman for his sole household . . . that is his civic establishment in Medical-School Street; thither and not elsewhere has his road led him. . . . Hark, a rap again! A musical woman's voice, refusing to be rejected: it is the Citoyenne who would do France a service. Marat, recognizing from within, cries, Admit her. Charlotte Corday is admitted."

The young heroine—for republican leaders are fair game, and their assassins are necessarily heroines and their voices "musical"—offered to give him some necessary information about the counter-revolution at Caen, and as he was occupied in making a note of her facts, she stabbed him with a large sheath knife (1792). . . .

Such was the quality of most of the leaders of the Jacobin party. They were men of no property—untethered men. They were more dissociated and more elemental, therefore, than any other party; and they were ready to push the ideas of freedom and equality to a logical extremity. Their standards of patriotic virtue were high and harsh. There was something inhuman even in their humanitarian zeal. They saw without humour the disposition of the moderates to ease things down, to keep the common folk just a little needy and respectful, and royalty (and men of substance) just a little respected. They were blinded by the formulæ of Rousseauism to the historical truth that man is by nature oppressor and oppressed, and that it is only slowly by law, education, and the spirit of love in the world that men can be made happy and free.

And while in America the formulæ of eighteenth-century democracy were on the whole stimulating and helpful because it was already a land of open-air practical equality so far as white men were concerned, in France these formulæ made a very heady and dangerous mixture for the town populations, because considerable parts of the towns of France were slums full of dispossessed, demoralized, degraded, and bitter-spirited people. The Parisian crowd was in a particularly desperate and dangerous state, because the industries of Paris had been largely luxury industries, and much of her employment parasitic on the weaknesses and vices of fashionable life. Now the fashionable world had gone over the frontier, travellers were restricted, business disordered, and the city full of unemployed and angry people.

But the royaltists, instead of realizing the significance of these Jacobins with their dangerous integrity and their dangerous grip upon the imagination of the mob, had the conceit to think they could make tools of them. The time for the replacement of the National Assembly under the new-made constitution by the "Legislative Assembly" was drawing near; and when the Jacobins, with the idea of breaking up the moderates, proposed to make the members of the National Assembly ineligible for the Legislative Assembly, the royalists supported them with great glee, and carried the proposal. They perceived that the Legislative Assembly, so clipped of all experience, must certainly be a politically incompetent body. They would "extract good from the excess of evil," and presently France would fall back helpless into the hands of her legitimate masters. So they thought. And the royalists did more than this. They backed the election of a Jacobin as Mayor of Paris. It was about as clever as if a man brought home a hungry tiger to convince his wife of her need of him. There stood another body ready at hand with which these royalists did not reckon, far better equipped than the court to step in and take the place of an ineffective Legislative Assembly, and that was the strongly Jacobin Commune of Paris installed at the Hôtel de Ville.

So far France had been at peace. None of her neighbours

had attacked her, because she appeared to be weakening herself by her internal dissensions. It was Poland that suffered by the distraction of France. But there seemed no reason why they should not insult and threaten her, and prepare the way for a later partition at their convenience. At Pillnitz, in 1791, the King of Prussia and the Emperor of Austria met, and issued a declaration that the restoration of order and monarchy in France was a matter of interest to all sovereigns. And an army of émigrés, French nobles and gentlemen, an army largely of officers, was allowed to accumulate close to the frontier.

It was France that declared war against Austria. The motives of those who supported this step were conflicting. Many republicans wanted it because they wished to see the kindred people of Belgium liberated from the Austrian yoke. Many royalists wanted it because they saw in war a possibility of restoring the prestige of the crown. Marat opposed it bitterly in his paper *L'Ami du Peuple,* because he did not want to see republican enthusiasm turned into war fever. His instinct warned him of Napoleon. On April 20th, 1792, the king came down to the Assembly and proposed war amidst great applause.

The war began disastrously. Three French armies entered Belgium, two were badly beaten, and the third, under Lafayette, retreated. Then Prussia declared war in support of Austria, and the allied forces, under the Duke of Brunswick, prepared to invade France. The duke issued one of the most foolish proclamations in history; he was, he said, invading France to restore the royal authority. Any further indignity shown the king he threatened to visit upon the Assembly and Paris with "military execution." This was surely enough to make the most royalist Frenchman a republican—at least for the duration of the war.

The new phase of revolution, the Jacobin revolution, was the direct outcome of this proclamation. It made the Legislative Assembly, in which orderly republicans (Girondins) and royalists prevailed, it made the government which had put down that republican meeting in the Champ de Mars and hunted Marat into the sewers, impossible. The insurgents gathered at the Hôtel de Ville, and on the tenth of August the Commune launched an attack on the palace of the Tuileries.

The king behaved with a clumsy stupidity, and with that

disregard for others which is the prerogative of kings. He had with him a Swiss guard of nearly a thousand men as well as National Guards of uncertain loyalty. He held out vaguely until firing began, and then he went off to the adjacent Assembly to place himself and his family under its protection, leaving his Swiss fighting. No doubt he hoped to antagonize Assembly and Commune, but the Assembly had none of the fighting spirit of the Hôtel de Ville. The royal refugees were placed in a box reserved for journalists (out of which a small room opened), and there they remained for sixteen hours while the Assembly debated their fate. Outside there were the sounds of a considerable battle; every now and then a window would break. The unfortunate Swiss were fighting with their backs to the wall because there was now nothing else for them to do. . . .

The Assembly had no stomach to back the government's action of July in the Champ de Mars. The fierce vigour of the Commune dominated it. The king found no comfort whatever in the Assembly. It scolded him and discussed his "suspension." The Swiss fought until they received a message from the king to desist, and then—the crowd being savagely angry at the needless bloodshed and out of control—they were for the most part massacred.

The long and tedious attempt to "Merovingianize" Louis, to make an honest crowned republican out of a dull and inadaptable absolute monarch, was now drawing to its tragic close. The Commune of Paris was practically in control of France. The Legislative Assembly—which had apparently undergone a change of heart—decreed that the king was suspended from his office, confined him in the Temple, replaced him by an executive commission, and summoned a National Convention to frame a new constitution.

The tension of patriotic and republican France was now becoming intolerable. Such armies as she had were rolling back helplessly towards Paris. Longwy had fallen, the great fortress of Verdun followed, and nothing seemed likely to stop the march of the allies upon the capital. The sense of royalist treachery rose to panic cruelty. At any rate the royalists had to be silenced and stilled and scared out of sight. The Commune set itself to hunt out every royalist that could be found, until the prisons of Paris were full. Marat saw the danger of a massacre. Before it was too late he tried to secure the establishment of emergency tribunals to filter the innocent from the guilty in this miscellaneous collection of schemers, suspects, and harmless gentlefolk. He was disregarded, and early in September the inevitable massacre occurred.

Suddenly, first at one prison and then at others, bands of insurgents took possession. A sort of rough court was consti-

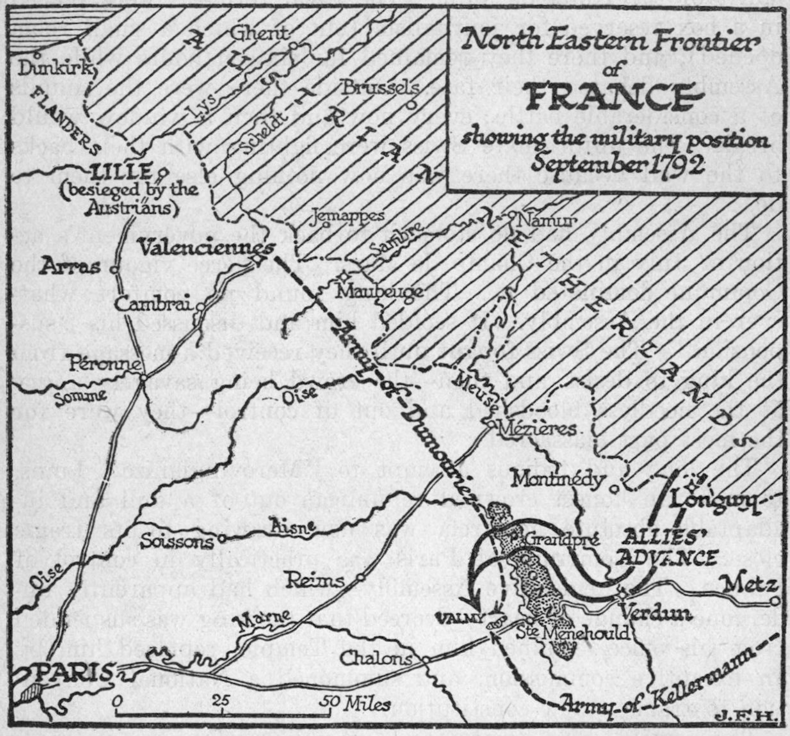

tuted, and outside gathered a wild mob armed with sabres, pikes, and axes. One by one the prisoners, men and women alike, were led out from their cells, questioned briefly, pardoned with the cry of "Vive la Nation," or thrust out to the mob at the gates. There the crowd jostled and fought to get a slash or thrust at a victim. The condemned were stabbed, hacked, and beaten to death, their heads hewn off, stuck on pikes, and carried about the town, their torn bodies thrust aside. Among others, the Princesse de Lamballe, whom the king and queen had left behind in the Tuileries, perished. Her head was carried on a pike to the Temple for the queen to see.

In the queen's cell were two National Guards. One would have had her look out and see this gristly sight. The other, in pity, would not let her do so.

Even as this red tragedy was going on in Paris, the French general Dumouriez, who had rushed an army from Flanders into the forests of the Argonne, was holding up the advance of the allies beyond Verdun. On September 20th occurred a battle, mainly an artillery encounter, at Valmy. A not very resolute Prussian advance was checked, the French infantry stood firm, their artillery was better than the allied artillery. For ten days after this repulse the Duke of Brunswick hesitated, and then he began to fall back towards the Rhine. This battle at Valmy—it was little more than a cannonade—was one of the decisive battles in the world's history. The Revolution was saved.

The National Convention met on September 21st, 1792, and immediately proclaimed a republic. The trial and execution of the king followed with a sort of logical necessity upon these things. He died rather as a symbol than as a man. There was nothing else to be done with him; poor man, he cumbered the earth. France could not let him go to hearten the emigrants, could not keep him harmless at home; his existence threatened her. Marat had urged this trial relentlessly, yet with that acid clearness of his he would not have the king charged with any offence committed before he signed the constitution, because before then he was a real monarch, super-legal, and so incapable of being illegal. Nor would Marat permit attacks upon the king's counsel. . . . Throughout Marat played a bitter and yet often a just part; he was a great man, a fine intelligence, in a skin of fire; wrung with that organic hate in the blood that is not a product of the mind but of the body.

Louis was beheaded in January, 1793. He was guillotined—for since the previous August the guillotine had been in use as the official instrument in French executions.

Danton, in his leonine rôle, was very fine upon this occasion. "The kings of Europe would challenge us," he roared. "We throw them the head of a king!"

§ 11

And now followed a strange phase in the history of the French people. There arose a great flame of enthusiasm for France and the Republic. There was to be an end to compromise at home and abroad; at home royalists and every form of disloyalty were to be stamped out; abroad France was to be the protector and helper of all revolutionaries. All Europe, all the world, was to become republican. The youth of France poured into the Republican armies; a new and wonderful song spread through the land, a song that still warms the blood like wine, the Marseillaise. Before that chant and the leaping columns of French bayonets and their enthusiastically served guns the foreign armies rolled back; before the end of 1792 the French armies had gone far beyond the utmost achievements of Louis XIV; everywhere they stood on foreign soil. They were in Brussels, they had overrun Savoy, they had raided to Mayence; they had seized the Scheldt from Holland. Then the French Government did an unwise thing. It had been exasperated by the expulsion of its representative from England upon the execution of Louis, and it declared war against England. It was an unwise thing to do, because the revolution which had given France a new enthusiastic infantry and a brilliant artillery, released from its aristocratic officers and many cramping traditions, had destroyed the discipline of its navy, and the English were supreme upon the sea. And this provocation united all England against France, whereas there had been at first a very considerable liberal movement in Great Britain in sympathy with the revolution.

Of the fight that France made in the next few years against a European coalition we cannot tell in any detail. She drove the Austrians for ever out of Belgium, and made Holland a republic. The Dutch fleet, frozen in the Texel, surrendered to a handful of cavalry without firing its guns. For some time the French thrust towards Italy was hung up, and it was only in 1796 that a new general, Napoleon Bonaparte, led the ragged and hungry republican armies in triumph across Piedmont to Mantua and Verona. An *Outline of History* cannot map out campaigns; but of the new quality that had come into war, it is bound to take note. The old professional armies had fought for the fighting, as slack as workers paid by the hour;

these wonderful new armies fought, hungry and thirsty, for victory. Their enemies called them the "New French." Says C. F. Atkinson,[1] "What astonished the Allies most of all was the number and the velocity of the Republicans. These improvised armies had in fact nothing to delay them. Tents were unprocurable for want of money, untransportable for want of the enormous number of wagons that would have been required, and also unnecessary, for the discomfort that would have caused wholesale desertion in professional armies was cheerfully borne by the men of 1793-94. Supplies for armies of then unheard-of size could not be carried in convoys, and the French soon became familiar with 'living on the country.' Thus 1793 saw the birth of the modern system of war—rapidity of movement, full development of national strength, bivouacs, requisitions and force as against cautious manœuvring, small professional armies, tents and full rations, and chicane. The first represented the decision-compelling spirit, the second the spirit of risking little to gain a little. . . ."

And while these ragged hosts of enthusiasts were chanting the Marseillaise and fighting for *La France*, manifestly never quite clear in their minds whether they were looting or liberating the countries into which they poured, the republican enthusiasm in Paris was spending itself in a far less glorious fashion. Marat, the one man of commanding intelligence among the Jacobins, was now frantic with an incurable disease, and presently he was murdered; Danton was a series of patriotic thunderstorms; the steadfast fanaticism of Robespierre dominated the situation. This man is difficult to judge; he was a man of poor physique, naturally timid, and a prig. But he had that most necessary gift for power, faith. He believed not in a god familiar to men, but in a certain Supreme Being, and that Rousseau was his prophet. He set himself to save the republic as he conceived it, and he imagined it could be saved by no other man than he. So that to keep in power was to save the republic. The living spirit of the republic, it seemed, had sprung from a slaughter of royalists and the execution of the king. There were insurrections: one in the west, in the district of La Vendée, where the people rose against the conscription and against the dispossession of the orthodox

[1] In his article, "French Revolutionary Wars," in the *Encyclopaedia Britannica*.

clergy, and were led by noblemen and priests; one in the south, where Lyons and Marseilles had risen and the royalists of Toulon had admitted an English and Spanish garrison. To which there seemed no more effectual reply than to go on killing royalists.

Nothing could have better pleased the fierce heart of the Paris slums. The Revolutionary Tribunal went to work, and a steady slaughtering began.[1] The invention of the guillotine was opportune to this mood. The queen was guillotined, most of Robespierre's antagonists were guillotined, atheists who argued that there was no Supreme Being were guillotined, Danton was guillotined because he thought there was too much guillotine; day by day, week by week, this infernal new machine chopped off heads and more heads and more. The reign of Robespierre lived, it seemed, on blood, and needed more and more, as an opium-taker needs more and more opium.

Danton was still Danton, leonine and exemplary upon the guillotine. "Danton," he said, "no weakness!"

And the grotesque thing about the story is that Robespierre was indubitably honest. He was far more honest than any of the group of men who succeeded him. He was inspired by a consuming passion for a new order of human life. So far as he could contrive it, the Committee of Public Safety, the emergency government of twelve which had now thrust aside the Convention, *constructed.* The scale on which it sought to construct was stupendous. All the intricate problems with which we still struggle to-day were met by swift and shallow solutions. Attempts were made to equalize property. "Opulence," said St. Just, "is infamous." The property of the rich was taxed or confiscated in order that it should be divided among the poor. Every man was to have a secure house, a living, a wife and children. The labourer was worthy of his hire, but not entitled to an advantage. There was an attempt to abolish *profit* altogether, the rude incentive of most human commerce since the beginning of society. Profit is the economic riddle that still puzzles us to-day. There were harsh laws against "profiteering" in France in 1793—England in 1919 found it necessary to make quite similar laws. And the Jacobin government not only replanned—in eloquent outline—

[1] In the thirteen months before June 1794, there were 1,220 executions; in the following seven weeks there were 1,376.—P. G.

the economic, but also the social system. Divorce was made as easy as marriage; the distinction of legitimate and illegitimate children was abolished. . . . A new calendar was devised, with new names for the months, a week of ten days, and the like—that has long since been swept away; but also the clumsy coinage and the tangled weights and measures of old France gave place to the simple and lucid decimal system that still endures. . . . There was a proposal from one extremist group to abolish God among other institutions altogether, and to substitute the worship of Reason. There was, indeed, a Feast of Reason in the cathedral of Notre-Dame, with a pretty actress as the goddess of Reason. But against this Robespierre set his face; he was no atheist. "Atheism," he said, "is aristocratic. The idea of a Supreme Being who watches over oppressed innocence and punishes triumphant crime is essentially the idea of the people."

So he guillotined Hébert, who had celebrated the Feast of Reason, and all his party.

A certain mental disorder became perceptible in Robespierre as the summer of 1794 drew on. He was deeply concerned with his religion. (The arrests and executions of suspects were going on now as briskly as ever. Through the streets of Paris every day rumbled the Terror with its carts full of condemned people.) He induced the Convention to decree that France believed in a Supreme Being, and in that comforting doctrine, the immortality of the soul. In June he celebrated a great festival, the festival of his Supreme Being. There was a procession to the Champ de Mars, which he headed, brilliantly arrayed, bearing a great bunch of flowers and wheat ears. Figures of inflammatory material, representing Atheism and Vice, were solemnly burnt; then, by an ingenious mechanism, and with some slight creakings, an incombustible statue of Wisdom rose in their place. There were discourses—Robespierre delivered the chief one—but apparently no worship. . . .

Thereafter Robespierre displayed a disposition to brood aloof from affairs. For a month he kept away from the Convention.

One day in July he reappeared and delivered a strange speech that clearly foreshadowed fresh prosecutions. "Gazing on the multitude of vices which the torrent of Revolution has rolled down," he cried, in his last great speech in the Convention, "I have sometimes trembled lest I should be soiled by the impure neighbourhood of wicked men. . . . I know that it is easy for the leagued tyrants of the world to overwhelm a single individual; but I know also what is the duty of a man who can die in the defence of humanity.'' . . .

And so on to vague utterances that seemed to threaten everyone.

The Convention heard this speech in silence; then when a proposal was made to print and circulate it, broke into a resentful uproar and refused permission. Robespierre went off in bitter resentment to the club of his supporters, and *re-read his speech to them!*

That night was full of talk and meetings and preparations for the morrow, and the next morning the Convention turned upon Robespierre. One Tallien threatened him with a dagger. When he tried to speak, he was shouted down, and the President jingled the bell at him. ''President of Assassins,'' cried Robespierre, ''I demand speech!'' It was refused him. His voice deserted him; he coughed and spluttered. ''The blood of Danton chokes him,'' cried someone.

He was accused and arrested there and then with his chief supporters.

Whereupon the Hôtel de Ville, still stoutly Jacobin, rose against the Convention, and Robespierre and his companions were snatched out of the hands of their captors. There was a night of gathering, marching, counter-marching; and at last, about three in the morning, the forces of the Convention faced the forces of the Commune outside the Hôtel de Ville. Henriot, the Jacobin commander, after a busy day was drunk upstairs; a parley ensued, and then, after some indecision, the soldiers of the Commune went over to the Government. There was a shouting of patriotic sentiments, and someone looked out from the Hôtel de Ville. Robespierre and his last companions found themselves betrayed and trapped.

Two or three of these men threw themselves out of a window, and injured themselves frightfully on the railings below without killing themselves. Others attempted suicide. Robespierre, it seems, was shot in the lower jaw by a gendarme. He was found, his eyes staring from a pale face whose lower part was blood.

Followed seventeen hours of agony before his end. He spoke never a word during that time, his jaw being bound up roughly in dirty linen. He and his companions, and the broken, dying bodies of those who had jumped from the windows, twenty-two men altogether, were taken to the guillotine instead of the condemned appointed for that day. Mostly his eyes were closed, but, says Carlyle, he opened them to see the great knife rising above him, and struggled. Also it would seem he screamed when the executioner removed his bandages. Then the knife came down, swift and merciful.

The Terror was at an end. From first to last there had been condemned and executed about four thousand people.

§ 12

It witnesses to the immense vitality and the profound rightness of the flood of new ideals and intentions that the French Revolution had released into the world of practical endeavour, that it could still flow in a creative torrent after it had been caricatured and mocked in the grotesque personality and career of Robespierre. He had shown its deepest thoughts, he had displayed anticipations of its methods and conclusions; through the green and distorting lenses of his preposterous vanity and egotism, he had smeared and blackened all its hope and promise with blood and horror, and the power of these ideas was not destroyed. They stood the extreme tests of ridiculous and horrible presentation. After his downfall, the Republic still ruled unassailable. Leaderless, for his successors were a group of crafty or commonplace men, the European republic struggled on, and presently fell and rose again, and fell and rose and still struggles, entangled but invincible.

And it is well to remind the reader here of the real dimensions of this phase of the Terror, which strikes so vividly upon the imagination and which has therefore been enormously exaggerated relatively to the rest of the revolution. From 1789 to late in 1791 the French Revolution was an orderly process, and from the summer of 1794 the Republic was an orderly and victorious state. The Terror was not the work of the whole country, but of the town mob which owed its existence and its savagery to the misrule and social injustice of the ancient régime; and the explosion of the Terror could have happened only through the persistent treacherous disloyalty of the royalists which, while it raised the extremists to frenzy, disinclined the mass of moderate republicans from any intervention. The best men were busy fighting the Austrians and royalists on the frontier. Altogether, we must remember, the total of the killed in the Terror amounted to a few thousands, and among those thousands there were certainly a great number of active antagonists whom the Republic, by all the standards of that time, was entitled to kill. It included such traitors and mischief-makers as Philip, Duke of Orleans of the Palais Royal, who had voted for the death of Louis XVI. More lives were wasted by the British generals alone on the opening day of what is known as the Somme offensive of July, 1916, than in the whole French revolution from start to finish. We hear so much about the martyrs of the French Terror because they were notable, well-connected people, and because there has been a sort of propaganda of their sufferings. But let us balance against them in our minds what was going on in the prisons of the world generally at that time. In Britain and America, while the Terror ruled in France, far more people were slaughtered for offences—very often quite trivial offences—against property than were condemned by the Revolutionary Tribunal for treason against the State. Of course, they were very common people indeed, but in their rough way they suffered. A girl was hanged in Massachusetts in 1789 for forcibly taking the hat, shoes, and buckles of another girl she had met in the street.[1] Again, Howard the philanthropist (about 1773) found a number of perfectly innocent people detained in the English prisons who had been tried and acquitted, but were unable to pay the gaoler's fees. And these prisons were filthy places under no effective control. Torture was still in use in the Hanoverian dominions of his Britannic majesty King George III. It had been in use in France up to the time of the National Assembly. These things mark the level of the age. It is not on record that anyone was deliberately tortured by the French revolutionaries during the Terror. Those few hundreds of French gentlefolk fell into a pit that most of them had been well content should exist for others. It was tragic, but not, by the scale of universal history, a great tragedy. The common man in France was more free, better off, and happier during the "Terror" than he had been in 1787.

The story of the Republic after the summer of 1794 be-

[1] Channing, vol. iii. chap. xviii.

comes a tangled story of political groups aiming at everything from a radical republic to a royalist reaction, but pervaded by a general desire for some definite working arrangement even at the price of considerable concessions. There was a series of insurrections of the Jacobins and of the royalists, there seems to have been what we should call nowadays a hooligan class in Paris which was quite ready to turn out to fight and loot on either side; nevertheless the Convention produced a government, the Directory of five members, which held France together for five years. The last, most threatening revolt of all, in October, 1795, was suppressed with great skill and decision by a rising young general, Napoleon Bonaparte.

The Directory was victorious abroad, but uncreative at home; its members were far too anxious to stick to the sweets and glories of office to prepare a constitution that would supersede them, and far too dishonest to handle the task of financial and economic reconstruction demanded by the condition of France. We need only note two of their names, Carnot, who was an honest republican, and Barras, who was conspicuously a rogue. Their reign of five years formed a curious interlude in this history of great changes. They took things as they found them. The propagandist zeal of the revolution carried the French armies into Holland, Belgium, Switzerland, south Germany, and north Italy. Everywhere kings were expelled and republics set up. But such propagandist zeal as animated the Directorate did not prevent the looting of the treasures of the liberated peoples to relieve the financial embarrassment of the French Government. Their wars became less and less the holy war of freedom, and more and more like the aggressive wars of the ancient régime. The last feature of Grand Monarchy that France was disposed to discard was her tradition of foreign policy, grasping, aggressive, restless, French-centred. One discovers it still as vigorous under the Directorate as if there had been no revolution.

§ 13

The ebb of this tide of Revolution in the world, this tide which had created the great Republic of America and threatened to submerge all European monarchies, was now at hand. It is as if something had thrust up from beneath the surface of human affairs, made a gigantic effort, and for a time spent itself. It swept many obsolescent and evil things away, but many evil and unjust things remained. It solved many problems, and it left the desire for fellowship and order face to face with much vaster problems that it seemed only to have revealed. Privilege of certain types had gone, many tyrannies, much religious persecution. When these things of the ancient régime had vanished, it seemed as if they had never mattered. What did matter was that for all their votes and enfranchisement, and in spite of all their passion and effort, common men were still not free and not enjoying an equal happiness; that the immense promise and air of a new world with which the Revolution had come, remained unfulfilled.

Yet, after all, this wave of revolution had realized nearly everything that had been clearly thought out before it came. It was not failing now for want of impetus, but for want of finished ideas. Many things that had oppressed mankind were swept away for ever. Now that they were swept away it became apparent how unprepared men were for the creative opportunities this clearance gave them. And periods of revolution are periods of action; in them men reap the harvests of ideas that have grown during phases of interlude, and they leave the fields cleared for a new season of growth, but they cannot suddenly produce ripened new ideas to meet an unanticipated riddle.

The sweeping away of king and lord, of priest and inquisitor, of landlord and taxgatherer and task-master, left the mass of men face to face for the first time with certain very fundamental aspects of the social structure, relationships they had taken for granted, and had never realized the need of thinking hard and continuously about before. Institutions that had seemed to be in the nature of things, and matters that had seemed to happen by the same sort of necessity that brought round the dawn and springtime, were discovered to be artificial, controllable, were they not so perplexingly intricate, and—now that the old routines were abolished and done away with—in urgent need of control. The New Order found itself confronted with three riddles which it was quite unprepared to solve: Property, Currency, and International Relationship.

Let us take these three problems in order, and ask what they are and how they arose in human affairs. Every human life is deeply entangled in them, and concerned in their solution. The rest of this history becomes more and more clearly the development of the effort to solve these problems; that is to say, so to interpret property, so to establish currency, and so to control international reactions as to render possible a world-wide, progressive, and happy community of will. They are the three riddles of the sphinx of fate, to which the human commonweal must find an answer or perish.

The idea of property arises out of the combative instincts of the species. Long before men were men, the ancestral ape was a proprietor. Primitive property is what a beast will fight for. The dog and his bone, the tigress and her lair, the roaring stag and his herd, these are proprietorship blazing. No more nonsensical expression is conceivable in sociology than the term "primitive communism." The Old Man of the family tribe of early palæolithic times insisted upon his proprietorship in his wives and daughters, in his tools, in his visible universe. If any other man wandered into his visible universe he fought him, and if he could he slew him. The tribe grew in the course of ages, as Atkinson showed convincingly in his *Primal Law,* by the gradual toleration by the Old Man of the existence of the younger men, and of their proprietorship in the wives they captured from outside the tribe, and in the tools and ornaments they made and the game they slew. Human society grew by a compromise between this one's property and that. It was largely a compromise and an alliance forced upon men by the necessity of driving some other tribe out of its visible universe. If the hills and forests and streams were not *your* land or *my* land, it was because they had to be *our* land. Each of us would have preferred to have it *my* land, but that would not work. In that case the other fellows would have destroyed us. Society, therefore, is from its beginnings the mitigation of ownership. Ownership in the beast and in the primitive savage was far more intense a thing than it is in the civilized world to-day. It is rooted more strongly in our instincts than in our reason.

In the natural savage and in the untutored man to-day—for it is well to keep in mind that no man to-day is more than four hundred generations from the primordial savage—there is no limitation to the sphere of ownership. Whatever you can fight for, you can own; women-folk, spared captive, captured beast, forest glade, stone pit or what not. As the community grew and a sort of law came to restrain internecine fighting, men developed rough and ready methods of settling proprietorship. Men could own what they were the first to make or capture or claim. It seemed natural that a debtor who could not pay up should become the property of his creditor. Equally natural was it that, after claiming a patch of land ("Bags I," as the schoolboy says), a man should exact payments and tribute from anyone else who wanted to use it. It was only slowly, as the possibilities of organized life dawned on men, that this unlimited property in anything whatever began to be recognized as a nuisance. Men found themselves born into a universe all owned and claimed, nay! they found themselves born owned and claimed. The social struggles of the earlier civilization are difficult to trace now, but the history we have told of the Roman republic shows a community waking up to the idea that they may become a public inconvenience and should then be repudiated, and that the unlimited ownership of land is also an inconvenience. We find that later Babylonia severely limited the rights of property in slaves. Finally, we find in the teaching of that great revolutionist, Jesus of Nazareth, such an attack upon property as had never been before. Easier it was, he said, for a camel to go through the eye of a needle than for the owner of great possessions to enter the kingdom of heaven. A steady, continuous criticism of the permissible scope of property seems to have been going on in the world for the last twenty-five or thirty centuries. Nineteen hundred years after Jesus of Nazareth we find all the world that has come under the Christian teaching persuaded that there could be no property in persons. There has been a turn-over in the common conscience in that matter. And also the idea that "a man may do what he likes with his own" was clearly very much shaken in relation to other sorts of property. But this world of the closing eighteenth century was still only in the interrogative stage in this matter. It had got nothing clear enough, much less settled enough, to act upon. One of its primary impulses was to protect property against the greed and waste of kings and the exploitation of noble adventurers. It was to protect private property that the Revolution began. But its equalitarian formulæ carried it into a criticism of the very property it had risen to protect.

How can men be free and equal when numbers of them have no ground to stand upon and nothing to eat, and the owners will neither feed nor lodge them unless they toil? Excessively—the poor complained.

To which riddle the Jacobin reply was to set about "dividing up." They wanted to intensify and universalize property. Aiming at the same end by another route, there were already in the eighteenth century certain primitive socialists—or, to be more exact, communists—who wanted to "abolish" private property altogether. The state (a democratic state was of course understood) was to own all property. It was only as the nineteenth century developed that men began to realize that property was not one simple thing, but a great complex of ownerships of different values and consequences, that many things (such as human beings, the implements of an artist, clothing, tooth-brushes) are very profoundly and incurably personal property, and that there is a very great range of things, railways, machinery of various sorts, homes, cultivated gardens, pleasure-boats, for example, which need each to be considered very particularly to determine how far and under what limitations it may come under private ownership, and how far it falls into the public domain and may be administered and let out by the state in the collective interest. On the practical side these questions pass into politics, and the problem of making and sustaining efficient state administration. They open up issues in social psychology, and interact with the enquiries of educational science. We have to-day the advantage of a hundred and thirty years of discussion over the first revolutionary generation, but even now this criticism of property is still a vast and passionate ferment rather than a science. Under the circumstances it was impossible that eighteenth-century France should present any other spectacle than that of vague and confused popular movements seeking to dispossess owners, and classes of small and large owners holding on grimly, demanding, before everything else, law, order, and security, and seeking to increase their individual share of anything whatever that could be legally possessed.

Closely connected with the vagueness of men's ideas about property was the vagueness of their ideas about currency. Both the American and the French republics fell into serious trouble upon this score. Here, again, we deal with something that is not simple, a tangle of usages, conventions, laws, and prevalent mental habits, out of which arise problems which admit of no solution in simple terms, and which yet are of vital importance to the everyday life of the community. The validity of the acknowledgment a man is given for a day's work is manifestly of quite primary importance to the working of the social machine. The growth of confidence in the precious metals and of coins, until the assurance became practically universal that good money could be trusted to have its purchasing power anywhere, must have been a gradual one in human history. And being fairly established, this assurance was subjected to very considerable strains and perplexities by the action of governments in debasing currency and in substituting paper promises to pay for the actual metallic coins. Every age produced a number of clever people intelligent enough to realize the opportunities for smart operations afforded by the complex of faiths and fictions upon which the money system rested, and sufficiently unsound morally to give their best energies to growing rich and so getting people to work for them, through tricks and tampering with gold, coinage, and credit. So soon as serious political and social dislocation occurred, the money mechanism began to work stiffly and inaccurately. The United States and the French Republic both started their careers in a phase of financial difficulty. Everywhere governments had been borrowing and issuing paper promises to pay interest, more interest than they could conveniently raise. Both revolutions led to much desperate public spending and borrowing, and at the same time to an interruption of cultivation and production that further diminished real taxable wealth. Both governments, being unable to pay their way in gold, resorted to the issue of paper money, promising to pay upon the security of undeveloped land (in America) or recently confiscated church lands (France). In both cases the amount of issue went far beyond the confidence of men in the new security. Gold was called in, hidden by the cunning ones, or went abroad to pay for imports; and people found themselves with various sorts of bills and notes in the place of coins, all of uncertain and diminishing value.

However complicated the origins of currency, its practical effect and the end it has to serve in the community may be stated roughly in simple terms. The money a man receives for his work (mental or bodily) or for relinquishing his property in some consumable good, must ultimately be able to purchase for him for his use a fairly equivalent amount of consumable goods. ("Consumable goods" is a phrase we would have understood in the widest sense to represent even such things as a journey, a lecture or theatrical entertainment, housing, medical advice, and so forth.) When everyone in a community is assured of this, and assured that the money will not deteriorate in purchasing power, then currency—and the distribution of goods by trade—is in a healthy and satisfactory state. Then men will work cheerfully, and only then. The imperative need for that steadfastness and security of currency is the fixed datum from which the scientific study and control of currency must begin. But under the most stable conditions there will always be fluctuations in currency value. The sum total of saleable consumable goods in the world and in various countries varies from year to year and from season to season; autumn is probably a time of plenty in comparison with spring; with an increase in the available goods in the world, the purchasing power of currency will increase, unless there is also an increase in the amount of currency. On the other hand, if there is a diminution in the production of consumable goods or a great and unprofitable destruction of consumable goods, such as occurs in a war, the share of the total of consumable goods represented by a sum of money will diminish and prices and wages will rise. In modern war the explosion of a single big shell, even if it hits nothing, destroys labour and material roughly equivalent to a comfortable cottage or a year's holiday for a man. If the shell hits anything, then that further destruction has to be added to the diminution of consumable goods. Every shell that burst in the recent war diminished by a little fraction the purchasing value of every coin in the whole world. If there is also an increase of currency during a period when consumable goods are being used up and not fully replaced—and the necessities of revolutionary and war-making governments almost always require this—then the enhancement of prices and the fall in the value of the currency paid in wages is still greater. Usually also governments under these stresses borrow money; that is to say, they issue interest-bearing paper, secured on the willingness and ability of the general community to endure taxation. Such operations would be difficult enough if they were carried out frankly by perfectly honest men, in the full light of publicity and scientific knowledge. But hitherto this has never been the case; at every point the clever egotist, the bad sort of rich man, is trying to deflect things a little to his own advantage. Everywhere, too, one finds the stupid egotist ready to take fright and break into panic. Consequently we presently discover the state encumbered by an excess of currency, which is in effect a non-interest-paying debt, and also with a great burthen of interest upon loans. Both credit and currency begin to fluctuate wildly with the evaporation of public confidence. They are, we say, demoralized.

The ultimate consequence of an entirely demoralized currency would be to end all work and all trade that could not be carried on by payment in kind and barter. Men would refuse to work except for food, clothing, housing, and payment in kind. The immediate consequence of a partially demoralized currency is to drive up prices and make trading feverishly adventurous and workers suspicious and irritable. A sharp man wants under such conditions to hold money for as brief a period as possible; he demands the utmost for his reality, and buys a reality again as soon as possible in order to get this perishable stuff, the currency paper, off his hands. All who have fixed incomes and saved accumulations suffer by the rise in prices, and the wage-earners find, with a gathering fury, that the real value of their wages is continually less. Here is a state of affairs where the duty of every clever person is evidently to help adjust and reassure. But all the traditions of private enterprise, all the ideas of the later eighteenth century, went to justify the action of acute-minded and dexterous people who set themselves to accumulate claims, titles, and tangible property in the storms and dislocations of this currency breakdown. The number of understanding people in the world who were setting themselves sincerely and simply to restore honest and workable currency and credit conditions were few and ineffectual. Most of the financial and speculative people of the time were playing the part of Cornish wreckers—not apparently with any conscious dishonesty, but with the completest self-approval and the applause of their fellow-men. The aim of every clever person was to accumulate as much as he could of really negotiable wealth, and then, and only then, to bring about some sort of stabilizing political process that would leave him in advantageous possession of his accumulation. Here were the factors of a bad economic atmosphere, suspicious, feverish, greedy, and speculative. . . .

In the third direction in which the Revolution had been unprepared with clear ideas, the problem of international relationships, developments were to occur that interacted disastrously with this state of financial and economic adventure, this scramble and confusion, this preoccupation of men's minds with the perplexing slipperiness of their private property and their monetary position at home. The Republic at its birth found itself at war. For a time that war was waged by the new levies with a patriotism and a zeal unparalleled in the world's history. But that could not go on. The Directory found itself at the head of a conquering country, intolerably needy and embarrassed at home, and in occupation of rich foreign lands, full of seizable wealth and material and financial opportunity. We have all double natures, and the French in particular seem to be developed logically and symmetrically on both sides. Into these conquered regions France came as a liberator, the teacher of Republicanism to mankind. Holland and Belgium became the Batavian Republic, Genoa and its Riviera the Ligurian Republic, north Italy the Cisalpine Republic, Switzerland was rechristened the Helvetian Republic, Mülhausen, Rome, and Naples were designated republics. Grouped about France, these republics were to be a constellation of freedom leading the world. That was the ideal side. At the same time the French government, and French private individuals in concert with the government, proceeded to a complete and exhaustive exploitation of the resources of these liberated lands.

So within ten years of the meeting of the States General, New France begins to take on a singular likeness to the old. It is more flushed, more vigorous; it wears a cap of liberty instead of a crown; it has a new army—but a damaged fleet; it has new rich people instead of the old rich people, a new peasantry working even harder than the old and yielding more taxes, a new foreign policy curiously like the old foreign policy disrobed, and—there is no Millennium.

XXXVII

THE CAREER OF NAPOLEON BONAPARTE

§ 1. *The Bonaparte Family in Corsica.* § 2. *Bonaparte as a Republican General.* § 3. *Napoleon First Consul, 1799-1804.* § 4. *Napoleon I. Emperor, 1804-14.* § 5. *The Hundred Days.* § 6. *The Map of Europe in 1815.*

§ 1

AND now we come to one of the most illuminating figures in modern history, the figure of an adventurer and a wrecker, whose story seems to display with an extraordinary vividness the universal subtle conflict of egotism, vanity, and personality with the weaker, wider claims of the common good. Against this background of confusion and stress and hope, this strained and heaving France and Europe, this stormy and tremendous dawn, appears this dark little archaic personage, hard, compact, capable, unscrupulous, imitative, and neatly vulgar. He was born (1769) in the still half-barbaric island of Corsica, the son of a rather prosaic father, a lawyer who had been first a patriotic Corsican against the French monarchy which was trying to subjugate Corsica, and who had then gone over to the side of the invader. His mother was of sturdier stuff, passionately patriotic and a strong and managing woman. (She birched her sons; on one occasion she birched Napoleon when he was sixteen.) There were numerous brothers and sisters, and the family pursued the French authorities with importunities for rewards and jobs. Except for Napoleon it seems to have been a thoroughly commonplace, "hungry" family. He was clever, bad-tempered, and overbearing. From his mother he had acquired a romantic Corsican patriotism.

Through the patronage of the French governor of Corsica he got an education first at the military school of Brienne and then at the military school of Paris, from which he passed into the artillery in 1785. He was an industrious student both of mathematics and history, his memory was prodigiously good, and he made copious note-books which still exist. These note-books show no very exceptional intelligence, and they contain short pieces of original composition—upon suicide and similar adolescent topics. He fell early under the spell of Rousseau; he developed sensibility and a scorn for the corruptions of civilization. In 1786 he wrote a pamphlet against a Swiss pastor who had attacked Rousseau. It was a very ordinary adolescent production, rhetorical and imitative. He dreamt of an independent Corsica, freed from the French. With the revolution, he became an ardent republican and a supporter of the new French régime in Corsica. For some years, until the fall of Robespierre, he remained a Jacobin.

§ 2

He soon gained the reputation of a useful and capable officer, and it was through Robespierre's younger brother that he got his first chance of distinction at Toulon. Toulon had been handed over to the British and Spanish by the Royalists, and an allied fleet occupied its harbour. Bonaparte was given the command of the artillery, and under his direction the French forced the allies to abandon the port and town.

He was next appointed commander of the artillery in Italy, but he had not taken up his duties when the death of Robespierre seemed likely to involve his own; he was put under arrest as a Jacobin, and for a time he was in danger of the guillotine. That danger passed. He was employed as artillery commander in an abortive raid upon Corsica, and then went to Paris (1795) rather down at heel. Madame Junot in her Memoirs describes his lean face and slovenly appearance at this time, "his ill-combed, ill-powdered hair hanging down over his grey overcoat," his gloveless hands and badly blacked boots. It was a time of exhaustion and reaction after the severities of the Jacobin republic. "In Paris," says Holland Rose, "the star of Liberty was paling before Mercury, Mars, and Venus"—finance, uniforms, and social charm. The best of the common men were in the armies, away beyond the frontiers. We have already noted the last rising of the royalists in this year (1795). Napoleon had the luck to be in Paris, and found his second opportunity in this affair. He saved the Republic—of the Directory.

His abilities greatly impressed Carnot, the most upright of the Directors. Moreover, he married a charming young widow, Madame Josephine de Beauharnais, who had great influence with Barras. Both these things probably helped him to secure the command in Italy.

We have no space here for the story of his brilliant campaigns in Italy (1796-97), but of the spirit in which that invasion of Italy was conducted we must say a word or two, because it illustrates so vividly the double soul of France and of Napoleon, and how revolutionary idealism was paling before practical urgencies. He proclaimed to the Italians that the French were coming to break their chains—*and they were!* He wrote to the Directory: "We will levy 20,000,000 francs in exactions in this country; it is one of the richest in the world." To his soldiers he said, "You are famished and nearly naked. . . . I lead you into the most fertile plain in the world. There you will find great towns, rich provinces, honour, glory, riches. . . ."

We are all such mixed stuff as this; in all of us the intimations of a new world and a finer duty struggle to veil and control the ancient greeds and lusts of our inherited past; but these passages, written by a young man of twenty-seven, seem to show the gilt of honourable idealism rubbed off at an unusually early age. These are the bribes of an adventurer who has brought whatever impulse of devotion to a great cause once stirred within him well under the control of his self-love.

His successes in Italy were brilliant and complete; they enormously stimulated his self-confidence and his contempt for the energy and ability of his fellow-creatures. He had wanted to go into Italy because there lay the most attractive task—he had risked his position in the army by refusing to take up the irksome duties of a command against the rebels in La Vendée—and there are clear signs of a vast expansion of his vanity with his victories. He had been a great reader of Plutarch's Lives and of Roman history, and his extremely active but totally uncreative imagination was now busy with dreams of a revival of the eastern conquests of the Roman Empire. He got the republic of Venice out of his way by cutting it up between the French and Austria, securing the Ionian islands and the Venetian fleet for France. This peace, the peace of Campo Formio, was for both sides a thoroughly scoundrelly and ultimately a disastrous bargain. The new republic of France assisted in the murder of an ancient republic—Napoleon carried his point against a considerable outcry in France—and Austria got Venetia, in which land in 1918 she was destined to bleed to death. There were also secret clauses by which both France and Austria were later to acquire south German territory. And it was not only the Roman push eastward that was now exciting Napoleon's brain. This was the land of Cæsar—and Cæsar was a bad example for the successful general of a not very stable republic.

Cæsar had come back to Rome from Gaul a hero and conqueror. His new imitator would come back from Egypt and India—Egypt and India were to be his Gaul. There was really none of the genius about which historians write so glibly in this decision. It was a tawdry and ill-conceived imitation. The elements of failure stared him in the face. The way to Egypt and India was by sea, and the British, in spite of two recent naval mutinies, whose importance Napoleon exaggerated, were stronger than the French at sea. Moreover, Egypt was a part of the Turkish empire, by no means a contemptible power in those days. Nevertheless he persuaded the Directory, which was dazzled by his Italian exploits, to let him go. An Armada started from Toulon in May, 1798, captured Malta, and had the good luck to evade the British fleet and arrive at Alexandria. He landed his troops hurriedly, and the battle of the Pyramids made him master of Egypt.

The main British fleet at that time was in the Atlantic outside Cadiz, but the admiral had detached a force of his best ships, under Vice-Admiral Nelson—as great a genius in naval affairs as was Napoleon in things military—to chase and engage the French flotilla. For a time Nelson sought the French fleet in vain; finally, on the evening of the first of August, he found it at anchor in Aboukir bay. He had caught it unawares; many of the men were ashore and a council was being held in the flag-ship. He had no charts, and it was a hazardous thing to sail into the shallow water in a bad light. The French admiral concluded, therefore, that his adversary would not attack before morning, and so made no haste in recalling his men aboard until it was too late to do so. Nelson, however, struck at once—against the advice of some of his captains.

One ship only went aground. She marked the shoal for the rest of the fleet. He sailed to the attack in a double line about sundown, putting the French between two fires. Night fell as the battle was joined; the fight thundered and crashed in the darkness, until it was lit presently by the flames of burning French ships, and then by the flare of the French flag-ship, the *Orient,* blowing up. . . . Before midnight the battle of the Nile was over, and Napoleon's fleet was destroyed. Napoleon was cut off from France.

Says Holland Rose, quoting Thiers, this Egyptian expedition was "the rashest attempt history records." Napoleon was left in Egypt with the Turks gathering against him and his army infected with the plague. Nevertheless, with a stupid sort of persistence, he went on for a time with this Eastern scheme. He gained a victory at Jaffa, and, being short of provisions, *massacred all his prisoners.* Then he tried to take Acre, where his own siege artillery, just captured at sea by the English, was used against him. Returning baffled to Egypt, he gained a brilliant victory over a Turkish force at Aboukir, and then, deserting the army of Egypt—it held on until 1801, when it capitulated to a British force—made his escape back to France (1799), narrowly missing capture by a British cruiser off Sicily.

Here was muddle and failure enough to discredit any general—had it been known. But the very British cruisers which came so near to catching him, helped him by preventing any real understanding of the Egyptian situation from reaching the French people. He could make a great flourish over the battle of Aboukir and conceal the shame and loss of Acre. Things were not going well with France just then. There had been military failures at several points; much of Italy had been lost, Bonaparte's Italy, and this turned men's minds to him as the natural saviour of that situation; moreover, there had been much speculation, and some of it was coming to light; France was in one of her phases of financial scandal, and Napoleon had not filched; the public was in that state of moral fatigue when a strong and honest man is called for, a wonderful, impossible healing man who will do everything for everybody. People, poor lazy souls, persuaded themselves that this specious young man with the hard face, so providentially back from Egypt, was the strong and honest man required—another Washington.

With Julius Cæsar rather than Washington at the back of his mind, Napoleon responded to the demand of his time. A conspiracy was carefully engineered to replace the Directory by three "Consuls"—everybody seems to have been reading far too much Roman history just then—of whom Napoleon was to be the chief. The working of that conspiracy is too intricate a story for our space; it involved a Cromwell-like dispersal of the Lower House (the Council of Five Hundred), and in this

affair Napoleon lost his nerve. The deputies shouted at him and hustled him, and he seems to have been very much frightened. He nearly fainted, stuttered, and could say nothing, but the situation was saved by his brother Lucien, who brought in the soldiers and dispersed the council. This little hitch did not affect the final success of the scheme. The three Consuls were installed at the Luxembourg palace, with two commissioners, to reconstruct the constitution.

With all his confidence restored and sure of the support of the people, who supposed him to be honest, patriotic, republican, and able to bring about a good peace, Napoleon took a high hand with his colleagues and the commissioners. A constitution was produced in which the chief executive officer was to be called the First Consul, with enormous powers. He was to be Napoleon; this was part of the constitution. He was to be re-elected or replaced at the end of ten years. He was to be assisted by a Council of State, appointed by himself, which was to initiate legislation and send its proposals to two bodies, the Legislative Body (which could vote, but not discuss) and the Tribunate (which could discuss, but not vote), which were *selected* by an appointed Senate from a special class, the "notabilities of France," who were elected by the "notabilities of the departments," who were elected by the "notabilities of the commune," who were elected by the common voters. The suffrage for the election of the notabilities of the commune was universal. This was the sole vestige of democracy in the astounding pyramid. This constitution was chiefly the joint production of a worthy philosopher, Sieyès, who was one of the three consuls, and Bonaparte. But so weary was France with her troubles and efforts, and so confident were men in the virtue and ability of this adventurer from Corsica, that when, at the birth of the nineteenth century, this constitution was submitted to the country, it was carried by 3,011,007 votes to 1,562. France put herself absolutely in Bonaparte's hands, and prepared to be peaceful, happy, and glorious.

§ 3

Now surely here was opportunity such as never came to man before. Here was a position in which a man might well bow himself in fear of himself, and search his heart and serve God and man to the utmost. The old order of things was dead or dying; strange new forces drove through the world seeking form and direction; the promise of a world republic and an enduring world peace whispered in a multitude of startled minds. Had this man any profundity of vision, any power of creative imagination, had he been accessible to any disinterested ambition, he might have done work for mankind that would have made him the very sun of history. All Europe and America, stirred by the first promise of a new age, was waiting for him. Not France alone. France was in his hand, his instrument, to do with as he pleased, willing for peace, but tempered for war like an exquisite sword. There lacked nothing to this great occasion but a noble imagination. And failing that, Napoleon could do no more than strut upon the crest of this great mountain of opportunity like a cockerel on a dunghill. The figure he makes in history is one of almost incredible self-conceit, of vanity, greed, and cunning, of callous contempt and disregard of all who trusted him, and of a grandiose aping of Cæsar, Alexander, and Charlemagne which would be purely comic if it were not caked over with human blood. Until, as Victor Hugo said in his tremendous way, "God was bored by him," and he was kicked aside into a corner to end his days, explaining and explaining how very clever his worst blunders had been, prowling about his dismal hot island shooting birds and squabbling meanly with an underbred gaoler who failed to show him proper "respect."

His career as First Consul was perhaps the least dishonourable phase in his career. He took the crumbling military affairs of the Directory in hand, and after a complicated campaign in North Italy brought matters to a head in the victory of Marengo, near Alessandria (1800). It was a victory that at some moments came very near disaster. In the December of the same year General Moreau, in the midst of snow, mud, and altogether abominable weather, inflicted an overwhelming defeat upon the Austrian army at Hohenlinden. If Napoleon had gained this battle, it would have counted among his most characteristic and brilliant exploits. These things made the hoped-for peace possible. In 1801 the preliminaries of peace with England and Austria were signed. Peace with England, the Treaty of Amiens, was concluded in 1802, and Napoleon was free to give himself to the creative statecraft of which France, and Europe through France, stood in need. The war had given the country extended boundaries, the treaty with England restored the colonial empire of France and left her in a position of security beyond the utmost dreams of Louis XIV. It was open to Napoleon to work out and consolidate the new order of things, to make a modern state that should become a beacon and inspiration to Europe and all the world.

He attempted nothing of the sort. He did not realize that there were such things as modern states in the scheme of possibility. His little imitative imagination was full of a deep cunning dream of being Cæsar over again—as if this universe would ever tolerate anything of that sort over again! He was scheming to make himself a real emperor, with a crown upon his head and all his rivals and school-fellows and friends at his feet. This could give him no fresh power that he did not already exercise, but it would be more splendid—it would astonish his mother. What response was there in a head of that sort for the splendid creative challenge of the time? But first France must be prosperous. France hungry would certainly not endure an emperor. He set himself to carry out an old scheme of roads that Louis XV had approved; he developed canals in imitation of the English canals; he reorganized the police and made the country safe; and, preparing the scene for his personal drama, he set himself to make Paris look like Rome, with classical arches, with classical columns. Admirable schemes for banking development were available, and he made use of them. In all these things he moved with the times, they would have happened—with less autocracy, with less centralization, if he had never been born. And he set himself to weaken the republicans whose fundamental convictions he was planning to outrage. He recalled the émigrés, provided they gave satisfactory assurances to respect the new régime. Many were very willing to come back on such terms, and let Bourbons be bygones. And he worked out a great reconciliation, a Concordat, with Rome. Rome was to support him, and he was to restore the authority of Rome in the parishes. France would never be obedient and manageable, he thought; she would never stand a new monarchy, without religion. "How can you have order in a state," he said, "without religion? Society cannot exist without inequality of fortunes, which cannot endure apart from religion. When one man is dying of hunger near another who is ill of surfeit, he cannot resign himself to this difference, unless there is an authority which declares—'God wills it thus: there must be poor and rich in the world: but hereafter and during all eternity the division of things will take place differently.'" Religion—especially of the later Roman brand—was, he thought, excellent stuff for keeping the common people quiet. In his early Jacobin days he had denounced it for that very reason.

Another great achievement which marks his imaginative scope and his estimate of human nature was the institution of the Legion of Honour, a scheme for decorating Frenchmen with bits of ribbon which was admirably calculated to divert ambitious men from subversive proceedings.

And also Napoleon interested himself in Christian propaganda. Here is the Napoleonic view of the political uses of Christ, a view that has tainted all French missions from that time forth. "It is my wish to re-establish the institution for foreign missions; for the religious missionaries may be very useful to me in Asia, Africa, and America, as I shall make them reconnoitre all the lands they visit. The sanctity of their dress will not only protect them, but serve to conceal their political and commercial investigations. The head of the missionary establishment shall reside no longer at Rome, but in Paris."

These are the ideas of a roguish merchant rather than a statesman. His treatment of education shows the same narrow vision, the same blindness to the realities of the dawn about him. Elementary education he neglected almost completely; he left it to the conscience of the local authorities, and he provided that the teachers should be paid out of the fees of the scholars; it is clear he did not want the common people to be educated; he had no glimmering of any understanding why they should be; but he interested himself in the provision of technical and higher schools because his state needed the services of clever, self-seeking, well-informed men. This was an astounding retrogression from the great scheme, drafted by Condorcet for the Republic in 1792, for a complete system of free education for the entire nation. Slowly but steadfastly the project of Condorcet comes true; the great nations of the world are being compelled to bring it nearer and nearer to realization, and the cheap devices of Napoleon pass out of our interest. As for the education of the mothers and wives of our race, this was the quality of Napoleon's wisdom: "I do not think that we need trouble ourselves with any plan of instruction for young females, they cannot be better brought up than by their mothers. Public education is not suitable for them, because they are never called upon to act in public. Manners are all in all to them, and marriage is all they look to."

The First Consul was no kinder to women in the Code Napoleon. A wife, for example, had no control over her own property; she was in her husband's hands. This code was the work very largely of the Council of State. Napoleon seems rather to have hindered than helped its deliberations. He would invade the session without notice, and favour its members with lengthy and egotistical monologues, frequently quite irrelevant to the matter in hand. The Council listened with profound respect; it was all the Council could do. He would keep his councillors up to unearthly hours, and betray a simple pride in his superior wakefulness. He recalled these discussions with peculiar satisfaction in his later years, and remarked on one occasion that his glory consisted not in having won forty battles, but in having created the Code Napoleon. . . . So far as it substituted plain statements for inaccessible legal mysteries his Code was a good thing; it gathered together, revised, and made clear a vast disorderly accumulation of laws, old and new. Like all his constructive work, it made for immediate efficiency, it defined things and relations so that men could get to work upon them without further discussion. It was of less immediate practical importance that it frequently defined them wrongly. There was no intellectual power, as distinguished from intellectual energy, behind this codification. It took everything that existed for granted. ("Sa Majesté ne croit que ce qui est."[1]) The fundamental ideas of the civilized community and of the terms of human co-operation were in process of reconstruction all about Napoleon—and he never perceived it. He accepted a phase of change, and tried to fix it for ever. To this day France is cramped by this early nineteenth-century strait-waistcoat into which he clapped her. He fixed the status of women, the status of labourers, the status of the peasant; they all struggle to this day in the net of his hard definitions.

So briskly and forcibly Napoleon set his mind, hard, clear, and narrow, to brace up France. That bracing up was only a part of the large egotistical schemes that dominated him. His imagination was set upon a new Cæsarism. In 1802 he got himself made First Consul for life with the power of appointing a successor, and his clear intention of annexing Holland and Italy, in spite of his treaty obligations to keep them separate, made the Peace of Amiens totter crazily from the very beginning. Since his schemes were bound to provoke a war with England, he should, at any cost, have kept quiet until he had brought his navy to a superiority over the British navy. He had the control of great resources for ship-building, the British government was a weak one, and three or four years would have sufficed to shift that balance. But in spite of his rough experiences in Egypt, he had never mastered the importance of sea power, and he had not the mental steadfastness for a waiting game and long preparation. In 1803 his occupa-

[1] Gourgaud quoted by Holland Rose.

tion of Switzerland precipitated a crisis, and war broke out again with England. The weak Addington in England gave place to the greater Pitt. The rest of Napoleon's story turns upon that war.

During the period of the Consulate, the First Consul was very active in advancing the fortunes of his brothers and sisters. This was quite human, very clannish and Corsican, and it helps us to understand just how he valued his position and the opportunities before him. Few of us can live without an audience, and the first audience of our childhood is our family; most of us to the end of our days are swayed by the desire to impress our parents and brothers and sisters. Few "letters home" of successful men or women display the graces of modesty and self-forgetfulness. Only souls uplifted, as the soul of Jesus of Nazareth was uplifted, can say of all the world, "Behold my mother and my brethren!" A large factor in the making of Napoleon was the desire to amaze, astonish, and subdue the minds of the Bonaparte family, and their neighbours. He promoted his brothers ridiculously—for they were the most ordinary of men. The hungry Bonapartes were in luck. Surely all Corsica was open-mouthed! But one person who knew him well was neither amazed nor subdued. This was his mother. He sent her money to spend and astonish the neighbours; he exhorted her to make a display, to live as became the mother of so marvellous, so world-shaking, a son. But the good lady, who had birched the Man of Destiny at the age of sixteen for grimacing at his grandmother, was neither dazzled nor deceived by him at the age of thirty-two. All France might worship him, but she had no illusions. She put by the money he sent her; she continued her customary economies. "When it is all over," she said, "you will be glad of my savings."

§ 4

We will not detail the steps by which Napoleon became Emperor. His coronation was the most extraordinary revival of stale history that it is possible to imagine. Cæsar was no longer the model; Napoleon was playing now at being Charlemagne. He was crowned emperor, not indeed at Rome, but in the cathedral of Notre-Dame in Paris; the Pope (Pius VII) had been brought from Rome to perform the ceremony; and at the climax Napoleon I seized the crown, waved the Pope aside, and crowned himself. The attentive reader of this *Outline* will know that a thousand years before this would have had considerable significance; in 1804 it was just a ridiculous scene. In 1806 Napoleon revived another venerable antiquity, and, following still the footsteps of Charlemagne, crowned himself with the iron crown of Lombardy in the cathedral of Milan. All this mummery was to have a wonderful effect upon the imagination of western Germany, which was to remember that it, too, had been a part of the empire of Charlemagne.

Napoleon as Emperor

The four daughter republics of France were now to become kingdoms; in 1806 he set up brother Louis in Holland and brother Joseph in Naples. But the story of the subordinate kingdoms he created in Europe, helpful though this free handling of frontiers was towards the subsequent unification of Italy and Germany, is too complex and evanescent for this *Outline*.

The pact between the new Charlemagne and the new Leo did not hold good for very long. In 1807 he began to bully the Pope, and in 1811 he made him a close prisoner at Fontainebleau. There does not seem to have been much reason in these proceedings. They estranged all Catholic opinion, as his coronation had estranged all liberal opinion. He ceased to stand either for the old or the new. The new he had betrayed; the old he had failed to win. He stood at last for nothing but himself.

There seems to have been as little reason in the foreign policy that now plunged Europe into a fresh cycle of wars. Having quarrelled with Great Britain too soon, he (1804) assembled a vast army at Boulogne for the conquest of England, regardless of the naval situation. He even struck a medal and erected a column at Boulogne to commemorate the triumph of this projected invasion. In some "Napoleonic" fashion the British fleet was to be decoyed away, this army of Boulogne was to be smuggled across the Channel on a flotilla of rafts and boats, and London was to be captured before the fleet returned. At the same time his aggressions in south Germany forced Austria and Russia steadily into a coalition with Britain against him. In 1805 two fatal blows were struck at any hope he may have entertained of ultimate victory, by the British Admirals Calder and Nelson. In July the former inflicted a serious reverse upon the French fleet in the Bay of Biscay; in October the latter destroyed the joint fleets of France and Spain at the battle of Trafalgar. Nelson died splendidly upon the *Victory*, victorious. Thereafter Napoleon was left with Britain in pitiless opposition, unattainable and unconquerable, able to strike here or there against him along all the coasts of Europe.

But for a while the mortal wound of Trafalgar was hidden from the French mind altogether. They heard merely that "storms have caused us to lose some ships of the line after an imprudent fight." After Calder's victory he had snatched his army from Boulogne, rushed it across half Europe, and defeated the Austrian and Russian armies at Ulm and Austerlitz. Under these inauspicious circumstances Prussia came into the war against him, and was utterly defeated and broken at the battle of Jena (1806). Although Austria and Prussia were broken, Russia was still a fighting power, and the next year was devoted to this unnecessary antagonist of the French, against whom an abler and saner ruler would never have fought at all. We cannot trace in any detail the difficulties of the Polish campaign against Russia; Napoleon was roughly handled at Pultusk —which he announced in Paris as a brilliant victory—and again at Eylau. Then the Russians were defeated at Friedland (1807). As yet he had never touched Russian soil, the Russians were still as unbeaten as the British; but now came an extraordinary piece of good fortune for Napoleon. By a mixture of boasting, subtlety, and flattery he won over the young and ambitious Tsar, Alexander I—he was just thirty years old —to an alliance. The two emperors met on a raft in the middle of the Niemen at Tilsit, and there came to an understanding.

This meeting was an occasion for sublime foolishness on the part of both the principal actors. Alexander had imbibed much liberalism during his education at the court of Catherine II, and was all for freedom, education, and the new order of the world—subject to his own pre-eminence. "He would gladly have everyone free," said one of his early associates, "provided that everyone was prepared to do freely exactly what he wished." And he declared that he would have abolished serfdom if it had cost him his head—if only civilization had been more advanced. He made war against France, he said, because Napoleon was a tyrant, to free the French people. After Friedland he saw Napoleon in a different light. These two men met eleven days after that rout; Alexander no doubt in the state of explanatory exaltation natural to his type during a mood of change.

Tsar Alexander I.

To Napoleon the meeting must have been extremely gratifying. This was his first meeting with an emperor upon terms of equality. Like all men of limited vision, this man was a snob to the bone, his continual solicitude for his titles shows as much, and here was a real emperor, a born emperor, taking his three-year-old dignities as equivalent to the authentic imperialism of Moscow. Two imaginations soared together upon the raft at Tilsit. "What is Europe?" said Alexander. "*We* are Europe." They discussed the affairs of Prussia and Austria in that spirit, they divided Turkey in anticipation, they arranged for the conquest of India, and indeed of most of Asia, and that Russia should take Finland from the Swedes; and they disregarded the disagreeable fact that the greater part of the world's surface is sea, and that on the seas the British fleets sailed now unchallenged. Close at hand was Poland, ready to rise up and become the passionate ally of France had Napoleon but willed it so. But he was blind to Poland. It was a day of visions without vision. Napoleon even then, it seems, concealed the daring thought that he might one day marry a Russian princess, a real princess. But that, he was to learn in 1810, was going a little too far.

After Tilsit there was a perceptible deterioration in Napoleon's quality; he became rasher, less patient of obstacles, more and more the fated master of the world, more and more intolerable to everyone he encountered.

In 1808 he committed a very serious blunder. Spain was his abject ally, completely under his control, but he saw fit to depose its Bourbon king in order to promote his brother Joseph from the crown of the two Sicilies. Portugal he had already conquered, and the two kingdoms of Spain and Portugal were to be united. Thereupon the Spanish arose in a state of patriotic fury, surrounded a French army at Baylen, and compelled it to surrender. It was an astonishing break in the French career of victory.

The British were not slow to seize the foothold this insurrection gave them. A British army under Sir Arthur Wellesley (afterwards the Duke of Wellington) landed in Portugal, defeated the French at Vimiero, and compelled them to retire into Spain. The news of these reverses caused a very great excitement in Germany and Austria, and the Tsar assumed a more arrogant attitude towards his ally.

There was another meeting of these two potentates at Erfurt, in which the Tsar was manifestly less amenable to the dazzling tactics of Napoleon than he had been. Followed four years of unstable "ascendancy" for France, while the outlines on the map of Europe waved about like garments on a clothesline on a windy day. Napoleon's personal empire grew by frank annexations to include Holland, much of western Germany, much of Italy, and much of the eastern Adriatic coast. But one by one the French colonies were falling to the British, and the British armies in the Spanish peninsula, with the Spanish auxiliaries, slowly pressed the French northward. All Europe was getting very weary of Napoleon and very indignant with him; his antagonists now were no longer merely monarchs and ministers, but whole peoples also. The Prussians, after the disaster of Jena in 1806, had set to work to put their house in order. Under the leadership of Freiherr von Stein they had swept aside their feudalism, abolished privilege and serfdom, organized popular education and popular patriotism, accomplished, in fact, without any internal struggle nearly everything that France had achieved in 1789. By 1810 a new Prussia existed, the nucleus of a new Germany. And now Alexander, inspired it would seem by dreams of world ascendancy even crazier than his rival's, was posing again as the friend of liberty. In 1810 fresh friction was created by Alexander's objection to Napoleon's matrimonial ambitions. For he was now divorcing his old helper Josephine, because she was childless, in order to secure the "continuity" of his "dynasty." Napo-

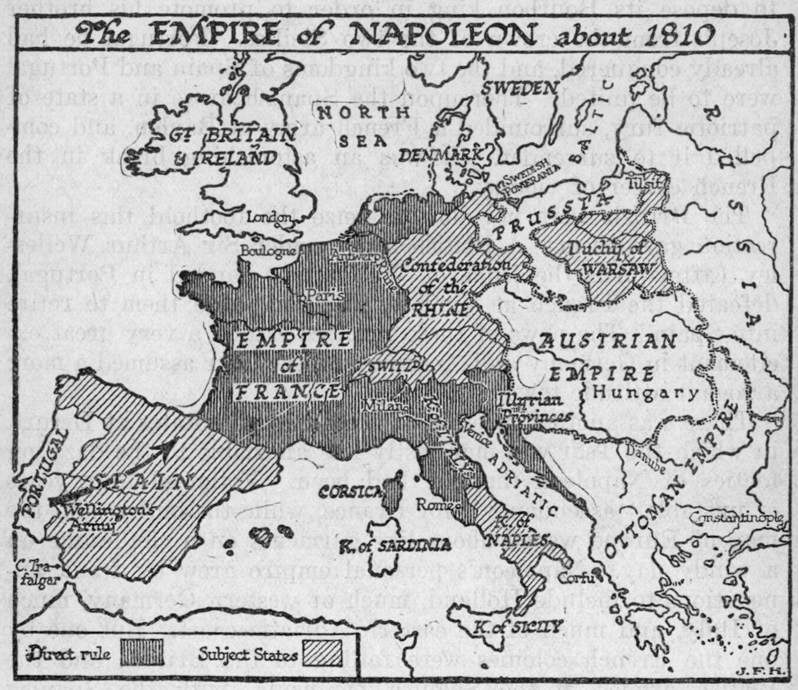

leon, thwarted of a Russian princess, snubbed indeed by Alexander, turned to Austria, and married the arch-duchess Marie Louise. The Austrian statesmen read him aright. They were very ready to throw him their princess. By that marriage Napoleon was captured for the dynastic system; he might have been the maker of a new world, he preferred to be the son-in-law of the old.

In the next two years this adventurer's affairs crumbled apace. Nobody believed in his pretensions any more. He was no longer the leader and complement of the revolution; no longer the embodied spirit of a world reborn; he was just a new and nastier sort of autocrat. He had estranged all free-spirited men, and he had antagonized the church. Kings and Jacobins were at one, when it came to the question of his overthrow. Only base and self-seeking people supported him, because he seemed to have the secret of success. Britain was now his inveterate enemy, Spain was blazing with a spirit that surely a Corsican should have understood; it needed only a breach with Alexander I to set this empire of bluff and stage scenery swaying toward its downfall. The quarrel came. Alexander's feelings for Napoleon had always been of a very mixed sort; he envied Napoleon as a rival, and despised him as an underbred upstart. Moreover, there was a kind of vague and sentimental greatness about Alexander; he was given to mystical religiosity, he had the conception of a mission for Russia and himself to bring peace to Europe and the world—by destroying Napoleon. In that respect he had an imaginative greatness Napoleon lacked. But bringing peace to Europe seemed to him quite compatible with the annexation of Finland, of most of Poland, and of great portions of the Turkish empire. This man's mind moved in a luminous fog. And particularly he wanted to resume trading with Britain, against which Napoleon had set his face. For all the trade of Germany had been dislocated and the mercantile classes embittered by the Napoleonic "Continental System," which was to ruin Britain by excluding British goods from every country in Europe. Russia had suffered more even than Germany.

The breach came in 1811, when Alexander withdrew from the "Continental System." In 1812 a great mass of armies, amounting altogether to 600,000 men, began to move towards Russia under the supreme command of the new emperor. About half this force was French; the rest was drawn from the French allies and subject peoples. It was a conglomerate army like the army of Darius or the army of Kavadh. The Spanish war was still going on; Napoleon made no attempt to end it. Altogether, it drained away a quarter of a million men from France. He fought his way across Poland and Russia to Moscow before the winter—for the most part the Russian armies declined battle—and even before the winter closed in upon him his position became manifestly dangerous. He took Moscow, expecting that this would oblige Alexander to make peace. Alexander would not make peace, and Napoleon found himself in much the same position as Darius had been in 2,300 years before in South Russia. The Russians, still unconquered in a decisive battle, raided his communications, wasted his army—disease helped them; even before Napoleon reached Moscow 150,000 men had been lost. But he lacked the wisdom of Darius, and would not retreat. The winter remained mild for an unusually long time—he could have escaped; but instead he remained in Moscow, making impossible plans, at a loss. He had been marvellously lucky in all his previous flounderings; he had escaped undeservedly from Egypt, he had been saved from destruction in Britain by the British naval victories; but now he was in the net again, and this time he was not to escape. Perhaps he would have wintered in Moscow, but the Russians smoked him out; they set fire to and burnt most of the city.

It was late in October, too late altogether, before he decided to return. He made an ineffectual attempt to break through to a fresh line of retreat to the south-west, and then turned the faces of the survivors of his Grand Army towards the country they had devastated in their advance. Immense distances separated them from any friendly territory. The winter was in no hurry. For a week the Grand Army struggled through mud; then came sharp frosts, and then the first flakes of snow, and then snow and snow. . . .

Slowly discipline dissolved. The hungry army spread itself out in search of supplies until it broke up into mere bands of marauders. The peasants, if only in self-defence, rose against them, waylaid them, and murdered them; a cloud of light cavalry—Scythians still—hunted them down. That retreat is one of the great tragedies of history.

At last Napoleon and his staff and a handful of guards and attendants reappeared in Germany, bringing no army with him, followed only by straggling and demoralized bands. The Grand Army, retreating under Murat, reached Königsberg in a disciplined state, but only about a thousand strong out of six hundred thousand. From Königsberg Murat fell back to Posen. The Prussian contingent had surrendered to the Russians; the Austrians had gone homeward to the south. Everywhere scattered fugitives, ragged, lean, and frost-bitten, spread the news of the disaster.

Napoleon's magic was nearly exhausted. He did not dare to

stay with his troops in Germany; he fled post haste to Paris. He began to order new levies and gather fresh armies amidst the wreckage of his world empire. Austria turned against him (1813); all Europe was eager to rise against this defaulting trustee of freedom, this mere usurper. He had betrayed the new order; the old order he had saved and revived now destroyed him. Prussia rose, and the German "War of Liberation" began. Sweden joined his enemies. Later Holland revolted. Murat had rallied about 14,000 Frenchmen round his disciplined nucleus in Posen, and this force retreated through Germany, as a man might retreat who had ventured into a cageful of drugged lions and found that the effects of the drug were evaporating. Napoleon, with fresh forces, took up the chief command in the spring, won a great battle at Dresden, and then for a time he seems to have gone to pieces intellectually and morally. He became insanely irritable, with moods of inaction. He did little or nothing to follow up the Battle of Dresden. In October the "Battle of the Nations" was fought round and about Leipzig, after which the Saxons, who had hitherto followed his star, went over to the allies. The end of the year saw the French beaten back into France.

1814 was the closing campaign. France was invaded from the east and the south; Swedes, Germans, Austrians, Russians, crossed the Rhine; British and Spanish came through the Pyrenees. Once more Napoleon fought brilliantly, but now he fought ineffectually. The eastern armies did not so much defeat him as push past him, and Paris capitulated in March. A little later at Fontainebleau the emperor abdicated.

In Provence, on his way out of the country, his life was endangered by a royalist mob.

§ 5

This was the natural and proper end of Napoleon's career. So this raid of an intolerable egotist across the disordered beginnings of a new time should have closed. At last he was suppressed. And had there been any real wisdom in the conduct of human affairs, we should now have to tell of the concentration of human science and will upon the task his treachery and vanity had interrupted, the task of building up a world system of justice and free effort in the place of the bankrupt

The TRAIL of NAPOLEON
1785-Entered Artillery
1795-"Whiff of grapeshot"
1799-First Consul
1804-Emperor
1815-Return from Elba
Showing the chief places of importance in his life
Note- The map does not attempt to show precise routes. Nor does it cover in detail all Napoleon's movements (e.g., various returns to Paris.)
J.F.H.
To St Helena
Surrendered to British
Rochefort 1815
BRITAIN
Boulogne 1804-5
Paris
Fontainebleau 1814
Return 1815
Waterloo 1815
SPAIN
PORTUGAL
C.Trafalgar 1805
Toulon
CORSICA b. 1769
Elba 1814
ITALY
Marengo 1800
Lodi 1796
Arcola
Campo Formio 1797
Ulm 1805
Jena 1806
Leipzig 1813
Ratisbon 1809
Wagram
Vienna
Austerlitz 1805
AUSTRIA
POLAND
Warsaw
Friedland
Tilsit 1807
Vilna
Smolensk 1812
Borodino
Moscow
RUSSIA
OTTOMAN EMPIRE
1798 Malta
Alexandria
Aboukir
Pyramids 1798
Cairo
Jaffa
Acre

ancient order. But we have to tell of nothing of the sort. Science and wisdom were conspicuously absent from the great council of the Allies. Came the vague humanitarianism and dreamy vanity of the Tsar Alexander, came the shaken Habsburgs of Austria, the resentful Hohenzollerns of Prussia, the aristocratic traditions of Britain, still badly frightened by the revolution and its conscience all awry with stolen commons and sweated factory children. No peoples came to the Congress, but only monarchs and foreign ministers; and though you bray a foreign office in the bloodiest of war mortars, yet will its diplomatic habits not depart from it. The Congress had hardly assembled before the diplomatists set to work making secret bargains and treaties behind each other's backs. Nothing could exceed the pompous triviality of the Congress which gathered at Vienna after a magnificent ceremonial visit of the allied sovereigns to London. The social side of the Congress was very strong, pretty ladies abounded, there was a galaxy of stars and uniforms, endless dinners and balls, a mighty flow of bright anecdotes and sparkling wit. Whether the two million dead men upon the battlefields laughed at the jokes, admired the assemblies, and marvelled at the diplomatists is beyond our knowledge. It is to be hoped their poor wraiths got something out of the display. The brightest spirit of the gathering was a certain Talleyrand, one of Napoleon's princes, a very brilliant man indeed, who had been a pre-revolutionary cleric, who had proposed the revolutionary confiscation of the church estates, and who was now for bringing back the Bourbons.

The allies, after the fashion of Peace Congresses, frittered away precious time in more and more rapacious disputes; the Bourbons returned to France. Back came all the remainder of the émigrés with them, eager for restitution and revenge. One great egotism had been swept aside—only to reveal a crowd of meaner egotists. The new king was the brother of Louis XVI; he had taken the title of Louis XVIII very eagerly so soon as he learnt that his little nephew (Louis XVII) was dead in the Temple. He was gouty and clumsy, not perhaps ill-disposed, but the symbol of the ancient system; all that was new in France felt the heavy threat of reaction that came with him. This was no liberation, only a new tyranny, a heavy and inglorious tyranny instead of an active and splendid one. Was there no hope for France but this? The Bourbons showed particular malice against the veterans of the Grand Army, and France was now full of returned prisoners of war, who found themselves under a cloud. Napoleon had been packed off to a little consolation empire of his own, upon the island of Elba. He was still to be called Emperor and keep a certain state. The chivalry or whim of Alexander had insisted upon this treatment of his fallen rival. The Habsburgs, who had toadied to his success, had taken away his Habsburg empress—she went willingly enough—to Vienna, and he never saw her again.

After eleven months at Elba Napoleon judged that France had had enough of the Bourbons; he contrived to evade the British ships that watched his island, and reappeared at Cannes in France for his last gamble against fate. His progress to Paris was a triumphal procession; he walked on white Bourbon cockades. For a hundred days, "the Hundred Days," he was master of France again.

His return created a perplexing position for any honest Frenchman. On the one hand there was this adventurer who had betrayed the republic; on the other the dull weight of old kingship restored. The allies would not hear of any further experiments in republicanism; it was the Bourbons or Napoleon. Is it any wonder that on the whole France was with Napoleon? And he came back professing to be a changed man; there was to be no more despotism; he would respect the constitutional régime. . . .

He gathered an army, he made some attempts at peace with the allies; when he found these efforts ineffectual, he struck swiftly at the British, Dutch, and Prussians in Belgium, hoping to defeat them before the Austrians and Russians could come up. He did very nearly manage this. He beat the Prussians at Ligny, but not sufficiently; and then he was hopelessly defeated by the tenacity of the British under Wellington at Waterloo (1815), the Prussians, under Blücher, coming in on his right flank as the day wore on. Waterloo ended in a rout; it left Napoleon without support and without hope. France fell away from him again. Everyone who had joined him was eager now to attack him, and so efface that error. A provisional government in Paris ordered him to leave the country; was for giving him twenty-four hours to do it in.

He tried to get to America, but Rochefort, which he reached, was watched by British cruisers. France, now disillusioned and uncomfortably royalist again, was hot in pursuit of him. He went aboard a British frigate, the *Bellerophon,* asking to be received as a refugee, but being treated as a prisoner. He was taken to Plymouth, and from Plymouth straight to the lonely tropical island of St. Helena.

There he remained until his death from cancer in 1821, devoting himself chiefly to the preparation of his memoirs, which were designed to exhibit the chief events of his life in a misleading and attractive light and to minimise his worst blunders. One or two of the men with him recorded his conversations and set down their impressions of him.

These works had a great vogue in France and Europe. The Holy Alliance of the monarchs of Russia, Austria, and Prussia (to which other monarchs were invited to adhere) laboured under the delusion that in defeating Napoleon they had defeated the Revolution, turned back the clock of fate, and restored Grand Monarchy—on a sanctified basis for evermore. The cardinal document of the scheme of the Holy Alliance is said to have been drawn up under the inspiration of the Baroness von Krüdener, who seems to have been a sort of spiritual director to the Russian emperor. It opened, "In the name of the Most Holy and Indivisible Trinity," and it bound the participating monarchs "regarding themselves towards their subjects and armies as fathers of families," and "considering each other as fellow-countrymen," to sustain each other, protect true religion, and urge their subjects to strengthen and exercise themselves in Christian duties. Christ, it was declared, was the real king of all Christian peoples, a very Merovingian king, one may remark, with these reigning sovereigns as his mayors of the palace. The British king had no power to sign this document, the pope and the sultan were not asked; the rest of the European monarchs, including the king of France, adhered. But the king of Poland did not sign because there was no king in Poland; Alexander, in a mood of pious abstraction, was sitting on the greater part of Poland. The Holy Alliance never became an actual legal alliance of states; it gave place to a real league of nations, the Concert of Europe, which France joined in 1818, and from which Britain withdrew in 1822.

There followed a period of peace and dull oppression in Europe over which Alexander brooded in attitudes of orthodoxy, piety, and unquenchable self-satisfaction. Many people in those hopeless days were disposed to regard even Napoleon with charity, and to accept his claim that in some inexplicable way he had, in asserting himself, been asserting the revolution and France. A cult of him as of something mystically heroic grew up after his death.

§ 6

For nearly forty years the idea of the Holy Alliance, the Concert of Europe which arose out of it, and the series of congresses and conferences that succeeded the concert, kept an insecure peace in war-exhausted Europe. Two main things prevented that period from being a complete social and international peace, and prepared the way for the cycle of wars between 1854 and 1871. The first of these was the tendency of the royal courts concerned, towards the restoration of unfair privilege and interference with freedom of thought and writing and teaching. The second was the impossible system of boundaries drawn by the diplomatists of Vienna.

The obstinate disposition of monarchy to march back towards past conditions was first and most particularly manifest in Spain. Here even the Inquisition was restored. Across the Atlantic the Spanish colonies had followed the example of the United States and revolted against the European Great Power system, when Napoleon set up his brother Joseph upon the Spanish throne in 1810. The Washington of South America was General Bolivar. Spain was unable to suppress this revolt, it dragged on much as the United States War of Independence had dragged on, and at last the suggestion was made by Austria in accordance with the spirit of the Holy Alliance, that the European monarchs should assist Spain in this struggle. This was opposed by Britain in Europe, but it was the prompt action of President Monroe of the United States in 1823 which conclusively warned off this projected monarchist restoration. He announced that the United States would regard any extension of the European system in the Western Hemisphere as a hostile act. Thus arose the Monroe Doctrine, which has kept the Great Power system out of America for nearly a hundred years, and permitted the new states of Spanish America to work out their destinies along their own lines. But if Spanish monarchism lost its colonies, it could at least, under the protection of the

Concert of Europe, do what it chose in Europe. A popular insurrection in Spain was crushed by a French army in 1823, with a mandate from a European congress, and simultaneously Austria suppressed a revolution in Naples. The moving spirit in this conspiracy of governments against peoples was the Austrian statesman, Metternich.

In 1824 Louis XVIII died, and was succeeded by that Count d'Artois whom we have seen hovering as an émigré on the French frontiers in 1789; he took the title of Charles X. Charles set himself to destroy the liberty of the press and universities, and to restore absolute government; the sum of a billion francs was voted to compensate the nobles for the château burnings and sequestrations of 1789. In 1830 Paris rose against this embodiment of the ancient régime, and replaced him by the son of that sinister Philip, Duke of Orleans, whose execution was one of the brightest achievements of the Terror. The other continental monarchies, in face of the open approval of the revolution by Great Britain and a strong liberal ferment in Germany and Austria, did not interfere in this affair. After all, France was still a monarchy. This young man, Louis Philippe (1830-48), remained the constitutional king of France for eighteen years. He went down in 1848, a very eventful year for Europe, of which we shall tell in the next chapter.

Such were the uneasy swayings of the peace of the Congress of Vienna, which were provoked by the reactionary proceedings to which, sooner or later, all monarchist courts seem by their very nature to gravitate. The stresses that arose from the unscientific map-making of the diplomatists gathered force more deliberately, but they were even more dangerous to the peace of mankind. It is extraordinarily inconvenient to administer together the affairs of peoples speaking different languages and so reading different literatures and having different general ideas, especially if those differences are exacerbated by religious disputes. Only some strong mutual interest, such as the common defensive needs of the Swiss mountaineers, can justify a close linking of peoples of dissimilar languages and faiths; and even in Switzerland there is the utmost local autonomy. Ultimately, when the Great Power tradition is certainly dead and buried, those Swiss populations may gravitate towards their natural affinities in Germany, France, and Italy. When, as in Macedonia, populations are mixed in a patchwork of villages and districts, the cantonal system is imperatively needed. But if the reader will look at the map of Europe as the Congress of Vienna drew it, he will see that this gathering seems almost as if it had planned the maximum of local exasperation. It destroyed the Dutch Republic, quite needlessly, it lumped together the Protestant Dutch with the French-speaking Catholics

of the old Spanish (Austrian) Netherlands, and set up a kingdom of the Netherlands. It handed over not merely the old republic of Venice, but all of North Italy as far as Milan to the German-speaking Austrians. French-speaking Savoy it combined with pieces of Italy to restore the kingdom of Sardinia. Austria and Hungary, already a sufficiently explosive mixture of discordant nationalities, Germans, Hungarians, Czecho-Slovaks, Jugo-Slavs, Rumanians, and now Italians, was made still more impossible by confirming Austria's Polish acquisitions of 1772 and 1795. The Polish people, being catholic and republican-spirited, were chiefly given over to the less civilized rule of the Greek-orthodox Tsar, but important districts went to Protestant Prussia. The Tsar was also confirmed in his acquisition of the entirely alien Finns. The very dissimilar Norwegian and Swedish peoples were bound together under one king. Germany, the reader will see, was left in a particularly dangerous state of muddle. Prussia and Austria were both partly in and partly out of a German confederation, which included a multitude of minor states. The King of Denmark came into the German confederation by virtue of certain German-speaking possessions in Holstein. Luxembourg was included in the German Confederation, though its ruler was also king of the Netherlands, and though many of its peoples talked French. Here was a crazy tangle, an outrage on the common sense of mankind, a preposterous disregard of the fact that the people who talk German and base their ideas on German literature, the people who talk Italian and base their ideas on Italian literature, and the people who talk Polish and base their ideas on Polish literature, will all be far better off and most helpful and least obnoxious to the rest of mankind if they conduct their own affairs in their own idiom within the ring-fence of their own speech. Is it any wonder that one of the most popular songs in Germany during this period declared that wherever the German tongue was spoken, there was the German Fatherland?

Even to-day men are still reluctant to recognize that areas of government are not matters for the bargaining and interplay of tsars and kings and foreign offices. There is a *natural and necessary political map of the world* which transcends these things. There is *a best way possible* of dividing any part of the world into administrative areas, and a best possible kind of government for every area, having regard to the speech and race of its inhabitants, and it is the common concern of all men of intelligence to secure those divisions and establish those forms of government quite irrespective of diplomacies and flags, "claims" and melodramatic "loyalties" and the existing political map of the world. The natural political map of the world insists upon itself. It heaves and frets beneath the artificial political map like some misfitted giant. In 1830 French-speaking Belgium, stirred up by the current revolution in France, revolted against its Dutch association in the kingdom of the Netherlands. The Powers, terrified at the possibility of a republic and of annexation to France, hurried in to pacify this situation, and gave the Belgiums a monarch from that rich breeding-ground of monarchs, Germany, Leopold I of Saxe-Coburg Gotha. There were also ineffectual revolts in Italy and Germany in 1830, and a much more serious one in Russian Poland. A republican government held out in Warsaw for a year against Nicholas I (who succeeded Alexander in 1825), and was then stamped out of existence with great violence and cruelty. The Polish language was banned, and the Greek Orthodox church was substituted for the Roman Catholic as the State religion. . . .

An outbreak of the natural political map of the world, which occurred in 1821, ultimately secured the support of England, France, and Russia. This was the insurrection of the Greeks against the Turks. For six years they fought a desperate war, while the governments of Europe looked on. Liberal opinion protested against this inactivity; volunteers from every European country joined the insurgents, and at last Britain, France, and Russia took joint action. The Turkish fleet was destroyed by the French and English at the Battle of Navarino (1827), and the Tsar invaded Turkey. By the treaty of Adrianople (1829) Greece was declared free, but she was not permitted to resume her ancient republican traditions. There is a sort of historical indecency in a Greek monarchy. But a Greek republic would have been dangerous to all monarchy in a Europe that fretted under the ideas of the Holy Alliance. A German king was found for Greece, one Prince Otto of Bavaria, slightly demented, but quite royal—he gave way to delusions about his divine right, and was ejected in 1862—and Christian governors were set up in the Danubian provinces (which are now Rumania) and Serbia (a part of the Jugo-Slav region). This was a partial concession to the natural political map, but much blood had still to run before the Turk was altogether expelled from these lands.

A little later the natural political map was to assert itself in Italy and Germany.

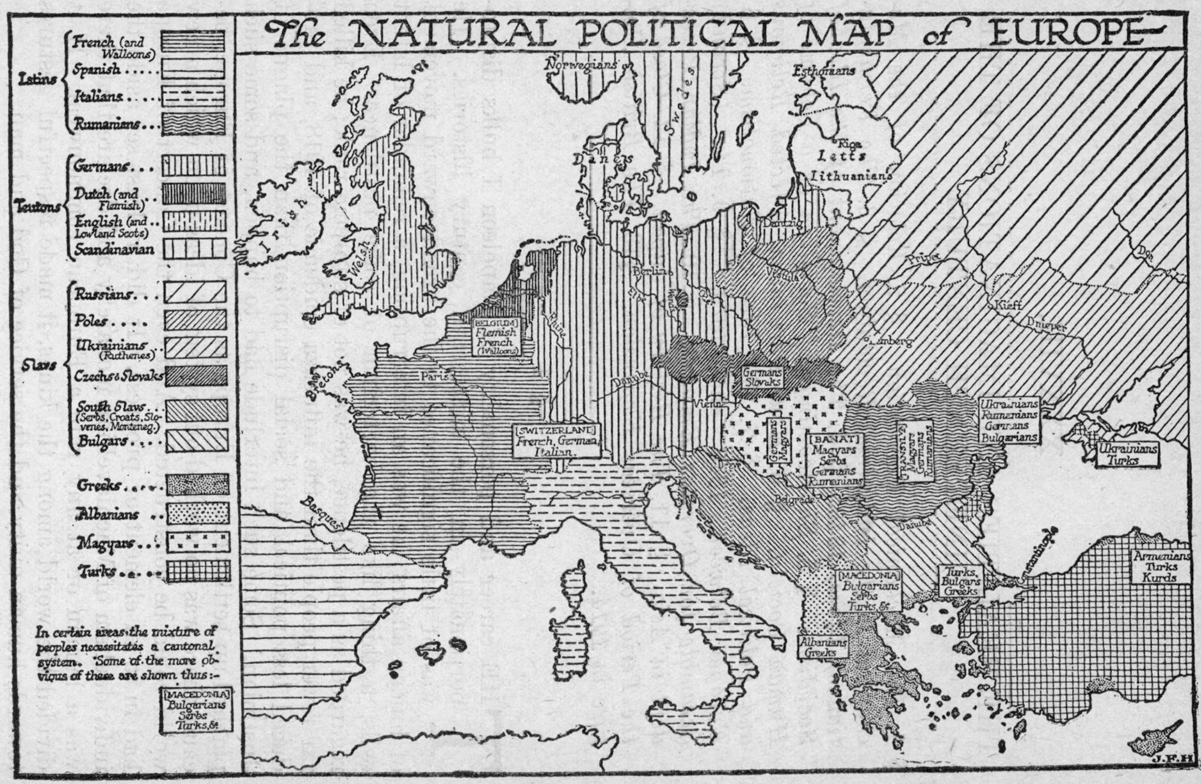
The NATURAL POLITICAL MAP of EUROPE
Latins
French (and Walloons)
Spanish
Italians
Rumanians
Teutons
Germans
Dutch (and Flemish)
English (and Lowland Scots)
Scandinavian
Slavs
Russians
Poles
Ukrainians (Ruthenes)
Czechs & Slovaks
South Slavs (Serbs, Croats, Slovenes, Monteneg.)
Bulgars
Greeks
Albanians
Magyars
Turks
In certain areas the mixture of peoples necessitates a cantonal system. Some of the more obvious of these are shown thus:-
[MACEDONIA] Bulgarians Serbs Turks, &c
Norwegians
Swedes
Danes
Esthonians
Riga
Letts
Lithuanians
Irish
Welsh
Bretons
Basques
Danzig
Berlin
Elbe
Wends
Vistula
Pripet
Don
Kieff
Dnieper
Lemberg
Rhine
Paris
Danube
Vienna
[BELGIUM] Flemish French (Walloons)
[SWITZERLAND] French, German, Italian.
Germans Slovaks
Germans Magyars
[BANAT] Magyars Serbs Germans Rumanians
[TRANSYL'A] Magyars Germans Rumanians
Ukrainians Rumanians Germans Bulgarians
Ukrainians Turks
Belgrade
Danube
Constantinople
[MACEDONIA] Bulgarians Serbs Turks, &c
Turks, Bulgars Greeks
Albanians Greeks
Armenians Turks Kurds
J.F.H

XXXVIII

THE REALITIES AND IMAGINATIONS OF THE NINETEENTH CENTURY

§ 1

THE career and personality of Napoleon I bulks disproportionately in the nineteenth century histories. He was of little significance to the broad onward movement of human affairs; he was an interruption, a reminder of latent evils, a thing like the bacterium of some pestilence. Even regarded as a pestilence, he was not of supreme rank; he killed far fewer people than the influenza epidemic of 1918, and produced less political and social disruption than the plague of Justinian. Some such interlude had to happen, and some such patched-up settlement of Europe as the Concert of Europe, because there was no worked-out system of ideas upon which a new world could be constructed. And even the Concert of Europe had in it an element of progress. It did at least set aside the individualism of Machiavellian monarchy and declare that there was a human or at any rate a European commonweal. If it divided the world among the kings, it made respectful gestures towards human unity and the service of God and man.

The permanently effective task before mankind which had to be done before any new and enduring social and political edifice was possible, the task upon which the human intelligence is, with many interruptions and amidst much anger and turmoil, still engaged, was, and is, the task of working out and applying a Science of Property as a basis for freedom and social justice, a Science of Currency to ensure and preserve an efficient economic medium, a Science of Government and Collective Operations whereby in every community men may learn to pursue their common interests in harmony, a Science of World Politics, through which the stark waste and cruelty of warfare between races, peoples, and nations may be brought to an end and the common interests of mankind brought under a common control, and, above all, a world-wide System of Education to sustain the will and interest of men in their common human adventure. The real makers of history in the nineteenth century, the people whose consequences will be determining human life a century ahead, were those who advanced and contributed to this fivefold constructive effort. Compared to them, the foreign ministers and "statesmen" and politicians of this period were no more than a number of troublesome and occasionally incendiary schoolboys—and a few metal thieves—playing about and doing transitory mischief amidst the accumulating materials upon the site of a great building whose nature they did not understand.

And while throughout the nineteenth century the mind of Western civilization, which the Renascence had released, gathered itself to the task of creative social and political reconstruction that still lies before it, there swept across the world a wave of universal change in human power and the material conditions of life that the first scientific efforts of that liberated mind had made possible. The prophecies of Roger Bacon began to live in reality. The accumulating knowledge and confidence of the little succession of men who had been carrying on the development of science, now began to bear fruit that common men could understand. The most obvious firstfruit was the steam-engine. The first steam-engines in the eighteenth century were pumping engines used to keep water out of the newly opened coal mines. These coal mines were being worked to supply coke for iron smelting, for which wood-charcoal had previously been employed. It was James Watt, a mathematical instrument maker of Glasgow, who improved this steam-pumping engine and made it available for the driving of machinery. The first engine so employed was installed in a cotton mill in Nottingham in 1785. In 1804 Trevithick adapted the Watt engine to transport, and made the first locomotive. In 1825 the first railway, between Stockton and Darlington, was opened for traffic. The original engine (locomotive No. 1, 1825) still adorns Darlington platform. By the middle of the century a network of railways had spread all over Europe.

Here was a sudden change in what had long been a fixed condition of human life, the maximum rate of land transport. After the Russian disaster, Napoleon travelled from near Vilna to Paris in 312 hours. This was a journey of about 1,400 miles. He was travelling with every conceivable advantage, and he averaged under five miles an hour. An ordinary traveller could not have done this distance in twice the time. These were about the same maximum rates of travel as held good between Rome and Gaul in the first century A.D., or between Sardis and Susa in the fourth century B.C. Then suddenly came a tremendous change. The railways reduced this journey for any ordinary traveller to less than forty-eight hours. That is to say, they reduced the chief European distances to about a tenth of what they had been. They made it possible to carry out administrative work in areas ten times as great as any that had hitherto been workable under one administration. The full significance of that possibility in Europe still remains to be realized. Europe is still netted in boundaries drawn in the horse and road era. In America the effects were immediate. To the United States of America, sprawling westward, it meant the possibility of a continuous access to Washington, however far the frontier travelled across the continent. It meant unity, sustained on a scale that would otherwise have been impossible.

The steamboat was, if anything, a little ahead of the steam-engine in its earlier phases. There was a steamboat, the *Charlotte Dundas,* on the Firth of Clyde Canal in 1802, and in 1807 an American named Fulton had a paying steamer, *The Clermont,* with British-built engines, upon the Hudson river above New York. The first steamship to put to sea was also an American, the *Phœnix,* which went from New York (Hoboken) to Philadelphia. So, too, was the first ship using steam (she also had sails) to cross the Atlantic, the *Savannah* (1819). All these were paddle-wheel boats, and paddle-wheel boats are not adapted to work in heavy seas. The paddles smash too easily, and the boat is then disabled. The screw steamboat followed rather slowly. Many difficulties had to be surmounted before the screw was a practicable thing. Not until the middle of the century did the tonnage of steamships upon the sea begin to overhaul that of sailing-ships. After that the evolution in sea transport was rapid. For the first time men began to cross the seas and oceans with some certainty as to the date of their arrival. The transatlantic crossing, which had been an uncertain adventure of several weeks—which might stretch to months—was accelerated, until in 1910 it was brought down, in the case of the fastest boats, to under five days, with a practically notifiable hour of arrival. All over the oceans there was the same reduction in the time and the same increase in the certainty of human communications.

Concurrently with the development of steam transport upon land and sea a new and striking addition to the facilities of human intercourse arose out of the investigations of Volta, Galvani, and Faraday into various electrical phenomena. The electric telegraph came into existence in 1835. The first underseas cable was laid in 1851 between France and England. In a few years the telegraph system had spread over the civilized world, and news which had hitherto travelled slowly from point to point became practically simultaneous throughout the earth.

These things, the steam railway and the electric telegraph, were to the popular imagination of the middle nineteenth century the most striking and revolutionary of inventions, but they were only the most conspicuous and clumsy firstfruits of a far more extensive process. Technical knowledge and skill were developing with an extraordinary rapidity, and to an extraordinary extent measured by the progress of any previous age. Far less conspicuous at first in everyday life, but finally far more important, was the extension of man's power over various structural materials. Before the middle of the eighteenth century iron was reduced from its ores by means of wood-charcoal, was handled in small pieces, and hammered and wrought into shape. It was material for a craftsman. Quality and treatment were enormously dependent upon the experience and sagacity of the individual iron worker. The largest masses of iron that could be dealt with under those conditions amounted at most (in the sixteenth century) to two or three tons. (There was a very definite upward limit, therefore, to the size of cannon.) The blast furnace arose in the eighteenth century, and developed with the use of coke. Not before the eighteenth century do we find rolled sheet iron (1728) and rolled rods and bars (1783). Nasmyth's steam hammer came as late as 1838. The ancient world, because of its metallurgical inferiority, could not use steam. The steam-engine, even the primitive pumping engine, could not develop before sheet iron was available. The early engines seem to the modern eye very pitiful and clumsy bits or ironmongery, but they were the utmost that the metallurgical science of the time could do. As late as 1856 came the Bessemer process, and presently (1864) the open-hearth process, in which steel and every sort of iron could be melted, purified, and cast in a manner and upon a scale hitherto unheard of. To-day in the electric furnace one may see tons of incandescent steel swirling about like boiling milk in a saucepan. Nothing in the previous practical advances of mankind is comparable in its consequences to the complete mastery over enormous masses of steel and iron and over their texture and quality which man has now achieved. The railways and early engines of all sorts were the mere first triumphs of the new metallurgical methods. Presently came ships of iron and steel, vast bridges, and a new way of building with steel upon a gigantic scale. Men realized too late that they had planned their railways with far too timid a gauge, that they could have organized their travelling with far more steadiness and comfort upon a much bigger scale.

Before the nineteenth century there were no ships in the world much over 2,000 tons burthen; now there is nothing wonderful about a 50,000-ton liner. There are people who sneer at this kind of progress as being a progress in "mere size," but that sort of sneering merely marks the intellectual limitations of those who indulge in it. The great ship or the steel-frame building is not, as they imagine, a magnified version of the small ship or building of the past; it is a thing different in kind, more lightly and strongly built, of finer and stronger materials; instead of being a thing of precedent and rule-of-thumb, it is a thing of subtle and intricate calculation. In the old house or ship, matter was dominant—the material and its needs had to be slavishly obeyed; in the new, matter has been captured, changed, coerced. Think of the coal and iron and sand dragged out of the banks and pits, wrenched, wrought, molten, and cast, to be flung at last, a slender, glittering pinnacle of steel and glass, six hundred feet above the crowded city!

We have given these particulars of the advance in man's knowledge of the metallurgy of steel and its results by way of illustration. A parallel story could be told of the metallurgy of copper and tin, and of a multitude of metals, nickel and aluminium to name but two, unknown before the nineteenth century dawned. It is in this great and growing mastery over substances, over different sorts of glass, over rocks and plasters and the like, over colours and textures, that the main triumphs of the mechanical revolution have thus far been achieved. Yet we are still in the stage of the firstfruits in the matter. We have the power, but we have still to learn how to use our power. Many of the first employments of these gifts of science have been vulgar, tawdry, stupid, or horrible. The artist and the adaptor have still hardly begun to work with the endless variety of substances now at their disposal.

Parallel with this extension of mechanical possibilities the new science of electricity grew up. It was only in the eighties of the nineteenth century that this body of inquiry began to yield results to impress the vulgar mind. Then suddenly came electric light and electric traction, and the transmutation of forces, the possibility of sending *power,* that could be changed into mechanical motion or light or heat as one chose, along a copper wire, as water is sent along a pipe, began to come through to the ideas of ordinary people. . . .

The British and the French were at first the leading peoples in this great proliferation of knowledge; but presently the Germans, who had learnt humility under Napoleon, showed such zeal and pertinacity in scientific inquiry as to overhaul these leaders. British science was largely the creation of Englishmen and Scotchmen[1] working outside the ordinary centres of erudition.[2] We have told how in England the universities after

[1] But note Boyle and Sir Wm. Hamilton as conspicuous scientific men who were Irishmen.

[2] It is worth noting that nearly all the great inventors in England during the eighteenth century were working men, that inventions proceeded from the workshop, and not from the laboratory. It is also worth noting that only two of these inventors accumulated fortunes and founded families.—E. B.

the reformation ceased to have a wide popular appeal, how they became the educational preserve of the nobility and gentry, and the strongholds of the established church. A pompous and unintelligent classical pretentiousness dominated them, and they dominated the schools of the middle and upper classes. The only knowledge recognized was an uncritical textual knowledge of a selection of Latin and Greek classics, and the test of a good style was its abundance of quotations, allusions, and stereotyped expressions. The early development of British science went on, therefore, in spite of the formal educational organization, and in the teeth of the bitter hostility of the teaching and clerical professions. French education, too, was dominated by the classical tradition of the Jesuits, and consequently it was not difficult for the Germans to organize a body of investigators, small indeed in relation to the possibilities of the case, but large in proportion to the little band of British and French inventors and experimentalists. And though this work of research and experiment was making Britain and France the most rich and powerful countries in the world, it was not making scientific and inventive men rich and powerful. There is a necessary unworldliness about a sincere scientific man; he is too preoccupied with his research to plan and scheme how to make money out of it. The economic exploitation of his discoveries falls very easily and naturally, therefore, into the hands of a more acquisitive type; and so we find that the crops of rich men which every fresh phase of scientific and technical progress has produced in Great Britain, though they have not displayed quite the same passionate desire to insult and kill the goose that laid the national golden eggs as the scholastic and clerical professions, have been quite content to let that profitable creature starve. Inventors and discoverers came by nature, they thought, for cleverer people to profit by.

In this matter the Germans were a little wiser. The German "learned" did not display the same vehement hatred of the new learning. They permitted its development. The German business man and manufacturer again had not quite the same contempt for the man of science as had his British competitor. Knowledge, these Germans believed, might be a cultivated crop, responsive to fertilizers. They did concede, therefore, a certain amount of opportunity to the scientific mind; their public expenditure on scientific work was relatively greater, and this expenditure was abundantly rewarded. By the latter half of the nineteenth century the German scientific worker had made German a necessary language for every science student who wished to keep abreast with the latest work in his department, and in certain branches, and particularly in chemistry, Germany acquired a very great superiority over her western neighbours. The scientific effort of the sixties and seventies in Germany began to tell after the eighties, and the Germans gained steadily upon Britain and France in technical and industrial prosperity.

In an Outline of History such as this it is impossible to trace the network of complex mental processes that led to the incessant extension of knowledge and power that is now going on; all we can do here is to call the reader's attention to the most salient turning-points that finally led the toboggan of human affairs into its present swift ice-run of progress. We have told of the first release of human curiosity and of the beginnings of systematic inquiry and experiment. We have told, too, how, when the plutocratic Roman system and its resultant imperialism had come and gone again, this process of inquiry was renewed. We have told of the escape of investigation from ideas of secrecy and personal advantage to the idea of publication and a brotherhood of knowledge, and we have noted the foundation of the British Royal Society, the Florentine Society, and their like as a consequence of this socializing of thought. These things were the roots of the mechanical revolution, and so long as the root of pure scientific inquiry lives, that revolution will progress. The mechanical revolution itself began, we may say, with the exhaustion of the wood supply for the ironworks of England. This led to the use of coal, the coal mine led to the simple pumping engine, the development of the pumping engine by Watt into a machine-driving engine led on to the locomotive and the steamship. This was the first phase of a great expansion in the use of steam. A second phase in the mechanical revolution began with the application of electrical science to practical problems and the development of electric lighting, power transmission, and traction.

A third phase is to be distinguished when in the eighties a new type of engine came into use, an engine in which the expansive force of an explosive mixture replaced the expansive force of steam. The light, highly efficient engines that were thus made possible were applied to the automobile, and developed at last to reach such a pitch of lightness and efficiency as to render flight—long known to be possible—a practical achievement. A successful flying-machine—but not a machine large enough to take up a human body—was made by Professor Langley of the Smithsonian Institute of Washington as early as 1897. By 1909 the aeroplane was available for human locomotion. There had seemed to be a pause in the increase of human speed with the perfection of railways and automobile road traction, but with the flying machine came fresh reductions in the effective distance between one point of the earth's surface and another. In the eighteenth century the distance from London to Edinburgh was an eight days' journey; in 1918 the British Civil Air Transport Commission reported that the journey from London to Melbourne, half-way round the earth, would probably, in a few years' time, be accomplished in that same period of eight days.

Too much stress must not be laid upon these striking reductions in the time distances of one place from another. They are merely one aspect of a much profounder and more momentous enlargement of human possibility. The science of agriculture and agricultural chemistry, for instance, made quite parallel advances during the nineteenth century. Men learnt so to fertilize the soil as to produce quadruple and quintuple the crops got from the same area in the seventeenth century. There was a still more extraordinary advance in medical science; the average duration of life rose, the daily efficiency increased, the waste of life through ill-health diminished.

Now here altogether we have such a change in human life as to constitute a fresh phase of history. In a little more than a century this mechanical revolution has been brought about. In that time man made a stride in the material conditions of his life vaster than he had done during the whole long interval between the palæolithic stage and the age of cultivation, or between the days of Pepi in Egypt and those of George III. A new gigantic material framework for human affairs has come into existence. Clearly it demands great readjustments of our social, economical, and political methods. But these readjustments have necessarily waited upon the development of the mechanical revolution, and they are still only in their opening stage to-day.

§ 2

There is a tendency in many histories to confuse together what we have here called the *mechanical revolution,* which was an entirely new thing in human experience arising out of the development of organized science, a new step like the invention of agriculture or the discovery of metals, with something else, quite different in its origins, something for which there was already an historical precedent, the social and financial development which is called the *industrial revolution.* The two processes were going on together, they were constantly reacting upon each other, but they were in root and essence different. There would have been an industrial revolution of sorts if there had been no coal, no steam, no machinery; but in that case it would probably have followed far more closely upon the lines of the social and financial developments of the later years of the Roman republic. It would have repeated the story of dispossessed free cultivators, gang labour, great estates, great financial fortunes, and a socially destructive financial process. Even the factory method came before power and machinery. Factories were the product not of machinery, but of the "division of labour." Drilled and sweated workers were making such things as millinery, cardboard boxes and furniture, and colouring maps and book illustrations, and so forth, before even water-wheels had been used for industrial processes. There were factories in Rome in the days of Augustus. New books, for instance, were dictated to rows of copyists in the factories of the book-sellers. The attentive student of Defoe and of the political pamphlets of Fielding will realize that the idea of herding poor people into establishments to work collectively for their living was already current in Britain before the close of the seventeenth century. There are intimations of it even as early as More's *Utopia* (1516). It was a social and not a mechanical development.

Up to past the middle of the eighteenth century the social and economic history of western Europe was in fact retreading the path along which the Roman State had gone in the three last centuries B.C. America was in many ways a new Spain, and India and China a new Egypt. But the political disunions of Europe, the political convulsions against monarchy, the recalcitrance of the common folk and perhaps also the greater accessibility of the western European intelligence to mechanical ideas and inventions, turned the process into quite novel directions. Ideas of human solidarity, thanks to Christianity, were far more widely diffused in this newer European world, political power was not so concentrated, and the man of energy anxious to get rich turned his mind, therefore, very willingly from the ideas of the slave and of gang labour to the idea of mechanical power and the machine.

The mechanical revolution, the process of mechanical invention and discovery, was a new thing in human experience, and it went on regardless of the social, political, economic, and industrial consequences it might produce. The industrial revolution, on the other hand, like most other human affairs, was and is more and more profoundly changed and deflected by the constant variation in human conditions caused by the mechanical revolution. And the essential difference between the amassing of riches, the extinction of small farmers and small business men and the phase of big finance in the latter centuries of the Roman Republic on the one hand, and the very similar concentration of capital in the eighteenth and nineteenth centuries on the other, lies in the profound difference in the character of labour that the mechanical revolution was bringing about. The power of the old world was human power; everything depended ultimately upon the driving power of human muscle, the muscle of ignorant and subjugated men. A little animal muscle, supplied by draft oxen, horse traction, and the like, contributed. Where a weight had to be lifted, men lifted it; where a rock had to be quarried, men chipped it out; where a field had to be ploughed, men and oxen ploughed it; the Roman equivalent of the steamship was the galley with its banks of sweating rowers. A vast proportion of mankind in the early civilizations was employed in purely mechanical drudgery. At its onset, power-driven machinery did not seem to promise any release from such unintelligent toil. Great gangs of men were employed in excavating canals, in making railway cuttings and embankments, and the like. The number of miners increased enormously. But the extension of facilities and the output of commodities increased much more. And as the nineteenth century went on, the plain logic of the new situation asserted itself more clearly. Human beings were no longer wanted as a source of mere indiscriminated power. What could be done mechanically by a human being could be done faster and better by a machine. The human being was needed now only where choice and intelligence had to be exercised. Human beings were wanted only as human beings. The *drudge,* on whom all the previous civilizations had rested, the creature of mere obedience, the man whose brains were superfluous, had become unnecessary to the welfare of mankind.

This was as true of such ancient industries as agriculture and mining as it was of the newest metallurgical processes. For ploughing, sowing, and harvesting, swift machines came forward to do the work of scores of men.[1] The Roman civilization was built upon cheap and degraded human beings; modern civilization is being rebuilt upon cheap mechanical power. For a hundred years power has been getting cheaper and labour dearer. If for a generation or so machinery has had to wait its turn in the mine, it is simply because for a time men were cheaper than machinery.[2]

Now here was a change-over of quite primary importance in human affairs. The chief solicitude of the rich and of the ruler in the old civilization had been to keep up a supply of drudges. As the nineteenth century went on, it became more and more plain to the intelligent directive people that the common man had now to be something better than a drudge. He had to be educated—if only to secure "industrial efficiency." He had to understand what he was about. From the days of the first Christian propaganda, popular education had been smouldering in Europe, just as it has smouldered in Asia wherever Islam has set its foot, because of the necessity of making the believer understand a little of the belief by which he is saved, and of enabling him to read a little in the sacred books by which his belief is conveyed. Christian controversies, with their competition for adherents, ploughed the ground for the harvest of popular education. In England, for instance, by the thirties and forties of the nineteenth century, the disputes of the sects and the necessity of catching adherents young had produced an abundance of night schools, Sunday schools, and a series of competing educational organizations for children, the

1 Here America led the old world.

2 In Northumberland and Durham in the early days of coal mining they were so cheaply esteemed that it was unusual to hold inquests on the bodies of men killed in mine disasters.

dissenting British schools, the church National Schools, and even Roman Catholic elementary schools. The earlier, less enlightened manufacturers, unable to take a broad view of their own interests, hated and opposed these schools. But here again needy Germany led her richer neighbours. The religious teacher in Britain presently found the profit-seeker at his side, unexpectedly eager to get the commonalty, if not educated, at least "trained" to a higher level of economic efficiency.

The second half of the nineteenth century was a period of rapid advance in popular education throughout all the Westernized world. There was no parallel advance in the education of the upper classes, some advance no doubt, but nothing to correspond, and so the great gulf that had divided that world hitherto into the readers and the non-reading mass became little more than a slightly perceptible difference in educational level. At the back of this process was the mechanical revolution, apparently regardless of social conditions, but really insisting inexorably upon the complete abolition of a totally illiterate class throughout the world.

The economic revolution of the Roman republic had never been clearly apprehended by the common people of Rome. The ordinary Roman citizen never saw the changes through which he lived, clearly and comprehensively as we see them. But the industrial revolution, as it went on towards the end of the nineteenth century, was more and more distinctily *seen* as one whole process by the common people it was affecting, because presently they could read and discuss and communicate, and because they went about and saw things as no commonalty had ever done before.

In this *Outline of History* we have been careful to indicate the gradual appearance of the ordinary people as a class with a will and ideas in common. It is the writer's belief that massive movements of the "ordinary people" over considerable areas only became possible as a result of the propagandist religions, Christianity and Islam, and their insistence upon individual self-respect. We have cited the enthusiasm of the commonalty for the First Crusade as marking a new phase in social history. But before the nineteenth century even these massive movements were comparatively restricted. The equalitarian insurrections of the peasantry, from the Wycliffe period onward, were confined to the peasant communities of definite localities, they spread only slowly into districts affected by similar forces. The town artisan rioted indeed, but only locally. The château-burning of the French revolution was not the act of a peasantry who had overthrown a government, it was the act of a peasantry released by the overthrow of a government. The Commune of Paris was the first effective appearance of the town artisan as a political power, and the Parisian crowd of the First Revolution was a very mixed, primitive-thinking, and savage crowd compared with any Western European crowd after 1830.

But the mechanical revolution was not only pressing education upon the whole population, it was leading to a big-capitalism and to a large-scale reorganization of industry that was to produce a new and distinctive system of ideas in the common people in the place of the mere uncomfortable recalcitrance and elemental rebellions of an illiterate commonalty. We have already noted how the industrial revolution had split the manufacturing class, which had hitherto been a middling and various sort of class, into two sections, the employers, who became rich enough to mingle with the financial, merchandizing, and land-owning classes, and the employees, who drifted to a status closer and closer to that of mere gang and agricultural labour. As the manufacturing employee sank, the agricultural labourer, by the introduction of agricultural machinery and the increase in his individual productivity, rose. By the middle of the nineteenth century, Karl Marx (1818-83), a German Jew of great scholarly attainments, who did much of his work in the British Museum library in London, was pointing out that the organization of the working classes by the steadily concentrating group of capitalist owners, was developing a new social classification to replace the more complex class systems of the past. Property, so far as it was power, was being gathered together into relatively few hands, the hands of the big rich men, the capitalist class; while there was a great mingling of workers with little or no property, whom he called the "expropriated," or "proletariat"—a misuse of this word—who were bound to develop a common "class consciousness" of the conflict of their interests with those of the rich men. Differences of education and tradition between the various older social elements which were in process of being fused up into the new class of the expropriated, seemed for a time to contradict this sweeping generalization; the traditions of the professions, the small employers, the farmer peasant and the like were all different from one another and from the various craftsman traditions of the workers; but with the spread of education and the cheapening of literature, this "Marxian" generalization becomes now more and more acceptable. These classes, who were linked at first by nothing but a common impoverishment, were and are being reduced or raised to the same standard of life, forced to read the same books and share the same inconveniences. A sense of solidarity between all sorts of poor and propertyless men, as against the profit-amassing and wealth-concentrating class, is growing more and more evident in our world. Old differences fade away, the difference between craftsman and open-air worker, between black coat and overall, between poor clergyman and elementary schoolmaster, between policeman and bus-driver. They must all buy the same cheap furnishings and live in similar cheap houses; their sons and daughters will all mingle and marry; success at the upper levels becomes more and more hopeless for the rank and file. Marx, who did not so much advocate the class-war, the war of the expropriated mass against the appropriating few, as foretell it, is being more and more justified by events.[1]

§ 3

To trace any broad outlines in the fermentation of ideas that went on during the mechanical and industrial revolution of the nineteenth century is a very difficult task. But we must attempt it if we are to link what has gone before in this history with the condition of our world to-day.

It will be convenient to distinguish two main periods in the hundred years between 1814 and 1914. First came the period 1814-48, in which there was a very considerable amount of liberal thinking and writing *in limited circles,* but during which there were no great changes or development of thought in the general mass of the people. Throughout this period the world's

[1] It is sometimes argued against Marx that the proportion of people who have savings invested has increased in many modern communities. These savings are technically "capital" and their owners "capitalists" to that extent, and this is supposed to contradict the statement of Marx that property concentrates into few and fewer hands. Marx used many of his terms carelessly and chose them ill, and his ideas were better than his words. When he wrote property he meant "property so far as it is power." The small investor has remarkably little power over his invested capital.

affairs were living, so to speak, on their old intellectual capital, they were going on in accordance with the leading ideas of the Revolution and the counter-revolution. The dominant liberal ideas were freedom and a certain vague equalitarianism; the conservative ideas were monarchy, organized religion, social privilege, and obedience.

Until 1848 the spirit of the Holy Alliance, the spirit of Metternich, struggled to prevent a revival of the European revolution that Napoleon had betrayed and set back. In America, both North and South, on the other hand, the revolution had triumphed and nineteenth-century liberalism ruled unchallenged. Britain was an uneasy country, never quite loyally reactionary nor quite loyally progressive, neither truly monarchist nor truly republican, the land of Cromwell and also of the Merry Monarch, Charles; anti-Austrian, anti-Bourbon, anti-papal, yet weakly repressive. We have told of the first series of liberal storms in Europe in and about the year 1830; in Britain in 1832 a Reform Bill, greatly extending the franchise and restoring something of its representative character of the House of Commons, relieved the situation. Round and about 1848 came a second and much more serious system of outbreaks, that overthrew the Orleans monarchy and established a second Republic in France (1848-52), raised North Italy and Hungary against Austria, and the Poles in Posen against the Germans, and sent the Pope in flight from the republicans of Rome. A very interesting Pan-Slavic conference held at Prague foreshadowed many of the territorial readjustments of 1919. It dispersed after an insurrection at Prague had been suppressed by Austrian troops.

Ultimately all these insurrections failed; the current system staggered, but kept its feet. There were no doubt serious social discontents beneath these revolts, but as yet, except in the case of Paris, these had no very clear form; and this 1848 storm, so far as the rest of Europe was concerned, may be best described, in a phrase, as a revolt of the natural political map against the artificial arrangements of the Vienna diplomatists, and the system of suppressions those arrangements entailed.

The history of Europe, then, from 1815 to 1848 was, generally speaking, a sequel to the history of Europe from 1789 to 1814. There were no really new *motifs* in the composition. The main trouble was still the struggle, though often a blind and misdirected struggle, of the interests of ordinary men against the Great Power system which cramped and oppressed the life of mankind.

But after 1848, from 1848 to 1914, though the readjustment of the map still went on towards a free and unified Italy and a unified Germany, there began a fresh phase in the process of mental and political adaptation to the new knowledge and the new material powers of mankind. Came a great irruption of new social, religious, and political ideas into the general European mind. In the next three sections we will consider the origin and quality of these irruptions. They laid the foundations upon which we base our political thought to-day, but for a long time they had no very great effect on contemporary politics. Contemporary politics continued to run on in the old lines, but with a steadily diminishing support in the intellectual convictions and consciences of men. We have already described the way in which a strong intellectual process undermined the system of Grand Monarchy in France before 1789. A similar undermining process was going on throughout Europe during the Great Power period of 1848-1914. Profound doubts of the system of government and of the liberties of many forms of property in the economic system spread throughout the social body. Then came the greatest and most disorganizing war in history, so that it is still impossible to estimate the power and range of the accumulated new ideas of those sixty-six years. We have been through a greater catastrophe even than the Napoleonic catastrophe, and we are in a slack-water period, corresponding to the period 1815-30. Our 1830 and our 1848 are still to come and show us where we stand.

§ 4

We have traced throughout this history the gradual restriction of the idea of property from the first unlimited claim of the strong man to possess everything and the gradual realization of brotherhood as something transcending personal self-seeking. Men were first subjugated into more than tribal societies by the fear of monarch and deity. It is only within the last three or at most four thousand years that we have any clear evidence that voluntary self-abandonment to some greater end, without fee or reward, was an acceptable idea to men, or that anyone had propounded it. Then we find spreading over the surface of human affairs, as patches of sunshine spread and pass over the hillsides upon a windy day in spring, the idea that there is a happiness in self-devotion greater than any personal gratification or triumph, and a life of mankind different and greater and more important than the sum of all the individual lives within it. We have seen that idea become vivid as a beacon, vivid as sunshine caught and reflected dazzlingly by some window in the landscape, in the teachings of Buddha, Lao Tse, and, most clearly of all, of Jesus of Nazareth. Through all its variations and corruptions Christianity has never completely lost the suggestion of a devotion to God's commonweal that makes the personal pomps of monarchs and rulers seem like the insolence of an overdressed servant and the splendours and gratifications of wealth like the waste of robbers. No man living in a community which such a religion as Christianity or Islam has touched can be altogether a slave; there is an ineradicable quality in these religions that compels men to judge their masters and to realize their own responsibility for the world.

As men have felt their way towards this new state of mind from the fierce self-centred greed and instinctive combativeness of the early palæolithic family group, they have sought to express the drift of their thoughts and necessities very variously. They have found themselves in disagreement and conflict with old-established ideas, and there has been a natural tendency to contradict these ideas flatly, to fly over to the absolute contrary. Faced by a world in which rule and classes and order seem to do little but give opportunity for personal selfishness and unrighteous oppression, the first impatient movement was to declare for a universal equality and a practical anarchy. Faced by a world in which property seemed little more than a protection for selfishness and a method of enslavement, it was as natural to repudiate all property. Our history shows an increasing impulse to revolt against rulers and against ownership. We have traced it in the middle ages burning the rich man's château and experimenting in theocracy and communism. In the French revolutions this double revolt is clear and plain. In France we find side by side, inspired by the same spirit and as natural parts of the same revolutionary movement, men who, with their eyes on the ruler's taxes, declared that property should be inviolable, and others who, with their eyes on the employer's hard bargains, declared that property should be abolished. But what they are really revolting against in each case is that the ruler and the employer, instead of becoming servants of the community, still remain, like most of mankind, self-seeking, oppressive individuals.

Throughout the ages we find this belief growing in men's minds that there can be such a rearrangement of laws and powers as to give rule and order while still restraining the egotism of any ruler and of any ruling class that may be necessary, and such a definition of property as will give freedom without oppressive power. We begin to realize nowadays that these ends are only to be attained by a complex constructive effort; they arise through the conflict of new human needs against ignorance and old human nature; but throughout the nineteenth century there was a persistent disposition to solve the problem by some simple formula. (And be happy ever afterwards, regardless of the fact that all human life, all life, is throughout the ages nothing but the continuing solution of a continuous synthetic problem.)

The earlier half of the nineteenth century saw a number of experiments in the formation of trial human societies of a new kind. Among the most important historically were the experiments and ideas of Robert Owen (1771-1858), a Manchester cotton-spinner. He is very generally regarded as the founder of modern Socialism; it was in connection with his work that the word "socialism" first arose (about 1835).

He seems to have been a thoroughly competent business man; he made a number of innovations in the cotton-spinning industry, and acquired a fair fortune at an early age. He was distressed by the waste of human possibilities among his workers, and he set himself to improve their condition and the relations of employer and employed. This he sought to do first at his Manchester factory and afterwards at New Lanark, where he found himself in practical control of works employing about two thousand people. Between 1800 and 1828 he achieved very considerable things: he reduced the hours of labour, made his factory sanitary and agreeable, abolished the employment of very young children, improved the training of his workers, provided unemployment pay during a period of trade depression, established a system of schools, and made New Lanark a model of better industrialism, while at the same time sustaining its commercial prosperity. He wrote vigorously to defend the mass of mankind against the charges of intemperance and improvidence which were held to justify the economic iniquities of the time. He held that men and women are largely the product of their educational environment, a thesis that needs no advocacy to-day. And he set himself to a propaganda of the views that New Lanark had justified. He attacked the selfish indolence of his fellow manufacturers, and in 1819, largely under his urgency, the first Factory Act was passed, the first attempt to restrain employers from taking the most stupid and intolerable advantages of their workers' poverty. Some of the restrictions of that Act amaze us to-day. It seems incredible now that it should ever have been necessary to protect little children of *nine* (!) from work in factories, or to limit the nominal working day of such employees to *twelve hours!*

People are perhaps too apt to write of the industrial revolution as though it led to the enslavement and overworking of poor children who had hitherto been happy and free. But this misinterprets history. From the very beginnings of civilization the little children of the poor had always been obliged to do whatever work they could do. But the factory system gathered up all this infantile toil and made it systematic, conspicuous, and scandalous. The factory system challenged the quickening human conscience on that issue. The British Factory Act of 1819, weak and feeble though it seems to us, was the Magna Carta of childhood; thereafter the protection of the children of the poor, first from toil and then from bodily starvation and ignorance, began.

We cannot tell here in any detail the full story of Owen's life and thought. His work at New Lanark had been, he felt, only a trial upon a small working model. What could be done for one industrial community could be done, he held, for every industrial community in the country; he advocated a resettlement of the industrial population in townships on the New Lanark plan. For a time he seemed to have captured the imagination of the world. The *Times* and *Morning Post* supported his proposals; among the visitors to New Lanark was the Grand Duke Nicholas who succeeded Alexander I as Tsar; a fast friend was the Duke of Kent, son of George III and father of Queen Victoria. But all the haters of change and all—and there are always many such—who were jealous of the poor, and all the employers who were likely to be troubled by his projects, were waiting for an excuse to counter-attack him, and they found it in the expression of his religious opinions, which were hostile to official Christianity, and through those he was successfully discredited. But he continued to develop his projects and experiments, of which the chief was a community at New Harmony in Indiana (U.S.A.), in which he sank most of his capital. His partners bought him out of the New Lanark business in 1828.

Owen's experiments and suggestions ranged very widely, and do not fall under any single formula. There was nothing doctrinaire about him. His New Lanark experiment was the first of a number of "benevolent businesses" in the world; Lord Leverhulme's Port Sunlight, the Cadburys' Bournville, and the Ford businesses in America are contemporary instances; it was not really a socialist experiment at all; it was a "paternal" experiment. But his proposals for state settlements were what we should call state socialism to-day. His American experiment and his later writings point to a completer form of socialism, a much wider departure from the existing state of affairs. It is clear that the riddle of currency exercised Owen. He understood that we can no more hope for real economic justice while we pay for work with money of fluctuating value than we could hope for a punctual world if there was a continual inconstant variability in the length of an hour. One of his experiments was an attempt at a circulation of labour notes representing one hour, five hours, or twenty hours of work. The co-operative societies of to-day, societies of poor men which combine for the collective buying and distribution of commodities or for collective manufacture or dairying or other forms of agriculture, arose directly out of his initiatives, though the pioneer co-operative societies of his own time ended in failure. Their successors have spread throughout the whole world, and number to-day some thirty or forty million of adherents.

A point to note about this early socialism of Owen's is that it was not at first at all "democratic." Its initiative was benevolent, its early form patriarchal; it was something up to which the workers were to be educated by liberally disposed employers and leaders. The first socialism was not a worker's movement; it was a master's movement.

Concurrently with this work of Owen's, another and quite independent series of developments was going on in America and Britain which was destined to come at last into reaction with his socialistic ideas. The English law had long prohibited combinations in restraint of trade, combinations to raise prices or wages by concerted action. There had been no great hardship in these prohibitions before the agrarian and industrial changes of the eighteenth century let loose a great swarm of workers living from hand to mouth and competing for insufficient employment. Under these new conditions, the workers in many industries found themselves intolerably squeezed. They were played off one against another; day by day and hour by hour none knew what concession his fellow might not have made, and what further reduction of pay or increase of toil might not ensue. It became vitally necessary for the workers to make agreements—illegal though they were—against such underselling. At first these agreements had to be made and sustained by secret societies. Or clubs, established ostensibly for quite other purposes, social clubs, funeral societies, and the like, served to mask the wage-protecting combination. The fact that these associations were illegal disposed them to violence; they were savage against "blacklegs" and "rats" who would not join them, and still more savage with traitors. In 1824 the House of Commons recognized the desirability of relieving tension in these matters by conceding the right of workmen to form combinations for "collective bargaining" with the masters. This enabled Trade Unions to develop with a large measure of freedom. At first very clumsy and primitive organizations and with very restricted freedoms, the Trade Unions have risen gradually to be a real Fourth Estate in the country, a great system of bodies representing the mass of industrial workers.

Arising at first in Britain and America, they have, with various national modifications, and under varying legal conditions, spread to France, Germany, and all the westernized communities.

Organized originally to sustain wages and restrict intolerable hours, the Trade Union movement was at first something altogether distinct from socialism. The Trade Unionist tried to make the best for himself of the existing capitalism and the existing conditions of employment; the socialist proposed to change the system. It was the imagination and generalizing power of

Karl Marx which brought these two movements into relationship. He was a man with the sense of history very strong in him; he was the first to perceive that the old social classes that had endured since the beginning of civilization were in process of dissolution and regrouping. His racial Jewish commercialism made the antagonism of property and labour very plain to him. And his upbringing in Germany—where, as we have pointed out, the tendency of class to harden into caste was more evident than in any other European country—made him conceive of labour as presently becoming "class conscious" and collectively antagonistic to the property-concentrating classes. In the Trade Union movement which was spreading over the world, he believed he saw this development of class-conscious labour.

What, he asked, would be the outcome of the "class war" of the capitalist and proletariat? The capitalist adventurers, he alleged, because of their inherent greed and combativeness, would gather power over capital into fewer and fewer hands, until at last they would concentrate all the means of production, transit, and the like into a form seizable by the workers, whose class consciousness and solidarity would be developed *pari passu* by the process of organizing and concentrating industry. They would seize this capital and work it for themselves. This would be the social revolution. Then individual property and freedom would be restored, based upon the common ownership of the earth and the management by the community as a whole of the great productive services which the private capitalist had organized and concentrated. This would be the end of the "capitalist" system, but not the end of the system of capitalism. State capitalism would replace private owner capitalism.

This marks a great stride away from the socialism of Owen. Owen (like Plato) looked to the common sense of men of any or every class to reorganize the casual and faulty political, economic, and social structure. Marx found something more in the nature of a driving force in his class hostility based on expropriation and injustice. And he was not simply a prophetic theorist; he was also a propagandist of the revolt of labour, the revolt of the so-called "proletariat." Labour, he perceived, had a common interest against the capitalist everywhere, though under the test of the Great Power wars of the time, and particularly of the liberation of Italy, he showed that he failed to grasp the fact that labour everywhere has a common interest in the peace of the world. But with the social revolution in view he did succeed in inspiring the formation of an international league of workers, the First International.

The subsequent history of socialism is chequered between the British tradition of Owen and the German class feeling of Marx. What is called Fabian Socialism, the exposition of socialism by the London Fabian Society, makes its appeal to reasonable men of all classes. What are called "Revisionists" in German Socialism incline in the same direction. But on the whole, it is Marx who has carried the day against Owen, and the general disposition of socialists throughout the world is to look to the organization of labour and labour only to supply the fighting forces that will disentangle the political and economic organization of human affairs from the hands of the more or less irresponsible private owners and adventurers who now control it.

These are the broad features of the project which is called Socialism. We will discuss its incompletenesses and inadequacies in our next section. It was perhaps inevitable that socialism should be greatly distraught and subdivided by doubts and disputes and sects and schools; they are growth symptoms like the spots on a youth's face. Here we can but glance at the difference between state socialism, which would run the economic business of the country through its political government, and the newer schools of syndicalism and guild socialism which would entrust a large measure in the government of each industry to the workers of every grade—including the directors and managers—engaged in that industry. This "guild socialism" is really a new sort of capitalism with a committee of workers and officials in each industry taking the place of the free private capitalists of that industry. The *personnel* becomes the collective capitalist. Nor can we discuss the undemocratic idea of the Russian leader Lenin, that a population cannot judge of socialism before it has experienced it, and that a group of socialists are therefore justified in seizing and socializing, if they can, the life of a country without at first setting up any democratic form of general government at all, for which sort of seizure he uses the Marxian phrase, a very incompetent phrase, the "dictatorship of the proletariat."

All Russia now is a huge experiment in that dictatorship.

The "proletariat" is supposed to be dictating the government of Russia through committees of workmen and soldiers, the Soviets, but as a matter of fact these Soviets have little or no real directive power. They assemble in meetings so big as to be practically mass meetings, and the utmost they can do is to give a general assent to the proceedings of the government. The Petersburg Soviet, which the writer visited in September, 1920, was a mass meeting of over three thousand people, incapable of any detailed criticism or direction of the Bolshevik government.[1]

§ 5

We are all socialists nowadays, said Sir William Harcourt years ago, and that is loosely true to-day. There can be few people who fail to realize the provisional nature and the dangerous instability of our present political and economic system, and still fewer who believe with the doctrinaire individualists that profit-hunting "go as you please" will guide mankind to any haven of prosperity and happiness. Great rearrangements are necessary, and a systematic legal subordination of personal self-seeking to the public good. So far most reasonable men are socialists. But these are only preliminary propositions. How far has socialism and modern thought generally gone towards *working out* the conception of this new political and social order, of which our world admittedly stands in need? We are obliged to answer that there is no clear conception of the new state towards which we vaguely struggle, that our science of human relationships is still so crude and speculative as to leave us without definite guidance upon a score of primarily important issues. In 1920 we are no more in a position to set up a scientifically conceived political system in the world than were men to set up an electric power station in 1820. They could not have done that then to save their lives.

The Marxist system points us to an accumulation of revolutionary forces in the modern world. These forces will continually tend towards revolution. But Marx assumed too hastily that a revolutionary impulse would necessarily produce an ordered state of a new and better kind. A revolution may stop half-way in mere destruction. No socialist sect has yet defined

[1] Wells, *Russia in the Shadows.*

its projected government clearly; the Bolsheviks in their Russian experiment seem to have been guided by a phrase, the dictatorship of the proletariat, and in practice, we are told, Trotsky and Lenin have proved as autocratic as the less intelligent but equally well-meaning Tsar, Alexander I. We have been at some pains to show from our brief study of the French revolution that a revolution can establish nothing permanent that has not already been thought out beforehand and apprehended by the general mind. The French republic, confronted with unexpected difficulties in economics, currency, and international relationships, collapsed to the egotisms of the newly rich people of the Directory, and finally to the egotism of Napoleon. Law and a plan, steadily upheld, are more necessary in revolutionary times than in ordinary humdrum times, because in revolutionary times society degenerates much more readily into a mere scramble under the ascendancy of the forcible and cunning.

If in general terms we take stock of the political and social science of our age, we shall measure something of the preliminary intellectual task still to be done by mankind before we can hope to see any permanent constructive achievements emerging from the mere traditionalism and adventuring that rule our collective affairs to-day. This Socialism, which professes to be a complete theory of a new social order, we discover, when we look into it, to be no more than a partial theory—very illuminating, so far as it goes—about property. We have already discussed the relationship of social development to the restriction of the idea of property. There are various schools of thought which would restrict property more or less completely. Communism is the proposal to abolish property altogether, or, in other words, to hold all things in common. Modern Socialism, on the other hand—or, to give it a more precise name, "Collectivism"—does clearly distinguish between personal property and collective property. The gist of the socialist proposal is that land and all the natural means of production, transit, and distribution should be collectively owned. Within these limits there is to be much free private ownership and unrestricted personal freedom. Given efficient administration, it may be doubted whether many people nowadays would dispute that proposal. But socialism has never gone on to a thorough examination of that proviso for efficient administration.

Again, what community is it that is to own the collective

property; is it to be the sovereign or the township or the county or the nation or mankind? Socialism makes no clear answer. Socialists are very free with the word "nationalize," but we have been subjecting the ideas of "nations" and "nationalism" to some destructive criticism in this *Outline*. If socialists object to a single individual claiming a mine or a great stretch of agricultural land as his own individual property, with a right to refuse or barter its use and profit to others, why should they permit a single nation to monopolize the mines or trade routes or natural wealth of the territories in which it lives, against the rest of mankind? There seems to be great confusion in socialist theory in this matter. And unless human life is to become a mass meeting of the race in permanent session, how is the community to appoint its officers to carry on its collective concerns? After all, the private owner of land or of a business or the like is a sort of public official in so far as his ownership is sanctioned and protected by the community. Instead of being paid a salary or fees, he is allowed to make a profit. The only valid reason for dismissing him from his ownership is that the new control to be substituted will be more efficient and profitable and satisfactory to the community. And, being dismissed, he has at least the same claim to consideration from the community that he himself has shown in the past to the worker thrown out of employment by a mechanical invention.

This question of administration, the sound and adequate bar to much immediate socialization, brings us to the still largely unsolved problem of human association; how are we to secure the best direction of human affairs and the maximum of willing co-operation with that direction? This is ultimately a complex problem in psychology, but it is absurd to pretend that it is an insoluble one. There must be a definite best, which is the right thing, in these matters. But if it is not insoluble, it is equally unreasonable to pretend that it has been solved. The problem in its completeness involves the working out of the best methods in the following departments, and their complete correlation:—

(i) *Education.*—The preparation of the individual for an understanding and willing co-operation in the world's affairs.

(ii) *Information.*—The continual truthful presentation of public affairs to the individual for his judgment and approval.

Closely connected with this need for current information is the codification of the law, the problem of keeping the law plain, clear, and accessible to all.

(iii) *Representation.*—The selection of representatives and agents to act in the collective interest in harmony with the general will based on this education and plain information.

(iv) *The Executive.*—The appointment of executive agents and the maintenance of means for keeping them responsible to the community, without at the same time hampering intelligent initiatives.

(v) *Thought and Research.*—The systematic criticism of affairs and laws to provide data for popular judgments, and through those judgments to ensure the secular improvement of the human organization.

These are the five heads under which the broad problem of human society presents itself to us. In the world around us we see makeshift devices at work in all those branches, ill coordinated one with another and unsatisfactory in themselves. We see an educational system meanly financed and equipped, badly organized and crippled by the interventions and hostilities of religious bodies; we see popular information supplied chiefly by a venal press dependant upon advertisements and subsidies; we see farcical methods of election returning politicians to power as unrepresentative as any hereditary ruler or casual conqueror; everywhere the executive is more or less influenced or controlled by groups of rich adventurers, and the pursuit of political and social science and of public criticism is still the work of devoted and eccentric individuals rather than a recognized and honoured function in the state. There is a gigantic task before right-thinking men in the cleansing and sweetening of the politician's stable; and until it is done, any complete realization of socialism is impossible. While private adventurers control the political life of the state, it is ridiculous to think of the state taking over collective economic interests from private adventurers.

Not only has the socialist movement failed thus far to produce a scientifically reasoned scheme for the correlation of education, law, and the exercise of public power, but even in the economic field, as we have already pointed out, creative forces wait for the conception of a right organization of credit and a right method of payment and interchange. It is a truism that the willingness of the worker depends, among other things, upon his complete confidence in the purchasing power of the currency in which he is paid. As this confidence goes, work ceases, except in so far as it can be rewarded by payment in goods. But there is no sufficient science of currency and business psychology to restrain governments from the most disturbing interferences with the public credit and with the circulation. And such interferences lead straight to the cessation of work, that is, of the production of necessary things. Upon such vital practical questions it is scarcely too much to say that the mass of those socialists who would recast the world have no definite ideas at all. Yet in a socialist world quite as much as in any other sort of world, people must be paid money for their work rather than be paid in kind if any such thing as personal freedom is to continue. Here, too, there must be an ascertainable right thing to do. Until that is determined, history in these matters will continue to be not so much a record of experiments as of flounderings.

And in another direction the social and political thinking of the nineteenth century was, in the face of the vastness of the mechanical revolution, timid, limited, and insufficient, and that was in regard to international relations. The reader of socialistic literature will find the socialists constantly writing and talking of the "State," and never betraying any realization that the "State" might be all sorts of organizations in all sorts of areas, from the republic of San Marino to the British Empire. It is true that Karl Marx had a conception of a solidarity of interests between the workers in all the industrialized countries, but there is little or no suggestion in Marxist socialism of the logical corollary of this, the establishment of a democratic world federal government (with national or provincial "state" governments) as a natural consequence of his projected social revolution. At most there is a vague aspiration. But if there is any logic about the Marxist, it should be his declared political end for which he should work without ceasing. Put to the test of the war of 1914, the socialists of almost all the European countries showed that their class-conscious internationalism was veneered very thinly indeed over their patriotic feelings, and had to no degree replaced them. Everywhere during the German war socialists denounced that war as made by capitalist governments, but it produces little or no permanent effect to denounce a government or a world system unless you have a working idea of a better government and a better system to replace it.

We state these things here because they are facts, and a living and necessary part of a contemporary survey of human history. It is not our task either to advocate or controvert socialism. But it is in our picture to note that political and social life are, and must remain, chaotic and disastrous without the development of some such constructive scheme as socialism *sketches,* and to point out clearly how far away the world is at present from any such scheme. An enormous amount of intellectual toil and discussion and education and many years—whether decades or centuries, no man can tell—must intervene before a new order, planned as ships and railways are planned, runs, as the cables and the postal deliveries run, over the whole surface of our earth. And until such a new order draws mankind together with its net, human life, as we shall presently show by the story of the European wars since 1854, must become more and more casual, dangerous, miserable, anxious, and disastrous because of the continually more powerful and destructive war methods the continuing mechanical revolution produces.

§ 6[1]

While the mechanical revolution which the growth of physical science had brought about was destroying the ancient social classification of the civilized state which had been evolved through thousands of years, and producing new possibilities and new ideals of a righteous human community and a righteous world order, a change at least as great and novel was going on in the field of religious thought. That same growth of scientific knowledge from which sprang the mechanical revolution was the moving cause of these religious disturbances.

In the opening chapters of this *Outline* we have given the main story of the Record of the Rocks; we have shown life for the little beginning of consciousness that it is in the still waiting vastness of the void of space and time. But before the end of the eighteenth century, this enormous prospect of the

[1] For a closely parallel view of religion to that given here, see *Outspoken Essays,* by Dean Inge, Essays VIII and IX on *St. Paul* and on *Institutionalism and Mysticism.*

past which fills a modern mind with humility and illimitable hope was hidden from the general consciousness of our race. It was veiled by the curtain of a Sumerian legend. The heavens were no more than a stage background to a little drama of kings. Men had been too occupied with their own private passions and personal affairs to heed the intimations of their own great destiny that lay about them everywhere.

They learnt their true position in space long before they placed themselves in time. We have already named the earlier astronomers, and told how Galileo was made to recant his assertion that the earth moved round the sun. He was made to do so by the church, and the church was stirred to make him do so because any doubt that the world was the centre of the universe seemed to strike fatally at the authority of Christianity.

Now, upon that matter the teller of modern history is obliged to be at once cautious and bold. He has to pick his way between cowardly evasion on the one hand, and partisanship on the other. As far as possible he must confine himself to facts and restrain his opinions. Yet it is well to remember that no opinions can be altogether restrained. The writer has his own very strong and definite persuasions, and the reader must bear that in mind. It is a fact in history that the teaching of Jesus of Nazareth had in it something profoundly new and creative; he preached a new Kingdom of Heaven in the hearts and in the world of men. There was nothing in his teaching, so far as we can judge it at this distance of time, to clash or interfere with any discovery or expansion of the history of the world and mankind. But it is equally a fact in history that St. Paul and his successors added to or completed or imposed upon or substituted another doctrine for—as you may prefer to think—the plain and profoundly revolutionary teachings of Jesus by expounding a subtle and complex theory of salvation, a salvation which could be attained very largely by belief and formalities, without any serious disturbance of the believer's ordinary habits and occupations, and that this Pauline teaching *did* involve very definite beliefs about the history of the world and man. It is not the business of the historian to controvert or explain these matters; the question of their ultimate significance depends upon the theologian; the historian's concern is merely with the fact that official Christianity throughout the world adopted St. Paul's view so plainly expressed in his epistles and so untraceable in the gospels, that the meaning of religion lay not in the future, but in the past, and that Jesus was not so much a teacher of wonderful new things, as a predestinate divine blood sacrifice of deep mystery and sacredness made in atonement of a particular historical act of disobedience to the Creator committed by our first parents, Adam and Eve, in response to the temptation of a serpent in the Garden of Eden. Upon the belief in that Fall as a fact, and not upon the personality of Jesus of Nazareth, upon the theories of Paul, and not upon the injunctions of Jesus, doctrinal Christianity built itself.

We have already noted that this story of the special creation of the world and of Adam and Eve and the serpent was also an ancient Babylonian story, and probably a still more ancient Sumerian story, and that the Jewish sacred books were the medium by which this very ancient and primitive "heliolithic" serpent legend entered Christianity. Wherever official Christianity has gone, it has taken this story with it. It has tied itself up to that story. Until a century and less ago the whole Christianized world felt bound to believe and did believe, that the universe had been specially created in the course of six days by the word of God a few thousand years before—according to Bishop Ussher, 4004 B.C. (The *Universal History*, in forty-two volumes, published in 1779 by a group of London booksellers, discusses whether the precise date of the first day of Creation was March 21st or September 21st, 4004 B.C., and inclines to the view that the latter was the more probable season.)

Upon this historical assumption rested the religious fabric of the Western and Westernized civilization, and yet the whole world was littered, the hills, mountains, deltas, and seas were bursting with evidence of its utter absurdity. The religious life of the leading nations, still a very intense and sincere religious life, was going on in a house of history built upon sand.

There is frequent recognition in classical literature of a sounder cosmogony. Aristotle was aware of the broad principles of modern geology, they shine through the speculations of Lucretius, and we have noted also Leonardo da Vinci's (1452-1519) lucid interpretation of fossils. A Frenchman, Descartes (1596-1650), speculated boldly upon the incandescent beginnings of our globe, and a Dane, Steno (1631-87), began the collection of fossils and the description of strata. But it was only as the eighteenth century drew to its close that the systematic study of geology assumed such proportions as to affect the general authority of the Bible version of that ancient Sumerian narrative. Contemporaneously with the *Universal History* quoted above, a great French naturalist, Buffon, was writing upon the Epochs of Nature (1778), and boldly extending the age of the world to 70,000 or 75,000 years. He divided his story into six epochs to square with the six days of the Creation story. These days, it was argued, were figurative days; they were really ages. There was a general disposition to do this on the part of the new science of geology. By that accommodating device, geology contrived to make a peace with orthodox religious teaching that lasted until the middle of the nineteenth century.

We cannot trace here the contributions of such men as Hutton and Playfair and Sir Charles Lyell, and the Frenchmen Lamarck and Cuvier, in unfolding and developing the record of the rocks. It was only slowly that the general intelligence of the Western world was awakened to two disconcerting facts: firstly, that the succession of life in the geological record did not correspond to the acts of the six days of creation; and, secondly, that the record, in harmony with a mass of biological facts, pointed away from the Bible assertion of a separate creation of each species straight towards a genetic relation between all forms of life, *in which even man was included!* The importance of this last issue to the existing doctrinal system was manifest. If all the animals and man had been evolved in this ascendant manner, then there had been no first parents, no Eden, and no Fall. And if there had been no fall, then the entire historical fabric of Christianity, the story of the first sin and the reason for an atonement, upon which the current teaching based Christian emotion and morality, collapsed like a house of cards.

It was with something like horror, therefore, that great numbers of honest and religious-spirited men followed the work of the English naturalist, Charles Darwin (1809-82); in 1859 he published his *Origin of Species by Means of Natural Selection,* a powerful and permanently valuable exposition of that conception of the change and development of species which we have sketched briefly in Chapter III; and in 1871 he completed the outline of his work with the *Descent of Man,* which brought man definitely into the same scheme of development with the rest of life.

Many men and women are still living who can remember the dismay and distress among ordinary intelligent people in the Western communities as the invincible case of the biologists and geologists against the orthodox Christian cosmogony unfolded itself. The minds of many resisted the new knowledge instinctively and irrationally. Their whole moral edifice was built upon false history; they were too old and set to rebuild it; they felt the practical truth of their moral convictions, and this new truth seemed to them to be incompatible with that. They believed that to assent to it would be to prepare a moral collapse for the world. And so they produced a moral collapse by not assenting to it. The universities in England particularly, being primarily clerical in their constitution, resisted the new learning very bitterly. During the seventies and eighties a stormy controversy raged throughout the civilized world. The quality of the discussions and the fatal ignorance of the church may be gauged by a description in Hackett's *Common-place Book* of a meeting of the British Association in 1860, at which Bishop Wilberforce assailed Huxley, the great champion of the Darwinian views, in this fashion.

Facing "Huxley with a smiling insolence, he begged to know, *was it through his grandfather or grandmother that he claimed his descent from a monkey?* Huxley turned to his neighbour, and said, 'The Lord hath delivered him into my hands.' Then he stood before us and spoke these tremendous words, 'He was not ashamed to have a monkey for his ancestor; but he would be ashamed to be connected with a man who used great gifts to obscure the truth.' " (Another version has it: "I have certainly said that a man has no reason to be ashamed of having an ape for his grandfather. If there were an ancestor whom I should feel ashamed in recalling, it would rather be a man of restless and versatile intellect who plunges into scientific questions with which he has no real acquaintance, only to obscure them by an aimless rhetoric and distract the attention of his audience from the real point at issue by eloquent digressions and skilled appeals to prejudice.") These words were certainly spoken with passion. The scene was one of great excitement. A lady fainted, says Hackett. . . . Such was the temper of this controversy.

The Darwinian movement took formal Christianity unawares, suddenly. Formal Christianity was confronted with a clearly demonstrable error in her theological statements. The Christian theologians were neither wise enough nor mentally nimble enough to accept the new truth, modify their formulæ, and insist upon the living and undiminished vitality of the religious reality those formulæ had hitherto sufficed to express. For the discovery of man's descent from sub-human forms does not even remotely touch the teaching of the Kingdom of Heaven. Yet priests and bishops raged at Darwin; foolish attempts were made to suppress Darwinian literature and to insult and discredit the exponents of the new views. There was much wild talk of the "antagonism" of religion and science. Now in all ages there have been sceptics in Christendom. The Emperor Frederick II was certainly a sceptic; in the eighteenth century Gibbon and Voltaire were openly anti-Christian, and their writings influenced a number of scattered readers. But these were exceptional people. . . . Now the whole of Christendom became as a whole sceptical. This new controversy touched everybody who read a book or heard intelligent conversation. A new generation of young people grew up, and they found the defenders of Christianity in an evil temper, fighting their cause without dignity or fairness. It was the orthodox theology that the new scientific advances had compromised, but the angry theologians declared that it was religion.

In the end men may discover that religion shines all the brighter for the loss of its doctrinal wrappings, but to the young it seemed as if indeed there had been a conflict of science and religion, and that in that conflict science had won.

The immediate effect of this great dispute upon the ideas and methods of people in the prosperous and influential classes throughout the westernized world was very detrimental indeed. The new biological science was bringing nothing constructive as yet to replace the old moral stand-bys. A real de-moralization ensued. The general level of social life in those classes was far higher in the early twentieth than in the early seventeenth century, but in one respect, in respect to disinterestedness and conscientiousness in these classes, it is probable that the tone of the earlier age was better than the latter. In the owning and active classes of the seventeenth century, in spite of a few definite "infidels," there was probably a much higher percentage of men and women who prayed sincerely, who searched their souls to find if they had done evil, and who were prepared to suffer and make great sacrifices for what they conceived to be right, than in the opening years of the twentieth century. There was a real loss of faith after 1859. The true gold of religion was in many cases thrown away with the worn-out purse that had contained it for so long, and it was not recovered. Towards the close of the nineteenth century a crude misunderstanding of Darwinism had become the fundamental mindstuff of great masses of the "educated" everywhere. The seventeenth-century kings and owners and rulers and leaders had had the idea at the back of their minds that they prevailed by the will of God; they really feared him, they got priests to put things right for them with him; when they were wicked, they tried not to think of him. But the old faith of the kings, owners, and rulers of the opening twentieth century had faded under the actinic light of scientific criticism. Prevalent peoples at the close of the nineteenth century believed that they prevailed by virtue of the Struggle for Existence, in which the strong and cunning get the better of the weak and confiding. And they believed further that they had to be strong, energetic, ruthless, "practical," egotistical, because God was dead, and had always, it seemed, been dead which was going altogether further than the new knowledge justified.

They soon got beyond the first crude popular misconception of Darwinism, the idea that every man is for himself alone. But they stuck at the next level. Man, they decided, is a social animal like the Indian hunting dog. He is much more than a dog—but this they did not see. And just as in a pack it is necessary to bully and subdue the younger and weaker for the general good, so it seemed right to them that the big dogs of the human pack should bully and subdue. Hence a new scorn for the ideas of democracy that had ruled the earlier nineteenth century, and a revived admiration for the overbearing and the cruel. It was quite characteristic of the times that Mr. Kipling should lead the children of the middle and upper-class British public back to the Jungle, to learn "the law," and that in his book *Stalky and Co.* he should give an appreciative description of the torture of two boys by three others, who have by a subterfuge tied up their victims helplessly before revealing their hostile intentions.

It is worth while to give a little attention to this incident in *Stalky and Co.*, because it lights up the political psychology of the British Empire at the close of the nineteenth century very vividly. The history of the last half century is not to be understood without an understanding of the mental twist which this story exemplifies. The two boys who are tortured are "bullies," that is the excuse of their tormentors, and these latter have further been incited to the orgy by a clergyman. Nothing can restrain the gusto with which they (and Mr. Kipling) set about the job. Before resorting to torture, the teaching seems to be, see that you pump up a little justifiable moral indignation, and all will be well. If you have the authorities on your side, then you cannot be to blame. Such, apparently, is the simple doctrine of this typical imperialist. But every bully has to the best of his ability followed that doctrine since the human animal developed sufficient intelligence to be consciously cruel.

Another point in the story is very significant indeed. The head master and his clerical assistant are both represented as being privy to the affair. They want this bullying to occur. Instead of exercising their own authority, they use these boys, who are Mr. Kipling's heroes, to punish the two victims. Head master and clergyman turn a deaf ear to the complaints of an indignant mother. All this Mr. Kipling represents as a most desirable state of affairs. In this we have the key to the ugliest, most retrogressive, and finally fatal idea of modern imperialism; the idea of a *tacit conspiracy between the law and illegal violence.* Just as Tsardom wrecked itself at last by a furtive encouragement of the ruffians of the Black Hundreds, who massacred Jews and other people supposed to be inimical to the Tsar, so the good name of the British Imperial Government has been tainted—and is still tainted—by an illegal raid made by Doctor Jameson into the Transvaal before the Boer War, by the adventures which we shall presently describe, of Sir Edward Carson and Mr. F. E. Smith (now Lord Birkenhead), in Ireland and by the tacit connivance of the British government in Ireland with the "reprisals" undertaken by the loyalists against the perpetrators of Sinn Fein outrages. By such treasons against their subjects, empires destroy themselves. The true strength of rulers and empires lies not in armies and navies, but in the belief of men that they are inflexibly open and truthful and legal. So soon as a government departs from that standard, it ceases to be anything more than "the gang in possession," and its days are numbered.

§ 7

We have already pointed out that there must be a natural political map of the world which gives the best possible geographical divisions for human administrations. Any other political division of the world than this natural political map will necessarily be a misfit, and must produce stresses of hostility and insurrection tending to shift boundaries in the direction indicated by the natural political map. These would seem to be self-evident propositions were it not that the diplomatists at Vienna evidently neither believed nor understood anything of the sort, and thought themselves as free to carve up the world as one is free to carve up such a boneless structure as a cheese. Nor were these propositions evident to Mr. Gladstone. Most of the upheavals and conflicts that began in Europe as the world recovered from the exhaustion of the Napoleonic wars were quite obviously attempts of the ordinary common men to get rid of governments that were such misfits as to be in many cases intolerable. Generally the existing governments were misfits throughout Europe because they were not socially representative, and so they were hampering production and wasting human possibilities; but when there were added to these universal annoyances differences of religion and racial culture between rulers and ruled (as in most of Ireland), differences in race and language (as in Austrian North Italy and throughout most of the Austrian Empire), or differences in all these respects (as in Poland and the Turkish Empire in Europe), the exasperation drove towards bloodshed. Europe was a system of governing machines abominably adjusted. From the stresses of this maladjustment the various "nationalist" movements that played so large a part in the history of the nineteenth century drew their driving force.

What is a nation? What is nationality? If our story of the world has demonstrated anything, it has demonstrated the mingling of races and peoples, the instability of human divisions, the swirling variety of human groups and human ideas of association. A nation, it has been said, is an accumulation of human beings who think they are one people; but we are told that Ireland is a nation, and Protestant Ulster certainly does not share that idea; and Italy did not think it was one people until long after its unity was accomplished. When the writer was in Italy in 1916, people were saying: "This war will make us one nation." Again, are the English a nation or have they merged into a "British nationality"? Scotchmen do not seem to believe very much in this British nationality. It cannot be a community of race or language that constitutes a nation, because the Gaels and the Lowlanders make up the Scotch "nation"; it cannot be a common religion, for England has scores; nor a common literature, or why is Britain separated from the United States, and the Argentine Republic from Spain? We may suggest that a nation is in effect any assembly, mixture, or confusion of people which is either afflicted by or wishes to be afflicted by a foreign office of its own, in order that it should behave collectively as if it alone constituted humanity. We have already traced the development of the Machiavellian monarchies into the rule of their foreign offices, playing the part of "Powers." The "nationality" which dominated the political thought of the nineteenth century is really no more than the romantic and emotional exaggeration of the stresses produced by the discord of the natural political map with unsuitable political arrangements.

Throughout the nineteenth century, and particularly throughout its latter half, there has been a great working up of this nationalism in the world. All men are by nature partisans and patriots, but the natural tribalism of men in the nineteenth century was unnaturally exaggerated, it was fretted and overstimulated and inflamed and forced into the nationalist mould. Nationalism was taught in schools, emphasized by newspapers, preached and mocked and sung into men. Men were brought to feel that they were as improper without a nationality as without their clothes in a crowded assembly. Oriental peoples who had never heard of nationality before, took to it as they took to the cigarettes and bowler hats of the west. India, a galaxy of contrasted races, religions, and cultures, Dravidian, Mongolian, and Aryan, became a "nation." There were perplexing

Tribal Gods — national symbols for which men would die — of the 19th Century
John Bull
Britannia
Germania
France
Cathleen ni Hoolihan

cases, of course, as when a young Whitechapel Jew had to decide whether he belonged to the British or the Jewish nation. Caricature and political cartoons played a large part in this elevation of the cult of these newer and bigger tribal gods—for such indeed the modern "nations" are—to their ascendancy over the imagination of the nineteenth century. If one turns over the pages of *Punch,* that queer contemporary record of the British soul, which has lasted now since 1841, one finds the figures of Britannia, Hibernia, France, and Germania embracing, disputing, reproving, rejoicing, grieving. It greatly helped the diplomatists to carry on their game of Great Powers to convey politics in this form to the doubting general intelligence. To the common man, resentful that his son should be sent abroad to be shot, it was made clear that instead of this being merely the result of the obstinacy and greed of two foreign offices, it was really a necessary part of a righteous inevitable gigantic struggle between two of these dim vast divinities. France had been wronged by Germania, or Italia was showing a proper spirit to Austria. The boy's death ceased to appear an outrage on common sense; it assumed a sort of mythological dignity. And insurrection could clothe itself in the same romantic habiliments as diplomacy. Ireland became a Cinderella goddess, Cathleen ni Houlihan, full of heartrending and unforgivable wrongs; young India transcended its realities in the worship of Bande Mataram.

The essential idea of nineteenth-century nationalism was the "legitimate claim" of every nation to complete sovereignty, the claim of every nation to manage all its affairs within its own territory, regardless of any other nation. The flaw in this idea is that the affairs and interests of every modern community extend to the uttermost parts of the earth. The assassination of Sarajevo in 1914, for example, which caused the great war, produced the utmost distress among the Indian tribes of Labrador because that war interrupted the marketing of the furs upon which they relied for such necessities as ammunition, without which they could not get sufficient food. A world of independent sovereign nations means, therefore, a world of perpetual injuries, a world of states constantly preparing for or waging war. But concurrently and discordantly with the preaching of this nationalism there was, among the stronger nationalities, a vigorous propagation of another set of ideas, the ideas of imperialism, in which a powerful and advanced nation was conceded the right to dominate a group of other less advanced nations or less politically developed nations or peoples whose nationality was still undeveloped, who were expected by the dominating nation to be grateful for its protection and dominance. This use of the word empire was evidently a different one from its former universal significance. The new empires did not even pretend to be a continuation of the world empire of Rome.

These two ideas of nationality and, as the crown of national success, "empire," ruled European political thought, ruled indeed the political thought of the world, throughout the latter half of the nineteenth century, and ruled it to the practical exclusion of any wider conception of a common human welfare. They were plausible and dangerously unsound working ideas. They represented nothing fundamental and inalterable in human nature, and they failed to meet the new needs of world controls and world security that the mechanical revolution was every day making more imperative. They were accepted because people in general had neither the sweeping views that a study of world history can give, nor had they any longer the comprehensive charity of a world religion. Their danger to all the routines of ordinary life was not realized until it was too late.

§ 8

After the middle of the nineteenth century, this world of new powers and old ideas, this fermenting new wine in the old bottles of diplomacy, broke out through the flimsy restraints of the Treaty of Vienna into a series of wars. By an ironical accident the new system of disturbances was preceded by a peace festival in London, the Great Exhibition of 1851.

The moving spirit in this exhibition was Prince Albert of Saxe-Coburg-Gotha, the nephew of Leopold I, the German king who had been placed upon the Belgian throne in 1831, and who was also the maternal uncle of the young Queen Victoria of England. She had become queen in 1837 at the age of eighteen. The two young cousins—they were of the same age—had married in 1840 under their uncle's auspices, and Prince Albert was known to the British as the "Prince Consort."

He was a young man of sound intelligence and exceptional education, and he seems to have been greatly shocked by the mental stagnation into which England had sunken. Oxford and Cambridge, those once starry centres, were still recovering but slowly from the intellectual ebb of the later eighteenth century. At neither university did the annual matriculations number more than four hundred. The examinations were for the most part mere *viva voce* ceremonies. Except for two colleges in London (the University of London) and one in Durham, this was all the education on a university footing that England had to offer. It was very largely the initiative of this scandalized young German who had married the British queen which produced the university commission of 1850, and it was with a view to waking up England further that he promoted the first International Exhibition which was to afford some opportunity for a comparison of the artistic and industrial products of the various European nations.

The project was bitterly opposed. In the House of Commons it was prophesied that England would be overrun by foreign rogues and revolutionaries who would corrupt the morals of the people and destroy all faith and loyalty in the country.

The exhibition was held in Hyde Park in a great building of glass and iron—which afterwards was re-erected as the Crystal Palace. Financially it was a great success. It made many English people realize for the first time that theirs was not the only industrial country in the world, and that commercial prosperity was not a divinely appointed British monopoly. There was the clearest evidence of a Europe recovering steadily from the devastation of the Napoleonic wars, and rapidly overtaking the British lead in trade and manufacture. It was followed directly by the organization of a Science and Art Department (1853), to recover, if possible, the educational leeway that Britain had lost.

The exhibition released a considerable amount of international talk and sentiment. It had already found expression in the work of such young poets as Tennyson, who had glanced down the vista of the future.

> "Till the war-drums throb'd no longer, and the battle-flags
> were furl'd.
> In the Parliament of man, the Federation of the world."

There was much shallow optimism on the part of comfortable people just then. Peace seemed to be more secure than it had been for a long time. The social gales of 1848 had blown, and, it seemed, blown themselves out. Nowhere had the revolution succeeded. In France it had been betrayed a second time by a Bonaparte, a nephew of the first Napoleon, but a much more supple man. He had posed as a revolutionary while availing himself of the glamour of his name; he had twice attempted raids on France during the Orleans monarchy. He had written a manual of artillery to link himself to his uncle's prestige, and he had also published an account of what he alleged to be Napoleonic views, *Des Idées Napoléoniennes* in which he jumbled up socialism, socialistic reform, and pacificism with the Napoleonic legend. The republic of 1848 was soon in difficulties with crude labour experiments, and in October he was able to re-enter the country and stand for election as President. He took an oath as President to be faithful to the democratic republic, and to regard as enemies all who attempted to change the form of government. In four years' time (December, 1852) he was Emperor of the French.

At first he was regarded with considerable suspicion by Queen Victoria, or rather by Baron Stockmar, the friend and servant of King Leopold of Belgium, and the keeper of the international conscience of the British queen and her consort. All this group of Saxe-Coburg-Gotha people had a reasonable and generous enthusiasm for the unity and well-being of Germany—upon liberal lines—and they were disposed to be alarmed at this Bonapartist revival. Lord Palmerston, the British foreign minister, was, on the other hand, friendly with the usurper from the outset; he offended the queen by sending amiable dispatches to the French President without submitting them for her examination and so giving her sufficient time to consult Stockmar upon them, and he was obliged to resign. But subsequently the British Court veered round to a more cordial attitude to the new adventurer. The opening years of his reign promised a liberal monarchy rather than a Napoleonic career; a government of "cheap bread, great public works, and holidays,"[1] and he expressed himself warmly in favour of the idea of nationalism, which was naturally a very acceptable idea to any liberal

[1] Albert Thomas in the *Encyclopaedia Britannica.*

German intelligence. There had been a brief all-German parliament at Frankfort in 1848, which was overthrown in 1849 by the Prussian monarchy.

Before 1848 all the great European courts of the Vienna settlement had been kept in a kind of alliance by the fear of a

second and more universal democratic revolution. After the revolutionary failures of 1848 this fear was lifted, and they were free to resume the scheming and counter-scheming of the days before 1789—with the vastly more powerful armies and fleets the first Napoleonic phase had given them. The game of Great Powers was resumed with zest, after an interval of sixty years, and it continued until it produced the catastrophe of 1914.

The Tsar of Russia, Nicholas I, was the first to move towards war. He resumed the traditional thrust of Peter the Great towards Constantinople. Nicholas invented the phrase of the "sick man of Europe" for the Sultan, and, finding an excuse in the misgovernment of the Christian population of the Turkish empire, he occupied the Danubian principalities in 1853. European diplomatists found themselves with a

question of quite the eighteenth-century pattern. The designs of Russia were understood to clash with the designs of France in Syria, and to threaten the Mediterranean route to India of Great Britain, and the outcome was an alliance of France and England to bolster up Turkey and a war, the Crimean War, which ended in the repulse of Russia. One might have thought that the restraint of Russia was rather the business of Austria and Germany, but the passion of the foreign offices of

France and England for burning their fingers in Russian affairs has always been very difficult to control.

The next phase of interest in this revival of the Great Power drama was the exploitation by the Emperor Napoleon III and the king of the small kingdom of Sardinia in North Italy, of the inconveniences and miseries of the divided state of Italy, and particularly of the Austrian rule in the north. The King of Sardinia, Victor Emmanuel, made an old-time bargain for Napoleon's help in return for the provinces of Nice and Savoy. The war between France and Sardinia on the one hand, and Austria on the other, broke out in 1859, and was over in a few weeks. The Austrians were badly beaten at Magenta and Solferino. Then, being threatened by Prussia on the Rhine, Napoleon made peace, leaving Sardinia the richer for Lombardy.

The next move in the game of Victor Emmanuel, and of his chief minister Cavour, was an insurrectionary movement in Sicily led by the great Italian patriot Garibaldi. Sicily and Naples were liberated, and all Italy, except only Rome (which remained loyal to the Pope) and Venetia, which was held by the Austrians, fell to the king of Sardinia. A general Italian parliament met at Turin in 1861, and Victor Emmanuel became the first king of Italy.

But now the interest in this game of European diplomacy shifted to Germany. Already the common sense of the natural political map had asserted itself. In 1848 all Germany, including, of course, German Austria, was for a time united under the Frankfort parliament. But that sort of union was particularly offensive to all the German courts and foreign offices; they did not want a Germany united by the will of its people, they wanted Germany united by legal and diplomatic action—as Italy was being united. In 1848 the German parliament had insisted that the largely German provinces of Schleswig-Holstein, which had been in the German Bund, must belong to Germany. It had ordered the Prussian army to occupy them, and the king of Prussia had refused to take his orders from the German parliament, and so had precipitated the downfall of that body. Now the King of Denmark, Christian IX, for no conceivable motive except the natural folly of kings, embarked upon a campaign of annoyance against the Germans in these two duchies. Prussian affairs were then very much in the hands of a minister of the seventeenth-century type, von Bismarck (count in 1865, prince in 1871), and he saw brilliant opportunities in this trouble. He became the champion of the German nationality in these duchies—it must be remembered that the King of Prussia had refused to undertake this rôle for democratic Germany in 1848—and he persuaded Austria to side with Prussia in a military intervention. Denmark had no chance against these Great Powers; she was easily beaten and obliged to relinquish the duchies. Then Bismarck picked a quarrel with Austria for the possession of these two small states. So he brought about a needless and fratricidal war of Germans for the greater glory of Prussia and the ascendancy of the Hohenzollern dynasty in Germany. German writers of a romantic turn of mind represent Bismarck as a great statesman planning the unity of Germany; but indeed he was doing nothing of the kind. The unity of Germany was a reality in 1848. It was and is in the nature of things. The Prussian monarchy was simply delaying the inevitable in order to seem to achieve it in Prussian fashion. That is why, when at last Germany was unified, instead of bearing the likeness of a modern civilized people, it presented itself to the world with the face of this archaic Bismarck, with a fierce moustache, huge jack boots, a spiked helmet, and a sword.

In this war between Prussia and Austria, Prussia had for an ally Italy; most of the smaller German states, who dreaded the schemes of Prussia, fought on the side of Austria. The reader will naturally want to know why Napoleon III did not grasp this admirable occasion for statecraft and come into the war to his own advantage. All the rules of the Great Power game required that he should. But Napoleon, unhappily for himself, had got his fingers in a trap on the other side of the Atlantic, and was in no position to intervene.

In order to understand the entanglement of this shifty gentleman, it is necessary to explain that the discord in interests between the northern and southern states of the American union, due to the economic differences based on slavery, had at last led to open civil war. The federal system established in 1789 had to fight the secessionist efforts of the confederated slave-holding states. We have traced the causes of that great struggle in Chapter XXXVI, § 6; its course we cannot relate here, nor tell how President Lincoln (born 1809, died 1865, president from 1861) rose to greatness, how the republic was cleansed from the stain of slavery, and how the federal government of the union was preserved. The story of President Lincoln is in itself a great epic of union and order threatened and saved, and it is with reluctance that it is treated so briefly here. But in this *Outline* we must cling closely to our main story.

For four long years (1861-65) this American civil war swung to and fro, through the rich woods and over the hills of Virginia between Washington and Richmond, until at last the secessionist left was thrust back and broken, and Sherman, the unionist general, swept across Georgia to the sea in the rear of the main confederate (secessionist) armies. All the elements of reaction in Europe rejoiced during the four years of republican dissension; the British aristocracy openly sided with the confederate states, and the British Government permitted several privateers, and particularly the *Alabama,* to be launched in England to attack the federal shipping. Napoleon III was even more rash in his assumption that after all the new world had fallen before the old. The sure shield of the Monroe Doctrine, it seemed to him, was thrust aside for good, the Great Powers might meddle again in America, and the blessings of an adventurous monarchy be restored there. A pretext for interference was found in certain liberties taken with the property of foreigners by the Mexican president. A joint expedition of French, British, and Spanish occupied Vera Cruz, but Napoleon's projects were too bold for his allies, and they withdrew when it became clear that he contemplated nothing less than the establishment of a Mexican empire. This he did, after much stiff fighting, making the Archduke Maximilian of Austria Emperor of Mexico in 1864. The French forces, however, remained in effectual possession of the country, and a crowd of French speculators poured into Mexico to exploit its mines and resources.

Bismarck

But in April, 1865, the civil war in the United States was brought to an end with the surrender of the great southern commander, General Lee, at Appomattox Court House, and the little group of eager Europeans in possession of Mexico found themselves faced by the victorious federal government in a thoroughly grim mood, with a large, dangerous-looking army in hand. The French imperialists were bluntly given the alternative of war with the United States or clearing out of America. In effect this was an instruction to go. This was the entanglement which prevented Napoleon III from interference between Prussia and Austria in 1866, and this was the reason why Bismarck precipitated his struggle with Austria.

While Prussia was fighting Austria, Napoleon III was trying to escape with dignity from the briars of Mexico. He invented a shabby quarrel upon financial grounds with Maximilian and withdrew the French troops. Then, by all the rules of kingship, Maximilian should have abdicated. But instead he made a fight for his empire; he was defeated by his recalcitrant subjects, caught, and shot as a public nuisance in 1867. So the peace of President Monroe was restored to the new world. There remained only one monarchy in America, the empire of Brazil, where a branch of the Portuguese royal family continued to reign until 1889. In that year the emperor was quietly packed off to Paris, and Brazil came into line with the rest of the continent.

But while Napoleon was busy with his American adventure, Prussia and Italy were snatching victory over the Austrians (1866). Italy was badly beaten at Custozza and in the naval battle of Lissa, but the Austrian army was so crushed by the Prussian at the battle of Sadowa that Austria made an abject surrender. Italy gained the province of Venetia, so making one more step towards unity—only Rome and Trieste and a few small towns on the north and north-western frontiers remained—and Prussia became the head of a North German Confederation, from which Bavaria, Württemberg, Baden, Hesse, and Austria were excluded.

Four years later came the next step towards the natural political map of Europe, when Napoleon III plunged into war against Prussia. A kind of self-destroying foolishness urged him to do this. He came near to this war in 1867 so soon as he was free from Mexico, by demanding Luxembourg for France; he embarked upon it in 1870, when a cousin of the king of Prussia became a candidate for the vacant throne of Spain. Napoleon had some theory in his mind that Austria, Bavaria, Württemberg, and the other states outside the North German Confederation would side with him against Prussia. He probably thought this would happen because he wanted it to happen. But since 1848 the Germans, so far as foreign meddling was concerned, had been in spirit a united people; Bismarck was merely imposing the Hohenzollern monarchy, with pomp, ceremony, and bloodshed, upon accomplished facts. All Germany sided with Prussia.

Early in August, 1870, the united German forces invaded France. After the battles of Wörth and Gravelotte, one French army under Bazaine was forced into Metz and surrounded there, and, on September 1st, a second, with which was Napoleon, was defeated and obliged to capitulate at Sedan. Paris found herself bare to the invader. For a second time the promises of Napoleonism had failed France disastrously. On September 4th, France declared herself a republic again, and thus regenerated, prepared to fight for existence against triumphant Prussianism. For though it was a united Germany that had overcome French imperialism, it had Prussia in the saddle. The army in Metz capitulated in October; Paris, after a siege and bombardment, surrendered in January, 1871.

With pomp and ceremony, in the Hall of Mirrors at Versailles, amidst a great array of military uniforms, the King of Prussia was declared German Emperor, and Bismarck and the sword of the Hohenzollerns claimed the credit for that German unity which a common language and literature had long since assured.

The peace of Frankfort was a Hohenzollern peace. Bismarck had availed himself of the national feeling of Germany to secure the aid of the South German states, but he had no grasp of the essential forces that had given victory to him and to his royal master. The power that had driven Prussia to victory was the power of the natural political map of Europe insisting upon the unity of the German-speaking peoples. In the east, Germany was already sinning against that natural map by her administration of Posen and other Polish districts. Now greedy for territory, and particularly for iron mines, she annexed a considerable area of French-speaking Lorraine, including Metz, and Alsace, which, in spite of its German speech, was largely French in sympathy. Inevitably there was a clash between German rulers and French subjects in these annexed provinces; inevitably the wrongs and bitterness of the subjugated France of Lorraine echoed in Paris and kept alive the passionate resentment of the French. . . .

The natural map had already secured political recognition in the Austrian Empire after Sadowa (1866). Hungary, which had been subordinated to Austria, was erected into a kingdom on an equal footing with Austria, and the Empire of Austria had become the "dual monarchy" of Austria-Hungary. But in the south-east of this empire, and over the Turkish empire, the boundaries and subjugations of the conquest period still remained.

A fresh upthrust of the natural map began in 1875, when the Christian races in the Balkans, and particularly the Bulgarians, became restless and insurgent. The Turks adopted violent repressive measures, and embarked upon massacres of Bulgarians on an enormous scale. Thereupon Russia intervened (1877), and after a year of costly warfare obliged the Turks to sign the treaty of San Stefano, which was, on the whole, a sensible treaty, breaking up the artificial Turkish Empire, and to a large extent establishing the natural map. But it had become the tradition of British policy to thwart "the designs of Russia"—heaven knows why!—whenever Russia appeared to have a design, and the British foreign office, under the premiership of Lord Beaconsfield, intervened with a threat of war if a considerable restoration of the Turks' facilities for exaction, persecution, and massacre was not made. For a time war seemed very probable. The British music-halls, those lamps to British foreign policy, were lit with patriotic fire, and the London errand-boy on his rounds was inspired to chant, with the simple dignity of a great people conscious of its high destinies, a song declaring that:

"We don't want to fight, but, by Jingo,[1] if we do,
We got the ships, we got the men, we got the munn-aye too" . . .

and so on to a climax:

"The Russ'ns shall not 'ave Con-stan-te-no - - - ple."

[1] Hence "Jingo" for any rabid patriot.

In consequence of this British opposition, a conference was assembled in 1878 at Berlin to revise the treaty of San Stefano, chiefly in the interests of the Turkish and Austrian monarchies, the British acquired the island of Cyprus, to which they had no sort of right whatever, and which has never been of the slightest use to them, and Lord Beaconsfield returned triumphantly from the Berlin Conference, to the extreme ex-

asperation of Mr. Gladstone, with what the British were given to understand at the time was "Peace with Honour."

This treaty of Berlin was the second main factor, the peace of Frankfort being the first, in bringing about the great war of 1914-18.

These thirty years after 1848 are years of very great interest to the student of international political methods. Released from their terror of a world-wide insurrection of the common people, the governments of Europe were doing their best to resume the game of Great Powers that had been so rudely interrupted by the American and French revolutions. But it looked much more like the old game than it was in reality. The mechanical revolution was making war a far more complete disturbance of the general life than it had ever been before, and the proceedings of the diplomatists were ruled, in spite of their efforts to disregard the fact, by imperatives that Charles V and Louis XIV had never known. Irritation with misgovernment was capable of far better organization and far more effective expression than it had ever been before. Statesmen dressed this up as the work of the spirit of Nationalism, but there were times and occasions when that costume wore very thin. The grand monarchs of the seventeenth and eighteenth centuries had seemed to be free to do this or that, to make war or to keep the peace, to conquer this province or cede that as they willed; but such a ruler as Napoleon III went from one proceeding to another with something of the effect of a man who feels his way among things unseen.

None of these European governments in the nineteenth century was in fact a free agent. We look to-day at the maps of Europe since 1814, we compare them with the natural map, and we see that the game the Great Powers played was indeed a game of foregone conclusions. Whatever arrangements they made that were in accordance with the natural political map of the world, and the trend towards educational democracy, held, and whatever arrangements they made contrary to these things, collapsed. We are forced, therefore, to the conclusion that all the diplomatic fussing, posturing, and scheming, all the intrigue and bloodshed of these years, all the monstrous turmoil and waste of kings and armies, all the wonderful attitudes, deeds, and schemes of the Cavours, Bismarcks, Disraelis, Bonapartes, and the like "great men," might very well have been avoided altogether had Europe but had the sense to instruct a small body of ordinarily honest ethnologists, geographers, and sociologists to draw out its proper boundaries and prescribe suitable forms of government in a reasonable manner. The romantic phase in history had come to an end. A new age was beginning with new and greater imperatives, and these nineteenth-century statesmen were but pretending to control events.

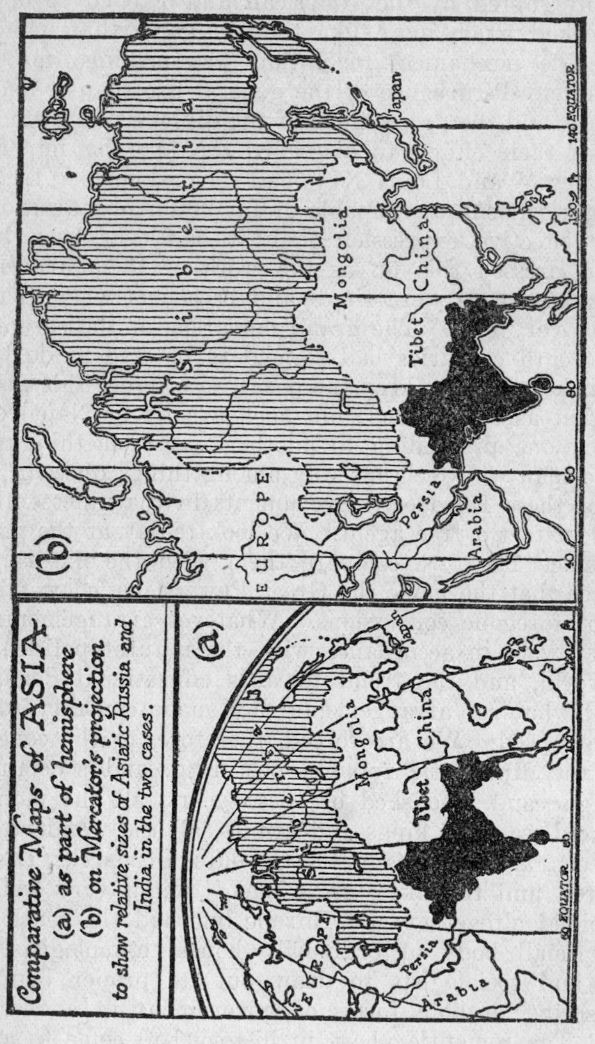

Comparative Maps of ASIA
(a) as part of hemisphere
(b) on Mercator's projection
to show relative sizes of Asiatic Russia and India in the two cases.

§ 9

We have suggested that in the political history of Europe between 1848 and 1878, the mechanical revolution was not yet producing any very revolutionary changes. The post-revolutionary Great Powers were still going on within boundaries of practically the same size and with much the same formalities as they had done in pre-revolutionary times. But where the increased speed and certainty of transport and telegraphic communications were already producing very considerable changes of condition and method, was in the overseas enterprises of Britain and the other European powers, and in the reaction of Asia and Africa to Europe.

The end of the eighteenth century was a period of disrupting empires and disillusioned expansionists. The long and tedious journey between Britain and Spain and their colonies in America prevented any really free coming and going between the home land and the daughter lands, and so the colonies separated into new and distinct communities, with distinctive ideas and interests and even modes of speech. As they grew they strained more and more at the feeble and uncertain link of shipping that joined them. Weak trading-posts in the wilderness, like those of France in Canada, or trading establishments in great alien communities, like those of Britain in India, might well cling for bare existence to the nation which gave them support and a reason for their existence. That much and no more seemed to many thinkers in the early part of the nineteenth century to be the limit set to overseas rule. In 1820 the sketchy great European "empires" outside of Europe that had figured so bravely in the maps of the middle eighteenth century, had shrunken to very small dimensions. Only the Russian sprawled as large as ever across Asia. It sprawled much larger in the imaginations of many Europeans than in reality, because of their habit of studying the geography of the world upon Mercator's projection, which enormously exaggerated the size of Siberia.

The British Empire in 1815 consisted of the thinly populated coastal river and lake regions of Canada, and a great hinterland of wilderness in which the only settlements as yet were the fur-trading stations of the Hudson Bay Company, about a third of the Indian peninsula, under the rule of the

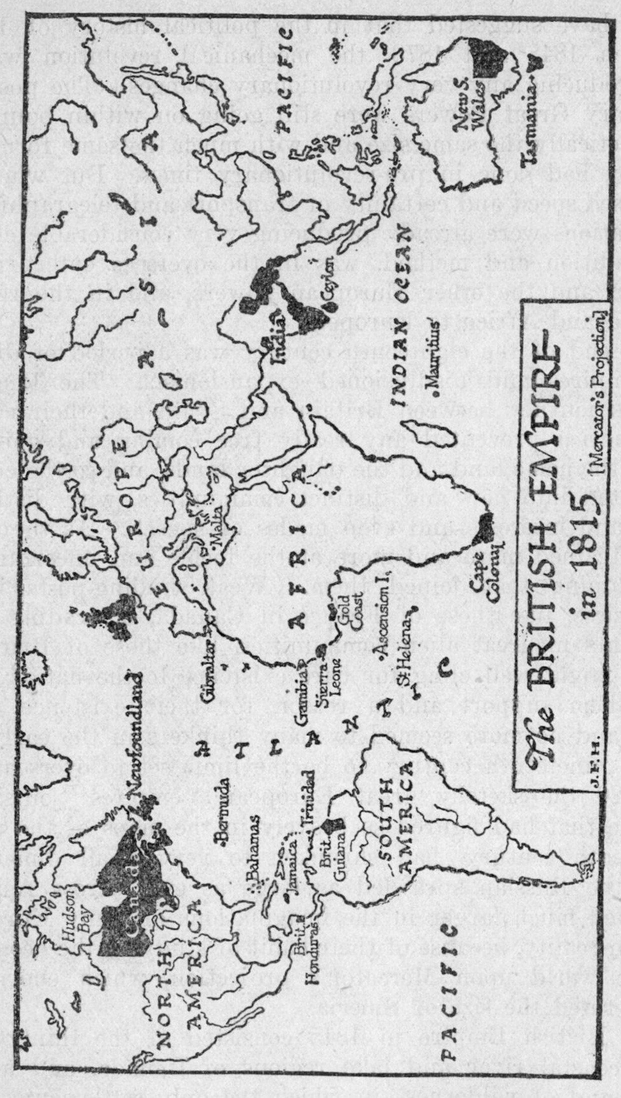
The BRITISH EMPIRE in 1815
[Mercator's Projection]
J.F.H.
NORTH AMERICA
Hudson Bay
Canada
Newfoundland
Bermuda
Bahamas
Jamaica
Brit. Honduras
Trinidad
Brit. Guiana
SOUTH AMERICA
PACIFIC
ATLANTIC
EUROPE
Gibraltar
Malta
Gambia
Sierra Leone
Gold Coast
Ascension I.
St. Helena
AFRICA
Cape Colony
ASIA
India
Ceylon
INDIAN OCEAN
Mauritius
PACIFIC
New S. Wales
Tasmania

East India Company, the coast districts of the Cape of Good Hope inhabited by blacks and rebellious-spirited Dutch settlers; a few trading stations on the coast of West Africa, the rock of Gibraltar, the island of Malta, Jamaica, a few minor slave-labour possessions in the West Indies, British Guiana in South America, and, on the other side of the world, two dumps for convicts at Botany Bay in Australia and in Tasmania. Spain retained Cuba and a few settlements in the Philippine Islands. Portugal had in Africa some vestiges of her ancient claims. Holland had various islands and possessions in the East Indies and Dutch Guiana, and Denmark an island or so in the West Indies. France had one or two West Indian Islands and French Guiana. This seemed to be as much as the European powers needed, or were likely to acquire of the rest of the world. Only the East India Company showed any spirit of expansion.

In India, as we have already told, a peculiar empire was being built up, not by the British peoples, nor by the British Government, but by this company of private adventurers with their monopoly and royal charter. The company had been forced to become a military and political power during the years of Indian division and insecurity that followed the break-up of India after the death of Aurangzeb in 1707. It had learnt to trade in states and peoples during the eighteenth century. Clive founded, Warren Hastings organized, this strange new sort of empire; French rivalry was defeated, as we have already told; and by 1798, Lord Mornington, afterwards the Marquis Wellesley, the elder brother of that General Wellesley who became the Duke of Wellington, became Governor-General of India, and set the policy of the company definitely upon the line of replacing the fading empire of the Great Mogul by its own rule. Napoleon's expedition to Egypt was a direct attack upon the empire of this British company. While Europe was busy with the Napoleonic wars, the East India Company, under a succession of governors-general, was playing much the same rôle in India that had been played before by Turkoman and such-like invaders from the north, but playing it with a greater efficiency and far less violence and cruelty. And after the peace of Vienna it went on, levying its revenues, making wars, sending ambassadors to Asiatic powers, a quasi-independent state, a state, however, with a marked disposition to send wealth westward.

In a previous chapter we have sketched the break-up of the empire of the Great Mogul and the appearance of the Mahratta states, the Rajput principalities, the Moslem kingdoms of Oudh and Bengal, and the Sikhs. We cannot tell here in any detail how the British company made its way to supremacy sometimes as the ally of this power, sometimes as that, and finally as the conqueror of all. Its power spread to Assam, Sind, Oudh. The map of India began to take on the outlines familiar to the English schoolboy of to-day, a patchwork of native states embraced and held together by the great provinces under direct British rule. . . .

Now as this strange unprecedented empire of the company grew in the period between 1800 and 1858, the mechanical revolution was quietly abolishing the great distance that had once separated India and Britain. In the old days the rule of the company had interfered little in the domestic life of the Indian states; it had given India foreign overlords, but India was used to foreign overlords, and had hitherto assimilated them; these Englishmen came into the country young, lived there most of their lives, and became a part of its system. But now the mechanical revolution began to alter this state of affairs. It became easier for the British officials to go home and to have holidays in Europe, easier for them to bring out wives and families; they ceased to be Indianized; they remained more conspicuously foreign and western—and there were more of them. And they began to interfere more vigorously with Indian customs. Magical and terrible things like the telegraph and the railway arrived. Christian missions became offensively busy. If they did not make very many converts, at least they made sceptics among the adherents of the older faiths. The young men in the towns began to be "Europeanized" to the great dismay of their elders.

India had endured many changes of rulers before, but never the sort of changes in her ways that these things portended. The Moslem teachers and the Brahmins were alike alarmed, and the British were blamed for the progress of mankind. Conflicts of economic interests grew more acute with the increasing nearness of Europe; Indian industries, and particularly the ancient cotton industry, suffered from legislation that favoured the British manufacturer. A piece of incredible folly on the part of the company precipitated an outbreak. To the Brahmin a cow is sacred; to the Moslem the pig is unclean. A new rifle, needing greased cartridges—which the men had to bite—was served out to the company's Indian soldiers; the troops discovered that their cartridges were greased with the fat of cows and swine. This discovery precipitated a revolt of the company's Indian army, the Indian Mutiny (1857). First the troops mutinied at Meerut. Then Delhi rose to restore the empire of the Great Mogul. . . .

The British public suddenly discovered India. They became aware of that little garrison of British people, far away in that strange land of fiery dust and weary sunshine, fighting for life against dark multitudes of assailants. How they got there and what right they had there, the British public did not ask. The love of one's kin in danger overrides such questions. There were massacres and cruelties. 1857 was a year of passionate anxiety in Great Britain. With mere handfuls of troops the British leaders, and notably Lawrence and Nicholson, did amazing things. They did not sit down to be besieged while the mutineers organized and gathered prestige; that would have lost them India for ever. They attacked often against overwhelming odds. "Clubs, not spades, are trumps," said Lawrence. The Sikhs, the Gurkhas, the Punjab troops stuck to the British. The south remained tranquil. Of the massacres of Cawnpore and Lucknow in Oudh, and how a greatly outnumbered force of British troops besieged and stormed Delhi, other histories must tell. By April, 1859, the last embers of the blaze had been stamped out, and the British were masters of India again. In no sense had the mutiny been a popular insurrection; it was a mutiny merely of the Bengal Army, due largely to the unimaginative rule of the company officials. Its story abounds in instances of Indian help and kindness to British fugitives. But it was a warning.

The direct result of the mutiny was the annexation of the Indian Empire to the British Crown. By the Act entitled *An Act for the Better Government of India,* the Governor-General became a Viceroy representing the Sovereign, and the place of the company was taken by a Secretary of State for India responsible to the British Parliament. In 1877, Lord Beaconsfield, to complete this work, caused Queen Victoria to be proclaimed Empress of India.

Upon these extraordinary lines India and Britain are linked

at the present time. India is still the empire of the Great Mogul, expanded, but the Great Mogul has been replaced by the "crowned republic" of Great Britain. India is an autocracy without an autocrat. Its rule combines the disadvantage of absolute monarchy with the impersonality and irresponsibility of democratic officialdom. The Indian with a complaint to make has no visible monarch to go to; his Emperor is a golden symbol; he must circulate pamphlets in England or inspire a question in the British House of Commons. The more occupied Parliament is with British affairs, the less attention India will receive, and the more she will be at the mercy of her small group of higher officials.

This is manifestly impossible as a permanent state of affairs. Indian life, whatever its restraints, is moving forward with the rest of the world; India has an increasing service of newspapers, an increasing number of educated people affected by Western ideas, and an increasing sense of a common grievance against her government. There has been little or no corresponding advance in the education and quality of the British official in India during the past seventy years. His tradition is a high one; he is often a man of exceptional quality, but the system is unimaginative and inflexible. Moreover, the military power that stands behind these officials has developed neither in character nor intelligence during the last century. No other class has been so stagnant intellectually as the British military caste. Confronted with a more educated India, the British military man, uneasily aware of his educational defects and constantly apprehensive of ridicule, has in the last few years displayed a disposition towards spasmodic violence that has had some very lamentable results. For a time the great war altogether diverted what small amount of British public attention was previously given to India, and drew away the more intelligent military men from her service. During those years, and the feverish years of unsettlement that followed, things occurred in India, the massacre of an unarmed crowd at Amritzar in which nearly two thousand people were killed or wounded, floggings and humiliating outrages, a sort of official's Terror, that produced a profound moral shock when at last the Hunter Commission of 1919 brought them before the home public. In liberal-minded Englishmen, who have been wont to regard their empire as an incipient league of free peoples, this revelation of the barbaric quality in its administrators produced a very understandable dismay. . . .

But the time has not yet come for writing the chapter of history that India is opening for herself. . . . We cannot discuss here in detail the still unsettled problems of the new India that struggles into being. Already in the Government of India Act of 1919 we may have the opening of a new and happier era that may culminate in a free and willing group of Indian peoples taking an equal place among the confederated states of the world. . . .

The growth of the British Empire in directions other than that of India was by no means so rapid during the earlier half of the nineteenth century. A considerable school of political thinkers in Britain was disposed to regard overseas possessions as a source of weakness to the kingdom. The Australian settlements developed slowly until in 1842 the discovery of valuable copper mines, and in 1851 of gold, gave them a new importance. Improvements in transport were also making Australian wool an increasingly marketable commodity in Europe. Canada, too, was not remarkably progressive until 1849; it was troubled by dissensions between its French and British inhabitants, there were several serious revolts, and it was only in 1867 that a new constitution creating a Federal Dominion of Canada relieved its internal strains. It was the railway that altered the Canadian outlook. It enabled Canada, just as it enabled the United States, to expand westward, to market its corn and other produce in Europe, and in spite of its swift and extensive growth, to remain in language and sympathy and interests one community. The railway, the steamship, and the telegraphic cable were indeed changing all the conditions of colonial development.

Before 1840, English settlements had already begun in New Zealand, and a New Zealand Land Company had been formed to exploit the possibilities of the island. In 1840 New Zealand also was added to the colonial possessions of the British Crown.

Canada, as we have noted, was the first of the British possessions to respond richly to the new economic possibilities the new methods of transport were opening. Presently the republics of South America, and particularly the Argentine Republic, began to feel, in their cattle trade and coffee growing, the increased nearness of the European market. Hitherto the chief commodities that had attracted the European powers into unsettled and barbaric regions had been gold or other metals, spices, ivory, or slaves. But in the latter quarter of the nineteenth century the increase of the European populations was obliging their governments to look abroad for staple foods; and the growth of scientific industrialism was creating a demand for new raw materials, fats and greases of every kind, rubber, and other hitherto disregarded substances. It was plain that Great Britain and Holland and Portugal were reaping a great and growing commercial advantage from their very considerable control of tropical and sub-tropical products. After 1871 Germany and presently France and later Italy began to look for unannexed raw-material areas, or for Oriental countries capable of profitable modernization.

So began a fresh scramble all over the world, except in the American region where the Monroe Doctrine now barred such adventures, for politically unprotected lands. Close to Europe was the continent of Africa, full of vaguely known possibilities. In 1850 it was a continent of black mystery; only Egypt and the coast were known. A map must show the greatness of the European ignorance at that time. It would need a book as long as this *Outline* to do justice to the amazing story of the explorers and adventurers who first pierced this cloud of darkness, and to the political agents, administrators, traders, settlers, and scientific men who followed in their track. Wonderful races of men like the pigmies, strange beasts like the okapi, marvellous fruits and flowers and insects, terrible diseases, astounding scenery of forest and mountain, enormous inland seas and gigantic rivers and cascades were revealed; a whole new world. Even remains (at Zimbabwe) of some unrecorded and vanished civilization, the southward enterprise of an early people, were discovered. Into this new world came the Europeans, and found the rifle already there in the hands of the Arab slave-traders, and negro life in disorder. By 1900, as our second map must show, all Africa was mapped, explored, estimated, and divided between the European powers, divided with much snarling and disputation into portions that left each power uneasy or discontented. Little heed was given to the welfare of the natives in this scramble. The Arab slaver was indeed curbed rather than expelled, but the greed for rubber, which was a wild product collected under compulsion by the natives in the Belgian Congo, a greed exacerbated by the pitiless avarice of the King of the Belgians, and the clash of inexperienced European administrators with the native population in many other annexations, led to horrible atrocities. No European power has perfectly clean hands in this matter.

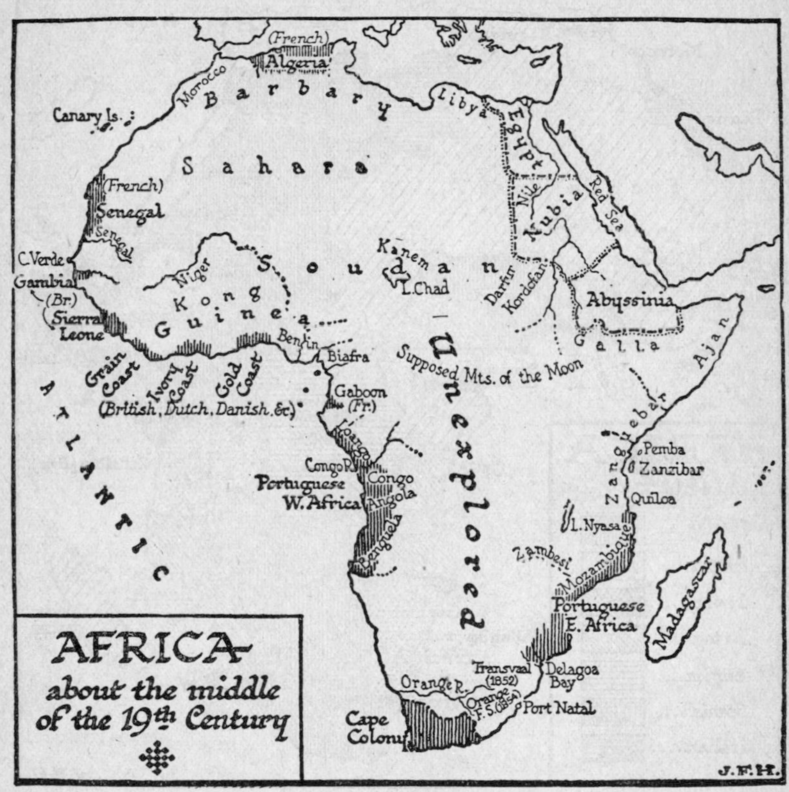

AFRICA about the middle of the 19th Century

We cannot tell here in any detail how Great Britain got possession of Egypt in 1883, and remained there in spite of the fact that Egypt was technically a part of the Turkish Empire, nor how nearly this scramble led to war between France and Great Britain in 1898, when a certain Colonel Marchand, crossing Central Africa from the west coast, tried at Fashoda to seize the Upper Nile. In Uganda the French Catholic and the British Anglican missionaries disseminated a form of Christianity so heavily charged with the spirit of Napoleon, and so finely insistent upon the nuances of doctrine, that a few years after its first glimpse of European civilization, Mengò, the capital of Uganda, was littered with dead "Protestants" and "Catho-

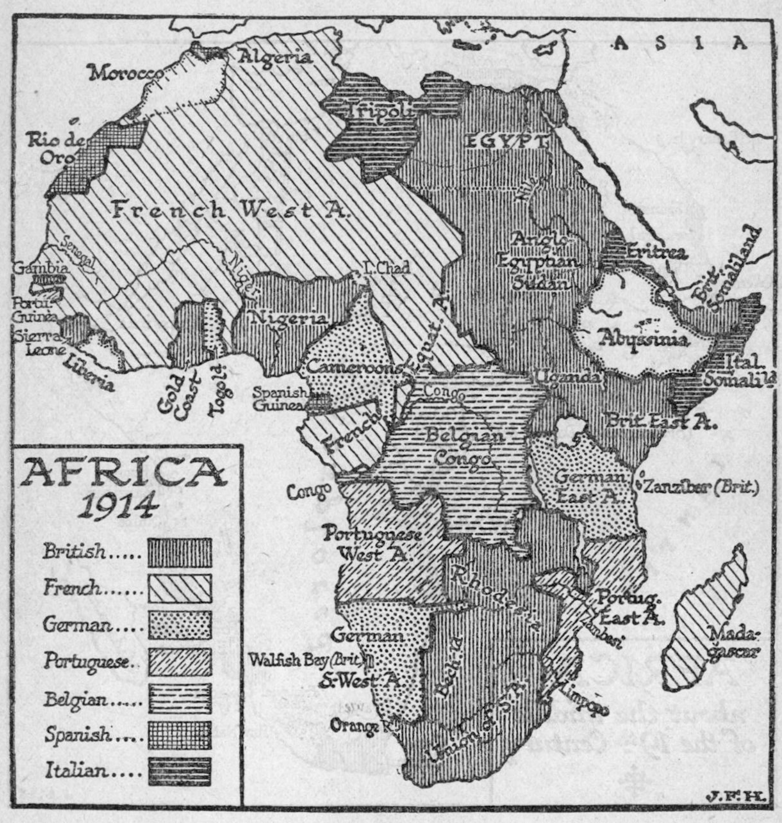

lics" extremely difficult to distinguish from the entirely unspiritual warriors of the old régime.

Nor can we tell how the British Government first let the Boers, or Dutch settlers, of the Orange River district and the Transvaal set up independent republics in the inland parts of South Africa, and then repented and annexed the Transvaal Republic in 1877; nor how the Transvaal Boers fought for freedom and won it after the Battle of Majuba Hill (1881). Majuba Hill was made to rankle in the memory of the English people by a persistent press campaign. A war with both republics broke out in 1899, a three years' war enormously costly to the British people, which ended at last in the surrender of the two republics.

Their period of subjugation was a brief one. In 1907, after the downfall of the imperialist government which had conquered them, the Liberals took the South African problem in hand, and these former republics became free and fairly willing associates with Cape Colony and Natal in a confederation of all the states of South Africa as one self-governing republic under the British Crown.

In a quarter of a century the partition of Africa was completed. There remained unannexed three comparatively small countries: Liberia, a settlement of liberated negro slaves on the west coast; Morocco, under a Moslem Sultan; and Abyssinia, a barbaric country, with an ancient and peculiar form of Christianity, which had successfully maintained its independence against Italy at the Battle of Adowa in 1896.

§ 10

It is difficult to believe that any large number of people really accepted this headlong painting of the map of Africa in European colours as a permanent new settlement of the world's affairs, but it is the duty of the historian to record that it was so accepted. There was but a shallow historical background to the European mind in the nineteenth century, hardly any sense of what constitutes an enduring political system, and no habit of penetrating criticism. The quite temporary advantages that the onset of the mechanical revolution in the west had given the European Great Powers over the rest of the old world were regarded by people, blankly ignorant of the great Mongol conquests of the thirteenth and following centuries, as evidences of a permanent and assured leadership. They had no sense of the transferability of science and its fruits. They did not realize that Chinamen and Indians could carry on the work of research as ably as Frenchmen or Englishmen. They believed that there was some innate intellectual drive in the west, and some innate indolence and conservatism in the east, that assured the Europeans a world predominance for ever.

The consequence of this infatuation was that the various European foreign offices set themselves not merely to scramble with the British for the savage and undeveloped regions of the world's surface, but also to carve up the populous and civilized countries of Asia as though these peoples also were no more than raw material for European exploitation. The inwardly precarious but outwardly splendid imperialism of the British ruling class in India, and the extensive and profitable possessions of the Dutch in the East Indies, filled the ruling and mercantile classes of the rival Great Powers with dreams of similar glories in Persia, in the disintegrating Ottoman Empire, and in Further India, China, and Japan. In the closing years of the nineteenth century it was assumed, as the reader may verify by an examination of the current literature of the period, to be a natural and inevitable thing that all the world should fall under European dominion. With a reluctant benevolent effort the European mind prepared itself to take up what Mr. Rudyard Kipling called "the White Man's Burthen"—that is to say, the lordship of the earth. The Powers set themselves to this enterprise in a mood of jostling rivalry, with half-educated or illiterate populations at home, with a mere handful of men, a few thousand at most, engaged in scientific research, with their internal political systems in a state of tension or convulsive change, with a creaking economic system of the most provisional sort, and with their religions far gone in decay. They really believed that the vast populations of eastern Asia could be permanently subordinated to such a Europe.

Even to-day there are many people who fail to grasp the essential facts of this situation. They do not realize that in Asia the average brain is not one whit inferior in quality to the average European brain; that history shows Asiatics to be as bold, as vigorous, as generous, as self-sacrificing, and as capable of strong collective action as Europeans, and that there are and must continue to be a great many more Asiatics than Europeans in the world. It has always been difficult to restrain the leakage of knowledge from one population to another, and now it becomes impossible. Under modern conditions world-wide economic and educational equalization is in the long run inevitable. An intellectual and moral rally of the

Asiatics is going on at the present time. The slight leeway of a century or so, a few decades may recover. At the present time, for example, for one Englishman who knows Chinese thoroughly, or has any intimate knowledge of Chinese life and thought, there are hundreds of Chinamen conversant with everything the English know. The balance of knowledge in favour of India may be even greater. To Britain, India sends students; to India, Britain sends officials, for the most part men untrained in scientific observation. There is no organization whatever for the sending of European students, as students, to examine and inquire into Indian history, archæology, and current affairs or for bringing learned Indians into contact with British students in Britain.

Since the year 1898, the year of the seizure of Kiau-Chau by Germany and of Wei-hai-wei by Britain, and the year after the Russian taking of Port Arthur, events in China have moved more rapidly than in any other country except Japan. A great hatred of Europeans swept like a flame over China, and a political society for the expulsion of Europeans, the Boxers, grew up and broke out into violence in 1900. This was an outbreak of rage and mischief on quite old-fashioned lines. In 1900 the Boxers murdered 250 Europeans and, it is said, nearly 30,000 Christians. China, not for the first time in history, was under the sway of a dowager empress. She was an ignorant woman, but of great force of character and in close sympathy with the Boxers. She supported them, and protected those who perpetrated outrages on the Europeans. All that again is what might have happened in 500 B.C. or thereabouts against the Huns.

Things came to a crisis in 1900. The Boxers became more and more threatening to the Europeans in China. Attempts were made to send up additional European guards to the Peking legations, but this only precipitated matters. The German minister was shot down in the streets of Peking by a soldier of the imperial guard. The rest of the foreign representatives gathered together and made a fortification of the more favourably situated legations and stood a siege of two months. A combined allied force of 20,000 under a German general then marched up to Peking and relieved the legations, and the old Empress fled to Sian-fu, the old capital of Tai-tsung. Some of the European troops committed grave atrocities upon the

Chinese civil population.[1] That brings one up to about the level of 1850, let us say.

There followed the practical annexation of Manchuria by Russia, a squabble among the powers, and in 1904 a British invasion of Tibet, hitherto a forbidden country. But what did not appear on the surface of these events, and what made all these events fundamentally different, was that China now contained a considerable number of able people who had a European education and European knowledge. The Boxer Insurrection subsided, and then the influence of this new factor began to appear in talk of a constitution (1906), in the suppression of opium-smoking, and in educational reforms. A constitution of the Japanese type came into existence in 1909, making China a limited monarchy. But China is not to be moulded to the Japanese pattern, and the revolutionary stir continued. Japan, in her own reorganization, and in accordance with her temperament, had turned her eyes to the monarchist west, but China was looking across the Pacific. In 1911 the essential Chinese revolution began. In 1912 the emperor abdicated, and the greatest community in the world became a republic. The overthrow of the emperor was also the overthrow of the Manchus, and the Mongolian pigtail, which had been worn by the Chinese since 1644, ceased to be compulsory. It continues, however, to be worn by a large proportion of the population.

At the present time it is probable that there is more good brain matter and more devoted men working out the modernization and the reorganization of the Chinese civilization than we should find directed to the welfare of any single European people. China will presently have a modernized practicable script, a press, new and vigorous modern universities, a reorganized industrial system, and a growing body of scientific and economic inquiry. The natural industry and ingenuity of her vast population will be released to co-operate upon terms of equality with the Western world. She may have great internal difficulties ahead of her yet; of that no man can judge. Nevertheless, the time may not be very distant when the Federated States of China may be at one with the United States of America and a pacified and reconciled Europe in upholding the organized peace of the world.

[1] See Putnam Weale's *Indiscreet Letters from Pekin*, a partly fictitious book, but true and vivid in its effects.

§ 11

The pioneer country, however, in the recovery of the Asiatic peoples was not China, but Japan. We have outrun our story in telling of China. Hitherto Japan has played but a small part in this history; her secluded civilization has not contributed very largely to the general shaping of human destinies; she has received much, but she has given little. The original inhabitants of the Japanese Islands were probably a northern people with remote Nordic affinities, the Hairy Ainu. But the Japanese proper are of the Mongolian race. Physically they resemble the Amerindians, and there are many curious resemblances between the prehistoric pottery and so forth of Japan and similar Peruvian products. It is not impossible that they are a back-flow from the trans-Pacific drift of the early heliolithic culture, but they may also have absorbed from the south a Malay and even a Negrito element.

Whatever the origin of the Japanese, there can be no doubt that their civilization, their writing, and their literary and artistic traditions are derived from the Chinese. They were emerging from barbarism in the second and third century of the Christian Era, and one of their earliest acts as a people outside their own country was an invasion of Korea under a queen Jingo, who seems to have played a large part in establishing their civilization. Their history is an interesting and romantic one; they developed a feudal system and a tradition of chivalry; their attacks upon Korea and China are an Eastern equivalent of the English wars in France. Japan was first brought into contact with Europe in the sixteenth century; in 1542 some Portuguese reached it in a Chinese junk, and in 1549 a Jesuit missionary, Francis Xavier, began his teaching there. The Jesuit accounts describe a country greatly devastated by perpetual feudal war. For a time Japan welcomed European intercourse, and the Christian missionaries made a great number of converts. A certain William Adams, of Gillingham, in Kent, became the most trusted European adviser of the Japanese, and showed them how to build big ships. There were voyages in Japanese-built ships to India and Peru. Then arose complicated quarrels between the Spanish Dominicans, the Portuguese Jesuits, and the English and Dutch Protestants, each warning the Japanese against the evil political designs of the others. The Jesuits, in a phase of ascendancy, persecuted and insulted the Buddhists with great acrimony. These troubles interwove with the feudal conflicts of the time. In the end the Japanese came to the conclusion that the Europeans and their Christianity were an intolerable nuisance, and that Catholic Christianity in particular was a mere cloak for the political dreams of the Pope and the Spanish monarchy—already in possession of the Philippine Islands; there was a great and conclusive persecution of the Christians, and in 1638 Japan with the exception of one wretched Dutch factory on the minute island of Deshima in the harbour of Nagasaki was absolutely closed to Europeans, and remained closed for over 200 years. The Dutch on Deshima were exposed to almost unendurable indignities. They had no intercourse with any Japanese except the special officials appointed to deal with them. During those two centuries the Japanese remained as completely cut off from the rest of the world as though they lived upon another planet. It was forbidden to build any ship larger than a mere coasting boat. No Japanese could go abroad, and no European enter the country.

For two centuries Japan remained outside the main current of history. She lived on in a state of picturesque feudalism enlivened by blood feuds, in which about five per cent. of the population, the *samurai,* or fighting men, and the nobles and their families, tyrannized without restraint over the rest of the population. All common men knelt when a noble passed; to betray the slightest disrespect was to risk being slashed to death by his *samurai.* The elect classes lived lives of romantic adventure without one redeeming gleam of novelty; they loved, murdered, and pursued fine points of honour—which probably bored the intelligent ones extremely. We can imagine the wretchedness of a curious mind, tormented by the craving for travel and knowledge, cooped up in these islands of empty romance.

Meanwhile the great world outside went on to wider visions and new powers. Strange shipping became more frequent, passing the Japanese headlands; sometimes ships were wrecked and sailors brought ashore. Through the Dutch settlement at Deshima, their one link with the outer universe, came warnings that Japan was not keeping pace with the power of the Western world. In 1837 a ship sailed into Yedo Bay flying a strange flag of stripes and stars, and carrying some Japanese sailors she had picked up far adrift in the Pacific. She was driven off by a cannon shot. This flag presently reappeared on other ships. One in 1849 came to demand the liberation of eighteen shipwrecked American sailors. Then in 1853 came four American warships under Commodore Perry, and refused to be driven away. He lay at anchor in forbidden waters, and sent messages to the two rulers who at that time shared the control of Japan. In 1854 he returned with ten ships, amazing ships propelled by steam, and equipped with big guns, and he made proposals for trade and intercourse that the Japanese had no power to resist. He landed with a guard of 500 men to sign the treaty. Incredulous crowds watched this visitation from the outer world, marching through the streets.

Russia, Holland, and Britain followed in the wake of America. Foreigners entered the country, and conflicts between them and Japanese gentlemen of spirit ensued. A British subject was killed in a street brawl, and a Japanese town was bombarded by the British (1863). A great nobleman whose estates commanded the Straits of Shimonoseki saw fit to fire on foreign vessels, and a second bombardment by a fleet of British, French, Dutch, and American warships destroyed his batteries and scattered his swordsmen. Finally an allied squadron (1865), at anchor off Kioto, imposed a ratification of the treaties which opened Japan to the world.

The humiliation of the Japanese by these events was intense, and it would seem that the salvation of peoples lies largely in such humiliations. With astonishing energy and intelligence they set themselves to bring their culture and organization up to the level of the European powers. Never in all the history of mankind did a nation make such a stride as Japan then did. In 1866 she was a mediæval people, a fantastic caricature of the extremist romantic feudalism; in 1899 hers was a completely Westernized people, on a level with the most advanced European powers, and well in advance of Russia. She completely dispelled the persuasion that Asia was in some irrevocable way hopelessly behind Europe. She made all European progress seem sluggish and tentative by comparison.

We cannot tell here in any detail of Japan's war with China in 1894-95. It demonstrated the extent of her Westernization. She had an efficient Westernized army and a small but sound fleet. But the significance of her renascence, though it was appreciated by Britain and the United States, who were already treating her as if she were a European state, was not understood by the other Great Powers engaged in the pursuit of new Indias in Asia. Russia was pushing down through Manchuria to Korea, France was already established far to the south in Tonkin and Annam, Germany was prowling hungrily on the look-out for some settlement. The three powers combined to prevent Japan reaping any fruits from the Chinese war, and particularly from establishing herself on the mainland at the points commanding the Japan Sea. She was exhausted by her war with China, and they threatened her with war.

In 1898 Germany descended upon China, and, making the murder of two missionaries her excuse, annexed a portion of the province of Shang-tung. Thereupon Russia seized the Liaotung peninsula, and extorted the consent of China to an extension of her trans-Siberian railway to Port Arthur; and in 1900 she occupied Manchuria. Britain was unable to resist the imitative impulse, and seized the port of Wei-hai-wei (1898). How alarming these movements must have been to every intelligent Japanese a glance at the map will show. They led to a war with Russia which marks an epoch in the history of Asia, the close of the period of European arrogance. The Russian people were, of course, innocent and ignorant of this trouble that was being made for them half-way round the world, and the wiser Russian statesmen were against these foolish thrusts; but a gang of financial adventurers surrounded the Tsar, including the Grand Dukes, his cousins. They had gambled deeply in the prospective looting of Manchuria and China, and they would suffer no withdrawal. So there began a transportation of great armies of Japanese soldiers across the sea to Port Arthur and Korea, and the sending of endless trainloads of Russian peasants along the Siberian railway to die in those distant battlefields.

The Russians, badly led and dishonestly provided, were beaten on sea and land alike. The Russian Baltic Fleet sailed round Africa to be utterly destroyed in the Straits of Tshushima. A revolutionary movement among the common people of Russia, infuriated by this remote and reasonless slaughter, obliged the Tsar to end the war (1905); he returned the southern half of Saghalien, which had been seized by Russia in 1875,

JAPAN
& the Eastern Coast of Asia
SIBERIA
Saghalien
Amur
MANCHURIA
Yezo
Vladivostok
MONGOLIA
SEA of JAPAN
Hondo (Nippon)
Tokio
Yokohama
LIAO-TUNG
KOREA
Pekin
Port Arthur
Tientsin
Wei-hai-wei
YELLOW SEA
SHANTUNG
Kiau-chau
Kioto
Osaka
Shikoku
Tsu-shima Strait
Nagasaki
Kiushiu
Hwang-ho
Nankin
CHINA
Shanghai
Hankau
Yang-tse-kiang
Lu-chu Is.
JAPANESE
Formosa
Si-kiang
Canton
Hong-kong
TONKIN
FRENCH
ANNAM
SOUTH CHINA SEA
Hainan
Philippine Is. (U.S.A.)
Luzon
Manila
Japanese...
Russian...
J.F.H.

evacuated Manchuria, resigned Korea to Japan. The White Man was beginning to drop his load in eastern Asia. For some years, however, Germany remained in uneasy possession of Kiau-Chau.

§ 12

We have already noted how the enterprise of Italy in Abyssinia had been checked at the terrible battle of Adowa (1896), in which over 3,000 Italians were killed and more than 4,000 taken prisoner. The phase of imperial expansion at the expense of organized non-European states was manifestly drawing to a close. It had entangled the quite sufficiently difficult political and social problems of Great Britain, France, Spain, Italy, Germany, and Russia with the affairs of considerable alien, unassimilable, and resentful populations; Great Britain had Egypt (not formally annexed as yet), India, Burmah, and a variety of such minor problems as Malta and Shanghai; France had cumbered herself with Tonkin and Annam in addition to Algiers and Tunis; Spain was newly entangled in Morocco; Italy had found trouble for herself in Tripoli; and German overseas imperialism, though its "place in the sun" seemed a poor one, derived what satisfaction it could from the thought of a prospective war with Japan over Kiau-Chau. All these "subject" lands had populations at a level of intelligence and education very little lower than those of the possessing country; the development of a native press, of a collective self-consciousness, and of demands for self-government was in each case inevitable, and the statesmen of Europe had been far too busy achieving these empires to have any clear ideas of what they would do with them when they got them.

The Western democracies, as they woke up to freedom, discovered themselves "imperial," and were considerably embarrassed by the discovery. The East came to the Western capitals with perplexing demands. In London the common Englishman, much preoccupied by strikes, by economic riddles, by questions of nationalization, municipalization, and the like, found that his path was crossed and his public meetings attended by a large and increasing number of swarthy gentlemen in turbans, fezes, and other strange headgear, all saying in effect: "You have got us. The people who represent your government have destroyed our own government, and prevent us from making a new one. What are you going to do with us?"

§ 13

We may note here briefly the very various nature of the constituents of the British Empire in 1914. It was and is a quite unique political combination; nothing of the sort has ever existed before.

First and central to the whole system was the "crowned republic" of the United British Kingdoms, including (against the will of a considerable part of the Irish people) Ireland. The majority of the British Parliament, made up of the three united parliaments of England, Scotland, and Ireland, determines the headship, the quality and policy of the ministry, and determines it largely on considerations arising out of British domestic politics. It is this ministry which is the effective supreme government, with powers of peace and war, over all the rest of the empire.

Next in order of political importance to the British States were the "crowned republics" of Australia, Canada, Newfoundland (the oldest British possession, 1583), New Zealand, and South Africa, all practically independent and self-governing states in alliance with Great Britain, but each with a representative of the Crown appointed by the Government in office;

Next the Indian Empire, an extension of the empire of the Great Mogul, with its dependent and "protected" states reaching now from Beluchistan to Burmah, and including Aden, in all of which empire the British Crown *and* the Indian Office (under Parliamentary control) played the rôle of the original Turkoman dynasty;

Then the ambiguous possession of Egypt, still nominally a part of the Turkish Empire and still retaining its own monarch, the Khedive, but under almost despotic British official rule;

Then the still more ambiguous "Anglo-Egyptian" Sudan province, occupied and administered jointly by the British and by the (British controlled) Egyptian Government;

Then a number of partially self-governing communities, some British in origin and some not, with elected legislatures and an appointed executive, such as Malta,[1] Jamaica, the Bahamas, and Bermuda;

Then the Crown colonies, in which the rule of the British Home Government (through the Colonial Office) verged on autocracy, as in Ceylon, Trinidad, and Fiji (where there was an appointed council), and Gibraltar and St. Helena (where there was a governor);

Then great areas of (chiefly) tropical lands, raw-product areas, with politically weak and under-civilized native communities, which were nominally protectorates, and administered either by a High Commissioner set over native chiefs (as in Basutoland) or over a chartered company (as in Rhodesia). In some cases the Foreign Office, in some cases the Colonial Office, and in some cases the India Office had been concerned in acquiring the possessions that fell into this last and least definite class of all, but for the most part the Colonial Office was now responsible for them.

It will be manifest, therefore, that no single office and no single brain had ever comprehended the British Empire as a whole. It was a mixture of growths and accumulations entirely different from anything that has ever been called an empire before. It guaranteed a wide peace and security; that is why it was endured and sustained by many men of the "subject" races—in spite of official tyrannies and insufficiencies, and of much negligence on the part of the "home" public. Like the "Athenian empire," it was an overseas empire; its ways were sea ways, and its common link was the British Navy. Like all empires, its cohesion was dependent physically upon a method of communication; the development of seamanship, ship-building, and steamships between the sixteenth and nineteenth centuries had made it a possible and convenient Pax—the "Pax Britannica," and fresh developments of air or swift land transport or of undersea warfare might at any time make it inconvenient or helplessly insecure.

[1] A new and much more liberal Maltese constitution was promulgated in June, 1920, practically putting Malta on the footing of a self-governing colony.

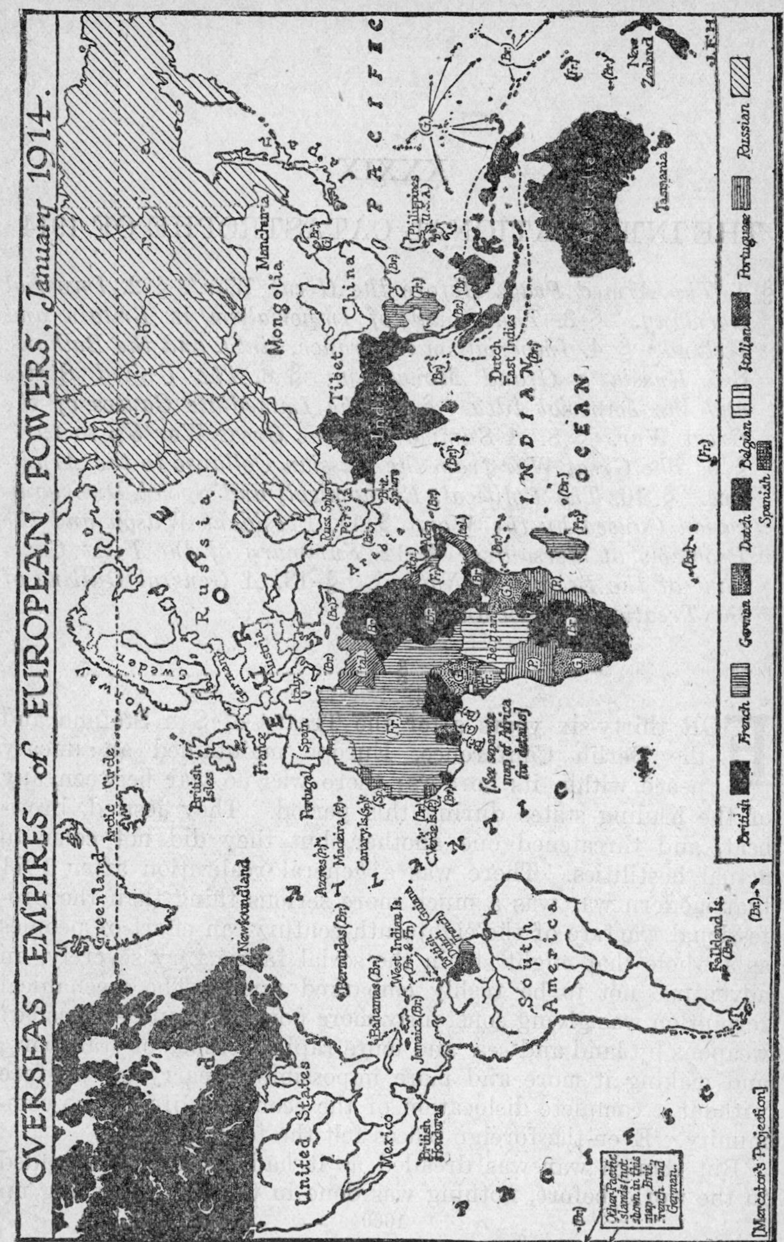
OVERSEAS EMPIRES of EUROPEAN POWERS, January 1914.
British
French
German
Belgian
Dutch
Spanish
Italian
Portuguese
Russian
[Mercator's Projection]
Other Pacific islands (not shown in this map) - Brit. French and German.
[See separate map of Africa for details]
INDIAN OCEAN
Arctic Circle
Greenland
Newfoundland
British Isles
France
Spain
Portugal
Italy
Germany
Austria
Sweden
Norway
Arabia
India
Tibet
China
Mongolia
Manchuria
Dutch East Indies
Philippines (U.S.A.)
Australia
Tasmania
New Zealand
United States
Mexico
British Honduras
South America
Falkland Is. (Br.)
Bermudas (Br.)
Bahamas (Br.)
Jamaica (Br.)
West Indian Is. (Br. & Fr.)
Azores (Pt.)
Madeira (Pt.)
Canary Is. (Sp.)
Belgian

XXXIX

THE INTERNATIONAL CATASTROPHE OF 1914

§ 1. *The Armed Peace Before the Great War.* § 2. *Imperial Germany.* § 3. *The Spirit of Imperialism in Britain and Ireland.* § 4. *Imperialism in France, Italy, and the Balkans.* § 5. *Russia a Grand Monarchy.* § 6. *The United States and the Imperial Idea.* § 7. *The Immediate Causes of the Great War.* § 8. *A Summary of the Great War Up to 1917.* § 9. *The Great War from the Russian Collapse to the Armistice.* § 10. *The Political, Economical, and Social Disorganization Caused by the War.* § 11. *President Wilson and the Problems of Versailles.* § 12. *Summary of the First Covenant of the League of Nations.* § 13. *A General Outline of the Treaties of 1919 and 1920.*

§ 1

FOR thirty-six years after the Treaty of San Stefano and the Berlin Conference, Europe maintained an uneasy peace within its borders; there was no war between any of the leading states during this period. They jostled, browbeat, and threatened one another, but they did not come to actual hostilities. There was a general realization after 1871 that modern war was a much more serious thing than the professional warfare of the eighteenth century, an effort of peoples as a whole that might strain the social fabric very severely, an adventure not to be rashly embarked upon. The mechanical revolution was giving constantly more powerful (and expensive) weapons by land and sea, and more rapid methods of transport; and making it more and more impossible to carry on warfare without a complete dislocation of the economic life of the community. Even the foreign offices felt the fear of war.

But though war was dreaded as it had never been dreaded in the world before, nothing was done in the way of setting up a federal control to prevent human affairs drifting towards war. In 1898, it is true, the young Tsar Nicholas II (1894-1917) issued a rescript inviting the other Great Powers to a conference of states "seeking to make the great idea of universal peace triumph over the elements of trouble and discord." His rescript recalls the declaration of his predecessor, Alexander I, which gave its tone to the Holy Alliance, and it is vitiated by the same assumption that peace can be established between sovereign governments rather than by a broad appeal to the needs and rights of the one people of mankind. The lesson of the United States of America, which showed that there could be neither unity of action nor peace until the thought of the "people of Virginia" and the "people of Massachusetts" had been swept aside by the thought of the "people of the United States," went entirely disregarded in the European attempts at pacification. Two conferences were held at The Hague in Holland, one in 1899 and another in 1907, and at the second nearly all the sovereign states of the world were represented. They were represented diplomatically, there was no direction of the general intelligence of the world to their deliberations, the ordinary common man did not even know that these conferences were sitting, and for the most part the assembled representatives haggled cunningly upon points of international law affecting war, leaving aside the abolition of war as a chimæra. These Hague Conferences did nothing to dispel the idea that international life is necessarily competitive. They accepted that idea. They did nothing to develop the consciousness of a world commonweal overriding sovereigns and foreign offices. The international lawyers and statesmen who attended these gatherings were as little disposed to hasten on a world commonweal on such a basis as were the Prussian statesmen of 1848 to welcome an all-German parliament overriding the rights and "policy" of the King of Prussia.

In America a series of three Pan-American conferences in 1889, 1901, and 1906 went some way towards the development of a scheme of international arbitration for the whole American continent.

The character and good faith of Nicholas II, who initiated these Hague gatherings, we will not discuss at any length here. He may have thought that time was on the side of Russia. But of the general unwillingness of the Great Powers to face the prospect of a merger of sovereign powers, without which permanent peace projects are absurd, there can be no sort of doubt whatever. It was no cessation of international competition with its acute phase of war that they desired, but rather a cheapening of war, which was becoming too costly. Each wanted to economize the wastage of minor disputes and conflicts, and to establish international laws that would embarrass its more formidable opponents in war-time without incommoding itself. These were the practical ends they sought at the Hague Conference. It was a gathering they attended to please Nicholas II, just as the monarchs of Europe had subscribed to the evangelical propositions of the Holy Alliance to please Alexander I; and as they had attended it, they tried to make what they conceived to be some use of it.

§ 2

The peace of Frankfort had left Germany Prussianized and united, the most formidable of all the Great Powers of Europe. France was humiliated and crippled. Her lapse into republicanism seemed likely to leave her without friends in any European court. Italy was as yet a mere stripling. Austria sank now rapidly to the position of a confederate in German policy. Russia was vast, but undeveloped; and the British Empire was mighty only on the sea. Beyond Europe the one power to be reckoned with by Germany was the United States of America, growing now into a great industrial nation, but with no army nor navy worth considering by European standards.

The new Germany which was embodied in the empire that had been created at Versailles was a complex and astonishing mixture of the fresh intellectual and material forces of the world, with the narrowest political traditions of the European system. She was vigorously educational; she was by far the most educational state in the world; she made the educational pace for all her neighbours and rivals. In this time of reckoning for Germany, it may help the British reader to a balanced attitude to recall the educational stimulation for which his country has to thank first the German Prince Consort and then German competition. That mean jealousy of the educated common man on the part of the British ruling class, which no patriotic pride or generous impulse had ever sufficed to overcome, went down before a growing fear of German efficiency. And Germany took up the organization of scientific research and of the application of scientific method to industrial and social development with such a faith and energy as no other community had ever shown before. Throughout all this period of the armed peace she was reaping and sowing afresh and reaping again the harvests, the unfailing harvests, of freely disseminated knowledge. She grew swiftly to become a great manufacturing and trading power; her steel output outran the British; in a hundred new fields of production and commerce, where intelligence and system was of more account than mere trader's cunning, in the manufacture of optical glass, of dyes and of a multitude of chemical products and in endless novel processes, she led the world.

To the British manufacturer who was accustomed to see inventions come into his works, he knew not whence nor why, begging to be adopted, this new German method of keeping and paying scientific men seemed abominably unfair. It was compelling fortune, he felt. It was packing the cards. It was encouraging a nasty class of intellectuals to interfere in the affairs of sound business men. Science went abroad from its first home like an unloved child. The splendid chemical industry of Germany was built on the work of the Englishman Sir William Perkin, who could find no "practical" English business man to back him. And Germany also led the way in many forms of social legislation. Germany realized that labour is a national asset, that it deteriorates through unemployment, and that, for the common good, it has to be taken care of outside the works. The British employer was still under the delusion that labour had no business to exist outside the works, and that the worse such exterior existence was, the better somehow for him. Moreover, because of his general illiteracy, he was an intense individualist: his was the insensate rivalry of the vulgar mind; he hated his fellow manufacturers about as much as he hated his labour and his customers. German producers, on the other hand, were persuaded of the great advantages of combination and civility; their enterprises tended to flow together and assume more and more the character of national undertakings.

This educating, scientific, and organizing Germany was the

natural development of the liberal Germany of 1848; it had its roots far back in the recuperative effort that drew its impulse from the shame of the Napoleonic conquest. All that was good, all that was great in this modern Germany, she owed indeed to her schoolmasters. But this scientific organizing spirit was only one of the two factors that made up the new German Empire. The other factor was the Hohenzollern monarchy which had survived Jena, which had tricked and bested the revolution of 1848, and which, under the guidance of Bismarck, had now clambered to the legal headship of all Germany outside Austria. Except the Tsardom, no other European state had so preserved the tradition of the Grand Monarchy of the eighteenth century as the Prussian. Through the tradition of Frederick the Great, Machiavelli now reigned in Germany. In the head of this fine new modern state, therefore, there sat no fine modern brain to guide it to a world predominance in world service, but an old spider lusting for power. Prussianized Germany was at once the newest and the most antiquated thing in Western Europe. She was the best and the wickedest state of her time.

The psychology of nations is still but a rudimentary science. Psychologists have scarcely begun to study the citizen side of the individual man. But it is of the utmost importance to our subject that the student of universal history should give some thought to the mental growth of the generations of Germans educated since the victories of 1871. They were naturally inflated by their sweeping unqualified successes in war, and by their rapid progress from comparative poverty to wealth. It would have been more than human in them if they had not given way to some excesses of patriotic vanity. But this reaction was deliberately seized upon and fostered and developed by a systematic exploitation and control of school and college, literature and press, in the interests of the Hohenzollern dynasty. A teacher, a professor, who did not teach and preach, in and out of season, the racial, moral, intellectual, and physical superiority of the Germans to all other peoples, their extraordinary devotion to war and their dynasty, and their inevitable destiny under that dynasty to lead the world, was a marked man, doomed to failure and obscurity. German historical teaching became an immense systematic falsification of the human past, with a view to the Hohenzollern future. All other nations were represented as incompetent and decadent; the Prussians were the leaders and regenerators of mankind. The young German read this in his school-books, heard it in church, found it in his literature, had it poured into him with passionate conviction by his professor. It was poured into him by all his professors; lecturers in biology or mathematics would break off from their proper subject to indulge in long passages of patriotic rant. Only minds of extraordinary toughness and originality could resist such a torrent of suggestion. Insensibly there was built up in the German mind a conception of Germany and its emperor as of something splendid and predominant as nothing else had ever been before, a godlike nation in "shining armour" brandishing the "good German sword" in a world of inferior—and very badly disposed—peoples. We have told our story of Europe; the reader may judge whether the glitter of the German sword is exceptionally blinding. Germania was deliberately intoxicated, she was systematically kept drunk, with this sort of patriotic rhetoric. It is the greatest of the Hohenzollern crimes that the Crown constantly and persistently tampered with education, and particularly with historical teaching. No other modern state has so sinned against education. The oligarchy of the crowned republic of Great Britain may have crippled and starved education, but the Hohenzollern monarchy corrupted and prostituted it.

It cannot be too clearly stated, it is the most important fact in the history of the last half century, that the German people was methodically indoctrinated with the idea of a German world-predominance based on might, and with the theory that war was a necessary thing in life. The key to German historical teaching is to be found in Count Moltke's dictum: "Perpetual peace is a dream, and it is not even a beautiful dream. War is an element in the order of the world ordained by God." "Without war the world would stagnate and lose itself in materialism." And the anti-Christian German philosopher, Nietzsche, found himself quite at one with the pious field-marshal. "It is mere illusion and pretty sentiment," he observes, "to expect much (even anything at all) from mankind if it forgets how to make war. As yet no means are known which call so much into action as a great war that rough energy born of the camp, that deep impersonality born of hatred, that conscience born of murder and cold-bloodedness, that fervour born of effort in the annihilation of the enemy, that proud indifference to loss, to one's own existence, to that of one's fellows, that earthquake-like soul-shaking which a people needs when it is losing its vitality."[1]

This sort of teaching, which pervaded the German Empire from end to end, was bound to be noted abroad, bound to alarm every other power and people in the world, bound to provoke an anti-German confederation and it was accompanied by a parade of military, and presently of naval, preparation that threatened France, Russia, and Britain alike. It affected the thoughts, the manners, and morals of the entire German people. After 1871, the German abroad thrust out his chest and raised his voice. He threw a sort of trampling quality even into the operations of commerce. His machinery came on the markets of the world, his shipping took the seas with a splash of patriotic challenge. His very merits he used as a means of offence. (And probably most other peoples, if they had had the same experiences and undergone the same training, would have behaved in a similar manner.)

The Emperor William II.

By one of those accidents in history that personify and precipitate catastrophes, the ruler of Germany, the emperor William II, embodied the new education of his people and the Hohenzollern tradition in the completest form. He came to the throne in 1888 at the age of twenty-nine; his father, Fred-

[1] These quotations are from Sir Thomas Barclay's article "Peace" in *the Encyclopaedia Britannica.*

erick III, had succeeded his grandfather, William I, in the March, to die in the June of that year. William II was the grandson of Queen Victoria on his mother's side, but his temperament showed no traces of the liberal German tradition that distinguished the Saxe-Coburg-Gotha family. His head was full of the frothy stuff of the new imperialism. He signalized his accession by an address to his army and navy; his address to his people followed three days later. A high note of contempt for democracy was sounded: "The soldier and the army, not parliamentary majorities, have welded together the German Empire. My trust is placed in the army." So the patient work of the German schoolmasters was disowned, and the Hohenzollern declared himself triumphant.

The next exploit of the young monarch was to quarrel with the old chancellor, Bismarck, who had made the new German Empire, and to dismiss him (1890). There were no profound differences of opinion between them, but, as Bismarck said, the Emperor intended to be his own chancellor.

These were the opening acts of an active and aggressive career. This William II meant to make a noise in the world, a louder noise than any other monarch had ever made. The whole of Europe was soon familiar with the figure of the new monarch, invariably in military uniform of the most glittering sort, staring valiantly, fiercely moustached, and with a withered left arm ingeniously minimised. He affected silver shining breastplates and long white cloaks. A great restlessness was manifest. It was clear he conceived himself destined for great things, but for a time it was not manifest what particular great things these were. There was no oracle at Delphi now to tell him that he was destined to destroy a great empire.

The note of theatricality about him and the dismissal of Bismarck alarmed many of his subjects, but they were presently reassured by the idea that he was using his influence in the cause of peace and to consolidate Germany. He travelled much, to London, Vienna, Rome—where he had private conversations with the Pope—to Athens, where his sister married the king in 1889, and to Constantinople. He was the first Christian sovereign to be a Sultan's guest. He also went to Palestine. A special gate was knocked through the ancient wall of Jerusalem so that he could ride into that place; it was beneath his dignity to walk in. He induced the Sultan to commence the reorganization of the Turkish Army upon German lines and under German officers. In 1895 he announced that Germany was a "world power," and that "the future of Germany lay upon the water"—regardless of the fact that the British considered that they were there already—and he began to interest himself more and more in the building up of a great navy. He also took German art and literature under his care; he used his influence to retain the distinctive and blinding German blackletter against the Roman type used by the rest of western Europe, and he supported the Pan-German movement, which claimed the Dutch, the Scandinavians, the Flemish Belgians, and the German Swiss as members of a great German brotherhood—as in fact good assimilable stuff for a hungry young empire which meant to grow. All other monarchs in Europe paled before him.

He used the general hostility against Britain aroused throughout Europe by the war against the Boer Republics to press forward his schemes for a great navy, and this, together with the rapid and challenging extension of the German colonial empire in Africa and the Pacific Ocean, alarmed and irritated the British extremely. British liberal opinion in particular found itself under the exasperating necessity of supporting an ever-increasing British Navy. "I will not rest," he said, "until I have brought my navy to the same height at which my army stands." The most peace-loving of the islanders could not ignore that threat.

In 1890 he had acquired the small island of Heligoland from Britain. This he made into a great naval fortress.

As his navy grew, his enterprise increased. He proclaimed the Germans "the salt of the earth." They must not "weary in the work of civilization; Germany, like the spirit of Imperial Rome, must expand and impose itself." This he said on Polish soil, in support of the steady efforts the Germans were making to suppress the Polish language and culture, and to Germanize their share of Poland. God he described as his "Divine Ally." In the old absolutisms the monarch was either God himself or the adopted agent of God; the Kaiser took God for his trusty henchman. "Our old God," he said affectionately. When the Germans seized Kiau-Chau, he spoke of the German "mailed fist." When he backed Austria against Russia, he talked of Germany in her "shining armour."

The disasters of Russia in Manchuria in 1905 released the spirit of German imperialism to bolder aggressions. The fear of a joint attack from France and Russia seemed lifting. The emperor made a kind of regal progress through the Holy Land, landed at Tangier to assure the Sultan of Morocco of his support against the French, and inflicted upon France the crowning indignity of compelling her by a threat of war to dismiss Delcassé, her foreign minister. He drew tighter the links between Austria and Germany, and in 1908, Austria, with his support, defied the rest of Europe by annexing from the Turk the Yugo-Slav provinces of Bosnia and Herzegovina. So by his naval challenge to Britain and these aggressions upon France and the Slavs he forced Britain, France, and Russia into a defensive understanding against him. The Bosnian annexation had the further effect of estranging Italy, which had hitherto been his ally.

Such was the personality that the evil fate of Germany set over her to stimulate, organize, and render intolerable to the rest of the world the natural pride and self-assertion of a great people who had at last, after long centuries of division and weakness, escaped from a jungle of princes to unity and the world's respect. It was natural that the commercial and industrial leaders of this new Germany who were now getting rich, the financiers intent upon overseas exploits, the officials and the vulgar, should find this leader very much to their taste. Many Germans who thought him rash or tawdry in their secret hearts, supported him publicly because he had so taking an air of success. *Hoch der Kaiser!*

Yet Germany did not yield itself without a struggle to the strong-flowing tide of imperialism. Important elements in German life struggled against this swaggering new autocracy. The old German nations, and particularly the Bavarians, refused to be swallowed up in Prussianism. And with the spread of education and the rapid industrialization of Germany, organized labour developed its ideas and a steady antagonism to the military and patriotic clattering of its ruler. A new political party was growing up in the state, the Social Democrats, professing the doctrines of Marx. In the teeth of the utmost opposition from the official and clerical organizations, and of violently repressive laws against its propaganda and against combinations, this party grew. The Kaiser denounced it again and again; its leaders were sent to prison or driven abroad. Still it grew. When he came to the throne it polled not half a million votes; in 1907 it polled over three million. He attempted to concede many things, old age and sickness insurance, for example, as a condescending gift, things which it claimed for the workers as their right. His conversion to socialism was noted, but it gained no converts to imperialism. His naval ambitions were ably and bitterly denounced; the colonial adventures of the new German capitalists were incessantly attacked by this party of the common sense of the common man. But to the army, the Social Democrats accorded a moderate support, because, much as they detested their home-grown autocrat, they hated and dreaded the barbaric and retrogressive autocracy of Russia on their eastern frontier more.

The danger plainly before Germany was that this swaggering imperialism would compel Britain, Russia, and France into a combined attack upon her, an offensive-defensive. The Kaiser wavered between a stiff attitude towards Britain and clumsy attempts to propitiate her, while his fleet grew and while he prepared for a preliminary struggle with Russia and France. When in 1913 the British government proposed a cessation on either hand of naval construction for a year, it was refused. The Kaiser was afflicted with a son and heir more Hohenzollern, more imperialistic, more Pan-Germanic than his father. He had been nurtured upon imperialist propaganda. His toys had been soldiers and guns. He snatched at a premature popularity by outdoing his father's patriotic and aggressive attitudes. His father, it was felt, was growing middle-aged and over-careful. The Crown Prince renewed him. Germany had never been so strong, never so ready for a new great adventure and another harvest of victories. The Russians, he was instructed, were decayed, the French degenerate, the British on the verge of civil war. This young Crown Prince was but a sample of the abounding upper-class youth of Germany in the spring of 1914. They had all drunken from the same cup. Their professors and teachers, their speakers and leaders, their mothers and sweethearts, had been preparing them for the great occasion that was now very nearly at hand. They were full of the tremulous sense of imminent conflict, of a trumpet call to stupendous achievements, of victory over mankind abroad, triumph over the recalcitrant workers at home. The country was taut and excited like an athletic competitor at the end of his training.

§ 3

Throughout the period of the armed peace Germany was making the pace and setting the tone for the rest of Europe. The influence of her new doctrines of aggressive imperialism was particularly strong upon the British mind, which was ill-equipped to resist a strong intellectual thrust from abroad. The educational impulse the Prince Consort had given had died away after his death; the universities of Oxford and Cambridge were hindered in their task of effective revision of upper-class education by the fears and prejudices the so-called "conflict of science and religion" had roused in the clergy who dominated them through Convocation; popular education was crippled by religious squabbling, by the extreme parsimony of the public authorities, by the desire of employers for child labour, and by individualistic objections to "educating other people's children." The old tradition of the English, the tradition of plain statement, legality, fair play, and a certain measure of republican freedom had faded considerably during the stresses of the Napoleonic wars; romanticism, of which Sir Walter Scott, the great novelist, was the chief promoter, had infected the national imagination with a craving for the florid and picturesque. "Mr. Briggs," the comic Englishman of *Punch* in the fifties and sixties, getting himself into highland costume and stalking deer, was fairly representative of the spirit of the new movement. It presently dawned upon Mr. Briggs as a richly coloured and credible fact he had hitherto not observed, that the sun never set on his dominions. The country which had once put Clive and Warren Hastings on trial for their unrighteous treatment of Indians, was now persuaded to regard them as entirely chivalrous and devoted figures. They were "empire builders." Under the spell of Disraeli's Oriental imagination, which had made Queen Victoria "empress," the Englishman turned readily enough towards the vague exaltations of modern imperialism.

The perverted ethnology and distorted history which was

persuading the mixed Slavic, Keltic, and Teutonic Germans that they were a wonderful race apart, was imitated by English writers who began to exalt a new ethnological invention, the "Anglo-Saxon." This remarkable compound was presented as the culmination of humanity, the crown and reward of the accumulated effort of Greek and Roman, Egyptian, Assyrian, Jew, Mongol, and such-like lowly precursors of its white splendour. The senseless legend of German superiority did much to exacerbate the irritations of the Poles in Posen and the French in Lorraine. The even more ridiculous legend of the superior Anglo-Saxon did not merely increase the irritations of English rule in Ireland, but it lowered the tone of British dealings with "subject" peoples throughout the entire world. For the cessation of respect and the cultivation of "superior" ideas are the cessation of civility and justice.

The imitation of German patriotic misconceptions did not end with this "Anglo-Saxon" fabrication. The clever young men at the British universities in the eighties and nineties, bored by the flatness and insincerities of domestic politics, were moved to imitation and rivalry by this new teaching of an arrogant, subtle, and forceful nationalist imperialism, this combination of Machiavelli and Attila, which was being imposed upon the thought and activities of young Germany. Britain, too, they thought, must have her shining armour and wave her good sword. The new British imperialism found its poet in Mr. Kipling and its practical support in a number of financial and business interests whose way to monopolies and exploitations was lighted by its glow. These Prussianizing Englishmen carried their imitation of Germany to the most extraordinary lengths. Central Europe is one continuous economic system, best worked as one; and the new Germany had achieved a great customs union, a Zollverein of all its constituents. It became naturally one compact system, like a clenched fist. The British Empire sprawled like an open hand throughout the world, its members different in nature, need, and relationship, with no common interest except the common guarantee of safety. But the new Imperialists were blind to that difference. If new Germany had a Zollverein, then the British Empire must be in the fashion; and the natural development of its various elements must be hampered everywhere by "imperial preferences" and the like. . . .

Yet the imperialist movement in Great Britain never had the authority nor the unanimity it had in Germany. It was not a natural product of any of the three united but diverse British peoples. It was not congenial to them. Queen Victoria and her successors, Edward VII and George V, were indisposed, either by temperament or tradition, to wear "shining armour," shake "mailed fists," and flourish "good swords" in the Hohenzollern fashion. They had the wisdom to refrain from any overt meddling with public ideas. And this "British" imperialist movement had from the first aroused the hostility of the large number of English, Welsh, Irish, and Scotch writers who refused to recognize this new "British" nationality or to accept the theory that they were these "Anglo-Saxon" supermen. And many great interests in Britain, and notably the shipping interest, had been built up upon free trade, and regarded the fiscal proposals of the new imperialists, and the new financial and mercantile adventurers with whom they were associated, with a justifiable suspicion. On the other hand, these ideas ran like wildfire through the military class, through Indian officialdom and the like. Hitherto there had always been something apologetic about the army man in England. He was not native to that soil. Here was a movement that promised to make him as splendidly important as his Prussian brother in arms. And the imperialist idea also found support in the cheap popular press that was now coming into existence to cater for the new stratum of readers created by elementary education. This press wanted plain, bright, simple ideas adapted to the needs of readers who had scarcely begun to think.

In spite of such support, and its strong appeal to national vanity, British imperialism never saturated the mass of the British peoples. The English are not a mentally docile people, and the noisy and rather forced enthusiasm for imperialism and higher tariffs of the old Tory Party, the army class, the country clergy, the music-halls, the assimilated alien, the vulgar rich and the new large employers, inclined the commoner sort, and particularly organized labour, to a suspicious attitude. If the continually irritated sore of the Majuba defeat permitted the country to be rushed into the needless, toilsome, and costly conquest of the Boer republics in South Africa, the strain of that adventure produced a sufficient reaction towards decency and justice to reinstate the Liberal Party in power, and to undo the worst of that mischief by the creation of a South African confederation. Considerable advances continued to be made in popular education, and in the recovery of public interests and the general wealth from the possession of the few. And in these years of the armed peace, the three British peoples came very near to a settlement, on fairly just and reasonable lines, of their long-standing misunderstanding with Ireland. The great war, unluckily for them, overtook them in the very crisis of this effort.

Like Japan, Ireland has figured but little in this *Outline of History,* and for the same reason, because she is an extreme island country, receiving much, but hitherto giving but little back into the general drama. Her population is a very mixed one, its basis, and probably its main substance, being of the dark "Mediterranean" strain, pre-Nordic and pre-Aryan, like the Basques and the people of Portugal and south Italy. Over this original basis there flowed, about the sixth century B.C.—we do not know to what degree of submergence—a wave of Keltic peoples, in at least sufficient strength to establish a Keltic language, the Irish Gaelic. There were comings and goings, invasions and counter-invasions of this and that Keltic or Kelticized people between Ireland, Scotland, Wales, and England. The island was Christianized in the fifth century. Later on the east coast was raided and settled by Northmen, but we do not know to what extent they altered the racial quality. The Norman-English came in 1169, in the time of Henry II and onward. The Teutonic strain may be as strong or stronger than the Keltic in modern Ireland. Hitherto Ireland had been a tribal and barbaric country, with a few centres of security wherein the artistic tendencies of the more ancient race found scope in metal-work and the illumination of holy books. Now, in the twelfth century, there was an imperfect conquest by the English Crown, and scattered settlements by Normans and English in various parts of the country. From the outset profound temperamental differences between the Irish and English were manifest, differences exacerbated by a difference of language, and these became much more evident after the Protestant Reformation. The English became Protestant; the Irish by a natural reaction rallied about the persecuted Catholic church.

The English rule in Ireland had been from the first an intermittent civil war due to the class of languages and the different laws of land tenure and inheritance of the two peoples. The rebellions, massacres, and subjugations of the unhappy island during the reigns of Elizabeth and James I we cannot tell of here; but under James came a new discord with the confiscation of large areas of Ulster and their settlement with Presbyterian Scotch colonists. They formed a Protestant community in necessary permanent conflict with the Catholic remainder of Ireland.

In the political conflicts during the reign of Charles I and the Commonweal, and of James II and William and Mary, the two sides in English affairs found sympathizers and allies in the Irish parties. There is a saying in Ireland that England's misfortune is Ireland's opportunity, and the English civil trouble that led to the execution of Strafford was the occasion also of a massacre of the English in Ireland (1641). Later on Cromwell was to avenge that massacre by giving no quarter to any men found under arms, a severity remembered by the Irish Catholics with extreme bitterness. Between 1689 and 1691 Ireland was again torn by civil war. James II sought the support of the Irish Catholics against William III, and his adherents were badly beaten at the battles of the Boyne (1690) and Aughrim (1691).

There was a settlement, the Treaty of Limerick, a disputed settlement in which the English Government promised much in the way of tolerance for Catholics and the like, and failed to keep its promises. Limerick is still a cardinal memory in the long story of Irish embitterment. Comparatively few English people have even heard of this Treaty of Limerick; in Ireland it rankles to this day.

The eighteenth century was a century of accumulating grievance. English commercial jealousy put heavy restraints upon Irish trade, and the development of a wool industry was destroyed in the south and west. The Ulster Protestants were treated little better than the Catholics in these matters, and they were the chief of the rebels. There was more agrarian revolt in the north than in the south in the eighteenth century.

Let us state as clearly as our space permits the parallelisms and contrasts of the British and Irish situation at this time. There was a parliament in Ireland, but it was a Protestant parliament, even more limited and corrupt than the contemporary British Parliament; there was a considerable civilization in and about Dublin, and much literary and scientific activity, conducted in English and centring upon the Protestant university of Trinity College. This was the Ireland of Swift, Goldsmith, Burke, Berkeley, and Boyle. It was essentially a part of the English culture. It had nothing distinctively Irish about it. The Catholic religion and the Irish language were outcast and persecuted things in the darkness at this time.

It was from this Ireland of the darkness that the recalcitrant Ireland of the twentieth century arose. The Irish Parliament, its fine literature, its science, all its culture, gravitated naturally enough to London, because they were inseparably a part of that world. The more prosperous landlords went to England to live, and had their children educated there. This meant a steady drain of wealth from Ireland to England in the form of rent, spent or invested out of the country. The increasing facilities of communication steadily enhanced this tendency, depleted Dublin and bled Ireland white. The Act of Union (January 1st, 1801) was the natural coalescence of two entirely kindred systems, of the Anglo-Irish Parliament with the British Parliament, both oligarchic, both politically corrupt in the same fashion. There was a vigorous opposition to the Union on the part not so much of the outer Irish as of Protestants settled in Ireland, and a futile insurrection under Robert Emmet in 1803. Dublin, which had been a fine Anglo-Irish city in the middle eighteenth century, was gradually deserted by its intellectual and political life, and invaded by the outer Irish of Ireland. Its fashionable life became more and more official, centering upon the Lord Lieutenant in Dublin Castle; its intellectual life flickered and for a time nearly died.

But while the Ireland of Swift and Goldsmith was part and lot with the England of Pope, Dr. Johnson, and Sir Joshua Reynolds, while there has never been and is not now any real definable difference except one of geography between the "governing class" in Ireland and in Britain, the Irish underworld and the English underworld were essentially dissimilar. The upward struggle of the English "democracy" to education, to political recognition, was different in many respects from the struggle of the Irish underworld. Britain was producing a great industrial population, Protestant or sceptical; she had agricultural labourers indeed, but no peasants. Ireland, with no coal, with a poorer soil and landlords who lived in England, had become a land of rent-paying peasants. Their cultivation was allowed to degenerate more and more into a growing of potatoes and a feeding of pigs. The people married and bred; except for the consumption of whisky when it could be got, and a little fighting, family life was their only amusement. Here are the appalling consequences. The population of Ireland

in 1785 was 2,845,932,
in 1803 was 5,536,594,
in 1845 was 8,295,061,

at which date the weary potato gave way under its ever-growing burthen and there was a frightful famine. Many died, many emigrated, especially to the United States; an outflow of emigration began that made Ireland for a time a land of old people and empty nests.

Now because of the Union of the Parliaments, the enfranchisement of the English and Irish populations went on simultaneously. Catholic enfranchisement in England meant Catholic enfranchisement in Ireland. The British got votes because they wanted them; the Irish commonalty got votes because the English did. Ireland was over-represented in the Union Parliament, because originally Irish seats had been easier for the governing class to manipulate than English; and so it came about that this Irish and Catholic Ireland, which had never before had any political instrument at all, and which had never sought a political instrument, suddenly found itself with the power to thrust a solid body of members into the legislature of Great Britain. After the general election of 1874, the old type of venal Irish member was swept aside, and the newly enfranchised "democracy" of Britain found itself confronted by a strange and perplexing Irish "democracy," different in its religion, its traditions, and its needs, telling a tale of wrongs of which the common English had never heard, clamouring passionately for a separation which they could not understand and which impressed them chiefly as being needlessly unfriendly.

The national egotism of the Irish is intense; their circumstances have made it intense; they were incapable of considering the state of affairs in England; the new Irish party came into the British Parliament to obstruct and disorder English business until Ireland became free, and to make themselves a nuisance to the English. This spirit was only too welcome to the oligarchy which still ruled the British Empire; they allied themselves with the "loyal" Protestants in the north of Ireland —loyal that is to the Imperial Government because of their dread of a Catholic predominance in Ireland—and they watched and assisted the gradual exasperation of the British common people by this indiscriminate hostility of the common people of Ireland.

The story of the relation of Ireland to Britain for the last half-century is one that reflects the utmost discredit upon the governing class of the British Empire, but it is not one of which the English commons need be ashamed. Again and again they have given evidences of goodwill. British legislation in relation to Ireland for nearly half a century shows a series of clumsy attempts on the part of liberal England, made in the face of a strenuous opposition from the Conservative Party and the Ulster Irish, to satisfy Irish complaints and get to a footing of fellowship. The name of Parnell, an Irish Protestant, stands out as that of the chief leader of the Home Rule movement. In 1886 Gladstone, the liberal British prime minister, brought political disaster upon himself by introducing the first Irish Home Rule Bill, a genuine attempt to give over Irish affairs *for the first time in history* to the Irish people. The bill broke the Liberal Party asunder; and a coalition government, the Unionist Government, replaced that of Mr. Gladstone.

This digression into the history of Ireland now comes up to the time of infectious imperialism in Europe. The Unionist Government, which ousted Mr. Gladstone, had a predominantly Tory element, and was in spirit "imperialist" as no previous British Government had been. The British political history of the subsequent years is largely a history of the conflict of the new imperialism, through which an arrogant "British" nationalism sought to override the rest of the empire against the temperamental liberalism and reasonableness of the English, which tended to develop the empire into a confederation of free and willing allies. Naturally the "British" imperialists wanted a subjugated Irish; naturally the English Liberals wanted a free, participating Irish. In 1892 Gladstone struggled back to power with a small Home Rule majority; and in 1893 his second Home Rule Bill passed the Commons, and was rejected by the Lords. It was not, however, until 1895 that an imperialist government took office. The party which sustained it was called not Imperialist, but "Unionist"—an odd name when we consider how steadily and strenuously it has worked to destroy any possibility of an Empire commonweal. These Imperialists remained in power for ten years. We have already noted their conquest of South Africa. They were defeated in 1905 in an attempt to establish a tariff wall on the Teutonic model. The ensuing Liberal Government then turned the conquered South African Dutch into contented fellow-subjects by creating the self-governing Dominion of South Africa. After which it embarked upon a long-impending struggle with the persistently imperialist House of Lords.

This was a very fundamental struggle in British affairs. On the one hand were the Liberal majority of the people of Great

Britain honestly and wisely anxious to put this Irish affair upon a new and more hopeful footing, and, if possible, to change the animosity of the Irish into friendship; on the other were all the factors of this new British Imperialism resolved at any cost and in spite of every electoral verdict, legally, if possible, but if not, illegally, to maintain their ascendancy over the affairs of the English, Scotch, and Irish and all the rest of the empire alike. It was, under new names, the age-long internal struggle of the English community; that same conflict of a free and liberal-spirited commonalty against powerful "big men" and big adventurers and authoritative persons which we have already dealt with in our account of the liberation of America. Ireland was merely a battleground as America had been. In India, in Ireland, in England, the governing class and their associated adventurers were all of one mind; but the Irish people, thanks to their religious difference, had little sense of solidarity with the English. Yet such Irish statesmen as Redmond, the leader of the Irish party in the House of Commons, transcended this national narrowness for a time, and gave a generous response to English good intentions. Slowly yet steadily the barrier of the House of Lords was broken down, and a third Irish Home Rule Bill was brought in by Mr. Asquith, the Prime Minister, in 1912. Throughout 1913 and the early part of 1914 this bill was fought and refought through Parliament. At first it gave Home Rule to all Ireland; but an Amending Act, excluding Ulster on certain conditions, was promised. This struggle lasted right up to the outbreak of the Great War. The royal assent was given to this bill after the actual outbreak of war, and also to a bill suspending the coming into force of Irish Home Rule until after the end of the war. These bills were put upon the Statute Book.

But from the introduction of the third Home Rule Bill onward, the opposition to it had assumed a violent and extravagant form. Sir Edward Carson, a Dublin lawyer who had become a member of the English Bar, and who had held a legal position in the ministry of Mr. Gladstone (before the Home Rule split) and in the subsequent imperialist government, was the organizer and leader of this resistance to a reconciliation of the two peoples. In spite of his Dublin origin, he set up to be a leader of the Ulster Protestants; and he brought to the conflict that contempt for law which is all too common a characteristic of the successful barrister, and those gifts of persistent, unqualified, and uncompromising hostility which distinguish a certain type of Irishman. He was the most "un-English" of men, dark, romantic, and violent; and from the opening of the struggle he talked with gusto of armed resistance to this freer reunion of the English and Irish which the third Home Rule Bill contemplated. A body of volunteers had been organized in Ulster in 1911, arms were now smuggled into the country, and Sir Edward Carson and a rising lawyer named F. E. Smith, trapped up in semi-military style, toured Ulster, inspecting these volunteers and inflaming local passion. The arms of these prospective rebels were obtained from Germany, and various utterances of Sir Edward Carson's associates hinted at support from "a great Protestant monarch." Contrasted with Ulster, the rest of Ireland was at that time a land of order and decency, relying upon its great leader Redmond and the good faith of the three British peoples.

Now these threats of civil war from Ireland were not in themselves anything very exceptional in the record of that unhappy island; what makes them significant in the world's history at this time is the vehement support they found among the English military and governing classes, and the immunity from punishment and restraint of Sir Edward Carson and his friends. The virus of reaction which came from the success and splendour of German imperialism had spread widely, as we have explained, throughout the prevalent and prosperous classes in Great Britain. A generation had grown up forgetful of the mighty traditions of their forefathers, and ready to exchange the greatness of English fairness and freedom for the tawdriest of imperialisms. A fund of a million pounds was raised, chiefly in England, to support the Ulster Rebellion, an Ulster Provisional Government was formed, prominent English people mingled in the fray and careered about Ulster in automobiles, assisting in the gun-running, and there is evidence that a number of British officers and generals were prepared for a pronunciamento upon South American lines rather than obedience to the law. The natural result of all this upper-class disorderliness was to alarm the main part of Ireland, never a ready friend to England. That Ireland also began in its turn to organize "National Volunteers" and to smuggle arms.

The military authorities showed themselves much keener in the suppression of the Nationalist than of the Ulster gun importation, and in July, 1914, an attempt to run guns at Howth, near Dublin, led to fighting and bloodshed in the Dublin streets. The British Isles were on the verge of civil war.

Such in outline is the story of the imperialist revolutionary movement in Great Britain up to the eve of the Great War. For revolutionary this movement of Sir Edward Carson and his associates was. It was plainly an attempt to set aside parliamentary government and the slow-grown, imperfect liberties of the British peoples, and, with the assistance of the army, to substitute a more Prussianized type of rule, using the Irish conflict as the point of departure. It was the reactionary effort of a few score thousand people to arrest the world movement towards democratic law and social justice, strictly parallel to and closely sympathetic with the new imperialism of the German junkers and rich men. But in one very important respect British and German imperialism differed. In Germany it centred upon the crown; its noisiest, most conspicuous advocate was the heir-apparent. In Great Britain the king stood aloof. By no single public act did King George V betray the slightest approval of the new movement, and the behaviour of the Prince of Wales, his son and heir, has been equally correct.

In August, 1914, the storm of the Great War burst upon the world. In September, Sir Edward Carson was denouncing the placing of the Home Rule Bill upon the Statute Book. On the same day, Mr. John Redmond, the leader of the Irish majority, the proper representative of Ireland, was calling upon the Irish people to take their equal part in the burthen and effort of the war. For a time Ireland played her part in the war side by side with England faithfully and well, until in 1915 the Liberal Government was replaced by a coalition, in which, through the moral feebleness of Mr. Asquith, the prime minister, this Sir Edward Carson figured as Attorney-General (with a salary of £7,000 and fees), to be replaced presently by his associate in the Ulster sedition, Sir F. E. Smith.

Grosser insult was never offered to a friendly people. The work of reconciliation, begun by Gladstone in 1886, and brought so near to completion, in 1914, was completely and finally wrecked.

In the spring of 1916 Dublin revolted unsuccessfully against this new government. The ringleaders of this insurrection, many of them mere boys, were shot with a deliberate and clumsy sternness that, in view of the treatment of the Ulster rebel leaders, impressed all Ireland as atrociously unjust. A traitor, Sir Roger Casement, who had been knighted for previous services to the empire, was tried and executed, no doubt deservedly, but his prosecutor was Sir F. E. Smith of the Ulster insurrection, a shocking conjunction. The Dublin revolt had had little support in Ireland generally, but thereafter the movement for an independent republic grew rapidly to great proportions. Against this strong emotional drive there struggled the more moderate ideas of such Irish statesmen as Sir Horace Plunkett, who wished to see Ireland become a Dominion, a "crowned republic" that is, within the empire, on an equal footing with Canada and Australia.

When in December, 1919, Mr. Lloyd George introduced his Home Rule Bill into the Imperial Parliament there were no Irish members, except Sir Edward Carson and his followers, to receive it. The rest of Ireland was away. It refused to begin again that old dreary round of hope and disappointment. Let the British and their pet Ulstermen do as they would, said the Irish. . . .

§ 4

Our studies of modern imperialism in Germany and Britain bring out certain forces common to the two countries, and we shall find these same forces at work in variable degrees and with various modifications in the case of the other great modern communities at which we shall now glance. This modern imperialism is not a synthetic world uniting movement like the older imperialism; it is essentially a *megalomaniac nationalism,* a nationalism made aggressive by prosperity; and always it finds its strongest support in the military and official castes, and in the enterprising and acquisitive strata of society, in new money, that is, and big business; its chief critics in the educated poor, and its chief opponents in the peasantry and the labour masses. It accepts monarchy where it finds it, but it is not necessarily a monarchist movement. It does, however, need a foreign office of the traditional type for its full development. Its origin, which we have traced very carefully in this book of our history, makes this clear. Modern imperialism is

the natural development of the Great Power system which arose with the foreign office method of policy, out of the Machiavellian monarchies after the break-up of Christendom. It will only come to an end when the intercourse of nations and peoples through embassies and foreign offices is replaced by an assembly of elected representatives in direct touch with their peoples.

French imperialism during the period of the Armed Peace in Europe was naturally of a less confident type than the German. It called itself "nationalism" rather than imperialism, and it set itself, by appeals to patriotic pride, to thwart the efforts of those socialists and rationalists who sought to get into touch with liberal elements in German life. It brooded upon the *Revanche*, the return match with Prussia. But in spite of that preoccupation, it set itself to the adventure of annexation and exploitation in the Far East and in Africa, narrowly escaping a war with Britain upon the Fashoda clash (1898), and it never relinquished a dream of acquisitions in Syria. Italy, too, caught the imperialist fever; the blood-letting of Adowa cooled her for a time, and then she resumed in 1911 with a war upon Turkey and the annexation of Tripoli. The Italian imperialists exhorted their countrymen to forget Mazzini and remember Julius Cæsar; for were they not the heirs of the Roman Empire? Imperialism touched the Balkans; little countries not a hundred years from slavery began to betray exalted intentions; King Ferdinand of Bulgaria assumed the title of Tsar, the latest of the pseudo-Cæsars, and in the shop-windows of Athens the curious student could study maps showing the dream of a vast Greek empire in Europe and Asia.

In 1913 the three states of Serbia, Bulgaria, and Greece fell upon Turkey, already weakened by her war with Italy, and swept her out of all her European possessions except the country between Adrianople and Constantinople; later in that year they quarrelled among themselves over the division of the spoils. Rumania joined in the game and helped to crush Bulgaria. Turkey recovered Adrianople. The greater imperialisms of Austria, Russia, and Italy watched that conflict and one another. . . .

§ 5

While all the world to the west of her was changing rapidly, Russia throughout the nineteenth century changed very slowly indeed. At the end of the nineteenth century, as at its beginning, she was still a Grand Monarchy of the later seventeenth-century type standing on a basis of barbarism, she was still at a stage where court intrigues and imperial favourites could control her international relations. She had driven a great railway across Siberia to find the disasters of the Japanese war at the end of it; she was using modern methods and modern weapons so far as her undeveloped industrialism and her small supply of sufficiently educated people permitted; such writers as Dostoievski had devised a sort of mystical imperialism based on the idea of Holy Russia and her mission, coloured by racial illusions and anti-Semitic passion; but, as events were to show, this had not sunken very deeply into the imagination of the Russian masses. A vague, very simple Christianity pervaded the illiterate peasant life, mixed with much superstition. It was like the pre-reformation peasant life of France or Germany. The Russian moujik was supposed to worship and revere his Tsar and to love to serve a gentleman; in 1913 reactionary English writers were still praising his simple and unquestioning loyalty. But, as in the case of the western European peasant of the days of the peasant revolts, this reverence for the monarchy was mixed up with the idea that the monarch and the nobleman had to be good and beneficial, and this simple loyalty could, under sufficient provocation, be turned into the same pitiless intolerance of social injustice that burnt the châteaux in the Jacquerie (see Chapter XXXIV, § 3) and set up the theocracy in Münster (Chapter XXXIV, § 3). Once the commons were moved to anger, there were no links of understanding in a generally diffused education in Russia to mitigate the fury of the outbreak. The upper classes were as much beyond the sympathy of the lower as a different species of animal. These Russian masses were three centuries away from such nationalist imperialism as Germany displayed.

And in another respect Russia differed from modern Western Europe and paralleled its mediæval phase, and that was in the fact that her universities were the resort of many very poor students quite out of touch and out of sympathy with the bureaucratic autocracy. Before 1917 the significance of the proximity of these two factors of revolution, the fuel of discontent and the match of free ideas, was not recognized in European thought, and few people realized that in Russia more than in any other country lay the possibilities of a fundamental revolution.

§ 6

When we turn from these European Great Powers, with their inheritance of foreign offices and national policies, to the United States of America, which broke away completely from the Great Power System in 1776, we find a most interesting contrast in the operation of the forces which produced the expansive imperialism of Europe. For America as for Europe the mechanical revolution had brought all the world within the range of a few days' journey. The United States, like the Great Powers, had world-wide financial and mercantile interests; a great industrialism had grown up and was in need of overseas markets; the same crises of belief that had shaken the moral solidarity of Europe had occurred in the American world. Her people were as patriotic and spirited as any. Why then did not the United States develop armaments and an aggressive policy? Why was not the stars and stripes waving over Mexico, and why was there not a new Indian system growing up in China under that flag? It was the American who had opened up Japan. After doing so, he had let that power Europeanize itself and become formidable without a protest. That alone was enough to make Machiavelli, the father of modern foreign policy, turn in his grave. If a Europeanized Great Power had been in the place of the United States, Great Britain would have had to fortify the Canadian frontier from end to end—it is now absolutely unarmed—and to maintain a great arsenal in the St. Lawrence. All the divided states of Central and South America would long since have been subjugated and placed under the disciplinary control of United States officials of the "governing class." There would have been a perpetual campaign to Americanize Australia and New Zealand, and yet another claimant for a share in tropical Africa.

And by an odd accident America had produced in President Roosevelt (President 1901-1909) a man of an energy as restless as the German Kaiser's, as eager for large achievements, as florid and eloquent, an adventurous man with a turn for world politics and an instinct for armaments, the very man, we might imagine, to have involved his country in the scramble for overseas possession.

There does not appear to be any other explanation of this

general restraint and abstinence on the part of the United States except in their fundamentally different institutions and traditions. In the first place the United States Government has no foreign office and no diplomatic corps of the European type, no body of "experts" to maintain the tradition of an aggressive policy. The president has great powers, but they are subject to the control of the senate, which again is responsible to the state legislatures and the people. The foreign relations of the country are thus under open and public control. Secret treaties are impossible under such a system, and foreign powers complain of the difficulty and uncertainty of "understandings" with the United States, a very excellent state of affairs. The United States is[1] constitutionally incapacitated, therefore, from the kind of foreign policy that has kept Europe for so long constantly on the verge of war.

And, secondly, there has hitherto existed in the States no organization for and no tradition of what one may call non-assimilable possessions. Where there is no crown there cannot be crown colonies. In spreading across the American continent, the United States had developed a quite distinctive method of dealing with new territories, admirably adapted for unsettled lands, but very inconvenient if applied too freely to areas already containing an alien population. This method was based on the idea that there cannot be in the United States system a permanently subject people. The first stage of the ordinary process of assimilation had been the creation of a "territory" under the federal government, having a considerable measure of self-government, sending a delegate (who could not vote) to congress, and destined, in the natural course of things, as the country became settled and population increased, to flower at last into full statehood. This had been the process of development of all the latter states of the Union; the latest territories to become states being Arizona and New Mexico in 1910. The frozen wilderness of Alaska, bought from Russia, remained politically undeveloped simply because it had an insufficient population for state organization. As the annexations of Germany and Great Britain in the Pacific threatened to deprive the United States navy of coaling stations in that ocean, a part of the Samoan Islands (1889) and the Sandwich Islands (Hawaii) were annexed (1898). Here for the first

[1] "Is," not "are." Since the Civil War the U. S. A. is one nation. A. C.

time the United States had real subject populations to deal with. But in the absence of any class comparable to the Anglo-Indian officials who sway British opinion, the American procedure followed the territorial method. Every effort was made to bring the educational standards of Hawaii up to the American level, and a domestic legislature on the territorial pattern was organized so that these dusky islanders seem destined ultimately to obtain full United States citizenship. (The small Samoan Islands are taken care of by a United States naval administrator.)

In 1895 occurred a quarrel between the United States and Britain upon the subject of Venezuela, and the Monroe Doctrine was upheld stoutly by President Cleveland. Then Mr. Olney made this remarkable declaration: "To-day the United States is practically sovereign on this continent, and its fiat is law upon the subjects to which it confines its interposition." This, together with the various Pan-American congresses that have been held, point to a real open "foreign policy" of alliance and mutual help throughout America. Treaties of arbitration hold good over all that continent, and the future seems to point to a gradual development of inter-state organization, a Pax Americana, of the English-speaking and Spanish-speaking peoples, the former in the rôle of elder brother. Here is something we cannot even call an empire, something going far beyond the great alliance of the British Empire in the open equality of its constituent parts.

Consistently with this idea of a common American welfare, the United States in 1898 intervened in the affairs of Cuba, which had been in a state of chronic insurrection against Spain for many years. A brief war ended in the acquisition of Cuba, Porto Rico, and the Philippine Islands. Cuba is now an independent self-governing republic. Porto Rico and the Philippines have, however, a special sort of government, with a popularly elected lower house and an upper body containing members appointed by the United States senate. It is improbable that either Porto Rico or the Philippines will become states in the Union. They are much more likely to become free states in some comprehensive alliance with both English-speaking and Latin America.

Both Cuba and Porto Rico welcomed the American intervention in their affairs, but in the Philippine Islands there was a demand for complete and immediate freedom after the Spanish war, and a considerable resistance to the American military administration. There it was that the United States came nearest to imperialism of the Great Power type, and that her record is most questionable. There was much sympathy with the insurgents in the states. Here is the point of view of ex-President Roosevelt as he wrote it in his *Autobiography* (1913):

"As regards the Philippines, my belief was that we should train them for self-government as rapidly as possible, and then leave them free to decide their own fate. I did not believe in setting the time-limit within which we would give them independence, because I did not believe it wise to try to forecast how soon they would be fit for self-government; and once having made the promise, I would have felt that it was imperative to keep it. Within a few months of my assuming office we had stamped out the last armed resistance in the Philippines that was not of merely sporadic character; and as soon as peace was secured, we turned our energies to developing the islands in the interests of the natives. We established schools everywhere; we built roads; we administered an even-handed justice; we did everything possible to encourage agriculture and industry; and in constantly increasing measure we employed natives to do their own governing, and finally provided a legislative chamber. . . . We are governing, and have been governing, the islands in the interests of the Filipinos themselves. If after due time the Filipinos themselves decide that they do not wish to be thus governed, then I trust that we will leave; but when we do leave, it must be distinctly understood that we retain no protectorate—and above all that we take part in no joint protectorate—over the islands, and give them no guarantee, of neutrality or otherwise; that in short, we are absolutely quit of responsibility for them, of very kind and description."

This is an entirely different outlook from that of a British or French foreign office or colonial office official. But it is not very widely different from the spirit that created the Dominions of Canada, South Africa, and Australia, and brought forward the three Home Rule Bills for Ireland. It is in the older and more characteristic English tradition from which the Declaration of Independence derives. It sets aside, without discussion, the detestable idea of "subject peoples."

Here we will not enter into political complications attendant upon the making of the Panama Canal, for they introduce no fresh light upon this interesting question of the American method in world politics. The history of Panama is American history purely. But manifestly just as the internal political structure of the Union was a new thing in the world, so, too, were its relations with the world beyond its borders.

§ 7

We have been at some pains to examine the state of mind of Europe and of America in regard to international relations in the years that led up to the world tragedy of 1914 because, as more and more people are coming to recognize, that great war or some such war was a necessary consequence of the mentality of the period. All the things that men and nations do are the outcome of instinctive motives reacting upon the ideas which talk and books and newspapers and schoolmasters and so forth have put into people's heads. Physical necessities, pestilences, changes of climate, and the like outer things may deflect and distort the growth of human history, but its living root is thought.

All human history is fundamentally a history of ideas. Between the man of to-day and the Cro-Magnard the physical and mental differences are very slight; their essential difference lies in the extent and content of the mental background which we have acquired in the five or six hundred generations that intervene.

We are too close to the events of the Great War to pretend that this *Outline* can record the verdict of history thereupon, but we may hazard the guess that when the passions of the conflict have faded, it will be Germany that will be most blamed for bringing it about, and she will be blamed not because she was morally and intellectually very different from her neighbours, but because she had the common disease of imperialism in its most complete and energetic form. No self-respecting historian, however superficial and popular his aims may be, can countenance the legend, produced by the stresses of the war, that the German is a sort of human being more cruel and abominable than any other variety of men. All the great states of Europe before 1914 were in a condition of aggressive nationalism and drifting towards war; the government of Germany did but lead the general movement. She fell into the pit first, and she floundered deepest. She became the dreadful example at which all her fellow sinners could cry out.

For long, Germany and Austria had been plotting an extension of German influence eastward through Asia Minor to the East. The German idea was crystallized in the phrase "Berlin to Bagdad." Antagonized to the German dreams were those of Russia, which was scheming for an extension of the Slav ascendancy to Constantinople and through Serbia to the Adriatic. These lines of ambition lay across one another and were mutually incompatible. The feverish state of affairs in the Balkans was largely the outcome of the intrigues and propagandas sustained by the German and Slav schemes. Turkey turned for support to Germany, Serbia to Russia. Rumania and Italy, both Latin in tradition, both nominally allies of Germany, pursued remoter and deeper schemes in common. Ferdinand, the Tsar of Bulgaria, was following still darker ends; and the squalid mysteries of the Greek court, whose king was the German Kaiser's brother-in-law, are beyond our present powers of inquiry.

But the tangle did not end with Germany on the one hand and Russia on the other. The greed of Germany in 1871 had made France her inveterate enemy. The French people, aware of their inability to recover their lost provinces by their own strength, had conceived exaggerated ideas of the power and helpfulness of Russia. The French people had subscribed enormously to Russian loans. France was the ally of Russia. If the German powers made war upon Russia, France would certainly attack them.

Now the short eastern French frontier was very strongly defended. There was little prospect of Germany repeating the successes of 1870-71 against that barrier. But the Belgian frontier of France was longer and less strongly defended. An attack in overwhelming force on France through Belgium might repeat 1870 on a larger scale. The French left might be swung back south-eastwardly on Verdun as a pivot, and crowded back upon its right, as one shuts an open razor. This scheme the German strategists had worked out with great care and elaboration. Its execution involved an outrage upon the law of nations because Prussia had undertaken to guarantee the neutrality of Belgium and had no quarrel with her, and it involved the risk of bringing in Great Britain (which power was also pledged to protect Belgium) against Germany. Yet the Germans believed that their fleet had grown strong enough to make Great Britain hesitate to interfere, and with a view to possibilities they had constructed a great system of strategic railways to the Belgian frontier, and made every preparation for the execution of this scheme. So they might hope to strike down France at one blow, and deal at their leisure with Russia.

In 1914 all things seemed moving together in favour of the two Central Powers. Russia, it is true, had been recovering since 1906, but only very slowly; France was distracted by financial scandals. The astounding murder of M. Calmette, the editor of the *Figaro,* by the wife of M. Caillaux, the minister of finance, brought these to a climax in March; Britain, all Germany was assured, was on the verge of a civil war in Ireland. Repeated efforts were made both by foreign and English people to get some definite statement of what Britain would do if Germany and Austria assailed France and Russia; but the British Foreign Secretary maintained a front of heavy ambiguity up to the very day of the British entry into the war. As a consequence, there was a feeling on the continent that Britain would either not fight or delay fighting, and this may have encouraged Germany to go on threatening France. Events were precipitated on June 28th by the assassination of the Archduke Francis Ferdinand, the heir to the Austrian Empire, when on a state visit to Sarajevo, the capital of Bosnia. Here was a timely excuse to set the armies marching. "It is now or never," said the German Emperor. Serbia was accused of instigating the murderers, and notwithstanding the fact that Austrian commissioners reported that there was no evidence to implicate the Serbian government, the Austro-Hungarian government contrived to press this grievance towards war. On July 23rd Austria discharged an ultimatum at Serbia, and, in spite of a practical submission on the part of Serbia, and of the efforts of Sir Edward Grey, the British Foreign Secretary, to call a conference of the powers, declared war against Serbia on July 28th.

Russia mobilized her army on July 30th, and on August 1st Germany declared war upon her. German troops crossed into French territory next day, and, simultaneously with the delivery of an ultimatum to the unfortunate Belgians, the big flanking movement through Luxembourg and Belgium began. Westward rode the scouts and advance guards. Westward rushed a multitude of automobiles packed with soldiers. Enormous columns of grey-clad infantry followed; round-eyed, fair young Germans they were for the most part—law-abiding, educated youngsters who had never yet seen a shot fired in anger. "This was war," they were told. They had to be bold and ruthless. Some of them did their best to carry out these militarist instructions at the expense of the ill-fated Belgians.

A disproportionate fuss has been made over the detailed atrocities in Belgium, disproportionate, that is, in relation to the fundamental atrocity of August, 1914, which was the invasion of Belgium. Given that, the casual shootings and lootings, the wanton destruction of property, the plundering of inns and of food and drink shops by hungry and weary men, and the consequent rapes and incendiarism follow naturally enough. Only very simple people believe that an army in the field can maintain as high a level of honesty, decency, and justice as a settled community at home. And the tradition of the Thirty Years' War still influenced the Prussian army. It has been customary in the countries allied against Germany to treat all this vileness and bloodshed of the Belgian months as though nothing of the sort had ever happened before, and as if it were due to some distinctively evil strain in the German character. They were nicknamed "Huns." But nothing could be less like the systematic destructions of these nomads (who once proposed to exterminate the entire Chinese population in order to restore China to pasture) than the German crimes in Belgium. Much of that crime was the drunken brutality of men who for the first time in their lives were free to use lethal weapons, much of it was the hysterical violence of men shocked at their own proceedings and in deadly fear of the revenge of the people whose country they had outraged, and much of it was done under duress because of the theory that men should be terrible in warfare and that populations are best subdued by fear. The German common people were bundled from an orderly obedience into this war in such a manner that atrocities were bound to ensue. They certainly did horrible and disgusting things. But any people who had been worked up for war and led into war as the Germans were, would have behaved in a similar manner.

On the night of August 2nd, while most of Europe, still under the tranquil inertias of half a century of peace, still in the habitual enjoyment of such a widely diffused plenty and

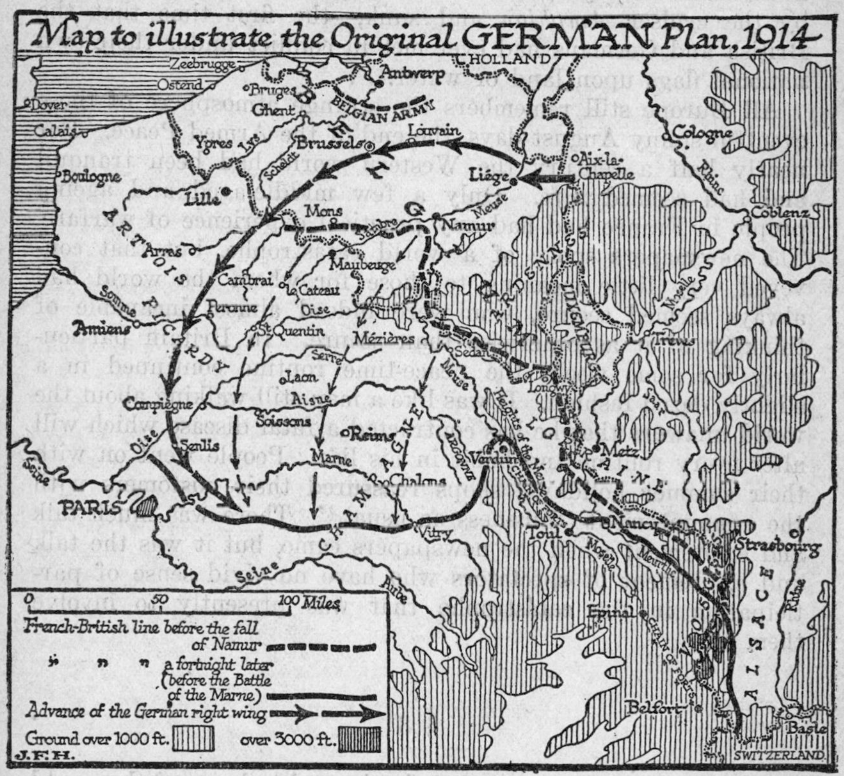

cheapness and freedom as no man living will ever see again, was thinking about its summer holidays, the little Belgian village of Visé was ablaze, and stupefied rustics were being led out and shot because it was alleged someone had fired on the invaders. The officers who ordered these acts, the men who obeyed, must surely have felt scared at the strangeness of the things they did. Most of them had never yet seen a violent death. And they had set light not to a village, but a world.

It was the beginning of the end of an age of comfort, confidence, and gentle and seemly behaviour in Europe.

So soon as it was clear that Belgium was to be invaded, Great Britain ceased to hesitate, and (at eleven at night on August 4th) declared war upon Germany. The following day a German mine-laying vessel was caught off the Thames mouth by the cruiser *Amphion* and sunk,—the first time that the British and Germans had ever met in conflict under their own national flags upon land or water. . . .

All Europe still remembers the strange atmosphere of those eventful sunny August days, the end of the Armed Peace. For nearly half a century the Western world had been tranquil and had seemed *safe*. Only a few middle-aged and ageing people in France had had any practical experience of warfare. The newspapers spoke of a world catastrophe, but that conveyed very little meaning to those for whom the world had always seemed secure, who were indeed almost incapable of thinking of it as otherwise than secure. In Britain particularly for some weeks the peace-time routine continued in a slightly dazed fashion. It was like a man still walking about the world unaware that he has contracted a fatal disease which will alter every routine and habit in his life. People went on with their summer holidays; shops reassured their customers with the announcement "business as usual." There was much talk and excitement when the newspapers came, but it was the talk and excitement of spectators who have no vivid sense of participation in the catastrophe that was presently to involve them all.

§ 8

We will now review very briefly the main phases of the world struggle which had thus commenced. Planned by Germany, it began with a swift attack designed to "knock out" France while Russia was still getting her forces together in the East. For a time all went well. Military science is never up to date under modern conditions, because military men are as a class unimaginative, there are always at any date undeveloped inventions capable of disturbing current tactical and strategic practice which the military intelligence has declined. The

German plan had been made for some years; it was a stale plan; it could probably have been foiled at the outset by a proper use of entrenchments and barbed wire and machine guns, but the French were by no means as advanced in their military science as the Germans, and they trusted to methods of open warfare that were at least fourteen years behind the times. They had a proper equipment neither of barbed wire nor machine guns, and there was a ridiculous tradition that the Frenchman did not fight well behind earthworks. The Belgian frontier was defended by the fortress of Liège, ten or twelve years out of date, with forts whose armament had been furnished and fitted in many cases by German contractors; and the French north-eastern frontier was very badly equipped. Naturally the German armament firm of Krupp had provided nutcrackers for these nuts in the form of exceptionally heavy guns firing high explosive shell. These defences proved therefore to be mere traps for their garrisons. The French attacked and failed in the southern Ardennes. The German hosts swung round the French left with an effect of being irresistible; Liège fell on August 9th, Brussels was reached on August 20th, and the small British army of about 70,000, which had arrived in Belgium, was struck at Mons (August 22nd) in overwhelming force, and driven backward in spite of the very deadly rifle tactics it had learnt during the South African War. The little British force was pushed aside westward, and the German right swept down so as to leave Paris to the west and crumple the entire French army back upon itself.

So confident was the German higher command at this stage of having won the war, that by the end of August German troops were already being withdrawn for the Eastern front, where the Russians were playing havoc in East and West Prussia. And then came the French counter-attack, strategically a very swift and brilliant counter-attack. The French struck back on their centre, they produced an unexpected army on their left, and the small British army, shaken but reinforced, was still fit to play a worthy part in the counter-stroke. The German right overran itself, lost its cohesion, and was driven back from the Marne to the Aisne (Battle of the Marne, September 6th to 10th). It would have been driven back farther had it not had the art of entrenchment in reserve. Upon the Aisne it stood and dug itself in. The heavy guns, the high explosive shell, the tanks, needed by the allies to smash up these entrenchments, did not yet exist.

The Battle of the Marne shattered the original German plan. For a time France was saved. But the German was not defeated; he had still a great offensive superiority in men and equipment. His fear of the Russian in the east had been relieved by a tremendous victory at Tannenberg. His next phase was a headlong, less elaborately planned campaign to outflank the left of the allied armies and to seize the Channel ports and cut off supplies coming from Britain to France. Both armies extended to the west in a sort of race to the coast. Then the Germans, with a great superiority of guns and equipment, struck at the British round and about Ypres. They came very near to a break through, but the British held them.

The war on the Western front settled down to trench warfare. Neither side had the science and equipment needed to solve the problem of breaking through modern entrenchments and entanglements, and both sides were now compelled to resort to scientific men, inventors, and such-like unmilitary persons for counsel and help in their difficulty. At that time the essential problem of trench warfare had already been solved; there existed in England, for instance, the model of a tank, which would have given the allies a swift and easy victory before 1916; but the professional military mind is by necessity an inferior and unimaginative mind; no man of high intellectual quality would willingly imprison his gifts in such a calling; nearly all supremely great soldiers have been either inexperienced fresh-minded young men like Alexander, Napoleon, and Hoche, politicians turned soldiers like Julius Cæsar, nomads like the Hun and Mongol captains, or amateurs like Cromwell and Washington; whereas this war after fifty years of militarism was a hopelessly professional war; from first to last it was impossible to get it out of the hands of the regular generals, and neither the German nor allied headquarters was disposed to regard an invention with toleration that would destroy their traditional methods. The tank was not only disagreeably strange to these military gentlemen, but it gave an unprofessional protection to the common soldiers within it. The Germans, however, did make some innovations. In February (28) they produced a rather futile novelty, the flame projector, the user of which was in constant danger of being burnt alive, and in April, in the midst of a second great offensive upon the British (second Battle of Ypres, April 17th to May 17th), they employed a cloud of poison gas. This horrible device was used against Algerian and Canadian troops; it shook them by the physical torture it inflicted, and by the anguish of those

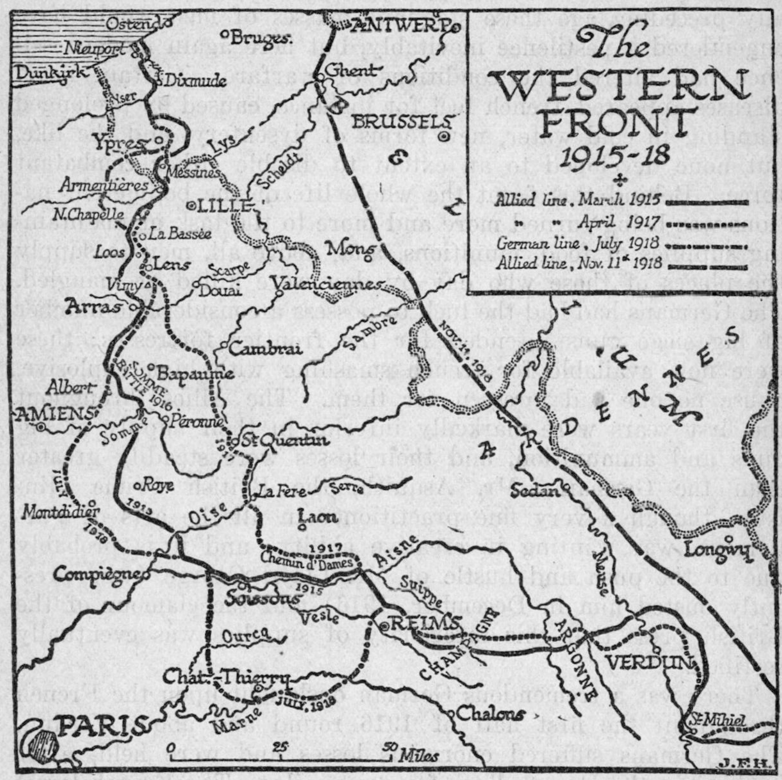

who died, but it failed to break through them. For some weeks chemists were of more importance than soldiers on the allied front, and within six weeks the defensive troops were already in possession of protective methods and devices.

For a year and a half, until July, 1916, the Western front remained in a state of indecisive tension. There were heavy attacks on either side that ended in bloody repulses. The French made costly but glorious thrusts at Arras and in Champagne in 1915, the British at Loos. From Switzerland to the North Sea there ran two continuous lines of entrenchment, sometimes at a distance of a mile or more, sometimes at a distance of a few feet (at Arras *e.g.*), and in and behind these lines of trenches millions of men toiled, raided their enemies, and prepared for sanguinary and foredoomed offensives. In any preceding age these stagnant masses of men would have engendered a pestilence inevitably, but here again modern science had altered the conditions of warfare. Certain novel diseases appeared, trench feet for instance, caused by prolonged standing in cold water, new forms of dysentery, and the like, but none developed to an extent to disable either combatant force. Behind this front the whole life of the belligerent nations was being turned more and more to the task of maintaining supplies of food, munitions, and, above all, men to supply the places of those who day by day were killed or mangled. The Germans had had the luck to possess a considerable number of big siege guns intended for the frontier fortresses; these were now available for trench smashing with high explosive, a use no one had foreseen for them. The Allies throughout the first years were markedly inferior in their supply of big guns and ammunition, and their losses were steadily greater than the German. Mr. Asquith, the British Prime Minister, though a very fine practitioner in all the arts of Parliament, was wanting in creative ability; and it is probably due to the push and hustle of Mr. Lloyd George (who presently ousted him in December, 1916) and the clamour of the British press that this inferiority of supplies was eventually rectified.

There was a tremendous German onslaught upon the French throughout the first half of 1916 round and about Verdun. The Germans suffered enormous losses and were held, after pushing in the French lines for some miles. The French losses were as great or greater. "*Ils ne passeront pas,*" said and sang the French infantry—and kept their word.

The Eastern German front was more extended and less systematically entrenched than the Western. For a time the Russian armies continued to press westward in spite of the Tannenberg disaster. They conquered nearly the whole of Galicia from the Austrians, took Lemberg on September 2nd, 1914, and the great fortress of Przemysl on March 22nd, 1915. But after the Germans had failed to break the Western front of the Allies, and after an ineffective Allied offensive made without proper material, they turned to Russia, and a series of heavy blows, with a novel use of massed artillery, were struck first in the south and then at the north of the Russian front. On June 22nd, Przemysl was retaken, and the whole Russian line was driven back until Vilna (September 2nd) was in German hands.

In May, 1915 (23rd), Italy joined the allies, and declared war upon Austria. (Not until a year later did she declare war on Germany.) She pushed over her eastern boundary towards Goritzia (which fell in the summer of 1916), but her intervention was of little use at that time to either Russia or the two Western powers. She merely established another line of trench warfare among the high mountains of her picturesque north-eastern frontier.

While the main fronts of the chief combatants were in this state of exhaustive deadlock, both sides were attempting to strike round behind the front of their adversaries. The Germans made a series of Zeppelin, and later of aeroplane raids upon Paris and the east of England. Ostensibly these aimed at depôts, munition works, and the like targets of military importance, but practically they bombed promiscuously at inhabited places. At first these raiders dropped not very effective bombs, but later the size and quality of these missiles increased, considerable numbers of people were killed and injured, and very much damage was done. The English people were roused to a pitch of extreme indignation by these outrages. Although the Germans had possessed Zeppelins for some years, no one in authority in Great Britain had thought out the proper methods of dealing with them, and it was not until late in 1916 that an adequate supply of anti-aircraft guns was brought into play and that these raiders were systematically attacked by aeroplanes. Then came a series of Zeppelin disasters, and after the spring of 1917 they ceased to be used for any purpose but sea scouting, and their place as raiders was taken by large aeroplanes (the Gothas). The visits of these latter machines to London and the east of England became systematic after the summer of 1917. All through the winter of 1917-18, London on every moonlight night became familiar with the banging of warning maroons, the shrill whistles of the police alarm, the hasty clearance of the streets, the distant rumbling of scores and hundreds of anti-aircraft guns growing steadily to a wild uproar of thuds and crashes, the swish of flying shrapnel, and at last, if any of the raiders got through the barrage, with the dull heavy bang of the bursting bombs. Then presently, amidst the diminuendo of the gunfire would come the inimitable rushing sound of the fire brigade engines and the hurry of the ambulances. . . . War was brought home to every Londoner by these experiences.

While the Germans were thus assailing the nerve of their enemy home population through the air, they were also attacking the overseas trade of the British by every means in their power. At the outset of the war they had various trade destroyers scattered over the world, and a squadron of powerful modern cruisers in the Pacific, namely, the *Scharnhorst,* the *Gneisenau,* the *Leipzig,* the *Nürnberg,* and the *Dresden.* Some of the detached cruisers, and particularly the *Emden,* did a considerable amount of commerce destroying before they were hunted down, and the main squadron caught an inferior British force off the coast of Chile and sank the *Good Hope* and the *Monmouth* on November 1st, 1914. A month later these German ships were themselves pounced upon by a British force, and all (except the *Dresden*) sunk by Admiral Sturdee in the Battle of the Falkland Isles. After this conflict the allies remained in undisputed possession of the surface of the sea, a supremacy which the great naval Battle of Jutland (May 1st, 1916) did nothing to shake. The Germans concentrated their attention more and more upon submarine warfare. From the beginning of the war they had had considerable submarine successes. On one day, September 22nd, 1914, they sank three powerful cruisers, the *Aboukir,* the *Hogue,* and the *Cressy,* with 1,473 men. They continued to levy a toll upon British shipping throughout the war; at first they hailed and examined passenger and mercantile shipping, but this practice they discontinued for fear of traps, and in the spring of 1915 they began to sink ships without notice. In May, 1915, they sank the great passenger liner, the *Lusitania,* without any warning, drowning a number of American citizens. This embittered American feeling against them, but the possibility of injuring and perhaps reducing Britain by a submarine blockade was so great, that they persisted in a more and more intensified submarine campaign, regardless of the danger of dragging the United States into the circle of their enemies.

Meanwhile, Turkish forces, very ill-equipped, were making threatening gestures at Egypt across the desert of Sinai.

And while the Germans were thus striking at Britain, their least accessible and most formidable antagonist, through the air and under the sea, the French and British were also embarking upon a disastrous flank attack in the east upon the Central Powers through Turkey. The Gallipoli campaign was finely imagined, but disgracefully executed. Had it succeeded, the Allies would have captured Constantinople in 1915. But the Turks were given two months' notice of the project by a premature bombardment of the Dardanelles in February, the scheme was also probably betrayed through the Greek Court, and when at last British and French forces were landed upon the Gallipoli peninsula in April, they found the Turks well entrenched and better equipped for trench warfare than themselves. The Allies trusted for heavy artillery to the great guns of the ships, which were comparatively useless for battering down entrenchments, and among every other sort of thing that they had failed to foresee, they had not foreseen hostile submarines. Several great battleships were lost; they went down in the same clear waters over which the ships of Xerxes had once sailed to their fate at Salamis. The story of the Gallipoli campaign from the side of the Allies is at once heroic and pitiful, a story of courage and incompetence, and of life, material, and prestige wasted, culminating in a withdrawal in January, 1916.

Linked up closely with the vacillation of Greece was the entry of Bulgaria into the war (October 12th, 1915). The king of Bulgaria had hesitated for more than a year to make any decision between the two sides. Now the manifest failure of the British at Gallipoli, coupled with a strong Austro-German attack in Serbia, swung him over to the Central Powers. While the Serbs were hotly engaged with the Austro-German invaders upon the Danube he attacked Serbia in the rear, and in a few weeks the country had been completely overrun. The Serbian army made a terrible retreat through the mountains of Albania to the coast, where its remains were rescued by an Allied fleet.

An Allied force landed at Salonika in Greece, and pushed inland towards Monastir, but was unable to render any effectual assistance to the Serbians. It was the Salonika plan which sealed the fate of the Gallipoli expedition.

To the east, in Mesopotamia, the British, using Indian troops chiefly, made a still remoter flank attack upon the Central Powers. An army, very ill provided for the campaign, was landed at Basra in the November of 1914, and pushed up towards Bagdad in the following year. It gained a victory at Ctesiphon, the ancient Arsacid and Sassanid capital within twenty-five miles of Bagdad, but the Turks were heavily reinforced, there was a retreat to Kut, and there the British army, under General Townshend, was surrounded and starved into surrender on April 29th, 1916.

All these campaigns in the air, under the seas, in Russia, Turkey, and Asia, were subsidiary to the main front, the front of decision, between Switzerland and the sea; and there the main millions lay entrenched, slowly learning the necessary methods of modern scientific warfare. There was a rapid progress in the use of the aeroplane. At the outset of the war this had been used chiefly for scouting, and by the Germans for the dropping of marks for the artillery. Such a thing as aerial fighting was unheard of. In 1916 the aeroplanes carried machine guns and fought in the air; their bombing work was increasingly important, they had developed a wonderful art of aerial photography, and all the aerial side of artillery work, both with aeroplanes and observation balloons, had been enormously developed. But the military mind was still resisting the use of the tank, the obvious weapon for decision in trench warfare.

Many intelligent people outside military circles understood this quite clearly. The use of the tank against trenches was an altogether obvious expedient. Leonardo da Vinci invented an early tank, but what military "expert" has ever had the wits to study Leonardo? Soon after the South African War, in 1903, there were stories in magazines describing imaginary battles in which tanks figured, and a complete working model of a tank made by Mr. J. A. Corry of Leeds, was shown to the British military authorities—who of course rejected it—in 1911. Tanks had been invented and re-invented before the war began. But had the matter rested entirely in the hands of the military, there would never have been any use of tanks. It was Mr. Winston Churchill, who was at the British Admiralty in 1915-16, who insisted upon the manufacture of the first tanks, and it was in the teeth of the grimmest opposition that they were sent to France. To the British navy, and not to the army, military science owes the use of these devices. The German military authorities were equally set against them. In July, 1916, Sir Douglas Haig, the British commander-in-chief, began a great offensive which failed to break through the German line. In some places he advanced a few miles; in others he was completely defeated. There was a huge slaughter of the new British armies. And he did not use tanks.

In September, when the season was growing too late for a sustained offensive, tanks first appeared in warfare. A few were put into action by the British in a not very intelligent fashion. Their effect upon the German was profound, they produced something like a panic, and there can be little doubt that had they been used in July in sufficient numbers and handled by a general of imagination and energy, they would have ended the war there and then. At that time the Allies were in greater strength than the Germans upon the Western front. The odds were roughly seven to four. Russia, though fast approaching exhaustion, was still fighting, Italy was pressing the Austrians hard, and Rumania was just entering the war on the side of the Allies. But the waste of men in this disastrous July offensive, and the incompetence of the British military command, brought the Allied cause to the very brink of disaster.

Directly the British failure of July had reassured the Germans, they turned on the Rumanians, and the winter of 1916 saw the same fate overtake Rumania that had fallen upon Serbia in 1915. The year that had begun with the retreat from Gallipoli and the surrender of Kut, ended with the crushing of Rumania and with volleys fired at a landing party of French and British marines by a royalist crowd in the port of Athens. It looked as though King Constantine of Greece meant to lead his people in the footsteps of King Ferdinand of Bulgaria. But the coast-line of Greece is one much exposed to naval action. Greece was blockaded, and a French force from Salonika joined hands with an Italian force from Valona to cut the king of Greece off from his Central European friends.

(In July, 1917, Constantine was forced to abdicate by the Allies, and his son Alexander was made king in his place.)

On the whole, things looked much less dangerous for the

Hohenzollern imperialism at the end of 1916 than they had done after the failure of the first great rush at the Marne. The Allies had wasted two years of opportunity. Belgium, Serbia, and Rumania, and large areas of France and Russia, were occupied by Austro-German troops. Counterstroke after counterstroke had failed, and Russia was now tottering towards a collapse. Had Germany been ruled with any wisdom, she might have made a reasonable peace at this time. But the touch of success had intoxicated her imperialists. They wanted not safety, but triumph, not world welfare, but world empire. "World power or downfall" was their formula; it gave their antagonists no alternative but a fight to a conclusive end.

§ 9

Early in 1917 Russia collapsed.

By this time the enormous strain of the war was telling hardly upon all the European populations. There had been a great disorganization of transport everywhere, a discontinuance of the normal repairs and replacements of shipping, railways, and the like, a using-up of material of all sorts, a dwindling of food production, a withdrawal of greater and greater masses of men from industry, a cessation of educational work, and a steady diminution of the ordinary securities and honesties of life. Nowhere was the available directive ability capable of keeping a grip upon affairs in the face of the rupture of habitual bonds and the replacement of the subtle disciplines of peace by the clumsy brutalities of military "order." More and more of the European population was being transferred from surroundings and conditions to which it was accustomed, to novel circumstances which distressed, stimulated, and demoralized it. But Russia suffered first and most from this universal pulling up of civilization from its roots. The Russian autocracy was dishonest and incompetent. The Tsar, like several of his ancestors, had now given way to a crazy pietism, and the court was dominated by a religious impostor, Rasputin, whose cult was one of unspeakable foulness, a reeking scandal in the face of the world. Beneath the rule of this dirty mysticism, indolence and scoundrelism mismanaged the war. The Russian common soldiers were sent into battle without guns to support them, without even rifle ammunition; they were wasted by their officers and generals in a delirium of militarist enthusiasm. For a time they seemed to be suffering mutely as the beasts suffer; but there is a limit to the endurance even of the most ignorant. A profound disgust for the Tsardom was creeping through these armies of betrayed and wasted men. From the close of 1915 onwards Russia was a source of deepening anxiety to her Western allies. Throughout 1916 she remained largely on the defensive, and there were rumours of a separate peace with Germany. She gave little help to Rumania.

On December 29th, 1916, the monk Rasputin was murdered at a dinner-party in Petrograd, and a belated attempt was made to put the Tsardom in order. By March things were moving rapidly; food riots in Petrograd developed into a revolutionary insurrection; there was an attempted suppression of the Duma, the representative body, attempted arrests of liberal leaders, the formation of a provisional government under Prince Lvoff, and an abdication (March 15th) by the Tsar. For a time it seemed that a moderate and controlled revolution might be possible—perhaps under a new Tsar. Then it became evident that the destruction of confidence in Russia had gone too far for any such adjustments. The Russian people were sick to death of the old order of things in Europe, of Tsars and of wars and great powers; it wanted relief, and that speedily, from unendurable miseries. The Allies had no understanding of Russian realities; their diplomatists were ignorant of Russian, genteel persons, with their attention directed to the Russian Court rather than Russia, they blundered steadily with the new situation. There was little goodwill among the diplomatists for republicanism, and a manifest disposition to embarrass the new government as much as possible. At the head of the Russian republican government was an eloquent and picturesque leader, Kerensky, who found himself assailed by the deep forces of a profounder revolutionary movement, the "social revolution," at home and cold-shouldered by the Allied governments abroad. His allies would neither let him give the Russian people land nor peace beyond their frontiers. The French and the British press pestered their exhausted ally for a fresh offensive, but when presently the Germans made a strong attack by sea and land upon Riga, the British Admiralty quailed before the prospect of a Baltic expedition in relief. The new Russian republic had to fight unsupported. In spite of their great naval predominance and the bitter protests of the great English admiral, Lord Fisher (1841-1920), it is to be noted that the Allies, except for some submarine attacks, left the Germans the complete mastery of the Baltic throughout the war.

The Russian masses were resolute to end the war. There had come into existence in Petrograd a body representing the workers and common soldiers, the Soviet, and this body clamoured for an international conference of socialists at Stockholm. Food riots were occurring in Berlin at this time, war weariness in Austria and Germany was profound, and there can be little doubt, in the light of subsequent events, that such a conference would have precipitated a reasonable peace on democratic lines in 1917 and a German revolution. Kerensky implored his Western allies to allow this conference to take place, but, fearful of a world-wide outbreak of socialism and republicanism, they refused, in spite of the favourable response of a small majority of the British Labour Party. Without either moral or physical help from the Allies, the "moderate" Russian republic still fought on and made a last desperate offensive effort in July. It failed after some preliminary successes and another great slaughtering of Russians.

The limit of Russian endurance was reached. Mutinies broke out in the Russian armies, and particularly upon the northern front, and upon November 7th, 1917, Kerensky's government was overthrown and power was seized by the Soviet Government, dominated by the Bolshevik socialists under Lenin, and pledged to make peace regardless of the Western powers. Russia passed definitely "out of the war."

In the spring of 1917 there had been a costly and ineffective French attack upon the Champagne front which had failed to break through and sustained enormous losses. Here, then, by the end of 1917, was a phase of events altogether favourable to Germany, had her government been fighting for security and well-being rather than for pride and victory. But to the very end, to the pitch of final exhaustion, the people of the Central Powers were held to the effort to realize an impossible world imperialism.

To that end it was necessary that Britain should be not merely resisted, but subjugated, and in order to do that Germany had already dragged America into the circle of her enemies. Throughout 1916 the submarine campaign had been growing in intensity, but hitherto it had respected neutral shipping. In January, 1917, a completer, "blockade" of Great Britain and France was proclaimed, and all neutral powers were warned to withdraw their shipping from the British seas. An indiscriminate sinking of the world's shipping began which compelled the United States to enter the war in April (6th) 1917. Throughout 1917, while Russia was breaking up and becoming impotent, the American people were changing swiftly and steadily into a great military nation. And the unrestricted submarine campaign for which the German imperialists had accepted the risk of this fresh antagonist, was far less successful than had been hoped. The British navy proved itself much more inventive and resourceful than the British army; there was a rapid development of anti-submarine devices under water, upon the surface, and in the air; and after a month or so of serious destruction, the tale of submarine sinkings declined. The British found it necessary to put themselves upon food rations; but the regulations were well framed and ably administered, the public showed an excellent spirit and intelligence, and the danger of famine and social disorder was kept at arm's length.

Yet the German imperial government persisted in its course. If the submarine was not doing all that had been expected, and if the armies of America gathered like a thunder-cloud, yet Russia was definitely down; and in October the same sort of autumn offensive that had overthrown Serbia in 1915 and Rumania in 1916 was now turned with crushing effect against Italy. The Italian front collapsed after the Battle of Caporetto, and the Austro-German armies poured down into Venetia and came almost within gunfire of Venice. Germany felt justified, therefore, in taking a high line with the Russian peace proposals, and the peace of Brest Litovsk (March 2nd, 1918) gave the Western allies some intimation of what a German victory would mean to them. It was a crushing and exorbitant peace, dictated with the utmost arrogance of confident victors.

All through the winter German troops had been shifting from the Eastern to the Western front, and now, in the spring of 1918, the jaded enthusiasm of hungry, weary, and bleeding Germany was lashed up for the one supreme effort that was really and truly to end the war. For some months American troops had been in France, but the bulk of the American army was still across the Atlantic. It was high time for the final conclusive blow upon the Western front, if such a blow was ever to be delivered. The first attack was upon the British in the Somme region. The not very brilliant cavalry generals who were still in command of a front upon which cavalry was a useless encumbrance were caught napping; and on March 21st, in "Gough's Disaster," the fifth British army was driven back in disorder. The jealousies of the British and French generals had prevented any unified command of the Allied armies in France, and there was no general reserve whatever behind Gough. Thousands of guns were lost, and scores of thousands of prisoners. Many of these losses were due to the utter incompetence of the higher command. No less than a hundred tanks were abandoned *because they ran out of petrol!* The British were driven back almost to Amiens. Throughout April and May the Germans rained offensives on the Allied front. They came near to a break through in the north, and they made a great drive back to the Marne, which they reached again on May 30th, 1918.

This was the climax of the German effort. Behind it was nothing but an exhausted homeland. The Allied politicians intervened in the quarrels of their professional soldiers, and Marshal Foch was put in supreme command of all the Allied armies. Fresh troops were hurrying from Britain across the Channel, and America was now pouring men into France by the hundred thousand. In June the weary Austrians made a last effort in Italy, and collapsed before an Italian counter-attack. Early in June Foch began to develop a counter-attack in the Marne angle. By July the tide was turning, and the Germans were reeling back. The Battle of Château Thierry (July 18th) proved the quality of the new American armies. In August the British opened a great and successful thrust into Belgium, and the bulge of the German lines towards Amiens wilted and collapsed. Germany had finished. The fighting spirit passed out of her army, and October was a story of defeat and retreat along the entire Western front. Early in November British troops were in Valenciennes and Americans in Sedan. In Italy also the Austrian armies were in a state of disorderly retreat. But everywhere now the Hohenzollern and Habsburg forces were collapsing. The smash at the end was amazingly swift. Frenchmen and Englishmen could not believe their newspapers as day after day they announced the capture of more hundreds of guns and more thousands of prisoners.

In September a great allied offensive against Bulgaria had produced a revolution in that country and peace proposals. Turkey had followed with a capitulation at the end of October, and Austro-Hungary on November 4th. There was an attempt to bring out the German Fleet for a last fight, but the sailors mutinied (November 7th).

The Kaiser and the Crown Prince bolted hastily, and without a scrap of dignity, into Holland. On November 11th an armistice was signed and the war was at an end. . . .

For four years and a quarter the war had lasted, and gradually it had drawn nearly everyone in the Western world, at least, into its vortex. Upwards of ten millions of people had been actually killed through the fighting, another twenty or twenty-five million had died through the hardships and disorders entailed. Scores of millions were suffering and enfeebled by under-nourishment and misery. A vast proportion of the living were now engaged in war work, in drilling and armament, in making munitions, in hospitals, in working as substitutes for men who had gone into the armies and the like. Business men had been adapting themselves to the more hectic methods necessary for profit in a world in a state of crisis. The war had become, indeed, an atmosphere, a habit of life, a new social order. Then suddenly it ended.

In London the armistice was proclaimed about midday on November 11th. It produced a strange cessation of every ordinary routine. Clerks poured out of their offices and would not return, assistants deserted their shops, omnibus drivers and the drivers of military lorries set out upon journeys of their own devising with picked-up loads of astounded and cheering passengers going nowhere in particular and careless whither they went. Vast vacant crowds presently choked the streets, and every house and shop that possessed such adornments hung out flags. When night came, many of the main streets, which had been kept in darkness for many months because of the air raids, were brightly lit. It was very strange to see thronging multitudes assembled in an artificial light again. Every-

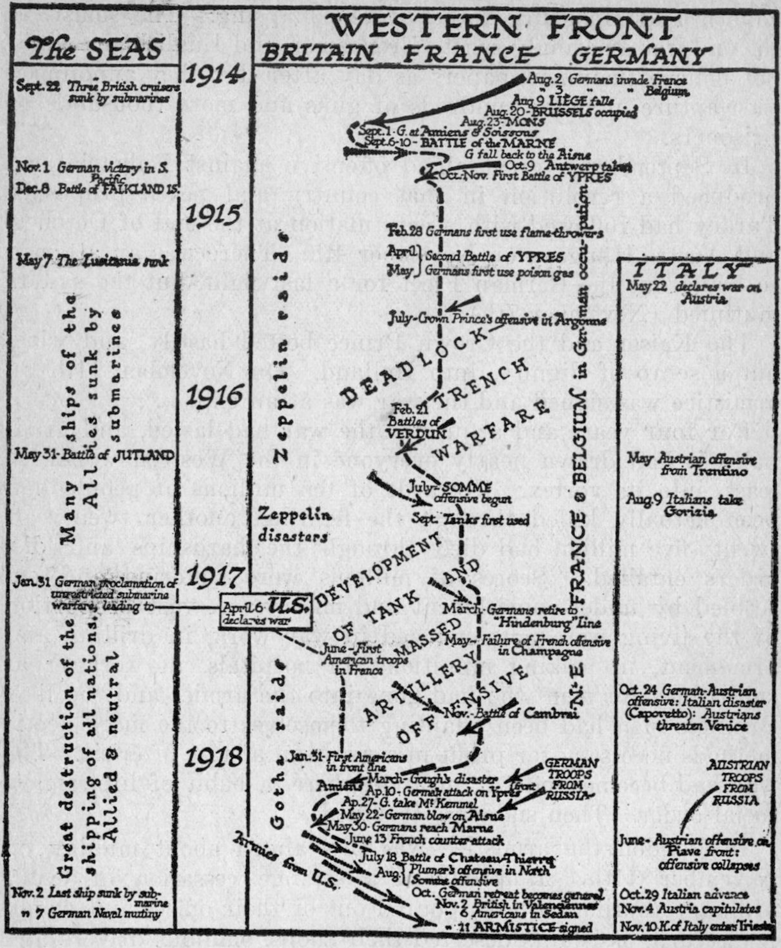

one felt aimless, with a kind of strained and aching relief. It was over at last. There would be no more killing in France, no more air raids—and things would get better. People wanted to laugh, and weep—and could do neither. Youths of spirit and young soldiers on leave formed thin noisy processions that shoved their way through the general drift, and did their best to make a jollification. A captured German gun was hauled from the Mall, where a vast array of such trophies had been set out, into Trafalgar Square, and its carriage burnt.

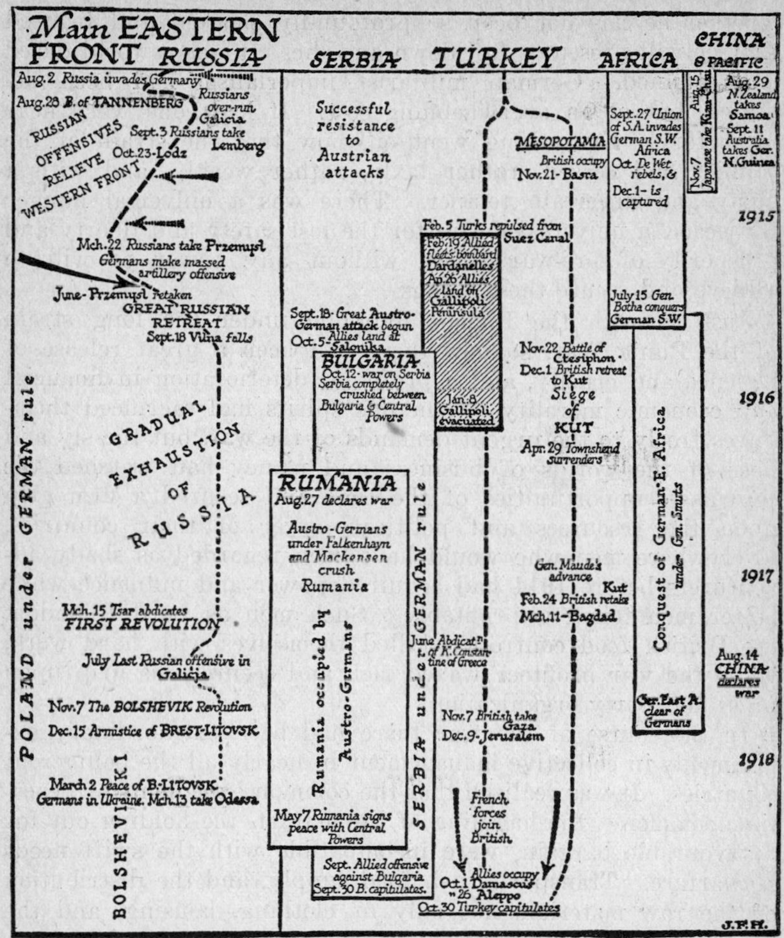

Squibs and crackers were thrown about. But there was little concerted rejoicing. Nearly everyone had lost too much and suffered too much to rejoice with any fervour.

§ 10

The world in the year after the great war was like a man who has had some vital surgical operation very roughly performed, and who is not yet sure whether he can now go on living or whether he has not been so profoundly shocked and injured that he will presently fall down and die. It was a world dazed and stunned. German militarist imperialism had been defeated, but at an overwhelming cost. It had come very near to victory. Everything went on, now that the strain of the conflict had ceased, rather laxly, rather weakly, and with a gusty and uncertain temper. There was a universal hunger for peace, a universal desire for the lost safety and liberty and prosperity of pre-war times, without any power of will to achieve and secure these things.

Just as with the Roman Republic under the long strain of the Punic War, so now there had been a great release of violence and cruelty, and a profound deterioration in financial and economic morality. Generous spirits had sacrificed themselves freely to the urgent demands of the war, but the sly and base of the worlds of business and money had watched the convulsive opportunities of the time and secured a firm grip upon the resources and political power of their countries. Everywhere men who would have been regarded as shady adventurers before 1914 had acquired power and influence while better men toiled unprofitably. Such men as Lord Rhondda, the British food controller, killed themselves with hard work, while the war profiteer waxed rich and secured his grip upon press and party organization.

In the course of the war there had been extraordinary experiments in collective management in nearly all the belligerent countries. It was realized that the common expedients of peacetime commerce, the haggling of the market, the holding out for a favourable bargain, were incompatible with the swift needs of warfare. Transport, fuel, food supply, and the distribution of the raw materials not only of clothing, housing, and the like, but of everything needed for war munitions, had been brought under public control. No longer had farmers been allowed to under-farm; cattle had been put upon deer-parks and grasslands ploughed up, with or without the owner's approval. Luxury building and speculative company promotion had been restrained. In effect, a sort of emergency socialist state had been established throughout belligerent Europe. It was rough-and-ready and wasteful, but it was more effective than the tangled incessant profit-seeking, the cornering and forestalling and incoherent productiveness of "private enterprise."

In the earlier years of the war there was a very widespread feeling of brotherhood and the common interest in all the belligerent states. The common men were everywhere sacrificing life and health for what they believed to be the common good of the state. In return, it was promised, there would be less social injustice after the war, a more universal devotion to the common welfare. In Great Britain, for instance, Mr. Lloyd George was particularly insistent upon his intention to make the after-war Britain "a land fit for heroes." He foreshadowed the continuation of this new war communism into the peace period in discourses of great fire and beauty. In Great Britain, there was created a Ministry of Reconstruction, which was understood to be planning a new and more generous social order, better labour conditions, better housing, extended education, a complete and scientific revision of the economic system. Similar hopes of a better world sustained the common soldiers of France and Germany and Italy. It was premature disillusionment that caused the Russian collapse. So that two mutually dangerous streams of anticipation were running through the minds of men in Western Europe towards the end of the war. The rich and adventurous men, and particularly the new war profiteers, were making their plans to prevent such developments as that air transport should become a state property, and to snatch back manufactures, shipping, land transport, the public services generally, and the trade in staples from the hands of the commonweal into the grip of private profit; they were securing possession of newspapers and busying themselves with party caucuses and the like to that end; while the masses of common men were looking forward naïvely to a new state of society planned almost entirely in their interest and according to generous general ideas. The history of 1919 is largely the clash of these two streams of anticipation. There was a hasty selling off, by the "business" government in control, of every remunerative public enterprise to private speculators. . . . By the middle of 1919 the labour masses throughout the world were manifestly disappointed and in a thoroughly bad temper. The British "Minister of Reconstruction" and its foreign equivalents were exposed as a soothing sham. The common man felt he had been cheated. There was to be no reconstruction, but only a restoration of the old order—in the harsher form necessitated by the poverty of the new time.

For four years the drama of the war had obscured the social question which had been developing in the Western civilizations throughout the nineteenth century. Now that the war was over, this question reappeared gaunt and bare, as it had never been seen before.

And the irritations and hardships and the general insecurity of the new time were exacerbated by a profound disturbance of currency and credit. Money, a complicated growth of conventions rather than a system of values, had been deprived within the belligerent countries of the support of a gold standard. Gold had been retained only for international trade, and every government had produced excessive quantities of paper money for domestic use. With the breaking down of the war-time barriers the international exchange became a wildly fluctuating confusion, a source of distress to everyone except a few gamblers and wily speculators. Prices rose and rose—with an infuriating effect upon the wage-earner. On the one hand was the employer resisting his demands for more pay; on the other hand, food, house-room, and clothing were being steadily cornered against him. And, which was the essential danger of the situation, *he had lost any confidence he had ever possessed that any patience or industrial willingness he displayed would really alleviate the shortages and inconveniences by which he suffered.*

In the speeches of politicians towards the close of 1919 and the spring of 1920, there was manifest an increasing recognition of the fact that what is called the capitalist system—the private ownership system that is, in which private profit is the working incentive—was on its trial. It had to produce general prosperity, they admitted, or it had to be revised. It is interesting to note such a speech as that of Mr. Lloyd George, the British premier, delivered on Saturday, December 6th, 1919. Mr. Lloyd George had had the education and training of a Welsh solicitor; he entered politics early, and in the course of a brilliant parliamentary career he had had few later opportunities for reading and thought. But being a man of great natural shrewdness, he was expressing here very accurately the ideas of the more intelligent of the business men and wealthy men and ordinary citizens who supported him.

"There is a new challenge to civilization," he said. "What is it? It is fundamental. It affects the whole fabric of society as we know it; its commerce, its trade, its industry, its finance, its social order—all are involved in it. There are those who maintain that the prosperity and strength of the country have been built up by the stimulating and invigorating appeal to individual impulse, to individual action. That is one view. The State must educate; the State must assist where necessary; the State must control where necessary; the State must shield the weak against the arrogance of the strong; but the life springs from individual impulse and energy. (Cheers.) That is one view. What is the other? That private enterprise is a failure, tried, and found wanting—a complete failure, a cruel failure. It must be rooted out, and the community must take charge as a community, to produce, to distribute, as well as to control.

"Those are great challenges for us to decide. *We* say that the ills of private enterprise can be averted. *They* say, 'No, they cannot. No ameliorative, no palliative, no restrictive, no remedial measure will avail. These evils are inherent in the system. They are the fruit of the tree, and you must cut it down.' That is the challenge we hear ringing through the civilized world to-day, from ocean to ocean, through valley and plain. You hear it in the whining and maniacal shrieking of the Bolshevists. You hear it in the loud, clear, but more restrained tones of Congresses and Conferences. The Bolshevists would blow up the fabric with high explosive, with horror. Others would pull down with the crowbars and with cranks—especially cranks. (Laughter.)

"Unemployment, with its injustice for the man who seeks and thirsts for employment, who begs for labour and cannot get it, and who is punished for failure he is not responsible for by the starvation of his children—that torture is *something that private enterprise ought to remedy for its own sake.* (Cheers.) Sweating, slums, the sense of semi-slavery in labour, must go. We must cultivate a sense of manhood by treating men as men. If I—and I say this deliberately—if I had to choose between this fabric I believe in, and allowing millions of men and women and children to rot in its cellars, I would not hesitate one hour. That is not the choice. Thank God it is not the choice. Private enterprise can produce more, so that all men get a fair share of it. . . ."[1]

Here, put into quasi-eloquent phrasing, and with a jest adapted to the mental habits of the audience, we have the com-

[1] *The Times*, December 8th, 1919.

mon-sense view of the ordinary prosperous man not only of Great Britain, but of America or France or Italy or Germany. In quality and tone it is a fair sample of British political thought in 1919. The prevailing economic system has made us what we are, is the underlying idea; and we do not want any process of social destruction to precede a renascence of society, we do not want to experiment with the fundamentals of our social order. Let us accept that. Adaptation, Mr. Lloyd George admitted, there had to be. Now this occasion of his speaking was a year and a month after the Armistice, and for all that period private enterprise had been failing to do all that Mr. Lloyd George was so cheerfully promising it would do. The community was in urgent need of houses. Throughout the war there had been a cessation not only of building, but of repairs. The shortage of houses in the last months of 1919 amounted to scores of thousands in Britain alone.[1] Multitudes of people were living in a state of exasperating congestion, and the most shameless profiteering in apartments and houses was going on. It was a difficult, but not an impossible situation. Given the same enthusiasm and energy and self-sacrifice that had tided over the monstrous crisis of 1916, the far easier task of providing a million houses could have been performed in a year or so. But there had been corners in building materials, transport was in a disordered state, and it did not *pay* private enterprise to build houses at any rents within the means of the people who needed them. Private enterprise, therefore, so far from bothering about the public need of housing, did nothing but corner and speculate in rents and sub-letting. It now demanded grants in aid from the State—in order to build at a profit. And there was a great crowding and dislocation of goods at the depôts because there was insufficient road transport. There was an urgent want of cheap automobiles to move about goods and workers. But private enterprise in the automobile industry found it far more profitable to produce splendid and costly cars for those whom the war had made rich. The munition factories built with public money could have been converted very readily into factories for the mass production of cheap automobiles, but private enterprise had insisted upon these factories being sold by the State, and would neither meet the public need itself nor let the State do so. So, too, with the

[1] Authorities vary between 250,000 and a million houses.

world in the direst discomfort for need of shipping, private enterprise insisted upon the shutting down of the newly constructed State shipyards. Currency was dislocated everywhere, but private enterprise was busy buying and selling francs or marks and intensifying the trouble. While Mr. George was making the very characteristic speech we have quoted, the discontent of the common man was gathering everywhere, and little or nothing was being done to satisfy his needs. It was becoming very evident that unless there was to be some profound change in the spirit of business, under an unrestrained private enterprise system there was little or no hope, in Europe at any rate, of decent housing, clothing, or education for the workers for two or three generations.

These are facts that the historian of mankind is obliged to note with as little comment as possible. Private enterprise in Europe in 1919 and 1920 displayed neither will nor capacity for meeting the crying needs of the time. So soon as it was released from control, it ran naturally into speculation, cornering, and luxury production. It followed the line of maximum profit. It displayed no sense of its own dangers; and it resisted any attempt to restrain and moderate its profits and make itself serviceable, even in its own interest. And this went on in the face of the most striking manifestations of the extreme recalcitrance on the part of the European masses to the prolonged continuance of the privations and inconveniences they suffered. In 1913 these masses were living as they had lived since birth; they were habituated to the life they led. The masses of 1919, on the other hand, had been uprooted everywhere, to go into the armies, to go into munition factories, and so on. They had lost their habits of acquiescence, and they were hardier and more capable of desperate action. Great multitudes of men had gone through such brutalizing training as, for instance, bayonet drill; they had learnt to be ferocious, and to think less either of killing or being killed. Social unrest had become, therefore, much more dangerous. Everything seemed to point to a refusal to tolerate the current state of affairs for many years. Unless the educated and prosperous and comfortable people of Europe could speedily get their private enterprise under sufficient restraint to make it work well and rapidly for the common good, unless they could develop the idea of business as primarily a form of public service and not primarily a method of profit-making, unless they could in their own interest achieve a security of peace that would admit of a cessation not only of war preparation, but of international commercial warfare, strike and insurrection promised to follow strike and insurrection up to a complete social and political collapse. It was not that the masses had or imagined that they had the plan of a new social, political, and economic system. They had not, and they did not believe they had. The defects we have pointed out in the socialist scheme (Chapter XXXVIII, § 5) were no secret from them. It was a much more dangerous state of affairs than that. It was that they were becoming so disgusted with the current system, with its silly luxury, its universal waste, and its general misery, that they did not care what happened afterward so long as they could destroy it. It was a return to a state of mind comparable to that which had rendered possible the debacle of the Roman Empire.

Already in 1919 the world had seen one great community go that way, the Russian people. The Russians overturned the old order and submitted to the autocratic rule of a small group of doctrinaire Bolshevik socialists, because these men seemed to have something new to try. They wrecked the old system, and at any cost they would not have it back. The information available from Russia at the time of writing this summary is still too conflicting and too obviously tainted by propagandist aims for us to form any judgment upon the proceedings and methods of the Soviet Government, but it is very plain that from November, 1917, Russia has not only endured that government and its mainly socialistic methods, but has fought for it successfully against anything that seemed to threaten a return to the old régime.

We have already (§ 5) pointed out the very broad differences between the Russian and the Western communities, and the strong reasons there are for doubting that they will move upon parallel lines and act in similar ways. The Russian peasants were cut off by want of education and sympathy from the small civilized community of prosperous and educated people which lived upon them. These latter were a little separate nation. The peasants below, under the really quite alien incitement of the Bolshevik socialists, have thrown that separate nation off and destroyed it. In the towns, and in the towns alone, communism rules (1920); the rest of Russia is now no more than a wilderness of barbaric peasantry. But there is much more unity of thought and feeling between class and class in the West than in Russia, and particularly in the Atlantic communities. Even if they wrangle, classes can talk together and understand each other. There is no unbroken stratum of illiterates. The groups of rich and speculative men, the "bad men" in business and affairs, whose freedoms are making the very name of "private enterprise" stink in the nostrils of the ordinary man, are only the more active section of very much larger classes, guilty perhaps of indolence and self-indulgence, but capable of being roused to a sense not merely of the wickedness but of the danger of systematic self-seeking in a strained, impoverished, and sorely tried world.

In one way or another it seems inevitable now that the new standard of well-being which the mechanical revolution of the last century has rendered possible, should become the general standard of life. Revolution is conditional upon public discomfort. Social peace is impossible without a rapid amelioration of the needless discomforts of the present time. A rapid resort to willing service and social reconstruction on the part of those who own and rule, or else a world-wide social revolution leading towards an equalization of conditions and an attempt to secure comfort on new and untried lines, seem now to be the only alternatives before mankind. The choice which route shall be taken lies, we believe, in western Europe, and still more so in America, with the educated, possessing, and influential classes. The former route demands much sacrifice, for prosperous people in particular, a voluntary assumption of public duties and a voluntary acceptance of class discipline and self-denial; the latter may take an indefinite time to traverse, it will certainly be a very destructive and bloody process, and whether it will lead to a new and better state of affairs at last is questionable. A social revolution, if ultimately the Western European States blunder into it, may prove to be a process extending over centuries; it may involve a social breakdown as complete as that of the Roman Empire, and it may necessitate as slow a recuperation.

§ 11

We have dealt with the social and economic disorder of the European communities, and the rapid return of the "class-war" to the foreground of attention, before giving any account of the work of world settlement that centred on the Peace Conference at Paris, because the worried and preoccupied state of everyone concerned with private problems of income, prices, employment, and the like goes far to explain the jaded atmosphere in which that Conference addressed itself to the vast task before it.

The story of the Conference turns very largely upon the adventure of one particular man, one of those men whom accident or personal quality picks out as a type to lighten the task of the historian. We have in the course of this history found it very helpful at times to focus our attention upon some individual, Buddha, Alexander the Great, Yuan Chwang, the Emperor Frederick II and Charles V and Napoleon I for example, and to let him by reflection illuminate the period in which he lived. The conclusion of the Great War can be seen most easily as the rise of the American President, President Wilson, to predominant importance in the world's hopes and attention, and his failure to justify that predominance.

President Wilson (born 1856) had previously been a prominent student and teacher of history, constitutional law, and the political sciences generally. He had held various professorial chairs, and had been President of Princeton University (New Jersey). There is a long list of books to his credit, and they show a mind rather exclusively directed to American history and American politics. He was mentally the new thing in history, negligent of and rather ignorant of the older things out of which his new world had arisen. He retired from academic life, and was elected Democratic Governor of New Jersey in 1910. In 1913 he became the Democratic presidential candidate, and as a consequence of a violent quarrel between ex-President Roosevelt and President Taft, which split the dominant Republican party, he became President of the United States.

The events of August, 1914, seem to have taken President Wilson, like the rest of his fellow-countrymen, by surprise. We find him cabling an offer of his services as a mediator on August 3rd. Then, for a time, he and America watched the conflict. At first neither the American people nor their President seem to have had a very clear or profound understanding of that long-gathered catastrophe. Their tradition for a century had been to disregard the problems of the Old World, and it was not to be lightly changed. The imperialistic arrogance of the German Court and the stupid inclination of the German military authorities towards melodramatic "frightfulness," their invasion of Belgium, their cruelties there, their use of poison gas, and the nuisance of their submarine campaign, created a deepening hostility to Germany in the United States as the war proceeded; but the tradition of political abstinence and the deep-rooted persuasion that America possessed a political morality altogether superior to European conflicts, restrained the President from active intervention. He adopted a lofty tone. He professed to be unable to judge the causes and justice of the Great War. It was largely his high pacific attitude that secured his re-election as President for a second term. But the world is not to be mended by merely regarding evil-doers with an expression of rather undiscriminating disapproval. By the end of 1916 the Germans had been encouraged to believe that under no circumstances whatever would the United States fight, and in 1917 they began their unrestricted submarine warfare and the sinking of American ships without notice. President Wilson and the American people were dragged into the war by this supreme folly. And also they were dragged into a reluctant attempt to define their relations to Old World politics in some other terms than those of mere aloofness. Their thoughts and temper changed very rapidly. They came into the war side by side with the Allies, but not in any pact with the Allies. They came into the war, in the name of their own modern civilization, to punish and end an intolerable political and military situation.

Slow and belated judgments are sometimes the best judgments. In a series of "notes," too long and various for detailed treatment in this *Outline*, thinking aloud, as it were, in the hearing of all mankind, President Wilson sought to state the essential differences of the American State from the Great Powers of the Old World. We have been at some pains in this history to make plain the development of these differences. He unfolded a conception of international relationships that came like a gospel, like the hope of a better world, to the whole eastern hemisphere. Secret agreements were to cease, "nations" were to determine their own destinies, militarist aggression was to cease, the seaways were to be free to all mankind. These commonplaces of American thought, these secret desires of every sane man, came like a great light upon the darkness of anger and conflict in Europe. At last, men felt, the ranks of diplomacy were broken, the veils of Great Power "policy" were rent in twain. Here with authority, with the strength of a powerful new nation behind it, was the desire of the common man throughout the world, plainly said.

Manifestly there was needed some over-riding instrument of government to establish world law and maintain these broad and liberal generalizations upon human intercourse. A number of schemes had floated in men's minds for the attainment of that end. In particular there was a movement for some sort of world league, a "League of Nations." The American President adopted this phrase and sought to realize it. An essential condition of the peace he sought through the overthrow of German imperialism was, he declared, to be this federal organ. This League of Nations was to be the final court of appeal in international affairs. It was to be the substantial realization of the peace. Here again he awakened a tremendous echo.

President Wilson was the spokesman of a new age. Throughout the war, and for some little time after it had ended, he held, so far as the Old World was concerned, that exalted position. But in America, where they knew him better, there were doubts. And writing as we do now with the wisdom of subsequent events, we can understand these doubts. America, throughout a century and more of detachment and security, had developed new ideals and formulæ of political thought, without realizing with any intensity that, under conditions of stress and danger, these ideals and formulæ might have to be passionately sustained. To her community many things were platitudes that had to the Old World communities, entangled still in ancient political complications, the quality of a saving gospel. President Wilson was responding to the thought and conditions of his own people and his own country, based on a liberal tradition that had first found its full expression in English speech; but to Europe and Asia he seemed to be thinking and saying, for the first time in history, things hitherto undeveloped and altogether secret. And that misconception he may have shared.

We are dealing here with an able and successful professor of political science, who did not fully realize what he owed to his contemporaries and the literary and political atmosphere he had breathed throughout his life; and who passed very rapidly, after his re-election as President, from the mental attitudes of a political leader to those of a Messiah. His "notes" are a series of explorations of the elements of the world situation. When at last, in his address to Congress of January 8th, 1918, he produced his Fourteen Points as a definite statement of the American peace intentions, they were, as a statement, far better in their spirit than in their arrangement and matter. This document demanded open agreements between nations and an end to secret diplomacy, free navigation of the high seas, free commerce, disarmament, and a number of political readjustments upon the lines of national independence. Finally in the Fourteenth Point it required "a general association of nations" to guarantee the peace of the world.

These Fourteen Points had an immense reception throughout the world. Here at last seemed a peace for reasonable men everywhere, as good and acceptable to honest and decent Germans and Russians, as to honest and decent Frenchmen and Englishmen and Belgians; and for some months the whole world was lit by faith in Wilson. Could they have been made the basis of a world settlement in 1919, they would forthwith have opened a new and more hopeful era in human affairs.

But, as we must tell, they did not do that. There was about President Wilson a certain egotism; there was in the generation of people in the United States to whom this great occasion came, a generation born in security, reared in plenty and, so far as history goes, in ignorance, a generation remote from the tragic issues that had made Europe grave, a certain superficiality and lightness of mind. It was not that the American people were superficial by nature and necessity, but that they had never been deeply stirred by the idea of a human community larger than their own. It was an intellectual but not a moral conviction, with them. One had on the one hand these new people of the new world, with their new ideas, their finer and better ideas, of peace and world righteousness, and on the other the old, bitter, deeply entangled peoples of the Great Power system; and the former were crude and rather childish in their immense inexperience, and the latter were seasoned and bitter and intricate. The theme of this clash of the raw idealist youthfulness of a new age with the experienced ripeness of the old, was treated years ago by that great novelist, Henry James, in a very typical story called *Daisy Miller*. It is the pathetic story of a frank, trustful, high-minded, but rather simple-minded American girl, with a real disposition towards righteousness and a great desire for a "good time," and how she came to Europe and was swiftly entangled and put in the wrong, and at last driven to welcome death by the complex tortuousness and obstinate limitations of the older world. There have been a thousand variants of that theme in real life, a thousand such trans-Atlantic tragedies, and the story of President Wilson is one of them. But it is not to be supposed, because the new thing succumbs to the old infections, that is the final condemnation of the new thing.

President Wilson

Probably no fallible human being manifestly trying to do his best amidst overwhelming circumstances has been subjected to such minute, searching, and pitiless criticism as President Wilson. He is blamed, and it would seem that he is rightly blamed, for conducting the war and the ensuing peace negotiations on strictly party lines. He remained the President representing the American Democratic Party, when circumstances conspired to make him the representative of the general interests of mankind. He made no attempt to forget party issues for a time, and to incorporate with himself such great American leaders as ex-President Roosevelt, ex-President Taft, and the like. He did not draw fully upon the moral and intellectual resources of the States; he made the whole issue too personal, and he surrounded himself with merely personal adherents. And a still graver error was his decision to come to the Peace Conference himself. Nearly every experienced critic seems to be of opinion that he should have remained in America, in the rôle of America, speaking occasionally as if a nation spoke. Throughout the concluding years of the war he had by that method achieved an unexampled position in the world.

Says Dr. Dillon:[1] "Europe, when the President touched

[1] In his book, *The Peace Conference.*

its shores, was as clay ready for the creative potter. Never before were the nations so eager to follow a Moses who would take them to the long-promised land where wars are prohibited and blockades unknown. And to their thinking he was that great leader. In France men bowed down before him with awe and affection. Labour leaders in Paris told me that they shed tears of joy in his presence, and that their comrades would go through fire and water to help him to realize his noble schemes. To the working classes in Italy his name was a heavenly clarion at the sound of which the earth would be renewed. The Germans regarded him and his humane doctrine as their sheet-anchor of safety. The fearless Herr Muehlon said: 'If President Wilson were to address the Germans, and pronounce a severe sentence upon them, they would accept it with resignation and without a murmur and set to work at once.' In German-Austria his fame was that of a saviour, and the mere mention of his name brought balm to the suffering and surcease of sorrow to the afflicted. . . ."

M. Clemenceau

Such was the overpowering expectation of the audience to which President Wilson prepared to show himself. He reached France on board the *George Washington* in December, 1918.

He brought his wife with him. That seemed no doubt a perfectly natural and proper thing to an American mind. Quite a number of the American representatives brought their wives. Unhappily a social quality, nay, almost a tourist quality, was introduced into the world settlement by these ladies. Transport facilities were limited, and most of them arrived in Europe with a radiant air of privilege. They came as if they came to a treat. They were, it was intimated, seeing Europe under exceptionally interesting circumstances. They would visit Chester, or Warwick, or Windsor *en route*—for they might not have a chance of seeing these celebrated places again. Important interviews would be broken off to get in a visit to some "old historical mansion." This may seem a trivial matter to note in a History of Mankind, but it was such small human things as this that threw a miasma of futility over the Peace Conference of 1919. In a little while one discovered that Wilson, the Hope of Mankind, had vanished, and that all the illustrated fashion papers contained pictures of a delighted tourist and his wife, grouped smilingly with crowned heads and such-like enviable company. . . . It is so easy to be wise after the event, and to perceive that he should not have come over.

Mr. Lloyd George

The men he had chiefly to deal with, for example M. Clemenceau (France), Mr. Lloyd George and Mr. Balfour (Britain), Baron Sonnino and Signor Orlando (Italy), were men of widely dissimilar historical traditions. But in one respect they resembled him and appealed to his sympathies. They, too, were party politicians, who had led their country through the war. Like himself they had failed to grasp the necessity of entrusting the work of settlement to more specially qualified men. "They were the merest novices in international affairs. Geography, ethnology, psychology, and political history were sealed books to them. Like the Rector of Louvain University, who told Oliver Goldsmith that, as he had become the head of that institution without knowing Greek, he failed to see why it should be taught there, the chiefs of State, having obtained the highest position in their respective countries without more than an inkling of international affairs, were unable to realize the importance of mastering them or the impossibility of repairing the omission as they went along. . . ."[1]

"What they lacked, however, might in some perceptible degree have been supplied by enlisting as their helpers men more happily endowed than themselves. But they deliberately chose mediocrities. It is a mark of genial spirits that they are well served, but the plenipotentiaries of the Conference were not

[1] Dillon.

characterized by it. Away in the background some of them had familiars or casual prompters to whose counsels they were wont to listen, but many of the adjoints who moved in the limelight of the world-stage were gritless and pithless.

"As the heads of the principal Governments implicitly claimed to be the authorized spokesmen of the human race, and endowed with unlimited powers, it is worth noting that this claim was boldly challenged by the people's organs in the Press. Nearly all the journals read by the masses objected from the first to the dictatorship of the group of Premiers, Mr. Wilson being excepted. . . ."[1]

The restriction upon our space in this *Outline* will not allow us to tell here how the Peace Conference shrank from a Council of Ten to a Council of Four (Wilson, Clemenceau, Lloyd George, and Orlando), and how it became a conference less and less like a frank and open discussion of the future of mankind, and more and more like some old fashioned diplomatic conspiracy. Great and wonderful had been the hopes that had gathered to Paris. "The Paris of the Conference," says Dr. Dillon, "ceased to be the capital of France. It became a vast cosmopolitan caravanserai teeming with unwonted aspects of life and turmoil, filled with curious samples of the races, tribes, and tongues of four continents who came to watch and wait for the mysterious to-morrow.

"An Arabian Nights' touch was imparted to the dissolving panorama by strange visitants from Tartary and Kurdistan, Korea and Aderbeijan, Armenia, Persia, and the Hedjaz—men with patriarchal beards and scimitar-shaped noses, and others from desert and oasis, from Samarkand and Bokhara. Turbans and fezes, sugar-loaf hats and head-gear resembling episcopal mitres, old military uniforms devised for the embryonic armies of new states on the eve of perpetual peace, snowy-white burnouses, flowing mantles, and graceful garments like the Roman toga, contributed to create an atmosphere of dreamy unreality in the city where the grimmest of realities were being faced and coped with.

"Then came the men of wealth, of intellect, of industrial enterprise, and the seed-bearers of the ethical new ordering, members of economic committees from the United States,

[1] Dillon. And see his *The Peace Conference,* chapter iii, for instances of the amazing ignorance of various delegates.

Britain, Italy, Poland, Russia, India, and Japan, representatives of naphtha industries and far-off coal mines, pilgrims, fanatics and charlatans from all climes, priests of all religions, preachers of every doctrine, who mingled with princes, field-marshals, statesmen, anarchists, builders-up and pullers-down. All of them burned with desire to be near to the crucible in which the political and social systems of the world were to be melted and recast. Every day, in my walks, in my apartment, or at restaurants, I met emissaries from lands and peoples whose very names had seldom been heard of before in the West. A delegation from the Pont-Euxine Greeks called on me, and discoursed of their ancient cities of Trebizond, Samsoun, Tripoli, Kerassund, in which I resided many years ago, and informed me that they, too, desired to become welded into an independent Greek Republic, and had come to have their claims allowed. The Albanians were represented by my old friend Turkhan Pasha, on the one hand, and by my friend Essad Pasha on the other—the former desirous of Italy's protection, the latter demanding complete independence. Chinamen, Japanese, Koreans, Hindus, Kirghizes, Lesghiens, Circassians, Mingrelians, Buryats, Malays, and Negroes and Negroids from Africa and America were among the tribes and tongues foregathered in Paris to watch the rebuilding of the political world system and to see where they 'came in.' . . ."

To this thronging, amazing Paris, agape for a new world, came President Wilson, and found its gathering forces dominated by a personality narrower, in every way more limited and beyond comparison more forcible than himself: the French Premier, M. Clemenceau. At the instance of President Wilson, M. Clemenceau was elected President of the Conference. "It was," said President Wilson, "a special tribute to the sufferings and sacrifices of France." And that, unhappily, sounded the keynote of the Conference, whose sole business should have been with the future of mankind.

Georges Benjamin Clemenceau was an old journalist politician, a great denouncer of abuses, a great upsetter of governments, a doctor who had, while a municipal councillor, kept a free clinic, and a fierce, experienced duellist. None of his duels ended fatally, but he faced them with great intrepidity. He had passed from the medical school to republican journalism in the days of the Empire. In those days he was an extremist of the left. He was for a time a teacher in America, and he married and divorced an American wife. He was thirty in the eventful year 1871. He returned to France after Sedan, and flung himself into the stormy politics of the defeated nation with great fire and vigour. Thereafter France was his world, the France of vigorous journalism, high-spirited personal quarrels, challenges, confrontations, scenes, dramatic effects, and witticisms at any cost. He was what people call "fierce stuff," he was nicknamed the "Tiger," and he seems to have been rather proud of his nickname. Professional patriot rather than statesman and thinker, this was the man whom the war had flung up to misrepresent the fine mind and the generous spirit of France. His limitations had a profound effect upon the conference, which was further coloured by the dramatic resort for the purpose of signature to the very Hall of Mirrors at Versailles in which Germany had triumphed and proclaimed her unity. There the Germans were to sign. To M. Clemenceau and to France, in that atmosphere, the war ceased to seem a world war; it was merely the sequel of the previous conflict of the Terrible Year, the downfall and punishment of offending Germany. "The world had to be made safe for democracy," said President Wilson. That from M. Clemenceau's expressed point of view was "talking like Jesus Christ." The world had to be made safe for Paris. "Talking like Jesus Christ" seemed a very ridiculous thing to many of those brilliant rather than sound diplomatists and politicians who made the year 1919 supreme in the history of human insufficiency.

(Another flash of the "Tiger's" wit, it may be noted, was that President Wilson with his fourteen points was "worse" than God Almighty. "Le bon Dieu" only had ten. . . .)

M. Clemenceau sat with Signor Orlando in the more central chairs of a semicircle of four in front of the fire, says Keynes. He wore a black frock-coat and grey suede gloves, which he never removed during these sessions. He was, it is to be noted, the only one of these four reconstructors of the world who could understand and speak both French and English.

The aims of M. Clemenceau were simple and in a manner attainable. He wanted all the settlement of 1871 undone. He wanted Germany punished as though she was a uniquely sinful nation and France a sinless martyr land. He wanted Germany so crippled and devastated as never more to be able to stand up to France. He wanted to hurt and humiliate Germany more than France had been hurt and humiliated in 1871. He did not care if in breaking Germany Europe was broken; his mind did not go far enough beyond the Rhine to understand that possibility. He accepted President Wilson's League of Nations as an excellent proposal if it would guarantee the security of France whatever she did, but he preferred a binding alliance of the United States and England to maintain, uphold, and glorify France under practically any circumstances. He wanted wider opportunities for the exploitation of Syria, North Africa, and so forth by Parisian financial groups. He wanted indemnities to recuperate France, loans, gifts, and tributes to France, glory and homage to France. France had suffered, and France had to be rewarded. Belgium, Russia, Serbia, Poland, Armenia, Britain, Germany, and Austria had all suffered too, all mankind had suffered, but what would you? That was not his affair. These were the supers of a drama in which France was for him the star. . . . In much the same spirit Signor Orlando seems to have sought the welfare of Italy.

Mr. Lloyd George brought to the Council of Four the subtlety of a Welshman, the intricacy of a European, and an urgent necessity for respecting the nationalist egotism of the British imperialists and capitalists who had returned him to power. Into the secrecy of that council went President Wilson with the very noblest aims for his newly discovered American world policy, his rather hastily compiled Fourteen Points, and a project rather than a scheme for a League of Nations.

"There can seldom have been a statesman of the first rank more incompetent than the President in the agilities of the Council Chamber." From the whispering darknesses and fireside disputes of that council, and after various comings and goings we cannot here describe, he emerged at last with his Fourteen Points pitifully torn and dishevelled, but with a little puling infant of a League of Nations, which might die or which might live and grow—no one could tell. This history cannot tell. We are at the end of our term. But that much, at least, he had saved. . . .

§ 12

This homunculus in a bottle which it was hoped might become at last Man ruling the Earth, this League of Nations as it was embodied in the Covenant of April 28th, 1919, was not a league of peoples at all; it was, the world discovered, a league of "states, dominions, or colonies." It was stipulated that these should be "fully self-governing," but there was no definition whatever of this phrase. There was no bar to a limited franchise and no provision for any direct control by the people of any state. India figured—presumably as a "fully self-governing state!" An autocracy would no doubt have been admissible as a "fully self-governing" democracy with a franchise limited to one person. The League of the Covenant of 1919 was, in fact, a league of "representatives" of foreign offices, and it did not even abolish the nonsense of embassies at every capital. The British Empire appeared once as a whole, and then India (!) and the four dominions of Canada, Australia, South Africa, and New Zealand appeared as separate sovereign states. The Indian representative was, of course, sure to be merely a British nominee; the other four would be colonial politicians. But if the British Empire was to be thus dissected, a representative of Great Britain should have been substituted for the Imperial representative, and Ireland and Egypt should also have been given representation. Moreover, either New York State or Virginia was historically and legally almost as much a sovereign state as New Zealand or Canada. The inclusion of India raised logical claims for French Africa and French Asia. One French representative did propose a separate vote for the little principality of Monaco.

There was to be an assembly of the League in which every member state was to be represented and to have an equal voice, but the working directorate of the League was to vest in a Council, which was to consist of the representatives of the United States, Britain, France, Italy, and Japan, with four other members elected by the Assembly. The Council was to meet once a year; the gatherings of the Assembly were to be at "stated intervals," not stated.

Except in certain specified instances the league of this Covenant could make only unanimous decisions. One dissentient on the council could bar any proposal—on the lines of the old Polish *liberum veto* (Chapter XXXV, § 7). This was a quite disastrous provision. To many minds it made the Covenant League rather less desirable than no league at all. It was a complete recognition of the unalienable sovereignty of states, and a repudiation of the idea of an overriding commonweal of mankind. This provision practically barred the way to all amendments to the league constitution in future except by the clumsy expedient of a simultaneous withdrawal of the majority of member states desiring a change, to form the league again on new lines. The covenant made inevitable such a final winding-up of the league it created, and that was perhaps the best thing about it.

The following powers, it was proposed, should be excluded from the original league: Germany, Austria, Russia, and whatever remains there were of the Turkish Empire. But any of these might subsequently be included with the assent of two-thirds of the Assembly. The original membership of the league as specified in the projected Covenant was: the United States of America, Belgium, Bolivia, Brazil, the British Empire (Canada, Australia, South Africa, New Zealand, and India), China, Cuba, Ecuador, France, Greece, Guatemala, Haiti, the Hedjaz, Honduras, Italy, Japan, Liberia, Nicaragua, Panama, Peru, Poland, Portugal, Rumania, the Serb-Croat-Slovene State, Siam, Czecho-Slovakia, and Uruguay. To which were to be added by invitation the following powers which had been neutral in the war: the Argentine Republic, Chile, Colombia, Denmark, Holland, Norway, Paraguay, Persia, Salvador, Spain, Sweden, Switzerland, and Venezuela.

Such being the constitution of the league, it is scarcely to be wondered at that its powers were special and limited. It was given a seat at Geneva and a secretariat. It had no powers even to inspect the military preparations of its constituent states, or to instruct a military and naval staff to plan out the armed co-operation needed to keep the peace of the world. The French representative in the League of Nations Commission, M. Leon Bourgeois, insisted lucidly and repeatedly on the logical necessity of such powers. As a speaker he was rather copious and lacking in "spice" of the Clemenceau quality. The final scene in the plenary session of April 28th, before the adoption of the Covenant, is described compactly by Mr. Wilson Harris, the crowded Banqueting Hall at the Quai d'Orsay, with its "E" of tables for the delegates, with secretaries and officials lining the walls and a solid mass of journalists at the lower end of the room. "At the head of the room the 'Big Three' *diverted themselves in undertones* at the expense of the worthy M.

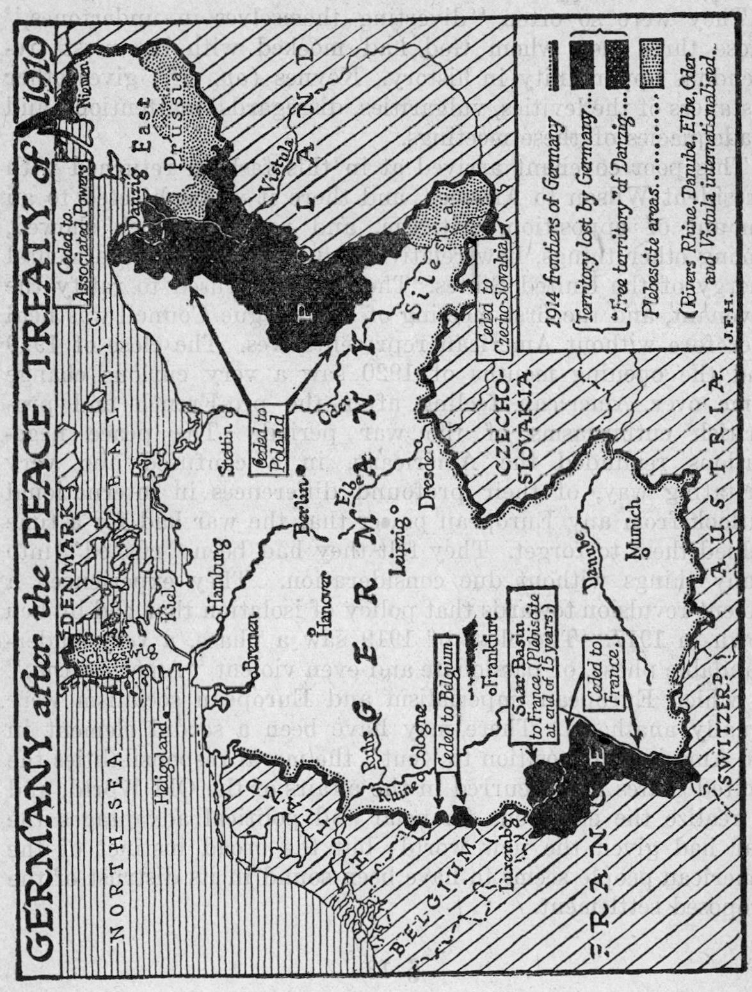
GERMANY after the PEACE TREATY of 1919
DENMARK
NORTH SEA
BALTIC
Heligoland
Schleswig
Kiel
Hamburg
Bremen
Stettin
Berlin
Hanover
Elbe
Oder
Leipzig
Dresden
Ruhr
Cologne
Rhine
Frankfurt
Munich
Danube
Danzig
East Prussia
Niemen
Vistula
Silesia
Ceded to Associated Powers
Ceded to Poland
Ceded to Czecho-Slovakia
Ceded to Belgium
Ceded to France.
Saar Basin. to France. (Plebiscite at end of 15 years.)
GERMANY
POLAND
CZECHO-SLOVAKIA
AUSTRIA
SWITZER^D
FRANCE
BELGIUM
HOLLAND
Luxembg
1914 frontiers of Germany
Territory lost by Germany...
"Free territory" of Danzig....
Plebescite areas..........
(Rivers Rhine, Danube, Elbe, Oder and Vistula internationalised.
J.F.H.

Bourgeois, now launched, with the help of what must have been an entirely superfluous sheaf of notes, on the fifth rendering of his speech in support of his famous amendments.''

They were so often ''diverting themselves in undertones,'' those three men whom God had mocked with the most tremendous opportunity in history. Keynes (*op. cit.*) gives other instances of the levities, vulgarities, disregards, inattentions, and inadequacies of these meetings.

This poor covenant arrived at in this fashion returned with President Wilson to America, and there it was subjected to an amount of opposition, criticism, and revision which showed, among other things, how relatively unimpaired was the mental energy of the United States. The Senate refused to ratify the covenant, and the first meeting of the League Council was held therefore without American representatives. The close of 1919 and the opening months of 1920 saw a very curious change come over American feeling after the pro-French and pro-British enthusiasms of the war period. The peace negotiations reminded the Americans, in a confused and very irritating way, of their profound differences in international outlook from any European power that the war had for a time helped them to forget. They felt they had been ''rushed'' into many things without due consideration. They experienced a violent revulsion towards that policy of isolation that had broken down in 1917. The close of 1919 saw a phase, a very understandable phase, of passionate and even violent ''Americanism,'' in which European imperialism and European socialism were equally anathema. There may have been a sordid element in the American disposition to ''cut'' the moral responsibilities the United States had incurred in the affairs of the Old World, and to realize the enormous financial and political advantages the war had given the new world; but the broad instinct of the American people seems to have been sound in its distrust of the proposed settlement.

§ 13

The main terms of the Treaties of 1919-20 with which the Conference of Paris concluded its labours can be stated much more vividly by a few maps than by a written abstract. We need scarcely point out how much those treaties left unsettled,

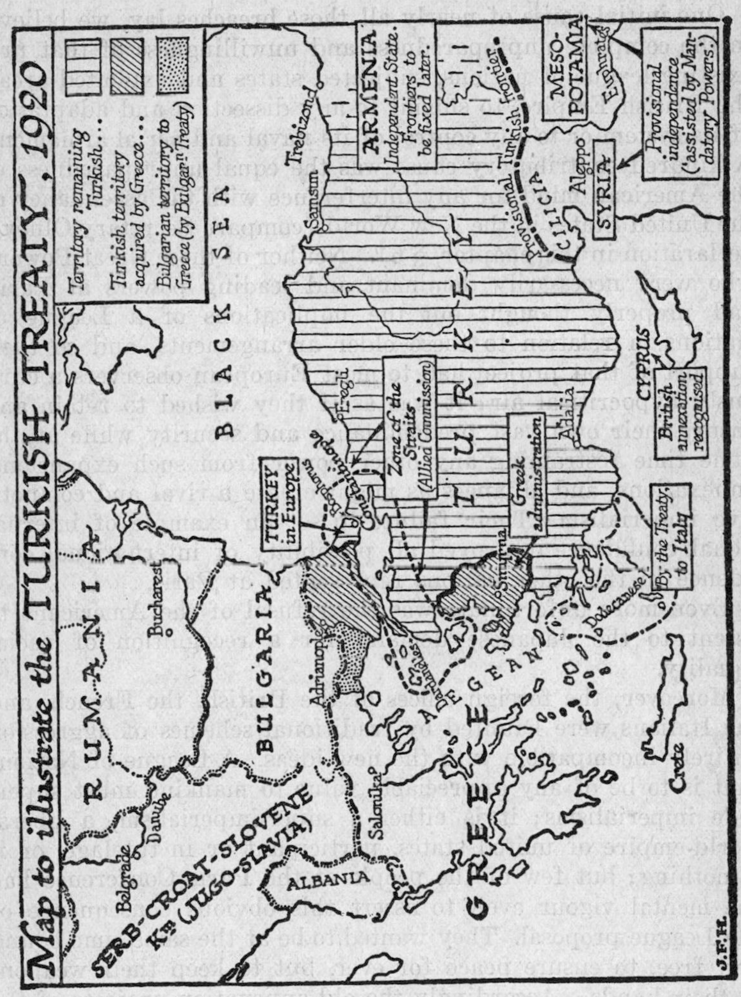
Map to illustrate the TURKISH TREATY, 1920
Territory remaining Turkish...
Turkish territory acquired by Greece...
Bulgarian territory to Greece (by Bulgar'n Treaty)
BLACK SEA
RUMANIA
Bucharest
Belgrade
Danube
BULGARIA
SERB-CROAT-SLOVENE Kᴰᴹ (JUGO-SLAVIA)
ALBANIA
Salonika
Adrianople
Constantinople
Bosphorus
Dardanelles
TURKEY in Europe
Zone of the Straits (Allied Commission)
Eregli
Samsun
Trebizond
ARMENIA Independent State. Frontiers to be fixed later.
TURKEY
Greek administration
Smyrna
Adalia
CILICIA
Provisional Turkish frontier
Aleppo
SYRIA
MESO-POTAMIA
Euphrates
Provisional independence ('assisted by Mandatory Powers.')
CYPRUS
British annexation recognised
By the Treaty, to Italy
Dodecanese
AEGEAN
GREECE
Crete
J.F.H.

but we may perhaps enumerate some of the more salient breaches of the Twelve that survived out of the Fourteen Points at the opening of the Conference.

One initial cause of nearly all those breaches lay, we believe, in the complete unpreparedness and unwillingness of that pre-existing league of nations, subjected states and exploited areas, the British Empire, to submit to any dissection and adaptation of its system or to any control of its naval and aerial armament. A kindred contributory cause was the equal unpreparedness of the American mind for any interference with the ascendancy of the United States in the New World (compare Secretary Olney's declaration in this chapter, § 6). Neither of those Great Powers, who were necessarily dominant and leading powers at Paris, had properly thought out the implications of a League of Nations in relation to these older arrangements, and so their support of that project had to most European observers a curiously hypocritical air; it was as if they wished to retain and ensure their own vast predominance and security while at the same time restraining any other power from such expansions, annexations, and alliances as might create a rival and competitive imperialism. Their failure to set an example of international confidence destroyed all possibility of international confidence in the other nations represented at Paris.

Even more unfortunate was the refusal of the Americans to assent to the Japanese demand for a recognition of racial equality.

Moreover, the foreign offices of the British, the French, and the Italians were haunted by traditional schemes of aggression entirely incompatible with the new ideas. A League of Nations that is to be of any appreciable value to mankind must supersede imperialisms; it is either a super-imperialism, a liberal world-empire of united states, participant or in tutelage, or it is nothing; but few of the people at the Paris Conference had the mental vigour even to assert this obvious consequence of the League proposal. They wanted to be at the same time bound and free, to ensure peace for ever, but to keep their weapons in their hands. Accordingly the old annexation projects of the Great Power period were hastily and thinly camouflaged as proposed acts of this poor little birth of April 28th. The newly born and barely animate League was represented to be distributing, with all the reckless munificence of a captive pope,

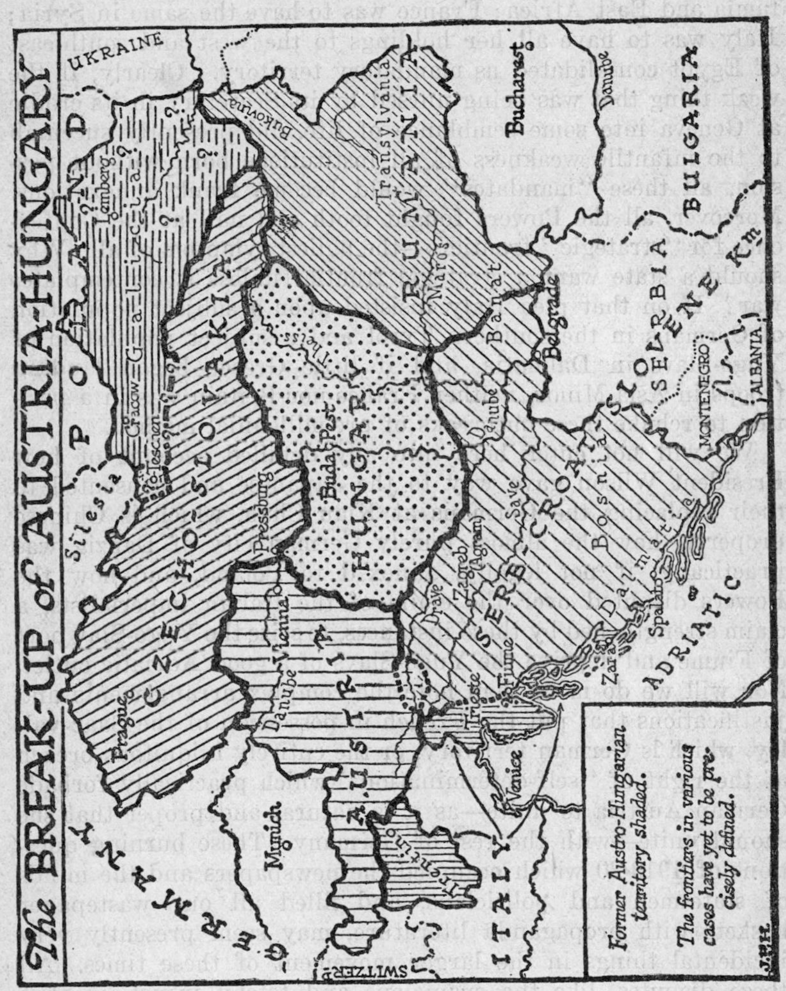
The BREAK-UP of AUSTRIA-HUNGARY
UKRAINE
POLAND
Lemberg
Galicia
Cracow
Teschen
Silesia
CZECHO-SLOVAKIA
Prague
Pressburg
Vienna
Danube
AUSTRIA
Munich
GERMANY
SWITZER-
Trentino
ITALY
Venice
Trieste
Fiume
Zara
Spalato
Dalmatia
ADRIATIC
Bosnia
SERB-CROAT-SLOVENE Km
Zagreb (Agram)
Drave
Save
Buda Pest
HUNGARY
Theiss
Danube
Banat
Belgrade
SERBIA
MONTENEGRO
ALBANIA
BULGARIA
Bucharest
Danube
RUMANIA
Transylvania
Maros
Bukovina
Former Austro-Hungarian territory shaded.
The frontiers in various cases have yet to be precisely defined.
J.F.H.

"mandates" to the old imperialisms that, had it been the young Hercules we desired, it would certainly have strangled in its cradle. Britain was to have extensive "mandates" in Mesopotamia and East Africa; France was to have the same in Syria; Italy was to have all her holdings to the west and south-east of Egypt consolidated as mandatory territory. Clearly, if the weak thing that was being nursed by its Secretary in its cradle at Geneva into some semblance of life, did presently succumb to the infantile weakness of all institutions born without passion, all these "mandates" would become frank annexations. Moreover, all the Powers fought tooth and nail at the Conference for "strategic" frontiers—the ugliest symptom of all. Why should a state want a strategic frontier unless it contemplates war? If on that plea Italy insisted upon a subject population of Germans in the southern Tyrol and a subject population of Yugo-Slavs in Dalmatia, and if little Greece began landing troops in Asia Minor, neither France nor Britain was in a position to rebuke these outbreaks of pre-millennial method.

We will not enter here into any detailed account of how President Wilson gave way to the Japanese and consented to their replacing the Germans at Kiau Chau, which is Chinese property, how the almost purely German city of Danzig was practically, if not legally, annex d to Poland, and how the Powers disputed over the claim of the Italian imperialists, a claim strengthened by these instances, to seize the Yugo-Slav port of Fiume and deprive the Yugo-Slavs of a good Adriatic outlet. Nor will we do more than note the complex arrangements and justifications that put the French in possession of the Saar valley, which is German territory, or the entirely iniquitous breach of the right of "self-determination" which practically forbade German Austria to unite—as it is natural and proper that she should unite—with the rest of Germany. These burning questions of 1919-20 which occupied the newspapers and the minds of statesmen and politicians, and filled all our wastepaper baskets with propaganda literature, may seem presently very incidental things in the larger movement of these times. All these disputes, like the suspicions and tetchy injustices of a weary and irritated man, may lose their importance as the tone of the world improves, and the still inadequately apprehended lessons of the Great War and the Petty Peace that followed it, begin to be digested by the general intelligence of mankind.

It is worth while for the reader to compare the treaty maps we give with what we have called the natural political map of Europe. The new arrangements do approach this latter more closely than any previous system of boundaries. It may be a necessary preliminary to any satisfactory league of peoples, that each people should first be in something like complete possession of its own household.

§ 14

A FORECAST OF THE NEXT WAR

The failure to produce a more satisfactory world settlement in 1919-20 was, we have suggested, a symptom of an almost universal intellectual and moral lassitude resulting from the overstrain of the Great War. A lack of fresh initiative is characteristic of a fatigue phase; everyone, for sheer inability to change, drifts on for a time along the lines of mental habit and precedent.

Nothing could be more illustrative of this fatigue inertia than the expressed ideas of military men at this time. It will round off this chapter in an entirely significant way, and complete our picture of the immense world interrogation on which our history must end, if we give here the briefest summary of a lecture that was delivered to a gathering of field-marshals, generals, major-generals, and the like by Major-General Sir Louis Jackson at the Royal United Service Institution in London one day in December, 1919. Lord Peel, the British Under-Secretary for War, presided, and the reader must picture to himself the not too large and quite dignified room of assembly in that building, and all these fine, grave, soldierly figures quietly intent upon the lecturer's words. He is describing, with a certain subdued enthusiasm, the probable technical developments of military method in the "next war."

Outside, through the evening twilight of Whitehall, flows the London traffic, not quite so abundant as in 1914, but still fairly abundant; the omnibuses all overcrowded because there are now not nearly enough of them, and the clothing of people generally shabbier. Some little way down Whitehall is a temporary erection, the Cenotaph, with its base smothered with a vast, pathetic heap of decaying wreaths, bunches of flowers, and the like, a cenotaph to commemorate the eight hundred thousand young men of the Empire who have been killed in the recent struggle. A few people are putting fresh flowers and wreaths there. One or two are crying.

The prospect stretches out beyond this gathering into the grey vastness of London, where people are now crowded as they have never been crowded before, whose food is dear and employment more uncertain than it has ever been. But let not the spectacle be one of unrelieved gloom; Regent Street, Oxford Street, and Bond Street are bright with shoppers and congested with new automobiles, because we must remember that everybody does not lose by a war. Beyond London the country sinks into night, and across the narrow sea are North France and Belgium devastated, Germany with scores of thousands of her infants dwindling and dying for want of milk, all Austria starving. Half the population of Vienna, it is believed unless American relief comes quickly, is doomed to die of hardship before the spring. Beyond that bleak twilight stretches the darkness of Russia. There, at least, no rich people are buying anything, and no military men are reading essays on the next war. But in icy Petrograd is little food, little wood, and no coal. All the towns of Russia southward as far as the snow reaches are in a similar plight, and in the Ukraine and to the south a ragged and dingy war drags to its end. Europe is bankrupt, and people's pockets rustle with paper money whose purchasing power dwindles as they walk about with it.

But now we will return to Sir Louis in the well-lit room at the United Service Institution.

He was of opinion—we follow the report in next morning's *Times*[1]—that we were merely on the eve of the most extensive modifications of the art of war known to history. It behoved us, therefore—us being, of course, the British and not the whole of mankind—to get on with our armaments and to keep ahead; a fine opening generalization. "It was necessary to develop new arms. . . . The nation which best did so would have a great advantage in the next war. There were people who were crying aloud for a reduction of armaments——"

(But there the Director of Trench Warfare and Supplies was wrong. They were just crying at the cenotaph, poor, soft,

[1] Checked by subsequent comparison with the published article in the *Jour. of the Roy United Service Institution*, vol. lxv, No. 457, February,

and stupid souls, because a son or a brother or a father was dead.)

Sir Louis believed that one of the greatest developments in the art of warfare would be brought about in mechanical transport. The tank he treated with ingratitude. These military gentlemen are ungrateful to an invention which shoved and butted them into victory almost in spite of themselves. The tank, said Sir Louis, was "a freak. . . . The outstanding feature" of the tank, he said, was that it made mechanical transport independent of the roads. Hitherto armies on the march had only been able to spoil the roads; now their transport on caterpillar wheels would advance in open order on a broad front carrying guns, munitions, supplies, bridging equipment, rafts, and men—and incidentally ploughing up and destroying hedges, ditches, fields, and cultivation generally. Armies would wallow across the country, leaving nothing behind but dust and mud.

So our imaginations are led up to the actual hostilities.

Sir Louis was in favour of gas. For punitive expeditions particularly, gas was to be recommended. And here he startled and disconcerted his hearers by a gleam of something approaching sentimentality. "It *might* be possible," he said, "to come to some agreement that no gas should be used which caused unnecessary suffering." But there his heart spoke rather than his head; it should have been clear to him that if law can so far override warfare as to prohibit any sort of evil device whatever, it can override warfare to the extent of prohibiting it altogether. And where would Sir Louis Jackson and his audience be then? War is war; its only law is the law that the maximum destruction of the forces of the enemy is necessary. To that law in warfare all considerations of humanity and justice are subordinate.

From gas Sir Louis passed to the air. Here he predicted "most important advances. . . . We need not trouble ourselves yet with flying destroyers of flying concrete forts, but in twenty years' time the Air Force Estimates might be the most important part of our preparations for war." He discussed the conversion of commercial flying machines to bombing and reconnaissance uses, and the need for special types of fighting machine in considerable numbers and always ready. He gave reasons for supposing that the bombers in the next war would not have the same targets near the front of the armies, and would secure better results by going further afield and bombing the centres "where stores are being manufactured and troops trained." As everyone who stayed in London or the east of England in 1917-18 knows, this means the promiscuous bombing of any and every centre of population. But, of course, the bombing of those 'prentice days would be child's play to the bombing of the "next war." There would be countless more aeroplanes, bigger and much nastier bombs. . . .

Sir Louis, proceeding with the sketch, mentioned the "destruction of the greater part of London" as a possible incident in the coming struggle. And so on to the culminating moral, that the highest pay, the utmost importance, the freest expenditure, must be allowed to military gentlemen. "The expense entailed is in the nature of an absolutely necessary insurance." With which his particular audience warmly agreed. And a certain Major-General Stone, a little forgetful of the source of his phrases,[1] said he hoped that this lecture "may be the beginning not of trusting in the League of Nations, but in *our own* right hand and *our* stretched-out arm!"

But we will not go on with the details of this dream. For indeed no Utopia was ever so impossible as this forecast of a world in which scarcely anything but very carefully sandbagged and camouflaged G.H.Q. would be reasonably safe, in which countless bombers would bomb the belligerent lands incessantly and great armies with lines of caterpillar transport roll to and fro, churning the fields of the earth into blood-streaked mud. There is not energy enough and no will whatever left in the world for such things. Generals who cannot foresee tanks cannot be expected to foresee or understand world bankruptcy; still less are they likely to understand the limits imposed upon military operations by the fluctuating temper of the common man. Apparently these military authorities of the United Service Institution did not even know that warfare aims at the production of states of mind in the enemy, and is sustained by states of mind. The chief neglected factor in the calculations of Sir Louis is the fact that no people whatever will stand such warfare as he contemplates, not even the people on the winning side. For as northern France, south-eastern Britain, and north Italy now understand, the victor in the "next war"

[1] Cp. Psalm cxxxvi.

may be bombed and starved almost as badly as the loser. A phase is possible in which a war-tormented population may cease to discriminate between military gentlemen on this side or that, and may be moved to destroy them as the common enemies of the race. The Great War of 1914-18 was the culmination of the military energy of the Western populations, and they fought and fought well because they believed they were fighting "the war to end war." They were. German imperialism, with its organized grip upon education and its close alliance with an aggressive commercialism, was beaten and finished. The militarism and imperialism of Britain and France and Italy are by comparison feeble, disorganized, and disorganizing survivals. They are things "left over" by the Great War. They have no persuasive power. They go on—for sheer want of wits to leave off. No European Government will ever get the same proportion of its people into the ranks and into its munition works again as the governments of 1914-18 did. Our world is very weak and feeble still (1920), but its war fever is over. Its temperature is, if anything, subnormal. It is doubtful if it will take the fever again for a long time. The alterations in the conditions of warfare are already much profounder than such authorities as Sir Louis Jackson suspect.[1]

[1] Here is another glimpse of the agreeable dreams that fill the contemporary military mind. It is from Fuller's recently published *Tanks in the Great War*. Colonel Fuller does not share that hostility to tanks characteristic of the older type of soldier. In the next war, he tells us: "Fast-moving tanks, equipped with tons of liquid gas . . . will cross the frontier and obliterate every living thing in the fields and farms, the villages, and cities of the enemy's country. Whilst life is being swept away around the frontier, fleets of aeroplanes will attack the enemy's great industrial and governing centres. All these attacks will be made, at first, not against the enemy's army . . . but against the civil population, in order to compel it to accept the will of the attacker."

For a good, well-balanced account of what modern war really means, see Philip Gibbs, *Realities of War*.

XL

THE NEXT STAGE OF HISTORY

§ 1. *The Possible Unification of Men's Wills in Political Matters.* § 2. *How a Federal World Government may Come About.* § 3. *Some Fundamental Characteristics of a Modern World State.* § 4. *What this World Might be were it under one Law and Justice.*

§ 1

WE have brought this *Outline of History* up to the threshold of our own times, but we have brought it to no conclusion. It breaks off at a dramatic phase of expectation. Nobody believes that the system of settlements grouped about the Treaty of Versailles is a permanent arrangement of the world's affairs. These Treaties were the end of the war and not the establishment of a new order in the world. That new order has now to be established. In social and economic as in international affairs we are in the dawn of a great constructive effort. The story of life which began inestimable millions of years ago, the adventure of mankind which was already afoot half a million years ago, rises to a crisis in the immense interrogation of to-day. The drama becomes ourselves. It is you, it is I, it is all that is happening to us and all that we are doing which will supply the next chapter of this continually expanding adventure of mankind.

Our history has traced a steady growth of the social and political units into which men have combined. In the brief period of ten thousand years these units have grown from the small family tribe of the early neolithic culture to the vast united realms—vast yet still too small and partial—of the present time. And this change in size of the state—a change manifestly incomplete—has been accompanied by profound changes in its nature. Compulsion and servitude have given way to ideas of associated freedom, and the sovereignty that was once concentrated in an autocratic king and god, has been widely diffused throughout the community. Until the Roman republic extended itself to all Italy, there had been no free community larger than a city state; all great communities were communities of obedience under a monarch. The great united republic of the United States would have been impossible before the printing press and the railway. The telegraph and telephone, the aeroplane, the continual progress of land and sea transit, are now insisting upon a still larger political organization.

If our *Outline* has been faithfully drawn, and if these brief conclusions are sound, it follows that we are engaged upon an immense task of adjustment to these great lines upon which our affairs are moving. Our wars, our social conflict, our enormous economic stresses, are all aspects of that adjustment. The loyalties and allegiances to-day are at best provisional loyalties and allegiances. Our true State, this state that is already beginning, this state to which every man owes his utmost political effort, must be now this nascent Federal World State to which human necessities point. Our true God now is the God of all men. Nationalism as a God must follow the tribal gods to limbo. Our true nationality is mankind.

How far will modern men lay hold upon and identify themselves with this necessity and set themselves to revise their ideas, remake their institutions, and educate the coming generations to this final extension of citizenship? How far will they remain dark, obdurate, habitual, and traditional, resisting the convergent forces that offer them either unity or misery? Sooner or later that unity must come or else plainly men must perish by their own inventions. We, because we believe in the power of reason and in the increasing good will in men, find ourselves compelled to reject the latter possibility. But the way to the former may be very long and tedious, very tragic and wearisome, a martyrdom of many generations, or it may be travelled over almost swiftly in the course of a generation or so. That depends upon forces whose nature we understand to some extent now, but not their power. There has to be a great process of education, by precept and by information and by experience, but there are as yet no quantitative measures of education to tell us *how much* has to be learnt or *how soon* that learning can be done. Our estimates vary with our moods; the time may be much longer than our hopes and much shorter than our fears.

The terrible experiences of the Great War have made very many men who once took political things lightly take them now very gravely. To a certain small number of men and women the attainment of a world peace has become the supreme work in life, has become a religious self-devotion. To a much greater number it has become at least a ruling motive. Many such people now are seeking ways of working for this great end, or they are already working for this great end, by pen and persuasion, in schools and colleges and books, and in the highways and byways of public life. Perhaps now most human beings in the world are well-disposed towards such efforts, but rather confusedly disposed; they are without any clear sense of what must be done and what ought to be prevented, that human solidarity may be advanced. The world-wide outbreak of faith and hope in President Wilson, before he began to wilt and fail us, was a very significant thing indeed for the future of mankind. Set against these motives of unity indeed are other motives entirely antagonistic, the fear and hatred of strange things and peoples, love of and trust in the old traditional thing, patriotisms, race prejudices, suspicions, distrusts—and the elements of spite, scoundrelism, and utter selfishness that are so strong still in every human soul.

The overriding powers that hitherto in the individual soul and in the community have struggled and prevailed against the ferocious, base, and individual impulses that divide us from one another, have been the powers of religion and education. Religion and education, those closely interwoven influences, have made possible the greater human societies whose growth we have traced in this *Outline;* they have been the chief synthetic forces throughout this great story of enlarging human co-operations that we have traced from its beginnings. We have found in the intellectual and theological conflicts of the nineteenth century the explanation of that curious exceptional disentanglement of religious teaching from formal education which is a distinctive feature of our age, and we have traced the consequences of this phase of religious disputation and confusion in the reversion of international politics towards a brutal nationalism and in the backward drift of industrial and business life towards harsh, selfish, and uncreative profit-seeking.

There has been a slipping off of ancient restraints; a real *de-civilization* of men's minds. We would lay stress here on the suggestion that this divorce of religious teaching from organized education is necessarily a temporary one, a transitory dislocation, and that presently education must become again in intention and spirit religious, and that the impulse to devotion, to universal service and to a complete escape from self, which has been the common underlying force in all the great religions of the last five and twenty centuries, an impulse which ebbed so perceptibly during the prosperity, laxity, disillusionment, and scepticism of the past seventy or eighty years, will reappear again, stripped and plain, as the recognized fundamental structural impulse in human society.

Education is the preparation of the individual for the community, and his religious training is the core of that preparation. With the great intellectual restatements and expansions of the nineteenth century, an educational break-up, a confusion and loss of aim in education, was inevitable. We can no longer prepare the individual for a community when our ideas of a community are shattered and undergoing reconstruction. The old loyalties, the old too limited and narrow political and social assumptions, the old too elaborate religious formulæ, have lost their power of conviction, and the greater ideas of a world state and of an economic commonweal have been winning their way only very slowly to recognition. So far they have swayed only a minority of exceptional people. But out of the trouble and tragedy of this present time there may emerge a moral and intellectual revival, a religious revival, of a simplicity and scope to draw together men of alien races and now discrete traditions into one common and sustained way of living for the world's service. We cannot foretell the scope and power of such a revival; we cannot even produce evidence of its onset. The beginnings of such things are never conspicuous. Great movements of the racial soul come at first "like a thief in the night," and then suddenly are discovered to be powerful and world-wide. Religious emotion—stripped of corruptions and freed from its last priestly entanglements—may presently blow through life again like a great wind, bursting the doors and flinging open the shutters of the individual life, and making many things possible and easy that in these present days of exhaustion seem almost too difficult to desire.

§ 2

If we suppose a sufficient righteousness and intelligence in men to produce presently, from the tremendous lessons of history, an effective will for a world peace—that is to say, an effective will *for a world law under a world government*—for in no other fashion is a secure world peace conceivable—in what manner may we expect things to move towards this end? That movement will certainly not go on equally in every country, nor is it likely to take at first one uniform mode of expression. Here it will find a congenial and stimulating atmosphere, here it will find itself antagonistic to deep tradition or racial idiosyncrasy or well-organized base oppositions. In some cases those to whom the call of the new order has come will be living in a state almost ready to serve the ends of the greater political synthesis, in others they will have to fight like conspirators against the rule of evil laws. There is little in the political constitution of such countries as the United States or Switzerland that would impede their coalescence upon terms of frank give and take with other equally civilized confederations; political systems involving dependent areas and "subject peoples" such as the Turkish Empire was before the Great War, seem to require something in the nature of a breaking up before they can be adapted to a federal world system. Any state obsessed by traditions of an aggressive foreign policy will be difficult to assimilate into a world combination. But though here the government may be helpful, and here dark and hostile, the essential task of men of goodwill in all states and countries remains the same, it is an educational task, and its very essence is to bring to the minds of all men everywhere, as a necessary basis for world co-operation, *a new telling and interpretation, a common interpretation, of history.*

Does this League of Nations which has been created by the covenant of 1919 contain within it the germ of any permanent federation of human effort? Will it grow into something for which, as Stallybrass says, men will be ready to "work wholeheartedly and, if necessary, *fight*"—as hitherto they have been willing to fight for their country and their own people? There are few intimations of any such enthusiasm for the League at the present time. The League does not even seem to know how to talk to common men. It has gone into official buildings, and comparatively few people in the world understand or care what it is doing there. It may be that the League is no more than a first project of union, exemplary only in its insufficiencies and dangers, destined to be superseded by something closer and completer as were the United States Articles of Confederation by the Federal Constitution. The League is at present a mere partial league of governments and states. It emphasizes nationality; it defers to sovereignty. What the world needs is no such league of nations as this nor even a mere league of peoples, but *a world league of men.* The world perishes unless sovereignty is merged and nationality subordinated. And for that the minds of men must first be prepared by experience and knowledge and thought. The supreme task before men at the present time is political education.

It may be that several partial leagues may precede any world league. The common misfortunes and urgent common needs of Europe and Asia may be more efficacious in bringing the European and Asiatic states to reason and a sort of unity, than the mere intellectual and sentimental ties of the United States and Great Britain and France. A United States of the Old World is a possibility to set against the possibility of an Atlantic union. Moreover, there is much to be said for an American experiment, a Pan-American league, in which the New World European colonies would play an in-and-out part as Luxembourg did for a time in the German confederation.

We will not attempt to weigh here what share may be taken in the recasting and consolidation of human affairs by the teachings and propaganda of labour internationalism, by the studies and needs of international finance, or by such boundary-destroying powers as science and art and historical teaching. All these things may exert a combined pressure, in which it may never be possible to apportion the exact shares. Opposition may dissolve, antagonistic cults flatten out to a common culture, almost imperceptibly. The bold idealism of to-day may seem mere common sense to-morrow. And the problem of a forecast is complicated by the possibilities of interludes and backwaters. History has never gone simply forward. More particularly are the years after a great war apt to be years of apparent retrocession; men are too weary to see what has been done, what has been cleared away, and what has been made possible.

Among the things that seem to move commandingly towards an adequate world control at the present time are these:—

(1) The increasing destructiveness and intolerableness of war waged with the new powers of science.

(2) The inevitable fusion of the world's economic affairs into one system, leading necessarily, it would seem, to some common control of currency, and demanding safe and uninterrupted communications, and a free movement of goods and people by sea and land throughout the whole world. The satisfaction of these needs will require a world control of very considerable authority and powers of enforcement.

(3) The need, because of the increasing mobility of peoples, of effectual controls of health everywhere.

(4) The urgent need of some equalization of labour conditions, and of the minimum standard of life throughout the world. This seems to carry with it, as a necessary corollary, the establishment of some minimum standard of education for everyone.

(5) The impossibility of developing the enormous benefits of flying without a world control of the air-ways.

The necessity and logic of such diverse considerations as these push the mind irresistibly, in spite of the clashes of race and tradition and the huge difficulties created by differences in language, towards the belief that a conscious struggle to establish or prevent a political world community will be the next stage in human history. The things that require that world community are permanent *needs,* one or other of these needs appeals to nearly everyone, and against their continuing persistence are only mortal difficulties, great no doubt, but mortal; prejudices, passions, animosities, delusions about race and country, egotisms, and such-like fluctuating and evanescent things, set up in men's minds by education and suggestion; none of them things that make now for the welfare and survival of the individuals who are under their sway nor of the states and towns and associations in which they prevail.

§ 3

The attainment of the world state may be impeded and may be opposed to-day by many apparently vast forces; but it has, urging it on, a much more powerful force, that of the free and growing common intelligence of mankind. To-day there is in the world a small but increasing number of men, historians, archæologists, ethnologists, economists, sociologists, psychologists, educationists, and the like, who are doing for human institutions that same task of creative analysis which the scientific men of the seventeenth and eighteenth century did for the materials and mechanism of human life; and just as these latter, almost unaware of what they were doing, made telegraphy, swift transit on sea and land, flying and a thousand hitherto impossible things possible, so the former may be doing more than the world suspects, or than they themselves suspect, to clear up and make plain the thing to do and the way to do it, in the greater and more urgent human affairs.

Let us ape Roger Bacon in his prophetic mood, and set down what we believe will be the broad fundamentals of the coming world state.

(i) It will be based upon a common world religion, very much simplified and universalized and better understood. This will not be Christianity nor Islam nor Buddhism nor any such specialized form of religion, but religion itself pure and undefiled; the Eightfold Way, the Kingdom of Heaven, brotherhood, creative service, and self-forgetfulness. Throughout the world men's thoughts and motives will be turned by education, example, and the circle of ideas about them, from the obsession of self to the cheerful service of human knowledge, human power, and human unity.

(ii) And this world state will be sustained by a universal education, organized upon a scale and of a penetration and quality beyond all present experience. The whole race, and not simply classes and peoples, will be *educated.* Most parents will have a technical knowledge of teaching. Quite apart from the duties of parentage, perhaps ten per cent. or more of the adult population will, at some time or other in their lives, be workers in the world's educational organization. And education, as the new age will conceive it, will go on throughout life; it will not cease at any particular age. Men and women will simply become self-educators and individual students and student teachers as they grow older.

(iii) There will be no armies, no navies, and no classes of unemployed people either wealthy or poor.

(iv) The world state's organization of scientific research

and record compared with that of to-day will be like an ocean liner beside the dug-out canoe of some early heliolithic wanderer.

(v) There will be a vast free literature of criticism and discussion.

(vi) The world's political organization will be democratic, that is to say, the government and direction of affairs will be in immediate touch with and responsive to the general thought of the educated whole population.

(vii) Its economic organization will be an exploitation of all natural wealth and every fresh possibility science reveals, by the agents and servants of the common government for the common good. Private enterprise will be the servant—a useful, valued, and well-rewarded servant—and no longer the robber master of the commonweal.

(viii) And this implies two achievements that seem very difficult to us to-day. They are matters of mechanism, but they are as essential to the world's well-being as it is to a soldier's, no matter how brave he may be, that his machine gun should not jam, and to an aeronaut's that his steering-gear should not fail him in mid-air. Political well-being demands that electoral methods shall be used, and economic well-being requires that a currency shall be used, safeguarded or proof against the contrivances and manipulations of clever, dishonest men.[1]

§ 4

There can be little question that the attainment of a federation of all humanity, together with a sufficient measure of social justice, to ensure health, education, and a rough equality of opportunity to most of the children born into the world, would mean such a release and increase of human energy as to open a new phase in human history. The enormous waste caused by military preparation and the mutual annoyance of competing great powers, and the still more enormous waste due to the under-productiveness of great masses of people, either because they are too wealthy for stimulus or too poor for efficiency, would cease. There would be a vast increase in the supply of human necessities, a rise in the standard of life

[1] See Wells, *The Salvaging of Civilization.*

and in what is considered a necessity, a development of transport and every kind of convenience; and a multitude of people would be transferred from low-grade production to such higher work as art of all kinds, teaching, scientific research, and the like. All over the world there would be a setting free of human capacity, such as has occurred hitherto only in small places and through precious limited phases of prosperity and security. Unless we are to suppose that spontaneous outbreaks of supermen have occurred in the past, it is reasonable to conclude that the Athens of Pericles, the Florence of the Medici, Elizabethan England, the great deeds of Asoka, the Tang and Ming periods in art, are but samples of what a whole world of sustained security would yield continuously and cumulatively. Without supposing any change in human quality, but merely its release from the present system of inordinate waste, history justifies this expectation.

We have seen how, since the liberation of human thought in the fifteenth and sixteenth centuries, a comparatively few curious and intelligent men, chiefly in western Europe, have produced a vision of the world and a body of science that is now, on the material side, revolutionizing life. Mostly these men have worked against great discouragement, with insufficient funds and small help or support from the mass of mankind. It is impossible to believe that these men were the maximum intellectual harvest of their generation. England alone in the last three centuries must have produced scores of Newtons who never learnt to read, hundreds of Daltons, Darwins, Bacons, and Huxleys who died stunted in hovels, or never got a chance of proving their quality. All the world over, there must have been myriads of potential first-class investigators, splendid artists, creative minds, who never caught a gleam of inspiration or opportunity, for every one of that kind who has left his mark upon the world. In the trenches of the Western front alone during the late war thousands of potential great men died unfulfilled. But a world with something like a secure international peace and something like social justice, will fish for capacity with the fine net of universal education, and may expect a yield beyond comparison greater than any yield of able and brilliant men that the world has known hitherto.

It is such considerations as this indeed which justify the concentration of effort in the near future upon the making of a new world state of righteousness out of our present confusions. War is a horrible thing, and constantly more horrible and dreadful, so that unless it is ended it will certainly end human society; social injustice, and the sight of the limited and cramped human beings it produces, torment the soul; but the strongest incentive to constructive political and social work for an imaginative spirit lies not so much in the mere hope of escaping evils as in the opportunity for great adventures that their suppression will open to our race. We want to get rid of the militarist not simply because he hurts and kills, but because he is an intolerable thick-voiced blockhead who stands hectoring and blustering in our way to achievement. We want to abolish many extravagances of private ownership just as we should want to abolish some idiot guardian who refused us admission to a studio in which there were fine things to do.

There are people who seem to imagine that a world order and one universal law of justice would end human adventure. It would but begin it. But instead of the adventure of the past, the "romance" of the cinematograph world, the perpetual reiterated harping upon the trite reactions of sex and combat and the hunt for gold, it would be an unending exploration upon the edge of experience. Hitherto man has been living in a slum, amidst quarrels, revenges, vanities, shames and taints, hot desires and urgent appetites. He has scarcely tasted sweet air yet and the great freedoms of the world that science has enlarged for him.

To picture to ourselves something of the wider life that world unity would open to men is a very attractive speculation. Life will certainly go with a stronger pulse, it will breathe a deeper breath, because it will have dispelled and conquered a hundred infections of body and mind that now reduce it to invalidism and squalor. We have already laid stress on the vast elimination of drudgery from human life through the creation of a new race of slaves, the machines. This—and the disappearance of war and the smoothing out of endless restraints and contentions by juster social and economic arrangements—will lift the burthen of toilsome work and routine work, that has been the price of human security since the dawn of the first civilizations, from the shoulders of our children. Which does not mean that they will cease to work, but that they will cease to do irksome work under pressure, and will work freely, planning, making, creating, according to their gifts and instincts. They will fight nature no longer as dull conscripts of the pick and plough, but for a splendid conquest. Only the spiritlessness of our present depression blinds us to the clear intimations of our reason that in the course of a few generations every little country town could become an Athens, every human being could be gentle in breeding and healthy in body and mind, the whole solid earth man's mine and its uttermost regions his playground.

In this *Outline* we have sought to show two great systems of development interacting in the story of human society. We have seen, growing out of that later special neolithic culture, the heliolithic culture in the warmer alluvial parts of the world, the great primordial civilizations, fecund systems of subjugation and obedience, vast multiplications of industrious and subservient men. We have shown the necessary relationship of these early civilizations to the early temples and to king-gods and god-kings. At the same time we have traced the development from a simpler neolithic level of the wanderer peoples, who became the nomadic peoples, in those great groups the Aryans and the Hun-Mongol peoples of the north-west and the north-east and (from a heliolithic phase) the Semites of the Arabian deserts. Our history has told of a repeated overrunning and refreshment of the originally brunet civilizations by these hardier, bolder, free-spirited peoples of the steppes and desert. We have pointed out how these constantly recurring nomadic injections have steadily altered the primordial civilizations both in blood and in spirit; and how the world religions of to-day, and what we now call democracy, the boldness of modern scientific inquiry and a universal restlessness, are due to this "nomadization" of civilization. The old civilizations created tradition, and lived by tradition. To-day the power of tradition is destroyed. The body of our state is civilization still, but its spirit is the spirit of the nomadic world. It is the spirit of the great plains and the high seas.

So that it is difficult to resist the persuasion that so soon as one law runs in the earth and the fierceness of frontiers ceases to distress us, that urgency in our nature that stirs us in spring and autumn to be up and travelling, will have its way with us. We shall obey the call of the summer pastures and the winter pastures in our blood, the call of the mountains, the desert, and the sea. For some of us also, who may be of a different lineage, there is the call of the forest, and there are those who would hunt in the summer and return to the fields for the harvest and the plough. But this does not mean that men will have become homeless and all adrift. The normal nomadic life is not a homeless one, but a movement between homes. The Kalmucks to-day, like the swallows, go yearly a thousand miles from one home to another. The beautiful and convenient cities of the coming age, we conclude, will have their seasons when they will be full of life, and seasons when they will seem asleep. Life will ebb and flow to and from every region seasonally as the interest of that region rises or declines.

There will be little drudgery in this better-ordered world. Natural power harnessed in machines will be the general drudge. What drudgery is inevitable will be done as a service and duty for a few years or months out of each life; it will not consume nor degrade the whole life of anyone. And not only drudges, but many other sorts of men and ways of living which loom large in the current social scheme will necessarily have dwindled in importance or passed away altogether. There will be few professional fighting men or none at all, no custom-house officers; the increased multitude of teachers will have abolished large police forces and large jail staffs, mad-houses will be rare or non-existent; a world-wide sanitation will have diminished the proportion of hospitals, nurses, sick-room attendants, and the like; a world-wide economic justice, the floating population of cheats, sharpers, gamblers, forestallers, parasites, and speculators generally. But there will be no diminution of adventure or romance in this world of the days to come. Sea fisheries and the incessant insurrection of the sea, for example, will call for their own stalwart types of men; the high air will clamour for manhood, the deep and dangerous secret places of nature. Men will turn again with renewed interest to the animal world. In these disordered days a stupid, uncontrollable massacre of animal species goes on—from certain angles of vision it is a thing almost more tragic than human miseries; in the nineteenth century dozens of animal species, and some of them very interesting species, were exterminated; but one of the first fruits of an effective world state would be the better protection of what are now wild beasts. It is a strange thing in human history to note how little has been done since the Bronze Age in taming, using, befriending, and appreciating the animal life about us. But that mere witless killing which is called sport to-day would inevitably give place in a better educated world community to a modification of the primitive instincts that find expression in this way, changing them into an interest not in the deaths, but in the lives of beasts, and leading to fresh and perhaps very strange and beautiful attempts to befriend these pathetic, kindred lower creatures we no longer fear as enemies, hate as rivals, or need as slaves. And a world state and universal justice does not mean the imprisonment of our race in any bleak institutional orderliness. There will still be mountains and the sea, there will be jungles and great forests, cared for indeed and treasured and protected; the great plains will still spread before us and the wild winds blow. But men will not hate so much, fear so much, nor cheat so desperately—and they will keep their minds and bodies cleaner.

There are unhopeful prophets who see in the gathering together of men into one community the possibility of violent race conflicts, conflicts for "ascendancy," but that is to suppose that civilization is incapable of adjustments by which men of different qualities and temperaments and appearances will live side by side, following different rôles and contributing diverse gifts. The weaving of mankind into one community does not imply the creation of a homogeneous community, but rather the reverse; the welcome and the adequate utilization of distinctive quality in an atmosphere of understanding. It is the almost universal bad manners of the present age which make race intolerable to race. The community to which we may be moving will be more mixed—which does not necessarily mean more interbred—more various and more interesting than any existing community. Communities all to one pattern, like boxes of toy soldiers, are things of the past rather than the future.

But one of the hardest, most impossible tasks a writer can set himself, is to picture the life of people better educated, happier in their circumstances, more free and more healthy than he is himself. We know enough to-day to know that there is infinite room for betterment in every human concern. Nothing is needed but collective effort. Our poverty, our restraints, our infections and indigestions, our quarrels and misunderstandings, are all things controllable and removable by concerted human action, but we know as little how life would feel without them as some poor dirty ill-treated, fierce-souled creature born and bred amidst the cruel and dingy surroundings of a European back street can know what it is to bathe every day, always to be clad beautifully, to climb mountains for pleasure, to fly, to meet none but agreeable, well-mannered people, to conduct researches or make delightful things. Yet a time when all such good things will be for all men may be coming more nearly than we think. Each one who believes that brings the good time nearer; each heart that fails delays it.

One cannot foretell the surprises or disappointments the future has in store. Before this chapter of the World State can begin fairly in our histories, other chapters as yet unsuspected may still need to be written, as long and as full of conflict as our account of the growth and rivalries of the Great Powers. There may be tragic economic struggles, grim grapplings of race with race and class with class. It may be that "private enterprise" will refuse to learn the lesson of service without some quite catastrophic revolution, and that a phase of confiscation and amateurish socialistic government lies before us. We do not know; we cannot tell. These are unnecessary disasters, but they may be unavoidable disasters. Human history becomes more and more a race between education and catastrophe. Against the unifying effort of Christendom and against the unifying influence of the mechanical revolution, catastrophe won—at least to the extent of achieving the Great War. We cannot tell yet how much of the winnings of catastrophe still remain to be gathered in. New falsities may arise and hold men in some unrighteous and fated scheme of order for a time, before they collapse amidst the misery and slaughter of generations.

Yet, clumsily or smoothly, the world, it seems, progresses and will progress. In this *Outline,* in our account of palæolithic men, we have borrowed a description from Mr. Worthington Smith of the very highest life in the world some fifty thousand years ago. It was a bestial life. We have sketched, too, the gathering for a human sacrifice, some fifteen thousand years ago. That scene again is almost incredibly cruel to a modern civilized reader.

Yet it is not more than five hundred years since the great empire of the Aztecs still believed that it could live only by the shedding of blood. Every year in Mexico hundreds of human victims died in this fashion: the body was bent like a bow over the curved stone of sacrifice, the breast was slashed open with a knife of obsidian, and the priest tore out the beating heart of the still living victim. The day may be close at hand when we shall no longer tear out the hearts of men, even for the sake of our national gods. Let the reader but refer to the earlier time charts we have given in this history, and he will see the true measure and transitoriness of all the conflicts, deprivations, and miseries of this present period of painful and yet hopeful change.

CHRONOLOGICAL TABLE

TO conclude this *Outline,* we give here a Table of Leading Events from the year 800 B.C. to 1920 A.D. Following that we give five time diagrams covering the period from 1000 B.C. onward, which present the trend of events in a graphic form.

It is well that the reader should keep in mind an idea of the true proportions of historical to geological time. The scale of the five diagrams at the end is such that by it the time diagram on page 142 would be about 8½ times as long, that is to say about 4 feet; that on page 47 showing the interval since the Eoliths, 555 feet, and that on page 11 representing the whole of geological time would be somewhere between 12 and at the longest and most probable estimate, 260 miles! Let the reader therefore take one of these chronological tables we give, and imagine it extended upon a long strip of paper to a distance of 55 feet. He would have to get up and walk about that distance to note the date of the painting of the Altamira caves, and he would have to go ten times that distance by the side of the same narrow strip to reach the earlier Neanderthalers. A mile or so from home, but probably much further away, the strip might be recording the last of the dinosaurs. And this on a scale which represents the time from Columbus to ourselves by three inches of space!

Chronology only begins to be precise enough to specify the exact year of any event after the establishment of the eras of the First Olympiad and the building of Rome.

About the year 1000 B.C. the Aryan peoples were establishing themselves in the peninsulas of Spain, Italy, and the Balkans, and they were established in North India. Cnossos was already destroyed, and the spacious times of Egypt, of Thotmes III, Amenophis III, and Rameses II were three or four centuries away. Weak monarchs of the XXIst Dynasty were ruling in the Nile Valley. Israel was united under her early kings;

Saul or David or possibly even Solomon may have been reigning. Sargon I (2750 B.C. of the Akkadian Sumerian Empire was a remote memory in Babylonian history, more remote than is Constantine the Great from the world of the present day. Hammurabi had been dead a thousand years. The Assyrians were already dominating the less military Babylonians. In 1100 B.C. Tiglath Pileser I had taken Babylon. But there was no permanent conquest; Assyria and Babylonia were still separate empires. In China the new Chow dynasty was flourishing. Stonehenge in England was already a thousand years old.

The next two centuries saw a renascence of Egypt under the XXII Dynasty, the splitting up of the brief little Hebrew kingdom of Solomon, the spreading of the Greeks in the Balkans, South Italy and Asia Minor, and the days of Etruscan predominance in Central Italy. We may begin our list of ascertainable dates with

B.C.

800. The building of Carthage.

790. The Ethiopian conquest of Egypt (founding the XXVth Dynasty).

776. First Olympiad.

753. Rome built.

745. Tiglath Pileser III conquered Babylonia and founded the New Assyrian Empire.

738. Menahem, king of Israel, bought off Tiglath Pileser III.

735. Greeks settling in Sicily.

722. Sargon II armed the Assyrians with iron weapons.

721. He deported the Israelites.

704. Sennacherib.

701. His army destroyed by a pestilence on its way to Egypt.

680. Esarhaddon took Thebes in Egypt (overthrowing the Ethiopian XXVth Dynasty).

667. Sardanapalus.

664. Psammetichus I restored the freedom of Egypt and founded the XXVIth Dynasty (to 610). He was assisted against Assyria by Lydian troops sent by Gyges.

608. Necho of Egypt defeated Josiah, king of Judah, at the Battle of Megiddo.

606. Capture of Nineveh by the Chaldeans and Medes. Foundation of the Chaldean Empire.

B.C.

604. Necho pushed to the Euphrates and was overthrown by Nebuchadnezzar II. Josiah fell with him.
586. Nebuchadnezzar carried off the Jews to Babylon. Many fled to Egypt and settled there.
550. Cyrus the Persian succeeded Cyaxares the Mede.
Cyrus conquered Croesus.
Buddha lived about this time. So also did Confucius and Lao Tse.
539. Cyrus took Babylon and founded the Persian Empire.
527. Peisistratus died.
525. Cambyses conquered Egypt.
521. Darius I, the son of Hystaspes, ruled from the Hellespont to the Indus.
His expedition to Scythia.
490. Battle of Marathon.
484. Herodotus born. Æschylus won his first prize for tragedy.
480. Battles of Thermopylæ and Salamis.
479. The Battles of Platæa and Mycale completed the repulse of Persia.
474. Etruscan fleet destroyed by the Sicilian Greeks.
470. Voyage of Hanno.
466. Pericles.
465. Xerxes murdered.
438. Herodotus recited his History in Athens.
431. Peloponnesian War began (to 404).
428. Pericles died. Herodotus died.
427. Aristophanes began his career. Plato born. He lived to 347.
401. Retreat of the Ten Thousand.
390. Brennus sacked Rome.
366. Camillus built the Temple of Concord
359. Philip became king of Macedonia.
338. Battle of Chaeronia.
336. Macedonian troops crossed into Asia, Philip murdered.
334. Battle of the Granicus.
333. Battle of Issus.
332. Alexander in Egypt.
331. Battle of Arbela.
330. Darius III killed.

B.C.

323. Death of Alexander the Great.
321. Rise of Chandragupta in the Punjab. The Romans completely beaten by the Samnites at the battle of the Caudine Forks.
303. Chandragupta repulsed Seleucus.
285. Ptolemy Soter died.
281. Pyrrhus invaded Italy.
280. Battle of Heraclea.
279. Battle of Ausculum.
278. Gauls' raid into Asia Minor and settlement in Galatia.
275. Pyrrhus left Italy.
264. First Punic War. (Asoka began to reign in Behar—to 227.) First gladiatorial games in Rome.
260. Battle of Mylæ.
256. Battle of Ecnomus.
246. Shi Hwang-ti became king of Ch'in.
242. Battle of Ægatian Isles.
241. End of First Punic War.
225. Battle of Telamon. Roman armies in Illyria.
220. Shi Hwang-ti became emperor of China.
     [Note that the date given to Shi Hwang-ti in the diagram on p. 142 is incorrect.]
219. Second Punic War.
216. Battle of Cannæ.
214. Great Wall of China begun.
210. Death of Shi Hwang-ti.
202. Battle of Zama.
201. End of Second Punic War.
200-197. Rome at war with Macedonia.
192. War with the Seleucids.
190. Battle of Magnesia.
149. Third Punic War. (The Yueh-Chi came into Western Turkestan.)
146. Carthage destroyed. Corinth destroyed.
133. Attalus bequeathed Pergamum to Rome. Tiberius Gracchus killed.
121. Caius Gracchus killed.
118. War with Jugurtha.
106. War with Jugurtha ended.
102. Marius drove back Germans.

B.C.

100. Triumph of Marius. (Wu-ti conquering the Tarim valley.)
91. Social war.
89. All Italians became Roman citizens.
86. Death of Marius.
78. Death of Sulla.
73. The revolt of the slaves under Spartacus.
71. Defeat and end of Spartacus.
66. Pompey led Roman troops to the Caspian and Euphrates. He conquered the Alani.
64. Mithridates of Pontus died.
53. Crassus killed at Carrhæ. Mongolian elements with Parthians.
48. Julius Cæsar defeated Pompey at Pharsalos.
44. Julius Cæsar assassinated.
31. Battle of Actium.
27. Augustus Cæsar princeps (until 14 A.D.).
4. True date of birth of Jesus of Nazareth.

A.D. Christian Era began.

6. Province of Mœsia established.
9. Province of Pannonia established. Imperial boundary carried to the Danube.
14. Augustus died. Tiberius emperor.
30. Jesus of Nazareth crucified.
37. Caligula succeeded Tiberius.
41. Claudius (the first emperor of the legions) made emperor by pretorian guard after murder of Caligula.
54. Nero succeeded Claudius.
61. Boadicea massacred Roman garrison in Britain.
68. Suicide of Nero. (Galba, Otho, Vitellius, emperors in succession.)
69. Vespasian began the so-called Flavian dynasty.
79. Titus succeeded Vespasian.
81. Domitian.
84. North Britain annexed.
96. Nerva began the so-called dynasty of the Antonines.
98. Trajan succeeded Nerva.
102. Pan Chau on the Caspian Sea. (Indo-Scythians invading North India.)

A.D.

117. Hadrian succeeded Trajan. Roman Empire at its greatest extent.

138. Antoninus Pius succeeded Hadrian. (The Indo-Scythians at this time were destroying the last traces of Hellenic rule in India.)

150. [About this time Kanishka reigned in India, Kashgar, Yarkand, and Kotan.]

161. Marcus Aurelius succeeded Antoninus Pius.

164. Great plague began, and lasted to the death of M. Aurelius (180). This also devastated all Asia.

180. Death of Marcus Aurelius.
(Nearly a century of war and disorder began in the Roman Empire.)

220. End of the Han dynasty. Beginning of four hundred years of division in China.

227. Ardashir I (first Sassanid shah) put an end to Arsacid line in Persia.

242. Mani began his teaching.

247. Goths crossed Danube in a great raid.

251. Great victory of Goths. Emperor Decius killed.

260. Sapor I, the second Sassanid shah, took Antioch, captured the Emperor Valerian, and was cut up on his return from Asia Minor by Odenathus of Palmyra.

269. The Emperor Claudis defeated the Goths at Nish.

270. Aurelian became emperor.

272. Zenobia carried captive to Rome. End of the brief glories of Palmyra.

275. Probus succeeded Aurelian.

276. Goths in Pontus. The Emperor Probus forced back Franks and Alemanni.

277. Mani crucified in Persia.

284. Diocletian became emperor.

303. Diocletian persecuted the Christians.

311. Galerius abandoned the persecution of the Christians.

312. Constantine the Great became emperor.

313. Constantine presided over a Christian Council at Arles.

321. Fresh Gothic raids driven back.

323. Constantine presided over the Council of Nicæa.

337. Vandals driven by Goths obtained leave to settle in Pannonia.

A.D.

337. Constantine baptized on his death-bed.
354. St. Augustine born.
361-3. Julian the Apostate attempted to substitute Mithraism for Christianity.
379. Theodosius the Great (a Spainard) emperor.
390. The statute of Serapis at Alexandria broken up.
392. Theodosius the Great emperor of east and west.
395. Theodosius the Great died. Honorius and Arcadius redivided the empire with Stilicho and Alaric as their masters and protectors.
410. The Visigoths under Alaric captured Rome.
425. Vandals settling in south of Spain. Huns in Pannonia, Goths in Dalmatia. Visigoths and Suevi in Portugal and North Spain. English invading Britain.
429. Vandals under Genseric invaded Africa.
439. Vandals took Carthage.
448. Priscus visited Attila.
451. Attila raided Gaul and was defeated by Franks, Alemanni, and Romans at Troyes.
453. Death of Attila.
455. Vandals sacked Rome.
470. Ephthalites' raid into India.
476. Odoacer, king of a medley of Teutonic tribes, informed Constantinople that there was no emperor in the West. End of the Western Empire.
480. St. Benedict born.
481. Clovis in France. The Merovingians.
483. Nestorian church broke away from the Orthodox Christian church.
493. Theodoric, the Ostrogoth, conquered Italy and became King of Italy, but was nominally subject to Constantinople.
(Gothic kings in Italy. Goths settled on special confiscated lands as a garrison.)
527. Justinian emperor.
528. Mihiragula, the (Ephthalite) Attila of India, overthrown.
529. Justinian closed the schools at Athens, which had flourished nearly a thousand years. Belisarius (Justinian's general) took Naples.

A.D.

531. Chosroes I began to reign.
543. Great plague in Constantinople.
544. St. Benedict died.
553. Goths expelled from Italy by Justinian. Cassiodorus founded his monastery.
565. Justinian died. The Lombards conquered most of North Italy (leaving Ravenna and Rome Byzantine). The Turks broke up the Ephthalites in Western Turkestan.
570. Muhammad born.
579. Chosroes I died.
(The Lombards dominant in Italy.)
590. Plague raged in Rome. (Gregory the Great—Gregory I—and the vision of St. Angelo.) Chosroes II began to reign.
610. Heraclius began to reign.
619. Chosroes II held Egypt, Jerusalem, Damascus, and had armies on Hellespont. Tang dynasty began in China.
622. The Hegira.
623. Battle of Badr.
627. Great Persian defeat at Nineveh by Heraclius. The Meccan Allies besieged Medina. Tai Tsung became Emperor of China.
628. Kavadh II murdered and succeeded his father, Chosroes II.
Muhammad wrote letters to all the rulers of the earth.
629. Yuan Chwang started for India. Muhammad entered Mecca.
632. Muhammad died. Abu Bekr Caliph.
634. Battle of the Yarmuk. Moslems took Syria. Omar second Caliph.
635. Tai Tsung received Nestorian missionaries.
637. Battle of Kadessia.
638. Jerusalem surrendered to Omar.
642. Heraclius died.
643. Othman third Caliph.
645. Yuan Chwang returned to Singan.
655. Defeat of the Byzantine fleet by the Moslems.
656. Othman murdered at Medina.
661. Ali murdered.

A.D.

662. Moawiya Caliph. (First of the Omayyad caliphs.)
668. The Caliph Moawiya attacked Constantinople by sea—Theodore of Tarsus became Archbishop of Canterbury.
675. Last of the sea attacks by Moawiya on Constantinople.
687. Pepin of Hersthal, mayor of the palace, reunited Austrasia and Neustria.
711. Moslem army invaded Spain from Africa.
714. Charles Martel, mayor of the palace.
715. The domains of the Caliph Walid I extended from the Pyrenees to China.
717-18. Suleiman, son and successor of Walid, failed to take Constantinople. The Omayyad line passed its climax.
732. Charles Martel defeated the Moslems near Poitiers.
735. Death of the Venerable Bede.
743. Walid II Caliph—the unbelieving Caliph.
749. Overthrow of the Omayyads. Abdul Abbas, the first Abbasid Caliph. Spain remained Omayyad. Beginning of the break-up of the Arab Empire.
751. Pepin crowned King of the French.
755. Martyrdom of St. Boniface.
768. Pepin died.
771. Charlemagne sole king.
774. Charlemagne conquered Lombardy.
776. Charlemagne in Dalmatia.
786. Haroun-al-Raschid Abbasid Caliph in Bagdad (to 809).
795. Leo III became Pope (to 816).
800. Leo crowned Charlemagne Emperor of the West.
802. Egbert, formerly an English refugee at the court of Charlemagne, established himself as King of Wessex.
810. Krum of Bulgaria defeated and killed the Emperor Nicephorus.
814. Charlemagne died, Louis the Pious succeeds him.
828. Egbert became first King of England.
843. Louis the Pious died, and the Carlovingian Empire went to pieces. Until 962 there was no regular succession of Holy Roman Emperors, though the title appeared intermittently.
850. About this time Rurik (a Northman) became ruler of Novgorod and Kieff.
852. Boris first Christian King of Bulgaria (to 884).

A.D.

865. The fleet of the Russians (Northmen) threatened Constantinople.
886. The Treaty of Alfred of England and Guthrum the Dane, establishing the Danes in the Danelaw.
904. Russian (Northmen) fleet off Constantinople.
912. Rolf the Ganger established himself in Normandy.
919. Henry the Fowler elected King of Germany.
928. Marozia imprisoned Pope John X.
931. John XI Pope (to 936).
936. Otto I became King of Germany in succession to his father, Henry the Fowler.
941. Russian fleet again threatened Constantinople.
955. John XII Pope.
960. Northern Sung Dynasty began in China.
962. Otto I, King of Germany, crowned Emperor (first Saxon Emperor) by John XII.
963. Otto deposed John XII.
969. Separate Fatimite Caliphate set up in Egypt.
973. Otto II.
983. Otto III.
987. Hugh Capet became King of France. End of the Carlovingian line of French kings.
1016. Canute became King of England, Denmark, and Norway.
1037. Avicenna of Bokhara, the Prince of Physicians, died.
1043. Russian fleet threatened Constantinople.
1066. Conquest of England by William, Duke of Normandy.
1071. Revival of Islam under the Seljuk Turks. Battle of Melasgird.
1073. Hildebrand became Pope (Gregory VII) to 1085.
1082. Robert Guiscard captured Durazzo.
1084. Robert Guiscard sacked Rome.
1087-99. Urban II Pope.
1094. Pestilence.
1095. Urban II at Clermont summoned the First Crusade.
1096. Massacre of the People's Crusade.
1099. Godfrey of Bouillon captured Jerusalem. Paschal II Pope (to 1118).
1138. Kin Empire flourished. The Sung capital shifted from Nanking to Hang Chau.

A.D.

1147. The Second Crusade. Foundation of the Christian Kingdom of Portugal.

1169. Saladin Sultan of Egypt.

1176. Frederick Barbarossa acknowledged supremacy of the Pope (Alexander III) at Venice.

1187. Saladin captured Jerusalem.

1189. The Third Crusade.

1198. Averroes of Cordoba, the Arab philosopher, died. Innocent III Pope (to 1216). Frederick II (aged four), King of Sicily, became his ward.

1202. The Fourth Crusade attacked the Eastern Empire.

1204. Capture of Constantinople by the Latins.

1206. Kutub founded Moslem state at Delhi.

1212. The Children's Crusade.

1214. Jengis Khan took Peking.

1215. Magna Carta signed.

1216. Honorius III Pope.

1218. Jengis Khan invaded Kharismia.

1221. Failure and return of the Fifth Crusade. St. Dominic died (the Dominicans).

1226. St. Francis of Assisi died. (The Franciscans.)

1227. Jengis Khan died, Khan from the Caspian to the Pacific, and was succeeded by Ogdai Khan.
Gregory IX Pope.

1228. Frederick II embarked upon the Sixth Crusade, and acquired Jerusalem.

1234. Mongols completed conquest of the Kin Empire with the help of the Sung Empire.

1239. Frederick II excommunicated for the second time.

1240. Mongols destroyed Kieff. Russia tributary to the Mongols.

1241. Mongol victory at Liegnitz in Silesia.

1244. The Egyptian Sultan recaptured Jerusalem. This led to the Seventh Crusade.

1245. Frederick II re-excommunicated. The men of Schwyz burnt the castle of New Habsburg.

1250. St. Louis of France ransomed. Frederick II, the last Hohenstaufen Emperor, died. German interregnum until 1273.

A.D.

1251. Mangu Khan became Great Khan. Kublai Khan governor of China.

1258. Hulagu Khan took and destroyed Bagdad.

1260. Kublai Khan became Great Khan. Ketboga defeated in Palestine.

1261. The Greeks recaptured Constantinople from the Latins.

1269. Kublai Khan sent a message of inquiry to the Pope by the older Polos.

1271. Marco Polo started upon his travels.

1273. Rudolf of Habsburg elected Emperor. The Swiss formed their Everlasting League.

1280. Kublai Khan founded the Yuan Dynasty in China.

1292. Death of Kublai Khan.

1293. Roger Bacon, the prophet of experimental science, died.

1294. Boniface VIII Pope (to 1303).

1295. Marco Polo returned to Venice.

1303. Death of Pope Boniface VIII after the outrage of Anagni by Guillaume de Nogaret.

1305. Clement V Pope. The papal court set up at Avignon.

1308. Duns Scotus died.

1318. Four Franciscans burnt for heresy at Marseilles.

1347. Occam died.

1348. The Great Plague, the Black Death.

1358. The Jacquerie in France.

1360. In China the Mongol (Yuan) Dynasty fell, and was succeeded by the Ming Dynasty (to 1644).

1367. Timurlane assumed the title of Great Khan.

1377. Pope Gregory XI returned to Rome.

1378. The Great Schism. Urban VI in Rome, Clement VII at Avignon.

1381. Peasant revolt in England. Wat Tyler murdered in the presence of King Richard II.

1384. Wycliffe died.

1398. Huss preached Wycliffism at Prague.

1405. Death of Timurlane.

1414-18. The Council of Constance. Huss burnt (1415).

1417. The Great Schism ended, Martin V Pope.

1420. The Hussites revolted. Martin V preached a crusade against them.

A.D.

1431. The Catholic Crusaders dissolved before the Hussites at Domazlice. The Council of Basle met.

1436. The Hussites came to terms with the church.

1439. Council of Basle created a fresh schism in the church.

1445. Discovery of Cape Verde by the Portuguese.

1446. First printed books (Coster in Haarlem).

1449. End of the Council of Basle.

1453. Ottoman Turks under Muhammad II took Constantinople.

1480. Ivan III, Grand-duke of Moscow, threw off the Mongol allegiance.

1481. Death of the Sultan Muhammad II while preparing for the conquest of Italy. Bayazid II Turkish Sultan (to 1512).

1486. Diaz rounded the Cape of Good Hope.

1492. Columbus crossed the Atlantic to America. Rodrigo Borgia, Alexander VI, Pope (to 1503).

1493. Maximilian I became Emperor.

1498. Vasco de Gama sailed round the Cape to India.

1499. Switzerland became an independent republic.

1500. Charles V born.

1509. Henry VIII King of England.

1512. Selim Sultan (to 1520). He bought the title of Caliph. Fall of Soderini (and Machiavelli) in Florence.

1513. Leo X Pope.

1515. Francis I King of France.

1517. Selim annexed Egypt. Luther propounded his theses at Wittenberg.

1519. Leonardo da Vinci died. Magellan's expedition started to sail round the world. Cortez entered Mexico city.

1520. Suleiman the Magnificent, Sultan (to 1566), who ruled from Bagdad to Hungary. Charles V Emperor.

1521. Luther at the Diet of Worms. Loyola wounded at Pampeluna.

1525. Baber won the battle of Panipat, captured Delhi, and founded the Mogul Empire.

1527. The German troops in Italy, under the Constable of Bourbon, took and pillaged Rome.

1529. Suleiman besieged Vienna.

A.D.

1530. Pizarro invaded Peru. Charles V crowned by the Pope. Henry VIII began his quarrel with the Papacy.
1532. The Anabaptists seized Münster.
1535. Fall of the Anabaptist rule in Münster.
1539. The Company of Jesus founded.
1543. Copernicus died.
1545. The Council of Trent (to 1563) assembled to put the church in order.
1546. Martin Luther died.
1547. Ivan IV (the Terrible) took the title of Tsar of Russia. Francis I died.
1549. First Jesuit missions arrived in South America.
1552. Treaty of Passau. Temporary pacification of Germany.
1556. Charles V abdicated. Akbar Great Mogul (to 1605). Ignatius of Loyola died.
1558. Death of Charles V.
1563. End of the Council of Trent and the reform of the Catholic Church.
1564. Galileo born.
1566. Suleiman the Magnificent died.
1567. Revolt of the Netherlands.
1568. Execution of Counts Egmont and Horn.
1571. Kepler born.
1573. Siege of Alkmaar.
1578. Harvey born.
1583. Sir Walter Raleigh's expedition to Virginia.
1601. Tycho Brahe died.
1603. James I King of England and Scotland. Dr. Gilbert died.
1605. Jehangir Great Mogul.
1606. Virginia Company founded.
1609. Holland independent.
1618. Thirty Years' War began.
1620. *Mayflower* expedition founded New Plymouth. First negro slaves landed at Jamestown (Va.).
1625. Charles I of England.
1626. Sir Francis Bacon (Lord Verulam) died.

A.D.

1628. Shah Jehan Great Mogul. The English *Petition of Right.*

1629. Charles I of England began his eleven years of rule without a parliament.

1630. Kepler died.

1632. Leeuwenhoek born. Gustavus Adolphus killed at the Battle of Lützen.

1634. Wallenstein murdered.

1638. Japan closed to Europeans (until 1865).

1640. Charles I of England summoned the Long Parliament.

1641. Massacre of the English in Ireland.

1642. Galileo died. Newton born.

1643. Louis XIV began his reign of seventy-two years.

1644. The Manchus ended the Ming dynasty.

1645. Swine pens in the inner town of Leipzig pulled down.

1648. Treaty of Westphalia. Thereby Holland and Switzerland were recognized as free republics and Prussia became important. The treaty gave a complete victory neither to the Imperial Crown nor to the Princes. War of the Fronde; it ended in the complete victory of the French crown.

1649. Execution of Charles I of England.

1658. Aurungzeb Great Mogul. Cromwell died.

1660. Charles II of England.

1674. Nieuw Amsterdam finally became British by treaty and was renamed New York.

1683. The last Turkish attack on Vienna defeated by John III of Poland.

1688. The British Revolution. Flight of James II. William and Mary began to reign.

1689. Peter the Great of Russia. (To 1725.)

1690. Battle of the Boyne in Ireland.

1694. Voltaire born.

1701. Frederick I first King of Prussia.

1704. John Locke, the father of modern democratic theory, died.

1707. Death of Aurungzeb. The empire of the Great Mogul disintegrated.

1713. Frederick the Great of Prussia born.

1714. George I of Britain.

A.D.

1715. Louis XV of France.

1727. Newton died. George II of Britain.

1732. Oglethorpe founded Georgia.

1736. Nadir Shah raided India. (The beginning of twenty years of raiding and disorder in India.)

1740. Maria-Theresa began to reign. (Being a woman, she could not be empress. Her husband, Francis I, was emperor until his death in 1765, when her son, Joseph II, succeeded him.)

Accession of Frederick the Great, King of Prussia.

1741. The Empress Elizabeth of Russia began to reign.

1755-63. Britain and France struggled for America and India. France in alliance with Austria and Russia against Prussia and Britain (1756-63); the Seven Years' War.

1757. Battle of Plassey.

1759. The British general, Wolfe, took Quebec.

1760. George III of Britain.

1762. The Empress Elizabeth of Russia died. Murder of the Tsar Paul, and accession of Catherine the Great of Russia (to 1796).

1763. Peace of Paris; Canada ceded to Britain. British dominant in India.

1764. Battle of Buxar.

1769. Napoleon Bonaparte born.

1774. Louis XVI began his reign. Suicide of Clive. The American revolutionary drama began.

1775. Battle of Lexington.

1776. Declaration of Independence by the United States of America.

1778. J. J. Rousseau, the creator of modern democratic sentiment, died.

1780. End of the reign of Maria-Theresa. The Emperor Joseph (1765 to 1790) succeeded her in the hereditary Habsburg dominions.

1783. Treaty of Peace between Britain and the new United States of America. Quaco set free in Massachusetts.

1787. The Constitutional Convention of Philadelphia set up the Federal Government of the United States. France

A.D.

discovered to be bankrupt. The Assembly of the Notables.

1788. First Federal Congress of the United States at New York.

1789. The French States-General assembled. Storming of the Bastille.

1791. The Jacobin Revolution. Flight to Varennes.

1792. France declared war on Austria. Prussia declared war on France. Battle of Valmy. France became a republic.

1793. Louis XVI beheaded.

1794. Execution of Robespierre and end of the Jacobin republic. Rule of the Convention.

1795. The Directory. Bonaparte suppressed a revolt and went to Italy as commander-in-chief.

1797. By the Peace of Campo Formio Bonaparte destroyed the Republic of Venice.

1798. Bonaparte went to Egypt. Battle of the Nile.

1799. Bonaparte returned. He became First Consul with enormous powers.

1800. Legislative union of Ireland and England enacted January 1st, 1801.

Napoleon's campaign against Austria. Battles of Marengo (in Italy) and Hohenlinden (Moreau's victory).

1801. Preliminaries of peace between France, England, and Austria signed.

1803. Bonaparte occupied Switzerland, and so precipitated war.

1804. Bonaparte became Emperor. Francis II took the title of Emperor of Austria in 1805, and in 1806 he dropped the title of Holy Roman Emperor. So the "Holy Roman Empire" came to an end.

1805. Battle of Trafalgar. Battles of Ulm and Austerlitz.

1806. Prussia overthrown at Jena.

1807. Battles of Eylau and Friedland and Treaty of Tilsit.

1808. Napoleon made his brother Joseph King of Spain.

1810. Spanish America became republican.

1811. Alexander withdrew from the "Continental System."

A.D.
1812. Moscow.
1814. Abdication of Napoleon. Louis XVIII.
1815. The Waterloo campaign. The Treaty of Vienna.
1819. The First Factory Act passed through the efforts of Robert Owen.
1821. The Greek revolt.
1824. Charles X of France.
1825. Nicholas I of Russia. First railway, Stockton to Darlington.
1827. Battle of Navarino.
1829. Greece independent.
1830. A year of disturbance. Louis Philippe ousted Charles X. Belgium broke away from Holland. Leopold of Saxe-Coburg-Gotha became king of this new country, Belgium. Russian Poland revolted ineffectually.
1832. The First Reform Bill in Britain restored the democratic character of the British Parliament.
1835. The word socialism first used.
1837. Queen Victoria.
1840. Queen Victoria married Prince Albert of Saxe-Coburg-Gotha.
1848. Another year of disturbance. Republics in France and Rome. The Pan-slavic conference at Prague. All Germany united in a parliament at Frankfort. German unity destroyed by the King of Prussia.
1851. The Great Exhibition of London.
1852. Napoleon III Emperor of the French.
1854. Perry (second expedition) landed in Japan. Nicholas I occupied the Danubian provinces of Turkey.
1854-56. Crimean War.
1856. Alexander II of Russia.
1857. The Indian Mutiny.
1858. Robert Owen died.
1859. Franco-Austrian war. Battles of Magenta and Solferino.
1861. Victor Emmanuel First King of Italy. Abraham Lincoln became President, U.S.A. The American Civil War began.
1863. British bombarded a Japanese town.
1864. Maximilian became Emperor of Mexico.

A.D.

1865. Surrender of Appomattox Court House. Japan opened to the world.

1866. Prussia and Italy attacked Austria (and the south German states in alliance with her). Battle of Sadowa.

1867. The Emperor Maximilian shot.

1870. Napoleon III declared war against Prussia.

1871. Paris surrendered (January). The King of Prussia became William I, "German Emperor." The Hohenzollern Peace of Frankfort.

1875. The "Bulgarian atrocities."

1877. Russo-Turkish War. Treaty of San Stefano. Queen Victoria became Empress of India.

1878. The Treaty of Berlin. The Armed Peace of thirty-six years began in western Europe.

1881. The Battle of Majuba Hill. The Transvaal free.

1883. Britain occupied Egypt.

1886. Gladstone's first Irish Home Rule Bill.

1888. Frederick II (March), William II (June), German Emperors.

1890. Bismarck dismissed. Heligoland ceded to Germany by Lord Salisbury.

1894-5. Japanese war with China.

1895. "Unionist" (Imperialist) government in Britain.

1896. Battle of Adowa.

1898. The Fashoda quarrel between France and Britain. Germany acquired Kiau-Chau.

1899. The war in South Africa began (Boer war).

1900. The Boxer risings in China. Siege of the Legations at Peking.

1904. The British invaded Tibet.

1904-5. Russo-Japanese war.

1906. The "Unionist" (Imperialist) party in Great Britain defeated by the Liberals upon the question of tariffs.

1907. The Confederation of South Africa established.

1908. Austria annexed Bosnia and Herzegovina.

1909. M. Bleriot flew in an aeroplane from France to England.

1911. Italy made war on Turkey and seized Tripoli.

1912. China became a republic.

A.D.

1913. The Balkan league made war on Turkey. Bloodshed at Londonderry in Ireland caused by "Unionist" gun running.

1914. The Great War in Europe began (for which see special time chart, pp. 1052-53).

1917. The two Russian revolutions. Establishment of the Bolshevik régime in Russia.

1919-20. The Clemenceau Peace of Versailles.

1920. First meeting of the League of Nations, from which Germany, Austria, Russia, and Turkey were excluded, and at which the United States was not represented.

And here our List of Events breaks off with a note of interrogation.

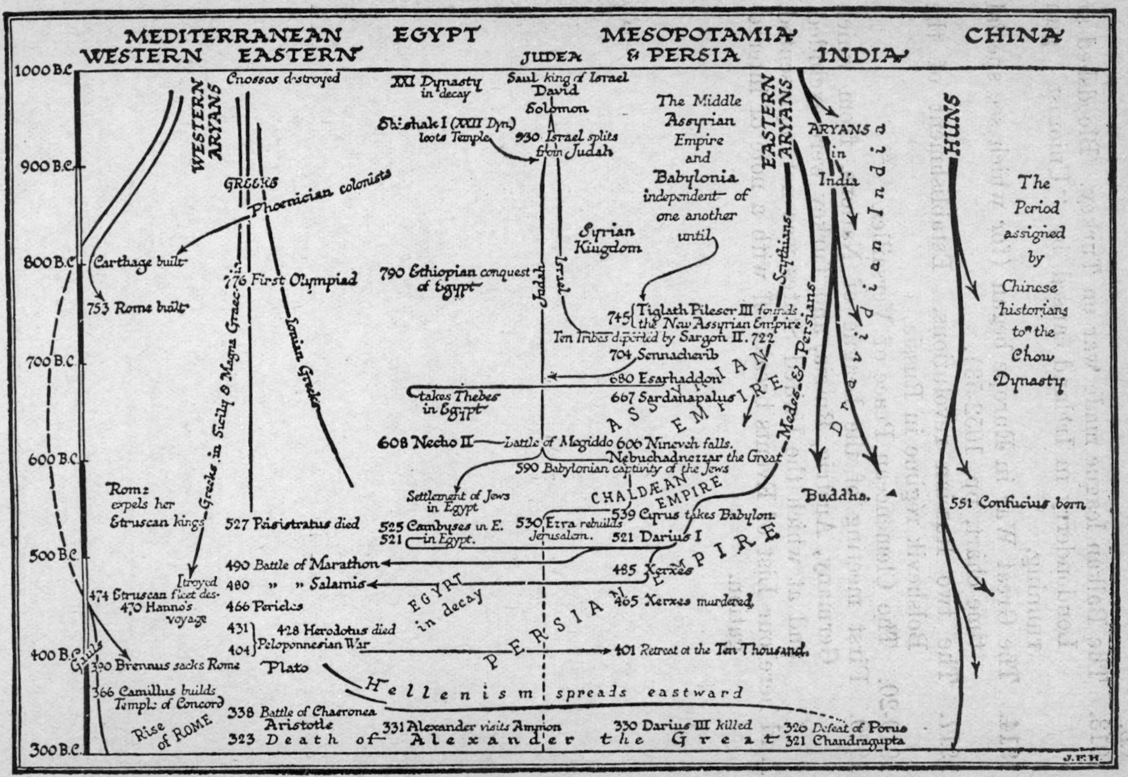

MEDITERRANEAN
WESTERN
EASTERN
EGYPT
JUDEA
MESOPOTAMIA & PERSIA
INDIA
CHINA
1000 B.C.
900 B.C.
800 B.C.
700 B.C.
600 B.C.
500 B.C.
400 B.C.
300 B.C.
WESTERN ARYANS
Cnossos destroyed
GREEKS
Phoenician colonists
Carthage built
753 Rome built
776 First Olympiad
Greeks in Sicily & Magna Graecia
Ionian Greeks
XXI Dynasty in decay
Shishak I (XXII Dyn.) loots Temple
Saul king of Israel
David
Solomon
930 Israel splits from Judah
Judah
Israel
The Middle Assyrian Empire and Babylonia independent of one another until
Syrian Kingdom
790 Ethiopian conquest of Egypt
745 Tiglath Pileser III founds the New Assyrian Empire
Ten Tribes deported by Sargon II. 722
704 Sennacherib
680 Esarhaddon
takes Thebes in Egypt
667 Sardanapalus
ASSYRIAN EMPIRE
608 Necho II
Battle of Megiddo
606 Nineveh falls.
Nebuchadnezzar the Great
590 Babylonian captivity of the Jews
Settlement of Jews in Egypt
CHALDÆAN EMPIRE
EASTERN ARYANS
Scythians
Medes & Persians
ARYANS in India
Dravidian India
Buddha.
HUNS
The Period assigned by Chinese historians to the Chow Dynasty
551 Confucius born
Rome expels her Etruscan kings
527 Peisistratus died
525 Cambyses in E.
521 in Egypt.
530 Ezra rebuilds Jerusalem.
539 Cyrus takes Babylon
521 Darius I
PERSIAN EMPIRE
490 Battle of Marathon
480 " " Salamis
485 Xerxes
465 Xerxes murdered
destroyed
474 Etruscan fleet des-
470 Hanno's voyage
466 Pericles
EGYPT in decay
431
404 Peloponnesian War
428 Herodotus died
401 Retreat of the Ten Thousand.
Gauls
390 Brennus sacks Rome
Plato
Hellenism spreads eastward
366 Camillus builds Temple of Concord
Rise of ROME
338 Battle of Chaeronea
Aristotle
331 Alexander visits Ammon
330 Darius III killed
326 Defeat of Porus
323 Death of Alexander the Great
321 Chandragupta
J.F.H.

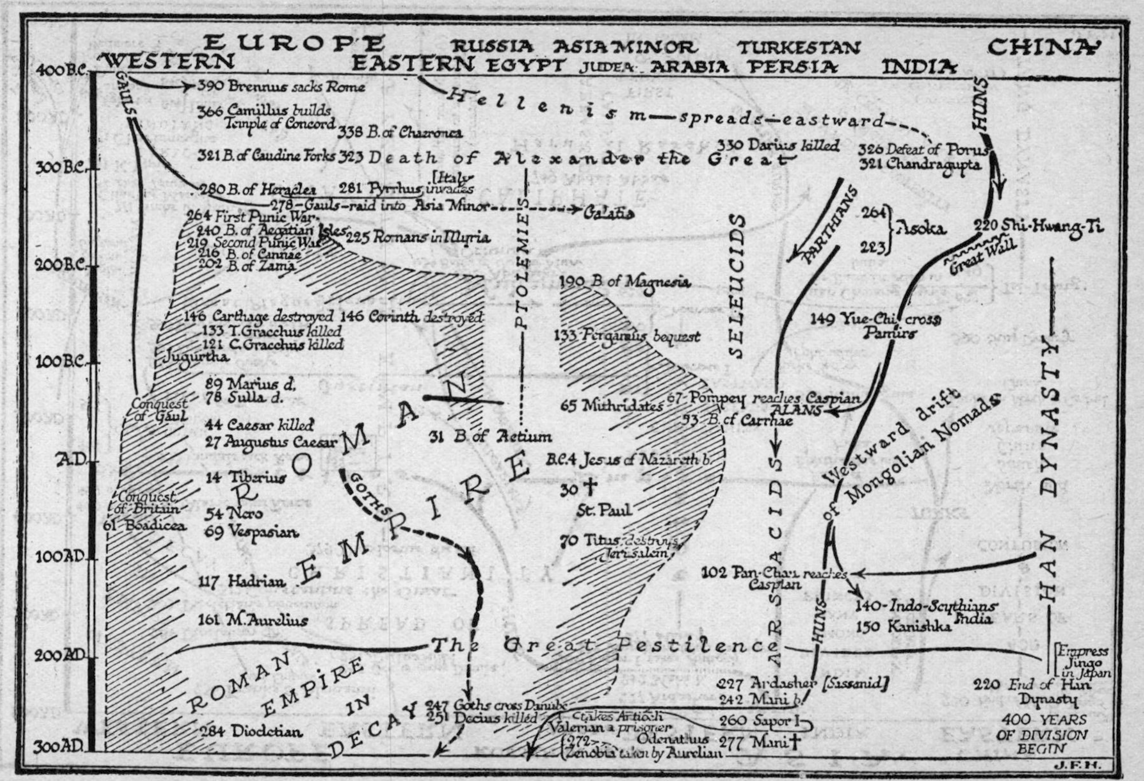
EUROPE
WESTERN
EASTERN
RUSSIA
EGYPT
ASIA MINOR
JUDEA
ARABIA
TURKESTAN
PERSIA
INDIA
CHINA
400 B.C.
300 B.C.
200 B.C.
100 B.C.
A.D.
100 A.D.
200 A.D.
300 A.D.
GAULS
390 Brennus sacks Rome
366 Camillus builds Temple of Concord
338 B. of Chaeronea
Hellenism—spreads—eastward
321 B. of Caudine Forks
323 Death of Alexander the Great
330 Darius killed
326 Defeat of Porus
321 Chandragupta
HUNS
280 B. of Heraclea
281 Pyrrhus invades [Italy
278—Gauls—raid into Asia Minor
Galatia
264 First Punic War
240 B. of Aegatian Isles
219 Second Punic War
216 B. of Cannae
202 B. of Zama
225 Romans in Illyria
PTOLEMIES
SELEUCIDS
PARTHIANS
264
223
Asoka
220 Shi-Hwang-Ti
Great Wall
190 B. of Magnesia
146 Carthage destroyed
146 Corinth destroyed
133 T. Gracchus killed
121 C. Gracchus killed
Jugurtha
133 Pergamus bequest
149 Yue-Chi cross Pamirs
HAN DYNASTY
89 Marius d.
78 Sulla d.
Conquest of Gaul
65 Mithridates
67 Pompey reaches Caspian
ALANS
53 B. of Carrhae
44 Caesar killed
27 Augustus Caesar
31 B. of Actium
ROMAN EMPIRE
B.C.4 Jesus of Nazareth b.
Westward drift of Mongolian Nomads
14 Tiberius
30 †
St. Paul
ARSACIDS
Conquest of Britain
61 Boadicea
54 Nero
69 Vespasian
GOTHS
70 Titus destroys Jerusalem
102 Pan-Chau reaches Caspian
117 Hadrian
140-Indo-Scythians India
150 Kanishka
161 M. Aurelius
The Great Pestilence
Empress Jingo in Japan
ROMAN EMPIRE IN DECAY
227 Ardasher [Sassanid]
242 Mani b.
220 End of Han Dynasty
247 Goths cross Danube
251 Decius killed
takes Antioch
Valerian a prisoner
Odenathus
260 Sapor I
400 YEARS OF DIVISION BEGIN
284 Diocletian
272 Zenobia taken by Aurelian
277 Mani †
J.F.H.

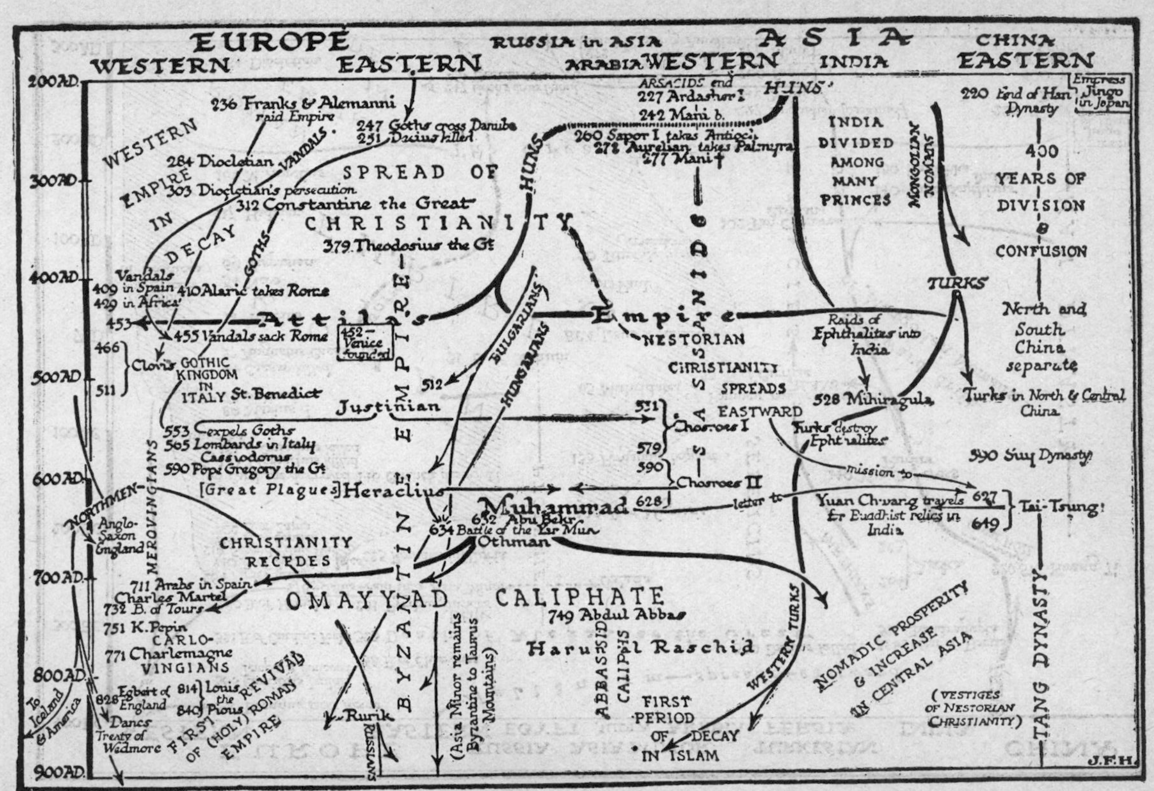
EUROPE
WESTERN
EASTERN
RUSSIA in ASIA
ARABIA
ASIA
WESTERN
INDIA
CHINA
EASTERN
200AD.
300AD.
400AD.
500AD.
600AD.
700AD.
800AD.
900AD.
236 Franks & Alemanni raid Empire
247 Goths cross Danube
251 Decius killed
WESTERN EMPIRE IN DECAY
284 Diocletian
303 Diocletian's persecution
312 Constantine the Great
SPREAD OF CHRISTIANITY
379 Theodosius the Gt
VANDALS
GOTHS
HUNS
Vandals 409 in Spain 429 in Africa
410 Alaric takes Rome
453
Attila's Empire
455 Vandals sack Rome
452 – Venice founded
466 511 Clovis
GOTHIC KINGDOM IN ITALY
St. Benedict
Justinian
512
553 expels Goths
565 Lombards in Italy
Cassiodorus
590 Pope Gregory the Gt
[Great Plagues]
Heraclius
BULGARIANS
HUNGARIANS
BYZANTINE EMPIRE
MEROVINGIANS
NORTHMEN
Anglo-Saxon England
CHRISTIANITY RECEDES
711 Arabs in Spain
Charles Martel
732 B. of Tours
751 K. Pepin
CARLO-VINGIANS
771 Charlemagne
Egbert of England
828
814 840 Louis the Pious
FIRST REVIVAL OF (HOLY) ROMAN EMPIRE
Danes
Treaty of Wedmore
To Iceland & America
Rurik
RUSSIANS
(Asia Minor remains Byzantine to Taurus Mountains)
ARSACIDS end
227 Ardashir I
242 Mani b.
260 Sapor I takes Antioch
278 Aurelian takes Palmyra
277 Mani †
SASSANID Empire
NESTORIAN CHRISTIANITY SPREADS EASTWARD
531 579 Chosroes I
590 628 Chosroes II
Muhammad
632 Abu Bekr
634 Battle of the Yarmuk
Othman
letter to
OMAYYAD CALIPHATE
749 Abdul Abbas
Haroun al Raschid
ABBASSID CALIPHS
FIRST PERIOD OF DECAY IN ISLAM
HUNS
INDIA DIVIDED AMONG MANY PRINCES
Raids of Ephthalites into India
528 Mihiragula
Turks destroy Ephthalites
mission to
Yuan Chwang travels for Buddhist relics in India
WESTERN TURKS
NOMADIC PROSPERITY & INCREASE IN CENTRAL ASIA
MONGOLIAN NOMADS
TURKS
220 End of Han Dynasty
Empress Jingo in Japan
400 YEARS OF DIVISION & CONFUSION
North and South China separate
Turks in North & Central China
590 Suy Dynasty
627 649 Tai-Tsung!
TANG DYNASTY
(VESTIGES OF NESTORIAN CHRISTIANITY)
J.F.H.

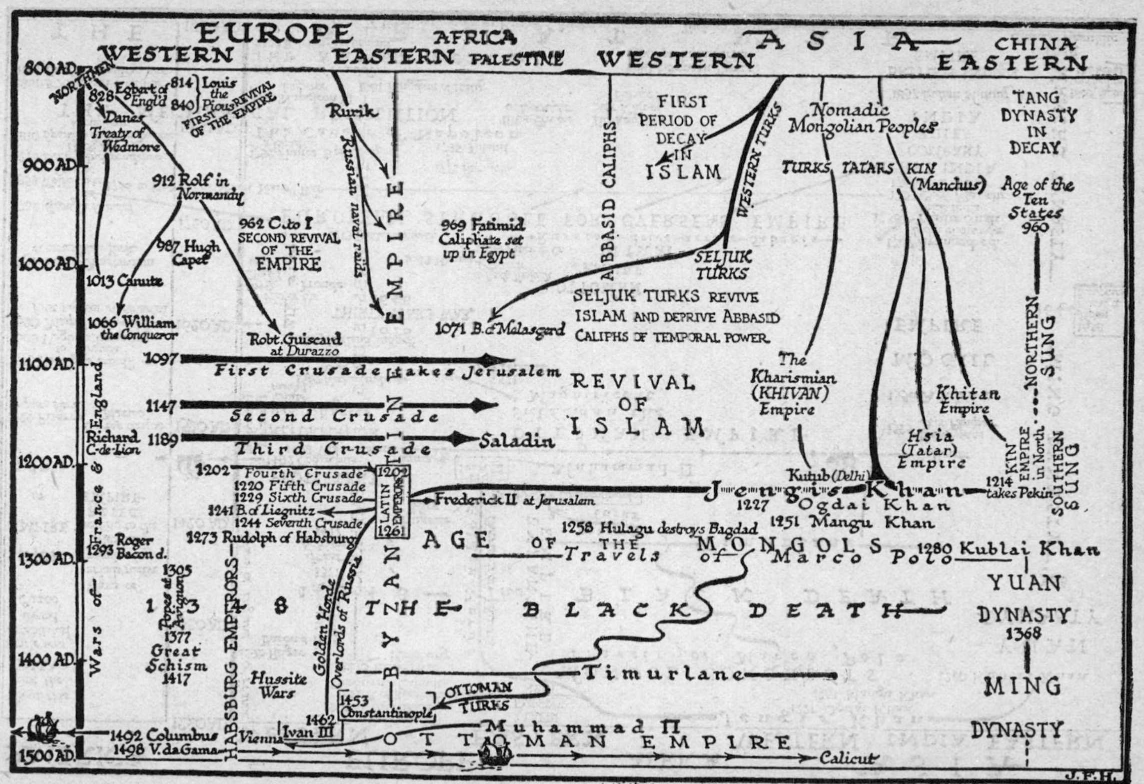
EUROPE
WESTERN
EASTERN
AFRICA
PALESTINE
ASIA
WESTERN
CHINA
EASTERN
800 A.D.
900 A.D.
1000 A.D.
1100 A.D.
1200 A.D.
1300 A.D.
1400 A.D.
1500 A.D.
NORTHMEN
828 Egbert of Engl'd
814 Louis the Pious 840
FIRST REVIVAL OF THE EMPIRE
Danes
Treaty of Wedmore
912 Rolf in Normandy
962 O. to I SECOND REVIVAL OF THE EMPIRE
987 Hugh Capet
1013 Canute
1066 William the Conqueror
Robt. Guiscard at Durazzo
Rurik
Russian naval raids
EMPIRE
969 Fatimid Caliphate set up in Egypt
1071 B. of Malasgerd
ABBASID CALIPHS
FIRST PERIOD OF DECAY IN ISLAM
WESTERN TURKS
SELJUK TURKS
SELJUK TURKS REVIVE ISLAM AND DEPRIVE ABBASID CALIPHS OF TEMPORAL POWER
Nomadic Mongolian Peoples
TURKS
TATARS
KIN (Manchus)
TANG DYNASTY IN DECAY
Age of the Ten States
960
NORTHERN SUNG
Khitan Empire
Hsia (Tatar) Empire
KIN EMPIRE in North
SOUTHERN SUNG
1214 takes Pekin
1097 First Crusade takes Jerusalem
1147 Second Crusade
1189 Third Crusade
Richard Cœur de Lion
Saladin
REVIVAL OF ISLAM
The Kharismian (KHIVAN) Empire
Wars of France & England
1202 Fourth Crusade
1220 Fifth Crusade
1229 Sixth Crusade
1241 B. of Liegnitz
1244 Seventh Crusade
1273 Rudolph of Habsburg
1293 Roger Bacon d.
1204 LATIN EMPERORS 1261
Frederick II at Jerusalem
Jenghis Khan
1227 Ogdai Khan
Kutub (Delhi)
1251 Mangu Khan
1258 Hulagu destroys Bagdad
1280 Kublai Khan
AGE OF THE MONGOLS
Travels of Marco Polo
YUAN DYNASTY
1368
MING DYNASTY
1305 Popes at Avignon
1377 Great Schism 1417
1348 THE BLACK DEATH
BYZANTINE
HABSBURG EMPERORS
Hussite Wars
Golden Horde
Overlords of Russia
Timurlane
OTTOMAN TURKS
1453 Constantinople
1462 Ivan III
Muhammad II
OTTOMAN EMPIRE
1492 Columbus
1498 V. da Gama
Vienna
Calicut
J.F.H.

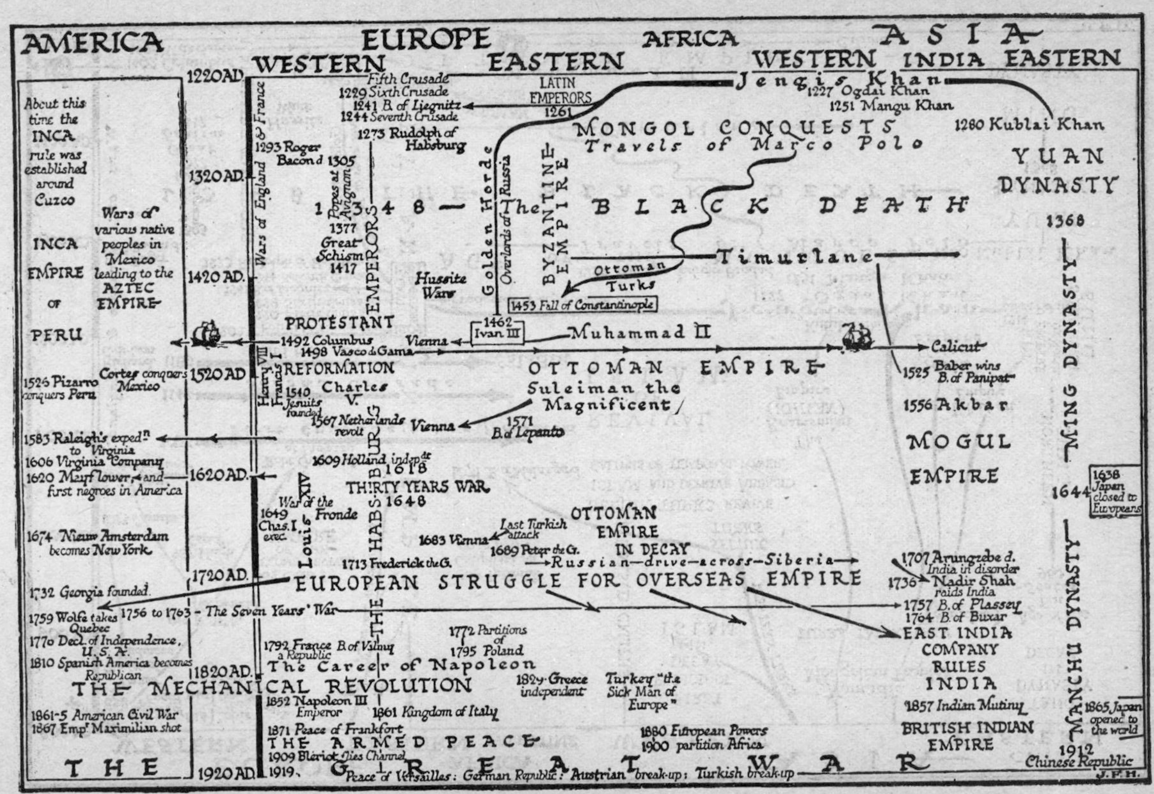
AMERICA
EUROPE
WESTERN
EASTERN
AFRICA
ASIA
WESTERN
INDIA
EASTERN
1220 AD.
1320 AD.
1420 AD.
1520 AD.
1620 AD.
1720 AD.
1820 AD.
1920 AD.
About this time the INCA rule was established around Cuzco
INCA EMPIRE of PERU
Wars of various native peoples in Mexico leading to the AZTEC EMPIRE
1526 Pizarro conquers Peru
Cortez conquers Mexico
1583 Raleigh's exped.n to Virginia
1606 Virginia Company
1620 Mayflower and first negroes in America
1674 Nieuw Amsterdam becomes New York
1732 Georgia founded
1759 Wolfe takes Quebec
1756 to 1763 - The Seven Years' War
1770 Decl. of Independence, U.S.A.
1810 Spanish America becomes Republican
THE MECHANICAL REVOLUTION
1861-5 American Civil War
1867 Emp.r Maximilian shot
THE ARMED PEACE
THE GREAT WAR
Wars of England & France
Fifth Crusade
1229 Sixth Crusade
1241 B. of Liegnitz
1244 Seventh Crusade
1273 Rudolph of Habsburg
1293 Roger Bacon d.
1305 Popes at Avignon
1377 Great Schism 1417
EMPERORS
1348 — The BLACK DEATH
Hussite War
1492 Columbus
1498 Vasco da Gama
PROTESTANT REFORMATION
Henry VIII
Francis I
1540 Jesuits founded
Charles V.
1567 Netherlands revolt
1609 Holland independ.t
1618 THIRTY YEARS WAR 1648
1649 Chas. I exec.
War of the Fronde
Louis XIV
THE HABSBURG
1713 Frederick the G.
EUROPEAN STRUGGLE FOR OVERSEAS EMPIRE
1792 France a Republic
B. of Valmy
The Career of Napoleon
1852 Napoleon III Emperor
1861 Kingdom of Italy
1871 Peace of Frankfort
1909 Blériot flies Channel
1919. Peace of Versailles: German Republic: Austrian break-up: Turkish break-up
LATIN EMPERORS
1261
Vienna
Golden Horde
Overlords of Russia
BYZANTINE EMPIRE
1453 Fall of Constantinople
1462 Ivan III
Muhammad II
OTTOMAN EMPIRE
Suleiman the Magnificent
1571 B. of Lepanto
Vienna
1683 Vienna
Last Turkish attack
1689 Peter the G.
OTTOMAN EMPIRE IN DECAY
Russian drive across Siberia
1772 Partitions of 1795 Poland
1829 Greece independent
Turkey "the Sick Man of Europe"
1880 European Powers 1900 partition Africa
Jengis Khan
1227 Ogdai Khan
1251 Mangu Khan
MONGOL CONQUESTS
Travels of Marco Polo
Ottoman Turks
Timurlane
1280 Kublai Khan
YUAN DYNASTY
1368
MING DYNASTY
Calicut
1525 Baber wins B. of Panipat
1556 Akbar
MOGUL EMPIRE
1707 Aurungzebe d. India in disorder
1736 Nadir Shah raids India
1757 B. of Plassey
1764 B. of Buxar
EAST INDIA COMPANY RULES INDIA
1857 Indian Mutiny
BRITISH INDIAN EMPIRE
1644
1638 Japan closed to Europeans
MANCHU DYNASTY
1865 Japan opened to the world
1912 Chinese Republic
J.F.H.

INDEX

KEY TO PRONUNCIATION

VOWELS

a as in far (far), father (fa' *thĕ*r), mikado (mi ka' dō).
ă „ „ fat (făt), ample (ămpl), abstinence (ăb' stin *ĕ*ns).
ā „ „ fate (fāt), wait (wāt), deign (dān), jade (jād).
aw „ „ fall (fawl), appal (a pawl'), broad (brawd).
ä „ „ fair (fär), bear (bär), where (hwär).

e „ „ bell (bel), bury (ber' i).
ĕ „ „ her (hĕr), search (sĕrch), word (wĕrd), bird (bĕrd).
ē „ „ beef (bēf), thief (thēf), idea (ī dē' *ă*), beer (bēr), casino (k*ă* sē' nō).

i „ „ bit (bit), lily (lil' i), nymph (nimf), build (bild).
ī „ „ bite (bīt), analyse (ăn' *ă* līz), light (līt).

o „ „ not (not), watch (woch), cough (kof), sorry (sor' i).
ō „ „ no (nō), blow (blō), brooch (brōch).
ö „ „ north (nörth), absorb (*ă*b sörb').
oo „ „ food (food), do (doo), prove (proov), blue (bloo), strew (stroo).

u „ „ bull (bul), good (gud), would (wud).
ŭ „ „ sun (sŭn), love (lŭv), enough (*ĕ* nŭf').
ū „ „ muse (mūz), stew (stū), cure (kūr).

ou „ „ bout (bout), bough (bou), crowd (kroud).
oi „ „ join (join), joy (joi), buoy (boi).

A short mark placed over **a**, **e**, **o**, or **u** (*ă*, *ĕ*, *ŏ*, *ŭ*) signifies that the vowel has an obscure, indeterminate, or slurred sound, as in: —

advice (*ă*d vīs'), current (kŭr' *ĕ*nt), notion (nō' sh*ŭ*n),
breakable (brā' k*ă*bl), sailor (sā' l*ŏ*r), pleasure (plezh' *ŭ*r).

CONSONANTS

"**s**" is used only for the sibilant "s" (as in "toast," tōst, "place," plās); the sonant "s" (as in "toes," "plays") is printed "z" (tōz, plāz).

"c" (except in the combinations "ch" and "*ch*"), "q" and "x" are not used.

b, d, f, h (but see the combinations below), k, l, m, n (see *n* below), p, r, t, v, z, and w and y when used as consonants have their usual values.

ch as in church (chĕrch), batch (băch), capriccio (ka prē' chō).
ch „ „ loch (lo*ch*), coronach (kor' o na*ch*), clachan (klă*ch*' an).

g „ „ get (get), finger (fing' gĕr).
j „ „ join (join), judge (jŭj), germ (jĕrm), ginger (jin' jĕr).

gh (in List of Proper Names only) as in Ludwig (lut' vigh).
hl („ „ „ „) „ „ Llandilo (hlăn dī' lō).
hw as in white (hwīt), nowhere (nō' hwär).

n „ „ cabochon (ka bō sho*n*'), congé (ko*n*' zhā).

sh „ „ shawl (shawl), mention (men' sh*ŭ*n).
zh „ „ measure (mezh' *ŭ*r), vision (vizh' *ŏ*n).

th „ „ thin (thin), breath (breth).
th „ „ thine (*th*īn), breathe (brē*th*).

The accent (') *follows* the syllable to be stressed.

INDEX

A

E

F

G

H

J

K

L

N

Q

R

W

X

Y

Z